THE OXFORD HANI

THUCYDIDES

THE OXFORD HANDBOOK OF
THUCYDIDES

Edited by
RYAN K. BALOT, SARA FORSDYKE,
and
EDITH FOSTER

OXFORD
UNIVERSITY PRESS

UNIVERSITY PRESS

Oxford University Press is a department of the University of Oxford. It furthers the University's objective of excellence in research, scholarship, and education by publishing worldwide. Oxford is a registered trade mark of Oxford University Press in the UK and certain other countries.

Published in the United States of America by Oxford University Press
198 Madison Avenue, New York, NY 10016, United States of America.

© Oxford University Press 2017

First issued as an Oxford University Press paperback, 2020

All rights reserved. No part of this publication may be reproduced, stored in a retrieval system, or transmitted, in any form or by any means, without the prior permission in writing of Oxford University Press, or as expressly permitted by law, by license, or under terms agreed with the appropriate reproduction rights organization. Inquiries concerning reproduction outside the scope of the above should be sent to the Rights Department, Oxford University Press, at the address above.

You must not circulate this work in any other form
and you must impose this same condition on any acquirer.

Library of Congress Cataloging-in-Publication Data
Names: Balot, Ryan K. (Ryan Krieger), 1969– editor of compilation. | Forsdyke, Sara, 1967– editor of compilation. | Foster, Edith (Edith Marie) editor of compilation.
Title: The Oxford handbook of Thucydides / edited by Ryan K. Balot, Sara Forsdyke, Edith Foster.
Description: New York, NY : Oxford University Press, [2017] | Includes bibliographical references and index. | Description based on print version record and CIP data provided by publisher; resource not viewed.
Identifiers: LCCN 2016019064 (print) | LCCN 2016018979 (ebook) | ISBN 9780199340385 (hardback) | ISBN 9780190053178 (paperback) |ISBN 9780199340392 (updf) | ISBN 9780190647742 (eBook) | ISBN 9780190647735 (online)
Subjects: LCSH: Thucydides. | Thucydides—Criticism and interpretation. | Thucydides—Political and social views. | Greece—Intellectual life—To 146 B.C. | Greece—Historiography.
Classification: LCC DF229.T6 (print) | LCC DF229.T6 O84 2017 (ebook) | DDC 938/.05092 [B]—dc23
LC record available at https://lccn.loc.gov/2016019064

Contents

Acknowledgments — ix
List of Contributors — xi
List of Abbreviations — xv
Map of Greece and the Aegean — xvii
Map of the Peloponnesus — xix
Map of Sicily — xxi
Map of the Mediterranean — xxiii

Introduction — 1

SECTION I THUCYDIDES AS HISTORIAN

1. Thucydides' Historical Method — 19
   SARA FORSDYKE

2. Thucydides on Early Greek History — 39
   HANS VAN WEES

3. The Pentecontaetia — 63
   LISA KALLET

4. Sparta and the Crisis of the Peloponnesian League in Thucydides' *History* — 81
   ELLEN G. MILLENDER

5. Thucydides on the Athenian Empire and Interstate Relations (431–404) — 99
   POLLY LOW

6. Thucydides on the Causes and Outbreak of the Peloponnesian War — 115
   ERIC W. ROBINSON

7. Thucydides on the First Ten Years of War (Archidamian War) — 125
   PETER HUNT

8. Mantinea, Decelea, and the Interwar Years (421–413 BCE) 145
   Cinzia Bearzot

9. Thucydides on the Sicilian Expedition 161
   Emily Greenwood

10. Thucydides on the Four Hundred and the Fall of Athens 179
    Andrew Wolpert

SECTION II THUCYDIDEAN HISTORIOGRAPHY

11. Writing History Implicitly through Refined Structuring 195
    Hunter R. Rawlings III

12. Scale Matters: Compression, Expansion, and Vividness in Thucydides 211
    W. Robert Connor

13. The Tree, the Funnel, and the Diptych: Some Patterns in Thucydides' Longest Sentences 225
    Jeffrey Rusten

14. Authorial Comments in Thucydides 239
    Mathieu de Bakker

15. Thucydides and Myth: A Complex Relation to Past and Present 257
    Rosaria Vignolo Munson

16. Speeches 267
    Antonis Tsakmakis

17. Characterization of Individuals in Thucydides' *History* 283
    Philip A. Stadter

18. Campaign and Battle Narratives in Thucydides 301
    Edith Foster

SECTION III THUCYDIDES AND POLITICAL THEORY

19. Was Thucydides a Political Philosopher? 319
    Ryan K. Balot

20. *Kinēsis*, Navies, and the Power Trap in Thucydides 339
    ARLENE W. SAXONHOUSE

21. Thucydides on Nature and Human Conduct 355
    CLIFFORD ORWIN

22. Thucydides and the Politics of Necessity 373
    MARK FISHER AND KINCH HOEKSTRA

23. The Regime (*Politeia*) in Thucydides 391
    S. N. JAFFE

24. Stasis in the War Narrative 409
    MICHAEL PALMER

25. Religion, Politics, and Piety 427
    PAUL A. RAHE

26. Thucydides on the Political Passions 443
    VICTORIA WOHL

27. Leaders and Leadership in Thucydides' *History* 459
    MARY P. NICHOLS

28. Thucydides and Crowds 475
    JOHN ZUMBRUNNEN

29. Thucydides, International Law, and International Anarchy 491
    ARTHUR M. ECKSTEIN

30. Xenophon as a Socratic Reader of Thucydides 515
    PAUL LUDWIG

31. Political Philosophy in an Unstable World: Comparing Thucydides and Plato on the Possibilities of Politics 531
    GERALD MARA

SECTION IV CONTEXTS AND ANCIENT RECEPTION OF THUCYDIDEAN HISTORIOGRAPHY

32. Thucydides' Predecessors and Contemporaries in Historical Poetry and Prose 551
    LEONE PORCIANI

33. Thucydides and His Intellectual Milieu 567
    ROSALIND THOMAS

34. Thucydides, Epic, and Tragedy 587
    TOBIAS JOHO

35. Thucydides and Attic Comedy 605
    JEFFREY HENDERSON

36. Thucydides and His Continuators 621
    VIVIENNE J. GRAY

37. Dionysius of Halicarnassus on Thucydides 641
    CASPER C. DE JONGE

38. Polybius and Sallust 659
    NICOLAS WIATER

39. Writing with Posterity in Mind: Thucydides and Tacitus on Secession 677
    CYNTHIA DAMON

40. Thucydides, Procopius, and the Historians of the Later Roman Empire 691
    CONOR WHATELY

Index Locorum 709
Subject Index 753

Acknowledgments

For their expertise, professionalism, and dedication, we would like to thank the many colleagues who have written essays for this volume. The editorial team at Oxford University Press, and above all Stefan Vranka, with Sarah Svendsen, Sarah Pirovitz, and John Veranes, has made significant contributions from the start; we are grateful for their confidence in us and for their hard work in seeing this volume through to completion. We also thank the production team, headed by Sasirekka Gopalakrishnan. Finally, we are grateful to Drew Stimson of the University of Michigan for his superb editorial assistance and we would especially like to thank the institutions that have supported us both financially and otherwise: the Institute for Advanced Studies at the University of Strasbourg, Case Western Reserve University, the University of Michigan, and the University of Toronto.

List of Contributors

Ryan K. Balot is Professor of Political Science and Classics at the University of Toronto.

Cinzia Bearzot is Professor of Greek History at the Catholic University in Milan.

W. Robert Connor is the former President and Director of the National Humanities Center in North Carolina and also former President of the Teagle Foundation in New York City.

Cynthia Damon is a Professor of Classical Studies at the University of Pennsylvania.

Mathieu de Bakker is University Lecturer of Ancient Greek at the University of Amsterdam.

Casper C. de Jonge is University Lecturer of Ancient Greek Language and Literature at Leiden University.

Arthur M. Eckstein is Professor of History and Distinguished Scholar-Teacher at the University of Maryland, College Park.

Mark Fisher is a Ph.D. candidate in Political Science at the University of California, Berkeley and soon to be Assistant Professor at Georgetown University.

Sara Forsdyke is Professor of Classical Studies and History at the University of Michigan.

Edith Foster is a Fellow at the Institute for Advanced Studies of the University of Strasbourg and a Senior Research Associate at Case Western Reserve University.

Vivienne J. Gray is Professor of Classics Emeritus at the University of Auckland, New Zealand.

Emily Greenwood is Professor of Classics at Yale University.

Jeffrey Henderson is the William Goodwin Aurelio Professor of Greek Language and Literature, and former Dean of the College and Graduate School of Arts and Sciences, at Boston University.

Kinch Hoekstra is the Chancellor's Professor of Political Science and Law and Affiliated Professor in Classics and Philosophy, at the University of California, Berkeley.

Peter Hunt is a Professor in the Department of Classics at the University of Colorado, Boulder.

S. N. Jaffe is an Assistant Professor of Political Science and International Affairs at John Cabot University and an Associate Researcher at the Berlin Thucydides Center of the Freie Universität Berlin.

Tobias Joho is Wissenschaftlicher Assistent at the Institut für Klassische Philologie of the University of Bern in Switzerland.

Lisa Kallet is Cawkwell Fellow in Ancient History, University College, Oxford.

Polly Low is Senior Lecturer in Ancient History at the University of Manchester.

Paul Ludwig is a member of the faculty at St. John's College in Annapolis, Maryland.

Gerald Mara is Affiliate Professor of Government at Georgetown University.

Ellen G. Millender is Professor of Classics and Humanities at Reed College.

Rosaria Vignolo Munson is the J. Archer and Helen C. Turner Professor of Classics at Swarthmore College.

Mary P. Nichols is Professor of Political Science at Baylor University.

Clifford Orwin is Professor of Political Science, Classics, and Jewish Studies and a Fellow of St. Michael's College and a Senior Fellow of Massey College at the University of Toronto.

Michael Palmer teaches Political Theory in the Honors College at the University of Maine.

Leone Porciani is Professor of Greek History at the University of Pavia.

Paul A. Rahe holds the Charles O. Lee and Louise K. Lee Chair in the Western Heritage at Hillsdale College.

Hunter R. Rawlings III is Professor of Classics and Interim President at Cornell University.

Eric W. Robinson is Professor of History at Indiana University.

Jeffrey Rusten is Professor of Greek literature at Cornell University.

Arlene W. Saxonhouse is the Caroline Robbins Professor of Political Science and Women's Studies and affiliated Professor of Classics at the University of Michigan.

Philip A. Stadter is Professor Emeritus of Classics at the University of North Carolina at Chapel Hill.

Rosalind Thomas is Dyson-Macgregor Fellow, Jowett Lecturer and Professor of Greek History, Balliol College, University of Oxford.

Antonis Tsakmakis is Associate Professor of Greek and Head of the Department of Classical Studies and Philosophy, University of Cyprus.

Hans van Wees is Grote Professor of Ancient History at University College, London.

Conor Whately is Associate Professor of Classics at the University of Winnipeg.

Nicolas Wiater is Lecturer in Classics at the University of St. Andrews.

Victoria Wohl is Professor of Classics at the University of Toronto.

Andrew Wolpert is an Associate Professor of Classics at the University of Florida.

John Zumbrunnen is Professor of Political Science, Faculty Director of Chadbourne Residential College and Director of the American Democracy Forum at the University of Wisconsin, Madison.

List of Abbreviations

ATL	B. D. Meritt, H. T. Wade-Gery, and M. F. McGregor. 1939–1953. *The Athenian Tribute Lists*. 4 vols. Princeton, NJ: American School of Classical Studies at Athens.
CT	S. Hornblower. 1991–2008. *A Commentary on Thucydides*. 3 vols. Oxford: Clarendon Press.
DK	H. Diels and W. Kranz, *Die Fragmente der Vorsokratiker*. 6th Edition, 1951. Berlin: Weidman.
FGrH	F. Jacoby et al. 1923–2199. *Die Fragmente der griechischen Historiker*. i–iii, Berlin; 1940–1958. Leiden: The Netherlands; 1998–. *FGrH*, iv, Leiden, Boston: Cologne.
EGM	R. L. Fowler. 2000–2013. *Early Greek Mythography*. i. *Text and Introduction*, ii. *Commentary*. Oxford: Oxford University Press.
HCT	A. W. Gomme, A. Andrewes, and K. J. Dover. 1945–1981. *A Historical Commentary on Thucydides*, i–v. Oxford: Clarendon Press.
IG I^3	D. Lewis, with L. Jeffery and E. Erxleben. 1981–1988. *Inscriptiones Graecae*. Vol. 1, 3rd ed., *Inscriptiones Atticae Euclidis anno anteriores*. Berlin.
IG II^2	J. Kirchner. 1913–1940. *Inscriptiones Graecae*. Vol. 2, 2nd ed., *Inscriptiones Atticae Euclidis anno posteriores*. Berlin.
Kassel-Austin	Rudolf Kassel and Colin Austin, eds. 1983–. *Poetae Comici Graeci* (*PCG*). 12 vols. Berlin and New York: De Gruyter.
ML	R. Meiggs and D. M. Lewis. 1988. *A Selection of Greek Historical Inscriptions: To the End of the Fifth Century B.C.* 2nd ed. Oxford: Oxford University Press.
RO	P. J. Rhodes and R. G. Osborne. 2003. *Greek Historical Inscriptions, 404–323 B.C.* Oxford: Oxford University Press.
TrGF	B. Snell, R. Kannicht, and S. Radt. 1985–2007. *Tragicorum Graecorum fragmenta*, i–ii^2, iii–v. Göttingen: Vandenhoeck & Ruprecht.
West	M. L. West. 2003. *Greek Epic Fragments from the Seventh to the Fifth Century BC*. Cambridge, MA: Harvard University Press.

Translations

Crawley   Robert B. Strassler, ed. *The Landmark Thucydides. A Comprehensive Guide to the Peloponnesian War.* New York: Free Press, 1996.

Lattimore   *The Peloponnesian War*, translated, with introduction, notes and glossary by Steven Lattimore. Indianapolis: Hackett Pub. Co. 1998.

Mynott   J. Mynott. *The War of the Peloponnesians and the Athenians.* Edited and Translated by Jeremy Mynott. Cambridge: Cambridge University Press, 2013.

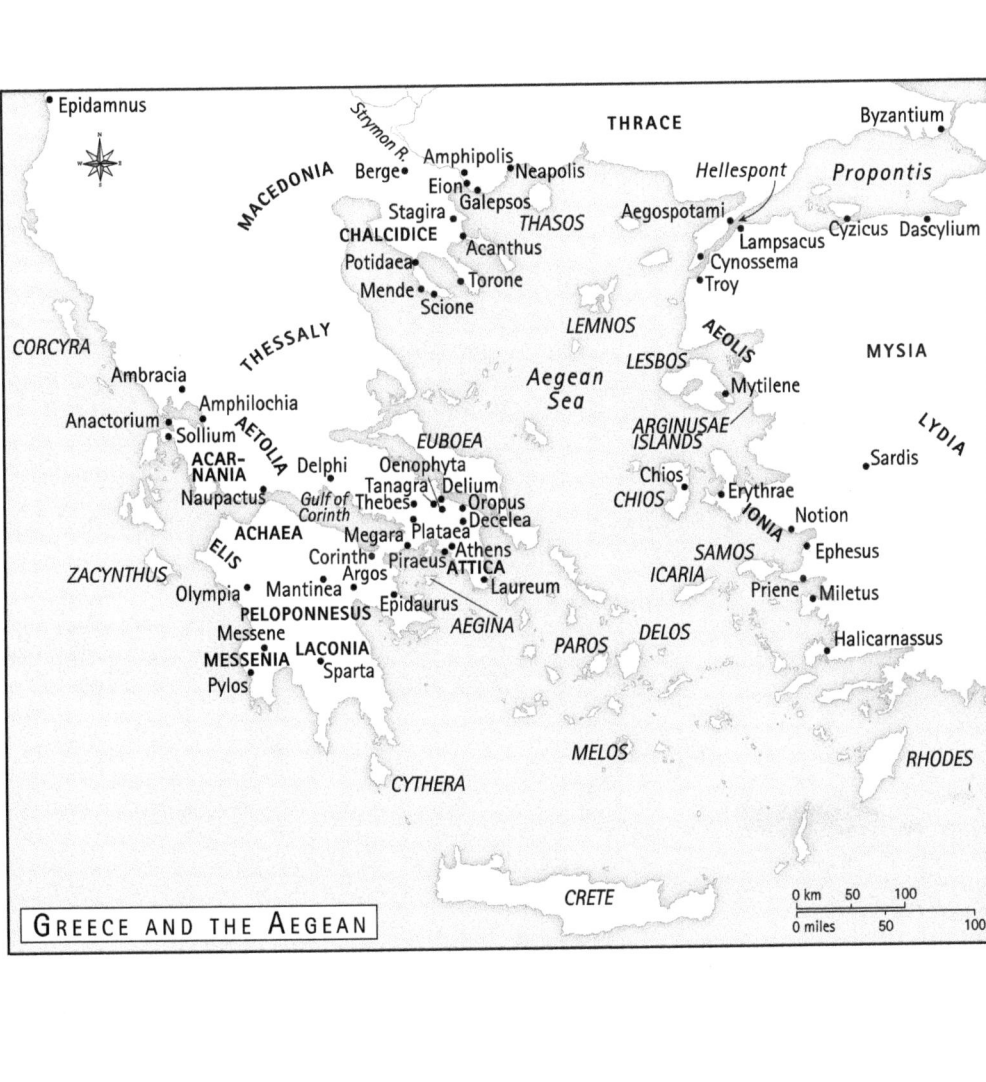

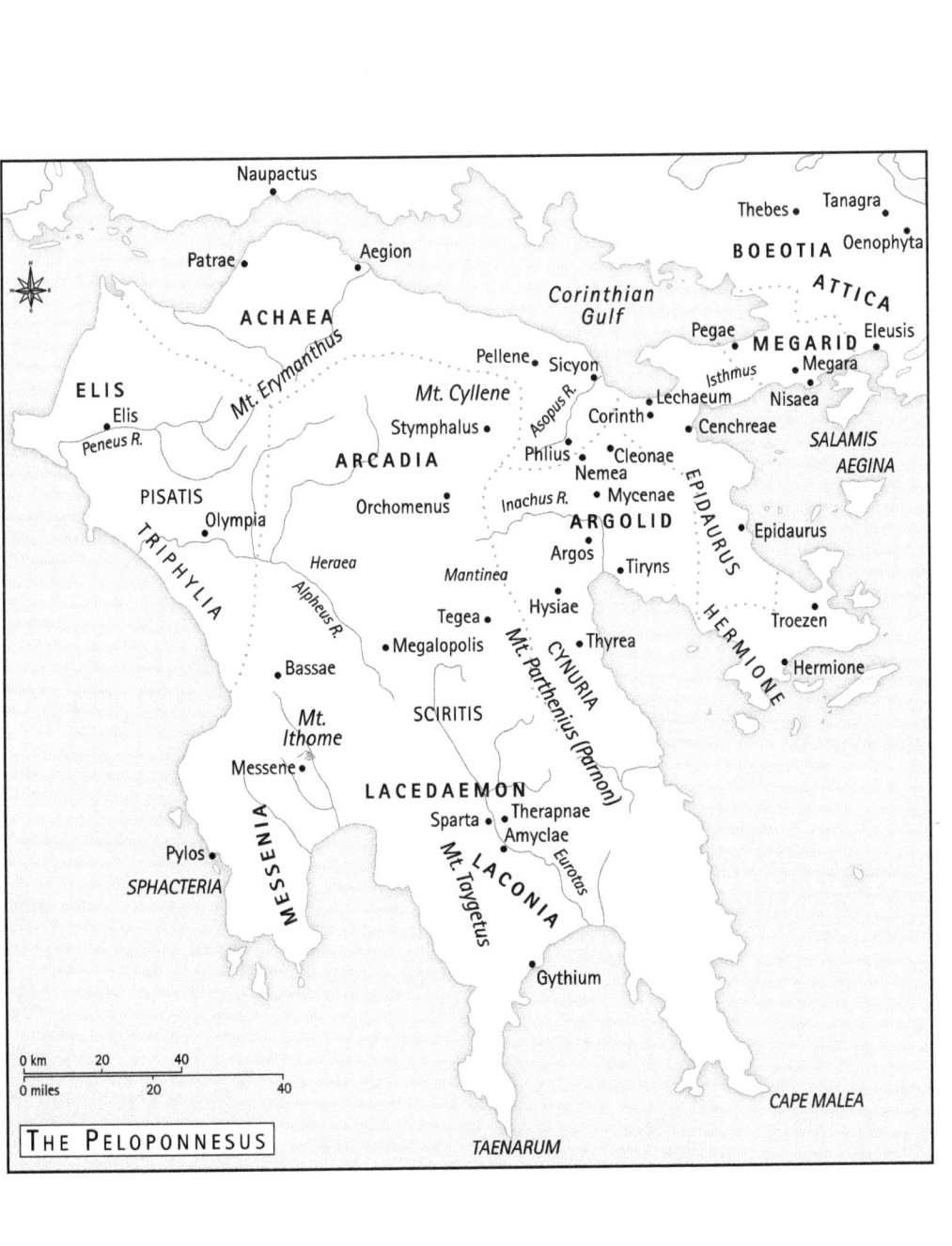

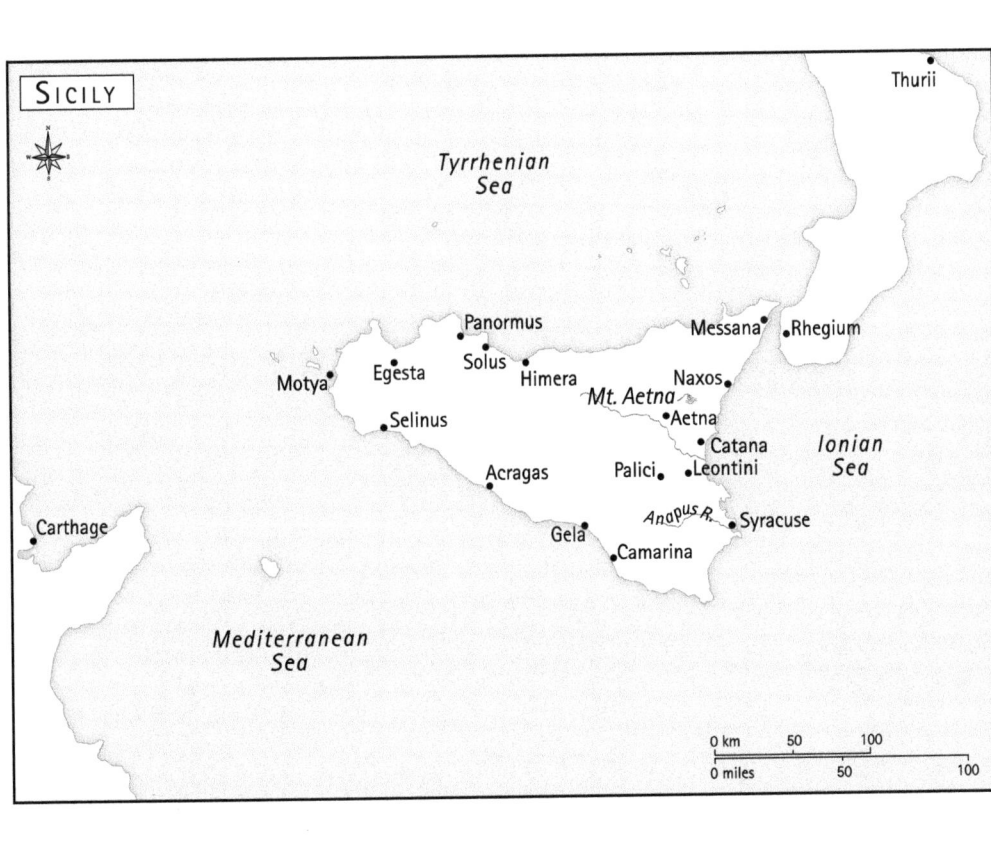

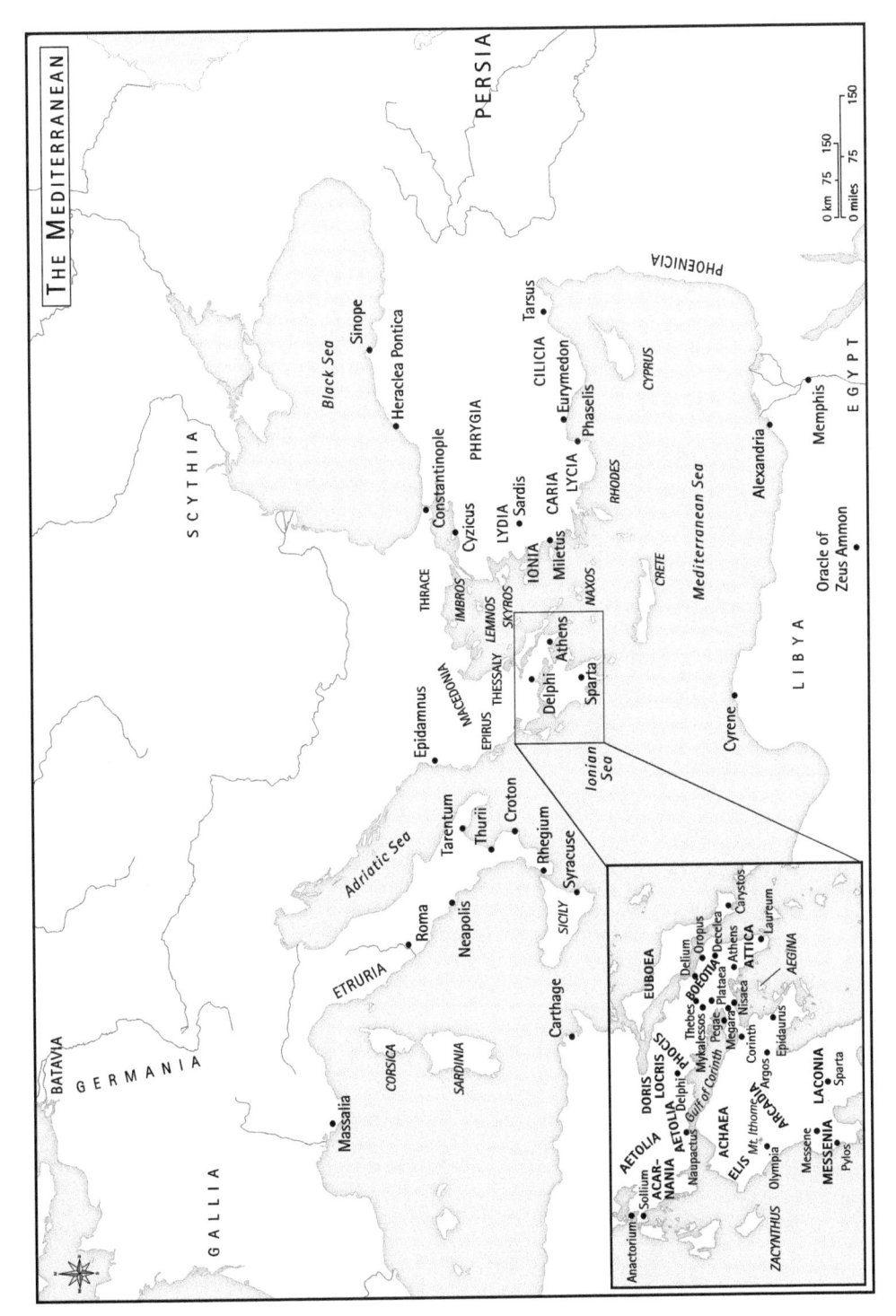

THE OXFORD HANDBOOK OF
THUCYDIDES

INTRODUCTION

In the past century, Thucydides' ideas of power, justice, and freedom have played a critical role in both political and academic discourse. From Thucydidean interpretations of the Cold War to contemporary debates about the so-called "Thucydides Trap," the Athenian historian has hardly ever disappeared from consciousness. We share the belief that we have much to gain from studying Thucydides' *History* and have assembled a range of chapters designed to provide an accessible and useful, but also suitably broad and deep, introduction to Thucydides' ideas. Our goal is to bridge traditionally divided disciplines in order to approach Thucydides' oeuvre as a whole, highlighting not only Thucydides' foundational role in the development of the practice of history but also his importance as a thinker and writer whose simultaneous depth and innovativeness have been the focus of intense literary and philosophical study since classical antiquity. Thus, our forty chapters focus on Thucydides as a historian, literary artist, and philosopher, while also elaborating upon his intellectual context and influence on other ancient thinkers.[1] The juxtaposition of historical, literary, philosophical, and reception studies will allow, we hope, for a better grasp of the whole of Thucydides' ambitious and complex project.

The first section, "Thucydides as Historian," analyzes Thucydides' historical methods and assesses the strengths and limits of his *History* in documenting and explaining the fifth-century Greek world and beyond. With a view to uncovering Thucydides' particular qualities as an historian, the first two chapters examine Thucydides' methods of historical inquiry. In the first chapter, "Thucydides' Historical Method," Sara Forsdyke weighs Thucydides' claims to have described what actually happened against the evidence for his authorial selectiveness, interpretation, and intervention. For all his rhetoric of factual accuracy, Thucydides shaped his account in ways that engage the emotions of his readers in order both to persuade and to move them. Forsdyke observes that Thucydides made explicit the difficulties of uncovering and evaluating historical evidence and shows how he developed methods of critical inquiry designed to reduce inaccuracies caused by partisanship and the imperfections of memory. Nevertheless, Forsdyke emphasizes that Thucydides was keen to rival the literary achievement of his predecessors (especially Homer and Herodotus), in part by maximizing the dramatic impact of his account. She concludes that while these two aspects of Thucydides' method

---

[1] Translations are the authors' own, unless otherwise specified.

are in tension, both are essential to the historical craft bequeathed by Thucydides to modern practitioners from Leopold von Ranke onwards.

In "Thucydides on Early Greek History," Hans van Wees examines the opening chapters of the work—known by scholars as the "Archaeology" (1.1–1.21)—and argues that its immediate purpose was to prove Thucydides' claim that the Peloponnesian War was the greatest war compared to previous wars. Van Wees suggests that Thucydides sought not only to establish the relative impoverishment of previous generations, but also to explain the role of resources and technology in driving growth. Furthermore, he points out that the Archaeology provides a developmental model of historical progress and an analytical history of power that was both innovative and influential. Yet Thucydides' originality and objectivity should not be overstated: according to van Wees, this model was based on Athenian perspectives on their own power at the time of the Peloponnesian War. The model itself required Thucydides to suppress evidence that did not fit. Van Wees concludes by arguing that Thucydides' account of early Greek history is inaccurate and can be corrected by using evidence from other sources, including Herodotus.

After exploring Thucydides' historical methods, we turn to the various aspects and stages of the war as he presents them. Of particular importance are Thucydides' selective coverage and emphases—questions that deserve investigation because of the possible gaps and distortions in his account. In certain cases, scholars are able to compare Thucydides' account with other contemporary evidence, including literary treatments and epigraphy. In other cases, authors illustrate the importance of evaluating Thucydides' positions critically and judging whether his representation of the war is plausible or convincing. In still other cases, scholars conclude that we have insufficient evidence either to confirm or to refute Thucydides' presentation. In general, the chapters in this section provide diverse assessments, occasionally criticizing Thucydides for his omissions and misguided emphases, but often vindicating his interpretations and explaining that his apparent partiality results from his special argumentative aims.

Lisa Kallet's chapter, "The Pentecontaetia," on Thucydides' account of the fifty years between the Persian and Peloponnesian Wars, falls into this latter category. Modern scholars have criticized this section of the history for its vague chronology and its failure to mention events such as the Peace of Callias or the transfer of the Delian League's treasury to Athens. Kallet argues that this criticism is ill founded, since it fails to take into account the purpose of the digression, which is not simply to provide a catalogue of events, but rather to provide support for Thucydides' own explanation of the cause of the war, namely, the growth of Athenian power and the fear that this growth induced in Sparta. She also argues that discrepancies between Thucydides' account and epigraphical sources for the war—which were once used to impugn Thucydides' accuracy—are often explicable by the different information provided by these two distinct types of evidence. Furthermore, as Kallet notes, the epigraphical evidence itself is currently being reassessed in light of a "tectonic shift" in scholarly dating and reconstruction.

Ellen Millender takes a more pessimistic stance on Thucydides' historical accuracy in a chapter that examines Thucydides' representation of the Spartans ("Sparta and the Crisis of the Peloponnesian League in Thucydides' *History*"). Millender argues that Thucydides fails to mention the sound strategic aspects of Spartan war policy and downplays Spartan successes. In particular, she suggests that Thucydides does not credit the Spartans with a serious naval policy. Such omissions reinforce Thucydides' presentation (in speeches and authorial comments) of the Spartans as cautious, fearful, and incapable of innovation. Thucydides' portrait of Sparta's relations with her allies, however, does seem to capture the ways in which Spartan defeats and failures of leadership undermined the unity of the Peloponnesian League during the Archidamian War. This unity was restored only with the decisive defeat of Athens and its allies at Mantinea in 418 BCE, a turning point whose significance Thucydides himself understood and acknowledged in his narrative.

In "Thucydides on the Athenian Empire and Interstate Relations," Polly Low takes a similarly critical position on Thucydides' treatment of the Athenian Empire. Low argues that the empire was a more complex phenomenon than is suggested by Thucydides' bleak portrait of the ruthless extension of power. By looking at a range of other sources, Low demonstrates that Thucydides' account of the machinery of empire and its development over time presents only a partial view. Furthermore, Low shows that on some topics, we are well informed neither by Thucydides nor other sources. Low concludes that "there is almost certainly another story of Athenian imperial development . . . to be told, even if we are not yet in a position to tell it."

The next three chapters provide a more positive assessment of Thucydides' historical account. Eric Robinson argues in "Thucydides on the Causes and Outbreak of the Peloponnesian War" that Thucydides' explanation of the "real cause" of the war is more convincing than the various competing accounts proffered by modern scholars. While not entirely discounting the explanatory power of the most prominent modern theories (including those at the opposite ends of a spectrum, such as G. E. M. de Ste. Croix's condemnation of the Spartans and Ernst Badian's indictment of the Athenians), Robinson shows that such one-sided explanations are less satisfactory than Thucydides' more balanced assessment, which is captured in the twin subjects of his explanatory sentence "the growth of the power of Athens" and "the alarm that this inspired in Sparta." Thucydides' point is that both Athens and Sparta were responsible for the outbreak of hostilities.

In his chapter on "Thucydides on the First Ten Years of War" Peter Hunt gives a largely positive assessment of the accuracy of Thucydides' account. Although Hunt finds minor mistakes and omissions, he argues that these do not have a significant effect on our understanding of the war. On the question of Thucydides' choice of emphasis, Hunt provides a more mixed evaluation. For example, on the one hand, Hunt suggests that Thucydides' emphasis on the conflict of a land versus a sea power (or as Hunt colorfully puts it "an elephant and whale") allows his readers to make sense of the myriad of disparate events that made up the first ten years of the war. On the other hand, Hunt criticizes Thucydides' claim that the Athenians would have won the war if it had not been for Pericles' successors, who abandoned his policy of refraining from expanding the empire during the war. Hunt points out that Periclean and post-Periclean leadership were not as different as Thucydides suggests, and, in any case, it is unclear how Athens could have won the war with an exclusively defensive strategy. Similarly, Hunt argues that Thucydides overplayed the breakdown of social mores resulting from the plague. In fact, the Athenians continued to pursue the war aggressively in ways that belie Thucydides' depiction of rampant lawlessness (see also Balot, "Was Thucydides a Political Philosopher?" chapter 19 in this volume).

Cinzia Bearzot discusses "Mantinea, Decelea, and the Interwar Years (421–413 BCE)" and argues that Thucydides was justified in his interpretation of the war as one long war rather than two wars interrupted by an unstable peace. Furthermore, Bearzot reads the distinctive features of this part of Thucydides' narrative (e.g., the presence of transcribed documents and the complex accounts of failed negotiations) not as signs of the incompleteness of the work, as some scholars have argued, but as support for Thucydides' argument that the peace was not a real peace. Finally, Bearzot shows that Thucydides' narrative of the interwar years is linked thematically to the rest of his account of the war and therefore contributes substantially to the unity of the work.

In her examination of the Athenian invasion of Sicily in "Thucydides on the Sicilian Expedition," Emily Greenwood adopts a more critical tone. Greenwood notes the largely Athenian focalization of Thucydides' narrative and the ways that it is shaped as an Athenian epic on the model of the *Iliad* and *Odyssey*, with the Athenians playing the part of both the Achaeans and Trojans in turn (see also Fisher and Hoekstra, "Thucydides and the Politics of Necessity," chapter 22 in this volume). Furthermore, Greenwood observes that the divergent experiences of different peoples in Sicily are left largely undocumented, and that a digression on the massacre of the people of Mycalessus, a small town in Boeotia, only underscores the lack of alternative perspectives in the rest of the narrative. Greenwood argues that Thucydides frames the war in Sicily as a transgressive act, even though he does not suggest that the tragic outcome was inevitable. Indeed, Greenwood notes that Thucydides uses several techniques to allow the reader to experience the uncertainty of events in "real time" even though the actual outcome of the war was known.

The section concludes with a chapter, "Thucydides on the Four Hundred and the Fall of Athens," by Andrew Wolpert, who argues that Thucydides was right to identify civil unrest, rather than the defeat in Sicily, as the cause of Athens' downfall. Focusing his analysis on the final incomplete book of the *History*, Wolpert suggests that despite modern criticism, Book 8 effectively explains both why the Athenians were able to hold out for almost ten years after their defeat in Sicily and also what new obstacles led to their ultimate defeat. Wolpert compares Thucydides' account of the oligarchy of the Four Hundred with that of the Aristotelian *Constitution of the Athenians* and shows how these two sources represent different perspectives that can be used to correct or supplement each other. Ultimately, however, Wolpert observes that Thucydides takes a far more negative view of the constitutional changes of 411, and argues that Thucydides' pessimistic view provides a better explanation for the short duration of the oligarchy.

The second section of this volume, "Thucydidean Historiography," comprises eight papers on the literary and rhetorical qualities of Thucydides' writing. Although these qualities were closely analyzed, and (as this volume shows) both admired and deprecated in ancient times, modern analysis of Thucydides' writing was delayed by the nineteenth- and early-twentieth-century tendency to define (for example, von Ranke) or to disparage (for example, Eduard Schwarz) Thucydides' *History* according to the standards of a modern conception of the historical sciences. These standards were developed by scholars who wished to claim for historical studies the same status and prestige as had by then accrued to the natural sciences, and were inimical to the literary analysis of ancient historiography. Their power began to evaporate after World War Two. Writers from war-torn nations (for example, Jacqueline de Romilly, Helmut Strasburger, Hans-Peter Stahl, and others) led the way, offering close readings that were attentive both to the complexities of Thucydides' style and also to how these complexities might be interpreted in order to approach Thucydides' meaning. In the following decades the pace of literary analysis of Thucydides and the other ancient Greek historians quickened considerably. Seminal works interpreted the text from the perspective of reader response theory (Connor 1984) and detailed the historian's techniques of persuasion (Woodman 1996). They cleared the field for further study and promoted a renewed focus on rendering close interpretation of Thucydides' writing accessible to the wider audience of readers and thinkers.

Further papers in this tradition are offered here, beginning with three chapters on the structure of Thucydides' *History* by Hunter Rawlings, W. R. Connor, and Jeffrey Rusten. Hunter Rawlings shows in "Writing History Implicitly through Refined Structuring" that the *History* displays many organizational options. In addition to dividing his account into seasons, Thucydides constructs parallelisms, juxtapositions, and antitheses on both a large and small scale. These may provoke the reader to compare, contrast, or relate entire episodes, sections of episodes, or words and clauses in particular sentences. For instance, a series of contrasted passages, such as the sequence of the Funeral Oration, the description of the plague, Pericles' final speech, and Thucydides' assessment of Pericles' life (2.35–65), which juxtapose diverse treatments of Periclean leadership and its contexts, may through its structure help the reader to understand Thucydides' view of Pericles and his role at Athens.

W. R. Connor's essay, "Scale Matters: Compression, Expansion, and Vividness in Thucydides," builds on this approach by providing an analysis of Thucydides' techniques of compression and expansion. Connor shows that Thucydidean sentences can be stripped down accounts of a sequence of events, but can also expand into elaborate constructions that include, for instance, superlatives, figures of speech, and the relation of vivid details. Likewise, longer passages can expand through narrative retardation, slowing down from an account according to summers and winters to become a narrative of day-by-day events; still other passages feature expansion through thematic repetition. As Rawlings also shows, sensitivity to such techniques can help us to reflect on Thucydides' purposes. If the length of an episode is proportionate to its significance, then it may be especially telling that Thucydides elaborates extensively upon episodes that might otherwise seem unimportant, such as (for instance) the Thracian attack on Mycalessus. Connor argues that such expansion is often an "indicator of intense suffering" (see also Forsdyke, "Thucydides' Historical Method," chapter 1 in this volume).

Jeffrey Rusten offers "The Tree, the Funnel, and the Diptych: Some Patterns in Thucydides' Longest Sentences," a further chapter on Thucydidean structure. All who have read Thucydides in close detail know the frustrations of trying to construe Thucydides' long sentences, which may be hundreds of words long and contain many interrelated parallel and subordinate clauses. Rusten's chapter analyzes three common types of long sentence in Thucydides, offering schematic charts of each sentence in order to explain both the overall structure and the relation of the clauses. His analysis is founded on Thucydides' presentation of the main action of each sentence: "tree" and "funnel" sentences represent the main action at the beginning and end, respectively, of a sentence; in "diptych" sentences "the main action is a hinge which opens to the reader two tableaus, a "before" and "after," and displays how they contrast with or mirror each other." Thucydides' accounts of complex events and many-layered motivations required a nuanced and subtle sentence structure, and sometimes great length. Rusten's chapter endeavors to make the historian's long sentences more approachable.

Rawlings, Connor, and Rusten address structures and devices that the reader must perceive and understand independently of any overt direction from the historian. However, Thucydides does offer authorial comments throughout the *History*. Mathieu de Bakker's chapter, "Authorial Comments in Thucydides," addresses the functions of Thucydides' authorial comments, pointing to their value for the evaluation of characters and events, as well as to their potential for framing the beginning and end of narrative episodes. Authorial comments may also highlight mythological or ethnographic observations; this fact suggests that interpreters of Thucydides should not slight these topics in their overall appreciation of Thucydides' priorities. Finally, de Bakker's chapter addresses the prominence of authorial comments in Book 8 of the *History*, arguing that Thucydides' presentation of the increasing fragmentation of Greece and of the conflicting interests of private individuals required firmer authorial control if it was not to become incoherent.

Rosaria Munson's chapter, "Thucydides and Myth: A Complex Relation to Past and Present," makes a related observation, showing that myth in Thucydides is subject to close authorial control. Indeed, she shows that Thucydides' speakers never refer to mythological figures or stories, so that the formation of mythical themes is restricted to the historian. Moreover, she explains a difference in attitude between Herodotus and Thucydides: whereas in Herodotus mythical material is the subject of narrative presentation, in Thucydides it may become the subject of argumentation, as, for instance, in the Archaeology. However, Thucydides also turns mythical material to other purposes. For instance, he employs mythological themes to support social analysis, as, for instance, in his treatments of the origins of the myths of the Athenian tyrannicides or of the Spartan commander Brasidas, passages that display how passionate attachments solidify into stories or rites that ultimately have significant political effects. In addition, he employs myth to evoke empathy, as when he weaves the story of Theseus' unification of Attica into his description of the Athenians' painful immigration from the outlying countryside in the face of the Spartan invasion of 431 BCE.

Antonis Tsakmakis's chapter on the speeches in Thucydides emphasizes their diversity and their "multifarious, dynamic relation to their narrative contexts, immediate or remote." Consolidating our sense of living in time with the war, the speeches do not rise above the limited conceptual horizons of the speakers. At the same time, they display a variety of speakers, audiences, themes, communicative situations, and effects, to mention only some of the criteria Tsakmakis reviews. To conclude "Speeches," Tsakmakis analyzes Thucydides' statements about how he composed the speeches (1.22.4), arguing that these statements are consistent with both the exercise of authorial control and also the dynamic historical responsiveness of the speeches we find in the *History*.

Philip Stadter's complementary chapter, "Characterization of Individuals in Thucydides' *History*," argues that Thucydides restricts his presentation of individuals to aspects that will help the reader to understand the course of the war. Stadter discusses in particular Pericles, Nicias, Alcibiades, Brasidas, and Thucydides, who features as a character in his own account. Stadter explores how Thucydides represents both their words and their deeds and delineates the networks of similar and contrasting traits that help us to understand their roles in the *History*.

Finally, Edith Foster's chapter on "Campaign and Battle Narratives in Thucydides" looks specifically at Thucydides' accounts of military actions in the war. Since campaign and battle narrative make up at least half of Thucydides' *History*, we can assume that these carefully formulated stories of warfare were a priority for the historian. The chapter discusses their function in the *History*, and to this end analyzes the prologues, actions, and speeches of the war narratives. Finally, it inquires into the usefulness and significance of Thucydides' campaign and battle accounts for the reader.

Foster's investigation of the "usefulness" of the *History* leads to the third section of this volume, "Thucydides and Political Theory." Should we think of Thucydides as both a historian and a political philosopher? As a writer who not only documented historical processes for a particular postwar audience, but also addressed general political questions for audiences of every time and place? Because of the universalizing ambitions of the *History*, Thucydides' own answer to such questions was, at least implicitly, affirmative. The third section of this volume is therefore devoted to interpreting the relationship between Thucydides' universalizing ambitions and the historical events that he described and explained. As he stated in his introduction (1.22), Thucydides discerned in the anarchic world of politics and warfare an inner logic that would remain stable, he anticipated, precisely because human nature itself is unchanging. Although Thucydides observed an apparently meaningless whirl of historical characters and events, he maintained that what he saw discloses permanent truths about humanity—if only the observer has keen enough vision to see them. Yet, as the first two parts of this volume reveal, interpreting history as it unfolds is almost impossibly difficult for spectators and political agents alike. Nature—including human nature—is not a generous parent who makes herself readily intelligible to her children. Hence, natural processes and human behavior require significant efforts of judgment and discernment. Within this framework Thucydides presents himself as a sophisticated educator and expositor, who proves superior not only to previous writers (such as Homer and Herodotus), but also to the statesmen and citizens who make political decisions within the *History* itself. Seemingly without effort, he glides from the particular to the universal and back again, and in doing so he purports to teach enduring lessons to those interested in human psychology and behavior as they are empirically found.

Thucydides wrote, of course, before disciplinary distinctions between history, historiography, and political theory were invented. Yet, given the shape of contemporary discourses in these fields, it is useful to begin again by re-establishing Thucydides' own view of himself as a preeminent theorist of lasting political questions. The third section's first essay is "Was Thucydides a Political Philosopher?" In it, Ryan K. Balot argues that Thucydides took up the foundational question of the good regime both in his remarks on Athens' mixed regime (8.97) and in his critical presentations of Athens and Sparta. Instead of imagining a naturally healthy polis, like Plato or Aristotle, Thucydides held up to scrutiny the arguments and actions of Athenians and Spartans, who believed that their cities, respectively, provided superior frameworks for human flourishing. Balot stresses that for Thucydides both Athenians and Spartans tended toward self-delusion. The Thucydidean world of suffering and incessant warfare suggests the likely falsity—and even dishonesty—of political idealism.

The next four essays treat the problems and questions that Thucydides himself presents as most fundamental to the understanding of politics in every time and place: power, human nature, necessity, and the regime. For Thucydides, politics is unthinkable apart from natural human drives to gain power and the constraints placed upon those drives either by the material world, by human nature, or by other human agents. In "*Kinēsis*, Navies, and the Power Trap in Thucydides," Arlene Saxonhouse shows that Thucydides, as for his translator Hobbes, power is kinetic rather than katastematic, or idle; the ambitious are constantly in motion, as the possession of power necessarily leads to the desire to expand power ceaselessly. Unlike Hobbes, however, Thucydides concretely illustrated this account of power by offering an "archaeology" of naval imperialism. The navy is the paradigmatic symbol of limitless aggression and therefore of unsatisfied aspirations. As Saxonhouse argues, the only remedy for power's frustrations is Thucydides' own enduring rational account of humanity's limitations and possibilities.

Developing Saxonhouse's theme of motion and rest, Clifford Orwin's chapter, "Thucydides on Nature and Human Conduct," situates Thucydides between "pre-Socratics," who were interested in the natural world at large, and "Socratics," who concerned themselves chiefly with ethics and politics. For Orwin, Thucydides dramatizes a contest between Athens and Sparta, which are respectively characterized by motion and rest. He thereby directs his readers' attention to large questions about justice, piety, and freedom, and their relationship to nature. Seen in this light, Thucydides' *History* constitutes a deep meditation on human responsibility in a world that both promises freedom to human beings and yet imposes harsh and apparently irresistible constraints on them. Thucydides' narrative, as Orwin shows, continually provokes readers to reflect on political life and its relationship to nature or the cosmos, without reassuring them that the cosmos is a purposeful or intelligible whole, and yet without denying the existence of patterns or regularities within it.

Orwin's expansive interpretation provides a helpful framework for Mark Fisher and Kinch Hoekstra's chapter, "Thucydides and the Politics of Necessity," which investigates human freedom and the diverse shapes of necessity in the *History*. When is "necessity" unambiguously compulsory, and when is it merely a self-serving artifact of international rhetoric—and how can political actors know the difference? While finding their way to a more optimistic conclusion than Orwin's ("Thucydides on Nature and Human Conduct," chapter 21 in this volume), Fisher and Hoekstra too appreciate the radically limited scope of our human capacity either to control desire or to predict and master contingency. With respect to these large questions of power, human psychology, and the cosmos, the "regime" (*politeia*) and its culture establish the political framework in which the transition from cause to consequence originates. Yet is Thucydides (like most other Greek political authors) convinced that this analytic category is the appropriate lens for exploring his central questions, or does he avoid consideration of internal dynamics in his eagerness to assimilate the activities of one regime to another in the international theater of war?

In initiating a series of discussions of the internal politics of Thucydides' diverse regimes, S. N. Jaffe offers "The Regime (*Politeia*) in Thucydides," a nuanced response that illustrates Thucydides' interest both in interstate dynamics and in the divergent cultural contexts that characterized the protagonists of his narrative. While Jaffe employs a broadly Aristotelian framework for distinguishing Thucydides' different regimes, he also pinpoints Thucydides' special interest in the rule of law and in what Jaffe calls "the rule of the wise." Jaffe interprets Thucydides as a quasi-Socratic theorist whose interests reach as far as identifying the best regime, without, however, neglecting the unstable and dangerous international environment in which any such regime will inevitably be located. Conversely, Michael Palmer's essay, "Stasis in the War Narrative," focuses on the seemingly inexorable disintegration of regimes throughout the *History*. Unlike many of his philosophical successors, however, Thucydides had no illusions about the possibilities of creating an enduringly healthy political world. Consequently, as Peter Euben (1990) once argued, one entry point into Thucydides' thinking about the good regime, or even the constituents of any regime, is to consider what falls apart during moments of civil conflict. Palmer's chapter explores Thucydides' various uses of the Greek word *stasis* (literally, a "standing") on his way to illuminating the full military and discursive parameters of the notorious conflict at Corcyra, as well as the impact of civil tensions and civil war at Athens. Palmer's distinctive contribution is to emphasize the role of individual leaders, such as Brasidas and Alcibiades— the first in potentially disrupting even-tempered Sparta, and the second in helping to remedy the problems created by civil tensions in the first place.

Further elaborating upon the operations of domestic politics, Paul Rahe addresses the role of "Religion, Politics, and Piety" in the *History*. "Politics and religion," or "civil religion," is a topic with which political theorists have begun to concern themselves in earnest, as the world's great monotheisms continue to expand, and as the liberal consensus on governmental neutrality increasingly finds itself under pressure. Building on the writings of Strauss and Orwin, Rahe distinguishes between the pious attitudes of the Spartans and the unconventionally irreligious attitudes of many Athenians, including its intellectuals and political leaders (not to mention Thucydides himself). His central question is whether political communities that abandon tradition, or long-standing attachments to ancestral gods and religious rituals, can withstand the pressing demands of warfare. That question may shed light on Thucydides' willingness to admire Sparta, despite his own apparent distaste for religious explanations and sensibilities—and on his ultimate ambivalence toward the startlingly innovative achievements of his native city.

The quest to view humanity through the lens of justice and necessity was rarely an exclusively cerebral one; instead, it was usually shot through with passions, which both informed and often disrupted ordinary political life. In exploring these connections, Victoria Wohl's essay, "Thucydides on the Political Passions," argues for the pervasiveness of politics throughout the *History*, even in the social construction of the passions, of rationality, and of their interrelations. Politics goes "all the way down" into human subjectivity and quintessentially manifests itself in Pericles' hyper-rationalistic approach to the passionate Athenian demos. The tense equilibrium between Periclean reason and demotic anger breaks down when Pericles dies, leaving the Athenians ever more subject to a self-destructive conspiracy of leaders and people, as post-Periclean Athens strives to satisfy acquisitive thirsts that are, in principle, unquenchable. Ultimately, Wohl proposes that Thucydides vindicates his own authority through opposing his historical rationality to the passions of war. In that sense, his own *logos* perpetuates the frequently tragic conflict between reason and passion that haunts Athenian politics throughout the war.

Any investigation of "passionate politics," and particularly Wohl's, naturally raises questions about the general relationship between leaders and ordinary citizens: how do leaders manage their citizens' passions? Are the passions of ordinary citizens merely chaotic and destabilizing, or do they also constitute an important medium through which citizens exercise political power? In order to address these and other questions of leaders and ordinary citizens, Mary Nichols and John Zumbrunnen focus, respectively, on leadership and on "crowds." Like Palmer on *stasis*, Nichols's essay, "Leaders and Leadership in Thucydides' *History*," highlights Thucydides' focus on the "great men" of his narrative, who are charged with the nearly impossible responsibility of cultivating, and then realizing in practice, a spirit of freedom among ordinary citizens. Intriguingly, Nichols finds three eminent Athenians and only one Spartan—Brasidas—worthy of consideration in this respect. Her account reveals the ways in which Thucydides teaches his readers to judge leaders on the basis of their capacity to shape the mores of their followers, not in accordance with standards internal to the regime itself, but rather with an eye to natural standards of human ethical and political potentiality.

Leaders make no sense without followers, as John Zumbrunnen's reconsideration of the crowd, or "mob" (*ochlos*), makes clear. With a special focus on the Athenian democracy, Zumbrunnen calls into question scholars' attempts either to attribute sophisticated epistemic capacities to the demos, à la Aristotle, or to envision crowds reductively as Platonic "many-headed beasts." Instead, Zumbrunnen argues in "Thucydides and Crowds" that the Athenian demos had the capacity to moderate and calm itself so that citizens could listen attentively to the arguments of speakers, and hence make effective judgments. The Athenians' capacity—and, indeed, their need—to listen to others suggests not a Thucydidean argument for the "wisdom of the masses," but rather a complex Thucydidean picture of the deliberative process that unfolds dynamically in the relations between the political elite and ordinary citizens.

Turning from internal political dynamics to "global" politics in "Thucydides, International Law, and International Anarchy," Arthur M. Eckstein addresses Thucydides' presentation of international relations and the causes of war. As Eckstein shows, Thucydides' own treatments of these issues should never be simply or unqualifiedly translated into terms familiar from later discourses. Instead, Thucydides' own examination of justice among states might lead to a rethinking of the categories that have come to seem familiar or natural. Viewing Thucydides as a model for later realists, but also qualifying the realist tradition, Eckstein argues that Thucydides presents international relations as an anarchic and inhospitable ecology characterized by violent conflict and continuous aggression. In his focus on the power of cities or states as collective units, and in his presentation of justice as a merely political or ideological construct, Thucydides is less interested in internal political relationships than readers may have thought.

Paul Ludwig's essay, "Xenophon as a Socratic Reader of Thucydides," by contrast, qualifies the ascription of realism to Thucydides: instead of being a thesis that Thucydides accepts, realism is a political outlook whose strengths and weaknesses Thucydides explores. Ludwig illustrates this main point through reading Thucydides in the light of his historical successor, Xenophon. As a Socratic thinker, and as a cautious and even elusive writer, Xenophon's focus on rational piety and ethical agency helps to bring out previously unnoticed ethical facets of Thucydides' own text. One key difference remains Xenophon's Socratic focus on human affairs—a domain entirely separate from the rest and motion of the natural world that (as Saxonhouse shows in "Kinēsis, Navies, and the Power Trap in Thucydides" and Orwin in "Thucydides on Nature and Human Conduct," chapters 20 and 21 in this volume) features subtly but significantly in Thucydides' text. On the other hand, Xenophon's investigation of piety, justice, and nobility leads readers to understand the persistence of these psychological factors even among those, such as the Athenian envoys at Melos, who most intransigently disclaim them. The relationship between the ethical and the political remains decidedly open as a result of the dialogue among Eckstein, Ludwig, and a number of earlier essays.

That openness, according to Gerald Mara's essay, "Political Philosophy in an Unstable World: Comparing Thucydides and Plato on the Possibilities of Politics," is precisely the posture that we should adopt as readers of Thucydides and Plato, who offer resources for what Mara calls "conversational political theory." Against those who would remove Plato from the turbulence of politics, and equally against those who regard Thucydides as a quasi-scientist of natural compulsions, Mara proposes that both authors invite dialogical responses to their texts—responses that also enable us to set their texts into a dialectical relationship with each other. They do so, in particular, through their multivocality: that is, their own self-conscious and critically informed presentation of diverse speeches, made on specific occasions and with specific intentions in mind, which invite their audiences to subject the characters' ideas to critical judgment. In elaborating this point, Mara shows that Plato and Thucydides can be read alongside each other, as mutually engaged participants in a conversation about the necessities of war and the epistemic significance of studying situations of extreme duress. For Mara, the activities of Thucydides and Plato as thinkers are continuous with the pragmatic judgments and historically situated conversations of both citizens and statesmen.

Mara's construction of the relationship between theory and practice is appropriately complex, given the mysteries that continue to surround Thucydides' own stance toward such issues. His reflections lead us outward, once again, to the largest questions of philosophy and political life. Should we conceive of the best human life as that of the actively engaged citizen or as that of the searcher for wisdom, remote from the world of politics? What role should a thinker or writer play with respect to civic education or political ideology? More specifically, is Thucydides himself friendly to the democratic project of open dialogue among citizens, or is he a stalwart critic of people power? Does he invite multiple responses to his own text, or does his apparently seamless narrative tend to shut down questioning and to establish the author's own voice as an authoritative political guide? Our way of approaching these questions says a great deal about our understanding of the teachings that might be available for audiences, classical or contemporary, of Thucydides' lasting historical and theoretical efforts. Our own theoretical engagement with his text leaves little doubt that Thucydides' universalizing ambitions, and his detailed interpretation of historical particularities, will continue to elicit thoughtful conversations among students of politics, now and in the future.

The fourth and final section of the volume, "Contexts and Ancient Reception of Thucydidean Historiography," seeks to place Thucydides in a variety of literary and intellectual contexts both before and after his time. The initial chapters show that Thucydides both drew on and diverged from his predecessors in his literary techniques as well as in his intellectual orientation. Despite his often critical stance, Thucydides was thoroughly immersed in the Greek literary tradition, including comedy, tragedy, and epic, as well as in the new intellectual movements of his own times, as represented above all by those traditionally called "sophists." For all of his immersion in that tradition, however, Thucydides was also an innovative thinker and writer whose thought and often idiosyncratic style were both reviled and revered by later writers. The chapters in this section treat Thucydides' reception in the Greco-Roman world and beyond, among historians who wrote in Greek and Latin, under both republican and monarchical constitutions, and before and after the advent of Christianity.

In surveying the works of Thucydides' predecessors and contemporaries, Leone Porciani's chapter, "Thucydides' Predecessors and Contemporaries in Historical Poetry and Prose," stresses a distinction between those on whom Thucydides relied for information (Homer, Hellanicus, and Antiochus) and those who were his "true predecessors" in methods and form (Hecataeus and Herodotus). Porciani diverges from recent scholarship that tends to see a fluid field of historical memory in the late fifth century, and instead asserts a stronger conception of generic boundaries than is currently fashionable. Furthermore, Porciani challenges recent attempts to discern in the *History* poetic allusions to Pindar, Mimnermus, and others, noting that the existence in Thucydides' text of poetic tropes such as "reversal" should not lead us to question the "genre-based specificities" of historical prose. Finally, and perhaps most controversially, Porciani suggests that the institution of the funeral oration—in which the past is seen as a vehicle for exalting the present—was a key part of the background that led to the emergence of the genre of history.

Rosalind Thomas, by contrast, argues for a looser set of generic conventions and shows in "Thucydides and His Intellectual Milieu" that Thucydides was part of a diverse group of individual thinkers ("sophists") who did not necessarily fit into neat categories of "philosopher," "rhetorician," "doctor," or "historian." Thucydides himself sometimes borrowed, sometimes criticized, and sometimes improved upon ideas in circulation at the time. For example, Thomas observes that Thucydides' account of the plague of 429 BCE featured a critique of both traditional ideas about the causes of disease and the latest medical theories. Yet in presenting his interpretation of the causes and social effects of war, he transfers ideas originally developed to describe the effect of disease on different individuals to explain the particular manifestations of civil war in the diverse circumstances of contemporary states. Furthermore, Thomas suggests that, in his emphasis on precision (*akribeia*), Thucydides signals his adherence to a principle central to the method of the early Hippocratics.

Similarly, Thomas shows that while Thucydides is often critical of deceptive rhetoric, he also demonstrates his deep familiarity with rhetorical techniques through the speeches he composed for his characters. Furthermore, Thomas argues that Thucydides used speeches such as those of the Plataean debate to experiment with radical ideas, including the overthrow of *nomos* in favor of the "natural" impulse to pursue self-interest. Despite such experiments, Thomas argues that Thucydides was not a moral relativist and that in fact his portraits of social decay such as the Corcyrean stasis imply that he valued the role of *nomoi* in holding communities together.

Tobias Joho's chapter, "Thucydides, Epic, and Tragedy," and Jeffrey Henderson's chapter, "Thucydides and Attic Comedy," explore not only Thucydides' debts to and differences from other writers of his own day, but also his creative adoption of patterns from the past. Joho begins by discussing Thucydides' adoption of Homeric structural mechanisms and continues with a comparative discussion of the poet's and the historian's strategic juxtapositions of longer and shorter narrative units. Joho's analysis complements the chapters of Rawlings ("Writing History Implicitly through Refined Structuring") and Connor ("Scale Matters: Compression, Expansion, and Vividness in Thucydides"), who also reflect on the ways in which Thucydides structures his material. Joho further addresses Thucydides' use of tragic irony, reversals, and narrative brinkmanship ("almost episodes"), strategies that were familiar from both epic and tragedy, before concluding with a discussion of Thucydides' use of Homer and tragedy in the Sicilian narrative. Overall, Joho's essay provides evidence for Thucydides' close familiarity and engagement with epic and tragic paradigms.

Jeffrey Henderson's chapter, "Thucydides and Attic Comedy," interprets Thucydides and the comic playwrights in the context of the contemporary personalities and events to which they responded. A dynamic relation between the two genres emerges. Henderson points, on the one hand, to comedy's engagement with political issues, and outlines "the narrative of Athens' decline after the death of Pericles" that is characteristic of both Attic Old Comedy and Thucydides. In addition, the comic and historiographic treatments of Athenian demagogues or of Athens' relation to her subject allies display important commonalities. On the other hand, Old Comedy's presentation of Pericles himself and of the causes of the war, for instance, differs from Thucydides' in important respects. Nevertheless, the relationship between the comic poets and the historian is closer than one might think, and Henderson argues that Thucydides often silently takes comic material into account when formulating his narrative.

The next series of chapters turn from Thucydides' predecessors and contemporaries to those who followed him, including both Greek and Roman writers. Vivienne Gray examines works that continued and completed Thucydides' unfinished history. Gray argues in "Thucydides and His Continuators" that although the authors of these works took Thucydides as their starting point, they did not adopt his narrative style or his outlook on the war. Xenophon, for example, whose *Hellenica* constitutes the first and only fully surviving continuation, not only extends his work beyond Thucydides' projected end point and thereby abandons his monographic focus on a single war, but also assumes a more determinately ethical perspective on events. Cratippus, on the other hand, both engaged in a sustained critique of Thucydides' inclusion of speeches and extended his narrative beyond Thucydides' end point. In doing so, Cratippus was able to end on a more positive note (the recovery of Athenian sea power c. 394 BCE) and is even said by ancient commentators to have glorified Athens. Moreover, Gray suggests that Theopompus' *Hellenica* was more influenced by Xenophon's completion of Thucydides than by Thucydides himself. The same may be true of the anonymous *Hellenica Oxyrhynchia*. Gray concludes her chapter with an analysis of Diodorus' continuation of Thucydides, and suggests that the Sicilian drew not only on Ephorus but also on several of the other continuators.

With the exception of Diodorus, Thucydides' continuators were writing for a Greek audience that was relatively close in time to the events depicted in Thucydides' *History*. Since we lack consistent evidence for Thucydides' influence in the early Roman Republic (but see Samotta 2012), our examination begins with the late republican period. Casper de Jonge's essay, "Dionysius of Halicarnassus on Thucydides," discusses Dionysius of Halicarnassus, a critic and historian who lived at Rome during the first century BCE and left behind several detailed discussions of Thucydides. De Jonge's paper highlights the importance of taking Dionysius' late republican readership into account. Dionysius' relationship to this audience is puzzling: Thucydides was popular among aristocratic late republican readers, including Dionysius' own patron. Nevertheless, Dionysius criticized Thucydides for his style and subject matter, although he praised the elder historian's devotion to the truth. De Jonge argues that this mixture of praise and blame can be understood if we remain aware of Dionysius' aims, and of the fact that both his conception of historical truth and also his style of rhetorical historiography differed from Thucydides'.

While De Jonge analyzes Dionysius' explicit assessment of the *History*, Nicolas Wiater investigates Thucydides' influence on republican historiography. Wiater's essay, "Polybius and Sallust," first reviews the effect of Thucydidean historical methods and conceptions of historical causation on Polybius, who composed his *Histories* in the second century BCE. Wiater then discusses the importance of Thucydides' example for Polybius' historiographical style. Moving forward to the first century BCE, Wiater introduces Sallust, a near contemporary of Dionysius of Halicarnassus. He begins with Sallust's famous imitations of Thucydidean style, particularly of Thucydides' density of expression and continues with an examination of passages that were adapted from Thucydides, pausing on Sallust's adaptation of Thucydides' description of the perversion of linguistic usage during the revolution at Corcyra. Wiater concludes that Thucydides' vocabulary and analytical categories offered Sallust a conceptual toolkit with which to interpret and describe the disintegrating Roman republic.

Whereas Polybius wrote in the middle republic, and Sallust wrote toward its end, Tacitus wrote in imperial times, and could by that time base his work on a long tradition of Roman historiography. Nevertheless, Cynthia Damon points out in "Writing with Posterity in Mind: Thucydides and Tacitus on Secession" that, from afar, Tacitus seems to be a Thucydidean. His focus on political and military affairs, his commitment to writing the truth about grim abuses of power, and his realistic grasp of imperial affairs, for instance, seem to suggest Thucydidean leanings. However, direct Thucydidean influence on Tacitus has rarely been traced; as Damon argues, to observe that an author stands in a certain tradition is not the same thing as the observation that one author read and studied another. In this chapter, Damon connects the two historians through a detailed review of their accounts of two revolutions, namely, Thucydides' account of the revolt of Mytilene from Athens and Tacitus' account of the revolt of the Batavians from Rome. She discerns Thucydidean structures and conceptual foundations without insisting on their priority for Tacitus, who may have transformed Thucydidean analyses to meet his own aims.

In the final chapter, "Thucydides, Procopius, and the Historians of the Later Roman Empire," Conor Whately describes Thucydides' influence on late antique historiography. Whately explores the imitation of Thucydidean language and structures among classicizing historians of the fifth and sixth centuries CE, and argues for the thoughtfulness and independence of their use of Thucydidean paradigms. Whately shows that Procopius' *History of the Wars of Justinian* provides both the most complete and the most interesting example of this thoughtful mimesis of Thucydides. Finally, Whately shows that Thucydides' influence passed into the early Middle Ages through the popularity of Procopius and his peers, fittingly ending the volume by introducing a largely unexplored epoch of Thucydidean influence.

While there is much more to be said about the reception of Thucydides in the early modern and modern period, such an extension of the volume would make an already long book unwieldy. We leave it to future scholars to explore this topic, along with other as yet unexamined avenues of research on Thucydides and his reception, and we close by drawing the reader's attention to the lively current discussions of the reception of Thucydides, including Harloe and Morley (2012), Fromentin et al. (2013), Meister (2013), Morley (2014), Morley and Lee (2015), and Thauer and Wendt (2015, 2016).

Ryan K. Balot, Sara Forsdyke, and Edith Foster

References

Connor, W. R. 1984. *Thucydides*. Princeton: Princeton University Press.
Euben, J. P. 1990. *The Tragedy of Political Theory: The Road Not Taken*. Princeton: Princeton University Press.
Fromentin, V., S. Gotteland, and P. Payen, eds. 2013. *Ombres de Thucydide : la réception de l'historien depuis l'antiquité jusqu'au début du XXe siècle : actes des colloques de Bordeaux, les 16-17 mars 2007, de Bordeaux, les 30-31 mai 2008 et de Toulouse, les 23-25 octobre 2008*. Bordeaux: Pessac, Ausonius.
Harloe, K., and N. Morley, eds. 2012. *Thucydides and the Modern World: Reception, Reinterpretation and Influence from the Renaissance to the Present*. Cambridge: Cambridge University Press.
Lee, C. M., and N. Morley, eds. 2015. *A Handbook to the Reception of Thucydides*. Chichester, West Sussex: John Wiley.
Meister K. 2013. *Thukydides als Vorbild der Historiker. Von der Antike bis zur Gegenwart*. Paderborn: Ferdinand Schöningh.
Morley, N. 2014. *Thucydides and the Idea of History*. London: I. B. Tauris.
Samotta, I. 2012. "Herodotus and Thucydides in Roman Republican Historiography." In *Thucydides and Herodotus*, edited by E. Foster and D. Lateiner, 345–78. Oxford: Oxford University Press.
Thauer, C. R., and C. Wendt, eds. 2015. *Thucydides and Political Order*. Vol. 1. Concepts of Order and the History of the Peloponnesian War. New York: Palgrave Macmillan.
Thauer, C. R., and C. Wendt, eds. 2016. *Thucydides and Political Order*. Vol. 2. Lessons of Governance and the History of the Peloponnesian War. New York: Palgrave Macmillan.
Woodman, A. J. 1996. *Rhetoric in Classical Historiography*. Portland: Areopagitica.

SECTION I

THUCYDIDES AS HISTORIAN

CHAPTER 1

THUCYDIDES' HISTORICAL METHOD

SARA FORSDYKE

> Now, what I want is, Facts. Teach these boys and girls nothing but Facts. Facts alone are wanted in life. Plant nothing else, and root out everything else. You can only form the minds of reasoning animals upon Facts: nothing else will ever be of any service to them. This is the principle on which I bring up my own children, and this is the principle on which I bring up these children. Stick to Facts, sir!
>
> Charles Dickens, *Hard Times*

As the recent boom in scholarship on Classical Reception attests, one cannot properly understand an ancient text without taking into account the ways that our current interpretations are based on past receptions (Porter 2008). In the case of Thucydides, perhaps no other reception has had such profound influence on our interpretation of his methods as those of the late nineteenth century, when the conception of history as a science emerged and Thucydides was hailed as the ancient forebear in this approach (Novick 1988; Muhlack 2011; Morley 2012). At this time, history was first being institutionalized as a university discipline, and many of the leading practitioners, such as Leopold von Ranke and Wilhelm Roscher, drew on Thucydides for the formulation of the methods of this new discipline (Morley 2012).

In what is now recognized as a one-sided interpretation, both Thucydides and von Ranke became known, especially in America, for an emphasis on history as the pursuit of the truth about the past, based on rigorous inquiry into the facts and free from any bias or partisanship (Iggers 1990, 2011; Novick 1988). While it is true, as we shall see, that Thucydides places emphasis on the impartial investigation of the facts, nevertheless, this interpretation of his methods underemphasizes not only the role of Thucydides' own judgments and interpretations, but also ignores the importance of narrative artistry in his presentation of the facts. While ancient critics already recognized literary "vividness," alongside the quest for the truth, as distinctive features of Thucydides' historical practice, it has taken until the second half of the twentieth century (with the notable exception of Cornford 1907) for modern scholars to give sufficient attention to these aspects of his craft.[1]

Arguably, this relatively recent focus on Thucydides' literary skill, fueled by postmodern skepticism about the idea of a "real" past that we can recover, has caused the pendulum to swing too far the other way. Consequently, the aim of this chapter is to achieve a balance between these two intertwined aspects of Thucydides' historical method. I shall suggest that Thucydides does indeed seek to distinguish himself on the basis of his accurate account of the past, yet for him this truthfulness is not a matter simply of uncovering facts that then speak for themselves. For Thucydides, the key to accuracy is his interpretation of the facts—the use of critical reasoning to assess the realities, especially about the causes of events. Furthermore, Thucydides wanted his readers *to experience events* as he perceived them and thereby also experience the validity of his interpretations of the past. In other words, Thucydides wished to show, not tell, his readers what happened.

Indeed, Thucydides invested a great deal of effort in the literary presentation of events, selecting and emphasizing those aspects that he thought essential to the truth about the past, and shaping in his presentation in order to provoke emotional responses that would induce his readers to accept his version of the past. This latter aspect of Thucydides' historical method brings his practice into line with those of his predecessors (especially Homer and Herodotus) from whom he vehemently attempted to distinguish himself. As we shall see throughout this chapter, despite Thucydides' claims to superiority, in fact, he drew heavily on the methods of inquiry and the literary techniques of those who preceded him.

Contemporary History, Evidence, and the Truth about the Past

The aspects of Thucydides' history outlined above—his quest for the truth and his rivalry with (as well as dependence on) his predecessors—are evident in the opening chapters, and indeed in the opening line of his work.

> Thucydides, an Athenian, composed the war between the Peloponnesians and Athenians, describing how they fought one another and, starting right away when the war began, expecting that it would be great and the most noteworthy of all previous wars. (1.1)

---

[1] For ancient critics, see Dion. Hal., *On Thucydides* 8; Lucian, *How to Write History*, with Canfora (2006); Plutarch, *On the Glory of the Athenians* 347a, with Walker (1993). For modern appreciation of Thucydides' literary craft, see (besides Cornford 1907), for example: Hunter (1973, 1982); Connor (1984); Rood (1998); Greenwood (2006); Grethlein (2010, 2012).

Just as Herodotus did before him, Thucydides proclaims his identity in the opening sentence and states his intention to write about how two peoples fought one another. While Herodotus, however, set out to write about "great and marvelous deeds," Thucydides seeks to surpass Herodotus' subject by stating that he writes about a war that is not only "great" but also "the most noteworthy of all previous wars." As becomes clear in subsequent pages, these previous wars include both the legendary Trojan War memorialized by Homer and the more recent Persian Wars that were the subject of Herodotus' *Histories*. In this regard, then, Thucydides seeks right from the outset of his work to establish his subject as greater than those that preceded him (Marincola 1997). This assertion of the greatness of his subject matter is only the first of many such claims throughout his work—a feature that, as we shall see, often involves the deployment of considerable literary and rhetorical embellishment, despite his own protestations that he has avoided such entertaining flourishes and has concerned himself only with discovering the truth (ἡ ἀλήθεια, τὸ σαφὲς) on the basis of the facts themselves (ἀπ' αὐτῶν τῶν ἔργων) (1.21–22).

Alongside this rhetorical boast of the greatness of his work in this first sentence, Thucydides lays claim to an important distinction of method from his predecessors. Whereas Homer and Herodotus wrote about events that took place before their own lifetimes, Thucydides tells us right away that he wrote about the war as it happened (1.1), a claim that he repeats in his "second introduction" midway through the work:

> The same Thucydides also wrote this account, in order (ἑξῆς), as each thing happened by summers and winters (ὡς ἕκαστα ἐγένετο κατὰ θέρη καὶ χειμῶνας), until the Spartans and their allies put an end to the empire of the Athenians and captured Piraeus and the Long Walls. (5.26.4–5)

While this statement is striking, once again it must be qualified. As just noted, for example, Thucydides' claim to write about a contemporary war is immediately followed by an inquiry into previous wars—that is, the remoter past—in order to prove that the current one was the greatest. Furthermore, although the bulk of Thucydides' account treats events from 431 through 411 BCE (when the account breaks off), the opening chapters are not the only digressions on earlier history (Munch 1935; Potou 2009). There are also significant digressions on the fifty years between the Persian and Peloponnesian War (the so-called Pentecontaetia, 1.89–117), the early history of Sicily (6.1–5) and the Pisistratid tyranny (6.54–59), as well as numerous smaller digressions on matters of legendary history (2.15, 2.68, 2.102, 3.96.1, 4.24.5, 6.2.1). It seems that Thucydides was not content to write contemporary history, but was keen to rival his predecessors and contemporaries also in their accounts of the remote past (see de Bakker, chapter 14, and Munson, chapter 15, in this volume).

There are several other ways in which Thucydides' claim to write contemporary history must be qualified. First of all, a key part of Thucydides' implicit argument regarding the superiority of contemporary history rests on his claim to have dated events more accurately. Indeed, Thucydides is openly critical of his predecessors for dating events by the year of magistrates in office (5.20.1–2) and in other imprecise ways (τοῖς χρόνοις οὐκ ἀκριβῶς, 1.97). Thucydides boasts that he uses a more refined system of dating events by summers and winters (2.1) and, in fact, in practice, sometimes indicates even more minute calibrations, such as the point within a season (that is, the beginning, middle, or end of summer or winter: for example, 5.52.1, 5.57.1). While already in ancient times critics noted that this system of dating imposed a rigidity on the narrative and made for choppy presentation (Dion. Hal., *On Thucydides* chapter 9), Thucydides clearly viewed it as an advance on the practices of his predecessors and contemporary rivals such as Hellanicus (1.97.2).

For Thucydides, this precise dating system was an essential motivation for his decision to write contemporary history since, as we have seen, he repeatedly claims to have written down each event as it happened in turn by summers and winters (1.1, 2.1, 5.26). But there are several indications that these characterizations of his practice are not entirely true. First of all, Thucydides inserts comments on later events at certain points in his narrative (for example. 2.65, 5.26, 6.15.4; cf. Dunn 2007, 116), and therefore it is clear that the surviving narrative is not simply an account of events told from the perspective of a person living through them at the time. Secondly, Thucydides himself acknowledges that he did not write down everything that happened, but lets slip at one point that he made "mention of only of those events that are especially worthy of record" (ἃ δὲ λόγου μάλιστα ἄξια ... τούτων μνησθήσομαι, 3.90.1; cf. 1.1.1). It is hard to believe that this judgment about the most noteworthy events was made entirely without the benefit of hindsight.

Finally, and most importantly, Thucydides admits that the difficulties of evidence were quite formidable, even for one doing contemporary history, and that therefore it was not always a straightforward process to write down what happened. Thucydides explicitly discusses the problem of evidence throughout his introduction, noting that, in both the case of the past and in that of contemporary events, it was difficult (χαλεπόν, 1.20.1, 1.22.1) to get accurate evidence (ἀκριβὲς σημεῖον, 1.10.1) and thereby determine the truth (ἡ ἀλήθεια, 1.20.3; cf. ἡ ἀκρίβεια, 1.22.1). While the reasons for the difficulties were slightly different in the case of the remote past compared to contemporary history, the problem of evidence persists in both cases. For the distant past, the remoteness in time (χρόνου πλῆθος, 1.1.3; cf. 1.20.1, 1.20.3) as well as the literary embellishments of the works of poets and prose chroniclers (1.21.1) meant that there was little reliable evidence. For contemporary events, Thucydides notes that even eyewitnesses tended to give different accounts of the events that they experienced because of partisanship (εὔνοια) or lapses of memory (μνήμη) (1.22.3).

Given these difficulties, Thucydides was compelled, as he tells us, to examine the evidence critically. Thucydides' verb of choice for this critical examination is σκοπεῖν (1.1.3; cf. 1.10.5, 1.22.4) but he uses a range of other verbs and phrases to suggest that he engaged in a careful and exhaustive examination of the evidence (τεκμήρια, σημεῖα). Moreover, he contrasts his rigor with the sloppy efforts of others. For example, he states that

> I did not think it right to write down the events of the war after learning them from whoever happened along, nor did I write them down as they seem to me to have

happened. Rather, even for events at which I myself was present, as well as those I heard about from others, I made an examination as far as possible with precision concerning each event (ὅσον δυνατὸν ἀκριβείᾳ περὶ ἑκάστου ἐπεξελθών). And it was toilsome work (ἐπιπόνως δὲ ηὑρίσκετο).... (1.22.2)

By contrast, Thucydides states that "men in general accept what they hear from their ancestors without testing it (οἱ ἄνθρωποι τὰς ἀκοὰς τῶν προγεγενημένων ... ἀβασανίστως ... δέχονται)" (1.20.1) and "for most men the pursuit of the truth is lacking in rigor (ἀταλαίπωρος τοῖς πολλοῖς ἡ ζήτησις τῆς ἀληθείας)" (1.20.3).

Despite Thucydides' explicit acknowledgement of the difficulties of evidence and his vivid description of his apparently Herculean labors, it is still rather unclear from these passages alone exactly what his process of critical examination entailed. What constitutes "evidence" for Thucydides and against what standard is it examined and tested? As we shall see from the following examples, Thucydides is sometimes able to uncover new pieces of evidence from his own personal observation (ὄψις), but, somewhat ironically, he relies largely on the evidence of oral tradition and hearsay (ἀκοή) and even Homeric poetry itself (of which he is so critical). Moreover, it is largely Thucydides' own judgment (γνώμη) of what is probable (εἰκός) that leads him to reconstruct what happened in one way rather than another. That is to say, it was not sufficient for Thucydides to discover "the facts" to find out the truth about what happened, but Thucydides' own judgments and interpretations played a vital role in his efforts to discover the truth about the past (cf. Kallet 2006, and earlier bibliography cited therein).

As noted above, in the opening chapters Thucydides digresses into the remote past to prove that his war is greater than any previous war.[2] In order to prove this greatness, he gathers evidence of various sorts, including his own personal observation (ὄψις) of current customs and conditions, oral traditions (ἀκοή), and Homeric poetry itself. For example, to prove that there were no settled populations in earliest times, he reasons that the differing fertility of different regions (known to him presumably from observation of current conditions) led to the movement of peoples (1.2). Similarly he infers the prevalence of piracy and weapon-bearing in ancient times from the continued existence of this way of life in certain regions in his own time, as well as the evidence of "the poets" who depict pirates as unashamedly admitting their profession (1.5–6). Moreover, Thucydides explicitly cites the evidence of Homer to prove his point that early Greece was weak in noting that Homer has no collective name for the Greeks. The absence of the word "Hellenes" in Homer then serves as the basis for his claim that the Greeks lacked unity and strength in early times (1.3; cf. Van Wees, chapter 2 in this volume, for a critique of Thucydides' reasoning here).

It is worth stressing, from these examples, that although Thucydides can be scathing in his criticism of the poets for their embellishment of the facts (1.21.1), he also often depends on these literary accounts to construct his own "more accurate" version. The

---

[2] On the opening chapters, or "Archaeology," and its methods, see Gehrke (1993); Tsakmakis (1995); Luraghi (2000); Rood (2006); and Van Wees, chapter 2 in this volume.

key difference for Thucydides is that he subjects these earlier accounts to critical examination against other pieces of evidence, including his own observations (ὄψις) and judgment of what was likely (εἰκός). The use of critical reasoning sometimes leads him to accept the evidence of Homer, and sometimes to reject it. For example, he argues strenuously that the physical remains of Mycenae visible in his own day should *not* be taken as proof that it was a powerful city compared to contemporary cities, since on the basis of physical remains alone, people today might overestimate Athens' power relative to that of the Spartans (1.10.1–2). Rather, Thucydides argues, it is reasonable (εἰκός) to trust Homer and to examine the actual power of cities (evident in Homer's catalogue of ships), rather than their physical appearance (1.10.3).

By contrast, in his account of early Sicilian history, Thucydides refuses to confirm the testimony of poets with regard to the earliest inhabitants of the island (6.1.2). Instead, he uses etymology to deduce that the Sikanoi were the first settlers of Sicily. Specifically, he argues that the island was first settled by people from the region of the river Sikania in Spain and that these settlers not only took their name from the river, but also originally called the island "Sikania." It is likely that Thucydides' knowledge of this early place name and its origins in Spain is derived from his familiarity with the now fragmentary work of the fifth-century Sicilian historian Antiochus (Luraghi 1991; cf. Tsamakis 1995, 166; Alonzo-Nunez 2000, 72; Pothou 2009, 134–41).

A final example will illustrate the way that Thucydides uses oral traditions (ἀκοή), physical evidence from personal observation (ὄψις), and reasoning from likelihood (εἰκός) to establish the truth about the past. In one of his digressions on earlier history, Thucydides aims to show that the Athenians do not speak accurately (ἀκριβὲς οὐδὲν λέγοντας) about events in the final years of the tyranny that existed some one hundred years before his own times (6.54–59; cf. 1.20 and recently, Meyer 2008). A key aspect of the Athenians' ignorance, according to Thucydides, is that they think that Hipparchus was tyrant when he was murdered by the pair of lovers, Harmodius and Aristogiton. In fact, Thucydides argues, Hipparchus was the younger brother of the tyrant, as is evident from both Thucydides' own better knowledge of oral tradition (ἀκοή) and from his use of reasoning from probability (εἰκός) about a piece of physical evidence that he himself has seen.

Thucydides notes that an inscription on the acropolis lists Hippias first of all the children of Pisistratus, and that only Hippias is recorded as having children of his own. On the basis of this observation (ὄψις), Thucydides reasons that "it is likely (εἰκός) that the oldest son married first" and that "it is furthermore not unreasonable (οὐδὲ τοῦτο ἀπεοικότως) that Hippias was listed first because he was the eldest and ruled as tyrant" (6.55.1–2). It is noteworthy that in this digression, Thucydides refers to hearsay or oral tradition (ἀκοή) as a source of knowledge three times (6.53.3, 6.55.1, 6.60.1), but also subjects this hearsay to testing against physical evidence (inscriptions) and his own critical reasoning (what is probable).

As has been widely discussed, much of the language and methods of critical enquiry is shared by Thucydides and other intellectuals of the second half of the fifth century, including historians, sophists, rhetoricians, and medical writers (Thomas 2000, 2006, and chapter 33 in this volume). For example, Herodotus refers to his methods using identical or similar terms to those used by Thucydides: hearsay (ἀκοή), personal observation (ὄψις), and judgment (γνώμη) (Luraghi 2001). Indeed, many of the historians/ethnographers of fifth-century Greece, including Hecataeus, Herodotus, and Thucydides, made extensive use of oral tradition, or what "is said" (λέγεται with Westlake 1977), yet also subjected these traditions to critical examination against other sources of knowledge (other oral and written sources, as well as their own personal observations) and made judgments about what was likely (εἰκός) to be true.[3]

It is worth commenting on Thucydides' rationale for needing to scrutinize for accuracy the accounts of eyewitnesses, since in this justification he introduces the idea of bias, which has played such an important role in the construction of the ideal of historical objectivity.

> It was difficult work because those who were present at each event did not report the same things about them, but rather they spoke according to their goodwill (εὐνοίας) towards either side or their memory (μνήμης). (1.22.3)

Thucydides' explicit recognition of the deficiencies of memory and particularly the distortions introduced by partisanship has been fundamental to his reputation as the founder of scientific or objective history until well into the twentieth century. On this interpretation, Thucydides' position—at least after 424—as an exile from his own city is taken as further evidence of his objectivity because, as he tells us, he had the leisure to be present on both sides of the conflict and better perceive events as a consequence of his leisure (5.26.5). Whether or not Thucydides achieved anything close to objectivity (an impossible ideal, according to most modern historians), there is no doubt that he sets out the ideal of impartiality in these passages and advocates a strongly critical attitude to eyewitness testimony, including his own. This recognition of the potential for bias can only have helped him approach historical truth, if not wholly obtain it.

If we turn now from discussion of Thucydides' methods in reconstructing events, to his treatment of formal speeches, we can see that there are both similarities and differences of method. As in the case of the events of the war, Thucydides notes how difficult it was for him and for others to remember exactly what was said in formal speeches:

> As for what each side said either right before the war or during the war itself, it was difficult to remember the precise words spoken (χαλεπὸν τὴν ἀκρίβειαν αὐτὴν τῶν λεχθέντων διαμνημονεῦσαι), both for me, when I myself heard them, and for others who reported them back to me from one place or another. (1.22.1)

Later in the work, Thucydides has his character Nicias acknowledge the same problem of memory regarding speeches when he wishes to send a message back to the Athenians

---

[3] Fowler (1996); Bertelli (2001); Luraghi (2001); Schepens (2011). Contrast Nicolai (2011) and Thomas (2000, 173n19), who believe that scholars have overestimated Hecataeus' rationalism.

about conditions in Sicily (Morrison 2004). Nicias does not trust that his words will be reported accurately, even in the relatively short time that it would take a messenger to cross from Syracuse to Athens.

> [Nicias] was afraid that the messengers would not report the reality of the situation (τὰ ὄντα), either because of their lack of skill in speech or their forgetfulness (μνήμης ἐλλιπεῖς γιγνόμενοι) or because they wished to please the mob. Therefore, he wrote a letter, believing that in this way most of all the Athenians would learn his argument (τὴν αὑτοῦ γνώμην), with nothing lost in transmission (μηδὲν ἐν τῷ ἀγγέλῳ ἀφανισθεῖσαν) and would deliberate on the basis of the truth (περὶ τῆς ἀληθείας). (7.8.2)

The problem of remembrance was therefore common to Thucydides and generals in the field like Nicias, who needed to ensure that his message reached the Athenians intact. In the case of the speeches of the war as a whole, however, Thucydides did not have the same ability as Nicias to make use of written documents. There were no transcripts of assembly debates at Athens, let alone speeches given in other states and in the field. As a result, Thucydides concedes that the speeches have been composed

> as it seemed to me (ὡς . . . ἂν ἐδοκοῦν ἐμοί) each speaker would say what was necessary for the occasion (ἕκαστοι περὶ τῶν αἰεὶ παρόντων τὰ δέοντα μάλιστ' εἰπεῖν), while holding as closely as possible to the whole argument of what was actually said (ἐχομένῳ ὅτι ἐγγύτατα τῆς ξυμπάσης γνώμης τῶν ἀληθῶς λεχθέντων). (1.22.1)

Scholars have subjected this sentence to extensive discussion, not least because there seems to be a tension between to the two halves of the sentence. What concerns us here, however, is that Thucydides admits the impossibility of knowing the precise words of the speeches, including those that he himself heard. As a consequence, he was forced to compose speeches according to what seemed to him to be "necessary for the business of persuasion—that is to say, the arguments needed to convince hearers to adopt the speaker's suggestions." (Marincola 2001, 78, citing Macleod 1983, 52; Tsakmakis, chapter 16 in this volume). While this admission seems radical according to the (unrealistic) strictures of the nineteenth-century notion of scientific history (that is, history based strictly on the evidence), it is in fact what most Greek and Roman historians did without apology. The difference with Thucydides is that he is explicit about his method, and that his approach to speeches is in some tension with his equally explicit—and even strident—claims to historical accuracy and truth (Hornblower 1997, 59).

While acknowledging some tensions here, it is important also to credit Thucydides for his openness about the difficulties and the compromises that he had to make. This transparency is evident throughout the work as Thucydides frequently reminds his readers of the gap between his account of speeches and what was actually said. For example, in his introductions to the speeches, he often writes that a speaker said "the following sort of thing" rather than that a speaker "gave the following speech" (for example, 3.36.6, 6.8.4,

6.32.3). Furthermore, Thucydides also explicitly acknowledges that his representations of assembly debates provide only a few of the speeches that were given at the time, and even specifies that he has selected for representation only the two most opposed positions (for example, 3.36.6, 6.32.3).

Thucydides' treatment of one of the major events of the war—the Battle of Mantinea in 418—provides an interesting parallel to his treatment of speeches insofar as he admits the impossibility of knowing the precise facts but nevertheless feels free to render the battle in a way that approximates or comes "as close as possible" to what actually happened. In this account, Thucydides acknowledges that he cannot give an accurate account of the numbers of troops on each side and—in a jab at Homer (Hornblower 2008, 180)—also criticizes the tendency of men to exaggerate.

> I was not able to write down accurately (γράψαι ... ἀκριβῶς) the numbers either of the individual contingents on each side or all of them together. For the number of the Spartans was unknown due to the secrecy of their political system, and the number of the others was untrustworthy (ἠπιστεῖτο) on account of the human tendency to exaggerate (τὸ ἀνθρώπειον κομπῶδες) with regard to their own forces. (5.68.2)

On the matter of Spartan secrecy, Thucydides similarly notes that it was difficult to learn the truth (τὴν ἀλήθειαν) about their casualties (5.74.3). Yet, on the other hand, Thucydides does not give up altogether on estimating the size of the armies, and in fact provides a detailed calculation (λογισμός) based on the size of the various divisions of the Spartan army (5.68.2–3). This detailed knowledge of the units and chain of command of the Spartan army (5.66.3–4) was presumably part of the rigorous investigations (despite Spartan secrecy) that he conducted in the Peloponnesus during the period of his exile (5.26.5). On this basis, he not only is able to provide a calculation of the size of the Spartan force, but also concludes his account of the entire battle with the claim that "such was the battle, or approximately such" (τοιαύτη καὶ ὅτι ἐγγύτατα τούτων) and confidently states that it was the "greatest battle among Greek states for a long time and involved the most highly reputed cities (ἀξιολογωτάτων πόλεων)" (5.74.1).

We can compare Thucydides' claim that his account of the Battle of Mantinea comes "as close as possible" to what actually happened to his similar claim that his speeches were "as close as possible to the whole argument of what was actually said." (1.22.1). While Thucydides does not tell us who his sources for the battle were, his account is focalized from the Spartan perspective and it is likely that he interviewed Spartans (Hornblower 2008, 180). Yet oral sources need to be examined critically, and even then one only approximates rather than reaches the truth. This example shows Thucydides once again using his critical reasoning to determine the truth about the past, or—as in the case of the speeches—as close as possible to the truth about the past.

A final aspect of Thucydides' explicit historical methodology (before we turn to his literary shaping) is his interest in causation and particularly his distinction between superficial and underlying or true causes (see Robinson, chapter 6 in this volume). Toward the end of his introduction, Thucydides makes clear that he is not only interested in describing *what* happened but also in explaining *why* it happened:

> The Athenians and the Peloponnesians started the war after breaking the Thirty-Years Peace that was made after the capture of Euboea. I wrote down first *the reasons that* they broke the Peace (διότι δ' ἔλυσαν τὰς αἰτίας προύγραψα) so that no one will ever in the future ask the cause (ἐξ ὅτου) of so great a war among the Greeks. (1.23.5)

As many have observed, Thucydides is original in neither his choice to write about war nor in his interest in the causes of war (Marincola 1999, 2006; Marincola et al. 2012). Herodotus also stated in his interest in explaining the "reason that (δι'ἣν αἰτίην) the Greeks and Barbarians fought one another" (preface) and spends a large part of his history explicating the deep cultural and political roots of the conflict. It even might be said that this interest in the causes of conflict goes back to Homer, who began his great poem about the quarrel between Achilles and Agamemnon with a call to the Muse to explain, "What god drove them to fight in bitter strife?" (*Iliad* 1.8).

Against this tradition of interest in the causes of conflict, however, Thucydides makes an explicit distinction between what he calls "the truest cause" and the openly cited causes proffered by each side.

> I think that the truest cause (τὴν ἀληθεστάτην πρόφασιν), but the one that was least cited openly (ἀφανεστάτην λόγῳ), was that the growth of Athens and the fear that it induced in the Spartans forced them to fight. The causes that were openly cited by both sides (αἱ δ' ἐς τὸ φανερὸν λεγόμεναι αἰτίαι) for the dissolution of the Peace treaty and the beginning of the war were as follows. . . . (1.23.6)

While Thucydides is very explicit about this distinction between true and alleged causes, it is important to recognize that his predecessors were also aware of this difference. Herodotus began his history with the diverging accounts of the hostility between Greeks and Barbarians, only to dismiss them in favor of his own understanding of the true cause of the hostilities:

> This is what the Persians and the Phoenicians say. I am not going to say that these things happened this way or some other way, but I after indicating who I know to have begun the wrongdoing against the Greeks will go forward in my narrative. . . . (1.5.3)

Interestingly, both Herodotus and Thucydides choose to give space in their narrative to the "alleged" causes of events, even if they themselves believe the "true" cause to be different. Indeed, immediately following his revelation of the "true" cause of the war (1.23), Thucydides launches into a narrative illustrating the alleged causes of the war— the disputes over Epidamnus (1.24–55) and Potidaea (1.56–65)—and then concludes with a reiteration of his earlier point that the true cause of the war was the Spartans' fear of the growth of Athens' power (1.88). Thucydides uses the terms *prophasis* and *aitia* in the same way as the medical writers, and it is clear that in this usage, as well as in other aspects of his terminology and methods, he is influenced by the medical writers (Rawlings 1976, Thomas 2006).

When we seek the basis of Thucydides' judgment about the "truest cause" of the war, we are forced again to acknowledge the role of his own judgments of what was likely (εἰκός) in the circumstances. While Thucydides does not provide an explicit formula for determining what was plausible in all circumstances, it is clear from passages throughout his work that one important principle is his view of human nature, and particularly the tendency for the strong to dominate the weak (see Saxonhouse, chapter 20, and Orwin, chapter 21, in this volume). This principle appears as the basis of his historical judgments already in his discussion of the legendary past when he reasons that Agamemnon was able to compel the other Greeks to follow him not because of the oath of Tyndareus, but rather because of their fear of his naval supremacy (1.9.3). Similarly, Thucydides provides a blunt analysis of the naval empire of King Minos of Crete, stating that:

> In the quest for gain, weak states put up with slavery to the stronger, and the powerful, who have surpluses, make the weaker states subjects. (1.8.3)

The idea of the domination of the weak by the strong guides Thucydides' reasoning not only about the King Minos and Agamemnon, but also the behavior of the protagonists in the Peloponnesian War, as Thucydides represents them (cf. Van Wees, chapter 2 in this volume). As Book 1 progresses we learn of the growth of Athenian power that threatens to enslave the Greek world, as well as Spartan fear of domination that ultimately leads them to declare war (see Robinson, chapter 6, and Kallet, chapter 3, in this volume). By the time we reach Book 5, the guiding principle of the behaviors of states is stated in its most raw form by the Athenians as they deal with the tiny island of Melos:

> We know as well as you do that in discussions of human affairs, justice enters only when there is a corresponding power to enforce it; but the powerful exact what they can, and the weak have to comply. (5.89, transl. Hornblower)

The parallels between the legendary past and the behaviors of states in the current war form the context for Thucydides' famous statement about the future value of his work. This statement also importantly illustrates the key role that Thucydides' understanding of human nature (τὸ ἀνθρώπινον) plays in his reasoning about what happened in the past:

> Perhaps the absence of the story-telling element in my accounts will make them less enjoyable. Yet it is enough that they will be judged useful to whoever wishes to examine the truth (τὸ σαφές) of these events that will recur in a similar way in future due to human nature (κατὰ τὸ ἀνθρώπινον). (1.22.4)

This emphasis on human nature places Thucydides' understanding of causes distinctly in the human realm (Thomas 2006, 87; Thomas, chapter 33, and Rahe, chapter 25, in this volume). Unlike Homer, who asked "what god" caused the strife between Achilles and Agamemnon (*Il.* 1.8), and unlike Herodotus, who frequently emphasizes the divine causes of events (Harrison 2000), Thucydides avoids supernatural explanations of events (cf. 5.26.3–4 with Thorburn 1999). While he does mention some apparently miraculous occurrences (see especially 1.23.2–3, discussed below, and 3.87.4, 4.52.1) and religious behavior (for example, the purification of Delos 3.104), he does not cite the gods as causes of these events or describe the gods as responsive to religious practice (Marinatos 1981; Hornblower 1992; Furley 2006).

These passages demonstrate the significant role that Thucydides' own judgment (γνώμη) of plausibility (εἰκός) based on human nature (τὸ ἀνθρώπινον) played in his interpretations of the causes of events. Moreover, when we consider that his judgment regarding causes influences his decision as to which events to include in his narrative, it becomes abundantly clear that he is not reconstructing the past strictly according to the facts. Rather, he is shaping the material according to his own judgment of what is likely to have happened, based on his own understanding of human nature.

For example, in his account of events in Sicily in the 420s, Thucydides states explicitly that he would relate only those events that were most worthy of record (3.90.1, cited above). One criterion of Thucydides' selection of events appears to be their role in illustrating what he believed to be the real reason for Athenian involvement in Sicily, namely, their desire to make the island subject to themselves:

> The Athenians sent [ships to Sicily] on the pretext (πρόφασις) of kinship, but really because they desired that grain not be brought from there to the Peloponnesus and also because they wished to perform a test to see if affairs in Sicily could come under their control. (3.86.4)

Summing up, it is clear that Thucydides' interpretations and judgments play an important role in determining the content of his history. It remains to demonstrate the ways that Thucydides gives the work literary form and shapes the emotions of his readers to align with his judgments and interpretations of the causes and significance of events.

Narrative Art, Emotions, and the Shaping of History

It is impossible, of course, to give full treatment to the topic of Thucydides' narrative art in this short chapter. Many excellent book-length studies, let alone chapters of this volume, have been devoted to this topic.[4] Yet it is important to emphasize that this aspect of Thucydides' craft is *part of his historical method*, since it is just as fundamental as his more explicit methodology regarding the process of historical research. Indeed, Thucydides believed that in order to convince his readers of the truth of his interpretations, they needed to experience events for themselves through his vivid representations. A few examples will illustrate how Thucydides artfully shapes episodes in his history to persuade his readers of his most striking claim, namely that the Peloponnesian War was the greatest war that ever took place.

We have already discussed how, at the outset of his history, Thucydides claims that his war is the greatest of all previous wars, and how he seeks to outdo his predecessors and contemporaries in both the greatness of his subject matter and the sophistication of his methods. Despite protestations to the contrary in his introduction (see 1.22.4, cited above), this rivalry extends to the literary quality of the work. That Thucydides succeeded in rivaling his predecessors in his literary brilliance was recognized already by the ancients. Indeed, Dionysius of Halicarnassus (see de Jonge, chapter 37 in this volume) wrote in the first century BCE:

> the special features of his style include compactness and solidity, pungency and severity, vehemence, the ability to disturb and terrify and above all emotional power (τὸ δεινὸν καὶ τὸ φοβερὸν ὑπὲρ ἅπαντα δὲ ταῦτα τὸ παθητικόν). (*On Thucydides* 8.24, Pritchett 1975, transl. S. Usher)

Similarly, F. M. Cornford, writing at the beginning of the twentieth century, viewed the obvious literary qualities of Thucydides' work as in conflict with his claim that it would be less enjoyable:

> If contemporaries were warned that the history would be "rather unattractive," what attraction would it retain for us today? Yet it does attract and move us strangely; and this appeal is a thing to be reckoned with and explained. (Cornford 1907, 80)

Many episodes illustrate the ability of Thucydides' narrative to "move us," and there have been numerous scholarly analyses of the brilliant literary features of such major episodes as the plague narrative, the sack of Plataea, the revolt of Mytilene, and the launching and destruction of the Sicilian expedition (see, for example, Finley 1967; Connor 1984; Grethlein 2010). Each of these episodes is retold with a vividness and immediacy that allows the reader to experience events themselves, including the peaks of Athenian ambition and the valleys of Athenian despair. Less frequently discussed, however, are the ways that Thucydides shapes even minor episodes of his history to echo and support his claim that his war was the greatest war that has taken place.

---

[4] See, for example, Cornford (1907); Hunter (1973, 1982); Connor (1984); Rood (1998); Greenwood (2006); Grethlein (2013b); in this volume, see especially Greenwood (chapter 9), Joho (chapter 34), and Connor (chapter 12).

As observed at the beginning of this essay, Thucydides elevates the subject of his history by claiming that the war was the most noteworthy of all previous wars (1.1.1). In stark contrast to the rigorously analytical methodological paragraphs that follow, moreover, he expands on this claim in the final paragraph of his introduction in a choice piece of rhetorical hyperbole:

> The length of this war was great (μέγα), and sufferings chanced to occur in Greece itself such as had not happened elsewhere in an equal amount of time (παθήματα τε ξυνηνέχθη γενέσθαι ἐν αὐτῷ τῇ Ἑλλάδι οἷα οὐχ ἕτερα ἐν ἴσῳ χρόνῳ). [In previous wars], there were not so many cities conquered and deserted . . . nor were so many men banished and murdered. . . . [In the present war] there were more frequent and stronger earthquakes, and more frequent eclipses, and great droughts among some and, as a result, famines and—that which did not the least harm and killed some portion of men—the plague. (1.23.2–3)

This passage is striking for its apparent conflict with Thucydides' own critique of embellishments and exaggerations just two paragraphs before (1.21.1). Even the fact that he comments on phenomena such as earthquakes, eclipses, famines, and plagues is jarring, since these subjects were often connected with popular belief about the role of the gods that Thucydides otherwise strictly avoids (see above). Moreover, this is not a one-time occurrence, since, elsewhere in the history, Thucydides emphasizes the degree of suffering as "the greatest" in various ways for events both great (for example, the Sicilian expedition 7.85.4, 7.87.5) and small (see episodes discussed below). As a result, the reader is constantly reminded of the theme of the greatness of the war, and more importantly, Thucydides repeatedly invests his account with emotional power (τὸ παθητικόν), thus stirring his readers' emotions and drawing them into the experience of the war.

This aspect of his work is especially clear in seemingly minor episodes in the war, and particularly in passages in which Thucydides draws out the suffering through the invention of characters and dialogue. In such episodes, it becomes manifest that Thucydides was not simply reporting what happened. Nor are his criteria for selecting "the most noteworthy events" simply based on the significance of events for illustrating his interpretation of the causes and outcome of the war. Rather, he also selects events for their dramatic potential, and invests them with emotional power through vivid detail, direct discourse, and evocative language.

Let us take two examples. The first falls in Thucydides' account of events in Amphilochia in 426–425 BCE. This region of northwest Greece was a minor theater of war, and the events that took place here had little impact on the major players in the war. The episode occurs in the aftermath of a battle between two minor players in the Peloponnesian War, the Ambraciots (supported by the Spartans) and Acarnanians (supported by the Athenians) (3.113). After an initial battle in which the Ambraciots are defeated by the Acarnanians, a second battle takes place between some Ambraciot reinforcements, who had arrived too late to participate in the first battle, and the Athenians, who had come in support of their allies the Acarnanians. This second group of Ambraciots is defeated by the Athenians just as a herald arrives from the survivors of the first group of Ambraciots in order to request permission to recover their dead.

In a remarkable mini-dialogue between the unnamed Ambraciot herald and an anonymous bystander, the enormity of the Ambraciot losses is dramatically revealed in a scene reminiscent of Sophoclean tragedy (Stahl 2003). As the Ambraciot herald gazes in wonder the number of arms lying on the battlefield, an anonymous bystander asks him why he is amazed, thinking he knows the outcome of the second battle. The herald estimates the number of dead to be 200, but the anonymous bystander responds in direct discourse that "these are not the weapons [of so few] but rather of more than one thousand" (3.113.4).

The herald then concludes, still in direct discourse, that then "the weapons do not belong to the men who fought with us," to which the bystander responds that the weapons do indeed belong to those men, "if you fought on Mount Idomene yesterday." The dialogue then speeds up, without any intervening indications of the speaker: "But we did not fight yesterday, but the day before during our retreat. And we fought these men who came with reinforcements from the city of the Ambraciots yesterday." The narrative then continues in the third person:

> The herald, when he heard this and realized that the reinforcements from the city had perished wholesale, lamenting and stunned by the enormity of the present disaster (ἀνοιμώξας καὶ ἐκπλαγεὶς τῷ μεγέθει τῶν παρόντων κακῶν), he went away without accomplishing anything and did not even request the corpses of the dead. For this catastrophe was the greatest of those that occurred in a single Greek city in the same number of days during this war (πάθος γὰρ τοῦτο μιᾷ πόλει Ἑλληνίδι ἐν ἴσαις ἡμέραις μέγιστον δὴ τῶν κατὰ τὸν πόλεμον τόνδε ἐγένετο). (3.113.6)

By representing this episode in the form of a dialogue in direct discourse, Thucydides dramatizes for his audience the herald's gradual realization of the extent of the Ambraciot losses. This literary technique, borrowed from Greek drama, is reminiscent of a messenger's speech, as H.-P. Stahl (2003, 134) has observed. As in Greek tragedy, this condensed recognition scene allows the audience to experience for themselves the protagonist's growing awareness of the extent of his own misfortune.

Furthermore, Thucydides' subsequent description in the third person of the herald's reaction to this realization is calculated to shock his audience so that their emotion echoes and replays the herald's own stunned amazement. By describing the herald as so overwhelmed that he forgets to request the corpses of the dead, Thucydides shocks his own audience, for whom the importance of proper burial of the dead was paramount (cf. the similar impact of Sophocles' *Antigone*, produced in the late 440s). This episode, moreover, recalls Thucydides' earlier description of the decline of funeral customs as a result of the plague (Thuc. 2.52.3-4; Stahl 2003, 134). Both this minor episode in Amphilochia and the plague narrative would have evoked emotions of shock and horror, and play a similar role in illustrating the larger theme of the fragility of human institutions in the face of the brutality of war.

The absence of burial is not the only the way that this minor episode is given emotional impact and woven into the larger themes of the history as a whole. Also significant is the language with which Thucydides emphasizes the enormity of the tragedy, since it recalls the introduction to his history where he expands on the greatness of the Peloponnesian War in relation to all other wars (1.23.2–3, cited above). In each passage, Thucydides claims that the sufferings that took place were unparalleled in the same space of time (ἐν ἴσῳ χρόνῳ, 1.23.2; ἐν ἴσαις ἡμέραις, 1.113.4). This method of emphasizing the greatness of suffering by claiming it was "the greatest" "in so short a time" or "in numbers of people affected" or "for such a small place"—turns out to be a favorite rhetorical technique of Thucydides, which he uses on several other occasions. This technique—a variety of hyperbole—is effective because it allows Thucydides both to stir the pity of his readers for the suffering involved in a particular episode of the history and at the same time to recall the larger theme of the greatness of the Peloponnesian War and, by implication, of his account of it.

A second example of Thucydides' use of minor episodes to support his interpretation of the greatness of the war occurs in the later part of the history, specifically Book 7, in the eighteenth year of the war, after the occupation of Decelea in Attica by the Spartans in 413. At this point in the war, the Athenians found themselves hard pressed by their enemies and hard up for cash. With the Spartan army occupying their territory, the Athenians had to import supplies from abroad, and were effectively fighting a war on two fronts, since they had already sent a large fleet to Sicily and had also to fight the Spartans in Greece, including in their own territory.

In these conditions, a group of 1,300 Thracian mercenaries, who were to have sailed to Sicily with the Athenians, arrived in Athens. Since they had reached Athens too late and the Athenians were in any case short of money, it was decided to send them back home. The Athenian Diitrephes was set in command over the mercenaries with instructions to escort them back to Thrace and to make use of the mercenaries to injure the enemy if possible on the way back.

This is the context of Thucydides' description of a brutal raid conducted by these mercenaries on the small town of Mycalessus in central Greece.

> The Thracians, attacking Mycalessus, destroyed both the houses and the temples. They murdered the people of the town, sparing neither the old nor the young, but killing everyone in turn whomever they encountered, including children and women. They even killed oxen and whatever other living thing they saw. For in fact the Thracian race, like most of the barbarian race, is very bloodthirsty in situations in which it has no fear. There was great confusion and every form of death (ἰδέα πᾶσα ... ὀλέθρου). They even attacked a school, the largest one there, and cut down all the students who happened to have just entered. This misfortune affecting the whole city was as great as any other (ξυμφορὰ τῇ πόλει πάσῃ οὐδεμιᾶς ἥσσων μᾶλλον ἑτέρας), and it occurred unexpectedly and with terrible effect (ἀδόκητός τε ἐπέπεσεν αὕτη καὶ δεινή).... A large portion of the population was lost. Such was the fate of Mycalessus and, considering the size of the city, it was worthy of pity as much as any other that took place during the war (τὰ μὲν κατὰ τὴν Μυκαλησσὸν πάθει χρησαμένην οὐδενὸς ὡς ἐπὶ μεγέθει τῶν κατὰ τὸν ἥσσον ὀλοφύρασθαι ἀξίῳ τοιαῦτα ξυνέβη). (7.29–30)

This episode is remarkable for several reasons. First, the raid, involving as it does some otherwise insignificant Thracian mercenaries in an otherwise insignificant town, was "peripheral to the war" and "a minor event that could easily have been omitted or relegated to a sentence or two" (Kallet 2001, 74). Instead, Thucydides chose to elaborate on this minor episode in high literary style. The phrase "every form of death," for example, is one we encounter in "purple" passages in the work, including Thucydides' account of the civil war at Corcyra and other episodes of high emotional intensity (cf. 1.109.1, 2.19.1, 3.81.5, 3.83.1, 3.98.3; cf. Flory 1988).

Furthermore, and most importantly, the language of the Mycalessus episode recalls the theme of the greatness of the suffering caused by the war, and in turn, the greatness of Thucydides' account of the war. Using the same rhetorical technique of hyperbole that he used in his account of the aftermath of the battle in Amphilochia and at the beginning of his work, Thucydides sums up his account of the brutal raid on Mycalessus by emphasizing its greatness relative to the small size of the city:

> this misfortune affecting the whole city was as great as any other (ξυμφορὰ τῇ πόλει πάσῃ οὐδεμιᾶς ἥσσων μᾶλλον ἑτέρας) and considering the size of the city, it was worthy of pity as much as any other that took place during the war (τὰ μὲν κατὰ τὴν Μυκαλησσὸν πάθει χρησαμένην οὐδενὸς ὡς ἐπὶ μεγέθει τῶν κατὰ τὸν πόλεμον ἧσσον ὀλοφύρασθαι ἀξίῳ τοιαῦτα ξυνέβη). (7.29–30)

By carefully selecting a criterion by which the extent of suffering can be shown in comparatively powerful light, Thucydides, like any good public speaker, is able to emphasize the importance of the subject matter at hand (compare Winston Churchill's fondness for hyperbole). Whether he is establishing the importance of the war itself, or of a single minor incident in the war, this technique allows Thucydides not only to evoke his readers' emotions in a powerful way, but also to create thematic unity across the myriad of major and minor incidents in the history. This is just one technique that illustrates the artistic unity of the work, but there are many others that one could explore in more detail if space permitted.

Conclusion

This chapter began by noting that the reception of Thucydides since the nineteenth century has been dominated by the idea of scientific or fact-based history. While not discounting Thucydides' efforts to establish the facts through critical examination of evidence, this chapter has aimed to provide a balanced presentation of his methods that also recognizes the role of interpretation as well as literary styling in his historical toolkit. Indeed, Thucydides' brilliant *combination* of methodological rigor, insight, and literary style has ensured that he has had a continuing impact on the practice of history. Moreover, as Kurt Raaflaub (2013, 2016) has recently argued persuasively, for Herodotus and Thucydides, fiction was necessary to convey historical insight—that is, elaboration and shaping of the past can impart a deeper historical truth than the dry narration of a series of facts. Good historical writing requires literary skill, and penetrating historical insight can be conveyed only through the selection and shaping of the past. On both these counts, Thucydides succeeded magnificently.

References

Alonzo-Nunez, J. M. 2000. *Die Archäologien des Thucydides*. Konstanz: Universitätsverlag Konstanz.
Bertelli, L. 2001. "Hecataeus: From Genealogy to Historiography." In *The Historian's Craft in the Age of Herodotus*, edited by N. Luraghi, 67–94. Oxford: Oxford University Press.
Burke, P. 1990. "Ranke the Reactionary." In *Leopold von Ranke and the Shaping of the Historical Discipline*, edited by G. G. Iggers and J. M. Powell, 36–44. Syracuse: Syracuse University Press.
Canfora, L. 2006. "Biographical Obscurities and Problems of Composition." In *Brill's Companion to Thucydides*, edited by A. Rengakos and A. Tsakmakis, 3–31. Leiden: Brill.
Connor, W. R. 1984. *Thucydides*. Princeton: Princeton University Press.
Cornford, F. M. 1907. *Thucydides Mythistoricus*. London: Edward Arnold. Reissued London: Routledge, 1965.
Dewald, C., and J. Marincola, eds. 2006. *The Cambridge Companion to Herodotus*. Cambridge: Cambridge University Press.
Dunn, F. M. 2007. *Present Shock in Late Fifth-Century Greece*. Ann Arbor: University of Michigan Press.
Finley, J. H. 1967. *Three Essays on Thucydides*. Cambridge: Harvard University Press.
Flory, S. 1988. "Πᾶσα ἰδέα in Thucydides." *American Journal of Philology* 109: 12–19.
Fowler, R. L. 1996. "Herodotus and His Contemporaries." *Journal of Hellenic Studies* 116: 62–87.
Furley, W. D. 2006. "Thucydides and Religion." In *Brill's Companion to Thucydides*, edited by A. Rengakos and A. Tsakmakis, 415–38. Leiden: Brill.
Gehrke, H.-J. 1993. "Thukydides und die Rekonstruktion des Historischen." *Antike und Abendland* 39: 1–19.
Greenwood, E. 2006. *Thucydides and the Shaping of History*. London: Duckworth.
Grethlein, J. 2010. *The Greeks and Their Past: Poetry, Oratory and History in the Fifth Century BCE*. Cambridge: Cambridge University Press.
Grethlein, J. 2013a. "The Presence of the Past in Thucydides." In *Thucydides between History and Literature*, edited by A. Tsakmakis and M. Tamiolaki, 91–118. Boston and Berlin: De Gruyter.
Grethlein, J. 2013b. "Democracy, Oratory and the Rise of Historiography." In *The Greek Polis and the Invention of Democracy: A Politico-cultural Transformation and Its Interpretations*, edited by J. P. Arnason et al., 126–43. Malden: Wiley-Blackwell.
Harloe, K., and N. Morley, eds. 2012. *Thucydides and the Modern World: Reception, Reinterpretation and Influence from the Renaissance to the Present*. Cambridge: Cambridge University Press.
Harrison, T. 2000. *Divinity and History: The Religion of Herodotus*. Oxford: Oxford University Press.
Hornblower, S. 1987. *Thucydides*. London: Duckworth.

Hornblower, S. 1992. "The Religious Dimension to the Peloponnesian War or What Thucydides Does Not Tell Us." *Harvard Studies in Classical Philology* 94: 169–97.
Hornblower, S. 1996. *A Commentary on Thucydides*. Vol. II, *Books IV–V.24*. Oxford: Clarendon.
Hornblower, S. 2008. *A Commentary on Thucydides*. Vol. III, *Books V.25–8.109*. Oxford: Clarendon.
Hunter, V. 1973. *Thucydides: The Artful Reporter*. Toronto: Hakkert.
Hunter, V. 1982. *Past and Process in Herodotus and Thucydides*. Princeton: Princeton University Press.
Iggers, G. G. 1990. "The Crisis of the Rankean Paradigm in the Nineteenth Century." In *Leopold von Ranke and the Shaping of the Historical Discipline*, edited by G. G. Iggers and J. M. Powell, 170–79. Syracuse: Syracuse University Press.
Iggers, G. G., ed. 2011. *The Theory and Practice of History: Leopold von Ranke*. London: Routledge.
Iggers, G. G., and J. M. Powell, eds. 1990. *Leopold von Ranke and the Shaping of the Historical Discipline*. Syracuse: Syracuse University Press.
Kallet, L. 2001. *Money and the Corrosion of Power in Thucydides: The Sicilian Expedition and Its Aftermath*. Berkeley: University of California Press.
Kallet, L. 2006. "Thucydides' Workshop of History and Utility Outside the Text." In *Brill's Companion to Thucydides*, edited by A. Rengakos and A. Tsakmakis, 335–68.
Lianeri, A. ed. 2011. *The Western Time of Ancient History: Historiographical Encounters with the Greek and Roman Pasts*. Cambridge: Cambridge University Press.
Luraghi, N. 1991. "Fonti e tradizioni nell' archaiologia siciliana (per una rilettura di Thuc. 6.2–5)." In *Hesperia 2: Studi sulla grecità di Occidente*, edited by L. Braccesi, 41–62. Rome: "L'Erma" di Bretschneider.
Luraghi, N. 2000. "Author and Audience in Thucydides' Archaeology: Some Reflections." *Harvard Studies in Classical Philology* 100: 227–39.
Luraghi, N. 2001. "Local Knowledge in Herodotus' Histories." In *The Historian's Craft in the Age of Herodotus*, edited by N. Luraghi, 138–60. Oxford: Oxford University Press.
Macleod, C. 1983. *The Collected Essays of Colin Macleod*. Oxford: Oxford University Press.
Marinatos, N. 1981. *Thucydides and Religion*. Königstein: Hain.
Marincola, J. 1997. *Authority and Tradition in Ancient Historiography*. Cambridge: Cambridge University Press.
Marincola, J. 1999. "Genre, Convention and Innovation in Greco-Roman Historiography." In *The Limits of Historiography: Genre and Narrative in Ancient Historical Texts*, edited by C. Kraus, 281–324. Mnemosune Supplement 191. Leiden: Brill.
Marincola, J. 2001. *Greek Historians*. Oxford: Oxford University Press.
Marincola, J. 2006. "Herodotus and the Poetry of the Past." In *The Cambridge Companion to Herodotus*, edited by C. Dewald and J. Marincola, 13–28. Cambridge: Cambridge University Press.
Marincola, J., et al. 2012. *Greek Notions of the Past in the Archaic and Classical Eras: History without Historians*. Edinburgh: Edinburgh University Press.
Meyer, E. 2008. "Thucydides on Harmodius and Aristogeiton, Tyranny and History." *Classical Quarterly* 58 (1): 13–34.
Morley, N. 2012. "Thucydides, History and Historicism in Wilhelm Roscher." In *Thucydides and the Modern World: Reception, Reinterpretation and Influence from the Renaissance to the Present*, edited by K. Harloe and N. Morley, 115–39. Cambridge: Cambridge University Press.

Morrison, J. V. 2004. "Memory, Time, and Writing: Oral and Literary Aspects of Thucydides' History." In *Oral Performance and Its Context: Orality and Literacy in Ancient Greece*, Vol. 5, edited by C. J. Mackie, 95–116. Leiden: Brill.

Muhlack, U. 2011. "Herodotus and Thucydides in the View of Nineteenth-Century German Historians." In *The Western Time of Ancient History: Historiographical Encounters with the Greek and Roman Pasts*, edited by A. Lianeri, 179–209. Cambridge: Cambridge University Press.

Münch, H. 1935. *Studien zu den Excursen des Thukydides*. Heidelberg: F. Bilabel.

Nicolai, R. 2011. "The Place of History in the Ancient World." In *A Companion to Greek and Roman Historiography*, edited by J. Marincola, 13–26. Malden: Wiley-Blackwell.

Novick, P. 1988. *That Noble Dream: The "Objectivity Question" and the American Historical Profession*. Cambridge: Cambridge University Press.

Porter, J. I. 2008. "Reception Studies: Future Prospects." In *A Companion to Classical Receptions*, edited by L. Hardwick and C. Stray, 69–81. Malden: Blackwell.

Pothou, V. 2009. *La place et le rôle de la digression dans l'oeuvre de Thucydide*. Historia Einzelschriften 203. Stuttgart: F. Steiner.

Pritchett, W. K. 1975. *Dionysius of Halicarnassus: On Thucydides*. Berkeley: University of California Press.

Raaflaub, K. A. 2013. "*Ktema es aiei*: Thucydides' Concept of 'Learning through History' and Its Realization in His Work." In *Thucydides between History and Literature*, edited by A. Tsakmakis and M. Tamiolaki, 3–21. Boston and Berlin: De Gruyter.

Raaflaub, K. A., 2016. "Die grosse Herausforderung. Herodot, Thukydides und die Erfindung einer neuen Form von Geschichtsschreibung." *Historische Zeitschrift* 302: 593–622.

Rawlings, H. R. 1975. *A Semantic Study of Prophasis to 400 BCE*. Wiesbaden: Steiner.

Rengakos, A., and A. Tsakmakis, eds. 2006. *Brill's Companion to Thucydides*. Leiden: Brill.

Rood, T. 1998. *Thucydides: Narrative and Explanation*. Oxford: Oxford University Press.

Rood, T. 2006. "Objectivity and Authority: Thucydides' Historical Method." In *Brill's Companion to Thucydides*, edited by A. Rengakos and A. Tsakmakis, 225–49. Leiden: Brill.

Schepens, G. 2011. "History and Historia: Inquiry in the Greek Historians." In *A Companion to Greek and Roman Historiography*, edited by J. Marincola, 39–55. Malden: Wiley-Blackwell.

Stahl, H.-P. 2003. *Thucydides: Man's Place in History*. Swansea: Wales Classical Press.

Thomas, R. 2000. *Herodotus in Context*. Cambridge: Cambridge University Press.

Thomas, R. 2006. "Thucydides' Intellectual Milieu and the Plague." In *Brill's Companion to Thucydides*, edited by A. Rengakos and A. Tsakmakis, 87–108. Leiden: Brill.

Thorburn, J. E. 1999. "Thucydides 5.26.3–5: The Verb ἰσχυρίζεσθαι and a Contrast in Methodology." *Classical Quarterly* 49 (2): 439–44.

Tsakmakis, A. 1995. *Thukydides über die Vergangenheit*. Tübingen: Narr.

Walker, A. 1993. "Enargeia and the Spectator in Greek Historiography." *Transactions of the American Philological Association* 123: 353–77.

Westlake, H. D. 1977. "ΛΕΓΕΤΑΙ in Thucydides." *Mnemosyne* 30: 345–62.

CHAPTER 2

THUCYDIDES ON EARLY GREEK HISTORY

HANS VAN WEES

THE introduction to Thucydides' history was wrong-headed and stylistically inept, according to the historian and literary critic Dionysius of Halicarnassus. This "proem" would have been much better, he thought, if Thucydides had not "stretched it out to 500 lines" but skipped straight from chapter 1 to chapter 21. So convinced was Dionysius that he proceeded to quote the whole of the remaining introductory text to show how well it read without the padding (*On Thucydides* 19–20). No modern reader will agree: the text that our critic wanted to edit out, a sweeping history of Greece known as the "Archaeology" (*archaiologia*, "account of ancient times"), is now universally regarded as a landmark of historical analysis.

But Dionysius did have a point: a more conventional introduction along the lines he preferred could have worked perfectly well. Thucydides could have begun with his claim that the Peloponnesian War was the "greatest" war ever fought (1.1.1–2), addressed the difficulty of finding reliable evidence (1.1.3, 1.21–22), and concluded that the Peloponnesian War was the greatest war because it lasted much longer than the previous greatest conflict, the Persian War, and involved "sufferings" (*pathēmata*) greater than ever before in the same span of time (1.23.1–3). Notable "sufferings" were certainly an important feature of Thucydides' narrative, dramatically evoked, carefully analyzed, or both, as in the case of civil war and plague (see Forsdyke, chapter 1 in this volume). So what need was there to insert a long account of early Greece?

The purpose of the Archaeology is to introduce another dimension of Thucydides' history: the analysis of power. The Archaeology defines the greatness of the Peloponnesian War not by the damage suffered but by the power deployed: the war involved greater military resources and larger numbers of Greeks than any other (1.1.1, 21.2).[1] Thucydides is not content merely to measure the scale of military power, but seeks to explain how it

---

[1] Some argue that in Thucydides' mind the scale of power and the scale of suffering were closely linked (Gomme 1945, 89–90), and that the ultimate purpose of the Archaeology is to explore the destructive consequences of armament (Foster 2010, 4–43), but there appears to be no hint at this link in the Archaeology itself. One may note that some of the "sufferings" listed are attributed to "barbarians"

came into being. Rather than a list of earlier, less impressive, wars, the Archaeology is an ambitious analysis of the growth of Greek power over nearly a millennium. This chapter explores both the nature and the factual reliability of Thucydides' model of historical development.

Military Resources and Modernity: Thucydides' Criteria of Development

Thucydides states that from the outset he expected the war to be a great conflict "on the evidence that both sides were at a peak of complete preparation (*paraskeuē*) for it" and the whole Greek world was being drawn in (1.1.1). The Archaeology expands on this statement and tries to demonstrate that "this movement (*kinēsis*) was the greatest among the Greeks and a part of the barbarians, indeed, one might say, among most of mankind" (1.1.2). The closing sentence of the Archaeology (1.21.2) states clearly that the war itself was "great" (contra Tsakmakis 1995, 41–45) but the choice of the word "movement" here, rather than simply "war," shows that Thucydides meant to include the preparation for war and mobilization of allies as "great" in their own right (Hammond 1952, 130–33). "Preparation" is a term often used by Thucydides, with a range of meanings difficult to render into English (Allison 1989): in a military context, it corresponds closely to "armament," both the process of getting ready to fight and the resulting resources made ready for war. The Archaeology thus aims to show that the armaments and allies gathered and deployed in 431 had never been surpassed.

The result is, according to some, a one-sided history "which leads from barbarism to the Athenian empire" (Romilly 1956, 285). Others see a scrupulously maintained balance between the development of Athens and Sparta (Allison 1989, 14–27; Tsakmakis 1995, 44–46). Neither view seems quite right. The histories of Athens and the Peloponnese (not just Sparta) are indeed juxtaposed and balanced quite carefully, but ultimately the two are structurally unequal because the growth of Greece is described almost entirely as a matter of moving closer and closer toward the military strengths of classical Athens, while the weaknesses of early Greece coincide exactly with the relative weaknesses of Peloponnesian armament at the start of the war, as identified by a series of speakers in Thucydides' account.

In 432 BCE, the "intelligent" Archidamus of Sparta (1.79.2) tells his people that they are "unprepared" to make war, and will need two or three years to get ready (1.80.3,

---

(1.23.2) or to natural and supernatural causes (1.23.3), so are not linked to Greek armament. Moreover, the Archaeology is closed off by ring composition at the end of 1.21 (e.g., Hornblower 1997, 59; Nicolai 2001, 264–66), and thus separated from the comments on suffering (contra e.g., Connor 1984, 30–31; Ellis 1991, 362–65, who identify a "ring" enclosing the whole of 1.1–23).

82.2, 5). They have better and larger land armies (1.81.1), but the Athenians "are highly experienced at sea and are very well equipped in every other way, with private and public wealth and ships and horses and weapons and a mass of people not matched in any other single place in Greece, and they also have many allies who pay tribute" (1.80.3, 81.4, 86.3). Sparta falls far short in number of ships, has no public funds, and its citizens are unwilling to contribute their own money (1.80.4), yet "war is largely not a matter of weapons, but of expenditure which enables the use of weapons" (83.2). Moreover, the Peloponnesians do not all share the same goals, and a war would serve only the "private interest" of some (1.82.5–6). A Corinthian speaker counters that the coastal and inland cities of the Peloponnese do, in the long run, have shared interests (1.120.2, 122.2, 124.1) and that Spartan leadership will ensure unity (1.120.1, 121.2; cf. 2.11.9). They insist that the Peloponnesians enjoy military superiority on land (1.121.2, 4), and will be able to find funds to create a navy, from the cities' own resources and by borrowing from the temple treasuries at Delphi and Olympia (1.121.3, 5); with practice they will eventually match Athenian naval skill (121.4). The Peloponnesians thus accept that their resources are inferior to those of Athens, even if they disagree on how serious their weaknesses are. Accordingly, they spend a year preparing for war (1.125.2), in part by raising ships and money from Sparta's allies in Italy and Sicily (2.7.2; cf. 1.82.1).

Armament is revisited in a speech attributed to Pericles, who says that the Peloponnesians may have a larger army (1.141.6, 143.5), but "they have no private or public money," and as a result can wage only brief wars against one another, no long wars overseas (1.141.3). Sustained warfare requires "surplus" (*periousia*), not ad hoc levies (141.5; 142.1). If the Peloponnesians somehow do raise funds to build a navy, they will still not have a chance to acquire naval expertise, or any access to professional crews (1.142.5–9, 143.2). Moreover, they "do not use a single Council hall" (1.141.6), so each state will pursue its own interests (1.141.7). In a second speech, Pericles sketches Athens' strengths, above all a large "surplus of money," mainly derived from tribute and other revenue from allies (2.13.2–5). This surplus funds a large and highly proficient navy (1.142.7), consisting of 300 triremes; in addition Athens has more than 30,000 troops, more than half of which guard 20 miles (178 *stadia*) of fortification wall (2.13.6–8). Thucydides notes shortly afterwards that the population of Attica had been politically unified since the days of the "intelligent" king Theseus, who had forced them to "use a single Council hall and *prutaneion*" (2.15.2), and that Pericles managed to preserve Athenian unity despite Sparta's best efforts to foment internal division (2.20.1–22.1).

This state of armament on both sides explains why the Archaeology is by and large interested in only two criteria of greatness and weakness: growing financial surpluses and navies, and increasing unification of Greek states under powerful leaders. These features of the Greek world are pursued as far back as the generation after the Flood. Thucydides does not adopt Herodotus' strategy of dismissing legends as beyond knowable history and confining himself to "the human age" (Hdt. 1.5-6; 3.122.2; cf. 2.118.1). Instead, he tackles tradition head on and argues that the military resources of the Greek world of his own day are even greater than those of the heroic past. The Archaeology thus represents history as a story of progress that culminates in a superior modern world, a conception that has been widespread in western culture since the nineteenth century but was unusual in antiquity.

Although modernity is measured primarily in scale of armament and degree of unification, the Archaeology also reflects a broader sense of "cultural" modernity felt by late fifth-century Athenians. For instance, comic plays of the 420s BCE mock as old-fashioned a certain hairstyle for men, which had fallen out of use sometime after the Persian War.[2] This kind of awareness of recent cultural change explains why Thucydides devotes a lengthy passage of the Archaeology to contemporary dress, which is otherwise barely relevant to his theme. After describing the traditional "luxurious" appearance of older Athenians, he notes that "the Lacedaemonians were the first to adopt moderate dress in the modern style" (τὸν νῦν τρόπον, 1.6.4). They were also the first to exercise naked rather than in loincloths, as was the Greek custom until "not many years" (οὐ πολλὰ ἔτη) ago, and still is the non-Greek custom (1.6.5). Thucydides' conclusion reveals why the apparent digression has been included: "one could point out many other ways in which the ancient Greek people lived in the same manner as barbarians do now" (1.6.6). In other words, habits of (un)dress illustrate how Greeks have continued to develop while other nations have stood still.

The idea that developments in Greece represent something fundamentally new in history helps explain why Thucydides claims that armament, alliances, and the war were the greatest "among most of mankind." To an extent, this claim is justified by some interventions by non-Greeks, especially the attacks in 429 BCE of a coalition of non-Greeks in the northwest as allies of Sparta (2.80–81) and of a huge Thracian army as allies of Athens (2.95–101), but such episodes hardly amounted to the participation of "most of mankind." If Thucydides meant, however, that most of the world had never witnessed such a mobilization of resources, his claim is less absurd (Hornblower 1997, 6, 62). Elsewhere, he hints at comparisons between Greek and other powers. The Thracians of the Odrysian empire are, he notes, the greatest power in the north, with a large army and "the greatest revenues of money" (2.97.5), but, we may understand, no navy. The Persian empire had been defeated, according to the Athenians, by the superiority of the smaller but better Greek fleet (1.73–5). According to another version, the Persians had lost because large military expeditions tend to "fail on foreign soil from a lack of supplies" (6.33.5–6; cf. 1.69.5), suggesting that even the Persians suffered from inadequate "preparation". A similar criticism is made by Thucydides himself of the Scythians who, if united, would have a greater army than either the Thracians or the Persians, "but they are not at all the equal of others in sound thinking or intelligence as far as their means of living are concerned" (2.97.6), that is, as nomads they have no surpluses of wealth to fund warfare. For different reasons, then, none of the greatest powers of Europe and Asia could match the sophistication of "modern" Greek, or at any rate Athenian, armament.

---

[2] Aristophanes, *Knights* 1324–34; *Clouds* 984–85. Also: Asios frag. 13 West; Heracleides of Pontus (cited by Athenaeus 512bc; Aelian *VH* 4.22).

Pacification and Unification: The Process of Development

The navy is the engine of growth for Thucydides. Navies pacify the seas, which leads to private and public material prosperity, which produces the funds to wage naval wars, which leads to the unification of states under the greatest naval power, which produces greater security and revenues for all, and so on in a virtuous circle of growth. The three main elements of this model—public finance, naval power, and political unification—are thus closely connected, but for clarity and convenience will be discussed separately.

The Growth of "Surplus" and Public Finance

Thucydides imagines that the earliest Greeks "had no strength in size of cities or other armament" (1.2.2), because their lives were constantly disrupted by violence. Plundering raids forced men to carry weapons at all times (1.5.1–6.2), "civil wars" (*staseis*) divided communities and made them vulnerable to outside attack (1.2.4, 6), and whole populations were forced to migrate away from danger (1.2.1). As a result, "they all used their own territory only as far as necessary for survival and they had no surplus of money and did not plant the earth, since they never knew when someone might attack and they were unfortified as well so another might take it from them" (1.2.2; cf. 1.6.1). The absence of planting does not mean that agriculture did not exist: the verb "to plant" (*phuteuein*) denotes cultivating vines, olives, and fruit trees, as opposed to grain.[3] Moreover, Thucydides refers to "power" derived from "good land" even at this very early stage (1.2.4). He evidently believed that the earliest Greeks were subsistence farmers but were unable to produce wine or olive oil, crops that require long-term investment (Marshall 1975, 32), on account of endemic violence.

Sea travel was not safe at this stage (1.2.2, 1.6.1), but it was possible: Thucydides stresses its importance in later stages of development, but never describes it as a new phenomenon; he merely says that it became more common (1.3.4, 5.1, 7.1, 13.1 and 5). However, "there was no trade" (*emporia*, 1.2.2), presumably because this would have involved primarily the exchange of high-value produce such as wine and olive oil by sea: in the beginning, violence curtailed both the use of trade routes and the production of commodities to be traded.

Conditions changed when Minos of Crete "acquired a navy" and used it to clamp down on "piracy" (*lēisteia*), i.e., seaborne plundering expeditions, a common and acceptable way to make a living at the time (1.5.1–2), which caused cities to be founded a long way from the sea (1.7). "The pirates, naturally (ὡς εἰκός), he cleared from the seas as much as he could, so that more revenues would come to him" (1.4; cf. 1.8.2). Thucydides may

---

[3] E.g. Hesiod *Works and Days* 22, 780–81; Xenophon, *Hellenica* 3.2.10; *Cyropaedia* 1.5.10.

have in mind the two actions undertaken by Athens near the start of the Peloponnesian War: the protection of Euboea from Locrian plundering raids in 431 (2.32) and the protection of merchant shipping from the Levant from attacks by Peloponnesian pirates in 430 (2.69.1). Such measures created a safer environment in which people could accumulate "greater surpluses of money" (1.7; cf. 1.8.3), and afford to build fortified settlements on coasts and isthmuses "for the sake of trade" (1.7). Evidently, a reduction of raiding made more profitable forms of production possible while the suppression of piracy at sea boosted trade, and both kinds of economic growth enabled Minos and others rulers to raise more taxes, duties, or tribute.

This image of Minos as a peacemaker is quite a departure from the Athenian legend that he was a despot who demanded tributes of human victims for the Minotaur (e.g., Hellanicus frag. 164 Fowler), or even from the Cretan version of the legend, which represented him as a straightforward conqueror, who did not expel the natives but integrated them into his navy (Hdt. 1.171.2–5). Whether Thucydides found his version in another source or formulated it himself, his picture of Minos reflects Athens' self-image as an enemy of pirates. In addition to the two anti-piratical actions already mentioned, Athens expelled the Dolopians from Scyros in 475 BCE (1.98.2), and in so doing eliminated a notorious pirates' nest, according to a later source (Plutarch, *Cimon* 8.3–6). In the mid-fifth century Athens is said to have tried to organize an international congress to discuss "how everyone might sail safely and keep the peace at sea" (Plut. *Pericles* 17.1). These claims may or may not be true (de Souza 1999, 26–30, 38–41), but the parallel with the policies attributed to Minos shows that they reflect a fifth-century *ideal* of sea power, which Minos had supposedly put into practice.

Not only is classical Athens foreshadowed here, but early Athens itself is imagined as playing a special role in the process of pacification. From the start, the city was an exception to the rule of violence: Attica had only "thin soil," but this lack of agricultural potential meant that civil war and migration did not occur (1.2.5); instead, exiles and migrants from the rest of Greece moved to Athens "because it was stable," so that the population grew (1.2.6). In view of their stability, it is no coincidence that "the Athenians were the first to put down iron," i.e., stopped carrying weapons in daily life, and, "relaxing their lifestyle, changed to something more luxurious" (1.6.3). The context suggests that this is supposed to have happened before the Trojan War. A plausible period for the adoption of more peaceful habits is the time of Theseus' unification of Attica, which put an end to internal wars (2.15.1–2).

Although financial resources were growing, they were still relatively small by the time of the Trojan War, Thucydides argues, and this limited the scale and effectiveness of Greek armies. He calculates that 102,000 Greeks came to Troy, but concludes that this is "not many, given that they were sent out from the whole of Hellas collectively" (1.10.5). More manpower would have been available but "lack of money" (ἀχρηματία) and "a shortage of supplies" (τῆς γὰρ τροφῆς ἀπορία) meant that Agamemnon brought only as many men as could be sustained from local resources, by raiding and by cultivating land in the Chersonese opposite Troy (1.11.1). "If they had come with a surplus of provisions," the Greeks would have overwhelmed Troy, but the manpower devoted to ad hoc provisioning undermined the war effort (1.11.2). All other Greek powers also remained "weak on account of a lack of money" (ibid.). Thus early Greece shared the most serious weakness in the armament of the contemporary Peloponnese, and suffered the same lack of supplies that in one version of events had caused the Persian invasion to fail. Athens, by contrast, was able to pay wages which its soldiers and rowers used to buy provisions from merchants or in local markets, or on occasion even from shiploads of supplies sent along by the city itself (Thuc. 6.21.2–22).

Thucydides states simply that "it is apparent" that a lack of finance forced the Greeks at Troy to cultivate their own food as well as raid for supplies. This is remarkable because, although raids are often mentioned (e.g., *Il.* 9.328–29; *Od.* 3.105–6), the epics say nothing about farming the Chersonese. I would suggest that this story was a local Athenian tradition, because an ancient commentator on Thucydides (1.11.1) explains that the cultivators "were led by Acamas and Antimachus," and Acamas was a son of Theseus, who ought to have been at Troy but, embarrassingly for the Athenians, was not mentioned in the *Iliad*. The story may thus have been invented in order to provide a respectable reason for Acamas' absence from the action, while simultaneously staking a claim to ownership of the Chersonese, which was colonized by Athens from c. 550 BCE onward (Hdt. 6.34–39).

After the Trojan War, Thucydides imagines, Greece once again suffered civil wars (1.12.2) and migrations, "so that they could not experience growth in tranquillity" (ἡσυχάσασαν αὐξηθῆναι, 1.12.1). It took a long time for Greece to be "stably pacified" again (1.12.4) and reach the next level of economic prosperity: people "engaged still more than previously in the acquisition of money" and "revenues became greater" (1.13.1). Corinth led the way: always "powerful in wealth" owing to transit trade by land, they made the most of the rise of seafaring: "acquiring their ships, they put down piracy and by providing a trading post (*emporion*) for land and sea, they kept their city powerful through revenues of money" (1.13.5). Again, the suppression of violence, especially maritime raiding, stimulates the growth of private and public wealth, especially through trade and taxes on trade.

At this point, the story of economic growth ends, but the story of the development of navies and the unification of Greek states continues, and accelerates.

Ships and Navies

For most of Greek history, navies consisted of the same type of ship used by pirates and raiders. Thucydides demonstrates this in detail for the vessels in the *Iliad*'s Catalogue of Ships, which mentioned crews of 120 and 50 men (*Il.* 2.510, 720–21), "indicating, it seems to me, the largest and the smallest," consisting of soldiers who did their own rowing (*Il.* 2.720–21), and leaving no room for passengers because their vessels were not "enclosed," i.e., with decks, but "built in a more piratical style in the ancient manner" (1.10.4). During the Trojan War and for many centuries thereafter, even the greatest navies were formed of such "pentekontors and long ships" (1.14.1, 3). The implied contrast is with the classical

Greek warship, the trireme, which had crew of 200, mostly specialist oarsmen, and enough room on deck for up to 40 "passengers" (Hdt. 6.15.1; Morrison et al. 2000, 107–26). The only advantage which early navies had over pirate fleets would thus have been their size, but Thucydides does not go into the details of their scale or organization.

After the first creation of a navy by Minos, the next major development took place only when the highest level of economic growth was reached:

> Greece equipped navies, and they embraced the sea more. The Corinthians are said to have been the first to handle matters relating to ships in much the same way as we do now, and triremes were first built in Greece at Corinth. (1.13.1–2)

Since Thucydides has told us very little about the nature of earlier navies, it remains obscure to what innovation, apart from the building of triremes, he refers. The verb "to handle" (μεταχειρίσαι), however, suggests a change in organization, and such a change would certainly have been necessary when triremes replaced pentekontors. Pentekontors were used in private raiding ventures, and early navies almost certainly consisted simply of privately owned ships mobilized for public expeditions, so that little central naval organization was required. The trireme, by contrast, with its large crew and small number of soldiers, was too expensive for almost all private ship owners and unsuitable for piratical activity. Building and maintaining triremes required public intervention, and this centralization of naval resources is surely what Thucydides had in mind (van Wees 2013).

The creation of navies is closely associated with the establishment of "tyrannies", "as revenues grew larger; previously there were hereditary kingships with agreed privileges" (1.13.1). The precise connection between tyrants and navies is left obscure, perhaps because Thucydides will later show tyrants in a negative light and does not want to give them credit for playing a positive role here, but the elliptically expressed idea is evidently that some individuals acquire so much wealth that they are able to acquire a position of greater power than traditional rulers were able to wield (Hornblower 1997, 42). Tyrannies thus represented a centralization of power, and this facilitated the development of modern navies.

The third stage of naval development involved the complete replacement of pentekontors by triremes, which had initially been built only in small numbers. This happened in Sicily and Corcyra c. 490 BCE (1.14.2), and at Athens shortly before 480 BCE, when Themistocles instigated expansion and modernization of the fleet (1.14.3), so that the Athenians "became naval people" (*nautikoi*, 1.18.2); he "was the first who dared propose that they embrace the sea" (1.93.3–4). In 480 BCE Athens contributed "a bit less than two-thirds" of 400 Greek vessels in total (1.74.1), i.e., 250 triremes, which for Thucydides was as large as the Athenian fleet ever became; he records that 250 ships, including 100 patrol vessels, was the highest number of Athenian ships at sea during the Peloponnesian War (3.17).

Straining to find any further naval development after the Persian War, Thucydides can only point to the trivial fact that triremes acquired "full-length decks" (1.14.3), and, as we have seen, to the high level of skill acquired by the Athenians in naval warfare (1.18.3). The most significant development after the Persian War was a new kind of political unity.

"Slavery for the Sake of Profit": The Unification of Greece

"It seems to me," says Thucydides (twice), that Greece was originally so divided that it did not even have the name "Hellas" yet, but each region was named after its own "tribe"; hence non-Greeks were not yet collectively known as "barbarians" either (1.3.2–3). This personal opinion is based on a skewed reading of the evidence, as we shall see, but the notion that Greece moved from extreme division and lack of any collective action to the point where the whole Greek world was involved in the Peloponnesian War is central to his model of history.

The first step towards unification was the spread of the name Hellenes from the subjects of Hellen, son of Deucalion, in Phthiotis (1.3.3) to other places, "as Hellen and his sons grew strong ... and they were brought in by the other cities to their benefit" (1.3.2). In other words, cities asked powerful outsiders for help, presumably to settle internal disputes or to provide military aid—much as Athens and Sparta later intervened in other states and brought these under their leadership (see e.g., 1.19; 1.75.2)—and this created a sense of unity.

Minos unified much of the Aegean by conquest, and expanded the Greek world by expelling native Carians from Cycladic islands and settling the first Greeks there (1.4; 1.8.2). This was only one example of a more general phenomenon: "for in their desire for profits the lesser put up with slavery to the stronger, and the more powerful with their surpluses made the smaller cities their subjects" (1.8.3). Thucydides here offers a striking vision of an international order that is based on coercion—rich cities convert their wealth into military power and conquer poorer cities—but is nevertheless materially advantageous even to the subjects. Political "slavery" is a price worth paying for greater security and prosperity. The contemporary parallels with the hierarchical leagues of Athens and Sparta are obvious, and the Athenians liked to stress that their alliance benefited all members (Thuc. 1.73.2–75.2).

The process of integration by force culminated in Agamemnon's leadership of all Greeks. "He predominated in power", contrary to the legend that said he merely led a coalition of his peers (1.9.1). "Because he had a stronger navy than the others," he assembled an army "not so much by asking favors as by inspiring fear" (1.9.3), and "we must infer from this expedition what the earlier ones were like" (1.9.4). In other words, unity was achieved by submission to the greatest naval power, and any earlier wars uniting part of Greece must also have been led by sea powers. Once again, Thucydides flags up this notion as his own (μοι δοκεῖ, twice, 1.9.2–3), and it is indeed unusual. A more obvious approach would have been to treat Agamemnon as a forerunner of Sparta's hegemonic position, achieved primarily by land-based expansion. This notion was cultivated by Sparta itself and reflected in Spartan cults for Agamemnon's son and his herald

Talthybius (Herodotus 1.67; 7.134, 159). Archaic poets even called Agamemnon king of Sparta (Stesichoros frag. 216; Simonides fr. 549 Page). Thucydides, however, ignores all this and makes Agamemnon a thalassocrat, like Athens.

After the Trojan War, the Greek world expanded. "The Athenians settled the Ionians and most of the islanders; the Peloponnesians most of Italy and Sicily and some places in the rest of Greece" (1.12.4). This formulation again departs from tradition, which linked the so-called Ionian migration from Athens with the migrations of Thessalians, Boeotians, and Dorians not long after the Trojan War. Thucydides notes the early dates of the latter, 60 and 80 years after the fall of Troy, and treats these movements as evidence of instability (1.12.1–3; cf. 1.2.3–6), but he does not date the Ionian migration, associates it with the much later colonization of southern Italy and Sicily (cf. 6.2.3, 5), and treats it as evidence of growth and prosperity (1.12.4; cf. 1.2.6). Thucydides does not mention the post–Trojan War migration of Aeolians at all, although he is aware of it (3.2.3; 7.57.5; 8.100.3). Migration traditions are thus manipulated to give the impression that Greek expansion was evenly shared between the protagonists of the Peloponnesian War: Athenians went east; Peloponnesians went west.

In this new, larger Greek world, the new, modern navies built by Corinth and others again coerced communities into larger political units. Polycrates, tyrant of Samos, "made the other islands subject" (1.13.6), the tyrants in Sicily also acquired considerable power (1.17), and generally naval warfare "increased strength in revenues of money and rule over others" (1.15.1). However, the tyrants did not use their funds and fleets as much as they might have done, because they were interested only in personal security and private wealth, so "they administered their cities as much as possible in safety," rather than wage war. The pursuit of self-interest also prevented unity among states: "everywhere, Greece was for a long time in a condition where it could achieve nothing conspicuous collectively, and individual cities were quite risk-averse" (ἀτολμοτέρα, 1.17). The inhibiting effect of self-interest is, as we have seen, repeatedly identified as a key Peloponnesian weakness in 431BCE, too.

Even more remarkable is Thucydides' claim that the main strength of the Peloponnesian coalition, its infantry army, had contributed nothing to the political unification of Greece.

> On land, no war took place that resulted in any increase in power. Such wars as did occur were all fought by cities against their own neighbors, and the Greeks did not venture out on foreign campaigns far from their own territory in order to conquer others. Subjects did not unite with the greatest cities, nor did the latter campaign together as equals, but they waged war by themselves, each against their neighbors (1.15.2).

This bold statement is in direct contradiction with what Thucydides himself says elsewhere about Sparta, which had "strength on land" (1.18.2) but lacked a navy and public funds, yet somehow "occupied two-fifths of the Peloponnese and led the whole of it as well as many external allies" (1.10.2), having put down tyrannical regimes across the

Greek world (1.18.1), and made itself "preeminent in power" in Greece by 480 BC (1.18.2). Sparta's role in Thucydides' model is not as an expansionist power in its own right, but as a facilitator of development in other states by removing the control of self-interested tyrants and so enabling the liberated cities to make full use of their financial and military potential. Sparta is able to intervene in this way, not because of its great army, but because it avoids all internal conflict. The Spartans have enjoyed "good order" and absence of tyranny for "a little more than 400 years until the end of the present war … and because of this they were able to regulate matters in other cities, too" (1.18.1). This radical denial of the role of land warfare shows just how crucial naval power is in Thucydides' thinking, along with political stability.

The final stages of political unification are the creation of Athens' league of former subjects of the Persian Empire, described in much more detail later (1.94–97.1), and the process by which the Greek world outside the Spartan and Athenian alliance systems gradually joined either side (1.18.2). One last time the superiority of Athenian power is emphasized. Sparta did not levy tribute, but imposed on their allies "an oligarchic regime orientated towards the Spartans alone" (1.19; cf. 1.144.2). Athens, by contrast, used its power to generate more money and military resources. "Over time, the Athenians took the ships from the cities … and ordered everyone to contribute money. And their individual armament for this war was greater than when they were at their most flourishing while the alliance was intact" (1.19). Despite the ambiguous wording, the general drift of Thucydides' argument makes its meaning clear enough: by 431 BC, Athens alone possessed greater resources than the whole Greek alliance had done at the time of the Persian War (Hornblower 1997, 56).

In short, navies pacify and unify the Greek world, by force but ultimately to the benefit of all, because greater stability and unity afford greater opportunities for individuals and cities to pursue "profits," albeit at the cost of political "slavery." This vision reflects Thucydides' perception at the start of the war that Athens' financial resources, armaments, and even aspects of its way of life represented a peak of power and modernity, while their opponents remained to some degree stuck in the past. Until summer 424 at least, most Athenians will have shared this view: "they thought nothing could stop them, and they would achieve the possible and the quite unfeasible alike, just as easily with great as with inadequate armament" (4.65.4); they even set their sights on the conquest of Carthage.[4] Soon after, the first military setbacks occurred, and Thucydides himself was exiled as a result, but even so the city remained in a position of great strength when the Peace of Nicias was concluded in 421. The Archaeology's criteria of historical progress had not yet been seriously undermined.

Athens' superiority was much less obvious after the failure of the Sicilian expedition in 413, let alone after the final defeat of the city, when Sparta had acquired public funds and a large navy thanks to Persian funding. After 413 or 404, one might have expected Thucydides no longer to see the Athenian empire as the culmination of Greek history. A less positive attitude to naval power and public finance can indeed be detected in

---

[4] Aristophanes, *Knights* 1303–304; cf. Thuc. 6.15, 90; Plut. *Pericles* 20.3.

the second part of his history (Kallet 2001). However, if the Archaeology was written not long after 421 BCE—the end of "the first war," as Thucydides originally conceived it before he decided to cover later events as well (5.24.2–26.4)—it is not surprising that in Thucydides' vision contemporary Athens was the model for all earlier powers, and ancient Athens a leading force for progress.

THE ARCHAEOLOGY AND EARLY GREEK HISTORY

Thucydides tries to persuade the reader that he was right to think, from the start, that the Peloponnesian War would be the greatest conflict ever. In order to do so, he needed to refer as much as possible to historical "facts" with which his audience was familiar, rather than rely on obscure or unorthodox traditions (Luraghi 2000), and to select and interpret his material in a way that supported his particular argument, rather than to give a balanced, comprehensive survey of history. The result is in many respects a seriously distorted account of early Greece.

The Skewed Chronology of Cultural History

Modern scholars have tended to accept Thucydides' argument that a collective "Hellenic" identity did not yet exist in Homer's time (especially Hall 2002, 125–34; Ulf 1996). Yet this is a clear instance of Thucydides' eagerness to play down the level of development in earlier ages getting the better of him. While it is true that Homer does not use "Hellenes" for all Greeks, it is incorrect to say that he has no single name for all Greece or the Greeks. In Homer, "Argos" often refers to the whole of Greece, rather than to the city of that name (e.g., *Il.* 1.30; 2.115; *Od.* 3.263; 4.99), and "Achaeans" is used almost 700 times as a collective designation of all Greeks (e.g., *Il.* 1.2; *Od.* 1.90); "Argives" (inhabitants of Argos) and "Danaans" (descendants of the daughters of Danaos) are also frequently used as a common name for all Greeks. Indeed, the Greeks at Troy are described as "Pan-Achaeans" (e.g., *Il.* 2.404; 7.73; 9.301; *Od.* 1.239; 14.369; 24.32), which implies a strong claim to shared identity. As Thucydides could have known, the poet Hesiod, generally regarded as a near-contemporary of Homer's, did already call the Greeks of his own day "Panhellenes" (*Works and Days* 527–28), yet usually called the Greeks of the Trojan War "Achaeans" (*Works and Days* 651–53; frags. 23(a).17; 165.14; 198.16; 204.47; cf. frag. 130 M.-W). Thucydides—and modern scholars—should have drawn the conclusion that for Homer and Hesiod the Greeks, although not yet all called Hellenes, were at the time of the Trojan War already a single ethnic group ("Achaeans") with a defined territory ("Argos") and shared descent from Danaos' daughters.

This misuse of Homer to support the historical model is compounded by the omission of Homeric evidence when it is in conflict with this model. The custom of bearing arms in daily life is crucial evidence for the theory that in the earliest phases of development violence was pervasive but was much reduced in the wake of Minos' elimination of piratical raiders. Yet Homer still portrays his heroes as being armed at home (*Od.* 4.307–11), at feasts (*Od.* 21.119; 22.74), at games (*Od.* 8.403–6) and at dances (*Il.* 18.597–98); they carry spears in public even for informal visits to the agora (*Od.* 20.124–57) and attendance at formal assemblies (*Il.* 2.42–47; *Od.* 2.2–14). Whether one takes this as evidence for the time of the Trojan War or the time of the poet, it does not fit the chronology of the model and is accordingly ignored. Instead, Thucydides cites "ethnographic" proof of his view: the Ozolian Locrians, Aetolians, and Acarnanians, as well as many non-Greeks, still "bear iron" today, a relic of what was once universal custom (1.5.3–6.2). This evidence had two advantages for Thucydides: it could not be chronologically fixed, and it was familiar to Athenian audiences in or shortly after 426 BCE, when Athens in alliance with Acarnanians and Ozolian Locrians attempted to conquer the Aetolians (Thuc. 3.94–98), whose "warlike" culture and habit of living "scattered far apart in unfortified villages" drew attention at the time (3.94.4; cf. 97.1).[5]

The true date of the change from "bearing iron" to a more relaxed and luxurious lifestyle, as described by Thucydides, is indicated by early Greek art. Men with swords and spears in nonmilitary contexts are commonly depicted in Late Geometric vase painting (c. 750–700 BCE); swords are still occasionally worn by men in "civilian" dress in art down to c. 650 and spears are carried by "civilians" in Attic vase painting as late as c. 530 BCE. Men stopped carrying swords when they adopted a new type of cloak, wrapped around the body in a way that severely restricted movement, and they stopped carrying spears when dress styles became still more luxurious (van Wees 1998). Thucydides' history of Greek dress is thus accurate in broad outline, but implies a date many centuries too early for the major change.

Conversely, the innovations attributed to the Spartans appear to be dated much too late. The narrative suggests that a moderate lifestyle was introduced at Sparta not long before luxurious dress and hairstyles were abandoned at Athens after the Persian War, and the introduction of athletic nudity is said to have occurred "not many years" ago. Yet Sparta's famous "austerity" was universally attributed to the reforms of Lycurgus, which Thucydides himself dates to "a little more than 400 years before the end of this war" (c. 825 BCE, if he means the Peace of Nicias; 1.18.1). As for Spartans exercising naked, the observation that athletes had previously worn loincloths "even at the Olympic games" (1.6.5) clearly alludes to the story that athletic nudity was invented by a sprinter at one of the earliest games, and Thucydides must have in mind the version in which this runner

---

[5] Similarly, Thucydides' evidence for Carians living in the Cyclades was a discovery of 426/5, when the Athenians purified Delos and found that "more than half" of the exhumed graves were Carian (1.8.1; Cook [1955, 267–69], shows that they mistook for "Carian" Greek burials of the Geometric period). The evidence from "the ancient poets" for the acceptability of piracy (1.5.2) included the *Homeric Hymn to Apollo* (452–55; also *Od.* 3.71–74; 9.252–55), later quoted at length (3.104), probably performed after the purification at the revived festival of Apollo.

was Acanthus of Sparta (Dion. Hal. 7.72.2–4). This event was normally dated as early as 720 BCE. "Not many years ago" is an odd way to describe three centuries, but rather than assume that Thucydides adopted an idiosyncratic date, we should recognize the phrase as a rhetorical gambit: it suits his model of progress to suggest that all things modern were recent innovations, and in a span of almost a millennium one can just about claim legitimately that 300 years is a relatively short time.[6]

When these changes really happened is a matter of debate. In Homer, boxers and wrestlers still wear loincloths (*Il.* 23.685, 710; *Od.* 18.67, 76), and the earliest naked athletes appear in art c. 650 BCE (McDonnell 1991), so this change is likely to have happened at about the same time as the abandonment of "bearing iron." The reforms attributed to Lycurgus, which established a uniform dress code and lifestyle at Sparta, however, have been assigned widely different dates by modern scholars: some make it around 650, but others favor a date around 550, and a few have argued for a still later date, c. 500 BCE (see van Wees 2017a; 2017b).

A Grudging History of Corinth

What Thucydides tells us about Minos, Agamemnon, and the heroic age derives from legends and epic poetry and is of little value as evidence for Bronze Age history. The Dorian, Ionian, and other migration stories, too, are in the realm of legend rather than Early Iron Age reality (MacSweeney 2013). Greek expansion into Italy and Sicily is the first unquestionably historical event, but although Thucydides later reveals a detailed knowledge of Greek settlement in Sicily (6.1–5), he does no more than touch upon it in the Archaeology. Much more significant for his model is the subsequent establishment of tyrannies and navies across the Greek world, and, for better or worse, his discussion of these developments has had a deep impact on modern accounts of the history of archaic Greece.

The potted naval history of Corinth that opens Thucydides' discussion poses particular problems of interpretation and chronology. It begins with the comment that the Corinthians "are said" to have been the first to create a "modern" navy (1.13.2), and continues:

> It is indeed apparent that Ameinias, a Corinthian shipwright, made four ships for the Samians; it is about 300 years before the end of this war that Ameinocles came to the Samians (13.3). The oldest naval battle of which we know was waged by Corinthians against Corcyraeans; this too is about 260 years down to the same time (13.4).

This is followed by a discussion of how Corinth had always benefited from trade even before sea travel was common, and had subsequently turned itself into a wealthy naval

---

[6] An alternative version made the athlete a Megarian (Pausanias 1.44.1; *IG* VII.52.5–6), but Thucydides apparently preferred the symmetrical juxtaposition of Athens and Sparta. Plato, *Republic* 452cd also dates the change "not long ago"; see further McDonnell (1991).

power (13.5). At first glance, it may seem that the first three sentences (1.13.2–4) list a series of events in chronological order, so that the first "modern" trireme navy was constructed before the export of ships to Samos, c. 721 BCE (if "the end of this war" refers to the Peace of Nicias), and the first naval battle, c. 681 BCE. However, this interpretation is difficult to reconcile with Thucydides' later statement that there were "few triremes" anywhere in Greece until c. 490 (1.14.1) and with the lack of contemporary evidence for triremes in Greece until the late sixth century BCE (e.g., Casson 1995, 43–81). Closer attention to the text suggests a different reading.

Thucydides does not make the claim in the first sentence about Corinthian priority on his own authority, but reports it as something that "is said" (λέγονται). Only here in the Archaeology do we find this noncommittal expression (Westlake 1977, 357–61; Rood 2006, 244–6), which contrasts sharply with the certainty and precision of the next two statements: "it is indeed apparent" (φαίνεται δὲ καὶ)[7] that Ameinocles went to Samos 300 years ago and "we know" (ἴσμεν) of a sea battle 260 years ago. In other words, Thucydides does not list three events of equal status in chronological order, but first reports a major claim that he uniquely avoids endorsing, and then moves on to cite a couple of firmly stated and dated "facts" about Corinth's naval history. Moreover, the vessels that Ameinocles built and those that fought the first naval battle are not explicitly triremes but simply "ships" (ναῦς; Meijer 1988). It is therefore possible that no chronological sequence is implied, but rather a contrast between Corinth's reputation as a great innovator in naval matters, and the lesser, conceivably earlier, naval achievements that Thucydides is prepared to accept as fact.

Corinth, more than Sparta, had been Athens' main enemy since 460 BCE (Thuc. 1.103.4), so it would not be surprising if Athenians wished to play down the pioneering role of the Corinthian navy. The Athenian version of the battle of Salamis claimed that the Corinthian ships had fled before the battle even started, whereas "the rest of Greece testifies" that they actually "fought among the foremost" (Hdt. 8.94). Corinth, for its part, tried to make political capital from having been a greater naval power than Athens by reminding the Athenians that once, before they became enemies, they had graciously let them have twenty vessels (Thuc. 1.41.2; Hdt. 6.89). Thucydides thus probably prefers not to endorse what "is said" so as not to lend support to Corinthian claims in a politically charged matter.

The other Corinthian achievements, by contrast, could be unambiguously accepted because, if anything, they were politically charged *against* Corinth. The first-ever naval battle was "waged by the Corinthians" (γίγνεται Κορινθίων), and is thus presented as an act of aggression against the Corcyraeans. Athens had made an alliance with Corcyra against Corinth in 434 (Thuc. 1.31–55), so the story of the battle may

---

[7] φαίνεται plus participle, "it is apparent," indicating certainty (as opposed to φαίνεται plus infinitive, "it seems," indicating uncertainty), is a favorite expression in the Archaeology: 1.2.2, 3.1, 9.4, 10.5, 11, 13.3, 14.1. Its significance is noted by Hornblower (1997, 44).

have circulated in contemporary political discourse as an example of long-standing Corinthian aggression against Athens' new ally (cf. Hdt. 3.48–53). As for Ameinocles, his shipbuilding is in itself hardly a spectacular historical feat, and one suspects that the point is rather that a Corinthian "came to the Samians" and worked "for the Samians." In 440 BCE, Athens had fought a hard war against Samos, and the Corinthians claimed credit for preventing a Peloponnesian intervention at the time, arguing that Athens should repay the favor by not intervening against Corinth in support of Corcyra (Thuc. 1.40.5, 41.2). Thucydides does not tell us how the Athenians countered that argument when they chose Corcyra's side, but one imagines that they would have seized upon any evidence of Corinth being friendly with Samos. The story of Ameinocles may have surfaced in that context.

On this reading, Thucydides gives no further clue to when the first modern trireme navy was created, since Ameinocles and the naval battle may well date to an earlier period, just as Corinth's revenues from trade by land, mentioned next, originate at a much earlier time. The sole indication of when public triremes were first constructed is the position of the episode after the colonization of Italy and Sicily, and at the same time as the rise of tyrants. Later sources tell us that Periander, tyrant of Corinth c. 625–585 BCE, "continually mounted expeditions and was warlike; he built triremes and made use of both seas," i.e., the Aegean and the Ionian sea (Nicolaus of Damascus *FGrH* 90 F 58.3; cf. Ephorus *FGrH* 70 F 179). His revenues from trade were so great that he never imposed any other form of taxation (Aristotle frag. 611.20 Rose). The centralization of power and revenues in Corinth under this tyrant fit Thucydides' model perfectly, and it is likely that the historian was aware of this tradition but preferred not to credit Periander explicitly, partly in order to remain vague about Corinth's main naval achievements and partly also because in his model tyrannical regimes were supposed to inhibit development, not act as a driving force for modernity.

We have no other evidence for the three naval achievements attributed to Corinth, but it seems plausible that Periander was the first to build public triremes, since his contemporary, the Egyptian Pharaoh Necho (610–594 BCE), built triremes in Egypt (Hdt. 2.159) and Corinth may have been part of a wider development. On Thucydides' dates, the first naval battle and Ameinocles' shipbuilding predated Periander and occurred under the oligarchy of the Bacchiads (to which he alludes at 1.24.2; 6.3.2).[8] A naval battle between Corinth and Corcyra at this time is possible, given that the two are said to have been enemies from the foundation of Corcyra onward (Hdt. 3.49; cf. Thuc. 1.25). Samos may have needed state-of-the-art ships (probably biremes, Casson 1995, 53–60) in the late eighth century to defend Samian settlers at Nagidus and Celenderis in Cilicia from Assyrian expansion; both contemporary Assyrian records and later Greek sources mention naval battles with "Ionians" in this region.[9]

---

[8] There is no justification for the common modern view that Thucydides' dates are based on unrealistically long forty-year generations and that these events happened much later.
[9] E.g. *State Archives of Assyria* 19 025; Abydenos *FGrH* 685 F 5; Berossos *FGrH* 680 F 7c.

The Stunted Growth of Ionia

The discussion of Corinth is followed by a brief account of Ionia, once again juxtaposing the Peloponnesian and Ionian power blocs. During the reigns of Cyrus and Cambyses (546–522 BCE), Ionians acquired large navies, though these included only "few triremes" (1.13.6, 14.1).

> When they fought against Cyrus they controlled the sea in their region for some time. And Polycrates, as tyrant of Samos under Cambyses, gained in naval strength and made the other islands his subjects and after capturing Rheneia dedicated it to Apollo Delios. The Phocaeans, settling Massalia, defeated the Carthaginians in a naval battle (1.13.6).

This selection of facts about Ionian naval power is best understood as a reflection of the particular interests of the Athenians. The Ionians' collective superiority to the Persians anticipates Athens' achievement during the Persian War. By contrast, Herodotus says that the Ionian cities were captured in sieges by land (1.161–62) and that the Persians under Cyrus had no fleet at all (1.143.1; cf. 151). Even allowing for Herodotus' hostility to Ionians (1.143–47, 153.3), it is hard to avoid the impression that Thucydides makes a lot of what may have been merely the lack of a Persian challenge at sea (Luraghi 2000, 235), in order to balance Corinth's naval achievements with a significant Ionian counterpart.

Polycrates gets short shrift compared to Herodotus' fulsome account of his deeds (3.39) and effusive obituary (3.122.2, 125.2). The sole achievement of Polycrates' career that Thucydides cares to note, the capture of the tiny island of Rheneia (recalled at 3.104.2), is hardly the best evidence of his power, and does not even rate a mention in Herodotus. The grudging recognition given to Polycrates, who could easily have been written up as a great Ionian pioneer, is presumably the result of a reluctance to give much credit to a tyrant or to Samos, Athens' recently defeated rival (cf. Irwin 2009). Competition between Athens and Samos explains why Thucydides singles out the dedication of Rheneia, twice: this gesture had been Polycrates' response to a partial purification of Delos by Athens under Peisistratus (Hdt. 1.64.2), and was in turn trumped by Athens' complete purification of Delos in 426 BCE.

Herodotus' version of Phocaean history emphasizes their earlier leading role in exploring the western Mediterranean, and their migration to Alalia on Corsica after Cyrus' conquest of Ionia (1.64–67). One can see why Thucydides chose not to use this material, because it involves defeat by the Persians, casts the Phocaeans in the role of pirates (1.163.2, 166.1), and ends with them suffering such losses in battle that they end up abandoning Alalia (1.166–67). Instead of piracy and defeat, Thucydides' narrative requires expansion and naval victory, which he duly provides by drawing on a Massaliot naval victory over Carthage, which was commemorated by a statue dedicated at Delphi (Paus. 10.18.7) and may have been well known, even if Herodotus chose not to mention it.

Scholars have usually taken the Phocaean "settling" of Massalia to refer to the city's original foundation, dated to 600 BCE (Timaeus *FGrH* 566 F 71), so that the episode would be too early to fit Thucydides' chronological scheme. However, "settling" (οἰκίζοντες) is as ambiguous in Greek as it is in English and does not necessarily mean the *first* settlement of a place. What Thucydides has in mind is probably Phocaeans emigrating after the Persian conquest and "settling" in a city they had founded earlier, as at Alalia (Hdt. 1.165.1, 166.1). Carthage may have intervened to stop increased piratical activity in the region, again as at Alalia. This interpretation is supported by a version of the story that explicitly dates the episode after the Persian conquest, and adds that it involved "a part" (*moira*) of the Phocaeans, i.e., the migrants split, some going to Alalia, others to Massalia (Paus. 10.8.6; cf. Isoc. 6.84). If Thucydides' choice of words suggests something grander—the foundation of an important city in the face of Carthaginian opposition—that is surely deliberate, and analogous to his inflation of minor successes against Persia into a fully fledged Ionian thalassocracy.

Despite the brevity of his remarks, Thucydides intends to suggest the emergence of a major naval power, with "Ionian affairs progressing towards greatness" (ἐπὶ μέγα, 1.16) when they were stopped by Persian expansion. Had their rise not been curtailed by external factors, the Ionians might apparently have achieved the kind of dominance later enjoyed by Athens. However, this is not the full story: Herodotus provides evidence which implies that Ionian (and Aeolian) naval power actually flourished under Persian rule.

Not all Ionian cities were subjected by Cyrus' generals, but Miletus made a treaty (Hdt. 1.141.4; 169.2) and the islanders "gave themselves up" (1.169.2), so that they retained the semi-independent status that they had occupied as allies of the Lydian kingdom (1.22.4, 27.5). This must mean that Polycrates built up his naval power while he was in effect a vassal of the Persian empire, though with enough independence to make an alliance with Egypt (3.39.2) and to raid Persia's other Aegean vassals. (The Persians did allow their Greek subjects considerable military freedom before 493 BCE: 6.42). Herodotus reports that Cambyses summoned the Ionians and Aeolians to provide ships for his campaign against Egypt in 525 BCE "because he regarded them as his slaves by inheritance" (2.1; cf. 3.1), but he implicitly suggests that Polycrates was not subject to this obligation: his story is that the tyrant secretly volunteered his ships to Cambyses as part of a devious scheme to get rid of political opponents (3.44). It seems clear that in reality Polycrates was indeed a vassal of Persia who was obliged to join the invasion of Egypt, and that it was the outbreak of hostilities between Persia and Egypt that put an end to his alliance with Egypt, rather than the Pharaoh's alarm at Polycrates' good fortune, as a famous folktale suggested (Hdt. 3.40-43).

Miletus, too, flourished as a Persian ally: by 500 BCE, it was "at its greatest peak and Ionia's showpiece" (Hdt. 5.28). Its rulers took a leading role in pushing Persian expansion across the Aegean, to the River Strymon in the north and Naxos in the center.[10] A vessel

---

[10] Histiaeus of Miletus is "given" Myrcinus on the Strymon (Hdt. 5.11), but this city lies farther west than the Persian conquest by land under Megabazus had yet reached (5.2, 10, 14–16), so its occupation must have involved naval military force (cf. 5.124–26). Naxos: Hdt. 5.30–34

from Mytilene was one of Cambyses' leading ships (3.13.1), a commander from Mytilene was one of Darius' most loyal advisers (4.97; 5.11, 38) and ships from Lesbos conquered Lemnos and Imbros for Persia (5.26). Even Athenian settlers in the Chersonese provided ships for Persian expeditions (4.137), presumably as dependent allies, a relation they also seem to have enjoyed with Lydia (6.37). If anything, the Persian conquest thus seems to have boosted Ionian naval power.

The first triremes in Ionia appear under Persian rule. Polycrates sent 40 triremes to Egypt in 525 BCE (Hdt. 3.44); Cambyses' Mytilenean flagship, too, was a trireme (implied at 3.14.4-5). Mytilene, Miletus and several of its neighbors in the Carian region provided ships for a fleet of 200 triremes (Hdt. 5.32-3, 37), and by 494 BCE, Samos had 60 triremes, Lesbos 70, Miletus 80 and Chios 100 (6.8). Athenian settlers in the Chersonese had 5 triremes (6.41). The contrast between the ubiquity of triremes in the Persian sphere of influence from 525 onward, and the exclusive use of pentekontors by Samos (Hdt. 3.39, 41; cf. 124) and Phocaea (1.163-64) until at least 540 BCE strongly suggests that Persian naval expansion under Cambyses, who "won Egypt and the sea" (3.34.4), was the catalyst for the spread of the trireme. The Persians may well have funded the building and equipment of triremes by their subjects and vassals, at least until the Ionian Revolt forced them to centralize control (van Wees 2013, 30-37, 147-48).

At a time when Athens led an alliance of Ionians and other eastern Greeks against the Persian Empire, the story of how these same cities had benefited from collaboration with the Persians was obviously not one that anyone wanted to hear. In Thucydides' case, it could further be argued that the story is irrelevant to his argument about the growing ability of Greek cities to engage in collective military action. However, what happened in Ionia under Persian rule is crucially important to his argument about the role of the trireme in modern navies and public finance, and his omission of this material distorts the historical picture.

Stagnation in Mainland Greece

Thucydides' cautious assessment of Corinth and his underestimation of the development of naval warfare in Ionia under Persian rule are as nothing compared to his devastating assessment of the insignificance of warfare in the archaic age: on land, nothing but border disputes, no wars that resulted in conquests or were fought by coalitions (1.15); in general, no wars, waged by tyrants, that showed any ambition beyond fighting neighboring cities (1.17). He allows two partial exceptions: the Lelantine War, and the wars of the tyrants in Sicily.

We have already noted that these claims contradict what Thucydides himself says about Sparta's acquisition of territory and power, and Herodotus' report that by 550 BCE "most of the Peloponnese was already subjected to the Spartans" (1.68.6). Although Thucydides argues that the Spartans were somehow able to overthrow tyrants because they were never ruled by a tyrant (cf. Hdt. 5.92α1-2, η5), it is obvious that in practice such interventions relied on military force. Thucydides' only specific example, the deposition of Hippias at Athens (1.18.1; 6.53.3, 59.4), involved four military actions according to Herodotus: two to oust the tyrant (5.63, 64) and two to support the new regime (5.72, 74–6). A fifth large expedition intended to restore Hippias did not get beyond the planning stage (Hdt. 5.90–93). Herodotus also notes the large expedition by Sparta and Corinth against Polycrates of Samos in 525 BCE (3.54–56). Plutarch lists numerous other tyrants taken down by Sparta: "the Cypselids at Corinth and Ambracia" (c. 580 BCE), Lygdamis of Naxos (c: 525–515), Aeschines of Sicyon (probably c. 550 BCE) and three otherwise unknown tyrants in Thasos, Phocis, and Miletus (*On the Malice of Herodotus* 21; *Mor.* 859a). An anonymous papyrus fragment (*FGrH* 105 F 1) attributes the putting down of tyrants to the campaigns of King Anaxandridas (c. 560–520 BCE), and the ephorate of Chilon (traditional date 556 BCE).

The reliability and details of this evidence are open to challenge, but since Thucydides himself says that Sparta's hegemony rested on having supportive regimes in allied cities, the replacement of popular tyrannies with oligarchies was surely an integral part of Sparta's "subjection" of the Peloponnese and therefore practiced for most of the sixth century (cf. Yates 2005; Cawkwell 1993). Interventions in Ambracia, Samos, Naxos, Thasos, and Miletus required naval expeditions, and some naval expeditions were directed even against targets that could have been reached by land: Athens in 512 (Hdt. 5.63) and Argos in 494 (6.76). Moreover, the dominant Ionian naval powers asked Sparta for military aid: Phocaea (Hdt. 1.141, 152), Samos twice (3.45–46, 148), and Miletus (5.49–51). The ships may have been provided by Corinth and other allies, but evidently archaic Sparta's military campaigns were more varied in kind and ambitious in scope than Thucydides' model could accommodate.

The same may be said of the wars fought by supposedly unadventurous tyrannical regimes. Herodotus, too, thought that Athens "began to grow" only after its tyrants were expelled: under their rule the Athenians were "no better in warfare than any of their neighbours, but when they were rid of the tyrants they became by far the foremost" (5.78; cf. 5.91). Yet Herodotus himself provided the evidence to disprove this claim: Peisistratus reconquered Sigeion on the Hellespont (5.94), and imposed a tyrant on Naxos (1.64). The Athenian occupation of Boeotia south of the Asopus (Hdt. 6.108) occurred in 519 BCE, i.e., under Hippias (Thuc. 3.68.5; cf. 3.55, 61). Thucydides later commends Peisistratus and Hippias for "completing their wars" without resorting to heavy taxation (6.54.5). Nor are the Athenian tyrants the only exception to the alleged rule: the naval power of Periander of Corinth is tacitly conceded in the Archaeology, and Polycrates of Samos is reluctantly given his due. Thucydides makes a further exception for "the tyrants in Sicily" i.e., Gelon and Hiero of Syracuse above all: "they advanced most in power" (1.17), were not overthrown by Sparta (1.18.1), and were the first (alongside Corcyra) to acquire large navies of triremes (1.14.2).

Later tradition credits the tyrants of Sicyon and Pheidon of Argos with a record of expansionist warfare, and Aristotle states as a rule that "in the old days" most tyrants came to power because they were successful generals as well as popular leaders (*Politics* 1305a7–15). Thucydides' and Herodotus' idea that tyrannical government inhibited warfare thus has very little to recommend it. The notion springs from hostility toward this type of regime, and in Thucydides' case also from the need to find a reason why earlier powers did not reach the same heights as contemporary Athens. In reality, archaic tyrants seem to have regarded wars of conquest as an effective way to achieve and maintain their position (van Wees 2003).

The reason why Thucydides acknowledges the military success and naval enterprise of the tyrants of Syracuse and Samos at all is no doubt that they were too famous to be ignored, as illustrated by Herodotus' comments about the "magnificence" of both (3.125.2). Rather than expose his model to criticism by omitting well-known evidence, he incorporated these figures in a minimal fashion. The same reason led him to acknowledge one exception to the rule that no wars were fought by coalitions of states, the Lelantine War: "the Greek world was divided to the greatest extent into alliances with either side for the war of the Chalcidians and Eretrians once upon a time" (ἐς τὸν πάλαι ποτὲ, 1.15.3). This conflict was very well known, and several of the allies were named by Herodotus (5.99) and Aristotle (*Pol.* 1289b38–39; frag. 98 Rose; cf. Plut. *Mor.* 760e–761a). The episode may have been of particular interest to Athens, which in 506 BCE occupied the territory of Chalcis (Hdt. 5.77). Rather than ignore this war, Thucydides noted it as an exception, and by dating it "once upon a time" suggested that it happened a very long time ago and was unlike anything seen since.

Modern scholars have tended to follow suit and dated the Lelantine War around 700 BCE, noting allusions to war in Euboea in the poems of Hesiod (*Works and Days* 650–60) and Archilochus (frag. 3 West). However, there is no good evidence that these early sources refer to the Lelantine War specifically. Moreover, a treaty banning the use of long-range missiles attributed to this war by Strabo (10.1.12) has been taken as evidence that it was a near-ritual border dispute, but Strabo also says that the objective was the Lelantine Plain (10.1.12; cf. Plut. *Mor.* 153f), which constituted the bulk of the territory of Chalcis, so the conflict must have been an attempt by Eretria to conquer its neighbor. So far from being an anomaly, the Lelantine War may have had much in common with Sparta's campaigns, as well as with other land-based wars involving coalitions of states mentioned in later sources, such as the First Sacred War, the campaigns of Pheidon of Argos, or the expansion of Sybaris in southern Italy. The evidence for all these conflicts is problematic, but not necessarily false (van Wees, 2017c). Thucydides' omission of these wars is dictated by his historical model, not proof that they never happened. His overall assessment of archaic wars waged on land or by tyrants as mere neighborly squabbles is highly questionable, evidently based on little more than his premise that only contemporary Athenian sea power was truly historically significant.

As for Athens itself, the idea that the city, like other mainland Greek states, had very few triremes and no naval tradition until Themistocles proposed his ship-building program (cf. Hdt. 7.144.2) is manifestly a caricature. For one thing, it ignores the Corinthian pioneers, who provided 40 triremes at Salamis in 480 BCE (Hdt. 8.1, 43) and had presumably been building up their "modern" navy since the days of Periander. The rest of the Greek fleet at Salamis consisted of hundreds of triremes and only a handful of pentekontors (Hdt. 8.43–48, 82), which implies that the trireme was established as the normal warship across mainland Greece well before the Persian War. The suggestion that

Athens built 200 triremes to wage war against a neighbor, Aegina, which supposedly itself had only a small fleet of pentekontors, is absurd. Nor is it credible that Athenians had not been "naval people" before 483 BCE, despite their well-attested overseas interests from c. 600 BCE onward. An alternative tradition plausibly claims that Athens built only 100 new triremes in 483 BCE and thus had up to 100 triremes already ([Aristotle] *Ath. Pol.* 22.7; Plut. *Themistocles* 4.2; Nepos, *Them.* 2.2.). Thucydides would have been aware of these points, but he chose to ignore them because for him the Athenian fleet represented modernity, and it suited him to treat it as a recent creation.

The true nature and size of mainland Greek fleets before the Persian War is hard to gauge, but one way of piecing together the evidence suggests that publicly owned trireme-based navies were established at Athens and elsewhere almost simultaneously with their emergence in Ionia, c. 525–500 BCE (e.g., van Wees 2013; Wallinga 2005; 1993).

Many features of the Archaeology reveal that it represents early Greek history as imagined by an Athenian, probably in the 420s, looking for forerunners of Athens at the peak of its power, while simultaneously trying to show that even the greatest of these forerunners never reached Athens' level. An effort is made to balance the histories of Athens' Ionian allies and its Peloponnesian opponents, but the second-greatest powers on each side, Corinth and Samos, rivals to Athens' naval power and formerly at a peak under the rule of tyrants, do not fit the model and are given relatively short shrift. Sparta gets credit for major contributions to cultural and political "modernity" by the introduction of an egalitarian lifestyle, athletic nudity, and the abolition of tyranny, but its methods of public finance and warfare are presented as old-fashioned and inadequate. Everything else that does not fit the model, such as expansionist warfare by land or internationally ambitious tyrants, is played down. Everything that represents modernity is presented as a very recent development, even if Greek tradition dated it centuries earlier and the true historical date may be generations earlier. However impressive as an intellectual feat, as an account of events and developments before the Persian War, the Archaeology is highly selective and often misleading.

References

Allison, J. W. 1989. *Power and Preparedness in Thucydides*. Baltimore: Johns Hopkins University Press.

Casson, L. 1995. *Ships and Seamanship in the Ancient World*. Baltimore: Johns Hopkins University Press.

Cawkwell, G. 1993. "Sparta and Her Allies in the Sixth Century." *Classical Quarterly* 43: 364–76.

Connor, W. R. 1984. *Thucydides*. Princeton: Princeton University Press.

Cook, R. M. 1955. "Thucydides as Archaeologist." *Annual of the British School at Athens* 50: 266–70.

de Souza, P. 1999. *Piracy in the Graeco-Roman World*. Cambridge: Cambridge University Press.

Ellis, J. R. 1991. "The Structure and Argument of Thucydides' Archaeology." *Classical Antiquity* 10 (2): 344–76.
Foster, E. 2010. *Thucydides, Pericles and Periclean Imperialism*. Cambridge: Cambridge University Press.
Gomme, E. 1945. *A Historical Commentary on Thucydides*, Vol. I. Oxford: Clarendon.
Hall, J. M. 2002 *Hellenicity: Between Ethnicity and Culture*. Chicago: University of Chicago Press.
Hammond, N. G. L. 1952. "The Arrangement of the Thought in the Proem and in Other Parts of Thucydides I." *Classical Quarterly* 2: 127–41.
Hornblower, S. 1997 *A Commentary on Thucydides*. Vol. I, *Books I–III*. Oxford: Clarendon.
Irwin, E. 2009 "Herodotos and Samos: Personal or Political?" *Classical World* 102 (4): 395–416.
Kallet, L. 2001. *Money and the Corrosion of Power in Thucydides*. Berkeley: University of California Press.
Luraghi, N. 2000. "Author and Audience in Thucydides' 'Archaeology': Some Reflections." *Harvard Studies in Classical Philology* 100: 227–39.
MacSweeney, N. 2013. *Foundation Myths and Politics in Ancient Ionia*. Cambridge: Cambridge University Press.
Marshall, M. H. B. 1975. "Urban Settlement in the Second Chapter of Thucydides." *Classical Quarterly* 25: 26–40.
McDonnell, M. 1991. "The Introduction of Athletic Nudity: Thucydides, Plato and the Vases." *Journal of Hellenic Studies* 111: 182–93.
Meijer, F. 1988 "Thucydides 1.13.2–4 and the Changes in Greek Ship-Building." *Historia* 37: 461–63.
Morrison, J., et al. 2000. *The Athenian Trireme*. 2d ed. Cambridge: Cambridge University Press.
Nicolai, R. 2001. "Thucydides' Archaeology: Between Epic and Oral Traditions." In *The Historian's Craft in the Age of Herodotus*, edited by N. Luraghi, 263–85. Oxford: Oxford University Press.
Romilly, J., de. 1956. *Histoire et raison chez Thucydide*. Paris, Les Belles Lettres.
Rood, T. 2006. "Objectivity and Authority: Thucydides' Historical Method." In *Brill's Companion to Thucydides*, edited by A. Tsakmakis and A. Rengakos, 225–49. Leiden and Boston: Brill.
Tsakmakis, A. 1995. *Thukydides über die Vergangenheit*. Tübingen, Gunter Narr Verlag.
Ulf, C. 1996. "Griechische Ethnogenese versus Wanderungen on Stämmen und Stammstaaten." In *Wege zur Genese griechischer Identität*, edited by C. Ulf, 240–80. Berlin: De Gruyter.
van Wees, H. 1998. "Greeks Bearing Arms." In *Archaic Greece: New Approaches and New Evidence*, edited by N. Fisher and H. van Wees, 333–78. London and Swansea: Classical Press of Wales.
van Wees, H. 2003. "Conquerors and Serfs." In *Helots and Their Masters in Laconia and Messenia*, edited by N. Luraghi and S. Alcock, 33–80. Washington, DC: Harvard University Press.
van Wees, H. 2013. *Ships and Silver, Taxes and Tribute: A Fiscal History of Archaic Athens*. London and New York, I.B. Tauris.
van Wees, H. 2017a. "The Common Messes." In *A Companion to Sparta*, edited by A. Powell. Malden: Wiley-Blackwell.
van Wees, H. 2017b. "Luxury, Austerity and Equality." In *A Companion to Sparta*, edited by A. Powell. Malden: Wiley-Blackwell.

van Wees, H., 2017c, 'The Lelantine War' and 'Early Greek Wars'. In *Encyclopedia of Ancient Battles*, edited by H. Sidebottom and M. Whitby. Malden: Wiley-Blackwell.

Wallinga, H. T. 1993. *Ships and Sea-Power before the Great Persian War*. Leiden, and Boston: Brill.

Wallinga, H. T. 2005. *Xerxes' Greek Adventure*. Leiden and Boston: Brill.

Westlake, H. D. 1977. "λέγεται in Thucydides. *Mnemosyne* 30: 345–62.

Yates, D. 2005. "The Archaic Treaties between the Spartans and Their Allies." *Classical Quarterly* 55: 65–76.

CHAPTER 3

THE PENTECONTAETIA

LISA KALLET

INTRODUCTION

THE term "Pentecontaetia" applies to the section in Thucydides' *History* treating the roughly fifty years (hence its name) between the end of the Persian Wars in 479 BCE and the beginning of the Peloponnesian War in 431 BCE (1.89–117). It also refers to that historical period, and it is as a source for that period that Thucydides is invariably faulted: confident judgments of what he should have included (based on modern assumptions of what a historian interested in the period would have written) are virtually *de rigueur*.

This appraisal, however, results in large part from misunderstandings of the fundamental aim of the Pentecontaetia. It is not a narrative survey intended to "cover," or even sketch, the period. It is principally an argument supporting a theory of causation; but, in typical Thucydidean style, it accomplishes this by using narrative strategies that require understanding before the excursus can properly be evaluated as a historical source. This chapter will elucidate Thucydides' aims and methods; in so doing, it will implicitly underscore just how very much he is not the "modernist" many commentators of this section still, despite long-standing awareness to the contrary (Loraux 1980 is the classic critique), seem to regard him as (reflected in the "should have," "would have" critical approaches).

PURPOSE AND NARRATIVE LOCATION OF THE EXCURSUS: 1.23.6 AND THE PENTECONTAETIA

The purpose of the Pentecontaetia directly stems from Thucydides' statement on the "true cause" (literally, "truest cause" (ἀληθεστάτη πρόφασις) of the Peloponnesian War.

> [The war] was begun by the Athenians and Peloponnesians with the dissolution of the Thirty Years' Treaty made after the conquest of Euboea. Regarding the question why they broke the treaty, I first give an account of their grievances and disputes, that no one may ever have to ask what circumstances plunged the Greeks into a war of such magnitude; the true cause, I believe, though it was least manifest, was that the Athenians, their power growing and instilling fear in the Spartans, forced them to go into the war (1.23.5–6).

Thucydides' explicit distinction between causes—"true" or underlying versus proximate or precipitating—is a historiographical pathbreaker. It also presupposes, given Thucydides' methodology (already illustrated amply, in the "Archaeology," 1.2–19), that evidence in support will follow; this is where the Pentecontaetia comes in, but not immediately, as he makes clear in the above quote. Its narrative location, some 2,000 lines later, as counted by the impatient critic Dion. Hal. (who thought it should have come right after Thucydides stated his view of the "true cause," *On Thucydides* 11), is delayed, "as so often in archaic and classical texts ... until the most effective point" (Stadter 1993, 43) in the narrative, precisely—and fittingly— when the Spartans have voted to declare war, "not so much," in Thucydides' view, "because they were persuaded by their allies, as much as because they feared the further growth of the power of Athens, seeing the greater extent of Greece already under their control" (1.88). This echo of the "true cause" opens the Pentecontaetia, which concludes with this summary:

> All these events of the Greeks against each other and the barbarians [including those concerning Corcyra, Corinth and Potidaea] took place in the fifty years' interval between Xerxes' retreat and the beginning of the present war. During this period the Athenians grounded their empire much more firmly, and advanced to a height of power. The Spartans, though fully aware of it, took few steps to prevent it, and remained inactive during most of the period, being traditionally slow to go to war except when compelled, and in the present instance being hampered by wars at home, until the growth of the power of the Athenians could no longer be ignored, and they were targeting their own alliance. They then felt that they could endure it no longer, but that the time had come for them to throw themselves heart and soul upon the hostile power, and break it, if they could, by commencing the present war (1.118.2).

The Pentecontaetia, then, will support the historian's personal view on the "true cause" of the war—a view bucking popular opinion, which would have been to blame Pericles, in convincing the Athenians not to rescind the Megarian Decree (1.140), or the Spartans, because they voted for war, and, as Thucydides has them concede at a later juncture, because they refused to accept the Athenians' offer of arbitration, and took responsibility for the Theban attack on Plataea at a time of peace (7.18.2). Just as the narrative of military events of the Pentecontaetia is about to get underway, however, Thucydides throws a bit of a curve by announcing that he will include some events that Hellanicus, an earlier contemporary, treated cursorily and with chronological imprecision (1.97). Ironically, these are precisely the areas for which scholars impugn Thucydides (e.g., Meiggs 1972, 445). Gomme (1959, 362) cast his criticism colorfully: "[Thucydides'] events float like sticks in water in an oblong bowl," with no linked relationship or significance that he could discern, signaling evidence of the digression's unfinished state; Gomme's attack ends with a helpful list of Thucydides' omissions (*HCT* I 365–70; see Rood 1998, 225–48; Stadter 1993 for stimulating correctives).

Chronology in Thucydides' Pentecontaetia

Ancient historians are frequently criticized when it comes to chronological reliability; Thucydides is no exception. An evaluation should depend first of all on relative chronology—does the historian get events in the right order? Thucydides' relative chronology has not been doubted (conceded even by Badian 1993, 76), but some precise dates are uncertain because he prefers vague terms such as "meanwhile," "later," and the like. Thus, we know the sequence of these events—the revolt of Naxos, the battle of Eurymedon, the revolt of Thasos and first colonization of Ennea Hodoi on the Strymon, the Peloponnesian earthquake, the helot and perioikic revolt against the Spartans as well as its duration, and the first expedition to Egypt—but not every precise date within that period. Diodorus might seem to offer assistance, since he places events within archon years, but they often just serve to highlight how problematic his chronological pegs are. It is not always clear whether all discrepancies should be traced back to his main source for the period, the fourth-century historian Ephorus, or Ephorus' source(s). (It has been argued that Hellanicus was Ephorus' source [Parker 2004]; and Thucydides' as well [Rainey 2004]; for Thucydides' view of Hellanicus, see above).

Thucydides is above all interested in the process by which Athenian power grew, and for that, relative chronology is key, but there is also an instance in the Pentecontaetia in which the exact sequence of events in parallel arenas of activity is crucial to establish. We can observe this "chronological investment" in his account of the circumstances that led to the transfer of hegemony from Sparta to Athens. In this case, he makes clear the precise temporal relationship between events in two parallel arenas (Byzantium and Sparta) at this critical historical moment (1.94).

The Origins of the Athenian *Archē*: "The Allies Begged Us...."

Athenians: "We did not acquire this empire by force. You [Spartans] were unwilling to prosecute the war and the allies came to us and begged us to take on the leadership" (1.75.2).

Mytilenaeans: "We became allies of the Athenians ... for the liberation of the Hellenes from the Persians" (3.10.3).

These speakers' perspectives should remind us, if reminding is needed, that the speeches Thucydides composes do not necessarily reflect his own views. In his account of the circumstances surrounding the origins of the empire, there is no idealism such as the Mytilenaeans, in the second quotation, express when they request Spartan assistance in their revolt in 427. In Thucydides' analysis, the outrageous, violent behavior of the Spartan commander Pausanias made the Greeks ask the Athenians to take over the leadership of the League, and his account of the new leaders' alacrity in reorganizing the League anew in accordance with their own interests undercuts the rhetorical agenda of the Athenians, in the first quotation, in which, at a congress at Sparta before the war, they deflect all agency in obtaining empire (1.95).

The core of the Pentecontaetia deals with the transfer of hegemony, the structural arrangements of the new league, its early activities, and its development into an empire in which Athens ruled over those very Greeks that joined the alliance. Emphases and selectivity lead to these conclusions, though in subtle ways. Simple questions, however, provide guidance: Why would the allies be willing to entrust themselves to the leadership of Athens? And, having done so, how and why did it happen that some 200 and more city-states were persuaded to turn over their monetary resources to Athens year after year? The answers get to the very heart of what constitutes Athenian power: they arrive as part of an intricate sequential argument.

Pausanias

Herodotus states baldly, referring to events in 478, that the Athenians "seized the pretext of Pausanias' *hubris* to take away the leadership of the alliance from the Spartans" (8.3.2).[1] In a nutshell, that makes the Athenians' takeover of the hegemony entirely opportunistic. What stands out about Thucydides' account is the different perspective: while both historians agree on Pausanias' behavior, the emphasis Thucydides gives to it and to the allies' reaction is conspicuous, especially because Thucydides himself is normally an economical writer. Consider his repeated attention to the allies' hatred of Pausanias. "*The violence of Pausanias* [all italics mine] had already begun to be disagreeable to the Hellenes, particularly to the Ionians and the newly liberated peoples. These resorted to the Athenians and requested them as their kinsmen to become their leaders, and *to stop any violence on the part of Pausanias*" (1.95.1). "It happened that Pausanias was recalled

---

[1] Another individual, Themistocles, and another theme, and factor in the growth of Athenian power—walls (and material culture generally)—figure prominently in Thucydides' Pentecontaetia (Foster 2010, 96–118): walls go up in Athens, marking the beginning of the rise of the city's power—and the first source of tension with Sparta in the post–Persian War period—and walls go down in allied cities, a punishment forced on those that risked revolt and failed in the endeavor, and comprised part of what transforms them into subjects, one by one: Naxos, Thasos, Chalcis, Samos, among others, Athens' naval dominance depended on its walls through the Athenians' ability to protect themselves from attacks from land and rule via the sea.

when the allies (except for Peloponnesians) changed over to the Athenians *because of their hatred of that man* (95.4); "The Athenians having thus succeeded to the supremacy by the voluntary act of the allies *through their hatred of Pausanias*, fixed which cities were to contribute money against the barbarian, which ships; their professed object being to retaliate for their sufferings by ravaging the king's country" (96.1). Finally, a passage later on, coming at the end of an extended excursus on Pausanias and Themistocles (further signaling his paramount interest in these two individuals): after describing at length Pausanias' medizing behavior (128–130), Thucydides concludes by reminding readers that "it was the very reason that the alliance went over to the Athenians" (1.130.2). The Spartans acquitted Pausanias of medism; Thucydides dissented: "[the charge] seemed the most clear-cut" (95.5).

Only a perverse reading of Thucydides' own treatment of the circumstances of the Athenian takeover, however, would see it as apologetic (Badian 1993, 132); it benefits, however, from context. Two years prior, there had been talk of the Athenians taking on the command of the naval arm of the Hellenic League; but the allies protested (8.3.1). It is not a priori evident that the Athenians' key role at Salamis would have offset uneasiness. When Pausanias' behavior made participation in the League intolerable, however, those allies in requesting that the Athenians take over, found it useful to cite their kinship with Athens (cf. Hdt. 9.106). Embedded in the context of Pausanias' behavior and the linkage Thucydides makes between it and the allies' request to Athens to become their leader leaves the reader no doubt that without the factor of Pausanias' behavior, that request would not have come.

This emphasis may also explain the interesting absence—deliberate, we may be sure—from Thucydides' account of another key player, Aristides. Plutarch represents Aristides' behavior in strong contrast to that of Pausanias, such that he, like the congenial Cimon (Plut., *Cim.* 6), wooed the allies over to the Athenian side (Plut., *Arist.* 23). This dimension would have diluted the central argument that above all it was Pausanias' medism that drove the allies into the Athenians' arms, nothing more, nothing less. There was nothing sentimental in this emergence of *archē*; for Thucydides, as for Herodotus, the Athenians got lucky—and they were ready (Davies 2013; Kallet 2013).

Tribute

At the end of his review of ancient history in the "Archaeology," Thucydides compresses the Pentecontaetia into a snapshot of the respective power bases of Sparta and Athens. He notes that after their alignment in the Hellenic League splintered and Athens became the head of the naval coalition, and Sparta the preeminent power on land, the sporadic military conflicts that marked the subsequent period until the Peloponnesian War gave the Athenians needed experience at sea. He concludes by stating simply that by that point each power had greater resources separately than the sum of their strength when the Hellenic League was united (1.19). He specifies the source of Athens' strength, which was tribute.

This foreshadows the "true cause," and the Pentecontaetia. It comes as no surprise, then, that the thematic centerpiece of the Pentecontaetia, namely, description and analysis of what enabled not only Athenian naval power, but also its continued growth (cf. the present participle in 1.23.6: *gignomenous*), is tribute. This explains the focus of the section of the excursus following the Athenians' takeover of the alliance.

> *The Athenians fixed the assessment* for the cities required *to contribute money*, and others ships against the barbarian. The specious reason *expressed for these contributions* was to ravage the King's land in retaliation for what they had suffered. The Hellenotamiai were then *for the first time established as an Athenian office, which collected the tribute—for that was the name given to the collection of the money. The first tribute was assessed at four hundred and sixty talents; and the treasury was on Delos*, where the meetings were held in the temple (1.96.1–2, my italics).

The cornucopia of detail about tribute—even down to the name, *phoros*, but more ominously, to the control over the funds by Athenians all along, despite the fact that the treasury will be on Delos—signposts what is unprecedented about this League: the institution of *phoros* will enable it to achieve *archē* and control allies against their will. Indeed, when Thucydides follows the meticulous attention to the structural aspects and arrangements of the *phoros*, after noting the change in leadership, with the statement that "*at first* the members were autonomous" (97.1), the clear implication is that the deprivation of autonomy will be tied to the payment of tribute. This will be confirmed shortly (1.99).

By the time Thucydides was writing, the term *phoros* was equated with subjugated status. When Thucydides specifies that *phoros* was what the monetary contribution was named from the start, we cannot know whether this was to signal that the repugnant term was used from the outset or, to mark it as a neutral term, distinguished from its Persian counterpart *dasmos* (cf. Murray 1966; Whitehead 1998; Raaflaub 2009). Whatever the case, justification, whether real or a pretext, would have been essential, and that justification highlights what was unique about this League in contrast to all other military alliances with which Greeks were familiar: the Athenians envisioned a standing navy, and offensive campaigns, year in, year out, not just defensive campaigns when required (Kallet-Marx 1993, 47). Greeks would need persuading on this point. Hence the *proschēma*: the promise of a return, namely, rewards from ravaging the King's land, which likely came with a reminder of the siege of Sestos and the fruits that it yielded (Hdt. 9.121; Plut., *Cim.* 9).

Second, by suggesting an ulterior motive (*proschēma*) for requiring annual monetary contributions (and ships), Thucydides might make us reasonably expect "but the real reason was," or the equivalent, such as in the case of the "true cause" (1.23.5–6; *cf.* 6.6.1); that none is explicit alerts us to look for an implicit contrast. Following the Athenians' campaign routes and targets supplies the answer (Rawlings 1977).

Hegemony to *Archē*: From Narration to Analysis, Implicit to Explicit Argument

Thucydides' narrative of the campaigns of the newly founded League is unadorned, even cursory. Eion (the westernmost Persian stronghold at the mouth of the Strymon) is captured, the inhabitants enslaved. The island of Skyros, captured, the inhabitants enslaved, the island settled by the Athenians. Then a war (*polemos*) against Karystos. Only in the case of Eion is there a hint why; but the whole account assumes geographical literacy and hindsight.

The capture of Eion benefited Athens, not the Delian League: it was an Athenian colony and *emporion* that Athenians saw as an Athenian victory, as attested by the dedication of three inscribed Herms celebrating it (Aesch. 3.183–85; Plut., *Cimon* 7.4–6; Thuc. 4.106). Thucydides will shortly (1.100.3) mention the expedition up the Strymon to colonize Ennea Hodoi, later Amphipolis. He notes its success, but then the disaster following when a major expedition (10,000, a suspiciously round number) went farther into the interior; the men were massacred; the colony failed. Skyros was a crucial transit station not only for long-distance trade from Thrace to Athens but from the Black Sea as well. Plutarch mentions that Skyros was used as a base for pirates; we cannot know whether it was significant that Thucydides omits that detail. Karystos controlled the only usable harbor on the southern end of Euboea, right across from Attica; the next stop was the Piraeus. The city, we learn from Herodotus, medized (though only after Artemisium, 8.66), but so did many others, and it had already paid the price, literally, when Themistocles took the Hellenic League fleet and extorted money from it after Salamis, after putting in at Andros and Paros (8.112, 121). That these were the first targets of the Athenians in control of the resources of the Delian League was no coincidence (Davies 1978, 77; 2013; Kallet 2013, 51–52).

Thucydides does not rely solely on implicit strategies. Soon after, when he reports the revolt of Thasos, he is nothing if not explicit: the islanders revolted because the Athenians were trying to seize control of their mainland possessions opposite the island, specifically, their *emporia* and their mine, that is, their profit-making commercial interests (1.100). The revolt, then, had a history Thucydides clues us into, with the geographical knowledge he assumes: Eion was the first target of the new League (a Parian-Thasian polis), thus, a first stage not only into the Strymon corridor, but also into the Thasian *peraia* to its east. This is what led to Thasos' revolt. Whereas the reader has had no explicit guidance in interpreting the Athenians' campaigns to this point, here Thucydides intends no ambiguity. When the two-year siege ended, the Athenians took over the possessions over which the war was fought and forced the Thasians to tear down their walls, hand over their ships, pay not only the cost of the siege, but also tribute for the future (1.101.3).

Athens' early targets by themselves implicitly help to explain why cities would revolt, but the language Thucydides uses for Naxos' condition post-revolt is also explicit: "Naxos was the first allied city to be enslaved contrary to custom, but afterwards it happened to others as circumstances arose" (1.98.4). Here the famous Thucydidean austerity gives way to emotive language as an introduction to the change in the character of the Athenians' control over their former allies. It is portentous and subtle: it combines (a) description—here is what the Athenians did as leaders of the League; (b) interpretation—they carried out a *war* on Karystos; they made *war on* ... and *enslaved* the Naxians; and (c) analysis: *this was the first time* it happened; it set a precedent. The following passage continues the analysis of growth by elaborating on the reasons for revolts and their connection to tribute and the increase in Athens' naval power and thus, its *archē*.

> Of all the causes of revolts, those connected with arrears of tribute and ships, and with failure to serve, were the chief; for the Athenians were severe and exacting, and made themselves offensive by applying compulsion to men who were neither accustomed to nor willing to labor continuously. In some other respects the Athenians were not the old popular rulers they had been initially; and if they had more than their fair share of service, it was correspondingly easy for them to suppress any that tried to revolt. For this the allies bore responsibility: their wish to get off campaigning made most of them arrange to pay their share of the expense in money instead of in ships, thereby to avoid having to leave their homes. Thus the Athenians were increasing their navy with the funds that the allies expended, while the allies, whenever they revolted, went into war lacking the resources, and the experience (1.99).

Since Thucydides charts development over time, we may question the reason for its placement there before the major Delian League victory over the Persians (strictly, the Phoenician navy), at the mouth of the Eurymedon River in Pamphylia in southern Asia Minor (1.100). In situating it thusly, Thucydides arguably makes that victory not so much a triumph of freedom over slavery, achieved by the Greeks under Athenian leadership over the Persians, as much as a battle between two rival empires.

The Development of Athenian Power: Two Themes

Expansion

The Pentecontaetia provides a bird's-eye view of Athenian movements over an increasingly broad geographical canvas from the Strymon River region in Thrace and the northwestern Aegean, to Egypt and Cyprus, then back to the Greek world, this time moving onto land, including the Peloponnese, then to the eastern Mediterranean yet again. This is no mere list of military expeditions. It is the story of imperial expansion by sea, then onto land, Sparta's sphere of control, and against or near to Sparta's allies (cf. 1.118).

The narrative sweep provides the interpretive umbrella that will contribute to the explanation of the "true cause" of the Peloponnesian War. In the sheer geographical expanse is the implicit notion of overextension in far-off places: while the Athenians attempt to take over land in central Greece and the Peloponnese, they also engage in major campaigns in Cyprus and Egypt (and the interior of Thrace) that ultimately fail. This will resonate when readers come to the account of the Sicilian expedition—at the beginning of his narrative of which, not coincidentally, Thucydides uses the phrase "true cause" (ἀληθεστάτη πρόφασις), to describe the real purpose of that expedition (6.6.1) in contrast to the ostensible one of answering an appeal for help from allies (Egestaeans and Leontinian exiles, 6.6, 19). These events in the Pentecontaetia, however, set the precedent.

In the case of the Athenians' expedition in Egypt (when they are already east in Cyprus, with 200 ships of their own and their allies), the request for aid comes from Inaros, the Libyan king, spearheading an Egyptian revolt (1.104; on the chronology, see Kahn 2008). Yet soon after he establishes the Athenian presence there Thucydides switches arenas, returning to the Greek world for four action-packed chapters. The Athenians had just settled the Messenians, who had been in revolt from the Spartans, at Naupactus, on the north shore of the Corinthian Gulf. Megara, in a war with Corinth, had defected from the Peloponnesian League, and gone over to Athens; the Corinthians were furious. There was fighting to be done, first, between the Corinthians and other Peloponnesians and Athenians, then a major, two-year war with the Aeginetans, who were subjugated and forced to tear down their walls, give up their fleet, and pay tribute. Next came the erection of the Long Walls at Athens. Sparta and Athens would engage at Tanagra and the Boeotians and Athenians at Oenophyta, both in Boeotia.

The construction of the eastern campaigns alongside the mainland, island, and Thracian campaigns as an overreach (analogous to the Sicilian expedition) is achieved through both dramatic presentation and recasting the Athenians' expedition in Egypt not entirely as a response to a request for assistance but above all as a campaign to conquer the country. In resuming the narrative of the eastern sphere of war, Thucydides notes that "every kind" of war occurred—a heightened mode of expression, and the first instance of a recurrent phrase to underscore excessive suffering and death in crisis (plague, stasis, senseless massacre at Mycalessus; see Flory 1988). Similarly, when he states that "at first the Athenians were masters of Egypt," it signals not only impending disaster, but also motives of conquest, such that answering a plea for assistance, like that of the Egestaeans in 415, is a mere cover for imperial expansion.

Thucydides did not have to spell out the fate of the Athenians and, presumably, their allies, in Egypt at the hands of a large Persian army: the Greeks were shut off on an island and besieged for a year and a half; then the Persians did what Persians do—in Herodotus, at least—and alter the natural world, by draining off the water around the island; they then captured the men on the island by foot. The six-year expedition failed (1.110). Yet, as soon as they had concluded a five-year truce with Sparta, the Athenians returned to the eastern Mediterranean under the command of Cimon with 200 of their own and allied ships. Campaigns took place in Cyprus (where Cimon died), Egypt, Phoenicia, and Cilicia, and, this time, battles were successful on both land and sea (1.112).

A casualty list from the tribe Erechtheis, from the early 450s, lists war dead from campaigns in Cyprus and Egypt—which we can relate to Thucydides' narrative—but also Phoenicia, unmentioned by Thucydides. The eastern campaigns, including that at Eurymedon, aimed at expanding Athens' power. They could have been told differently. Eurymedon could have been highlighted as a Delian League triumph. The Cypriote and Egyptian campaigns could have been presented as Delian League campaigns. Thucydides' version of the last was an Athenian expedition of conquest displaying power, audacity, failure, and resilience—much like the Sicilian expedition and its aftermath (see 2.65.11–13; 8.1–3).

Revolts

Revolts signify empire. Members of a free alliance do not "revolt," but subjects in an empire do. There is no mistaking the linkage when Thucydides states baldly that Naxos was "the first ally to be enslaved, and then, others fell victim as circumstances arose"; he did not need to add that others fell victim to the same treatment—narrative overkill for Thucydides, one might have thought. The ending of the Pentecontaetia, the revolt of Samos, makes the case cogently.[2]

The trouble on Samos that culminated in its revolt in 440/39 (1.115.2–117) is the last event treated in the Pentecontaetia proper (although Thucydides explicitly mentions the events concerning Corcyra and Potidaea that he had already covered, and "other circumstances that led to the war" in 118.1, thus including them in the period, a fact too easily overlooked in critiques of his account). The Samian revolt began with a long-standing, nonetheless, garden-variety conflict with Miletus over Priene that blossomed into a revolt, and contained factionalism within Samos itself. But this was not just any revolt, and Athens' response was not an ordinary response— rather, Thucydides' decision about how to write it up was not like the narration of other revolts in the Pentecontaetia. Gomme, in commenting on how well the war with Samos revealed "the true nature of the Athenian 'empire,'" seems to have recognized the aptness of the revolt as an ending for the Pentecontaetia (1959, 351; Wecowski 2013). In a significant respect, the revolt of Samos and the Athenian response marked a renewed "imperial moment" (for the phrase, see Kagan 2010; and Samos' apt choice of Naxos in that volume), a demonstration of an aggressive empire, in evidence even after the disasters in Egypt, the failures of land expansion, and the loss of Megara and its harbors.

---

[2] Megara is the exception, the one city during this period whose revolt the Athenians could do nothing about, 1.114; one wonders whether Pericles took that failure personally, as commander in charge—an implicit teaser Thucydides slips in?

This revolt demonstrated the power of the *archē* for these reasons: Samos, one of the three "guardians of the empire" (*Ath. Pol.* 24.2), unlike tributary subjects that lacked a fleet, or other means of defense, had a large navy. Moreover, the Athenians were easily able to enlist their other two ship-contributing allies, Chios and Lesbos, to join their own fleet. Persians figure conspicuously in this episode. The Persian satrap of Ionia, Pissouthnes, not only freed Samian hostages whom the Athenians had placed on Lemnos, but also led 700 *epikouroi* (mercenaries) against Samos. The threat of the Phoenician navy was significant enough to make Pericles leave with sixty ships south down the Carian coast. Both Athenians and Persians were willing and ready to intervene in the stasis at Samos; there was evidently plenty of unfinished business that the Samian revolt highlights.

The narrative strategy by which Thucydides insinuates the larger meaning of this closing episode is important. He throws at the reader a dizzying cascade, not of talents of silver expended, but of ship numbers: sixty initially arrive from Athens, sixteen then splinter off here and there; forty-four, under all ten generals, defeat the Samians' seventy in battle, including twenty transports. Forty more arrive from Athens, and twenty-five from Chios and Lesbos; but then sixty leave on the news that the Phoenician fleet was on its way, five Samian ships having gone to fetch it. Another forty come from Athens under three generals, and twenty, under two generals, and another thirty ships from Lesbos and Chios—all these in the space of twenty-six *Oxford Classical Texts* lines. Pericles looms large in this episode as the only general here named: "Pericles and nine others" (for the phrasing, see Dover 1960), though five others are named further along (including one Thucydides, probably not the historian; for likelier candidates see Gomme 1959 *ad loc.*).

Revolts can demonstrate power, but the coalescence of all these factors in the revolt of Samos—war between cities in the *archē*, one of which had its own navy, and revolted; stasis within that city, one side of which procured Persian aid—made it a brilliant test case of the state of Athens' imperial might several years before the outbreak of war. Furthermore, that the Athenians were able to command the two other privileged islands in the *archē* (Chios and Lesbos) to join in the suppression of the revolt was a clear indication of Athens' ability to command allegiance even from those that had defensive power.

By the conclusion of the Pentecontaetia, readers know that tribute fuels Athens' empire and, therefore, that a ready supply of capital fueled by revenue underpins the rapidity with which the Athenians can deploy a total of 160 ships when needed, even after previous losses; Thucydides' narrative choice of cataloguing numbers and the rapid deployments of ships, rather than talents, makes the point crisply, and neatly. But money and expense are never far away: in relating the settlement following the end of the siege, Thucydides notes that it included an order to repay the entire cost of the war in fixed installments. An inscription (ML 55; Fornara 133, with a new fragment) preserves three payments totaling 1,400 talents made by the Treasury of Athena to the ten generals, sources that are compatible with Thucydides' account (following Lewis 1981); a treaty with the island followed after (on the date, Matthaiou 2014, 162–63, if he is correct in accepting Thucydides' possibly tight chronology).

The Growth of Athenian Power: The Evidence of Inscriptions

Epigraphy is nonpareil as evidence in general. In this case, it consists of numerous decrees, mostly fragmentary, emanating straight from the Athenian *ekklēsia*, telling us precious details about Athens' dealings with its empire during this period when neither Thucydides nor other narrative sources aim to provide a comprehensive account; and that aside, decrees usually reveal what literary historians do not care to, for whatever reason. Whether these different kinds of evidence dovetail, clash, or do not speak to one another at all, is of paramount interest to the historian of the Athenian empire. In this case, Thucydides neither defends the empire nor its agents; we would expect decrees of the Athenian *ekklēsia* to reflect and represent through their rhetoric a different attitude.

Sometimes they dovetail, as in the case of the removal of the treasury from Delos to Athens. From Thucydides we learn the initial location; we know about the transfer from Plutarch but not its date (*Per.* 12.1; cf. *Arist.* 25.3). Epigraphic evidence (a fragment of a tribute quota list containing chronologically precise information, *IG* I^3 285, fr. 1) fixes the date when the Athenians first paid the one-sixtieth (the *aparche*) into Athena's treasury to 454/3, thus providing the *terminus ante quem*, at least, for the transfer of the treasury. The connection with the construction of the Parthenon a few years hence may not be coincidental. Here epigraphy closes a gap, bringing together literary sources with their different purposes and interests and allows us to see how viewing those together with the linchpin piece of evidence can be fruitful.

It used to be the case that inscriptions virtually clinched a reconstruction of the mid-fifth century history of the empire. The orthodox view is owed to the editors of the so-called tribute lists (Meritt et al. 1950), consisting chiefly of the hundreds of inscribed fragments of *aparchai* lists, the record that the Hellenotamiai made to the city's accountants of the one-sixtieth dedicated to Athena from the annual tribute; the first fifteen years were inscribed on one huge stele (the *Lapis Primus*). The narrative of the reconstruction was published in 1950 (*ATL* Vol. 3); Meiggs (1972) contributed important articles, synthesized in his *Athenian Empire*, still the main handbook in English. A number of decrees of the Athenian assembly dealt with empire-wide issues, such as difficulty with tribute collection, or pertained to specific cities, usually in the case of revolt—the Chalcis decree (ML 52; Fornara 103; OR 131), the Erythrae decree (ML 40; Fornara 71; OR 121)—and were interpreted as demonstrating the completed "transformation" from League to Empire, as well as revealing problems in maintaining a firm hand (see Meiggs 1972, 152–74). Signs of disaffection or crisis in the epigraphic record could be married with the collapse of the Egyptian campaign after Cimon's death in Cyprus, and the revolts on Euboea and of Megara. Most important, in their concern with tribute collection, and revolts, they dovetailed, and in very concrete terms, with Thucydides' analysis of the circumstances and the means by which the Athenians were able to increase their rule with the "allies" paying for their very subjection (1.99).

The difference between writing about the Pentecontaetia in the twenty-first century in contrast to the twentieth is that epigraphic dating and reconstructions have undergone a tectonic shift caused by the removal of a technical epigraphical deterrent, the form of the letter sigma, that was thought to have gone out of fashion by 446. One inscription with the older style sigma—a treaty or renewal of a treaty with Sicilian Egesta (ML 37; Fornara 81; OR 166)—contains both the old-style sigma and an archon's name in the prescript (legible with the aid of enhanced laser photography), which means it could now be dated securely (to 418 BCE), a rarity for inscriptions of this period. One consequence has been a "domino-effect" (Papazarkadas 2009, 78), that is, the wholesale downdating to the 420s of the lot of inscriptions that formed the vital peg in the "growth of empire" reconstructions during the Pentecontaetia. In fact, this period is when the main dissenter of the Athenian tribute-list orthodoxy, Harold Mattingly (1996), had insisted all the documents dated to the mid-fifth century should be placed. But treating the inscriptions as a virtual unit, an approach whereby all inscriptions that *could* be placed in the 420s BCE *should* be (Papazarkadas 2009), is too extreme. It is essential to scrutinize the arguments for dating each document on its own merits (Rhodes 2008, 2014).

The fragments of lists of the *aparchai* of the period 454/3–432 have allowed the reconstruction that over those years well over 200 cities, perhaps more, paid some 400 talents in imperial revenue. Thucydides has Pericles state as a fact that some 600 talents of silver came in annually from the empire, "for the most part of tribute" (Thuc. 2.13.3). These data aroused skepticism over Thucydides' figure of 460 talents for the first assessment of tribute, on the grounds that League membership initially would have comprised fewer members than in the mid-fifth century—a not unreasonable assumption. A recurrent fallacy informing the history of the Athenian empire, however, is that assessments and payments of tribute should correspond. One records a decision; the other records what was implemented. We have ample confirmation, in fact, that assessments and collection did not harmonize.

A case in point is that by 430, the northeast mainland city of Methone had been in negotiations with Athens over certain debts to the city (ML 65; Fornara 128; OR 150). Its date of entry into the *archē* is unknown, but for it to have arrears by that date it would have been in the *archē* at least for the previous assessment period (and the fragmentary condition of "lists" make it impossible to argue that it was or wasn't a longer-standing member). Yet the Athenians considered Methone's loyalty so important that they not only forgave its arrears, but also for the future required the city to pay only the *aparchē*. This was not the only instance of such individualized arrangements. Rubrics denoting late payments, or partial payments (Lepper 1962; Meiggs 1972, 249–52) in the *aparchai* lists, for example, also are useful for highlighting the difference between assessment and collection.

One inscription with parallels to the Samian conflict concerns arrangements between Athens and the nearby coastal city of Erythrae (mentioned above, difficult of analysis because it is lost, its contents therefore based on a facsimile, also now lost, though a different facsimile has been discovered, Malouchou 2014). The city appears to have been in stasis, with exiles who had medized constituting one faction. As in the case of Samos (1.115), Athens intervened and imposed constitutional change, specifically, a council (*boulē*) of 120 men, selected by lot. (Epigraphic and literary evidence are equally important for understanding Athens' practice of establishing democracies, which was not at all consistent; see Brock 2009). The decree illustrates the typical blend of imperial authority, whether legal, political, economic, or military, infringing on local autonomy characteristic of much of the epigraphic record of the Athenian empire. In addition, reference to the Persians, as in the case of the Samian stasis and revolt, underscores the pressures on communities that both empires, the Athenian and the Persian, exerted that were exacerbated at times of stasis.

In Thucydides, the Athenians, appearing at a Spartan assembly before the war, bristle at—unless they boast of?— their reputation for forcing their allies to come to Athens to litigate: they see this as a privilege that other empires—read Persia—do not grant and for which they do not deserve to be hated (Thuc. 1.77; cf. [Xen.] 1.17). An inscription traditionally dated to the 460s or 450s, concerning the judicial relations between Athens and Phaselis (ML 31; Fornara 68; OR 120), for which the arguments for moving to the 420s do not yet appear conclusive, allows—or compels—the Phaselians to litigate certain cases in Athens "just like the Chians" at the polemarch's court. It is possible to interpret this as a privilege granted to the Phaselians in return for their joining the League/*archē* around the time of the battle of Eurymedon, when their trade networks in the eastern Mediterranean would have been cut off and they would have had to have reoriented their networks to the west (Bresson 2008, 113–15).

It is difficult to maintain the reconstruction of "crisis" and "transformation" solely on the epigraphic record anymore. It is not that those particular decrees that projected power (and heavy-handedness)—"transformation"—but that also reflected weakness in the administrative machinery—"crisis"—no longer could fit this period, but that the criteria and the arguments no longer better suit this period than the first decade of the Peloponnesian War. For example, one inscription that had been a mainstay of the "hardening" of empire, Cleinias' proposal of a new procedure for the collection of tribute to prevent theft en route to Athens (ML 46; Fornara 98; OR 154), is now best dated to 425/4. The decree recording the terms of the settlement with Chalcis mentioned above complements Thucydides' reference to the revolt on Euboea and may well still belong in 446; it attests unequivocally to a "hardened" *archē*, not unfamiliar to readers of Thucydides. While this decree, and others like it, do not use the language of subjugation and slavery (Low 2005), they get their point across nonetheless.

The View from Sparta

There have been characterizations of the Spartans before the Pentecontaetia begins, by the Corinthians (1.68–71), and by two Spartans, King Archidamus (1.80–85) and an ephor, Sthenelaïdas (1.86). They serve to reflect the portrait of Spartans in 432. In the Pentecontaetia, the Spartans' attitudes and actions are represented as variable, to the point of inscrutability. We wonder, then, about the Spartans' position vis-à-vis the Athenians.

A checklist ends up with more questions than answers. Were they hostile, or friendly? Aggressive, or uneasy? They were suspicious of the Athenians' wall building, happy to have them take over the League; ready to invade Attica at the request of the Thasians, but unwilling to be bribed by Artaxerxes to invade Attica several years later. Thucydides presents the only confrontation between the two powers, the Spartan victory at Tanagra, as occurring simply because the Spartans were confounded by their inability to chart a safe route home after campaigning in Doris (1.107–108). But then there was Pleistoanax's aborted invasion, and the threat of war when the Samians revolted. Sparta had a keen interest in Delphi (the Second Sacred War) during the five-year truce, but after they restored the city to the Delphians, the Athenians ousted them and put the Phocians in charge. Sparta did not respond. An odd history, if the aim of the Pentecontaetia is to afford a coherent understanding of Spartan-Athenian relations during the Pentecontaetia.

The View from Corinth

What Thucydides does pinpoint clearly and unambiguously is the injury to Corinth during this period. Close allies before 460, the Corinthians and Athenians became enemies in 460 when Megara joined the Athenian *archē* because of war with its neighbor Corinth. This ignited Corinth's "intense hatred" for Athens (1.103.4). The following, detailed by Thucydides, did not help: the Athenians gained control of Megara's two harbors; made an alliance with Argos just south of Corinth; captured and brought into the *archē* the nearby island of Aegina; settled the Messenians at Naupactus, on the north shore of the Gulf, now with a main naval station there took Corinth's possession Chalcis just to the west at the mouth of the Gulf; attacked Sicyon, Corinth's immediate neighbor; and took possession of a good part of Achaea in the north Peloponnese. From Corinth's perspective, whatever the Athenians' relations with Sparta were during this period, more locally the Athenians were putting a chokehold around them.

Conclusion

At the beginning of this chapter I noted historians' tendency to judge Thucydides' Pentecontaetia by their own standard of what those interested in demonstrating Athens' rise to power should include; when they find fault, they might take the view that if Thucydides had had the chance he would have revised and improved the excursus, according to these standards. Even if not taking an extreme view like some, that the events in the excursus are just raw data in a barren narrative landscape, put in these bald terms, the historiographical anachronism is obvious. Readers legitimately, however, lament the absence of more, better, different details about this period than Thucydides provides.

We might pose the question, then: What is lost, given the purpose(s) of the Pentecontaetia, by not having a reference to the Peace of Callias? What is lost by not having a reference to the transfer of the treasury of the Delian League? If we take the first, to say that Thucydides should have explicitly mentioned the Peace of Callias is to correct him. If we assume a Peace was concluded, then Thucydides knew about it. The attention accorded Pissouthnes' activity and the advance of the Phoenician navy in the closing episode of the Pentecontaetia is itself a very Thucydidean way of making the point about the so-called Peace: it was a non-starter.

As for the removal of the League treasury, in one respect, it made no practical difference: Athenians controlled the funds when they appointed themselves its treasurers in 478. We might reflect, however, on one of the anecdotes Plutarch preserves (*Per.* 12), once the treasury had been moved, about the propriety of its use on rebuilding the temples burnt by the Persians. The Parthenon building accounts show that the Hellenotamiai contributed funds in ten of the years (Pope 2000, 63; Kallet-Marx 1989). Greeks associated monumental buildings with power. Thucydides, ever the contrarian, disagreed: "one should not examine the appearance of cities rather than their power" (1.10), this in a comment on the false association people made between temples and power.

Having suggested ways of looking at these two (in)famous examples of omissions, we might ask what then the excursus accomplishes in the light of its expressed aims. It makes clear what is so very different about Athens' power and that that power had the potential for increase, even with setbacks. It answers the question how the Athenians were able to achieve naval *archē*, an instrument of control of other Greeks that, through the injection of money to fund the navy and the costs of empire generally, was paid for by those very Greeks. The rest, in a sense, might be icing were it not for the necessity also to establish the Athenians' aims, having taken over the leadership of the alliance and reorganized it on their own terms. While Thucydides describes a process of hardened control over allies who became "subjects" through their tributary status, the Pentecontaetia makes short shrift of the modern reconstruction of "free alliance" only gradually transforming into "empire" by mid-century in accordance with interpretations of epigraphic evidence. Thucydides has a shorter honeymoon; the "enslavement" of Naxos is unequivocal, as is the rapacious appropriation of the Thasian *peraia*.

His interpretative lens on the period, in other words, helps us understand choices. Although he prepares the reader repeatedly for the bipolar conflict before the Peloponnesian War begins, the excursus itself is intended to help us understand the bold, untethered nature of Athenian naval power (for which the Corinthians' characterization in 1.70 is a good introduction), including how it affects Sparta's allies—perhaps more than Sparta itself; in fact, the account of the period presents a more complex tripolar, and multi-sphered world. To that extent, the Pentecontaetia may try to do too much, not too little.

References

Badian, E. 1993. *From Plataea to Potidaea: Studies in the History and Historiography of the Pentecontaetia*. Baltimore: Johns Hopkins University Press.
Bresson, A. 2008. *L'économie de la Grèce des cites: II. Les espaces de l'échange*. Paris:
Brock, R. 2009. "Did the Athenian Empire Promote Democracy?" In *Interpreting the Athenian Empire*, edited by J. Ma, N. Papazarkadas, and R. Parker, 149–66. London: Duckworth.
Davies, J. K. 1978. *Democracy and Classical Greece*. London: Colin.
Davies, J. K. 2013. "Corridors, Cleruchies, Commodities, and Coins: The Pre-history of the Athenian Empire." In *Handels- und Finanzgebaren in der Ägäis im 5. Jh. v. Chr. : Trade and Finance in the 5th c. BC Aegean World* (BYZAS 18), edited by A. Slawisch, 1–24. Istanbul: Ege Yayınları.
Dover, K. J. 1960. "ΔΕΚΑΤΟΣ ΑΥΤΟΣ." *JHS* 80: 61–77.
Flory, S. 1988. "Pasa Idea in Thucydides." *AJP* 109:12–19.
Fornara, C. 1977. *From Archaic Times to the End of the Peloponnesian War*. Edited and translated by C. Fornara. Baltimore: John Hopkins University Press.
Foster, E. 2010. *Thucydides, Pericles and Periclean Imperialism*. Cambridge: Cambridge University Press.
Gomme, A. W. 1959. *A Historical Commentary on Thucydides*. Vol. I. Oxford: Clarendon.
Kagan, D. 2010. "Pericles, Thucydides and the Defense of Empire." In *Makers of Ancient Strategy. From the Persian Wars to the Fall of Rome*, edited by V. Hanson, 31–57. Princeton: Princeton University Press.
Kahn, D. 2008. "Inaros' Rebellion against Artaxerxes I and the Athenian Disaster in Egypt." *CQ* 58: 424–40.
Kallet, L. 2013. "The Origins of the Athenian Economic *Arche*." *JHS* 133: 43–60.
Kallet-Marx, L. 1993. *Money, Expense, and Naval Power in Thucydides'* History 1–5.24. Berkeley: University of California Press.
Lepper, F. A. 1962. "Some Rubrics in the Tribute Quota Lists." *JHS* 82: 25–55.
Lewis, D. M., ed. 1981. *Inscriptiones Graecae*. Vol. I, *Inscriptiones Atticae Euclidis anno anteriores*. 3rd ed. Berlin: De Gruyter.
Loraux, N. 1980. "Thucydide n'est pas un collègue." *Quaderni di Storia* 12: 55–81.
Low, P. 2005. "Looking for the Language of Athenian Imperialism." *JHS* 125: 93–111.
Ma, J., N. Papazarkadas, and R. Parker, eds. 2009. *Interpreting the Athenian Empire*. London: Duckworth.
Malouchou, G. E. 2014. "A Second Facsimile of the Erythrai Decree (*IG* I³ 14)." In *ΑΘΗΝΑΙΩΝ ΕΠΙΣΚΟΠΟΣ: Studies in Honour of Harold B. Mattingly*. Athens: Hellenike Epigraphike Hetaireia, edited by A. P. Matthaiou and R. K. Pitt, 73–96. Athens: Hellenike Epigraphike Hetaireia.
Marginesu, G., and Ath. A. Themos. 2014. "Ἀνέλοσαν ἐς τὸν πρὸς Σαμίος πόλεμον." In *ΑΘΗΝΑΙΩΝ ΕΠΙΣΚΟΠΟΣ: Studies in Honour of Harold B. Mattingly*. Athens: Hellenike Epigraphike Hetaireia, edited by A. P. Matthaiou and R. K. Pitt, 170–84. Athens: Hellenike Epigraphike Hetaireia.

Matthaiou, A. P. 2014. "The Treaty of Athens with Samos (*IG* I³ 48)." In *ΑΘΗΝΑΙΩΝ ΕΠΙΣΚΟΠΟΣ: Studies in Honour of Harold B. Mattingly*. Athens: Hellenike Epigraphike Hetaireia, edited by A. P. Matthaiou and R. K. Pitt, 141–69. Athens: Hellenike Epigraphike Hetaireia.

Matthaiou, A. P., and R. K. Pitt, eds. 2014. *ΑΘΗΝΑΙΩΝ ΕΠΙΣΚΟΠΟΣ: Studies in Honour of Harold B. Mattingly*. Athens: Hellenike Epigraphike Hetaireia.

Mattingly, H. B. 1996. *The Athenian Empire Restored: Epigraphic and Historical Studies*. Ann Arbor: University of Michigan Press.

Meiggs, R. 1972. *The Athenian Empire*. Oxford: Clarendon.

Moroo, A. 2014. "The Erythrai Decrees Reconsidered: *IG* I³ 14, 15, 16." In *ΑΘΗΝΑΙΩΝ ΕΠΙΣΚΟΠΟΣ: Studies in Honour of Harold B. Mattingly*. Athens: Hellenike Epigraphike Hetaireia, edited by A. P. Matthaiou and R. K. Pitt, 97–120. Athens: Hellenike Epigraphike Hetaireia.

Meritt, B. D., H. T. Wade-Gery, and M. F. McGregor. 1950. *The Athenian Tribute Lists*. Vol. 3. Princeton: American School of Classical Studies at Athens.

Murray, Oswyn. 1966. "Ο ΑΡΧΑΙΟΣ ΔΑΣΜΟΣ." *Historia* 15: 142–56.

Papazarkadas, N. 2009. "Epigraphy and the Athenian Empire: Reshuffling the Chronological Cards." In *Interpreting the Athenian Empire*, edited by J. Ma, N. Papazarkadas, and R. Parker, 67–88. London: Duckworth.

Parker, V. 2004. "The Historian Ephorus: His Selection of Sources." *Antichthon* 38: 29–50.

Pope, S. A. 2000. "Financing and Design: The Development of the Parthenon Program and the Parthenon Building Accounts." In *Miscellanea Mediterranea*, edited by R. R. Holloway, 61–70. Archaeologia Transatlantica 18. Providence: Center for Old World Archaeology and Art, Brown University.

Raaflaub, K. 2009. "Learning from the Enemy." In *Interpreting the Athenian Empire*, edited by J. Ma, N. Papazarkadas, and R. Parker, 89–124. London: Duckworth.

Rainey, S. 2004. "Thucydides, 1.98–118, Diodorus, 11.60–12.28, and Their Common Source." *Athenaeum* 92: 217–236.

Rawlings, H. R., III. 1977. "Thucydides on the Purpose of the Delian League." *Phoenix* 31: 1–8.

Rhodes, P. J. 2008. "After the Three-Bar Sigma Controversy: The History of Athenian Imperialism Reassessed." *CQ* 58: 501–506.

Rhodes, P. J. 2014. "What Remains of Periclean Imperialism?" In *ΑΘΗΝΑΙΩΝ ΕΠΙΣΚΟΠΟΣ: Studies in Honour of Harold B. Mattingly*. Athens: Hellenike Epigraphike Hetaireia, edited by A. P. Matthaiou and R. K. Pitt, 39–50. Athens: Hellenike Epigraphike Hetaireia.

Rood, T. 1998. *Thucydides: Narrative and Explanation*. Oxford: Clarendon.

Stadter, P. A. 1993. "The Form and Content of Thucydides' Pentecontaetia (1.89–117)." *GRBS* 34: 35–72.

Whitehead, D. 1998. "'Ο ΝΕΟΣ ΔΑΣΜΟΣ: 'Tribute' in Classical Athens." *Hermes* 128: 173–88.

CHAPTER 4

SPARTA AND THE CRISIS OF THE PELOPONNESIAN LEAGUE IN THUCYDIDES' *HISTORY*

ELLEN G. MILLENDER

THUCYDIDES' work on the Peloponnesian War is one of our most important sources not only on classical Sparta in general but also on the Peloponnesian League, the alliance that contributed significantly to Sparta's status as a leading Greek power from its inception in the sixth century to its dissolution in the fourth. Much of Thucydides' information on Sparta's relationship with its allies in this league occurs in his treatment of the Archidamian War and its aftermath in the first five books of his *History*. In this section of his work, in which he sharply contrasts Spartan conservatism and Athenian dynamism, Thucydides at once illuminates the effects of Sparta's struggle with Athens on its hegemonic status and reveals his understanding of the roots of Sparta's dominance in the Peloponnesus. Right from the start of his analysis of the course of their struggle, Thucydides portrays the Spartans as cautious, fearful, and incapable of innovation—especially in terms of military policy and strategy. This military inadaptability, according to Thucydides, not only undermined the Peloponnesian war effort but also, more importantly, contributed to allied disaffection and the destabilization of Spartan hegemony in the Peloponnesus.

Both themes under consideration—Sparta's military malaise and its consequently hobbled hegemony—are explicit in Thucydides' account of the debate held at Sparta in 432 (1.66–88). Thucydides here, as elsewhere in his text, provides a window onto the events through orations that combine, to varying degrees, actual speeches, his own views on the leading considerations that influenced political decisions and behavior during the war, and popular currents of thought in late-fifth-century Athens (cf., especially, Garrity 1998). Through the four speeches delivered at the meetings of the Spartan Assembly and the Peloponnesian League, Thucydides explores the national character of

Athens and Sparta in order to demonstrate that the Peloponnesian War was the inevitable clash between two vastly different types of society. Thucydides has the aggrieved Corinthians introduce this series of speeches with an urgent plea for Spartan resistance to Athenian aggression (1.68–71). Instead of focusing on their complaints against Athens, however, Thucydides' Corinthians critique the Spartans' conservatism, passivity, and ignorance of the profound differences between themselves and the Athenians. In the process the Corinthians erect a polarity between Athenian initiative and Spartan obsolescence, a polarity that comes to a head in their call for an end to Spartan inertia (1.71.2–3):

> As we have just shown, your ways are old-fashioned as compared with theirs. Just as in the arts, innovations must always prevail. And though undisturbed customs are best for the city at peace, those who are compelled to respond to many situations have need of much invention. For this very reason Athens, because of its vast experience, has been carried further than you on the path of innovation.

The angered Corinthians, however, offer the Spartans little in the way of concrete demands for changes in Spartan foreign policy or instructions concerning the logistics of a concerted Peloponnesian response to Athenian aggression. Instead, they opaquely advise the Lacedaemonians to follow the Athenians' example of enterprise without explaining what such innovation entails (cf. Legon 1973, 161; Crane 1992, 227; Foster 2010, 82–83).

While scholars have argued that the Corinthians here point to Sparta's need to make political changes in order to compete with Athens (cf. Hornblower 1991, 115–16; Millender, forthcoming), their attack on the Lacedaemonians' old-fashioned ways also likely embraces the issue of military adaptation—i.e., the Spartans' inability to change militarily in order to meet the hegemonic challenge posed by Athens. The Corinthians spend much of their speech critiquing the Spartans' unwillingness to use their military might to curb Athenian aggression (1.69, 71) and suggest that such indecision and inaction likewise characterized the Lacedaemonians' response to the Persian invasion in the early fifth century (1.69.5). Particularly noteworthy is their call for Spartan action and their threat to look for alliance elsewhere—likely among the Argives, the Spartans' main rivals in the Peloponnesus (1.71.4–5). Here the Corinthians reveal the most dangerous consequence of the Spartans' failure to mount an effective military response to Athenian aggression: a crisis in confidence and growing belief among Sparta's allies that the Lacedaemonians were incapable of providing effective leadership of the Peloponnesus (cf., especially, 1.69, 71.5).

As he traces the course of the Archidamian War down to the Peace of Nicias of 421 through the first five books of his *History*, Thucydides bears out the Corinthians' fears in his almost wholly negative treatment of Spartan strategy and operations. More particularly, through his depictions of the various Spartans who crafted and prosecuted the Peloponnesian war effort, Thucydides reveals his own belief that the Lacedaemonians proved to be particularly unwilling—or perhaps inept—students of warfare. And it was the Spartans' failures in the field that, in Thucydides' eyes, most damaged their relations with their allies and thereby compromised the integrity of the Peloponnesian League.

This chapter will investigate Thucydides' portrait of Spartan military obsolescence and its geopolitical ramifications by first considering Thucydides' largely negative treatment of Spartan military strategy and performance during the Archidamian War. As we shall see in the first two sections of this study, Thucydides stresses Spartan military failures and even seems to underemphasize—and perhaps ignore—the potentially successful and innovative aspects of Spartan strategy. The final two sections of the chapter will then analyze Thucydides' depiction of the Spartans' increasingly troubled relations with their allies until their victory at Mantinea in 418 restored both their military reputation and the integrity of the Peloponnesian League.

"The Same Men Then and Now": The Spartans' Technological Rut

The most adroit students of war in Thucydides' *History* are the Athenians, who, according to the Corinthians, profoundly differ from the Spartans in their daring, innovation, and expansive cast of mind (1.70.2–4; cf. Forde 1989, 17–21; Taylor 2010, 9–10, 15–19, 21–22). The Athenian envoys at the debate in 432 likewise present their fellow countrymen as particularly adaptive in their ability to meet the exigencies of war by correlating their character to their present circumstances. Forced to face the Persians on their own, the Athenians effectively reconceived their very identity and broke with the Greeks' foundational ties to the land by abandoning their *polis* and destroying their household property (1.74.2). Thucydides provides a similar characterization of the Athenians in his *Archaeology* (1.18.2), where he recounts the Athenians' transformation into seamen (ναυτικοί) in response to the looming Persian invasion (cf. Forde 1989, 22–25; Foster 2010, 40–41; Taylor 2010, especially, 9–10, 14, 22–26).

According to the Corinthians, it is now the Spartans' turn to learn from and adapt in response to war—this time the imminent struggle with the Athenians (1.71.3). They call on the Spartans to borrow a page from the Athenians' textbook and leave behind their obsolete ways and embrace the penchant for invention so well exploited by their Athenian enemies (cf. Foster 2010, 82; Crane 1998, 221). In his account of the final two speeches delivered at the debate, Thucydides examines the feasibility of such a change in Spartan character and suggests that the Spartans' learning curve was steep indeed.

One might argue, on the contrary, that the next speaker, the Eurypontid King Archidamus II, offers an intelligent estimation of the challenges that a Spartan declaration of war on Athens would entail (1.80–85.2; cf. Moxon 1978; Foster 2010, 92–93). Archidamus, moreover, echoes both Thucydides (cf. 1.13–15) and Pericles (cf. 1.141.2–44; 2.62.2–3) in his understanding of the profound difference between land-based and sea-based power as well as the economic advantages that sea powers necessarily possess (1.80–81; cf. 1.82.1, 83.2; see Stahl 2003, 53–54). Archidamus, like Pericles in his later speeches, also realizes that the traditional tactics of invasion and devastation would never allow the Spartans to exploit against Athens their superior hoplite force (1.81.2–6; cf. 1.143.4, 2.62.2–3)—even though he continues to countenance the efficacy of such an attack on Athenian land (1.82.2–4). Archidamus even admits to the limited nature of Sparta's superiority in hoplite tactics, given the dependence of infantry on sufficient funding (1.83.2). Archidamus, moreover, demonstrates what may seem to be an ability to think outside traditional Spartan parameters in his advice to the Spartans both to seek allies among Greeks and non-Greeks and to build up the Peloponnesians' naval and financial resources (1.82.1). Finally, Archidamus envisions the eventuality of a vastly different kind of war based on a policy of fomenting rebellion among Athens' allies and predicated on the development of a strong Peloponnesian fleet (1.81.3–4).

Archidamus nevertheless understands the Corinthians' call to action only on a military level and ignores the Corinthians' demand for a change in Spartan character. He primarily configures the profound differences between Athens and Sparta in materialist terms (cf. 1.80.3–4, 83.2–3) and does not appear to share—or perhaps to comprehend fully—the Corinthians' belief that it was the Athenians' uniquely innovative character that lay at the root of Athens' power (cf. Crane 1998, 211; Foster 2010, 91–92). Archidamus, rather, indulges in a lengthy eulogy of Sparta's rigid conservatism (1.84–85.1), in which he characterizes his fellow Spartans as hidebound and even distrustful of education—an attitude that he considers essential to the Lacedaemonians' excellence at war and deliberation (1.84.3):

> We are good at both war and deliberation because we are well-ordered; warlike because self-control is largely based upon a sense of honor, and a sense of shame is largely based on courage. And we are good at deliberation because we are educated with too little learning to despise the laws and too rigorously trained in self-control to disobey them. And we are trained to avoid being too clever in useless matters— such as being able to produce in words an excellent criticism of the enemy's preparations and then failing to proceed against them with equal success in practice.

As his proud analysis of Sparta's strengths makes clear, Thucydides' Archidamus rejects the Corinthians' demand for a change in Spartan character and mocks any educational practices that could threaten traditional Spartan values. If we are to believe Archidamus, Spartan character, once it has been joined by sufficient material resources (cf. 1.80–81), will prove more than capable of challenging Athens' supremacy (cf. Crane 1998, 211, 221).

Perhaps even more revealing is Archidamus' claim that "it is not necessary to suppose that human beings differ much from one another but that the best are the ones educated in the severest school" (1.84.4). As the Corinthians demonstrate in their earlier speech, the Athenians profoundly differ from their Lacedaemonian opponents on many levels— most importantly in the former's military adaptability and flexibility. In his speech at the assembly, Archidamus employs a far more limited form of redefinition in his attempt to put a positive spin on the Corinthians' complaints of Spartan lethargy and caution.

Instead of a call for more dynamism or any kind of change, Archidamus simply repackages these entrenched Spartan qualities as "sensible moderation" (1.84.1–2: σωφροσύνη ἔμφρων). In the same spirit Archidamus concludes his speech with a call to adhere to Sparta's ancestral practices, which have always benefited the Lacedaemonians and thus, he seems to assume, will meet the challenge of Athenian aggression (1.85.1).

We meet an even less promising student of war in the final speaker at the debate at Sparta, the otherwise unknown Spartan ephor, Sthenelaïdas, who delivers a fiery harangue that convinces the Spartans to vote in favor of war with Athens (1.86; cf. Bloedow 1981 and 1987; Allison 1984). At first glance, Sthenelaïdas' call for immediate action against Athens seems to counter the portrait of a slow and cautious Sparta that figures so prominently in the other speeches delivered at the debate (cf. Crane 1998, 216, 220). Upon more careful inspection, however, Sthenelaïdas turns out to be even more reactionary than the Eurypontid king. The ephor's laconic claim to sufficient money, ships, and horses parallels Archidamus' materialistic focus and ignorance of the need for a change in Spartan character. But unlike Archidamus, the ephor reveals a staggering lack of understanding concerning the different resources enjoyed by both sides and an unwillingness—or inability—to conceive of the new policies and strategies that will be necessary to tackle Athens' imperial threat.

The ephor, rather, appears mired in the past, as suggested by his praise of the Spartans as "the same men then [i.e., during the Persian Wars] and now" (1.86: ἡμεῖς δὲ ὁμοῖοι καὶ τότε καὶ νῦν ἐσμέν). The ephor's use of the term ὁμοῖοι, in addition, makes a striking nod to the ideology of the *Homoioi* ("the peers") that underpinned the Spartan *politeia* and that promoted the uniformity and discipline in Spartan life more explicitly praised by Archidamus in his earlier speech at the debate (cf. 1.84–85.1). Armed with this "sameness," along with its focus on the past and insistence on conformity, Sthenelaïdas intends to combat the individuality and versatility that Pericles' Athens encouraged in its citizens (cf. 2.41.1). The fact that the unimaginative ephor proves more persuasive than his—albeit slightly—more farsighted king suggests that Thucydides' Corinthians have won a Pyrrhic victory at the conclusion of the debate at Sparta in 432. They may have achieved their immediate end in the Spartan Assembly's vote that the Thirty Years' Treaty had been broken (cf. 1.87–88), but their demand for Spartan innovation seems unrealizable.

In his account of their later speech at the second congress of their allies, Thucydides has the Corinthians accordingly ratchet down their expectations for the Peloponnesian force (1.120–24; cf. Taylor 2010, 39; Foster 2010, 136–37). Granted, they understand the random nature of war and, accordingly, the need to adapt technologically to changing circumstances (1.122.1). The adaptation that the Corinthians envisage here, however, differs markedly from their earlier demand for change. This time, rather than highlighting differences in national character, the Corinthians echo Archidamus' earlier focus on issues of material strength. They call for investment in sea power with help from allied resources and funds in Olympia and Delphi, and they also hope to lure away Athens' sailors with the offer of higher pay (1.121.3, 5). Despite their own naval experience and expertise, the Corinthians appear to be no different from the Peloponnesian farmers whom Pericles later derides. They, too, fail to grasp the enormity of the education that the Peloponnesians will have to undertake to compete on the seas with Athens' ever improving sailors—an education that Pericles describes as a skill (τέχνη) that demands much study and time (1.142.6–9; cf. 1.141.3; see Edmunds 1975, 24–29). And it is Pericles' predictions that seem to bear fruit, when Thucydides starkly informs us that the Peloponnesians' first salvo in the war, almost a year later in 431, consisted of the most old-fashioned of tactics: an invasion of Attica (1.125).

It should not be surprising to find at the head of this invasion the Spartan King Archidamus II (2.10–23), whose earlier speech demonstrates his attachment to this traditional strategy (1.82.2–4), despite his (or rather Thucydides') awareness of its likely inefficacy (cf. 1.81.2–6; see Moxon 1978, 14–15; Pelling 1991, 126–29). Scholars have argued that Archidamus actually pursued a shrewd strategy in his invasions of Attica in 431 and 430, both of which aimed to pressure the Athenians into accepting pitched battle and came close to success (2.21.2–22.1, 59–65.3; cf. Bloedow 1983). In the end, however, Archidamus' stubborn adherence to this tactic (2.11.1) and conviction in the Athenians' attachment to their land (2.11.6–8; cf. 1.82.2–4) failed to counter the reality of Pericles' unusually adaptable Athenians (cf. 2.14, 16.2; see Taylor 2010, 61, 64).

Whatever the merits of Archidamus' strategy in the early years of the Archidamian War, Thucydides provides a largely negative account of the invasion of 431. Although the Spartans initially showed energy in the planning of this invasion (2.10), Thucydides' description of the expedition emphasizes the gradual dissipation of this initiative through the slow progress and repeated delays of the Peloponnesian army (cf. Westlake 1968, 126–30). His account of the invasion opens with a speech delivered by Archidamus, which once again portrays the king as a conservative, plodding leader (2.11). Archidamus begins by repeating the Corinthians' claims concerning the Peloponnesian force's experience and size (2.11.1; cf. 1.121.2). As in his speech at the earlier debate (cf. 1.80.1, 85.1), Archidamus prizes the experience that comes with age (2.11.1) and urges the Spartans not to fall short of their fathers' standards (2.11.2; cf. Pelling 1991, 126; Crane 1998, 222). In the same vein, Archidamus asks his soldiers to live up to their reputation (2.11.2) and to consider the glory or shame they will bring to their forebears (2.11.9). Archidamus then concludes with a call for the Spartans to maintain the same traditional values that he extols in his earlier speech: order and obedience (2.11.9).

Following Archidamus' speech with its "back to the past" call for action, Thucydides provides a negative account of the expedition that focuses on its slowness and ineffectiveness. After the delay caused by the Spartan king's attempt to reopen negotiations (2.12.1–4), Thucydides claims that the expedition continued to lose its impetus as the Peloponnesians sluggishly mustered at the Isthmus (2.18.3; cf. 2.13.1), slowly progressed toward Attica, and then inexplicably wasted valuable time at Oenoe (2.18.3–4). However sound the strategic reasons behind the Peloponnesians' attempt to capture Oenoe might have been, Thucydides fails to note them and appears to have exaggerated the extent of the delay involved (cf. Westlake 1968, 126). He rather focuses on the Peloponnesian troops' harsh criticism of Archidamus' lackluster leadership, even if he does not explicitly endorse it (2.18.2–5; cf. Cartledge and Debnar 2006, 571).

Archidamus' later decision to remain at Acharnae almost managed to induce the Athenians to come out to battle in defense of their land (2.21.2–22.1). Thucydides, however, continues to stress the passive nature of this plan through his attempt to account for Archidamus' reasons for not advancing into the plain in the immediate vicinity of Athens (2.20; cf. Westlake 1968, 129–30). His account of the invasion then concludes with a simple reference to its failure to force the Athenians into battle and a vague description of the Peloponnesians' further plundering which, like the campaign itself, seems to have run out of steam (2.23). Thucydides' later account of the Peloponnesians' second invasion of Attica in 430 similarly undercuts Archidamus' military skills, this time through its relative brevity (2.47.2, 55–56.1, 57), as does his description of the last invasion of Attica led by Archidamus in the spring of 428 (3.1–3).

All in all, Thucydides' accounts of Archidamus' invasions of Attica highlight this king's failures, downplay any success that attended them, and focus upon the conservative nature of both the king and Spartan tactics (cf. Westlake 1968, 132). Thucydides' even starker accounts of the later invasions in 427 (3.26), in 426 (3.89.1), and in 425 (4.2.1), in turn, underline the Spartans' adherence to this stale and seemingly ineffective tactic. His lack of information on—and presumably lack of interest in—these invasions is even more noteworthy, if, as Thomas Kelly (1982, 48, 50) has argued, the invasion of 427 was not simply another infeasible attempt to bring the Athenians to their knees but primarily aimed to distract the Athenians while the Peloponnesians sent a fleet across the Aegean to Lesbos (cf. 3.25–26). Kelly (1982, 50) believes that the Spartans' invasion of Attica in the spring of 425 was part of a similarly ambitious plan to divert the Athenians' attention while the Peloponnesians attempted to send a fleet to gain control of Corcyra (cf. 4.2.3, 3.1, 8.2). Whether or not he understood their strategic value, Thucydides not only fails to connect the dots between these invasions and other components of the Spartans' overall war plan but also actually uses these invasions to point out the stunning lack of military progress that the Spartans achieved in the first part of the war. In aggregate, these invasions did little more than show the Spartans that Athens could not be reduced by invasion and that new tactics were seriously in order.

Sparta's Famous Hoplites "at Sea"

Throughout his account of the Archidamian War, Thucydides depicts the Spartans as even less adept at naval warfare. Thucydides, moreover, arguably provides a selective and skewed portrait of Spartan naval activity—despite his own awareness of Sparta's serious attempt to challenge Athens' supremacy at sea (cf. Moxon 1978; Kelly 1979 and 1982; Krentz 1997, 66). As his text reveals, the agricultural devastation of Attica did not remain the cornerstone of Spartan strategy against Athens (*contra* Brunt 1965; Kagan 1974, 18–24). In fact, the Spartans put a fleet into action no fewer than six times during this phase of the war: once in 430 to Zacynthus (2.66), twice in 429 against the Athenians in the Corinthian Gulf (2.80–92), twice in 427 to Lesbos (3.15–16, 25–33.1) and Corcyra

(3.69, 76–81.1), and again in 425 to Corcyra (4.2.3, 3.1). In 426 the Spartans also founded a colony at Heraclea Trachinea as a potential naval base against Euboea (3.92). These naval expeditions were notoriously unsuccessful, but Kelly (1982, 53–54; cf. Krentz 1997, 66–67) suggests that Thucydides at the very least did not realize the complexity of Spartan naval strategy during the Archidamian War.

While scholars may debate both the relative merits of the Spartans' naval policy in the early years of the war and Thucydides' grasp of Spartan strategy, Thucydides' consistently negative portrait of Spartan naval activity points to his belief that the Spartans (and their allies) were turning out to be the poor students of warfare—and especially of naval skill (τέχνη)—that Pericles predicted in his first speech to the Athenians (cf. 1.142.6–9). The Spartans' challenges at sea become clear in Thucydides' account of the Peloponnesians' naval encounter with the Athenians under Phormio in the Corinthian Gulf in 429 (2.80–92). According to Thucydides, Phormio correctly predicted that the Peloponnesian ships would behave more like a hoplite army than a navy and would prove unable "to maintain their formation, like a force on land" (2.84.2; cf. Flory 1993, 118). The wind that he had anticipated blew in from the gulf, sent the Peloponnesian ships into confusion, and made them a ripe target for Athens' swift and successful attack (2.84.2–4). After recounting this defeat, Thucydides emphasizes the Spartans' unwillingness—or inability—to learn from their mistakes (2.85.2; cf. Stahl 2003, 85–86):

> The Spartans, especially since this was their first attempt at a sea battle, found it greatly contrary to their calculations, and so far from thinking that their own navy was deficient, believed that some form of cowardice had occurred, not taking into consideration the long experience of the Athenians as compared to their own brief practice.

The Lacedaemonians, instead, responded in anger to this loss by sending to their admiral Cnemus and his fleet an advisory commission with orders to prepare for another battle at sea (2.85.1). In a later speech, these advisors and the other Peloponnesian commanders admit to the campaign's poor strategy—sailing as if for a fight on land rather than a battle at sea—and lack of proper preparation. They also concede that lack of experience may have played a part in their loss at sea (2.87.2). In the end, however, they still view the defeat as the result of bad luck (2.87.2) and their courage as more than a match for Athenian skill (2.87.3–9; cf. 1.121.4; see Crane 1998, 226–27; Stahl 2003, 87–88). While they discount cowardice as a factor in their defeat at sea—very likely in order to bolster morale (2.87.3), these leaders harp on courage as the key to a Spartan victory. They claim that they will prepare for battle, not with a rethinking of strategy, but rather in such a way as "to allow no one an excuse for playing the coward" (2.87.9; cf. 2.85.2).

Phormio's speech likewise emphasizes the Spartans' rigid adherence to hoplite tactics and consequent failure to become true ναυτικοί (seamen). After mocking the Spartans' reliance on their numbers and claim to a monopoly on bravery, Phormio critiques their inappropriate tactics (2.89.2): "They are confident for no other reason than the success that their experience in land fighting usually gives them, and which they think will do the same for them at sea." Thucydides, it is true, notes Phormio's fear of a confrontation in a confined space that could allow the Peloponnesian navy to exploit its greater number of ships and turn a sea battle into an infantry encounter (2.89.8). The Spartans in the end, more importantly, lured the Athenians into the Corinthian Gulf, where they won a partial victory through their experience in hoplite tactics (2.90). Indeed, as Stewart Flory (1993, 118) has noted, Thucydides describes the Peloponnesian navy as if it were a hoplite phalanx, formed up in four lines, with the right wing in the lead as they began to sail along the inside of the gulf (2.90.1).

While this engagement would seem to have validated the Spartan naval commissioners' earlier counsel (cf. 2.87.3–9), the Spartans soon realized that Athenian naval experience was far more formidable than they had imagined (2.91). Thanks to the superior skill displayed by one of their vessels, the Athenians managed to turn the tables on their opponents and routed the Spartan fleet by creating panic among the less experienced, and yet overconfident, Peloponnesians (2.91.4):

> As a result of this unexpected and unlikely event, panic gripped the Peloponnesians, who at the same time sailed up in pursuit in disorder because of their victory. Some of them dropped their oars and stopped sailing in their desire to wait for the main part of the fleet, a dangerous thing to do considering the short distance from the enemy's prows, while others, through their ignorance of the area, ran aground in the shallows.

The Athenians then fell upon the Peloponnesians, captured a number of their ships, and regained their own ships that had been disabled and towed away (2.92.1–2). As if to rub salt in the wound, Thucydides explicitly claims that the Peloponnesians' mistakes and disorder allowed the Athenians to make short work of their navy (2.92.1).

Thucydides' treatment of this naval encounter suggests that the Spartans' expertise in hoplite tactics, while it had its advantages, proved unsuited to naval warfare and was no match for the Athenians' skill and unique ability to adapt to changing circumstances (cf. Crane 1998, 227–28; Flory 1993, 119). Under pressure, even the Spartans' renowned ability to remain in formation foundered. Thucydides also suggests that war at sea demanded a more innovative kind of leader than the Spartan Timocrates, who committed suicide after the sinking of his ship—as if he were the quintessential Spartiate officer taking his life after letting down the hoplite phalanx (cf. Millender 2016, 180) rather than a naval advisor (2.92.3; cf. 2.85.1).

Thucydides again emphasizes the hurdles that the Spartan students of seamanship had to overcome in his ensuing account of the Peloponnesian plan to attack the Peiraeus when it was unguarded in 429/8 (2.93–94). While one may credit the Spartans Cnemus and Brasidas for such an innovative and bold strategy, Thucydides immediately robs the Spartans of responsibility for this plan by attributing it to unspecified Megarian "instructors" (2.93.1). Despite Thucydides' belief that the plan was achievable (2.93.3), fear of danger and concern about the direction of the wind allegedly led the Peloponnesians to confine their activity to Salamis. There they captured the fortress and squadron of ships that blocked the entrance to Megara and caused great consternation at Athens before returning with their prisoners and plunder to Nisaea (2.93.4–94.3). Thucydides, it should be noted, fails to comment on the Peloponnesians' daring relief of the naval blockade of Megara or the Athenians' panicked response (cf. Pearson 1936, 48). Instead, he focuses on the failure of the attempt and explicitly puts the blame for this lost opportunity on the Spartans' inability to accomplish a feat that "might easily have been achieved if they had been willing to keep their nerve" (2.94.1).

Even more damning is Thucydides' treatment of the Spartans' later expedition in aid of the Mytilenians' revolt from Athens. Here Thucydides provides a vivid illustration of Spartan torpor and fear as well as one of his most explicitly hostile portrayals of Spartan leadership (3.15–16, 25–33.1; on Thucydides' portrait of Alcidas, see, especially, Roisman 1987). Although they prepared a fleet to send to Mytilene under Alcidas in the summer of 428 (3.16.3), this expedition did not take place until the following summer (3.26.1). Thucydides then focuses on the slowness of its progress through the accumulation of terms and phrases denoting delay (3.27.1, 29.1)—perhaps unfairly emphasizing Alcidas' fear and caution and overlooking the factors that likely contributed to Alcidas' delay, such as the Spartans' difficulties in rounding up ships from their allies (cf. Roisman 1987, 393–96, 403; see also Kelly 1982, 47). According to Thucydides, the fleet, after a leisurely voyage around the Peloponnesus, finally arrived at Delos and eventually reached Embatum in Erythrae about seven days after the surrender of Mytilene (3.29). Despite this setback, a certain Elian by the name of Teutiaplus—again rather than one of the Spartan leaders—advised the Peloponnesians to sail immediately to Mytilene and to take advantage of the Athenians' relaxed vigilance following the Mytileneans' surrender (3.30; cf. Gomme, *HCT* 2.291–93; Lateiner 1975). Alcidas instead clung to the one idea that he had—to return home as quickly as possible (3.31.1–2). In both his refusal to improvise and his flight (3.31.2–33.1), Alcidas exhibited the same base fear and lack of enterprise that earlier had led to the Spartans' abandonment of their plan to seize the Peiraeus (cf. Westlake 1968, 143–45; Lateiner 1975, 178, 182). As Joseph Roisman (1987, 397–400), however, rightly notes in his attempt to redeem Alcidas, Thucydides'—or his sources'—hostile portrait of Alcidas here ignores the risks inherent in both Teutiaplus' plan and the Ionians' advice to capture an Ionian city or the Aeolic city of Cyme (3.31).

Caution, fear, and Alcidas' lack of imagination likewise appear to have derailed the Spartans' later attempt to exploit the revolution in Corcyra (3.69, 76–81.1), which concluded with another hasty flight homeward (cf. Kelly 1982, 47; Roisman 1987, 409–11). In his narrative of these events, Thucydides adds that Alcidas and the Peloponnesians were so consumed by their wish to avoid being seen by the Athenians that they ceased to be an effective fleet, sailing close to shore at night and then hauling their ships across the isthmus at Leucas (3.81.1). Alcidas, like the other Lacedaemonians featured thus far in the *History*, proved incapable of the kind of adaptability that Sparta's Corinthian allies in 432 saw as absolutely necessary if Sparta was to offer an effective challenge to Athens' hegemony (1.71.2–3).

The Hegemon That Was No Hegemon: Loss of the "Home-Field Advantage" and Allied Discontent

Through his treatment of the Peloponnesians' ineffective invasions of Attica and repeated failures at sea, Thucydides demonstrates that the Spartans and their allies had little to show for their efforts both on land and at sea during the first stage of the Peloponnesian War. Particularly troubling was the fact that Sparta repeatedly performed poorly on land, where it traditionally had the ancient equivalent of a home-field advantage, as Thucydides highlights in his accounts of its losses in Acarnania in 429 (2.80–82) and in Amphilochian Argos in 426/5 (cf. 3.102.5–7, 105–113). Sparta's greatest and most humiliating defeat, however, occurred in 425, when the Athenian Demosthenes occupied Pylos, and the Spartans' subsequent failure to drive the Athenians from their territory led to the entrapment of a Peloponnesian force on the island of Sphacteria (4.3–15). The Spartans again proved incapable of adapting to a new military situation—a complete reversal of the norm according to Thucydides—as they failed to dislodge the Athenians in their attack from the sea, while the Athenians successfully fought on land (4.12.2–3). The Athenian general Cleon's later capture of the hoplite force trapped on Sphacteria, which included among its 292 survivors 120 Spartiates, further revealed the limitations of Sparta's hoplite expertise and the dangers that military inflexibility posed to Spartan prestige and hegemony (4.28–40).

As Thucydides makes clear, the disaster on Sphacteria, along with other examples of incompetence and slowness, severely undermined the Spartans' vaunted reputation as a land power with an unrivalled army (5.28.2, 75.3; cf. 4.12.3). The Spartans, to be fair, did not completely fail to adapt to the exigencies of war, as Thucydides reveals in his, albeit brief, nod to their development of a cavalry and a force of archers in 424 in response to Athens' successes at Pylos, Sphacteria, and Cythera (4.55.2). Thucydides, nevertheless, immediately undercuts this admission by noting how contrary these changes were vis-à-vis the Spartans' usual practice and how irresolute they became in the face of the unfamiliar kind of warfare they were waging with the Athenians (4.55.2). The Spartan Brasidas also made serious inroads into Athens' sphere of influence in his Thraceward campaign of 424–422. Thucydides, however, repeatedly contrasts Brasidas with other Spartan leaders, in terms of his energetic, imaginative, and enterprising leadership (4.81, 84.2, 108.6; cf. Westlake 1968, 148, 150–58). Brasidas' gains, moreover, occurred far from the main site of operations—the Peloponnesus—and do not appear to have countered the disaffection among Sparta's allies that increased exponentially over the course of the Archidamian War.

Indeed, as Thucydides repeatedly points out, the diminution of Sparta's military reputation entailed an inverse uptick in allied resentment that threatened to destabilize the Peloponnesian League. Such allied discontent, of course, was already strong before the outbreak of the war, as Thucydides demonstrates in his account of the Corinthian envoys' demand that Sparta step up and act as a proper hegemon or else forfeit its "friends and kinsmen" (1.71.4–7):

> So let your sluggishness end here. Now assist your allies and especially the Potidaeans, as you promised, and invade Attica at once lest you betray friends and kinsmen to their bitterest enemies and drive the rest of us in despair to some other alliance. If we did so, we would be doing nothing wrong either before the gods who witnessed our oaths or before men who perceive the situation. For those who break a treaty are not the ones who go over to others because they have been left in the lurch but those who do not help those to whom they swore their oaths. But if you are willing to show energy, we will stand by you; for neither would it be sanctioned for us to make a change, nor would we find other allies with whom we have such close bonds. For these reasons choose the right course and strive to lead the Peloponnesus in its full greatness handed down to you by your fathers.

What exactly the Corinthians mean in their reference to oaths, treaties, and "some other alliance" has given rise to continuing scholarly debate, as has almost every aspect of the Peloponnesian League—particularly the nature of the League's "constitution" as well as the extent of Sparta's sway over its allies (for bibliography see Bolmarcich 2005, 5–6, nn. 1–5 and 2008, 66, nn. 7–11). Whether this league was a hegemonic symmachy under Spartan control (cf., especially, Larsen 1932, 1933, and 1934; De Ste. Croix 1972, 96–124, 339–40) or rather a more loosely organized body of states under limited Spartan domination (Bolmarcich 2008, 66; cf. Lendon 1994; Yates 2005) remains a hotly disputed issue. Whichever way they lean, scholars have long recognized the severity of the fractures that the League experienced during at least the first stage of the Peloponnesian War and the fault lines in the League that Thucydides highlights in his *History*.

According to Thucydides, allied criticism was already strong in 431 in response to Archidamus' sluggish invasion of Attica (2.18.2–5). The Spartans' debacle in the territory of Amphilochian Argos in 426/5 (cf. 3.102.5–7, 105–113) could only have exacerbated such allied discontent, in light of the poor leadership exhibited by both the slain Eurylochus, who failed to maintain order among his troops (3.108), and Menedaïus, who left many of his allies in the lurch in his haste to return to Sparta (3.109–11). In his detailed treatment of this event, Thucydides claims that the Athenian Demosthenes and his Acarnanian allies made a secret agreement that allowed the Spartan Menedaïus, his Mantinean forces, and other leading Peloponnesians to retreat in order to weaken the Spartans' Ambraciot allies and to discredit the Spartans and the Peloponnesians with their allies in that region (3.109.1–2). After Menedaïus and the others made their ignominious getaway, the Ambraciots were slaughtered to such a degree (3.110–12) that Thucydides describes the destruction of their forces as "the greatest disaster that fell upon any single Hellenic city in an equal number of days during the war" (3.113.6).

The combination of poor military performance and improper hegemonic behavior must have been particularly galling to Sparta's allies, given the Spartans' increasing reliance on allied soldiers as a result of their chronic *oliganthrōpia* (cf. Millender 2006, 248–53 and 2016, 178–79, 190; see also Cawkwell 1983, 385–94; Cartledge 1987, 37–43). Indeed, while their allies received a major blow, the Spartans lost only two of the three citizens who went out with the 3,000 Peloponnesian allies (cf. 3.100, 109.1). The fact that the bulk of such military disasters fell on the allies seems not to have been lost on the Spartans' Mantinean allies, the only Peloponnesians who maintained discipline as their force scattered in disarray (3.108.3). While Thucydides does not specifically mention any disaffection on the part of the Mantineans, James Capreedy has noted that when we next encounter the Mantineans in the *History*, they are engaged in a conflict (423/2 BCE) that signals both their interest in acquiring their own sphere of influence in Arcadia and the beginning of their disaffiliation from Sparta (4.134; cf. 5.29.1, 33 and Capreedy 2014, 356–57; on Sparta's relationship with Mantinea, see Amit 1973, 121–82; on the Arcadian *poleis*, see Nielsen 1996 and 2002).

The Spartans' failure to make even a dent in Athens' control of the sea during this period and their losses at Pylos and Sphacteria in 425 could have only further undermined their military reputation and hegemonic status. The infamous surrender of the Spartans on Sphacteria sent shock waves through their fellow Greeks, who had believed that no form of compulsion could induce the Spartans to surrender their arms rather than fight to the death (Thuc. 4.40). To add insult to injury, the Spartans repeatedly demonstrated their willingness to put their own needs—specifically, their desire to recover the Spartiates captured on Sphacteria—before the interests of their allies (cf., especially, 4.15). After the Athenians' initial victory at Pylos and blockade of Sphacteria, the Spartans so desperately sought a truce that they unilaterally turned over to Athens approximately sixty Peloponnesian warships, which the Athenians later refused to return (4.16–23.1). The Spartans thereby deprived themselves and their allies of any possibility of taking on Athens at sea (cf. Kelly 1982, 51–52). Their allies, who had contributed those ships, suffered the brunt of Spartan ineptitude once again. Thucydides suggests that the Spartans were aware of possible allied discontent (cf., e.g., 4.22.3, 5.14.4), but their continuing obsession with regaining Pylos and the Spartiate prisoners far outweighed any concern for their allies (4.41.3, 108.7, 117; 5.15).

As Thucydides demonstrates, allied disaffection reached the boiling point with the Spartans' later negotiations for peace with Athens in 422/1. The Spartans' desire to come to terms with Athens angered a number of their most powerful allies, who voted against peace (5.17.2) and continued to reject the treaty (5.22.1, 25.1, 30, 35.3). Even though the Spartans assumed that their alliance with Athens would quell allied discontent (5.22.2), a number of Sparta's allies viewed the conclusion of this peace treaty as a betrayal of their interests (5.27.2, 29.2–3). Distrust in Sparta's concern for the welfare of the Peloponnesus (5.27.2) and disdain for Sparta's military reputation (5.28.2) spread and began to pose a serious threat to Spartan hegemony, as state after state began to consider alliance with Sparta's main foe in the region, Argos (5.27–30). Ultimately, Mantinea, Elis, and Corinth entered into alliance with Argos (5.29–31); the Spartans' Boeotian and Megarian allies also seriously considered this alliance (5.32.5–7, 36–38); and the Argives, Mantineans, and Eleans later concluded a treaty with the Athenians in 420 (5.43.3–48.1).

The Battle of Mantinea and the Restoration of Spartan Hegemony

According to Thucydides, the Spartans finally took steps to stop the spread of disaffection and instability in the Peloponnesus through success on the battlefield against the Argives and their allies in midsummer 418. The Spartans demonstrated the geopolitical importance that they attached to this battle in their decision to send out under the Eurypontid King Agis II a full force that included helots (5.57.1). Success in this battle would send a powerful message not only to those states that were either actively involved in or contemplating revolt but also to those allies who sent large contingents to accompany the Spartans, including the Tegeans, the Phliasians, the Boeotians, and the Corinthians (5.57.2). While this battle never took place (5.60.1), those Spartans who were eager for war gained a second chance to restore their preeminence in the Peloponnesus later that summer at Mantinea. As Thucydides notes, the Spartans again realized the necessity for military action when they learned that another of their key allies, Tegea, was on the point of defecting to the Argive alliance (5.64.1). The gravity of the situation is again underlined by the Spartans' immediate decision to take the field with their entire force of citizens and helots on an unprecedented scale (5.64.2).

In his relatively detailed account of the ensuing battle, Thucydides makes it clear that the Spartans at Mantinea simultaneously resuscitated their tarnished military reputation and provided for both current and erstwhile allies a powerful reminder of the dangers that disloyalty to Lacedaemon entailed (5.66–74; cf. Lazenby 1985, 125–34; Schwartz 2009, 259–60; Millender 2016, 187–89). All of the participants on the field that day were treated to a spectacle of Spartan military expertise that fully demonstrated Xenophon's claim that the Spartans were the only professional practitioners of the craft of war in Hellas (*Lac. Pol.* 13.5; cf. Hdt. 7.102–104; Plut. *Pel.* 23.4; see Hodkinson 2006, 129–30; Millender 2016, 168–69). The Spartan hoplites' superior training and organization were especially apparent in their ability to snatch a victory out of Agis' sudden decision to move some of his regiments to the left to keep the Mantineans from outflanking the left wing of his force. According to Thucydides, this hastily conceived tactical maneuver created a hole in Agis' line and enabled the Mantineans, together with their Arcadian allies and the thousand picked troops from Argos (cf. 5.67.2), to rout the Spartans on the left. Despite this initial loss, the rest of the Spartan force eventually broke the entire Argive line and later rescued the defeated left wing of Agis' army (5.71–73).

The Spartans' overwhelming victory put to rest the Argives' claims to supremacy in the Peloponnesus and quashed the Athenians' attempts to contest both the Spartans' hegemony in the region and preeminence on the field (cf. 5.69.1). At the same time, the Spartans demonstrated the folly of the disaffected Mantineans, who witnessed the defeat and flight of their recently acquired Argive and Athenian allies (5.73.3). As Thucydides' narrative demonstrates, everyone on the field that day learned that Sparta was still the greatest land power in Hellas and the only viable hegemon in the Peloponnesus, despite its military missteps during the Archidamian War (5.75.3; cf. 5.28.2):

> By this one action they did away with the reproaches leveled against them by the Hellenes at this time, whether for cowardice because of the disaster on the island, or for incompetence and slowness on other occasions. For it now seemed that although they had been worsted by fortune, they were still the same men in spirit.

The battle of Mantinea, however, provided more dividends than the simple restoration of Sparta's sullied reputation. Thucydides reveals that the Spartans used their military superiority and consequent victory to bring about structural changes in the Peloponnesus that were aimed to create greater stability in the region and to restore their dominance over their allies. At the conclusion of the battle, Thucydides tells us, the victorious Lacedaemonians slaughtered many of the fleeing Mantineans but allowed the privileged thousand picked Argives to get away safely (5.73.3). Not surprisingly, the following winter witnessed the conclusion of a peace treaty and alliance between Sparta and a now pro-Spartan Argos (5.76–80; cf. Hanson 1999, 207; Ruzé 2006, 270–71). Once the Argives had abandoned their alliance with Mantinea, Athens, and Elis (5.78), the Mantineans had no choice but to come to terms with Sparta and were forced to give up the cities under their control (5.81; cf. Funke 2009, 6–10).

As Thucydides' Alcibiades seems to have understood, Sparta's control of the Peloponnesian League rested first and foremost on its ability to outperform its fellow Greeks on the battlefield. The central role that military superiority on land played in the Spartans' relations with their allies explains their decision to risk their all on the result of one day's fighting at Mantinea in 418 (6.16.6), just as it did later at Nemea and Coronea in 394 (Xen. *Hell.* 4.2.9–23, 3.15–21). This reading, of course, does not deny the variety of obligations that bound the Spartans and their allies and the likelihood that the Spartans maintained leverage over their allies by a variety of means, including interference in their allies' domestic political arrangements (cf. Bolmarcich 2005; Yates 2005). Thucydides' account of the Spartans' relations with their allies during the Archidamian War, however, suggests that the key to their domination of their allies, as well as allied grumbling, disaffection, and outright revolt, lay in the Spartans' ability to demonstrate their right to their reputation as the supreme land power in mainland Greece. This "simple exercise of physical power," to quote Sarah Bolmarcich (2005, 6), was in reality anything but simple.

Indeed, Thucydides' account of the battle of Mantinea shows just how effective a tool victory in hoplite warfare could be, both ideologically and politically. Success in this kind of conflict—the most performative and theatrical form of Greek warfare—reminded allies and enemies alike of Sparta's lone ability to protect and police its sphere of influence (Millender 2016). On a more practical level, the Spartan hoplites at Mantinea vividly destroyed the enemy on the field and effectively quashed the political aspirations of disgruntled allies and opposing states alike (cf. Connor 1988; Hanson 2000, 222; Millender 2016, 187–89). Indeed, the Peloponnesus remained essentially quiet and stable for the remainder of the Peloponnesian War. After Sparta finally secured its hegemonic authority with Athens' defeat, the Spartans' imperialistic ambitions precipitated the Corinthian War (395–386) and led to increasing violations of their allies' autonomy after the conclusion of the King's Peace in 386. Despite the resulting disaffection of Sparta's allies, the Peloponnesian League remained largely intact until the Spartans' humiliation on the battlefield of Leuctra in 371 made its dissolution inevitable.

References

Allison, J. W. 1984. "Sthenelaidas' Speech: Thucydides 1.86." *Hermes* 112: 9–16.
Amit, M. 1973. *Great and Small Poleis: A Study in the Relations Between the Great Powers and the Small Cities in Ancient Greece*. Collection Latomus 134. Brussels: Peeters Publishers.
Bloedow, E. F. 1981. "The Speeches of Archidamus and Sthenelaidas at Sparta." *Historia* 30: 129–43.
Bloedow, E. F. 1983. "Archidamus the 'Intelligent' Spartan." *Klio* 65: 27–49.
Bloedow, E. F. 1987. "Sthenelaïdas the Persuasive Spartan." *Hermes* 115: 60–66.
Bolmarcich, S. 2005. "Thucydides 1.19.1 and the Peloponnesian League." *GRBS* 45: 5–34.
Bolmarcich, S. 2008. "The Date of the 'Oath of the Peloponnesian League.'" *Historia* 57: 65–79.
Brunt, P. A. 1965. "Spartan Policy and Strategy in the Archidamian War." *Phoenix* 19: 255–80.
Capreedy, J. 2014. "Losing Confidence in Sparta: The Creation of the Mantinean Symmachy." *GRBS* 54: 352–78.
Cartledge, P. A. 1987. *Agesilaos and the Crisis of Sparta*. London and Baltimore: Duckworth.
Cartledge, P. A., and P. Debnar. 2006. "Sparta and the Spartans in Thucydides." In *Brill's Companion to Thucydides*, edited by A. Rengakos and A. Tsakmakis, 559–87. Leiden: Brill.
Cawkwell, G. L. 1983. "The Decline of Sparta." *CQ* 33: 385–400.
Connor, W. R. 1988. "Early Greek Land Warfare as Symbolic Expression." *Past & Present* 119: 3–29.
Crane, G. 1992. "The Fear and Pursuit of Risk: Corinth on Athens, Sparta and the Peloponnesians (Thucydides 1.68–71, 120–21)." *TAPA* 122: 227–56.
Crane, G. 1998. *Thucydides and the Ancient Simplicity: The Limits of Political Realism*. Berkeley, Los Angeles, and London: University of California Press
De Ste. Croix, G. E. M. 1972. *The Origins of the Peloponnesian War*. London: Duckworth.
Edmunds, L. 1975. *Chance and Intelligence in Thucydides*. Cambridge: Harvard University Press.
Flory, S. 1993. "The Death of Thucydides and the Motif of 'Land on Sea.'" In *Nomodeiktes: Greek Studies in Honor of Martin Ostwald*, edited by R. M. Rosen and J. Farrell, 113–23. Ann Arbor: University of Michigan Press.
Forde, S. 1989. *The Ambition to Rule: Alcibiades and the Politics of Imperialism in Thucydides*. Ithaca and London: Cornell University Press.
Foster, E. 2010. *Thucydides, Pericles, and Periclean Imperialism*. Cambridge: Cambridge University Press
Funke, P. 2009. "Between Mantinea and Leuctra: The Political World of the Peloponnese in a Time of Upheaval." In *The Politics of Ethnicity and the Crisis of the Peloponnesian League*, edited by P. Funke and N. Luraghi, 1–14. Cambridge and London: Harvard University Press.
Garrity, T. F. 1998. "Thucydides 1.22.1: Content and Form in the Speeches." *AJP* 119: 361–84.

Gomme, A. W., A. Andrewes, and K. J. Dover. 1945–1981. *A Historical Commentary on Thucydides*. 5 vols. Oxford: Oxford University Press.

Hanson, V. D. 1999. "Hoplite Obliteration: The Case of the Town of Thespiae." In *Ancient Warfare: Archaeological Perspectives*, edited by J. Carman and A. Harding, 203–17. Stroud: Sutton Publishing.

Hanson, V. D. 2000. "Hoplite Battle as Ancient Greek Warfare: When, Where, and Why?" In *War and Violence in Ancient Greece*, edited by H. van Wees, 201–32. Swansea: Classical Press of Wales.

Hodkinson, S. 2006. "Was Classical Sparta a Military Society?" In *Sparta & War*, edited by S. Hodkinson and A. Powell, 111–62. Swansea: Classical Press of Wales.

Hornblower, S. 1991. *A Commentary on Thucydides, Volume I: Books I-III*. Oxford: Oxford University Press.

Kagan, D. 1974. *The Archidamian War*. Ithaca and London: Cornell University Press.

Kelly, T. 1979. "Peloponnesian Naval Strength and Sparta's Plans for Waging War against Athens in 431 B. C." In *Studies in Honor of Tom B. Jones*, edited by M. A. Powell Jr. and R. H. Sack, 245–55. Kevelaer: Verlag Butzon und Bercker and Neukirchen-Vluyn: Neukirchener Verlag.

Kelly, T. 1982. "Thucydides and Spartan Strategy in the Archidamian War." *American Historical Review* 87: 25–54.

Krentz, P. 1997. "The Strategic Culture of Periclean Athens." In *Polis and Polemos: Essays on Politics, War, and History in Ancient Greece in Honor of Donald Kagan*, edited by C. D. Hamilton and P. Krentz, 55–72. Claremont: Regina.

Larsen, J. A. O. 1932. "Sparta and the Ionian Revolt: A Study of Spartan Foreign Policy and the Genesis of the Peloponnesian League." *CP* 27: 136–50.

Larsen, J. A. O. 1933. "The Constitution of the Peloponnesian League." *CP* 28: 257–76.

Larsen, J. A. O. 1934. "The Constitution of the Peloponnesian League. II." *CP* 29: 1–19.

Lazenby, J. F. 1985. *The Spartan Army*. Warminster Aris and Phillips.

Lateiner, D. 1975. "The Speech of Teutiaplus (Thuc. 3.30)." *GRBS* 16: 175–84.

Legon, R. 1973. "The Megarian Decree and the Balance of Greek Naval Power." *CP* 68: 161–71.

Lendon, J. E. 1994. "Thucydides and the 'Constitution' of the Peloponnesian League." *GRBS* 35: 159–77.

Millender, E. G. 2006. "The Politics of Spartan Mercenary Service." In *Sparta & War*, edited by S. Hodkinson and A. Powell, 235–66. Swansea: Classical Press of Wales.

Millender, E. G. 2016. "The Greek Battlefield: Classical Sparta and the Spectacle of Hoplite Warfare." In *The Topography of Violence in the Greco-Roman World*, edited by W. Riess and G. Fagan, 162–94. Ann Arbor: University of Michigan Press.

Millender, E. G. Forthcoming. "Νόμιμα ἀρχαιότροπα καὶ ἄμεικτα: Thucydides' Alienation of Spartan Kingship." In *Thucydides and Sparta*, edited by A. Powell and P. Debnar. Swansea: Classical Press of Wales.

Moxon, I. 1978. "Thucydides' Account of Spartan Strategy and Foreign Policy in the Archidamian War." *Rivista storica dell'antichità* 8: 7–26.

Nielsen, T. H. 1996. "A Survey of Dependent *Poleis* in Classical Arkadia." In *More Studies in the Ancient Greek Polis*, edited by M. H. Hansen and K. A. Raaflaub, 63–105. Stuttgart: Franz Steiner Verlag.

Nielsen, T. H. 2002. *Arkadia and Its Poleis in the Archaic and Classical Periods*. Hypomnemata 140. Göttingen: Vandenhoeck & Ruprecht.

Pearson, L. 1936. "Propaganda in the Archidamian War." *CP* 31: 33–52.

Pelling, C. B. R. 1991. "Thucydides' Archidamus and Herodotus' Artabanus." In *Georgica: Greek Studies in Honour of George Cawkwell*, BICS 58, edited by M. A. Flower and M. Toher, 120–42. London: University of London.

Roisman, J. 1987. "Alkidas in Thucydides." *Historia* 36: 385–421.

Ruzé, F. 2006. "Spartans and the Use of Treachery Among Their Enemies. In *Sparta & War*, edited by S. Hodkinson and A. Powell, 267–85. Swansea Classical Press of Wales.

Schwartz, A. 2009. *Reinstating the Hoplite: Arms, Armour, and Phalanx Fighting in Archaic and Classical Greece*. Stuttgart: Franz Steiner Verlag.

Stahl, H.-P. 2003. *Thucydides: Man's Place in History*. Swansea: Classical Press of Wales.

Taylor, M. 2010. *Thucydides, Pericles, and the Idea of Athens in the Peloponnesian War*. Cambridge: Cambridge University Press.

Westlake, H. D. 1968. *Individuals in Thucydides*. Cambridge: Cambridge University Press.

Yates, D. C. 2005. "The Archaic Treaties between the Spartans and Their Allies." *CQ* 55: 65–76.

CHAPTER 5

THUCYDIDES ON THE ATHENIAN EMPIRE AND INTERSTATE RELATIONS (431–404)

POLLY LOW

THE principal subject of Thucydides' history is, by his own account, "the war fought against each other by the Peloponnesians and the Athenians" (1.1.1). This narrative, however, is inextricably tied up with the story of the growth and decline of Athens' imperial power. Thucydides therefore provides us with one of the earliest, and certainly one of the most influential, analyses of the Athenian Empire (or Delian League), and also of the wider context of Greek interstate relations in this period. But his presentation of these subjects, though compelling, is not comprehensive, nor—of course—is it objective. It is fortunate, therefore, that this is an area in which we are relatively well supplied with alternative sources of evidence, both literary and (especially) epigraphic. These sources may not always rival the immediacy or excitement of Thucydides' narrative, but they do deserve our attention, not just (or ideally, not at all) to fill in "gaps" in the Thucydidean version (cf. Jowett 1881, lxxviii), but also to provide a check on or corrective to Thucydides' distinctive, and distinctively bleak, assessment of the interstate politics of the fifth century. This is not to say, of course, that the epigraphic (or literary) evidence is any more objective than Thucydides' account, but rather that it can provide an alternative perspective on the structures and activities of the Athenian Empire (and of interstate politics more widely), and shed light on some significant Thucydidean omissions.

A few preliminary comments on the nature of the non-Thucydidean evidence will be useful. As already noted, there is some contemporary (or near-contemporary) literary evidence: some information can be gleaned from Athenian comedy, and the "Old Oligarch"s' *Constitution of the Athenians* has much to say, or to allege, about the workings of the Empire (Osborne 2004). Fourth-century literary texts (particularly Isocrates, but other orators and historians, too) also offer occasional observations on both the glories and the excesses of the fifth-century past (Meiggs 1972, 397–403). Of the material evidence, the most important subcategory—arguably a category in its own right—is the epigraphic record of the Empire (and of interstate politics more widely): inscribed texts of treaties and other diplomatic agreements; regulations for the management of the Empire (or of its constituent parts); honorific decrees for those active in interstate politics in various ways; and financial records, especially the "Tribute Quota Lists" (often abbreviated to "Tribute Lists" or "ATLs"), which record the proportion of allied tribute dedicated to the goddess Athena each year. (The key epigraphic material, with very helpful explanatory notes, can be consulted in Osborne 2000.) The epigraphic evidence is, therefore, a rich source of information about the Empire and attitudes toward it, although it does have two significant limitations. The first is one of perspective: the record of Greek inscriptions in this period is overwhelmingly dominated by Athens, and so the epigraphic evidence does not, for the most part, get us any closer than does the literary material (including Thucydides) to a non-Athenian view of fifth-century interstate politics. The second limitation is more technical, but more pressing for those who want to use inscriptions as a foil to Thucydides' account of the development of the Empire: a large number of these texts, including some of the ones that seem most crucial to understanding changes in Athenian imperial practice cannot be securely dated by objective criteria (although it was, until relatively recently, thought that they could be, and various theories about the reliability of Thucydides' narrative were constructed on that basis: for the current state of the debate, see Rhodes 2008, Papazarkadas 2009). We will return to the problem of diachronic change later, but must begin by outlining the structure and systems of the Empire, as they operated during the Peloponnesian War.

Running the Empire

How did the Athenian Empire work? Thucydides' (explicit) answer to that question, given at 1.96, is a very brief one: the alliance was made up of states who wanted to continue to fight the Persians; some of those states made contributions in ships, others in money (that is, tribute); the contributions of tribute were managed by a board of Athenian officials established for this purpose, the *Hellenotamiai*. There was also a council of members of the alliance, which, in the early years of the organization, met to agree on the League's policy, although allied input into League decision-making was, Thucydides implies at 1.97.1, a short-lived phenomenon. Indeed, we almost never see, in Thucydides or anywhere else, any evidence for the activities of the allied council. Gomme et al. (1945–1981, 1.280) suggest that it had ceased to operate by 454 (if not earlier), while Hornblower (1991–2008, 1.146) believes that meetings might have continued until the 430s. Such speculation, however, can be based only on the silence of the sources, and on Athens' approach to other aspects of the management of the Empire (the scanty evidence is discussed by Culham 1978).

Thucydides' implication, at 1.97.1 and elsewhere, is that the running of the Athenian Empire was, from an early stage (and certainly by the time of the Peloponnesian War), almost entirely in Athenian hands: the Athenians were responsible for shaping the alliance's policies, and for ensuring that those policies were carried out. Scattered references in Thucydides' text, and more particularly in non-Thucydidean (and especially epigraphic) evidence, allow us to add a little color and detail to that picture, although it must be said at the outset that our picture of the administration of the Empire is very far from complete. No one source gives us an account of the whole system, so we are left trying to assemble an overview from geographically and chronologically scattered snippets of evidence.

The Aristoteleian *Athenaion Politeia* claims (24.3) that the Empire provided employment for 700 officials stationed outside Athens (that is, it seems safe to infer, in the cities that were members of the Empire). But this figure is (even by the standards of ancient statistics) particularly unreliable: the transmitted text is not secure at this point (Rhodes 1993, 305), nor is there any reason to believe that the total originally given by the author, whatever it was, would have been based on a strictly accurate census; modern estimates for the numbers of officials extend both well below (Balcer 1976, 258 suggests a figure of about 416 for the period of the Pentacontaetia) and above (Constantakopoulou 2013, 39–40) the Aristoteleian figure.

But if absolute numbers are hard to come by, the general pattern is relatively clear. We can distinguish between two types of Athenian official: those sent to maintain a long-term presence in some allied states (it should be emphasized that not all states, and perhaps not even the majority, would have had such officials), and those dispatched from Athens on specific missions. The precise duties of the former category of official are hard to pin down—they tend to be referred to by the catch-all label *archontes* ("magistrates")—but when they appear in our sources they are associated, for example, with attempts to ensure that regulations are enforced (e.g., ML 45, §§1 and 3); with administration of the tribute (e.g., *IG* I³ 282, B.I, lines 11–12); and on one occasion with the distribution of grain (*IG* I³ 62, lines 5–6; Balcer 1976, 271–7). Resident garrison-commanders (*phrourarchoi*) could also be included in this category, and can be found performing functions that suggest that their duties extended beyond the purely military: citizens of Erythrae, for example, are (probably; the text is heavily restored at the relevant point) required to swear an oath of loyalty (to Athens) in front of the *phrourarchos* (*IG* I³ 15, line 38, with Balcer 1976, 277–79; on garrisons in the Empire, see Nease 1949).

In addition to (and sometimes instead of) these permanent officials, the Athenians also made use of visiting magistrates, such as *episkopoi* ("inspectors"), like those sent to supervise the initial enforcement of the Athenian regulations for Erythrae (ML 40, lines 13–14; for further discussion and examples: Balcer 1976, 258–69; 1977), or heralds (*kerukes*) dispatched to announce new regulations (e.g., ML 45, §9), or a new tribute assessment (e.g., ML 69, lines 4–6). It is this second sort of official whose omnipresent meddlesomeness is ridiculed in Aristophanes' *Birds* (1021–57), although it is worth noting that the joke here seems to lie not just in the fact that Athenian imperial control was so extensive that even a brand new city (not to mention a city located in the sky) could not escape its reach, but also in that, in spite of this, the Athenians could not count on being able to exercise the sort of close control that would, for example, stop a disgruntled citizen from defecating on a *stēlē* on which Athenian regulations were inscribed (*Birds* 1054).

Even allowing for the distortions of Aristophanic humor, this picture of the nature of Athenian management of the Empire during the Peloponnesian War seems broadly correct: what we find is a rather inconsistent mixture of direct interventionism and remote or delegated (and therefore, sometimes, imperfect) control. The underlying reason for this lies, in part, in the nature of the Empire's development: Athenian officials were not deployed systematically, but rather in response to specific crises (above all in response to revolts) or—and particularly later in the century—to implement individual (albeit Empire-wide) pieces of legislation. But there are also issues of resource, and of practicality. It is unclear how willing Athenians would have been to be sent away from home on such missions: a decree imposing regulations on Miletus includes a clause that forbids any eligible Athenian from refusing to be sent to Miletus to serve as *archon* there (*IG* I^3 21, lines 5–6). It seems reasonable to infer from this that it might not always have been easy to persuade Athenians to undertake such roles. On the other side of the equation, hostility to an Athenian interloper, even if not ending in outright violence (as in the Aristophanic example) might well have made the imposition of Athenian regulations (by Athenian officials) problematic.

The Athenians did, however, have access to an alternative source of manpower: namely, local officials (such as the local *archontes* required to enforce the Standards Decree in cities where no Athenian official was present: ML 45, §4), and local supporters of Athenian power, especially those who held the position of *proxenos* (an untranslatable term, but one whose duties are roughly equivalent to those of an Honorary Consul: Herman 1987, 130–42; for a catalogue of Athens' fifth-century *proxenoi*, see Walbank 1978). These men, whose obligations were broadly defined as being to do "good things" for the Athenians, seem likely to have acted as the first line of Athenian imperial control in many cities (Meiggs 1949). In return, they were offered both privileges and protection by the Athenians. That the latter might have been particularly necessary is seen by (for example) the fact that one of the first acts of the oligarchic (and anti-Athenian) party in the Corcyrean *stasis* was to murder the Athenian *proxenos*, a certain Peithias (3.70.6; Peithias is in fact described by Thucydides as *etheloproxenos*, "volunteer *proxenos*," a label not attested elsewhere and not explained by Thucydides, but perhaps intended to emphasize that his cooperation with the Athenians was spontaneously offered rather than based on any hereditary obligation).

Thucydides is aware of the existence (and the potentially inflammatory role) of these agents of imperial control (both Athenian and non-Athenian), but they do not receive any sustained attention in his narrative: the presence of Athenian *archontes* at Samos, for example, is noted only at the point where they are captured and handed over to a local Persian governor (1.115.5). He is, if anything, even less informative on the nature of the regulations that those officials might have been attempting to impose. We do find occasional references to specific interventions (the imposition of democracy at Samos, for example: 1.115.3; the mass confiscation of land after the Mytilene revolt: 3.50), and allusions to wider policies (such as the Athenian ambassadors' brief discussion of their legal policy toward the allies at 1.77.1). But the bigger picture, again, has to be pieced together from other evidence. From this, it is possible to establish two broad modes of action. The first is reactive, and narrowly targeted in response to a particular crisis (a revolt, or a change of political regime). In such cases, we see the Athenians imposing on particular cities regulations that restrict certain aspects of their behavior. This might be (as at Erythrae: ML 40) the creation of a system of democratic governance; or (as at Chalkis: ML 52) limitations on a city's judicial autonomy; or (as at Hestiaea: 1.114.3, with $IG\ I^3$ 41) expulsion of the original population and establishment of a new Athenian settlement in its place (such settlements could also, of course, function as a further means of Athenian control in the regions in which they were located: Brunt 1966, 84).

The second variety of regulation is more proactive, and (at least in intention) encompasses the entire Empire. There seem to have been some judicial regulations that applied to all cities ([Xen] *Ath. Pol.* 1.16; for further examples, see De Ste. Croix 1961), and by the last quarter of the fifth century (if not earlier) all cities were obliged to participate in and bring offerings to some of the major Athenian festivals (Panathenaia: ML 46, lines 41–43; Dionysia: Σ. Aristophanes *Acharnians* 504; Eleusis: ML 73, line 14; generally on religion in the Empire, see Parker 1996, 142–51). Most notorious of all is the Athenian attempt (alluded to in the passage of Aristophanes' *Birds* discussed above, but more extensively preserved in a series of epigraphic fragments: ML 45, the so-called Standards Decree) to impose a single (Athenian) set of standards for coinage, weights, and measures across the Empire. (Lewis 1997 remains a useful brief discussion of this decree and its significance, although new epigraphic discoveries since he wrote have changed the picture slightly: the decree is now more firmly dated in the 420s, and new fragments show that there were at least two different versions of the text in circulation.)

The epigraphic evidence gives us a (relatively) clear sense of the content of these regulations, but leaves room for considerable uncertainty about their intention. Should these be seen as potentially beneficial measures, which would facilitate trade for all allied states (as Figueira 1998 attempts to argue for the Standards Decree), or ensure the allies' access to legal protection (as Thucydides has his Athenian ambassadors claim at 1.77), or moderate the potential violence of domestic conflict within allied cities (Forsdyke 2005, 205–39)? Or, alternatively, should they be viewed as essentially repressive instruments, intended to allow the Athenians to exercise their power as directly (and, in the case of the Standards Decree, as profitably) as possible? We cannot rule out the possibility that some allies might have benefited from these measures (and we will return to this point below), but the harsh penalties for noncompliance that the regulations often include surely suggest that the Athenians anticipated some resistance to their imposition.

These decrees, therefore, provide useful information—and rather more information than Thucydides gives us—about the practical measures by which the Athenians ran their empire. They also, albeit more ambiguously, reveal something about Athens' attitude to imperial power, and in particular the issue of how, and in whose interests, it should be exercised. The question of how far the epigraphic representation of this latter theme can be made to align with the Thucydidean picture of Athenian imperial development and imperial ideology is a complex one, which will be addressed in more detail below. Before turning to that problem, however, it is necessary to spend some time thinking about the piece of imperial machinery to which Thucydides gives the most prominence: the tribute (*phoros*).

Tribute and Its Significance

The Athenian decision to levy financial contributions—tribute—from its allies is presented by Thucydides as an innovation: he offers an explanation of the term, and notes that it requires a new board of magistrates to administer it (1.96.1–2). What he does not explicitly say, but perhaps expected his audience to know, is that the levying of tribute was, until this point, most closely associated with Persian imperial practice: tribute, that is, carries more than merely financial implications (Murray 1966, 150; Kallet-Marx 1993, 45–57; Whitehead 1998, 178–81), and the payment of tribute becomes a potent symbol of subjection to Athens. It is used by Thucydides in his catalogue of forces at the Sicilian expedition, for example, to distinguish between different categories of Athenian ally (7.57), and those few islands (two, by the time of the outbreak of the war) that still made contributions in ships rather than tribute are treated as having a particularly privileged status in the Empire (1.19). That the Mytileneans, in spite of this status, nevertheless chose to revolt from Athens is singled out by Cleon as a reason that Athenian retribution for their disloyalty should justifiably be severe (3.39). This view of tribute as a primary marker of imperial subjection is not restricted to Thucydides: Athens' public display of the tribute is pointed to by Isocrates (8.82) as something for which the fifth-century Empire was particularly hated; in the fourth century, the Athenians give an explicit commitment *not* to levy *phoros* from their new alliance (RO 22, line 24).

But tribute also, of course, had a practical function: it was a major source of revenue for the Athenians, and its timely and effective collection was a matter of increasing concern during the Peloponnesian War. Thucydides does provide some (apparently) hard figures for Athens' income from the tribute: 460 talents at the League's foundation (1.96.2), rising to 600T by the outbreak of the war (2.13.3). Both of these figures, however, are problematic, because neither can easily be made to fit with the figures for tribute payment that are extrapolated from the Tribute Quota Lists. These inscribed records do not exist for the earliest years of the Empire (when the tribute was still stored on Delos), but it has been estimated that the total yearly tribute recorded from 453 (the earliest extant list) to 433 never exceeded 400T (ML, pp. 87–88). Thucydides' figures (for both 478 and 432) therefore seem too high—in the latter case quite significantly so—and this anomaly has caused considerable scholarly discomfort (see the discussions in Gomme et al. 1945–1981, 1.273–9, 2.17–19; Hornblower 1991–2008, 1.145–6, 252–3). The transmitted text seems secure in both cases, which leaves as possible explanations either that Thucydides has got his figures wrong (or, perhaps more plausibly, is including under the label of "tribute" income that actually came from other allied sources), or that the inscribed Quota Lists themselves give a misleading impression of tribute payments. The latter option is not impossible: the lists are very poorly preserved, and the figures derived from them are the product of a significant amount of modern reconstruction. It is worth remembering, too, that the lists do not record actual payments, but rather the proportion of income that, having arrived at Athens by a certain point in the year, was dedicated to the goddess Athena: tribute that was paid late, or for some reason never reached Athens at all, would not be included in the lists (Constantakopoulou 2013, 34–37).

But if Thucydides (or his speakers) is exaggerating the amount of revenue received from tribute, this would in fact not be completely out of line with the picture that emerges from other sources. The epigraphic evidence in particular shows that the Athenians were anxious to collect all the revenue they deemed to be owed to them, and also to maximize that revenue as much as possible—and both of these concerns appear to have intensified during the Peloponnesian War. A decree of 426 (ML 68) revises the procedures for collecting tribute, setting up a board of officials (*eklogeis*: "collectors") in every city, and establishing systems for monitoring the delivery of the money and punishing those cities that failed to pay. (The inscribed decree was decorated with carvings of bags stuffed with money [Lawton 1995, no. 1], a gesture that seems revealing of the Athenians' willingness to celebrate the financial benefits of empire.) The following year, a further decree was passed (ML 69), again attempting to ensure that income from tribute was maximized, and setting out a notably ambitious list of states from which tribute was to be collected (see further below). These decrees give us far more detail about the mechanics of tribute collection than we see in Thucydides, and reveal how complex and problematic a process the administration of the tribute must have been. But they are not inconsistent with what Thucydides does tell us (or suggest to us) about the centrality of tribute to Athens' imperial project, and to its pursuit of the war; ML 69 is explicit, in fact, that those assessing the tribute must ensure that the Athenians "have sufficient money for the war" (line 46).

In view of all this, Athens' decision (in 413) to replace the tribute with a 5% tax "on all seaborne traffic" is noteworthy, and it is not surprising to find that Thucydides reports this move at a key point in his narrative (7.28, between his descriptions of the creation of the Spartan fort at Deceleia, and the murderous rampage of Athens' Thracian mercenaries at Mycalessus). Kallet (2001, 136–40) has emphasized that Thucydides intends this decision to be read in the context of the looming crisis in Athens' imperial power. Thucydides reports that the Athenians believed that the tax would generate more income than the tribute: we do not have enough data to know if they were correct, although the general tone of Thucydides' account has been read to suggest that he thought they were not (Kallet 2001, 137, noting his characterization of the Athenians as "lusting after victory"); that is, the decision is (for Thucydides) evidence not just of Athenian greed, but also of the irrationality that such greed provoked. Whether or not we accept Thucydides' (implied) analysis of the motivation for the change from *phoros* to taxation, it is clear that this was a significant change in policy—which makes it frustrating that we have so little evidence for its effect (financial or otherwise) on the Empire. A comment in

Aristophanes (*Frogs*, line 363) suggests that the tax was still being collected in 405, and there is no clear evidence that tribute was ever reintroduced (although no absolute proof that it was not); but we do not know how much income was generated by the tax, nor do we have any sense of whether it was seen by the allies as more or less of an imposition (whether economic or symbolic) than the tribute. The financial basis of the Empire clearly underwent a significant change in 413, but the current state of our knowledge makes it very hard to know whether we should see this as a retreat toward a more narrowly "economic" approach to imperial power (Kallet 2001, 196) or, rather, a shift to a parallel but distinct mode of imperial exploitation (Figueira 2005).

The Empire in the Peloponnesian War: Stability or Change?

The critical period for the establishment of Athens' imperial power was (for Thucydides) the Pentacontaetia (see Kallet, see chapter 3 in this volume). Nevertheless, as we have already seen, it is clear that the Empire did not remain unchanged during the Peloponnesian War. The pattern of the early years of the war is, in Thucydides' narrative, one of consolidation (in line with Pericles' reported advice at 1.144.1 and 2.65.7); of its middle years, of attempted expansion (notably in Sicily); and in the closing parts of the narrative, of incipient collapse (the very last days of the Empire are, of course, not recorded in the *History*, but the wave of defections described at 8.5–28 clearly signals the beginning of the end). This model should be treated with a degree of caution, since even in Thucydides' narrative, we see evidence for expansion (and attempted expansion) during the Archidamian War: we could note, for example, the annexation of Aegina (and expulsion of its native population: 2.27), the excursions into Lycia and Caria in 430/29 (2.69, with Keen 1993), the attacks on Minoa (3.51), the (failed) attempt to incorporate Melos into the Empire in 426 (3.91.1–3, and, further West, attempts to establish a foothold in Locri (3.99, 103; on all these, see Hunt, chapter 7 in this volume). The poor state of preservation of the Tribute Quota Lists after about 430 makes it difficult to trace with confidence any changes either in overall membership of the Empire in this period or in the amount of tribute received from it, although it is possible to identify some evidence for the extension of Athenian control during the war: the appearance in the lists of the mid-420s of cities once under the protection of Mytilene, for example, must reflect the expansion of Athens' direct power in that region after the suppression of the Mytilenean revolt (Meiggs 1972, 533).

We are, then, not particularly well informed about the exact size of the Athenian Empire during this period. About 248 states appear on the Quota Lists overall, but no more than about 190 are listed in any single year. In part, this discrepancy probably does reflect a constant background of defections from and additions to the Empire (the changes in the presence or absence of a number of Thracian cities in the 430s, for example, are likely to echo shifts in relations between those cities and their two powerful potential protectors, Athens and the Macedonian king Perdiccas: Meiggs 1972, 250); but in many cases an absence from the list might simply mean that the tribute from that community for that year was, for some reason, not recorded (Constantakopoulou 2013, 37–38).

Where we do find clearer evidence for a quite dramatic expansion in the scope of the Empire is in a different sort of tribute list: the tribute assessments, which record not what the Athenians actually received in tribute, but what they hoped to obtain. Of these, the best preserved is the assessment of 425/4 (ML 69), which expresses an intention to extract tribute (and lots of it: about 1460T in total) from about 410 cities. The problem, though, lies in knowing exactly what this list is evidence for: does it indicate an actual (and quite significant) increase in the size of the Empire by the mid-420s, or is it rather evidence of an increase in Athenian ambition (or, less sympathetically, wishful thinking)? That the latter is more likely to be the case is suggested above all by one notable inclusion in the list of assessed cities: Melos (line 65)—a state that, as readers of Thucydides know only too well, was not finally suppressed by the Athenians until a decade later.

The problem of interpreting this particular text brings us to a larger—and still unresolved—question: did the ideology of Athenian imperialism undergo any significant change during the Peloponnesian War? Or, to put it in more simplistic terms, did the Empire become more brutal, or more nakedly "imperialistic" as the war progressed? There are some reasons to believe that Thucydides thought so. Taking a cue from Thucydides' observation (in the context of the Corcyrean *stasis*) that "war runs a violent school" (3.82.2; tr. Hammond 1989), it can be tempting to trace a progression during the war, from Athens' avoidance (just) of resorting to mass murder as a means of controlling the rebellious Mytileneans (3.49.4), via the slaughter at Melos (5.116.4), to the final, fatal, overextension into Sicily (where the brutal logic of imperial expansion is chillingly set out in the speech of the ironically named Euphemus: 6.82–87). Alternatively (or additionally; the explanations need not be mutually exclusive), a shift in practice could be linked to changes in Athens' domestic leadership: the restraint of Pericles gives way to the demagogic excesses of Cleon and those who follow him.

But this model of steady decline from "Periclean" restraint to later excess risks oversimplifying a more complex picture. True, Thucydides himself (at 2.65) claims that leaders after Pericles pushed Athens' imperial policies in distinctly new (and more dangerous) directions, but several modern commentators have wondered if Thucydides' narrative of post-Periclean foreign policy really supports that claim (for an overview of the problems, see Hornblower 1991–2008, 1.346–8), while others have noted that non-Thucydidean sources place far less weight on Pericles' death as a turning point (Azoulay 2014, 127–36). It is also possible to point to a number of instances of imperial brutality even before Pericles' death: the dispossession of the Hestiaeans in 447/6 (1.114.3) and of the Aeginetans in 432 (2.27), or the suppression of the revolt of Samos in in 440/39 (1.115–17; Plutarch, *Pericles* 25.8 reports a version of these events that associates Pericles in particular with violent reprisals against the rebellious Samians).

The evidence of inscriptions has often been deployed in an attempt to expand (or refute) the Thucydidean picture. The epigraphic record undoubtedly provides some support for the view that Athenians were keen to expand their empire during the war (or, on a more cynical reading, were happy to delude themselves about the extent of their power). We have already noted a key piece of evidence for this in the tribute reassessment decree of 425/4 (ML 69), a text that seems to complement the Thucydidean picture of an Empire whose ambitions—whether under the stress of war, or because they lacked the guiding hand of a restrained political leader—were starting to spiral out of control.

The difficulty, though, lies in establishing whether this expansionist and exploitative approach to empire can be so neatly restricted to the 420s and later, and it is at this point that the uncertainty over the dating of many key inscriptions becomes relevant. The assessment decree (ML 69) is securely dated to 425/4, but a number of other decrees, which seem to show a similarly aggressive approach to the running of the Empire, are less easy to place. These include measures that impose stringent regulations on individual states (e.g., *IG* I^3 21: a decree imposing legal and other restrictions on Miletus), as well as attempts to introduce Empire-wide controls and obligations—a move that in itself might seem to suggest a change in attitude to Empire (that is, a shift toward seeing it, precisely, as an Empire, to be managed as a whole, rather than as a collection of more or less discrete interstate entanglements). Significant examples in this latter category include ML 46, a decree of "strongly imperial flavour" (ML, p. 120) concerned with tribute payment; ML 73, a decree that (among other things) compels all allied states to send first fruits to the sanctuary of Demeter at Eleusis; and, most notoriously, ML 45, the Standards Decree, in which the Athenians attempt to impose their own currency, weights, and measures across the Empire, with extremely severe punishments for those who fail to comply. The dates of all of these decrees can be established only from circumstantial evidence. If placed in the 420s they would provide good support for the existence of a post-Periclean shift in Athenian imperial practice and ideology—but it is far from clear that they can all be dated to this period; in fact, the growing consensus (represented most clearly in Rhodes 2008, table 1) is that they are scattered quite widely from the 440s down to the 420s. Attempting to construct a rigid model for imperial development on the basis of such evidence would be unwise, at least given the current state of our knowledge. For now, the best that can be done is (as always) to read Thucydides with caution, and in the knowledge that there is almost certainly another story of Athenian imperial development in the Peloponnesian War to be told, even if we are not yet in a position to be able to tell it.

Attitudes toward Empire

The Athenian Empire that we see in Thucydides' *History* is a coercive and oppressive structure, a fact that is acknowledged by the Athenians (e.g., by Pericles at 2.63, or by Cleon at 3.37), resented by the members of the Empire (according to, e.g., the rebellious

Mytileneans: 3.9–14), and exploited (with varying degrees of initiative or success) by the Spartans (as, e.g., by Brasidas at 4.85–87). The Athenians do, it is true, make occasional attempts to present themselves in a more positive light (e.g., in the speech of the ambassadors at Sparta at 1.73–78), but the overall Thucydidean picture of the Athenian Empire is of an essentially unpopular organization, held together only by force or the threat of force. This picture can seem hard to challenge—it is supported not just by the speeches, but also by the narrative: Thucydides tells us of revolts (and the brutal suppression of those revolts, as at Mytilene); forced incorporation into the Empire (as at Melos); and of the rapidity with which states seize their chance to escape from imperial control as soon as Athenian power starts to crumble toward the end of the war.

It would be perverse to deny that the Empire must have been highly unpopular in some places and periods. As well as the revolts mentioned by Thucydides, there is epigraphic evidence for unrest (and more) in the decrees that reimpose Athenian control on rebellious allies (e.g., ML 40 on Erythrae; ML 52 on Chalkis); some defections can also be traced by the disappearance of states from the Tribute Quota Lists: see, e.g., Meiggs 1972, 562–65 for the case of Miletus). Later literary sources also support the view of the empire as an organization driven by fear and hatred: Xenophon (*Hellenica* 2.2.3), for example, memorably describes the Athenians' fear (on losing the war) that those abuses which they had inflicted on the Greeks would be imposed on them in turn. That such discomfort about fifth-century imperial behavior was more widely felt is suggested by the "Prospectus" of Athens' fourth-century multilateral alliance (RO 22), which includes guarantees not to impose garrisons, not to confiscate land, not to levy tribute, and not to violate the freedom and autonomy of member states: not, in short, to do the various things that (according to Thucydides and others) made the fifth-century Empire so detested.

Nonetheless, it is worth asking whether the loathing of the Empire was as universal as it can sometimes appear. The impact of imperial rule on the domestic politics of the member states should be considered here. Thucydides himself notes that the Empire tended to support (and to be supported by) democratic factions in the subject states (3.82.1, 7.55.2); it has been suggested that this fact, combined with Thucydides' lukewarm views on Athens' own democracy (or at least some aspects of it), might have increased his tendency to see the Empire in mostly negative terms. Thucydides emphasizes the ways in which imperial power impinged on the freedom of the Greeks, and it is hard to deny that this is true at the level of interstate interaction. But it could be argued (and is argued, most influentially by De Ste. Croix 1954/5; cf. Bradeen 1960, Romilly 1966) that the Empire promoted freedom within states by supporting democratic governments; as a result (the argument goes), far from being hated by all, Athenian rule might even have been actively welcomed by many, particularly those who favored democratic government. In support of this view, it is possible to point to the fact (which Thucydides noted) that the revolt at Mytilene was undermined (in the first instance) by the refusal of "the people" (*demos*) at Mytilene to continue to support a rebellion led by "the ruling classes" (*dunatous*: 3.27.3). The Athenians' documented imposition of democratic rule as a response to rebellion, at Erythrae and elsewhere, is also relevant (examples are catalogued by Brock 2009, 153–55). It is possible to overemphasize the extent of Athens' support for democracy (Brock 2009,161 notes that there is a strong degree of pragmatism in Athenian policy in this matter), but those individuals or factions who benefited from it would presumably have been more inclined to tolerate, or even welcome, Athenian leadership as a result.

Other factors that might have encouraged support for the Empire should also be considered. The Athenian use of *proxenoi*—trusted individual citizens of subject states—as agents of imperial control has been noted, as has the fact that the position of these men could be precarious. But when things were going well, to be an Athenian *proxenos* was surely beneficial, bringing enhanced status for the officeholder both at home and elsewhere in Greece (it is worth noting that the special protection offered by Athens to these men extended, at least in theory, over "as many cities as the Athenians ruled": on the formula, see Meiggs 1972, 425–27). Some cities received special trading or legal concessions (Phaselis is granted special legal privileges: ML 31; Methone is offered protection from Macedonian intervention, as well as the right to import grain from Byzantium: ML 65). Finally, the possibilities for participation in major Athenian religious festivals, and for cultivation of kinship connections and other ties of interstate *xenia*, might have been seen by at least some individuals or states as positive opportunities rather than oppressive impositions (see, for example, the apparently voluntary gift, from a community on the island of Carpathos, of wood to be used in constructing a temple of Athena: *IG* I^3 1454; on kinship ties in the Empire, see Fragoulaki 2013, 209–81). It is possible that some or all of these factors might have made Athenian imperial control a largely positive experience for some, but in trying to move from plausible speculation to firm conclusions, we are seriously hampered by the absence of non-Athenian perspectives on the question. Nonetheless, it is always worth remembering that Thucydides' largely bleak view of the nature of empire for those ruled by it need not necessarily have been universally shared; at the very least, it is essential to acknowledge that there must have been considerable variation in the impact of empire on its subjects, as states, and as individuals; and in both economic and political terms.

Empire and Interstate Relations

Thucydides presents the Athenian Empire as an organization that distorts and disrupts the traditional patterns and norms of Greek interstate politics. A line is crossed at an early point, in the "enslavement" of Naxos (1.98.4: "quite contrary to normal practice"), and from then onward it can seem that the Athenians, though they might claim to be doing "nothing contrary to human nature" (1.76.2) in establishing their rule over the Greeks, do not feel any need to operate according to the normal conventions of interstate politics.

Nonetheless, it is clear that those conventions exist, and that, even if they are sometimes broken (and not only by the Athenians), they still provide a framework for relations between states, both within and outside the Empire (as, rightly, emphasized by Sheets 1994; see also Low 2007, 77–128). States continued to make treaties with one another during this period, binding themselves to both specific and more open-ended commitments. A good example is the treaty reported by Thucydides at 5.47, which establishes a multilateral alliance between the Athenians, Argives, Mantineans, and Eleans, together with the existing allies of each party. (An inscribed copy of the same treaty is also partially preserved: *IG* I³ 83; Hornblower 1991–2008, 3.110–12 gives a useful account of the relationship between the Thucydidean and inscribed versions.) The treaty demonstrates a number of conventional features: it is made for a finite, though extended, period (one hundred years: an unusually long time, perhaps to be taken as more or less synonymous with "eternity," but not unparalleled: an early treaty, ML 17, has the same time frame); it sets out a series of negative (mutual nonaggression) and positive (assistance in the case of invasion) obligations between the treating parties; and it is guaranteed by the mutual swearing of oaths, and by the erection of inscribed copies of the agreement both in local sanctuaries, and in the Panhellenic sanctuary at Olympia.

It is tempting to add that another characteristic feature of this treaty is that it fails (two years later, at 5.79, the Argives can be found making a fifty-year treaty with the Spartans). But it would be a mistake to conclude from this that all treaties were meaningless. Not only is it the case that our sources (not just Thucydides) tend always to be more interested in agreements that fail than those that work, but it is also notable that— even in Thucydides—it is clear that breaking a treaty was thought to have consequences for the party responsible. Thucydides, as we might expect, places little weight on the possible religious implications of treaty breaking (although Xenophon, by contrast, is adamant that the Spartan collapse of the fourth century proved that the gods punished those who violated their treaty oaths: *Hellenica* 5.4.1), but he does show that states were worried about being blamed for causing a treaty to fail. He notes, for example, the Athenians' careful annotation of the treaty *stēlē* of the Peace of Nicias with an addendum making it clear that the Spartans broke the treaty before the Athenians did (5.56.3); he also draws attention to the Spartans' anxiety that they were thought to have been at fault for the outbreak of the Archidamian war (because they had ignored a treaty provision that required disputes to be referred to arbitration: 7.18.3).

A similar pattern applies to the use (and abuse) of "diplomats" in this period: the heralds, ambassadors, and other messengers who ensured that communication between states could continue even when they were at war. Here, too, Thucydides reports some notable breaches of the principle that such men should be inviolable: Athens' capture and execution of the Peloponnesian envoys en route to Persia is a conspicuous example (2.67). But, once more, we should assume that these actions are noteworthy precisely because they are exceptional; elsewhere in Thucydides, we find envoys performing their tasks without difficulty. Athenian ambassadors speak at Sparta (1.73–78), and Spartan envoys address the Athenian assembly (4.17–20), as do multiple representatives from Sicilian *poleis* (6.8, 19), and elsewhere (Mosley 1973, 78–79 has more examples; we could also note the regular appearance of ambassadors in Aristophanes' versions of Peloponnesian War diplomacy in, for example, *Acharnians* or *Lysistrata*). A grave monument from Athens shows that when foreign ambassadors did come to harm (in this case, the inscription emphasizes, by accident), they would be granted an honorific burial by their host city (*IG* II² 5224: the monument is for two Corcyrean ambassadors, who probably died in the last third of the fifth century).

Finally, interpersonal connections remain an important tool of interstate politics throughout (and beyond) the Peloponnesian War. The role of the *proxenos* as an agent of imperial control has already been noted, but *proxenia* was not an exclusively imperial phenomenon; many (perhaps most) Greek states seem to have made use of these men to help maintain, or even enhance, their interstate relations (we see both Argive and Spartan *proxenoi* in action in the diplomatic maneuvers of 418, for example: 5.59.5, 76.3). Interpersonal connections could operate on a less formal level, too: the orator Andocides claimed that he took advantage of an old friendship with the Macedonian royal house to secure a supply of oar spars for the Athenian fleet in 411 (Andoc. 2.11); toward the end of the century, the Athenians set up inscribed honors (*IG* II² 174) for Epicerdes of Cyrene, who had succeeded—presumably by exploiting some local contacts—in securing the release of Athenians still imprisoned in the stone quarries of Syracuse. This sort of exploitation of interpersonal ties is not always very visible in Thucydides' narrative of events (though it can sometimes be discerned: see Herman 1990), but enough survives to show how important it must have been as a mechanism of interstate politics in this period, both within and beyond the Athenian Empire (the wider phenomenon is discussed by Mitchell 1997).

Conclusion: Thucydides' Empire

Thucydides creates for us an exceptionally vivid picture of the nature of Athenian imperialism during the Peloponnesian War. Empire, in the Thucydidean view, becomes a destructive addiction: once the Athenians are committed to amassing this power, it becomes too dangerous to let it go (as Pericles warns them: 2.63.2); but the violence and exploitation required to keep the Empire afloat cannot be sustained indefinitely. This picture of the Empire (and of imperialism more generally) is compelling, and Thucydides was certainly not the only ancient commentator who was attracted to it. Isocrates, in the fourth century, likens the lure of empire to that of a bad love affair: "it turns the heads of those who are besotted by it, and is in its nature like courtesans, who entice their victims to love but destroy those who indulge this passion" (8.103).

What is sometimes lost in Thucydides' account, though, is some of the complexity of the business of running an empire, particularly in time of war. Thucydides focuses our attention on the moments of acute crisis and drama: the triremes racing to Mytilene (3.49), the standoff at Melos (5.85–116), the loss of Euboea (8.96). But there must also have been (and we can sometimes perceive, especially in the epigraphic evidence) a constant strain involved in keeping the Empire running, in responding to local crises, and, in particular, in ensuring a steady flow of income. The Athenians' ability to keep this organization together for (by the standards of Greek interstate politics) a remarkably long time is, if not necessarily admirable, at least worthy of notice.

Thucydides' picture of interstate politics, likewise, can make for persuasive, if depressing, reading: this is a world where treaties are abandoned with barely a thought, where envoys are murdered, where deception is commonplace. Such events undoubtedly did occur, and it may well be that the power disparities of the fifth century made it easier for some states—Athens, above all—to get away with violations of interstate conventions that would have been impossible in other periods. But even among the upheavals of the Peloponnesian War, we should not assume that the Greek states operated in a system of complete anarchy. Our picture of the world of interstate politics in this period needs to leave some space for a less dramatic, but no less complex, pattern of interstate interactions: interpersonal ties, religious constraints, and kinship links—as well, certainly, as greed and self-interest—all combined to shape the behavior of states and their citizens in the last decades of the fifth century.

REFERENCES

Azoulay, V. 2014. *Pericles of Athens*. Translated by J. Lloyd. Princeton: Princeton University Press.
Balcer, J. M. 1976. "Imperial Magistrates in the Athenian Empire." *Historia* 25: 257–87.
Balcer, J. M. 1977. "The Athenian Episkopos and the Achaemenid 'King's Eye.'" *AJPh* 98: 252–63.
Bradeen, D. W. 1960. "The Popularity of the Athenian Empire." *Historia* 9: 257–69.
Brock, R. 2009. "Did the Athenian Empire Promote Democracy?" In *Interpreting the Athenian Empire*, edited by J. Ma, N. Papazarkadas, and R. Parker, 149–66. London: Duckworth.
Brunt, P. A. 1966. "Athenian Settlements Abroad in the Fifth Century B.C." In *Ancient Society and Institutions: Studies Presented to Victor Ehrenberg on His 75th Birthday*, edited by E. Badian, 71–92. Oxford: Blackwell.
Constantakopoulou, C. 2013. "Tribute, the Athenian Empire and Small States/Communities in the Aegean." In *Trade and Finance in the 5th Century B.C. Aegean World*, edited by A. Slawisch, 25–42. Istanbul: Ege Yayınları.
Culham, P. 1978. "The Delian League: Bicameral or Unicameral?" *AJAH* 3: 27–31.
De Ste. Croix, G. E. M. 1954–1955. "The Character of the Athenian Empire." *Historia* 3: 1–41.
De Ste. Croix, G. E. M. 1961. "Notes on Jurisdiction in the Athenian Empire, II." *CQ* 11: 268–80.
Figueira, T. J. 1998. *The Power of Money: Coinage and Politics in the Athenian Empire*. Philadelphia: University of Pennsylvania Press.
Figueira, T. J. 2005. "The Imperial Commercial Tax and the Finances of the Athenian Hegemony." *Incidenza dell' Antico* 3: 83–133.
Forsdyke, S. 2005. *Exile, Ostracism, and Democracy: The Politics of Expulsion in Ancient Greece*. Princeton and Oxford: Princeton University Press.
Fragoulaki, M. 2013. *Kinship in Thucydides: Intercommunal Ties and Historical Narrative*. Oxford: Oxford University Press.
Gomme, A. W., A. Andrewes, and K. J. Dover. 1945–1981. *A Historical Commentary on Thucydides*. 5 vols. Oxford: Clarendon.
Hammond, M. 1989. *Thucydides. The Peloponnesian War. A New Translation*. Oxford: Oxford University Press.

Herman, G. 1987. *Ritualised Friendship and the Greek City*. Cambridge: Cambridge University Press.
Herman, G. 1990. "Treaties and Alliances in the World of Thucydides." *PCPS* 36: 83–102.
Hornblower, S. 1991–2008. *A Commentary on Thucydides*. 3 vols. Oxford: Clarendon.
Jowett, B. 1881. *Thucydides*. Vol. 2. Oxford: Clarendon.
Kallet-Marx, L. 1993. *Money, Expense and Naval Power in Thucydides' History, 1–5.24*. Berkeley, Los Angeles, and London: University of California Press.
Kallet, L. 2001. *Money and the Corrosion of Power in Thucydides: The Sicilian Expedition and Its Aftermath*. Berkeley, Los Angeles, and London: University of California Press.
Keen, A. G. 1993. "Athenian Campaigns in Karia and Lykia during the Peloponnesian War." *JHS* 113: 152–57.
Lawton, C. A. 1995. *Attic Document Reliefs: Art and Politics in Ancient Athens*. Oxford: Clarendon.
Lewis, D. M. 1997. "The Athenian Coinage Decree." In *Selected Papers in Greek and Near Eastern History*, edited by J. Rhodes, 116–39. Cambridge: Cambridge University Press.
Low, P. A. 2007. *Interstate Relations in Classical Greece: Morality and Power*. Cambridge: Cambridge University Press.
Meiggs, R. 1949. "A Note on Athenian Imperialism." *CR* 63: 9–12.
Meiggs, R. 1972. *The Athenian Empire*. Oxford: Clarendon.
Mitchell, L. G. 1997. *Greeks Bearing Gifts: The Public Use of Private Relationships in the Greek World, 435–323 BC*. Cambridge: Cambridge University Press.
Mosley, D. J. 1973. *Envoys and Diplomacy in Ancient Greece*. Historia Einzelschriften 22. Wiesbaden: Steiner Verlag.
Murray, O. 1966. "*Ho Archaios Dasmos*." *Historia* 15: 142–56.
Nease, A. S. 1949. "Garrisons in the Athenian Empire." *Phoenix* 3: 102–11.
Osborne, R. G. 2000. *The Athenian Empire*. 4th ed. London: London Association of Classical Teachers.
Osborne, R. G. 2004. *The Old Oligarch: Pseudo-Xenophon's "Constitution of the Athenians."* London: London Association of Classical Teachers.
Papazarkadas, N. 2009. "Epigraphy and the Athenian Empire: Re-shuffling the Chronological Cards." In *Interpreting the Athenian Empire*, edited by J. Ma, N. Papazarkadas, and R. Parker, 67–88. London: Duckworth.
Parker, R. C. T. 1996. *Athenian Religion: A History*. Oxford: Clarendon.
Rhodes, P. J. 1993. *A Commentary on the Aristotelian* Athenaion Politeia. Revised ed. Oxford: Clarendon.
Rhodes, P. J. 2008. "After the Three-Bar Sigma Controversy: The History of Athenian Imperialism Reassessed." *CQ* 58: 500–506.
Romilly, J. de. 1966. "Thucydides and the Cities of the Athenian Empire." *BICS* 13: 1–12.
Sheets, G. A. 1994. "Conceptualizing International Law in Thucydides." *AJPh* 115: 51–73.
Walbank, M. B. 1978. *Athenian Proxenies of the Fifth Century B.C.* Toronto: Stevens.
Whitehead, D. M. 1998. "*Ho Neos Dasmos*: 'Tribute' in Classical Athens." *Hermes* 126: 173–88.

CHAPTER 6

THUCYDIDES ON THE CAUSES AND OUTBREAK OF THE PELOPONNESIAN WAR

ERIC W. ROBINSON

Thucydides speaks clearly and forthrightly about what he sees as the causes of the devastating war starting in 431 BCE between the Athenians and the Spartans (what we call the Peloponnesian War). He declares as follows at 1.23.5–6:

> διότι δ᾽ ἔλυσαν, τὰς αἰτίας προύγραψα πρῶτον καὶ τὰς διαφοράς, τοῦ μή τινα ζητῆσαί ποτε ἐξ ὅτου τοσοῦτος πόλεμος τοῖς Ἕλλησι κατέστη. τὴν μὲν γὰρ ἀληθεστάτην πρόφασιν, ἀφανεστάτην δὲ λόγῳ, τοὺς Ἀθηναίους ἡγοῦμαι μεγάλους γιγνομένους καὶ φόβον παρέχοντας τοῖς Λακεδαιμονίοις ἀναγκάσαι ἐς τὸ πολεμεῖν.

> To the question of why the Athenians and the Peloponnesians broke the treaty, I answer by placing first an account of their grounds of complaint and points of difference, that no one may ever have to ask the immediate cause which plunged the Hellenes into a war of such magnitude. However, the real cause, though the least spoken of, I consider to be the growth of the power of Athens, and the alarm this inspired in Sparta, which made war inevitable. (Crawley translation in Strassler 1996, modified.)

The context is significant. Thucydides has just finished introducing his history and arguing that, compared to earlier times and conflicts, this war was the greatest ever fought by Greeks. He is about to begin his narrative of the events leading up to the war's outbreak. But before he does so, he wants to make sure his readers do not confuse the upcoming description of "grounds of complaint and points of difference" (τὰς αἰτίας ... καὶ τὰς διαφοράς) with what he judges to be the true, underlying cause of the war (τὴν ... ἀληθεστάτην πρόφασιν). So he spells it out here, emphasizing the combination of the growth of Athenian power and the fear this inspired among the Spartans in compelling the participants to war.

But this prominent declaration was not enough for Thucydides. Later in the same book, after he has narrated the various flashpoints of conflict in the mid-to-late 430s BCE and reached a climax with the war debate in Sparta in 432, Thucydides inserts this brief reminder, at 1.88:

ἐψηφίσαντο δὲ οἱ Λακεδαιμόνιοι τὰς σπονδὰς λελύσθαι καὶ πολεμητέα εἶναι οὐ τοσοῦτον τῶν ξυμμάχων πεισθέντες τοῖς λόγοις ὅσον φοβούμενοι τοὺς Ἀθηναίους μὴ ἐπὶ μεῖζον δυνηθῶσιν, ὁρῶντες αὐτοῖς τὰ πολλὰ τῆς Ἑλλάδος ὑποχείρια ἤδη ὄντα.

The Spartans voted that the treaty had been broken, and that war must be declared, not so much because they were persuaded by the arguments of their allies, as because they feared the growth of the power of the Athenians, seeing most of Hellas already subject to them. (Crawley translation)

Still not done with the question, Thucydides moves directly from this statement to the so-called Pentecontaetia, his summary narrative of the growth of the Athenian Empire and Athenian interactions with the Spartans in the decades following the Persian Wars of 480–479 BCE. Immediately after this disquisition, at 1.118.2, Thucydides restates in even greater detail his thesis on the true causes of the war:

...ἐν οἷς οἱ Ἀθηναῖοι τήν τε ἀρχὴν ἐγκρατεστέραν κατεστήσαντο καὶ αὐτοὶ ἐπὶ μέγα ἐχώρησαν δυνάμεως, οἱ δὲ Λακεδαιμόνιοι αἰσθόμενοι οὔτε ἐκώλυον εἰ μὴ ἐπὶ βραχύ, ἡσύχαζόν τε τὸ πλέον τοῦ χρόνου, ὄντες μὲν καὶ πρὸ τοῦ μὴ ταχεῖς ἰέναι ἐς τοὺς πολέμους, ἢν μὴ ἀναγκάζωνται, τὸ δέ τι καὶ πολέμοις οἰκείοις ἐξειργόμενοι, πρὶν δὴ ἡ δύναμις τῶν Ἀθηναίων σαφῶς ᾔρετο καὶ τῆς ξυμμαχίας αὐτῶν ἥπτοντο. τότε δὲ οὐκέτι ἀνασχετὸν ἐποιοῦντο, ἀλλ᾽ ἐπιχειρητέα ἐδόκει εἶναι πάσῃ προθυμίᾳ καὶ καθαιρετέα ἡ ἰσχύς, ἢν δύνωνται, ἀραμένοις τόνδε τὸν πόλεμον.

During this interval the Athenians succeeded in placing their empire on a firmer basis, and themselves advanced their power to a very great height. The Spartans, though fully aware of it, opposed it only for a little while, but remained inactive during most of the period, being of old slow to go to war except under the pressure of necessity, and in the present instance being hampered by wars at home. Finally, the growth of the Athenian power could no longer be ignored as their own confederacy became the object of its encroachments. They then felt that they could endure it no longer, but that the time had come for them to throw themselves heart and soul upon the hostile power, and break it, if they could, by commencing the present war. (Crawley translation)

Let us take note of some key features of Thucydides' striking thesis. First, as many have remarked upon, the historian explicitly contrasts the "truest" (ἀληθεστάτην) causes of the war with other, more frequently and openly alleged ones. It is not that the "grounds of complaint and points of difference" are without explanatory value for him. Thucydides surely would not have bothered with his lengthy accounts of the prewar affairs at Epidamnus, Corcyra, and Potidaea if it had been all meaningless. Rather, he wants his readers to understand that the deeper, underlying causes that he has identified mattered even more. This is a momentous contrast to draw. As Simon Hornblower (1991, 65) says, "the explicit formulation of a distinction between profound and superficial causes is arguably Thucydides' greatest contribution to later history-writing."

Other important features of his thesis are its balance and lack of moralizing. In each of the three statements quoted above, Thucydides carefully balances the parts played by Athens and Sparta. Athens' fearsome imperial power looms large as a driving force for war, but equally prominent and inextricably connected is Sparta's bellicose reaction. Nor does any bitterness or sense of blame attach to Thucydides' pronouncements. In none of the three statements or their immediate context does he cast aspersions on one side or the other for their behavior. Elsewhere in his history Thucydides shows himself quite willing to apply a strong moral conscience to his story (e.g., on Athenian failings after Pericles' death at 2.65, or the evils of civil war at 3.82–84), but he holds it in abeyance here.

Finally, and related to this last point, is Thucydides' emphasis on the inevitability of the war. His Greek at the end of 1.23.6 resists easy translation into English because Thucydides has failed to provide a direct object for the verbal phrase "compelled to war" (ἀναγκάσαι ἐς τὸ πολεμεῖν): we expect to see "the Spartans" or "the Athenians and the Spartans" or even just "them," and if we had such a supplied direct object we could emphasize the actions of a particular city or cities in initiating the conflict. By *not* providing a direct object for "compel" (ἀναγκάσαι), Thucydides instead emphasizes the compulsion itself—that is, his own abstract formulation that the twinned forces of growing Athenian power and an alarmed Sparta together *forced* the war to happen (Ostwald 1988, 2–4).

Scholarly Controversies

Thucydides' direct statement (and repeated restatement) of his carefully considered thesis has not prevented scholars from disagreeing heatedly about the war's causes and the proper interpretation of Thucydides' views on the matter. Indeed, according to Martin Ostwald, "it is difficult to think of any single passage in ancient Greek literature that has given rise to more intense controversy than Thucydides' statement on the causes of the Peloponnesian War" at 1.23.6 (1988, 1).

In times past the arguments often pivoted around the issue of the manner of composition of Thucydides' history (Romilly 1963, 3–10, 370–72; Andrewes 1959). Was the statement at 1.23.6 (and the other two that follow) later insertions into a text a younger Thucydides had started to prepare before the result of the war was known? If so, how should this affect our valuation of one or the other line of thinking? But from the last half of the twentieth century forward, scholars have moved on from the old clash of "Analysts" and "Unitarians." The latter (those who wish to treat the history as a unity, not a collection of clearly separable "strata") seem to have prevailed, both regarding this issue and more generally in Thucydidean studies (see Hornblower 2008, 1–4). Thus more recent scholars, while willing to admit that different parts of the history very likely were composed at different times, regard Thucydides' thought and method as comprehensible *in toto* and prefer not to create multiple Thucydides-es to argue with and over.

The main question remains, then: is Thucydides' stated thesis correct? If not, what *really* caused the war?

Interestingly, most of those who have tackled this question have ended up rejecting Thucydides' explanation, or at least significantly changing its emphasis. (An exception: Cawkwell 1997.) This common scholarly move is possible only because of the wealth of information about the war and its buildup that Thucydides himself provides—his account is so rich and detailed that many have sought to use it to contradict the author's own thesis. There are other, briefer, sources of information as well, of course: Diodorus' centuries-later universal history devotes the better part of two books to the conflict; a number of Plutarch's Roman-era biographies of Greek statesmen bear directly upon it; from contemporary authors the comedies of Aristophanes occasionally provide useful bits of evidence, including on the question of the war's outbreak; and, naturally, there are many inscribed documents from the second half of the fifth century that directly or indirectly bear on the war, especially as concerns Athens. All of these sources (and others) provide additional information that scholars have used to help build new interpretations. But none comes close to Thucydides in terms of depth of attention or weight of authority brought to the question of the war's onset.

Various alternative causes have been alleged over the years, with greater or lesser success. For a time in the twentieth century, for example, it was popular to point to economics and trade as having driven the participants to battle. Whether the thesis involved greedy merchants in the Piraeus, grain-hungry Peloponnesians, or a trade competition between Corinth and Athens, each suffers from a decided lack of evidence and few if any adherents nowadays (for a critical overview, see Kagan 1969, 347–49).

In contrast, condemning Athenian policies has proven to be an enduringly popular approach. Whether because of Athens' long-standing imperial expansion (everywhere from the Aegean to Thrace to Boeotia to Aegina to southern Italy), or the actions of Pericles and others in the years immediately prior to the war, or both, many scholars have fingered the Athenians as chief culprits (e.g., Rhodes 1987; Badian 1993; Kagan 2009, 35–74) This diverges from Thucydides' thesis because of the stress the ancient historian laid on the balanced role of Athens and Sparta remarked upon above. Nevertheless, it arguably represents the smallest departure from the author's statements. After all, even in Thucydides' formulation, the growth and exercise of Athenian power is necessarily prior to any Spartan reaction to it. And Thucydides certainly expends much effort in his history forwarding the issue of Athenian imperialism both before and during the war (Romilly 1963). Dionysius of Halicarnassus, writing in the first century BCE, summarized Thucydides as having said that the growth of Athenian power was the true cause of the war (*Thucydides* 10). To blame Athens primarily, then, is to take a relatively small step from Thucydides' stated view.

So what suggests Athenian culpability beyond the empire itself? One can start with the fact that many contemporary Athenians blamed Pericles and his policies for the war.

Thucydides indicates as much at 2.59.2, when he says "the Athenians" blamed Pericles for persuading them to go to war, which matches his presentation of Pericles' convincing his fellow citizens not to cave in to Spartan demands with his speech at 1.139–45. Further evidence for Athenian blame of Pericles can be found using non-Thucydidean sources. In two different wartime comedies Aristophanes makes jokes showing that some Athenians, at least, held Pericles at fault for starting the war, most particularly by promoting the Megarian Decree (*Acharnians* 515–39; *Peace* 601–27.) Congruent points of view are reflected in later authors (Plutarch, *Pericles*, 31–32; Diodorus 12.38–39).

Central to this line of argument is the Megarian Decree. The Athenians issued this decree (or decrees, on which see Brunt [1951] 1997, with Hornblower 1991, 110–112) in the years before the war in order to punish the Sparta-allied Megarians by denying them access to the markets and ports of Athens and its allies. This amounted to a primitive sort of trade embargo, the first of its kind, and one that had painful effect if we can believe the implications in Aristophanes' *Acharnians* and in Thucydides. (For a famously heterodox view of the decree, see de Ste. Croix 1972, 225–89). It was a clever device to use because a novel act like a trade embargo can hardly have been envisaged by the Thirty Years' Peace, which guaranteed protection of the allies of each side only from actual attack. But perhaps it was too clever: while the Megarian Decree surely represented no technical violation of the treaty, it did violate its spirit, which made the move highly provocative.

Modern historians have often remarked that Thucydides seems to want to downplay the significance of this decree. He never discusses the circumstances of its enactment, and he barely mentions its existence until 1.139, where he reveals that during final negotiations the Spartans offered to back off from war if Athens revoked this single decree—a striking admission of its importance. The natural supposition is that Thucydides wished to say as little as possible about the Megarian Decree because it seems to undermine his claim that the long-standing growth of Athenian power and Spartan fear of it caused the war, not the complaints of allies over a grievance like this. If so, he was right to be concerned: the decree represents a powerful reason to doubt Thucydides' thesis.

Connected to this line of argument is the general level of provocation and intransigence displayed by the Athenians and, above all, Pericles, on the eve of the war. Donald Kagan has argued persuasively that, for all the brilliance of Thucydides' insight into long-term versus immediate causes, the truth is that the war was *not* inevitable. The Thirty Years' Peace was thoughtfully negotiated and meant to last; episodes following it (like Athens' Panhellenic foundation of Thurii and Corinth's argument to leave Athens undisturbed as it quelled the Samian rebellion) show that the treaty was working, and that it was possible, in ancient Greece as in more modern times, for peace between hostile states or alliances to endure and not end in world-destroying war. If Pericles and the Athenians of the late 430s had better gauged Peloponnesian reactions to provocative moves like the Megarian Decree, Athens' Corcyrean alliance, and its ultimatum to Potidaea, or had shown a willingness to compromise at the very end, war could have been avoided. (Kagan 1969; 2009, 23–74)

Scholars usually make these kinds of arguments for Athenian culpability while accepting the basic reliability (though not perfection) of Thucydides as a reporter. Ernst

Badian, however, takes a radically different view in arguing for Athenian guilt: for him, Thucydides shows himself to be an *entirely* biased reporter, one who distorts events and twists motives, disregarding truth whenever he can get away with it, in order to promote a pro-Athenian agenda and make it seem that the Spartans, jealous of Athenian power, ruthlessly started the war. Badian sees signs of this agenda (signs all previous Thucydides scholars somehow completely missed) in the portrayal of the Spartans as feckless and dishonest, in the suppression of damaging information like the exact terms of the Thirty Years' Peace, and misrepresentation of events like the Spartan vote in 432, which was surely just a vote that Athens had violated the treaty, not a vote for war (Badian 1993).

Scholars have rightly challenged many aspects of Badian's approach (e.g., Meyer 1997, 35–39). Among its problems is his selective and unpersuasive reading of the tone of Thucydides' account. For example, Badian sees a blatantly partisan portrayal of the Spartans as devious and untrustworthy, but fails to acknowledge that Thucydides often goes out of his way to show the Athenians behaving as badly or even worse (e.g., 1.72–86; 1.90–92). Of course it is true that Thucydides argues for a thesis and sometimes arranges events and speeches conveniently to support that thesis. But such does not render him a fiendishly biased reporter/historian bent on exonerating his homeland. Indeed, we know what Thucydides' text looks like when he engages in a hatchet job (see his treatment of fellow Athenian Cleon, especially in Book 5): it bears no resemblance to his discriminating picture of Athenians and Spartans provoking and responding to each other as tensions built over time.

As popular as it has been to find fault with Athenian prewar policies, some scholars have, on the contrary, identified the Spartans as bearing chief responsibility for the war. The most prominent of these is G. E. M. de Ste. Croix. His monumental tome *The Origins of the Peloponnesian War* (with its forty-seven appendices [!], 1972) engages in an exhaustive, step-by-step refutation of points used to blame the Athenians for the outbreak of hostilities. Athens' decision to ally with neutral Corcyra fell within its treaty rights even as Athens bent over backward to avoid trouble with Corinth as a result of it; Corinth, not Athens, was the provocateur in the events at Corcyra, and was again when it sent military aid to Potidaea (which, though a Corinthian colony, had been a member of Athens' empire for years and "must certainly" have been listed as such in the Thirty Years' Peace, 79); nor did the Megarian Decree in any way violate the treaty. Thus Athens acted repeatedly and consistently within its rights. In contrast, the Spartans, egged on by their allies, shattered the terms of the peace by refusing to submit their differences to arbitration and instead invading Attica. Indeed, as de Ste. Croix emphasizes, Thucydides shows that years later the Spartans believed themselves to have been more at fault for causing the war: "They considered that the offense had been more on their own side" (Crawley translation, 7.18.2; ... ἐν γὰρ τῷ προτέρῳ πολέμῳ σφέτερον τὸ παρανόμημα μᾶλλον γενέσθαι ...).

De Ste. Croix attributes the Spartan zeal for war to a number of factors, including their mistaken belief that they would win easily (Thuc. 4.85.2, 5.14.3, and 7.28.3), and, even more, Sparta's unique vulnerability as a polity: its massive slave population of helots. Because of the potential for a crippling helot rebellion, Sparta "could not take risks which an ordinary Greek State might afford: she could not allow another city to reach a position of power from which it could threaten either herself or her allies" (291). Thus, according to de Ste. Croix, Thucydides was right to emphasize Sparta's fear in causing the war, though we must understand Sparta's *own culpability* in creating that fear: "The Helot danger was the curse Sparta had brought upon herself, an admirable illustration of the maxim that a people which oppresses another cannot itself be free" (292).

Moralizing aside, de Ste. Croix is right to highlight the confidence many Spartans felt about winning the war they were starting, and the special problem the helots represented. Corinth's threat to spark secessions from the Peloponnesian League if Sparta failed to act to defend its allies (a threat acted upon years later, 5.27–38) would have weighed especially heavily on the Spartans because of the way they relied on the League to shield their land, with its restive slave population, from outside incursion. And the emphasis De Ste. Croix places on Sparta and its allies' direct responsibility for beginning the hostilities, when they could have sought arbitration according to the treaty or further negotiations, seems justified. On the other hand, his lengthy attempt to dismiss the significance of the Megarian Decree fails to convince. Whatever one makes of de Ste. Croix's grand and tortured argument about the purpose of the decree (it was not about commerce at all, but merely aimed at humiliating the Megarians), it fails to remove the force of Thucydides' statement at 1.139 that in Sparta's final negotiations with Athens, the decree was the only real sticking point—and thus that an Athenian concession here would have prevented the war. Periclean and Athenian intransigence on this point is just as striking as before.

In the end, one might well judge that the chief accomplishment of De Ste. Croix's defense of Athenian policy and impugning of Sparta's has been not to remove Athens from the hot seat, but to restore an almost Thucydidean balance to the issue—de Ste. Croix has made it harder to ignore the very real Spartan bellicosity that turned allies' grievances and mutual tensions into open warfare in 431 BCE.

But might one see chief culpability lying with a third party? Corinth's provocative behavior in the years leading up to the war has certainly drawn attention, both by Thucydides and by scholars seeking to unravel the war's true causes (e.g., Tritle 2010, 11–43; Kagan 1969 ["Theirs is the greatest guilt..." 354]). The Corinthians, who Thucydides claims conceived a "bitter hatred" (τὸ σφοδρὸν μῖσος) for Athens during the "First" Peloponnesian War (1.103.4), precipitated the crises over Corcyra and Potidaea and played the leading role in goading their ally Sparta into confrontation with Athens, especially if we can believe the two speeches Thucydides has them deliver at the two meetings of Spartans and allies right before the war. Perhaps Corinth's constant stirring of the pot of war deserves the greatest censure.

One might argue, however, that the sort of blame game we have seen scholars engage in—the Athenians were the evildoers! No, the Spartans were worse! No, it was the dastardly Corinthians!—not only becomes tiresome, but also is unworthy of the sophisticated historical account Thucydides has given us. Perhaps we should look to different, less accusatory approaches to the issue.

Victor Davis Hanson (2005, 8–16) offers one such broader view. For him the buildup to war and the rising fear felt by the Spartans had less to do with specific Athenian transgressions than it did the nature of Athens itself: "Athenianism" represented not just imperialism, he claims, but a new force for "globalization" driven by Athens' "proselytizing and expansionary" democracy (13–14). This revolutionary democratic ideology was poison to staid, conservative Sparta, which saw itself losing out to Athens' new kind of society and power. The Spartans reacted emotionally and violently against it, bringing on the war.

Part of what animates Hanson's thinking is his explicit linking of the modern United States of America, a globalizing democracy to be sure, with ancient Athens (8–9). Whatever one thinks of this comparison, the main drawback to Hanson's claim about the war's cause is the complete lack of evidence for it: nowhere in Thucydides or any other ancient source is it even hinted that Athenian *democracy* drove the Spartans or their allies to war, as opposed to manifest Athenian power or provocative policies. Nor do the flashpoints of the late 430s (the Corcyrean alliance, Megarian Decree, Potidaea) have much to do with constitutional conflict. Moreover, the idea (simply assumed by Hanson) that Athens was driven to spread democracy with a kind of messianic zeal becomes impossible to maintain after careful consideration of the evidence (see Robinson 2011, chapter 4).

A fresh approach with more promise comes from J. E. Lendon. In *Song of Wrath* (2010; see also Lendon 2007) Lendon argues that the confrontation between Sparta and Athens that ultimately exploded into war amounted to a classic dispute over rank. Sparta had long held the top position among Greek states, a primacy secured through its superior hoplite soldiers and domination of the Peloponnesian League, and signaled clearly to all by Sparta's consensus selection as leader of the Greeks banding together to resist Persia in 480. Athens was of old a secondary power at best, but one whose status rose precipitously during and after the Persian Wars. With the glory it earned in that conflict and the burgeoning power it showed in mastering an Aegean empire, Athens had ascended to the point where it could now challenge Sparta's hegemony. This way of thinking about the rivalry of Sparta and Athens was natural for the notoriously competitive ancient Greeks, steeped as they were in classics like Homer's *Iliad* in which such rank-consciousness is pervasive.

Lendon fruitfully reviews the history of Spartan-Athenian relations from the Persian Wars down to 431 by using the lens of rank and shows how well it explains otherwise curious situations and behaviors, like the odd combination of Athenian subservience to Spartan leadership with prickly resentment of other rivals for positions of honor (Syracuse, Tegea) during the Persian Wars; compare this with the fierce resentment imperial Athens later showed when, bypassing an opportunity to lord it over Sparta during the helot rebellion of the 460s, it followed Cimon's plea to aid its rival—only to be humiliatingly snubbed. This ultimately resulted in the First Peloponnesian War. Lendon's thesis is also aided by the language that Thucydides puts in Pericles' mouth during the speech he gives to dissuade the Athenians from giving in to Sparta's final demands: Athens simply must reject them, because "a firm refusal will make them clearly understand that they must treat you as equals (ἀπὸ τοῦ ἴσου)" (1.140.5, Crawley translation). The whole speech reeks of the notion that Athens was past bowing before Spartan superiority, and would (indeed, *must*) go to war before doing so again.

Lendon's recasting of the outbreak of the war as a contest of rank offers a new and useful way to frame the conflict. That Thucydides does not present things in such a way himself is no impediment: as scholars have long perceived, Thucydides consciously offers a revisionist opinion of the war's causes with his highly abstracted notion of Athenian power triggering Spartan fear to compel war. Moreover, a rank-based approach can explain the otherwise bizarre Periclean (and Athenian) intransigence at the end, when a small concession over the Megarian Decree could have averted war. This came not from mindless provocation or pride: the Athenians made their stand for the reasons Pericles gives, that the *manner* of Sparta's demand (an ultimatum) made it impossible for Athens to back down and retain what it saw as its fully merited equal standing relative to Sparta.

Of course, one can find ways to criticize the "contest of rank" thesis. Thucydides' language given to Pericles at 1.140 may suit the idea very well, but what of other occasions? The one Athenian speech and two Spartan speeches delivered during the Spartan war congress (Thuc. 1.73–86) presented excellent occasions to reveal a status rivalry—and yet they do not. The Athenian speaker seems at pains to justify the Athenian Empire's existence and warns of the danger of war; King Archidamus notes the difficulties the Spartans would have in making an immediate attack and advises caution; the ephor Sthenelaïdas scratches his head at the Athenian speaker's fancy, boastful words and urges war as the only honorable course to protect their allies. None of the speakers paints the conflict as one over status, or even references the rank of one side or the other. Nor do the non-Thucydidean sources (Aristophanes, Diodorus) hint at an overarching status rivalry lying behind the war's outbreak. Thus, as intuitively appealing as the rank theory is, one cannot help noticing how much reading it back into the sources is necessary to see it in operation.

Conclusions

It is hard not to admire the beauty and force of Thucydides' formulation of the war's causes. The notion that the growth of Athenian power alarmed Sparta to the point where the two juggernauts were set on a deadly collision course is thoughtful and elegantly neutral, and accords well with what we know of fifth-century history. One may reasonably disagree with Thucydides, of course, as many modern scholars have. And yet, when they do so, Thucydides' own rich account usually figures prominently in their crafting. Those who see Athenian misbehavior driving the war's outbreak can make a powerful case, but this is in large part because Thucydides is complicit in its making, with his relentless focus on the creation and maintenance of an aggressive Athenian Empire. Those putting primary responsibility on the Spartans or Corinthians lean heavily on Thucydides' narrative of the final few years of tension and the Peloponnesian decision to launch the war. New theories such as Lendon's contest of rank face the difficult task of being judged against Thucydides' persuasive and inevitably better documented thesis.

Scholars will no doubt continue to seek more satisfying answers to the tantalizing question of what caused the Peloponnesian War. In developing these ideas they will have as both essential resource and formidable hurdle the account of the war's first historiographical interpreter.

References

Andrewes, A. 1959. "Thucydides and the Causes of the War." *Classical Quarterly* 9: 223–39.
Badian, E. 1993. "Thucydides and the Outbreak of the Peloponnesian War: A Historian's Brief." In *From Plataea to Potidaea*, by E. Badian, 125–62. Baltimore: Johns Hopkins University Press.
Brunt, P. A. (1951) 1997. "The Megarian Decree." In *Studies in Greek History and Thought*, by P. A. Brunt, 1–16. Oxford: Oxford University Press.
Cawkwell, G. 1997. *Thucydides and the Peloponnesian War*. London: Routledge.
De Ste. Croix, G. E. M. 1972. *The Origins of the Peloponnesian War*. London: Duckworth.
Gomme, A. W. 1945. *A Historical Commentary on Thucydides*, Vol. I. Oxford: Clarendon.
Hanson, V. D. 2005. *A War Like No Other*. New York: Random House.
Hornblower, S. 1991. *A Commentary on Thucydides*. Vol. I, *Books I–III*. Oxford: Clarendon.
Hornblower, S. 2008. *A Commentary on Thucydides*. Vol. III, *Books 5.25–8.109*. Oxford: Clarendon.
Kagan, D. 1969. *The Outbreak of the Peloponnesian War*. Ithaca: Cornell University Press.
Kagan, D. 2009. *Thucydides: The Reinvention of History*. New York: Viking.
Lendon, J. E. 2007. "Athens and Sparta and the Coming of the Peloponnesian War." In *The Cambridge Companion to the Age of Pericles*, edited by L. J. Samons II, 258–81. New York: Cambridge University Press.
Lendon, J. E. 2010. *Song of Wrath*. New York: Basic Books.
Meyer, E. 1997. "*The Outbreak of the Peloponnesian War* after Twenty-Five Years." In *Polis and Polemos. Essays on Politics, War, and History in Ancient Greece in Honor of Donald Kagan*, edited by C. D. Hamilton and P. Krentz, 23–54. Claremont: Regina.
Ostwald, M. 1988. *ANAΓKH in Thucydides*. Atlanta: Scholars.
Rhodes, P. J. 1987. "Thucydides on the Causes of the Peloponnesian War." *Hermes* 115: 154–65.
Robinson, E. W. 2011. *Democracy beyond Athens. Popular Government in the Greek Classical Age*. Cambridge: Cambridge University Press.
Romilly, J. de. (1947) 1963. *Thucydides and Athenian Imperialism*. Translated by P. Thody. Oxford: Blackwell.
Strassler, R. B., ed. 1996. *The Landmark Thucydides*. New York: Touchstone.
Tritle, L. A. 2010. *A New History of the Peloponnesian War*. Malden: Wiley-Blackwell.

CHAPTER 7

THUCYDIDES ON THE FIRST TEN YEARS OF WAR (ARCHIDAMIAN WAR)

PETER HUNT

Introduction

THIS appraisal of Thucydides as a historian of the Archidamian War treats two sets of topics.[1] First and more obvious, historians should get their facts right—a criterion Thucydides himself emphasizes repeatedly (Thuc.1.20–1.22, 1.23.5–6, 6.54–55). Accordingly, the first section considers a variety of external checks on Thucydides' accuracy. The second section considers several cases in which scholars have criticized or praised Thucydides for the way he structures, emphasizes, plays down, or omits events or trends. Of course, these two categories, though heuristically useful, sometimes blend into each other: for example, overemphasis beyond a certain level is a mistake. Rather than attempting to encompass the justly famous speeches, debates, or descriptions in which Thucydides explores concepts such as power, morality, decision-making, and the limits of prediction, this chapter will focus narrowly on Thucydides' account of the war—including the plague, which damaged Athenian military power more than anything else (Thuc. 3.87.2).

Accuracy

Although we have no other independent account of the Peloponnesian War with which to compare Thucydides' history, over the generations scholars have found

---

[1] See Lewis (1992) for an authoritative treatment of the war; Lendon (2010) provides recent bibliography and an overall interpretation in terms of competition between states over rank. All dates are BCE.

a variety of ways to check Thucydides' accuracy. In particular, we can compare his account with contemporary comedy, other historians (for a few sections), Persian records, Greek inscriptions, and the topography of Greece. Some of this evidence can only be consistent with Thucydides, but does not have probative value: for example, the battle of Amphipolis *could* have taken place as Thucydides describes it, given the topography of the area (Pritchett 1965, 1980). Other types of evidence—e.g., inscriptions—may confirm or disconfirm Thucydides' account more directly. Although historians have found a few mistakes, the results of these investigations are generally reassuring.

Aristophanes

The plays of Aristophanes provide the source closest to Thucydides in time, place, and—to a surprising extent, given their genres—subject matter (see Henderson, chapter 35 in this volume). We possess four complete plays of Aristophanes from the period of the Archidamian War: the *Acharnians* (425), the *Knights* (424), the *Wasps* (422), and *Peace* (421). Although Aristophanes wrote comedies, his plays are replete with topical political and military references, the vast majority of which either confirm or can easily be reconciled with Thucydides' account of the war—but on the Megarian Degree, see Robinson, chapter 6 in this volume.

Aristophanes is plainly reacting to and finding humor, sometimes bitter, in the same war and events that Thucydides describes. He often presents the view from below, while Thucydides gives the commanders' perspective: for example, Thucydides reports the numbers, generals' names, and goal of an expedition, whereas Aristophanes focuses on the muster lists and the hated command "come with three days' rations" (Aristophanes, *Acharnians* 197 with Olson 2002, 132; *Peace* 312). Like Thucydides, Aristophanes' *Acharnians* repeatedly represents the devastation of the Attic countryside, the migration within the walls, and the resentment these events evoked. We also find references consistent with Thucydides' descriptions of many of the campaigns of the early war. Examples are legion and include several references to the capture of the Spartans at Pylos, both Cleon's role in this event and the peace offers that followed (*Knights* 54–57, 1052–53, 1058–59, 1166–67, 1201; *Peace* 664–67), a celebration of the role of the cavalry on a shipborne campaign against Corinth (Aristophanes, *Knights* 595–610 with Thucydides 4.42–44), a reference to the sacking of the town of Prasia (Aristophanes, *Peace* 242–43 with Thuc. 2.56.5), and one to the siege of Scione (*Wasps* 210 with Thuc. 4.129–33).

The cast of characters is also reassuringly similar in Thucydides and Aristophanes: Pericles, Cleon, Laches, and Lamachus are prominent in both. The most striking exception to this general congruence is Hyperbolus. Aristophanes mocked him in *Wasps* (422) and ranked him as Athens' preeminent politician in *Peace* (421). Eupolis attacked Hyperbolus in 421 (Rusten 2006, 551), and *ostraka* against him survive (Smarczyk 2006, 518). But Thucydides, who clearly loathed Hyperbolus, does not mention this leading

Athenian politician until he was killed in exile in 411 after having been ostracized (Thuc. 8.73.3 with Hornblower 2008, hereafter *CT*, 3.968–972).

Campaigns in Sicily

Thucydides narrates Athens' earlier interventions in Sicily (427–425) in small sections, which provide little context for the events described. This treatment suits the typical patterning of the first half of Thucydides' history, where the appeal of chronological precision often trumps continuity of narrative (see Forsdyke, chapter 1 in this volume; cf. Dewald 2005, 3–4). Thucydides' lack of attention to Sicilian affairs masks, whether deliberately or not, the extent to which Athenian—and even Spartan—interests there were long-standing: the Sicilian expedition was not the unprecedented and almost inexplicable foolishness that Thucydides depicts (*CT* 3.5–12; see also Fragoulaki 2013, 291–316). A papyrus fragment of a Sicilian historian (*FGrHist* 577F2) describes events of summer 426 in enough detail to highlight how scanty and poorly balanced is Thucydides' account: "he [Thucydides] recorded the inconclusive petty warfare of the late summer and winter while passing over the more impressive capture of the five Locrian triremes in the earlier part of the year" (Bosworth 1992, 49). Thucydides' scanty treatment of Sicilian affairs in the Archidamian War may serve the literary purpose of setting up the great Sicilian disaster, but this mistake does not: the decision to go to Sicily and the consequent disaster would hardly read differently, depending on whether the acute reader could or could not call to mind the five Locrian ships of 426. More mundane alternatives, easy to imagine but impossible to prove, provide more likely explanations for this bobble.

The Persian Ambassador

The Athenians captured Artaphernes, a Persian ambassador on the way to Sparta, and the assembly eventually decided to send their own embassy to accompany him back to the Persian king, Artaxerxes (Thuc. 4.50). These ambassadors, however, turned back when they learned that Artaxerxes had died. We know from Babylonian documents that Artaxerxes died between December 424 and February 423, about a full year past the point in Thucydides' narrative where he reports this series of events, in winter 425. Has Thucydides misdated an assembly in Athens or provided an anachronistic explanation for the return of the embassy? A consideration of the way Thucydides structures his narrative provides a better explanation (*CT* 2.100–101). Thucydides wisely did not break up his one-paragraph account of the capture of the ambassador, his trip to Athens, the Athenian decision and abortive embassy, and its return. Thucydides reported the whole affair at one time in his overall narrative, that of the first event, the capture of the ambassador: a case of narrative *prolepsis*. For whatever reasons, the last event in the sequence did not take place until a full year later, at which point Artaxerxes had indeed died.

Inscriptions

Thucydides worked during a period when documentation on stone of government decisions and finances was increasing. This development sometimes permits modern historians an independent check on his account of the war. Most surviving inscriptions support, or are consistent with, Thucydides' history (Smarczyk 2006, 522). Some of the most striking confirmations (e.g., the treaty among the Athenians, Eleans, Argives, and Mantineans) and some of the most problematic cases (e.g., the treaty between Athens and Egesta, if dated to the year of Antiphon [e.g., Dawson 1996]) fall outside the period of the Archidamian War. One inscription ($IG\ I^3$ 364, lines 19–21) does allow us to correct the name of one of two commanders of an expedition to Corcyra listed by Thucydides. He probably confused two different men with the same patronymic (Smarczyk 2006, 519; *CT* 1.95 on Thuc. 1.51.2). Why Thucydides does not mention the third general on the inscription is obscure, but possibilities are easy to imagine: e.g., he fell sick and didn't go.

In contrast to this one discrepancy, Simon Hornblower's comparison of Thucydidean names with those known from other sources, especially inscriptions, has proved reassuring: for example, when Thucydides names an otherwise unknown Thessalian or Boeotian, the person at least turns out to have an attested Thessalian or Boeotian name (*CT* 2.102–107)—see below on Athenian financial inscriptions, in "Athenian Finances."

Topography, Battle Narratives, and Pylos

Topography allows for a check on the accuracy of Thucydides' battle and campaign narratives. Given the (reconstructed) ancient landscape, can the action have taken place as and where Thucydides says it did? Historians have long pursued this approach with generally encouraging results: for example, ten chapters of W. Kendrick Pritchett, *Studies in Ancient Greek Topography* (1965–1992) treat Thucydides, and Dietram Müller's relatively recent *Topographisch-geographisches Bildlexikon zum Geschichtswerk des Thukydides* (2013) provides maps, photos, and bibliography on hundreds of places mentioned in Thucydides. Thucydides' account has repeatedly not been disproved. He does not aspire to a rich geographic understanding of events and mainly limits himself to what the reader must know to understand the course of events (Funke and Haake 2006), but, in this goal, he is generally successful.

One unsettling case is his description of the geography of Pylos and the bay of Navarino. His account of the campaign provides many geographic and other details and appears well informed. Nevertheless, that Thucydides makes three mistakes in his description of the geography and relates an impractical Spartan battle plan makes it likely that he did not take the considerable trouble of visiting the place himself (Rubincam 2001, 82–83 endorsing Gomme et al., hereafter, *HCT* 3.484). Two of his mistakes are relatively minor; the problem is the width of the southern entrance into Navarino Bay. Thucydides describes this as "a passage for eight or nine ships," but the narrowest point is about three-quarters of a mile, so Thucydides has underestimated the number of ships that could pass through, perhaps by a factor of ten. Thucydides also relates a Spartan plan to block off tightly—*buzēn*—the two entrances to the bay, but this southern entrance is too wide for this to work given Spartan resources (Thuc. 4.8.7, 4.13.4; cf. Thuc. 7.59.3). Scholars have offered various explanations of these two mistakes (e.g., Wilson 1979; Bauslaugh 1979; contra Rubincam 2001; *CT* 2.159–160; Sears 2011). Overall, I prefer Loren Samons's (2006) explanation that Thucydides got these consistent pieces of misinformation—the Spartan plan and the narrow entrance—from Spartan sources, among whom all sorts of tendentious versions of their plans and the subsequent naval battle were likely after their defeat. Thucydides claims that he did not just believe the first person he heard and that he compared and weighed separate accounts (Thuc. 1.22.2–3). It is not surprising that Thucydides was not able to do this successfully for every detail in his history—and even in what seems to be a rare botch he expressed the width of the southern entrance with an alternative number, "eight or nine," which suggests considerable uncertainty (Rubincam 2001, 81).

Thucydides is thus detected in a few mistakes. Unsurprisingly, he was not perfect. When it comes to evaluating how much weight to put on these inaccuracies, two contrary perspectives are illuminating. On the one hand, there is no way to check the vast majority of the information Thucydides provides. The mistakes historians have detected come from the small subset of his material where we happen to have another source with which to correct him. If, for example, we had more inscriptions and other contemporary histories of the Archidamian War, we would doubtless discern other inaccuracies in Thucydides. On the other hand, simple confirmations of basic facts are historically uninteresting and attract little attention. I deliberately mentioned in "Aristophanes" above that Aristophanes confirms that Cleon got the credit for the victory of Pylos, but few treatments of Thucydides' accuracy would bother with such an obvious point. Historians are liable, rather, to focus on the problematic cases, and this selection bias makes for an excessively negative picture. Balancing these two contrary perspectives is difficult. Comparison with other ancient historians, whose evaluation for accuracy is generally subject to the same two tendencies, puts Thucydides near the top of the list. For example, the contrast between Thucydides and Xenophon, whose history picked up where Thucydides left off, is stark (e.g., Cawkwell 1966).

EMPHASIS AND NEGLECT

The variety and geographic extent of Athenian and Spartan activity during the Archidamian War was huge: sieges, blockades, sea battles, and land campaigns with hoplites, cavalry, peltasts, archers, and slingers; theaters of combat from the coast of Thrace and Ionia to Sicily. Hostility between oligarchic and democratic factions in many city-states complicated the war with an internal political dimension, of which both sides took advantage. On the one hand, Thucydides' treatment reflects this complexity and variety: one analysis of the structure of his account of the Archidamian War

(2.1–5.24) distinguishes 119 separate episodes (Dewald 2005, 35). On the other hand, Thucydides imposed order on the variegated, massive, and amorphous mass of events that constituted the Archidamian War with the narrative choices he made. Since the war often involved several simultaneous campaigns or series of actions, even putting events in order required choices. More important, Thucydides had to decide what trends or events to play down or omit entirely and what to include or emphasize, especially in the speeches, both during and before the war, that shape the reader's perception of key patterns and issues. He may also have emphasized or played down events for reasons less conscious and rational and thus have produced a picture of the Archidamian War that either his contemporaries or historians today would consider distorted. This section treats several cases in which Thucydides highlights or neglects certain trends or events. It considers whether these choices were justified and what other views were possible or even preferable. It considers the patterns he discerned in events and his manner of explaining events.

The Elephant and the Whale

Even before his war narrative begins, Thucydides shapes the reader's expectations by reporting predictions of the war's likely course (Thuc. 1.121–1.123, 1.141.2–1.144.1). The most important element in Athens' war plans was a negative one: they refused to go out to fight a battle with the main Peloponnesian army even when it devastated Attica (Thuc. 2.65.7; cf. 1.143.4, 2.21.1–2.22.1). Consequently, when the Spartans did the obvious and attacked the territory of their enemy, Athens endured five invasions of Attica, costly and humiliating but not decisive. They also avoided a set battle with the Theban army, as evidenced by their failure to try to relieve Plataea even when the Spartans and most of their allies were far away (cf. Hornblower 2007, 141–44, contra West 2003). Even when the Athenians became more aggressive and confident later in the war, the battle at Delium was unintended (Thuc. 4.90.4).

Thucydides portrays this refusal of battle as a controversial and unexpected decision and attributes it to Pericles' advice. He reports that many Athenians did, in fact, want to sally out and fight, but Pericles (somehow) restrained them (Thuc. 2.21.2–2.22.2 with Christensen and Hansen 1989; Rusten 1989, 129; *CT* 1.275–76; cf. 2.11.6–8). But this strategic decision was probably not as innovative as Thucydides implies; rather, its roots went back to Themistocles (Krentz 1997, 61–65). Famously, Athens did not fight a land battle against the Persians in 480, when they gave up the city itself to be sacked; nor did they fight when Pleistoanax, the Spartan king, marched into Attica in 446 (Thuc. 1.114.2). These events provided precedents for the Athenian decision in 431. In addition, so the argument goes, the Long Walls had been built at great expense and effort for this very purpose, so that the Athenians could refuse battle and retreat behind the walls with their supplies from the sea secure.

The reason for building the Long Walls was not, however, quite so simple: they provided security without a battle, but also in the event of a lost battle. In the First

Peloponnesian War, the Athenians chose to fight several major land battles, including Tanagra (457) against the Spartans, Oenophyta (457), and Coronea (447/6)—the last of which certainly took place after the Long Walls had been built. It was not certain whether they would attempt the same in 431 or withdraw into the city without fighting. Thucydides may exaggerate the innovation involved in Pericles' avoidance of land battle, but it was a real choice.

On the positive side, Pericles advised the Athenians to use their naval power against Sparta (Thuc. 1.143.4). A prerequisite for this was the maintenance of Athenian naval superiority. Unlike the Athenians, the Spartans intended to contest their enemy's element: at the start of the war they had a plan to muster 500 triremes in all (Thuc. 2.7.2 with Kelly 1982 and *CT* 1.244). Nevertheless, at no point in the Archidamian War did the Peloponnesians actually muster a navy willing and able to oppose Athens' experienced and large force in a major battle. For example, the Spartans promised to support the revolt of Mytilene (428–427), a crucial opportunity, but its fleet was too small, just fifty-three triremes, and arrived too late to save Mytilene. It then fled rather than risk being caught at sea by the Athenians (Thuc. 3.29–3.33).

Athens used their naval superiority to harm Sparta and its allies with raids and attacks launched from its navy. Under oar, triremes could easily travel ninety miles in a day (Morrison et al. 2000, 102–106), so the Peloponnesians had no way to anticipate the attacks and were far from having the manpower to protect their whole coast. The size and ambitions of these attacks varied, with the largest involving 100 triremes and 4,000 hoplites (Thuc. 2.56.1–2). The goals and results of the naval attacks varied from case to case. The Athenians sacked Prasia on the coast of Laconia (Thuc. 2.56.5) and captured the island of Cythera (Thuc. 4.53–4). They devastated many other areas, made many hasty retreats, and risked a few small set battles, which they sometimes won and sometimes lost.

Modern experience would suggest a blockade as a typical way to deploy superior naval power. Ancient triremes, however, needed to put into land each night, whereas merchant ships did not. Unless there was a bottleneck, such as the Hellespont, or unless it was a matter of a single city (Thuc. 1.116.2, 3.18.5), triremes were not capable of cutting off trade (Gomme 1933; cf. Thuc. 3.86.4 with De Ste. Croix 1972, 216–17; cf. Lewis 1992, 388). Grain prices were volatile (Lys. 22.14), so the operations of the Athenian navy doubtless drove up prices in nearby enemy cities. Nor should we underrate attempts to cut off trade to individual cities. The squadron in Naupactus had a considerable ability to disrupt Corinthian trade from the West, and the Athenians captured Minoa and built a base there to interfere with Megarian shipping (Thuc. 3.51.2, 4.67.3). No Athenian blockade could starve Peloponnesian farmers into submission, but it could make life more difficult for some cities.

Thucydides put the land-power versus sea-power aspect of the war into the high relief it probably deserves (cf. Thuc. 4.12.3). His narrative, however, reveals a more complicated situation and hence a busy war: both Sparta and Athens were inventive and determined about doing as much as they could within the limitations imposed by their opponent's power.

Whenever possible without risk of a major battle, the Athenians took advantage of geography and the seasons to make attacks by land. Even during the invasions of Attica, quick cavalry attacks limited the ravaging of the region by preventing the Peloponnesians from spreading out over the countryside (Hunter 2005). On a larger scale, they invaded Megarian territory each year, presumably before and after the Peloponnesian army invaded Attica (Thuc. 4.66.1; cf. Thuc. 2.31.3). They intervened in Acarnania and Amphilocia, apparently too distant or unimportant to provoke a major Peloponnesian response.

Conversely, the Athenian navy could not be present always and everywhere in superior numbers, a reality that allowed the Peloponnesians opportunity for naval actions. Corinth's access to the west coast of Greece was the most troublesome for distant Athens. Phormio managed to defeat two larger Peloponnesian fleets with his small squadron of twenty Athenian ships based in Naupactus (Thuc. 2.83–92). Nevertheless, before and even after these battles, the Peloponnesian navy continued to operate off the west coast whenever the Athenians did not have a major navy there (Thuc. 2.33.1, 2.66, 3.76–3.80, 4.2.3). When a large Athenian navy did come west, the Peloponnesians displayed considerable ingenuity to avoid battle (Thuc. 3.80.2–3.81.1 with *HCT* 2.367; Thuc. 4.8.2). Athenian naval superiority became complete only after Pylos in 425, a turning point in the war at sea that Thucydides does not stress. Upon a questionable pretext, the Athenians refused to give back the sixty ships that the Spartans handed over during the truce before the attack on the island and capture of the men (Thuc. 4.16.1, 4.23.1). [2] After Pylos, we hear of no more Peloponnesian naval operations during the Archidamian War.

Despite all these actions by Athens on land and Sparta on sea, duly reported by Thucydides, the prewar predictions and Pericles' advice help the reader to stay focused on the big picture. Behind all the detail, the reader keeps in mind the essential point that this was a war between "an elephant and a whale," a land power and a sea power, neither willing to risk a decisive battle in the other's element. Thucydides is not a modern academic historian; nevertheless, he succeeds brilliantly at finding and highlighting patterns in numerous, various, and complicated events.

The Failure of Athenian Leadership

Another Thucydidean pattern in the events of the war is more controversial and probably tendentious. Pericles advised the Athenians not to add to the empire during the war or risk the city (Thuc. 2.65.7; cf. 1.144.1 and 2.13.2). And, according to Thucydides, the Athenians would have prevailed if they had followed this advice. After Pericles' death, however, competing demagogues and overconfidence led Athens to take needless risks and eventually caused Athens' defeat (Thuc. 2.65.7–10). The expedition to Sicily is

---

[2] This incident must have provoked considerable resentment among Sparta's allies, who provided ships, especially Corinth: all their expensive triremes had been sacrificed to Athenian double-dealing and Sparta's desire to get back the Spartiates on Pylos. Thucydides does not mention this resentment here or when he describes the reasons for Corinth's refusal to swear to the Peace of Nicias (Thuc. 5.30.2).

obviously foremost in Thucydides' mind and beyond the scope of this chapter (Thuc. 2.65.11; see Greenwood, chapter 9 in this volume). But Pericles had died in 429: when did the Athenians begin to attempt conquests and take risks contrary to Pericles' judgment, endorsed by Thucydides?

Unfortunately, Pericles' criteria of caution and non-conquest are hard to apply to the many and varied initiatives the Athenians took in the Archidamian War, both before and after his death (Holladay 1978). For example, there are a host of borderline cases: small but strategically advantageous acquisitions such as Thronium and Minoa (Thuc. 2.26.2; 3.51); fortification of an outpost as opposed to conquest, such as Methana (Thuc. 4.45.2); and conquest or attempted conquest of islands, Cythera and Melos (Thuc. 3.91.1–3, 4.53–54).

Thucydides' distinction between Pericles' caution and the rashness of Athens after he died is too tidy. Nevertheless, the Athenians attempted two land campaigns in 424, which were risky and clearly contrary to Pericles' advice not to expand the empire. The Athenians tried to take advantage of internal dissension and thus to win over both Megara and Boeotia (424), areas they had not controlled since the years of their midcentury land empire (Thuc. 1.103.4, 1.108.3, 1.113–1.114). As it happened, the Megarian campaign ended with partial success, the capture of Megara's port Nisaia, but not the city itself (Thuc. 4.66–74); the Boeotian campaign ended with a costly defeat at Delium (Thuc. 4.89–4.101.2). By far, the most important and successful campaign in the Archidamian War was the fortification of Pylos, another action hard to classify in terms of Pericles' advice (Holladay 1978, 399–402), but one that clearly did not fit the pattern of Athenian actions in the first two years of the war under Pericles. Had the Athenians not made the attempt—and gotten lucky by capturing the Spartans on Sphacteria and taking all the ships of the Peloponnesian navy—the war would have seemed likely to drag on indefinitely. Without taking some such risks, how did Pericles plan to win? Or did he just hope that Athens could survive, "win through" (*CT* 1.230 on Thuc. 1.144.1)? That Thucydides does not explicitly answer such a basic question is best explained by his admiration for Pericles; it renders unpersuasive his interpretation of the war in terms of a failure of leadership.

The Helots

Relative to other important historical patterns in the war, the participation of helots is not incorporated into the main trends of Thucydides' narrative (cf. Lewis 1977, 27–28). Intelligent Athenians, such as Pericles, knew that inciting revolt among the helots in Messenia could be a potent tactic against the Spartans, as it turned out to be. It was after several years based in Naupactus and campaigning with the Messenian exile community settled there by the Athenians (Thuc. 1.103.3, 3.94.3–3.98, 3.102, 3.107.1–3.114.2) that Demosthenes proposed establishing a base on Pylos to be manned by them. His goal was to incite rebellion, something the Messenian exile community in Naupactus cannot have failed to recommend—though Thucydides neglects to mention this. Thucydides is not reticent about the importance of this threat (Thuc. 4.41.3, 4.55.1, 5.14.3; Rhodes 1998, 234 even implies that he exaggerates it; cf. Paradiso 2004 and Harvey 2004 on Thuc. 4.80), but it is conspicuously absent from any of the speeches, plans, or discussions that shape the reader's judgment of what events were really important. I have argued that the topic was an awkward one: the slave-owning Athenians were not keen to incite a "slave rebellion," according to the Spartan description of helots as slaves (Hunt 1998, 62–82). It is probably not a coincidence that Thucydides omits the name of Komon, one of the rare occasions we can supplement Thucydides with a name from another source. Komon was the commander of the Messenians of Naupactus and led a contingent up cliffs to take the Spartans at Sphacteria from behind and force their surrender (Thuc. 4.36.1 with *CT* 2.191; Paus. 4.26.2).

Brasidas was allowed to recruit 700 helots for his long campaign in the North (Thuc. 4.80.5), an effort that resulted in the defection of fifteen Athenian allies including rich and strategically located Amphipolis (Thuc. 4.108.1). Sparta may normally have preferred not to use helots this way, since they were part of the Spartans' agricultural work force and ended up getting their freedom as a reward for service. At this juncture, however, with raids from Pylos and Cythera, the Spartans feared a general revolution of the sort that had happened after the earthquake of the 460s (Thuc. 1.101.2–1.103.3, 4.55.1). They were happy to send vigorous young helot men a long way away (Thuc. 4.80.2). Unlike Peloponnesian citizen farmers, unwilling to campaign out of season, these helots—and the 1,000 mercenaries whom Brasidas also mustered—could go on the long expeditions needed to reach Athenian allies by land. Thucydides is far from highlighting this tactic in any of the speeches before the war predicting its course, or in any of Brasidas' battlefield speeches, or in his own voice. I have argued that this reticence is partly due to the ideological problem presented when helots—slaves, according to the Spartans—acted as soldiers, something that only brave free men should be capable of, and especially when they played a decisive role in the war (Hunt 1998, 53–62).

Athenian Finances

Any Periclean plan to defeat or even to outlast the Spartans depended on the Athenians being able both to afford years of naval warfare, an expensive proposition, and to support an army abroad whenever an extended siege, also a costly process, was necessary. These were not just military necessities, but also helped many Athenians displaced from their farms to make a living (Rosivach 2011). Donald Kagan, for example, accepts a high estimate of the cost of the Peloponnesian War, about 2000 talents per year, and estimates that the Athens would have run out of money within four years (1974, 36–40). But the cost of the war is hard to estimate: the average length of naval campaigns is the most recalcitrant issue and is much less than the eight-month average Kagan uses (Rosivach 1985). So a priori arguments about Athenian finances fail.

Two important Athenian inscriptions—the tribute reassessment decree of 425 (*IG* I³ 71 = ML #69) and the *Logistai* Inscription (*IG* I³ 369 = ML #72), which records loans to Athens from the sacred treasuries—provide important evidence about Athenian finances during the Archidamian War. Unfortunately, the relationship between these inscriptions and Thucydides' account of the Athenian finances—with Thuc. 3.17 problematic in itself—is controversial and notoriously difficult. There are several key points on which historians differ to greater or smaller degrees and hence numerous different reconstructions (Pritchard 2015, section 4.1 with bibliography), but in this brief treatment I will distinguish two basic positions.

According to the first, the high cost of the war, reflected in the loans Athens took out from the sacred treasuries, drove the city into grave financial difficulties. Even though the Athenians tripled the tribute rate in 425, financial pressure continued and contributed to their desire to make peace in 421 (Samons 2000, 208–10). Despite Thucydides' usual interest in the material basis of warfare, he does not give these difficulties due attention, perhaps because they put Pericles' intransigence toward the Spartans and his optimism about the course of the war in a bad light (e.g., *CT* 1.341; cf. Luginbill 2011, 127–31, contra Foster 2012). The second reconstruction plays down the significance of the loans from the sacred treasuries and questions the efficacy, significance, and necessity of the reassessment decree of 425 (Kallet-Marx 1993, 164–70, 191–98; cf. *CT* 2.94–99). The war was admittedly expensive, but Athens possessed a sufficient reserve throughout. Thucydides consistently emphasizes the importance of money and would not have neglected to discuss extreme measures had they ever become necessary—Pericles or no Pericles. With these two overarching perspectives in mind, let us now turn to the epigraphic evidence itself.

The accounts of the *Logistai*, inscribed in late 422 or 421 (Samons 2000, 215), recorded the outstanding loans taken from sacred treasuries on the Acropolis, those of Athena and of the Other Gods. To modern thinking, borrowing from a sacred treasury seems a sign of desperation, but in the classical Greek world, it was a typical way of financing expenditures beyond a state's usual annual budget (Giovannini 2008). In the Athenian case, the loans began at the very start of the war, well before Athens could have been in any financial difficulty. These loans do, however, reflect large expenditures on the war and, almost certainly, funded military spending beyond Athens' annual revenue (e.g., *CT* 2.97–98 even after Kallet-Marx 1993). The loans had not been paid down by the time of the *Logistai* Inscription, nor did the lending ever stop entirely, so the simplest assumption is that the Athenians were spending their entire annual revenue and using these loans to cover the rest of their expenses (Samons 2000, 210n179; contra Kallet-Marx 1993, 195).

The loans thus represent a considerable reduction of the Athenians' monetary reserves, which seem to have consisted largely of these sacred treasuries. They began the war with 6,000 talents (Thuc. 2.13.3). They locked up 1,000 talents of this amount in a special reserve in the event of an attack on the city by sea (Thuc. 2.24.1). The *Logistai* Inscription shows that the Athenians borrowed from the treasuries—i.e., they spent—about 4,800 talents (ML #72, p. 217) beyond their annual revenues. Although we cannot simply subtract 4,800 from 5,000—since some borrowing occurred before Pericles' enumeration at Thuc. 2.13.3—the Athenians did not have much of a reserve at the end of the war.

It is in this context that historians have traditionally interpreted the reassessment decree of 425. This dealt at length with the procedure for collecting the tribute and takes a harsh line in order to assure the collection of funds. It also assigns the new level of tribute that cities owed to Athens. Not all the letters of the grand total are preserved, but of the options allowed by the extant letters, epigraphers restore 1,460 talents. Their choice follows from the increases in tribute required of some regions whose figures are preserved: for example, the tribute of the cities in the Hellespont triples (ML #69, 193). 1,460 talents is much higher than the total seen on the extant Athenian tribute lists from earlier periods, sums that peak at around 388 talents in 433/2 before the war (*ATL* 3.334; cf. the 600 talents of Thuc. 2.13.3 with *HCT* 2.17). Literary sources also mention, but do not date, increases to a high level of tribute, 1,200 or 1,300 talents (Andocides 3.9 ≈ Aeschines 2.175; Plut., *Arist.* 24.3–5; cf. Aristophanes, *Wasps* 656–60 with a total Athenian income of 2,000 talents). Accordingly, some historians attribute the increases in the reassessment of 425 to the imminent depletion of the Athenian treasury and wonder why Thucydides did not mention either the crisis or its (attempted) solution: "the strangest of all omissions in Thucydides" (*HCT* 3.500; contra Kallet-Marx 1993, 165–66. See Pritchard 2015, section 4.1; Lendon 2010, 467–69, n68, for recent bibliography).

A partial explanation may lie in the fact that we do not possess tribute lists or reassessments for earlier in the war. Russell Meiggs (1972, 331) suggests that the tribute may have been raised in a series of steps; consequently, the reassessment decree of 425 may not have been such an innovation. If the loans from the treasury of Athena approximately made up the deficit between war expenses and revenue, the decline in the loans per year of 1,100 talents from 1,300 in 430/29 to 200 in 428/7 (ML #72, 217) may, in part, reflect an increase in tribute because of reassessments in 430 and 428, for which there is some epigraphic evidence (*ATL* iii.69–70, 352). This line of reasoning does not entirely get Thucydides off the hook: if there was a large increase in tribute, whether at one time or in steps, we would have preferred him to have mentioned it.

Another observation, however, can supplement this partial explanation: an assessment decree is not the same as a record of tribute actually received. Cities that never paid tribute—e.g., Melos!—are listed on the reassessment decree of 425; more than twice as many cities are listed as paid tribute in any one year. Even a city that was definitely a tribute-paying subject of Athens could appeal its tribute: it was in the context of such disputes that Antiphon wrote speeches for Lindus and Samothrace (Gagarin 2002, 161). Kallet argues that Thucydides does not mention the reassessment decree, because it was not effective (Kallet-Marx 1993, 166–170). Her general contention, that Thucydides' consistent interest in wealth and power makes it unlikely that he would have omitted something important, has a circular aspect to it, but may be true nonetheless (169). So perhaps the increase in tribute was neither as sudden nor as great as it seems—nor perhaps that surprising a policy during an expensive war.

The one place that Thucydides directly discusses Athenian financial difficulties during the Archidamian War is problematic. In his account of the events of 428, Thucydides emphasizes the financial difficulties that the Athenians were facing (Thuc. 3.17): they had manned up to 250 ships in a single summer (at about a talent per ship per month, not to mention the cost of building and equipping them) and the 3,000 hoplites besieging Potidaea had been paid well (costing an even talent per day in total); these expenses used up Athenian funds. This discussion fits well after a deliberate and formidable display of Athenian power and wealth: the Athenians raised a fleet of 100 and raided the Peloponnese at will without moving any forces from the siege of Mytilene, which the Spartans had been hoping to relieve (Thuc. 3.16). The discussion is soon followed by a notice that the Athenians, for the first time, imposed a capital tax on themselves to raise money (Thuc. 3.19.1), arguably a more drastic step than increasing the amount that others, their allies, had to pay.

Unfortunately, scholars from at least the mid-nineteenth century have objected to aspects of Thucydides' discussion in 3.17. Most crucially, it does not seem that the Athenians had 250 ships in action at any time that fits the passage (Steup 1869, 351–54). Thus some have considered 3.17 a late and incompetent interpolation (Steup 1869, 350; Rhodes 1994, 190–91) and others believe it is a misplaced draft version and belongs earlier in the narrative, between 2.56 and 2.57 (Adcock 1925, 321; cf. Lewis 1992, 385). Given that the passage is Thucydidean otherwise and fits well between the display of power before and the capital tax after, Thucydides may either have made a mistake here, or an error or omission in his narrative prevents us from squaring 250 ships with his reported deployments (cf. *CT* 1.400–401).

If the passage is genuine, Thucydides discusses Athenian financial troubles relatively early in the war. This timing is consistent with the declining size of the loans from Athena's treasury, as noted, and with increases in tribute in 430 and 428 rather than only in 425: by 428 Athens' revenue may have been larger and its deficit much smaller. Furthermore, although it is hard to estimate Athenian military expenses, they may well have declined after 428 when the Peloponnesians failed to challenge Athens at sea even to support Mytilene. In 425, the campaign of Pylos resulted in the capture (by sharp diplomatic practice) of the entire Peloponnesian fleet, so Athens no longer needed to man large navies at all. The capture of the Spartiates on Sphacteria allowed Athens to prevent further invasions of Attica by threatening to kill their prisoners (Thuc. 4.41.1). This carried huge benefits for the Athenian economy (cf. Dem. 1.27) and consequently less need for them to provide employment in the navy. These military considerations as well as the inscriptional evidence suggests that the notices in Thucydides 3.17 and 3.19 occur near the end of Athens' financial difficulties and are not a harbinger of increasing problems. Consistent with this interpretation, Thucydides gives a variety of reasons that the Athenians were ready to make peace in 421, but does not include financial difficulties among them (Thuc. 4.117, 5.14.1–2; cf. Thuc. 6.26.2; Andoc. 3.8; Kallet-Marx 1993, 179–180; contra Samons 2000, 211).

The Plague

Thucydides devotes considerable attention to the plague that struck Athens in two main waves, in 430–429 and then again in 427 (Thuc. 2.47–2.54; 3.87.1–3). It was no surprise: by a wide margin Athens lost more men to the plague than in any battle during the Archidamian War (Thuc. 3.87.3).

Thucydides' description of the course of the disease is detailed and the vocabulary he uses is large and overlaps with that used by ancient medical writers (Page 1953; contra Parry 1969; cf. Thuc. 2.49.3 with Thomas 2006, 98). The goal of applying modern medical expertise to diagnose the disease from Thucydides' description has been tempting, but hopeless, since at least 1835 (Holladay and Poole 1979, 282–95). Even if Thucydides were completely accurate in his own terms, we cannot easily equate Thucydides' terms with equivalent symptoms as classified by a modern doctor (e.g., Thuc. 2.49 with HCT 2.154–56; CT 1.321–22). Ancient doctors did not even look for many of the symptoms that modern doctors would have considered diagnostic, such as swollen lymph nodes. More fundamental, a disease is caused by the relationship between a microbe and its human host. Microbes evolve relatively quickly and even their human hosts can change considerably over 2,000 years; consequently, a disease of 430 would not be the same as that disease today (Holladay and Poole 1979, 282–86). In many well-known cases, a microbe causes dramatically different symptoms—e.g., attack different organs—as it and its host population change over time. These a priori objections are borne out in practice: different teams or authors have proposed almost thirty different diseases (Papagrigorakis et al. 2006a, 208, Table 1), but none of these fits Thucydides' description perfectly.

In Kerameikos, a mass grave of 150 people in five layers of bodies, mainly without intervening dirt and with a relatively small number of cheap grave goods, has been dated to the late fifth century and is most plausibly interpreted as containing plague victims, probably of low social status (Baziotopoulou-Valavani 2002, 199–201). This provides an external piece of evidence consistent with Thucydides' plague and, in part, justifies his dismay at the neglect of traditional funeral rites (Thuc. 2.52.4).[3] But Thucydides goes further and claims that the plague ushered in immorality, extreme individualism, a *carpe diem* attitude, and a loss of faith in the gods (Thuc. 2.53) and we can believe that he observed this in a few individuals. But one has only to imagine oneself as a common soldier on the several-month naval expedition to attack Potidaea, on which more than a quarter of the hoplites died of plague (Thuc. 2.58.3), to question Thucydides' generalization: most people did not have the option of indulging in lawless enjoyment of the moment. Indeed, in everything that Thucydides reports about Athenian actions in the years before and after the plague—which is a lot—we see no change in mores but rather the continued intense and aggressive pursuit of the war,

---

[3] Unfortunately, an attempt to determine the disease from bacterial DNA isolated from the skeletons' dental pulp was not persuasive (Shapiro and Rambaut 2006; contra Papagrigorakis et al. 2006a and Papagrigorakis et al. 2006b).

the prerequisite for which was a strong spirit of communal cohesion and individual self-sacrifice.

When it comes to the plague's effect on religious feeling, William Furley (2006, 431–33) sees "an uneasy mix of attitudes," but skepticism and amorality were not the main components in that mix. Rather than undermining religion, Alexander Rubel argues persuasively, the plague resulted in a turning toward religion (2014, 46–63; cf. Mikalson 1984). For example, Diodorus Siculus claims that the purification of Delos was a result of the plague and of the fear that an affronted divinity was responsible for it (Diod. Sic. 12.58.6; Thuc. 3.104 with CT 1.519; Rubel 2014, 61–62). The plague narrative serves a literary purpose (Woodman 1988, 32–40) and has been immensely influential to subsequent plague narratives in Western literature (e.g., Crawfurd 1914; Rubincam 2004). What it does not do is to confront with ugly reality the idealized picture of Athens in Pericles' funeral oration. Rather, Thucydides' description of the moral decay occasioned by the plague is no less of a distortion than the most high-flown phrases of the funeral oration that precede it.

Thucydides deserves admiration for a different reason. Individuals probably noticed contagion well before recorded history and Thucydides makes it clear that some people were afraid to approach plague victims for fear of catching the disease (Thuc. 2.51.5). Nevertheless, the historian himself deserves the credit of being the first writer clearly to operate within the model of contagion, something that was not formally proposed again until the sixteenth century and not fully accepted until the nineteenth century. His observation of acquired immunity was also an important first (Thuc. 2.51.6 with Holladay and Poole 1979, 295–300; Holladay 1987, contra Solomon 1985).

The Peace of Nicias

After a one-year truce and after an expedition under Cleon suffered a defeat at the battle of Amphipolis (Thuc. 5.7–5.10), the Athenians and Spartans conducted negotiations and agreed to the Peace of Nicias in early spring 421, about ten years after the first act of war—the attack on Plataea. Thucydides' explanations for the antagonists' willingness to make peace are clear and satisfying. They fall into two categories (5.14–15 and 5.16–17; cf. 4.117).

First, he treats the collective feelings of the Athenians and Spartans, respectively (Thuc. 5.14). The defection of northern allies and the outcomes of the battles of Delium and Amphipolis had damaged the Athenians' excessive self-confidence deriving from their successes, Pylos in particular. For their part, the Spartans had thought that a few invasions of Attica would reduce Athens to submission, but instead they had suffered the capture of their men on Sphacteria, helot unrest, and raids from Pylos and Cythera. Future prospects remained grim: there was no way to tell how much trouble the helots could cause, and a thirty-year treaty with Argos was set to expire. Without a plausible victory scenario and with Attica now immune to invasion, to continue the war would just mean further delay in getting their prisoners back (Thuc. 4.117.2). Thucydides depicts both the Spartans and Athenians as rational calculators whose predictions about the future have become more realistic with the experience of war. Now that their overoptimistic assessments of the likely costs and benefits of further fighting had come down to earth and approximated each other, they were able to make mutually acceptable compromises (cf. Blainey 1973, 56).

Thucydides also gives weight to the motivations of individual Spartan and Athenian leaders: the pro-war Brasidas and Cleon had both died at the battle of Amphipolis; for their own reasons, Pleistoanax the Spartan king and Nicias the Athenian statesman both favored peace (5.16). It is no surprise that the opinions of a Spartan war hero and a king play a large role in Spartan policy; it is more surprising that Thucydides represents the views of two politicians, determined by selfish personal motives, as crucial to Athenian policy. Thucydides exaggerates the influence of Pericles, in part by giving him several unopposed speeches, but also in his own voice (Thuc. 2.65.8-10; cf. Azoulay 2014, 137-56). At the end of the Archidamian War, too, Thucydides puts a great deal of weight on the power of individuals within the democracy (see also Tsakmakis 2006 and Gribble 2006; cf. Westlake 1968).

Since with a few exceptions, the peace terms mainly required a return to the status quo ante, it might seem that the war was basically drawn—or unfinished, as Thucydides famously insists (Thuc. 5.26.2-3). But, already in Thucydides we find signs that the Spartans were considered to have come off worse (Thuc. 5.75.3; 7.18.2). And, despite Thucydides, Athenian tradition sometimes considered the Archidamian War as a separate entity and, not surprisingly, viewed the Peace of Nicias as a great success for Athens (Plato, *Menexenus* 242 c-e; Andocides 3.8-9 ≈ Aeschines 2.175; cf. Plutarch, *Nicias* 9.6-97).

Several factors explain this verdict about what appears a drawn war. First, other than Archidamus himself, most Spartans expected to win the war and considered anything less a loss, an opinion shared by most of Greece (Thuc. 1.81.6, 1.122.4, 4.85.2, 5.14.3, 7.28.3; cf. Lendon 2010, 371-81). Even the Athenian view may have been similar. Since the overall tendency of Pericles' strategy was defensive and opposed to more aggressive and risky plans, his victory aims were probably also conservative, the preservation of the Athenian empire and a war painful enough to Sparta to discourage future interference. The Athenians had achieved these goals.

Second, Sparta did not just declare war on Athens; its avowed goal was to liberate Greece from Athenian tyranny (Thuc. 1.139.3, 2.8.4). At the war's end, the Athenian empire was barely diminished and Sparta had manifestly failed. Indeed, Sparta had to sit by while Athens recaptured and punished city-states that had revolted at Sparta's instigation.

Third, states commonly regard their wars as defensive and thus drawn wars drift into the win category (Blainey 1973, 58). For Pericles and the Athenians, the Archidamian War was a defensive war (Thuc. 1.140.2-1.141.1, 1.144.2), and thus maintaining the status quo ante counted as a win. Some Spartans, too, thought the war's purpose was the defense of their allies and friends (Thuc. 1.68-69, 1.71.4, 1.79, 1.86), especially Corinth, Megara, and Aigina. But these allies could not have regarded the war as a successful defense. During the war the Athenians recaptured Potidaea and took and retained

Sollium and Anactorium, cities linked to Corinth in different ways; they took and kept the port of Megara; they dispossessed and exiled the Aiginetans. Certainly, since neither Megara nor Corinth agreed to the Peace of Nicias—and the Aiginetan refugees had not even been safe at Thyrea (Thuc. 4.57), Sparta's friends and allies did not feel well defended. Athenians later bragged that they had defeated Sparta in this war; according to Thucydides, they had merely survived the first round (Thuc. 5.25–26).

Conclusion

Even accurate historians may fail to impress because of what they include or do not, what they stress or do not, what patterns in events they bring out, and what sort of historical explanations they offer. To a large extent these are areas in which Thucydides shines. He may have played down the roles of helots as a resource and a liability for Sparta, but his reticence is typical of classical Greek historians—as I have argued elsewhere (1998). The case that he neglected Athens' financial difficulties to whitewash Pericles has not been proved, the documentary evidence notwithstanding. Thucydides' emphasis on the contrast between the land power of Sparta and the naval power of Athens allows us to see a crucial pattern in what would otherwise be a crowded and chaotic mass of events. His explanation of Athenian mistakes and of its eventual defeat in terms of a failure of leadership after Pericles is notoriously controversial and difficult to understand—if that is not putting it too generously. On the other hand, his description of the motivations behind the Peace of Nicias is admirably concise, clear, and persuasive—and consistent with his emphasis elsewhere on the primacy of calculations of advantage. As a historian of the Archidamian War, he comes off very well on the whole, not to mention those passages on which his reputation as a literary figure and as a political philosopher rests.

References

Adcock, F. E. 1925. "On Thucydides III, 7." *Cambridge Historical Journal* 1 (3): 319–22.
Azoulay, Vincent. 2014. *Pericles of Athens*. Translated by Janet Lloyd; foreword by Paul Cartledge. Princeton: Princeton University Press.
Bauslaugh, Robert A. 1979. "The Text of Thucydides IV 8.6 and the South Channel at Pylos." *Journal of Hellenic Studies* 99: 1–6.
Baziotopoulou-Valavani, E. 2002. "A Mass Burial from the Cemetery of the Kerameikos." In *Excavating Classical Culture: Recent Archaeological Discoveries in Greece*, edited by Maria Stamatopoulou and Marina Yeroulanou, 187–202. Oxford: Beazley Archive and Archaeopress.
Blainey, Geoffrey. 1973. *The Causes of War*. New York: The Free Press.
Bosworth, A. B. 1992. "Athens' First Intervention in Sicily: Thucydides and the Sicilian Tradition." *Classical Quarterly* 42(1): 46–55.

Cawkwell, G. L. 1996. "Introduction." In *Xenophon: A History of My Times*, edited by G. L. Cawkwell, 7–48. Harmondsworth: Penguin.
Christensen, J., and Mogens Hansen. 1989. "What Is Syllogos in Thukydides 2.22.1?" In *The Athenian Ekklesia*, ii, edited by Mogens Hansen, 195–212. Copenhagen: Museum Tusculanum Press.
Connor, W. Robert. 1984. *Thucydides*. Princeton: Princeton University Press.
Crawfurd, Raymond. 1914. *Plague and Pestilence in Literature and Art*. Oxford: Clarendon.
Dawson, Stuart E. 1996. "The Egesta Decree Ig I3 11." *ZPE* 112: 248–52.
De Ste. Croix, G. E. M. 1972. *The Origins of the Peloponnesian War*. London: Duckworth.
Dewald, Carolyn J. 2005. *Thucydides' War Narrative: A Structural Study*. Berkeley and Los Angeles: University of California Press.
Foster, Edith. 2012. "Review of Robert D. Luginbill, Author of Illusions: Thucydides' Rewriting of the History of the Peloponnesian War." *BMCR* 2012.03.16.
Fragoulaki, Maria. 2013. *Kinship in Thucydides: Intercommunal Ties and Historical Narrative*. Oxford: Oxford University Press.
Funke, Peter, and Matthias Haake. 2006. "Theaters of War: Thucydidean Topography." In *Brill's Companion to Thucydides*, edited by Antonios Rengakos and Antonis Tsakmakis, 369–84. Leiden: Brill.
Furley, William D. 2006. "Thucydides and Religion." In *Brill's Companion to Thucydides*, edited by Antonios Rengakos and Antonis Tsakmakis, 415–38. Leiden: Brill.
Gagarin, M. 2002. *Antiphon the Athenian: Oratory, Law, and Justice in the Age of the Sophists*. Austin: University of Texas Press.
Giovannini, Adalberto. 2008. "The Parthenon, the Treasury of Athena and the Tribute of the Allies." In *The Athenian Empire*, edited by Polly Low, 164–84. Edinburgh: Edinburgh University Press.
Gomme, A. W. 1933. "A Forgotten Factor of Greek Naval Strategy." *JHS* 53: 16–24.
Gomme, A. W., A. Andrewes, and K. J. Dover. 1945–1981. *A Historical Commentary on Thucydides*. Oxford: Clarendon.
Gribble, David. 2006. "Individuals in Thucydides." In *Brill's Companion to Thucydides*, edited by Antonios Rengakos and Antonis Tsakmakis, 439–68. Leiden: Brill.
Harvey, David. 2004. "The Clandestine Massacre of the Helots (Thucydides 4.80)." In *Spartan Society*, edited by Thomas J. Figueira, 199–217. Swansea: The Classical Press of Wales.
Holladay, A. J. 1978. "Athenian Strategy in the Archidamian War." *Historia* 27: 400–27.
Holladay, A. J. 1987. "Thucydides and the Recognition of Contagion: A Reply." *Maia* 39: 95–6.
Holladay, A.J., and J. C. F. Poole. 1979. "Thucydides and the Plague of Athens." *Classical Quarterly, New Series* 29(2): 282–300.
Hornblower, Simon. 1991–2008. *A Commentary on Thucydides*. 3 vols. Oxford: Clarendon.
Hornblower, Simon. 2007. "Thucydides and Plataian Perjury." In *Horkos: The Oath in Greek Society*, edited by Alan H. Sommerstein and Judith Fletcher, 138–47. Exeter: Bristol Phoenix.
Hunt, Peter. 1998. *Slaves, Warfare, and Ideology in the Greek Historians*. Cambridge: Cambridge University Press.
Hunter, J. Hugh. 2005. "Pericles' Cavalry Strategy." *Quaderni Urbinati di Cultura Classica* 81(3): 101–108.
Kagan, Donald. 1974. *The Archidamian War*. Ithaca and London: Cornell University Press.
Kallet-Marx, Lisa. 1993. *Money, Expense, and Naval Power in Thucydides' History 1–5.24*. Berkeley and Los Angeles: University of California Press.

Kelly, Thomas. 1982. "Thucydides and Spartan Strategy in the Archidamian War." *American Historical Review* 87(1): 25–54.
Krentz, Peter. 1997. "The Strategic Culture of Periclean Athens." In *Polis and Polemos: Essays on Politics, War, and History in Ancient Greece in Honor of Donald Kagan*, edited by Charles D. Hamilton and Peter Krentz, 55–72. Claremont: Regina.
Lendon, J. E. 2010. *Song of Wrath: The Peloponnesian War Begins*. New York: Basic Books.
Lewis, D. M. 1992. "The Archidamian War." In *Cambridge Ancient History*, edited by D. M. Lewis, J. Boardman, J. Davies, and M. Ostwald. Vol. V, *The Fifth Century*, 370–432. Cambridge: Cambridge University Press.
Lewis, David M. 1977. *Sparta and Persia*. Leiden: Brill.
Luginbill, Robert D. 2011. *Author of Illusions: Thucydides' Rewriting of the History of the Peloponnesian War*. Newcastle upon Tyne: Cambridge Scholars.
Meiggs, Russell. 1972. *The Athenian Empire*. Oxford: Clarendon.
Meritt, B. D., H. T. Wade-Gery, and M. F. McGregor. 1939–1953. *The Athenian Tribute Lists*. 4 vols. Princeton: American School of Classical Studies at Athens.
Mikalson, Jon. D. 1984. "Religion and the Plague in Athens, 431–423 B.C." In *Studies Presented to Sterling Dow on His Eightieth Birthday*, edited by Kent J. Rigsby, 10, 217–225. Durham: Duke University Press.
Morrison, J. S., J. F. Coates, and N. B. Rankov. 2000. *The Athenian Trireme: The History and Reconstruction of an Ancient Greek Warship*. 2nd ed. Cambridge: Cambridge University Press.
Müller, Dietram. 2013. *Topographisch-geographisches Bildlexikon zum Geschichtswerk des Thukydides*. Wiesbaden: Chelmos Verlag.
Olson, S. Douglas. 2002. *Aristophanes: Acharnians*. Oxford: Oxford University Press.
Page, D. L. 1953. "Thucydides' Description of the Great Plague at Athens." *Classical Quarterly* 47:97–119.
Papagrigorakis, Manolis, Christos Yapijakis, Philippos N. Synodinos, and Effie Baziotopoulou-Valavani. 2006a. "DNA Examination of Ancient Dental Pulp Incriminates Typhoid Fever as a Probable Cause of the Plague of Athens." *International Journal of Infectious Diseases* 10: 206–14.
Papagrigorakis, Manolis, Christos Yapijakis, Philippos N. Synodinos, and Effie Baziotopoulou-Valavani. 2006b. "Insufficient Phylogenetic Analysis May Not Exclude Candidacy of Typhoid Fever as a Probable Cause of the Plague of Athens (Reply to Shapiro et Al.)." *International Journal of Infectious Diseases* 10: 335–36.
Paradiso, Annalisa. 2004. "The Logic of Terror: Thucydides, Spartan Duplicity and an Improbable Massacre." In *Spartan Society*, edited by Thomas J. Figueira, 179–98. Swansea: The Classical Press of Wales.
Parry, Adam. 1969. "The Language of Thucydides' Description of the Plague." *BICS* 16: 106–18.
Pritchard, David. 2015. *Public Spending and Democracy in Classical Athens*. Austin: University of Texas Press.
Pritchett, Kendrick. 1965–1992. *Studies in Ancient Greek Topography*. Vols. 1–8. Berkeley and Los Angeles: University of California Press.
Pritchett, W. Kendrick. 1965. "Amphipolis." In *Studies in Ancient Greek Topography*. Vol. 1, 30–45. Berkeley and Los Angeles: University of California Press.
Pritchett, W. Kendrick. "Amphipolis Restudied." In *Studies in Ancient Greek Topography*, Vol. 3, by W. Kendrick Pritchett, 298–346. Berkeley and Los Angeles: University of California Press, 1980.

Rengakos, Amtonios, and Antonis Tsakmakis, eds. 2006. *Brill's Companion to Thucydides*, Leiden: Brill.

Rhodes, P. J. 1994. *Thucydides: History III*. Warminster: Aris and Phillips.

Rhodes, P. J. 1998. *Thucydides: History IV.1–V.24*. Warminster: Aris and Phillips.

Rosivach, Vincent. 1985. "Manning the Athenian Fleet, 433–426." *American Journal of Ancient History* 10:41–66.

Rosivach, Vincent. 2011. "State Pay as War Relief in Peloponnesian-War Athens." *Greece & Rome* 58(2): 176–83.

Rubel, Alexander. 2014. *Fear and Loathing in Ancient Athens: Religion and Politics During the Peloponnesian War*. Translated by Michael Vickers and Alina Piftor. Durham: Acumen Publishing.

Rubincam, Catherine. 2004. "The Topography of Pylos and Sphacteria and Thucydides' Measurement of Distance." *Journal of Hellenic Studies* 121, (2001): 77–90.

Rubincam, Catherine. 2004. "Thucydides and Defoe: Two Plague Narratives." *International Journal of the Classical Tradition* 11(2): 194–212

Rusten, Jeffrey S. 1989. *Thucydides: The Peloponnesian War, Book II*. Cambridge: Cambridge University Press.

Rusten, Jeffrey S. 2006. "Thucydides and Comedy." In *Brill's Companion to Thucydides*, edited by Antonios Rengakos and Antonis Tsakmakis, 547–58. Leiden: Brill.

Samons, Loren. J. 2000. *Empire of the Owl: Athenian Imperial Finance*. Vol. 142, Historia Einzelschriften. Stuttgart: Franz Steiner.

Samons, L. J. 2006. "Thucydides' Sources and the Spartan Plan at Pylos." *Hesperia* 75(4): 525–540.

Sears, Matthew. 2011. "The Topography of the Pylos Campaign and Thucydides Literary Themes." *Hesperia* 80: 157–68.

Shapiro, Beth, Andrew Rambault, and Thomas P. Gilbert. 2006. "No Proof That Typhoid Caused the Plague of Athens." *International Journal of Infectious Diseases* 10:334–45.

Smarczyk, Bernhard. 2006. "Thucydides and Epigraphy." In *Brill's Companion to Thucydides*, edited by Antonios Rengakos and Antonis Tsakmakis, 495–522. Leiden: Brill.

Solomon, Jon. 1985. "Thucydides and the Recognition of Contagion." *Maia: Rivista di Letterature Classiche* 3:21–23.

Steup, Julius. 1869. "Ein Einschiebsel Bei Thukydides." *RhM* 24: 350–61.

Thomas, Rosalind. 2006. "Thucydides' Intellectual Milieu and the Plague." In *Brill's Companion to Thucydides*, edited by Antonios Rengakos and Antonis Tsakmakis, 87–108. Leiden: Brill.

Tsakmakis, Antonis. 2006. "Leaders, Crowds, and the Power of the Image: Political Communication in Thucydides." In *Brill's Companion to Thucydides*, edited by Antonios Rengakos and Antonis Tsakmakis, 161–87. Leiden: Brill.

West, Stephanie. 2003. "ΟΡΚΟΥ ΠΑΙΣ ΕΣΤΙΝ ΑΝΩΜΥΜΟΣ: The Aftermath of Plataean Perjury." *Classical Quarterly* 53(2): 438–47.

Westlake, H. D. 1968. *Individual in Thucydides*. Cambridge: Cambridge University Press.

Wilson, John. 1979. *Pylos 425 BC: A Historical and Topographical Study of Thucydides' Account of the Campaign*. Warminster: Aris and Phillips.

Woodman, A. J. 1988. *Rhetoric in Classical Historiography: Four Studies*. London: Croom Helm.

CHAPTER 8

MANTINEA, DECELEA, AND THE INTERWAR YEARS (421–413 BCE)

CINZIA BEARZOT

This chapter examines Thucydides' account of the interwar years. It discusses the introductory sections (5.25–26) and sequentially considers the events from the Peace of Nicias to the occupation of Decelea. The main thesis developed in the chapter is that Thucydides' account of the interwar years is thematically linked with the work as a whole and thus contributes to rather than detracts from the unity of the work. Indeed, the transcription of documents and the detailed accounts of failed negotiations, unstable coalitions, and the machinations of Alcibiades are part of Thucydides' deliberate design to prove that the peace was not a real peace and that the war, just like his work, was a unified whole.

An Unstable Truce and the Unity of the War

Let us begin by examining how Thucydides introduces the interwar period, and in particular the ways that he marks the phases of a war while still arguing for the war as a unified whole. Thucydides is our main source for these years, and is the only one who provides a general picture of this period (Hose 2006). Diodorus, mainly relying on Ephorus, offers a brief selection of events including the peace of Nicias (12.74–76), the battle of Mantinea (12.78–79), and the breaking of the truce in 413 (13.8). Plutarch, in his *Life of Alcibiades*, obviously focuses on Alcibiades rather than providing a general account.

Thucydides' account of the "interwar" years (421–413) begins at 5.25, after the transcription of the text of the Peace of Nicias (5.23–24). This peace marks the end of the "first war," which lasted for ten years (5.24.2), and is generally known as the "Archidamian War" after the Spartan King Archidamus who led the annual invasions of Attica during this period (Diod. 12.75.1 calls it the "Peloponnesian War"; on periodization, see Strauss 1997; Parmeggiani 2011, 458–78).

The end of the "ten-years war" (*ho dekete polemos*) is mentioned again immediately below (5.25.1) and there Thucydides also anchors the date with references to the ephor Pleistolas and the archon Alcaeus. Thucydides evidently wants to create the sense of an accomplished narration and of the opening of a new phase. He does this despite the fact that there are indeed elements of continuity with the preceding narrative. For example, Thucydides uses the terminology employed while recounting the beginning of the war (Rood 2004, 84–88) and characterizes the period as an "unstable truce" (*anokōchē ou bebaios*). This period lasted six years and ten months (on this figure see Hornblower 2008, 43–44) between the peace concluded after the ten years' war, the breach of the peace treaty and the resumption of open hostilities (*phaneros polemos*: 5.25.1-3). Thus the chapter introduces the reader to the theme of the unity of the war, as present in 5.26.

Thucydides provides some cues that can help us to understand the structure of the narration of the interwar years, an account that has been much criticized and that, in the old (and in some cases outdated) controversy between unitarian and separatist critics (Connor 1984, 3–19; Dewald 2005, 1–22), has been considered a sign of incompleteness or, in any case, of lack of revision.

At 5.25.1 Thucydides reports that immediately after the signing of the peace, the Corinthians "tried to unsettle the arrangements" (*diekinoun ta pepragmena*: translation by Lattimore 2002). The language of "upheaval" (*kinēsis*: a term applied to the entire war at 1.1.2) evokes the breach of the peace treaty of 446, a breach that in 431 led to the outbreak of the Peloponnesian War (Connor 1984, 142), and marks the beginning of the process that will lead to the resumption of open hostilities. Immediately thereafter, Thucydides refers indeed to the disorder (*tarachē*) between Sparta and its allies (both *tarachē* and *anarchia* in the Peloponnesus are mentioned in Diod. 12.77.4). At 5.25.2 the historian portrays the growing climate of suspicion of Athens against Sparta for breach of the terms of peace (see 5.35.2). The same theme of suspicion dominates Thucydides' account of the 462/1 turning point (1.102) that led to a period (461–446) also affected by creeping war. The notion of "unstable truce" (5.25.3) does finally present the interwar years not as a period of peace but of instability until the resumption of open hostilities. Thus, 5.25 is shaped so as to demonstrate the thesis presented at 5.26, according to which the period after 421 was in fact a time of creeping war. This impression is accentuated by the theme of the quarrels (*diaphorai*), introduced at 5.26.6 and recurring in subsequent chapters. The wish to highlight the extreme precariousness of the peace agreement signed in 421 has also been recognized in the peculiar characteristics of the narrative of Book 5, which consists of simple units, rapidity in rhythm, and density in content (Rood 2004, 83–108; Dewald 2005, 115–143).

The authorship of 5.26 (the "Second Preface") has been attributed to Xenophon by L. Canfora. The difficulty of attributing to Xenophon what the author of the chapter says of himself (in particular, the strategy at Amphipolis) has led Canfora to conclude that Xenophon speaks here *in persona Thucydidis* (Canfora 2006). In contrast, other scholars have recognized Thucydides' typical argumentative pattern, the same that can be observed at 1.21–22 (Lang 2011, first published in 2002; Hornblower 2008, 44–45). In any case, the chapter, written after the end of the war and the fall of Athens (5.26.1), is dominated by awareness of the unity of the conflict. Thucydides argues that the interim period (*hē dia mesou xumbasis*) cannot indeed be considered peace (*eirēnē*) since the two sides did not comply with the terms of the peace. Furthermore, Thucydides notes, there were clashes between Mantinea and Epidaurus and both sides committed faults (*hamartēmata*). From the point of view of Athens, moreover, the allies in Thrace remained enemies and the Boeotians observed a truce renewed every ten days (5.26.2: Hornblower 2008, 47–48). Thucydides therefore concludes that the war lasted for twenty-seven years and included the first ten years' war, the "suspicious truce" (*hupoptos anokōchē*) and the subsequent war that goes here undefined (5.26.3; see 8.11.3). Chapter 26 closes by introducing the themes of the quarrels after 421 (*diaphora*), the breach of the treaty, and the hostilities that followed (5.26.6). Thucydides' insistence on convincing the reader of his interpretation is here manifest: *kinēsis, tarachē, hupopsia,* and *diaphora* are the keywords that pervade the introductory chapters to the interwar years, and characterize them as years of "cold war" destined to lead again to open war.

The introduction to the "interwar" years, therefore, shows signs of unity with the work as a whole, and therefore should not be taken as an indication of incompleteness or of two separate works that were only later clumsily stitched together.

Diplomacy in the Peloponnesus

This section considers Thucydides' account in the chapters 5.27–5.43. Thucydides is specifically interested in diplomatic activity, which involved "third parties" such as Corinth, Argos, Mantinea, Elis, Boeotia, and Megara, as it allows him to corroborate his thesis of the unity of the war by emphasizing the unstable (*ou bebaios*) character of the peace and the resulting climate of mutual suspicion. The historian pays particular attention to the Peloponnesian side, overlooking (or relegating to extremely brief notes) other war fronts, such as the northern and the micro-Asiatic ones (Hornblower 2008, 56–57), and the events in Athenian home politics; he explores the difficult balance of power in the Peloponnesus and highlights widespread intolerance toward Sparta and its hegemony. This narrow focus may be a result of the kind of information that Thucydides had available for this period. In an autobiographical note of the Second Preface, Thucydides recalls that during his exile he found himself "present at the activities of both sides, especially the Peloponnesians." It is likely therefore that he had Corinthian (Stroud 1994), Spartan, or Argive sources (Hornblower 2006, 615–28; Hornblower 2011, 139–152).

The Peace of Nicias was not ratified by the Boeotians, Corinthians, Eleans, and Megarians, who were concerned about the clause that allowed the Spartans and Athenians to amend the treaty if like-minded (5.18.11), regardless of the opinion of their allies (5.29.3; see Diod. 12.75.4). Immediately after the conclusion of peace, the Corinthian ambassadors left Sparta and headed to Argos (5.27), where they talked unofficially with some magistrates. In their opinion, when signing the peace the Spartans had in view the subjugation (*katadoulōsis*) of the Peloponnesus (see 29.3: the propagandistic nature of this issue has been emphasized); the duty of saving the Peloponnesus had now fallen upon the Argives, who should lead a defensive coalition (*epimachia*) based on autonomy and equal rights; widespread hatred of the Spartans would ensure the success of the enterprise. By embracing this initiative, the Corinthians bring into question the legitimacy of Spartan hegemony, as already done in 432 (1.68–71), and embody the same role of promoters of the war that they had played after 435.

The proposals of the Corinthians were welcomed (5.28) by the Argives (the thirty-year peace signed with Sparta in 451 was expiring (see 1.115.1; 4.133.2; 5.14.4; Paus. 5.23.4), and they hoped to be able to restore their ancient hegemony over the Peloponnesus (see Hdt. 1.1 and 1.82; Diod. 12.75.6–7), and by several other Greek city-states (the Panhellenic tone is particularly strong in Diod. 12.75.2 and 5). Regardless of the fact that the Corinthians had asked to avoid involving the demos, the Argives communicated the project to the *archai* (probably the *boulē*) and the assembly. In this way, Thucydides immediately highlights an element of tension between the Corinthians and Argives, namely, political and constitutional differences, that will subsequently induce the former to withdraw from the coalition.

The reasons that led the Mantineans and Eleans to join the defensive alliance (5.29–31) rest on a view of the Peloponnesus as agitated by disputes (*diaphorai*). Mantinea and its allies were motivated by the democratic orientation of Argos, a historical enemy (*diaphoros*) of Sparta, and the wish to maintain their control over Arcadia (see 5.33.1). Their defection caused most Peloponnesians to follow their example, due to anger (*orgē*) toward Sparta, and fear of subjugation as preannounced by the Corinthians (5.29). The Eleans, in enmity (*diapheromenoi*) with Sparta about Lepreon, first allied with the Corinthians and then with the Argives (5.31.1–5). They were followed by the Corinthians and the Chalcidians of Thrace (5.31.6). After the conclusion of the alliance, there began to take shape the first difficulties. The allies failed to ensure the support of the Boeotians and Megarians, who, being oligarchic, preferred Sparta to Argive democracy. The democratic nature of the alliance clearly engendered distrust. Thucydides paints a picture of considerable instability, which only worsens with the continuation of the account.

Thereafter Thucydides follows the diplomatic path that led to the Quadruple Alliance among Argos, Mantinea, Elis and Athens. Chapter 5.35, which has a recapitulative nature (Hornblower 2008, 82–83), above all resumes the theme of mutual suspicion between the Athenians and Peloponnesians (35.2–4) for breach of the treaty. Although Thucydides concludes that in the summer of 421, "there was peace and regular communication between the two sides" (5.35.8; see 35.2), the truce was beginning to show signs of failure and, as anticipated by Thucydides (5.14.4, 5.22.2), there loomed the possibility of the involvement of Athens in the internal disputes of the Peloponnesus. Not surprisingly, the Athenians were present, along with the Boeotians and Corinthians, at the meeting held at Sparta in the winter of 421/20.

At the end of the meeting, two of the new Spartan ephors, Cleobulos and Xenares, launched a diplomatic initiative: with the help of the Boeotians and Corinthians, they tried to bring the Argives into alliance with Sparta and to exclude Athens from the agreement among the Peloponnesian states (5.36; the chapter is rich in textual difficulties: Hornblower 2008, 84–87). This initiative, which had a markedly personal character, according to Thucydides, revitalized the Spartan pro-war party. The plan, however, failed (5.37–38).

In the following chapters, Thucydides outlines the crisis of the Corinthian project (also defined a "failure": Westlake 1940; *contra* Kagan 1960) because of decreasing conviction on the part of the Argives. At the beginning of the war season of 420, the Argives "became fearful they would be isolated" (5.40.1) and therefore they sent Eustrophos and Aeson as ambassadors to enter into an agreement with Sparta (5.40). Different reasons may explain the concerns of Argos: the durability of the agreement between Sparta and Athens, a bond that deprived the democratic alliance they led of Athenian support; the disengagement of Corinth; and the presence, at Argos, of pro-Spartan forces (5.40.3).

Therefore, Argos reached a compromise with Sparta that provided for the signing of a fifty-year truce and for the resolution of the territorial dispute on the district of Cynuria (5.41; see 5.14.4). Thucydides reports that the Spartans "had the terms written down" (5.41.3: *xunegrapsanto*), which he paraphrases carefully with traces of technical terminology. Since the draft was never approved, or therefore published, Thucydides must have drawn this piece of information from Peloponnesian documentation gathered during the years of his exile (5.26.5: Bearzot 2003, 275–76).

With the renewed agreement between the Argives and Sparta, the project of the Corinthians seemed to run aground. A new series of disputes (*diaphorai*) revived, however, the prospects of a war that would include the Athenians. Consequently, the leaders of the war party in Athens gained new strength (5.43.1).

Several scholars believe that this part of Thucydides' account, as most of Book 5, should be considered unfinished (Hornblower 1987, 136–143; Hornblower 2008, 1–4 and 55–57) and that it is confused, boring and unsatisfactory with respect to the selection of facts. Several factors contribute to create a sense of confusion: textual unclarity, unsatisfactory information provided by Thucydides, and lack of clarity about the positions of the parties involved (the representatives of the different cities act personally and in secret; pretexts hide the true motives of their actions). Yet, on closer inspection, the sense of confusion may also originate from Thucydides' wish to highlight the complexity of a hectic diplomatic activity and the consequences of the opposed policies of the factions (Connor 1984, 141–157; see below, in "Transcription of Documents," for further discussion), in line with the general idea of war as a "violent teacher" that shatters the communities (3.82.2).

Alcibiades and the Resumption of War

At 5.43 the focus of the account shifts to Athens, and in particular to Alcibiades. His intervention in the Peloponnesian disputes (*diaphorai*) to facilitate the resumption of the war against Sparta perfectly exemplifies the role of individual initiative as a factor shaping history (Westlake 1968; Gribble 2006).

Alcibiades is here presented for the first time (see 6.15–16 and 6.89), and Thucydides' introduction of this historical figure deserves attention. After mentioning Alcibiades' young age and illustrious family ancestry, Thucydides enumerates his motivations, both the political ones (he favored siding with Argos) and the personal ones (Alcibiades was indeed offended because the Spartans had negotiated the peace with Nicias and Laches, in spite of the fact that his own family boasted an ancient relation of proxeny with Sparta). In doing so, the Spartans had overlooked the help that he himself had granted to the prisoners at Sphacteria—the latter element in any case ignored in Book 4. It must be pointed out that Thucydides very likely considered Alcibiades' personal motivations as prevailing (see 8.47.1 and Plut., *Alc.* 14.2; Hornblower 2008, 101). Alcibiades accused the Spartans of bad faith and of having signed the treaty with the aim of destroying the Argives and isolating the Athenians; once he had stirred the dispute (*diaphora*), he privately (*idiai*) urged the Argives to seek an alliance with the Mantineans and Eleans (5.43.2–3; the allusion is to Alcibiades' *xenoi* [guest-friends]; see 6.61.3 and Diod.).

The development of a dispute (*diaphora*) between Sparta and Athens led the Argives to incline toward Athens again. They trusted in their ancient friendship (perhaps the 462/1 alliance) and in their common democratic political orientation (the same motivation is attributed to the Mantineans at 5.29.2). The Argives sent ambassadors to Athens, accompanied by others from Elis and Mantinea. The Spartans Philocharidas, Leon, and Endius also arrived in Athens. Endius was Alcibiades' *xenos* (8.63: an agreement between the two has even been hypothesized: Kagan 1981, 60–77) and had been sent over to prevent the alliance between Athens and Argos. The Spartans required the restitution of Pylos, but also apologized for having signed an alliance with the Boeotians (5.44). Fearing that the Spartan ambassadors might convince the people to reject the alliance with Argos, Alcibiades resorted to manipulation and plotted a deception (*mēchanē*), persuading the ambassadors to say nothing of their autocratic appointment, so as to arouse the anger of the people (5.45: Tuci 2013). Because of the adjournment of the assembly until the following day, Nicias had the chance to send an embassy, whose only result was, however, the renewal of oaths sworn in the Peace of Nicias. The Athenians, offended by this conduct, concluded the so-called Quadruple Alliance (5.46). Thucydides fully transcribes the treaty at 5.47 and, remarkably, comparison between Thucydides' version and the epigraphic text (*IG* I^3, 83) reveals his accuracy and fidelity to the original, despite some minor discrepancies (Pouilloux 1987, 309. For a transcription of treaties by Thucydides, see the section "Transcription of Documents").

In any case, the Peace of Nicias was not renounced by either party. Thus, the main consequence of these events was the disengagement of the Corinthians, who did not want to join either the new coalition that included Athens, or the one that had been concluded among the Argives, Eleans, and Mantineans. On the contrary, the Corinthians intended to maintain the defensive nature of the previous treaty (see 5.27.6 and 31.6), and thus turned again toward Sparta (5.48; the "return" of the Corinthians to the Spartan side closes the ring opened at 5.27.2). The coalition led by Argos thus lost a member of exceptional importance.

THE OLYMPIC CRISIS OF 420

Chapters 49–50 are devoted to the 420 Olympic crisis in which the Spartans were excluded from the Games. This was a real Olympic "excommunication," like the one that at Delphi triggered the Third Sacred War (Sordi 1984a, 1984b; Hornblower 2000). The crisis was the outcome of the Spartan-Elean conflict that began with the clashes over the control of Lepreon, in Tryphilia, and lasted, as it seems, until the defeat of the Eleans by the Spartans at the beginning of the fourth century.

Thucydides narrates the premises to these events at 5.31 and 34.1. A territorial dispute between the Eleans and Lepreans had been submitted to the arbitration of the Spartans, who had pronounced themselves in favor of the Lepreans. As the Eleans did not abide by the arbitration, the Spartans sent to Lepreum their hoplites first and, later, settled there the newly enfranchised citizens (*neodamodeis*) and the helots that had fought with Brasidas in Chalcidice. The Eleans imposed a fine to the Spartans for having sent hoplites into Lepreum during the Olympic truce. The Spartans pleaded that the imposition was unjust, saying that when they sent off the hoplites, the truce had not yet been proclaimed in Sparta. The Eleans then declared that they were willing to waive the fine if the Spartans would restore Lepreum; as the Spartans did not consent to this proposal, the Eleans offered that the Spartans should at least swear before the Greeks that they would pay the fine at a later date. This offer was also refused and the Spartans were excluded from the temple and thus prevented from sacrificing or competing in the Olympic Games.

The condition of international isolation in which Sparta found itself because of this episode is confirmed by the Thessalians' attack to Heraclea in Trachis (5.51.1–5.52.2) as well as by Alcibiades' intervention in the Peloponnesus, when he sided with the Argives and their allies (5.52.2). The fall in prestige that the Spartans suffered is confirmed by the reaction of Argos, which at the end of the summer of 420 tried to convince the Corinthians to join the anti-Spartan alliance, and promoted the war against Epidaurus. However, in the two years that followed, Sparta was able to successfully restore the unity of the Peloponnesus under its own leadership. This was probably a consequence of the intervention of the Athenians, which spread the fear that Athens, and not Argos, would replace Sparta as hegemon over the Peloponnesus.

Alcibiades in the Peloponnesus

In 5.52–6 Thucydides highlights the personal commitment of Alcibiades in the Peloponnesus. He intervened in the years 420 and 419 to strengthen the alliance and oppose Corinth. He also fomented the war against Epidaurus, summoned (perhaps) a conference in Mantinea and, upon his return to Athens at the end of the summer, persuaded the Athenians to inscribe on the stele of the Peace of Nicias that the Spartans did not keep their oaths (5.56.3: see Smarczyk 2006, 505–6).

At the end of the summer of 420, Argos resumed its political and diplomatic initiative, beginning with an unsuccessful appeal to Corinth (5.50.5). Simultaneously, Alcibiades intervened in the Peloponnesus (5.52.2). His army swept through the country and he "settled various business of the alliance." In addition, he initiated the building of long walls from Patras to the sea, and designed the fortification of Rhium (which, however, was hindered by the Corinthians and Sicyonians). The objective was to attain stable control over the Gulf of Corinth. In the following summer (419), Argos waged war against the Epidaurians (one of the clues to the unity of the war mentioned at 5.26.2) on a pretext (*prophasis*: 5.53): the Epidaurians had not sent the offering, because of the temple of Apollo Pythaeus, controlled by the Argives. This conflict was part of a project inspired by Alcibiades. Thucydides comments that the Argives and Alcibiades believed that the control of Epidaurus was essential both to obtain the neutrality of Corinth and to ensure communication between Argos and Athens via Aegina. During this war, a conference was held at Mantinea upon the invitation of the Athenians (an event that confirms their interest in the Peloponnesus: 5.55.1).

Alcibiades evidently sought to build a stable anti-Spartan allied force in the Peloponnesus, continuing a project of Themistocles (Forrest 1960; see O'Neil 1981 and Hornblower 1991, 220 [who are more prudent]; Ar. *Eq.* 465–467 assigns also to Cleon a project for allying with Argos), and aimed to curb the leading role of the Corinthians. The influence of Corinth on the fate of the anti-Spartan coalition appears to be connected with the fact that, while Argos could deal individually with the democratic states of anti-Spartan tradition, it struggled to harmonize with oligarchic states, such as the Boeotians and Megarians. Corinth, however, could not be suspected of being pro-Athenian and could ensure that the coalition would secure the freedom of the Peloponnesus, avoiding the shift from Spartan to Athenian control. For this reason, in 420 the Argives attempted to gain the support of Corinth, and after failing to obtain it, tried to ensure its neutrality. Alcibiades' interventionism conforms therefore to a well-articulated strategic plan (Kagan 1981, 78–84; Luraghi 2013) that reveals a clear view of the Peloponnesian balance of power, and appears to be connected also to the personal relations of Alcibiades himself, whose guest-friends (*xenoi*) were both Argive (6.61.3) and Spartan (Endius: 8.6.3). The fact that at 6.29.3 Thucydides reports that the Argives and some of the Mantineans were serving in the campaign against Sicily only for Alcibiades's sake is further confirmation of the solidity of the ties that he had established in the Peloponnesus.

Troubles in Argos

Thucydides' account of the fourteenth and fifteenth years of the war (5.57–5.83) is devoted to the resumption of the war against Epidaurus, the battle of Mantinea, and the internal troubles in Argos.

The expedition led by the Spartans and their allies against Argos ended avoiding military confrontation *in extremis* (5.57–5.60): as the armies were on the point of engaging at Nemea, two Argives, Thrasyllus, one of the five *stratēgoi*, and Alciphron, a Spartan *proxenos*, negotiated with Agis so as to avoid battle (5.59.5). Thucydides considers this initiative, as well as Agis' decision to accept a truce for four months after consulting with only one of the magistrates who were accompanying him (5.60.1), to be of a personal nature. These circumstances reveal the fragility of the internal balance of Argos, where the democratic government was evidently not able to handle the project launched in 421 (Kagan 1962). The truce crippled Spartan military action, and prompted the anti-Spartan capture of Orchomenus in Arcadia; it also certainly had political motivations, and exposed both Thrasylos and Agis to the suspicion of their fellow citizens (5.60.5–6; 5.63; see Diod. 12.78.4–6). Also in this case, the internal political tensions heavily interfered with the international context.

At 5.61.1–2 Thucydides describes a meeting at Argos, in which the Athenians persuaded the Argives to break the truce with the Spartans and to resume the war. Alcibiades was there as an ambassador (*presbeutēs*; Diod. 12.79.1 narrates that Alcibiades was present as a private citizen, *idiōtēs*, because of the friendly ties that he had with the Eleans and Mantineans). Orchomenus was attacked with success but shortly afterward disagreements arose within the coalition on the continuation of the war (5.62). The Eleans wanted to attack Lepreum, while the Mantineans wished to attack Tegea; the Argives and Athenians sided with the Mantineans, and the Eleans withdrew (the Eleans were about 3,000 men; lack of their support did perhaps affect the outcomes of the battle of Mantinea), while Tegea was preparing a democratic coup. The account highlights the tensions within the anti-Spartan coalition, the rift between the cities of the Peloponnesus, and the inadequacy of Argos. These were indeed the circumstances of which Alcibiades, once again personally engaged in the Peloponnesus, intended to take advantage.

At 5.64 the account of the battle of Mantinea begins. The territory of Mantinea was invaded by the Spartans after receiving news of the possible defection of Tegea and the narration concludes at 5.75.6, spanning the entire summer of 418. The battle, which Thucydides considers the greatest among those fought among the Greeks for a very long time (5.74.1), allows the historian to provide information on how the Spartan army operated (5.66), as well as on the deployment of the two parties involved, in particular on the Argive chosen men (*logades*, 5.67; see 5.76.2 and 5.81.2; Diod. 12.75.7 and 80.2 highlight their role at Mantinea, thanks to a merge of excerpts from Thucydides' work by Ephorus, or perhaps thanks to further intelligence) and on the number of soldiers engaged

(5.68: Thucydides notices here, as at 5.74.3, the difficulty of obtaining information from the Spartan field; see Forsdyke, chapter 1 in this volume, for further discussion).

The description of the battle of Mantinea (5.70–74) reveals excellent intelligence, and almost seems to assume a paradigmatic value (Connor 1984, 144). The battle concludes the chain of events that began with Pylos and is assigned a significant role in the narration (Rood 2004, 61–63; Stahl 2006, 320–38). The victory of Sparta reaffirmed its military superiority and restored its prestige: Sparta was relieved of the accusations of cowardice (*malakia*) for Pylos and of lack of deliberation (*aboulia*) and sluggishness (*bradutēs*), which re-echo those of the Corinthians in 432 (5.75.3). On the other hand, Alcibiades would however still claim as a success the fact of having prompted the major powers of the Peloponnesus to war and of having endangered the position of the Spartans (6.16.6; see Plut. *Alc*. 15.1).

At the beginning of winter, Sparta proposed an agreement with Argos, which was well received by the pro-Spartan faction. The proposal, discussed in the presence of Alcibiades (once again personally involved in the Peloponnesus; see 5.61.2), persuaded the Argives to abandon their alliance with Athens, Mantinea, and Elis, and join the Spartan coalition (5.76). Thucydides transcribes the draft of the agreement at 5.77, and its approved version at 5.79 (the transcription of these almost identical texts is puzzling: see discussion below in "Transcription of Documents"); also in this case, the documentary material originates from the Peloponnesian area that Thucydides could access during his exile (5.26.5). As a result of the alliance, Argos was brought under full Spartan control (5.80).

At the end of the winter of 418/7, a coup put down the democracy at Argos and a pro-Spartan oligarchy was established (5.81.2). The special corps of the Thousand, set up in 421 by selecting hoplites on the basis of physical strength and wealth (Diod. 12.75.7), formed, it seems, the core of the antidemocratic revolutionaries (Diod. 12.80.2–3). Thucydides, who is primarily interested in the international context, provides few details on the regime of the Thousand, whereas other sources (Diod. 12.80.2–3, Plut. *Alc*. 15.2; Paus. 2.20.2; Aen. Tact. 17.2–4; Arist. *Pol*. 5.1304a) mention strong internal tensions and violence. The oligarchy did not last long: in 417/6 the Argive democrats regained control of the city with the help of the Athenians (82.2–6). One may wonder whether Alcibiades was behind the resumption of cooperation between Argos and Athens (an agreement signed in the summer of 416 is attested in *IG* I^3 86): this is in effect what Plutarch says (*Alc*. 15.4–5).

The Capture of Melos

At 5.84.1 the account of the sixteenth year of the war (416/5) begins. This year was marked by the events related to Melos and the preparation of the Sicilian expedition. Although this apparently entails a change in subject, Book 5 does still focus on the problem of the relations between the strong and the weak (in the Peloponnesus and on the islands).

The colonial theme (the relations between Melos and Sparta), for example, anticipates the Sicilian question. The attack on Melos, moreover, could be seen as revenge against Sparta for Mantinea. Finally, the need to recall the tensions between Athens and Melos in 426 serves to support the thesis of the unity of the war (Hornblower 2008, 215–225).

At 5.84.1 Thucydides narrates Alcibiades' expedition to Argos and the arrest of 300 pro-Spartans who were deported to the islands (see 6.61). This account shows that Alcibiades' commitment in favor of Argos did not cease even after the failure of the internal democratic crisis in 418–417.

Immediately afterward, Thucydides reports on the expedition against Melos, which, being a Spartan colony, did not intend to submit to the Athenians, "unlike the rest of the islanders" (5.84.2; see 3.91.2, about the 426 attack: they "were islanders, yet unwilling to be their subjects or join their alliance").

Thucydides' account of the long dialogue between the Athenians and Melians before capitulation (5.85–113) conveys a bitter reflection on the outcomes of Athenian imperialism, which at this point was utterly indifferent to any values. From the very beginning of the episode, the Athenians refuse to consider ethical or legal arguments: disparity between the parties requires indeed that discussions proceed solely on the basis of the useful (*to chrēsimon*), which coincides with the interest (*to sumpheron*) of the strongest. In the end, the Melians relied on "fortune from the gods" (5.104), and the Athenians argued that the exercise of domination by the strongest over the weakest is a natural necessity that cannot conflict with divine law.

Melos capitulated in the winter of 415 and was treated extremely harshly, as had happened to Histiaea, Potidaea, Aegina, Mytilene, Torone, and Scione. The men were put to death, the women and children were sold for slaves, and a cleruchy of 500 men (5.116.2–4) was sent to the island. According to the speech *Against Alcibiades* ([Andoc.] 4) and re-echoed by Plutarch (*Alc.* 16.6), Alcibiades expressed the opinion that the Melians should be enslaved ([And.] 4.22). Despite Thucydides' silence, this is consistent with Alcibiades' anti-Spartan orientation and his defense of the empire as an instrument of power.

Book 5 concludes with the end of the siege on Melos and the fate of the island, in the winter of 415. Here Thucydides concludes the account begun at 5.27, an account that is focused, on the one hand, on the disputes (*diaphorai*) in the Peloponnesus, the dialectics of hegemony/autonomy, the role of the third parties, and the development of diplomatic activity that was often inconclusive. On the other hand, his account manifests a specific interest in the figure of Alcibiades and in his project of a stable democratic and anti-Spartan alliance in the Peloponnesus.

Transcription of Documents

The transcription of documents is characteristic of the part of Thucydides' work that we are considering. As early as at 4.16, Thucydides furnishes a large account of the negotiations in 425 between Athens and Sparta about the Spartan soldiers stranded on the island of Sphacteria (see 4.20.1 for the Athenian answer), which he paraphrases with traces of technical terminology (Hornblower 1996, 116; 359). This reference is followed by the series of transcriptions of Books 5 and 8: a first group of six treaties dated between 423 and 418 (four concerning Athens, two concerning the Peloponnesus) and a second group of three treaties between Sparta and Persia between 412 and 411. In no case does the historian provide hints about the origin of his intelligence: autopsy of the original inscriptions and readings of archival copies or transcriptions by mediators often have a similar degree of probability (Smarczyk 2006, 502).

The density of transcribed documents in Books 5 and 8 has been interpreted as an indicator of incompleteness. In the controversy between unitarian and separatist critics, such density has furnished arguments in favor of the former. Yet, it has not been demonstrated that transcribing texts was unacceptable at a stylistic level (Canfora 2006, 26–29). Furthermore, transcribed documents can also be found in Books 1, 6, and 7, which are not considered as lacking in final revision.

With the emergence of the narratological perspective, scholars have generally inclined to relate the inclusion of documents in historical accounts to a conscious methodological innovation (Hornblower 1996, 113–122: however, from the alleged "methodological turning point" at 4.117, Thucydides does not consistently opt for inserting documents), and to emphasize its precise narrative function. The specific style of this part of the work would be the result of a deliberate choice aimed at highlighting the difficulty of assessing a hectic time of "apparent peace" yet of substantial war; even more so as Book 5 contains also very elaborate parts, such as the Melian Dialogue and the account of the battle of Mantinea (Connor 1984; Rood 2004, 83; Dewald 2005).

A continuous reading of Thucydides' work from 4.117 to 5.83 clearly shows that, in order to make comprehensible the complex historical events occurring between 423 and 417, the historian often needs to allude to the content of the treaties concluded in this period (and in particular to the Peace of Nicias). The main objective of transcription could therefore be the intent of providing exhaustive data capable of making perspicuous the rather confused and contradictory actual development of the events recounted, characterized as they were by the difficulty of achieving stable agreements. Indeed, the transcription of documents covers precisely the period of the "suspicious truce," which was marked by nonobservance of the terms so carefully set forth in official documentation. Thus, it is likely that Thucydides deemed it useful to provide the reader with information for a thorough comparison between the frantic diplomatic activity of those years and the evolution of the actual relations between the parties. Thucydides employs transcriptions both as a narrative device (as they are fixed points in the progression of events, or serve the aim of emphasizing the instability of the agreements reached: Connor 1984, 144–157) and as a historiographical tool (to allow an accurate comparison between the legal/diplomatic situation and the claims of the parties involved). It is also possible that Thucydides intended to complete, through documentary material, intelligence that was scarce in other respects, perhaps because of the difficulty of interviewing an adequate number of eyewitnesses (Bearzot 2003).

Sicily and Peloponnesus

At 6.1 the account of the Sicilian expedition, which dominates Books 6 and 7, begins. Thucydides does not, however, fail to provide links to the events narrated in Book 5.

Alcibiades was involved in the cooperation between the Peloponnesus and Sicily in Books 6 and 7. At the beginning of the seventeenth year of the war (415/14), Thucydides includes three direct speeches, two by Nicias (6.9–14 and 6.20–23) and one by Alcibiades (6.16–18), that are particularly rich in interesting allusions. Nicias, who opposed the expedition, emphasizes that the project was likely to ignore the enemies in Greece and attract others (6.10.1); the pacts were uncertain (the adjective *bebaios* evokes the definition of "uncertain truce" at 5.25.3) and one had to strengthen the empire before aspiring to extend it (6.10.2–3). In his reply, Alcibiades—presented as eager to become general, conquer Sicily and Carthage and attain personal advantages (6.15.2; see 6.12.2)—claims to have done well, despite the apparent failure, for having put Sparta in a critical situation (6.16.6: about how Thucydides distances himself from this opinion, see Hornblower 2008, 347–348) and deprived the Peloponnesians of their hope of defeating Athens (6.17.8). Besides maintaining the validity of his Peloponnesian policy, Alcibiades precisely presents it as consistent with the expedition to Sicily under the common objective of humbling the Peloponnesians. Hermocrates too urged the Syracusans to send an embassy to Sparta and Corinth, to ask them to come to their aid as soon as possible and to launch war in Greece (6.34.3), drawing a link between the war at home and the war in the West (see also 6.73.1–2). Remarkably, this linkage reoccurs several times in the account of the Sicilian expedition and in related speeches: see, for example, Hermocrates at 6.80.1; Euphemus at 6.84.1 and 87.1; the ambassadors from Syracuse and Corinth at Sparta (6.88.7–8) and Alcibiades on the same occasion (6.88.10).

Alcibiades in Sparta: The Occupation of Decelea

Alcibiades continues to be the protagonist of the subsequent events, even after the scandal of the Herms and his involvement in the subsequent investigation. The story is well known. The mutilation of the Herms was considered part of an antidemocratic conspiracy fomented by Alcibiades' intrigues (6.27.3, 60.1). During the investigation, Alcibiades was denounced for having parodied the Eleusinian Mysteries. Thucydides seems to believe that these accusations were unfounded and artfully magnified by the enemies of Alcibiades (6.28.2). Nevertheless, Alcibiades' tendency to transgression, which was at odds with a democratic way of life, as well as his ambition contributed to foster the suspicion that he was leaning toward tyranny (6.15.3–4; 6.60.1).

Alcibiades asked to be tried immediately but it was decided to let him sail. According to Thucydides, his enemies wanted to proceed against him on graver charges, which would be more easily made up during his absence. Probably, it was also feared that the morale of the soldiers would be affected, and that the allied contingents personally tied to Alcibiades would abandon the enterprise (6.29.3, 61.5). Thucydides is thus convinced of the groundlessness of the accusations, which he considers to be of a political nature.

In June 415 the fleet arrived in Catania; shortly thereafter, the ship *Salaminia* arrived from Athens, under instruction to bring Alcibiades back to Athens to be judged. The ship of Alcibiades followed the *Salaminia* up to Thurii; there he escaped and reached the Peloponnesus. The Athenians found him guilty, and sentenced him to death *in absentia*.

Although Alcibiades feared the Spartans "because of his activities in the Mantinean affair" (6.88.9), he nonetheless decided to head to Sparta, where he arrived in the winter of 415/14. Thucydides reports the speech with which Alcibiades addressed the assembly (6.89–92). First of all, he justified himself for having fomented the anti-Spartan agreement among Argos, Mantinea, Elis and Athens—saying that the Spartans, preferring to negotiate with his enemies, had discredited him: Thucydides confirms, through Alcibiades' words themselves, the opinion expressed at 5.43—and for his ties with democracy, ties due to family tradition and political necessity. Then, Alcibiades gave the Spartans advice on how to conduct the war: they should help the Syracusans in order to prevent the conquest of Sicily and Italy by Athens and a subsequent attack on the Peloponnesus; then they should occupy Attica permanently, fortifying Decelea, and undermine the foundations of the Athenian empire (6.91.6).

The occupation of Decelea closes the interwar years and opens the last phase of the war. The first piece of information about Decelea is at 6.91.6: in Sparta, Alcibiades points out that, among the advantages for the Spartans, there is the possibility of tapping the riches of Attica and depriving the Athenians of their revenues.

The Spartans were persuaded, and began to fortify Decelea at the end of the winter of 414 (6.93.2). The fortification of Decelea (and the invasion of Attica by Agis; according to Diod. 13.9.1, Alcibiades was with Agis) is mentioned again at 7.19.1, at the beginning of the nineteenth year of the war (413/12). Other pieces of information are at 7.27.3–5 and 28, where Thucydides specifies the difficulties caused by the occupation of Decelea—now the base of enemy operations—which had led to losses in wealth and men. Occupation had also cut off communications with Euboea through the Euripus and forced the Athenians to import everything by sea, thereby turning the city into a fortress under siege. The Athenians were condemned to exhausting guard duty on the city walls and, above all, were engaged in a fierce two-front war (7.28.3; see 6.1.1). Occupation-related difficulties accentuated financial fragility and reduced the revenues. The inflow of tribute had so declined that it had to be replaced with a five percent tax on imports by sea (see Low, chapter 5 in this volume, for discussion of the implications of this shift).

This dramatic description, which finds a parallel at 8.1 (regarding the reactions to the arrival in Athens of the news of the defeat of Sicily), closes the account of the interwar years, fully corroborating the thesis of the unity of the war as set forth at 5.26. The uncertain truce occurring after 421 was in fact not only characterized by creeping war but also led indeed to a two-front war (the Decelean/Ionian war and the Sicilian Expedition), through a process in which human decision and fortune (*tuchē*, i.e., man's inability to control events) are inextricably intertwined (Connor 1984; Hornblower 1987).

References

Bearzot, C. 2003. "L'uso dei documenti in Tucidide." In *L'uso dei documenti nella storiografia antica*, edited by A. M. Biraschi, P. Desideri, S. Roda, and G. Zecchini, 267–314. Naples: Edizioni Scientifiche Italiane.

Canfora, L. 2006. "Biographical Obscurities and Problems of Composition." In *Brill's Companion to Thucydides*, edited by A. Rengakos and A. Tsakmakis, 3–31. Leiden and Boston: Brill.

Connor, W. R. 1984. *Thucydides*. Princeton: Princeton University Press.

Dewald, C. 2005. *Thucydides' War Narrative*. Berkeley: University of California Press.

Forrest, W. G. 1960. "Themistokles and Argos." *CQ* 10: 221–41.

Gribble, D. 2006. "Individuals in Thucydides." In *Brill's Companion to Thucydides*, edited by A. Rengakos and A. Tsakmakis, 439–68. Leiden and Boston: Brill.

Hornblower, S. 1987. *Thucydides*. London: Duckworth.

Hornblower, S. 1991. *A Commentary on Thucydides*. Vol. I., *Books I–III*. Oxford: Clarendon.

Hornblower, S. 1996. *A Commentary on Thucydides*. Vol. II, *Books IV–V.24*. Oxford: Clarendon.

Hornblower, S. 2000. "Thucydides, Xenophon, and Lichas: Were the Spartans Excluded from the Olympic Games from 420 to 400 B.C.?" *Phoenix* 54: 212–25.

Hornblower, S. 2006. "Thucydides and the Argives." In *Brill's Companion to Thucydides*, edited by A. Rengakos and A. Tsakmakis, 615–28. Leiden and Boston: Brill.

Hornblower, S. 2008. *A Commentary on Thucydides*. Vol. III, *Books 5.25–8.109*. Oxford: Clarendon.

Hornblower, S. 2011. *Thucydidean Themes*. Oxford: Oxford University Press.

Hose, M. 2006. "Other Sources." In *Brill's Companion to Thucydides*, edited by A. Rengakos and A. Tsakmakis, 669–90l. Leiden and Boston: Brill.

Kagan, D. 1960. "Corinthian Diplomacy after the Peace of Nicias." *AJPh* 81: 291–310.

Kagan, D. 1962. "Argive Politics and Policy after the Peace of Nicias." *CPh* 57: 209–18.

Kagan, D. 1981. *The Peace of Nicias and the Sicilian Expedition*. Ithaca and London: Cornell University Press.

Lang, M. L. 2011. "Thucydidean Thought." In *Thucydidean Narrative and Discourse*, By M. L. Lang; edited by J. S. Rusten and R. Hamilton, 113–16. Ann Arbor: Michigan Classical Press. (Originally published in 2002 in *Mnemosyne* 55: 200–203.)

Lattimore, S., ed. 1998. *The Peloponnesian War*. By Thucydides. Indianapolis and Cambridge: Hackert.

Luraghi, N. 2013. "Lo storico e la sua guerra: Tucidide e la grande strategia della guerra del Peloponneso." In *American Legacy: La SISM ricorda Raimondo Luraghi*, 1–19. Rome: Società Italiana di Storia militare.

O'Neil, J. L. 1981. "The Exile of Themistokles and Democracy in the Peloponnese," *CQ* n.s. 31: 335–46.

Parmeggiani, G. 2011. *Eforo di Cuma: Studi di storiografia greca*. Bologna: Patron.

Pouilloux, J. 1987. "L'épigraphie et l'objectivité historique de Thucydide." In *Stemmata. Mélanges de philologie, d'histoire et d'archéologie grecques offerts à Jules Labarbe,* edited by T. Hackens, J. Servais, B. Servais-Soyez, 305–15. Liège-Louvain-la-Neuve: L'Antiquité classique.

Rengakos, A., and A. Tsakmakis, eds. *Brill's Companion to Thucydides.* Leiden and Boston: Brill.

Rood, T. 2004. *Thucydides: Narrative and Explanation.* Oxford: Clarendon.

Smarczyk, B. 2006. "Thucydides and Epigraphy." In *Brill's Companion to Thucydides,* edited by A. Rengakos and A. Tsakmakis, 495–522. Leiden and Boston: Brill.

Sordi, M. 1984a. "Le implicazioni olimpiche della guerra d'Elide." In *Problemi di storia e cultura spartana,* edited by E. Lanzillotta, 143–59. Rome: G. Bretschneider.

Sordi, M. 1984b. "Il santuario di Olimpia e la guerra d'Elide." In *I santuari e la guerra nel mondo classico,* edited by M. Sordi, 20–30. Milan: Vita & Pensiero.

Stahl, H.-P. 2006. "Narrative Unity and Consistence of Thought. Composition of Event Sequences in Thucydides." In *Brill's Companion to Thucydides,* edited by A. Rengakos and A. Tsakmakis, 301–34. Leiden and Boston: Brill.

Strauss, B. S. 1997. "The Problem of Periodization: The Case of the Peloponnesian War." In *Inventing Ancient Culture: Historicism, Periodization and the Ancient World,* edited by M. Golden and P. Toohey, 165–75. London and New York: Routledge.

Stroud, R. S. 1994. "Thucydides and Corinth." *Chiron* 24: 267–304.

Tuci, P. A. 2013. "*Hesychia* spartana e *neoteropoiia* ateniese: Un caso di manipolazione nelle trattative per le alleanze del 420 a.C." In *La cultura a Sparta in età classica (Aristonothos* 8), edited by F. Berlinzani, 71–104. Trento: Tangram Edizioni Scientifiche.

Westlake, H. D. 1940. "Corinth and the Argive Diplomacy." *AJPh* 61: 413–21.

Westlake, H. D. 1968. *Individuals in Thucydides.* Cambridge: Cambridge University Press.

CHAPTER 9

THUCYDIDES ON THE SICILIAN EXPEDITION*

EMILY GREENWOOD

THUCYDIDES' narrative of the Athenian expedition to Sicily in Books 6 and 7 of his *History* poses similar interpretative problems to those raised by the larger war between the Athenians and the Peloponnesians that supplies the broader historical context and narrative frame for the expedition. In both cases, although we have other sources for some of the events and material in question, Thucydides' artful narrative shapes our understanding of the conflict. On the one hand we have history—the total history of the war in Sicily between 415 and 413 BCE and all of the events that contributed to and influenced the course of this conflict; and on the other hand we have history-text, or narrativized history—the version of this conflict that Thucydides relates in his *History*. The former (the total history) exists only speculatively, as a tantalizing theoretical figment: the sum total of everything that pertained to this conflict and that would, in its total form, be unnarratable. Understanding the structure of Thucydides' narrative and the politics and poetics of his representation of this conflict is therefore crucial and requires that we simultaneously read and unread Thucydides: that we read him to uncover the structure and logic of his narrative of the war, and that we unread him to identify the limits of his account.[1]

The interpretative problems sketched in the introductory paragraph apply to Thucydides' *History* in its entirety, and are common to all historical narratives. Books 6 and 7 pose an additional challenge, as they were composed as part of a larger narrative

---

* I would like to thank Sara Forsdyke for improving comments on this chapter.
[1] Excellent sequential accounts and analyses of the events and narrative of Books 6 and 7 exist. Connor (1984, 158–209) offers a close analysis of the language and structure of Thucydides' narrative in the context of the work as a whole. More recently, Hawthorn (2014, 165–201) discusses Thucydides' historical interpretation in Books 6 and 7, with an emphasis on political analysis and critique. Stahl (2003) has an excellent discussion of the relationship between the speeches in Books 6 and 7 and the narration of events (173–88; a revised version of Stahl 1973), and a discussion of the way in which Thucydides structures the narrative in these books around a series of "crisis points" (2003, 189–222).

work but also exhibit a very high degree of internal coherence and narrative autonomy (see Dewald 2005, Chapter 6). At the historiographical level, as a war within a war—an account of a war that is completed within a war that is ongoing—Books 6 and 7 frame the reader's experience and encourage reflection on both writing and reading the history of a war (Stahl 2003, 187). At the historical level, Thucydides suggests that this second, embedded war, which put the Athenians in a state of "double war" (*diplous polemos*), is emblematic of the Athenians' aggressive and ambitious imperialism in this period and their poor economic and logistical planning in the last decade of the war (see Kallet 2001 on Thucydides' critique of Athenian economic planning and poor calculation of power).

The first interpretative step for us as readers of Thucydides is to address the question of the kind of narrative that we think we are reading in Books 6 and 7 of the *History*. The title of this chapter follows well-established convention in referring to the subject of Books 6 and 7 of Thucydides' *History* as "the Sicilian Expedition." There is some support for this label in Thucydides; at 2.65.11 he refers to the campaign in Sicily as "the voyage/expedition to Sicily" (ὁ ἐς Σικελίαν πλοῦς), but as a blanket description for a two-year conflict in Sicily, it warrants scrutiny. Thucydides' narrative of the Athenian invasion of Sicily is largely focalized through the Athenians. After a brief excursus on the history, geography, and ethnography of Sicily at the beginning of Book 6 (Chapters 2–5, the so-called *Sikelika*), Thucydides begins his narrative of the war in Sicily with a paired debate between the Athenian politicians Nicias and Alcibiades, based on the assembly meetings in which the Athenians took the decision to send an expedition to Sicily (6.8–26). The military expedition is debated in response to a plea for intervention from notional Egestaian allies, and as an opportunity to expand the empire with the immediate mission to assist the Egestaians as a convenient pretext (the latter argument is made by Alcibiades at 6.18.4). The account of the assembly debates is followed by an account of the mutilation of the herms in Athens (6.27–29), which Thucydides treats both in terms of its impact on Athenian morale and as an example of the distracted quality of the Athenians' collective deliberation. Next we share the perspective of the inhabitants of Athens, themselves watched by any foreigners in the city, watching the departure of the expedition from the Piraeus (6.30.2–6.31.1):

> The local people were seeing off their own, whether friends, relatives, or sons, all departing in hope and tears: hope for conquests to come, and tears for those they might never see again, as they took to heart how far from their native land the voyage was taking them.[2]

This passage implants a clear narrative trajectory and expectation of *nostos*, which is finally fulfilled and disappointed at the end of Book 7 (7.87.6), where Thucydides comments that "few out of many made the return voyage home" (ὀλίγοι ἀπὸ πολλῶν ἐπ' οἴκου ἀπενόστησαν; see Allison 1997, 512–514 for a close analysis of the Homeric resonances of the verb ἀπονοστέω). As many scholars have remarked, the use of the verb

---

[2] Unless otherwise stated, all translations of Thucydides in this chapter are taken from Mynott (2013).

ἀπονοστέω recalls the references to the *Odyssey* at the beginning of Book 6 of the *History*. At 6.2.1, Thucydides mentions that the Cyclopes and Laestrygonians are said to have been the oldest inhabitants of Sicily. Stavros Frangoulidis has drawn attention to the Odyssean symmetry at the beginning and end of the Sicilian narrative and suggested that the symmetry establishes a "heroic frame" for the narrative (1993, quoting from p. 102). Other scholars have endorsed this idea of the Athenian invasion of Sicily as a post-Homeric epic, with evocations of both the *Iliad* and the *Odyssey* and the Athenians as Achaeans in the initial stages of the narrative, setting out to conquer "'Trojan' Sicily," before themselves becoming Trojans, as the besiegers become the besieged (Mackie 1996; Allison 1997; Hornblower 2008, 711–713 on 7.75.5).[3] In Thucydides' telling, this epic war in Sicily is entirely an Athenian epic, with the Athenians as both aggressors and victims. Once the Athenians have arrived in Sicily, their experience is privileged over that of the Syracusans and their allies. We largely follow the progress of the war through their psychology and emotions, with occasional shifts of perspective to what the Syracusans were thinking and feeling. The very tendency to refer to the events of summer 415 to summer 413 BCE as the "Sicilian Expedition" is a legacy of this Athenian focalization. If we adopt the perspective of the Syracusans and the other peoples of Sicily who were dragged into a two-year war, it makes little sense to refer to this as the "Sicilian Expedition." Instead, "war of aggression" or "hostile invasion" would be more appropriate.

Although Thucydides does focalize sections of the narrative of Books 6 and 7 through Syracusans, most notably the general Hermocrates (see especially his speeches at 6.32.3–41.4, and 6.76.1–80.5), and gives us brief sketches of Syracusan group-thinking and morale, there is no attempt to explain or understand the conflict in light of the longer history of Syracuse and the Syracusans' cultural identity (see Zahrnt 2006). It is also notable that Thucydides twice describes the Syracusans as "similar in nature" (*homoiotropoi*) to the Athenians (7.55.2, 8.96.5; at 7.55.2 the reference is to *poleis* in the plural (πόλεσι ... ὁμοιοτρόποις), but it is clear that Syracuse is the primary referent). We might even go further and say that, insofar as the *History* offers us a postmortem on a failed ideal of Athens, then while the Syracusans and their allies were the actual enemy, Thucydides' deeper interest is in the Athenians confronting themselves and their own natures in Sicily.[4]

The implications of this focalization and what alternative versions of the Sicilian expedition might look like are evident when we turn to Diodorus Siculus' account of the invasion of Sicily, written in the first century BCE (see Hornblower 2008, 10 on Diodorus' "discrepant version"). In his account of the climactic sea battle in Syracuse (Thuc. 7.70–71), Diodorus flips the point of view that we find in Thucydides, focusing instead on the dramatic perspective of the Syracusans on the home front and their stakes in the battle.

---

[3] Hornblower (2008) suggests that in conceiving of the defeated Athenians as Trojans, Thucydides was influenced by both literary and visual depictions of the fall of Troy.

[4] For a broader historical discussion of Athens and Syracuse as "twin *poleis*," see Ober (2015, 219–20, and chapter 8 generally).

Diodorus describes the Syracusan families watching and even participating in the decisive battle in the harbor at Syracuse, with the ramparts of the city providing an amphitheater for the battle in the bay (13.14.4–13.16.7).

Although Diodorus inverts Thucydides' focus on the Athenians, his Syracusan focalization repeats the Thucydidean emphasis on the collision of two great powers—Athens and Syracuse—while playing down the interests and experiences of all of the other political communities and peoples involved in the war, whether voluntarily or involuntarily. Thucydides gives us a catalogue of all the different peoples involved in the war (7.57–59.1), reminiscent both of Homer's catalogue of ships and Herodotus' catalogue of the Greek forces at the battle of Salamis (Hdt. 8.43–8; see Hornblower 2008, 655), and prefaces it by emphasizing the great ethnic and geographical diversity of the combatants:

> This gathering represented the greatest number of nationalities (ἔθνη) ever assembled at a single city, with the exception of course of the overall totals involved in this war with the cities of the Athenians and Spartans. (7.56.4)

However, for all that Thucydides enumerates some fifty-two different nationalities in his catalogue, from Acarnanians to Zacynthians, readers are seldom given glimpses into the imagined mindset and emotions of these other peoples. Instead, they are mostly viewed from the exterior, as accessories to the conflict. An example of fleeting, distributed focalization occurs at 6.69.3, where Thucydides considers the divergent motivation of the Athenians, their independent allies, and their subject allies, but here too the Athenians are distinguished from the others, who are treated *en bloc*, as defined by the nature of their relationship to the Athenian empire.

An obvious exception is the digression on the disaster that befell the polis of Mycalessus in Boeotia, narrated at 7.29. Thucydides describes how Mycalessus was attacked by Thracian mercenaries under the command of the Athenian general Diitrephes, who was escorting them back to Thrace because the Athenians, who had initially contracted their services to join a relief expedition to Sicily, no longer needed them (the Thracians arrived too late to sail with the expedition). "So disaster struck the whole city and was the worst ever suffered, so sudden was it and terrible" (7.29.5), "part of the population of Mycalessus was completely wiped out. Such was the fate of Mycalessus, which in relation to its size suffered a calamity as grievous as any in the war" (7.30.3). Scholars have pointed to the role that the digression on Mycalessus plays in illustrating the enormous human suffering that resulted from the Atheno-Peloponnesian War—an observation that Thucydides makes at 1.23.1–4 (see Stahl 2003, 136–37). Following Robert Connor (1984, Appendix 7), Lisa Kallet has analyzed the digression on Mycalessus in light of Thucydides' digression at 7.27–28 on the Athenians' flawed financing and logistical planning at this juncture in the war. In Kallet's analysis, the account of the massacre at Mycalessus serves both to depict the larger theme of human suffering in the war, and to tie the moral responsibility for this instance of suffering to poor fiscal decisions made by the Athenians (2001, 120–26, and 140–46).

This striking digression, which relates the suffering of a polis—Mycalessus—that is peripheral to the war, serves to highlight the fact that the differential ways in which the Atheno-Peloponnesian war (and the Sicilian phase of the war) was experienced and suffered by different peoples drawn into the conflict go largely undocumented. If we think about the wars that Thucydides did not write, there were as many different potential versions of the war as there were different nationalities involved, not to mention that attitudes to the war diverged within the same ethnic and political communities.

The Exemplarity Problem

Within the *History*, intertextual correspondences set up the Athenians' defeat in Sicily as the negative *paradeigma* (object lesson, example) to others which the Melians warn them of in the dialogue in Book 5 (5.90): "in defeat, encountering great retribution, you may become an example to others" (my translation; see Greenwood 2006, 23–24 for discussion). Toward the end of Book 7, the description of the Athenians' state of mind unmistakably echoes the very traits that they had scorned in the Melians in Book 5 as they have desperate recourse to hope and fortune. In a speech of encouragement before the final sea battle in the harbor of Syracuse, Nicias exhorts his troops to "remember the uncertainty of war, and prepare to renew the fight in the hope that fortune (τύχη) may swing our way too" (7.61.3). Correspondingly, in his speech of encouragement before the final sea battle, Gylippus reassures the Syracusans and their allies that "[the Athenians] are so overwhelmed by their troubles and under such pressure in their present quandary that they are reduced to the desperate condition of trusting more to luck (τύχη) than preparation" (7.67.4). The Athenians' dependence on τύχη here recalls the Melians' dependence on τύχη at 5.104, 5.112.2, and 5.113.

For readers of Thucydides in the twenty-first century, many of whom harbor strong postcolonial and anti-imperial sympathies (the present writer included), it is tempting to read the fate of the Athenians in Sicily as payback for imperial aggression, as part of a broader anti-imperial parable. Stated in these terms, such an interpretation seems crudely anachronistic, but translated into the normative expectations of Greek interstate relations in the second half of the fifth century BCE, the Athenians' approach to empire is excessive and aggressive and perverts established standards of reciprocity-based morality (see Low 2007, especially pp. 222–233 on Thucydides as a source for the discourse of Athenian interstate relations). The famous passage in Xenophon's *Hellenica*, describing the Athenians' sleepless night when they received the news of the defeat of the Athenian navy at Aegospotami in 405 BCE, fearing that they would suffer the kind of treatment that they had meted out to other Greeks, confirms the Athenians' sense of their own transgression of Greek interstate norms (*Hell.* 2.2.3).

There is ample material in Books 6 and 7 to support a strong critique of Athenian imperialism. Thucydides conveys his unequivocal authorial judgment that this was an imperialist war of aggression, and that the Athenians had the objective of conquering

Sicily (and from there Carthage) as a step toward the conquest of the entire Greek world and proximate territories (6.6.1, and 6.15.2). Elsewhere, the critique of Athenian imperialism is focalized through individual speakers, all hostile to Athens in different ways: Hermocrates (6.33.2, 6.76.2), Alcibiades (6.90.2), and Gylippus (7.66.2). But it is problematic to conclude from Thucydides' representation of these debates that the Athenian demos understood itself to be voting for a military expedition to conquer Sicily and extend its empire. As Geoffrey Hawthorn remarked in a discussion of the decision-making process in the Athenian assembly that led to the Sicilian expedition, "apart from Nicias and perhaps a few others, the 'Athenians' may in some sense have wanted to subjugate Sicily. But it would be too strong to say that they were determined to do so and too strong to say that they weren't. They were, one might say, in a mood to see' (Hawthorn 2014, 165).

The question of Athenian imperialism in Books 6 and 7 gains another dimension when we consider the ways in which Thucydides' representation of the Sicilian expedition recalls the Persian invasions of Greece as described by Herodotus—particularly the second invasion under Xerxes (see Rood 2009 [originally 1999], and Harrison 2000). As Kurt Raaflaub has argued, Athenian intervention in Sicily in 427–424 BCE influenced Herodotus' narration of the second Persian invasion of Greece in Books 7–9 of the *Histories*, suggesting that Athenian imperialism in Sicily had become the model for thinking about and criticizing the excesses of empire as a geopolitical phenomenon.[5] Insofar as Thucydides writes a critique of Persian imperialism and displays a wary sense of the ways in which the Athenians were repeating similar patterns of expansion, we might also consider Thucydides' treatment "post-imperial," leaving aside the question of whether an allusion to the Athenians' loss of their empire at the end of the Peloponnesian War also lurks behind Thucydides' critique of Athenian imperialism in Books 6 and 7.

Versions of a post-imperial reading of the Sicilian expedition circulated in the fourth century BCE, as Athenians reflected on the losses of a once preeminent ancestral Athens. In the pamphlet *On the Peace*, written in the context of the Social War of 357–355 BCE, Isocrates offers a scathing retrospective on Athenian imperialism in Sicily (in the context of the Athenians' imperious behavior toward their allies in the present day):

> For they reached such a degree of neglect of their own possessions and of covetousness of the possessions of other states that when the Lacedaemonians had invaded our territory and the fortifications at Decelea had already been built, they manned triremes to send to Sicily and were not ashamed to permit their own country to be cut off and plundered by the enemy while dispatching an expedition against a people who had never in any respect offended against us. Nay, they arrived at such a pitch of folly that at a time when they were not masters of their own suburbs they expected to extend their power over Italy and Sicily and Carthage. And so far did they outdo all

---

[5] Raaflaub (2002); Raaflaub adduces a series of parallels between Herodotus' account of the second Persian invasion of Greece and Athenian imperialism in Sicily in 427–424 BCE.

mankind in recklessness that whereas misfortunes chasten others and render them more prudent our fathers learned no lessons even from this discipline.

> On the Peace, 84–85; translated by George Norlin, Loeb Classical Library, Isocrates Vol. 2

Thucydides certainly frames the Athenians' invasion of Sicily as transgressive imperialism, but he invites his readers to adopt a double consciousness that is simultaneously aware of the disaster in store for the Athenians and the multiple tragic ironies that result, while at the same time recognizing that the failure of the expedition was contingent on pragmatic human decision-making. At 2.65.11, Thucydides makes the pointed claim that the Sicilian expedition was "not so much a mistake of judgement (γνώμης ἁμάρτημα) about the enemy they were attacking as a failure on the part of those sending the men abroad to follow up this decision with further support for them." Reading Thucydides' account of the expedition in Books 6 and 7, we might add other factors such as *kairos* (the right thing happening at the right time), the weather, and a bundle of other unpredictables that together constitute *tuchē*—the chance element in human affairs. Far from presenting Athenian defeat as inevitable, Thucydides calls attention to the opportunities for victory (see Rood 1998, 160–61 for discussion of this passage, and pp. 159–99 for an analysis of Thucydides' attitude to Athens' defeat in Sicily). The clearest incidence of counterfactual possibilities, counter-narratives, and the potential for other endings occurs at Book 7, Chapter 2, where the Athenians are close to completing their wall to encircle Syracuse (in summer 414 BCE). At 7.2.1 the Corinthian commander Gongylus arrives to find the Syracusans about to debate withdrawal from the war in their assembly and is just in time to intervene and talk them round. Thucydides emphasizes the fortuitous nature of Gongylus' arrival by pointing out that Gongylus left Corinth last, but arrived in Syracuse first (7.2.1). Gongylus' timely intervention is then reinforced by the arrival of Gylippus:

> He [Gylippus] happened to come at the critical moment when the Athenians had completed about a mile of their double wall to the Great Harbour and had only a short stretch left to reach the sea, which they were still working on.... So close did the Syracusans come to disaster. (7.2.4)

> ἔτυχε δὲ κατὰ τοῦτο τοῦ καιροῦ ἐλθὼν ἐν ᾧ ἑπτὰ μὲν ἢ ὀκτὼ σταδίων ἤδη ἀπετετέλεστο τοῖς Ἀθηναίοις ἐς τὸν μέγαν λιμένα διπλοῦν τεῖχος, πλὴν κατὰ βραχύ τι τὸ πρὸς τὴν θάλασσαν (τοῦτο δ' ἔτι ᾠκοδόμουν), ... παρὰ τοσοῦτον μὲν αἱ Συράκουσαι ἦλθον κινδύνου.

Robert Connor has described this sentence as "one of the most astonishing in the *Histories*" (1984, 187). As Hans-Peter Stahl has suggested in an important discussion of Books 6 and 7, these "almost situations" lay bare the "crisis points" or "hinges" of history in Thucydides' thought—junctures at which events could have turned out differently (see Stahl 2003, 189–222; and pp. 201–216 for a discussion of the arrival of Gongylus and Gylippus). The extremely fortuitous nature of Gongylus' arrival, and the subsequent timely arrival of Gylippus, have aroused scholars' suspicions, leading to the suggestion that Thucydides has played tricks with time and perhaps even invented the coincidence of Gongylus' arrival and the assembly meeting (Hawthorn 2014, 188). What is unmistakable is Thucydides' insistence that a possible Athenian breakthrough was thwarted by a chance concatenation of events.

The flip side to the argument that Thucydides resists the inevitability of Athenian defeat, writing against hindsight, is the observation that the Athenians took a huge risk and made themselves vulnerable to factors that they could neither predict nor control. In his first speech in the assembly debate at the beginning of Book 6, Nicias describes the city as "running the greatest risk in its history" (μέγιστον δὴ τῶν πρὶν κίνδυνον ἀναρριπτούσης, 6.13.1). It is notable that the vocabulary of risk (κινδυνεύω and its cognates) and reckless daring (τόλμα) clusters around the Athenians in Books 6 and 7, echoing their characterization in earlier books of the *History*. Although we are given hints that things could have turned out differently in Sicily, with a slight shift in political leadership and different circumstances on the ground, there is also an insinuation that the Athenians' intractable natures are also to blame. While the Athenians might conceivably have conquered Sicily in a counterfactual scenario, ultimately the narrative confirms the truism that the only sure way to have avoided a colossal disaster would have been not to invade in the first place (Nicias articulates a version of this truism at 6.11.4).

However, the critique of imperialism does not apply exclusively to the Athenians, although they are the primary aggressors. As Simon Hornblower has pointed out, the Athenian attempt to colonize Sicily is part of a larger history of attempts to annex Sicily, including an attempt by the Spartans in 510 BCE (2008, 10). Moreover, there is also a sense that the Syracusans are just as eager as the Athenians to annex parts of Sicily (Harrison 2000, 87).

A Double War

A sticking point in Thucydidean interpretation is the elision of the historical phenomenon that scholars refer to as the Peloponnesian war with Thucydides' representation and narrativization of this war. There are many different aspects to this debate, not least the historical question of whether the conflict that Thucydides treats as a single war was actually two distinct wars, separated by a false Peace (the Archidamian War of 431–421, and the Iono-Decelean War of 414–404, with the intervening Peace of Nicias of 421–415, which was characterized by ongoing conflict). Thucydides himself addresses this debate at 5.26.1–4, before reaffirming that it was essentially a single, continuous war (for the debate about the periodization of the Peloponnesian War, see Strauss 1997, and Bearzot, chapter 8 in this volume). Within this larger debate, Books 6 and 7 raise interesting historiographical questions about how Thucydides narrates a war within a war and how he mediates between the "epic" dimensions of the Sicilian campaign and the larger war, of which it was a particular phase and that is also described in totalizing, epic terms (1.1 and 1.23.1–3).

As is often observed, the opening sentence of the *History* collapses the distinction between Thucydides' narrative and the war of which it is a narrative, leading to the construct of Thucydides' narrative as the war ("Thucydides of Athens wrote the war of the Peloponnesians and the Athenians"—Θουκυδίδης Ἀθηναῖος ξυνέγραψε τὸν πόλεμον τῶν Πελοποννησίων καὶ Ἀθηναίων; see Loraux 1986, Edmunds 1993, and Bakker 2006 for discussion). As Egbert Bakker has argued, qualifying Nicole Loraux's discussion of this passage, "the war is more than mere subject matter to which the text 'refers.' The war as Thucydides' work presents it, perhaps its very existence, is bound up with its very writing" (2006, 111). This sense is reaffirmed at 1.21.2, where Thucydides' use of the phrase *ho polemos houtos* / ὁ πόλεμος οὗτος (the deictic pronoun *houtos* implies "this war that you have in front of you") merges his narrative of the war and the war that it signifies (see Bakker 2006, 118).

Readers who reach the end of Thucydides' account are aware of one gaping contradiction in the co-identification of text and war: namely, that the end of Thucydides' work is not commensurate with the end of the actual war in 404, breaking off instead in the narration of events that took place in 411 BCE. Books 6 and 7 open up another structural tension, by introducing a parallel war to that of the main frame. At 6.1.1, Thucydides remarks that most Athenians "were unaware that they were taking on a war on almost the same scale as that against the Peloponnesians" (οὐ πολλῷ τινὶ ὑποδεέστερον πόλεμον ἀνῃροῦντο ἢ τὸν πρὸς Πελοποννησίους). The motif of the double war intensifies as the narrative of the Sicilian campaign proceeds. At 7.18.2 Thucydides introduces the term "double war" (διπλοῦν τὸν πόλεμον), focalized through the Spartans, who draw comfort from the fact that the Athenians are being stretched by having to fight two wars. Subsequently, at 7.28.3, Thucydides refers to the pressure on the Athenians of having "two wars" (δύο πολέμους) at the same time (7.28.3–4).

> And now, against all reasonable expectation, in the seventeenth year after the first such invasion, and already war-worn in every way, they should go to Sicily and undertake another war on the same scale as the one they already had with the Peloponnese.
>
> καὶ τὸν παράλογον τοσοῦτον, … ὥστε ἔτει ἑπτακαιδεκάτῳ μετὰ τὴν πρώτην ἐσβολὴν ἦλθον ἐς Σικελίαν ἤδη τῷ πολέμῳ κατὰ πάντα τετρυχωμένοι, καὶ πόλεμον οὐδὲν ἐλάσσω προσανείλοντο τοῦ πρότερον ὑπάρχοντος ἐκ Πελοποννήσου.

Given the very close identification between Thucydides' work and the war (*polemos*) fought between the Athenians and the Peloponnesians, the introduction of a second *polemos* threatens to upset the integrity of Thucydides' narrative as a coherent account of a single war. But, as I will suggest here, this war that is subordinate to the main war is itself integral to Thucydides' reconstruction of the dynamic and changeable nature of the war as it unfolded.

At 1.1 Thucydides claims that his narrative of the war is based on a continuous record of the progress of the war. Clearly, there is a tension between Thucydides' claim to have written the war in real time and the revised, retrospective narrative that we now read. One way in which Thucydides reconciles this tension is by depicting the continuous revision of participants' expectations as the war played out, writing in hindsight but reproducing the real-time experience of war (see the discussion of Thucydides' "experiential narrative" below in "*Ho Paralogos*: The Unpredictability of War and Narrative Suspense"). Books 6 and 7 conform to this pattern. They offer a narrative of an entire war: the ending of this embedded war could not be more total or conclusive—πανωλεθρίᾳ (7.87.6)—and Thucydides employs a string of superlatives to convey the totality of defeat. But meanwhile the main war continues, subsuming the Sicilian disaster within its remit. The Sicilian campaign is the greatest except for the other war, "this war" (*hode ho polemos*)—this one that Thucydides is writing, as he keeps on reminding the reader. As Thucydides claims at 7.56.4, the campaign in Sicily "represented the greatest number of nationalities ever assembled at a single city, with the exception of course of the overall totals involved in this war with the cities of the Athenians and Spartans" (ἔθνη γὰρ πλεῖστα δὴ ἐπὶ μίαν πόλιν ταύτην ξυνῆλθε, πλήν γε δὴ τοῦ ξύμπαντος λόγου τοῦ ἐν τῷδε τῷ πολέμῳ πρὸς τὴν Ἀθηναίων τε πόλιν καὶ Λακεδαιμονίων).[6] At the conclusion to his narrative of the campaign in Sicily, Thucydides reasserts the primacy of the main war, commenting that this action (ἔργον/*ergon*, apparently referring to the final phase of the campaign in Sicily) "was the most momentous of any in this war" (ξυνέβη τε ἔργον τοῦτο [Ἑλληνικὸν] τῶν κατὰ τὸν πόλεμον τόνδε μέγιστον, 7.87.5). Here the Sicilian *polemos* that has occupied our attention for two books is folded into and subordinated to the *polemos* that is the subject of the work as a whole.

Ho Paralogos: The Unpredictability of War and Narrative Suspense

In the text of the *History* as we have it, bearing in mind its incomplete state, the two-war theme is a key driver of narrative suspense, allowing readers to experience the unpredictability and open-ended nature of war. As a highly self-contained narrative of a campaign that is presented as a full-scale war, Books 6 and 7 disrupt the sense of the inevitable trajectory of the work, depicting an expedition that defies the expectations of the internal observers in the *History*. We have seen Thucydides' judgement that the Athenians' actions in prosecuting a double war (one in Attica and one in Sicily) utterly confounded the calculations of the other Greeks (τὸν παράλογον τοσοῦτον ποιῆσαι, 7.28.3; see above in "A Double War"). Thucydides puts the same noun, *ho paralogos* ("the

---

[6] Also cited in the opening section of this essay above.

incalculable element"), in the mouth of Athenian envoys, addressing the Spartan assembly about the risk of impending war in the Summer of 432 BCE, narrated in Book 1 of the *History*. There the Athenian representatives warn the Spartans to "think in advance about how unpredictable war can be before you find yourselves involved in one" (τοῦ δὲ πολέμου τὸν παράλογον, ὅσος ἐστί, πρὶν ἐν αὐτῷ γενέσθαι προδιάγνωτε, 1.78.1–2).

Although readers come to Thucydides knowing the end of his *History*, or having access to knowledge of how the war ended, by drawing attention to the different phases of the conflict and the constantly disappointed/surprised expectations of those involved, the war within the war shuffles our expectations and hints at alternative histories and the contingency of the war as we know it. The outcome of this second, embedded war is foreknown by Thucydides' readers, both intra-textually (the Athenians' defeat in Sicily is flagged up in a famous prolepsis at 2.65.11–12), and extra-textually. Yet the denouement of the narrative exploits the participants' ignorance of how it would unfold. Throughout Books 6 and 7, narrative focalization is distributed between two poles: narratorial foresight (based on hindsight) on the one hand, and actor ignorance on the other hand. The gap between these two poles opens up ironic distance that contributes so richly to the tragic texture of the Sicilian campaign.

As Egbert Bakker has demonstrated in an analysis of the modulation of tense and aspect in Thucydidean narrative, pivotal episodes in the final stages of Thucydides' narrative of the Sicilian campaign are narrated predominantly in the imperfect tense, which participates in "the discourse of the observer" and "present[s] the action as experienced (the incompleteness of the action being a natural consequence of the point of view adopted)" (1997, 42–43). This is particularly true of the narrative of the final naval battle in the harbor at Syracuse (7.70–71), the retreat of the Athenians, including the scene in which they break camp (7.75), and their slaughter at the Assinarus River (7.84–85.1).

Building on Egbert Bakker's work on Thucydides' manipulation of tense to convey the experience of past events as they unfolded, Jonas Grethlein has argued that Thucydides counterbalances the teleological determinism of a war whose outcome is already known, by means of an "experiential narrative" that reactivates the presentness of the past as it was experienced by historical actors (2013, 29–52, developing Grethlein 2010, 248–51). One of the narrative devices used to restore the experientiality of the past is "sideshadowing," the signaling of other possible outcomes that lay open in the past (a term introduced by Morson 1994). For Grethlein, Gylippus' fortuitous arrival, and Thucydides' remark that "so close did the Syracusans come to disaster" (see above in "The Exemplarity Problem") constitutes an instance of counterfactual "sideshadowing" (2010, 250).

The double-war motif, which is reflected in the structure of the narrative as Thucydides effectively pauses the narrative of the main war to narrate this other, simultaneous war, means that the end of the war in Sicily, resulting in total annihilation for the Athenians, is a misleading and premature ending (see Hornblower 2008, 744 on the end of the Sicilian narrative at 7.87 as a "false closure"). The Athenians rally and resume their war effort, and resurrect the city that is metaphorically fallen at the end of Book 7, as Nicias had predicted in his words of encouragement to the troops at 7.77.7: ". . . if you get to escape the enemy ... the Athenians among you will get to raise up again the great power of their fallen city" (ἢν νῦν διαφύγητε τοὺς πολεμίους, ... οἱ Ἀθηναῖοι τὴν μεγάλην δύναμιν τῆς πόλεως καίπερ πεπτωκυῖαν ἐπανορθώσοντες). Again the reader has to revise expectations, keeping time with the combatants and contemporary observers across the Greek world who had to constantly revise their projections of the length of the war and the Athenians' ability to withstand Spartan military superiority (see, for example, 5.14.3, 7.28.3, 8.2.1). After the double war scenario narrated in Books 6 and 7, which defied Greeks' expectations of how the ongoing conflict would unfold, at the beginning of Book 8 the narrative continues but the conflict is reset: "So both sides were engaged in these activities and were busily equipping themselves for war just as though they were only now beginning it" (8.5.1), and while losses accumulate and alliances shift, and the psychological impact of previous victories and defeats shapes morale, the war is constantly renewed. In fact, as many scholars have observed, at 8.96.1–2 Thucydides downgrades the scale of the disaster in Sicily in the context of the news about the revolt of Euboea in the summer of 411 BCE:

> When the news from Euboea reached Athens the sense of shock there was greater than ever before. Neither the disaster in Sicily, great though it seemed to be at the time, nor any other event had ever scared them as much.
>
> Τοῖς δὲ Ἀθηναίοις ὡς ἦλθε τὰ περὶ τὴν Εὔβοιαν γεγενημένα, ἔκπληξις μεγίστη δὴ τῶν πρὶν παρέστη. οὔτε γὰρ ἡ ἐν τῇ Σικελίᾳ ξυμφορά, καίπερ μεγάλη τότε δόξασα εἶναι, οὔτε ἄλλο οὐδέν πω οὕτως ἐφόβησεν.

Tragic Emplotment

The Sicilian expedition is often described as "ill-fated," which is just one way in which scholars have assimilated Thucydides' tragic emplotment of the war. While Thucydides resists the implication that the outcome of the Sicilian expedition is a foregone conclusion and that it is somehow fated, he nonetheless exploits Athenian tragedy and Greek tragic thought more broadly (especially tragic thought in Homer) to imbue what happened to the Athenians in Sicily in a tragic light. In a well-known analysis of the final sea battle in the harbor at Syracuse (7.70–71), Jacqueline de Romilly stressed the way in which Thucydides employs both pathos of structure (e.g., expectation and reversal of expectation), and pathos of description (scenes of suffering and lamentation) in order to affect his readers and to convey the experience of those watching disaster unfold (2012, 95–102; originally 1967). The description of the Athenians breaking camp as they prepare to retreat inland is similarly graphic and theatrical, as Thucydides describes how the Athenians were tormented by the spectacle of their own suffering (7.75.2–3):

> And what was so terrible about the situation was not just the fact that they were retreating after losing all their ships, and that in place of high hopes they and the

city were now in mortal danger; but in the very act of leaving the camp behind each of them also had to suffer torments of sight and mind. The bodies of the dead were unburied, so anyone seeing a friend lying there was reduced to a mixture of grief and fear, and the living who were left behind sick and wounded were far more distressing to their living comrades than were the dead, and were in a more wretched state than those who had already lost their lives.

The description of the suffering continues, with further pitiful details, before concluding with the statement that "this was certainly the greatest reversal (μέγιστον διάφορον) that ever befell a Greek army" (7.75.7), and yet in the same sentence Thucydides notes that the survivors bore their sufferings, mindful of worse suffering that might lie ahead.

Historiography and Surviving Disaster

Notwithstanding the generic influence of tragedy and the strong vein of tragic thought that runs through Books 6 and 7, Thucydides is not writing a tragedy. Thucydides' *History* writes through disaster, with a high degree of intellectual positivism, insisting on the importance of critical and analytical detachment and on learning from failure and disaster, not as a facile exercise, but as a continuous endeavor. The narrative of Books 6 and 7 offers an important case study of a finite war within a war. As a two-year campaign, as opposed to the twenty-seven-year conflict of which it was a phase, the Sicilian expedition was easier to circumscribe and to analyze. Although the reason for the unfinished state of the *History* is not known, it is possible that the lack of completion reflects the difficulty and unwieldiness of narrating the conflict in its entirety.

As we saw with the "exemplarity" problem, while Thucydides' authorial self-presentation is didactic and lays claim to superior insight into the events that he narrates, it is not always clear what lessons he would have us learn. Perhaps the overriding historiographical insight offered in Books 6 and 7 is the precariousness of the accurate facts in a context in which different individuals and interest groups appropriate the discourse of truth and put rhetorical pressure on their audiences as they attempt to interpret the situation and deliberate accordingly. This is particularly evident in the speeches. At 6.33.1, the Syracusan general Hermocrates defends his point of view by saying that he speaks from a position of clearer knowledge than any other (ἐμαυτὸν σαφέστερόν τι ἑτέρου εἰδὼς) and claims to know the truth (τὸ δὲ ἀληθές) about the Athenians' motives, as opposed to the pretext (πρόφασις) for the expedition (a verbal echo of Thucydides' language about the "truest cause of the war" at 1.23.6, and the "truest motive" for the invasion of Sicily at 6.6.1). At 6.91.1, in the course of a self-interested and tendentious account of affairs in Athens and his role in them, Alcibiades tells the Spartan assembly that "you have now heard from the person with the best inside knowledge (παρὰ τοῦ τὰ ἀκριβέστατα εἰδότος) exactly what the intentions were behind the expedition now in progress," (6.91.1). The efficacy of Alcibiades' rhetoric is confirmed when Thucydides describes the Spartans' credulous reaction to this speech, "judging that they had been listening to the one man who really knew the facts (νομίσαντες παρὰ τοῦ σαφέστατα εἰδότος ἀκηκοέναι)" (6.93.1–2). The Spartan general Gylippus employs similarly scientific vocabulary at 7.67.4 when he assures the Syracusans and their allies about the poor state of Athenian morale: "And there is one thing you can be quite sure of—and we have this on our best authority . . ." (τὸ δ' ἀληθέστατον γνῶτε ἐξ ὧν ἡμεῖς οἰόμεθα σαφῶς πεπύσθαι). In the mouths of these politicians, the use of the adjectives ἀκριβής (accurate), σαφής (clear), and ἀληθής (true) provide uncanny echoes of Thucydides' description of his historical project.[7] Thucydides privileges *akribeia* (accuracy) as the quality that he strives for in his historical research (1.22.2, 1.22.2, 5.26.5, 6.55.1) and associates its absence with ignorance about the past (6.54.1). And when it comes to characterizing his own intellectual project, Thucydides singles out the ability to construct a clear picture (*to saphes*) of past events as the overriding quality and virtue of his painstaking account (1.22.4).

It is not that Hermocrates, Nicias, and Gylippus lack insight, but the high stakes of the military context translate into exaggerated truth claims. The competition for truth in the political arena is highlighted by Nicias' letter (7.11–14), sent back to Athens as a dispatch from the field, which is framed as an attempt by a politician to educate his target audience (the Athenian assembly) so that they can deliberate about the truth (μαθόντας τοὺς Ἀθηναίους βουλεύσασθαι περὶ τῆς ἀληθείας, 7.8.2)—a striking formulation. The language of instruction is repeated in the letter itself (μαθόντας ὑμᾶς, 7.11.2), as is the claim to be revealing the truth (τὸ ἀληθὲς δηλῶσαι, 7.15.1). Like Hermocrates and Gylippus, Nicias also uses the language of clarity (σαφῶς εἰδότας, 7.14.4). Nicias' attempt to improve communication with the Athenian audience through the use of a written briefing recalls his pessimistic rhetoric in his speeches to the assembly debate at Book 6, where he is resigned to the powerlessness of his arguments as he faces the culture of political debate in Athens and the Athenians' mood (6.9.3). But even this attempt to establish ideal conditions for deliberation fails and its failure shows up the value of Thucydides' work as an account of past events that is relevant and useful for understanding both the past and events in the future (see Greenwood 2006, 76–81 for a more extensive discussion of the relationship between Nicias' letter and Thucydides' *History*).

Thucydides' intellectual positivism—the idea that, in the domain of intellectual inquiry it is possible to attain a higher standard of truth and accuracy—is achieved at some remove from the political institutions that shaped day-to-day existence for his readers. As far as we can tell, the majority of the *History* was written in exile; at any rate, Thucydides accredits the tranquility of exile with his ability to produce the kind of work that he has (5.26.5–6). As Elton Barker has pointed out, there are limits to the insight that

---

[7] ἀκριβής and ἀληθής are used substantively; σαφής is used adverbially (σαφέστατα). Gylippus also uses the positive degree of the adverb, σαφῶς.

Thucydides offers his readers, since they are mired in the political communities about which they are reading, with all their shortcomings. In Barker's words, Thucydides' readers are embroiled in a real life "crisis of interpretation" (2009, 203–63, quoting from p. 263).

It is part of the conative nature of Thucydides' historical research to present us both with ideals of historical inquiry and examples of the obstacles to a clear account of the past. An example of the former is Thucydides' presentation of his careful, archival research to establish an accurate account of the assassination of Hipparchus and the tyranny of Hippias (6.54–59). Thucydides' disclosure at 7.59, about the difficulty of establishing what happened in the chaotic night battle at Epipolae (7.44.1) stands in stark contrast:

> The Athenians were now getting so confused and bewildered that it was difficult to learn from either side in any detail how events continued. In daytime things are clearer, of course, but even then individual participants scarcely know what is happening right by them, let alone across the whole field of action. But in a night-battle—and this was the only one involving significant forces in this particular war—how could anyone know anything for sure?

And yet Thucydides circumvents the obscurity of his reports by offering what is ostensibly an accurate account of the chaos, although chaos, by its very nature, defies narration (see Greenwood 2006, 36). This is a case in which the watchful reader must out-Thucydides Thucydides.

Conclusion

This chapter began by emphasizing the selectivity of Thucydides' account and considering the war in Sicily that Thucydides *did not* write. An obvious consideration is the other sources for the Sicilian expedition that tell us things that Thucydides does not, whether through omission or ignorance.

Aristophanes' *Birds*, produced in 414 BCE, offers a comic critique of the Sicilian expedition—then in its first year—as a ridiculously ambitious colonization project. In the period following the Sicilian expedition, Aristophanes' *Lysistrata* (411 BCE) testifies to the war-weariness of the Athenian population, focalized through its women, and makes mocking reference to the assembly debates in which the decision to launch the expedition was taken (lines 390–392). The briefest comparison of Thucydides and these two plays of Aristophanes reveals vast spheres of experience that Thucydides does not touch upon (the almost total neglect of woman's participation in warfare is just one example).

Had they survived, the *Sikelika* (*Sicilian history*) of the Syracusan historian Philistus in the fourth century BCE would have offered us a fascinating counter-narrative to

Thucydides, albeit in a historian who was himself influenced by Thucydides. Likewise is Timaeus of Tauromenion, who wrote in the fourth and third centuries BCE and produced his own history of Sicily, and who is both criticized and cited by Plutarch as a source on the Sicilian expedition. Diodorus Siculus, writing in the first century BCE, also used Timaeus' account and, as discussed above, gives us an alternative, Sicilian focalization for the expedition.

When it comes to later writers, Plutarch's *Life of Nicias* points to the problem: no subsequent writers were able to rival Thucydides for sheer narrative power and, where their accounts overlapped with subject matter treated by Thucydides, were both derivative and in competition with him (*Nic.* 1). And yet, in the eyes of many subsequent reading communities, Plutarch's version of Greek (and Roman) history, told through the lives of famous men, proved more accessible and readable than Thucydides' *History*. His *Life of Nicias* preserves for us many details that did not make it into Thucydides' account, as well as variant accounts of some of the details (e.g., at *Nic.* 28.4 Plutarch cites Timaeus for an alternative version of how Demosthenes and Nicias died, a version he contrasts with that given in Thucydides and Philistus). Plutarch also gives us an epilogue to the end of Thucydides' narrative of the Sicilian Expedition, by discussing the fate of the Athenian prisoners (Chapter 29), and a more novelistic version of how the news of the defeat reached Athens (Chapter 30). The narrative of Books 6 and 7 is a demonstration of the exemplarity of Thucydides' *History* and the pitfalls that this exemplarity poses for historical interpretation.

References

Allison, J. W. 1997. "Homeric Allusion at the Close of Thucydides" Sicilian Narrative.' *American Journal of Philology*, 118(4): 499–516.

Bakker, E. J. 1997. "Verbal Aspect and Mimetic Description in Thucydides." In *Grammar as Interpretation: Greek Literature in Its Linguistic Contexts*, edited by E. J. Bakker, 7–53. Mnemsoyne Supplement 171. Leiden: Brill.

Bakker, E. J. 2006. "Contract and Design." In *Brill's Companion to Thucydides*, edited by A. Rengakos and A. Tsakmakis, 109–29. Leiden: Brill.

Barker, Elton T. E. 2009. *Entering the Agon: Dissent and Authority in Homer, Historiography and Tragedy*. Oxford: Oxford University Press.

Connor, W. R. 1984. *Thucydides*. Princeton: Princeton University Press.

Dewald, C. 2005. *Thucydides' War Narrative: A Structural Study*. Berkeley: University of California Press.

Edmunds, Lowell. 1993. "Thucydides in the Act of Writing." In *Tradizione e innovazione nella cultura greca: Da Omero all' età ellenistica; Scritti in onore di Bruno Gentili*, edited by R. Pretaogstini, 831–52. Rome: Gruppo Editoriale Internazionale.

Frangoulidis, S. A. 1993. "A Pattern from Homer's *Odyssey* in the Sicilian Narrative of Thucydides." *QUCC* 44: 95–102.

Greenwood, Emily. 2006. *Thucydides and the Shaping of History*. London: Duckworth.

Grethlein, J. 2010. *The Greeks and Their Past: Poetry, Oratory and History in the Fifth Century BCE*. Cambridge: Cambridge University Press.

Grethlein, J. 2013. *Experience and Teleology in Ancient Historiography: "Futures Past" from Herodotus to Augustine*. Cambridge: Cambridge University Press.

Harrison, T. 2000. "Sicily in the Athenian Imagination: Thucydides and the Persian Wars." In *Sicily from Aeneas to Augustus: New Approaches in Archaeology and History*, edited by Christopher Smith and John Serrati, 84–106. Edinburgh: Edinburgh University Press.

Hawthorn, G. 2014. *Thucydides on Politics: Back to the Present*. Cambridge: Cambridge University Press.

Hornblower, S. 2008. *A Commentary on Thucydides*. Vol. III, *Books 5.25–8.109*. Oxford: Clarendon.

Kallet, L. 2001. *Money and the Corrosion of Power in Thucydides: The Sicilian Expedition and Its Aftermath*. Berkeley: University of California Press.

Loraux, N. 1986b. "Thucydide a écrit la Guerre du Péloponnèse." *Métis* 1: 139–61.

Low, Polly. 2007. *Interstate Relations in Classical Greece*. Cambridge: Cambridge University Press.

Mackie, C. J. 1996. "Homer and Thucydides: Corcyra and Sicily." *Classical Quarterly* 46 (1): 103–13.

Morson, G. S. 1994. *Narrative and Freedom: The Shadows of Time*. New Haven: Yale University Press.

Mynott, J., ed. and trans. 2013. *The War of the Peloponnesians and the Athenians*, by Thucydides. Cambridge: Cambridge University Press.

Norlin, George (1929) *Isocrates Vol. II*. Edited and Translated by George Norlin. Loeb Classical Library. Cambridge: Harvard University Press.

Ober, Josiah. 2015. *The Rise and Fall of Classical Athens*. Princeton: Princeton University Press.

Perrin, B. 1996 *Plutarch Lives*. Vol. 3, *Pericles and Fabius Maximus, Nicias and Crassus*. Translated by Bernadotte Perrin. Cambridge. [Translation originally published in 1916.]

Raaflaub, K. A. 2002. "Herodot und Thukydides: Persischer Imperialismus im Lichte der athenischen Sizilienpolitik." In *Widerstand-Anpassung-Integration: Die griechische Staatenwelt und Rom; Festschrift für Jürgen Deininger zum 65. Geburtstag*, edited by N. Ehrhardt and L.-M. Günther, 11–40. Stuttgart: Franz Steiner Verlag.

Romilly, J. de. 2012. *The Mind of Thucydides*, translated by Elizabeth Rawlings. Edited and with an introduction by Hunter R. RawlingsIII and Jeffrey Rusten. Ithaca: Cornell University Press. [First published as *Histoire et raison chez Thucydide*, 1967].

Rood, T. 1998. *Thucydides: Narrative and Explanation*. Oxford.

Rood, T. 2009. "Thucydides' Persian Wars." In *Oxford Readings in Classical Studies: Thucydides*, edited by J. Rusten, 148–75. Oxford: Clarendon.

Stahl, H.-P. 1973. "Speeches and Course of Events in Books Six and Seven of Thucydides." In *The Speeches in Thucydides: A Collection of Original Studies*, edited by P. A. Stadter, 60–77. Chapel Hill: University of North Carolina Press.

Stahl, H.-P. 2003. *Thucydides: Man's Place in History*. Swansea: Classical Press of Wales.

Strauss, B. S. 1997. "The Problem of Periodization: The Case of the Peloponnesian War." In *Inventing Ancient Culture: Historicism, Periodization, and the Ancient World*, edited by M. Golden and P. Toohey, 165–75. London and New York: Routledge.

Zahrnt, Michael. 2006. "Sicily and Southern Italy in Thucydides." In *Brill's Companion to Thucydides*. edited by A. Rengakos and A. Tsakmakis, 629–55. Leiden: E. J. Brill.

CHAPTER 10

THUCYDIDES ON THE FOUR HUNDRED AND THE FALL OF ATHENS

ANDREW WOLPERT

> Although they had lost a great portion of the fleet in Sicily as well as other armed forces and had thrown the city into civil war, nevertheless they held out for [ten] years more against their former enemies as well as the Sicilians and many of their allies who had risen up against them, and later Cyrus, the son of the Great King, who funded the Peloponnesian fleet, and they did not surrender until they were overcome by the private conflicts which they carried out against themselves. So many were the reasons Pericles had foreseen that the city would easily prevail over the Peloponnesians unaided in the war.
>
> Thucydides 2.65.12–13

BOOK 8 is incomplete. It ends abruptly in the middle of a sentence, lacks speeches, and even has some sections that are in a rough form, suggesting that Thucydides may have intended to revise or expand them (see Gomme et al. 1981, 369–75; Hornblower 2008, 1053–54). For a conclusion, one must turn instead to a brief summary statement on the final years of the war that appears in Book 2 after Pericles' last speech. Although Thucydides' readers cannot help regretting that he left his work unfinished, they should be grateful that he made it through the middle of 411 BCE to write about the revolt of Athenian allies, the overthrow of the Athenian democracy by the Four Hundred, and their removal from power. It is difficult enough to understand why Thucydides places so much emphasis in 2.65 on private conflicts to explain the Athenian defeat.[1] If his history had stopped at the end of Book 7 with the destruction of the Athenian fleet in Syracuse, it would have been too easy for his readers to dismiss the significance of the last stage of the war and to conclude instead that defeat was inevitable after Sicily. Even

---

[1] For Thucydides' explanation of the Athenian defeat, see Romilly (1965); Gomme et al. (1981, 423–24); Connor (1984, 62–63); Kagan (1987, 417–26); Foster (2010, 216–18); Taylor (2010, 271–74).

in its incomplete form, Book 8 shows why Thucydides was right to believe that the defeat in Sicily was not enough to force Athens to surrender to Sparta and how civil unrest changed Athens and caused the Athenians to lose the Peloponnesian War.

Although the Spartans had the upper hand and the war was fought entirely on Athenian land and the territory of her subjects, the Athenians were able to hold out for nearly another decade because the Spartans were still hampered by their inability to act decisively. Discord within its leadership and among its allies prevented Sparta from following up on the victory in Sicily. The Spartans were now on the offensive, but they could not end the war, because Persia would not give them its full support, the cities of Ionia and the Hellespont were unable to act in concert, and the Athenians still exhibited some of the same resilience that they had displayed in the early years of the war. At the same time, Book 8 reveals that there was a fundamental change in the dynamics of the war, a change that caused Thucydides to attribute so much importance to internal discord for the Athenian defeat. Shell-shocked by the loss of their forces in Sicily, the Athenians began to doubt themselves and hesitated to take the steps that were necessary to prevent the dissolution of their empire. As they shed some of those characteristics, for which they were famous and that in the eyes of Pericles had helped turn Athens into a great naval empire, they became susceptible to internal unrest that would eventually be their undoing. The Four Hundred swiftly seized power and their rule quickly collapsed because Athens could not stop its allies from revolting. Some of the oligarchs may have had serious political convictions. However, they came to power with such ease not because the bulk of the Athenians shared their concerns about the democracy. Instead, most Athenians were concerned first and foremost about the survival of their city. The oligarchs held out to them the vain hope that Athens could win the war if they handed over the state to the Four Hundred. Those who knew better were eliminated, so the Athenians did not have the wherewithal to stop the Four Hundred from gaining power. Because they failed to make good on their promises and proved themselves to be dangerous traitors, the Four Hundred were just as quickly overthrown. So when the narrative abruptly ends in the middle of 411, Athens was in a better position than at any other point in Book 8, but the seeds for her downfall had also been sown. By examining the revolt of Athenian allies, the rise of the Four Hundred, and their removal from power, I will show how this tension pervades the final book of Thucydides.

The Revolt of Athenian Allies

Thucydides begins Book 8 by describing how all of Greece expected the war to soon be over (8.2.1–2). Although this expectation is understandable after Sicily, it was quickly proven to be wrong. True to form, the Spartans were slow to follow up on their victory. Athenian allies may have been eager to revolt, but none of them wanted to be the first to challenge Athens. So the last chapter of the war begins on a false note: the end is not as near as everyone thinks. For Cornford (1907, 244), the book falls flat. Because Book 7 is filled with so much *pathos* and Thucydides gives his readers the impression that Sicily sealed Athens' fate, Book 8 cannot help standing out as a poor epilogue. The city merely limped along until finally it could no longer withstand Sparta with Persian support. For Hornblower (1987, 145–50), the disconnect between the finality of the Athenian defeat in Book 7 and her recovery in Book 8 reveals that Thucydides changed his views about the role of individuals for the course of history. Alcibiades' leadership after Sicily, especially at the Battle of Cyzicus, caused Thucydides to emphasize impersonal forces less and individuals more (see also Westlake 1968). Book 8 may be incomplete, but it is possible that some of its incongruities were intentional. They need not be proof that the book lacks the historian's artistry or reflects a fundamental change in his methods or his views. Elsewhere Thucydides exploits the tension between expectations and outcomes to draw his readers' attention to changes, developments, and patterns in the war (Connor 1984, 210–13, 30–37). By beginning Book 8 in such a jarring fashion, Thucydides emphasizes the significance of the Athenian recovery. Most cities would have been compelled to surrender after suffering such a defeat. However, Athens was unlike any other Greek city. The Athenians would still exhibit some of the resilience that the Corinthians attributed to them (1.70.5–6). So the work now focuses on the reasons that the Athenians were able to hold out, how the city recovered in spite of the magnitude of the defeat in Sicily, and what the nature was of the new obstacles that the Athenians were facing.

In hindsight, the pause in fighting that took place in 413 is not surprising. Neither side was prepared for the next stage of the war, because the Athenian defeat in Sicily was so much worse than anyone could have expected. When news of the destruction of the fleet first reached Athens, the Athenians were stunned and could not believe the reports. Once they had overcome their initial shock, they prepared for an attack that they thought was imminent by gathering together whatever timber, funds, and equipment they could find. They did their best to secure Euboea and their other allies. Yet, they did not draw from the reserve funds, which were intended for such an emergency, because they did not want to make a bad situation worse by squandering their remaining resources. Just as they had done after the plague in 430, they began to hesitate and doubt themselves and their leaders. They elected a board of *probouloi* (advisors) who were given special authority to prepare motions for the assembly (8.1.1–3). The Athenians seem to have lost confidence in their ability to handle the emergency through established democratic procedures and institutions. Hagnon, the father of Theramenes, and Sophocles, the tragic playwright, are the only known *probouloi*. Both men had served the city well and had proven themselves to be loyal democrats, and there was not yet public talk of changing the constitution. The Athenians created this temporary board so that they could respond quickly to any pressing emergency that should arise. Lysias claims that the *probouloi* conspired against the democracy (12.65), but he is probably referring to their later service on the board of *sungrapheis* when they were reappointed in 411 and charged with the task of drafting a new constitution (*Ath. Pol.* 29.2). Therefore, it would be a mistake to view the election of the *probouloi* in 413 as representing the beginning of the oligarchic movement.[2] Still, their election suggests that the Athenians had serious doubt about their ability to withstand Sparta, and conspirators would later use such doubt to overthrow the democracy.

The Spartans prepared a fleet by seeking contributions from their allies, but they had difficulty deciding on a strategy. They received emissaries from Euboea, Lesbos, and Chios as well as competing requests for military support from Tissaphernes and Pharnabazus, the Persian satraps of Ionia and the Hellespont, who were eager to expel Athenian forces so they could collect tribute once again from the Greek cities in their territories. The Spartans decided first to assist Erythrae and Chios because of the ships and resources the Chians could provide, but an earthquake forced them to reduce their assistance to five triremes (8.5, 6). This was hardly the way to begin a major offensive that could challenge Athenian control of the Aegean. So when the winter of 413/412 came to an end, Athenian allies may have been ready to revolt, but the empire remained intact and the Spartans had accomplished very little.

In the summer of 412, the Spartans began again in earnest. They sent a fleet to Chios, which was intercepted by the Athenians before it could leave the Peloponnesian coast and was defeated in a battle at Spiraeum, a deserted Corinthian fort near Epidaurus. The remaining ships were prevented from sailing out of the harbor. The Spartans were so disheartened by their defeat that they refused to send reinforcements and even wanted to recall the forces that they had already sent out (8.8–11). Unfortunately for Athens, Alcibiades, who was still in King Agis' good graces, rushed out with a small contingent before news of the Spartan defeat could reach Chios. When he arrived, he told the Chians that additional forces were on their way. This trickery was enough to entice Chios to revolt, and now that Peloponnesian forces were active in the area, revolt spread to Erythrae and Clazomenae. The Peloponnesian fleet was welcomed when it arrived in Teos and Miletus, the Persians began negotiating a treaty with Sparta, and revolutions broke out in other cities, including Methymna and Mytilene. When the Athenians learned about Chios, they immediately voted to use their reserve funds and sent a fleet. They began an extended campaign to regain Chios and secured Samos by helping the Samian people overthrow the oligarchy and establish a democracy (8.12–22). For the rest of the war, Samos served as a base for Athenian operations, and the Samian people remained loyal to Athens even after the Battle of Aegospotami.

The Athenians began to make some headway by recovering Lesbos and defeating the Peloponnesian forces at Miletus, but the damage was already done (8.23–25). Upon the arrival of reinforcements, which Alcibiades had persuaded the enemy to send, the Athenian commanders decided to follow Phrynichus' advice and return to Samos rather than risk a battle (8.26–27). Thucydides praises Phrynichus for his caution (8.27.5). A victory would have helped the Athenians regain control of their empire, but they were outnumbered, and a defeat so soon after Sicily seemed too risky. However, Thucydides overstates the risks of such a battle and ignores the losses the Athenians suffered because of Phrynichus' retreat (Kagan 1987, 67–68). By ending the blockade of Miletus, the

---

[2] Ostwald (1986, 339–43); cf. Jameson (1971); contra Hignett (1952, 269); Harris (1990, 268); Munn (2000, 134–35).

Athenian campaign against Chios faltered and the Spartans mobilized their fleet. Rhodes revolted, Amorges was surrendered to Persia, and Peloponnesian forces later entered the Hellespont. Thucydides may have been right to praise Pericles for his conservative strategy at the start of the war when the empire was intact and it was uncertain whether a Spartan failure to defeat Athens might cause defection within the Peloponnesian League. Athens was facing a very different situation after Sicily, when its empire was in a state of revolt. By delaying to act decisively, the Athenians lost their chance to contain the revolutions breaking out among their allies and gave their enemy time to gather more forces. So for the remainder of the war, they responded with mixed results to the revolutions that continued to break out throughout their empire as Peloponnesian forces arrived with assistance.

Although Sparta now had a plan of action, it could not be fully executed, because of the inadequacy of Persian aid, disagreement within its leadership and among its allies, and an inability to defeat an Athenian fleet except when it was significantly outnumbered or at a considerable disadvantage. Part of the problem was that Sparta had too much area that it needed to cover from the Hellespont to Ionia, and the subject cities of Athens were unwilling to carry out operations beyond their own territories (Westlake 1979). In the winter of 412/411, Chios denied a request from the Spartan admiral Astyochus to provide Lesbos with military support. Astyochus retaliated by withholding aid from Chios until Athenian fortifications on the island were almost finished (8.32, 40). The Spartans lost confidence in Astyochus and sent him a board of advisors, which included Lichas. The board was to oversee the admiral's actions and was instructed to replace him with Antisthenes if necessary (8.38.3–4, 39.2). In the meantime, Alcibiades fell out of favor with King Agis. He fled to Tissaphernes and advised the satrap to reduce the support provided to the Peloponnesian forces so that Persia could regain control over the Aegean and the coast of Asia Minor once the Athenians and the Spartans had weakened one another through a war of attrition (8.45–46). Tissaphernes welcomed such advice because Lichas had already angered the satrap by opposing terms of a treaty that Chalcideus and Therimenes had previously negotiated (8.43.3–4). Whether the final version of the treaty with Persia was any better than the earlier drafts, Sparta still had to concede Asia Minor to the Great King. The treaty stipulated that Persia would provide pay for Peloponnesian sailors and furnish the King's fleet for joint operations, but even these concessions served Persian interests (8.58). They insured that the Spartans would not become so strapped for money that they would have to plunder his territory to pay their troops (8.57.1).[3]

The Rise of the Four Hundred

The Athenians failed to capitalize on the political disarray hampering Spartan military effort because they soon became enmeshed in more serious internal discord of their own. Thucydides gives a negative portrayal of the oligarchs. He emphasizes the

---

[3] For Spartan negotiations with Persia and the differences in the drafts of the treaty, see Lévy (1983); Lewis (1977, 83–107); Hornblower (2008, 800–801, 854–55, 924–25).

political machinations and the campaign of violence that they carried out to overthrow the democracy. The *Athēnaiōn Politeia*, by contrast, presents them in a more positive light by focusing mainly on the motions that the conspirators presented to the assembly and by highlighting how they were responding to doubts that their fellow citizens had about the merits of their democracy. The genres and the aims of the two authors explain some of the differences (Westlake 1973, 196). Thucydides focuses on Athenian civil unrest only as it relates to the Peloponnesian War while the *Athēnaiōn Politeia* is primarily concerned with the constitutional history of Athens. As a result, their accounts are in some ways complementary and can be used together to fill in the gaps and omissions that exist in each (Hornblower 2008, 945–46; cf. Harris 1990, 25).

For example, we know from Thucydides (as discussed above in "The Revolt of Athenian Allies") that a board of *probouloi* were first elected in 413 shortly after the Athenians learned about Sicily (8.1.3). The *Athēnaiōn Politeia* explains that the board had ten members but neglects to mention when or how the *probouloi* were appointed (29.2). It is also possible to use one account to correct the other. Thucydides mentions that ten *sungrapheis* were elected in 411 with full powers to draft laws and bring to the assembly whichever motions they believed would best serve the city (8.67.1). The *Athēnaiōn Politeia*, by contrast, states that twenty *sungrapheis* were elected in 411 to work in conjunction with the ten *probouloi* (29.2). It is likely that Thucydides provides the wrong number of *sungrapheis* (Rhodes 1981, 372–73; Ostwald 1986: 369; Hornblower 2008: 948–49). Whether the board consisted of ten or thirty members is in itself of minor significance. However, by neglecting to mention that the ten *probouloi* were reappointed to work with twenty newly appointed *sungrapheis,* Thucydides fails to reveal how the oligarchs coopted a democratically elected board in order to legitimize the radical proposals that the *sungrapheis* would present to the assembly (Gomme et al., 1981, 164–65).

There are other differences between Thucydides and the *Athēnaiōn Politeia* that are more serious and clearly go beyond minor omission because of the genre of the work or error from the sources. They present the Four Hundred so differently that the two accounts cannot be fully reconciled.[4] The *Athēnaiōn Politeia* states that the Five Thousand were elected and ratified the constitution of the Four Hundred (30.1, 32.1), while Thucydides suggests that the Four Hundred refused to convene the Five Thousand or even publish their registers (8.89.2, 92.11, 93.2). More problematic are the "constitution of the present" and "the constitution of the future," which the *Athēnaiōn Politeia* discusses in great detail (30–31), but are completely absent from Thucydides. Ultimately one must decide whether to agree with Thucydides that the Four Hundred were opportunists who seized power through a campaign of violence when Athens was weak or with the *Athēnaiōn Politeia* that Sicily caused many Athenians to begin to doubt the merits of their democracy. Thucydides has not always fared well in modern debates. Westlake

---

[4] Although Thucydides' account shows how the oligarchs relied on ideology, propaganda, and even democratic procedures to gain control of the city, he clearly depicts violence as the essential weapon in their arsenal (contra Taylor 2002).

(1973, 196–98) believes that Thucydides' negative view of the oligarchs caused him to emphasize their violence, while the omissions in the *Athēnaiōn Politeia* are from the use of sources that were favorable to the Four Hundred. Harris (1990, 267–72) concludes that Thucydides' views on the downfall of Athens influenced his narrative of the Four Hundred. Shear (2011, 20–21) suggests that lawsuits brought against the Four Hundred after they were overthrown led Thucydides to emphasize civil unrest and ignore the constitutional debate.

It is possible that Thucydides wrote his account while he was still in exile, and he relied on information from informants who fled Athens after the Four Hundred were overthrown (see Gomme et al. 1981, 251–54). However, this does not make his account less credible, and it does not explain why he neglected to mention the measures that oligarchs proposed or chose to present them so unfavorably. If former members of the Four Hundred were his main source, he would have had plenty of information on their legislation, and he would have been more likely to give them a positive spin. There is, however, no reason to assume that any omission is necessarily from a lack of information because of his exile. For example, Thucydides neglects to name Phrynichus' assassins (8.92.2). This does not prove that he wrote his history before the assassins were publicly honored (see Meiggs and Lewis 1988, 260–63; Lys. 13.70–72; Lycurg. *Leoc.* 1.112). He may have decided not to include additional information about Phrynichus' assassination, in order to keep his readers focused on the events of 411 as they were unfolding (Hornblower 2008, 1019–21; contra Gomme et al. 1981, 309–10). Thucydides' account of the Four Hundred certainly has limitations, weaknesses, and deficiencies, but the same is also true of the *Athēnaiōn Politeia*. In the end, Thucydides' version is to be preferred because he offers a more compelling explanation for the reasons that the oligarchy was so short lived, as a review of his narrative of the Four Hundred shows.

Thucydides begins his discussion on the overthrow of the democracy by describing how the conspirators had competing private motives, personal agendas, and ideological biases that caused them to join forces. Yet again, Alcibiades was the catalyst. Not content to remain in Tissaphernes' court as an advisor to the satrap, he attempted to orchestrate his return by telling influential Athenians stationed at Samos that he could secure Persian aid if the Athenians would dissolve the democracy and recall him. He was received favorably by some trierarchs and other prominent men, some of whom were already considering how they could overthrow the democracy (8.47). They approved the plan because they wanted to gain control of the government, they would personally benefit from the King's aid since they bore the greatest expenses for the war, and they believed that with Persian support Athens could defeat Sparta (8.48.1). The hope of Persian pay was enough to keep the rank and file quiet (8.48.3). Only Phrynichus distrusted Alcibiades. He thought Alcibiades was looking only after his own interests, Athenian allies were not any less likely to revolt if the Athenians changed their constitution, and overtures to Persia were useless (8.48.4–6). He was correct, but he failed to warn his fellow citizens about the mistakes that they were about to make. Phyrnichus' hatred for Alcibiades and fear that the democrats would welcome him back caused

Phrynichus to become a zealot oligarch only after Alcibiades fell out of favor with the conspirators by failing to win over Tissaphernes (8.68.3).[5]

Once the conspirators had made sufficient progress in the camp, they sent Pisander and other envoys to Athens to gather support for their cause. The envoys presented their plan to the assembly, which relented because Pisander told the Athenians that they could always change the government back and Athens was in such dire straits the Athenians were willing do whatever was necessary to avoid losing the war. Pisander had generals who might oppose their plan removed from their command, and he rallied political associations (*sunōmosiai*) that were hostile to the democracy (8.53–54). He then left Athens to negotiate unsuccessfully with Tissaphernes. The political associations prepared for his return to Athens by killing a number of prominent democrats, including Androcles, and anyone who openly expressed opposition to them. These violent acts so terrified the Athenians that they refused to speak out in public against the conspirators because they assumed their numbers were larger than they actually were (8.65–66). Far from being implausible, Thucydides' account explains quite clearly why the oligarchs were met with so little resistance when Pisander returned to Athens in the summer of 411 to overthrow the democracy.

An assembly was called at which the *sungrapheis* were elected with full power to bring forward any motion that they believed would help Athens. Then at the next meeting of the assembly, which was held at Colonus, outside of the walls of Athens, the *sungrapheis* presented their proposals. The Four Hundred were elected without any opposition, and they were granted the power to govern Athens and convene the Five Thousand as they deemed appropriate (8.67, 69.1). Because Colonus is so close to the city, it is unlikely that fear of the Spartan army stationed at Decelea kept Athenians away from the meeting (Gomme et al.1981: 165–67; Taylor 2002: 103–104). Still, a meeting of the Athenian assembly at such an unprecedented location would have been highly symbolic and would have given the Athenians the impression that its outcome was a fait accompli (Lang 1948, 280–81; Kagan 1987, 147–49). After the meeting, the Four Hundred, armed with daggers and accompanied by 120 youths, went to the Council of Five Hundred. They dismissed the councilors and took over the chamber unopposed (8.69.3–4). If one examines each step of their campaign in isolation, it is surprising how easy it was for the Four Hundred to carry out their conspiracy when they had so few supporters.

If instead one considers their entire campaign in its totality, the ease with which they accomplished their goals becomes understandable. Thucydides suggests the oligarchs did not encounter active resistance from the rest of the population, because they carried out a well-organized and sustained war against the democracy on many fronts. They used ideology, violence, terror, and grassroots networks to prevent the

---

[5] Phrynichus attempted to prevent Alcibiades' return by colluding with Astyochus (8.50–51). It is not entirely clear how he thought his scheme would work, but he somehow was able to avoid being accused of treason for his secret correspondences with the enemy (see Kagan 1987, 124–30).

democrats from mobilizing an effective resistance. Athens was especially vulnerable because the majority of the population was in so much despair after the defeat in Sicily and was even clinging to the vain hope that the conspirators might actually be able to secure Persian aid. Finally, many of the most ardent supporters of the democracy could not help because they were away from Athens serving in the navy stationed at Samos.

The Removal of the Four Hundred

Although the sailors did not object when the conspirators first proposed their plan, their subsequent actions show that the rise and fall of the Four Hundred hinged on them. When they learned that the oligarchs had seized control of Athens, many of them wanted to sail home to restore the democracy, but they chose to stay in Ionia because the Peloponnesian fleet was active in the area. Thrasybulus and Thrasyllus emerged as the leaders of the democratic forces, which swore oaths of allegiance to the democracy, generals and captains suspected of treason were replaced, and the sailors declared themselves to be the *dēmos* and the city to be in a state of revolt (8.75.1–2, 76.2–3). Alcibiades now offered his services to the democratic forces and won their good will. Thucydides even praises him for preventing them from sailing back to Athens, because a departure of the fleet from Ionia would have resulted in mass revolts among the allies (8.86.4). The Four Hundred sent envoys to Samos in an effort to win over the navy. When they returned to Athens unsuccessful and the Four Hundred learned that the navy was working with Alcibiades, dissension arose within their ranks between the extremists and the moderates. Theramenes and his supporters attempted to win the goodwill of the people by calling on his colleagues to hand over the government to the Five Thousand (8.89). In contrast to the *Athēnaiōn Politeia*, which presents Theramenes as a moderate working to help his fellow citizens (28.5), Thucydides suggests the Four Hundred collapsed because of personal rivalries within their own ranks (8.89.3). He may be going too far in denying political motivations for Theramenes' actions. However, supporters and collaborators of the Thirty subsequently exaggerated the extent to which Theramenes can be viewed as a moderate in order to justify their own actions during the civil war.[6]

Because the navy refused to cooperate with the Four Hundred and there was now dissension within the ranks of the oligarchs, the extremists—Phrynichus, Aristarchus, Pisander, and Antiphon—were willing to agree to peace with Sparta on any terms. They began to construct a defensive wall in Eëtioneia. Theramenes accused them of building this structure so the Spartan navy could enter the Piraeus (8.90.1–3). Phrynichus was then assassinated in the agora, and hoplites imprisoned one of the generals in the

---

[6] For the myth of Theramenes, see Harding (1974); Lehmann (1976, 282–88); Engels (1993).

Piraeus. Theramenes was sent to the Piraeus to restore order, but instead called on the hoplites to destroy the wall (8.92). Finally, there was a general panic when news came to Athens that Euboea had revolted. As Thucydides explains, Sparta could have ended the war by sailing against the Piraeus. This maneuver would have forced the Athenian navy to return to Athens and the Athenians would have lost control of Ionia and the Hellespont (8.96). The Spartans, however, kept to their old ways and failed to follow up on the victory in Euboea. Fearing for their safety, the Athenians were now quick to act. For the first time since the start of the civil war, they called for a meeting of the assembly in the Pnyx. The Athenians deposed the Four Hundred, the Five Thousand were placed in power, and Pisander along with some other leading oligarchs fled to the Spartan camp at Decelea (8.97–98).

The problem with the constitutional debate in the *Athēnaiōn Politeia* is that it cannot explain why the rule of the Four Hundred lasted only four months. Some conspirators were certainly serious in their efforts to reform the Athenian constitution (see Osborne 2003; Shear 2011, 41–53). However, their discussions remained private until 411, and these private conversations had very little impact on the events leading up to the rule of the Four Hundred. This is why Thucydides does not mention Pythodorus' involvement in the motions presented to the Athenian assembly (*Ath. Pol.* 29.2) and ignores Cleitophon's rider (*Ath. Pol.* 29.3). These omissions were not a result of Thucydides' disinterest in the inner workings of the Athenian democracy. The content of these motions could not help him explain to his reader why the assembly voted in favor of the oligarchs' demands. The Athenians were in a desperate situation that made them willing to do whatever was necessary to prevent a Spartan victory. After the Four Hundred came to power, the Athenians realized that the oligarchs could not win the war and even believed that the Four Hundred were willing to betray Athens to the enemy. So the Athenians immediately rallied together to depose the Four Hundred, and their rule quickly came to an end. More than anything else, the vain hope that Persia might become an Athenian ally and the absence of the most ardent supporters of the democracy from Athens explain why the oligarchs gained control of the city so easily. Still, the conspirators had to cow the Athenians by carrying out a campaign of terror and violence.

Nevertheless, 411 was an important year for the debate on the Athenian constitution because it marks the point when private discussions among the opponents of the democracy were brought to light. After the democracy was restored, democrats responded in kind with their own search for the *patrios politeia*. Then when the Thirty came to power under the same pretense as the Four Hundred, the constitutional debate was only heightened (Wolpert 2002, 35– 42). This explains why the *Athēnaiōn Politeia* places so much emphasis on these constitutional maneuvers. The author relies on sources that transposed a highly contentious public debate from the fourth century onto the events of 411. Thucydides, by contrast, writing shortly after the Four Hundred, rightly calls attention to the public fears and private agendas that made Athens so vulnerable to revolution and the violence that prevented loyal democrats from stopping the oligarchs.

The Fall of Athens

In light of Thucydides' assessment of Pericles in Book 2, his effusive praise of the Five Thousand cannot help be startling to his readers:

> Not least remarkable is the fact that for the first time in my lifetime the Athenians clearly enjoyed good government. It was a judicious blend geared to the interests of the few and the many, and this fact first buoyed up the city after the wretched condition into which it had fallen.[7]

The accomplishments of the Athenians under the Five Thousand pale in comparison to their achievements under Pericles' leadership. Most contemporary Athenians must not have shared Thucydides' views about the Five Thousand; otherwise, they would not have restored the full democracy shortly after the Battle of Cyzicus in 410.[8] This is yet further proof that Thucydides was right about the reasons that the Four Hundred came to power. The Athenians were not suddenly interested in having an extensive public debate on their constitution when at any moment the enemy could be marching against the city. They were vulnerable to revolution because they were afraid of losing the war. They saw Sparta helping Athenian allies to revolt and working with Persia to defeat them, and they no longer had resources in reserve to hold Sparta off. Because of their victory at Cyzicus, they regained such confidence in themselves and their war effort that they restored the full democracy. The transition probably occurred without any serious opposition. They had under the Four Hundred demanded that the oligarchs hand over the government to the Five Thousand as a way of secretly advocating for democracy (8.92.11). After Cyzicus, there was now no longer a reason for such secrecy.

In the context of Book 8, Thucydides' praise of the Five Thousand is understandable. As Connor (1984, 227) explains, "The easy inference that if democracy has proved pernicious, oligarchy must be beneficial is implicitly shattered through the [Thucydides'] treatment of the Athenian oligarchs. The book even goes one step further, in pointing to an alternative to both democracy and oligarchy." Thucydides' objections to the Four Hundred did not stop him from giving Phrynichus and Antiphon the praise that he thought they deserved (8.27.5, 68.1–2). Personal interests may have motivated Alcibiades to work with Sparta, Persia, and even Athenian oligarchs. Yet Thucydides acknowledges that Alcibiades saved the city and even helped the democratic cause by preventing the navy from abandoning Ionia (8.86.4). He refuses to view politics as monolithic or use rigid taxonomies to explain how people and organizations operate.

---

[7] 97.2, translated in Ostwald (1986, 395 n. 199). For the bibliography on Thucydides' political views, see Ober (1998, 52–53 n. 1).

[8] In response to De Ste. Croix (1956) and Sealey (1967, 111–32), Rhodes (1972) argues convincingly that the intermediate regime of the Five Thousand restricted political rights to men of hoplite status and therefore cannot be considered a full democracy.

The actions of individuals appear prominently in Book 8 not because Thucydides changed his views on historical causation (see Stadter, chapter 17 in this volume), but because conflict and dissension were now the driving forces of the war. The book also shows that Sicily did not cause Athens to surrender to Sparta. The Athenians still could have escaped defeat if they had been able to overcome their own differences and work together to pursue the best interests of the city. This is why Thucydides praises the constitution of the Five Thousand (see Jaffe, chapter 23 in this volume). He saw in the intermediate regime a way for the Athenians to move beyond past extremism and factionalism that threatened to destroy Athens. However, the actions of the Four Hundred were too deleterious for the Athenians to overcome. A residue of distrust and suspicion remained among the Athenians long after the oligarchs were deposed. Fear that some of their fellow citizens might still be harboring opposition to the democracy (and even plotting against it) caused them to put on trial the generals who led the forces at Arginusae. Athens was as a result left with inexperienced commanders for the fleet that fought at Aegospotami. So the Four Hundred may have ruled for only four months, but their rule lasted long enough to seal Athens' fate.

Book 8 is challenging to Thucydides' readers not only because it is incomplete, but also because the war changed fundamentally after Sicily. Athens could no longer win, but it was not yet defeated. Sparta could have quickly ended the war if it had responded immediately after the destruction of the Athenian fleet in Sicily or if it had sent its navy to Athens after the revolt of Euboea. Yet Sparta was still not prepared to act decisively. Although Athenian allies were eager to revolt, they were afraid to risk the consequences and were unable to act in concert. Athens might have been able to contain or even prevent revolutions from breaking out within the empire if it had responded quickly to the new threats that emerged after Sicily. Fear, hesitation, and delay weakened Athens and caused it to succumb to a civil war that unleashed destructive forces that could not be contained. Still, the Athenians proved themselves to be resilient in the face of adversity. They continued to withstand Sparta and were able to recover many of their allies. The war changed after Sicily, but the Athenians and Spartans responded to the new threats and dangers in surprisingly familiar ways.

REFERENCES

Connor, W. Robert. 1984. *Thucydides*. Princeton: Princeton University Press.
Cornford, Francis McDonald. 1907. *Thucydides Mythistoricus*. London: Edward Arnold.
De Ste. Croix, G. E. M. 1956. "The Constitution of the Five Thousand." *Historia* 1956: 1–23.
Engels, Johannes. 1993. "Der Michigan-Papyrus über Theramenes und die Ausbildung des 'Theramenes-Mythos.'" *ZPE* 99: 125–55.
Foster, Edith. 2010. *Thucydides, Pericles, and Periclean Imperialism*. Cambridge: Cambridge University Press.
Gomme, A. W., A. Andrewes, and K. J. Dover. 1981. *An Historical Commentary on Thucydides*. Vol. 5, *Book VIII*. Oxford: Clarendon.
Harding, Phillip. 1974. "The Theramenes Myth." *Phoenix* 28: 101–11.

Harris, Edward Monroe. 1990. "The Constitution of the Five Thousand." *HSCP* 93: 243–80.
Hignett, Charles. 1952. *A History of the Athenian Constitution to the End of the Fifth Century B.C.* Oxford: Clarendon.
Hornblower, Simon. 1987. *Thucydides*. Baltimore: Johns Hopkins University.
Hornblower, Simon 2008. *A Commentary on Thucydides*. Vol. 3, *Books 5.25–8.109*. Oxford: Clarendon.
Jameson, Michael H. 1971. "Sophocles and the Four Hundred." *Historia* 20: 541–68.
Kagan, Donald. 1987. *The Fall of the Athenian Empire*. Ithaca: Cornell University Press.
Lang, Mabel. 1948. "The Revolution of the 400." *AJP* 69: 272–89.
Lehmann, Gustav. 1976. "Ein Historiker namens Kratippos." *ZPE* 23: 265–88.
Lévy, Edmund. 1983. "Les trois traités entre Sparte et le Roi." *BCH* 107: 221–41.
Lewis, David M. 1977. *Sparta and Persia*. Leiden:Brill.
Meiggs, Russell, and David Lewis, eds. 1988. *A Selection of Greek Historical Inscriptions to the End of the Fifth Century B.C.* Rev. ed. Oxford: Clarendon.
Munn, Mark H. 2000. *The School of History: Athens in the Age of Socrates*. Berkeley: University of California Press.
Ober, Josiah. 1998. *Political Dissent in Democratic Athens: Intellectual Critics of Popular Rule*. Princeton: Princeton University Press.
Osborne, Robin. 2003. "Changing the Discourse." In *Popular Tyranny: Sovereignty and Its Discontents in Ancient Greece*, edited by Kathryn A. Morgan, 251–72. Austin: University of Texas Press.
Ostwald, Martin. 1986. *From Popular Sovereignty to the Sovereignty of Law: Law, Society, and Politics in Fifth-Century Athens*. California: University of California Press.
Rhodes, P. J. 1981. *A Commentary on the Aristotelian Athenaion Politeia*. Oxford: Clarendon.
Romilly, Jacqueline de. 1965. "L'optimisme de Thucydide et le jugement de l'historien sur Périclès (Thuc. II 65)." *REG* 78: 557–75.
Sealey, Raphael. 1967. *Essays in Greek Politics*. New York: Manyland Books.
Shear, Julia L. 2011. *Polis and Revolution: Responding to Oligarchy in Classical Athens*. Cambridge: Cambridge University Press.
Taylor, Martha C. 2002. "Implicating the *Demos*: A Reading of Thucydides on the Rise of the Four Hundred." *JHS* 122: 91–108.
Taylor, Martha C. 2010. *Thucydides, Pericles, and the Idea of Athens in the Peloponnesian War*. Cambridge: Cambridge University Press.
Westlake, H. D. 1968. *Individuals in Thucydides*. Cambridge: Cambridge University Press.
Westlake, H. D. 1973. "The Subjectivity of Thucydides: His Treatment of the Four Hundred at Athens." *Bulletin of the John Rylands University Library* 56: 193–218.
Westlake, H. D. 1979. "Ionians in the Ionian War." *CQ* 29: 9–44.
Wolpert, Andrew. 2002. *Remembering Defeat: Civil War and Civic Memory in Ancient Athens*. Baltimore: Johns Hopkins University Press.

SECTION II

THUCYDIDEAN HISTORIOGRAPHY

CHAPTER 11

WRITING HISTORY IMPLICITLY THROUGH REFINED STRUCTURING

HUNTER R. RAWLINGS III

Aims, Method, and Audience

In a few passages in his own name (1.1, 1.20–23, 2.48, 5.20, 5.26, 6.54–60), Thucydides self-consciously reveals his aims and methods, and his intended audience. In doing so, he contrasts his principles and procedures with those of his predecessors, among whom he probably had Herodotus chiefly in mind, since the latter also wrote a lengthy account of a major war, a work that was apparently well-regarded by a wide audience. Herodotus had made clear his own method of writing history in statements such as this one (2.123.1): "Whoever finds such stories credible, let him make use of the things said by the Egyptians. It is a principle underlying my entire *logos* that I write down the things reported by each witness in the oral tradition." Thucydides directly answers that procedure in these words (1.22.2): "As for the actual events of this war, I did not think it appropriate to write down what I learned from any sources that came my way, nor even what appeared to me to have happened, but I subjected both what I myself saw, and what I heard from others, to the most stringent tests of accuracy in each case. I went to great pains to find my facts, since those who were present at each event did not say the same things about them, but instead reported as their bias or memory determined." In addition to asserting the superiority of his critical analysis of oral sources, Thucydides extols the value of written sources on several occasions: see particularly 6.54–59 and 7.8–10.

Similarly, Thucydides distinguishes his purpose and his material from those pursued by his predecessors. They "turn to whatever material lies at hand," and their "search for the truth is careless" (1.20.3). They put their accounts together "motivated more by pleasing their audience than by attending to the truth, since much of their material has from the passage of time won its way to the dubious status of myth." He, on the other hand, has "founded his facts on the clearest evidence," and the reader "would not go wrong by trusting his account" (1.21.1).[1]

Finally, Thucydides claims a different readership: "Perhaps the lack of mythic material in my account will appear rather unappealing to the listening audience; but if those (few) who will want to study the clear truth of what happened and is going to happen again in similar or related form according to the human condition judge my account useful, it will be sufficient [for my purposes]. It has been composed as an enduring possession to be read (heard) over time rather than as a competition-piece to be read (heard) on the spot" (1.22.4).

In ancient Greece almost all "reading" entailed listening to someone read a text aloud. I take the verb "to be heard" in the last sentence as equivalent to our "reading," and construe it with both phrases, "possession to be heard over time," and "competition-piece to be heard on the spot." (I make the case for this new interpretation of 1.22.4 in Rawlings 2016.) Thucydides emphasizes that he writes for an elite audience, a discriminating audience that will want to study the truth rather than indulge in immediate listening pleasure. In a number of passages, he stipulates what his "ideal reader" is to do with his text. In 1.10.5, 1.21.2, 1.22.4, 2.48.3, 5.20.2, and 5.68.1–2 the verb is *skopein*, "to study," "to consider"; in 1.23.5, 5.26.2, 5.26.3, and 6.55.1 he uses other intellectually active verbs of "judging," "seeking," "discovering," "judging right," and "knowing." Thucydides thus asks his reader to think about what he is reading, to consider historical questions, to make judgments about events and issues as they appear in his account.

Explicit Structure

With this kind of careful and engaged reader in mind, Thucydides makes it clear that he is not going to construct a loose-jointed narrative aimed at listening pleasure. He announces the organizing principle for his narrative in 2.1, at the outset of his account of the war itself: "[The war] has been written sequentially, as each event occurred, by summer and winter." He repeats this principle in his so-called second introduction, 5.26: "The same Thucydides the Athenian has also written the following account sequentially, as each event occurred, by summers and winters, until the Lacedaemonians and their allies ended the empire of the Athenians, and occupied the Long Walls and the Piraeus." The historian also marks the end of each year in his account, twelve times explicitly with his own name, in "tag lines" of this type: "And the winter ended, and the (ninth) year of this war which Thucydides composed."

This emphasis on treating events *in sequence by season* contrasts sharply with the work of Herodotus, which was organized around *logoi*, stories about peoples and places that came up in the course of Herodotus' broad scan of ancient civilizations. Note, for

---

[1] On first person statements in Thucydides, see de Bakker, chapter 14 in this volume; for Thucydides' concept of truth, see de Jonge, chapter 37 likewise in this volume.

example, this passage in 2.35.1: "I go along lengthening the *logos* about Egypt, since it has the most wonders and presents physical structures beyond description over the entire land; for these reasons more will be said about it" (similarly, cf. 3.60.1 on Samos). And see 1.95.1: "From here my *logos* goes on to inquire about Cyrus, who this man is who destroyed the rule of Croesus, and about the Persians, in what way they took the leadership of Asia." And in 4.30.1, "I wonder (in fact from the beginning my *logos* sought after additions)...." In the last two passages the *logos* has an active role, almost as if it had a will of its own apart from the author Herodotus. The story tells itself, meandering as it sees fit.

In these passages Herodotus reveals the expansive nature of his narrative, his openness to supplements and digressions that naturally occur in the course of his account, his acquiescence in the story's natural progression from point to point. Herodotus' *logoi* span huge realms of space and time, crossing borders and generations with ease, and they provide encyclopedic information about customs, landmarks, and political and military events. The author's skill in storytelling, and the reader's pleasure in listening to stories that comprehensively describe regions and peoples and the histories of dynasties, dictate the shape of Herodotus' account (though we shall see at the end of this chapter that Herodotus significantly altered that structure when he came to the culminating section of his work, Xerxes' invasion of Greece).

Thucydides is far more stringent in his selectivity, and he insists upon rigid control of his narrative: he focuses all his attention upon the war, omitting most cultural and natural material and limiting digressions to a minimum; he maintains a rigorous chronology by treating events in the order in which they occurred, and by generally interrupting narratives of operations in discrete theaters of the war when a season ends, then resuming them in the next one.

The result is concentration upon one war as the sole subject, upon narrative discipline and compactness, upon exclusion of extraneous material, and upon strict structuring of time and space. As I mentioned before, audience pleasure in extended, ramifying stories is sacrificed in this scheme. The gains are in historiographical precision and in narrative intensity: the reader is led to pay attention to each discrete episode the historian chooses to present.

THE USE OF SYNTACTICAL STRUCTURE TO CREATE IMPLICIT MEANING

Within these narrative confines, how does Thucydides present history to his elite reader? For the most part, he does so implicitly, not explicitly. As Thomas Hobbes notably said in his note "To the readers" of his translation of Thucydides, "But *Thucydides* is one, who, though he never digresse to read a Lecture, Morall or Politicall, upon his owne Text, nor enter into mens hearts, further then the actions themselves evidently guide him, is yet accounted the most Politique Historiographer that ever writ. The reason whereof I take to bee this: He filleth his Narrations with that choice of matter, and ordereth them with that Judgement, and with such perspicuity and efficacy expresseth himself, that, as *Plutarch* saith, he maketh his *Auditor* a *Spectator*." Structure, then, not overtly offered opinion, marks Thucydides' method and reveals his purpose: to enable the reader to study history and thereby detect its complex and recurring patterns. Hence it is structure that the careful reader must observe and delineate in Thucydides' text.

Thucydides designs his text on multiple levels, from the smallest to the largest scale. As every reader of Thucydides' Greek quickly recognizes, his sentences evince to an extreme degree the characteristic Greek *men . . . de* construction, the balanced antithesis of parallel elements. In Thucydides' case, the formal syntax very often contrasts the specific elements of *appearance* on the one hand, and of *reality* on the other. As Adam Parry (1981) cogently argued in his Ph.D. dissertation, Thucydides relentlessly exposes the difference between words and deeds, between opinion and fact, between openly expressed pretexts and underlying motives, between intention and results, between conception and actuality. He thus highlights the ways in which human language (*logos* in Greek) attempts to describe or to control reality (*ergon* in Greek), and often winds up failing to do so. Many of Thucydides' sentences portray this effort, and he regularly uses several synonyms of *logos* and *ergon* to draw the telling contrast between words and deeds. The most striking such statements are put into the mouths of political leaders who betray their own disingenuousness through dishonest rhetoric, which is made manifest to the careful reader through syntactical clues. Cleon's speech to the Athenian Assembly in 3.37–40 (see especially chapter 38) is particularly noteworthy: he assaults the use of sophisticated rhetoric by other political leaders in language that is itself highly antithetical and cleverly paradoxical: Thucydides thus makes Cleon condemn himself out of his own mouth!

Here, then, at the level of the sentence, is a telling example of Thucydides' use of structure to reveal meaning to close readers.[2] The historian saw the Peloponnesian War not simply as an intense military conflict, but as a wrecker of civilized norms. His famous analysis of civil war (3.82–84), cited by John Adams and other American Founders as a warning against societal breakdown, deconstructs the ways in which political factions pervert language to achieve their ends. In chapter 82 he demonstrates this perversion in sentences of condensed incongruity. "They willfully changed the accepted relationship between words and reality: reckless audacity came to be considered the courage of an ally; prudent hesitation, specious cowardice; moderation was considered to be a cover for weakness; an intelligent perspective became an incapacity to commit to anything. Frantic violence constituted manliness; cautious plotting a justifiable means of self-defense" (3.82.4; modified Crawley translation).

Here Thucydides *evinces* revolutionary slogans in the structure of his language, thereby giving the reader a palpable taste of extremism. Rhetoric exposed is politics grasped: the reader comes to know the nature of revolution through careful attention to

---

[2] On the structure of Thucydides' complex sentences, see Rusten, chapter 13 in this volume.

language itself. Thucydides' tightly controlled antitheses leave an indelible impression in his readers' consciousness. Structure produces meaning, all the more so if we remember that almost all of Thucydides' "readers" were listeners, in the sense that they were listening to someone read a text aloud to a small group. The sound of the sentence made the act of "reading" more intense and vivid than in our case, which is generally solitary and silent. "Close reading" by Thucydides' elite audience meant group reading that no doubt led to discussion and enhanced appreciation of the form as well as of the meaning of the prose. For contemporary examples of such group reading, see Xenophon, *Memorabilia* 1.6.14; Plato, *Theatetus*, opening passage; *Parmenides*, 127b–d; *Phaedo*, 97bc–98b; *Phaedrus*, 228a–b.

THE USE OF ARCHITECTURAL PARALLELISM TO CREATE IMPLICIT MEANING

Just as Thucydides uses structure at the micro level of the sentence to unveil fundamental aspects of human nature, so he employs parallelism at the macro level of the entire work to draw the perceptive reader's attention to recurring patterns in history. Thucydides divides his twenty-seven-year-long war into two ten-year wars with a precarious, essentially meaningless truce in the middle (see 5.26 for his delineation of these periods). As I argued in 1981, the historian draws numerous parallels between the two periods of "open war," and signals the parallelism by means of recurring phrases, cross-references, and explicit and implicit comparisons among cities, leaders, and situations in the two periods of constant conflict. The historiographical advantage of thus defining and highlighting two wars of Homeric length is patent: Thucydides amplifies his central claim that "his" war is the greatest in Hellenic history, far surpassing those described by Homer and Herodotus in length, intensity, destruction, and significance.

The division into "Books" that we see in our texts of Thucydides is not the historian's own and, in fact, there were three different divisions of his work in antiquity, all the product of Alexandrian scholars. In considering Thucydides' own architecture, then, we should not be distracted by the Book division of the text. We should instead attend to the historian's own markers. When we do so, we note, first of all, a remarkable degree of correspondence between the introductions to the two ten-year wars, best seen schematically in Figure 1.

The parallelism in treatment is particularly poignant in the repeated use of key terms for causality, in the provision of ancient background, in the placement of major speeches, and in the focus upon related but contrasting Athenian leaders of the two wars, Pericles in the first, Nicias and Alcibiades in the second. Symmetry between groups of speeches (Figure 2) is especially striking because the historian had considerable latitude in including or not including polished speeches in his text. That Thucydides chose to create complex rhetorical sets addressing similar

Book 1		Book VI, 1–93	
Introduction and Archaeology of mainland Greece	1–19	Introduction and Archaeology of Sicily	1–5
Methodology and *alethestate prophasis*	20–23	*Alethestate prophasis*	6–7
Corcyraean Question Speeches of Corcyraeans and Corinthians at Athens: should Athens ally with Corcyra? The real question: the coming war with Sparta. In a second assembly the Athenians reverse their earlier decision and accept the alliance	24–55	Sicilian Question Speeches of Nicias and Alcibiades at Athens: should Athens support her ally Egesta? The real question: the conquest of Sicily Nicias fails to persuade the Athenians to change their minds	8–26
The problem of Potidaea Troubles in the Athenian Empire	56–66	Preparations for the expedition The incident of the Herms Internal dissension in Athens	27–32
Conference at Sparta Speeches of: Corinthians Athenians Archidamus Spartan ephor	67–88	Conference at Syracuse Speeches of: Hermocrates Athenagoras Syracusan general	33–41
The Pentecontaetia How a unified, aggressive and resilient Athens acquired her empire	89–118	The Athenians in Sicily The Athenians are hesitant and militarily ineffective because of dissension among the generals	42–52
The second conference at Sparta: Speech of the Corinthians	119–125		
Pericles charged by Sparta with blood guilt Digression on Pausanias and Themistocles, one Spartan, one Athenian	126–139	Alcibiades charged by Athens with sacrilege Digression on Harmodius and Aristogeiton and their effect on Hippias' tyranny	53–61
		The Athenians before Syracuse: Nicias fails to follow up his advantage and the Athenians lose their opportunity to end the war quickly with a victory	62–75
		Conference at Camarina Speeches of: Hermocrates Euphemus, an Athenian	76–88
Pericles' speech at Athens calling for war against Sparta	140–144	Alcibiades' speech at Sparta calling for war against Athens	89–92
Summary of the speech's effect: *Arche* of the first ten-year war	1.145–2.1	Summary of the speech's effect: *Arche* of the second ten-year war	93

FIGURE 1 Parallel Structures, Books 1 and 6.

I				VI	
Corcyraeans (32–36)		Athens		Nicias	(9–14)
Corinthians (37–43)				Alcibiades	(16–18)
				Nicias	(20–23)
Corinthians (68–71)				Hermocrates	(33–34)
Athenians (73–78)		Sparta	Syracuse	Athenagoras	(36–40)
Archidamus (80–85)				Syracusan general	(41)
Spartan ephor (86)					
Corinthians (120–124)		Sparta	Camarina	Hermocrates	(76–80)
				Euphemus	(82–87)
Pericles (140–144)		Athens	Sparta	Alcibiades	(89–92)

FIGURE 2 Parallel Speeches, Books 1 and 6.

topics at parallel places in the two ten-year wars reveals his purpose: to create in the reader's mind the strong impression that a major war is again beginning, and that comparison of the choices confronted and decisions made by the respective leaders on the two sides will uncover important lessons of history. History is repeating itself but, as is common in Thucydides, with unexpected twists and ironic results. For the Athenians, Syracuse is a more difficult opponent than Sparta; and Nicias and Alcibiades are not Pericles.

When the two wars actually begin (2.1, 6.94), we continue to find markers of Thucydidean comparison and contrast. Though he had less latitude for historiographical choice in composing the accounts of the wars themselves than he did in his introductions to the wars, Thucydides still employed parallelism in those accounts. Once Alcibiades has departed from the Athenian expedition to Sicily, Thucydides focuses upon the figure of Nicias as the principal leader of the Athenian force there, and draws implicit comparisons with Pericles in the "first war." The reader cannot help noting that Pericles and Nicias receive parallel speeches, both direct and indirect, as well as general assessments upon their deaths. One can note this similarity schematically. Pericles is given an indirect speech to the Athenian Assembly in 2.13; Nicias has his letter to the Assembly read in 7.11–15. Both detail the resources Athens has for its coming conflict. In 2.35–46 Pericles presents his formal Funeral Oration; in 7.61–64 and 7.69.2, Nicias gives his informal talks to his soldiers. In 2.60–64 Pericles offers his stirring exhortatory speech after the plague; in 7.77 Nicias pleads with his soldiers after the defeat of the Athenian fleet in the Great Harbor of Syracuse. In 2.65 Thucydides writes his political assessment of Pericles at his death; in 7.86 Thucydides gives his personal assessment of Nicias at his death.

In Pericles' case, Thucydides emphasizes commitment to the public good and the extraordinary power of masterful rhetoric; in that of Nicias, Thucydides stresses assiduous attention to private success, which he tries to meld with public honor, and the failure of his weak rhetoric to persuade the Athenians to adopt his policy prescriptions. Pericles is the sole and indispensable leader of Athens in the opening years of the first war; Nicias vies for authority with Alcibiades, fails to thwart the expedition to Sicily (though having given two speeches early in Book Six), tries to resign his command, and gives a weak address to his fellow soldiers just before the final battle in Syracuse. His death is characterized as pathetic, in contrast to the heroic obituary Thucydides bestows upon Pericles.

Another telling comparison drawn by the historian is that between Athens in the first war and Syracuse in the second. In the first part of his narrative it is Athens that is the democratic innovator, the dynamic exemplum of naval power; in the second part, it is Syracuse, which even becomes the "new Athens" in its inventiveness and energy: see, for example, 7.28 and 55 for evocations of this development. Thucydides gradually bestows upon Syracuse a number of key Athenian characteristics that had been central to his theme of power in the first part of his history, and thus impresses upon the reader how the Athenian invasion and attempted encirclement of Syracuse actually enable the Syracusans to learn from their enemy, to implement bold new naval practices, and to surpass the Athenians in bravado, eventually defeating them through superior tactics, skill, and force of will.

While Thucydides draws some of these comparisons explicitly, most of them are implicit in the structuring of the narrative in Books 1 and 2 on the one hand, and in Books 6 and 7 on the other. The placement of speeches, the focus of attention upon similar characteristics of cities and leaders, and narrative parallelism tacitly reveal patterns in the history of the war and deepen the reader's understanding of what is transpiring in relationship to what has already transpired. In Books 3 and 8 further direct contrasts appear, particularly in chapters devoted to revolts of Athenian subjects and to civil wars, the first in Corcyra, the second in Athens itself. Thucydides was clearly alert to opportunities to make such structural points. One can even speculate that his structuring of the last events of the first part of the war was influenced by his knowledge of the last years of the overall war: the highly contrived and unusually designed Melian Dialogue may owe its unique form (and perhaps its prediction of the future—see 5.91) to the dialogue we know that the victorious Spartans and Corinthians held to determine the Athenians' fate following their final siege and surrender in 404 BCE. Though we do not have the end of Thucydides' account of the war, we might divine its shape by noting his narrative choices in comparable places in the first part of his war. He was fond of parallelism, particularly when it revealed the ironies of history.

Ring Composition

While syntactical and architectural form define Thucydidean structure at the micro and macro levels, respectively, ring composition sometimes shapes episodes of moderate scale in the narrative. W. Robert Connor (1984) has identified rings in the Archaeology, in the central sections of Books 2 and 3, and in parts of Books 6 and 7, and other scholars have detected elaborate, highly articulated rings in the text as well. Thucydides employs the pattern A, B, C, C, B, A, occasionally with subdivisions, to conduct his narrative through chiastically related stages. This kind of repetition in reverse produces typically Thucydidean symmetry-with-contrast, akin to the parallelism-with-*variatio* that characterizes his prose style at the sentence level.

What does Thucydides want to achieve with ring composition? It is not always clear that he has a conscious purpose, but certainly in several instances he deepens or creates implicit comparisons and contrasts. For example, Connor shows (Appendix Seven, p. 258) how in 7.26-31 Thucydides artfully links the episodes of Decelea and Mycalessus by composing a small ring that begins in 7.26.2 and ends in 7.31.1. The account of the Spartan fortification of Decelea in 7.27.3-28.4 details the damage done to the Athenians by the year-round occupation of that Attic site. In 7.29-30 Thucydides depicts the late arrival and dismissal of Athens' Thracian allies, followed by the atrocity that the rejected Thracians commit in the small town of Mycalessus. Decelea and Mycalessus occupy similar places in the two parts of the ring.

Thucydides emphasizes at length the enormous financial harm the year-round occupation of Decelea caused the Athenians. At Mycalessus he dwells upon the horrible and senseless murders of school children by savage barbarians. Connor argues that Thucydides thereby suggests the "incommensurability of two thematic systems within the work—financial resources/expenditures and human resources/expenditures" (1984, 258). In other words, chiasmus produces *implicit ethical meaning.*

In a more sophisticated and elaborate ring structure in 6.53-61 (Connor, Appendix Six, p. 257), Thucydides demonstrates how the Athenians' misinterpretation of their famous tyrannocide leads to their disastrous mistreatment of Alcibiades at the outset of the Sicilian Expedition, Athens' ambitious and ultimately ruinous invasion of the city of Syracuse. In this case Thucydides makes several points at once: the Athenians do not know their own history, the tyrannocide was a ludicrous act committed by sex-crazed lovers for purely private reasons against a good political regime, and the Athenians' mistaken views of history led to paranoia in 416 BCE, hence to suspicion against Alcibiades, their most successful general. Their expulsion of Alcibiades accordingly contributes to the failure of the Sicilian Expedition, and the Athenians draw precisely the wrong historical parallel. Thucydides reveals the real one, namely, that when Athens mistreats its effective leaders, it pays a huge price. Thucydides thus not only makes a strong historical point, but he also demonstrates a historiographical one of deep significance: getting history right matters.

Juxtaposition as a Literary Means of Producing Ironic Effects

Thucydides is famous for his striking juxtapositions: Pericles' great Funeral Oration (the only one of many annual funeral speeches the historian chooses to give us), with its high praise of Athenian character, followed by the Plague passage, which accentuates the degradation of Athenian character under stress; the Melian Dialogue (the only such formal dialogue in the text), full of Athenian hubris, followed immediately by the beginning of Thucydides' account of the Sicilian Expedition, the "total disaster" that led to Athens' eventual defeat and downfall; the parallel literary treatments of the Plataean and Mytilenean episodes in Book 3, the first ending with a Spartan, the second with an Athenian atrocity.

In each case it is Thucydidean *choice* that is notable. His narrative explicitly and consistently reports consecutive events in specific theatres, by season; but the further structuring of the narrative is completely a matter of authorial decision. Formal devices such as major speeches and dialogues evince the writer's own emphasis, ultimately his purpose. Thucydides' purpose is clearly to make the reader reflect upon the ironies and paradoxes and pretences of history, the gaps between the ideal and the real, the gaps between avowed rationales and underlying motivations.

How should we view Thucydides' heavy emphasis upon the reversal of the very Athenian values and characteristics Pericles praises (2.37–41) in the Funeral Oration only a few lines later in the Plague? After all, the historian seems to go out of his way to undercut memorable phrases he has just given to Pericles: ". . . the Athenian would easily present a self-sufficient individual under the broadest circumstances and with the most versatile grace" (2.41.1); "no individual at all proved to be self-sufficient, no matter how strong or weak, but all perished alike, though cared for with every regimen" (2.51.3). Is it Thucydides' intent to mock Periclean optimism and idealism? To evoke pity in the reader?

Perhaps the next juxtaposition helps to answer the conundrum: following his account of the Plague, Thucydides gives Pericles another speech, his final one in the *History*. In it Pericles is made to say that a great city must stand up bravely to its human opponents and bear stoically its divinely caused setbacks, and that the only thing the Athenians have not foreseen in the war is the Plague; all else they have predicted and surmounted. This is what citizens of a great polis do, says Pericles. The way to respond to the Plague, then, is to redouble efforts, not give in to doubt and fear. Immediately after this speech, Thucydides renders his final judgment on Pericles' foresight, personal qualities and public policies, one full of praise for Pericles and of sharp disapproval of the capabilities and loyalty of those who followed him in the leadership of Athens. Does this mean that we know how Thucydides wants us to think about the juxtaposition of Funeral Oration and Plague, or about the Periclean approach to war? I think not. Such tensions and uncertainties, emphasized by structure, are not simple or transparent. They constitute the complexity and depth of the *History*, characteristics that the sensitive reader takes for what they are: expressions of the historian's artistic ability and intellectual seriousness. History's most important lessons are hard to fathom, and open to different interpretations by different readers.

Verbal Linkages

In her influential book *Histoire et raison chez Thucydide*, published in 1956, J. de Romilly uncovered another structuring technique in the text, what she called *fils conducteurs*, "guiding threads." She also used the term "*enchainements*," "chains" or "linkages," to describe the verbal connections Thucydides created to unify his text at small and large scale:

> He is not content with noting a summary relationship between events, attaching them, for the most part, to a common idea; he is careful, in the very choice of words and phrases, to give to these relationships an almost mathematical rigor. Similar elements assume a similar form; the conclusions match the plans. Whatever succeeds or fails, repeated or changed, stands out self-evidently without needing to be expressed.
>
> E. Rawlings's translation of Romilly 2012, p. 16

Romilly traced these linkages through large segments of text, demonstrating how Thucydides consistently used the same key terms to describe similar features in different episodes. It is the precision of his repetitive diction that Romilly has identified and found remarkable, even among Greek writers fond of such devices. His purpose was always to draw the reader's attention to historical patterns, paradigms that enable rigorous comparison and contrast. The patterns are products of Thucydidean reasoning:

> As a result a vast field is opened for the subtlety of the author. The verbal comparisons may not suggest important words or important ideas, but they always establish connections, they unify. They bring together grammatical phrases of any kind, marking parallelisms and suggesting interpretations.
>
> E. Rawlings's translation of Romilly 2012, p. 19

The more one pursues these long threads in Thucydides' text, the more one sees Thucydides' mind at work: drawing connections, compelling comparisons, building a unified web of history for the reader to contemplate and study. The effect is not only unity, but also *abstraction*: analytical reasoning produces complex structuring. Thucydides distills historical events down to their essence, then links them via their common elements, which are highlighted for the reader by identical words and phrases. The historian thereby *creates* meaning, or at least enhances and brings out the meaning intrinsic in the events themselves. Again the method is implicit, not explicit: the author renders few candid judgments of his own; he enables the reader to come to judgments seemingly on her own. But she has been led to enlightenment by a subtle and deep-reasoning writer who uses multiple literary structures to make history intelligible.

"Units of Action" in Thucydides

Another way of analyzing structure is to look at how the historian designed individual episodes in the war. Carolyn Dewald (2005) studied what she calls "units of action": these are the "beads" or building blocks of the narrative segments that constitute episodes in Thucydides' *History*. She finds that in the first ten-year war known as "Archidamian" by scholars, these building blocks are remarkably similar from episode to episode. In her Appendix A, she portrays these units of action schematically for Books 2 through 5, Chapter 24, demonstrating that the basic patterns repeat one another throughout this part of the *History*. The lead sentence of each episode paints a simple picture of the new event, the next sentences extend the narrative, the following ones give a more complex picture, further units often return to a simple picture, and so on through the episode. The result is a "linear, paratactic progression of units" through each year, "the string, or thematic unity of the whole, often remaining tacit or implicit in the way the sequence of segments unrolls" (2005, xi).

To narrate the period following the Archidamian War, Dewald argues, Thucydides gradually abandoned this tight structure in favor of an increasingly hypotactic style "that integrates and subordinates many narrative strands into a larger unified and complex whole" (xii). "The whole narrative has become a single, unified account, and all actions are described as parts of it" (157). Dewald is cautious in assigning reasons for this major change, but tentatively concludes that Thucydides' perception of the war altered as it continued for a much longer time than anyone, including the historian himself, had foreseen: "he fashioned a new and much more complicated kind of narrative in the service of getting down for us, his readers, what he saw, in all its multiple interconnections" (163).

There is no doubt that the Sicilian Expedition (our Books 6 and 7) evinces a highly focused authorial vision: it subsumes all other events in mainland Greece and the Aegean to a degree unique in Thucydides' work. It is also true that Book 5, Chapters 25–116 and Book 8 are differently organized from the other books of the *History*: they strike many readers as less unified, less consistent in structure, for whatever reasons (radically diverse reasons have been proposed). Thucydides clearly regards the Athenian adventure in Sicily as the greatest event of his war, and its conclusion as the greatest defeat in Greek history (see the end of Book 7). He implicitly designs his account of it as a literary parallel to Herodotus' portrayal of Xerxes' failed expedition to Greece, even repeating Herodotus' rare term for "total destruction" in his summary of the expedition (7.87.6). It is worth noting that Herodotus had similarly altered the structure of his narrative when he came to describe the invasion of Greece: after composing an episodic account of world history, replete with digressions and leaps from place to place and from era to era in his first six books, he wrote a unified narrative of Xerxes' expedition in Books 7 and 8. It is fair to say that Books 6 and 7 in Thucydides, and Books 7 and 8 in Herodotus constitute thematic culminations of the two works, and that their organizing principles reflect that role. Form indicates historiographical meaning.

Reader Response and Focalization

Robert Connor (1984) and, more recently, Timothy Rood (1998) have written excellent books further elucidating Thucydides' artful relationship with his readers. Connor pursued a sequential reading of the text from beginning to end in order to demonstrate that the historian consistently involved the reader in the work by building expectations, creating tensions, and then subverting or even contraverting the reader's assumptions in the subsequent narrative. The result is "a progression of thought and feeling" (18) that makes the *History* endlessly intense and unsettling for a discerning reader. This is yet another implicit device in Thucydides' literary toolkit, a very subtle one that puts complex structuring to use in and between episodes.

A poignant example is the way in which Thucydides portrays the promises and assurances the Spartan general Brasidas gives to Athenian subjects in the northern region of Greece in order to persuade them to revolt from Athenian rule. As Thucydides portrays the allies' growing enthusiasm for the general's rhetoric and their anticipation of imminent liberty, he also hints to the reader that Brasidas' arguments are at least partially specious, and that Spartan commitment to the "freedom of the Greeks" is unreliable.[3] As events unfold in the text, the Athenian allies whom the clever Brasidas tempts to revolt are going one way and the reader the other. This divergence is common in Thucydides, who often enables his readers to see things his "characters" do not. This double vision characterizes his method, which consistently makes the reader form judgments about the honesty of public rhetoric, the accuracy of leaders' predictions, and the limits of human understanding.

Connor and others also demonstrate how Thucydides subverts his own text on occasion. At the end (Chapter 50) of the Mytilenean episode in Book 3, just when the reader heaves a sigh of relief at the last-minute rescue of the population of Mytilene from Cleon's original motion to kill all the adult males and sell the women and children into slavery, Thucydides reports dryly that a new resolution by Cleon passed the Athenian Assembly to put to death the prisoners sent previously to Athens by the General Paches as "most responsible for the revolt (they were a little over a thousand)." The number comes as a surprise, as Connor emphasizes (1984, 86, with footnote 18), because the reader has just been led to a completely different mood by the dramatic portrayal of the arrival of the second ship from Athens with orders to spare the populace. I would add that Thucydides had told us about these prisoners several times before (Chapters 28, 35, and 36) in terms that suggested they were not numerous: they are described as "those in power," "those treating with the Lacedaemonians," and "those Mytilenean men Paches

---

[3] On Brasidas in Thrace, see also Foster, chapter 18 in this volume.

sent to Athens from Tenedos." Thucydides withheld their number until now to gain effect. What kind of effect? Moral shock.

Jeff Rusten (2015) reveals how Thucydides similarly changes registers in his preface. Chapters 1–19 of Book 1 make the case that the resources held by the two sides in the Peloponnesian War far exceeded those available to Greeks in all prior conflicts. This constitutes Thucydides' argument for the superiority of "his war" to all previous ones. Rusten points out that

> ... chapter 23 does not confirm or reflect or link to any of the overt themes of 1.2–19 ... (money, ships, walls)... rather, it subverts them, in part by stressing supernatural events, but especially by revealing that the upcoming war will contain unmatched examples of the failures of the denigrated predecessor-enterprises in 1.1–19—lack of food, ... a war that goes on too long, ... stasis, ... murders, ... exiles, ... cities emptied of their populations...." (2015, 38).

Thucydides undercuts the notion of "greatness" with a list of sufferings endured in the Peloponnesian War, and thus defines war as tragedy, not glory. Again the implicit point is a moral one.

Timothy Rood dissected Thucydidean literary method by noting subtle shifts in narrative speed, frequency, and order. Rood studies devices such as analepsis, "a narration of a story-event at a point in the text after later events have been told," and prolepsis, "a narration of a story-event at a point before earlier events have been mentioned" (1998, 11, quoting G. Genette). He also looks closely at "focalization," Genette's term for the locus of perception from which a story is presented. The sum of these analytical methods is a narratological approach to the text, one that investigates in great detail and, at the minutest level, authorial control of the pace and movement and perspective of the account.

The result, once more, illuminates Thucydides' astonishing skill in composition and the subtlety of his literary design. Even apparently bare, straightforward narrative betrays, under Rood's acute analysis, "patterns of disappointed expectation and misunderstanding, the difficulty of reading events" (1998, 99), and reveals paradoxes that deepen the reader's appreciation of events. Themes emerge from Thucydides' account at every turn and force themselves upon the reader's consciousness: by inducing the reader constantly to *interpret*, Thucydides gives *implicit meaning* to history. The levels of structuring seem almost limitless in Thucydides' text, so artful is his rhetorical sophistication.

This is what Hobbes, citing Plutarch, meant by "making his auditor a spectator." Thucydides' readers are engaged in an intellectual and ethical dialectic, much as are the readers of Plato. Which arguments convince, the Athenians' or the Melians', in the "terrible Melian Dialogue" at the end of Book 5? Who proposes the better punishment for the Mytileneans' crime, Cleon or Diodotus, in the Athenian Assembly in Book 3? Who is right about the Sicilian Expedition, Nicias or Alcibiades, at the beginning of Book 6? What is the meaning of the complicated Pylos episode in Book 4? Unlike Polybius, for example, Thucydides eschews didacticism, always preferring the implicit method, always making the reader do the work of choosing. Structure rules.

References

Connor, W. R. 1984. *Thucydides*. Princeton: Princeton University Press.
Crawley, R. 1951. *Thucydides. The Peloponnesian War*. New York: Random House.
Dewald, C. 2005. *Thucydides' War Narrative: A Structural Study*. Berkeley: University of California Press.
Genette, G. 1990. "Fictional Narrative, Factual Narrative." *Poetics Today* 11: 755–74.
Hobbes, T. 1629/1989. *The Peloponnesian War. Thucydides: The Complete Hobbes Translation*. David Grene, ed. Chicago: University of Chicago Press.
Parry, A. 1981. *Logos and Ergon in Thucydides*. New York: Harvard University Press.
Rawlings, H. R. 1981. *The Structure of Thucydides' History*. Princeton: Princeton University Press.
Rawlings, H. R. 2016. "KTEMA TE ES AIEI ... AKOUEIN." *Classical Philology* 111 (2): 107–116.
Romilly, J. de. 1956. *Histoire et raison chez Thucydide*. Paris: Les Belles Lettres.
Romilly, J. de. 2012. *The Mind of Thucydides*. Translated by E. T. Rawlings. Ithaca: Cornell University Press. [First published as *Histoire et raison chez Thucydide*.]
Rood, T. 1998. *Thucydides: Narrative and Explanation*. Oxford: Oxford University Press.
Rusten, J. 2015. "*Kinesis* in the Preface to Thucydides." In *Kinesis: The Ancient Depiction of Gesture, Motion, and Emotion*, edited by C. A. Clark, E. Foster, and J. P. Hallett, 27–40. Ann Arbor: University of Michigan Press.

CHAPTER 12

SCALE MATTERS

Compression, Expansion, and Vividness in Thucydides

W. ROBERT CONNOR

INTRODUCTION

SCALE matters and in Thucydides it not only matters, it perplexes. In antiquity it puzzled Dionysius of Halicarnassus, or rather provoked his condemnation of Thucydides as lazy:

> ... In the elaboration (*exergasia*) of his chapters he is rather careless, either giving more space to matters that demand less or else indolently treating in a cursory manner matters that require more detailed treatment.... (Dionysius of Halicarnassus *On Thucydides* 13, translated by W. K. Pritchett)

Before joining Dionysius in his criticisms we need to ask *how* expansion and contraction are achieved in Thucydides' work, that is, what techniques are used—and why. And while we are at it, we must ask what effects such changes of scale have on the alert reader of this extraordinary work.

The investigation of scale in Thucydides cannot be detached from what can be made out about rhetorical theory in his day. Scale was a matter of concern among contemporary rhetoricians, as may be inferred from Plato's comments about various teachers of rhetoric:

> Tisias and Gorgias ... made small things seem great and great things small by the power of speech, ... and ... invented conciseness (*suntomia*) of speech and measureless length on all subjects ... And once when Prodicus heard these inventions, he laughed and said that he alone had discovered the art of proper speech, that discourses should be neither long nor short, but of reasonable length (*metria*). (*Phaedrus* 267 b, translated by H. N. Fowler, modified)

This concern with the proper length of a speech is also reflected in the Funeral Oration, where Thucydides has Pericles refer to commonly held views about scale:

> ... The friend [of a deceased warrior] who is familiar with every facet of the story may think that some point has not been set forth with that fullness which he wishes and knows it to deserve. (2.35.2) (Here and in most places in this essay I follow the translation of R. Crawley).

It is not, perhaps, a great leap from the orator's podium to the historian's study. Indeed, A. J. Woodman (1988), among others, has shown in some detail the similarities between Thucydides' narrative technique and the instruction offered by his contemporaries, the Sophists. There are, moreover, striking resemblances between Thucydides' practice and some of the doctrines set forth by rhetoricians of a much later date. For that reason, I have added references to the useful collection of material in Lausberg 1998 whenever they seem apposite.

Yet, caution is in order, since the rhetoricians did not always agree with one another, nor do their rules adequately characterize Thucydidean practice. Thucydides' account of the Peloponnesian War does not, for example, show many signs of being shaped by Prodicus' Goldilocks-like preference for a "just right" balance between fullness and compression. Scale in Thucydides varies greatly from episode to episode; the challenge is to determine why and to what effect

Nor will it do to emphasize Thucydides' "conciseness" (*suntomia*), without looking closely at passages where actions are described with great detail and vividness. To be sure, Thucydides' work contains many passages written with great conciseness, for example:

> ... Eurylochus lodged the hostages in Kytinion, in Doris, and advanced upon Naupactus through the country of the Locrians. On his way he seizes Oineon and Eupalion, two of the towns that refused to join him. Arriving in the territory of Naupactus, and having now been joined by the Aetolians, the army laid waste the land and took the suburb of the town, which was unfortified; and after this they seize Molykreion, also a Corinthian colony subject to Athens. (3.102.1)

Every stage of the operation presented opportunities for expansion—more precise chronological indicators, closer attention to the army's route, or the presentation of vivid details. The narration is clear; fast paced; unencumbered by speeches, sensory detail, or stylistic embellishment. If we take such passages as a baseline for gauging scale in Thucydides' writing, many passages will be equally succinct, a few more highly compressed, and some greatly expanded.

Variation in scale is especially striking when two ostensibly similar situations are treated in different ways, as, for example, in the Athenian punishments of Aegina and of Mytilene. Mytilene fills fourteen chapters of Book 3, including the famous debate between Cleon and Diodotus, and culminates in a life-or-death race of triremes with conflicting orders to the Athenian commander there—the result is a hairbreadth escape for the Mytilenean citizenry, but death for the ringleaders of the rebellion (3.50.1). Here scale is reinforced by intertwining the Mytilene and Plataean episodes in a complex structure (Connor 1984, 253), as if in a hall of mirrors.

By contrast, Thucydides' treatment of the Aeginetans is of a different order of magnitude, and occurs in a loose sprawl of narrative. After a succinct account of the expulsion of the Aeginetans from their native island and their relocation to Thyrea in the Peloponnese (2.27), the story temporarily stops, to be resumed in Book 4 (Chapters 56–57). There it seems at first just another incident in Athenian naval operations in the region: they sack and burn Thyrea. The Athenian commanders capture some of the Aeginetans and send them to Athens, where, along with a Spartan commander and prisoners from Cythera, they were put to death (4.57.4). The report of these operations is powerful but succinct, taking just twenty-eight lines in the Oxford Classical Text, a small fraction of the space devoted to Mytilene. To be sure, Thyrea (though not Aegina) had less strategic value than Mytilene, but that may not be the full explanation of the differences in treatment. A similar discrepancy in scale emerges if one compares this account of the Aeginetans with that of the Melians at the end of Book 5. Since Melos was not of great strategic significance, something else must account for the attention it receives.

Variations in scale are not uncommon in Thucydides, as Carolyn Dewald's book (2005) makes clear. To understand the significance of such variation, however, we need to examine the techniques of expansion and compression in the work, and observe the contexts in which they occur and the effects that follow from them.

Methods of Expansion and Compression

Compression

Let us begin with compression, and with a caution: Thucydides may have passed quickly over some episodes because he did not yet have the detailed information he was always looking for; that may be the case, for example, at the beginning of Book 8. For a long time he was an exile, cut off from some sources of information. His work, moreover, is incomplete, and in some places clearly lacking final revision. In other places, however, the compression is clearly deliberate:

> During the same summer different operations were carried on by the different belligerents in Sicily; by the Siceliots themselves against each other, and by the Athenians and their allies. I shall however confine myself to the actions in which the Athenians took part, choosing the most important (*logou malista axia*). (3.90.1)

Compression, however, is not simply omission. It can also be a way of advancing the author's interpretation of events. Indeed, in Thucydides the scale of an episode is often an indicator of its importance. A fully detailed account, as we shall see, mirrors the importance of an episode; per contra, brevity can signal that an ostensibly important event is less significant than commonly thought. That seems to be the message in the contrast drawn between the Persian and the Peloponnesian wars:

> The Median war, the greatest achievement of past times, yet found a speedy decision in two actions by sea and two by land. The Peloponnesian war was prolonged to an immense length, and long as it was it was short without parallel for the misfortunes it brought upon Hellas. (1. 23.1)

The first of these two sentences is a tour de force of compression. It uses the grammatical form of the dual to reduce two Persian attacks, quite different in nature and separated by a decade, into two pairs of battles, two infantry and two naval. By minimizing the Persian wars, Thucydides in effect magnifies the significance of his own subject matter.

The comparison advances the goal of the introductory section of the work, the so-called Archaeology, by emphasizing the greatness of Thucydides' subject matter. Once this greatness is well established, Thucydides can turn to another goal, demonstrating the growth of Athenian power in the years between the Persian and the Peloponnesian wars. Compression, in other words, is a way of advancing Thucydides' goals, and also helps him avoid a potential conflict between these goals. The battle fought near the river Eurymedon in the mid-460s BCE was one of the largest and most dramatic battles of the fifth century. This Athenian victory is a useful indicator of the growth of Athenian power, but its presentation must not be allowed to distract the reader from the recognition that the Peloponnesian War was even greater. Thucydides deals with this problem by providing only the basic facts without adding an exact chronology or vivid details. Nor does he discuss the strategic rationale for the battles, or their military and diplomatic consequences:

> Next we come to the actions by land and by sea at the river Eurymedon, between the Athenians with their allies, and the Medes, when the Athenians won both battles on the same day, under the command of Cimon son of Miltiades and captured and destroyed the whole Phoenician fleet, consisting of two hundred vessels. (1.100.1)

The narrative then moves directly on to the rebellion of Thasos and other events in the Thraceward region, told at considerably greater length (1.100.2–101.2) than the Eurymedon account. At this point Thucydides provides succinct but adequate indication of the goals of Athenian operations, and the sensational detail of a secret Spartan promise to invade Attica. By the time we have read about Thasos, Eurymedon is almost eclipsed.

Other methods of compression are used as well, for example, the evocation of earlier passages, as in the account of the revolt of Scione in 4.120.3 where Brasidas "spoke to the same effect as at Acanthus and Torone," but added further arguments. The effect is to avoid redundancy and speed the reader ahead to another speech by Brasidas (4.126) and to the vivid narrative that follows.

A similar technique, allusion, can also yield useful results. In his treatment of the Megarian Decree, the episode that many have considered the spark that set off the great war, Thucydides never gives a full account of the matter; instead he introduces the decree obliquely: we first hear of it through an allusion in a speech of Corinthian ambassadors seeking to avert a conflict with Athens:

> It were, rather, wise [for you Athenians] to try to counteract the unfavorable impression that your conduct toward Megara has created. For kindness opportunely shown has a greater power of removing old grievances than the facts of the case may warrant. (1.42.2)

This allusive presentation allows Thucydides to mention the *cause célèbre* without magnifying its significance or undermining his thesis that "the truest *prophasis* I consider to be the one which was least talked about—that the Athenians were growing great . . ." (1.23.6). Compressing the Megarean affair into allusions is a skillful way of advancing Thucydides' interpretive agenda.

Thucydides is not alone in such uses of compression. Ancient rhetoricians gave considerable attention to "minimization." (Much of the evidence is collected by Lausberg 1998, sec. 259 and 1070.1; see also Aristotle *Rhetoric* 2.18.4, Bekker 1870, p. 1391b.) Some of these writers refer to it as *to meioun*, contrasting it with *to auxein*, to augment or expand. The *Rhetoric for Alexander*, preserved among the works of Aristotle, however, uses what seems to me a more revealing term, *tapeinōsis*, "lowering" or "minimization," when discussing "the minimization of creditable qualities and the amplification of discreditable ones" (1425b 37, translated by Rackham). Quintilian (*Inst.* 8.3.48) and many other rhetoricians treated such "lowering" as a matter of style (Lausberg 1998, sec. 1238.1), that is the use of low-class speech, but the *Rhetoric for Alexander* seems to view it more broadly, and more in keeping with Thucydidean attention to the scale of the narrative.

These techniques of minimization help Thucydides avoid a trap into which orators and rhetoricians sometimes fall—by attempting to refute views with which they disagree, inadvertently calling attention to them. His pattern is to pass over them as quickly as possible.

Behind the techniques of compression which we have observed in Thucydides can be detected a tacit mimetic principle—that the scale of presentation should be proportionate to the significance of the episode within Thucydides' interpretive framework. If this suggestion is correct, matters Thucydides considered minor should receive little space, even if commonly regarded as highly important. Conversely, increased scale should be a way of emphasizing what Thucydides deemed most significant. This suggestion can be tested by examining episodes in which Thucydides' techniques of expansion are put to use.

Expansion

Thucydides' techniques of expansion can shape long sections of the text, or require only a few deft words. In either case their effects can be significant. For example, the staccato effect of a string of coordinating conjunctions, can "make even small things great" (Demetrius, *On Style* 54, cf. 63). The effect of such polysyndeton can be greater than that achieved by subordination, as some ancient rhetoricians (Lausberg 1998, sec. 686) were well aware, and as modern readers can readily detect: for example, in the staccato opening of the speech of Archidamus in 1.80. Similarly, the addition of a short phrase, such as "in the ninety-third year after they became allies of the Athenians"—can increase the force of an otherwise formulaic phrasing, in this case the rounding-off formula in 3.68.5 for the end of the siege of Plataea. The expansion drives home the failure of the Athenians to rescue their loyal ally. Another form of expansion, the addition of a superlative, can underline the significance of an ostensibly routine operation, as in 2.31.2, when Thucydides notes that the Athenian expedition of 431 BCE was the largest (*megiston dē*), thereby emphasizing the observation that follows, that the city was still at its height and had not yet been afflicted by the plague.

Litotes (Lausberg 1998, sec. 586–88), in some ways a mirror image of the superlative, can be used in similar ways, as when, in the account of the Corcyrean *stasis* (3.81.5), the phrase "nothing that did not happen" (*ouden hoti ou xunebē*), makes the point that everything possible *did* happen. Thucydides then adds a pleonasm (Lausberg 1998, sec. 859) "and even more." There are many more such "figures of speech," or *tropoi*, that result in expansion in Thucydides, not least hyperbaton (or *huperbasis*), as we shall soon see.

To the modern reader such tropes, or figures of speech, (Lausberg 1998, sec. 552–98), may seem strained and pointless, at best a trivial ornament. Among the ancients, however, they came to be recognized as means of making a presentation more compelling. They do this in part by setting the emotional register of a passage that often depends less on word choice than on the arrangement of the words chosen. Hence figures of speech can signal the intensification of emotion in a passage, and help bring it to life in the minds and hearts of the audience. In Thucydides such figures are not decorative; the shaping of language is closely tied to the shaping of reader reaction to situations Thucydides deemed of great significance.

Expansion through such tropes regularly achieves the mimetic effect we have expected—it increases the scale of important episodes. Big matters (*ta megala*) receive big treatment. In Thucydides, however, greatness is not identical with strategic significance. Sometimes ostensibly minor episodes are greatly expanded, especially, it turns out, when they involve great suffering (*pathos*).

It is important, then, as we examine the other end of the spectrum of expansionary techniques, that is, those that involve more than a few words or brief turns of phrase, to be alert to the question of what Thucydides presented as truly great about the war. The most obvious of these larger-scale expansions are speeches, dialogues, addresses to troops or political assemblies, represented as direct quotation, or paraphrased in indirect discourse. Such speeches often occur in contrasting pairs (antilogies), as in the debates determining the fate of Plataea and Mytilene in Book 3, or sometimes in a triad, as when the Athenians argue about the Sicilian expedition in 6.9–23. The triad underlines the strategic significance of the decision, but expansion through direct discourse can also heighten the pathos of a passage. As Dionysius of Halicarnassus noted,

Thucydides' writing in some expanded passages "makes the suffering appear so cruel, so terrible, so piteous, as to leave no room for historians or poets to surpass him" (*Thuc.* 15).

The following sections of this essay will concentrate on three other forms of expansion (day-by-day narrative, vividness, and "reprise") in the work, and then examine the cumulative effect of expansionary techniques in one major episode.

Day-by-Day Narration

Thucydides can compress into a sentence or two military operations that must have taken several days, weeks, or even a whole campaign season, as he does in his account of the fourth Peloponnesian invasion of Attica (3.1). Such passages reflect the routine of war and let the reader move on to more revealing matters. Sometimes, however, Thucydides' narrative becomes more granular, providing a day-by-day or even hour-by-hour account. That is the case, for example, in the buildup to the account of the Corcyrean *stasis* in 3.70 ff. At first, events flow without chronological indicators, but that changes in 3.72.3 with "Night coming on. . . ." Day-by-day narrative follows: "The next day passed in skirmishes" (3.73.1); "After a day's interval" (3.74.1); "On the next day" (3. 75.1). And with day-by-day narrative comes tense shifts, in and out of the historical present. The ancient rhetoricians (Lausberg 1998, sec. 814, relying on Quintilian *Institutes* 9.2.41) called such shifting of tenses *metastasis* and recognized its close connection to vividness (*enargeia*), as can be seen in the account of the battle between the oligarchs and the demos in the city of Corcyra itself:

> After a day's interval hostilities recommence and the demos is victorious . . . the women also valiantly assisted, pelting with tiles from the house and they endured the din of battle with a fortitude beyond their sex. . . .. Towards dusk the oligarchs . . . set fire to the houses around the market-place, and the lodging-houses . . . (3.74.1–2)

Expansion through day-by-day narration allows the inclusion of sensory detail, and hence for increased vividness, the next mode of expansion to be examined.

Vividness (*Enargeia*, Latin *Evidentia*)

Vivid sensory detail is not restricted to day-by-day narrative. One finds it, for example, in the description of the plague in Athens, with bodies piled one upon another and with half dead people reeling in the streets and converging on the fountains in their desperate search for water (2.52.2). Such vividness came to be thought characteristic of the work:

> The most effective historian is the one who makes his narrative like a painting by giving a visual quality to the sufferings and characters. Thucydides certainly always strives after this vividness (*enargeia*) in his writing, eagerly trying to transform

his reader into a spectator and to let the sufferings (*pathē*) that were so shocking (*ekplēktika*) and disorienting (*taraktika*) to those who beheld them have a similar effect on those who read about them. (Plutarch *De glor. Ath.* 3, *Moralia* 347a)

Ancient rhetoricians, and more recently Woodman (1988) and Zanker (1981), recognized the value and emotional power of "vividness" (Lausberg 1998, sec. 810–19). It provided a way to make the reader into an eyewitness. In doing so, it depends on *phantasia*, the ability to call up visual images, a capacity that Longinus describes as "where, inspired by strong emotion, you seem to see what you describe and bring it . . . before the eyes of your audience" (*On the Sublime* 15.2, translated by Fyfe). Quintilian shows that process in action:

> Shall we not turn [daydreaming] to our advantage? I make a complaint that a man has been murdered; shall I not bring before my eyes everything that is likely to have happened when the murder occurred? Shall not the assassin suddenly sally forth? Shall not the other tremble, cry out, supplicate or flee? Shall I not behold the one striking, the other falling? Shall not the blood, and paleness, and last gasp of the expiring victim present itself fully to my mental view? 32. Hence will result that *enargeia*, which is called by Cicero "illustration" and "evidentness," which seems not so much to narrate as to exhibit, and our feelings will be moved not less strongly than if we were actually present at the affairs of which we are speaking. (Quintilian *Inst.* 6.2.30ff., translated by Watson)

Enargeia is clearly a powerful tool for the orator and advocate. For the historian it is a way of enhancing his authority, since readers who feel themselves to be eyewitnesses are ready to believe what they have been made to see. And seeing it is, for while the other senses have their place, vision is preeminent. As Aristotle noted, ". . . hearing is a duller perception than sight, and consequently the effects (*pathē*) arising from it are superficial . . . But since sight is the most vivid (*enargeitatēs ousēs*) of all the senses, the effects produced by it are correspondingly great (*Problemata* 7. 886b 33 ff., translated by Hett, modified).

To be sure, other senses also contribute to the vividness of Thucydidean narrative. Sound has a powerful role, as in the loud noise (*psophos*), which induced the panic at Lekythos (4.115.3), the shout (*boē*) in 4.34.2, and the crashing together of ships (*ktypos*) in 7.70. These can create consternation, *ekplēxis*. Thirst (e.g., 2.52.2) is powerful as well; and smell is perhaps the worst of all (7.87.2), or is it the taste of cannibalism (2.70.1)?

In Thucydides' day how fully developed was rhetorical theory about *enargeia* and similar techniques, and to what extent was he guided by it? One must be very cautious since the use of *enargeia* in the criticism of poetry cannot be attested before the second century BCE, as Zanker (1981, 306 f.) has shown. Still, the earliest appearance of the word, in Plato's *Politicus* 277c, suggests that not long after Thucydides the term was in use as a way of evaluating speech.

There is, moreover, a connection between vivid narration and one feature of Thucydides' distinctive approach to investigating the past and presenting it to his readers—his emphasis on *akribeia*, getting the details right. The importance of *akribeia* and related terms in Thucydides' methodology has been recognized in Thucydidean studies: for example, in Crane (1996). Although Thucydides does not use *akribeia* to characterize the narrative that results from his investigations, the *enargeia* of his account may be a byproduct of *akribeia*; that is, the hard work of getting the details right may also yield the material needed for a vivid account. Demetrius may hint at that in his treatise on style:

> ... vividness ... arises from an exact narration (*ex akribologias*), overlooking no detail and cutting out nothing." (Sec. 208, translated by Fyfe)

Reprise

Sometimes Thucydides' treatment of an episode seems to come close to completion and then start again with new intensity. By analogy to music, one might call this "reprise," not, however, as exact repetition, but as resumption after an apparent culmination or near resolution. From time to time Thucydidean narratives seem to approach completion, then resume, restating and intensifying themes already introduced and developed. The defeat of the Athenians by the Aetolians near Aegitium (3.98) provides a good illustration. The description of the defeat culminates in the words "and falling into pathless gullies and places that they were unacquainted with, thus they perished (*diephtheironto*; 3.98.1, lines 18f. of the OCT). It would be easy to complete this episode with a rounding-off formula and move on to the operations at Naupactus (3.98.5). Instead, Thucydides expands the story of the defeat, recounting in detail the flight of the Athenians. Once again we see the Aetolian javelins in action (*esakontizontes*, line 21, cf. *esēkontizon* in line 8) and again hear of the "perishing" (*diephtheiron* in line 22). The theme of losing one's way is also repeated (*tēn hodōn hamartanontas*, line 23); this time they end up in a wood "which had no ways out, and which was soon fired and burnt round them by the enemy" (lines 24f.). At this point Thucydides steps back and generalizes "every form of flight and destruction afflicted the army of the Athenians" (3.98.3), adding the casualty figures and then an emphatic superlative, "these were the best men (*beltistoi dē andres*) in this war from the city of the Athenians to have perished (*diephtharēsan*)" 3.98.4, line 31).

A similar structure can be seen in the account of the slaughter at Mycalessus in 7.29f.: the horror builds in two long sentences (7.29.3), the first with a series of genitive absolutes, the second with polysyndeton. The reader sees what happened at dawn the day the Thracians attack the unsuspecting town:

> ... bursting into Mycalessus [the Thracians] sacked the houses and temples, and murdered (*ephoneuon*) the inhabitants, sparing neither youth nor age but killing all they fell in with, one after the other, children and women, and even beasts of burden, and whatever else they saw with life in it. ...

Surely that was enough horror, and enough space for the story of a single day in a small town of no strategic significance. And, indeed, Thucydides seems to pause, as if about to generalize and then move on to a new episode: "The Thracian race, as is often the case with barbarians, is most bloodthirsty when its confidence is high" (7.29.4). But then the horror resumes and intensifies:

> And then no small (*ouk oligē*) confusion reigned and every form of destruction; and they fell upon (*epipesontes*) a boys' school, the largest that there was in the place, into which the children had just gone, and cut them all to pieces (*katekopsan*).

Then come the real markers of the extremity of the event:

> The disaster falling upon the whole town was unsurpassed in magnitude (*oudemias hēssōn*), unapproached by any (*mallon heteras*) in suddenness and horror. (7.29.5)

The grammatical structure continues the polysyndeton of 7.29.4, adding litotes and a ring marked by *epipesontes* in line 17 and *epepeson* in line 20 (cf. lines 4–5). The power of the passage comes largely, I am convinced, from the resumption of vivid detail and the pace of the narrative: the story comes at us fast, ferociously, repeatedly, as the attack did to the people who lived—and died—in Mycalessus.

But the story is still not over. Theban allies of Mycalessus moved swiftly against the booty-laden Thracians, chase them (the tense switches to the historic present in *katadiōkousin* (7.30.1, line 23) and kill many of them. When the casualties on both sides are recounted, Thucydides again sums up the disaster, echoing 7.29.5, ". . . a calamity, for its extent, as lamentable as any that happened in the war" (7.30.3). The sentence combines a litotes (literally, "less than none") with two complex, expanded separations of words that logically or grammatically belong together, *hyperbata*. The sentence cannot adequately be rendered in English, but encapsulates the disproportionate scale of the *pathos* that Mycalessus experienced.

The Mycalessus episode raises a double question: why such emphasis on a strategically minor operation, and why the reprise and all the features of elaborate style? Since the use of reprise as well as some of the vocabulary and stylistic traits of this passage recur in the account of the Sicilian disaster, a fresh look at that story may help answer these questions.

The Withdrawal from Syracuse (7.73–87)

After the Athenians' defeat at Syracuse they are forced to withdraw by land in increasingly desperate condition. The description is one of the fullest in Thucydides, bringing together many of the techniques of expansion that we have already discussed, but which can now be seen to reinforce one another and act synergistically. Much of the story is presented in day-by-day narrative (". . . they now decided to stay also the following day (7.74.1) . . . the removal of the army took place upon the second day after the sea-fight" (7.75.1). With greater chronological detail comes added sensory detail: sight, of course, but also sound. As the Athenian troops find they must leave behind their disabled comrades, we hear the cries and laments:

> These fell to entreating and bewailing until their friends knew not what to do, begging them to take them and loudly calling to each individual comrade or relative whom they could see, hanging upon the necks of their tent-fellows . . . calling again and again upon heaven and shrieking as they were left behind. (7.75.4)

Such sensory vividness confronts the reader with the suffering already experienced (*peponthotas*) and the prospect of even worse still to come (*pathōsin*, 7.75.4). Thucydides even breaks from his usual aversion to similes and likens the sufferings of the army to that of a besieged city (7.75.5). Soon Nicias is shouting (*boēi*, 7.76.1) words of encouragement to the dispirited army; his words are reported in direct discourse (7.77).

After that the sound goes dead. Vision, however, reaches a new intensity as the Athenian troops, exhausted and dehydrated, pushed on to the river Assinarus:

> Forced to huddle together, they fell against and trod down one another, some dying immediately (*euthus diephtheironto*) upon the javelins, others getting entangled together and stumbling over the articles of baggage, without being able to rise again. Meanwhile the opposite bank, which was steep, was lined by the Syracusans, who showered missiles down upon the Athenians, most of them drinking greedily and heaped together in disorder in the hollow bed of the river. The Peloponnesians also came down and butchered them, especially those in the water, which was thus immediately spoiled (*euthus diephtharto*), but which they went on drinking just the same, mud and all, bloody as it was, most even fighting to have it. (7.84.3–5)

The passage works to a large extent by having the reader's eyes follow the weapons hurled down at the frantic Athenians in the river bed; then we see on one bank the Syracusans shooting their missiles from above (*anōthen*); then the focus returns to the river bed and the chaos among the Athenians. Then from the other bank the Peloponnesian troops made their descent (*epikatabantes*). The focus shifts from the slitting of throats (*esphazon*) to the water, spoiled as it was, and then to the mud, turning red with blood, to the Athenian troops fighting one another for it, then to their bodies piled up, like the dead from the plague (7.85.1, cf. 2.52.2). Rarely is such vivid and appalling detail found in a historical account.

Up to this point the narrative of the episode has all been in past tenses, but when the situation is clearly hopeless—even to Nicias—the tense shifts, just for a second, to the more vivid historical present, as Nicias hands himself over (*paradidōsi* 7.85.1) to the Spartan commander, Gylippus.

In Thucydides' work the culmination of a narrative is often marked by a superlative, and in 7.85.4 that pattern seems to sum up the disaster—"...this was the greatest slaughter..." (*pleistos gar dē phonos houtos*, line 26f.). The superlative is expanded and made more emphatic by being surrounded by litotes (*ouk oligon* in line 26, and *oudenos elassōn* in line 27).

It's all over. The story could now be drawn to a swift completion, perhaps with a casualty count or a few words on the execution of Nicias and his colleague, Demosthenes. Instead there is a reprise—one more, even more appalling episode, the fate of those who were captured and imprisoned in the quarries of Syracuse:

> Crowded in a narrow hole, without any roof to cover them, the heat of the sun and the stifling closeness of the air tormented them during the day, and then the nights which came on autumnal and chilly, made them ill by the violence of the change; besides, as they had to do everything in the same place for want of room, and the bodies of those who died of their wounds or from the variations in the temperature, or from similar causes, were left heaped together one upon another, intolerable stench arose; while hunger and thirst never ceased to afflict them, each man during eight months having only half a pint of water and a pint of corn given him daily. In short, no single suffering (*kakopathēsai*, cf. 87.2, line 10) to be apprehended by men thrust into such a place was spared them. (7.87.1–2)

The details are conveyed in polysyndeton; there are fifteen coordinating connectives (*te* and *kai*) in these lines. Again there is no hint of sound, but the visual detail is vivid; nor does the narrative spare us the stench of rotting bodies. As the unit draws to a close we once again encounter a Thucydidean superlative, full of irony, "this was the greatest (*megiston*) Hellenic achievement (*ergon*) of any in this war, or, in my opinion, in Hellenic history" (7.87.5, line 16 of the OCT). This superlative is followed by two more, in assonance: ". . .most glorious (*lamprotaton*) to the victors, and most calamitous (*dustuchestaton*) to the conquered (line 18 f.). These are surrounded by the repeated litotes *ouden hoti ouk* in lines 10 and 21.

Thucydides has used almost all his expansionary techniques in his account of Athens' Sicilian disaster. It is rare to find such fullness, such *enargeia*, such compelling development of a central theme, *pathos*, the Athenians' suffering, and in a wider sense the power of war to turn active into passive, and take away any illusion of control.

Without this "reprise" the Sicilian narrative would still create in its reader, I believe, an emotional mimesis of the sufferings the Athenians endured. But the reprise brings some of the themes of the preceding chapter, the thirst of the Athenians, for example (7.84.2 and 7.87.2), to a new level of intensity.

Conclusion: A Mimetic Principle at Work?

> Still, it is extremely foolish to argue about the length or brevity of writings, for what we should value, I suppose, is not their extreme brevity or prolixity, but what they do best (*ta beltista*). (Plato, *Laws* IV 722a f., translated by R. G. Bury, modified)

A few years ago the agent of an artist friend of mine urged her to start painting on larger canvases. When she did so, the effect was stunning. The increase in scale let light assert itself, drew the viewer into the painting, brought the landscapes more fully to life. The change was qualitative, not quantitative.

"Scale matters," we say, and in Thucydides too it makes possible qualitative change, not just more, more intense. It's a form of risk taking, *kindynos*. Longinus noted that when he commented on Thucydidean risk taking. He saw Thucydides as

> ... making the audience terrified for the total collapse of the sentence and compelling them from sheer excitement to share the speaker's risk: then unexpectedly after a great interval, the long-lost phrase turns up, pat at the end so that he astounds them all the more by the sheer reckless audacity of his *hyperbaseis*. (22.4, translated by Fyfe, modified)

Behind such writing stands a mimetic principle. The text imitates the emotional effects of its subject matter. The scale is mimetic as well; what is great in the subject matter demands greatness of scale. That's true, of course, for the major battles, especially those that are turning points in the war. But there are other types of greatness in the war and these deserve treatment in proportion to their significance.

So, it follows that we must ask: what was Thucydides' understanding of greatness? One important line of inquiry is provided by the way he uses the adjective *megas* (meaning big or great, especially vertically). Its superlative *megistos* is particularly revealing. That is evident from the outset when Thucydides refers to his expectation that this war would be a great one, indeed the greatest *kinēsis*, disturbance (1.1.1–2).

The theme of greatness is restated in 1.23, clarifying what Thucydides meant in those earlier sentences. Now it is explicit:

> The Peloponnesian war was prolonged in length (*mēkos*) and scale (*mega*), and sufferings (*pathēmata*) came about in it for Greece, without parallel in a comparable amount of time. Never had so many cities been taken and laid desolate, here by the barbarians, here by the parties contending (the old inhabitants sometimes being removed when their cities were captured); never was there so much banishment and blood-shedding, now on the field of battle, now through *stasis*. Old stories of occurrences handed down by tradition, but scarcely confirmed by experience, suddenly ceased to be incredible; there were earthquakes of unparalleled extent and violence; eclipses of the sun occurred with a frequency unrecorded in in previous times; there were great droughts in sundry places and consequent famines, and that most calamitous and destructive visitation, the sickness of plague. (1.23.1–3)

This passage starts with, then moves beyond conventional measures of greatness—length and size of military operations—and ends with a catalogue of *pathēmata*, not just "sufferings," but things that happen over which humans have no control. This understanding of greatness, combined with the mimetic principle that the scale of treatment should be proportionate to the significance of the episode, explains why certain episodes are accorded extensive treatment even though they are not of great strategic significance. The measure of greatness is *pathos*, not military might. Expansion of scale makes it possible to bring the reader face to face with and see with vividness the moments where *pathos* appears in all its aspects—suffering of those swept into the war, their loss of control, and the emotion of the sympathetic reader. *Pathos* is Thucydides' distinctive and ultimate measure of greatness.

Pathos seems to intensify as the war goes on. It's powerful enough in the account of the plague in the second book, no less so in that of the Corcyrean *stasis* in Book 3. It is implicit in the story of Mytilene and of its counterpart Melos, and culminates in Book 7 with the account of Mycalessus and of the Sicilian disaster. And while we can only extrapolate, would it not be the story of Athens itself—defeat, suffering, the loss of autonomy and control, if Thucydides' story of the war had been completed?

Such a way of writing is Thucydides' genre changer, the feature that most sharply distinguishes his work from his predecessors'. To be sure, it is not inconsistent with Greek rhetorical theory, as we understand it from later writers. Thucydides' goal, however, is not praise or blame, acquittal or conviction, adoption of one policy rather than another. By controlling scale and all that goes along with such control he has, I believe, moved his narrative, and his readers, beyond rhetoric, from *peithō* to *pathos*. . .

References

Bekker, I. ed. 1831-1870. *Aristotelis Opera*. Berlin: Georg Reimer.
Bury, R. G. trans. 1926. *Plato: Laws*. Cambridge: Harvard University Press.
Connor, W. R. 1984. *Thucydides*. Princeton: Princeton University Press.
Crane, G. 1996. *The Blinded Eye: Thucydides and the New Written Word*. Lanham: Rowman and Littlefield.
Crawley, R. trans. 1951. *Thucydides: The Peloponnesian War*. New York: The Modern Library.
Dewald, C. 2005. *Thucydides' War Narrative*. Berkeley: University of California Press.
Fowler, H. N. trans. 1914. *Plato: Euthyphro, Apology, Crito, Phaedo, Phaedrus*. Cambridge: Harvard University Press.
Fyfe, W. H. 1995. *Aristotle: Poetics. Longinus: On the Sublime. Demetrius: On Style*. Cambridge, MA: Harvard University Press.
Hett, W. S. trans. 1927. *Aristotle: Problems Volume I*. Cambridge: Harvard University Press.
Lausberg, H. 1998. *Handbook of Literary Rhetoric*. Translated by Matthew T. Bliss et al. Leiden, Brill.
Pritchett, W. K. trans. and comm. 1975. *Dionysius of Halicarnassus: On Thucydides*. Berkeley: University of California Press.
Rackham, H. trans. 1936. *Aristotle: Problems Volume II and Rhetoric to Alexander*. Cambridge: Harvard University Press.
Roberts, W.R. trans. 1927. *Demetrius: On Style*. Cambridge: Harvard University Press.
Watson, J. S. trans. 1909. *Quintilian's Institutes of Oratory*. London: G. Bell.
Woodman, A. J. 1996. *Rhetoric in Classical Historiography*. Portland: Areopagitica.
Zanker, G. 1981. "Enargeia in the Ancient Criticism of Poetry." *Rheinisches Museum* 124: 297–311.

CHAPTER 13

THE TREE, THE FUNNEL, AND THE DIPTYCH

Some Patterns in Thucydides' Longest Sentences

JEFFREY RUSTEN

"What is the matter with the man, that he writes like that?" So wrote R. G. Collingwood (1952, 29) of Thucydides' notoriously difficult style. Dionysius of Halicarnassus (*Thuc.* 55, cf. de Jonge 2011, and chapter 37 in this volume) was more precise in his objections: "[We might] imitate those constructions whose brevity, impressiveness, vehemence, intensity, grandeur and the related virtues are obvious to everyone; but neither admire nor imitate those which are baffling, hard to understand, in need of linguistic commentary, and whose figuration is tortured and apparently ungrammatical."

Although Thucydides' excessive brevity is often criticized as here (see also Denniston 1952, 21), he is also faulted for his long sentences: "ideas which are hyperbatic and intricate and desire to express many things abruptly and take a long time to reach their conclusions" (Dion. Hal., *Thuc.* 52), and for arguments that "become twisted and intricate and hard to untangle." (Letter to Ammaeus 16, with reference to Thuc. 2.37.4). Indeed, a late-twentieth-century translation of Thucydides claims increased accuracy precisely because it retains his long sentences, without splitting them up (Lattimore 1998).

All these statements would suggest that length in itself may be a criterion for selecting Thucydidean sentences for stylistic analysis, and in fact many of his longest sentences (usually 100 words or more; I began with those collected by Yaginuma 1988 and 2000, 75–77, although the details of his analysis in Japanese are inaccessible to me)[1] are structured in quite distinctive ways. Three types of sentence stand out because they mass numerous subordinate clauses (mostly circumstantial participles and relative clauses) separately from an isolated main verb (or cluster of verbs). According to this

---

[1] Thanks to Kurt Pipa for assistance with Yaginuma's writings.

verb's position in the sentence, the main action is presented as either an initial fact to be explicated and complicated (the "tree"), or as the final culmination of a complex of motives or observations (the "funnel"), or as a hinge that opens to the reader two tableaux, a "before" and "after," and displays how they contrast with or mirror each other (the "diptych").

ARTICULATION AND SUBORDINATION: READING THUCYDIDES' LONG SENTENCES

The analyses in the following sections show the separate cola on each line, with progressive indentations indicating each level of subordination—a successive colon's subordination is indicated by placement below and to the right of its predecessors; alternatively, being placed to their left means it belongs to a higher level of syntax. Only the cola on the extreme left margin are independent clauses. Sometimes, however, coordinating sentence particles (τε/καί, γάρ, μέν/δέ) are placed alone on a separate line to clarify the controlling structure.

This visualization does not employ common distortions to clarify the sentences: it never alters word order, omits words, draws connective or dividing lines, or underlines or capitalizes words. Instead it separates cola for comprehension, to show levels of subordination by simple indentation (leftmost for main clauses), and to indicate whatever cohering phrases are separated by hyperbaton, not by re-arranging words, but by placing them at the same indentation, to show that they belong to the same level of subordination. To follow the word order of the entire sentence, read row-by-row, left to right. To follow the levels of syntactic subordination, read column-by-column from the top down for the entire first column; for each column thereafter read the subordinate phrase or phrases between the higher-level elements to the left on which they depend.

I should add that the appended *translations* make no attempt to reproduce either the word order or the levels of subordination, and often translate subordinate clauses as independent sentences and alter their order.

Sophisticated readers will notice immediately that, despite my application of the word "tree" to one of these types, my procedure is completely unrelated to the syntactic markup known as "treebanking," which is clearly defined, especially as it applies to Thucydides, in Mambrini 2013.[2] My analysis is by comparison more subjective and impressionistic, and is centered on a feature that syntactic markup seems largely to filter out of its descriptions, namely the order in which words are placed.

---

[2] Thanks to Eleni Bozia for helping clarify my thoughts here.

The Tree: Initial Single-Verb Long Sentences

This sentence type has been noticed both in antiquity and among modern critics of Thucydides. Denniston (1952, 66-7) noted it as particularly Thucydidean, although he mistakenly thought it identical with the "historical period" mentioned by Demetrius (*On Style* 19)—rather, it resembles most closely Demetrius' "dialogic" period, which is exemplified in Demetrius by the first sentence of Plato's *Republic*, famously thought in antiquity to be the end-product of careful revisions (cf. Dion. Hal. *de Comp verb* 25, Quint. 8.6.64, Diog. Laert. 3.37):

> κατέβην
>   χθὲς
>   εἰς Πειραιᾶ
>   μετὰ Γλαύκωνος τοῦ Ἀρίστωνος
>   προσευξόμενός
>   τε
>   τῇ θεῷ
>   καὶ ἅμα
>   τὴν ἑορτὴν
>   βουλόμενος θεάσασθαι
>   τίνα τρόπον ποιήσουσιν
>   ἄτε νῦν πρῶτον ἄγοντες.

FIGURE 1 Plato, Republic 1, 327a.

> I went down yesterday to the Piraeus, with Glaucon, son of Ariston; I was going to pray to the goddess, and also wanted to watch how they would carry out the festival, since they were holding it for the first time.

The sentence is grammatically complete in the first few words, but the speaker's motivations are appended in causal participles, and the second of these is expanded with a further clause that moves away from him to the performers of the ritual who will be the focus of the next sentence, after which the third sentence (see note three for the full quotation) will close the ring (προσευξόμενός ... θεάσασθαι /προσευξάμενοι καὶ θεωρήσαντες) and reverse the opening movement (κατέβην ... μετὰ Γλαύκωνος / ἀπῇμεν πρὸς τὸ ἄστυ); the opening has been merely a prelude to the encounter to come.[3]

---

[3] 327a: κατέβην χθὲς εἰς Πειραιᾶ μετὰ Γλαύκωνος τοῦ Ἀρίστωνος προσευξόμενός τε τῇ θεῷ καὶ ἅμα τὴν ἑορτὴν βουλόμενος θεάσασθαι τίνα τρόπον ποιήσουσιν ἄτε νῦν πρῶτον ἄγοντες. καλὴ μὲν οὖν μοι

Thucydides' opening sentence is longer (and will resonate more widely in his text), but similarly structured:

> Θουκυδίδης Ἀθηναῖος ξυνέγραψε τὸν πόλεμον
>   τῶν Πελοποννησίων καὶ Ἀθηναίων,
>   ὡς ἐπολέμησαν πρὸς ἀλλήλους,
>   ἀρξάμενος εὐθὺς καθισταμένου
>   καὶ ἐλπίσας
>   μέγαν τε ἔσεσθαι
>   καὶ ἀξιολογώτατον τῶν προγεγενημένων,
>   τεκμαιρόμενος
>   ὅτι ἀκμάζοντές
>   τε
>   ἦσαν ἐς αὐτὸν ἀμφότεροι παρασκευῇ τῇ πάσῃ
>   καὶ
>   τὸ ἄλλο Ἑλληνικὸν
>   ὁρῶν
>   ξυνιστάμενον πρὸς ἑκατέρους,
>   τὸ μὲν εὐθύς
>   τὸ δὲ καὶ διανοούμενον

FIGURE 2 Thucydides 1.1.

Thucydides of Athens composed the war the Peloponnesians and Athenians fought against each other. He started as soon as it broke out, since he foresaw it would be important, and most noteworthy of all before it. This deduction was based on the peak of every aspect of preparedness reached by both entrants, and the observation that the remaining Greek peoples were joining one side or the other, either from its outbreak or planning it later.

The main verb is followed by two participles that are not parallel in sense (ἀρξάμενος is temporal, ἐλπίσας is causal), the second of which is in turn explained by two further participles introducing subordinate clauses, and the second of these is elaborated still more. (For more detailed discussion of its context, see Rusten, in preparation). Far from being a "flaccid" (Denniston 1952, 67) structure, it moves the reader from the foregrounded simple action back into its motivations and precursors—the participles are in reverse chronological order—which will lead to a parallel between rational prediction of the future and reconstruction of the past in the τεκμήρια of 1.2–20 (on which see Rusten, in preparation).

The same structure produces a different effect in a sentence from the Funeral Oration (2.43.1–2):

καὶ ἡ τῶν ἐπιχωρίων πομπὴ ἔδοξεν εἶναι, οὐ μέντοι ἧττον ἐφαίνετο πρέπειν ἣν οἱ Θρᾷκες ἔπεμπον. [327β] προσευξάμενοι δὲ καὶ θεωρήσαντες ἀπῆμεν πρὸς τὸ ἄστυ.

> καὶ οἵδε μὲν προσηκόντως τῇ πόλει τοιοίδε ἐγένοντο·
>   τοὺς δὲ λοιποὺς
> χρὴ
>   ἀσφαλεστέραν μὲν εὔχεσθαι,
>   ἀτολμοτέραν δὲ μηδὲν ἀξιοῦν
>   τὴν ἐς τοὺς πολεμίους διάνοιαν ἔχειν,
>   σκοποῦντας μὴ λόγῳ μόνῳ τὴν ὠφελίαν,
>   ἥν ἄν τις
>   πρὸς οὐδὲν χεῖρον αὐτοὺς ὑμᾶς εἰδότας
>   μηκύνοι,
>   λέγων
>   ὅσα
>   ἐν τῷ τοὺς πολεμίους
>   ἀμύνεσθαι]
>   ἀγαθὰ ἔνεστιν,
>   ἀλλὰ μᾶλλον
>   τὴν τῆς πόλεως δύναμιν καθ' ἡμέραν ἔργῳ θεωμένους
>   καὶ ἐραστὰς γιγνομένους αὐτῆς,
>   καὶ
>   ὅταν ὑμῖν μεγάλη δόξῃ εἶναι,
>   ἐνθυμουμένους
>   ὅτι
>   τολμῶντες
>   καὶ γιγνώσκοντες τὰ δέοντα
>   καὶ ἐν τοῖς ἔργοις αἰσχυνόμενοι
>   ἄνδρες αὐτὰ ἐκτήσαντο,
>   καὶ
>   ὁπότε καὶ πείρᾳ του σφαλεῖεν,
>   οὐκ οὖν καὶ τὴν πόλιν γε τῆς σφετέρας ἀρετῆς ἀξιοῦντες
>   στερίσκειν,]
>   κάλλιστον δὲ ἔρανον αὐτῇ προϊέμενοι.

FIGURE 3 Thucydides 2.43.1-2 (107 words).

Now these men, in kinship to the city, matched this description. And those remaining behind, in your determination against the enemy, must pray for better survival, but decide on no less daring. Do not study what you will gain from a single speech that might dwell on what you yourselves know just as well, the advantages inherent in resisting our enemies. Instead of that, immerse yourselves daily in the city's actual power—fall under its spell—and when you realize its magnitude, then think that it was acquired by men who dared, who knew what to do, and would have been ashamed not to do it. If their attempt at anything ever was defeated they did not suddenly decide to withhold from the city their own bravery; they lavished on it the finest contribution of all.

After ἔχειν there is no further infinitive dependent on χρὴ. Instead, διάνοιαν is expanded with accusative participles that develop its contents and motivation, and these are themselves sometimes expanded, as Pericles directs hearers away from his own speech and toward deepening their perception of the city's importance, the men who acquired it, and the gift to the city of their lives. As Trédé (1975) well observes, the initial main clause in these structures is the trunk from which grow the branches that fill out the action, its "ramifications."

The tree structure can also be exploited formally, as in 6.43.1, the description of Athenian forces crossing over from Corcyra to Sicily (133 words), where two initial verbs are followed by 110 words of datives of military accompaniment expanded by parentheses, all organized by μέν/δέ.

The Funnel: Long Sentences that Culminate in their Final Verb(s)

The opposite structure, where a main verb is deployed at the end of a sequence of participles and other subordinate clauses detailing motives and circumstances, has long been noted as a characteristically Thucydidean narrative device (cf. Schneider 1974; Lang 1995), and often the last main verb in these sequences is a decisive one (1.20.2 ἀπέκτειναν; 2.42.4 ἀπηλλάγησαν; 2.65.10–12 ἐταράχθησαν; 2.65.12 ἐσφάλησαν). In some cases Thucydides pushes this structure to the limit by maximizing the preceding subordinate clauses before funneling them all into a single decisive action.

One such sentence describes the thinking of the Spartans just before they executed the surrendered Plataeans (3.68.1, ninety words):

οἱ δὲ Λακεδαιμόνιοι δικασταὶ
  νομίζοντες
    τὸ ἐπερώτημα σφίσιν ὀρθῶς ἕξειν,
      εἴ τι ἐν τῷ πολέμῳ ὑπ' αὐτῶν ἀγαθὸν πεπόνθασι,
  διότι
    τόν τε ἄλλον χρόνον ἠξίουν δῆθεν
      αὐτοὺς κατὰ τὰς παλαιὰς Παυσανίου μετὰ τὸν Μῆδον
      σπονδὰς ἡσυχάζειν
    καὶ ὅτε ὕστερον
      πρὸ τοῦ περιτειχίζεσθαι
    [ἃ]προείχοντο αὐτοῖς κοινοὺς εἶναι κατ' ἐκεῖνα,
      ὡς οὐκ ἐδέξαντο,
  ἡγούμενοι
    τῇ ἑαυτῶν δικαίᾳ βουλήσει ἔκσπονδοι ἤδη ὑπ' αὐτῶν κακῶς πεπονθέναι
  αὖθις τὸ αὐτὸ ἕνα ἕκαστον παραγαγόντες καὶ ἐρωτῶντες,
    εἴ τι Λακεδαιμονίους καὶ τοὺς ξυμμάχους ἀγαθὸν ἐν τῷ πολέμῳ δεδρακότες
    ὁπότε μὴ φαῖεν,
ἀπάγοντες ἀπέκτεινον
καὶ ἐξαίρετον ἐποιήσαντο οὐδένα.

FIGURE 4 Thucydides 3.68.1 (90 words).

The Spartan judges thought that the question posed to the Plataeans, whether Spartans had been done any good by the Plataeans during the war, would be correct. They claimed they had long kept asking the Plataeans to abstain from war in accordance with the old treaty of Pausanias after the Persian war. Later, before they laid siege to them, when they offered them neutrality on that basis and they did not accept, they considered that because their proposal had been lawful they had been dismissed from the treaty, and had accordingly suffered injury from them. They rounded them up one by one and put to them the same question, whether they had done anything good for the Spartans and their allies during the war. When they said no, they led him them away and killed them. They made no exceptions.

The Plataeans and Thebans have made direct speeches justifying their position; here the Spartans' participial motivation (see again Schneider 1974 and Lang 1995) contains their legalistic self-justification (though undermined by δῆθεν) for framing the case in this way. The passage illustrates the Athenians' acid put-down of Spartan morality in the Melian dialogue (1.106.3).

The background to a Spartan decision is characterized differently in another funnel sentence at 5.17.2, which is about peace negotiations and a treaty with Athens (124 words):

```
καὶ
    τόν τε χειμῶνα τοῦτον ἦσαν ἐς λόγους
    καὶ πρὸς τὸ ἔαρ ἤδη
        παρασκευή τε προεπανεσείσθη
            ἀπὸ τῶν Λακεδαιμονίων
                περιαγγελλομένη κατὰ πόλεις ὡς <ἐς> ἐπιτειχισμόν,
                    ὅπως οἱ Ἀθηναῖοι μᾶλλον ἐσακούοιεν,
καὶ
    ἐπειδὴ
        ἐκ τῶν ξυνόδων ἅμα πολλὰς δικαιώσεις προενεγκόντων ἀλλήλοις
    ξυνεχωρεῖτο
        ὥστε
                    ἃ ἑκάτεροι πολέμῳ ἔσχον
                ἀποδόντας
            τὴν εἰρήνην ποιεῖσθαι,
            Νίσαιαν δ' ἔχειν Ἀθηναίους
                        (ἀνταπαιτούντων
                γὰρ
                    Πλάταιαν
            οἱ Θηβαῖοι ἔφασαν
                    οὐ βίᾳ,
                    ἀλλ' ὁμολογίᾳ
                                αὐτῶν προσχωρησάντων
```

FIGURE 5 Thucydides 5.17.2 (124 words).

```
                                               καὶ οὐ προδόντων
                    ἔχειν τὸ χωρίον,
              καὶ οἱ Ἀθηναῖοι τῷ αὐτῷ τρόπῳ τὴν Νίσαιαν),
        τότε δὴ
              παρακαλέσαντες τοὺς ἑαυτῶν ξυμμάχους
        οἱ Λακεδαιμόνιοι,
              καὶ ψηφισαμένων
                    πλὴν Βοιωτῶν καὶ Κορινθίων καὶ Ἠλείων καὶ
                    Μεγαρέων
              τῶν ἄλλων
                    ὥστε καταλύεσθαι
                          (τούτοις δὲ οὐκ ἤρεσκε τὰ πρασσόμενα),
        ποιοῦνται τὴν ξύμβασιν
        καὶ ἐσπείσαντο πρὸς τοὺς Ἀθηναίους
        καὶ ὤμοσαν,
        ἐκεῖνοί τε πρὸς τοὺς Λακεδαιμονίους,
        τάδε·
```

FIGURE 5 Continued

During this winter they entered into talks; as spring approached the Spartans sent messages to their cities to solicit an advance offensive buildup ostensibly for a permanent fortification, so that the Athenians would take the talks more seriously. And at the point when, after conferences in which many demands were put forward at once against each other, they reached an agreement to make peace after the return of the territories each side had gained during the war, except that Athens would keep Nisaea (when they asked for Plataea back the Thebans said they possessed the territory not by force but by a treaty of submission and not betrayal, so the Athenians said the same thing about Nisaea), at that point the Spartans, after a conference of their allies where, with the exception of Boeotians, Corinthians, Eleans, and Megarians (who objected to the terms) all the rest voted to make an end, executed the accord, and made a formal treaty with the Athenians and took an oath, as did the Athenians to the Spartans, in the following words. [The exact terms and names of the oath-takers follow.]

Note the following features:

- A long process with some detail is disposed of in a single sentence.
- Spartans are the subject throughout, although negotiations and treaty are reciprocal.
- Two initial verbs (τε/καί) govern the opening Spartan gambit (thirty words).
- The rest of the sentence ("when … then indeed") concludes with a trio of verbs all referring to the same act of peacemaking. But here the circumstances prior to the agreement—a Spartan feint at a new stage of permanent war, disputes over the terms (leading to an exception for Athens), allies refusing to accept—seem less to lead up to the peace than to undermine it.

A similar, but shorter structure fills in the background for the description of the execution of Nicias at 7.86.4.

Diptych Structures

The two previous structures are striking in their rigor and length, but hardly unique to Thucydides—indeed, it is precisely because they are standard in other historians and orators that they are notable in the otherwise stylistically eccentric historian. But a third structure seems much more original and may be Thucydides' own invention. One could say it puts together the two previous ones, with a verb-initial sentence motivating, planning, or in some other way setting up the action of part one, which is then unrolled and played out with a decisive verb in the second part. Yet the beginning or end (and the position of the verb) is less important than the turning point in the middle, which is strongly marked as a logical or temporal hinge.

The most notable example is the exquisitely structured showdown between the forces of Brasidas and the Athenians at 4.73, a moment of high suspense that unrolls as follows: a small Athenian force executes a plot to enter Megara with the help of sympathizers inside the walls; their initial trick fails, but they have already taken the seaport of Nisaea, and hope that internal events at Megara may still go their way (69.1). Meanwhile, the Spartan Brasidas has rushed to the area with a large force; his own initial request to enter and defend Megara has also been rebuffed, since both factions inside the city decide to keep still and see what will happen between the two major powers outside the walls (ἡσυχάσασι τὸ μέλλον περιιδεῖν, 71.2).

```
μετὰ δὲ τοῦτο
Βρασίδας καὶ τὸ στράτευμα ἐχώρουν
        ἐγγυτέρω τῆς θαλάσσης
        καὶ τῆς τῶν Μεγαρέων πόλεως,
καὶ
        καταλαβόντες χωρίον ἐπιτήδειον
        παραταξάμενοι
ἡσύχαζον,
        οἰόμενοι
                σφίσιν ἐπιέναι τοὺς Ἀθηναίους
        καὶ
                τοὺς Μεγαρέας
        ἐπιστάμενοι
                περιορωμένους
                        ὁποτέρων ἡ νίκη ἔσται.
καλῶς δὲ ἐνόμιζον σφίσιν ἀμφότερα ἔχειν,
        ἅμα μὲν
                τὸ μὴ ἐπιχειρεῖν προτέρους μηδὲ μάχης καὶ κινδύνου ἑκόντας ἄρξαι,
                ἐπειδή γε ἐν φανερῷ ἔδειξαν ἑτοῖμοι ὄντες ἀμύνεσθαι,
                καὶ αὐτοῖς ὥσπερ ἀκονιτὶ τὴν νίκην δικαίως ἂν τίθεσθαι,
```

FIGURE 6 Thucydides 4.73 (253 words).

                    ἐν τῷ αὐτῷ δὲ
                            καὶ πρὸς τοὺς Μεγαρέας ὀρθῶς ξυμβαίνειν·
                                                    (εἰ
                                    μὲν γὰρ
                                            μὴ ὤφθησαν ἐλθόντες,
                                    οὐκ ἂν ἐν τύχῃ γίγνεσθαι σφίσιν,
                                    ἀλλὰ σαφῶς ἂν
                                            ὥσπερ ἡσσηθέντων
                                    στερηθῆναι εὐθὺς τῆς πόλεως·
                                    νῦν δὲ κἂν τυχεῖν αὐτοὺς ᾿Αθηναίους μὴ βουληθέντας
                                            ἀγωνίζεσθαι,
                                                    ὥστε ἀμαχητὶ ἂν περιγενέσθαι αὐτοῖς ὧν ἕνεκα
                                                            ἦλθον.)
ὅπερ καὶ ἐγένετο.
οἱ γὰρ Μεγαρῆς,
            ὡς οἱ ᾿Αθηναῖοι
                    ἐτάξαντο μὲν παρὰ τὰ μακρὰ τείχη ἐξελθόντες,
                    ἡσύχαζον δὲ καὶ αὐτοὶ μὴ ἐπιόντων,
                    λογιζόμενοι καὶ οἱ ἐκείνων στρατηγοὶ
                            μὴ ἀντίπαλον εἶναι σφίσι τὸν κίνδυνον,
                                    ἐπειδὴ καὶ τὰ πλείω αὐτοῖς
                                            προυκεχωρήκει,
                                    ἄρξασι μάχης πρὸς πλέονας αὐτῶν
                                    ἢ λαβεῖν νικήσαντας Μέγαρα
                                    ἢ σφαλέντας τῷ βελτίστῳ τοῦ ὁπλιτικοῦ
                                            βλαφθῆναι,
                            τοῖς δὲ
                                    ξυμπάσης τῆς δυνάμεως καὶ τῶν
                                            παρόντων
                                    μέρος ἕκαστον κινδυνεύειν εἰκότως ἐθέλειν
                                            τολμᾶν,
                    χρόνον δὲ ἐπισχόντες
                    καὶ ὡς οὐδὲν ἀφ' ἑκατέρων ἐπεχειρεῖτο,
                    ἀπῆλθον πρότερον οἱ ᾿Αθηναῖοι ἐς τὴν Νίσαιαν
                    καὶ αὖθις οἱ Πελοποννήσιοι
                            ὅθενπερ ὡρμήθησαν,
οὕτω δὴ
            τῷ μὲν Βρασίδᾳ αὐτῷ
            καὶ τοῖς ἀπὸ τῶν πόλεων ἄρχουσιν
οἱ τῶν φευγόντων φίλοι Μεγαρῆς,
            ὡς ἐπικρατήσαντι
            καὶ
                    τῶν ᾿Αθηναίων οὐκέτι ἐθελησάντων μάχεσθαι,
            θαρσοῦντες μᾶλλον
ἀνοίγουσί τε τὰς πύλας
καὶ
            δεξάμενοι
                    καταπεπληγμένων ἤδη τῶν πρὸς τοὺς ᾿Αθηναίους πραξάντων
ἐς λόγους ἔρχονται.

FIGURE 6 Continued

After this [i.e., after an indecisive battle between Boeotian and Athenian cavalry] Brasidas and his army advanced closer to the sea and Megara, occupied a suitable area and formed for battle, but remained still. They thought that the Athenians were attacking them, and they knew that the Megarians were waiting to see which side would have the victory. They believed the situation was in their favor in two ways: firstly that they must not attempt to be first to initiate battle and its risk unless forced, since they had clearly shown that they were ready to defend themselves and that the victory might be fairly assigned to them as if uncontested; at the same time, that it was turning out successfully for them as to the Megarians since, had they not been conspicuous in coming there, chance might not be coming into play for them, rather they would have immediately lost the city just as clearly as if defeated; but now the Athenians might themselves chance to be unwilling to join the contest, so that what the Peloponnesians had come to accomplish might fall into their hands without any fighting.

This is precisely what happened.

Now the Megarians—after the Athenians had come out and formed for battle beside the long walls, but themselves too remained still when the enemy did not attack, because their generals too made a calculation: since the greater part of their plan had been successful, if they initiated a fight against their superior numbers it was not an equivalent risk for them between taking Megara if they won, and suffering the deaths of the elite of the hoplites if they were defeated; whereas for the other side it made sense for each fraction of those actually present out of the entire force to take a chance on being willing to dare a battle. They waited for a while, and when nothing was attempted by either side, were the first to withdraw to Nisaea, as did the Peloponnesians in response, to the point from which they had advanced—it was then that those Megarians who were friends of the exiles had more confidence, while those who had negotiated with Athens were devastated, since the Athenians were no longer going to fight. They opened up the gates to Brasidas himself as the victor and to the commanders from the other cities, and welcomed them and entered into negotiations.

Although it is a unit, this structure consists of three sentences, the first and last of 119 and 131 words, respectively. The first sentence has two main verbs at the beginning, then sets up an indirect statement with ἐνόμιζον that continues for its final seventy-seven words.

The third sentence, after naming its subject (the Megarians), embarks on a subordinate causal clause with a different subject (the Athenians) that is so long (eighty-five words) that the Megarians are nearly forgotten before we finally return to them with οὕτω δή, and now splits them into two groups (οἱ τῶν φευγόντων φίλοι Μεγαρῆς and τῶν πρὸς τοὺς Ἀθηναίους πραξάντων), of which only the first is the subject.

The middle sentence has just three words, but controls the entire unit. Not only does it shift the focus from Brasidas' calculations to the Athenians, but it also indicates that the former's predictions will come true, and, after the δέσις of the situation, initiates its λύσις.

Furthermore, the structural intricacy is marked by repetitions and synonyms both within the alternative calculations of the first part (μάχης/ἀμαχητί, ὥσπερ ἀκονιτὶ τὴν νίκῃ/ἀμαχητί, ἐν φανερῷ/σαφῶς, ἂν ἐν τύχῃ γίγνεσθαι/κἂν τυχεῖν), and especially between the parallel actions and calculations of the first and second part:

παραταξάμενοι/ ἐτάξαντο
ἡσύχαζον/ἡσύχαζον δὲ καὶ αὐτοὶ (also in the buildup to this sentence at 4. 71.1)
ἐπιέναι/μὴ ἐπιόντων
ἡ νίκη/ νικήσαντας
ἐπιχειρεῖν/οὐδέν . . . ἐπεχειρεῖτο
κινδύνου/τὸν κίνδυνον, κινδυνεύει
μάχης . . . ἄρξαι/ἄρξασι μάχης.
ἕτοιμοι ὄντες, κἂν τυχεῖν . . . μὴ βουληθέντας ἀγωνίζεσθαι/κινδυνεύειν
εἰκότως ἐθέλειν τολμᾶν, οὐκέτι ἐθελησάντων μάχεσθαι
ἡσσηθέντων/σφαλέντας

Just as Athens' attempt on Megara is the hinge of the reversal in this section from Athens' successes to its failures (Babut 1981, 427), so Thucydides presents the detailed turning point as hinging on Brasidas' strategic insight. Indeed, this moment is so important that Brasidas himself will embellish it in a later speech (4.85.7) and be rebuked by Thucydides for exaggeration (4.108.5; see Foster, chapter 18 in this volume).

Other sentences, which cannot be discussed in detail here, show that Thucydides favors the diptych form for moments of high drama:

1.133: The ephors carry out a sting on Pausanias (134 words).
8.90.1: Activities of the Athenian oligarchs (104 words plus forty words).
8.99: The Peloponnesians decide to work with Pharnabazus instead of Tissaphernes (100 words before οὕτω δή, sixty-seven words after it).

No two examples are precisely alike, but all present the diptych and its hinge as vividly as the Brasidas-Athens standoff, and repay close analysis. Note that they are spread throughout the history but, unlike the "Tree" and "Funnel" structures studied above, they occur only in the narrative.

References

Collingwood, R. G. 1946. *The Idea of History*. Oxford: Clarendon.
De Jonge, C. C. 2011. "Dionysius of Halicarnassus and the Scholia on Thucydides' Syntax." In *Ancient Scholarship and Grammar: Archetypes, Concepts, and Contexts*, edited by S. Matthaios, F. Montanari, and A. Rengakos, 451–78. New York: De Gruyter.
Denniston, J. D. 1952. *Greek Prose Style*. Oxford: Clarendon.
Lang, M. 1995. "Participial Motivation in Thucydides." *Mnemosyne* 48: 48–65. (Reprinted in Lang et al. 2011.)
Lang, M., J. Rusten, and R. Hamilton, eds. 2011. *Thucydidean Narrative and Discourse: Essays by Mabel Lang*. Ann Arbor: Michigan Classical Press.
Lattimore, S., trans. 1998. *Thucydides: The Peloponnesian War*. Indianapolis: Hackett.

Mambrini, F. 2013. "Thucydides 1.89–118: A Multi-layer 'Treebank.'" *Center for Hellenic Studies Research Bulletin* 1 (2), http://nrs.harvard.edu/urn-3:hlnc.essay:MambriniF.Thucydides_1.89-118_Multi-layer_Treebank.2013

Rusten, J. 2015. "*Kinêsis* in Thucydides' Preface." In *Kinesis: Essays for Donald Lateiner on the Ancient Depiction of Gesture, Motion, and Emotion,* edited by C. A. Clark, E. Foster, and J. P. Hallett, 27–40. Ann Arbor: University of Michigan Press.

Rusten, J., in preparation. *Commentary on Book One of Thucydides.* Greek and Latin Classics Series. Cambridge: Cambridge University Press.

Schneider, C. 1974. *Information und Absicht bei Thukydides: Untersuchung zur Motivation des Handelns.* Hypomnemata 41. Göttingen: Vandenhoeck & Ruprecht.

Trédé, M. 1975. "Les causes multiples et l'organisation de la période chez Thucydide." In his *Association Guillaume Budé Actes IX Congrès,* 166–76. Paris.

Yaginuma, S. 1988. "Toukyudidesu Chōbun Ni Tsuite" ("On Thucydides' Long Sentences.") *Bungei gengo kenkyu: Bungeihen* 15: 1–28.

Yaginuma, S. 2000. *Toukyudidesu no buntai no kenkyū (The Study of Thucydides' Style),* Tokyo: Iwanami Shoten.

CHAPTER 14

AUTHORIAL COMMENTS IN THUCYDIDES

MATHIEU DE BAKKER

Introduction

At the outset of the fifth year of the Peloponnesian war Thucydides records a string of earthquakes in Athens, Euboea, and Boeotia (3.87.4; 89.1). He mentions a simultaneous surge of the sea that destroys parts of the coastal regions in the Euboean Gulf (3.89.2–3). He reports a similar combination of tsunami and seismic activity on the island of Peparethus (modern-day Skopelos, 3.89.4), and ends with the following observation:

> And I (ἔγωγε) think that the cause of this phenomenon is that the earthquake in the area where its shock was most violent makes the sea withdraw and when it suddenly returns with more force causes the flooding to take place. Without an earthquake I do not think (οὐκ . . . μοι δοκεῖ) that such an event could ever happen. (3.89.5)

This authorial comment upon the forces of nature stands out in Thucydides' work, which rarely strays away from the themes of human action, fortune, and suffering. At first glance it looks like a typically Herodotean afterthought (e.g., Hdt. 2.156.2, 3.115.1–2), in which the emphatic personal pronoun ἔγωγε suggests that the historian seeks to distance himself from those who account for the tsunami as an independent—divinely inspired?—phenomenon. Are polemical reasons enough, however, to merit such an exceptional authorial observation? Thucydides' account of the war is highly focused and selective, and he rarely expresses opinions on subjects that bear no apparent relevance to his larger project. Can we find clues that place his comment within a wider perspective?

At the end of his introduction, Thucydides underlines the magnitude of his subject, arguing that the suffering that befell Greece during the war was without precedent (1.23.1). He claims that the war's atrocities coincided with unparalleled portents and natural calamities, as Greece was struck by more (frequent and violent) earthquakes, solar eclipses, droughts, and famines than ever before. On top of those came the plague, which affected a major part of its population (1.23.3). Although the historian does not claim a causal relationship, he implies that the exceptional events of the war should be seen in coherence with its accompanying natural phenomena.

In the narrative context of Thucydides' tsunami comment, the coherence between natural and human events is thematized. Athens faces another outbreak of the plague, with devastating effects upon its troops (3.87.1–3). Meanwhile, the earthquakes that occur across Greece (3.87.4) make the Spartan king Agis decide to cancel his invasion of Attica (3.89.1). In the intervening paragraph Thucydides relates how the Athenians who are campaigning in Sicily are not able to sail against the Aeolian Islands because of drought (3.88.1), and mentions the volcano on Hiera, one of the archipelago's members (3.88.3). Volcanic activity recurs in a later instalment of Athens' first Sicilian expedition, when Mount Etna erupts for the third time since the Greeks colonized Sicily (3.116.1–2). Thucydides structures his narrative in such a way that these natural phenomena frame the closure of the fifth (3.88.4) and sixth (3.116.3) year of his war.

Although Thucydides' personal comment upon the causal relationship between earthquake and tsunami may appear isolated, it ties in with the implication of coherence between human and natural events that is suggested at the end of his introduction and highlighted in this part of the narrative. When the civil war in Corcyra escalates because of the involvement of Sparta and Athens (3.72–81, 3.82.1), and when the Athenians scale up their war with their first deployment to Sicily (3.86), military activity across the Greek world can no longer be seen in isolation, and it looks as if the forces of nature operate in harmony, orchestrating an ominous background against which this increase in activity unfolds. Thucydides' tsunami comment thus hints at an underlying explanatory model in which all events in the cosmos are interdependent. In his world, suffering caused by human action is bound to be paralleled by natural calamities. Although he never voices this principle explicitly, he weaves references to the forces of nature into his narrative and thereby suggests that they act in some form of "concomitance" with human events.[1]

This chapter addresses instances in the *Histories*' narrative where the author surfaces in person to evaluate the events he describes, as well as the effects of these evaluations upon the ways in which his rich and complex historiography can be received. A first type of these authorial comments is embedded in or framed by the verb forms δοκέω "I think" or δοκεῖ μοι "it seems to me" (e.g., the tsunami comment above). A second type marks the introduction or closure of episodes or accompanies prominent actors when they enter or leave the narrative. A third type consists of "metanarrative references" (Munson 2012, 255) that reflect upon the credibility of the information in the narrative by, for instance, ascribing it to an anonymous source with λέγεται "it is said." Thucydides uses these evaluative comments more sparsely than Herodotus, but since they reveal the author's attitude to his subject matter, they function as valuable pointers to the interpretation of the events as they are staged in the narrative. Often, they can be connected to ideas that Thucydides raises in his longer authorial essays, in particular those

---

[1] For the term, see Munson (2015, 43).

at the outset of his project: the Archaeology (1.2–19), his essay on method (1.20–22), and his observations upon the magnitude and cause of the war (1.23).

Thucydides is often praised for the ways in which his narrative stimulates his reader to become an eyewitness of the events as they unfolded in the past (cf. Kurke 2000, 150). Recent research has revealed that the historian employs a host of narrative techniques to heighten this "experientiality" of his narrative.[2] A strategic use of tenses and moods, detailed description, the representation of speeches, and thoughts ascribed to the actors are all means by which Thucydides "immerses" his reader in the text, so as to impart experiences the outcome of which the actors cannot predict. As Grethlein points out, in such a narrative authorial intrusions like ana-and prolepses and comments are scarce, and judgments preferably obliquely embedded, for instance in words and thoughts of the actors (Grethlein 2013, 18–19).

Thucydides' narrative, however, is not exclusively "experiential." Rood, for instance, argues that the historian's occasional admissions of uncertainty and his emphasis upon the difficulty or inability to find out the truth about the past also serve rhetorical ends, since they lend credibility to the many parts of the narrative in which these methodological issues are smoothed over (Rood 2006, 237). Rood pays attention to passages where Thucydides' personal engagement surfaces, and defines his historiographical *persona* as Janus-faced, diagnosing "a tension between reticent detachment and passionate engagement, between the democratic impulse to let readers make what they will of the narrative and the rigid sense of authority that pervades the narrative" (Rood 2006, 249).

Following Rood's approach one could characterize Thucydides' narrative as a multilayered composition in which the author shifts gears between various stylistic and narratological registers, some of which enable him to present his views in more overt authorial ways. From an interpretative perspective, it is by making themes recur in passages of different registers that Thucydides underlines their saliency. In this respect, much attention has been paid to the interaction between his narrative and the speeches of his actors.[3] In this chapter I argue that despite their scarcity his authorial evaluative comments play an important role in this interaction, too, and deserve equal weight with the speeches and the narrative in the interpretation of his work.[4]

---

[2] Grethlein (2013). See Allan (2007, 2013) for a description of these techniques from a formal-linguistic point of view.
[3] *Inter alia* by Stahl (1966); Hunter (1973); Macleod (1983); Connor (1984); Rood (1998); Morrison (2006); Pelling (2009); Stahl (2009).
[4] Earlier studies of the way(s) in which Thucydides' authorial *persona* surfaces in his work are Pearson (1947); Loraux (1986); Gribble (1998); Rood (2004, 2006). In writing this chapter I took Gribble's and Rood's work as point of departure. Both embed their views within a helpful narratological framework and acknowledge the rhetorical function of the authorial comments.

Programmatic Authorial Comments

Authorial comments are regularly found at the beginning of episodes, or in their initial chapters. They usually carry a programmatic function, specifying or confining the theme(s) of the episode that follows. As was seen above, the narrative that follows the account of Corcyraean *stasis* opens with the story of Athens' first deployment to Sicily. Here, at the beginning of the sixth year of the war, Thucydides notes that, as to Sicilian affairs, he will mention only

> the most important actions (λόγου μάλιστα ἄξια) that the Sicilian allies undertook with the help of the Athenians (μετὰ τῶν Ἀθηναίων οἱ ξύμμαχοι) and that their enemies undertook against the Athenians. (3.90.1)

His choice of words implies that he has omitted wars between the Sicilians themselves in which Athens was not involved. This admission of selectivity is unusual[5] and can be interpreted as an excuse for not inserting a more comprehensive account of Sicilian affairs. It thereby conforms to the rhetorical ploy of *anticipatio*, by which an orator seeks to preempt an objection of his opponent by raising it himself (and playing it down) in anticipation. The comment, however, has an intriguing side effect, as it makes the reader aware that Athens is at this stage playing only a supporting role in Sicily (observe that the Sicilians and not the Athenians are the grammatical subject of the sentence), as opposed to its deep involvement in the war in Greece itself. Indeed, we subsequently learn that Athenian activities are limited to the Sicilian coasts, its nearby islands, and the defense of its ally Rhegium. Thucydides seals his narrative of Athens' first Sicilian campaign with the observation that "afterwards the Greeks in Sicily fought one another *without the Athenians on land*" (4.25.12, my italics). Thus he heightens his reader's awareness that—as to Sicilian affairs—the Athenians are so far only able to scratch the surface with their fleet and in spite of later reinforcements (3.115) lack the manpower to become more deeply engaged. Their relative insignificance in Sicilian warfare is grossly out of tune with the expectations of the Athenians at home, who dispatch the first naval force with the subjection of Sicily in mind (3.86.4). Accordingly, they punish the admirals on their return, "assuming that they were bribed into a retreat whilst it was possible for them to subject Sicily" (4.65.3). This discrepancy between Athenian expectations and Sicilian reality on the ground is further thematized in the narrative of Athens' second, larger Sicilian campaign (Books 6–7).

Programmatic authorial comments may also hint at polemical reasons for the insertion of an episode or the choices made in its presentation. Thucydides begins his digression on the events between the Persian and Peloponnesian Wars (the *Pentekontaetia*) by indicating that he will focus upon the growth of the Athenian empire ("the Athenians

---

[5] Cf. Hornblower (1987, 37) and *Comm. ad loc.*

came in such a way into the situation in which their power grew" 1.89.1). He repeats the announcement of this aim at 1.97.2, where he also points out that his predecessors neglected the period, whereas his contemporary Hellanicus dealt with it only briefly and inaccurately. As in the case of the first Sicilian campaign, these announcements of selectivity frame a larger, compositional goal.

At the end of the *Pentekontaetia*, Thucydides states that these were all (ξύμπαντα) the actions that the Greeks undertook against one another and against foreigners in the approximately fifty years between Xerxes' retreat and the beginning of this war (1.118.2). At first glance, this statement may seem at odds with his opening announcements, as it mentions Greece in general, but not the growth of Athens. It can, however, also be read as an evaluative summary: since almost all events that are mentioned in the preceding digression are Athenian acts of interference, aggression, and expansion, the digression serves to justify Spartan fear of the Athenians. It is this fear that in the first place triggers the insertion of the digression, which explains, by showing the growth of Athenian power, how it came to pass that "they [the Spartans] saw that the majority of Greece was already under their [the Athenians'] sway (ὑποχείρια ἤδη ὄντα)" (1.88).

At the end of his introduction (1.23.6), Thucydides diagnoses this fear as "the truest cause, but least avowed in words" (τὴν ... ἀληθεστάτην πρόφασιν, ἀφανεστάτην δὲ λόγῳ, 1.23.6). There, he presents his diagnosis as resulting from personal analysis (observe ἡγοῦμαι "I am of the opinion," 1.23.6), whereas in 1.88 Spartan fear is mentioned as a *fait accompli*, substantiated by the ensuing digression, which focuses wholly on Athens' expansion as experienced by the Spartans and the other Greeks. Thucydides thus combines authorial comments (1.23.6 and 1.97.2), explanatory suggestions (1.88), and a selective approach in the digression, to persuade his reader of the accuracy of his analysis that Athens' empire building in the preceding decades gave rise to Spartan fear and thereby caused the war. The placement and content of his authorial comments in the opening book point to an argumentative structure that resembles forensic oratory. Thucydides initially expresses his claim about the war's cause as his own opinion (1.23.6), and thereupon delivers evidence in the *Pentekontaetia* that enables him to postulate his initial claim as an unquestionable fact.[6]

Programmatic, too, but in a different way, are Thucydides' character judgments, which are often brief and usually accompany the introduction of an actor or are inserted into the context of his most prominent performance.[7] Most judgments tend to praise the actors in general terms for qualities such as "intelligence" (ξύνεσις) or "excellence" (ἀρετή). They thereby frame the actor's subsequent words and deeds, and encourage the reader to consider the effects of these characteristics upon the current situation presented in the narrative. Thucydides, for instance, praises the character of Hermocrates, a leading politician in Syracuse, at a crucial junction in the Sicilian

---

[6] My analysis here is based upon Westlake (1955) and Connor (1984, 42–47).
[7] On the characterization of individuals in Thucydides see Westlake (1968); Gribble (2006); de Bakker (2013).

episode, when the city has lost its first major battle to the Athenians (6.69–71), and organizes an assembly to discuss the situation:

> He was in every way a remarkably intelligent man (ξύνεσιν οὐδενὸς λειπόμενος), and in the war had not only shown the qualities that come from experience but also won a name for his personal courage (ἀνδρείᾳ ἐπιφανής). (6.72.2)

In Hermocrates' subsequent harangue Thucydides shows how these characteristics relate to the situation at hand. Hermocrates' intelligence surfaces in his analysis of the defeat (6.72.3–4), which Thucydides makes coincide with his own evaluation (6.69.1). Both author and actor ascribe the rout to a lack of organization and experience, which undermined an otherwise unrelenting fighting spirit on the part of the Syracusan defenders. Hermocrates adds concrete suggestions to make the command structure of the Syracusan army more effective and to improve its combat skills and gear (6.72.4–5). Helped by his reputation for courage, he convinces his fellow citizens to adopt the entire (πάντα, 6.73.1) set of motions. In doing so he makes the Syracusans determined to continue resistance, and significantly contributes to the further course of events. Thus Thucydides, through a strategic placement of authorial comments upon Hermocrates' character, points his reader toward an interpretation of the episodes that follow, in which the Syracusan statesman maintains a leading role. Furthermore, the comments also allow his reader to re-evaluate Hermocrates' earlier performance, when he had played a decisive role in the foundering of Athens' first Sicilian campaign by persuading the other Sicilians to end their infighting and come to terms at a conference in Gela (4.58–65, where Thucydides represents Hermocrates' proposal in a direct speech). With his reappearance in the narrative of Athens' second Sicilian campaign, Hermocrates emerges more and more as a man of action in battle and diplomacy (cf. 6.75.4 at Camarina), and as a formidable opponent to the Athenians, who more or less face the equivalent of Pericles, whom Thucydides had introduced as "the first of the Athenians, most capable of speaking and acting" (1.139.4).[8]

Given that Thucydides presents himself as a historian in an authoritative relation to his material (observe his claim to have persistently conducted empirical research in his essay on methodology, 1.22.2), the programmatic pointers in his narrative on themes, selection, and character can be considered his most effective rhetorical tool for guiding his reader.

Authorial Comments as Asides

Authorial comments inserted in the course of an episode do not carry the same programmatic function as comments found at the outset. At first sight, these comments

---

[8] For parallels between Pericles and Hermocrates, see Raaflaub (2006, 221).

appear as footnotes or asides, as illustrated by the tsunami comment discussed above. As they often stray beyond the themes of warfare and military action, however, they contain clues to the historian's methodology and views upon the world. Here I will focus on oracles, ethnography, and the legendary past. Whereas in Herodotus' *Histories* oracles usually propel the narrative, ethnography is given ample attention, and the legendary past is regularly discussed or evoked, Thucydides has pushed these topics to the fringes of his work and usually refers to them in his asides. But the presence, content, and placement in the narrative of these asides are so significant that they should be included in this chapter.

Thucydides mentions various oracles and portentous sayings in his work and in some cases discusses their content.[9] He usually abstains from committing himself to their divine authority by, for instance, ascribing the oracle to an (anonymous) source. This is exemplified by the oracle that the Spartans receive when they ask whether it is better to wage war against Athens:

> And, as is reported, (ὡς λέγεται), the god answered to them that they [the Spartans] would win the war if they fought hard, and that he would assist them, both invited and uninvited. (1.118.3)

This oracle is mentioned again at the end of Thucydides' essay on the plague, where the historian describes its effects upon the citizens of Athens (2.54.4), who believe that they have understood the way in which Apollo has, in causing the plague, assisted the Spartans. In the same chapter, Thucydides mentions another oracular saying of which the elders "claimed" (φάσκοντες, 2.54.2) that it had been chanted already for a long time:

> The Doric War will come and the plague (λοιμός) will join it. (2.54.2)

The historian points out that the exact words of the oracle were disputed, as some believed the correct reading to be "famine" (λιμός) and not "plague" (λοιμός). The plague in Athens, however, made people decide in favour of λοιμός, though Thucydides admits that a future coincidence of war and famine might make them change their minds (2.54.3). In discussing these oracles, Thucydides tacitly acknowledges their importance, as they influence popular morale during the war, but he also highlights the extent to which their value depends upon the responses of their recipients (cf. Grethlein 2013, 29). He himself provides an example of this when he discusses the oracle that warned against settlement in the Pelargikon area of Athens:

> And to me the oracle seems to have come to pass in a sense contrary to what one expected. For the misfortunes that befell the city were not caused by its illegal settlement, but its settlement became inevitable because of the war, and although the

---

[9] On Thucydides and oracles see Powell (1979); Marinatos (1981); Dover (1988).

oracle did not mention the latter, it knew in advance (προῄδει) that the place would never become settled for a good purpose. (2.17.2)

Thucydides presents himself here as a clever interpreter, preferring rationalistic explanation to superstition. Thereby the reader is reminded of his authority and encouraged to apply similar critical facilities in analyzing the past. Nonetheless, he does not deny the oracle its predictive faculty, which has led to speculations about Thucydides' belief in oracles in general. Thucydides' claim that the oracle had advance knowledge (προῄδει) should not, however, be taken as indicative of his personal religious views.[10] He merely credits the oracle with proper common sense, as it professes that accursed ground will only become inhabited under extreme circumstances.

A second subject that Thucydides treats in his authorial asides is ethnography. This appears to be an innovation over earlier historians, who either dealt with ethnography exclusively (e.g. Hecataeus *periodos gēs*) or inserted long ethnographic essays in their works (Herodotus). Thucydides' focus remains fixed upon the war, and only rarely does he make ethnographical observations. An exception is found in his essay about the war of the Odrysians against the Macedonians (2.95–101). In this part of the narrative Thucydides pays attention to the geography of the Odrysian empire in Thrace in a manner that resembles Herodotus (cf. Hornblower 2004, 181; Munson 2012, 244–246). Observe, for instance, the adoption of the so-called hodological perspective, i.e. the view of the wandering traveler, in describing the layout of the area, typically expressed by the dative (x) or made explicit by the measurement of an area in temporal units as a traveler would count them (y)[11]:

> (x) ... next, if you cross (ὑπερβάντι) the Haemus, the Getae... (2.96.1)
> (y) And over land a well-equipped man (ἀνὴρ εὔζωνος) will complete the journey from Abdera to the Danube in eleven days. (2.97.1)

Furthermore, he makes observations about the customs of the Thracians, indicating that some of their tribes "wore daggers" (2.96.2; 98.4), and saying of the Odrysians that

> they had established a custom contrary to that of the Persian royalty and in line with that of the other Thracians: to take gifts rather than give them. (2.97.4)

This last comment explains the rise to power of the Odrysian monarchs (2.97.4–5). Their huge income enables them to levy an enormous army from the tribes, which attracts even more autonomous Thracians in search of booty, until it reaches a size, "as is said" (λέγεται), of no fewer than 150,000 soldiers and cavalry (2.98.3). In spite of this mass, which makes the Greeks in the area look fearfully to the Northeast, the effects of

---

[10] For discussion and references, see Hornblower (whose opinion I follow), *Comm. ad loc.*
[11] For the "hodological" perspective in Herodotus, see Purves (2010, chap. 3 and 4).

the expedition are minimal. Plagued by a shortage of provisions and harsh weather, the Odrysian king, Sitalces, hastily withdraws after a settlement is reached (2.101.5–6).

As the effects of Sitalces' expedition upon the course of the war in Greece are slight, Thucydides' exceptional attention to ethnographical elements in this passage asks for an explanation. It has been plausibly suggested that Thucydides knew the area well because his ancestors came from Thrace, and that he wished to establish his authority with a detailed account of its geography and the customs of its people (Hornblower, *Comm. ad* 2.95–101). But it cannot be excluded that he had other motives for dwelling upon the Odrysian campaign at such length. First, it was Athens' involvement in the area that caused the entire expedition to happen, since the city wanted Sitalces' help to quell the Chalcidian war (2.95.2). If we are willing to interpret, with Rusten (2015), Thucydides' introductory κίνησις … μεγίστη (1.1.2) as referring to the unprecedented "mobilization" that the war brought about, Sitalces' sizeable campaign offers a poignant example and also proof that this "mobilization" affected "part of the non-Greek people" (μέρει τινὶ τῶν βαρβάρων, 1.1.2). But the story also underlines the potential danger of Athenian involvement with less civilized peoples who are accustomed to take rather than to give and who still carry their weapons upon them—in contrast to the Athenians themselves, who were the first to lay them down (1.6.3). Sitalces' expedition risks spiraling out of control and it is only because of its logistic backfiring that further destabilization of the area can be prevented. This destabilization of the area is anyway highlighted by Thucydides' choice of verb (he "made [them] move," ἀνίστησιν, 2.96.1; cf. 96.3) to describe the way in which Sitalces levies his army. He thereby makes the campaign resemble a migration of Thracian tribes into areas closer to the Greek world, with potentially devastating effects.

A third subject that recurs in authorial asides are traditions about the Greek legendary past. As commentators have pointed out, Thucydides accepted these as essentially historical, though, like his predecessor Herodotus, he approached them with a critical mind.[12] An example of his approach is his warning not to confuse Teres, father of Thracian king Sitalces, with the mythical Thracian king Tereus:

> This Teres has nothing in common with the Tereus who married Pandion's daughter from Athens. He [Tereus] lived in Daulia, a place in modern-day Phocis where Thracians dwelled at the time, and it was in that area that the women committed their crime upon Itys (many poets too have nicknamed the nightingale the bird of Daulia), and it is evident (εἰκός) that Pandion contracted the marriage for his daughter at this moderate distance with an eye on mutual assistance rather than at a distance of so many days in the land of the Odrysians. But Teres did not even have the same name. … (2.29.3)

Thucydides makes his reader aware that the Thracian kings Teres and Tereus are not to be confused. This exceptional, corrective aside may have had polemical intentions. It is possible that he targets the Athenian *vox populi*, just as he elsewhere finds fault with his

---

[12] See Hornblower, *Comm. ad* 1.9–11; Rhodes, *Comm. ad* 1.3.1.

fellow citizens for a limited or biased understanding of their past. Fundamental in this respect is the opening paragraph of his digression on method (1.20), where he blames the majority of the Greeks for slackness in their search for the truth. Athenian ignorance about the Pisistratids and the assault upon Hipparchus is offered as poignant example there, and later elaborated in a digression that frames Thucydides' account of the scandal of the Hermae and the recall of Alcibiades from his command in the Sicilian expedition (6.54–59).

Thucydides' approach to the ancient legend of Tereus resembles the rationalism that is typical of Herodotus. He does not reject its content, but provides evidence (based on what the poets say and upon plausibility, εἰκός) that Pandion's daughter married Tereus (not Teres) from Phocis, which was near enough to provide support to the Athenian king. His version of the legend thereby conforms with his view of Greece's early past as expounded in the Archaeology, where the past is characterized by frequent migrations throughout a violent world (1.2.1) and the absence of different names for "Greeks" and "barbarians" (1.3.3), which explains why an Athenian king would marry off a daughter to a Thracian peer. Migrations, violence, and Greco-barbarian relationships recur in other, similar, asides on Greek legend, such as the references to the foundations of Amphilochian Argos (2.68.3–5) and Acarnania (2.102.5–6) by the sons of Amphiaraus from Argos. According to legend, they took part in the second, successful expedition against Thebes, and afterwards murdered their mother in revenge of their father. Exiled from Argos, they moved to the Greek Northwest, where they established colonies that had to cope with a volatile non-Greek population in their hinterlands. In the case of Macedonia, Thucydides explains how the Temenids—also exiles from Argos (cf. Hdt. 8.137.1)—carved out a large coastal territory for themselves by driving out several barbarian tribes (2.99.3–6).[13]

Other references to the Greek legendary past befit the historian's general themes in a similar way. In the Archaeology, he presents the Cretan king Minos as the first to establish a thalassocracy in the Aegean. He thereby launches the theme of concomitance between progress in naval developments and rule over others (observe ἦρξε "he [Minos] ruled," 1.4) and anticipates the growth of Athens' empire as expounded later in the *Pentekontaetia* (see above). In the case of Agamemnon, Thucydides further elaborates this theme, claiming that in his view (μοι δοκεῖ, 1.9.3) it was the fear of the king's naval superiority that motivated the other Greeks to ally themselves and partake in the expedition against Troy (1.9.1–4). Again, Athens comes to mind, whose superiority inspires fear, not only in its enemies (e.g., Sparta's fear 1.23.6), but also in its subordinate allies, as evidenced by Pericles' and Cleon's appeal to the Athenians to consider their ruling over the empire a tyranny (respectively 2.63.2 and 3.37.2).

Taken together, the asides on the legendary past that punctuate Thucydides' narrative of the first years of the war, as well as his observations in the Archaeology, have in common that they seek to strip the remote past of its heroic veneer and instead present it as a forerunner of contemporary history in its instability and violence. Powerful tribes and cities like the Odrysians, the Macedonians, Amphilochian Argos, and Acarnania all became allied to Athens, as a consequence of which some of the worst massacres in the war took

---

[13] See Munson, chapter 15 in this volume for Scione and the rest.

place, such as the massive defeat and killing of the Ambracian armies—"the single most severe disaster that happened to one Greek city in this war" (3.113.6)—and the needless slaughter of the inhabitants (men, women, children, and cattle alike) of Mycalessus by a band of Thracian mercenaries (7.29–30, on which see also below). It is tempting to assume that Thucydides, as an echo to these gruesome events, evokes the darker sides of Greek legends in his authorial asides.[14] Also in the Theseus digression, Thucydides hints at violence, when he states that Theseus, on becoming "powerful" (δυνατός), "forced" (ἠνάγκασε) the Athenians to use "one city" (2.15.2).

Thucydides looks back upon the war as a period of enormous loss and increasingly primitive violence and finds that human behavior is essentially the same, whether in the legendary past or more recently. This relates to the statement at the end of his essay on methodology, that his work is a "possession for ever" (κτῆμα ... ἐς αἰεί, 1.22.4) from which one can learn, as human nature will not change and will respond identically to similar events in the future. His message is one of profound pessimism on the nature of mankind, with little hope for enlightenment in the future.

In sum, Thucydides' asides upon oracles, ethnography, and the legendary past generally concern uncertainty about the future, changeability, instability, (forced) migration, and violence. They also question the nature of "civilized" Greeks, spatially, in relation to the neighboring non-Greek peoples like the Thracians, and temporally, against the backdrop of a violent legendary past. It is tempting to assume that Thucydides uses these comments to create a tension with the ideas of "Athenian Enlightenment" as proclaimed by orators like Pericles in their *Epitaphioi*. Whereas the latter approach past and present with an emphasis upon unchangeable Athenian core values such as individual liberty, autarchy, and selflessness, Thucydides hints at a long-standing tradition of greed, coercion, displacement, and internecine warfare, themes that are introduced in his Archaeology and subsequently elaborated. It may not be a coincidence that most of his authorial asides are found in the context of the narrative of the early Archidamian War, where their contrastive effect with the optimistic and patriotic Periclean oratory is most strongly felt.

Authorial Comments as Afterthoughts

The authorial evaluations that Thucydides places at the end of narrative episodes have in common that they single out an actor, an event, or a set of events for their unique or extraordinary character. This is exemplified by Thucydides' encomiastic judgment of Themistocles (1.138.3), which is placed at the end of the digression about his fate after the

---

[14] Bowie (2012) observes a similar narrative strategy in Herodotus' account of Xerxes' march to Greece. In his Mycalessus account Thucydides singles out the Thracian attack upon a school, in which all boys are massacred (7.29.5). I thank Maurits de Leeuw for pointing out to me in a private comment that the infanticide theme also features in the Tereus myth (2.29.3, see above), also in a Thracian context. Observe, too, in this respect, the geographical proximity of Daulia to Mycalessus.

Persian war (1.135.2–138). The historian uses six superlatives to praise his foresight and extemporizing talents. On the one hand, this judgment may serve as a response to his predecessor Herodotus, whose portrait of Themistocles is complicated by incidents of corruption and concealed self-enrichment (cf. Moles 2010, 35; Blösel 2012, 232–36). On the other hand, it anticipates the already mentioned introduction of Pericles (1.139.4) as "the first of the Athenians, most capable of speaking and acting," who is presented as heir to the Athenian naval politics that Themistocles had set in motion.

In the cases of Pericles and Nicias, the most successful Athenian generals of their generation, Thucydides awards character judgments (respectively 2.65 and 7.86.5) as epitaphs after their deaths. His praise of Pericles is part of a longer argument about the ultimate causes of Athens' defeat (2.65, discussed below), whereas Nicias is pitied at the end of the Sicilian episode as

> a man who, of all Hellenes in my time (ἐπ' ἐμοῦ), least deserved to come to so miserable an end because of his way of life, which he conducted wholly in accordance with high standards. (7.86.5, see Hornblower *ad loc.* for a discussion of the ambiguities in the Greek. I follow Dover's interpretation, *ad loc.*)

Rood (1998, 185), who convincingly argues that these words do not contain the slightest irony or scorn, compares their pathos to Thucydides' evaluation of the indiscriminate act of slaughter that was committed by Thracian mercenaries in the town of Mycalessus (7.29–30):

> Such was the fate that befell Mycalessus, which is worthy to be lamented (ὀλοφύρασθαι) second to none (οὐδενός … ἧσσον) of the calamities of this war if you regard the size of the city. (7.30.3)

Poignant in this comment is the verb "lament" (ὀλοφύρασθαι), which Thucydides elsewhere uses in the context of the Athenian Funeral Oration. There Pericles claims that he seeks "to encourage, not lament" (οὐκ ὀλοφύρομαι μᾶλλον ἢ παραμυθήσομαι, 2.44.1, cf. 2.34.4) the parents of the fallen Athenians. Pericles' optimistic message contrasts with the sadness that speaks from Thucydides' comment on Mycalessus, from the killing of whose women and children no comfort can be derived. It also reminds the reader that the incident should be seen as a side effect of the alliance between Athens, the self-proclaimed head of civilization, and Thracian tribes, a race of which Thucydides claims that it is "most murderous (φονικώτατον), equal to the most uncivilised barbarians, whenever it felt confidently in charge" (7.29.4).

More such superlative expressions are found in the comment that closes off Thucydides' Sicilian narrative, which further increases the pathos already evoked by his judgment of Nicias:

> It so happened that this was the greatest (μέγιστον) deed of this war, and, to my mind, also of the Greek deeds about which we know from hearsay. For the victors

it was a most glorious (λαμπρότατον) result, and for those who lost utterly disastrous (δυστυχέστατον). For they were defeated in every respect and after enduring enormous misery they went down, as the saying goes, "in total destruction" (πανωλεθρίᾳ), their infantry, their navy, in short everything, and only a few out of many made it home. (7.87.5–6)

Owing to their position at the end of episodes, authorial statements like the foregoing resemble funerary epigrams for those who have died prematurely. They appeal to the reader to pause and reflect in pity upon the deceased, who deserved a better fate, and, more generally, upon the loss and suffering that was caused by the war (cf. Ossipova 2001). In this way they also fulfil a rhetorical function in that they testify to the unprecedented magnitude of the war as it was announced at the end of the introduction to his work (1.23.1–3).

Authorial Comments in Book 8

Authorial comments are more frequently found in the post-Sicilian part of the *Histories*. Here, Thucydides qualifies the revolt of Chios against Athens as an error (8.24.5), and later explains why Athens failed to obtain the loyalty of its allies when the city was in civil turmoil (8.64.5). He also evaluates the effects of oligarchy in Athens, with positive evaluations of the characters of its leaders (8.68). In the narrative of the standoff between the oligarchs in the city and the democrats aboard the fleet at Samos, he fits in the suggestion that Athens would have lost Ionia and the Hellespont if Alcibiades had not discouraged the fleet from leaving Samos and attacking the oligarchs at home (8.86.4–7). Thucydides' voice also emerges from the wings to praise the constitution of Five Thousand that replaced the oligarchic Four Hundred in Athens:

And at least for the first time in my life Athens was evidently well governed. (8.97.2)

The relation between this observation and Thucydides' attitude towards Periclean democracy has been much debated (for an overview, see Hornblower *ad loc.*). Less attention has been paid however to its placement in the midst of the narrative of the collapse of the Athenian empire. While Athens is torn apart in the conflict between oligarchs and democrats, and the fleet at Samos sides with the latter, the Spartans sail around Sounion and defeat an underprepared Athenian fleet near Eretria. The consequent loss of Euboea leads to a "consternation greater than ever before" in Athens (ἔκπληξις μεγίστη δὴ τῶν πρὶν παρέστη, 8.96.1). Thucydides motivates his superlative by summing up the dire situation: the city in "civil strife" (*stasis*), the fleet unavailable, Athens has now lost the most valuable asset of its remaining empire. The rhetorical question that follows—one of only two in the *Histories*—raises the pathos of his argument: "how could it not be natural that they lost courage?" (πῶς οὐκ εἰκότως ἠθύμουν; 8.96.2). A scenario, formulated as a counterfactual, follows, that highlights the danger to Athens' survival. If the Spartans had seized the opportunity and immediately put pressure upon the city, they would have forced it to give up its positions in the Aegean, and the end of the war would have been imminent (8.96.4). By drawing out the fate that the Athenians fear, the historian evokes an emotional response, even though history for the moment takes a different path.

After Thucydides' emotionally colored description of Athens' dire situation, his positive assessment of the constitution of the Five Thousand has a tragic ring. Like Herodotus' Croesus, the Athenians turn out to be late learners. Their attempts to remedy their constitution will not suffice, as Thucydides makes clear immediately afterwards, when a group of fugitive oligarchs around Pisander offer Athens another blow by betraying the fortress at Oenoe to the Boeotians (8.98.1–3). Thucydides mentions the loss of Oenoe when he seals off his narrative of Athenian *stasis*, once more inviting his reader to reflect upon the ways in which the political turmoil in Athens damages its interests elsewhere:

> In this way the Boeotians captured and seized Oenoe, and the oligarchy in Athens and the conflict (στάσις) ended. (8.98.4)

Rounding off what may well have been meant to be the first installment of his account of political turmoil in Athens (the war would still continue for another seven years), Thucydides elaborates the cause of Athens' downfall as announced after Pericles' death, where, in a unique prolepsis, he had stated that the city would ultimately succumb to internal conflicts (2.65.12, see below). The constitution of the Five Thousand arrived too late to remedy the situation, and despite good intentions those responsible were not capable of turning the tide.

Exceptional is Thucydides' assessment of the enigmatic role of Tissaphernes in the non-appearance of the Phoenician fleet that is stationed at Aspendus.[15] Whereas the historian elsewhere remains tacit about the process of fact-finding and presents a polished narrative, he this time admits it is difficult to find out Tissaphernes' motives and makes some rare metanarrative comments:

> It is not told in the same way (λέγεται δὲ οὐ κατὰ ταὐτό) and it is not easy to know with what plan he went to Aspendos and, upon arriving there, failed to bring the ships. (8.87.2)

After discrediting the rumor that the Phoenician fleet had not been there at all, Thucydides—in a manner that resembles Herodotus' use of variant versions—mentions three different ways in which others seek an answer to his question, and rounds off with his own analysis:

> It seems however most plausible (σαφέστατον) to me that he held back the fleet to cause delay and hindrance to the Greeks, so as to create damage as long as he stayed

---

[15] I rely here upon Munson's more elaborate analysis of this passage (2012, 270–74).

there, and postponed his return, and a balance in power, so that he would not make one of the two parties the stronger by swearing allegiance to one of them. (8.87.4)

With this observation Thucydides elaborates his earlier analysis of Tissaphernes' tactic of "wearing down both sides" (τρίβειν ἀμφοτέρους, i.e., both Athens and Sparta, 8.56.2—a policy that was recommended to him by Alcibiades, 8.46.1). Rood (2006, 247) ascribes to the uncertainty about Tissaphernes' motives a dramatic effect, by which Thucydides seeks to undermine the impression of Alcibiades' influence upon the satrap. His uncertainty may, however, also be meant to highlight the danger of Persian involvement in Greek affairs. Both parties woo the Persians, whose grandees become increasingly willing to commit themselves to the warring parties. The involvement of a powerful foreign player in the Aegean board game raises the war to a new level of complexity, in particular as Persian motives are more difficult to gauge (and research) than those of the Greek participants.

The increase of authorial comments gives Thucydides' post-Sicilian narrative a more personal color. This may result from an intense post-war debate about the causes of Athens' demise, to which Thucydides may have wished to contribute (think, for instance, about his positive qualification of the leading oligarchs (8.68), who hardly play a role in his narrative). On another view, however, his more overt personal engagement ties in with the increasingly personal nature that warfare seems to take in this part of the *Histories*, which focuses more than before upon powerful individuals who act primarily in their own interests, and upon behavior that leads to fragmentation across the Hellenic world and an increasingly complex war.[16] This individualization of the war was announced in the pivotal evaluation of Pericles' role in Athens (2.65), where Thucydides had explained that after Pericles' death the city was governed primarily along the lines of *personal* glory and interests (κατὰ τὰς ἰδίας φιλοτιμίας καὶ ἴδια κέρδη), which brought respect and wealth to individuals when successful, but harmed the state when things went wrong (2.65.7). In the case of the Sicilian episode, it was due to *personal* slander in the city (κατὰ τὰς ἰδίας διαβολάς, 2.65.11) that the position of the army was "made weaker," and later, during the civil turmoil (*stasis*), it was the *personal* conflicts (τὰς ἰδίας διαφοράς, 2.65.12) that made the city succumb to its foreign enemies. It appears that Thucydides needed a more overtly authorial writing manner to capture the increasing complexity and individualization in the last decade of the war, and to highlight the importance of these developments in his explanation of how it came about that Athens fell.

Conclusion

Postmodern Thucydides, no longer objective as was once believed, wrote a book about recent history by which he meant to persuade its reader of his pessimistic view

---

[16] Cf. Munson (2012, 272–73): "Thucydides' efforts to be an objective observer become particularly strenuous throughout Book 8, where special interests and fragmented actions multiply . . . all these interventions are part of the same balancing act and effort not to be seduced by one view or the other."

of war and human nature. One of his most persuasive means for guiding his reader in the interpretation of his writing are his authorial comments. Despite their relative scarcity, they are interconnected among one another, and also tie in with the narrative sections, the descriptive catalogues, the speeches, and the longer authorial essays (in particular the Archaeology). This connectedness is illustrated by the comments in his post-Sicilian narrative of Book 8, which encourage the reader to relate the chaotic events in Greece to Thucydides' overall analysis of Athens' defeat as announced after Pericles' death (2.65).

Depending on their position the comments can have different functions. When they anticipate an episode, they mostly have a programmatic function, and point the reader to themes that should be taken into account in the evaluation of what follows. Authorial comments within the episode offer themselves as asides, in that they deal with topics that are traditional to the historiographical genre but that Thucydides has sacrificed in favour of his greater goal of describing the war. The asides, however, show his awareness of the role of superstition, of "other" worlds, and of Greek legends as backdrops to contemporary events. Especially in the narrative of the early years of the war these comments throw a critical light upon the utopian discourse professed by Pericles in his funeral oration, and question Athenian assumptions of superiority in civilization and morale. Comments that round off episodes usually mark their extraordinary character, and bear witness to Thucydides' claim of the war's unparalleled magnitude (1.23.1–3).

Finally, authorial comments belong to the argumentative register of the historian and thereby determine the interpretation of the narrated events they accompany. Their presence sustains Thucydides' monumental rhetorical enterprise, with its gripping narrative and the elevated language of its speeches. Just as Thucydides considered the physical world around him to be held together by complex and coherent ties, so he composed his work, tightly weaving together his own thoughts and those of his actors in parallel or contrastive patterns against the background of the events of the war that he selected for commemoration.

References

Allan, R. J. 2007. "Sense and Sentence Complexity: Sentence Structure, Sentence Connection, and Tense-Aspect as Indicators of Narrative Mode in Thucydides' *Histories*." In *The Language of Literature: Linguistic Approaches to Classical Texts*, edited by R.J. Allan and M. Buijs, 93–121. Leiden: Brill.

Allan, R. J. 2013. "History as Presence: Time, Tense and Narrative Modes in Thucydides." In *Thucydides between History and Literature*, edited by A. Tsakmakis and M. Tamiolaki, 371–90. Berlin and Boston: De Gruyter.

de Bakker, M.P. 2013. "Character Judgements in the *Histories*: Their Function and Distribution." In *Thucydides between History and Literature*, edited by A. Tsakmakis and M. Tamiolaki, 23–40. Berlin and Boston: De Gruyter.

Blösel, W. 2012. "Thucydides on Themistocles: A Herodotean Narrator?" In *Thucydides and Herodotus*, edited by E. Foster and D. Lateiner, 215–40. Oxford: Oxford University Press.

Bowie, A. 2012. "Mythology and the Expedition of Xerxes." In *Myth, Truth, and Narrative in Herodotus*, edited by E. Baragwanath and M. P. de Bakker, 269–86. Oxford: Oxford University Press.

Connor, W. R. 1984. *Thucydides*. Princeton: Princeton University Press.

Dover, K. J. 1965. *Thucydides: Book VII*. Oxford: Oxford University Press.

Dover, K. J. 1988. "Thucydides on Oracles." In *The Greeks and their Legacy*, vol. 2, by K. J. Dover, 65–73. Oxford: Blackwell.

Grethlein, J. 2013. *Experience and Teleology in Ancient Historiography:"Futures Past" from Herodotus to Augustine*. Cambridge: Cambridge University Press.

Gribble, D. 1998. "Narrator Interventions in Thucydides." *JHS* 118: 41–67.

Gribble, D. 2006. "Individuals in Thucydides." In *Brill's Companion to Thucydides*, edited by A. Rengakos and A. Tsakmakis, 439–68. Leiden and Boston: Brill.

Hornblower, S. 1987. *Thucydides*. London: Duckworth.

Hornblower, S. 1991–2008. *A Commentary on Thucydides*. 3 vols. Oxford: Clarendon.

Hornblower, S. 2004. *Thucydides and Pindar: Historical Narrative and the World of Epinikian Poetry*. Oxford: Oxford University Press.

Hunter, V. J. 1973. *Thucydides: The Artful Reporter*. Toronto: University of Toronto Press.

Kurke, L. 2000. "Charting the Poles of History: Herodotos and Thoukydides." In *Literature in the Greek and Roman Worlds: A New Perspective*, edited by O. Taplin, 133–55. Oxford: Oxford University Press.

Loraux, N. 1986. "Thucydide a écrit la guerre du Péloponnèse." *Mètis* 1: 139–61.

Macleod, C. 1983. *The Collected Essays of Colin Macleod*. Oxford: Oxford University Press.

Marinatos, N. 1981. "Thucydides and Oracles." *JHS* 101: 138–40.

Moles, J. 2010. "Narrative and Speech Problems in Thucydides Book 1." In *Ancient Historiography and Its Contexts, Studies in Honour of A. J. Woodman*, edited by C. S. Kraus, J. Marincola, and C. Pelling, 15–39. Oxford: Oxford University Press.

Morrison, J. V. 2006. "Interaction of Speech and Narrative in Thucydides." In *Brill's Companion to Thucydides*, edited by A. Rengakos and A. Tsakmakis, 251–77. Leiden and Boston: Brill.

Munson, R. V. 2012. "Persians in Thucydides." In *Thucydides and Herodotus*, edited by E. Foster and D. Lateiner, 241–77. Oxford: Oxford University Press.

Munson, R. V. 2015. "Natural Upheavals in Thucydides (and Herodotus)." In *Kinesis: Essays for Donald Lateiner on the Ancient Depiction of Gesture, Motion, and Emotion*, edited by C. Clark, E. Foster, and J. Hallett, 41–59. Ann Arbor: University of Michigan Press.

Ossipova, O. V. 2001. "Nicias' 'Eulogy' in Thucydides (7.86.5) and Greek Epitaphs." *Vestnik Drevnei Istorii* 237 (2): 113–118.

Pearson, L. 1947. "Thucydides as Reporter and Critic." *TAPA* 78: 37–60.

Pelling, C. B. R. 2009. "Thucydides' Speeches." In *Oxford Readings in Classical Studies*, edited by J. S. Rusten, 176–87. Oxford: Oxford University Press. Originally published 2000, in *Literary Texts and the Greek Historian*, by C. B. R. Pelling, 112–22. London and New York: Routledge.

Powell, A. 1979. "Thucydides and Divination." *BICS* 26: 45–50.

Purves, A. C. 2010. *Space and Time in Ancient Greek Narrative*. Cambridge: Cambridge University Press.

Raaflaub, K. A. 2006. "Thucydides on Democracy and Oligarchy." In *Brill's Companion to Thucydides*, edited by A. Rengakos and A. Tsakmakis, 189–221. Leiden and Boston: Brill.

Rhodes, P. J. 2014, trans. *Thucydides: History Book 1; Introduction, Translation and Commentary*. Oxford, Havertown, PA: Aris and Phillips.

Rood, T. 1998. *Thucydides: Narrative and Explanation*. Oxford: Oxford University Press.

Rood, T. 2004. "Thucydides." In *Narrators, Narratees, and Narratives in Ancient Greek Literature,* edited by I. J. F. de Jong, R. Nünlist, and A. Bowie, 115–28. Leiden and Boston: Brill.

Rood, T. 2006. "Objectivity and Authority: Thucydides' Historical Method." In *Brill's Companion to Thucydides,* edited by A. Rengakos and A. Tsakmakis, 225–49. Leiden and Boston: Brill.

Rusten, J. S. 2015. "*Kinesis* in the Preface to Thucydides." In *Kinesis: Essays for Donald Lateiner on the Ancient Depiction of Gesture, Motion, and Emotion,* edited by C. Clark, E. Foster, and J. Hallett, 27–40. Ann Arbor: University of Michigan Press.

Stahl, H.-P. 1966. *Die Stellung des Menschen im geschichtlichen Prozess.* Munich: C. H. Beck.

Stahl, H.-P. 2009. "Speeches and the Course of Events in Books Six and Seven of Thucydides." In *Thucydides: Oxford Readings in Classical Studies,* edited by J. S. Rusten, 341–58. Oxford: Oxford University Press. Originally published 1963. *The Speeches in Thucydides. A Collection of Original Studies with a Bibliography,* edited by P. A. Stadter, 60–77. Chapel Hill: University of North Carolina Press.

Westlake, H. D. 1955. "Thucydides and the Pentekontaetia."*CQ* 5 n.s.: 53–67.

Westlake, H. D. 1968. *Individuals in Thucydides.* Cambridge: Cambridge University Press.

CHAPTER 15

THUCYDIDES AND MYTH

A Complex Relation to Past and Present

ROSARIA VIGNOLO MUNSON

THUCYDIDES' no-fiction contract with his readers is the strictest among prose writers down to his times (cf. Morgan 2011, 559). He intends his history to be a "possession for ever" for those who want to know the past and deliberate about the future. But in order for a report of world events to be useful, it needs to be vetted for accuracy (*to saphes*) and must exclude the *muthōdes*—that is to say, the mythical and fabulistic in a broad sense (1.22.2–4).[1] Thucydides will narrate a war that occurred during his own lifetime, for the painstaking research of which he can count on himself as a participant and on the interrogation of others who witnessed both events and speeches (1.22.1–2).

Thucydides, however, paves the way for his statement of this methodological program with a survey starting from a remote past, accessible through poetic traditions that represent the most disheartening repository of whatever is distorted, unverified, exceedingly magnified, embroidered, or merely entertaining—in a word, *muthōdes*. One of the reasons for undertaking this survey is no doubt to demonstrate that it cannot be done in a satisfactory way (1.13; 20.1; 21.1) and to discredit previous attempts. But the formal manner in which Thucydides attaches the excursus to his initial statement of purpose gives a better clue: he needs to de-provincialize his war. The conflict between the Athenians and the Peloponnesians was the greatest in history, he announces (1.1). This claim should be taken seriously, in spite of the fact that people always claim that the war they personally experienced was greatest, at least until they forget, at which point they revert to the celebration of past deeds (1.21.2). Thucydides' "Archaeology"—as we conventionally call it[2]—intends to demonstrate that in fact things were smaller in the past: from rude and brutish beginnings, societies grow to be more prosperous and

---

[1] For the meaning of the term see Flory (1985); Saïd (2011, 78).
[2] 1.1–19. On this section, see especially Gomme (1945, 91–157); Hammond (1952); Romilly (1956, 240–98); Connor (1984, 20–32); Rusten (2006); Luraghi (2000); Nicolai (2001); Hornblower (1991, 7–56); Foster (2010, 8–43).

complicated. Their greater resources and power also produce greater wars, and specifically the latest and greatest is the one Thucydides is about to describe.

But the argument is not as superficial as all that. Thucydides' main rivals here are Homer and Herodotus, the poet who immortalized the most paradigmatic ancient war in the imaginary of the Greeks, and the researcher whose narrative of the Persian Wars ranged over an unparalleled extension of time and space. Thucydides competes with both by inserting his own subject matter into a comparably broad heroic and world-historical context. His attempt does not completely succeed—references to *barbaroi* and descriptions of ethnographic particulars tend to remain rather local, just as the claim at 1.2 that the Peloponnesian War affected "most men both Greek and non-Greek" is somewhat unconvincing. But as he tries, he is also teaching the admirers of his two predecessors a lesson on how to deal with legendary material, if one must. In this section of the Archaeology, therefore, the remote past is the object not of narrative but of argumentation, marked by the vocabulary of hearsay, opinion, and proof (Romilly 1956, 242). Here are just the first two examples in this passage of the type of metanarrative that Thucydides usually avoids in his subsequent account of the war:

> It is evident (φαίνεται) that in ancient times the land that is now called Hellas was not inhabited by settled populations. (1.2.1)
> Not least also the following demonstrates to me (δηλοῖ δέ μοι) the weakness of the ancients. . . . (1.3.1)

In tracing the evolution of the Greek world during the heroic age, Thucydides uses the poetic tradition and combines it with material (or "archaeological") observation and reasoning. He seems deliberately to avoid describing his own activity by means of typical Herodotean terms such as ἀκοή ("hearsay") ὄψις ("eyewitness"), and γνώμη ("opinion," "interpretation"), not to mention ἱστορίη ("research"), yet his form of discourse is here exceptionally close to the one Herodotus favors throughout his work. At the same time, and in spite of avowals of uncertainty about the possibility of accuracy in this sphere, Thucydides posits a much greater continuity between the heroic age and historical times than Herodotus does (Luraghi 2000, 234; Munson 2012, 197). This attitude is partly a consequence of Thucydides' general disregard of transcendence (including the divine apparatus of epic sagas, which he of course eliminates); but it also represents an extension of the basic principle that at any time or any place human nature remains the same (1.22.4). The idea that human beings have always responded to their environment with economic and political motives similar to those of his contemporaries—love of gain, prestige, and fear being permanent causes of action (see 1.76.2; 1.23.6) —allows Thucydides to derive by analogy a plausible (εἰκός) reconstruction of the past by interpreting whatever evidence is available through his knowledge of the forces that shape the present.

The method is circular because the reconstruction of the remote past is in turn designed to anticipate the historical patterns operative in the narrative present. Thus, on the basis of some unspecified ἀκοή (1.4.1), the reign of the mythical Minos of Crete, who "as it is likely" (ὡς εἰκός) fought piracy to protect his revenues, is reshaped on the model of the Athenian thalassocracy;[3] but at the same time Minos is also presented as the earliest historical precedent of how power is inherently connected with ships and money, how the stronger will submit to the weaker, and how the resulting arrangement, if ably managed, will serve the economic interests of both ruler and ruled (1.8.2–4). Agamemnon is a somewhat less successful paradigm of naval empire (Zali 2011, 22–25): he must have enjoyed the command of the sea to be able to lead the first common Greek enterprise (reconstruction of the past; 1.3.1 and 4; 1.9.1–4), but the Trojan War also implicitly demonstrates (1.11–12.1) how hegemonic powers can overextend themselves and eventually revert to chaos and ruin (foreshadowing of the future).

Since one of Thucydides' aims in the Archaeology is evidently to introduce themes that will recur in the rest of the work, one has to wonder why Thucydides' *speakers* hardly ever bring the heroic age to bear either in order to prove generalizations about the workings of history or for the purpose of supporting specific claims. Thucydides reports that the inhabitants of Scione say that their city was originally settled by Achaeans stranded on their way back from Troy (4.120.1), and that the Corcyreans boast of their connection with the Homeric Phaeacians—no doubt for the purpose of devaluing the role of their historical motherland, Corinth (1.25.4; Hornblower 1996, 63). He shows the political nature of this type of popular mythmaking when he cites a case that originated in the recent and easily documentable past: after the death of Brasidas, Amphipolis declared the Spartan general as its *oikist*, obliterating all monuments of the Athenian Hagnon having founded the city (5.11.1; cf. 4.102.3). But these are exceptions: Thucydides' speeches do not contain explicit references to the heroic age.[4] In Herodotus, where the opposite is the case (see Hdt. 1.1–5, 5.94, 7.150; 7.159; 7.161.3; 9.116; Grethlein 2010, 158–86; Zali 2011, 5–8), an especially allusive episode concerns a quarrel that broke out between Tegeans and Athenians over the honor of occupying a privileged position in the Panhellenic army that is about to confront the Persians at Plataea (Hdt. 9.25–26). In their contest of words, which in the economy of Herodotus' text foreshadows the hegemonic struggles among the Greeks that will flare up more destructively after the Persian Wars, the two sides enumerate their respective benefactions to Greece through the ages (cf. Munson 2001, 219–20). The Tegeans recall that it was one of their own who challenged and defeated in a duel Hyllus the son of Heracles, thereby delaying the return of the Heraclids to the Peloponnese for one hundred years (Hdt. 9.25). The Athenians, before magnifying their historical victory at Marathon, boast of how they provided refuge to the exiled Heraclids, buried the dead in the war of the Seven against Thebes, defeated the Amazons who invaded Attica, and distinguished themselves in the expedition to Troy

---

[3] On the meaning of ἀκοή, see Hornblower (1991, 22). Thucydides' unique use of the expression ὧν ἀκοῇ ἴσμεν in this passage combines Herodotean vocabulary to form a non-Herodotean expression; this suggests an allusion to (and disagreement with) Herodotus' account of Minos at 1.171 and 3.122; see Hornblower (1991, 19–20). On Minos in Herodotus and Thucydides in the light of current mythological traditions, see Irwin (2007); Munson (2012, 201–12).

[4] At 5.105 the Athenians allude, albeit skeptically, to divine rather than heroic myth in support of their "might is right" historical rule.

(Hdt. 9.26). It is hard to know whether ancient Greek negotiators ever really talked in these terms when they needed to get things done, but in the sphere of epideictic rhetoric, at least, the Athenian catalogue of deeds starting from the heroic age conforms to a model reflected by highly conventional fourth-century funeral orations such as those of Lysias and Demosthenes, or the imitation of the genre in Plato's *Menexenus* (Loraux 1986, 60–76; Grethlein 2010, 105–25).

In Thucydides, by contrast, Pericles' Funeral Oration omits the catalogue of past deeds altogether, but begins with a preamble that makes clear that his *epitaphios* will not entirely follow the usual format (2.35–36.2). Pericles' brief allusion to the Athenian myth of autochthony, another usual theme of funeral orations, resembles the allusion in the narrator's own voice in the Archaeology to the extent that it takes all the myth out of it.[5] Pericles privileges contemporary accomplishments: today's Athenians "do not need the praise of Homer or of anyone else who will give momentary pleasure with verses, but whose interpretation of facts will be destroyed by truth" (οὐδὲν προσδεόμενοι οὔτε Ὁμήρου ἐπαινέτου οὔτε ὅστις ἔπεσι μὲν τὸ αὐτίκα τέρψει, τῶν δ' ἔργων τὴν ὑπόνοιαν ἡ ἀλήθεια βλάψει, 2.41.4). Similarly, the Athenian envoys at Sparta justify their right to empire on the basis of their accomplishments in the Persian War and the circumstances that followed, but they decline to rehearse ancient events, evidence for which comes from hearsay of words rather than from the listeners' eyewitness (παλαιὰ ... ὧν ἀκοαὶ μᾶλλον λόγων μάρτυρες ἢ ὄψις τῶν ἀκουσομένων, 1.73.1). The Athenians at Melos and Euphemus at Camarina both suggest in different ways that the mention of past deeds is a common practice but that, under the circumstances, it would be out of place (5.89; 6.83.2; Zali 2011, 19). Thucydides, in other words, consistently draws attention to the fact that he will neither let his speakers borrow his own pragmatic reconstruction nor allow them to include the heroic past in their arguments in the traditional way.

The frequent use of the device of *praeteritio* by Thucydides' speakers throws into higher relief the polemical nature of Thucydides' own confrontation with stories that "have won their way into the mythical" (ἐπὶ τὸ μυθῶδες ἐκνενικηκότα, 1.21.1). In the first ten chapters of the Archaeology (1.2–11) we find about twenty negations designed to rectify erroneous ideas about the heroic age.[6] Hypothetical sentences (e.g., 1.10.2; 11.2) have a similar function. Homer—for the likes of whom fifth-century Athens has no use

---

[5] See Pelling (2009, especially 476–78). Pericles simply says that "the same people have always occupied this land, and each generation has kept it free until this day through their excellence" (2.36.1). Thucydides in the Archaeology refers to autochthony only as the result of a disadvantage: Attica was always inhabited by Athenians because the infertility of the land did not encourage settlers from abroad (1.2.4). But there was a wealth of mythical narratives involving Erechtheus/Erychthonius about Athenians being "sons of their soil," with the implication of racial superiority over other groups of Greeks. See especially Loraux (1986, 148–50, 193, 277–78).

[6] See also 2.29.3, designed to deny the notion that Teres (father of Sitalces, who was king of the Odrysian Thracians in 431 BCE) was a descendant of the brutal mythical Thracian king Tereus (who married the Athenian princess Procne and defiled her sister Philomela: Aeschylus, *Suppliants* 60–68; cf. Ovid, *Metamorphoses*. 6.424–84). Hornblower (1991, 287) suggests that Thucydides is here correcting Hellanicus, but a connection between Teres and Tereus may have been made more generally by the Athenian public at the time of Athenian involvement with the Odrysian ruling family.

(2.41.4)—is nevertheless indispensable for the Trojan War (1.10.3), on whose occurrence per se no Greek author ever cast any doubt. Homer has value especially as an "involuntary" source, as when he unwittingly shows that the Greeks used to have no common name (1.3.3) or that there was a time when piracy used to be an acceptable activity (1.5.2; cf. Romilly 1956, 246). Yet, being a performer and a poet, he may be ranked among those who lack integrity or practical sense.[7]

In Thucydides' opinion (μοι δοκεῖ), for example, Agamemnon gathered the armament for the Trojan War "*not so much* (οὐ τοσοῦτον) because Helen's suitors were bound by oaths to her father Tyndareus, but because he (Agamemnon) was superior in power" (1.9.1). It is interesting to note that Thucydides, unlike Herodotus and many others among his own contemporaries, neither disputes nor discusses the role of Helen as a cause of the war. (Could he have believed that a woman's abduction was the "truest reason" for the first Panhellenic expedition in history?[8]) He does not, either, entirely deny the importance of the suitors' oath.[9] But his "not so much x but y" form of discourse minimizes the idealistic motive in favor of a more pragmatic, and less heroic, explanation.

To corroborate his point, Thucydides valorizes a non-Homeric tradition, defined as "what those Peloponnesians say who have received in memory from their ancestors the most reliable information" (λέγουσι δὲ καὶ οἱ τὰ σαφέστατα Πελοποννησίων μνήμῃ παρὰ τῶν πρότερον δεδεγμένοι, 1.9.2). Here the cautionary force of λέγουσι is blunted by the relative credibility (σαφές, which is the opposite of the *muthōdes*, 1.22.4) of the purely genealogical (and therefore romance-free) account of how the Pelopids wrested from the Perseids the dominion over the Peloponnese and adjacent islands. But the proof-value of what Thucydides is ready to trust is limited,[10] and any further inference on his part is just that, an inference: it is because Agamemnon inherited his power that, again "in my opinion"(μοι δοκεῖ, at 1.9.3), he was able to make the expedition, "relying *not* on good will as much as on fear" (οὐ χάριτι τὸ πλέον ἢ φόβῳ, 1.9.3). This partially demythologized version based on negation better fits the causal model by which Thucydides interprets history throughout his work: power, and especially naval power, is the basis of all great enterprises, from Minos of Crete (1.8) to fifth-century Athens, and the fear that power inspires is a fundamental motive for action.

---

[7] 1.21.1. Herodotus more forgivingly attributes Homer's inaccuracies to the special requirements of the epic genre (2.116).

[8] On women in Thucydides, see Hornblower's amusing note at 1.6.3, the passage where Thucydides discusses Greek change of dress: "This is a rare excursus into 'social history'. Hdt. (V 88) had described a change in the dress of Athenian women (from 'Doric' to 'Ionic') . . . Th. on the other hand seems to be concerned only with men, that is from 'Ionic' to 'Doric' (. . .). Thucydides is not necessarily contradicting Hdt., since they are concerned with different sexes; but it is characteristic of Hdt. that on this issue he shows interest in women and characteristic of Thucydides that he does not, even in a chapter which in other respects ranges widely for him" (Hornblower 1991, 25–26). Thucydides' general disregard for the historical role of women, of course, greatly narrows the available mythical repertoire. I am grateful to Edith Foster for this insight.

[9] On the significance of oaths in Thucydides, see Lateiner (2012).

[10] Cf. note 14.

Thucydides' negations and his speakers' exclusions of heroic age material that all their listeners would have shared go hand in hand with his open mistrust of common beliefs. One of the most conspicuous features of the *History* is its insistence on the unreliability of ordinary people. Both narrator and speakers maintain several times that "the Athenians"—that is to say, the sovereign assembly—are prone to making impulsive decisions, change their minds overnight, or commit serious errors of policy that lead to disastrous results or, if not, it is only because of sheer luck (see especially 2.65). This sort of popular instability is the result of the ebb and flow of collective emotions such as public anger, private grief, fear, exaltation, pity or, in general, passion (ὀργή),[11] but it also has an intellectual aspect: people tend to hold mistaken ideas both about (more or less) faraway places and about the (more or less remote) past. In the chapters of the Archaeology that detail his painstaking method of research, Thucydides observes that "men accept from one another traditions (ἀκοάς) of past events, even traditions that are local to their own country, without putting them to the test of fire (ἀβανίστως)" (1.20.1). Even relatively recent episodes of Greek history become distorted, including, among other things, the role of Athens' so-called tyrannicides, who did not actually kill the tyrant, as most people think, but his younger brother (1.20.2). In Book 6, Thucydides exceptionally chooses to expand on the misconceptions concerning this particular event, specifying that Harmodius and Aristogiton did not liberate Athens from an already oppressive regime, but made the tyranny harsher, and did not do what they did for ideological or political reasons, but on account of an amorous incident (ἐρωτικὴν συντυχίαν, 6.54.1). He does so for a special reason: the resilience of the tyranny after the action of the tyrannicides was discussed as an alarming precedent in the streets of Athens at the time of the mutilation of the Herms on the eve of the expedition to Sicily, that is to say, in the "present" of Thucydides' narrative. This was one case when the incorrect memory of the demos (πιστάμενος ... ἀκοῇ, 6.53.3; μιμνησκόμενος ὅσα ἀκοῇ ἠπίστατο, 6.60.1) actually affected political action. The Athenians' misunderstanding of history (an intellectual shortcoming) came together with their emotional fragility ("passion": see αὐτῶν ὀργιζομένων, 6.60.2), leading them to exaggerate the import of a distracting affair in the present and, as a result, to handicap an enterprise (already ill planned) in the imminent future.[12] Here and throughout his work the aim of Thucydides' corrections is not to improve the knowledge of a broad and diverse audience of fellow Greeks (which is arguably what Herodotus is trying to do). He rather speaks *about* the masses (τὸ πλῆθος), not to them. He represents their ignorance to a restricted readership that he hopes will benefit from what the past can teach.

But there are chinks in the armor of Thucydides' criticism of popular or poetic myth, both at the intellectual and at the emotional levels. After reproaching the Athenians

---

[11] ὀργή denotes the public's momentary anger, e.g., at 1.140.1, 2.11.4, 2.60.1.

[12] On the multiple thematic connections between Thucydides' Harmodius and Aristogiton references and their surrounding narrative, see Hornblower (2008, 433–53) and Meyer (2008), with extensive bibliographies. See also Rawlings (1981, 110–11, 257–58). The documentary evidence for the popular perception of the tyrannicides has been discussed most recently by Ferrario (2014, 18–25).

for making the expedition to Sicily "most of them being inexperienced about its size or the number of its populations, both Greek and non-Greek" (6.1.1), he inserts an ethnographical survey in which he reports without irony the *poetic* traditions that Cyclopes and Laestrygones are the mythical ancestors of the earliest native inhabitants (6.2.1); in the same section, he is also not reluctant to derive the Elymians of Eryx and Egesta from Trojan refugees (6.2.3).[13] Mostly, however, Thucydides' occasional deference to tradition (if we can call it that) has to do with empathy. Thucydides' war is "great" for many reasons, including the unprecedented resources it mobilized, but also, notably, on account of the great *pathēmata* that accompanied it (1.23.1–3). I have argued elsewhere that in the face of the tremendous sufferings so suddenly and inexplicably brought about by the war and the plague, Thucydides' resistance to widespread mythical thinking in response to oracles and signs gives way to a humbler approach (cf. Munson 2015). In the area of mythical *narratives*, let us consider especially the following passage, where Thucydides explains the acute feeling of separation and loss experienced by the Athenians when they had to move from their farms and seek protection in the city in the imminence of the first Peloponnesian invasion of Attica (2.14.2–15):

> It was painful for them to move, because they had always been used to live in the country. From the most ancient times (ἀπὸ τοῦ πάνυ ἀρχαίου) this was true of the Athenians more than any other people. For under Cecrops and the early kings until Theseus, Attica had always been inhabited in separate towns, each with its own town hall and magistrates; when there was no danger, they did not go to the king for deliberations but governed themselves and took counsel on their own. Some of them even made war against the king, as the Eleusinians with Eumolpus against Erechtheus. But when the kingship passed on to Theseus, who was both intelligent and powerful, he reordered the region by eliminating, among other things, the counsel chambers and offices of the various towns. Consolidating them into the city we have now, with a single council house and town hall, he "synoecized" all the citizens. And although they each administered their property as before, Theseus compelled them to have only one polis, which became great, once all were counted as its citizens; as such it was bequeathed by Theseus to posterity (μιᾷ πόλει ταύτῃ χρῆσθαι, ἣ ἁπάντων ἤδη ξυντελούντων ἐς αὐτὴν μεγάλη γενομένη παρεδόθη ὑπὸ Θησέως τοῖς ἔπειτα).

Thucydides goes on to recall that a city festival celebrated "even to this day" (ἔτι καὶ νῦν) testifies to the synoecism as a landmark event in Athenian history; he provides evidence (τεκμήριον) that previously Athens had been a more compact urban center, somewhat secondary to the inhabitants of greater Attica, by noting the current location of the city's most ancient sanctuaries (ἱερὰ ἀρχαῖα) and the spring from which, since ancient times, it is believed (ἔτι ἀπὸ τοῦ ἀρχαίου ... νομίζεται), the Athenians draw water before weddings and other rituals (2.15.3–5). His method here is similar to his use

---

[13] On the cluster of Homeric references in Thucydides' Sicilian (and Corcyrean) narratives, see Mackie (1996). On other references to myths of ancient descent, see Fragoulaki (2013, 55).

of visible signs of material culture in support of limited points in the Archaeology.[14] But the Theseus tradition in the passage quoted from 2.14.2–15)—this he reports in a distinctly different way than he does the *akoai* about his two other paradigmatic heroic figures, Minos and Agamemnon.[15] Here we find no cautionary markers, skeptical disclaimers, discussion of proofs, or indication that "ancient events are impossible to ascertain on account of the lapse of time" (τὰ ἔτι παλαίτερα σαφῶς μὲν εὑρεῖν διὰ χρόνου πλῆθος ἀδύνατα, 1.1.3). The reason is that the importance of this story has not so much to do with historical truth as with the way in which it reflects the Athenians' collective emotions and the meaning Thucydides attributes to their displacement in 431.

The somewhat fabulistic introduction of Theseus as a wise and powerful leader (γενόμενος μετὰ τοῦ ξυνετοῦ καὶ δυνατός) who put Athens on its way to greatness also connects the heroic age to the more recent past and to the present of the narrative by recalling Thucydides' praise of Themistocles and his political successor Pericles.[16] The evacuation of Attica at the time of the second Persian War, which Thucydides recalls precisely in this narrative (2.16.1), had been promoted by Themistocles. Now, at the beginning of the Peloponnesian War, the Athenians were physically moving again, troubled and depressed for having to abandon their property and their old way of life in the country demes (2.16.1–2). Somewhat like Themistocles and Pericles, Theseus had forced (ἠνάγκασε, 2.15.2) the Athenians to leave behind a part of themselves. He acted against public inclination but for the public good, so as to bequeath to posterity a united city that proceeded to become great (μιᾷ πόλει . . . ἣ ἁπάντων . . . μεγάλη γενομένη παρεδόθη). The memory of Theseus would not indeed have been out of place in Pericles' Funeral Oration, but Thucydides reserves it for himself, as a metaphor for the tension between consequential leadership and popular sentiment in a narrative of suffering, in which "greatness" is a profoundly ambivalent goal. This represents, perhaps, his most complete surrender to *to muthōdes*.

References

Connor, W. R. 1984. *Thucydides*. Princeton: Princeton University Press.
Flory, S. 1990. "The Meaning of τὸ μὴ μυθῶδες (1.22.4) and the Usefulness of Thucydides' History." *CJ* 85 (3): 193–208.

---

[14] For example, at 1.8.1 where the ancient Carian tombs found at Delos can only serve as evidence that Carians originally lived there, and not for the more important point that Minos expelled Carian pirates from the islands.

[15] Thucydides (like Herodotus) establishes no connection between Theseus and Minos. See note 3, end.

[16] Thucydides praises Themistocles for his innate ξύνεσις and δύναμις (1.138.3) and he calls Pericles λέγειν καὶ πράσσειν δυνατώτατος (1.139.4), adding that the city "became greatest under his leadership" (ἐγένετο ἐπ᾽ἐκείνου μεγίστη, 2.65.5). ξύνεσις is implicitly attributed to Pericles in both passages, and especially at 1.140.1 (in Pericles' own speech) and 2.34.6. See Gomme (1956, 49); Hornblower (1991, 124–25).

Ferrario, S. B. 2014. *Historical Agency and the "Great Man" in Classical Greece.* Cambridge: Cambridge University Press.

Foster, E. 2010. *Thucydides, Pericles, and Periclean Imperialism.* Cambridge: Cambridge University Press.

Fragoulaki, M. 2013. *Kinship in Thucydides: Intercommunal Ties and Historical Narrative.* Oxford: Oxford University Press.

Gomme, A. W. 1945. *A Historical Commentary on Thucydides.* Vol. I. Oxford: Oxford University Press.

Gomme, A. W. 1956. *A Historical Commentary on Thucydides.* Vol. II. Oxford: Oxford University Press.

Grethlein, J. 2010. *The Greeks and Their Past: Poetry, Oratory and History in the Fifth Century BCE.* Cambridge: Cambridge University Press.

Hammond, N. G. L. 1952. "The Arrangement of the Thought in the Proem and in Other Parts of Thucydides I." *CQ* 2: 127–41.

Hornblower, S. 1991. *A Commentary on Thucydides.* Vol I, *Books I–III.* Oxford: Clarendon.

Hornblower, S. 1996. *A Commentary on Thucydides.* Vol II, *Books IV–V.24.* Oxford: Clarendon.

Hornblower, S. 2008. *A Commentary on Thucydides.* Vol III, *Books 3.25–8.109.* Oxford: Clarendon.

Irwin, E. 2007. "The Politics of Precedence. First 'Historians' on First 'Thalassocrats.'" In *Debating the Athenian Cultural Revolution: Art, Literature, Philosophy, and Politics, 430–380 BC*, edited by R. Osborne, 188–223. Cambridge: Cambridge University Press.

Lateiner, D. 2012. "Oaths: Theory and Practice in the *Histories* of Herodotus and Thucydides." In *Thucydides and Herodotus*, edited by E. Foster and D. Lateiner, 154–84. Oxford: Oxford University Press.

Loraux, N. 1986. *The Invention of Athens.* Cambridge: Harvard University Press.

Luraghi, N. 2000. "Author and Audience in Thucydides' Archaeology." *HSCP* 100: 227–39.

Mackie, C. J. 1996. "Homer and Thucydides: Corcyra and Sicily." *CQ* 46 (1): 103–13.

Meyer, E. A. 2008. "Thucydides on Harmodius and Aristogeiton, Tyranny, and History." *CQ* 58 (1): 13–34.

Morgan, J. R. 2011. "Fiction and History: Historiography and the Novel." In *A Companion to Greek and Roman* Histotiography, edited by J. Marincola, 553–64. Malden: Blackwell.

Munson, R.V. 2001. *Telling Wonders: Ethnographic and Political Discourse in the Work of Herodotus.* Ann Arbor: University of Michigan Press.

Munson, R. V. 2012. "Herodotus and the Heroic Age: The Case of Minos." In *Myth, Truth, and Narrative in Herodotus*, edited by E. Baragwanath and M. de Baker, 195–212. Oxford: Oxford University Press.

Munson, R. V. 2015. "Natural Upheavals in Thucydides (and Herodotus)." In *Kinesis: Essays for Donald Lateiner on the Ancient Depiction of Gesture, Motion, and Emotion*, edited by C. A. Clark, E. Foster, and J. P. Hallett, 41–59. Ann Arbor: University of Michigan Press.

Nicolai, R. 2001. "Thucydides' Archaeology: Between Epic and Oral Traditions." In *The Historian's Craft in the Age of Herodotus*, edited by N. Luraghi, 263–85. Oxford: Oxford University Press.

Pelling, C. 2009. "Bringing Autochthony Up-to-Date: Herodotus and Thucydides." *CW* 102 (4): 471–83.

Rawlings, H. R. 1981. *The Structure of Thucydides' History.* Princeton: Princeton University Press.

Romilly, J. de. 1956. *Histoire et raison chez Thucydide*. Paris: Les Belles Lettres.

Rusten, J. 2006. "Thucydides the Prehistorian." In *Ten Years of the Agnes Kirsopp Lake Michels Lectures at Bryn Mawr*, edited by S. B. Faris and L. E. Lundeen, 135–47. Bryn Mawr: Bryn Mawr Commentaries.

Zali, V. 2011. "Agamemnon in Herodotus and Thucydides: Exploring the Historical Uses of a Mythological Paradigm." *Electra* no. 1: 61–98. http://electra.lis.upatras.gr/index.php/electra/article/view/57/56. Date accessed: 2 January 2015.

CHAPTER 16

SPEECHES

ANTONIS TSAKMAKIS

It was Thucydides who inaugurated the systematic insertion of set speeches in Greek and Roman (but also Byzantine, Medieval, and even later) historiography.[1] After Thucydides, from Xenophon to Voltaire and Schiller, political and military historiography occasionally allowed its main heroes to address large audiences or influential individuals and groups with lengthy and elaborate speeches. However, no historian has been more renowned for such speeches than Thucydides. His speeches have been studied, imitated, paraphrased, or translated more than any other part of his work (and more than any other historian's speeches)—not as historical sources, but as rhetorical artifacts and examples of intense theoretical reasoning. Only in the twentieth century did the study of Thucydidean speeches for their own sake give way to a literary approach that takes account of the interplay between speeches and narrative.[2]

Direct speech entered Greek historiography under the influence of a long-standing narrative tradition. More than two-fifths of the *Iliad* consists of direct discourse, ranging from brief statements or verbal exchanges to formal speeches delivered in public. In contrast to this flexible use of speech in epic poetry and Herodotus, Thucydides kept other types of direct discourse, such as conversational dialogue, to a minimum,[3]

---

[1] I express my thanks to Edith Foster and Katerina Mikellidou for their helpful comments.

[2] On Thucydides after the Renaissance, see Pade (2006); Iglesias-Zoido (2015). R. Zahn (1934) was the first to study in detail a Thucydidean speech as a part of the work's design. For the military exhortations, cf. Luschnat (1942), which treated them as an organic component of the work and highlighted the connections between them and the narrative.

[3] These are mainly debates or statements that emphasize the failure of communication before war establishes itself: the *Melian Dialogue* (5.85–111) between the Athenians and Melians is a battle of concise, astute statements, whose organization as a sophistic combat prefigures its inconclusiveness; five passages in direct discourse, distributed in three episodes with escalating tension (the middle passage consisting of a report of the Athenians' reply to the Plataeans), dramatize in an almost Herodotean ampleness the diplomatic dialogue between Archidamus and the Plataeans at the beginning of the Spartan campaign in Boeotia (2.71–74; on such clusters of speeches in Herodotus cf. Lang 1984, 132–41); a memorable *mot* by a Spartan envoy who had not been received by the Athenians seals the collapse of any effort toward an understanding and the outbreak of hostilities: "this day will be the beginning of great misfortunes for the Hellenes" (2.12.3; cf. Hdt. 5.30.1; 5.97.3). Finally, in 3.113 an Ambracian herald becomes aware of a disaster,

and composed (mainly) public speeches according to the guidelines and practices of the art of rhetoric as practiced in fifth-century Athens. His two preferred types of oratory are deliberative speeches delivered prior to a crucial decision, and battle exhortations, which are usually introduced by forms of the verbs παραινῶ or παρακελεύομαι instead of λέγω. Only one speech pair (by the Plataeans and Thebans, 3.61–67) is usually classified as forensic oratory (although this designation misrepresents its affinities to the political orations; note also that contrary to regular judicial practice, the "defense speech" by the Plataeans comes first), while Pericles' Funeral Oration (2.35–46) belongs to the epideictic genre. All speeches are thematically related to the work's central and exclusive theme, the war.[4]

In Homeric epic, public speeches and public arguments about important political issues function as a means of exploring and confirming shared ethical and political principles within a community, for example, in a conference of commanders or in the *agora*. While the decision-making authority belongs to the person highest in the hierarchy, Homeric speeches nevertheless reflect the importance of public communication and consent in the early Greek polis. Later in time, Herodotus explicitly praises "equality in speech" as an important factor for Athens' political and military progress (ἰσηγορίη as the opposite of tyranny: 5.78); yet he does not reproduce entire assembly speeches in direct speech. (Themistocles' speech to the Athenians in 8.109 is the unique example of an Athenian leader addressing—and persuading—"the Athenians.") As in Homer, important decisions are often preceded by intensive discussion in a small circle, where direct speech contributes to the vividness of the scene and to the dramatic tension of the narrative; it also highlights the topic under discussion as important. The speeches held during the consultation about Xerxes' plan to invade Greece are the most illustrious example (Hdt. 7.5–25). Like all speeches in his work, they lack historicity. However, they reveal the rationale behind the decision to go to war and serve the delineation of character. In any case, they suggest to the reader the interpretation and evaluation of events in a rather unambiguous manner. For instance, a primary function of the implicit focus on Xerxes (as a speaker or audience of other persons' speeches in this scene) is to expose his failure properly to appraise warnings and flattery.[5]

---

in the course of a dialogue with a stranger that is very akin to a tragic stichomythia; cf. Stahl (1966, 134–35). The climax of the scene is the abandonment of the shocked herald's initial intention to ask for the corpses of the deceased.

[4] Cf. 1.21.1: the speeches of the work were delivered "either before they entered the war, or during it." The peculiar character of the Funeral Oration is discussed by Orwin (1994, 15–29), who emphasizes the salience of the theme of empire in this speech. Speeches are absent in both Book 5 and Book 8. In his penetrating discussion of Book 5, Rood (1998) remarks that ". . . the lack of speech tellingly points to a pattern of repeated failure: talk was plentiful and unproductive; expansion would tell us little. Proposals are not even reported indirectly: they were predictable and futile. When many interrelated issues were at stake in each conference, we should not be surprised that Thucydides does not select one for paradigmatic treatment" (p. 91).

[5] On "political" speeches in Homer see Hölkeskamp (2000); on speeches in Herodotus (and Thucydides) Scardino (2007); Zali (2014), which points out that debate mostly fails on both the Persian and the Greek sides—but for different reasons (166–168). On indirect report in both historians: Scardino (2012). On Herodotus' association of *isēgoria* with Athens' achievements, see Tamiolaki (2010, 226–28).

During this same debate, Xerxes' uncle Artabanus idealistically represents the expression of various people's opinions as a heuristic tool whereby a better decision could be taken (7.10α1). Nevertheless: in Herodotus, arguments and persuasion represent only surface explanations. Xerxes, he notes, would have become king after Darius, even if he had not had the best arguments against his stepbrother Artobazanes, because his mother "Atossa had all the power" (7.3.4). In Thucydides, too, despite their prominence in the narrative, the impact of speeches on decisions is not guaranteed, and their contribution to the reader's understanding of the addressees' decision is rather indirect. The first two speeches (the speeches by the Corcyraeans and the Corinthians in Athens, 1.32–43) are delivered in an Assembly that failed to take a conclusive decision, as is explicitly made clear in the postscript to the antilogy:

> When the Athenians had heard both out, two assemblies were held. In the first there was a manifest disposition to listen to the representations of Corinth; in the second, public feeling had changed, and an alliance with Corcyra was decided on, with certain reservations. It was to be a defensive not an offensive, alliance. It did not involve a breach of the treaty with the Peloponnesus: Athens could not be required to join Corcyra in any attack upon Corinth. But each of the contracting parties had a right to the other's assistance against invasion, whether of his own territory, or that of an ally. For it began now to be felt that the coming of the Peloponnesian War was only a question of time, and no one was willing to see a naval power of such magnitude as Corcyra sacrificed to Corinth; though if they could let them [i.e., the Corcyraeans and Corinthians] weaken each other by mutual conflict, it would be no bad preparation for the struggle which Athens might one day have to wage with Corinth and the other naval powers. At the same time the island seemed to lie conveniently on the coasting passage to Italy and Sicily.
>
> Translations of block quotations are by Richard Crawley.

This passage not only allows the reader to become aware of the force and the dangers inherent in rhetoric (the Athenians were not able to take a decision immediately; they were oscillating during two meetings), but also emphasizes its limits. Both speeches seem to have been taken seriously by the audience, but neither side was completely successful. The final decision shows that arguments from both speeches were valued as important (Corinthians: "respect the treaties, the customs, our rights over our allies"; Corcyraeans: "don't let our navy be controlled by your enemies"). Presumably, the postscript echoes opinions expressed in the speeches that were delivered by Athenian speakers in both assembly meetings, but not included by the historian. At the same time, the narrative postscript to the antilogy invites the external audience, Thucydides' readers, to compare their own responses to the speeches with the Athenians' final decision. The reference to future operations in Italy and Sicily (a point made by the Corcyraeans and especially emphasized by the narrator, as well) signifies that full appreciation of the speeches requires the knowledge of the whole war and its narrative (and vice versa, the speeches prepare the introduction of later events—which is a Homeric technique).[6]

---

[6] On Homeric techniques in Herodotus and Thucydides, see Rutherford (2012). For an analysis of the Athenians' response to the speeches by the Corcyraeans and Corinthians, cf. Foster (2010, 55–64).

Additional information is therefore sometimes needed to make the decisions of particular addressees fully intelligible. The historical importance of the speeches held at the Congress of the Peloponnesian League in Sparta (1.68–78) is diminished by the narrator's comment that the Spartans declared war on Athens "not so much because they were persuaded by the arguments of the allies, as because they feared the growth of the power of the Athenians" (1.88). Although Athenian aggressiveness had been explicitly denounced by the Corinthian speakers and is openly exhibited in the Athenians' speech, the reader needs the Pentecontaetia (1.89–118, a narrative of the events between the end of the Persian Wars and Peloponnesian War) fully to appreciate the Spartans' fears regarding the escalation of Athenian imperialism. The final decision about going to war is taken in a meeting of the Spartans "by themselves" (1.79.1) after the inclusion of a further pair of contrasting orations by the king Archidamus and the ephor Sthenelaïdas (1.80–86). The impact of these latter speeches is also undermined by a significant piece of information: the ephor, having completed his speech, applied a tactical trick during the vote (1.87).

There are also decisions that seem to ignore the speeches that precede them. The Camarinaeans decided to remain neutral in the conflict between Syracuse and Athens, since they thought that this involved the least risk for them. The speeches by the Syracusan Hermocrates and the Athenian Euphemus (6.82–87) are not necessary for understanding this decision, apart from the fact that they illustrate the Athenians' difficulty in maintaining the support of Sicilian cities. Are these speeches therefore superfluous? To the reader they provide two contrasting, comprehensive appraisals of Athenian expansionism and the renewal of war.

This example shows how speeches that are unable to convince others to adopt the political or military policies for which they argue nevertheless carry out important functions in the economy of the work. They not only provide essential historical information on various aspects of reality, but also uncover beliefs and attitudes, highlight arguments and emotions, explore possibilities and expectations, and introduce themes and perceptions. Thus, the cluster of four speeches held at Sparta (1. 68–87) introduces the reader to the situation in Greece at the eve of the war: the speeches touch upon the problems and challenges to which the two blocks were exposed, they suggest how these challenges were evaluated by each side, and they indicate the tensions within each League. They also reveal and comment on the divergent mentalities of Athenians and Spartans, just as they reveal the different approaches and schools of thought within Sparta, and much else.

In general, Thucydides' speeches provide deeper insights into the mechanics of political processes and historical causality.[7] They also demonstrate how rhetoric can influence the course of events, how various people may or may not respond to rhetoric itself

---

[7] Although the experience of the past is critically discussed in Thucydides' speeches, they do not serve as retrospective narratives of past events (unlike Homeric speeches and some speeches in later historiography—see e.g., Polydamas' speech in Xenophon's *Hell.* 6.1.4–16).

or to the challenges of a critical moment,[8] and how a leader can interact with the people. Lastly, they provide tools for an informed response to the narrative and suggest models to make human behavior more intelligible. Speeches in Thucydides have a dynamic quality. Their importance is neither local nor speculative; they broaden the reader's perspective in a way that potentially influences the reading of the whole narrative (or of any part of it). Thus, they form part of a dialectic process. They do not necessarily contain ultimate truths, but they are necessary for a synthetic perception of reality and for a genuinely critical approach toward the events. Speakers argue, theorize, project their ideas onto the future; the work as a whole probes the validity of their efforts.

Speeches in classical historiography are not the authentic orations that were delivered by historical actors. They rather serve a historian's historiographical and philosophical aims. In this respect, the principles behind their composition may well be in dissonance with Aristotle's assessment that historiography deals with the particular ("what Alcibiades"—a Thucydidean protagonist—"did or suffered," *Poetics* 9.1451b11; one could add: "and what he said"), whereas tragedy deals with universal matters (καθόλου). The Aristotelian type of objective historiography does not (and cannot) exist in a pure form. But while modern historiography is primarily concerned with *what* happened in the past, and *why* it happened (its ideals being to offer comprehensive information and to show the causal relations between events), classical historiography is no less interested in illustrating *how* things happened—another debt to the narrative tradition of the Greeks. It is not, therefore, surprising that ancient historians frequently yielded to the temptations of artistry to stimulate aesthetic responses or to suggest exemplarity.

In Thucydides, speeches are seemingly the point at which the narrator disappears and the narrative is maximally aligned with its referent, the "story" itself (thus seeming to be historically "accurate," but also "concrete"—concerned with the particular). Although speeches express particular points of view, they are used by Thucydides in a way that contradicts verisimilitude[9] and challenges the reader to delve into fundamental questions about mankind, society, politics, and history. If set speeches in historiography pretend to be "inserted" texts, spoken by a speaker other than the narrator, this ultimately provides an alibi for the freedom of their composition.[10] The particular becomes a means for raising abstract questions and, in this sense, Thucydides' speeches invite the reader to take a rather philosophical glance at the world. The speeches are less an effort to serve accuracy and to dramatize historical narrative in a manner that

---

[8] Cf. Schmitz (2010).

[9] They are shorter than real speeches, more uniform in language, very complex in style, sophisticated in thought. Further indications used by various scholars as arguments against the historicity of Thucydides' speeches are discussed by Hornblower (1987, 55–66), which cautiously concludes that these indications cannot be regarded as proofs.

[10] Cf. Laird (1999, 150–52), on the impossibility of preserving "objective reality" in historiography: reality consists of events and utterances; historiography reports about constructed facts and reproduces speech. "In that no live utterance can ever be reproduced in a narrative, historiography must be regarded, if not as invention, then at least as a kind of improvisation" (152). Cf. also Hansen (1998, 46) on military exhortations: "the battle exhortation is essentially a historiographic fiction and not a rhetorical fact."

inevitably would be incomplete and distorting (and thus, in Platonic terms, "τρίτον ἀπὸ τῆς ἀληθείας"); without being an idealist before Plato, but rather an intellectualist, Thucydides constantly attempts to link the particular to more general concepts, and he treats individuals, actions, situations, and events in terms of abstract notions and archetypical properties.

Alcibiades, for example, who was prosecuted in Athens and had fled to Sparta, in his speech before the Spartans (6.89–92) reasonably endeavors to defend his earlier policy towards Sparta and also to justify the betrayal of his own city in order to forestall possible reservations about his moral integrity. But he goes one step further when he presents himself as a "lover of the city" (φιλόπολις, three times in 6.92.2–4), arguing that his struggle against his opponents within Athens reflects his patriotic attitude. The exaggerated emphasis on such a sophistic claim could hardly serve the purpose of securing the benevolence of his former enemies. Instead, Alcibiades' claims should be assessed against the narrative context. From one perspective his claims need to be read against what the reader already knows about Alcibiades and his selfish motives: this language of "loving the city" may ironically foreshadow his future involvement in Athenian politics, especially his role in the overthrow of democracy in 411 and his subsequent recall. Within the work's largest economy, the adjective also invites the reader to compare Alcibiades to Pericles, who had used the same adjective about himself (2.60.5; it is significant that Pericles did not betray the city in any way, although he was faced with the hostility of the masses). At the same time, however, Thucydides urges the reader to reflect on a general matter, namely, on the relation between the individual and the city, a topic of special interest for orators, tragic and comic poets, and philosophers in classical Athens.[11]

The special value of Thucydides' speeches derives from the fact that they are related to real-life situations (unlike, e.g., tragic *agōnes logōn*) and also meet the expectations of a contemporary audience that was familiar with the discussion of puzzling theoretical issues and acute practical dilemmas in speech form. Speeches, however, were not expected to be documents; moreover, accuracy and exhaustiveness would not necessarily be an advantage (or their lack a disadvantage). Thucydides seems to have been fully aware of the paradox: "true but not authentic"—and anticipates his readers' concerns about the antinomies pertaining to his speeches in the so-called methodological chapter (1.22, where he specifies the general principles he has been following in the course of his research and of the composition of his work). The label "ὅσα λόγῳ εἶπον ἕκαστοι" ("as to the speeches which were made by different men") seems to refer (in this context) to the

---

[11] The same question was treated, e.g., by Plato in the *Crito*. It is probable that, like Platonic dialogues, Thucydides' work was intended to be studied in schools of rhetoric and philosophy or in gatherings of an educated elite audience that included prospective politicians. The speeches were probably among the parts that served as starting points for the discussion of wide-ranging topics, historical, political, and moral. Thucydides' work could be also used as a basis for rhetorical exercises. The above mentioned conflict between Corcyra and Corinth and the debate at Athens suggested an ideal pedagogical opportunity for students composing contrasting speeches, as they could have been delivered by Athenians in the assembly meetings. On Thucydides' audiences, cf. Morrison (2007).

set speeches, and signals Thucydides' commitment to the historicity of the speeches he includes. Speeches are treated as deeds, a practice that reflects the importance of rhetorical communication in Thucydides' world—and especially in his native city, democratic classical Athens (accordingly, the reader assumes that the speeches are included in the notion of ἔργα in 1.21.2, where ἔργον is coextensive with the subject matter of the entire work). Unsurprisingly, the historian first confirms the difficulty of reporting discourse accurately—not so much because he was expected to have done this, but rather in order to suggest that accuracy would have been his target even in the speeches, if this were feasible (it should be noted that the new practice of publishing speeches by contemporary orators made this idea less strange than in earlier periods): "χαλεπὸν τὴν ἀκρίβειαν αὐτὴν τῶν λεχθέντων διαμνημονεῦσαι ἦν ἐμοί τε ὧν αὐτὸς ἤκουσα καὶ τοῖς ἄλλοθέν ποθεν ἐμοὶ ἀπαγγέλλουσιν" ("some I heard myself, others I got from various quarters; it was in all cases difficult to carry them word for word in one's memory . . .").

Although Thucydides adopts the terminology of forensic rhetoric to describe the establishment of truth[12] (thus implying that he is following the highest possible standards of meticulous investigation), he refers to the possibility of accurate reporting of speeches only to deny it, and to use it as a foil to his alternative practice: "ὡς δ' ἂν ἐδόκουν μοι ἕκαστοι περὶ τῶν αἰεὶ παρόντων τὰ δέοντα μάλιστ' εἰπεῖν ἐχομένῳ ὅτι ἐγγύτατα τῆς ξυμπάσης γνώμης τῶν ἀληθῶς λεχθέντων, οὕτως εἴρηται" (". . . my habit has been to make the speakers say what was in my opinion demanded of them by the various occasions, of course adhering as closely as possible to the general sense of what they really said"). Thucydides' positive statements are full of vagueness and ambiguity (1.22.1).[13] Moreover, ἐδόκουν μοι establishes Thucydides' subjective perspective. Placed, however, after his authoritative criticism of poets, logographers (1.21.1), and his contemporaries (1.20), and also after the sovereign argumentation *in propria persona* in the Archaeology, the historian's announcement of his procedure is not likely to be heard with dissatisfaction; the reader will rather welcome it at this very point.

Expressions like ἕκαστοι and τῶν αἰεὶ παρόντων even here foreground the concrete and the particular, and suggest accuracy: Thucydides' rhetoric is masterfully calculated. The term δέοντα ("what is required") alludes to a rhetorical ideal (this is exactly what a speaker would also have claimed to pursue). In consequence of his stated procedure, the author is also able to defend contrasting views—from a historical point of view this practice may be a compromise, but from a rhetorical as well as a philosophical perspective it adds to the value of his work. As deeds, Thucydides' speeches are historical (they were truly delivered), but at the same time they are free from each speaker's weaknesses and limitations: they are—Thucydides assures us—expert speeches of exemplary quality.[14]

---

[12] Cf. Tsakmakis (1998).
[13] Cf. Pelling (2000, 115–18); Porciani (2007), which is the most recent comprehensive discussion of the problems of the passage.
[14] The exemplary character of Thucydides' speeches has sometimes been overemphasized; see e.g., Leimbach (1985) on the exhortations. Leimbach believes that every speech corresponds to a different model type, appropriate for a specific situation.

What is, then, left from what was really said? Indeed very little is guaranteed (though Thucydides occasionally *can* offer more)[15]—a flaunting adjective placed in a conative expression and accompanied by a superlative adeptly fabricates the impression that Thucydides will provide the advertised accuracy: ἐχομένῳ ὅτι ἐγγύτατα τῆς ξυμπάσης γνώμης τῶν ἀληθῶς λεχθέντων. ξύμπασα combines abstraction and generality ("overall," "on the whole"); on the one hand, it points toward the opposite of accuracy and precision; still, it is restrictive enough to exclude whatever detail would contradict each speaker's ideas. Thus, it signals the author's commitment to truth and reality (in the way that truth is present in a summary or a conclusion), but not to factual precision. γνώμη is a further vague term; it is what a person has in mind, and it is according to this content that its meaning can be further specified ("view," "opinion," and "purport" are legitimate renderings, but it is not the choice among them that matters in the present context); γνώμη (derived from γιγνώσκω) is usually not a property of a speech; the speech is rather the vehicle of a person's γνώμη—Thucydides' unconventional construction creates again a sense of vagueness (which contradicts, and is concealed by, the rhetorically drastic claim "as close as possible"). At the same time, the passive expression τῶν ἀληθῶς λεχθέντων (as τὰ ἔργα τῶν πραχθέντων in the next paragraph) again suggests objectivity, since it suppresses any subjective focus. Thucydides' rhetoric is efficient: while he promises so little (in terms of positivist, scientific ideals) he proves to proclaim exactly the opposite.[16] All in all, the blend of subjective and objective elements can vary according to the available information, or according to Thucydides' desire to highlight certain themes or motives, but not least because not every speaker who happened to be active at a crucial historical moment was equally skilled as a speaker. Ultimately, the degree of authenticity of the speeches is one aspect of an overarching question, namely, how much of what gives life to Thucydides' principal heroes is "Thucydidean."

Rhetorical aptitude is a skill for which specific individuals are explicitly praised by Thucydides: above all Pericles, a model in every respect who claims to be "second to no man either in knowledge of the proper policy or in the ability to expound it" (2.60.5; see also 1.138.3 on Themistocles); Brasidas, called "not a bad speaker for a Spartan" (4.84.2)—his speeches, however, are "seductive" (4.88.1); Antiphon, whose admirable apology could not save his life (8.68.1-2). Conversely, Nicias is shown to disregard the καιρός, the right moment to speak, and thus he elicits the result opposite from the one he intended (6.24).

Nevertheless, speakers frequently express their reservation toward the impact of rhetoric. Thucydides occasionally confirms that speeches can be deceitful; military

---

[15] See e.g., Marincola (2001, 79–81) on Thucydides' flexibility in composing his speeches.

[16] The indefiniteness of ξύμπασα γνώμη τῶν ἀληθῶς λεχθέντων may also have been favored by the fact that some speeches are attributed to more than one speaker (2.87: Cnemus, Brasidas, Peloponnesian generals—7.66-68: Peloponnesian generals and Gylippus); other speeches may incorporate positions defended by several different speakers, since Thucydides includes no more than one speech for each side. Finally, Thucydides was elected general in the year 424, and he might have addressed the ecclesia either this year or before. Is it not reasonable to assume that some thoughts expressed by Pericles (whose policy he admittedly endorsed) or even Diodotus in their speeches echo Thucydides' own speeches?

rhetoric employs the topical argument that preparations or qualities such as skill and boldness are more important than the commander's words of encouragement (6.68.1). It is true that different audiences display different attitudes to rhetoric. The Athenians are prone to succumbing to the "pleasure of logos." Cleon's criticism of the citizens who long for aesthetic pleasure instead of judicious reasoning (3.38.7) is exaggerated, but not unjustified: the Athenians are shown in the narrative to be guided by emotion rather than reason, and this is connected to their notorious volatility. Thus, in the Corcyraean debate they take a reasonable decision (under Pericles' influence?), but this happens only in a second assembly, a day after they have listened to the speeches we read; in the Mytilenaean debate the scene has already moved to the second day of deliberation (3.36), and we watch the Athenians revise a decision that they took the day before in extreme anger. Finally, the Sicilian debate ends with the complete domination of passion. This time, Nicias is unable to initiate a revision, although he is given a second speech in the same debate (a unique case in Thucydides). Pericles can control the Athenian masses: his first speech (1.140–144) is a triumph—Thucydides highlights this by not including any speeches by other Athenians and by not even mentioning Pericles' opponents while he was alive. Pericles' last speech (2.60–64), however, has only a temporary impact on his audience, as it simply postpones his condemnation by the agitated masses who blame him for their distress. Cleon, too, progressively loses the game against his fellow citizens: although he is introduced as the "most able to persuade the people" among his contemporary Athenians (3.36.6), his one and only direct speech in the work is a failure. Later, he manages to manipulate the Assembly in his effort to reject the Spartans' plea for peace (4.22); yet, he is finally trapped by his own slanders and maneuvering in the Assembly and is sent against his will to Pylos (4.27–28).

Equally remarkable is the People's change of mood regarding Alcibiades as soon as he leaves Athens. What Cleon said in the meetings about the peace and Pylos, but also the discussions that led to Alcibiades' removal from office and recall to Athens, are reported in indirect discourse, meaning that whole scenes are rendered from the narrator's point of view. This enables Thucydides to suggest an unambiguous characterization of the persons and to enforce his desired interpretation upon the events. This also happens for example, with Pericles, whose favorable presentation at the beginning of the war (2.12–13) largely relies on the indirect reporting of his considerations and statements.[17] The same narrative strategy prevails throughout Book 8, where no direct speeches are found, perhaps for the same reason: to allow Thucydides to put forward his own evaluation of a turbulent period and of the persons involved in the narrative.[18] Besides, the lack of speeches may reflect the atmosphere of the period—decisions were now taken secretly,

---

[17] Cf. also Foster (2010, 173–74).
[18] Cf. also Debnar (2013, 284): "Indirect discourse, with its ability to blur boundaries—not only between thought and speech, but also between discourse and narrative, as well as between Thucydides' own judgments and those of historical agents—seems especially well suited to this phase of the war." Scardino (2012) has shown that indirect speeches can display exactly the same rhetorical properties as direct speeches.

and public deliberation was replaced by conspiratorial meetings, open violence, and underhanded agreements.[19]

Despite the great number of speeches in Thucydides' *History* and the similarities they share, almost every speech is unique and remarkable. There is a high degree of diversity regarding the speakers (their nationality, capacity, personal character, views, interests, intentions and sincerity; their past, their reputation, and their degree of involvement in the narrative), their counterparts (political rivals or enemies), the audience (nationality, size, and function: citizens, magistrates, soldiers, military officers; disposition and receptivity), the balance of power between speakers or between speaker and audience, the concrete circumstances and the issue at stake, the degree of autonomy of the speech occasion within the narrative, the background information provided before the speech, and the concluding remarks about its effects.[20] Envoys speaking away from their city often remain unnamed (this possibly does justice to the fact that more than one person might have defended their city's views with a speech or during informal talks and negotiations, but it also avoids focusing on individuals: envoys could have had ties to the city they were sent to, and for this very reason they easily came under suspicion, if something went wrong; it is not coincidental that Thucydides named the two representatives of the Plataeans before the Spartan judges: one of them was not only called Lakōn, but was also a proxenos of Sparta). Some military speeches are attributed to more than one person (see n. 16); in one instance there is an indication of the iterative character of a speech (Pagondas, 4.91), other generals were moving between the troops while addressing them (hence, we can assume that not everybody was listening to the same speech (Hippocrates, 4.94.2; Nicias, 7.76.). Hippocrates had addressed only half his army when his enemies attacked. Some speeches answer or seem to answer others (as a part of an antilogy, of the same narrative section, or in remote parts of the work), while many speakers guess, know, or claim that they know what is happening on the opposite side.

The topics addressed in the speeches also vary significantly; most speeches are directly concerned with war: if it is to be avoided (or not), how and why; which side to take and according to which criteria; how to succeed in it; how to treat enemies or revolting allies; how to justify present and past aggressiveness, enmity, neutrality, treason. Hermocrates and Athenagoras even discuss whether reports about Athens' expedition to Sicily are to be trusted: this exceptional case requires an exceptional postscript (6.41): Thucydides adds that an unnamed general concludes the assembly by chastizing Athenagoras' abusive speech and asking the city to focus on the actual situation, as Hermocrates had advised. (On the Athenian side, Nicias had vainly appealed to the *prytanis* to use his

---

[19] See Connor (1984, 210–30), against the once dominant analytic view, according to which Book 8 is incomplete and speeches might have been planned for its final revision. Dionysius of Halicarnassus criticized the historian because the first book contains numerous speeches but is poor in deeds ("πράξεις"), while the opposite happens in Book 8 (*Thuc.* 15–16). In fact, Thucydides never claims that he cites the most important speeches, or speeches by the best speakers, nor does he in any way reveal the criteria for his selections.

[20] Morrison (2006); Pavlou (2013).

authority in the same manner and become the "healer" of a city that was suffering from its overdose of democracy, where speaking made everything possible, 6.14).

In contrast to Herodotus' praise of *isēgoria*, for Thucydides freedom of speech does not promise success. In the same vein, speeches are neither the best nor the most straightforward way to explain decisions, to justify victory or defeat; in Thucydides' universe it is not sufficient to speak well, to be persuasive, to tell the truth. Thucydides' speeches are not to be assessed according to their practical success with their primary audience. Some speeches are entirely futile, such as the Plataeans' apology before the Spartans after their surrender. The representatives of the captives deliver a speech whose length (second only to the Funeral Oration) is disproportional to the size of their primary audience (five Spartan judges) and their prospects of success (the speakers acknowledge that they are confronted with a preconceived verdict). Apart from the tragic potential of their situation, which appeals to the human feelings of the reader, the Plataeans locate their case within a broad historical perspective. They warn the Spartans that a massacre will permanently stain their future reputation (3.58.2: βραχὺ γὰρ τὸ τὰ ἡμέτερα σώματα διαφθεῖραι, ἐπίπονον δὲ τὴν δύσκλειαν αὐτοῦ ἀφανίσαι; "our lives may be quickly taken, but it will be a heavy task to wipe away the infamy of the deed"), and they also stress that they deserve to be treated in accordance with their past: they played an active role in the salvation of Greece during the Persian Wars, unlike their Theban prosecutors (whom they oblige to justify their dishonorable medism in their reply). In the Plataeans' view, history is instrumental not only for the making of their identity but also for the ways in which others are expected to treat them. The debate recapitulates—against the background of Herodotus—a significant past, and explores on equal terms the possible significance of the present. Rhetoric engages both in the rewriting of the past and in the identification of the present:

> οὐ πρὸς τῆς ὑμετέρας δόξης, ὦ Λακεδαιμόνιοι, τάδε, οὔτε ἐς τὰ κοινὰ τῶν Ἑλλήνων νόμιμα καὶ ἐς τοὺς προγόνους ἁμαρτάνειν οὔτε ἡμᾶς τοὺς εὐεργέτας ἀλλοτρίας ἕνεκα ἔχθρας μὴ αὐτοὺς ἀδικηθέντας διαφθεῖραι, φείσασθαι δὲ καὶ ἐπικλασθῆναι τῇ γνώμῃ οἴκτῳ σώφρονι λαβόντας, μὴ ὧν πεισόμεθα μόνον δεινότητα κατανοοῦντας, ἀλλ' οἷοί τε ἂν ὄντες πάθοιμεν καὶ ὡς ἀστάθμητον τὸ τῆς ξυμφορᾶς ᾧτινί ποτ' ἂν καὶ ἀναξίῳ ξυμπέσοι (3.59.1)

> it were not to your glory, Spartans, either to offend in this way against the common law of the Hellenes and against your own ancestors, or to kill us, your benefactors, to gratify another's hatred without having been wronged yourselves: it would be more to your glory to spare us and to yield to the impressions of a reasonable compassion; reflecting not merely on the awful fate in store for us, but also on the character of the sufferers, and on the impossibility of predicting how soon misfortune may fall even upon those who deserve it not.

Thucydides' rhetorical speeches not only mediate between past, present, and future, but also mediate between possibility and reality, between the human intellect and the swiftly changing circumstances. They are part of a process in which "the course of things is as arbitrary as the plans of man" (ἐνδέχεται γὰρ τὰς ξυμφορὰς τῶν πραγμάτων οὐχ ἧσσον ἀμαθῶς χωρῆσαι ἢ καὶ τὰς διανοίας τοῦ ἀνθρώπου; Pericles in his first speech, 1.140.1).

Despite the diverging opinions, arguments, and interests expressed in Thucydides' speeches, all speakers more or less share or are seriously confronted with political realism as a dominant ideological assumption; Nicias' attempt to encourage his men before the final disaster by introducing a "Herodotean" theory according to which the gods put limits to excessive success and unendurable suffering, so that therefore optimism is required, only underlines his desperate situation and reveals his helplessness (7.77). The Plataeans' appeal for a balance between reason and emotion (οἴκτῳ σώφρονι) ultimately exposes the Spartans' pragmatism, as they will slaughter the captives in order to please the Thebans, whom they believe they need more. However, the Plataeans' proposal is an essential contribution to the quest for a balance between realism and humanism, between necessity and morality, which is a trademark of Thucydides' endeavor. Most of his speakers, however, are extreme pragmatists; for many particular reasons humanist sympathies are rarely detected among their particular points of view.

Although the language of all speakers is unmistakably "Thucydidean" (only the inserted documents of treaties violate the rule of stylistic uniformity), slight variations of linguistic preference reveal the author's desire for stylistic differentiation according to the speaker, the audience, the topic, and the communicative aim of each speech.[21] Thus, the high frequency of coherence particles such as γὰρ and οὖν to be found in Pericles' speeches may reflect the constructive character of his rhetoric. On the contrary, Cleon (characterized as the most violent but also most persuasive Athenian politician of his days, 3.36.6, and a demagogue, 4.21.3) and Athenagoras (also a "most persuasive leader of the demos," 6.35.2) try to impress their audiences through the emphatic force of particles that are otherwise rare in Thucydides (τοι, οὔκουν, δὲ δή, δῆτα, τοιγάρτοι, ἦ πού γε δή). Speeches addressed to a Spartan audience have a lower average of words per period: Archidamus (18.7 words per period), Sthenelaïdas (19.1), Mytilenaeans (20.3), Corinthians (20.7), Alcibiades (21.3); the average number in the total corpus of speeches is about 24. Alcibiades' Spartan speech is carefully structured, with audience-friendly indications of its parts, heading, summaries, and transitions. Its three parts are equal in length, and the central part is subdivided into two equal sections. Alcibiades' cooperative stance unveils the medium of rhetoric to appease the well-known mistrust of his Spartan audience toward rhetoric. In contrast, Brasidas' speech to the Acanthians (4.89–92) seeks to achieve the opposite aim: to overwhelm the audience and make them

---

[21] Unlike the letter of Nicias from Sicily (7.8), which was read by the secretary to the Athenian ecclesia, and is regularly compared to the speeches, but is free from rhetorical adornments, speeches make regular use of figures, especially antithesis. Sound effects also seem to be important in the speeches, especially in the Funeral Oration (2.37.1 begins with a hexameter; cf. also the juxtaposition of four double vowels in 2.36.1 τὴν γὰρ χώραν οἱ αὐτοὶ αἰεὶ οἰκοῦντες ..., where the hiatuses evoke the idea of temporal length and other qualities).

surrender (this speech is full of contrastive focus: "don't do A, but B"; "my aim is not X but Y").²²

If Thucydides' antilogies (and, by implication, all speeches) substantiate the Protagorean principle that "for every issue there are two contradictory discourses" (DL 9.51 = 80 B 6a DK), Brasidas' style reflects an attempt to use the power of logos according to Gorgias' maxim (82 B 11.13 DK) that logos is able to replace one opinion (δόξα) by another (at will). Nonetheless, as everything within this sophistic approach, logos inevitably relativizes itself, too. The overwhelming presence of speech in Thucydides (both through the practice of including speeches and in theoretical expositions within them) is capped by an awareness of its limitations. Thucydides' narrative is about what happened; the speeches demonstrate human efforts to influence or rework what happened. Their significance points beyond the situation: the evaluation of a decision or action, the characterization of a leader or community, the understanding of historical causality. They can be read and interpreted as studies (or parts of a study) on the possibilities of action and communication, on the power of reason, on the manifestation and concealment of particular interests and points of view. As Colin MacLeod put it, ". . . his characters cannot be simply models of wisdom . . . the rhetoric which they employ. . . is for the historian a way of discovering to his readers the limits, or the failures, as well as the powers, of reasoning; and in this exposure of human weakness Thucydides' work is both rationalistic and tragic, an analysis of human error, be it corrigible or otherwise."²³

REFERENCES

Connor, W. R. 1984. *Thucydides*, Princeton: Princeton University Press.
Crawley R. 1951. *Thucydides. The Peloponnesian War*, New York: Random House.
Debnar P. 2013. "Blurring the Boundaries of Speech: Thucydides and Indirect Discourse." In *Thucydides between History and Literature*, edited by A. Tsakmakis and M. Tamiolaki, 271–85. Berlin and Boston: De Gruyter.
Foster, E. 2010. *Thucydides, Pericles, and Periclean Imperialism*. Cambridge: Cambridge University Press.
Hansen M. H. 1998. "The Little Grey Horse: Henry V's Speech at Agincourt and the Battle Exhortation in Ancient Historiography."*Histos* 2: 46–63. http://www.dur.ac.uk/Classics/histos/1998/hansen.html
Hölkeskamp, K.-J. 2000. "Zwischen Agon und Argumentation: Rede und Redner in der archaischen Polis." In *Rede und Redner: Bewertung und Darstellung in den antiken Kulturen*, edited by C. Neumeister and W. Raeck. Möhnesee: Bibliopolis.
Hornblower, S. 1987. *Thucydides*. London: Johns Hopkins University Press.

---

²² Tompkins (1972) was the first to study the divergence of stylistic preferences in Thucydidean speeches. On Cleon see Tsakmakis-Kostopoulos (2011).
²³ Macleod (1983, 64).

Iglesias-Zoido, J. C. 2015. "The Speeches of Thucydides and the Renaissance Anthologies." In *A Handbook to the Reception of Thucydides*, edited by C. Lee and N. Morley, 43–60. Malden and Oxford: Wiley.

Laird, A. 1999. *Powers of Expression, Expressions of Power: Speech Presentation and Latin Literature*. Oxford: Oxford University Press.

Lang, M. 1984. *Herodotean Narrative and Discourse*. Cambridge and London: Harvard University Press.

Luschnat, O. 1942. *Die Feldherrnreden im Geschichtswerk des Thucydides*. Leipzig: Dieterich.

Leimbach, R. 1985. *Militärische Musterrhetorik: Eine Untersuchung zu den Feldherrnreden des Thukydides*. Stuttgart: Steiner.

MacLeod, C. 1983. *Collected Essays*. Oxford: Oxford University Press.

Marincola, J. 2001. *Greek Historians*. Greece and Rome: New Surveys in the Classics 31. Oxford: Oxford University Press.

Morrison, J. V. 2006. "Interaction of Speech and Narrative in Thucydides." In *Brill's Companion to Thucydides*, edited by A. Rengakos and A. Tsakmakis, 251–77. Leiden and Boston: Brill.

Morrison, J. V. 2007. "Thucydides' *History* Live: Reception and Politics." In *Politics of Orality*, edited by C. Cooper, 217–33. Leiden and Boston: Brill.

Orwin, C. 1994. *The Humanity of Thucydides*. Princeton: Princeton University Press.

Pade, M. 2006. "Thucydides' Renaissance Readers." In *Brill's Companion to Thucydides*, edited by A. Rengakos and A. Tsakmakis, 779–810. Leiden-Boston: Brill.

Pavlou, M. 2013. "Attributive Discourse in the Speeches in Thucydides." In *Thucydides between History and Literature*, edited by A. Tsakmakis and M. Tamiolaki, 409–33. Berlin and Boston: De Gruyter.

Pelling, C. 2000. *Literary Texts and the Greek Historian*. London: Routledge.

Porciani, L. 2007. "The Enigma of Discourse: A View of Thucydides." In *A Companion to Greek and Roman Historiography* edited by J. Marincola, 328–35. Malden: Blackwell.

Rood, T. 1998. *Thucydides. Narrative and Explanation*. Oxford: Oxford University Press.

Rutherford, R. 2012. "Structure and Meaning in Epic and Historiography." In *Thucydides and Herodotus*, edited by E. Foster and D. Lateiner, 13–38. Oxford: Oxford University Press.

Scardino C. 2007. *Gestaltung und Funktion der Reden bei Herodot und Thukydides*. Berlin: De Gruyter.

Scardino C. 2012. "Indirect discourse in Herodotus and Thucydides." In *Thucydides and Herodotus*, edited by E. Foster and D. Lateiner, 67–96. Oxford: Oxford University Press.

Schmitz, T.A. 2010. "The Mytilene Debate in Thucydides." In *Stimmen der Geschichte*, edited by D. Pausch, 45–65. Berlin and New York. De Gruyter.

Stahl, H.-P. 1966. *Thukydides: Die Stellung des Menschen im geschichtlichen Prozeß*, Munich. (English translation, Stahl, H.-P. 2003. *Thucydides: Man's Place in History*. Swansea: Classical Press of Wales.)

Tamiolaki M. 2010. *Liberté et esclavage chez les historiens Grecs classiques*. Paris: Presses de l'Université Paris-Sorbonne

Tompkins, D. P. 1972. "Stylistic Characterization in Thucydides: Nicias and Alcibiades." In *Studies in Fifth Century Thought and Literature*, edited by Adam Parry, 181–214. Yale Classical Studies 22. Cambridge: Cambridge University Press.

Tsakmakis, A. 1998. "Von der Rhetorik zur Geschichtsschreibung: Das Methodenkapitel des Thukydides (1.22.1–3)", *RhM* 141: 239–55.

Tsakmakis, A., and Y. Kostopoulos. 2011. "Cleon's Imposition on His Audience." In *Thucydides—A Violent Teacher? History and Its Representations*, edited by G. Rechenauer and V. Pothou, 171–83. Goettingen. V&R unipress.

Zahn, R. 1934. *Die erste Periklesrede (Thukydides I 140–144: Interpretation und Versuch einer Einordnung in den Zusammenhang des Werkes*. Borna and Leipzig: R. Noska.

Zali, V. 2014. *The Shape of Herodotean Rhetoric: A Study of the Speeches in Herodotus' Histories with Special Attention to Books 5–9*. Leiden: Brill.

CHAPTER 17

CHARACTERIZATION OF INDIVIDUALS IN THUCYDIDES' *HISTORY*

PHILIP A. STADTER

PAGONDAS, an otherwise unknown Theban commander, in the winter of 424/3 roused his Boeotian colleagues to attack an Athenian army that had earlier invaded Boeotian territory, but in large part already left. Thucydides reports his speech in direct discourse (4.92). Pagondas denounced the Athenians for their aggression, greed, and desire to enslave others, and called the army to defend their country as their fathers had at Coronea. Enflamed by his words, the Boeotians attacked and overwhelmed the Athenians, who lost some 1000 hoplites, their general Hippocrates, and a large number of light armed troops (4.101.2). Thucydides neither offers background for Pagondas nor makes any attempt to characterize him or distinguish him from his fellows, except through his speech and action, which effectively convey his patriotism and energy. Yet Pagondas' initiative and leadership were immensely significant: this was not a minor skirmish but a shocking loss for Athens. Coupled with the fall of Amphipolis to Brasidas that same winter (4.106), the defeat was a major factor in the Athenian decision to make peace in 422/1 (5.14.1). For one brief moment, Thucydides shines a spotlight on Pagondas—and never mentions him again. Pagondas' personal enterprise and speech are not part of a biographical construct, but are essential to the history of the war.

The case of Pagondas exemplifies a fundamental principle: what we see of the words and deeds of individuals in Thucydides' *History of the Peloponnesian War* should be read chiefly in terms of their importance for understanding that war in all its complexity.[1] The corollary is that Thucydides ruthlessly suppresses personal details of

---

[1] For Thucydides' treatment of individuals, see Westlake (1968); Gribble (1999, 159–213; 2006); and De Bakker (2013) and their bibliographies. Hornblower (1991–1996) and (2008) offer insight and essential information on all the individuals discussed in this paper. Throughout, this paper treats Thucydides' treatment of these persons, not their actual character.

family, political activity, and social position except when they are directly relevant to his account. Unlike Plutarch, he offers no background history of Pericles' political battles or Alcibiades' youthful pranks (cf. Gribble 2006: 440). The Spartan debate on going to war offers a clear example. We hear nothing of the political controversies that lay behind King Archidamus' speech advising caution or the ephor Sthenelaïdas' words exhorting the Spartans to war (1.80–85, 86). The latter's motion sets the war on its course, and we need know no more. The description of Archidamus as intelligent (ξυνετός, 1.79.2) is immediately confirmed by his speech's careful analysis of the difficulties of confronting Athens. Moreover, Archidamus' wariness is later apparent both in his speech (2.11) and his actions (2.18–20, 23), when he hopes that the invasion he leads will convince the Athenians to yield. But Thucydides is silent on internal politics at Sparta as well as the personal background of the king and the ephor. His rule is to present the characteristics and personalities of leading actors insofar as they contribute to understanding the war's complexities. His focus, as he states at 1.22.4, is to offer a clear picture (τὸ σαφές) of events as they manifest the human situation (τὸ ἀνθρώπινον), and he will not be led into gossip or storytelling (τὸ μυθῶδες) for its own sake.

This does not mean that he suppressed all individual characterization. On the contrary, Thucydides uses several methods to direct the reader's attention to features of character that influence the course of the war. We may list five techniques: (1) speeches, direct and indirect, attributed to leading actors; (2) Thucydides' own authorial comments; (3) opinions of other actors; and (4) participial modifiers and other subordinate clauses that specify the observations or reasoning behind given actions (cf. Lang 1995). Finally, the narrative itself constantly exposes the interpretations and choices that leaders have made to the hard light of fact. The congruence or gap between what was proposed or acted upon, and what actually followed, reveals foresight and decisiveness as well as wishful thinking and deception (conscious or unconscious). Thucydides' presentation of leaders thus draws the reader into the historical moment, while the interplay of these techniques allows a remarkable degree of nuance, even ambiguity, of interpretation.

As in the cases already mentioned, speeches offer a special opportunity to convey both the choices of leaders and the emotions of the participants. Often Thucydides is content to assign speeches to some collective body: "the Corinthians" or "the Corcyraeans." Only seventeen persons are allotted direct speeches in the *History*, and of these speakers, eleven, including Pagondas and Sthenelaïdas, have only one speech each (West 1973, 7–15). However, a few major figures stand out. Pericles, Hermocrates, and Brasidas deliver three each, and Alcibiades two. Nicias is conspicuous with six, all in Books 6 and 7, and Archidamus with five, three of these forming part of the negotiations before the siege of Plataea.[2] All these actors played major, continuing roles in the war. Their speeches not only present arguments for action, but also reveal character and

---

[2] Pericles 1.140–44, 2.35–46, 60–64 (and note also his indirect speech at 2.13); Hermocrates 4.59–64, 6.33–34, 76–80; Brasidas 4.85–87, 126, 5.9; Alcibiades 6.16–18, 89–92; Nicias 6.9–14, 20–23, 68, 7.11–15 (a letter), 61–64, 77; Archidamus 1.80–85, 2.11, 72.1, 72.3, 74.2.

motivations, contradictions and inner conflicts. When the historian supplements them with his own comments and indications of motivation, as often, he establishes a vibrant tension between the author's "objective" viewpoint and the speaker's "subjective" words. Granted that the words themselves are chosen to serve the historian's purpose as well as the speaker's, this dynamic creates a rich texture, illuminating both the individuals and their effect on the progress of the war.

In what follows, I shall consider how Thucydides presents three outstanding Athenians leaders whose characters strongly affected the course of the war: Pericles (with a brief look at his successor Cleon), Nicias, and Alcibiades. Two other commanders, the Spartan Brasidas and Thucydides himself, also merit attention. The similar traits and significant contrasts of these men's characters weave a network of behaviors that helps clarify why the war progressed as it did.

Pericles

Pericles appears during the Pentecontaetea as a successful general, leading expeditions to the Corinthian gulf and Euboea, defending Attica from a Peloponnesian invasion, and crushing the revolt of Samos.[3] These campaigns, especially the last, demonstrated both Athens' strength and dynamism and Pericles' leadership. As war loomed, Thucydides explains that the Spartans attacked Pericles indirectly, through an ancestral curse, because "he was most powerful of those in his time and while leading the city he opposed the Lacedaemonians in every way. In particular, he did not allow the city to yield, but urged the Athenians to fight" (1.127.2–3). Thucydides explains that Pericles was "connected to the curse through his mother," one of the few statements on parentage in his history (Alcibiades' ancestry will be another, cf. 5.43.2). A few chapters later, Thucydides once more notes his influence: "the first of the Athenians at that time, most powerful both to speak and to act" (ἀνὴρ κατ' ἐκεῖνον τὸν χρόνον πρῶτος Ἀθηναίων, λέγειν τε καὶ πράσσειν δυνατώτατος, 1.139.4). These comments set the stage for his first speech, in which his position is unequivocal: "I continue to have the same opinion, not to yield to the Peloponnesians" (1.140.1). The speech sets out the reasons to resist, and most importantly, the resources that Athens commands and that permit her to confront Sparta and her allies. The Athenians accept his exhortation and the war he urges (1.145.1). The speech provides a window into Pericles' character: fiercely proud of Athens, unwilling to be cowed by Spartan threats, confident in his own intellectual analysis, and endowed with the gift of persuasive rhetoric to overwhelm all opposition. His strategic analysis is not unique, for the speech of King Archidamus at Sparta saw the

---

[3] 1.111.2 (Corinthian gulf); 114.1, 3 (Euboea and Eleusis); 116.1, 3; 117.2 (Samos). Among the many works on Thucydides' treatment of Pericles, see Vogt (2009) with Strasburger (2009, 218–19); Westlake (1968, 23–42); Greenwood (2006, 68–80); Foster (2010); Christodoulou (2013).

same strengths and weaknesses in the two opponents, but Archidamus was presented as more cautious, more aware of the uncertainties of war (1.80–85.2).

Pericles' willingness to sacrifice his personal wealth for the greater good becomes apparent when he promises to donate to the state any lands or property that the invading Peloponnesians might spare from destruction in order to put him in a bad light (2.13.1). The indirect speech that follows first explains Pericles' dual strategy of abandoning Attica and focusing on the sea and then provides a detailed account of Athens' enormous resources (2.13.2–8). However, Thucydides' account of the sufferings of the Athenians who were forced to huddle within the walls (2.14–17) offers a contrasting view, suggesting that Pericles' unfeeling, even ruthless, devotion to Athens' imperial role has a dark side. The historian also sets Pericles' own magnificent vision of the glory of Athens, blending democracy and imperial rule, as expressed in his funeral oration (2.35–46), against the reality of plague-ridden Athens (2.47.2–54). Without explicit statement by the author, these juxtapositions create a multidimensional portrait of Pericles' personality and policy.

In 430 the desperate Athenians were ready to treat for peace (2.59.2), but Pericles reaffirmed his utter confidence in his own strategy and his willingness to sacrifice individual wealth for the good of the polis. Pericles rebuked the Athenians in his third speech, again reported in direct discourse, for inconsistency and because they, in contrast to himself, put personal goods before public ones (2.60–64). Thucydides ascribes to Pericles this revealing statement about himself:

> You are angry with me, a man second to no one in understanding what should be done and in explaining it, and additionally both devoted to the city and above money. For the one who understands but cannot explain is as bad as the one who never imagined what should be done. The one who possesses both qualities, but with ill will to the city, would not speak well for her interests. Finally, the one who possesses these qualities, but can be won by money, would sell everything for that. (2.60.5–6)

These are the qualities that made Pericles exceptional in Thucydides' eyes as well. In the chapter that follows this speech (2.65), Thucydides offers his readers a report on the Athenians' response to Pericles and an extended commentary on his qualities as compared with those of his successors. The Athenians, we learn, reacted ambivalently: they relieved their frustration at their personal suffering by fining him, but accepted his guidance of the city. Noting that Pericles died not long after, Thucydides confirms Pericles' effectiveness as a leader, based on three qualities: his status (ἀξίωμα), his judgment (γνώμη), and his willingness to forego personal gain ("being obviously completely unbribable, διαφανῶς ἀδωρότατος," 2.65.8). The historian's denunciation of the leaders who followed is severe: their personal ambitions and desire for gain led them to please the Athenians with empty promises or flattery. Their competition led to infighting and mutual slander, until open factional conflict eventually broke out (2.65.11–13). Nevertheless, Pericles' analysis of Athens' strengths (ἡ πρόνοια αὐτοῦ ἡ ἐς τὸν πόλεμον) was confirmed by the city's ability to resist its enemies for so long.

These comments, considering not only Pericles' character and strategy, but also the years that would follow, down past the Sicilian disaster to Athens' final defeat, set Pericles' leadership and vision of Athens as a keystone in Thucydides' narrative. The particular blend of Pericles' character, combining judgment, integrity, and persuasiveness, determined Athens' course and offered a plan for winning. But the historian reveals also how little Pericles understood the power of individual ambition and greed. Although he could prescribe a recipe for success, he could not guarantee it, for the collective character of the Athenians, and the individual characters of their leaders, could not continue in the path he began. In Pericles' third speech, Thucydides notes already the effect of the plague and the war on the statesman: he is still equally convinced of his strategic analysis, but he now concedes that not all can be planned in advance, for divine powers (τὰ δαιμόνια) may intervene (2.64.2). Further, he recognizes that Athens will be hated by its so-called allies, so that it may be called a tyrant city, and that in the last analysis, "all things are born to diminish" (2.64.3). Thucydides' history will trace the course of this diminishment, in Athens' leaders and in the city itself.

In this way Thucydides presents Pericles' leadership through authorial comments and quoted speeches (direct or indirect) that focus attention on his individual role. At the same time, the historian's comments on character introduce issues that will be central to the historical narrative. The comparison with later Athenian leaders at 2.65 extends its scope down to Athens' defeat in 404. Every successive leader at Athens should be measured against Pericles' standard.

Cleon

Phormio and other Athenian generals stand out for their military successes, but are not political figures, and so not directly comparable to Pericles. The demagogue Cleon is more apposite. When the narrative first brings him forward, ready to deliver a speech demanding the death sentence for all the Mytilenean rebels, Thucydides comments directly on his character: "he was the most violent (βιαιότατος) of the citizens and at that time by far the most persuasive with the people" (3.36.6). The ability to lead through persuasion was a Periclean virtue, and the following speech (3.37–40) plays with some Periclean phrases, but the speech's attack on democratic discussion and its unreasoning exhortation to the most violent reprisals contrasts strongly with Periclean policy. In this case, Diodotus' rather sophistic argument for limiting punishment so as to retain allied support (3.42–48) fits Pericles' plan more closely. Diodotus' character is not developed, and the historian offers neither background nor comment on this speaker beyond the notice that he had already opposed execution in the prior debate. Cleon, however, returns to the narrative to confront Nicias over Pylos. Thucydides criticizes him for his demagoguery, using participial phrases (γνοὺς twice, ὁρῶν) to express Cleon's recognition of the need to attack Nicias to maintain his own position (4.21.3, 27.3–5). Quite surprisingly, after being sent as a co-commander to Pylos, he is able to bring home a number of Spartan captives. However, when he attempts to deal with Brasidas in Thrace, he is outmaneuvered and killed at Amphipolis. Thucydides is outspoken on Cleon's vicious character, affirming after his death: "He fiercely opposed peace, considering (νομίζων) that with calm his own crimes would be more apparent and his calumnies less credible" (5.16.1, cf. 4.27.3–4). He clearly considered Cleon the first of the demagogues who led Athens away from Periclean policy, ascribed his successes more to luck than to foresight, and thought his death overdue. Perhaps Thucydides was secretly pleased that Cleon had not succeeded at Amphipolis, where he himself had failed.

Nicias

The deaths of Cleon and his Spartan opponent Brasidas at Amphipolis eliminated the two chief supporters of the war and allowed Nicias to negotiate the peace that bore his name. Thucydides' narrative up to the Sicilian Expedition presents Nicias as "the most successful campaigner of his contemporaries" (5.16.1), but, unlike Cleon or Brasidas, a man eager to make peace. Thucydides explains Nicias' motivation:

> Nicias wished to preserve his good fortune (εὐτυχία) while he was free from harm and honored, and hoped for the present that both he and his fellow citizens would be relieved of trouble, and for the future that he would leave a good reputation as someone who had never failed the city. He thought that this could come about by keeping out of danger and entrusting himself to fortune (τύχη) as little as possible, and that peace offered freedom from danger. (5.16.1)

Far from becoming more confident, thanks to his victories, Nicias felt a dread of the unpredictable future. When he was chosen as co-commander for an expedition to Sicily with whose scope and purpose he completely disagreed, this dread was augmented by a fear of the irrationality of the Athenian assembly. From then until his death, the trajectory of his life gives a personal focus to the tragedy of the Sicilian Expedition, while Alcibiades, who had urged the expedition, finds himself completely free of its burdens, and pursues his own extraordinary path. Key moments reveal clearly Nicias' determining part in the Sicilian narrative: the debate before the Sicilian Expedition, Nicias' letter to the Athenians after the attempt to build a siege wall had failed, and the successive stages of the disastrous retreat.[4]

In the spring of 416, the Athenians decided to undertake an expedition to Sicily to help allies there, and "to order everything in Sicily as they thought best for Athens" (6.8.2). Nicias, appointed along with Alcibiades as one of the commanders, asked that the decision be reconsidered, "thinking (νομίζων)," as Thucydides reports, "that the city had not deliberated rightly, but with a slight and specious pretext was aiming

---

[4] See Rood (1998, 182–201), Gribble (2006, 459–62).

at the whole of Sicily, an enormous task" (6.9.4). Nicias' speech (6.9–14) rehearses the many reasons why the expedition was a bad idea, displaying a Periclean rational analysis of Athens' situation. But where Pericles was aggressively self-confident, even when attacked (cf. 2.60.5–6), Nicias' speech is full of hesitation, "packed with concessions and reversals" (Tompkins 1972, 185). He defends himself as speaking neither from fear for himself or his property nor from desire for honor, but simply as a good citizen. Yet he seems to believe from the outset that he will not be able to change the Athenians' mindset: he will speak what he thinks best, but "against your character (τοὺς τρόπους τοὺς ὑμετέρους) any words of mine would be weak" (6.9.3). Nicias here is shown to have neither the self-assurance, nor the rhetorical power, nor the political stature of a Pericles (cf. Hornblower 2008, 320–23 to 6.9–23). He may have been surprised by the assembly's decision, as he had been by Alcibiades' tricking of the Spartan ambassadors and opposition to the peace treaty in 420, and so was less prepared to confront the expedition's supporters. In any case, his frustration with Alcibiades' private behavior and public policies bursts out in a personal attack on his opponent, which Alcibiades will turn against him. Thucydides here shows us Nicias characterizing both the Athenians and Alcibiades; in the following speech Alcibiades will respond to him, characterizing Nicias and giving his own view of the Athenians. Their exchange of reproaches is another indication of the intrusion into political discourse of emotions that Pericles had been able to contain.

Thucydides has a dual purpose in reporting the speech: on the one hand, to explore Nicias' character, on the other, and more importantly, to set out the challenges that Athens will face in Sicily, all of which will prove in the event truer than even the pessimistic Nicias suspects (cf. Stahl 1973, 65–69). Nicias shares much of Pericles' prescience, but, at least as Thucydides presents him, does not have the character to win over his fellow citizens. His situation may reflect that of many other Athenians who were dismayed by the assembly's rashness, but unable to impede it.

Even after Alcibiades' powerful response, Nicias tries again, in a second speech (6.20–23). His tone-deaf perseverance is counterproductive, since his attempt to frighten the Athenians with the enormous number of ships and men that would be required only inflames them more and leads them to commit far more resources than they can actually afford (as he has pointed out), so that when the expedition does fail, Athens will not be able to recover its former strength. Throughout, Nicias is unable to face down the assembly, despite his clear awareness of the dangers, or even to escape his assignment, as he obviously would like to do. His offer to surrender his office at 6.23.3 is similar to the one he made to Cleon in 425 (4.28.3) and, as we shall see, to his later request to be relieved of his command in his letter of winter 414–413 (7.15.1).[5]

Thucydides thus ties Nicias' character to the course of the war and the ultimate failure in Sicily. Nicias does not cause the defeat, and in fact sees clearly the enormous risks the city is taking, but he cannot support his farsighted wisdom with the strength of

---

[5] Nicias' multiple efforts to resign are striking: there are no other known incidents of an Athenian commander asking to be relieved. Cf. Tompkins (2016).

character, the social status,[6] the rhetorical skill, or the sensitivity to the moods of the assembly that could have prevented it. The paradox is that he must suffer for his inability to persuade or to set a new and independent course.

Nicias' clear understanding of the decisions that needed to be made conflicts with his deep fear of telling the truth to the Athenians (7.14.4). Even in his strongest attempt to influence them, his letter of late summer 414, Thucydides shows his hesitation and irresolution (cf. Greenwood 2006, 76–81). After setting out the dire situation, Nicias still offers two alternatives: either to recall their troops, or to send out a force as large as the first one had been—and with it, a replacement for himself (7.15.1). Of course, Nicias dearly wishes the former, but his character will not allow him to say so, nor will he insist on resigning, although his sickness demands that he be relieved. He is both afraid of the Athenians and ruled by his sense of honor, which required that he not abandon the post assigned him, or seem a quitter. Even when he is most desperate, his alternatives convey the sense that success is possible. This is the same tactic he had tried in the initial debate on sending the expedition, and it is equally disastrous.

Tracing the progress of the retreat, Thucydides records Nicias' attempts to avoid the inevitable: the hesitant initial decision to leave, the lunar eclipse and the consequent fatal delay, his desperate and futile exhortations to the troops, and finally his surrender and Thucydides' postmortem evaluation. Nicias' fear returns as an important factor in the narrative when the generals consult about a possible retreat and again when the eclipse leads Nicias to postpone the Athenian removal for another month. Although Thucydides himself tends to exclude consideration of the divine from his history, his comment that "he was in fact excessively given to divination and that sort of thing" (7.50.4), seems less condemnatory than rueful, in contrast to Plutarch, who sharply criticizes Nicias' superstition (*Nic.* 4.1–2, 23.1–24.1). Nicias' fear of *tuchē* comes back to haunt him, and the very effort to respect the gods' will leads to disaster.

From this point on, Nicias attempts fruitlessly to reverse his fate. His exhortations to his troops are both noble and pathetic: "Men make the city and not empty walls or ships" (7.77. 7). The soldiers are the city, and their defeat will be a presage of the ultimate defeat of Athens. After his surrender, even two other factors that might have helped him personally, his money and his contacts with pro-Athenian Syracusans, turn against him. The latter fear that he may reveal their dealings, while others fear that his wealth may allow him to escape, so he is summarily executed. Thucydides' decision to reserve his presentation of Nicias' religious scruples and his wealth until late in his narrative heightens the drama of the account. Nicias had said, "I have seemed second to no one in good fortune (εὐτυχία), personally and otherwise" (7.77.2). The reader now realizes that Nicias' good fortune included his wealth, at the very moment when it finally leaves him.

Thucydides ends Nicias' story with a moving epitaph: "And so he died for such a reason or a very similar one, certainly the least worthy of the Greeks of my time to come to such a degree of misfortune (δυστυχία), because his whole way of life (ἐπιτήδευσις) was directed toward virtue (ἀρετή)" (7.86.5). Some readers have thought Thucydides ironic

---

[6] Both Pericles and Alcibiades come from old aristocratic families.

here, but surely he is not. We should see rather a comparison with Alcibiades, whose license (παρανομία) and disgraceful habits (ἐπιτηδεύματα, 6.15.4) contrast dramatically with Nicias' virtue-oriented life. Unlike Alcibiades, Nicias had conducted his life, to use his own words, "with much devotion toward the gods, and justly and without reproach toward men" (7.77.2). He should not have met such an end.

Nicias' noble but weak leadership led to the disaster he had foreseen. Thucydides' account of the Sicilian campaign ends with the suffering of the Athenian prisoners and the destruction of Athens' hopes: "of many, few returned home" (7.87.6).

Alcibiades

The historian provides an unusually full introduction to Alcibiades' entrance into his narrative in summer 420 (5.43).[7] He was young, too young to have authority in most cities, the reader learns, but of a distinguished family. He preferred an alliance with Argos rather than with Sparta, but also opposed the existing Spartan-Athenian treaty "from pride and competitiveness." The account of his motives reveals his background and character: the Spartans had scorned his youth and not respected his efforts to renew the Spartan proxeny that his grandfather had renounced, even though Alcibiades had shown his pro-Spartan feelings by caring for the Spartan prisoners from Sphacteria. Rejected by Sparta, he turned against the treaty and supported one with Argos. Thucydides' presentation invites comparison with Pericles. Alcibiades, like Pericles, could claim both an ancestral Spartan connection and the status (ἀξίωμα) of a noble family. But whereas Pericles acted to preserve Athens' independence of action, Alcibiades, Thucydides tells us, undermined the peace with Sparta more from personal motives than civic, "believing himself slighted on every side" (5.43.3). This is the first of many occasions when his competitiveness and desire for recognition will seriously affect the course of the war.

In narrating Alcibiades' intrigues to establish the Argive alliance, Thucydides shows us a politician who combines the instability of youth with aristocratic pride. He gets his way by cleverness, deception, and the use of his family's high standing in the city. He appears shrewd but has no long-range plan. The historian refuses to elaborate on why he might have thought an alliance with Argos was better, beyond distrust of the Spartans. After he won approval for the alliance, Alcibiades stirred up opposition to Sparta in the Peloponnese, until this policy suffered a major setback with Sparta's victory at the battle of Mantinea in 418 (5.70–74).

Three years later, Alcibiades' championing of the Sicilian Expedition was a pivotal point in Athens' fortunes in the Peloponnesian War. Thucydides goes out of his way to tie the initial success and ultimate failure of the expedition to Alcibiades' character. The historian employs three major elements: first, he shows Nicias' personal attack on

---

[7] On Thucydides' treatment of Alcibiades, see especially Gribble (1999, 158–213).

Alcibiades, then his own authorial opinion at 6.15, and finally Alcibiades' self-defense and exhortation to war (6.16–18).

Nicias denounced Alcibiades as young, eager to be admired for the horses he breeds, and in debt, pursuing private splendor at the cost of the public good (6.12.2). His criticism is picked up and expanded by Thucydides, who introduces Alcibiades' speech with an account of his character and actions that is more far-reaching than that which prefaced his first appearance (6.15, cf. 5.43). The historian begins with the reasons for his support of the expedition, confirming Nicias' strictures:

> He wished to block Nicias both as his political opponent and also because of the attack he had made upon him in the speech, and besides he was exceedingly eager for (ἐπιθυμῶν) a command by which he hoped to capture Sicily and Carthage, and personally to gain in wealth and reputation (χρήμασί τε καὶ δόξῃ) by means of his successes (εὐτυχήσας. (6.15.2).

Alcibiades' motives, Thucydides states forcefully, were political rivalry and pursuit of extraordinary military success (conquest of Sicily and Carthage!) that could bring him wealth and honor. Like Nicias, Alcibiades also desires to have good fortune (εὐτυχία), but in a markedly different way. It is striking that Thucydides considers it so important to inform his readers of Alcibiades' personal motives even before presenting his speech, for fear perhaps that the speech itself would not sufficiently reveal Alcibiades' egoism and disregard for the welfare of the city as a whole. Thucydides then traces the disastrous effect of Alcibiades' personal life on the city:

> For the position (ἀξιώματι) he held among the citizens led him to indulge his desires (ἐπιθυμίαις) beyond what his means would bear, both in keeping horses and other expenditure, and this later on had not a little to do with the ruin of the Athenian state. Alarmed at the magnitude of the license (παρανομίας) in his own life and habits, and at the attitude (διανοίας) that he showed in everything he undertook, the mass of the people marked him as an aspirant to tyranny (ὡς τυραννίδος ἐπιθυμοῦντι) and became his enemies (πολέμιοι); and although in his public life he conducted military affairs very well (κράτιστα), in his private life his habits (ἐπιτηδεύμασιν) gave offense to everyone, so that they entrusted affairs to other hands, and thus soon ruined the city. (6.15.3–4)

Thucydides' remarks on Alcibiades show a progression from political rivalry, through desire for military and thus financial success, to the underlying self-indulgence requiring expenditure beyond his means, motivated by his desire for glory. Thus, as Gribble remarks (2006, 463), "the private sphere, the individual, is allocated a direct causal importance." Coupled with these factors are his flouting of convention and way of thinking.[8] Thucydides explains neither expression, although Plutarch gives many examples of the former, and Alcibiades' speech suggests elements of the latter.

---

[8] These Thucydides later connects directly to the accusations of Alcibiades' enemies (6.28.2: "giving as evidence his other undemocratic license in his practices").

Thucydides sets out the dilemma: the Athenians' judgment of Alcibiades' character alienated them from him, but by entrusting the city to others, they destroyed Athens. In this estimation, Alcibiades' character, not his military skill or lack of it, had the most lasting effect on the course of the war. His extraordinary inventiveness and ambition were offset by the self-indulgence, quite un-Periclean, of his life. The evaluations at 2.65 and 6.15 tie the characters of Pericles and Alcibiades together, forming an interpretative network and offering "signposts within the narrative" (cf. De Bakker 2013, 35).

Alcibiades' reply to Nicias' attack radiates aggressive self-confidence: "The things for which I am notorious bring honor to my ancestors and myself, and profit to my country" (6.16.1). However, it is not just Nicias' attack he is rejecting, but the studied opinion of the historian as well. His arguments for the expedition will be in large part disproved by events. The whole speech, 6.16–18, abounds with exaggeration, boasting, and deception, and it is unnecessary to provide further examples. Yet Alcibiades' enthusiastic, if self-centered and deluded, support for the war was shared by most of the Athenians: "a passion fell upon all as a body to set sail" (καὶ ἔρως ἐνέπεσε τοῖς πᾶσιν ὁμοίως ἐκπλεῦσαι, 6.24.3). Here, as often, the Athenians' enthusiasm seems to reflect Alcibiades' ambition for conquest and personal wealth as well as his boundless confidence of success in whatever he attempted. Alcibiades is a true representative of the ever optimistic and dynamic Athenian spirit described by the Corinthians before the war began (1.68–71; cf. Connor 1984, 39–41, 168). This is the spirit Nicias had tried unsuccessfully to tame with his speeches.

Even more revealing, perhaps, of the contradictory impulses in Alcibiades' character is the speech that he delivered later in the same year after he had escaped enemies at home by fleeing to Sparta (6.89–92).[9] Whereas before he was a cheerleader for Athenian greatness, he now denounces the city and its leaders, who had sentenced him to death *in absentia*. His words are completely self-centered, hostile to the governing group at Athens and the very idea of democracy, and brilliantly aware both of what the Spartans wished to hear and of the best ways to hurt his own city. Alcibiades had already destroyed Athens' hopes to win over Messana when he betrayed the pro-Athenians there to the Syracusans (6.74.1). The steps he urged at Sparta, to send a Spartan commander to Syracuse, to resume the war, and to fortify Decelea in Attica, would be devastating to Athens, whether they were planned independently by the Spartans or not. His account of the democracy and his own relation to Athens is the very opposite of Pericles': he sees democracy as a means, not a goal, and the city not as a community of citizens, but the possession of an individual. The sophistic reasoning he uses to defend his previous hostility to Sparta and his present hostility to Athens, redefining the meaning of "patriotic" (φιλόπολις), cannot hide the fact that he clearly is a traitor, and a vicious one at that.

---

[9] Thucydides, in his digression on the tyrannicides and his accounts of the Hermocopidae and mysteries affairs, goes to great lengths to show that Alcibiades' exile resulted from misinformation, hostile politicians, and an enraged and frightened populace, as well as his own unbridled lifestyle (6.27–29; 6.53–61.4). Cf. Stahl (2003, 1–11); Pelling (2000, 18–25); and Hornblower (2008 *ad loc*).

Once more, Alcibiades' brilliant but unreliable character shapes the course of the war and contributes to Athens' ultimate defeat.

Alcibiades' speech at Sparta is so brilliant, and so antithetical to the Periclean ideal of patriotism, that one wonders whether it is not in large part Thucydides' own creation, meant to illustrate Alcibiades' amoral cleverness. Yet it fits well with Alcibiades' characterization as so far presented. It is not clear, however, to what extent Thucydides' harsh judgment of Alcibiades reflects personal feeling or resentment, influenced by his own experience of rejection and exile, rather than an objective analysis.[10]

Thucydides reports that the same self-centered duplicity continues after the defeat in Sicily as Alcibiades attempts to play off four parties against one another: the Spartans, Tissaphernes, the Athenians on Samos, and the Four Hundred in Athens. The situation in the Aegean was extremely complex, and Alcibiades appears as a kind of juggler, trying to keep all the different interests in some kind of balance, with the aim of securing his own safety and eventually his return to Athens. Given all the competing characters and purposes, Thucydides prefers to present Alcibiades' character and that of Tissaphernes, Astyochus, Pisander, and others through indirect speech and his own interjections and interpretations, rather than by direct speech.

Alcibiades' attempts to use Tissaphernes for his own purposes were of special interest. The historian records Alcibiades' advice to Tissaphernes, to play one combatant off against the other (8.45–46), then wryly comments on his motivation: "he was preparing his return to his fatherland, knowing that, if he did not destroy it (εἰ μὴ διαφθερεῖ αὐτήν), it would be possible at some point for him, through persuasion, to return" (8.47.1). Is that qualification, "if he did not destroy it," Alcibiades' thinking, or Thucydides' hypothesis? In any case it shows Alcibiades in a very harsh light: he is willing to risk the ruin of Athens to achieve his goal. The Athenian assembly, Thucydides had said (6.15.4), would ruin Athens by rejecting Alcibiades, but Alcibiades himself did all he could to weaken the city. The reader feels a tension between what Alcibiades could accomplish if he were to be accepted by the Athenians and the damage he has caused. Thucydides' words both characterize Alcibiades and reveal the impact of his character on the decisions of the democrats on Samos and the oligarchs in Athens, and ultimately on the outcome of the war.

In his narrative of this period, Thucydides draws attention to Alcibiades' wily scheming, confirming Phrynichus' denunciation of his motives (8.48.4) and calling attention to his many false, self-serving statements and boastful exaggerations (8.81.2–3). When later in summer 411 Alcibiades successfully persuaded the Athenians on Samos not to attack their mother city, Thucydides voices his approval, but with a bite: "*for the first time* (πρῶτον τότε), it seems, he profited the city as much as anyone" and adds, "no one else would have been capable of restraining the crowd" (8.86.4–5). This extraordinary statement puts in perspective all Alcibiades' previous dealings: they have never helped the

---

[10] Thucydides' presentation of Themistocles' suggestion to Xerxes that he could help subjugate Greece (1.138.2) seems quite different. De Bakker 2013 suggests also the importance of postwar recriminations on Thucydides' interpretation of the part played by key figures such as Alcibiades.

city. The statement applies to Alcibiades' action, but as we have seen, his actions grew out of his character.

The *History* breaks off in the course of summer 411, and so we cannot learn how Thucydides might have presented Alcibiades' character in the light of his return to Athens, his generally successful campaign in Ionia between 410 and 406, and his second exile. It may be that in this section Thucydides would have shown not only that "he conducted military affairs very well" (6.15.4) but also that his character had changed. But throughout the extant narrative, from Alcibiades' first entrance when supporting the Argive alliance, through his role in encouraging, leading, and ultimately destroying the Sicilian Expedition, to his negotiations in the Aegean, he has been portrayed by Thucydides, through his direct and indirect speeches, his actions, his motives, and the author's comments, as ingenious and persuasive, but unreliable, dangerous, and deceptive. He had the ability to do great things, but more often than not his actions were directed primarily to his own glory. After he was accused and outlawed in the Hermocopidae scandal, his reaction was to strike back against Athens in every way he could. His flouting of custom and his ambitious attitude (his παρανομία and διανοία) gave his enemies the excuse to attack, and also fueled his revenge. He thus served as a prime example of that struggle for honor and power within the city that followed Pericles' death, a struggle that Thucydides saw as leading to its ruin (cf. 2.65. 10–12, 6.15.4).

Brasidas

The Spartan commander Brasidas radically challenged Athens' position in the region of Thrace and weakened its whole empire. Thucydides blends authorial comment, reports of others' reactions, selection of detail, dramatic narrative, and speeches to create a portrait of a courageous and decisive commander.[11] On his first appearance at Methone in 431, Thucydides notes, he acted so swiftly and successfully that he was given special honors at Sparta (2.25). Thereafter the historian tracks Brasidas' actions as dynamic advisor to the cautious commanders Cnemus (2.85–93) and Alcidas (3.69, 76–80). Later, his rapid action thwarted an Athenian attack on Megara (4.70–74.1). Finally, on a mission to help the Chalcideans, he raced (δρόμῳ, διέδραμε, 4.78.5, 79.1) north through Thessaly before pro-Athenian forces could stop him. Thucydides reports the opinions of the Spartans who dispatched him and of those in Thrace who awaited his aid (4.81), characterizing him through the observations of others. For the former, he was "a doer" (δραστήριος), and extremely useful on campaigns. The latter found him just and moderate, and so were easily persuaded to revolt from Athens. Brasidas' speech to the Acanthians, combining persuasion, deception, and threats, demonstrates the effectiveness of his appeals

---

[11] On Thucydides' portrait of Brasidas, see Hornblower (1996, 38–61) and Howe (2005). Cf. also Westlake (1968, 60–85); Hunter (1982, 119–75); Greenwood (2006, 24–33).

to Athens' allies (4.85–87).[12] Later, his tactical skill and moderation permitted him to win over the major city of the district, Amphipolis (4.103–106) as well as lesser cities. At his death, the Amphipolitans named him founder and hero, a testimony to the admiration he inspired (5.11).[13] His surprising and extremely successful campaign in the north had two major effects, Thucydides notes: the Spartans won cities that could be used as bargaining chips in negotiating a treaty, and much later, after Athens' defeat in Sicily, the allies of Athens were more willing to entrust themselves to Sparta because of the nobility and good sense (ἀρετὴ καὶ ξύνεσις) he had shown. Thucydides adds dryly, "He was the first [Spartan] to go out and show himself noble in all respects, and left a strong hope that all the rest would be similar" (4.81.2–3). As Connor has observed (1984, 131), the point of Thucydides' comments "is not to affirm Brasidas' virtues but to lead the reader to an appreciation of their long-run importance, the creation among Athens' allies of a climate of opinion favorable to the Spartans." His dynamic character dramatically altered the course of the war (cf. De Bakker 2013, 25–26).

Thucydides

Brasidas' daring generalship and persuasiveness affected Thucydides directly. The historian in fact figures not only as "author of the war" (1.1: ξυνέγραψε τὸν πόλεμον), as is evident in the prefatory statements (1.1–23, 5.26) and the regular authorship notices at year end, but as a historical agent as well. Readers gain some idea of his character and can speculate about its effect on the view of the war put forward in his narrative. We learn not only that Thucydides was an extremely conscientious, theoretically sophisticated observer and historian, but also that he himself had suffered in the war. His bare notices of himself invite the reader's scrutiny. He reports that he was a survivor of the plague at Athens (2.48.3), leading many to conclude that he brought the same acute observation and tragic sensibility to his description of the plague as he did to his history. In addition, as a military commander in winter 424/3 he was not able to act quickly enough to save Amphipolis from Brasidas' attack (4.104.4–107.1). The Athenians punished him with exile, and it was twenty years before he could return. He records these facts with a Stoic terseness, yet we may suppose that they left traces in his history. Though his exile had the happy result for us that it gave him access to both sides of the conflict (5.26.5), the experience of command and rejection certainly must have colored his attitude toward other commanders who suffered rejection or its threat, most notably perhaps Nicias and Alcibiades, but also Pericles. The Athenian assembly could be quite harsh with

---

[12] Thucydides notes "he was not a bad speaker, for a Lacedaemonian" (4.84.2). The Acanthians found his speech "seductive" (4.88.1), though Thucydides notes later that it was "attractive but untrue," (4.108.4). Brasidas spoke also at Torone and Scione (4.114.3–5, 120.3). Thucydides comments on the foolishness of those revolting (4.108.4) and later recalls the harsh fate of Scione after it fell to Athens (5.32.1).

[13] Cf. also 4.121.1, his honors at Scione.

its generals. It had fined Pericles (2.65.3), exiled Pythodorus and Sophocles, and fined Eurymedon in 424 (4.65.3). As we saw, Nicias had lived in fear of its wrath. Thucydides shared also with these three men great wealth: the riches and influence derived from his rights to work gold mines in the area led Brasidas to act unexpectedly swiftly to capture Amphipolis (4.105.1). As with Nicias, Thucydides' wealth proved on this occasion a negative factor.

Thucydides' response to exile was quite different from that of Alcibiades: whereas the latter allied himself with Athens' enemy, Thucydides chose to remain on the sidelines, to observe and compose his history.[14] He knew also the instability of fortune: neither Nicias' inability to save the Sicilian Expedition nor Alcibiades' failures at Andros and Notium would have seemed strange to the man who had lost Amphipolis by perhaps a few hours. No doubt he also regretted that he had not had the foresight to see the need to stay closer as Brasidas advanced on the city. Foresight, fortune, and fickleness in fact became three significant motifs that shape and reveal the character of leaders in his history.

Conclusion

Characterization is an essential instrument in Thucydides' narrative tool chest. His history is meant to help understand the human situation, or how humans act (1.22.4), and this meant understanding the motivations of major figures and how their natures affected their words and actions, which in turn shaped the course of the Peloponnesian War. Thucydides provides exceptional detail about the men whose characters are examined in this chapter, since they play such an important part in the narrative of the war, weaving a web of similarities and contrasts that unites them. Pericles' confidence in Athens' strength and his pride in its accomplishments led him to resist the Peloponnesians' ultimatums and design a strategy of restraint on land and aggression by sea, which he realized through persuasive rhetoric and unyielding determination. Thus the war began. Nicias' awareness of the dangers of war to himself and his city and his fear of its uncertainty led him to make peace in spring 421, to defend the peace when the Athenians grew frustrated with the Spartans, and to oppose the expedition against Sicily. His character helped forge a peace, but could not reduce Athenian resentments and ambitions. Instead, his fear of the Athenian assembly and his desire to show himself a good citizen led to a crushing defeat at Syracuse. Alcibiades' youth, aristocratic birth, and genuine talents, combined with self-centered pride, amoral competitiveness, and disdain for others' opinions, allowed him many interim successes but no final victory. Always his willingness to spend extravagantly to win extraordinary success led him to risk more than he or Athens could sustain. His Argive policy led to much disturbance,

---

[14] Cf. the case of Themistocles, who stayed apart from Greek affairs, though under Persian protection, and perhaps even preferred to commit suicide rather than work for Persia against Greece (1.138.4).

but was defeated by Agis' Spartans at Mantinea. His magnetic personality persuaded the Athenians to attack Sicily, but his wild behavior led them to exile him, a major blow to his project's success. In exile, anger and offended pride led him to urge Athens' enemy to action; later, after he had fled Sparta, his deceptions weakened both cities. Thucydides' *History* breaks off, leaving the reader in suspense as to how this mercurial figure would shape the future narrative. However, in his overviews of Pericles and Alcibiades as leaders at 2.65.12 and 6.15.4, the historian had already signaled the significant role the ambitions and passions of individuals would play in Athens' defeat.

References

Christodoulou, P. 2013. "Thucydides' Pericles: Between Historical Reality and Literary Representation." In *Thucydides between History and Literature*, edited by A. Tsakmakis and M. Tamiolaki, 225–54. Berlin: De Gruyter.
Connor, W. R. 1984. *Thucydides*. Princeton: Princeton University Press.
De Bakker, M. P. 2013. "Character Judgements in the Histories: Their Function and Distribution." In *Thucydides between History and Literature*, edited by A. Tsakmakis and M. Tamiolaki, 23–40. Berlin: De Gruyter.
Foster, E. 2010. *Thucydides, Pericles, and Periclean Imperialism* Cambridge: Cambridge University Press.
Greenwood, E. 2006. *Thucydides and the Shaping of History*. London: Duckworth.
Gribble, D. 1999. *Alcibiades and Athens: A Study in Literary Presentation*. Oxford: Clarendon.
Gribble, D. 2006. "Individuals in Thucydides." In *Brill's Companion to Thucydides*, edited by A. Rengakos and A. Tsakmakis, 439–68. Leiden and Boston: Brill.
Hornblower, S. 1991–1996. *A Commentary on Thucydides*. Vols. I–II. Oxford: Clarendon.
Hornblower, S. 2008. *A Commentary on Thucydides*. Vol. III. Oxford: Clarendon.
Howie, J. G. 2005. "The Aristeia of Brasidas: Thucydides' Presentation of Events at Pylos and Amphipolis." In *Papers of the Langford Latin Seminar 12: Greek and Roman Poetry, Greek and Roman Historiography*, edited by F. Cairns, 207–84. Cambridge: Francis Cairns.
Hunter, V. 1982. *Past and Process in Herodotus and Thucydides*. Princeton: Princeton University Press.
Lang, M. 1995. "Participial Motivation in Thucydides." *Mnemosyne* 48: 48–65.
Pelling, C. 2000. *Literary Texts and the Greek Historian*. London: Routledge.
Rood, T. 1998. *Thucydides: Narrative and Explanation*. Oxford: Oxford University Press.
Rusten, J., ed. 2009. *Thucydides: Oxford Readings in Classical Studies*. Oxford: Oxford University Press.
Stahl, H.-P. 1973. "Speeches and Course of Events in Books Six and Seven of Thucydides." In *The Speeches in Thucydides*, edited by P. A. Stadter, 60–77. Chapel Hill: University of North Carolina Press. (Reprinted in Rusten 2009, 341–58.)
Stahl, H.-P. 2003. *Thucydides: Man's Place in History*. Swansea: Classical Press of Wales. (English version of Stahl, 1966, *Thukydides: Die Stellung des Menschen im historischen Prozess*. Zetemata. Munich).
Strasburger, H. 2009. "Thucydides and the Political Self-Portrait of the Athenians." In *Thucydides: Oxford Readings in Classical Studies*, edited by J. Rusten, 191–219.

Oxford: Oxford University Press. Translated by Rusten from "Thukydides und die politische Selbstdarstellung der Athener." Originally published in *Hermes* 86 (1958): 17–40.

Tompkins, D. P. 1972. "Stylistic Characterization in Thucydides: Nicias and Alcibiades." *YClS* 22: 181–214.

Tompkins, D. P. 2016. "The Death of Nicias: No Laughing Matter." In *Clio and Thalia, Essays on the Connections between Comedy and Historiography in Fifth Century Athens*, edited by E. Baragwanath and E. Foster, *Histos*, Supplement 6.

Vogt, J. 2009. "The Portrait of Pericles in Thucydides." In *Thucydides: Oxford Readings in Classical Studies,* edited by J. Rusten, 220–37. Oxford: Oxford University Press. Translated by Rusten from "Das Bild des Perikles bei Thukydides." Originally published in *Historische Zeitschrift* 182 (1956): 249–66.

Westlake, H. D. 1968. *Individuals in Thucydides*. Cambridge: Cambridge University Press.

CHAPTER 18

CAMPAIGN AND BATTLE NARRATIVES IN THUCYDIDES

EDITH FOSTER

It seems natural to us that Thucydides should devote most of his book (cf. Hunt 2006, 395) to campaigns and battles, since he is telling the story of a war. But this feeling is somewhat deceptive. Thucydides does not describe battles because they happened, but rather because he considers them useful for understanding the war, and also warfare in general. Although there are about eighty-three battle narratives in Thucydides (Paul 1989, 308), most campaigns and battles are merely referenced or only briefly described.

Moreover, to take Thucydides' campaign and battle narratives for granted misses their ingenuity. They were something new, and offered postwar Athenians an opportunity that had not existed for any previous generation, namely, to read (or hear) a detailed account and analysis of the political and military events that had brought about their present situation. If campaign and battle descriptions account for more than half of the text of the *History*, I suggest that this proportion may partly originate as a response to the Athenian reader's interest in knowing about and discussing those events, however traumatic.

This chapter focuses on Thucydides' account of the Spartan and Athenian campaigns to Thrace and Boeotia in 4.76–5.14. Comparisons to other Thucydidean campaigns and battles will be found in both the body of the argument and the notes. Overall, we will suggest some answers to the following questions: What are the aims of Thucydides' campaign and battle narratives? What questions do they answer? How do the campaign and battle narratives function in the *History* as a whole? In examining these questions, this chapter will look at the prologue, actions, and speeches of the selected section of text.

Introducing Campaign and Battle Narratives

The text between 4.76 and 5.14 falls into two parts. In the first part (4.76–116), Thucydides offers alternating descriptions of the Athenians' failed campaign to Boeotia and Brasidas' successful campaign to Thrace, in which he captures the cities of Acanthus, Amphipolis, and finally Torone. The second part (4.117–5.11) begins with a truce, which quickly fragments. Further Athenian allies revolt to Brasidas, and the renewed fighting culminates in a decisive battle, at which the Athenians fail to reclaim the city of Amphipolis. These campaign stories begin with prologues at 4.76–81 and 4.117, and end with a description of the resulting circumstances, including the "Peace of Nicias" (5.14ff.).

The campaign stories of 4.76–5.14 lead through a series of battles to a decisive battle. This structure is common in Thucydides. For instance, his account of the prewar events begins with a description of the circumstances (1.24–28) that lead to the battle at Leukimme (1.29–30), defeat in which only sharpens the Corinthians' determination to renew the fight (1.31). The story culminates in the much more detailed narrative of the Corinthians' near defeat at Sybota (1. 46–55). An opposing example occurs in Book 2, where Phormio confirms his first victory with a second at 2.80–2.92. Likewise, in Book 3, Demosthenes leads two battles in Acarnania, at the second of which his Ambraciot enemies are utterly crushed (3.105–114). The Pylos narrative (4.2–41) of Book 4 also includes two main battles narratives, leading to the climactic defeat and capture of the Spartans on Sphacteria. Similarly, in Book 5 the campaign narrative that ends with the battle of Mantinea begins with the vivid story of an aborted Spartan campaign to Argos (5.58–60), continues with an account of further Argive attacks on Spartan allies, begins again with the more determined Spartan campaign to Tegea (5.64) and ends with the lengthy narrative of the battle of Mantinea, in which the Spartans reclaim the reputation they had lost at Pylos (5.65–73). In Books 6 and 7, a series of battles (6.98, 100, 101–103, 7.3–4) at Syracuse unexpectedly leads to the Syracusan victory that prevents Athenian circumvallation; most famous of all are the three final naval battles at Syracuse that lead to Athens' decisive defeat at 7.70–71. In short, the carefully selective campaign narratives frequently lead to climactic battles; likewise, and as we shall see, each individual battle story is composed to lead to the point of no return that decides victory and defeat. These structures form the reliable skeleton of large swathes of the text, so that we can assert from the beginning that campaign and battle narratives have an important structural function for the plot of the *History*. It is also possible to observe that the repeated pattern has a psychological basis: the expectation that the outcome of each battle will have consequences that determine the further course of events draws us through the campaign narratives to their conclusions.

Important campaign stories in the *History* begin with a prologue of some kind. These prologues are quite various in form, and some of them—for instance, the lengthy introduction to the Sicilian *logos*—are unique. However, we can also discern common types.

Like the campaign narratives we will review in this chapter, some prominent campaign stories begin with analytical descriptions of the events and motivations that caused the two sides to be fighting with particular forces in a particular place at a particular time (e.g., 1.56–61, 4.2–6, 4.76–81, 8.1–4). Other, usually shorter, prologues introduce only the active party's motivations and forces (e.g., 2.80, 3.86, 5.57).

Still other prologues include representations of thoughtful planning (cf., e.g., 3.94.2–5, 4.29–31, 4.66, 4.76, 7.42). Further representations of planning, which often resume or respond to the representations offered in the prologues, may play an important role during the subsequent battle stories (cf., e.g., 1.62.3–4, 2.84.2, 3.107.3, 5.65.4). Thucydides' use of depictions of planning to introduce his battle and campaign narratives contributes to the famous sense of "speed" of Thucydidean battle narrative, since once the reader knows the plan or plans, the battle events are readily perceived and can unroll in swift order (cf. Romilly 2012, 25–27). Moreover, depictions of planning allow readers to perceive the success or failure of each side's intentions, as well as of their efforts.

The prologue to the campaigns under discussion in this chapter, found at 4.76–81, introduces the thoughts, motivations, and circumstances of both sides, before starting the narration of their interrelated campaigns: in addition to the functions I have just mentioned, prologues often invite a comparison between the combatants. This comparison is continued throughout the story, since an important aspect of Thucydidean impartiality, and simultaneously of the interest of the campaigns, is created by continuously alternating the focus of the account between the competing parties (Romilly 2012, 29–33).

In this case the prologue begins with Athens and by establishing the reality of Athens' Boeotian campaign. It starts by informing the reader that the Athenian general Demosthenes arrived at Naupactus with forty ships in the summer of 424 BCE (76.1). Thucydides then explains that the Athenians, together with individuals who include exiles from two Boeotian cities, Thebes and Orchomenus, have developed a plan for taking control of Boeotia. On a set day, so the plan goes, the conspirators will betray the towns of Siphae and Coronea to Athenian forces, and the Athenians will capture a third site, namely, the temple of Apollo at Delium. By capturing these places the Athenians plan to split Theban forces so that they can more easily harass individual Boeotian cities. They hope that they will in this way "easily" (76.5), if perhaps gradually, extend their influence over Boeotia.

Other than to lay it before us, Thucydides does not assess or characterize this plan, perhaps because he has already explicitly commented on the Athenians' aggressive and overconfident attitudes in the period since their victory over the Spartans at Pylos (cf. 4.41.4, 4.65.3–4). Neither does he reintroduce Demosthenes, hero of the Pylos narrative (cf. 4.2.2–4.41) or his less famous colleague Hippocrates. In addition, he offers no comment on the Athenian plan to capture a temple, although he specifies that this was their aim (4.76.4). As commonly, the end of the introduction returns to its beginning, explaining that Demosthenes is at Naupactus to raise allied troops for the attack on Boeotia, just as Hippocrates will lead a force from Athens itself. They are preparing for the appointed day (77.1 and 2).

The immediately subsequent introduction to the Spartan campaign begins *in medias res*. "At the same time" (78.1) as Demosthenes and Hippocrates are making their Boeotian arrangements, the Spartan general Brasidas has arrived at Heracleia in Trachis with 700 Helot hoplites and 1,000 mercenaries. Brasidas has called upon friends in the region to lead him through Thessaly to Thrace. When he and his friends are stopped by other Thessalians, who are friendly to Athens and "want the opposite" (78.3) of the Thessalians leading him, he scores the first of his many rhetorical conquests, convincing the opposing Thessalians that they have no reason not to let him pass (78.4). Despite this victory he takes nothing for granted, and literally runs (78.5, 79.1) through Thessaly until he is across the border with Macedon. This swift dramatic story introduces Brasidas into the action of the campaigns, and begins the contrast between Athens and Sparta: Brasidas has stolen a march while the Athenians plan.

Both parts of the prologue thus begin by showing that the action of a campaign is underway, and both back away from action to provide explanations (cf. Dewald 2005): just as Thucydides had explained Demosthenes' presence at Naupactus, he now explains the reasons for Brasidas' presence in the north. Brasidas has been summoned by Perdiccas, king of Macedon. Perdiccas has more than one motivation for calling on the Spartans. Most of all, he wants them to help him fight his neighbor, Arrhabaeus. However, fear of Athens' currently aggressive mood also motivates both Perdiccas and the Athenian allies who are calling upon Spartan aid together with him (cf. 1.57.2–5).

Normally, the Spartans would respond to such overtures very slowly, if at all, but in the present situation they share their suppliants' desire to stop Athens. They hope (4.80.1) to prevent further Athenian attacks on the Peloponnesus by sending an army to Athens' restive northern allies, who have offered to subsidize the expedition. Moreover, the Spartans also have further motivations. For instance, they want to rid themselves of the strongest helots, whose rebellions they must ceaselessly fear, but especially now that Pylos has been captured; finally, Brasidas was eager to go.

These motivations seem straightforward enough, but in fact this paragraph of introduction is dense, ironic, and anachronic. It has included a foreboding story (*katalepsis*) of how at some past time the Spartans had freed, but then "disappeared" 2000 of the best, and therefore most threatening, helots (4.80.3; see Paradiso 2004; Cartledge and Debnar 2006, 565), and ends with a suggestive discussion of the hopes Brasidas' character would for long inspire among the Athenian allies (*analepsis*). Thucydides tells us that Brasidas' "justice and moderation" (1.81.2) frequently caused Athens' allies to revolt (although he also took some cities by stealth) so that the Spartans ultimately had cities to trade against relief from aggression against the Peloponnesus. He joins these observations to an analysis of the period after his *History* breaks off in 411: later on, he says, after the Sicilian campaign, Brasidas' "courage and intelligence" (81.2) continued to cause goodwill toward Sparta, and established a "firm hope" (81.3) that other Spartans would be similar. Only the most important ironies of these statements can be mentioned here: in fact, Sparta quickly snuffed out the allies' hopes for freedom (as Thucydides mentions, the cities were traded back), so that the characterization of Brasidas and the hopes that he inspired are a reproach not only to Athens, but also to Sparta (cf. Orwin 1994, especially 80–81, and Connor 1984, especially 129–132).

The prologue thus connects the ensuing campaign narratives to a deeper analysis of the war. However, it mainly provides the information necessary for understanding the immediate situation, and establishes a contrast between the opposing powers. As we saw, Athens' plan is complex, concrete, and has an aggressive aim, upon which Thucydides makes no comment. In contrast, the Spartans have a number of defensive aims, and do not have a plan, just an idea that they should try to detach Athens' allies in the north. For them, everything relies on one man, who will use whatever opportunities the situation provides. Brasidas, whose death will seal the end of this section of the text, has received a correspondingly extensive and complex introduction. Moreover, Thucydides discusses the motivations for Sparta's decisions at some length. Perhaps he allows Athens' plan to speak for itself because it is typical for this period, whereas Sparta's actions are a departure from her post-Pylos quiescence (cf. 4.55), so that the internal and external causes of Sparta's movements require description.

Finally, the prologue also reminds us of more permanent motivations. Hope is important for all participants: the Athenians hope "easily" to subdue Boeotia, the Spartans hope to stop Athenian attacks on the Peloponnesus, and the allies hope that Sparta will turn out to be more principled than Athens. Fear, by contrast, characterizes Perdiccas and Athens' allies, namely, those parties resisting Athenian control or invasion. Whether motivated by hope or fear, all parties are bound by the laws of power. Both the Boeotian exiles who are calling on Athens and also the Macedonian king and Athenian allies who appeal to Sparta are trying to use the great powers for their own ends, and are in fact influencing their policies and actions (Hawthorn 2014, 81–83). But as the explanation of Sparta's subsequent actions showed, the greater powers are not offering help in order to serve the interests of others. The prologues establish the reader in the network of political, military, and social complications that is typical of every campaign, but also has particular characteristics on each occasion. They do not, however, foreshadow the unpredictable events of the battles themselves.

Delium

Thucydides' narrative of the campaign events includes both battles and speeches, which we will examine in the following two sections of this paper, beginning with three battles: the battles at Delium, Torone, and Amphipolis.

The battle at Delium is well-known to military historians as one of only two set hoplite battles between Greek forces described in Thucydides, the other being the battle of Mantinea (5.57–75). The story begins in 4.89, where the reader discovers that the initiation of Athens' plan to conquer Boeotia was both botched and betrayed, so that Siphae and Coroneia remained in Theban hands. Only the occupation of the temple at Delium was carried out: Hippocrates brought the entire army of the Athenians to Delium and constructed a fortified wall around the sanctuary in about two and a half days (4.90.1–3). The Athenians then set guards at Delium and the main army withdrew about ten stades, back to the borders of Attica (4.90.4).

Thucydides juxtaposes this invasion story with the representation of a Boeotian speech. Although most of his eleven colleagues are willing to let the Athenians withdraw, the Boeotarch Pagondas is not willing to do so, and fervently reminds his countrymen that the Athenians in particular must be punished for their incursions if all Boeotia is not to be conquered (4.92). Thucydides tells us that Pagondas' speech convinced his countrymen, and with this enters upon the introduction to the battle itself, outlining the movements of each side in typical alternating order. He relates that Pagondas swiftly led the assembled Boeotian troops to the Athenian position, but remained behind a hill where the Athenians could not see him, and there organized his forces (4.93.1). In the next sentence we hear that when Hippocrates heard about the Boeotian movements he came to the battle site from Delium, leaving 300 cavalry to guard the temple, and also to help in the battle, whenever opportunity should arise (4.93.2).

Back to the Boeotians, who station men to stop this force (4.93.3), getting ahead of Hippocrates' idea. When they are ready, they appear over the crest of the hill, both to the Athenians and to the reader, with sudden and emotive vividness, enacting (cf. Hornblower 2008, 36) Athenian consternation at being compelled to confront the force their initial plan had hoped, but failed, to split into three. The Boeotians have 7,000 hoplites, 10,000 light armed troops, 1,000 cavalry, and 500 peltasts (93.3). Thucydides explains where the peoples of the Boeotian federation are disposed along the left, middle, and right of the battle line and that the Thebans, who are on the right flank, have chosen to line up their phalanx twenty-five men deep (93.4). The names, numbers, and clear positions make for vivid clarity (*enargeia*) in respect to everything that spells trouble for Athens: the Boeotians have the physical advantage of occupying higher ground and the moral advantage of suddenly appearing with a dishearteningly large and united force, against whose unusual formation the Athenians have no counter strategy.

Thucydides now returns to the Athenians, who also have about 7,000 hoplites. They line up opposite their enemy, eight deep along their whole front, with cavalry on both flanks; they have no light armed troops to speak of, since these had returned to Athens after fortifying Delium (94.1). Thucydides briefly delays the beginning of the battle through representing the Athenian general Hippocrates' short exhortation to his outnumbered troops (for speeches, see the final section of this chapter), but the Thebans sing their paean and attack from the hill before Hippocrates can speak to half of his army. The Athenians respond by running toward their enemy, and the battle narrative begins (96.1).

Thucydides' accounts of battle are bound to disappoint readers who seek Homeric descriptions of hand-to-hand combat with their accompanying lengthy scenes of mutilation and death, and on the other hand also those who seek technical descriptions of hoplite warfare. Thucydides offers neither of these types of narrative, although he proves that he could have offered both.[1] He aims instead for the representation of the psychology and experience of men and commanders in massed battles. In this story, for

---

[1] For more detail on the technical problems of hoplite fighting, see, for example, 5.71. For descriptions of agony in battle, not directly Homeric, since they pertain to groups, see, for example, 4.34.2–3 or 7.44.3–8. For a description of an individual wounding (Brasidas), see 4.12.1.

instance, Thucydides tells us that when the armies met, there was for everyone "a fierce battle and shoving of shields" (96.2). He then tells us that the Thebans' allies, who were stationed on the left side of their line, were losing (96.3–4). Here the Thespians were stationed among the others. Their force was isolated and surrounded by the Athenian right, who cut them down hand to hand, and also kill some of each other in the confusion caused by the encirclement. No other aspect of the fighting on this side of the battle is mentioned.

In contrast to his account of these memorable events, which are, however, less important for understanding the battle outcome, Thucydides' subsequent sentences focus directly on the causes of the Athenian defeat. He reports that the Theban right is defeating the Athenians (96.4). Then Pagondas briefly reappears to issue this battle narrative's only command, namely, to order the cavalry forces that had remained hidden behind the hill to attack the Athenians who were defeating his left side. His tactic is fully successful, perhaps mainly because the Athenians make a mistake: they believe that a new army has come to attack them, and fall into a panic (96.5). However, at this point it occurs to the reader that Pagondas had ensured before the battle that Hippocrates' cavalry would not be able to help him at this moment.

The remainder of the account (96.6–9) is devoted to explaining how the Athenian force falls into disarray, so that dispersed groups of soldiers flee to wherever they think they can save themselves.[2] The Boeotians "follow them killing" (96.8), especially with their cavalry and with the cavalry of the Locrians, which had arrived just as the Athenians were routed; fortunately for the surviving Athenians, the battle was fought in the late afternoon, and darkness soon makes their escape somewhat easier. Upon their return to the battlefield the Boeotians set up the usual victory trophy and strip the Athenian corpses (97.1; cf. Lateiner 1977). They do not return these corpses when the Athenians request them, but rather require the Athenians first to evacuate the Delium temple. When the Athenians do not do this, they keep the corpses until they can expel the Athenians from their fortification with fire and force, and then finally give them back, about seventeen days after the battle. Approximately 1,000 Athenians have died, and about 500 Thebans (4.101.1).[3]

This is Thucydides' narrative of the battle at Delium. It offers a clear explanation for Athens' defeat: the Athenians were winning on the right and losing on the left until Pagondas' surprise cavalry attack, which forms the turning point of the narrative, caused the victorious Athenian right to panic and thus the whole Athenian army to fall into disorder. This report of the collapse of Athenian morale and then organization

---

[2] Both atrocities (e.g. such as killing one's own men or one's allies by accident, or the entrapment and slaughter of inferior or defeated forces) and errors of recognition are regular elements of Thucydidean battle narrative. For atrocities similar to this one, cf. for example, 1.50.1, 1.105.3–4. The most famous description of the destruction of a fleeing force is from 7.78–87, but cf., for example, 3.98.3–4, 3.108.3, 3.112.7, 7.44.7. The Delium story references three errors of cognition: 4.89.1, 96.3 and 96.5; cf. the discussion of Cleon's errors at Amphipolis, below.

[3] On Thucydides' story of Athenian defeat at Delium and its relation to the post-war Athenian audience, cf. Foster, forthcoming.

reflects Thucydides' analysis of battle, in which such reversals of morale are a key factor in defeat.[4] Overall, the account explains why the Athenians lost so badly. In addition, the prominent references to the slaughter of the Thespians, to Athenian deaths by friendly fire, and to the errors, panic, and desperate flight of the retreating Athenians show the experiences and psychological states of those who were there. Thucydides spares his Athenian readers the cruelty neither of their own deeds nor of their defeat. Thucydidean battle narrative is anything but a glorification of war.

Torone

Or is it? What of the suspenseful descriptions of Brasidas' conquests of Acanthus, Amphipolis, or Torone, or of his adventures with Perdiccas (4.124–128), in which stories Thucydides shows that Brasidas is able to activate a combination of military decisiveness and diplomatic acumen that overwhelms all opponents? Stories of Athenian defeat are often linked to the overarching theme of the defeat of Athens (cf. 7.43.7 for an echo of the battle at Delium). By contrast, stories that emphasize success show intelligence, careful planning, versatility, energy, and luck; they may be thought to over-praise and over-emphasize the role of commanders such as Demosthenes, Phormio, or Brasidas (cf. e.g., Hornblower 1996, 38–61), and moreover to represent a hopeful view of warfare.[5] What is their function in the *History*?

Torone was captured at dawn. The success of the venture depended on the reliability of Brasidas' contacts inside the city and the bravery of seven of his men, who entered the city at night with Brasidas' partisans, captured and prepared key entrances, and then brought in a further number of Brasidas' men, so that the city was already occupied when Brasidas and his army swiftly entered and made for the high points of the city (4.110–112).

Brasidas' entry was tantamount to its capture and forms the turning point of the story, since no one in the city was able to offer significant opposition. Although some of the fifty Athenians guards sleeping in the agora were killed, most fled either to their two ships or to a fort called Lekythos, which was situated on a narrow height above the city. The ignorant majority of citizens awakened to utter confusion (4.113.1). Having achieved secure control of Torone, Brasidas exercised his by then famous moderation, announcing to the Athenians that they and any Toronaean sympathizers who were with them could leave Lekythos without damage, and to the Toronaeans themselves that no one

---

[4] Cf. the final battle in the harbor at Syracuse, after which the Athenians are morally, not physically, defeated (7.72.3–4) and the reversals of moral after Epipolae (7.46), at Naupactus (2.91.4–92.1), or on Sphacteria (4.34.1, 35.1).

[5] Cf., for example, Phormio's victories at Naupactus (2.83–92), or Gylippus' successes at Syracuse. Moreover, some campaign narratives seem to offer no assessment of the events, and may therefore seem to be blamably neutral about aggressive warfare. Cf. from many examples, such as 2.79 or 4.53–54. On this type of narrative, see especially Rood (1998, 225ff.).

need fear disadvantages from him, so long as they all now stay true to their alliance with Sparta (4.114). On the other hand, he does not offer the Toronaeans a choice about accepting this alliance.

The first phase of fighting is now over. A second phase begins when the Athenians at Lekythos do not leave, and Brasidas attacks them. The situation provokes the historian to offer one of his vivid descriptions of a few defenders energetically holding off a much larger force (cf., e.g., 2.2–7, 2.75–77, 3.20–22). The Athenians secure themselves for a day by shooting from the houses inside the fort, but on the next day they perceive that Brasidas intends to use a machine to blow fire at them. They build a wooden tower to increase the range of their defense, but carry up so many stones and jars of water that it crashes to the ground. This is the turning point: the noise of the tower's collapse causes those Athenians who are not nearby to believe that Brasidas has entered the fort, with the result that they flee to the ships and the forward defenders are compelled to follow them. Brasidas kills any who were left behind, and then dedicates the entire area to Athena, believing, says Thucydides, that his capture of Lekythos "happened by some means other than human agency" (4.116.2).

The story of the capture of Torone exhibits Thucydides' famous capacity to make the reader feel present at the events: the account offers many opportunities for the imagination, leading us along, for instance, with the men who enter the city and secure the gates at night (4.110.2), suggesting the impatient suspense of those left outside as they creep closer and closer, showing the exact arrangements made inside the city while they are waiting (111.2) and finally explaining the fire signal that sets the army running into the opened gates or climbing up beams that had been left leaning on the outer wall (112.2). Such details draw the reader's sympathy and interest and help create the suspense that drives the story to its outcome.

At any point, of course, Brasidas' men in the city might have been discovered, or something else might have gone wrong (cf. the events at 4.135.1). However, it did not. Thucydides' stories of successful warfare show first of all what really happened: some commanders and forces were both lucky and effective, and could cause decisive damage to their enemies. In terms of the larger narrative, Thucydides contrasts Brasidas' partly lucky successes at Amphipolis, Acanthus, and Torone with the story of Athens' partly unlucky defeat in its quite similar campaign to Boeotia. In a world at war, he tries to explain to his Athenian readers the roles of both luck and skill in creating military outcomes. A further exposition of why some commanders can succeed where others fail is offered in Thucydides' narrative of the battle for Amphipolis.

Amphipolis

So far this section has discussed the battle between the Athenians and the Boeotians at Delium and the Spartan conquest of Torone. In these stories Pagondas and Brasidas were essential to victory, but not particularly prominent in the story of the actual fighting, where the actions and experiences of ordinary soldiers got closer narrative description. By contrast, the story of Cleon and Brasidas' battle at Amphipolis contrasts the generals' thoughts, feelings, and actions at some length.

The battle of Amphipolis was the last major battle between Athens and Sparta before the so-called Peace of Nicias in 421; the story of this battle, in which Athens is decisively defeated and both generals die, represents the final climax of our interrelated campaign narratives. Its focus on the character and thoughts of the two generals helps to create the sense that we have reached the moment to which the long series of battles has been leading: we are brought close to their minds before they die and their characters can have no further effect on policy (cf. 5.16.1). However, the Amphipolis story also completes the campaign events foreseen in the prologue; after it, the narrative breaks off in favor of authorial explanations of the circumstances that led to the Peace of Nicias (5.14–17).

The Amphipolis story begins with a lengthy (5.6–8) presentation of the forces, preparations, and initial movements of each side, during which Thucydides exhibits Brasidas' thoughtful caution and ability to interpret his enemy's movements, while simultaneously showing Cleon's inability to think about his enemy. Representations of Cleon's futile autopsy reveal his incapacity: Cleon repeatedly views the battlefield, but rather than perceiving his present enemy, he sees only what pertains to his own aims (5.7.3–4, cf. 5.10.3).[6] Lacking caution, Cleon has also moved into a position advantageous to Brasidas, who decides to attack before any reinforcements can come to help him. The next chapter (5.9) contains Brasidas' exhortation (*parainesis*) to his troops (for analysis of speeches, see below). Brasidas' plan, presented in the exhortation, is now clear to the reader. He will first attack with 150 men, hoping to panic the unprepared Athenians, and his main force will attack second, hoping to come upon an army that is already disorganized.

Thucydides shows that this plan works perfectly, not because it had to, since the Athenians have a better army and an equal number of men, but because Cleon is entirely unable to predict it. Brasidas remains hidden to Cleon until it is too late, and even when Cleon sees Brasidas, he still thinks that he can walk away. Impatient and inexperienced, Cleon compounds his army's problems through retreating in an incompetent way (5.10.4). Brasidas sees this disorganization and points out the meaning of the Athenian movements to the men around him (10.5) before the double attack begins.

The battle is depicted in swift paratactic clauses: Brasidas and his advance force attack, running out from Amphipolis, and turn the Athenian line; his army follows immediately. The two successive surprise attacks throw the Athenians into confusion and their left side flees. Now Brasidas is wounded and Cleon is killed. The right side of the Athenian army mounts a fierce defense, but is finally routed by the enemy cavalry. This is the end; as frequently, an account of the consequences follows. The cavalry hunts the fleeing men (10.5). Brasidas is carried off the field and dies (although he does live to hear that his men won, 10.11), the corpses are stripped, a trophy set up (10.12), the Athenian corpses returned, and the (very unequal) dead counted (11.2); the combatants either go

---

[6] Cf. Greenwood (2006, 24–33); Rood (1998, 83ff.).

home or settle into their new position (11.3). The paragraph is unusual only for its digression on the post-mortem honors accorded to Brasidas at Amphipolis (5.11.1).

At this point, one can point out more confidently that Thucydidean battle narrative does not glorify warfare as such, however detailed or suspenseful the battle narratives may be: Thucydides never omits to record the terrible things that happen to people during and after battles. While Brasidas is shown to be a much better general than Cleon, it is hard to see how a story in which so many conscripted (5.8.2) Athenians and allies die, and Brasidas himself, not gloriously, but as a result of a random missile (5.10.8) also dies, would seem to an Athenian audience to praise warfare.

Moreover, even this battle story does not boast the emotional intensity found in the final battle narratives of Athenian defeat in Book 7, which any study of campaigns and battles in Thucydides must mention. Most famous is Thucydides' narrative of the final sea battle between Athenian and Syracusan forces (7.69.3–7.72). In this battle account Thucydides depicts the fierce fighting and then turns to the perceptions of the infantry waiting on the shore, showing their sufferings as they watch the massive battle and its many individual events. They respond to momentary victories with shouts and prayers, to perceived defeats with curses and groans, to a combat hanging in the balance by twisting their bodies to and fro with the action, and finally with a universal and united wailing when they see the Athenians defeated (7.71.3–7). By writing in this way, Thucydides brings the reader or listener to terrors of the battlefield with intense immediacy.

Thucydides' battle narratives first of all answer these questions. What happened? Who won, who lost, and why? In addition, they answer questions about leadership: how do good and bad commanders think and act? Not only luck and experience, but also versatile intelligence made Brasidas effective against the Athenians, who prided themselves on possessing this attribute to a far greater degree than Spartans (cf. 2.41.1). Thucydides, however, persistently shows that no one group has a monopoly on such characteristics (cf. the Syracusan Hermocrates, in Books 6 and 7). Finally, the battle narratives transmit something of what it was like to be present. This aspect of the narratives is not foreseen in the prologues, which do not prepare the reader for the slaughter of the Thespians at Delium or the agony of the men watching from the shore in Sicily. The battle narratives thus deploy representations that depart from analysis and are intended to produce unmitigated emotional effects that have often been compared to tragedy: pathos, suspense, remorse, and horror.

Speeches in Campaign and Battle Narratives

Although Pagondas and Hippocrates also hold important speeches, Brasidas is the main speaker in the campaign narratives we are examining. He makes several political speeches and also delivers two military exhortations. Like Nicias at Syracuse, for instance, or Alcibiades in Ionia, he takes a leading role in both the political and the military events of the successive campaigns.

The importance of Brasidas' speeches can perhaps be illustrated through reviewing the story of his conquest of Acanthus, most of which is composed of Brasidas' speech to the Acanthians (4.85–87). In chapter 84, he arrives with his army in time to threaten the vulnerable grape harvest, and the Acanthians are persuaded to hear him. His speech, which emphasizes that the Spartans have come, belatedly but really, to free the Greeks from the Athenians (4.85), advertises that the Spartans swore to allow the cities to remain autonomous and that Brasidas himself has no intention of supporting any faction within the city (4.86.1–5, cf. Babut 1981, 431–434). However, he also makes it clear that the Acanthians have little real choice: if they do not submit, he will compel them to do so (4.87.2–3). Brasidas' combination of promises and threats achieves its intended result: Acanthus revolts from Athens (88). The conquest of Acanthus, then, is achieved almost without military action (although not without credible threat of such action), and relies on Brasidas' rhetorical skill at least as much as on his generalship. Thereafter, this same speech, with additions appropriate to each context, effectively consolidates Brasidas' military success at Torone (4.114.3), and confirms his hold over the enthusiastic Scionaeans (4.120.3). Brasidas' persuasive powers are crucial to the success of his campaigns.

Brasidas' two exhortations have an even more immediate military function. In one (4.126), he convinces a mixed force of Greeks who have been abandoned by their Macedonian allies and are about to be attacked by the Illyrians, a tribe generally believed to be fierce warriors, that a safe retreat is possible. In the other (5.9), as we have seen, Brasidas is inside Amphipolis, sharing his plan for attacking Cleon with a force of men raised on the spot. In both cases he begins by addressing all the men as Peloponnesians, and also explains why the Peloponnesians are superior (4.126.1–2; 5.9). The speeches then proceed to address the situation: the first one explains why the men should not be concerned about the fact that the Macedonians have abandoned them, describes the kind of attack they can expect from the Illyrians, and finally argues that the men will not need to fear this attack if they respond energetically and stay in good order. The second speech outlines Cleon's mistakes and the opportunity these represent, and then Brasidas' plan to attack with a few men first. It ends with commands to follow orders and be brave, and a representation of what the Athenians will do to Brasidas' men if they lose.

Thucydides is considered to be the writer who perfected the employment of military exhortations in historiography (cf. Zali 2014, 237ff.), so that a short analysis of these speeches is warranted. Military exhortations are an attempt directly to influence the morale of a fighting force. Like other successful military exhortations in Thucydides (cf., e.g., Demosthenes at 4.10, Phormio at 2.89, or Gylippus at 7.66), Brasidas' speeches create confidence primarily through showing that he has a useful analysis of the situation and a plan to meet the challenges (cf. Luschnat 1942). Brasidas' speeches also create confidence through appealing to the men's common "Peloponnesian" character, building unity from a claim of shared virtue if no other basis exists. Finally, Brasidas addresses his men's fears. In the case of the Illyrian attack, he argues strongly, even using mockery (4.126.5), that fear of the Illyrians is groundless. At Amphipolis, using the opposing strategy, he emphasizes that loss will mean death or slavery to Athens, but says this only after he has shown that he thinks his plan can work.

Perhaps the greatest difference between Brasidas' military exhortations and his political speeches is that in the military exhortations he tells no lies. At Acanthus, Torone, and Scione, Brasidas had repeated that the Spartans swore to allow the cities their autonomy. But the Spartans quickly sent supervisors (4.132.3). In addition, he had argued that the Athenians would not come to face him in Thrace, since they had been afraid of his smaller forces in a previous engagement at Megara (4.85.7, cf. 114.3, 120.3). In fact, Brasidas had outnumbered the Athenians at Megara (cf. 4.67.1, 72.2, and 68.5). Thucydides remarks on this deception and the fact that it gave Athens' rebellious allies false confidence (4.108.5). By contrast, Thucydides' narrative presentation "guarantees" Brasidas' military exhortations both before and afterward. I suggest that the coherence between narrative and speech enacts Brasidas' military reliability, and allows the reader to sense the confidence which moved the men on the ground.

Like the deceptions of Brasidas' political speeches, the arguments of exhortations that are predictive of failure in a battle are confuted by the narrative context (cf. Tsakmakis and Themistokleous 2013). On the cusp of the battle of Delium, the Athenian general Hippocrates delivers a military exhortation to his Athenian troops. He argues to his soldiers that they will free Attica from the annual Peloponnesian attacks if they win, since the Peloponnesians will not attack Attica without the Boeotian cavalry (95.2). In addition, they will conquer Boeotia, living up to the achievement of their forefathers at Oenophyta (95.3). However, the attacks on Attica had already been prevented, since Cleon had sworn in the previous year to kill the 292 Spartan prisoners captured at Pylos if the Spartans attacked again (4.41.1). Moreover, Hippocrates' talk of victory at Oenophyta ignores Athens' subsequent defeat at Coroneia, after which the very Boeotians whom the Athenians are now fighting had reclaimed their land (cf. 1.107–8 and 114; 4.92.6). Hippocrates' speech also contrasts to successful exhortations in that he presents no battle plan or reassuring information to his troops, but can only adjure them to be brave: the fact that his speech is cut off by Pagondas' attack speaks more loudly than his words (contra Leimbach 1985, 72, with Hansen 1998 on the historicity of the exhortations).

Conclusion

Much has perforce been neglected here: Although we have been able to discuss some chance atrocities, as well as errors of cognition and perception, Thucydides' emphasis on the role of chance as a cause of events (cf. Babut 1981, 423), has not received the attention it requires. In addition, Thucydides' references to natural circumstances (e.g., stormy weather: 4.103.5, darkness 4.110.1, topography: 4.113.2) have been given short shrift. Moreover, there was little discussion of Thucydides' focus on technology. For example, the detailed description of the Athenian fortification at Delium (4.90.2–3) displays the Athenians' willingness to destroy a sacred landscape in order to achieve their aims. The equally detailed description of the device with which the Boeotians expel the Athenians from this fortification shows their opposing determination (they will burn down the sanctuary, rather than allowing the Athenians to stay; cf. Miles 2014 for the meaning), as well as advances in war technology: at the siege of Plataea, the Peloponnesians had counted on a favorable wind to spread fire, and therefore failed (cf. 2.77.5). The Theban device, which uses bellows, ensures that they will not repeat that failure (4.100.2–4). One suspects that the descriptions of the Athenian fortification and the Theban fire machine answer each other: the Boeotians win all the battles in the Delium narrative: military, rhetorical, and technical.

Finally, Thucydides' remarks on past history also had to be ignored. In the campaign narratives we discussed, Thucydides offers emotionally resonant descriptions of the historical geography of Amphipolis (4.102), the Acte peninsula (site of Torone, 4.109), and Scione (4.120), calling up their storied pasts and ancient dignity for an Athenian audience that had lost Amphipolis and destroyed both Torone and Scione (5.3.4 and 5.32.1; cf. Xen. *Hell.* 2.2.3).

However, the chapter did try to keep Thucydides' Athenian contemporaries in mind. As was mentioned at the outset of this chapter, Thucydides for the first time wrote for readers who could remember the depicted events. He aimed to provide a discussable account of the war he thought was most interesting to talk about (1.1) and perhaps particularly to offer his Athenian readers, who were poorly informed (cf. Hunt 2010), an explanation for the causes of Athens' defeat. Aside of this particular aim, he frequently emphasizes that all parties decided to go to war without fully understanding what could, and probably would, happen (e.g., at 2.8, 4.65.4, 4.108.4, 6.1.1 [with 6.6.1], or 6.31.1). An aspect of the usefulness of his history (1.22.4) would be to prepare readers of any era for the consequences of such decisions.

He does this, as we saw, by showing that the often terrible events are the results of human hopes and plans. This is another innovation. Thucydides reduced war to human decisions, passions, and capacities, eliminating the divine forces active in Homer and Herodotus. By cutting war down to size, he accomplished a tremendous service to humanity, firmly establishing a non-metaphysical attitude toward warfare and war leaders. Brasidas may believe (or advertise to others who believe) that divine forces intended his victory at Lekythos (4.116.2); Thucydides shows that a weak and over-burdened tower fell down.

This reduction of war to a manifestation of human psychology had consequences for the structure of the *History*. The lengthy campaign stories reflect Thucydides' analysis of the human causes of the events, and their underlying function is to provoke us to try to understand that analysis. At the same time, his exploration of the experience of battles and campaigns shows that the reality of battle escapes analysis or prediction, and is frequently uncontrollably tragic.

References

Babut, D. 1981. "Interprétation historique et structure littéraire chez Thucydide: remarques sur la composition du livre iv." *Bull. assoc. G. Budé* 40: 417–39.
Cartledge, P., and P. Debnar. 2006. "Sparta and the Spartans in Thucydides." In *Brill's Companion to Thucydides*, edited by A. Rengakos and A. Tsakmakis, 559–87. Leiden: Brill.
Connor. 1984. *Thucydides*. Princeton: Princeton University Press.
Dewald, C. 2005. *Thucydides' War Narrative*. Berkeley and Los Angeles: University of California Press.
Foster, E. 2012. "Thermopylae and Pylos, with Reference to the Homeric Background." In *Thucydides and Herodotus*, edited by E. Foster and D. Lateiner, 185–215. Oxford: Oxford University Press.
Foster, E., forthcoming. "Military Defeat in Fifth Century Athens: Thucydides and his Audience." In *War Losses in the Ancient World*, edited by Jessica Clark and Brian Turner. Leiden: Brill.
Greenwood, E. 2006. *Thucydides and the Shaping of History*. London: Duckworth.
Hansen M. H. 1998. "The Little Grey Horse: Henry V's Speech at Agincourt and the Battle Exhortation in Ancient Historiography." *Histos* 2: 46–63. http://research.ncl.ac.uk/histos/documents/1998.02HansenTheLittleGreyHorse4663.pdf
Hawthorn, G. 2014. *Thucydides on Politics: Back to the Future*. Cambridge: Cambridge University Press.
Hornblower, S. 1996. *A Commentary on Thucydides*. Vol. II, *Books IV–V.24*. Oxford: Clarendon.
Hornblower, S. 2008. *A Commentary on Thucydides*. Vol. III, *Books 5.25–8.109*. Oxford: Clarendon.
Hunt, P. 2006. "Warfare." In *Brill's Companion to Thucydides*, edited by A. Rengakos and A. Tsakmakis, 385–414. Leiden: Brill.
Hunt, P. 2010. "Athenian Militarism and the Recourse to War." In *War, Democracy, and Culture in Classical Athens*, edited by D. Pritchard, 225–42. Cambridge: Cambridge University Press.
Lateiner, D. 1977. "Heralds and Corpses in Thucydides." *CJ* 71 (2): 97–106.
Leimbach, R. 1985. *Militärische Musterrhetorik: Eine Untersuchung zu den Feldherrnreden des Thukydides*. Stuttgart: Steiner.
Luschnat, O. 1942. *Die Feldherrnreden im Geschichtswerk des Thukydides*. Leipzig: Dieterich.
Miles, M. 2014. "Burnt Temples in the Landscape of the Past." In *Valuing the Past in the Greco-Roman World: Proceedings from the Penn-Leiden Colloquia on Ancient Values VII*, edited by James Ker and Christoph Pieper, 111–45. Leiden: Brill.
Orwin, C. 1994. *The Humanity of Thucydides*. Princeton: Princeton University Press.
Paradiso, Annalisa. 2004. "The Logic of Terror: Thucydides, Spartan Duplicity, and an Improbable Massacre." In *Spartan Society*, edited by Thomas Figueira, 179–98. Swansea: Classical Press of Wales.
Paul, G. M. 1989. "Two Battles in Thucydides." *Echos du Monde Classique/Classical Views* xxxi, n.s. 6:307–12.
Romilly, J. de. 2012. *The Mind of Thucydides*. Edited by H. Rawlings and J. Rusten. Ithaca: Cornell University Press.
Rood, T. 1998. *Thucydides: Narrative and Explanation*. Oxford: Oxford University Press.
Tsakmakis, A., and C. Themistokleous. 2013. "Textual Structure and Modality in Thucydides' Military Exhortations." In *Thucydides between History and Literature*, edited by A. Tsakmakis and M. Tamiolaki, 391–408. Berlin: De Gruyter.
Zali, V. 2014. *The Shape of Herodotean Rhetoric: A Study of the Speeches in Herodotus' History, with Special Attention to Books 5–9*. Leiden: Brill.

SECTION III

THUCYDIDES AND POLITICAL THEORY

CHAPTER 19

WAS THUCYDIDES A POLITICAL PHILOSOPHER?

RYAN K. BALOT

THE answer to this question is obviously "no," if the reader has in mind a traditional conception of the political philosopher as a writer who offers a detailed vision of good human lives lived within a good (or even the best) society.[1] My contention is that Thucydides was, like Machiavelli, aware of such constructs but critical of them. He regarded them as "utopias," which could be seen upon reflection to be both self-destructive and harmful to others. To probe the weaknesses of these illusions, he emphasized *to akribes*, "accuracy," or "precision" (e.g., 1.10.1, 6.54.1). Through accurately presenting the motivations of his characters, and through investigating historical causation with clear vision, Thucydides put on display his contemporaries' self-delusions and distortions, even as he explained why human beings are persistently attached to their own hopes and desires. Through his engagement with these issues, his *History* can be seen to enter into debates with political philosophy as traditionally construed. Thucydides' distinctive contribution was to argue that history itself, properly understood, is superior to philosophy as a source of truth about the human condition.

THUCYDIDES' UTOPIA?

When searching for a positive political ideal in the *History*, scholars have often been disappointed. What we have is slender: Thucydides' praise for the Athenian "regime of the Five Thousand," which makes a brief appearance in Book 8. Thucydides says that this regime embodied a "moderate blend" that served the interests of the few and the

---

[1] The author is grateful to Clifford Orwin and Seth Jaffe for careful commentaries on the present chapter. On Thucydides' status as a thinker and writer, see Euben (1977); Ober (2001); Orwin (1994), especially 172–73.

many (8.97.2). This regime, he says, helped the Athenians to recover from their recent troubles—for example, the oligarchic revolution of 411 BC, most immediately, but also their devastating failure in Sicily.

Thucydides shows strikingly little interest in this regime. He explains neither its inner workings nor his admiration for it; he says only that, under this regime, the Athenians governed themselves well for the first time in his lifetime. With this minimalist claim, Thucydides leaves open the possibility that mixed regimes might be wholly ineffective in other cities; equally, other imaginable political orders could prove superior to them either in Athens or elsewhere. He does not defend the regime against the charge that it was transitory and gave way almost immediately to a populist democracy (cf. 8.68.2). By contrast, other theorists of the "mixed regime," such as Plato, Aristotle, Polybius, and Cicero, elaborated upon the concept in great detail, describing its strengths and weaknesses, legislating the appropriate types of mixture, and locating it precisely within taxonomies of diverse regimes. More importantly, the canonical political philosophers would have provided a thick description of this regime—one that explained its embodiment of justice and its capacity to enable citizens to live well. If we call to mind Aristotle's descriptions of the "good regime," mixed or otherwise, in the *Politics* (see Balot 2015), then the contrast with Thucydides' few sentences on the Five Thousand could not be sharper. Thucydides devoted his attention to other things, such as civic convulsion, international instability, the questions of justice and power, and the relationship between speech (*logos*) and deed (*ergon*).

Yet even if Thucydides avoided utopianism, the political philosophers of the fourth century, such as Xenophon, Isocrates, Plato, and Aristotle, had read his work carefully. Thucydides' own explanation of his purposes makes more intelligible their enthusiastic engagement with the *History*. Thucydides began the *History* by modestly asserting that he "wrote up" (*xunegrapse*, 1.1.1) the war between Athens and Sparta. He later said, less modestly, that his war was history's greatest war (1.1.2) and that his ambition was to offer an account that would be permanently useful (1.22.4). His accurate writing might be less enjoyable than that of others because it lacks a "fabulous" (*to ... muthōdes*, 1.22.4) character; he will provide no story from the heroic past, with characters whose relation to divinity (for example) makes them greater than ordinary; his characters are familiar human types, recognizable to us all, individuals whom we can visualize and with whom we can perhaps empathize (cf. Connor 1984, 16–17; Romilly 2012, 95; Strauss 1964, 139–40). Rather, the self-proclaimed sober historian states his intention as follows:

> It will be adequate if my work is judged helpful by all those who wish to look clearly at what has happened and what is likely to happen in the future, or something close to that, given what human beings are like. It is laid up as a possession forever, rather than as a contest-piece intended for its immediate audience (1.22.4).

Thucydides did not inquire into history as an antiquarian, convinced that historical knowledge is per se desirable. Exploring the past, he declares, is instructive; his *History* is meant to teach its readers. True, everything will look and even be different, depending on its time and place (3.82, 7.44), not to mention the acuity of the observer (cf. 1.10, 5.26.5). In fact, Thucydides' own account of the ancient past—his "Archaeology" (1.2–20)—reveals that he was aware, as we might expect, of profound historical discontinuities in the evolution from the remote past to the living present; and he had no reason to believe that the political regimes or the technologies or beliefs of his own day would endure permanently. The link between past and future is human nature, or the ways of human beings. Human beings—what they are and what they do—are the philosophical focus of Thucydides' work. Thucydides' universalizing ambition to distill and grasp *to anthrōpinon*, "humanness," lifts his work out of its deep immersion in historical particularity and justifies a philosophical interpretation, albeit not one that will settle itself inflexibly in either the universal or the particular realm (cf. Hobbes 1975, 15).[2]

In what ways, then, is Thucydides' *History* supposed to help us understand the events of past and future, in light of human nature? Does Thucydides offer a philosophical "teaching" that can be captured in a series of clear and interlocking theses? Or does he provide another sort of advice or education with regard to the lasting questions of the human condition?

A World of War

It is obvious, but easily neglected, that Thucydides chose to uncover the human essentials through recounting and analyzing a war between Athens and Sparta. Encouraging his readers to feel the weight of this great convulsion, the exiled general made the case that his twenty-seven-year war was a single, meaningful unit; the peace that interrupted it was not a genuine cessation of hostilities (5.26; cf. 1.18.3). This argument is reminiscent of the views of the Platonic character Cleinias, a Dorian, who declares at the beginning of the *Laws* that cities are always at war with one another, whether ordinary people know it or not (*Leg.* 625d–e). War is the rule rather than the exception. Thucydides invites us to consider that violent conflict, or at least its ever-present possibility, may be the unavoidable horizon within which human beings must order their lives.

Thucydides does not ignore the distinction between war and peace. He speaks, almost wistfully, of times of peace (e.g., 2.65.5, 3.82.2, 3.104.3–6), and he pinpoints the formal commencement of the war, when Athens and Sparta began to communicate only through heralds (2.1). His characters take such formalities seriously, even long after the fact (e.g., 7.18.2). Given the novelty of Pericles' strategy, moreover, the Athenians themselves experienced the Peloponnesian War differently from the preceding time of peace

---

[2] Compare Hobbes: Thucydides "so clearly set before men's eyes the ways and events of good and evil counsels, that the narration itself doth secretly instruct the reader, and more effectually than can possibly be done by precept" (Hobbes 1975, 18).

(2.14–16, 2.61), as did Greeks in other cities, who were emboldened to seek help from the great powers in order to destroy their domestic political rivals (3.82.1) or to liberate themselves from Athens (2.8.4–5, 3.2.1, 4.108.3). After describing a long period of continual motion and resettlement, Thucydides identifies a time when peace and relative security characterized "archaic" Greece, although that period of stability was hardly more than the basis for colonization and imperial ventures (1.12–14). At the same time, nothing in Thucydides' story of the past qualifies his belief, to use Heraclitus' language, that "war is the father of all" (DK 22 B 53), even if certain characters propose (for their own reasons) that peace is a blessing (e.g., 4.62). However great it may be, the present war merely expands the violence and suffering of previous wars (1.23, 7.87.5), a point illustrated by Thucydides' accounts of the Archaeology and the Pentecontaetia, not to mention his discussion of early Sicily (6.1–5). All of these episodes were filled with persistent attacks and counterattacks; the build-up of military power for the sake of aggression against outsiders; and the ceaseless migration of suffering peoples in search of peace and stability. Despite the suffering involved, people are attracted to war, especially when they know nothing of it (2.8.1, 6.24; cf. 4.59.2). Even Sparta, the regime presented as being most "at rest" in a world of motion (cf. Strauss 1964, 155–57, 160; Orwin, chapter 21 in this volume), was constantly at war.

The *History* is Thucydides' only book, and so there is nowhere else to look for his account of humanity. Why does Thucydides believe that the human condition is defined by war and not peace—or, more modestly, that war is more revealing of human essentials than peace? Thucydides neither asks nor answers such questions abstractly. He confines himself to the analysis of war, much as Machiavelli purposefully confined himself to the analysis of politics and power and in the process ignored traditional subjects such as God, the soul, the miseries of hell, and so on (Strauss 1958, 31). In Thucydides' presentation, war is uniquely revealing of humanity, in that it both displays in high relief and then strips away characteristic human delusions. In doing so, war reveals humanity's deepest passions and drives—an experience that is often disquieting and necessarily limited in its prospects. In large part, those essential human elements explain the persistence of warfare itself: the self-aggrandizing ambitions of leaders, the craven and yet aggressive obedience of their followers, the desires and the imprudence that lead to disastrous mistakes. The world of Thucydides, the world of war, is a tragic world; if Sophocles had been a historian, then he would have written Thucydides' *History* (see Williams 1993, 161–64; Shanske 2007, 69–118; Geuss 2005, 219–33). The chief reason, in fact, that historical accuracy will not be pleasurable (1.22.4) is precisely that the world itself is more likely to cause sorrow or regret than delight. Equally, however, war lays bare the stubborn and courageous resilience of ordinary human beings, who push themselves to survive the worst misfortunes and to carry on together. If they are lucky, then they might attain some measure of decency, stability, material sufficiency, and honesty. Thucydides explores these issues, and the question of the "best regime," chiefly by concentrating on his book's two protagonists, Athens and Sparta.

Athens, City on a Hill?

Unlike Plato and Aristotle, Thucydides offered a grim story of political origins, one based on the phenomena of history rather than optimistic pronouncements about human beings' natural dispositions to associate with one another or to fulfill their most worthwhile or distinctive human capacities. In actual fact, and despite Homeric and other legends, early Greece did not exist; the past is an undifferentiated history of forced migrations, conflict over fertile land, piracy, and poverty (1.2–12). Its keynote was suffering. Cities were placed on hills—on an "acropolis," the highest geographical point—because hills were essential to establishing a military stronghold (cf. 2.15.3–6 with 4.32.3–4, 4.36, 5.7.3–4). Athens, however, occupied a singular position in Thucydides' reconstruction of earlier epochs, not because it was a flourishing regime, but rather because the undesirability of Attica meant that it alone had no need for defense in its earliest incarnations (1.2). Hence, by contrast with his philosophical successors, Thucydides did not present politics as a "natural growth," a framework within which human beings could realize their potential or achieve their "flourishing" condition (*eudaimonia*). But he did concern himself with investigating the political significance of utopian speculations about politics, whose rough outlines he discerned in the public discourses of his own day.

Imagine reading a work that described a flourishing society based on the rule of law. Its fundamental principles are freedom and equality. Its citizens are open, tolerant, and respectful. Political offices are assigned strictly on the basis of merit. Private homes are beautiful; festivals are celebrated continuously and at public expense. This society is cosmopolitan. Its citizens are courageous and well informed. They love beauty; they philosophize. They participate knowledgeably in politics. This society is worthy of great devotion and personal sacrifice. This society is the best society; it is a model for all others.

Obviously, the foregoing is a summary of Pericles' Funeral Oration in the *History*. Its substance is indisputably utopian, even if utopias are typically more remote from reality than this one, and even if utopias are usually presented in written works rather than in public speeches. In this oration, the Athenian leader celebrates democratic Athens as the best society (2.35–46). Pericles argues that, in dying for their city, the fallen soldiers revealed a devotion that was both outstanding and yet proportionate to the benefits they enjoyed as citizens. The Athenians had created an exemplary city (2.37), and they not only embraced freedom, equality, and appropriate pleasures, but also revered the law and emphasized the education of the citizens' character (2.37–40). Athens was an entirely new kind of city that did justice both to human action and to human rationality. Most importantly, according to Pericles, Athens provided an institutional and cultural context in which the Athenians could lead self-chosen lives that fully developed their potential for human grace and excellence. In order to make those lives possible, the city provided security from external aggression without demanding that its citizens conform to the rigid standards of manliness and the compulsory sense of shame that were characteristic of Sparta. In the process of establishing civic solidarity, Athens perfectly harmonized ideals that were traditional opposites: legal order with personal freedom, meritocracy with equality, bravery in war with political deliberation (Balot 2001 and 2014; Manville 1997).

Pericles seems to jumble together a number of ideas: that the Athenians are already admirable; that they should strive to live up to the ideals that he evokes, with the implication that more work is needed; and, finally, that he is describing the Athenians' *nature* in some unspecified sense. He is presenting a potentially toxic mixture of the descriptive and the normative, and he is trading on the concept of nature to do so. Thucydides' text is designed to reveal, at a minimum, and among other things, that the Athenian political realities did not match up to Pericles' vision. Throughout his speeches, Pericles shows himself to be uncompromisingly attached to promoting the dignity and greatness of his city, construed in a specifically militaristic or imperialistic sense. He scoffs at the thought of yielding to Sparta's demands (1.140–141; cf. 1.127). He insists on the primacy of honor, glory, and imperial achievement, and he encourages the Athenians to internalize their ancestors as models and even rivals (1.144.3–4, 2.36, 2.41, 2.61.4, 2.63–64). These traditional, militaristic ideas conflict with the peaceful and pleasurable lives that Pericles evokes in his funeral oration, with its emphasis on festivals, individual freedom, political deliberation, and philosophy (2.38–2.40). Pericles' interpretation of democracy as a citizen-based meritocracy of virtue (2.37.1) sits uneasily with Thucydides' own statement that "Periclean democracy" is an oxymoron, since Pericles was directing affairs (2.65.8–9). The fact was that, because of the democracy's freedoms and its exuberance, Athens' forces had long been centrifugal, and it took a Pericles (or Themistocles: 1.93.3–8 or Theseus: 2.15.2) to keep the city unified and healthy.

These objections are not only abstract and philosophical; rather, the distance between Pericles' utopia and Athens' behaviour reveals itself more and more concretely over the course of the war. As Pericles himself had indicated, deeds (*erga*) reveal the truth more clearly than words (*logoi*), even if our knowledge of deeds must be mediated through language (2.35.1; Ober 1998, 52–63, 83–89, 93–94; Parry 1981). For example, just after praising Pericles' leadership (2.65), Thucydides records that the Athenians got hold of several Peloponnesian ambassadors, whom they received as prisoners from the Thracian prince Sadocus (2.67). Fearing the Corinthian Aristeus, they killed them all without giving them a trial or a chance to speak and threw their bodies into a pit; characteristically, they justified (*dikaiountes*) their action as one of proportionate revenge for earlier Spartan misbehavior (2.67.4). Perhaps only the Athenians were perverse enough to embrace their barbarism as an expression of delicate principle. Thucydides records many other similar cases, whether famous or seemingly trivial. While he draws attention to the Athenians' destruction of Melos (5.116.2–4), he merely mentions that their devastation of Scione equally involved massacring the adult men and enslaving the women and children (5.32.1; cf. their treatment of the Mendaeans at 4.130.6–7).

Thucydides invites his readers to set these episodes against the Athenians' own self-promoting and self-exculpatory speeches abroad, whose arguments go well beyond Pericles' Funeral Oration. On the one hand, the Athenians frequently argue, with

Pericles, that they are more virtuous than others and that they are "worthy" of their power (1.76.2). They are more just, more dedicated to law, and more moderate than others who have taken positions of power (1.76.2–4). They are benefactors of Hellas (6.87.3). On the other hand, the Athenians excuse themselves by declaring that nature has compelled them to act as they have done (1.75–76, 5.105.2; cf. 6.83); other estimable speakers, such as Hermocrates of Syracuse, voice similar views, to the effect that the strong rule wherever they can (4.61.3–6). Although Thucydides' account punctures the Athenians' pretensions to exceptional virtue, he is inclined to accept the Athenian view that they are no worse—though certainly no better—than others (cf. Orwin 1994, 193–202; Balot 2015; Hoekstra and Fisher, chapter 22 in this volume). But it is important that their resemblance to others does not excuse them.[3] To the contrary, Thucydides does not minimize the suffering brought on by Athenian ambitions—including the suffering of the Athenians themselves (cf. 1.113, 2.47–54, 3.49–50, 3.112–113, 7.86–87). Instead, he invites his readers to sympathize with the other Greeks' desire to be "free" (2.8.4–5, 3.9–14, 3.46.5–6, 4.108.3, 4.121, 4.123, 5.82; cf. 4.108.4–7, 8.48.4–7). The most "civilized" Greeks draw ever closer to the barbaric Thracians, who destroyed a school full of children at Mycalessus, along with all the adults and even the farm animals (7.29–30; compare 7.87 with 7.30). The implication is not that the Athenians (or Thracians) had no choice in these matters, but that they could have done far better, even if they did only what most people would do in similar situations.

Thucydides concerned himself equally with "accuracy" in domestic politics. In the case of the Athenian democracy, readers come to appreciate that post-Periclean democracy is beset by certain distinctive perversities. First, despite the democratic ideals of freedom, independent thought, and innovation, the demos itself was susceptible to the angry pugnacity and self-aggrandizement that Greek culture had traditionally embraced. Nothing else explains their attraction to Cleon's angry traditionalism (3.36.6, 3.40). The appeal of traditional manliness enabled Cleon to crush the Spartan proposals to make peace in 425 BCE (4.21–23), but it also forced him, through a surprising turn of events, to become the general at Pylos (4.27–29). Although Cleon's command at Pylos later proved successful, Thucydides presents his original offer to take over the command as insane, albeit thrust upon him by his rhetorical gibes against Nicias' lack of manliness (4.39.3, 4.27.5; cf. 4.28.5).[4] More importantly, the Athenians' dedication to traditional honor led them to undertake the Sicilian Expedition, after a debate in which anxieties about cowardice shut down free speech (6.24.4). Pericles' own inflammation of the Athenians' anger and his manipulation of their easily provoked sense of manly self-respect even led them to start the war itself (1.140–41). It is worth noting, however,

---

[3] Note 6.54: Thucydides says that the Athenians are "no better than others" (translated by Warner 1972, adapted) at recalling their own history, a comment that gains in sharpness because the Athenians prided themselves on their intellectual superiority to others. As they were no better, so too were they no worse.

[4] Unfortunately for the Athenians, Cleon's success led him to become overconfident and hence to make critical mistakes at Amphipolis, and in turn he lost his own life and squandered those of 600 exceptional soldiers (5.1–10, especially 5.7).

that the "doves" of Athenian politics, above all Nicias, were hardly more admirable, since they possessed only a simplistic and self-obsessed understanding of the importance of peace (cf. Nicias at 5.16.1, 5.46.1, and below).

Second, as Diodotus points out, the Athenian deliberative process is hardly underwritten by the rationalism evoked by Pericles. Rather, it is shot through with suspicion and dishonesty:

> It has become the rule also to treat good advice honestly given as being no less under suspicion than bad, so that a man who has something rather good to say must tell lies in order to be believed, just as a man who gives terrible advice must win over the people by deception. Because of these suspicions, ours is the only city that no one can possibly benefit openly, without deception, since if anyone does good openly to the city, his reward will be the suspicion that he had something secretly to gain from this. (3.43; translated by Woodruff 1993)

In a climate of fear and uncertainty—which is inevitable in a world of war—democratic citizens cannot help being suspicious of their leaders' integrity. Thucydides documents a number of examples of leaders who betray their fellow citizens (2.2–2.3, 4.76, 4.110.1, 5.116.3, 6.89–92, 8.14.1–2; 8.50–51); the people's suspicions were, apparently, often justified. Less dramatically, Athenian leaders often formulated policies in order to protect their own reputations or interests (2.65.10–11: post-Periclean leaders in general; 4.27.3–28: Cleon; 5.16.1: Cleon and Nicias; 5.43: Alcibiades; 5.46: Nicias; 6.15.2: Alcibiades; 7.48–49: Nicias; 8.50–1: Phrynichus)—a fact that helps to explain Pericles' proposed donation of his country properties, just in case the invading Spartans did not ravage them (2.13.1). Oligarchic coups were a persistent threat even at Athens (1.107.4, 8.47–48; cf. 8.45–98), and, according to Thucydides, even the misguided suspicion of threats that did not genuinely exist could lead to harmful consequences, as in the city's treatment of Alcibiades (6.15.4, 6.27–29, 6.53, 6.60; though cf. 6.89, 8.6.3). In the case of Diodotus ("the gift of the god"), however, Thucydides encourages his readers to see that through explicitly appealing to self-interest, narrowly understood, Diodotus persuades the Athenians to choose a course that is merciful and even perhaps just (see Mara 2008, 57–59, 251–52). But the strategy of deceiving the people for their own good misfired badly when Nicias tried to impress the demos with the difficulty of the Sicilian Expedition, only to intensify their longings and to make their eventual defeat all the more devastating (6.19–25, 7.87). What readers might infer is both the necessity of democratic suspicions and the vulnerabilities that they set in motion.

Third, even when the people seem to be decidedly in power, they often turn out to be unaware of their leaders' ways of stage-managing their Assembly debates. A case in point is the "Argive Alliance," which was arranged through the manipulations of Alcibiades. Thucydides introduced Alcibiades in his narrative of the events of 420 BCE, just after the Peace of Nicias, offering a detailed story of intrigue among the various Peloponnesians, the Athenians, and the Boeotians. Indignant at the Spartans' treatment of him, and taking advantage of the opportunity provided by disputes over Panactum,

Alcibiades secretly invited the Argives to make the case for an alliance at Athens (5.42–43; cf. 6.89). He tricked the Spartan ambassadors into discrediting themselves in front of the Athenian Assembly (5.44–46). Over the objections of Nicias the peacemaker, whose "face" was at stake (5.46.4), the Athenians voted for an alliance with the Argives, Mantineans, and Eleans (5.46.5–47). To be sure, the prudence of making this alliance may be in doubt, considering the quick triggers of all the Greek cities involved (cf. 5.49–50), the expanded involvement of Alcibiades in the Peloponnese (5.52–53), and the consequential battle of Mantinea (especially 5.75). What is not in doubt is the undue and undemocratic influence of leaders such as Alcibiades, who waited until 411 BCE to perform a memorable service to his country (8.86.4), and whose political outlook was fatally shaped by self-regard (5.43, 6.15–16, 6.89, 8.47; cf. 6.12.2 for Nicias' accusation of Alcibiades on this score, and 8.50–51 for a good example of Phrynichus acting along the same lines).

While Thucydides certainly mentions these intrigues in order to illustrate the Athenians' lack of self-understanding, he is not always critical of leaders, such as Pericles, who take similar action that proves advantageous to the city (2.22). In fact, Thucydides suggests, either explicitly or implicitly, that great individuals—such as Theseus, Peisistratus, Themistocles, and Pericles—made Athens as great as it was, not the demos (cf. Strauss 1964, 211–213). On the contrary, the ordinary democratic citizens were often responsible for limiting or even destroying the activities of great individuals (e.g., Alcibiades at 6.15, Antiphon at 8.68). Even those who opposed the democracy, whether ultimately or only occasionally, were worthy of admiration and often, though not always, helped Athens (Phrynichus, 8.27; Antiphon, 8.68; Alcibiades, 8.86).

Fourth, if the Athenians did not understand that democracy qua people-power is ineffective, then they also failed to appreciate the ambiguities of their admiring and inclusive vision of the demos itself. These ambiguities emerge clearly from Thucydides' account of the affair of the Herms (6.27–28). On the eve of the Sicilian Expedition, the stone statues of the god Hermes were defaced throughout the city—an act of vandalism that awakened deep religious fears and anxieties about the destruction of the democracy (6.27–28). Athenians may have respected the law profoundly, as Pericles had said, but Alcibiades' enemies used the occasion to bring untimely legal charges against him, just as he was setting out to command the Athenian ships. Although Alcibiades offered to stand trial immediately, Thucydides says, his enemies intrigued to delay the proceedings in order to inflame the Athenians and to make even graver accusations against him (6.29). While Alcibiades and the other generals were at work in Sicily, the Athenians imprisoned a number of their top citizens (*tous chrēstous*, 6.53.2, cf. 6.60.2: *axiologoi anthrōpoi*) on the basis of allegations made by "worthless individuals" (*ponērōn anthrōpōn*, 6.53.2). Fearful and angry, the Athenians became more and more "savage," Thucydides says (6.60.2), a term that echoes the savagery in full bloom during periods of intense civic convulsions, such as the Athenian plague (2.52–53) or the Corcyraean civil war (3.81.4–3.82). What finally released the pressure was that one of these "worthy" prisoners (Andocides; cf. Hornblower 2008, 453) agreed to accept immunity in order to make public accusations against the others—whether truly or not, Thucydides says, we will never know. Without much additional thought, the Athenians accepted the story, freed those who were not accused, and put on trial the others, ultimately executing every one of them. They were less committed to the truth than to using a number of their fellow citizens as scapegoats in order to calm their anxieties. The city "profited" (*ōphelēto*, 6.60.5) from this turn of events, Thucydides remarks.

In recounting this story both accurately and parsimoniously, Thucydides made several telling points. First, politics, or at least democratic politics, might be ugly enough to benefit from the unjust sacrifice of the few to the many. In moving on from the episode of the Herms, the Athenians antagonized a number of the better citizens and showed that the demos included and protected not everyone, but only those not exposed to political intrigue or allegation. Without special commentary, Thucydides provoked his readers to reflect that this event not only undermined the Athenians' inclusive image of themselves, but also told against the arguments for democratic inclusiveness advanced by the Syracusan Athenagoras (6.39).

Second, the Athenians, including Pericles, lacked a dedication to the truth, because of the combustible mixture of fear and ambition that defined the city. Not being committed to the truth, the Athenians who lawlessly executed their top citizens destroyed Pericles' idealized dedication to the law (2.37). It was significant for their deliberations that they did not take time to understand the truth: for example, with regard to history—the history of Sicily (6.1–6) or the history of the tyrannicides (1.20, 6.53–61, though cf. 6.53), much less the history of the Trojan War (1.9–11). They were easily deceived with regard to the money promised them by the Egestaeans, who had summoned them to Sicily (6.46). Thucydides' criticism is not deliberately aimed at a grand-scale and supposedly Platonic "cowardice before reality" (to use Nietzsche's famous phrase). Instead, his own dedication to the truth in the sense of "accuracy" is more mundane—a fact about it that explains its lasting grip on readers, whatever their ontological commitments.[5] The truth that the Athenians failed to understand is the truth of history, not the truths that may lie behind or above the phenomena (for Thucydides' effort to nail down factual details, and his abhorrence of exaggeration, see 3.113.6, 5.68.2).

The fifth and final point is that the supposedly virtuous and self-directing demos refused to accept responsibility for its own decisions. Implicitly, at least, Thucydides began to indict the Athenians on this score early in the war, when the suffering Athenians momentarily turned against Pericles—for having convinced them to declare war in the first place (2.59, 2.65.3; cf. 2.21, and 8.1.2, on those who recommended the Sicilian Expedition)! The Athenians wanted political power and imperial glory without accepting any of the responsibilities that necessarily accompany them. Related to their "immaturity" and hypocrisy in this respect was an unwillingness to tolerate commanders who proved unable to carry out the Athenian Assembly's decisions as stated. Suspicions typically reached an intense pitch when leaders campaigning far away accepted more lenient terms than the demos had hoped for, as in the generals' decision to accept less

---

[5] For praise of Thucydides' honesty, as opposed to Platonic cowardice, see especially Williams (1993); Geuss (2005, 219–233); Hawthorn (2014).

than unconditional surrender at Potidaea (2.70), or in other generals' decision to accept peace in Sicily in 424 BCE (4.65). Because of the Athenians' success at Pylos, in particular, according to Thucydides, the demos had begun to believe that its power was invincible and so decided to banish two generals and to fine a third, on the grounds that their troops could have taken Sicily altogether (4.65; cf. 3.98). Thucydides makes it clear that the demos was not often in a good position to judge such commanders: whatever the status of his speech after the Athenian defeat at Epipolae, Nicias plausibly contrasts commanders and troops on the ground, who possess local knowledge, with voters in the Athenian Assembly, who rely on hearsay and prejudicial speeches (7.48). Thucydides himself, of course, might have been especially sensitive to these questions because of his own banishment after Amphipolis, where he arrived too late to defend the city against Brasidas' forces—though, according to Thucydides, he did everything that he could possibly have done in the circumstances (4.102–8, 5.26.5–6). The Athenians' commanders were unfairly punished for being incapable of mastering the war's contingencies.

It would be unfair to say that these problems are distinctively democratic, but Thucydides highlights them at Athens, particularly, because the Athenian case vividly and poignantly illustrates the distance between self-idealization and practice in the world of war. Yet what sort of critique does Thucydides thereby provide? His presentation might show only that the Athenians failed to live up to their ideals—not that the ideals themselves were misguided. In fact, history cannot tell us, all by itself, what is worthy of admiration. History might tell us what is possible or realistic, and it might inform us as to what works and what does not. But charging only that the Athenians failed to enact their own ideals would be a great concession to the Athenians' democratic eudaimonism. For Thucydides would then be admitting that the Athenians had, indeed, constructed a normatively compelling ideal—which is an admirable accomplishment in its own right.

What other kinds of criticism might the historian level against the Periclean utopia? Perhaps his idea was that Pericles' vision led to less rather than greater understanding of the world, that it ignored the ineluctable suffering of war—both the suffering of Athenians themselves and the suffering caused by the Athenians. If Pericles had attended more closely to those elements of the human experience, then he might have thrown open the questions of justice and injustice for the Athenians' consideration. Instead of promoting a salutary form of Athenian self-questioning, however, Pericles magnified Athens for an audience of Athenians. His speech thereby served to undergird the Athenians' imperialistic and exploitative way of life, by articulating and rationally defending Athenian ideals, and by ignoring inconvenient facts about the world of war and our human responses to it. Pericles' utopian self-image not only failed to constitute self-knowledge, but also kept the Athenians from looking at themselves honestly. Such, at any rate, is Thucydides' presentation. The Athenians might respond that the funeral oration was simply one moment of political life that could be balanced by many others, including the funerary ritual as a whole, the Athenians' theatrical and festival experiences, and the other contexts of public oratory and the variegated activities of citizenship.

Intriguingly, though, Thucydides discerns in the Athenian democracy other sources of strength—reasons to admire Athens that go beyond and mostly fall outside the case that the Athenians make on their own behalf. The chief characteristic that Thucydides highlights is resilience. After their defeat in Sicily, for example, the Athenians understandably grew terrified; but they reacted, not by becoming demoralized, but rather by taking swift and prudent action. They began to ready a new fleet, to work with their allies, and to undertake political reform, including the election of older citizens as counselors (8.1; cf. 2.65.12). Thucydides says explicitly that in this respect they acted like all democracies: once they are terrified, they get themselves into shape (8.1.4). As the Corinthians had predicted early on (1.70), the Athenians immediately carried out their plan to rebuild (8.4). When the Chian oligarchs, under the influence of Alcibiades, decided to revolt, the Athenians recognized the seriousness of their situation and initiated a sequence of excellent strategic decisions to relieve Chios (8.15). Even when they lost control of Euboea—a loss that provoked the greatest fear ever in Athens, according to Thucydides—the city still sent out twenty ships and undertook the political reforms that established the mixed regime of 411 BCE (8.96–97). Toward the very end of the *History* (8.106), in fact, Thucydides reports that the Athenians had recovered both from Sicily and from the oligarchic revolution and began to think that they could achieve final victory. What is most amazing about Athens is its capacity to carry on through the war despite its own extraordinary suffering (7.27–28; cf. 1.121).

Managing their suffering effectively with sound judgment and resilience, and without panicking (cf. 8.94, 8.96–97, along with the Athenians' reaction to Brasidas' successes in Thrace, 4.108)—that capacity, Pericles had said in his final words in the *History*, was characteristic of the strongest (*kratistoi*) cities and individuals (2.64). Having examined the action of the work, we can recognize that this resilience is a Thucydidean redefinition of courage, one that rivaled and in his view proved superior to the understanding of courage that Pericles himself had offered in the Funeral Oration (2.40.2–3), since the style of courage admired in the Funeral Oration was better suited to the Athenians' imperialistic projects. Thucydidean resilience was appropriate to the world of war and suffering that he had come to know through history. The Athenians, above all, exemplify this attribute. Consider their general willingness, despite their suffering, to remain within the city for the duration of the war, along with their capacity to endure defeat and calamity right through to the bitter end (2.65.12, with Hoekstra and Fisher, chapter 22 in this volume; 7.27–28).

One neglected example of the Athenians' courage, in just this sense, is their recovery from the plague (2.47–54), from which they suffered so heavily (2.50). Scholars have often argued that this dramatic scene serves to undermine the optimism and rationalism of the Periclean Funeral Oration with which it is juxtaposed (e.g., Monoson and Loriaux 1998, 288–90). While there is truth in that judgment, it is more central to Thucydides' purposes to show that despite the gory details (2.49), the Athenians continued to prosecute the war with full energy (2.56–57, 2.69, 2.79–94); they were not as worn down as the Mytileneans proclaimed (3.13.3; cf. 3.16–3.17). The Athenians manifested the same resilience during the second outbreak of the plague (3.87–88). They expended extraordinary energy without slipping into the civil tensions that were characteristic of the Corcyraean civil war (3.82–83). No political cabal used the opportunity to destroy its political enemies, even when the Spartans had attacked Salamis and had plans to sail into the Piraeus (2.93–94). By comparison with civil conflict elsewhere, it is trivial to blame the Athenians for using one another's funeral pyres (2.52.4) or spending money on pleasure (2.53; see Balot, 2016).

On the basis of this analysis, we may infer three points. First, that in Thucydides' view it is impossible to fulfill the eudaimonistic ideal, because the world is characterized by war, which typically has a harmful impact on domestic political life. Second, precisely because of war's omnipresence, any effort to project a political ideal of manliness and rational control will fail to do justice to our vulnerability to suffering. Pericles' oration neglected the virtue of resilience and the primacy of endurance. And so Pericles not only advanced a misguided ideal, but also failed to recognize the goodness of Athens for what it was. Third, even if Thucydides himself often expresses and invites traditionally disapproving reactions when he mentions Athenian wrongdoing, he leaves readers uncertain about whether conventional ideas of justice and decency are compatible with the world of war as he represents it.

Sparta, Moderate and Decent?

Sparta had no funeral oration, no comparable institution of self-examination—a significant fact in itself. Yet Sparta too is introduced by an able speaker (atypically for a Spartan: cf. 4.17.2, 4.84), King Archidamus, who offers an extended reflection on Sparta's claim to be the best regime (1.80–85). Even if the Athenians saw themselves as cultivating every sort of excellence, it was Sparta, not Athens, that had always been celebrated for its devotion to virtue (cf. 4.40). In the fourth century, however, Isocrates, Plato, and Aristotle leveled well-known criticisms at Sparta and its admirers. We will see that already in the fifth century Thucydides laid the foundations for their arguments through his disquietingly "accurate" presentation of this unusual regime and its many public illusions.

Before the beginning of the war, in the course of urging moderation on his hawkish fellow citizens, King Archidamus explained in general terms why the Spartans should not feel themselves vulnerable to the criticisms of their allies, such as Corinth, who accused them of dullness and excessive hesitation, and yet, simultaneously, of a hypertrophied concern for their own profit and welfare. Archidamus credits the Spartans with being prudent and sound members of a permanently free and well-regarded city (1.84.1–2). With the help of Thucydides' artistry, Archidamus anticipates Pericles' exaltation of Athenian virtue by arguing that the Spartans are both brave in war and judicious in their deliberations, precisely because their way of life is unusually well ordered (1.84.3). Moreover, in an anticipatory response to Pericles' comments on the Athenians' exceptional rationality, Archidamus argues that the Spartans have good judgment because of their respect for the law, their self-control, and their decent appreciation of chance and contingency—principles that have not been corrupted by any excessive, even sophistic education (1.84.3–4). The traditional, law-abiding, disciplined, and moderate Spartans, he implies, intentionally avoid Athenian freedoms because those freedoms are self-indulgent rather than liberal, corrosive rather than healthy. The austere Spartans are least inclined to indulge in excessive confidence in the midst of success, just as they are too steady to become demoralized after suffering setbacks.

Thucydides' readers must fill out Archidamus' remarks by appreciating both how Spartans perceive themselves elsewhere in the text and how others (including their chief critics) represent the Spartans. The Corinthians, for example, speak of the deep confidence that Spartans have in their own way of life, which produces sōphrosunē, along with a kind of conservatism (1.68–70). Although those spokesmen are not necessarily trustworthy, it is possible to hear echoes of the Spartans' own positive self-understanding lying beneath their criticisms of Spartan ignorance and slowness. Equally, when Pericles praises Athens for natural courage rather than courage produced through rigorous training (2.39; cf. 1.121), he is alluding to the strict educational system and the virtues (especially martial ones) of which the Spartans were so proud, as Spartan generals often suggest (2.11, 2.87.4–59, 5.9.9, 5.69.2), and which other Greeks tended both to admire (4.40; cf. 5.72.2) and to fear (cf. 4.34.1). The Spartans have a proud tradition of liberating others from oppression (1.18.1, 1.122–24, 2.8.4, 4.85–87) and of showing pious devotion to the gods (1.118.3, 1.123, 5.50, 5.54–55). In a world of war, which turns out to be subject to contingency in ways that Pericles did not foresee, the Spartans' traditional discipline and caution may seem to constitute a sound basis for political life—especially if those qualities lead the city to display courage and justice in exemplary ways.

Almost immediately after Archidamus' speech, however, any sympathy for Sparta along these lines drains away, as the Spartans decide to go to war without considering the Athenian offer of arbitration (1.86–88; cf. 1.78, 1.85). Thucydides shows the ephor Sthenelaïdas making a speech that stirs up the Spartans' sense of righteous indignation at Athenian aggression (1.86–87)—one that appealed at a deeper level, Thucydides says, to the Spartans' fear (1.88, 1.23.6). Through an irregular voting procedure, Sthenelaïdas shamed the opponents of war into voting against their better judgment; the Spartan Assembly not only violated the terms of the treaty and thus disrespected the law, but also undermined Archidamus' appeal to their traditional caution and their "wisdom in council" (Balot 2014, 124–25, 207–9). The Spartans deceived themselves into thinking that their behavior expressed a serious-minded dedication to both justice and piety, even though they remained dimly aware, for a long time, that they were acting unjustly (7.18). Strikingly, the Spartans had been willing to listen to others' criticisms of Sparta and, at least in Archidamus' speech, to respond to them reflectively; but Sthenelaïdas' speech, and the subsequent vote, showed not only that Sparta lacked judiciousness, but also remained beholden to traditional, and typically misguided, notions of shame, honor, and manliness. It was generally true, as Demosthenes later pointed out (20.106), that Spartans themselves could not criticize Sparta. Right away—not to mention thereafter—the Spartans' behavior and attitudes failed to match up to the fullest appreciation of Sparta that could be offered; the royal author of this appreciation was soon criticized for his weakness, slowness, and lack of patriotism (2.18; cf. the similar treatment of Pleistoanax at 2.21.1, 5.16–17 and of Agis at 5.60, 5.63, 5.65).

This early interplay, and ultimately conflict, between speech and deed sets the stage for Thucydides' general portrayal of the Spartans as self-ignorant and hypocritical: the Spartans deluded themselves into thinking that they were members of a republic of virtue, when, in fact, Sparta's self-image (not to mention its behavior) was both harmful to others and self-destructive (cf. 1.122). Thucydides' salient point is that the Spartans themselves believed in the so-called "Spartan mirage," with the result that they could not critically understand their limitations or remedy their defects. Instead of seeking self-knowledge, therefore, the Spartans remained fundamentally at odds with themselves. Thucydides draws attention to two chief sources of dissonance or disharmony in the Spartans' national experience, both of them intimately connected to the courage and justice that Sparta claimed for itself. Courage or "manliness" (*andreia*) was Sparta's hallmark (2.87.4–5, 2.89.2, 4.12, 4.40, 4.126.2, 5.9.9, 5.72.2). Yet, as Plato and Aristotle asked most directly (*Leg.* 625c–638b; *Pol.* 2.9.1271b1–11, 7.14.1333b5–40), *should* courage be a city's chief virtue? If so, then the enticements of manliness in its most belligerent and toxic expression will often override the claims of more significant virtues such as justice and prudence—an outcome to which the Sthenelaïdas episode draws attention, and one that recurs throughout the war (3.68, 5.83).

Whatever its location in the hierarchy of virtues, moreover, should courage, of all things, be motivated by ignorance, shame, and even fear (Millender 2002; Balot 2014, 209–11)? Pericles had pointed out the implausibility of that idea when he described Athenian courage as an expression of democratic wisdom (2.40). Yet, for a city that prized courage or manliness above all other virtues (e.g. 2.87.4–5, 4.12), Thucydides identified numerous decisions and behaviors that were motivated by the Spartans' unwarranted fear. Reasonable judgments can perhaps differ over the Spartans' fear of growing Athenian power (1.23.6, 1.88), but not all Spartan fears could be rationally justified. Most concretely, the Spartans were afraid to attack the Piraeus, even though opportunities kept presenting themselves; however capable they were of conceiving an audacious plan, the Spartans made excuses and failed to execute their designs because of the dangers they would face (2.9–94, 8.96). Their slowness turned out to be an expression of cowardice rather than prudence, contrary to Archidamus, and as Thucydides repeatedly stresses (3.27, 3.29, 3.31, 3.33; cf. 1.74, 3.109), although occasionally, he says, they simply lacked the energy to execute their plans (4.13). Either way, they could hardly liberate others, such as the Mytileneans, when they behaved so listlessly (3.27). Piety was often an excuse for cowardice (3.89, 5.82.3, 5.116, 6.95, 8.6.5). The Spartans were prone to panic when they confronted unexpected turns of events (2.91), because their courage was limited to what they knew—hoplite battle regulated by the Hellenic rules of war—and they lacked the capacity to adapt to novel circumstances (3.33–36; cf. Ober 2015). When such circumstances arose, the Spartans could occasionally recover their self-confidence and act decisively, as they did just before the Battle of Mantinea, and even more during the battle itself (5.64–74). Most generously, then, one might charge that Spartan courage was typically outmoded and inappropriate to the circumstances; but that charge indicates that Spartan traditionalism itself was defective, in that it failed to produce an adequate expression of its most admired virtue. A more genuine and adequate courage, by contrast, was displayed not only in the larger designs of the Athenians (e.g., 1.73–74), but also in smaller-scale incidents such as the Plataeans' daring escape—from a Spartan siege—during the night (3.20–24). In a world characterized by "motion," Spartan traditionalism is singularly inappropriate (8.96.5; cf. 7.57). Archidamus' speech did nothing to open the Spartans' eyes to this conspicuous liability.

Yet, because of its traditionalism, Sparta would seem to be a first-rate candidate for embodying the resilience that, as we saw above, Thucydides favored because of the contingencies and misfortunes of the world of war. As Archidamus had said, Sparta both prizes and actually exhibits the moderation that enabled its citizens to keep themselves calm during success (4.18, 8.24.4). In practice, however, the Spartans were not equally able to recover from setbacks. Particularly after their soldiers were captured on Sphacteria, the Spartans were demoralized—in part because they faced an innovative enemy whose tactics, strategy, and outlook they failed to comprehend, and in part because they could not, despite their self-image, handle fortune's blows, even though they had anticipated them in the abstract (4.55–57). The Spartans' lack of self-understanding, and their excessive elevation of courage as a virtue, led them to misinterpret defeats as expressions of cowardice rather than chance or lack of experience (2.85.2). More importantly, though, the Spartans lacked the resilience that Thucydides shows to be characteristic of Athens. In the face of defeat, Spartans typically become demoralized and despair about the future (2.86.6, 8.11.3). Their traditionalism did not prepare them to endure misfortune with equanimity; rather, they spent much of the war demoralized, uncertain of themselves (cf. 5.54–55), and anxious to make peace (cf. 4.81.2, 5.13–15, 5.60). They did, however, finally cast off their irresolution at the Battle of Mantinea and successfully restore their reputation and self-confidence (5.75.3), only to continue to show fear, irresolution, and hesitancy shortly thereafter (e.g., in their relations with Argos at 5.82), especially whenever they confronted new contexts or opportunities (e.g., 8.96).

If there was anything, or anyone, capable of counteracting the Spartans' hesitations and irresolution, it was their general Brasidas, Sparta's most successful commander in the *History* (4.81). The context for the appearance of this meritorious general (cf. 2.25) is that, on Thucydides' showing, Sparta rarely produced, and was unlikely to produce, visionary leaders (4.81.3): over and over we see the irresolution of kings such as Pleistoanax (2.21.1, 5.16–17) and Agis (e.g., 5.60, 5.63, 5.65) and generals such as Alcidas (3.27; cf. Strauss 1964, 212–213). The city's wisest leaders, such as Archidamus, enjoyed less authority than they should have had, because their moderation came into conflict with the Spartans' traditional machismo (cf. 1.87–88, 2.18). On the other hand, men of outsized ambition often came to a bad end: most notably, the regent Pausanias, whose intrigues with both Persians and helots (1.131–133) led Sparta's officials to starve him to death (1.134). Pausanias illustrated through his self-indulgence in the pleasures and temptations of Persia that Sparta's mercilessly backward culture was unsatisfying to those with great desires or aspirations (cf. 1.130, 1.132); as an outstanding individual

(1.138.6), Pausanias was continually recalled to Sparta (1.131) and subjected to the surveillance of the home government.

With Brasidas, not a member of the royal family, things were different because he was both wise and energetic, and, to some extent at least, he put into practice the Spartans' self-proclaimed liberation of the Greeks (4.81, 4.87, 4.108), though at times this "liberation" consisted only of installing very narrow oligarchies friendly to Sparta (4.74, 4.132.3; cf. 3.62). His successes in the northern theater were dazzling, admired even by the Athenian soldiers (5.7.2). But they were impermanent because, as Thucydides points out, the leading Spartans were jealous of him, and they simply wanted to end the war (4.108.7). Sparta's internal tensions over decisions of war and peace, particularly among its leaders, come to the surface surprisingly frequently, as individuals were shown to be motivated by their own personal concerns rather than the common good (cf. 5.15–17 with 5.39). A recipient of heroic honors in Amphipolis (5.11, cf. 4.121), Brasidas should have been an Athenian; Sparta badly needed, but could not make full use of, a great man who would press his advantage—something Spartans typically failed to do, even as victorious hoplites (5.73). More often than not, as in Sicily, the Spartans were followers who mistook themselves for leaders.[6]

Spartan courage made sense, if at all, only when an un-Spartan leader took charge; Sparta's claim to justice never made sense. In fact, the city's chief source of internal disharmony derived from its hypocrisy in relation to justice. Despite Thucydides' reference to the Spartans' stable regime, their unity, and their internal strength (1.18.1), they were at odds with themselves whenever justice was at issue. Although they persistently and explicitly affirmed their dedication to justice (1.86–88; cf. 4.86), the Spartans constructed a social system based on the exploitation of helots—state-owned serfs, mostly from Messenia, who had been enslaved during Sparta's earlier wars of expansion in the Peloponnese (1.101). In one sense Sparta and Athens were equally "slave societies"; but the Spartans, the Messenians, and the other Greeks recognized differences between enslaving fellow Greeks and enslaving non-Greeks. The Spartans' treatment of the helots belied their reputation for piety and justice, if only it could have been brought to light accurately. In the past, they had executed helot suppliants (1.128.1), while during the present war, as it seems, they executed some 2000 helots who expected to be emancipated for their good service (cf. the question asked of the Plataeans at 3.52, 3.68), precisely because these men were the most spirited and hence the most likely to revolt (4.80). Strikingly, the Spartans kept their methods of execution a secret and did not even attempt a public explanation or justification (4.80.4); thus they confessed their injustice.

Their hypocrisy in these respects also gave rise to civil tension. Because the helots could revolt or ally with Sparta's enemies, and because of their implacable hatred of the Spartans (4.3.3), the Messenians posed a constant threat to the stability of Spartan society (1.101–2, 1.132.4, 3.54.5, 4.41, 4.55, 4.80, 5.14.3, 5.23.3) and to Sparta's interests in the war (4.36, 4.41). As Aristotle later pointed out (*Pol.* 5.2.1302a24–31), injustice was the

---

[6] It is useful in this connection to note the impact of Alcibiades' appearance at Sparta, starting with his speech at 6.89–92 and the Spartans' reactions to it at 6.93.

principal cause of revolution. On the other hand, it was hypocritical of the Spartans to pose as liberators of the other Greeks from Athens, when they were the leading imperialists of the Peloponnese (1.10.2, 1.76); viewed from this perspective, the Athenians were, ironically, also liberators of their fellow Greeks, the Messenians, from Spartan domination (4.41, 5.91). So great were Sparta's anxieties about revolution that the Spartans went so far as to disenfranchise the soldiers captured on Sphacteria, at least for a time, on the grounds that their loss of face might motivate them to cause trouble (5.34.2).

On the other hand, although Sparta capitalized upon its reputation as a liberator and upon popular hatred of Athens (1.18.1, 2.8.4–5), the Spartans' treatment of other Greeks, even apart from the Messenians, was often decidedly unjust and destructive. Whenever they captured citizens of enemy or even neutral states at sea, they killed them (2.67.4); their general Alcidas also typically killed neutrals (3.32; as did the Athenians, 5.116). The Spartans helped others only when it suited them; even when it did suit them, they were ineffective in carrying out their plans (3.27–33, 3.55; cf. 5.105.3–4, 5.112–113).

The most outstanding example of Sparta's destruction of its own congratulatory self-image was its treatment of Plataea (cf. 3.57). Having been attacked by Thebes, the Plataeans recovered control of their city and awaited a siege with the help of an Athenian garrison of eighty men (2.6, 2.78). An invading Peloponnesian army approached the city during the summer of 429 BCE. Although he was apparently reasonable in the early negotiations, Archidamus found ways to twist history, religion, and oaths to the gods to Sparta's advantage, in order to justify besieging Plataea (2.74). The Spartans' inept siege maneuvers lived up to the city's self-chosen reputation of dim-wittedness (2.75–78, 3.19–24). Eventually the starving inhabitants surrendered, whereupon the Spartans sent five judges to determine their fates. They asked simply whether the Plataeans had helped the Spartans and their allies during the war (3.52.4, 3.68.1); in other words, justice was equivalent to Sparta's good (3.56; cf. Orwin 1994, 70–78 with 5.105.3–4, 5.112–113). A more effective policy, which incurred less hatred, was that of Brasidas: to forgive past alliances with Athens, on the grounds that cities had no experience of Sparta (4.114.4). At all events, the traditionalistic Spartans cared less about Greek traditions of freedom fighting—in which Plataea, of course, had played a storied role—than initial appearances would suggest. The crowning touch is that the Spartans constructed a temple to Hera, along with lodgings for the existing temple, out of the roofs, doors, and walls of the executed Plataeans (3.68.3). The image deftly captures Sparta's level of dedication to piety, justice, and liberation. Thucydides comments that Sparta took action against Plataea in order to please Thebes, which was useful to its interests—temporarily (3.68.4).

Conclusion: Thinking Realistically about the World

At the beginning of the final book, Thucydides analyzed the Chians' decision to revolt. Prompted by the roguish Alcibiades, who had been banished from Athens, they calculated that Athens' defeat in Sicily and the rising fortunes of its enemies made the time right (8.14). The Athenians responded with unexpected vigor and threw the Chians into a defensive position when their large slave population began to revolt (8.40). Even so, the Chians enjoyed many successes with Spartan help throughout 411 BCE, and the outcome remained in doubt when Thucydides' text breaks off. Interestingly, Thucydides respected the Chians' decision, even if they were mistaken in thinking that Athens was incapable of fighting back (8.24). They might have made the wrong decision, judging in retrospect, but Thucydides says that they did not make their decision through overconfidence or desire or misguided hope (8.24.5). In that respect their decision stood in contrast to the decisions of certain northern Greeks to ally themselves with Brasidas, since those decisions were based on hopes and wishes and distorted applications of rationality (4.108.4), just as Diodotus had predicted (3.45). Thucydides does not worship success. Rather, he admires undistorted and dispassionate political prudence, which involves respect for life's unpredictability (8.24.4–5).

Rationality may be "at risk" because of contingency, as interpreters have recently suggested (Williams 1993, 163–64; Geuss 2005, 225; Hawthorn 2014, 235; Hornblower 2010, 6–7), but for Thucydides that point is obvious. More important is a rationality that also understands its own limits. This more adequate conception of rationality or prudence is, on Thucydides' showing, essential to politics conducted within a world of war—all the more so because conventions are likely to fail, as they did during the civil war at Corcyra (3.82–83). Religious oaths, legal constraints, social shame—none of these standard features of culture can pose an effective barrier to suffering or destruction. By contrast, political prudence can survive such moments of social breakdown and therefore provide us with the best opportunity to live decently in an environment that is inevitably hostile (cf. Farrar 1988, 189). Even if no "best regime" can secure humanity's flourishing in a world of war, then at least prudent leaders, who open their followers to a more adequate self-understanding, may be able to moderate suffering. In Thucydides' presentation, that goal is as ambitious as politics should be.

References

Balot, Ryan K. 2001. "Pericles' Anatomy of Democratic Courage." *American Journal of Philology* 122.4: 505–25.
Balot, Ryan K. 2014. *Courage in the Democratic Polis: Ideology and Critique in Classical Athens.* New York: Oxford University Press.
Balot, Ryan K. 2015. "Philosophy and 'Humanity': Reflections on Thucydidean Piety, Justice and Necessity." In *In Search of Humanity*, edited by Andrea Radasanu, 17–36. Lanham: Lexington.
Balot, Ryan K. 2016. "Civic Trust in Thucydides' *History*." In *Thucydides and Political Order: Concepts of Order and the History of the Peloponnesian War*, edited by Ernst Baltrusch, Christian R. Thauer, and Christian Wendt, 151–73. New York: Palgrave Macmillan.
Connor, W. R. 1984. *Thucydides*. Princeton: Princeton University Press.
De Ste. Croix, G. E. M. 1954. "The Character of the Athenian Empire." *Historia* 3: 1–41.
Euben, J. Peter. 1977. "Creatures of a Day: Thought and Action in Thucydides." In *Political Theory and Praxis: New Perspectives*, edited by Terence Ball, 28–56. Minneapolis: University of Minnesota Press.

Farrar, Cynthia. 1988. *The Origins of Democratic Thinking: The Invention of Politics in Classical Athens*. Cambridge: Cambridge University Press.

Geuss, Raymond. 2005. "Thucydides, Nietzsche, and Williams." In *Outside Ethics*, by Raymond Geuss, 219–33. Princeton: Princeton University Press.

Hawthorn, Geoffrey. 2014. *Thucydides on Politics: Back to the Present*. Cambridge: Cambridge University Press.

Hobbes, Thomas. (1629) 1975. "Of the Life and History of Thucydides." In *Hobbes's Thucydides*, edited by Richard Schlatter. New Brunswick: Rutgers University Press.

Hornblower, Simon. 2008. *A Commentary on Thucydides*. Vol III, *Books 5.25–8.109*. Oxford: Oxford University Press.

Hornblower, Simon. 2010. *Thucydidean Themes*. Oxford: Oxford University Press.

Manville, P. B. 1997. "Pericles and the 'Both/and' Vision for Democratic Athens." In *Polis and Polemos*, edited by Charles D. Hamilton and Peter Krentz, 73–84. Claremont: Regina.

Mara, Gerald. 2008. *The Civic Conversations of Thucydides and Plato*. Albany: State University of New York Press.

Millender, Ellen G. 2002. "Herodotus and Spartan Despotism." In *Sparta: Beyond the Mirage*, edited by Anton Powell and Stephen Hodkinson, 1–61. London and Swansea: Classical Press of Wales.

Monoson, S. Sara, and Michael Loriaux. 1998. "The Illusion of Power and the Disruption of Moral Norms." *American Political Science Review* 92.2: 285–297.

Ober, Josiah. 1998. *Political Dissent in Democratic Athens: Intellectual Critics of Popular Rule*. Princeton: Princeton University Press.

Ober, Josiah. 2001. "Thucydides Theoretikos/Thucydides Histor: Realist Theory and the Challenge of History." In *War and Democracy: A Comparative Study of the Korean War and the Peloponnesian War*, edited by David McCann and Barry S. Strauss, 273–306. Armonk and London: Sharpe.

Ober, Josiah. 2015. *The Rise and Fall of Classical Greece*. Princeton: Princeton University Press.

Orwin, Clifford. 1994. *The Humanity of Thucydides*. Princeton: Princeton University Press.

Parry, Adam. 1981. *Logos and Ergon in Thucydides*. New York: Arno.

Romilly, Jacqueline de. (1956) 2012. *The Mind of Thucydides*. Translated by Elizabeth Trapnell Rawlings; edited by Hunter R. Rawlings III and Jeffrey S. Rusten. Ithaca and London: Cornell University Press.

Shanske, Darien. 2007. *Thucydides and the Philosophical Origins of History*. New York: Cambridge University Press.

Strauss, Leo. 1958. *Thoughts on Machiavelli*. Chicago: University of Chicago Press.

Strauss, Leo. 1964. *The City and Man*. Chicago: Rand McNally.

Warner, R., trans. 1972. *The History of the Peloponnesian War*, by Thucydides. Harmondsworth: Penguin.

Williams, Bernard. 1993. *Shame and Necessity*. Berkeley: University of California Press.

Woodruff, Paul, trans. 1993. *Thucydides on Justice, Power, and Human Nature*. Indianapolis: Hackett.

CHAPTER 20

KINĒSIS, NAVIES, AND THE POWER TRAP IN THUCYDIDES

ARLENE W. SAXONHOUSE

In his introductory paragraph Thucydides tells us that in anticipation of a great war, he wrote down the events of what he refers to as the greatest movement—*kinēsis autē megistē*—ever to occur. At first he says among the Greeks, but then qualifies himself to add, on second thought, that it was the greatest movement among most of mankind as a whole. To support his prediction that this will be a momentous war, more worthy of report than any other, he affirms that each side in the conflict had reached its peak (*akmazontes*) with a full complement of military resources. The section that immediately follows the introductory paragraph, the so-called Archaeology, explains what had been entailed in reaching that peak by chronicling how some of the cities of Greece transformed themselves from weak and scattered associations into powerful ones possessing the resources to control—or, more generously in John Finley's language, "unify" (1967, 87–89)—other cities and resist the incursions of foreigners.

While the story Thucydides writes down is of the conflict between the Athenians and the Peloponnesians and while he emphasizes that both sides had reached their peak, the Archaeology is peculiarly one sided in its portrayal of the ascent to the cities' "peak." I shall argue that this "one side-ness" gives a distinct perspective on the nature of power as understood by Thucydides, leading to what I shall call "the power trap," the situation in which the possession of power demands that those with power search ceaselessly for more—and then more. Having power traps the one with power in an endless searching for more. Thucydides' most astute student, Thomas Hobbes, compared the power of a man as "like to fame, increasing as it proceeds; or like the motion of heavy bodies, which the further they go, make still more haste" such that all mankind experience "a perpetual and restless desire of power after power that ceaseth only in death" (1994, Chapter 10, 58). The language of power for Thucydides, as for Hobbes, cannot be separated from the language of motion, and this connection underlies the conflict between the two cities that have reached their peak. For us the language of "having reached a peak" might suggest a static moment in time. For Thucydides it is just a point in the ceaseless search for more power. As Romilly expresses it, "[A]ny state or individual, if powerful enough, has a natural desire to expand its authority ... The wish to rise exists by itself just as naturally as the wish to survive" (1977, 20–21). The constant movement, though, cannot be sustained. For Hobbes that movement ends only in the death of the individual or the creation of a leviathan; for Thucydides the movement ends with the defeat of the city. No leviathan is offered as an escape from the endless pursuit of power for the cities of Thucydides' *History*. In contrast, the author expects that his own work will be an everlasting possession (*ktēma ... es aiei*, 1.22.4), outlasting the powerful cities about which he writes. It is the well-crafted word that has the capacity to endure over time and escape the perpetual motion as cities pursuing power over others cannot.

As Hobbes understood well when he wrote about the natural condition of mankind, not every man must seek power after power for all to be drawn into the vortex of conflict. So too with Thucydides: not all cities share in the constant motion of a naval power such as Athens, but it is the Athenian model that determines the behavior of all other cities. The Athenians famously affirm that their pursuit of power is nothing exceptional. While they claim that all cities display this drive (see especially 1.76.2 and 5.105.2), whether rightly or wrongly, the mere fact that some are so driven means that all must seek power lest they become subject to those having the resources to enslave or destroy them. *Kinēsis* dominates Thucydides' landscape.[1] Escape from that world is found only by eschewing the usual accouterments of power in the everlasting speech of the historian.

THE BACKSTORY OF POWER/ THE ARCHAEOLOGY

In the beginning, the Greek peninsula was a land marked by powerlessness, providing only a fragile existence for its inhabitants. There were no secure dwellings; peoples were forced by those with superior numbers to abandon the lands in which they had previously lived; there was no trade; there were no cities of any size. As Thucydides elaborates, during this early period of powerlessness people "lived off their own land just at subsistence level and neither produced any surplus goods nor planted the ground, since they had no walls and never knew when some invader might come to rob them" (1.2.2).[2] In order to highlight the weakness of those ancient times, Thucydides points to the absence of any "common action" or even common name (1.3.1–2). The peoples inhabiting what later became Greece "because of their individual weakness and their

---

[1] See Connor (1984, 21n4) for a discussion of the use of the word *kinēsis* in Greece at this time.
[2] I use the translation of Thucydides by Mynott (2013) with occasional modifications for the longer quotations. Translations of short passages are my own.

lack of contact with each other, failed to achieve anything together before the Trojan War" (1.3.4). And even the Trojan War was a "comparatively small [expedition] by our standards" (1.10.3). In addition, Thucydides writes, look at those places where people still live "by the old ways," meaning that they bear arms as did the men in all of Greece in previous ages "since their settlements were unprotected and travel between them was unsafe, and so they got used to carrying weapons in their everyday life" (1.6.1). The life of man in Thucydides' early Greece was like the life of man in Hobbes's state of nature, insecure—a realm of constant fear, or we can say poor, nasty, brutish, and short.

With reference to the Athenians and the unique story of how they became the power they did, Thucydides provocatively suggests that it was the poverty of their soil. Where the soil is rich, invasions from outsiders are frequent, as are internal conflicts arising from the inequalities of power that accompany the unequal possession of the land. With its infertile soil Athens escaped such internal and external challenges, providing a safe haven for those expelled from richer lands. These new inhabitants, cast out of their own cities, increased the population of Athens so much that she became a "mother country" to colonies in Ionia, indicating a strength and stability not experienced elsewhere. And as a result of that increased security, Thucydides notes, the Athenians were the first of the Greeks "to put aside their [individual] arms and adopt a more relaxed and comfortable lifestyle" (1.6.3).

Of the two warring powers, the Athenians receive first mention in the account of the movement from prehistory to contemporary times when people felt sufficiently safe so that they could put aside their arms. Thucydides mentions that the customs of both cities changed with this increased sense of security. The Spartans, for instance, abandoned their old-fashioned style of dress (1.6.4), but in describing the attributes that contributed to the accumulation of power that allowed men to lay aside their arms, Thucydides highlights just those factors that mark Athens and not Sparta. We learn why Athens became secure and strong, but not why Sparta did.

First, Thucydides writes of the importance of a navy. He credits Minos with establishing the first navy. His navy enabled him to become "master over most of what is now called the Hellenic Sea"; in addition, it allowed him to install his sons as rulers and expel the original inhabitants of the Cyclades. More important, his navy enabled him to rid the seas of the pirates who had prevented trade and thus thwarted the acquisition of capital (1.4.5, 1.8.2). Cities located on the coast were now free from the threat of pirate raids and "more able to pursue the acquisition of wealth and lived in greater security" (1.8.3). The weaker cities, desiring more material wealth, accepted the rule of the stronger cities that with the advantage of increased resources were able to subdue those weaker cities.

Thucydides' analysis of Minos' power and the consequences of his building a navy then influences his reading of the Trojan War. It was neither the oath of Tyndareus nor any sentiments of loyalty that brought together the forces amassed for the recapture of Helen. Rather, Thucydides explains, it was fear—fear of Agamemnon's power—that brought together the host of ships joining him on the expedition to Troy. Whence this power, though? Thucydides relies on Homer to answer this question. Homer describes Agamemnon as "lord over many islands and the whole of Argos" and Thucydides deduces that since Mycenae was based on the mainland, Agamemnon must have had a strong navy. As the king of Mycenae, he could not have ruled over "many" islands without a sizeable navy (1.9.4). Not only did Agamemnon have the largest contingent of ships at Troy, but it was also precisely that contingent that gave him the power to lead the Greeks to Troy. Possession of ships determined power. Thucydides thinks almost in reverse. Agamemnon was powerful; therefore, he must have had a navy. Homer's evidence supports this conclusion.

Tracing the history that followed the return of the forces from Troy as Greece continued its trajectory toward a more civilized and stable condition where men could live unarmed, Thucydides continues to identify the navy and the resulting increased revenues and material possessions as crucial to the increasing power (*dunastōteras*) of Greece (1.13.1). Minos may have had the first navy, but Thucydides credits Corinth with developing modern shipbuilding techniques and in particular identifies the Corinthian shipwright, Ameinocles, who built ships not only for the Corinthians but also for the Samians more than 300 years before the end of the Peloponnesian War (1.13.3). Strategically located on the Isthmus, Corinth could take advantage of those Greeks of old who traveled for trade more by land than by sea and became the city referred to by the poets as "wealthy Corinth" (1.13.5). When commerce moved to the seas and away from land transportation, the Corinthians with their ships were in a position to clear the seas of the pirates and "by offering a market both by land and sea they made their city powerful enough through the income produced" (1.13.5). The Ionians followed the example of Crete and Corinth, built their own navies, and became strong enough to resist to the Persian King, for a while at least. And Polycrates of Samos "was able through his sea power to make various islands subject to him" (1.14.6).

Despite all this attention to naval power, navies before the Persian Wars were still limited to a few ships, and even after Themistocles famously persuaded the Athenians to build "the ships with which they actually fought their sea battles" Thucydides adds that "even these were not completely decked over" (1.16.3). Concluding his summary of the development of and the rising importance of the Greek navies, Thucydides remarks that "those who actively developed them ... strengthened their positions greatly in terms of revenue and dominion over others, especially those who had insufficient land of their own and who sailed against the islands and subjugated these" (1.15.1). As with Corinth, what mattered was the revenue garnered through trade, not land. The Archaeology, filled with reports of navies, contrasts the lively expansion of power enjoyed by naval powers to those bound to the land: "But on land not a single war took place from which any new power accrued" (1.15.2). Therefore, Thucydides might have asked, why should he bother discussing the uninteresting and uneventful acquisition of power on land? And he doesn't.

Along with the development of naval strength as key to the growth of power in the prehistory of the Peloponnesian War is the building of walls. The absence of walls made the early cities susceptible to the raids by those pirates who roamed the seas. With the rise of the navies making seafaring safer, cities that "were starting to have more ample resources" built on the coastline and "fortified [themselves] with walls" (1.7).

Walls offered further security so that the inhabitants not fearing raids could enjoy the increased wealth coming from the trade in which they now could freely engage. When the Athenians return to their city from the ships after the retreat of the Persians, they immediately engage in rebuilding the "city and its walls" (1.89.3), so important are they to them. And to highlight that importance Thucydides devotes the three following chapters (1.90–92) to the diplomatic chicanery in which Themistocles engaged in order to give the Athenians sufficient time to rebuild the walls. The construction of the walls contributes mightily to Athens being at her peak when the war breaks out. Navies, wealth (resources that did not come from land), walls: these fill the narrative that Thucydides tells of the emergence of the world in which the war about which he is to write occurs and they all portend the magnitude of that war.

The history of Sparta surfaces only briefly in this backstory. For Sparta there were no walls, there was no navy, and the material resources were slight. When Thucydides takes a break in the sequential narrative in Chapter 10 to reflect on the inadequacy of sight as a guide to historical knowledge, he remarks on the great power of both Athens and Sparta. But, he notes, if future generations were to look at the monuments left behind long after the demise of each city, the observers would see little left by the Spartans, in contrast to the monuments remaining in Athens. These men of the future "would find it hard to believe that Sparta's power matched its reputation," even though "the Spartans occupy two-fifths of the Peloponnese and are leaders of the whole of it as well as many allies beyond it" (1.10.2). The factors that may have led to Sparta's ascent to such territorial power are curiously absent from Thucydides' survey of early Greek history. We do read that "though it [Sparta] went through the longest known period of civil strife after its present inhabitants . . . had taken possession of it," it nevertheless enjoyed many years of good government (*eunomia*) avoiding the tyrannies that surfaced in other cities (including Athens) and that after their 400 years of enjoying the same regime the Spartans were sufficiently strong (*dunamenoi*) to arrange their own affairs as well as that of other cities (1.18.1). Thucydides makes it seem that the static, unchanging (boring?) *eunomia* put Sparta at her peak, but it is a story he (by contrast with Herodotus) feels no need to develop.[3]

Thucydides moves almost seamlessly from his discussion of the prehistory of Greece to the Persian wars, when the Spartans were the "pre-eminent power" and assumed the leadership of the Greek alliance against the Persians, whereas the Athenians, abandoning the physical city of temples and homes, became a city that defended itself by going down into the ships. While we are prepared for the Athenians' retreat into their ships from the prior mention of her navy, it is only the unchanging political regime that gives any clue as to why the Spartans were the preeminent power in the Peloponnese. Sparta's power evokes even more puzzlement, given Thucydides' comments about

---

[3] Strauss (1964, 146) has quite a different take on this; he finds that Sparta's power lies in her moderation despite her prosperity. In part this may be because Strauss focuses on the Archaeology as Thucydides' affirmation of the weakness of olden times rather than as an exploration of the accumulation of those resources that make cities powerful.

Agamemnon's power and how he, coming from landlocked Mycenae, *must* have had a navy in order to inspire fear in the other cities and to have the resources to lead the expedition to Troy. Landlocked Sparta had no such navy, at least until the very end of the war, after Thucydides' own narrative ends.

The backstory recounted in the Archaeology, then, is the story of the rise of navies and their contribution to the transformation of Greece from the chaotic world lacking even a unifying name to the complex political associations that immediately precede the Peloponnesian War. It is a tale that confirms the weakness of previous times and the greatness of the powers that will engage in the war that he records. But in his telling Sparta, though receiving occasional mention to contrast her history with that of Athens, is largely absent from the theoretical framing that the Archaeology offers with regard to the rise of power in Greece. Thucydides' modeling of the emergence of power in Greece does not include Sparta.

I want to argue that the Archaeology ignores the story of the Spartan rise to power because it is Athens' story with its dependence on the navy that provides the dynamic force to the history that Thucydides chronicles. Mere acquisition of power without the perpetual motion entailed in having a navy leaves static the relations between cities and is not worth writing down. The story that interests Thucydides is not static like Sparta. Rather, like the war that Thucydides anticipates, it is all about the motion captured by the lively Athenian ships. The Archaeology as preface with its equation of power and navies sets the stage for understanding power as inexorably connected with movement—*kinēsis*—and therefore with war.

Spartan Power—or the Absence Thereof—and Athenian Motion

At the end of Book 1 Thucydides presents the first of Pericles' three speeches. This one is to encourage the Athenians to stand firm in their resistance to the demands that the Spartans are making of the Athenians with regard to Potidaea, Aegina, and the Megarian Decree. Among Pericles' arguments for resisting those demands is the catalogue of the Spartans' weaknesses relative to strength of the Athenians. In essence, Pericles recites the Archaeology in reverse identifying what the Spartans lack: the walls, navy and material resources that Athens (and the Corinthians) acquired as Greece moved from chaos to order. First, Pericles explains that the Peloponnesians work the land themselves and do not have the private or public resources (*chrēmata*) available to engage in a war. Indeed, "they have no experience of protracted overseas wars because their own campaigns against one another are kept brief by the fact of their poverty" (1.141.3). Pericles elaborates on how the Spartans' poverty will hinder their ability to carry on war, how the Peloponnesians are not sufficiently united to take prompt action, how—as before the settlement of cities described in the Archaeology—they attend to their private interests rather than the common concerns (1.141.4–7). Emphasizing these points, he repeats that the "biggest" hindrance for the Peloponnesians is their lack of wealth, and adds that their efforts to build a wall or outfit a navy should not cause any concern (1.143.1). With the Athenians poised to attack, the Spartans may be able to build a few forts, but they could not fortify defensive walls. Further, as farmers unfamiliar with the sea, they will never be able to achieve anything worthwhile (*axion*, 1.142.7).[4]

The security that Pericles assures the Athenians they have as they inevitably bring on war comes specifically from the power they have acquired with their navy, their wealth and their walls, just those assets Thucydides highlighted in his story of Greece's march toward a civilized life. Both sides in the conflict that is about to occur may have reached their "peak," as Thucydides writes in his introductory paragraph, but it is the Athenians who have garnered the resources and power that goes with those resources that should ensure their success in the war—a war that they, in the end, will lose.

The Corinthians' speech in Book 1 explores the psychologies of cities whose power derives from navies and those—forgotten about in the Archaeology—whose power comes from their land forces. The Corinthians have arrived at Sparta with the goal of spurring the Spartans to recognize the need to stop what seems to be the ever-increasing number of cities in Greece that are falling under Athenian control. They chastise the Spartans for their lethargy, their attachment to *hēsuchia*, the quiet life; at the same time the Corinthians vividly portray the energetic Athenians. It is the latter who merely have to think a thought for that thought almost instantaneously to become a deed. Spartan indolence, in contrast, has allowed, the Corinthians complain, the Athenians to build up her power: "You are responsible, allowing them first to strengthen (*kratunai*) and later to build the wall" (1.69.1). Once the energetic Athenians actively acquired this power, they enslaved, as the Corinthians phrase it, the Greek cities. Now, the Corinthians demand, it is time to stop the ever-moving, ever-expanding Athenians.

In order to incite the Spartans into action, the Corinthians paint a portrait of the Athenians that reveals what a formidable opponent they have become, at the same time that they show how weak the Spartans are. The contrast that the Corinthians emphasize lies not so much in the relative possession of material resources that Pericles and Archidamus emphasize, but in the psychologies of the two cities. The city bound to the land is characterized by "antiquated" practices (1.71.2); it "dithers" and "hesitates" (71.1); it reacts defensively; it never leaves home (1.70.4); it is "passive" (1.69.4).[5] The inhabitants of the city that has become a naval power are "natural innovators"; they are "bold beyond their means" (1.70.2); they "are always after getting more ... and think of leisure (*hēsuchia apragmon*) as a greater disaster than irksome toil" (1.70.8).

---

[4] Archidamus in his efforts to dissuade the Spartans from going to war makes much the same argument as Pericles with regard to the Spartans' lack of resources and naval skills (1.80.3–4).

[5] The historical adequacy of this description of the Spartans by the Corinthians must, of course, be questioned, given Spartan hegemony over so much of the Peloponnese. The claims must be understood in terms of the rhetorical intentions of the Corinthians [and Thucydides' emphasis on the Spartan attention to controlling the helot resistance to the exclusion of discussions of Spartan supremacy in the Peloponnese (1.101–3)].

Let me emphasize the connection the Corinthians make between the restlessness that is characteristic of Athens and the possession of the navy. The navy is itself a source of constant motion traversing the moving seas and congruent with the character of the Athenians as described by the Corinthians. Taking to their ships, the Athenians are often carried far from their home city. In their rebuke to the Spartans, the Corinthians note that while they, the Spartans, remain at home, the Athenians are always abroad, seeking gain "by going away (*apousiai*)" (1.70.4), traveling from one spot to another. With their navy the Athenians are distinguished by this pattern of constant motion as they sail from one success to another, acquiring power after power. "If they fail to go and achieve something they have planned on doing they believe they have been deprived of what was already theirs," but if they succeed, "they count that a small gain compared with future prospects." Failure does not hinder their forward motion; rather, "they redirect their hopes to make good the loss elsewhere" (1.70.7).

Summing up their view of the Athenians, the Corinthians pithily state, "They have been born to allow quiet (*hēsuchian*) neither to themselves nor to others" (1.70.8). Always in motion, the Athenians prevent others from living a quiet life such as the Spartans have done for 400 years. The Athenians' ceaseless energy forces others to move. *Kinēsis* is the word that substitutes for war in the introductory paragraph. *Kinēsis* marks the life of the Athenians, the city with ships. The static, unexercised power of the Spartans, as the Corinthians present it, simply allowed the Athenians the space to remain in motion, acquire more resources, and become so powerful that, the Corinthians warn, they are on the brink of "enslaving all of Greece" (1.69.1).

The (Inescapable) Power Trap

Once the war has begun and the Athenians are stressed by the destruction of their lands by the Spartans and the devastation of the Plague, they not only blame Pericles for their suffering but also are eager to sue for peace. Pericles in his third speech does not so much defend himself, though he does that too, as try to persuade the Athenians to persevere in their commitment to the war. This he does in part by again identifying the importance of the navy to their efforts—the navy that makes the loss of their lands and their homes little more than the loss of gardens and ornaments, easily replaced precisely because of the advantages they garner from their navy. "There is no one to stop your sailing the world's seas—neither the Great King of Persia nor any other people on earth" (2.62.2). The speech, though, is more than exhortation; it is also a warning about what will happen if they do not continue in the war that has now begun. The power and the empire they have acquired with their navy have put them in a position that demands constant vigilance. That vigilance can never cease. "And do not suppose that what is at stake here is a simple issue of freedom versus slavery. On the contrary, it is also about loss of empire and the danger from the hatred your empire has brought you" (2.63.1). And he reminds the Athenians, "Nor can you now give up possession of the empire, should anyone be frightened by the present situation and try to make a manly virtue of non-involvement (*apragmonsunē*)" (2.63.2). The power acquired with their navy has become a burden that controls their actions. They cannot escape its demands. There is no release from the constant search for more power, for once power has been acquired over others, the city is always faced with the challenge of those who would resist. The navy embodies motion, but the power that the navy ensures demands the unceasing movement that the Corinthians found in the Athenian psyche. Motion is not only a psychological trait. It is a political and military necessity.

In the Funeral Oration Pericles had spoken dismissively about the *apragmon*, the citizen who is not involved in the life of the city, calling such a man "useless (*achreios*)" (2.40.2). In contrast, he praised the fully engaged warrior who faced death for the city. In Pericles' third speech the *apragmon* is not simply the uninvolved and therefore useless citizen; he is the one who persuades others not to pursue the war in which Athens is engaged, who fails to acknowledge that Athens ("like a tyranny") cannot rest in the pursuit and preservation of power without destroying the itself. The *apragmon* himself would by himself not be saved. He must join with those who are energetic in the movements of the war. Such a citizen is of no benefit to a city that rules, Pericles says, only to one that is a subject state that "seeks safety in submission" (2.63.3). In this third speech, Pericles insists that the powerful city must maintain that activity about which the Corinthians had spoken; that constant engagement is not simply a part of the Athenian character, but a necessity lest the city become subject to her former subjects. Brash Alcibiades in Book 6, as he eggs on the Athenians to embark on the ill-fated Sicilian campaign, repeats Pericles' admonitions: "It is not an option for us to set limits to the empire like accountants; on the contrary, since we are in this situation we are forced to take active initiatives against some cities and keep our grip on the rest, because there is a danger that if we do not take others into our empire we shall fall into theirs." And noting the peculiar situation of Athens, he adds the warning that "you cannot take the same passive stance as other states might, that is unless you are also going to change your whole style of life to match theirs as well" (6.18.3).

Once power has been obtained, there is no rest—meaning there will always be war or the potential for war. But without that acquisition of power chronicled in the Archaeology, we would remain in a world of subsistence living, of migrations of peoples because of fear rather than conquest, of small and insecure settlements. Therein lies the tragedy of Thucydides' *History*, where Athens and her navy define the terms of political engagements. The acquisition of power demands movement, which almost by definition means war. But without that acquisition we are left in the miserable life portrayed in the prehistory described in the Archaeology.

Other speeches in the *History* capture Pericles' and Alcibiades' portrayal of the power trap (see especially Cleon's at 3.37), but perhaps it is the speech of an unknown Athenian with the pleasant name of Euphemus in Book 6 that elaborates most vividly on the pressures to pursue the power that then places constraints on its possessor. Euphemus speaks before the Ionian Camarinians in order to persuade them to continue their alliance with the Athenians rather than shift their support to Syracuse. In doing so, he offers the Camarineans a story about why the Athenians acquired their empire. Looking to the period after the Persian invasions, he explains that the Athenians were concerned about the number of the Dorians in the Peloponnese and their proximity to Athens. The Athenians needed to consider how they could best ensure that they did not become subject to the Peloponnesians. In other words, the Athenians, perhaps correctly, fearing slavery and imagining the Peloponnesians to be motivated like themselves and driven on by an unending pursuit of power, understood that they themselves needed to become powerful. Fearing the power of others, they pursued power themselves. And becoming powerful themselves they needed to preserve and not yield that power; they could do so only by pursuing more power. They were caught in the power trap. And so, Euphemus explains, the Athenians acquired a fleet, allowing them to be free from the "empire and hegemony (*archēs kai hēgemonias*)" (6.82.3) of the Spartans. As Euphemus spells it out, the only justification for the Spartans to be giving the Athenians orders "rather than we them" was that they (the Spartans) were "the dominant force (*meizon ischuoun*) at the time" (6.82.3). To protect themselves from becoming subjects of the Spartans, they built their fleet. With their ships built to defend themselves against the Spartans, the Athenians could then maintain their hegemonic status over the islands that had previously been ruled by the Persian King, giving them in turn the power (*dunamin echontes*, 6.82.3) to protect their own. Though those islands over which they gained power were inhabited by Ionians, Euphemus claims that the Athenians were not wrong to "enslave (*dedoulōsthai*)" them, as the Syracusans had suggested they were in their appeal for Camarinian support. The Ionian islands had not defended their "mother-country" and thus they had "willed their own enslavement and wanted to do the same to us" (6.82.4). One or the other—the Athenians or those living on the islands—would be enslaved. There was no option that did not involve the pursuit of power by one or the other or both. Had the Athenians been passive, had they wallowed in Spartan indolence, practiced *apragmonsunē* and not sought power and the control over others, they would themselves have become the slaves of the Spartans or of Ionian islanders whom, Euphemus now admits without shame, they have enslaved.

And so the Athenians, Euphemus claims, "deserve, are worthy of (*axios*)" their empire. But that worth, he seems to say, comes only from acting as they must, given the necessary movement of cities to acquire power. Euphemus offers justifications that match those of the Athenians who spoke at Sparta before the war began, citing the ships contributed by the Athenians in the fight to resist the Persian king and the commitment they made to the endeavor to repel the invading armies (1.74), but Euphemus moves beyond the fine words of freedom and the embellishments of the Athenians at Sparta to add another dimension: "We have it [the empire] because we sought to strengthen ourselves (*ischuos oregomenoi*) against the Peloponnesians" (6.83.1). The Athenians acted for their own safety, protecting themselves against the dangers that threatened them, namely, subjection to the rule of another city, first the islands and then Sparta. Though the Athenians control the seas, they have arrived in Sicily and specifically at Camarinia, Euphemus claims, seeking support from Camarina because of a concern with their own safety. Euphemus becomes blunt; no euphemisms for Euphemus: "We hold our empire in Greece out of fear, and it is fear that brings us here with our friends to establish our security" (6.83.4). The Athenians' widespread power offers no escape from the power trap. It only tightens the spring.

Thucydides' story of Athens is of a naval power whose constant motion forces it to remain in motion, to pose threats to the freedom of those who remain quiet. The Corinthians had blamed Spartan quiescence for the expanding power of the Athenians and the enslaving of the allies. Not to move, not to pursue power is to abandon oneself and one's allies to the mastery of others—or, on occasion, to destruction. In the brief story Thucydides tells of the city of Mycalessus, he presents the tragic consequences writ small of the failure to acknowledge the pursuit of power that affects every city, even those that avoid such a pursuit. In the midst of describing the activities of the Spartans, Athenians, and Syracusans in Sicily during the summer of the nineteenth year of the war at the beginning of Book 7, Thucydides takes us very briefly to events in Greece when the Athenians were struggling at great expense to retain control of Deccleia and to bring in supplies from Euboea. They were, Thucydides writes, "financially crippled" (7.28.4). As a result, Thracian swordsmen who had intended to join the Athenian forces in Sicily had been sent back to Thrace, their one drachma a day pay too costly for the Athenians under their current financial constraints. Under the leadership of the Athenian general Diitrephes, the Thracian swordsmen made an assault on the small town of Mycalessus. Thucydides is at pains to capture the pathos of this attack, noting that the attackers "spared neither young nor old but killed everyone in their path as they came on them—women and children, even beasts of burden and any other living thing they set eyes on." And he adds, "total mayhem ensued, and death and destruction came in every form. They even burst in on a boys' school . . . just after the pupils had entered it, and they massacred them all." In one of the remarkably few openly personal comments on the events of the war, Thucydides writes, "Disaster struck the whole city and was the worst ever suffered, so sudden was it and so terrible (*deinē*)" (7.29.3–5).

The pathos Thucydides evokes, though, must be qualified. Thucydides remarks that the Mycalessians "were off their guard (*aphulaktous*)" and that "their walls were weak, in some places dilapidated and in others built to no great height." Further, "the gates had been left open because they felt they had nothing to fear" (7.29.3). In other words, they imagined themselves living outside the power trap. They did not see the need for the acquisition of the resources that led other cities to have power. Their lack of preparation for a possible invasion by others showed their failure to comprehend the understanding of human nature that Thucydides was so eager to communicate and that Hobbes had learned so well: the pursuit of power by some necessitates the pursuit of power by all. The Mycalessians should have been sufficiently insecure to seek power for themselves. They escaped the power trap only by ignoring it and thus brought devastation to themselves. Early in the *History*, after the speeches urging the Spartans to go to war or to avoid putting themselves into a war they could not control, Thucydides interjects his own analysis of the causes of the war. The war occurred because the Spartans were fearful of the Athenians' power, fearful that they like the citizens of the islands in the Aegean would become the servants of Athens. In the single sentence that constitutes Chapter 88 of Book 1, Thucydides writes, "The Spartans voted that the treaty had been broken and that they must go to war, not so much because they were persuaded by the speeches of their allies as because they feared a further growth in the power of the Athenians, seeing that most of Greece was already subject to them." Not to fear the pursuit of power by others would be to welcome the fate that awaited the unwalled, unguarded Mycalessians.

The movement described in the Archaeology away from chaos and weakness to a civilized life entailed the acquisition of power by some, but that very acquisition came to control the cities of Greece, granting quiet to none. The tragedy is not only that all the children in the schoolroom were killed, awful enough as that was. The tragedy is that it is the nature of power to require not only the constant movement of those who have it, but also that—as the Corinthians said of the Athenians—power denies rest to all. The power that brings civilization to the Greek peninsula also necessitates the pursuit of power after power by all, leading inevitably to the movement that is war. Orwin writes that Thucydides' sympathy for the victims of power captures his "humanity" (1994, 9). I would suggest that we are all the victims of power and thus deserving of Thucydides' sympathy. The world in which we live is one created—figuratively or not—by the navy of the Minos, by the shipbuilding of Ameinocles, by the fleet of the Athenians.

Memory and the Escape from the Power Trap

While the failure to pursue power leads to the submission to others (or worse, as in the case of Mycalessus), the pursuit of power itself cannot—in the end—be endless. It brings its own strategic flaws to plague the powerful city. Pericles—who in his first speech had assured the Athenians of their military superiority because of their navy, who had spoken of the resilience necessary to resist the demands of the Spartans, who had affirmed that Athens ruled as a tyrant and could not give up power without becoming a slave to others—also urged the Athenians to moderate the restlessness that had brought them such power. Thus, he advised—to no avail, as it turns out—the Athenians to "keep quiet (*hēsuchazontas*)" while they care for the fleet and not add on to the empire by war or endanger the city (2.65.7). But what he advises is precisely what the Athenians cannot do. The quiet—the leisure that the Spartans practiced, at least according to the Corinthians—does not come easily to a city that lives through its navy. The new adventure Sicily offers when the Egestaeans come asking for aid is hard to resist. Nicias urges in un-Athenian fashion restraint and he does so in language we would expect not to be readily accepted by the Athenians. He complains about the brevity of the consideration to men who merely have to think a thought for it to be accomplished (6.9.1). He warns men of whom the Corinthians say that "for them alone to hope for something is to have it, such is their speed in executing their plans" (1.70.7), that their "haste is untimely" (6.9.3). It is the enthusiasm and energy of Alcibiades that appeals to the Athenians as he eggs them on: "We can hope to puncture the pride of the Peloponnesians when they see we so resent our current inactivity (*hēsuchian*) . . . for we shall be masters of the sea" (6.18.4). Urging them to eschew Nicias' (Spartan) policy of "non-intervention (*apragmonsunē*)," he asks them to hold on to their "traditional good practices" and "take the city further forward (*prosagagein*)" (6.18.6). Concluding his exhortation, he reminds the Athenians that "a city which is accustomed to activity would be very quickly destroyed by a change to inactivity" and that the greatest security lies in maintaining their character (*ethē*) and traditions (*nomoi*) and how they live (*politeuōsin*) (6.18.7).

In Thucydides' analysis of the failure of the Sicilian campaign, it is not the drive toward expansion about which Pericles had warned and which Alcibiades encourages that brings about the losses there, but the failure of leadership by the individuals who, as Thucydides writes, "engaged in personal intrigues over the leadership of the people and so blunted the effectiveness of the forces in the field" (2.65.11) and who therefore failed to acknowledge the centrality of Alcibiades to any success in Sicily (Forde 1989, 7). Simply having walls, wealth, and a navy does not ensure success in the search for power after power. Power in those terms may be the motive force, but skill and effective leadership are essential to enable the city to maintain that motion over time. That the Athenians with their naval power allow no rest to others is no assurance that they will be able to keep themselves forever in motion. It is a fact that Pericles recognizes well.

In his third speech, even after he has spoken forcefully about the importance of continued movement and the threat that inaction poses for the city, and immediately after he has boasted that Athens has acquired the "greatest power (*dunamin megistēn*) up until this time," Pericles acknowledges that the power the Athenians have acquired will not last forever, "for all things by nature become smaller (*elassousthai*)" (2.64.3). At that point memory will replace the physical power over others that Athens once had in deed. Unlike the power that comes from navies, memory does not depend on constant motion in order to maintain itself. Indeed, memory must remain unmoved, static in the mind over generations and millennia. Memory is the answer to the power trap for Pericles, as it is for Thucydides.

In his Funeral Oration, Pericles praises the efforts of those who came before, especially the fathers who gained possession (*ktēsamenoi*) of the empire that the current generation now enjoys, but even more so, he praises the current generation who have increased (*epēuxēsamen*) the polis to such an extent that Athens now has the resources to be self-sufficient in war and in peace (2.36.3).[6] The story of Athens, as Pericles presents it, is one of expansion, consistent with Thucydides' theme of power as motion. Even so, Pericles imagines for the citizens he is trying to energize that moment in the future when Athens may no longer exist. In his third speech he tells them that while

---

[6] Mynott has difficulty with *epēuxēsamen*, since Pericles suggests that the fathers had brought the empire to its current state, but the language of "increasing" is important, for it captures the notion that power (or empire) does not stand still, that it is a process of continual expansion—that ceaseth only in death.

"to be hated and unpopular in the short term has been the common experience of all those who have presumed to rule over people other than themselves; the wise decision is to accept the odium in pursuit of the larger purpose. For hatred is short lived," he says looking toward the future, "but the brilliance of the present deeds shines on to be remembered in everlasting glory." And so he exhorts his audience to fix their "minds on achieving that fine future to come and on incurring no present shame, and commit yourselves to both objectives" (2.64.5) (See also Romilly 1977, 7). In his Funeral Oration, beloved by so many, detailing the beauty of the city he leads, Pericles acknowledges that the unending pursuit of power must eventually end in death for the city. And so he speaks of the men who have died in seeking to preserve Athens' power, promising them the "unaging praise (*agērōn epainon*)" that they have gained along with "forever-to-be-remembered (*aieimnēstos*) fame" (2.43.2). The acquisition of empire and the continuous pursuit of power after power that accompanies it are caught in the warp of time where leadership matters; memories can escape that time warp and live forever.

So too does Thucydides' *History*, at least in Thucydides' own anticipation that he is producing a possession that will last forever. The product he creates with his words has a permanence that the empire acquired by a navy and under the impetus of the unending search for power can never produce, as even its most ardent advocate recognizes. The acquisition of navies, of walls, of material sets the city on the path to motion and brings with it the need for others to acquire the resources to protect themselves from the pursuit of power by their adversaries. The cycle of power acquisition and the motion that it entails informs the history Thucydides writes. But the history itself acquires its own power absent walls, navies, and material resources. Its power lies in enabling others to see clearly (1.22.4) the workings of power in the world around them. The restless politics of acquisition dims before the permanence of the speech of the book Thucydides chose to write. It lasts forever, as the cities enmeshed in the power trap do not. Neither Thucydides nor Pericles controls the way those memories and that history will remain present for future generations, but once established, they each imagine—and imagine correctly—that the search for power after power that plagued and continues to plague political life would for them cease as everlasting memory replaces conquest and empire.

References

Connor, W. Robert. 1984. *Thucydides*. Princeton: Princeton University Press.
Finley, John. (1942) 1967. *Thucydides*. Ann Arbor: University of Michigan Press.
Forde, Steven. 1989. *The Ambition to Rule: Alcibiades and the Politics of Imperialism in Thucydides*. Ithaca: Cornell University Press.
Hobbes, Thomas. (1651) 1994. *Leviathan*, ed. with Introduction and Notes by Edwin Curley. Indianapolis: Hackett.

Mynott, Jeremy, ed. and trans. 2013. *The War of the Peloponnesians and the Athenians*. By Thucydides. Cambridge Texts in the History of Political Thought. Cambridge: Cambridge University Press.
Orwin, Clifford. 1994. *The Humanity of Thucydides*. Princeton: Princeton University Press.
Romilly, Jacqueline, de. 1977. *The Rise and Fall of States According to Greek Authors*. Jerome Lectures. Ann Arbor: University of Michigan Press.
Strauss, Leo. 1964. *The City and Man*. Chicago: University of Chicago Press.

CHAPTER 21

THUCYDIDES ON NATURE AND HUMAN CONDUCT

CLIFFORD ORWIN

In earlier writings I expounded a somewhat "Socratic" Thucydides. I stressed the centrality of the regime for him and his dialectical (not merely antithetical) presentation of opposing viewpoints. In these respects, I argued, he anticipated crucial teachings ascribed to Socrates and explored by his admirers. (On the many parallels between Thucydides and Plato, see Gerald Mara's contribution to this volume.)

Concerning nature, however, and its implications for understanding human conduct, the two outlooks appear to diverge. The Socratics promote philosophy as the best way of life, which is to say one according to nature. Thucydides, by contrast, is silent as to a life according to nature. His reticence suggests a nature less gracious than that extolled by the Socratics. Even so, I will argue, his project displays a crucial "methodological" parallel with theirs. For him as for them, the study of the human or political things (including therefore much that "pre-Socratic" thinkers would have dismissed as conventional) requires (and permits) no turn away from the natural ones.[1]

NATURE AS OBSTACLE AND ALIBI: THUCYDIDES' "ATHENIAN THESIS"

As suggested, the most obvious difference between Thucydides' presentation of nature and that of the Socratics is that he eschews "teleology." However enigmatic the political proposals of Plato and Aristotle, it is clear that their understandings of nature support a transpolitical ambition. In Aristotelian terms, the *phusis* of each being implies its *telos*

---

[1] I am grateful to David O. Davies, Mohan Mathaen, Brad Inwood, and Ryan K. Balot for comments and advice, and indebted to the pioneering effort of Gerald Proietti (1992).

or completion. For human beings this *telos* comprehends both practical and theoretical virtue. Aristotle is of course aware that few natural beings (including human ones) approach that perfection of which the best of their species are capable. With his usual tact, however, he pronounces that while nature wishes for the best, she cannot always achieve it (*Politics* 1254b–1255a, 1255b), often rather leaving us in confusion. He concedes that any presumption of nature's goodness demands also an admission of her weakness. Still, insofar as intention may be imputed to nature she aims at our perfection. By presenting the fullest and most satisfying human life as that according to nature, the Socratics encourage gratitude to her.

Thucydides' presentation of nature strikes a very different note. Consider two of his best-known formulations.

> And during the *stasis* the cities suffered such acts of rage as occur and will always occur for so long as men have the same nature, if sometimes more terribly and sometimes less, varying in their form as each change of fortune dictates. (3.82.1)

> From what is reputed of the gods and what is manifest of human beings, we conclude that always, by a necessity of nature, they rule to the limits of their power. (5.105.2) (Translations from Thucydides are my own)

Thucydides offers the first of these statements in his own name; the second he ascribes to the Athenian envoys to the Melians. Neither comment suggests that human nature inclines us toward perfection. In the first, nature serves to ground a prediction of the inevitable recurrence of the most terrible evils that human beings inflict on one another. In the second, it figures not as an impetus to virtue but as an alibi for our chronic failure to achieve it. The passages agree in depicting human nature not as a friend to lofty aspirations but as an impediment to them.

The quotation from the Athenian envoys to Melos falls into a sequence of pronouncements (all but one of which Thucydides ascribes to anonymous spokesmen for the Athenians) that cast nature as an excuse for conduct that might otherwise appear transgressive. In three of the instances noted, the norms violated are those of justice; in the fourth, those of piety. All these speakers pronounce a tension between *phusis* and *nomos*: the demands of nature, presented as overmastering necessities, prevail over those of convention. The envoys to Melos go so far as to speak of the natural inevitability of imperial expansion as itself a *nomos* (the normal term for law or convention) (5.105.2): they do so to underscore how invariably it overrides *nomos* in the usual sense.

While the earliest proponents of this argument justifying empire, the Athenian envoys to Sparta, specify those natural motives to which they ascribe overmastering force—fear, honor, and profit or advantage (1.75.3, 1.76.2)—later ones don't bother. Indeed, to do so seems superfluous, given that these motives originally specified as compelling (and therefore exculpatory) include all the usual incentives to rule. There is no case of rule, actual or attempted, that lacks sufficient excuse. Abstention from it is too much to demand of human nature, although we may still distinguish between more or less just instances of rule in the sense of harsher and gentler ones (1.76.3–4, 77.1–5; cf. 5.111.4).

As this line of argument is to be found primarily in the mouths of Athenian characters, I will follow Leo Strauss (1964, 183) in calling it the "Athenian thesis."

THE DOUBTFUL REACH OF NATURE: CONTRADICTIONS IN THE ATHENIAN THESIS

The Athenian thesis presents nature in a decidedly ambiguous light. To act "according to nature" or under the sway of universal compulsion is to act the same as, and therefore no worse than, other men. This argument from nature is welcome to the Athenians because it excuses their empire. Yet compulsion as such is unwelcome to human beings (even as empire is unwelcome to its subjects). And no true Athenians could be satisfied with the claim that they, their city, and their empire are merely no worse than others.

In fact, both the envoys to Sparta and those to Melos insist on the superiority of Athens. They agree with Pericles in presenting the empire as attesting to Athens' *virtues*, which they of course do not present as compelled. These include her superior justice, which unlike that of weaker cities (who clamor for justice because it suits their interests) is genuine, and is so precisely in being irreducible to any of the three alleged compulsions. The envoys to Melos similarly pride themselves on Athens' prudence and her "measured" (*metrios*) treatment of her inferiors (5.111.4). They too cling to an implicit distinction between a realm of natural compulsion and one of residual freedom within which Athenians continue to display their virtue. At the very least, all spokesmen for Athens from the beginning of the work to its end insist on her *reasonableness* as a virtue for which she deserves credit.

Nothing so attests to the confusion of the Athenians on the issue of (natural) compulsion as the claim of the envoys to Sparta that honor qualifies as such a compulsion (1.75.3). Here they are clearly at odds with the Pericles of the Funeral Oration, who eschewing any mention of compulsion presents the Athenian empire as a freely chosen project, motivated by an *erōs* for the city evoked by its bestowal of eternal renown on each and every of its citizens (2.43). This Sunday-best presentation of the empire deliberately evades the delicate question of its justice; in this and quite a few other respects it won't bear careful scrutiny. The speech of the envoys presents a different problem. In displaying their irresoluteness as to whether fear or honor is the primary compulsion grounding the Athenian empire (cf. 1.75.3 with 1.76.2), they assimilate the seemingly less compulsory to the more so. In so doing they attest above all to just how keenly and deeply they experience the thirst for honor. It may be that by honor (the word for which, *timē*, can also be translated "office") the envoys mean primarily the precedence enjoyed by the imperial power: as an ad for a candy bar once declared, "when you're this big, they call you Mister." Yet, in fact, the envoys seek to establish their honor in a loftier sense, by asserting their unique *worthiness* of empire. What justifies their empire is less the natural compulsion to exercise it (which allegedly presses equally on all cities) than the virtue to which it attests and that they declare to be unique to Athens.

Yet what is the status in nature of this concern with virtue, which, however defective or confused its expression, defines what is best in Athens? The envoys acknowledge this problem precisely by declaring honor a compulsion, and therefore natural even as fear is natural. Yet it is as demeaning as it is unpersuasive to assimilate a concern with honor (culminating in pride in one's virtue) to the merely feral passion of fear. It is also ultimately fatal to such concern, for by its reductionism it opens the way to a debunking of honor (5.111.3–4; cf. the absence of any consideration of honor from the speech of Euphemus, the final exponent of the Athenian thesis in a therefore truncated version [6.81–87], and the reasoning of Phrynichus at 8.27). This problem in the Athenians' self-understanding suggests the necessity of an ampler understanding of nature, one capable of grounding the appeal of the just and noble, although these are irreducible to the useful, let alone the compulsory. By displaying this difficulty, Thucydides again points forward toward Plato and Aristotle.

Thucydides on the Defectiveness of Nature

For the Socratics, true to the etymology of *phusis,* nature is growth (and its inevitable concomitant, decay). We cannot conceive it as simply voluntary or "free": the plant does not ripen as the plant that it is because it has willed or decided to do so. Nor, on the other hand, do we think of this process in terms of compulsion, as if someone or something had forced that plant to be a rose and to attain gorgeous maturity as one. Only if the rose grew into something strange, something unroselike or merely stunted, would we ask what had compelled this unfortunate outcome.

That is to say that Plato and Aristotle do raise this question about almost every human being: why do we almost all fall so short of the highest human possibilities? They answer that it is either because we are defective by nature or that we are the products of defective conventions; indeed, that most of us are both of these. For just as both thinkers see the vast majority of laws as defective, so also do they see outstanding human natures as rare. Again, while nature's intentions are of the best, she lacks the means of accomplishing them. She guides us toward a perfection that she almost never provides us the means of attaining.

Thucydides' critique of nature appears more stringent still. The problem isn't that nature fails to provide us with goals. She does so with a vengeance: we experience these goals as compulsions. Yet as already suggested, the fact that we so experience them already implies a certain restlessness with them. Precisely by alleging their necessity to excuse our pursuit of them, we acknowledge them as problematic. As Colin Macleod

(1974, 395) remarked of the envoys to Melos, "There is no pride in [their] statement [of their motives for their invasion], for they claim to be doing only the inevitable...."

Of what, then, are the Athenians proud? As we have seen, of their virtue, and of the empire insofar as it displays it. Yet this claim (and the Periclean vision of the empire that supports it) is undermined by their invocation of the thesis. For what is the thesis but a recurrent excuse for the failure of the Athenians to live up to a standard of justice that they themselves acknowledge? The Athenians yearn to persuade others (to say nothing of themselves) that they are justified in conduct that their enemies denounce as brazen: that their motives for empire (which are anybody's motives for empire) must be deemed truly compulsory. For only as compulsory will they justify. That the Athenians feel compelled to defend themselves by means of the thesis thus attests to the abiding (may we say natural?) appeal of justice to human beings.

Praiseworthy (and choiceworthy for its own sake) would be to contain the pursuit of rule within reasonable bounds, to heed the necessary no more than necessary. This the Athenians claim to do. Even if by the time of the Melian Dialogue the alleged prudence or measure of Athens has largely replaced her justice, the envoys continue to assert Athens' superior virtue, in which they vainly seek to school the Melians.

The great difficulty confronting all the Athenian exponents of the thesis is that while they present nature as compelling us to injustice they continue to defer to virtue (therefore including justice) as the natural standard for human beings. The promptings of nature emerge as disharmonious, admitting of no apparent resolution. Worse, as the expositions proceed in the course of the work and the logic of the argument becomes clearer, the realm of virtue retreats evermore before necessity. The focus on the naturalness of the necessary/compulsory threatens to leave virtue high and dry, ungrounded and unprotected.

The Socratics propose to defend nature by solving this problem. As we have already noted, they deny that nature offers no more than the infernal din of those passions that press on us as necessities. She also gently nudges us toward perfection and happiness. Inevitably, nature so understood is highly complex, and it would be safer to understand classical "teleology" as provisional than as dogmatic.

The Athenian Thesis Expanded: Diodotus and Hermocrates

The envoys to Melos may appear the most intransigent exponents of the Athenian thesis. They are not its most thoughtful ones. That distinction falls to the Athenian Diodotus and the Syracusan Hermocrates. These are arguably the characters in the work whose understanding most approaches that of Thucydides himself. Like the more conventional spokesmen for the thesis, Diodotus and Hermocrates stress the power of what we would call psychological compulsions. Yet they move beyond them in their articulation of these. The others have presented human societies as compelled by nature to seek certain goals. At the same time they have depicted them as free to pursue these goals reasonably and perhaps even virtuously in other senses. So conceived, nature's sway will not seem altogether oppressive, or the case for human dignity entirely compromised.

Diodotus and Hermocrates, by contrast, come very close to casting the city as a madhouse. Their speeches are extraordinarily complex, repaying close analysis and defying brief summary. In their very artfulness they underscore the crucial role of reason in guiding society. Yet for both speakers it is primarily because societies are so irrational that such care is required in addressing them.

Diodotus undertakes to defend the defeated Mytileneans against harsh retaliation by the Athenians. The Athenians cannot but view this revolt of the most privileged among their subjects as not only gratuitous but treacherous. Therefore, Diodotus can hope to evoke sympathy for them only by extenuating transgression as such. "All are by nature prone to transgress, whether acting individually or in common (*idia kai dēmosia*), and there is no law that can prevent it" (3.45.3). There is, Diodotus asserts, no condition of human life, be it poverty, its daring fed by compulsion, or plenty, whose craving for more (*pleonexia*) arises from arrogance and presumption, that is not in the grip of some fatal passion. "Hope also, and longing (*erōs*), the latter leading to ruin and the former following closely behind," beckon us to our destruction, as does fortune, which by unpredictably gracing a few deludes all to venture.

> ... [To which delusion] cities are even more prone than individuals, for they contend for the greatest things, freedom and empire, and because each individual, when acting with all his fellows, exaggerates his strength beyond all reason. In a word it is impossible, and only the most naïve would suppose that, harsh laws or any other terror will deter human nature once it is fully resolved on something. (3.45.6–7)

Hopefulness, treated as a pathology, is the theme common to the speeches of Diodotus and Hermocrates. Both begin from the Athenian thesis but extend it. Diodotus plays on the dual meaning of the Greek *hamartēma* ("miss," used of both errors and transgressions) to reinterpret all transgression as error, whether as regards the end or the means. In his hands, then, the thesis becomes a general theory of human irrationality, thus anticipating Thucydides' great reader Hobbes. Hermocrates too, in probing the unfailing attractiveness of war despite the universal recognition of it as an evil, points to the universal tendency of cities to rely on whatever factors exaggerate their prospects of victory (4.62).

Neither Diodotus nor Hermocrates denies the possibility of sober second thoughts: indeed, each seeks to foster them. But both present this opportunity as commonly arising only as a result of initial fecklessness. Cities shoot first (most often themselves in the foot or the head) and ask questions later. Acting as they do for the highest stakes under great duress and amid a bog of uncertainties, they cannot be expected to get things right the first time. Neither speaker presents the process of deliberation as strictly bound to fail, or cities as therefore under strict natural compulsion to err. But reason emerges from their speeches as so flickering a light that human beings bereft of it seem worthy less of anger than of pity. Here these speakers agree with Nicias, his gods, and very likely Thucydides himself (cf. 4.108.2).

When Diodotus calls freedom and empire the "two greatest things," that is not to imply that our pursuit of them is likely to bring us happiness. The "greatest things" do not gladden but madden. As the most unhinging of goals they entrain the most evils for victim and agent alike. Diodotus promotes not freedom and empire (which hardly require his endorsement) but moderation in their pursuit. He implies that not they but the clearsightedness to which they are so often fatal is, if not the "greatest" thing, at least the most salutary. While the "greatest things" are to be preferred to their alternative (subjection to the power of others), their goodness is highly qualified. (On prudence as the crucial good for Thucydides, see also Ryan K. Balot, chapter 19 in this volume.)

Yet does such clearsightedness imply a distinct way of life? As we mentioned earlier, the biggest question in comparing Thucydides and the Socratics is that of a natural way of life. If Thucydides endorsed some such life, his world would look much more like theirs. There you would find your naturally indicated peak; there would be the *telos* otherwise lacking. But I can find no such life in Thucydides, no resolution, even in principle or for the very few, of the problem posed by human nature. He surely refrains from promoting philosophy as a distinct way of life.

This difference between Thucydides and Plato is reflected in their respective treatments of *erōs*. To be sure, the *Republic* presents *erōs* as thoroughly ambiguous: the philosopher, the best of men, is moved by it, but so is the worst of men, the so-called tyrannical soul. As there are different parts of the soul that predominate in different types of soul, so there are different types of *erōs*. Still, Plato praises *erōs* as, at the very least, one possible way to philosophy.

Thucydides agrees with Plato both that our natures are highly susceptible to *erōs* and that this is problematic. In fact, no *erōs* emerges from his work as salutary. It is Pericles' invocation of *erōs* in the Funeral Oration that most anticipates Plato's presentation of it as ambiguously a longing for the supremely beautiful and for immortality for oneself. (In Pericles' presentation *erōs* seems to fill both these bills, while also binding the citizen to the city.) Thucydides' mentions of *erōs* in his own name serve to debunk this view. In Diodotus' speech, as we have seen, *erōs* figures with its handmaiden hope as the great human spoiler. Judging from the sole example to which Thucydides calls our attention, *erōs* leads nowhere in private matters beyond sexual congress with the desired object, with all the attendant jealousies and rivalries such as may also corrupt the public realm (6.54–59). In public matters proper, as Diodotus suggests, it will very likely lead to shipwreck. Nor do its ends prove as sublime as that preached by Pericles. He had invoked an *erōs* for Athens itself because its power underwrote a perpetual memory of the virtue of its citizens (2.43.1). Instead, the Athenians will conceive an *erōs* for the conquest of Sicily (the only one that Thucydides imputes to them as a people) (6.24.3). And while perpetuity figures in this *erōs* also, it is the perpetuity of pay that the many at Athens expect the island to yield them. The contrast could not be clearer—or more ludicrous.[2] (On

---

[2] On *erōs* in Thucydides see the excellent treatment in Ludwig (2002, 121–69).

Thucydides' treatment of *erōs*, see also Victoria Wohl, chapter 26, and Ryan K. Balot, chapter 19, in this volume.)

THE ATHENIAN THESIS AND THE OUTLOOK OF THUCYDIDES

Does Thucydides subscribe to the Athenian thesis? We might just as soon that he didn't. Not just the adversaries of Athens but common sense will bristle at the thesis as self-serving. Isn't it all too typical of us to contrive excuses for precisely our least excusable conduct? Can we really lay all such conduct at the door of nature? And doesn't any such blanket alibi, by denying our ultimate responsibility for our actions, deprive them (and us) of their dignity?

Thus far, then, experience supports the opponents of the thesis (and of Athens). Still, the thesis recurs so often in the work, so forcefully articulated and with so many nuances and variations, that we can't dismiss the possibility that Thucydides acquiesces in it. His own statement at 3.82.1—the first of the two texts quoted at the beginning of this essay—lends further credence to this possibility. Just as the apologists for the Athenian empire insist that the sway of stronger over weaker is only to be expected because grounded in our common nature, so Thucydides himself asserts of the even more egregious outrages of *stasis*. Yes, the *pleonexia* (greed) and *philotimia* (ambition) of the factional leaders were responsible for the violence of the *stasis* (3.82.8), but were the factional leaders responsible for their *pleonexia* and *philotimia*? Thucydides doesn't reprove the excesses of the partisans as the enemies of Athens typically reprove her imperialism. Rather, he resembles the spokesmen for the thesis in ascribing such atrocities to an only too predictable interplay between human nature and political circumstance. (On Thucydides' treatment of *stasis*, see Michael Palmer, chapter 24 in this volume.)

This view of *stasis* once granted, it seems only too plausible to cast the case of empire in similar terms. Be that as it may, Thucydides offers no statement on this question in his own name parallel to the one on *stasis*. His characters (including both proponents and opponents of the Athenian thesis) express their opinions on this as on other matters, but we cannot begin by imputing any of these opinions to Thucydides. The question is whether Thucydides' account as a whole, in its subtle interplay of speeches (*logoi*) and deeds (*erga*), serves to vindicate the thesis.

The most convincing refutation of the thesis would be a persuasive counterexample. Proponents of the thesis present their case as wholly empirical. It is because no society has ever been known to respect justice so much as to refrain from ruling others that we may conclude that to do so would be to rise above human nature. (It goes without saying that many have refrained from ruling others from the same motives of fear, honor, or advantage that under more favorable circumstances would have inclined them to pursue power). The first question facing us, then, is whether the narrative provides any such counterexample.

In fact, it provides only counterfeit ones. Of the cities arrayed against Athens, all claim to act in contradiction with the thesis, but none does so. From the noxious hypocrisy of the Corinthians and the Thebans and the creeping expansionism of regional powers like Mytilene and Syracuse to the Spartan and Chian preoccupation with problems at home that preclude adventurous policies abroad, there is no city in Thucydides whose conduct rebuts the thesis.

But does the want of such a persuasive counterexample suffice to vindicate the thesis? Not entirely. For this deficiency in justice, even if general, is subject to various interpretations—of which "nature made me do it" is only one and not necessarily the most compelling. Thucydides compels us to consider as well a much older Hellenic explanation of the human propensity to transgress. That is our *hubris*, or impiety, for which we have no one to blame but ourselves. For piety commands blamelessness not only toward the gods but also toward other human beings (7.77.2): Zeus was the patron and enforcer of justice. Such is the outlook of the most important character in Thucydides, the ill-starred Athenian commander Nicias. As he and his men begin their much too delayed retreat from Sicily, having already suffered terrible evils and anticipating still worse to come, he reflects on their likely standing with the gods.

> [Perhaps our misfortunes] may be lightened. The enemy has enjoyed all possible good fortune, and if by our campaign we have incurred blame before one of the gods, we have already suffered ample punishment. For others there have been who have attacked their fellows, and having done what human beings will do, have not suffered more than they could bear. We may then plausibly (or fairly, *eikos*) expect kinder treatment from the divine (for surely by now we are more deserving of pity than rancor). (7.77.3–4)

Nicias edges toward the Athenian thesis but stops well short of it. As the spokesman for the older piety, he eschews the novel notion of nature and any alibi founded on it. By maintaining human culpability, Nicias implies the absence of compulsion in the respect crucial for piety—precisely our freedom to refrain from transgression. For without such freedom the very notion of transgression becomes incoherent, and with it that of divine punishment.

At the same time, Nicias recognizes, as all who are truly pious must, the fragility of piety including his own. (Was he too not swept up in the unjust folly of the Sicilian project, for all his initial resolve to oppose it?) As undertakings like the Sicilian one amply attest, "men will do as men do." Hence the plausibility of Nicias' hope that in their very justice the gods will limit the punishment of the Athenians to the sufferings already inflicted on them.

Nicias imagines both gods and men who enjoy freedom from natural compulsion: men, who being free to act justly or unjustly, may justly be held to account, and gods who are not only free to judge us but on whose justice we may rely. He rejects the position of the Athenian envoys to Melos, who subject the gods to natural necessity even as they do human beings. Nicias agrees with those envoys that transgression is the rule among human beings. Unlike them, he struggles to maintain piety and justice as obligations incumbent on us, weak reeds though we are.

As Thucydides nowhere explicitly endorses the Athenian thesis that empire is excusable as a natural compulsion, so he nowhere explicitly endorses the contrary claim of piety. Nicias' hopes from the gods are rudely dashed: only destruction awaits him, along with the rest of his host. Perhaps the gods prove more demanding than he supposes: applying justice with rigor, they have found the Athenians wanting. Or perhaps the heavens are vacant, and the fate of the Athenians simply follows from the natural course of human events.

The Catalogue of the Contingents (7.57) as Commentary on the Athenian Thesis

One statement of Thucydides puts a certain distance between him and the Athenian thesis, thereby suggesting also a certain agreement with Nicias. This is 7.57, which catalogues the forces present on the respective sides at the climactic engagement of the Sicilian Expedition, the battle in the Great Harbor of Syracuse.

> [These were the forces that made war in Sicily, whether to conquer the island or to defend it,] standing with one another not so much out of right (*dikē*) or kinship, but rather as matters fell out for each regarding compulsion or advantage. (7.57.1)

Thucydides proceeds to classify the various contingents according to this final pair of motives. These prove parallel to a second dichotomy, between willing participants and unwilling ones. The criteria that Thucydides applies are commonsensical: only those qualify as compelled who have been dragged along against their will (or who would have been, had that will been lacking, because constrained as subjects or clients to participate whether they like it or not). These include not only the subject allies of Athens (including some nominally independent ones, 7.57.5, 7), but, on the other side of the battle, the Sicyonians from Peloponnese, who accompany their fellow Dorians only under compulsion (7.58.3; cf. 5.81.6). They also include, however, the Italiot cities of Thurii and Metapontum, allies of Athens because their democratic regimes, recently begotten in *stasis*, depend on her continued support (7.57.11). Here the harsh exigencies of self-preservation under which any regime labors qualify as no less constraining than the iron grip of a hegemon. (On the centrality of the regime for Thucydides, see Seth Jaffe, chapter 23 in this volume.)

Those classified as constrained, however, include two whose participation is subjectively most willing. The first of these are the Plataeans, survivors of an extinct city who are languishing in exile at Athens, who contend against the murderous Thebans to avenge the destruction of their city. Then there are the Corcyraeans, motivated by their inveterate hatred of the Corinthians. Thucydides nonetheless classifies both groups as constrained, presumably because so dire was their dependence on Athens that they could not have declined to accompany her. The Argives, by contrast, while equally allies of Athens, he counts among the willing combatants, their motives being mercenary: presumably Athens was in no position to compel so large and distant an ally to participate. These examples serve to underline that what Thucydides means by compulsion or constraint is so in the most tangible and concrete (and therefore indisputable) of senses. No reasonable observer would hold it against the Plataeans, Corcyraeans, Thurians, or Metapontines that they had accompanied the Athenians: it was otherwise with the Argives.

Willing, by contrast, is the participation of all who act from some version of advantage (*xumpheron*). As Thucydides here employs this term it is an umbrella covering a wide range of motives. All mercenaries enrolled in the expedition are deemed to fight no less willingly than the Argives. (A very special case are the Acarnanians, who while paid to participate do so primarily from affection for the Athenian commander Demosthenes.) So, finally, are all other independent cities that came to war in Sicily whichever the side and whatever the reason. Those deemed willing thus include even Camarina, which supports her predatory Syracusan neighbor to avoid her reprisal should she prove victorious [cf. 6.88.]) Thucydides implies that the participation of all these cities (however many may have found themselves between the same rock and hard place as Camarina) remains willing because subject only to their autonomous reckoning of the relevant advantages and risks. Like the Argives and the other mercenary contingents, these cities decide for themselves: however exigent their situations otherwise, no hegemon compels them. Such is evidently also the principle that Thucydides applies to Syracuse herself. While he comments that of all the cities, she faced the greatest danger from the invasion (7.58.4), neither does he range her among the cities that fought Athens under constraint. If anything, the suggestion is that her supreme danger heightened her willingness. Free to decide whether fear supported resistance to the Athenians or capitulation to them, Syracuse could hardly plead that either course was compulsory (nor would she have wished to decline credit for her decision to resist).

At the head of the list of the willing stand the Athenians themselves (7.57.2). Actuated as they have been by the hope of perpetual pay, a love of foreign sights, and a by now long-departed confidence in the expedition's safety (6.24), who could deem their participation unwilling? Thucydides' statement that an erōs for the expedition seized the Athenians must be taken as an emphatic statement not of the necessity but of what we might call the overpowering willingness of the enterprise. That which a city is only too ready to do qualifies thereby not as compulsion or constraint but its opposite, whereas the Athenian spokesmen at Sparta had classified as compelling that very thirst for gain that later infuses the Sicilian Expedition, Thucydides, as we have seen, restricts that term to cases of external constraint.

Thucydides thus both contrives this conspicuous opportunity to endorse the Athenian thesis and declines it. This isn't to say that he altogether disowns it. In developing his dichotomy of constraint or compulsion on the one hand and interest in the broad sense on the other, he acquiesces in the "realism" of the thesis. Those cities not acting under constraint because subservient to the interest of others act on some interest of their own, be it fear, honor, interest in its narrow sense, hatred, or (exceptionally, as with the Acarnanians) affection.

Nor does Thucydides here construe compulsion as narrowly as those of his characters who reject the Athenian thesis. These would certainly have contested his claim that the Italiot allies of Athens had acted under constraint because subject to the harsh exigencies of maintaining their democratic regimes. Partisans of oligarchy all, they would never accept democracy as an excuse for anything or anything as an excuse for democracy (cf. Alcibiades' attempt to cope with this difficulty before a Spartan audience at 6.89.3–6). Consider also in this connection the Thebans' implacable rejection of the claim of the Plataeans to have had no choice but to become and remain allies of the Athenians (3.60–67). In their vindictive tirade the Thebans imply that that no Athenian ally is ever such by necessity, the better course of opposing Athens (and acquiescing in the hegemonic ambitions of Thebes) remaining always open to it. (That is also to say that no ally of Thebes is such by necessity, but always by that wise and virtuous choice in which the Boeotians other than the Plataeans supposedly acquiesce so freely. What greater bliss than to be dominated by the Thebans?) It is no small part of Thucydides' humanity to recognize the limited options (and hence the limited accountability) of weaker cities like Plataea so exposed to the rigors of necessity. As 7.57–58 makes clear, Thucydides recognizes certain cases of fear (those supporting the constraints that the stronger impose on the weaker) as tantamount to necessity. If the proponents of the Athenian thesis may be held to exaggerate the sway of compulsion in politics, so the opponents of the thesis minimize it. Yet absolute necessity evades us: the Melians, after all, weak as they were, were not compelled to surrender to the Athenians. "The very least one would have to say is that there are different kinds of compulsion" (Strauss 1964, 210)—and, equally, different kinds or degrees of willingness. (On the range and ambiguities of Thucydides' treatment of necessity, see also Kinch Hoekstra and Mark Fisher, chapter 22 in this volume.)

Of a piece with Thucydides' implicit defense of the Plataeans from the charges of the Thebans is his staunch rejection of all such vindictiveness as follows from rejection of the Athenian thesis. He evinces not a trace of indignation against those Athenians and others whose participation in the invasion of Sicily is so greedily willing. He resembles Nicias—and Nicias' gods—in knowing men too well to be scandalized at their overreaching. Perhaps Nicias and those gods of his are right as well that we shouldn't excuse such behavior as naturally compulsory for human beings. Better to say with Nicias rather that they are only too prone to it (which implies, as Nicias has suggested in his final speech, an extenuation, although not an excuse).

Motion and Rest

No reader of Thucydides can fail to note the recurrence throughout his work of the dyad of motion (*kinêsis*) and rest (*hêsuchê*). Nor will our task let us ignore this shaggy, unkempt pair. For in Thucydides' presentation it marks the intersection of human nature with nature as such.

Thucydides begins by describing the war as the greatest motion ever known among the Hellenes (1.1.2), which as such presupposed centuries of accumulation of rest. In its beginnings, most of what was later Hellas had known only motion. For that very reason there had been no great motions, only swarming, sound and fury signifying nothing. Although this unrest extended even to the uprooting of entire peoples, that too was a petty event: the players changed locations; the game remained the same. Existence was hand to mouth. Rest or stability (including the emergence of cities, the necessary condition of any great motion, such as the present war) had been achieved only with the passage of much time. An exception was Attica, a rocky terrain coveted by none. There a large population gathered, fed by the constant upheaval elsewhere. Granted rest, the Athenians prospered, grew, and finally began to send out colonists. This is Thucydides' first mention of the kind of motion that depended on antecedent rest. (On motion and Thucydides' treatment of earliest times, see also Arlene W. Saxonhouse, chapter 20 in this volume.)

As the work proceeds, this theme merges with Thucydides' other great themes. If we are to believe the Corinthian envoys to the First Spartan Conference, the Athenians are a people in perpetual motion (born, as these envoys say, to take no rest themselves and to leave none to others ([1.70.9]). Sparta, by contrast, to whom the Corinthians are appealing for aid, is a city at rest, that companion of justice, but has become mired in it: now Sparta must bestir herself and put herself in motion before it is too late to repel the Athenian motion (1.71). Motion will recur in the discussion of *stasis* at 3.82–83: not only do the cities sink into frantic self-destructive motion to which all rest and stability fall prey, but also *stasis* itself is described as a motion (3.82.1), in this parallel to the war itself.[3] So too of the two leaders who vie for primacy at Athens after the death of Cleon, Nicias promotes a policy of rest, Alcibiades one of motion (5.16.1, 6.9–18).[4]

Rest and motion thus figure as recurring terms of Thucydides' presentation of political life. Yet Thucydides' most intriguing reference to rest is not exclusively or primarily political. At 5.26, in a kind of second beginning to the work, Thucydides explains how he managed to write it. He tells of the rest he enjoyed due to his exile from Athens following the loss of Amphipolis. Here rest refers first of all to Thucydides' circumstances: to the leisure that his exile had imposed on him. Yet it also seems a metaphor for that contemplation in the service of a stable and nonpartisan understanding of (and

---

[3] On the issue of *stasis* as pervading Thucydides' work as a whole, see Price (2001).
[4] On the opposition between Nicias and Alcibiades (but also between Nicias and Pericles) in this regard, see Burns (2012, 221–23).

amidst) the din of the greatest motion. Or is that contemplation itself to be understood as a species of motion? Like the other examples of human rest in the work, Thucydides' exile furnished the opportunity for an activity; are we to conceive of that activity as a motion?

Signs and Portents

When it comes to rest and motion, politics discloses just the half of it: the distinctively human half. Thucydides also calls our attention to a wide range of nonhuman happenings amenable to analysis in these terms. These include eclipses, volcanic eruptions, earthquakes, tidal waves, and flash floods. We would call these natural phenomena, but that already attests to our tutelage to modern science. Thucydides' characters and readers, like other ordinary Hellenes of their day (and long after), viewed such matters not as "natural" but as divine. They were expressions of the gods' concern with us (often of their displeasure, but displeasure is still concern). Since all gods are most visible when hostile (cf. Aristophanes, *Knights* 30–35), it was disruptions of every kind—earthquakes, volcanoes, storms, plagues—that Hellenes most associated with the divine. Seeing the gods as movers and shakers, they for that very reason prayed to them for rest.

Nowhere does Thucydides explicitly repudiate this view. He sometimes defers to it. At 1.23.3, for instance, in contending that the war he has recorded was the greatest one, he adduces what great disturbances had accompanied it, on land and sea and in the heavens as well as among and within cities. Without actually mentioning the gods—so obtrusive in the accounts of such events offered by his rivals Homer and Herodotus—Thucydides nods in their direction. A murmur of the divine pervades his work, inconclusive but welcome to readers for whom no account of the human would be complete without reference to the divine.

Of such events traditionally ascribed to the gods, the most significant for Thucydides' narrative are the plague that strikes Athens in the second year of the war (2.47–54) and the lunar eclipse that occurs during the Sicilian expedition (7.50). Public opinion among the relevant Athenians ascribes both events to divine agency.

In the plague the despondent Athenians see the hand of Apollo, the Homeric sender of plagues and an avowed ally of Sparta in the war (2.54.4; cf. 1.118.3). Thucydides does not comment on this verdict, but his own account tends to subvert it. He declares his ignorance of how the plague began, and offers only hearsay evidence as to where (2.48). Even so he undercuts the suggestion that this fatal irruption had reflected divine hostility to the Athenians. Not only was the plague as lethal to nonhuman creatures as to human ones (2.50: a fact he notes as particularly unusual), but it had afflicted several other peoples before falling on Athens (2.48). Nor was this even the first known instance of it (2.47.3). Given its wide dissemination elsewhere, no divine malice is needed to account for its having finally reached Athens through her bustling port of Piraeus (2.48.2; cf. Pericles' recent boast in his Funeral Oration that there is no product from anywhere that does not make its way to Athens [2.38.2]). Apollo would be a sorry archer indeed if he had aimed this shaft at the Athenians in particular.

The eclipse that befalls the Sicilian Expedition proves a disaster of a different sort. Unlike the plague, it is not intrinsically an important evil. In itself it poses no obstacle to the planned (and urgent) Athenian withdrawal from Syracuse. There follows nonetheless the postponement of that plan for thrice nine days, on the authority of the diviners attached to the expedition (on "thrice nine," cf. 5.26.3). The common soldiers support this delay, as does Nicias, the one of the commanders of the armada who is resplendent for his piety (and who thus immobilizes his colleagues). As a result the Athenian and allied host, which could still have escaped mostly intact, will meet with eventual annihilation (7.87.5–6). Thucydides remarks drily that Nicias "was somewhat too attached to divination" (7.50.4), thus hinting at the proper degree of attachment to it. If the plague is an evil by its nature, the eclipse is one due only to the convention of its divinity.

Thucydides doesn't state explicitly that celestial events as such should be deemed natural rather than divine. As already noted, he defers to the divine in his way. He does note, however, of a certain solar eclipse that it occurred at the beginning of the lunar month, "which appears to be the one and only time this can happen" (2.28). He repeats this point at 4.52.1 (he who repeats himself only rarely). Must we understand the gods' capacity to signal their will to us as hostage to the lunar calendar? (On Thucydides' treatment of piety, see also Paul Rahe, chapter 25 in this volume.)

As Alcmaeon Wandered

Thucydides' most evocative treatment of rest and motion in the nonhuman realm features a figure from the misty past, Alcmaeon son of Amphiaraus (2.102). Thucydides introduces him while expounding an event of the third winter of the war. Rather than besiege the hostile town of Oeniadae in Acarnania, the Athenians decide to withdraw: the town, Thucydides explains, was inaccessible in winter because surrounded by water at that season. He might have stopped there. He proceeds to offer an account of the general topography of the area—to which he then appends the tale of Alcmaeon, a seemingly superfluous footnote to an already superfluous excursus.

From the first of these accounts we learn that from time immemorial the turbid river Achelous has deposited sediments at its mouth at Oeniadae, one already populated by a chain of small islands. As a result the islands have by Thucydides day almost ceased to be such. They have grown into what during the dry season was or would soon be a single mass comprising the mainland, the former islands, and the alluvial deposits.

Alcmaeon strays into these wetlands as a matricide, having slain his mother in retribution for her betrayal of his father. The Delphic god, ruling that Alcmaeon's offense had polluted the entire world, had forbidden him to settle anywhere on it. Thus outcast from the society of gods and men, Alcmaeon had wandered. After many years he arrived at the mouth of the Achelous. Observing the process of the emergence of land out of water, he reckoned that an area sufficient to support life might have arisen since the time of his transgression. So there he settled, and through his son Acarnan begot the local tribe of that name.

In this account drawn from the epic tradition, the natural process of the formation of the delta is invoked to explain the fulfillment or circumvention of an oracle. Thucydides will not vouch for this part of the story, which he presents merely as belonging to "what is said of Alcmaeon." His own account is entirely empirical, evidently based on his own observation. Unlike the epic version, it features not the interplay of god and man but merely that of rest and motion. The rushing river chips away at its banks, carrying off dissolved bits of rest (earth), which it will eventually reconstitute as such through its alluvial deposits. What prevents the silt of these deposits from dispersing over a wider area (i.e., what grants them rest or compels them to rest) is the staunch resistance of the Echades, the chain of small islands at the river's mouth. By confining the river's exit to the sea to narrow and winding channels, they force it to disgorge its burden. Having done so they gather that earth to themselves, encroaching still more on the river and hampering its motion yet further.

For most of the Achelous' course, motion appears to triumph over rest as water bears away earth. At the final stage, however, the process is reversed, as earth reclaims its own from its rival, forcing it to become its collaborator. This is a wonderful parable of a world conceived as an equilibrium between motion and rest maintained only by the conflict of the two of which now one and now the other appears to have the better. At 3.89.1–5 (his account of the inundations at Atalanta and Peparethus during the sixth year of the war) Thucydides offers counterbalancing examples of the sea encroaching on the land. He ascribes these inundations to earthquakes, to motions racking (and shaping) the domain of apparent stability or rest. Here as elsewhere it is not merely the opposition but the interplay or interaction of motion and rest that shapes the Thucydidean cosmos.

As for the Delphic god, he plays no role in this outcome so fortunate for Alcmaeon. (Here, at least, "what is said of Alcmaeon" agrees with Thucydides' observations.) No deity will intervene to end the wandering of the fugitive, but silt enough will do so. Ritual purification yields to natural process. What Auden said of poetry we may say of the god: he makes nothing happen. To appreciate the full force of this example we must recall that Alcmaeon's counterpart in the Attic epic tradition was Orestes. Thucydides hints at a world in which rest and motion have replaced the gods as first principles. This passage shows him at both his most serious and his most playful.

THE NATURAL LAW AND THE DIVINE LAW

Yet we do not do the gods justice if we consider the reinterpretation of the world as a natural interplay of motion and rest as implying simply their debunking and dismissal. Strauss (1964, 161) suggests that if "the divine law properly understood is the interplay of motion and rest, [then] one must study [Thucydides'] work in the light of the question of how that divine law is related to the divine law in the ordinary sense."

Much later in his essay (190) Strauss returns to this question.

> Taking the question of right entirely by itself, i.e. disregarding the gods altogether, one may say that there is a kinship between injustice and motion and between justice and rest, but that just as rest presupposes motion and issues in motion, justice presupposes injustice and issues in injustice. It is precisely for this reason that human beings seek support for right in the gods or that the question of right cannot be considered entirely apart from the question concerning the gods.

Strauss thus links Thucydides' concern with the question of the gods in the ordinary sense with that interplay of rest and motion that he has earlier conjectured was the "divine law properly understood." Paradoxically, "taking the question of right entirely by itself, disregarding the gods altogether" yields the conclusion that "this question cannot be considered entirely apart from the question concerning the gods." The inevitable weakness of justice in a world with no "gods" but rest and motion and as such indifferent to our deepest human longings explains the inseparability of the issue of justice from that of the divine. It is therefore precisely Thucydides' teaching on nature that supports Strauss's seemingly enigmatic conclusion (241) that he "open[s] [us] to the full impact of the all-important question which is coeval with philosophy although the philosophers do not frequently pronounce it—the question *quid sit deus.*"

Human Nature and Nonhuman Nature

Thucydides could not have contemplated human nature without considering how it was related to the rest of nature. He could not have raised the question of human action without posing that of its relation to action or motion generally. It is this question to which his treatment of rest and motion ventures a provisional answer.[5]

While irreducible to the subpolitical,[6] politics is continuous with it in manifesting rest and motion. It participates in a natural dynamic that Thucydides shows to be neither wholly unintelligible to us nor wholly subject to our control. Is this the ultimate truth of which the "Athenian thesis" is an intuition? Nature issues in torrents that (as in the case of the river Achelous) it sometimes limits by dikes of its own, but Thucydides does not anticipate Machiavelli by exhorting us to erect dikes of our own (cf. also 4.75.2 with the *Prince*, Chapter 25). The war and the *stasis* that accompanies it are the outcomes

---

[5] My thanks to Brad Inwood for the suggestion that of known "pre-Socratic" thinkers the one to whose account of the cosmos Thucydides appears to owe the most is Empedocles. On Thucydides' relation to the natural science of his time see also Rosalind Thomas, chapter 33 in this volume.

[6] Cf. Proietti (1992, 192–93).

of human decisions, but they overwhelm the power of decision. They are the work of agents but they overwhelm the power of agency. The wise statesman will recognize that political life is never fully within the grasp of the actors.

Human nature as it discloses itself in politics thus reflects nature as we can observe it otherwise. Or we could state this the other way around: Thucydides offers evidence that the rest of nature mirrors politics. He clearly rejects the dismissal of the political as such as conventional. He encourages us to approach nature as a whole through that part of it that is most accessible to us. What we can grasp of the nonhuman realm confirms its continuity with the human. Whatever Thucydides' differences with the Socratics, here is another way in which he anticipates them.

References

Balot, Ryan K. 2015. "Philosophy and 'Humanity': Reflections on Thucydidean Piety, Justice and Necessity." In *In Search of Humanity*, edited by Andrea Radasanu, 17–36. Lanham: Lexington.
Burns, Timothy W. 2012. "Nicias in Thucydides and Aristophanes Part I: Nicias and Divine Justice in Thucydides," *Polis* 29 (2): 217–33.
Ludwig, Paul W. 2002. *Eros and Polis: Desire and Community in Greek Political Theory*. Cambridge: Cambridge University Press.
Macleod, C. W. 1974. "Form and Meaning in the Melian Dialogue." *Historia* 23: 385–400.
Price, Jonathan J. 2001. *Thucydides and Internal War*. Cambridge: Cambridge University Press.
Proietti, Gerald. 1992. "The Natural World and the Political World in Thucydides' History." In *Law and Philosophy: Essays in Honor of George Anastaplo*, edited by John A. Murley et al., 184–94. Athens: Ohio University Press.
Strauss, Leo. 1964. *The City and Man*. Chicago: Rand McNally.

CHAPTER 22

THUCYDIDES AND THE POLITICS OF NECESSITY

MARK FISHER AND KINCH HOEKSTRA

THUCYDIDES' Pericles concludes his first speech to the Athenian assembly with a rousing call to arms: "You must know that it is a necessity to be at war—and we will have opponents who are less eager if we accept it more willingly—and that, for both a private individual and a city, the greatest honors result from the greatest risks" (1.144.3).[1] As rhetorically powerful as this exhortation is, Pericles might seem fundamentally confused about the nature of necessity. As the sovereign judge of Athenian policy, the assembled citizen body may presently decide against this war by offering the concessions that the Spartans demand, and even to follow Pericles' counsel will be a choice the Athenians have made. In claiming that "it is a necessity to be at war (*anankē polemein*)," does Pericles deny this choice? It seems not, for Pericles is exhorting them to make one choice and not another. In what sense, then, is the war necessary?

These tensions are not just a mismatch between a speech and its practical context. Having insisted that war is a necessity, Pericles himself immediately turns to the vocabulary of freely chosen action. "We will have opponents who are less eager," he says, "if we accept it more willingly (*hekousioi mallon*)." This seems to imply that the Athenians might choose to resist what he has just identified as necessary, though it would be imprudent for them to do so. But necessity seems to render such prudential judgment moot. Pericles then insists that the Athenians will make themselves eligible for "the greatest honors (*megistai timai*)" by confronting "the greatest risks (*megistōn kindunōn*)," which in this case means to "accept more willingly" a war that is necessary. If the Athenians are confronting the greatest dangers willingly, we might understand how their valor could win them honor. But if they confront these dangers because they have to? We usually think that people deserve neither praise nor blame for what they do necessarily.

---

[1] All translations are our own unless otherwise noted. We gratefully acknowledge the assistance of Ryan K. Balot, Seth Jaffe, Derin McLeod, Nikolaos Papazarkadas, and Darien Shanske.

How are we to make sense of Pericles' call to win honor by freely choosing a necessary war? Given Thucydides' reverence for Pericles' intellectual abilities (1.139.4, 2.65.8), it is unlikely that he is presenting him as incoherent. Perhaps Thucydides is instead depicting Pericles' gift for political rhetoric, the art of persuading an audience of one's counsel. How better to convince the Athenian people to go to war than by persuading them that it is at the same time necessary, prudent, and honorable? Thucydides' own claim that the war was necessary (1.23.6; cf. 1.88.1), however, primes us to see that there is more to Pericles' rhetoric than mere manipulation.

Pericles' exhortation to war presents the modern reader with puzzles concerning the nature of necessitated action, a central category throughout Thucydides' work. The upshot may not be that he misunderstands what we mean by necessity, but that we misunderstand what he means by it. Attending both to Thucydides' text and to his intellectual context can resolve these puzzles and illuminate the meanings of political necessity therein. It can also help us to recognize claims of necessity that are in harmony with choice, responsibility, and honor.

Necessity and Choice

As in English, claims of necessity in ancient Greek could be made by using a number of different words and indicating a number of different senses. In speaking of necessity, ancient Greeks frequently used the noun *anankē* and its related verb, adverb, and adjective. These words are usually translated unproblematically as "necessity," "to necessitate," etc., though sometimes "constraint" or "compulsion" is more appropriate. There are also other ways to refer to necessity in Greek. There are the impersonal verbs *chrē* and *dei*, both of which assert a need for some thing or some action. There are verbal adjectives and verbs in the imperative mood. There is the word *akōn*, which means that one's action is against one's wishes, and marks that one is acting according to some constraining necessity.

In Greek literature before Thucydides, the forces said to necessitate are diverse: physical constraint, the gods, military or political command, natural phenomena such as storms, imminent threat to one's life or one's family, poverty, persuasive speech, hunger, lust. In surveying such claims, we can see that many writers were comfortable speaking of actions as necessitated both when they were voluntary (*hekōn*) and when they were involuntary or undertaken unwillingly (*ouch hekōn*, *akōn*). These cases seem to be importantly different, however. In certain circumstances, there is literally nothing one can do to escape the force of an overpowering wind, an attacking enemy, or a swelling wave. In these cases of "hard necessity," one can resist with all of one's might and still get swept away. For the Greeks as for us, however, most claims that it is necessary for someone to do something are not claims of this type. Instead, they describe intentional action constrained in some significant way by powers over which one has little or no control. Most claims to necessity, that is, involve an action that is both *hekōn*, voluntary, and *akōn*, against one's wishes. We can call such a claim one of *practical necessity*, being a claim about what must be done in the circumstances one is in, given one's commitments and character. For example, it is in this way that the Trojan men are necessitated to stay and fight the approaching Achaeans outside the city wall (*Iliad* 8.57). With their wives and children inside, the Trojans do not fight involuntarily, for example by being physically forced to fight; they choose to fight because they see no real alternative. Indeed, Homer's Greek suggests they *yearn* to fight (8.56, *memasan*). Surrendering their families to rape and slavery does not present itself as an option for them: it is not just that they prefer on balance to fight and quite possibly die, but that in some sense they must do so. They ardently choose what they must choose.

This talk of necessitated choice will look confused to those modern readers who assume that when there is necessity, there is no choice, and vice versa. Even in those cases that appear most like hard necessity, however, we see that Thucydides is describing necessitated choice, not necessity precluding choice. Thus, for instance, in the final use of an *ananke* word in the text, Thucydides relates that Mindarus was forced (*anankastheis*) to put into port at Icarus after he was caught in a storm (8.99.1). Thucydides is not saying that the storm drove Mindarus into port as a matter of hard necessity. He is instead saying that, because of the storm, Mindarus was compelled to make for port and seek safety rather than carrying on to his destination.

Martin Ostwald (1988, 7–19), in a notable word study of *ananke*, has convincingly argued that there is not a single case of hard necessity to be found associated with this term in Thucydides. He concludes that Thucydides adhered to an understanding of necessity that Ostwald (like von Fritz before him) calls "psychological" and that we might label "interpretive": for Thucydides, necessity was the result of beliefs and attitudes that led agents to think they had but one course of action open to them. Mindarus' commitment to the preservation of his fleet and his belief that the storm threatened this go unmentioned by Thucydides, but they must be assumed if the claim to necessitation is to make sense. In other cases, Thucydides more clearly spells out the underlying conditions of practical necessitation. For instance, it was the combination of the Mytileneans' desire to revolt from Athens, Athenian awareness of their plan, and Mytilenean unpreparedness that forced (*anankasthentes*) them to revolt before they were ready (3.2.1–3.4.2). Both the force of circumstances and the agent's aims and beliefs (not least about these circumstances) were essential to account for the necessitated action.

NECESSITY, NATURE, AND THE SUPERNATURAL

It is important not to misstate the implications of Ostwald's conclusion, which do not extend to a general claim that a conception of necessary causation is absent from Thucydides. Thucydides clearly endorses and employs the idea of what we would call a necessary cause. In explaining a series of tidal waves in 426 BCE, for instance, he identifies earthquakes as their cause (*aition*), concluding that "without an earthquake, it seems to me, such a thing would not have happened" (3.89.5). But Thucydides does not characterize this kind of causal relationship in the language of necessity, though we habitually do so. In this way, Thucydides implicitly but consistently differentiates between the causal forces at work in the natural world and the necessity that compels human action through human judgment.

If the meaning of necessity in Thucydides' text is not equivalent to the modern conception of causal determinism, we might think that there is instead a more ancient and prescientific idea at work: necessity as supernaturally determined fate. Thucydides would have known this conception of necessity well from its prominence in myth, epic, and tragedy. In this milieu, *Ananke* was sometimes represented as a divinity. In visual art, Necessity is winged but intently walking in the same direction as a strong wind (Sidorova 2001, 34 and plate 30, lekythos dated to c. 470–460 BCE). In a self-consciously archaic myth, Plato (*Republic* 10 617b-e; cf. Aeschylus?, *Prometheus Bound* 515–16, 103–105, 936) identifies Necessity as the mother of the Fates, one of whom says that each person is responsible for and necessarily bound to his or her own choice of life. The tragic vision depended on conceptions of Fate darkly unspooling according to Necessity. Oedipus must live out his fate, as must Achilles, Odysseus, and Ajax. Humans must, by the nature of their condition, be ruled by the gods. Yet, in epic and tragedy, human life is depicted as overdetermined, agents freely choosing their way to divinely determined ends. Given the richness of this association between necessity, choice, and divine determination, we might profitably wonder whether this sense is at work in Thucydides' text.

Ultimately, however, there is no reason to think that Thucydides believed in supernatural necessitation or used this understanding of necessity. The idea does appear at least once in the text. Responding to the plague, and repudiating accusations that his policies were to blame for it, Pericles exhorts: "One must endure the acts of gods as a matter of necessity (*anankaiōs*)" (2.64.2). The similarity of this statement to lines in the Homeric Hymn to Demeter (147) and Aeschylus' *Persae* (293) suggests that this was a deeply traditional sentiment (see also Sophocles, *Philoctetes* 1316–17; Euripides, *Phoenissae* 382, 1763). We can understand why Pericles would have drawn on this rhetoric in this situation, especially given the strong association between plague and divine resentment in the traditional Greek worldview. But there is no evidence to suggest that Thucydides himself adopted a supernatural explanation of the plague, or of any other aspect of the war. His references to necessity surveyed above are to choices constrained by human circumstances and beliefs, not the cryptic workings of the divine.

There is one important conception of necessity that sits awkwardly with the paradigm of practical necessitation, however, and resembles tragic overdetermination in important respects. In the Melian Dialogue, most famously, the Athenians contend that a natural imperative compels all people to rule whenever they have the power to do so (5.105.2; cf. 4.61.5). The universality of the claim for this "necessity of nature" (*phuseōs anankaias*) distinguishes it from context-dependent claims of chosen practical necessity.

There is something recognizably tragic about this framing of a psychological drive in terms of necessity. In the surviving works of Euripides we find with particular frequency the claim that *erōs*, or lust, acts on humans as a necessitating force. This claim is importantly different, of course: *erōs* is not only a compelling physical urge, but also the tool with which Aphrodite achieves her ends. The necessity of lust is supernatural, as a number of Euripidean characters claim (Jason, Phaedra's nurse, Helen), not just psychological. In this way it looks to be "harder" than if it were only a psychological impulse, for one is acting under the compulsion of an external and implacable force, the god's command. It would seem to be an unavoidable fate, overpowering even the most determined efforts to escape it.

Euripides nonetheless depicts characters who struggle against this simultaneously psychological and supernatural necessity. Phaedra, for instance, refers to her desire for her son-in-law Hippolytus, as well as the ruin that it is causing her, as occurring without either of them intending it (*Hippolytus* 319, *philos m' apollus' ouch hekousan ouch hekōn*). Phaedra's lust looks to be a case of hard necessity, imposed as it is by an implacable goddess. Yet Hippolytus is entirely unyielding in the face of *erōs* and Phaedra valiantly resists acting on her urges, holing up in the palace and trying to starve herself to death. Although neither escape Aphrodite's ultimate plan for them, both characters demonstrate that lust, however controlling it may feel, is a different kind of compulsion from external, physical necessitation.

In Euripides' *The Trojan Women*, performed in the spring of 415 BCE, a few months after the Athenian conquest of Melos (surely a significant context for that performance, despite the doubts of Erp Taalman Kip [1987] and others), we see the supernatural necessity of *erōs* being directly contested. Here, Helen faces off against Hecuba in an *agōn* over the former's culpability for the war (906–1032). Helen pleads that she cannot be held responsible for running off with Paris: Aphrodite gave her as a prize, and when Paris came to Sparta, he had Aphrodite's powers at hand, acting as her appointed avenger (*alastōr*). How could she resist? How could she be blamed for failing to resist?

> Why did I do it? What made me run away from home
> with the stranger, and betray my country and my hearth?
> Challenge the goddess then; show your strength greater than Zeus'
> who has the other gods in his power, and still is slave
> to Aphrodite alone! Shall I not be forgiven? (946–50, translated in Lattimore 2012)

In the same scene, Hecuba characterizes Zeus as a "natural necessity," or *anankē phuseos* (886), a phrase very similar to that of Thucydides' Athenians in Melos (5.105.2). Nonetheless, she dismisses the idea that Helen's lust is supernaturally determined and to be forgiven on account of its necessity. Helen and Hecuba dramatically present necessity's two faces: the powerful force that constrains us to act in a certain way, and yet, because of this, also the powerful excuse that can be used to try to justify our wrongful actions. Their *agōn* suggests that the exculpatory power of psychological urges was, at the very least, contested in Athens during the final decades of the fifth century.

Even before the Melian affair, to justify or deflect attention from wrongdoing by arguing from the necessity of nature could be derided as chicanery. In the famous debate in which a personified Unjust Argument confutes and converts his rival Just Argument, Aristophanes has Unjust Argument explain his techniques:

> I will go on from there to the necessities of nature (*tas tēs phuseōs anankas*). You've erred, you've fallen in love, you've had a bit of an affair, and then you've been caught. You're done for, because you're not able to argue. But if you become my pupil you can indulge your nature, leap and laugh, think nothing shameful. If by chance you are seized as an adulterer, this is what you will reply to the husband: that you have done nothing wrong (*hōs ouden ēdikēkas*). Then make reference to Zeus, saying that even he is unable to resist lust and women, and how can you, a mortal, be stronger than a god? (*Clouds* 1075–82, modified from Sommerstein 1982; cf. Gorgias, *Helen* 6–21)

Necessities drive history as they drive tragedy, but the glib application of necessity as a universal solvent of all responsibility is recognized as pernicious farce. When Thucydides attributes to the Athenians at Melos an appeal to a comprehensive justification for acting on natural impulses, Athenian audiences had long been laughing at such self-serving rationalizations of injustice.

Necessity, Responsibility, and Character

Despite his conviction that people share a common human nature (2.50.1, 3.82.2, [3.84.2]; cf. 1.22.4, 5.68.2), Thucydides recognized that different communities possessed and cultivated different collective characters (8.96.5), which in turn influenced how their members interpreted and pursued their interests. Thus, despite the universal pull of self-interest, the diversity of political cultures precluded any universal model of human nature that could explain human action in all of its variability and specificity. To account for why individuals or groups acted as they did in a given situation, Thucydides suggests that it is crucial to know something about their particular character, not just that they are humans pursuing their interests.

Thucydides frames the Athenians and Spartans as peoples of disparate national characters already in the Archaeology, but the most vivid portrait of this contrast comes in the Corinthians' speech at the Spartan congress (1.68–71). The Athenians are portrayed as a recklessly active people, wanting what they don't have and constantly trying to get it. For them, to pursue one's interests means to try to acquire more. The Spartans, on the other hand, are portrayed as inactive and conservative, a people preoccupied with keeping what they already have. Both groups feel the pull of nature's necessity, but they feel it pull in different directions. The Corinthians thus characterize the Athenians and Spartans as fundamentally different in how they respond to necessity when it is felt. The

Spartans dither, refraining from doing what they must for as long as they can (1.70.2). The Athenians, on the other hand, pursue what is necessary (*ta deonta*) as keenly as if they were going to a festival (1.70.8). While the Corinthians have a practical motive to paint such contrasting pictures of these collective personalities, Thucydides himself endorsed the contrast and employed it to great explanatory effect (see especially 8.96.5).

A number of political theorists have identified contrasting outlooks on necessitated action and the demands of justice as the most important difference between the Spartans and the Athenians. According to Clifford Orwin (1994), the Spartans maintain that humans have the choice to act justly or not and therefore always bear the burden of moral responsibility for their actions. The Athenians, however, characteristically hold that necessity defines the human condition, as the strong are compelled by fear, honor, and expediency to rule over the weak. The compulsion of these psychological forces, Orwin's Athenians suggest, exculpates them from injustice committed on behalf of the empire, as it does anyone driven to action by such forces. Given that they claim that fear, honor, and expediency are ubiquitous motivations for political action, this "Athenian thesis" suggests to Orwin a radical loss of moral responsibility from the political world.

Whether or not Thucydides blamed the Athenians would thus seem to hinge on whether he believed that they had to act as they did. The previous section suggested, however, that Thucydides and his readers may have doubted the natural necessity of ruling whenever one has the power to do so, thus leaving rulers responsible for their rule. Moreover, there is reason to think that an assumption of the broad incompatibility of necessity and responsibility is either a modern projection onto Thucydides' text, or a generalization of a position that would have been seen as tendentious. Consider again the context of Athenian tragedy, which frequently presents characters who live out their lives according to the necessity of a divine plan and are nevertheless held responsible for their actions. Although Oedipus, for example, is compelled by the gods to murder his father and commit incest with his mother, he is deeply shamed by these actions, and the gods punish all of Thebes for his transgressions with a devastating plague. For Oedipus, necessity and responsibility form a tragic union, not an antithetical pair (Williams 1993, especially chapter 6; for an application to Thucydides, see Balot 2015, 23–26). Sophocles' presentation of Oedipus suggests that Thucydides and his contemporaries could hold the Athenians responsible even for necessitated transgressions.

In thinking of Thucydides as a sort of tragic critic of Athenian democracy, it is important to remember that in fifth-century Greek culture, tragic necessity was not only a vehicle for blame. It was also a vehicle for honor and greatness. The capacity to endure supernaturally necessitated sufferings was a cardinal virtue of the Greek hero, both in Homeric epic and Athenian tragedy, as was the capacity to cause great suffering for others. One of the epithets of Odysseus, for instance, was *polutlas*, "much-enduring" or "much-suffering," and he can claim to have endured as much hardship as anyone (*Odyssey* 7.211–12). Achilles, likewise, endures god-sent sufferings over the course of the *Iliad*; his very name suggests grief or pain (*achos*) (Nagy 1979, 69–93), while his fame depends on his own destruction (*Iliad* 9.410–16). As a tragic hero, Thucydides' Athenians, even if compelled, would be eligible not only for blame, but everlasting glory.

Can such a tragic perspective be found in Thucydides' text? It is tempting to move from the argument that Thucydides innovates by extending the scientific approach of the Hippocratic medical writers to social and political action (cf. Cochrane 1929, Ober 2006, Thomas 2012) to the idea that he sought to break radically from the methods and explanatory structures of the literary tradition. The latter position appears to gain support from Thucydides' early polemic against previous prose writers and poets (1.21–22). But Thucydides is very specific about his objection: they distorted their accounts in order to make them more attractive for their audiences (1.21.1). As a result, they were inaccurate and unreliable. Thucydides' major contribution is to be that he will privilege accuracy over the qualities that make a work immediately pleasing (1.22.4). We find here no censure of traditional modes of heroic explanation or evaluation.

Far from wholly rejecting a heroic or tragic perspective, Thucydides shows from his very first sentence that his work is motivated by and oriented to greatness. He asserts that he began the project of recording the war because he "expected it to be great (*megan*) and more worthy of account (*axiologōtaton*) than any before it" (1.1.1). This expectation, he explains, was based upon the buildup to the war being "the greatest mobilization (*kinēsis megistē*: see Rusten 2015) among the Greeks and some part of the barbarians; one might say, among the greater part of humankind" (1.1.2). Thucydides, like his predecessors, chose to write about a great war, thinking greatness most worthy of account. His war differed from theirs most importantly, he says, because it was even greater than any before it—an affirmation that only confirms that he shares with prior authors of great wars the heroic metric of value.

Following soon after this opening characterization of the war's greatness, Thucydides continues to work in a recognizably tragic mode, underlining the relationship between superlative greatness and unsurpassed suffering:

> Of earlier events, the greatest to have happened was the Persian War, and yet that was swiftly decided by two naval battles and two land battles. The length of this war was far greater, and more suffering (*pathēmata*) was endured by the Greeks in this than in any comparable period of time. For never had so many cities been laid waste once captured, either by the barbarians or by the Greeks warring against each other . . . nor had there been so many men exiled and murdered, some due to war and others to civil strife. (1.23.1–2)

This passage has given commentators pause (e.g., Connor 1984, 30–32), suggesting to them that Thucydides must be subverting the traditional understanding of greatness by making it synonymous with suffering. Thucydides may indeed innovate in how he frames the suffering of this war, but the connection between greatness and suffering is neither new nor subversive. Epic and tragedy had always focused on the fearsome mental and physical traumas of greatness, and the greatest of heroes are marked out by exceptional suffering: Heracles, Oedipus, Achilles, Hector, Odysseus. Thucydides' primary theme of greatness and suffering is characteristic of the heroic worldview, though like other authors in early Greek literature he has a distinctive approach to it. Integral to

Thucydides' innovation is his deep reflection on the *dēmos* itself as heroic, as the collective takes on the power, honor, and depravity of the heroic king (see Hoekstra 2016 on this theme).

Glory, greatness, and suffering again reinforce one another in Thucydides' analysis of Athenian defeat after the death of Pericles (2.65.5–13). Thucydides lauds Pericles for leading Athens to its greatest height during peacetime and for accurately understanding its capacities in times of war. For proof that Athens really was as great as Pericles had said it was, and that the Athenians were capable of outlasting the Spartans as he said they could, Thucydides points to the extraordinary amount of suffering that they were able to endure before being overcome:

> Having suffered ruin in Sicily, in the greater part of the navy, and in other war materials as well, and with the city already in a state of civil strife, [the Athenians] nevertheless endured against their original enemies for [eight] more years, and with them the Sicilians as well, and against the still greater number of tributary allies who rebelled, and later against Cyrus, the son of the Persian King, who joined as ally against them and provided money for the Peloponnesians to build a navy, and they did not give in until they were led by personal quarrels to attack themselves and were finally defeated. (2.65.12; cf. 2.64.3)

Thucydides' style here accentuates the almost endless amount of endurance that the Athenians demonstrated before they were vanquished at last. With each relentless clause of this protracted sentence, stretched to its syntactical limits with lists and additions, the Greek reader feels each successive blow that landed on Athens. It is thus all the more impressive that the Athenians endured for years against these mounting odds. Their unremitting opponents cannot break the Athenians, and the passage leaves open the possibility that they could have held out against their external enemies indefinitely if they had not turned on themselves. And Thucydides further suggests that the Athenians even endured civil war for some time, adding to the awesomeness of their resilience. Thucydides demonstrates that the Athenians, pitted against the greater part of the known world, and eventually against themselves, far exceeded any of the figures of epic and tragedy in the capacity for heroic endurance. It was fitting that, in the greatest of wars, the greatest of heroes should fall.

Necessity, Imperialism, and Injustice

Some have perceived an underlying principle that unites the Athenians' arguments concerning the relationship between empire, necessity, and justice. This principle is thought to be revealed in the Athenians' first speech in the work, at the Spartan Congress. The Athenians there assert the maxim that "one is altogether blameless when looking after oneself (*to xumpheronta . . . eu tithesthai*) amid the greatest dangers" (1.75.5). This is a premise of the Athenians' argument that they are not to be blamed for their empire. The Athenians argue that they are in "the greatest dangers" precisely because of their empire, as the imperial subjects are hostile and rebellious. Should they lose imperial control, they would face the immediate revenge of their former subjects, and fear of this prospect compels them (like any other autocratic ruler) to maintain their rule (1.75.4; cf. 1.75.1–3). The Athenians contend that hatred of their rule itself compels them to continue it, and that they are absolved of any associated injustice because of the grave risk they face.

This argument echoes elsewhere in the text (e.g., 2.63.1–3, 3.37.2), but we should be wary of identifying it as the essential Athenian position. For the text suggests that there may not be an essential Athenian argument, as the Athenians' claims repeatedly change in both subtle and significant ways. This is especially notable when we look at the work as a whole, but is even true within the speech at Sparta itself.

Prior to arguing for the necessity of maintaining their empire, the Athenians argue that it was necessary to acquire it. The source of the necessity to acquire empire was not, as it could not then have been, the hatred of the imperial subjects. Rather, the Athenians argue, they found themselves confronted by the confluence of three different circumstances that gave them no choice but to take the empire: the Persian threat, Sparta's departure from the anti-Persian alliance, and the invitation to replace the Spartans as leader of this alliance (1.75.2). In this situation, they argue, they were forced (*katēnankasthēmen*) to establish their empire, "first by fear, then by honor, and finally by advantage (*ōphelias*)" (1.75.3). Pointing to the perilous situation that they were in, as well as the motivating force of fear, the Athenians look here to be making an argument from practical necessity. The inclusion of honor and advantage as necessitating forces, however, makes this argument an unusually encompassing one. Rather than using the argument from necessity for its reductive clarity, identifying a single value or aim such as self-preservation to trump all others, it suggests that the acquisition of empire was overdetermined for the Athenians by overlapping claims of practical necessity. This suggestion is simultaneously rendered doubtful by claiming that sources of action that appear to be optional (such as advantage) truly necessitate.

This emphasis on fear, honor, and advantage is picked up when the Athenians argue for the natural necessity of the rule of the strong over the weak:

> We have done nothing amazing or deviant from normal human behavior if we accepted an empire that was being given and did not give it up, overcome (*nikēthentes*) by the greatest—honor, fear, and advantage; nor in turn are we the first to do such a thing, but rather it has always been the case that the weaker are coerced (*kateirgesthai*) by the stronger. (1.76.2)

The participle *nikēthentes*, here translated as "overcome," suggests the hard necessity of coercion through physical domination. Thucydides accentuates this suggestion with the adjectival phrase "the greatest" (*tōn megistōn*), which identifies who has overcome the Athenians. In making the adjective modify a noun, as English demands, many translators look ahead to what sits in apposition: honor, fear, and advantage. They thus suggest that we read this as "greatest motivations." Modern editors of Thucydides' Greek text have also tried to define *tōn megistōn* by inserting a "three" (*triōn*) into the adjectival phrase. But both attempts at greater specificity undercut the rhetorical magnification suggested by the Greek: *tōn megistōn*, left by itself, puts the reader in mind of the greatest possible conquerors, the most potent forces of the natural, supernatural, and human world. These psychological forces are thus depicted as if they were the hardest of necessities, suggesting that the Athenians would not be any less responsible for their actions if forced by the hand of god. The Athenians paint themselves as at once the stronger and the weaker party, coerced to coerce.

The Athenians build onto this argument from natural necessity a claim that they should be commended for the justice that they have demonstrated in the administration of their empire. "They are worthy of praise," they assert, "who are more just than their present power requires of them when following human nature and ruling over others" (1.76.3). But this move would seem to contradict the ubiquitousness of necessity in imperial life and the consequent exculpation of imperial injustice. If the Athenians are capable of the ethical responsibility needed to be just, how can they claim to be excused of all injustice?

We do not find a clear and programmatic statement of the Athenians' position in their speech at Sparta, but rather three different arguments that overlap even as they are at odds with one another. This pattern of parallelism, tension, and overdetermination is characteristic of the ways in which the Athenians argue from necessity, both in individual speeches and across the text. Despite echoes in theme and form, their arguments are always changing.

Pericles offers a fine example of this pattern. In his third speech, he too argues that it is practically necessary to maintain the empire, but he does so to different ends. Like the Athenians in Sparta, he insists that it is prohibitively dangerous to give up the empire, on account of the animosity their rule has engendered (2.63.1). But Pericles does not use this argument to excuse Athenian wrongdoing. Rather, he boldly says to the Athenians, "you already hold your empire like a tyranny, one that seems unjust to take but perilous to let go" (2.63.2). Pericles suggests that the Athenians must stay the course even if it was embarked upon unjustly.

Another argument from practical necessity that Pericles gives is based on honor rather than self-preservation. The logic of the argument is simple: the Athenians must stand up to the Spartans and fight because their freedom and honor are at stake (1.140.2, 1.141.1; cf. 2.63.1). To give in to the Spartans' demands is tantamount to becoming their slaves, Pericles argues, placing the honor that the Athenians had accrued since the Persian Wars on the line. The Athenians cannot give this up, Pericles asserts, and thus there is no choice but to fight.

With this argument, Pericles again departs from the simple idea that necessity exculpates, and he does so in a heroic register. He begins his first speech with the imperative "you must not yield (*mē eikein*) to the Peloponnesians," and this thought echoes throughout his two assembly speeches (1.140.1, 1.141.1, 2.64.3; cf. 2.60.1, 2.61.1). As Bernard Knox (1964, 15–17) noted, the refusal to yield (*eikein*) is characteristic of the

Sophoclean hero. Pericles insists that in following the compelling force of honor and refusing to yield, the Athenians are acting admirably and deserve praise (2.61.1). "It seems right (*eikos*) for you to stand up for the honor (*tōi timōmenōi*) the city receives from ruling an empire, honor that glorifies you all," he tells the Athenians, "and for you not to shrink from the labors, or not to pursue the honors (*tas timas*)" (2.63.1). Pericles makes clear that the Athenians effectively must follow the pull of honor, which requires stubbornly heroic action liable to praise and blame. He states that the Athenians will win everlasting glory for themselves by standing up to the Spartans, becoming the envy of every active man (2.64.3–5). At the same time, Pericles accepts that they will incur blame for this course of action. Men of an idle disposition will disparage the project, he suggests, and contemporaries will find the Athenians odious. Pericles suggests that this blame is not simply nullified by Athenian necessity. It will be greatly overshadowed by Athenian glory in the future, however, and is therefore worth incurring (2.64.4–5).

In the Melian Dialogue, the Athenians do reject blame for their empire. They dismiss justice and injustice altogether, as irrelevant to a party so superior in power (5.89.1). To the Melians' characterization of them as unjust, the Athenians reply only in terms of necessity, not deigning to specify whether such necessity means that what they are doing is just, merely excusable, or beyond categories of culpability. In addition to their argument from "necessity of nature" discussed above, the Athenians depend on the idea that the hatred of their subjects practically necessitates aggressive actions to maintain their empire (5.91.1, 5.97.1). They assert that their subjects interpret the persistence of Melian neutrality as a symbol of Athenian weakness, making their rule over these subjects less secure. The Athenians thus claim to be compelled by their fear of their subjects to subdue the Melians even though they pose no immediate physical threat. Unlike both Pericles and the Athenians at Sparta, therefore, the Athenians at Melos insist (5.95.1, 5.97.1) that the argument for the necessity of maintaining empire implies a further imperative of imperial expansion.

In the Sicilian Debate, Alcibiades articulates another argument for the practical necessity of imperial expansion based on self-preservation. As others do, Alcibiades argues that the empire is in a constant state of existential threat. He does not, however, identify the imperial subjects as the source of this threat. He instead asserts that the Athenian empire's future existence is critically threatened by other imperial powers like themselves, as each seeks to absorb the others (6.18.2–3; cf. 2.63.1, 5.91.1). All aspiring or established imperial powers, Alcibiades suggests, are on a collision course with one another in a contest for survival and supremacy. In such a world, preemptive action against potentially threatening powers such as Syracuse is necessary (*anankē*), "for we are in danger of being ruled by others if we do not rule" (6.18.3). Alcibiades is silent on the question of whether this necessity exculpates the Athenians. Like Pericles before him, Alcibiades is not concerned with the justice of Athenian action, but with convincing the Athenians that they must go to war.

In contrast, Athenians elsewhere agree with their representatives at Sparta that necessity exculpates. Yet these are not straightforward reiterations of the Athenian position in Sparta. For example, Cleon argues that the Mytileneans could be forgiven for their rebellion if they had been forced to revolt by the necessity of their situation, but in fact they revolted out of hubris and therefore deserve punishment (3.39.2–6). Rather than appealing to necessity to excuse the Athenians, Cleon uses it as a foil to accuse the Mytileneans, thus harnessing necessity in a different way to justify the use of Athenian imperial power.

Perhaps the strongest claim of the exculpatory force of necessity comes in the affair of the Athenian occupation of the sanctuary of Apollo at Delium. The Athenians assert that "it is reasonable (*eikos*) that anything done because of a formidable military threat is forgivable, even before the god; for altars are a place of refuge for those who commit involuntary errors (*akousiōn hamartēmatōn*), and we reserve the name 'crime' for those bad deeds that were uncompelled (*tois mē anankēi kakois*)" (4.98.6; cf. 3.40.1). This is another articulation of the idea that whatever is done in the face of imminent physical threat is coerced and therefore excusable. The Athenians extend the exculpatory scope of the claim even further with their claim that the god would pardon action thus compelled. Unlike the Athenians in Sparta, the Athenians at Delium are not concerned with justifying their empire at large, and this argument makes no reference to the structural sources of practical necessity inherent in empire. Rather, the Athenians are defending themselves against very specific charges relating to their occupation of Delium, and the threat they face is a superior Boeotian army waiting to engage them in battle. In speaking about the necessity that they act under, then, they are not speaking about the necessities felt by stronger powers at all. Rather, they take up the position of the weaker power, of men who are staring death in the face.

As this should make clear, there is a conspicuous diversity in the Athenians' arguments from necessity. These arguments do not consistently feature exculpation, empire, or the same source of necessity. What is less clear is what Thucydides is doing amid all of this variety. Is there supposed to be a right version of this argument that many Athenians get wrong? Are we seeing the Athenians change their understanding as they become increasingly drunk on power? Or are we simply seeing the Athenians make whatever arguments they can, given the different situations that they are in?

Rhetorical Necessity

The variability of Athenian appeals to necessity leads to the suspicion that their underlying commitment is not to a particular view of necessity, but to saying what they think will best bring about their aims in speaking. Interpretations of Thucydides offered in the last fifty years would have us wonder further whether the appeal to necessity (and to reality more generally) is just a powerful rhetorical move in an ineluctably discursive universe. For most of the twentieth century, Thucydides was presented as focused on *erga* rather than *logos*, scientifically seeking to report the truth of events and excavate the underlying realities of power. On this view, the speeches in the text were seen as either epiphenomenal or—in some cases—as revealing authorial belief. More recently,

Thucydidean scholarship took a linguistic turn. The speeches came to be read less as statements of the speakers' or author's belief and more as rhetorical constructions by Thucydidean characters. Even Thucydides' presentation of the *erga* of the war is a *logos*, it was emphasized, and he uses his own speech to manipulate the reader's expectations and emotional states (Stahl 1966; Parry 1969, 1972; Connor 1977). It may be tempting to conclude that Thucydides gives us *logos* all the way down, that even his own apparent objectivity is but the adoption of "an authorial stance, a device, a mode by which the author presented himself to the reader" (Connor 1984, 6, 8).

Early in his work, Thucydides states that the speeches he relates are some mixture of the actual policy (*gnōmē*) of the historical speaker and his own judgment of "what was most necessary for each speaker to say" (1.22.1, *ta deonta malist' eipein*). This reveals little about the logic driving Thucydides' own contribution. He says that the speeches were written according to "what was most necessary" but apparently leaves open the meaning or kind of necessity. Colin Macleod (1983, 52) has suggested that Thucydides' Greek is not as vague as it seems. Referring to Gorgias' *Helen* (2) and Plato's *Phaedrus* (234e6), Macleod maintains that *ta deonta eipein* specifically refers to the sophistic art of saying what was necessary to persuade an audience. On this reading, Thucydides programmatically reveals to his reader that the speeches are constructed according to a logic of rhetorical necessity.

Some claims of necessity within the speeches are themselves readily describable as rhetorical necessities. Speakers frequently make reference to the necessity that they say certain things, or that they say them in a particular way. The Corinthians begin with an emphatic assertion that it is necessary to respond to the Corcyraeans' accusations against them and to prove that they are in the right (1.37.1). Diodotus states that one must lie in order to be believed in the Athenian assembly (3.43.2). The Melians say that it is necessary to argue in terms of interest as the Athenians demand (5.90.1). In beginning his speech in Sparta, Alcibiades insists that it is first necessary to address the slanders made against him (6.89.1). Rhetorical necessity of this kind is similar to the practical necessity of which examples were given earlier, though the necessitating end is not self-preservation or honor in the first instance, but the need to persuade or otherwise motivate one's audience.

Such persuasion is always in the service of further aims, however, and the need to persuade an audience can even be a straightforward case of the practical necessity of self-preservation. In the case of the Melians, for instance (and in some way too for the Plataeans), persuasion could have meant survival. Those who failed to persuade were instead sentenced to death by their audience. Death is not confined to discourse, and whatever the nature of Thucydides' project, it must depend on a conviction that such actions and events occurred not merely in speech but in deed. The consequences are not only discursive, but discourse has real consequences. Indeed, that is *why* Thucydides gives us the *logoi* of historical actors, and why he gave us his own *logos*, which he hoped above all else would be useful for future readers (1.22.4).

Were we to take Thucydides' speakers at their word, we might be astonished at their view of the pervasiveness of constraints on action. It is clear, however, that necessity is frequently invoked because it is thought to be rhetorically effective. We have suggested that a tragic conception of necessity that is compatible with responsibility is at work in Thucydides' text. Nonetheless, the Athenians and others sometimes draw on a judicial conception of responsibility precluded by necessity: defending against accusations of injustice, they claim necessity to disavow responsibility and avert the consequences of blame. In addition, speakers sometimes claim necessity when exhorting their audience to do something. To convince people that they face a situation of practical necessity is to make them believe that they have only one choice open to them; and this is not merely to describe but to create a situation of practical necessity. Believing that they must, they must.

None of this implies that the speakers in Thucydides who make necessity claims are all or only deploying them to manipulate their audience in such ways. Nor does it mean that necessity is merely rhetorical for Thucydides. During his own narration of the war's events, Thucydides often writes of people who are practically necessitated. We have no good reason to doubt the sincerity of Thucydides when he describes the practical necessitation of Mindarus, or invokes necessity in his own voice on other occasions. He so describes a range of hard realities that drive human decisions, as when the long-besieged Potidaeans are driven to cannibalism (2.70.1), Theseus compelled the residents of rural Attica to accept the rule of the city of Athens (2.15.2), and the Athenian subjects before the war find themselves in pressing circumstances (1.99.1). And in his analysis of *stasis*, Thucydides more generally identifies necessity as a characteristic feature of war, providing an explanation immediately grounded in the realities of conflict for why claims of necessity are so pervasive in his work (3.82.2).

Thucydides recognized that necessities were frequent in political life, especially in the contexts of empire and war. Necessity remains the product of straitened circumstances, however, as found above all in war (3.82.2). Such circumstances mean that there is greater motivation to make claims of necessity regardless of their truth, but also that more claims of necessity may truthfully be made.

Necessity, War, and History

We can finally return to Pericles. We wondered at the outset about the consistency of Pericles' counsel to the Athenians to choose what was necessary. This should now appear as an unproblematic claim of practical necessity. We also asked about the coherence of his assertion that the Athenians stood to gain honor by willingly pursuing a war that was necessary. We are now in a position to read Pericles' claim as an exhortation to act heroically in the face of necessity. But we may still wonder about the truth status of Pericles' claim that the war was in fact a necessity.

It is apparent why it would have been rhetorically advantageous for Pericles to frame the war in terms of necessity. Whether or not it was necessary, if he could bring the Athenians to believe that it was, they would have no choice but to follow him to war.

It may be tempting to assume that Pericles did not believe the claim, but exhorted the Athenians to war for his own ends or his perception of theirs. But Thucydides gives us good reason to think otherwise. He directly characterizes Pericles as a leader of superlative integrity (2.65.8), for instance; and most importantly, he offers a claim about the cause of the war that reinforces Pericles' own.

Emphasizing that it is a statement of personal belief (*hēgoumai*), Thucydides identifies "the truest cause" of the war in terms of necessity: "The Athenians were becoming great and causing fear in the Lacedaemonians, which necessitated (*anankasai*) war" (1.23.6). Commentators have long debated whether Thucydides here attributes responsibility for the war to Athens or Sparta. Ostwald (1988, 1–5), however, has convincingly argued that Thucydides had neither city in mind individually, but both together. It was the combination of Athenian greatness and Spartan fear that made war unavoidable, as it made it practically necessary for each city to confront the other.

Thucydides' identification of the truest cause is abbreviated, and later in the text he elaborates these basic elements. For example, it emerges that Pericles himself is critical to Athenian greatness (2.65.5), as well as serving a more direct role in necessitating the war. Athenian character and circumstance also contributed significantly to Athenian greatness, and to the necessity of war. The Athenians were active, competitive, and—as they brilliantly displayed in the Persian Wars—heroically stubborn. Their acquisition, defense, and expansion of the empire bred conflict with the Spartan alliance, to which they also refused to submit. Character and circumstance thus combined to compel the Athenians to confront the Spartans. Thucydides' Pericles sees this clearly and articulates this realization in such a way that the Athenians can see it clearly, too. Pericles plays a vital role in compelling the Athenians to war by teaching them to see the necessities already inherent in their situation.

We might profitably wonder whether this characterization of what Pericles is doing for the Athenians can help us understand what Thucydides is doing for his reader. Thucydides states that his goal was to write a work that would be judged "useful" (1.22.4, *ōphelima*). Interpreters have long disagreed over what this means. For much of the twentieth century, and also by some recent scholars, it was thought that Thucydides wrote with the intention of providing a manual for political leaders (Finley 1942, 50; cf. Ober 2006, Raaflaub 2013). In Thucydides, according to this interpretation, one was to find the fundamental patterns or necessary laws shaping political life, the recognition of which was to allow agents to control the political process of their own day. On the other hand, there have been more pessimistic interpretations of Thucydides. Parry (1981, 103–13) and Stahl (2003, chapter 2) argue, for instance, that Thucydides' usefulness was not practical but strictly intellectual, helping his reader see the past "clearly" (1.22.4). Others (cf. Connor 1984, Hawthorn 2014) go further, suggesting that Thucydides denied there were enduring patterns to be seen in human affairs, and that he taught his reader to recognize instead the subtle hand of chance and contingency, as well as the folly of those who tried to control the flow of events with reductive theory.

Like Pericles, Thucydides sought to teach his audience to see the necessities inherent in their situations. This recognition is intellectual, but has immediate practical consequences. Such readers will judge differently, causing them to act differently, causing politics to unfold differently. Most forcefully, if they believe themselves to be compelled, they will be compelled. Yet, necessity is not presented as a problem that can be solved. Rather, it is something to be endured, and which it is praiseworthy to endure. But necessity is best and most laudably endured when it is accurately identified as such. In this, Thucydides' text promises to be of great use to its reader.

In helping his readers to recognize necessity at work, Thucydides can compel them to action. In this sense, the text itself can necessitate. Yet it must then be true that the text possesses liberatory power as well. Just as Pericles is able to compel his audience by persuading them that they are compelled, so Thucydides can release his audience from compulsion when showing them that they are not necessitated in the way that they thought they were. Recognizing again and again that the Athenians and others did not have to do all that they did, Thucydides' readers can be freed from making similar mistakes. They can also be freed from the manipulations of political leaders who falsely invoke necessity for their own ends. Practical necessity follows from believing that there is only one choice; practical liberty follows from realizing that there are other ways to go.

References

Balot, R. 2015. "Philosophy and 'Humanity': Reflections on Thucydidean Piety, Justice, and Necessity." In *In Search of Humanity: Essays in Honor of Clifford Orwin*, edited by A. Radasanu, 17–35. New York and London: Lexington.
Cochrane, C. N. 1929. *Thucydides and the Science of History*. London: Oxford University Press.
Connor, W. R. 1977. "A Post-Modern Thucydides?" *Classical Journal* 72: 289–98.
Connor, W. R. 1984. *Thucydides*. Princeton: Princeton University Press.
Erp Taalman Kip, A. M. van 1987. "Euripides and Melos." *Mnemosyne* 40: 414–19.
Finley, J. 1942. *Thucydides*. Cambridge: Harvard University Press.
Hawthorn, G. 2014. *Thucydides on Politics: Back to the Present*. Cambridge: Cambridge University Press.
Hoekstra, K. 2016. "Athenian Democracy and Popular Tyranny." In *Popular Sovereignty in Historical Perspective*, edited by R. Bourke and Q. Skinner, 15–51. Cambridge: Cambridge University Press.
Knox, B. 1964. *The Heroic Temper: Studies in Sophoclean Tragedy*. Berkeley and Los Angeles: University of California Press.
Lattimore, R., trans. 2012. *The Trojan Women*. In *Euripides III*, 3rd ed., edited by M. Griffith and G. Most. Chicago: University of Chicago Press.
Macleod, C. 1983. *Collected Essays*. Oxford: Clarendon.
Nagy, G. 1979. *The Best of the Achaeans: Concepts of the Hero in Archaic Greek Poetry*. Baltimore: Johns Hopkins University Press.
Ober, J. 2006. "Thucydides and the Invention of Political Science." In *Brill's Companion to Thucydides*, edited by A. Rengakos and A. Tsakmakis, 131–59. Leiden: Brill.
Orwin, C. 1994. *The Humanity of Thucydides*. Princeton: Princeton University Press.
Ostwald, M. 1988. *ANAΓKH in Thucydides*. Atlanta: Scholars.

Parry, A. 1969. "The Language of Thucydides' Description of the Plague." *Bulletin of the Institute of Classical Studies* 16: 106–118.

Parry, A. 1972. "Thucydides' Historical Perspective." *Yale Classical Studies* 22: 47–61.

Parry, A. (1957) 1981. Logos *and* Ergon *in Thucydides*. New York: Arno.

Raaflaub, K. 2013. "*Ktēma es aiei*: Thucydides' Concept of 'Learning through History' and Its Realization in His Work." In *Thucydides between History and Literature*, edited by A. Tsakmakis and M. Tamiolaki, 3–22. Boston and Berlin: De Gruyter.

Rusten, J. 2015. "*Kinesis* in the Preface to Thucydides." In *Kinesis: The Ancient Depiction of Gesture, Motion, and Emotion*, edited by C. A. Clarke, E. Foster, and J. P. Hallett, 27–40. Ann Arbor: University of Michigan Press.

Sidorova, N. 2001. *Corpus Vasorum Antiquorum, Russia: Pushkin State Museum of Fine Arts, Moscow, Fascicule IV, Attic Red-Figured Vases*. Translated by Tatyana Budkova. Rome: L'Erma di Bretschneider.

Sommerstein, A., trans. 1982. *Clouds*. The Comedies of Aristophanes 3. Warminster: Aris & Phillips.

Stahl, H.-P. (1966) 2003. *Thucydides: Man's Place in History*. Swansea: The Classical Press of Wales.

Thomas, R. 2012. "Thucydides' Intellectual Milieu and the Plague." In *Brill's Companion to Thucydides*, edited by A. Rengakos and A. Tsakmakis, 87–108. Leiden: Brill.

Williams, B. 1993. *Shame and Necessity*. Berkeley and Los Angeles: University of California Press.

CHAPTER 23

THE REGIME (*POLITEIA*) IN THUCYDIDES

S. N. JAFFE

Introduction

This chapter offers a preliminary articulation of the issue of the regime (*politeia*) in the *History*. *Politeia* is a key concept for all ancient political thought. After a discussion of the importance of domestic politics for Thucydides' account of the Peloponnesian War, the chapter outlines how Thucydides presents the regimes of the one, the few, and the many. The conclusion offers more speculative claims about three political orders—or effective principles of rule—that Thucydides himself endorses, including the mixed regime at Athens of the eighth book.

Why the Regime Matters

The *History* is famous for its unsparing portrayal of intercity relations in Hellas amidst the pressures and uncertainties of a great war. But what about domestic politics? What of the characters of the many regimes appearing in Thucydides' pages? Historical writing, as practiced today, involves the description and explanation of the causes and consequences of past events, with an emphasis on historical particularity or on the idiosyncrasies of time and place. Thucydides himself focused on the generation-long struggle between Athens and Sparta, a war that convulsed not only the Hellenic cities but also a considerable part of the non-Greek world (1.1.2).[1] His "method," however, is different from that of the contemporary historian (Orwin 1989); for Thucydides claims that his account of a particular war reveals a universal understanding of war and politics.

---

[1] Translations are drawn from Strassler 1996.

The Peloponnesian War is then a paradigmatic war, and Thucydides' account of it is designed to bring out what is illustrative or representative.

Thucydides' effort to depict the permanent features of international politics, which bind events together and make them meaningful, presupposes an initial discernment and then a coherent vision of what is important and what is not in human affairs—an account of how human nature manifests itself in the recurrent experiences of the human condition. Since human nature is shaped and organized *within* communities, every political order in Thucydides' book represents a historically conditioned manifestation of this nature. Consequently, to grasp the foreign policy of cities—to understand "war"—we must first acknowledge that human beings are organized within distinct communities.

To understand these communities within the framework of Thucydides' universalizing ambitions, it is crucial to interpret not only his depiction of various regimes but also his evaluation of them. Which regimes are good or successful, and is it possible to offer statesmen useful advice about them (cf. 1.22.4)? Does Thucydides consider Sparta, a closed society, the best regime because of its eventual victory in the Peloponnesian War? Or does he favor Athens instead, a cosmopolitan city, which produces more glittering individuals than Sparta, but which ultimately loses the war because its domestic common good dissolves into private interest seeking? Or is it neither of these? Could it be that Thucydides reflects only on the advantages and disadvantages of different political orders, without decisively judging which regime is better? Even if Thucydides does have universal ambitions, the answers to these questions may turn out to be highly situational or circumstantial. In investigating the diverse regimes of the *History*, then, we need to inquire about what makes a city well adapted to meeting the challenges of its strategic environment.

Domestic Politics at First Glance

Readers quickly encounter multiple regimes in the *History*—kingships, oligarchies, democracies, mixed regimes, and tyrannies—and all of them are in motion amidst the unrest of the long war. Thucydides reveals the inner workings of these diverse regimes in three main ways. First, he narrates certain domestic events in detail and leaves it to his readers to grasp the significance of the episodes for themselves. Second, Thucydidean characters at times refer to the internal life of cities or praise or criticize a regime type; readers are invited to assess these opinions with reference to the action of the war itself. Third and finally, Thucydides offers occasional commentary in his own voice, as opposed to the more implied commentary of his narrative. As the work unfolds, Thucydides leads his readers to appreciate the interrelationships among these varied presentations of domestic political life.

First are those moments when Thucydides himself brings regime dynamics into the foreground. To give the main examples, there is the account of the plague at Athens in Book 2 (2.47–2.59); the description and commentary on the revolution at Corcyra in Book 3 (3.70–3.84); and the presentation of the Athenian domestic scene in Book 8, where the Athenians progressively slide into faction or *stasis*, culminating in the oligarchic revolution of 411 BCE.[2] These episodes are principally examined in relation to the broader conflict and illustrate the deforming pressures of war on domestic politics, and the way in which civil discord—or internal disunity—affects the prosecution of the wider war. Thucydides' theme in these episodes is political breakdown.[3]

Second, Thucydidean characters sometimes discuss the characters of particular cities or even of a specific regime type. In Book 1, for example, Corinthian envoys compare and contrast the "ways" (*tropoi*) of the Athenians and the Spartans (1.70). Archidamus, a Spartan king, whom Thucydides introduces just after the Corinthian speech, corroborates elements of the Corinthian presentation in his own person. He also praises Sparta's distinctive regime and education, while Pericles, in the Funeral Oration, asserts that it is the democratic regime itself (*politeia*), along with the ways and practices of the Athenians, which represent the living sources of Athenian imperial power (2.36.4). Still later in the work, a Syracusan demagogue, Athenagoras, publicly reflects on the class tensions experienced by his democracy (6.36–6.40); and an Athenian, Phrynichus, criticizes oligarchy, only to become its partisan subsequently (cf. 8.48.6–8 with 8.68.3). Moreover, during his narrative of the civil war at Corcyra, Thucydides himself reproduces the characteristic claims, counterclaims, and slogans of oligarchs and democrats alike (3.82.8).[4]

Third and finally, Thucydides himself occasionally comments on certain regimes, corroborating (or refuting) the claims of his characters. In the eighth book, for example, he explicitly confirms elements of the Corinthian comparison of the opposing ways of Athens and Sparta, while suggesting that Athens and Syracuse are similar, in large part because the two cities are democratic (8.96.5). Thucydides also takes pains to emphasize that the specter of tyranny drives the Athenian *dēmos* into paroxysms of paranoia and anger. In Book 6, he digresses to discuss the Peisistratid tyranny as a means of explaining the popular furor against Alcibiades at the time of the Sicilian expedition; for, as he notes there, the *dēmos* feared that Alcibiades aspired to become a tyrant (6.15.2–4, 6.28.2, 6.53.1–3. 6.60.1–2, and 6.61.1). Perhaps the most revelatory Thucydidean statement, however, is his claim that the regime of the Five Thousand at Athens, a mixed regime, was the best at Athens during his lifetime—a remark that may come as a surprise, since he had personally witnessed the flourishing of Periclean Athens (8.97.2).[5]

Scholarly approaches to these issues can be divided into two principal camps. For the first, the central question is the character of Thucydides' own politics, particularly with

---

[2] For an account of the relation between the style and substance of Book 8, see Connor (1984, 210–30); for a provocative theoretical elaboration of its meaning, see Forde (1989, 116–75).

[3] For the most comprehensive treatment of *stasis* in the *History*, see Price 2001.

[4] With regard to this passage (and others), Saïd (2013, 204) argues that Thucydides demonstrates a clear distrust of ideologically marked terms, and so refuses to side with partisan definitions of either democracy or oligarchy. Mitchell (2016, 57–58, 65) maintains that Thucydides is inviting his readers to reflect on the instability of political language itself, and to recognize that the opposition between oligarchy and democracy is more apparent than real.

[5] In the second book, Thucydides emphasizes that the Athenians eventually lose the war because the city descends into faction or *stasis* (2.65.7–11).

regard to his allegiance to Athens and its empire (Connor 1984, 237–242); an unavoidable question in such approaches is whether or not Thucydides is a Periclean.[6] For adherents of the second approach, the focus is on the Athenian democracy itself, which is conceived of as a resource for theorizing about the possibilities and limits of democracy in our own era.[7]

Fewer scholars, however, raise the question of whether we can uncover the logic of Thucydides' own presentation of various regimes or of his account of domestic politics generally. Raaflaub (2006) maintains that Thucydides is deeply opposed to both radical democracy and radical oligarchy, while Edmunds (1975) argues that Thucydides' famous presentation of the inversion of traditional virtues during the revolution at Corcyra betrays a predilection for oligarchic (or Spartan) virtues, one revelatory of an Archaic pattern of thought. Orwin (1994, especially 193–206), following Strauss (1964), makes the case that the primary opposition in the *History* is not between democracy and oligarchy but rather between Athens and Sparta. There remains a question, however, as to whether Athens and Sparta are representative of their different regime types. Pope (1988) asserts that the principal binary for Thucydides is between tyranny and the decision-making of free citizens, regardless of whether those citizens are "the few" or "the many." Finally, Saïd (2013) scrutinizes the various terms that designate the masses in the *History*, including whether they are used neutrally, positively, or negatively. She makes the case that the examples of rule praised by Thucydides—that of Pericles, the regime of the Five Thousand, and the reign of the Peisistratids—are all praised, at least in part, because the interests of the masses are taken into account.[8]

With these perspectives in mind, we are in a position to examine how Thucydides presents the rule of the many, the few, and the one. Given the sheer historical detail of the *History*, the treatment in this chapter will necessarily remain schematic, and it will be useful to sharpen the discussion by investigating the extent to which Thucydides' account of the different regimes is representative and illustrative, or, alternatively, if it remains uncompromisingly particular.

The Regime of the Many and the Regime of the Few

In his account of democracy and oligarchy, Thucydides focuses above all on domestic stability, or, relatedly, on the manner in which democracies and oligarchies are

---

[6] For a recent canvassing of the Thucydides-Pericles question and a perceptive account of the differences between the men, see Foster 2010.

[7] Mara 2008; Zumbrunnen 2008; see Lee 2015 for a synthetic account of the Thucydides and democracy debates.

[8] See also Mitchell (2016, 67–68) who argues that Thucydides' account of the "political vocabularies" of democracy and oligarchy finds a kind of culmination in the mixed regime of the eighth book, where these vocabularies generate new meanings which facilitate a healthier blend of the interests of the many and the few.

susceptible to *stasis* or faction (Fliess 1959, 622). In addition to whatever dangers are posed by the ascension to power of one faction or the other, revolution risks prolonged and enervating factional struggle, a compromised foreign policy, and even the possibility of tyranny. Tyranny and revolution are the chief internal dangers that oligarchies and democracies both face (Kokaz 2001, 100).

For all of their differences, democrats and oligarchs share a common hostility to tyranny. This theme emerges already in the first pages of the *History*. In the Archaeology, Thucydides presents the Spartans as inventing or discovering the common good, which is based on equality among citizens (1.6.4). Even if oligarchs and democrats have different understandings of equality, the common good and civic equality characterize Hellenic political life generally and represent distinctively Hellenic innovations (Orwin 1994, 31). Pope (1988, 278–82), who has tracked the use of national collectives in the work—the Athenians, the Spartans, the Corinthians, among others—has discovered that while such collectives are surprisingly common in reference to Hellenic cities, oligarchic and democratic alike, they are virtually *never* used by Thucydides of the Persians and other non-Greeks, among whom citizenship and active decision-making were not central. It is therefore reasonable to suppose, with Pope, that oligarchy and democracy were more similar than they were different for Thucydides, especially when compared to despotism. Tyranny, in other words, represents an equal challenge to oligarchic and democratic claims of citizen equality, and also to oligarchic and democratic claims to self-rule.

In addition to the threat of tyranny, democracies and oligarchies face the ever-present danger that outside powers will foment domestic strife by exacerbating the normally muted differences between rival elements within the city. According to Thucydides, external war *inevitably* aggravates divisions within cities; in times of peace cities do not have the same opportunity, incentive, or pretext for engaging in factional struggle (3.82.1). Divisions within cities always exist, of course, but these can become dangerously activated—that is, rendered pathologically salient—by the shifting balance of external forces, or by the blandishments of opportunists on the doorstep.[9] Thucydides also reveals a progressively corrosive logic to the progression of faction or *stasis* itself, which heightens party distinctions by magnifying hatred and enmity, and which pushes civil strife toward ever more terrifying extremes (3.82.6). Throughout the *History*, disunity is presented as a perennial political problem (1.2.4). Moreover, the destruction of a city's common good, whether oligarchic or democratic, has clear implications for the foreign policy of the afflicted city, for unity is a condition of the effective use of power. A divided city is far less capable of meeting the demands of its strategic circumstances than a unified one.

---

[9] Various conflicts between oligarchic and democratic factions became activated by the Peloponnesian war itself, by the fact that Sparta supported oligarchy and Athens democracy (see 3.47.2–3, 3.82.1; and Cogan 1981). In other words, the significance of the many-few distinction grew over the latter half of the fifth century BCE as a result of the Peloponnesian War (Pope 1988, 282; Johnson Bagby 2011).

The English philosopher Thomas Hobbes, who translated the *History* into English in 1629, captures something of the Thucydidean view of political order when he asserts in *Leviathan* that all forms of government perform the same elemental function, if more or less effectively: they provide a foundational security for the community (Hobbes 1994, 120). In this light, the city itself represents a protection from external threats as well as a bulwark against internal ones. Security is the precondition of every other good.[10] Hence, maintaining political order across time becomes an important standard for assessing the (relative) health of actual regimes—a yardstick for judging the success or failure of cities in the *History*.

For Thucydides, in other words, a "best" regime, whatever its ideological allegiances, is one that (at a minimum) safeguards its people, principally by maintaining its political integrity in the face of the contrivances of its neighbors and the blows of fortune. Such cities can be conquered or destroyed, of course, but adherence to a shared conception of the common good gives citizens the best chance of survival. Pericles expresses a similar view when, in his final speech, he claims that the private individual needs the city more than the city needs any individual (2.60.2–4). Hermocrates' speech at Gela about the critical importance of Sicilian unity in the face of opportunistic Athenian meddling in Sicilian affairs makes a parallel argument, although in the context of deliberations about the shared interests of all Sicilians. Hermocrates explicitly compares the situation in Sicily to a civil war (4.64.4–5).

Stability does not guarantee victory in war, of course, but instability will almost assuredly doom a city. According to Thucydides, Athens does not lose the Peloponnesian War because the city's power is insufficient to win it, but instead because the Athenians succumb to civil strife, and so cannot wield their great power effectively (2.65.7–13).[11] Overall, Thucydides explores the ways in which external war contributes to internal war, but also the ways in which cities (or factions within them) foolishly invite civil war. It may be for this reason that he equally opposes *radical* democracy and *radical* oligarchy, as Raaflaub (2006) suggests, for the very word "radical" suggests *stasis*, the alienation of the rival faction, and so the incipient danger of civil strife.

The issue of the domestic virtues that conduce to stability raises the interesting interpretive possibility that the distinctive "ways" (*tropoi*) of Athens and Sparta might relate to their regime types, for Athens is of course a democracy and Sparta an oligarchy.[12] When Edmunds (1975) terms certain dispositions "Athenian" or "Spartan," he is referring to those places in the *History* where the theme of the character (*tropos*) of a city is explicitly raised, or when the actions of a city (or its citizens) correspond to an earlier

---

[10] On the caretaking of the body as an essential element of regime stability, see Orwin (2016).
[11] Loraux 2006 offers a provocative account of Athenian *stasis*.
[12] One of the few monographs devoted to national character in Thucydides, albeit with a different focus than this chapter is Luginbill (1999); Johnson Bagby (2011) helpfully canvasses the ideological constituents of national character; Zumbrunnen (2008) offers an interpretation that emphasizes the highly rhetorical (and so contestable) nature of the appeals to an "essential" Athenian character.

statement about a city's character. This term, *tropos*—way, manner, or character—is a precursor to the comprehensive articulation of the regime of later Greek thought. Yet Thucydides and his characters do not use the term to describe oligarchy or democracy as distinct forms of government, but rather to depict the specific behaviors of the Athenians, Spartans, and Syracusans.

The Athenians are quick, daring, and aggressive in their pursuit of profit, while the Spartans are their opposites—cautious and slow, intent on preserving what they already have (1.70.1–9). The differing characters of the two cities are first introduced in the prefatory Archaeology (1.6), but the contrast is significantly expanded in the second Corinthian speech of the first book (1.70), and it runs throughout the entire *History* (8.96.5). These episodes support the claim that the principal regime opposition in the *History* is in fact that between Athens and Sparta (Orwin 1994, 192). Crucially, Thucydides himself confirms elements of Corinth's presentation in his eighth book, where he notes that the Athenians and Syracusans share a similar way or manner (*homoiotropos*, 8.96.5).

This Thucydidean confirmation which contrasts Athens and Sparta and strongly emphasizes the similarity between Athens and Syracuse, suggests that the *History's* account of Athens is representative of democracy altogether. In fact, a thematic movement of the sixth and seventh books is the progressive change in the Syracusan character to one resembling the daring Athenian manner. Moreover, just as the Persian invasion was a spur to the development of the Athenian character, the Athenian invasion of Sicily proves a spur to a revolution in Syracuse's ways. Perhaps not every democracy behaves like imperial Athens—here one might think of Thucydides' account of democratic Argos (or indeed of Syracuse itself prior to the Athenian invasion)—but the character of imperial Athens is clearly bound up with the democratic possibility itself.

Could Sparta be equally representative of another regime type? Sparta is a highly unusual *polis*, an apparently sui generis oligarchy, with a class of Spartan citizens, a council of elders, two hereditary kingships, a rotating board of ephors, and a large enslaved Helot population. Although Aristotle suggests that some consider the Spartan regime to be a mixed one—due to its blending of a monarchical element, the double kingship, with a board of ephors and its Spartiate class—it nonetheless seems more accurate to characterize the regime as an oligarchy, defined, essentially, by the Spartiate class (*Politics* II.3 1265b35–40). Thucydides himself emphasizes the longstanding *eunomia* of the regime, a term that was an oligarchic watchword of the fifth century (1.18.1). Sparta moreover demonstrates a clear and long-standing affinity for oligarchies, exerting control over her allies in the Peloponnesus through the installation of friendly oligarchical regimes (1.19), while also generally supporting oligarchic factions throughout the Peloponnesian War itself (3.82.1).

Consequently, the cautious disposition of the Spartan regime may represent an extreme oligarchic possibility, just as Athenian daring represents a democratic one. Like his Athens, then, Thucydides' Sparta may in fact be an ideal type. Oligarchs are generally more inclined to conservatism than democrats, precisely because they are (properly) fearful of revolution stirred up by the disenfranchised and disaffected.[13] The Spartans, for their part, are permanently on guard against the possibility of a helot uprising.

In the eighth book, Thucydides emphasizes that the Chians and the Spartans are the only cities in his estimation that successfully combine moderation with prosperity. In a later passage, he darkly hints that this moderation is the product of each city's large slave population, which acts as a salutary check on foreign policy adventurism (cf. 8.24.4 with 8.40.2). This fear of a slave revolt is also a shaping factor in the development of the political culture of these cities (regarding Sparta, see especially Thucydides' important statement at 4.80.3). The prevention of rebellion from below, be it of the *demos* or of slaves, comprises an element of the common good of the ruling class.[14] Yet it would be hard to admire this moderation as a simple virtue of the regime, for it appears to be the result of a merely prudential calculation. Despite the fact that the historical source of Sparta's moderation is her slaves, the Spartan education strongly emphasizes moderation, meaning that while certain traits can have their origins in a city's strategic circumstance, they can eventually become genuine virtues (see 1.79.2, 1.84, and 1.86.2).

How do Thucydidean characters evaluate democracy and oligarchy?[15] In the sixth book, Athenagoras, a Syracusan demagogue, in the middle of a partisan and ill-informed speech, extols the solid virtues of the democratic regime. He emphasizes its inclusiveness and the ability of the *dēmos* to judge the right course of action. In the Funeral Oration, Pericles presents imperial (democratic) Athens as an almost perfect regime, in which all equally serve the state, but each serves it according to his distinctive talents and abilities (2.37.1). According to Pericles, Athens is both a democracy and a meritocracy. Athenagoras, in contrast to Pericles, is a deeply unsympathetic figure whose advice is clearly foolish. The reader knows that the Athenians are sailing for Sicily in force, but Athenagoras claims that the specter of such a threat has been raised by Hermocrates solely for the purpose of an oligarchic plot (6.36.1–2, 6.38.2–5, 6.40.1–2; and Andrews 2009).

Nonetheless, Athenagoras offers an interesting, if not entirely persuasive, rejoinder to the (presumably oligarchic) claim that the wise or the wealthy merit rule. He argues that it is in fact the *dēmos* that judges best and indeed stands for the entire city, whereas oligarchy represents only a part (cf. 2.40.1, where Pericles make a related point about the people's ability to judge). Oligarchy brings the people many dangers, he says, but takes more than its fair share of the city's goods; it is only democracy that serves the interest of the whole city, for the *dēmos* encompasses the whole (6.39.1–2). As to the plausibility of

---

[13] This fear accounts for the common cause between oligarchic parties in different cities. It is also why Sparta establishes oligarchies in the Peloponnesus to increase her political control (1.19). Oligarchs, of whatever caliber or stripe, invariably claim to be the "best men" (cf. 3.82.8, 6.39, and 8.48.6).

[14] In his presentation of the revolution at Corcyra, Thucydides notes that the slaves join forces with the people—their natural allies?—while the wealthy are assisted by mercenaries (3.73).

[15] For an illuminating genealogical account of the development of the concept of the free citizen as it developed in the contentious debate between democrats and oligarchs, see Raaflaub 1983, which situates various passages from the *History* within this broader conversation.

these claims, Pericles himself makes statements about the fickleness of the mob, which is tossed about by its emotions. These statements raise questions about the actual ability of the people to judge properly for themselves; the reader can also find evidence for believing that Thucydides himself endorses this Periclean skepticism about the multitude (cf. 1.140.1, 2.59.1–3, and 2.65.1–4). Diodotus, a later Athenian speaker, even goes so far as to claim that the only way to serve a democratic city is to deceive it (3.43.3).

As provocative as these arguments may be, the speakers' disagreements lead to little resolution of the basic question. Even if democracy encompasses the whole people and oligarchy only a part, if the people are truly poor judges of their own interests, then the figure of the statesman in democratic times becomes of vital importance. Thucydides' endorsement of Pericles at 2.65 suggests that this is in fact his view. Above all, he praises Pericles for leading the people instead of being led by them (2.65.8).

With regard to oligarchies, in the eighth book, an Athenian, Phrynichus, maintains that oligarchic parties are harsher and more immoderate than the gentler *dēmos* (8.48.6; see also Orwin 1994, 187–188; and Forde 1989, 130–139).[16] But the action of the war significantly qualifies this assertion. Thucydides makes it clear that the bloody revolution at Corcyra ended only when the *democrats* had liquidated the oligarchic class (3.81.2–5 and 4.46–48). Neither the few nor the many prove to be gentle or public spirited when they experience the deforming pressures of civil war (3.82.2). Thucydides also explicitly remarks that the logic of an oligarchic revolution sows the seeds of its own destruction, for the presumptive superiority of the few to the many leads each oligarch to think of himself as superior to every other. The logic of oligarchy, in other words, ultimately points toward tyranny, or to the breakdown of the oligarchic common good itself (8.89.3).[17] In certain circumstances, however, the collective fear of revolution from below can inoculate oligarchical orders against this tendency—indeed, Thucydides hints that vaunted Spartiate equality has its origins in precisely this fear (cf. 1.6.4 with 1.18.1 and 4.80.3)

Thucydides evaluates the regimes of the few and the many by how well these political orders maintain their common goods and realize their strategic interests amidst the pressures of war. Democratic regimes are more broadly inclusive than oligarchic ones, but the quality of their strategic judgment fully hinges upon the quality of their statesmen because of the pervasive fickleness of the multitude (see, for example, 2.65.4; and Hunter 1988).[18] Unlike democratic regimes, which have to fear only oligarchical (or tyrannical) conspiracies, oligarchic orders are threatened by revolution from below and from within the ruling class itself. They are therefore less stable than democratic ones.[19]

---

[16] This same Phrynichus will later become a partisan of oligarchy out of his dislike of Alcibiades, who, he claims, cares neither for democracy nor for oligarchy but only for that regime which will reconcile him with Athens, while those in the city itself should do their utmost to avoid *stasis* (8.48.4).

[17] Mara 2015 (324) asserts that in the eighth book oligarchy is presented as incompatible with citizenship itself.

[18] Thucydides does *not* make comparable remarks about the fickleness of the few.

[19] Aristotle makes the same point about the relative stability of democracies (*Pol.* V.1. 1302a7–10).

The Rule of One, Tyranny, and Kingship

For Aristotle, the rule of one for the sake of the ruler's own interest is tyranny, while rule by one for the sake of the common advantage is kingship (*Pol.* III.4.1279a26–1279b10). For Thucydides, by contrast, kingship and tyranny appear related to stages of political development, one revelatory of certain differences between Hellenes and barbarians. Distinguished by the citizen equality originally introduced by the Spartans (1.3.3, 1.5.3, and 1.6), the Hellenes have advanced beyond the barbarian form of communal organization, which is the hereditary kingship of a powerful military figure.

Kings in the *History* occur only in the ancient Hellenic context, except, notably, at Sparta, but frequently in the contemporary barbarian world (note, for example, Perdiccas 1.57.2; Sitalces, 2.29.3–4). The first peoples were barbarians, and so the original Hellenes resemble the contemporary barbarians (1.6.6). The world is of full of peoples at uneven stages of political development. Tyrants, for their part, appear only in the Hellenic cities of the *History*, primarily in the two or three generations before the Peloponnesian war, and their appearance is tied to the rise of wealth (1.13.1). Contemporary tyrants make only rare appearances (but see, for instance, 2.30.1 and 2.33.1).

Historically, of course, "tyranny" was always not a term of obloquy.[20] While Thucydides himself uses the term in a more descriptive sense, his characters, by contrast, generally speak disparagingly of tyrants, who violate that equality which is so central to Greek citizenship.[21] All cities view the corruption of their citizens as dangerous, but the Spartans, who take their citizen equality to an extreme, view the corruption of their citizens' way of life as a special concern. Thucydides' treatment of the medizing of Pausanias makes this abundantly clear (1.6.4 with 1.95.7, 1.130.1–2, 1.132.2). The Athenians, who are more ostensibly open to differing forms of private life (Pericles: 2.37.2, 2.39.1; Nicias: 7.69.2), nonetheless fear that Alcibiades aspires to a tyranny, in large part because of his extravagant lifestyle (6.15.3–4).

Consequently, citizens who are thought to aspire to one-man rule are viewed with deep hostility and suspicion. Early in the *History*, Thucydides says that the Hellenic tyrants were concerned principally with their own security and advantage, and with the increase of their private houses. Consequently, they were conservative in their policies, and so their cities did little that was daring or worthy of report (yet compare this with the Sicilian tyrants: 1.14.2 and 1.17). This portrait of the tyrants is sharply contrasted with the subsequent citizen levies of mainland Greece, who fought the Persian and Peloponnesian wars—great Hellenic events made possible by the deposition of the tyrants, which the Spartans made their task in the years before the Persian invasion

---

[20] For an illuminating discussion of the trope of the tyrant in the classical period, see Forsdyke 2009. For an account of tyranny in the *History*, see Dreher (2016), who furnishes a useful list of all of the tyrants mentioned by name, along with textual references (92–93).

[21] The Corinthians castigate the Athenians for being a tyrant city at 1.122.3 and 1.124.3. Pericles, Cleon, and Euphemus embrace the designation (cf. 2.63.2, 3.37.2, 6.85.1).

(1.18.1). In his later account of the Peisistratids at Athens, however, Thucydides corrects (or at least qualifies) his earlier presentation of the tyrants from the Archaeology. In Book 6, the Peisistratids are presented as public spirited and as intelligent leaders. They not only adorn the city of Athens but also fight its wars (6.54.5).

In light of his positive evaluation of the Athenian tyrants, it is intriguing that Thucydides saw Athens under Pericles as a rule (*archē*) by the city's first citizen (2.65.9).[22] This presentation is the likely source of the Hobbesian claim that Thucydides is a proponent of monarchy, like himself (Hobbes 1994, lvi). Certainly, if Pericles held any sort of kingship, it was not a legal or institutional one, for Pericles "ruled" solely on the basis of his ability to persuade the *dēmos*. Thucydides moreover presents him as intransigently devoted to Athens. Pericles himself takes pains to emphasize his public spiritedness, not only in his deeds but also in his final speech, which implies that he felt vulnerable to suspicion (cf. 2.13.1 with 2.61.5–7).[23] Moreover, the mythical figure of the Athenian king Theseus also makes an appearance in Book 2, and he is presented as laying down the foundation of the city's later power through his political unification of Attica (2.15.2). His actions appear prescient and public spirited, like those of his non-royal successors, Themistocles and Pericles.

Thucydides' view of one-man rule is surely less hostile than that of his characters. Everything, however, depends upon the quality of the man who helms the ship of state. The fraught question of Thucydides' attitude to the mercurial and treacherous Alcibiades is bound up with these issues (see Forde 1989; Gribble 1999; Palmer 1982). In principle, Thucydides does not oppose the rule of a single preeminent man, though he may be skeptical of the abilities of any particular aspiring tyrant: for example, the unsuccessful aspirant Cylon (1.126.6).

Three Principles of Political Rule

What principles of political rule does Thucydides himself favor?[24] With regard to its production of capable individuals, Athens is surely the finest city in the *History*—no other city can boast so many talented citizens—but Athens loses the Peloponnesian War because of civil strife. Sparta, by contrast, is a better collective than Athens, for the Spartan constitution, the source and fount of Spartan power, inoculates her citizen levy against faction within its ranks; but, with the notable exception of Brasidas (and perhaps Gyllipus), Spartan leaders are less talented than their Athenian counterparts (1.18.1).[25] Each principal city can therefore make a partial but justified claim

---

[22] For the argument that Thucydides' presentation of the Peisistratids is not actually as positive as commentators have generally thought, see Dreher (2016, 93–96).
[23] The Spartans certainly attempt to undermine him domestically (1.127.1).
[24] Johnson Bagby 2011 (132–39) offers a synthetic vision of Thucydides' own politics as it relates to various regimes types.
[25] Thucydides makes clear that prior to the institution of the Spartan constitution, Sparta suffered from civil strife for an *extremely* long period of time.

to political excellence.[26] I conclude this chapter by proposing that there are three principles of political rule that Thucydides himself endorses. These orders manifest solid virtues but also corresponding vices or disadvantages. There is, in Thucydides' account, no simply best regime. Instead, Thucydides presents his readers with various forms of political virtue, each of which can make genuine claims to different kinds of communal excellence. These forms of rule are not the same as democracy or oligarchy—or indeed as Athens and Sparta. Instead, they capture those essential elements or traits that Thucydides singles out for praise in Athens, Sparta, and various other regimes.

The Rule of the Wise

The first form of rule that Thucydides approves of is the rule of a wise or prudent man, what we can call the rule of (political) wisdom. Throughout the *History*, he demonstrates a strong affinity for the figure of the talented statesman and general. The extraordinary praise of Themistocles at 1.138 makes this clear. Themistocles is presented as uniquely able to do the necessary (or needful) things at every moment (*ta deonta*). He also foresees and prepares for a vast increase in Athenian power (1.93.3). Thucydides' presentation of kingship is characterized by a lively awareness that great kings, such as Theseus, can serve the long-term interests of their people (2.15.2). Two non-Athenians, Brasidas and Hermocrates, also come in for high praise (4.81.2; 6.72.2). While Thucydides surely recognizes that the rule of a single man can be less stable than other forms of rule—and so dangerous on precisely this account—single rulers can do great good for their cities, as the Peisistratids did for Athens.

A wise leader makes the best decisions for his people in whatever situation they find themselves, while the quality of the city's strategy is dependent on the soundness of his strategic judgment. Apprehending the threats, opportunities, and constraints of his circumstance, he deftly chooses the best course of action. Yet the life of a single individual, no matter how outstanding, is fragile: Themistocles died of illness; Pericles, the preeminent Athenian of his generation, from plague; and Brasidas, the greatest of Spartan generals, in battle (1.138.4, 2.65.6, 5.10.11). There is no guarantee that another talented statesman or general will replace the one that has fallen. Indeed, Thucydides explicitly traces Athenian decline to the squabbles for popular preeminence among Pericles' successors (2.65.10–11).

A great leader (or general) can achieve spectacular results for his city. While Athens facilitates the development of such men more than any other city, the presence or absence of such a leader at the right moment is ultimately the product of chance and (in the case of democracies) of the people's ability to recognize their genius and to trust in

---

[26] Rahe (1996, 139) makes a related point. The virtues and vices of the two regimes are sides of a single coin: "Yet it is precisely because Athens gives relatively free rein to the potential for greatness inherent in human nature, that it is Athens, not Sparta, that loses all sense of measure and falls apart."

their counsel. There is, however, a different form of rule that more fully arms a regime against fortune, but that makes spectacular success less likely.

The Rule of Law

In addition to the rule of wisdom, which is more at home in Athens than Sparta, Thucydides highlights the benefits of the absolute rule of law, which characterizes the Spartan regime. Once again, he maintains that the Spartan regime avoids tyranny and *stasis* because of its *eunomia*, or good order (1.18.1). Every regime has its laws and customs, of course, which it categorically demands that its citizens obey, but Sparta's good order requires a far more complete subordination of the individual to the community than any other city in the *History*. All Spartiates are equally slaves to Spartan law, whose necessities every citizen is harshly educated to obey from earliest childhood (1.84.4, 2.39.1). This education facilitates the unity of the ruling Spartiate class and cultivates an abiding trust amongst its members. For later fourth-century Greek philosophers, the character of the law is itself inextricably tied to regime type, but Thucydides emphasizes not the character of the law per se, but instead the intensity of the attachment to the law itself as a bulwark against domestic instability and fortification of a city's attachment to its common good. The Athenian Cleon's polemical assertion that "bad laws that are never changed are better for a city than good ones that have no authority" captures something of this Thucydidean position (3.37.3).[27] Relatedly, in their speech at Sparta, the Corinthians refer to Sparta's laws as unmoved (1.71.3).

During the civil war at Corcyra, however, the paradigm of *stasis* in the *History*, Thucydides makes it clear that all respect for law broke down along with social trust (3.82.6, 3.83.1). Instead of remaining unmoved, law itself was overwhelmed by the ascendant passions of the factional parties. In Book 1, the Corinthians note that the Spartans' trust in their constitution and way of life is the living source of their moderation (1.68.1), while the Spartan King Archidamus furnishes the clearest articulation of the reverential Spartan attitude toward their constitution and ancestral practices (1.84). It is Spartiate equality, enshrined and enforced by law, nourished by trust, and cemented by fear of the Helots, that keeps Sparta moderate in prosperity (4.80.3, 8.24.4, 8.40.2).[28]

Finally, because Sparta's *eunomia* does not rely upon a single individual, it represents a partial inoculation against fortune, for the regime can withstand the loss of any individual, no matter how outstanding. Yet there are also disadvantages to this form of political life. In contrast to the rule of a single prudent individual, the law is deaf to the

---

[27] But with a distinctly Athenian twist, for presumably no Spartan would suggest that an existing law was bad.
[28] Sparta's social cohesion and law-abidingness are also bound up with piety, for the Spartans clearly believe that the gods punish lawbreakers. This made clear in the seventh book, when Thucydides reveals that the Spartans viewed the capture of their men on Sphacteria as divine chastisement for their violation of the Thirty Years' Peace (7.18.2).

specifics of circumstance. Instead of relying upon individual or collective judgment, as the Athenians generally do (2.40.2)—and as a wise ruler assuredly does—the Spartans struggle to grasp what the law demands at every moment.

When it offers little in the way of guidance, or little in the way of how to apply a general principle to a particular circumstance, the Spartans are usually at a loss. Consequently, they fail to act quickly to grasp at favorable opportunities, a fault for which the Corinthians rightly condemn them, as Thucydides himself agrees (1.70.1–4 with 8.96.5). Sparta may not be capable of pressing her advantages, and she may make strategic or tactical errors (8.96.5), but the regime's conservatism means that these mistakes are unlikely to be fatal. The Thucydidean suggestion appears to be that these disadvantages are amply compensated for by the maintenance of the city's unity across time.[29]

Overall, the *History*'s Athens–Sparta comparison reveals extreme forms of political development: the flourishing of individuality, on the one hand (Athens), and the subordination of individual judgment to the authority of community, on the other (Sparta). Both Athens and Sparta, then, are representative or illustrative of more general political possibilities, which have real advantages but also corresponding disadvantages.

The Regime of the Five Thousand at Athens

The regime of the Five Thousand at Athens is the third and final form of political rule that Thucydides himself favors: a species of mixed regime. Unlike the homogeneity of the Spartiate ruling class, however, the ruling class in a mixed regime is heterogeneous. At 8.97.2, Thucydides remarks that the regime of the Five Thousand at Athens, established as a consequence of the shock following the revolt of Euboea, was the best at Athens of his lifetime.[30] A mixed regime, which becomes a major theoretical preoccupation of later Greek thought (Hahm 2009), not only satisfies the interests of oligarchs and democrats alike, but also gratifies their respective desires for honor. It represents, then, a mixture of the interests and aspirations of rich and poor alike.[31] Despite Thucydides' praise for this regime, it was not long lasting. While a mixed regime has obvious advantages, we can raise the question of whether such a regime, particularly a newly formed one, is actually better than an entrenched—and so presumably more stable—democracy or oligarchy, given Thucydides' own unremitting emphasis on domestic stability.[32]

---

[29] One wonders if Thucydides would have revised these views if he had been able to observe the fate of Sparta in the fourth century.

[30] For an incisive interpretation of 8.97, see Connor (1984, 227–30), particularly n34.

[31] Saïd (2013, 206) argues that the passage "... only calls for an equal attention paid to the interests of the elite and those of the masses."

[32] Mara (2015, 325) usefully remarks, given the short life-span of this regime, that "... Thucydides' evaluation might be read less as a decisive verdict on regime forms and more as the recognition of the importance of questions that are continually in need of attention."

According to Thucydides, the architects of the regime of the Four Hundred and ultimately of the Five Thousand at Athens were among the ablest Athenians, even the city's finest men (8.68). His overall suggestion is that a mixed regime offers some of the advantages of the rule of the wise, by encouraging the participation of the best (which a radical democracy discourages), and something of the stabilizing effects of the rule of law.[33] Stability is achieved not by a complete and total subordination to a common way of life, as it is at Sparta, but instead through the deft balancing of oligarchic and democratic interests.

A mixed regime therefore insulates a city from civil strife by involving all of the major elements of the city in political rule—the rich, the middling element, and the best—without tilting too far in the direction of the inconstant rule of the many or of the oppressive rule of the few. It satisfies (some of) the distinctive interests of heterogeneous elements within the broader community. Over the long run, a regime of this sort promises greater stability and success than either oligarchy or democracy, for it represents not only a mix of the rule of the few and the rule of the many, but also a blend of political wisdom and domestic stability. To pull the thematic threads together, we suggest that a mixed regime not only avoids the already mentioned vices of the rule of the many and the rule of the few, but it also blends the virtues of the rule of wisdom with those of the rule of law. It shares, in other words, some of the virtues of those other forms of political rule that Thucydides himself endorses.

Thucydides on the Regime

The issue of domestic politics goes to the heart of Thucydides' ambitions as an analyst of political life. Unlike Plato and Aristotle, who begin with an emphasis on the just individual and on the health of domestic political life, and whose unremitting focus is on the best regime, Thucydides begins from the widest and most extreme political perspective—international struggle during a Panhellenic war—and works his way down into cities and their constituent elements. Above all, he emphasizes the worst degradation of civic life: civil war. The *History*'s focus is not on an abstractly perfect city at peace—or on the virtues bound up with the highest flourishing of the soul—but instead on imperfect cities fighting a long war, and on the virtues requisite for surviving it.

Thucydides vividly shows his readers that every city exists within the broader currents of international politics, and that the exigencies of foreign policy make constant and pressing demands upon domestic political life, while at the same time exacerbating divisions within cities. War may be for the sake of peace, as Aristotle maintains (*Pol.*

---

[33] Thucydides depicts many brilliant and public-spirited Athenians, but his praise of Antiphon at 8.68.1 suggests that some of the best men were deterred from participating in democratic public life.

1333a3), but how durable is peace itself? What are citizens entitled to expect from politics, given human nature and the recurrent experiences of the human condition?

Thucydides' emphasis on war over peace, as opposed to the Socratic one on peace over war, explains why the regime plays a comparatively subordinate role in his *History*. He explores the regime as it pertains to successful or unsuccessful foreign policy, where strategic judgment and domestic stability are of paramount importance. Whether Plato and Aristotle intend their best regimes to be practicable, whether they intend them to stimulate political hopes or to chasten them, Thucydides expects less from politics than they do.

References

Andrews, James. A. 2009. "Athenagoras, Stasis, and Factional Rhetoric (Thucydides 6.36–40)." *Classical Philology* 104 (1): 1–12.

Balot, Ryan, ed. 2009. *A Companion to Greek and Roman Political Thought*. Chichester and Malden: Wiley-Blackwell.

Cogan, Mark. 1981. "Mytilene, Plataea, and Corcyra: Ideology and Policy in Thucydides, Book Three." *Phoenix* 35 (1): 1–21.

Connor, W. R. 1984. *Thucydides*. Princeton: Princeton University Press.

Dreher, Martin. 2016. "*Turannis* in the Work of Thucydides." In *Thucydides and Political Order: Concepts of Order and the History of the Peloponnesian War*, edited by Christian R. Thauer and Christian Wendt, 87–109. London: Palgrave MacMillan.

Edmunds, Lowell. 1975. "Thucydides' Ethics as Reflected in the Description of Stasis (3.82.83)." *Harvard Studies in Classical Philology* 79: 73–92.

Fliess, Peter J. 1959. "Political Disorder and Constitutional Form: Thucydides' Critique of Contemporary Politics." *Journal of Politics* 21 (4): 592–623.

Forde, Steven. 1989. *The Ambition to Rule: Alcibiades and the Politics of Imperialism in Thucydides*. Ithaca: Cornell University Press.

Forsdyke, Sara. 2009. "The Uses and Abuses of Tyranny." In *A Companion to Greek and Roman Political Thought*, edited by Ryan K. Balot, 231–46. Chichester and Malden: Wiley-Blackwell.

Foster, Edith. 2010. *Thucydides, Pericles, and Periclean Imperialism*. Cambridge: Cambridge University Press.

Gribble, David. 1999. *Alcibiades and Athens: A Study in Literary Presentation*. Oxford: Clarendon.

Hahm, David E. 2009. "The Mixed Constitution in Greek Thought." In *A Companion to Greek and Roman Political Thought*, edited by Ryan K. Balot, 178–98. Chichester and Malden: Wiley-Blackwell.

Hobbes, Thomas. 1994. *Leviathan: With Selected Variants from the Latin Edition of 1668*, edited by Edwin Curley. Indianapolis: Hackett.

Hunter, Virginia. 1988. "Thucydides and the Sociology of the Crowd." *Classical Journal* 84 (1): 17–30.

Johnson Bagby, Laurie M. 2011. "Thucydides and the Importance of Ideology." In *On Oligarchy*, edited by David Tabachnick and Toivo Koivukoski, 110–39. Toronto: University of Toronto Press.

Kokaz, Nancy. 2001. "Between Anarchy and Tyranny: Excellence and the Pursuit of Power and Peace in Ancient Greece." *Review of International Studies* 27: 91–118.

Lee, Christine. 2015. "Thucydides and Democratic Horizons." In *A Handbook to the Reception of Thucydides*, edited by Neville Morley and Christine Lee, 332–51. London: Wiley Blackwell.

Loraux, Nicole. 2006. *The Divided City: On Memory and Forgetting in Ancient Athens*. New York: Zone.

Luginbill, Robert Dean. 1999. *Thucydides on War and National Character*. Boulder: Westview.

Mara, Gerald. 2008. *The Civic Conversations of Thucydides and Plato: Classical Political Philosophy and the Limits of Democracy*. Albany: SUNY Press.

Mara, Gerald. 2015. "Thucydides and the Problem of Citizenship." In *A Handbook to the Reception of Thucydides*, edited by Neville Morley and Christine Lee, 313–31. London: Wiley Blackwell.

Mitchell, Lynette. 2016. "Greek Political Thought in Ancient History." *Polis, The Journal for Ancient Greek Political Thought* (Special Issue: *Approaches and Methods in Greek Political Thought*, edited by Ryan K. Balot) 33.1: 52–70.

Morley, Neville, and Christine Lee, eds. 2015. *A Handbook to the Reception of Thucydides*. London: Wiley Blackwell.

Orwin, Clifford. 1989. "Thucydides' Contest: Thucydidean 'Methodology' in Context." *Review of Politics* 51: 345–64.

Orwin, Clifford. 1994. *The Humanity of Thucydides*. Princeton: Princeton University Press.

Orwin, Clifford. 2016. "Beneath Politics: Thucydides on the Body as the Ground and Limit of the Political Regime." In *Thucydides and Political Order: Concepts of Order and the History of the Peloponnesian War*, edited by Christian R. Thauer and Christian Wendt, 113–27. London: Palgrave MacMillan.

Palmer, Michael. 1982. "Alcibiades and the Question of Tyranny in Thucydides." *Canadian Journal of Political Science* 15 (1): 103–24.

Pope, Maurice. 1988. "Thucydides and Democracy." *Historia: Zeitschrift für Alte Geschichte* 37 (3): 276–96.

Price, Jonathan J. 2001. *Thucydides and Internal War*. Cambridge: Cambridge University Press.

Raaflaub, Kurt. A. 1983. "Democracy, Oligarchy, and the Concept of the 'Free Citizen' in Late Fifth Century Athens." *Political Theory* 11 (4): 517–44.

Raaflaub, Kurt. A. 2006. "Thucydides on Democracy and Oligarchy." In *Brill's Companion to Thucydides*, edited by Antonios Rengakos and Antonis Tsakmakis, 189–222. Leiden: Brill.

Rackham, H., trans. 1944. *Politics*, by Aristotle. Cambridge: Harvard University Press.

Rengakos, Antonios, and Antonis Tsakmakis, eds. 2006. *Brill's Companion to Thucydides*. Leiden: Brill.

Rahe, Paul A. 1996. "Thucydides' Critique of Realpolitik." In *Roots of Realism*, edited by Benjamin Frankel, 105–41. London: Frank Cass.

Saïd, Suzanne. 2013. "Thucydides and the Masses." In *Thucydides between History and Literature*, edited by Antonis Tsakmakis and Melina Tamiolaki, 199–224. Berlin and Boston: De Gruyter.

Strauss, Leo. 1964. *The City and Man*. Chicago: University of Chicago Press.

Tabachnick, David, and Toico Koivukoski, eds. 2011. *On Oligarchy*. Toronto: University of Toronto Press.

Thauer, Christian R., and Christian Wendt, eds. 2016. *Thucydides and Political Order: Concepts of Order and the History of the Peloponnesian War*. London: Palgrave MacMillan.

Thucydides. 1996. *The Landmark Thucydides: A Comprehensive Guide to the Peloponnesian War*, edited by Robert B. Strassler. New York: Free Press.

Tsakmakis, Antonis, and Melina Tamiolaki, eds. 2013. *Thucydides between History and Literature*. Berlin and Boston: De Gruyter.

Zumbrunnen, John. 2008. *Silence and Democracy: Athenians Politics in Thucydides' History*. University Park: Pennsylvania State University Press.

CHAPTER 24

STASIS IN THE WAR NARRATIVE

MICHAEL PALMER

According to Thucydides, to adapt a remark of Leo Strauss on tyranny (1991, 22), *stasis* is a phenomenon coeval with political life.[1] That Thucydides is the "realist" among the myriad "idealists" of ancient Greek thinkers is such a common observation that it obviates citation. I shall refrain from translating Thucydides' term *stasis* (usually translated "civil war" or "revolution") until we have determined what he means by it through careful examination of those events in the *War* narrative that he, himself, calls *staseis* (the plural of *stasis*). In this, I follow Connor (1984, 96n39): "English 'factionalism' is too tame, and 'civil strife,' 'civil war,' 'revolution,' and 'class warfare' have the wrong connotations." Thucydides mentions at least forty instances of *stasis* in the narrative, and the word appears perhaps hundreds of times.

Stasis before Corcyra

The first mention of *stasis* in Thucydides appears in Book 1, Chapter 2, sentence 4, in the so-called Archaeology, "account of olden times"; he tells us that in the time of nascent "Hellenic" ("civilized") life, the cities that became most powerful on account of their "excellent land" (*aretēn gēs*) destroyed themselves with *staseis*. I note this early reference in order to emphasize that *stasis* is a paramount preoccupation of Thucydides throughout his entire narrative, not only in the famous passages on it. As a result, as Price (2001, 333) has remarked, "This [early mention of *stasis*] enables the reader to appreciate the fullest extent of the war's destruction: the primary casualty . . . was Hellas itself." As Price

---

[1] For the text of Thucydides, I have used the Oxford Classical Text Edition (Thucydides 1976). Translations are mine, except where otherwise noted. I have transliterated all Greek words, including those from secondary sources.

also observes, the Archaeology serves as proof that the war between the Peloponnesians and the Athenians is the "greatest disturbance" (*kinēsis . . . megistē*) that ever affected Hellas, and is thus worthy of Thucydides' life-long study; the war's importance makes the narrative a "possession for always" (*ktēma te es aiei*, 1.22.4) for the few who genuinely desire "the truth" (*tēs alētheias*, 1.20.3). Price's argument is that the guiding thread of the narrative is *stasis*, that "the analysis of *stasis* contains Thucydides' own fullest, most concentrated and profoundest reflections on historical truths."[2]

Stasis at Corcyra

The Corcyreans had been in a condition of *stasis* ever since captives were taken by the Corinthians in the two sea battles off Epidamnus; allegedly (*logō*) their friends had simply paid for their freedom, but really (*ergō*) they had been bribed to betray Corcyra to the Corinthians (3.70.1). The *stasis* at Corcyra begins before the war proper has begun. The first thing the returned prisoners did was to bring Pithias, a voluntary *proxenos* of Athens and leader of the *dēmos*, up on charges of conspiring to enslave the Corcyreans to the Athenians (70.3). The trial ended in acquittal, and Pithias retaliated by charging the wealthiest of his accusers with committing a sacrilege, of which they were convicted, whereupon they took refuge at some temples (70.4–5). These men, realizing that both they and their plot were in dire jeopardy, suddenly rushed upon the council house and murdered Peithias and about three score other councilors and private individuals, while a few of their enemies gained refuge on the Attic ship still in the harbor (70.6).

The conspirators' next step was to compel (*ēnankasan*) the Corcyrean Assembly to agree that henceforth they should stand neutral between the two major sides in the war; this would best prevent their enslavement to Athens. They also immediately sent envoys to forestall action against themselves, but the Athenians arrested them, and put them and their Corcyrean fugitives together on the island of Aegina. Meanwhile, with the arrival of a Lacedaemonian ship at Corcyra, the factions split apart, each gaining control of strategic places on the island and one of its two main harbors (71–72.3). The next day, the two parties skirmished, and secured allies: the democrats, from their slaves; the oligarchs, hiring mercenaries (73). Two days later, there was a battle won by the *dēmos*, in which even the women participated, which participation was, according to Thucydides, "beyond nature" (*para phusin*) (74). Now the Athenian general Nicostratus arrived with twelve ships and five hundred Messenian hoplites, and negotiated a settlement between the factions: twelve oligarchic leaders should face trial (they immediately fled); the rest should make peace with one another and be allied with Athens (75.1). The

---

[2] Price (2001, 11) says, "When Thucydides writes in the *stasis* model that 'every form of evil-doing arose in the Hellenic world because of the *staseis*' (*dia tas staseis*, 3.83.1)" he indicates that the "evil-doing," if it originated in the *staseis* and was typical of them, was nevertheless not limited to them: "*dia tas staseis* is not the same as *en tais stasesi*" (Price 2001, 273).

dēmos then began to berate their enemies, who went to a temple as suppliants (75.3); the *dēmos* armed themselves and, but for Nicostratus' intervention, would have butchered the oligarchs (75.4), about 400 of whom went to the temple of Hera, but the *dēmos* persuaded them to settle on a nearby island instead (75.5). I think the most important thing to notice at this point in Thucydides' presentation is his close attention to the use and abuse of the sacred things, such as temples.

A few days later, Alcidas, with Brasidas as adviser, arrived with fifty-three ships, preparing to sail on Corcyra (76). This threw the Corcyrean "many" (*hoi polloi*) into a panic; they manned sixty ships as quickly as they could equip them, while the commanders of the Athenian ships wished to leave the scene (77.1). But when their ships approached the Peloponnesians, two deserted to the enemy, and war broke out between the factions on the others, so that all order dissolved (77.2). This prompted the Peloponnesians to set twenty ships against the Corcyreans and the rest against the Athenians, including the two Athenian sacral state ships, the *Salaminia* and the *Paralos* (77.3). A battle ensued, in which the disordered Corcyreans were ineffectual, and the Athenians fought cautiously, trying to throw the enemy into confusion by sailing in an enclosing circle around them (3.78.1). The Peloponnesians responded by bringing their whole force together in a line and advancing on the Athenians (78.2). The Athenians slowly retired, and the battle ended (78.3–4).

The Peloponnesians did not press their advantage; they returned to their harbor, taking thirteen captured Corcyrean ships with them; nor did they venture to attack the much-alarmed city, although "it is said" that Brasidas advised Alcidas to do so; meanwhile, the Corcyrean *dēmos*, fearing that the enemy *would* attack them, persuaded some of the oligarchs to board the ships with them; the next day, the Athenian general Eurymedon arrived with sixty ships (80.2).

At this point, Alcidas fled for home (81.1). The Corcyrean *dēmos* promptly proceeded to kill as many of their personal enemies as they could get their hands on, as well as the oligarchs they had persuaded to man their ships; they persuaded those in the temple of Hera to submit to trial, and immediately condemned them all to death (81.2). Most of the suppliants, however, refused trial, once they had realized what was happening, preferring to take their own lives, hanging themselves, or cutting their throats with arrows (81.3). This extreme conflict continued throughout the week that Eurymedon remained with his ships (81.4). Every form (*idea*) of death ensued, and other horrors that are wont to occur, our author tells us, occurred: fathers slew sons; men were murdered impiously (81.5). In brief, the worst kinds of evils were perpetrated, and the Athenians just watched.

The extremes to which the factions went seemed so bad because this was among the first that later disrupted (*ekinēthē*) the entire Hellenic world, and the leaders of the *dēmos* desired to call in the Athenians; the oligarchs, the Peloponnesians. In peacetime, they would have had no pretext (*prophasis*), but now that Athens and Sparta were at odds with each other, they did (82.1). So the cities fell upon a calamitous number of *staseis*, such as happen "and always will," Thucydides writes, on account of "human nature"; in peaceful and prosperous (*agathous*) times both cities and private individuals have gentler thoughts (*gnōmas*) than when faced with necessity (*anankas*). But war is a "violent school teacher" (*biaios didaskalos*), and human beings stoop to their circumstances in a passionate temper (*orgas*) (82.2).³ I take Thucydides to mean that war teaches men to be excessively violent.

Thus the cities began to suffer *staseis*, and the ones that came later were worse than the one at Corcyra, because factions learned from the earlier *staseis* how to behave more effectively in the later ones, inventing new, more monstrous, modes of attack and revenge (82.3). Along with the deeds (*erga*), the normal meaning of words changed to match them; or, it would be more precise to say that the words retained their traditional meanings, but the ways they were applied were transformed: reckless "daring" (*tolma*) or "manliness" (*andreia*) came to mean party loyalty; "prudence" (*to sōphron*) came to mean unmanly cowardice; to be very "clever" (*zuneton*) meant to be useless in action; rash impulsiveness meant to be a real man, while caution became a euphemism for shirking one's tasks (82.4). The hothead was always trusted; his rival (even on his own side), suspect; the executer of a plot was clever, but one who could anticipate a plot was even cleverer; whoever sought to avoid having to do either was disloyal to his party and afraid; in short, evildoers, and especially those who turned others into evildoers, were most highly prized (82.5). Blood ties were weaker than party ones, for the true partisan was willing "to dare" (*tolman*), and these deeds were not enacted for the public good, but for the sake of "greed" or "getting more" (*pleonexia*); contrary to normally trusted sacred law, oaths were the occasion for general "lawlessness" (82.6).

The "cause" (*aitia*) of all this was desire to rule and "love of glory" (*philotimian*) inspired by the "love of victory" (*philonikein*), which leads to ruling, and *pleonexia*. The *stasis* leaders on each side in the cities used euphemisms, such as "political equality for all under law (*isonomias*)" or "reasonable (*sōphronos*) aristocracy," feigning to care for the public good, but really caring only about dominating the city, seeking vengeances even more terrible, beyond any sense of "justice" (*dikaiou*), passing unjust death sentences or committing other acts of violence, glutting their momentary and fluctuating passions. Odious deeds covered by pretenses were highly praised; any sort of piety was scorned. Anyone who wished to remain neutral was continually destroyed by both factions, either because of the extreme degree of hostility between the two factions, or jealousy that neutrals might survive. The notion seems to be that the adversaries, who were risking their lives for their vision of what the regime should be, could not abide anyone distancing himself from the struggle, and living to enjoy the fruits of it (82.8). Simple nobility or goodwill were scorned out of existence, while antagonism and mistrust prevailed (83.1); for no assurances nor any oaths carried any weight, so security was considered hopeless (83.2). Generally, those of weaker intelligence prevailed, boldly resorting to action, not wanting to fall prey to fine words and ingenious plots (83.3). On the other

---

³ Price (2001, 24) explains, "The word *gnōmē* here embraces the variety of meanings of the word: mental disposition, thought, judgment and purpose ... a decision or conviction reached after careful thought and deliberation. By contrast, *orgai* are strong emotions, passions which circumvent or overwhelm rational processes," and notes (26n39) that the "concise remarks of Strauss" in Strauss (1964) can "unravel some of the complexities." He also points us to Edmunds (1975).

hand, their more intelligent opponents fell prey to the delusion that they had plenty of time to outwit their inferiors, so they perished in disproportionate numbers (83.4).

It is widely debated whether or not Chapter 84 is authentic, but to forgo dealing with it would be to presume I knew the answer to this question, which I do not; indeed, I'm not certain that anyone does or even can. If authentic, it is the longest passage in Thucydides' own name in the narrative, and it seems uncharacteristically to engage in broad "ethical" judgments. I am hesitant to speculate about why Thucydides should choose to do this; I'll simply say that decent readers are somewhat reassured about the human condition by this reprieve from unmitigated horror.

It was at Corcyra, he tells us, that most of these acts of extreme daring were first committed, the sort of acts committed by human beings who are under the powerful influence of *hubris* rather than any kind of "moderation" (*sōphrosunē*), once given the opportunity, contrary to any sort of "accepted justice" (*para dikēn*), when they seek release from their habitual poverty, and are overcome by desire to take their neighbors' goods (84.1). At the "critical moment" (*kairon*) when the city is in utter confusion, "human nature" (*anthrōpeia phusis*), which tends to commit injustice when it can, and now triumphant over the laws, delighted in displaying its uncontrollable angry passions; for surely no man, our author judges, would place vengeance before piety (*hosiou*), and gain before innocence of injustice, were he not overwhelmed by the mighty power of envy (*to phthonein*) (84.2). In fact, human beings seeking vengeance never hesitate to abrogate the usually accepted rules, even though they need them in quieter times (84.3).

At the beginning of Chapter 85, Thucydides almost repeats the opening sentence of Chapter 84. Such were the angry passions that the Corcyreans indulged in, and Eurymedon sailed away (85.1). Later, however, about 500 of the Corcyrean fugitives on the island (of the oligarchic faction) got to the mainland, seized some forts, established a base, and having already ravaged the people on the island, created a famine in the city (85.2). After failing to persuade Lacedaemon or Corinth to restore them to power, they secured boats and crossed back to the island, now numbering about 600 (85.3). They burned their boats, to force themselves to stick the course, and after building a fort on Mount Istone, they proceeded to destroy the people in the city, and dominate the land (85.4). Later in the narrative, we learn that the Corcyrean *stasis* ended with the complete victory of the democrats, that is, the complete destruction of the oligarchs.

Thomas Hobbes was probably the most important student Thucydides ever had. The question is, does Thucydides teach the same thing that Hobbes teaches? Hobbes certainly thought so, but the correct answer is "No." What's the difference? The answer lies in Thucydides' different posture before this grim scenario of Corcyra: resignation. But before what does he resign himself? His account of the plague that eviscerated Athens in the first year of the war is harrowing—the lawlessness that pervaded the city, the abandonment of all the things that were considered noble, even of the concern for sacral burial of those who perished—but it pales in comparison to what the man-made plague of *stasis* reveals about "human nature."

What happened at Corcyra was the epitome of what happened in the Hellenic world during this war (3.82), but Thucydides says explicitly that as horrendous as what happened at Corcyra was, it turned out to be just the beginning of what *staseis* wreaked in Hellas. As it is, his attempt to describe what is perhaps ineffable leads to some of the most difficult and controversial Greek sentences in his book. There was what Nietzsche would call a "trans-valuation of all values." Thucydides emphasizes the permutations that occurred in the social significance of words, the result of which was political, social, and moral chaos, because while words retained their traditional meanings, they were employed in completely new and perverse ways. There was a complete triumph of "daring" (that most Athenian characteristic) over "moderation" (that most Spartan characteristic). Concern for any sort of justice was overcome by the yearning for angry vengeance, and even sacred oaths were unable to impose any limits on what human beings were willing to do. Thoroughly evil men were praised for their cleverness, while people of any decency and moderation were scoffed at as fools. Contracts were nothing but pretexts (*prophaseis*) for betrayal. Thucydides remarks the dissolution of even family bonds, and the utter abandonment of any laws, human or divine.

Here is where Thucydides offers his famous personification of war: it is a "violent schoolmaster" (*biaios didaskalos*): a teacher about violence, via violence. Nevertheless, we should remember it is a teacher; in fact, it was Thucydides' own teacher, especially concerning human nature. War is a teacher because war brings necessity (*anankē*) to bear on human affairs (*erga*). *Stasis*, the most violent of human phenomena, teaches Thucydides that whatever restraints may forestall it are sacred (even if only metaphorically). It is of paramount importance to recognize that Thucydides says explicitly that his account of *stasis* is to teach us how things will always be in human life. He does not think for a moment that his having written this account will affect the future in any way. These horrors cannot be eliminated or even ameliorated by the writing of books, or by any other means. Thucydides leaves to others the futile attempt to change the world; his aspiration is to understand it. Thucydides utterly lacks the extreme "hopefulness" that is characteristic of most of the modern political philosophers in the tradition of Machiavelli, Bacon, Hobbes, and Locke. (There are, of course, exceptions: Burke and Tocqueville come immediately to mind.)

The Prospect of *Stasis* at Sparta

Thucydides famously tells us that Sparta was the only city in Hellas that avoided *stasis* during this war, and had a regime that had not changed its laws in 400 years (1.18.1). Aruguably, however, Thucydides shows us in the narrative that Sparta faced the prospect of *stasis* during the war (Palmer 2015). Everything revolved around the Spartans' outstanding commander, Brasidas, and the army of helots with which he set out for the Thraceward regions (4.70.1, 79–80; see Westlake [1968, 149n4] on the term "Thraceward") to liberate Athens' allied cities there. Sparta had faced helot revolts before, but never the combination of a helot revolt and a brilliant Spartan commander who was willing and able to lead them in full-blown internal war with the city; one might compare the much less successful attempt of Pausanias to set himself up as the "Great King" of the Spartans by betraying all of Greece to the "Great King" of Persia. Pausanias lacked the "intelligence," "speed," "measuredness," "farsightedness," and "virtue" of Brasidas—he was the furthest thing one could imagine from a man "energetic in every way," "a good man in all respects," or a "just" man, all qualities Thucydides attributes to Brasidas (2.25.2, 4.81.2–3, 4.84.2, 4.87.4, 4.106, 4.108.3). In short, Pausanias was a typical brutish Spartan (1.94–95; 128.2–35.1), while Brasidas was a remarkable human individual. Brasidas' expedition to "liberate the Greeks" was simultaneously his opportunity to "liberate" *himself* from Sparta, without which he could be a king. Hornblower (1996, 458) goes so far as to call Brasidas "superhuman."

Brasidas was not only more "Athenian" than "Spartan," but he also displayed *only* what were the very *best* qualities of "Athenianism" (cf. Nichols, chapter 27 in this volume). What are we shown of his truly remarkable achievements and virtues? We see that he was a man who, even in antiquity, was compared with Homer's Achilles. In his first appearance in Thucydides' *War*, he earns the *unique* honor of being the *only* individual in the narrative ever to be noted for having won special honors for his bravery from *any* city, yet the leading Spartans are envious of his great abilities: he is suspected of something at Sparta, and with good reason. His Thraceward expedition itself—the greatest undertaking attempted by either side during the so-called "Archidamian War"—was "most of all" at his own initiative. Brasidas displays "speed" and "daring" throughout, knows the value of the element of "surprise," "sudden moves," and always acts "at the critical moment," as he leads an ever growing army that becomes ever more personally loyal to him, an army with no Spartans in it, but numerous heavily armed helots, an innovation in the Spartan *nomoi*, their customary constitutional ways. We should note the great significance of the fact that this instance of the Spartans' arming helots as hoplites and sending them out with Brasidas—at least up to this point in their history—seems to have been unique. The available evidence indicates that the *neodamodeis*, who were helots liberated for military service, did not arise as a regular practice in Sparta until after Brasidas' death. Brasidas' career led to regime change at Sparta. True, the practice of arming slaves for battle in warfare was not so uncommon in other parts of the Greek world, and later in Rome, but this was the first time it had ever been done in Sparta, which itself constituted a change in the Spartan regime.

Brasidas is "prudent" without being "moderate"; he is, rather, "measured," like the best of the Athenians, in all his speeches and deeds. Here there is much confusion, due to the neglect by most of Thucydides' commentators of the care with which he uses the distinction between the two Greek words *sōphrosunē* ("moderation") and *metrion* ("measuredness"), each of which *can* be translated as "moderation," but should never be confused when one is reading Thucydides. In referring to his Spartans, he invariably uses "moderation"; in referring to his Athenians, invariably "measuredness."[4] The only Spartan to whom he ever attributes "measuredness" is Brasidas. He is the only man in Thucydides ever called "energetic in everything he did." He is the only man in Thucydides ever

---

[4] I first explained and utilized this distinction in Palmer (1982a).

called "just." He is among fewer than a handful of human beings attributed with "virtue" (*aretē*) by Thucydides.[5] Of all the human beings who are ever pronounced "virtuous" by Thucydides, with the exception of the Athenians' Pisistratid tyrants, he is the *only* one *also* attributed with "intelligence," and *no* other individual in Thucydides is *ever* said to be "just" *and* "a good man in all respects," not even Pericles. The unique appearance of the word "gentleness" (*praotēs*) in the narrative occurs in Thucydides' description of Brasidas, and he is the only person who ever publicly sacrifices to Athena. These attributions compel the discerning reader to recognize that Brasidas was, in Thucydides' view, a man of the rank of Themistocles, Theseus, the Pisistratid tyrants, Pericles, Demosthenes, Hermocrates, and Phrynichus, even superior to some of these. I maintain that the two apparently divergent assessments by Thucydides of Brasidas' "virtues" are not discrepant, but cumulative. In his first assessment of Brasidas (4.81), he characterizes Brasidas as held at Sparta to be "energetic" (*drastērion*) in everything he undertook, as showing himself to be "just and measured" (*dikaion kai metrion*) toward the cities he caused to revolt from Athens, and that the "virtue and intelligence" (*aretē kai xunesis*) he displayed at this time was later favorable to the Lacedaemonians, for he was "considered a good man in all he did" (*doxas einai kata panta agathos*), which left behind the (mistaken) hope that the other Lacedaemonions were like him. In the second assessment (4.108.2–3), he attributes only showing himself to be "measured" (*metrion*), comments on his "gentleness" (*praotēta*) toward the cities that revolted to him, and mentions that he lied to some of the cities (108.5). This leads most commentators to note that "justice" especially is dropped from the second assessment, and to draw invidious inferences from this fact. I, however, understand the lying to be not a "correction" of the first eulogy, but precisely an example of his "measuredness": war requires a prudent general to tell lies, and I would note that Plato's Socrates in *The Republic* (382c–d) condones lying in three circumstances, and that the instances of Brasidas' lying meets two of them, while the third in not relevant.

Brasidas' speech at Acanthus is one of the most remarkable speeches in the *War*, which becomes the prototype for most of his other speeches, and which emphasizes his dedication to "the liberation of the Greeks." True, Brasidas may lie, as regards the Spartans' having sworn an oath that "liberation" is the purpose of his expedition, but let us not forget that he also swears his *own* solemn oaths that this is his mission (4.86.2).

During the one-year truce in the war, we see that the Spartans' alleged *cause de guerre* was a complete fraud, but it may not have been for Brasidas. As Orwin (1994, 80) comments, "Brasidas' ambitions may exceed those of Sparta. He may well intend a vast extension of her influence, through a new confederacy of former Athenian allies, as much Brasidean as Spartan." At Scione, Brasidas is publicly crowned with a golden crown and declared "The Liberator of Greece"; privately, he is decked with the garlands of an Olympic victor, and "ritual offerings" are made to him. Brasidas possessed the magnificent virtue that Themistocles (and Thucydides himself) possessed: to be able to see even into the most distant possibilities of a given situation. Also, no other man in the

---

[5] For an exhaustive annotated analysis of Thucydides' use of the word *aretē*, see Palmer (1989).

fifth-century BCE was ever received in a foreign city as enthusiastically as Brasidas, with the sole exception of Themistocles. My point here is to emphasize that Thucydides' presentation of Brasidas' career serves to show how close Sparta came to full-blown *stasis* during this war.

Brasidas makes the only speech in the war that distinguishes "Greek" or "civilized" life from "barbarism." At Amphipolis, he completely destroys Cleon and his army in perhaps his "shrewdest," most "daring," and "bravest" military action, which results in his heroic death. He is entombed in the most solemn of ceremonies, with his monument placed in the center of a fenced-off "sacred precinct," after which sacrifices are made to him at least as to a hero (a demigod in ancient Greece), according to some manuscripts, even as to a god. He is declared the city's founder, and annual games are established in his honor. He is the first man in recorded Greek history to be publicly named the "savior" of a city.

The dark cloud that hangs over Brasidas' reputation is that while he went around the Thraceward region liberating cities, from the point of view of the regime at home, these were mere bargaining chips that the Spartans intended to return to the Athenians in exchange for their prisoners taken at Sphacteria, and that afterwards these cities were very harshly punished. But I suggest that had Brasidas lived, he would not have permitted the betrayal of these cities. One argument in support of this contention emerges clearly if we ask the following question: Why is Ischagoras sent out from Sparta with an army, during the truce, to go to Brasidas, when Brasidas' earlier request for them to send one to him had been denied because the leading Spartiates were jealous of his success (see 4.108.6–7)? Imagine Brasidas with a large army of helots who were personally loyal to him, once having established for himself "a new confederacy of former Athenian allies" (Orwin, 1994, 80), marching on Sparta with his battle-hardened hoplites, wearing his golden crown as "The Liberator of Greece," and promising the helots in the Peloponnese their freedom! Can there be any doubt that the Spartans would have had on their hands a helot revolution that far surpassed that of 464? This time, would their increasingly disaffected allies have come to her rescue?[6]

I believe that Thucydides invites us to consider the possibility that Brasidas aspired to found a new regime in Sparta, one in which he would enjoy the status Alcibiades craved in Athens: the status of Pericles.[7] Thucydides' account of the career of Brasidas is his teaching on the prospect of *stasis* at Sparta, which was prevented only by the untimely and chance death of Brasidas at the battle of Amphipolis. What we learn from Thucydides' presentation of the career of Brasidas is that full-blown *stasis* might have come to even as stable a regime as Sparta's: the great strength of Sparta's regime is trust amongst the leading Spartiates; the advent of a truly remarkable human being at Sparta, in itself, posed a threat to the stability of that regime.

---

[6] For an extensive annotated analysis of Thucydides' treatment of the career of Brasidas, see Palmer (2015, 65–85).

[7] For elaboration on Alcibiades' ambitions, see Palmer (1982b); for Thucydides' judgment of Pericles' career, see Palmer (1982a).

Stasis at Athens

Book 8 introduces a remarkable number of outstanding Athenian individuals, all of whom are highly praised, and all of whom have a dark side to their characters. Thucydides gives very high praise to men such as Alcibiades (not introduced in Book 8, of course, but which he dominates); Phrynichus, who betrays the Athenians, and later all the Greeks; Antiphon, who is so suspected by the *dēmos* that he cannot even speak in the assembly; Pisander, an inveterate liar; and Theramenes, a traitor to both the democracy and the oligarchy. In this book, the most extreme form of *stasis* almost comes to Athens.

Their spectacular defeat in Sicily was so great that at first the Athenians refuse to believe it; then they become angry at the men who spoke in favor of it, and at the soothsayers and diviners who had led them to believe they would conquer Sicily; they were in the greatest fear and consternation they had ever been; their resources were depleted; they thought safety was hopeless; they expected an immediate enemy attack on the city, and the full revolt of their allies. In this extreme danger, as the *dēmos* is wont to do, they put aside their complaints about the current structure of the city's regime, considered the common danger, and were ready to order everything aright (8.1).

Nevertheless, *stasis* came home to Athens, and Thucydides' narration of the politics of the Athenian *stasis* is more detailed even than his analysis of the Corcyrean one. Thucydides marks the *stasis* at Athens as beginning with the decision of the trierarchs and most powerful men in the fleet stationed on Samos to overthrow the democracy (8.47.1–2). We should note that these events coincide with Alcibiades having just fled Sparta and become adviser to Tissaphernes, and to his beginning to help out Athens again (8.46), seeking to maneuver his way to restoration to Athens (8.47). Nobody trusts Alcibiades, but he has an amazing ability to get people to think that someone else of whom they have need trusts him. On this point, Phrynichus seems to have been the most astute of the conspirators. His chief concern is the breakout of full-blown *stasis*, and he judged Alcibiades to care no more for oligarchy than he did for democracy, an attitude that Thucydides says "really was the case" (*hoper kai ēn*, 8.48.4). Alcibiades, the ward of Pericles, wanted the status in Athens that Pericles had enjoyed when for many years under his leadership she was "in name (*logō*) a democracy, but in fact (*ergō*) the rule of the first man" (2.65.9).

In any event, the conspirators prepared to send Pisander to Athens to negotiate Alcibiades' recall and the overthrow of the democracy (8.49). This caused Phrynichus, fearing for his own safety, to undertake a scheme to try to get the others to turn on Alcibiades (8.50.1). He twice tries unsuccessfully to conspire with Astyochus, the Lacedaemonian naval commander, against Alcibiades, but Astyochus remains loyal to Alcibiades, loyalty that led Alcibiades to write a letter to the army at Samos, urging death for Phrynichus (50.2–4). Phrynichus was now "extremely afraid," being in the "greatest danger (*megistō kindunō*)," so he wrote to Astyochus again, essentially offering him the opportunity to destroy the entire Athenian army (50.5). Chapter 51 details how Phrynichus, for once—temporarily—completely outmaneuvered Alcibiades. After this, Alcibiades continued to ply Tissaphernes, assiduously (*prothumōs*) (52). Meanwhile, Pisander and others from Samos arrived at Athens, outlined the whole situation, and urged the recall of Alcibiades and the alteration of the democracy to win over the Persian king and defeat the Peloponnesians (53.1). Many of Alcibiades' enemies spoke against his recall, as did the priests, on account of the profanation of the Mysteries, for which the democracy had banished him, loudly calling upon the gods; but Pisander dealt with each in turn, asking what other hope (*ētina elpida*) the city had (53.2). Remarkably, he persuaded them, and then told them plainly (*saphōs*), in the only portion of a speech in direct discourse in all of Book 8, "We can only achieve our goals if we adopt a more moderate (*sōphronesteron*) form of government, giving more of the ruling to the few ... and deliberate more about our safety than about our form of government, and we must recall Alcibiades, for he is the only man alive who can effect this" (53.3).

The *dēmos* initially took this advice harshly, but Pisander brought them around (emphasizing *sōtēria*, 54.1). Pisander and ten others were selected to deal with Tissaphernes and Alcibiades as they thought best (54.2). They discharged Phrynichus of his duties (54.3). Before he left the city, Pisander visited the political clubs and urged them to overthrow the democracy (54.4). Later, after convoluted tactics were practiced by Alcibiades, who was concerned that his weak situation vis-à-vis Tissaphernes would be exposed, he made such outrageous demands on the oligarchs that Pisander had no choice but to angrily return to Samos (8.56).

We cannot, of course, detail all the complicated events of the last year of the war that Thucydides relates, most of which affected the *stasis* at Athens. The most remarkable thing to note, if one compares the account of the *stasis* at Corcyra and the *stasis* at Athens, is that the former really had no potential, even, to significantly affect the outcome of the war, whereas if full-blown *stasis* at Athens had run its full course, the war would have ended years before it in fact did.

The first act of the young oligarchs was to murder Androcles, the main leader of the *dēmos*, and the man held most responsible for the charges that had originally gotten Alcibiades tried and sentenced to death, *in absentia*; they thought that murdering his political enemy would please Alcibiades, and induce him to make Tissaphernes their friend; some others were also secretly killed (65.2). The conspirators then purported to establish a regime called the Five Thousand, but this regime was nothing more than a facade (65.3). What was most conducive to the success of the conspirators was that no one really knew if the Five Thousand existed, and if they did, who they were; and in fact there were among the conspirators men whom no one would ever have suspected; the ignorance of the *dēmos* caused general distrust in the city, because fellow citizens feared sharing any concerns with another from fear that he might belong to the Five Thousand (8.66). The establishment of a strict oligarchy was now openly proposed by Pisander, but he still referred to a citizen body of the Five Thousand (8.67–68.1). According to Thucydides, the real architect of the revolution was Antiphon, a man of virtue (*aretē*); in fact, a man of such outstanding ability that the *dēmos* was so suspicious of him that he could not even speak in the Assembly; nevertheless, working behind the scenes, he could be the most useful man in Athens in advising anyone in any situation (68.1). Later, Thucydides says, when on trial for his life, Antiphon gave the best defense speech (*apologia*) of the times, but was put to death anyway (68.2). We cannot help thinking of the historical Socrates' trial here. (Was Thucydides aware of it? It is difficult to think he was not.) Phrynichus was in favor of oligarchy, because he thought an oligarchy would never recall Alcibiades (68.3). But Theramenes was first among those who attempted the overthrow of the democracy. Consequently, since it was conducted by so many very intelligent men (*andrōn pollōn kai xunetōn*), the conspiracy, difficult as it was, not unreasonably (*ouk apeikotōs*) succeeded; it was quite something, after almost a century since the overthrow of the tyrants, to deprive the Athenians of their freedom (68.4), especially because they had been accustomed, ever since their victory in the Persian Wars, to subjecting (*archein*) others, not being subjected themselves (*archein* is the word used for ruling and empire). The Athenians in Thucydides' presentation are the city most desirous of being a "tyrant" over their empire, as Cleon had called them (3.72.2), echoing Pericles himself (with the qualification that Pericles has said "like a tyranny" (2.63.2), and the city most afraid of tyranny. This led them to banish their greatest benefactor before this war, Themistocles, and arguably their greatest potential benefactor in this one, Alcibiades.

The strict oligarchy of the so-called Four Hundred was then installed: with the Assembly dissolved, some of those who were to rule entered the Council, and with the 120 youths, they discharged the Councilors (8.69). No disturbance arose in the city, so they assumed office, taking care to pay all due respect to the traditional prayers, sacred rituals, and all things concerning the gods (8.70.1). They then made overtures to King Agis, wishing to negotiate a peace treaty and end the war (70.2). For various mistaken reasons, King Agis refuses to negotiate with the envoys from the Four Hundred. Instead, he tries to taunt the Athenians into a battle, approaching their very walls. When his tactics fail, he is willing to negotiate a peace treaty with the Four Hundred, so they sent envoys to Lacedaemon (8.71). The Athenians also sent word to Samos that they were working for the good of the whole city, and that the Five Thousand really existed; they feared the navy at Samos would never consent to a narrow oligarchy in Athens (8.72). A reaction against the oligarchy had already begun in the navy, but some of the leaders of those who had earlier risen up against it (cf. 8.21) were now persuaded by Pisander to change sides and join the conspiracy—about 300 of them. But the popular party was aware of these schemes, and notified Leon and Diomedon, two *stratēgoi*, the trierarch Thrasybulus (who later led the struggle to overthrow the Thirty Tyrants) and the hoplite leader Thrasyllus, and also the men on the *Paralos*, so that when the 300 traitors attacked, they were defeated, thirty of them put to death, the rest granted amnesty and permitted to share in the democracy (8.73). The point I would emphasize here is that at critical moments in the Athenian *stasis* there are neutral men, or sensible men, or prudent and measured men, for example, Alcibiades, who intervene to prevent the *stasis* from developing into a full-blown one.

Chaireas, very enthusiastic for the change in government (8.74.1), was on the *Paralos*, and he went to the army and told them many exaggerated and false things about what was happening to the city, especially to their women and children (8.74). On hearing these things, the soldiers wanted to stone to death all who had been chief promoters of the oligarchy, but men of a more neutral position dissuaded them, reminding them of the nearby presence of their real enemies, the Peloponnesians (8.75.1). Next, Thrasybulus and Thrasyllus, who had been chief leaders of the pro-democratic party, made everyone, including all Samians of military age, take the most solemn oaths that they would fight to the end for the democracy, convinced that should the Four Hundred or the enemy army prevail it would mean complete destruction for them (8.75.2–3). So the struggle was now intense. The army dismissed its generals and held new elections of captains and generals, among them Thrasybulus and Thrasyllus, who encouraged them with many reasons not to be disheartened: they were a greater number than the oligarchs, had control of the whole navy to get supplies, a democratic city at Samos as good as Athens, control of the Piraeus, and above all, they only had to recall Alcibiades and (they mistakenly thought) he could provide them with an alliance with the Persian King; if all else failed, they could simply leave with their ships and settle elsewhere (8.76); thus they encouraged and comforted one another (8.77).

In the meantime, the leaders at Samos, especially Thrasybulus, succeeded in bringing Alcibiades to Samos under amnesty (8.81.1). Thucydides gives Alcibiades a speech in indirect discourse in which he generally complains about how badly Athens has treated him, and makes exaggerated, even false, claims about their need for the aid of Tissaphernes and how only he could secure it (81.2–3). The Athenians immediately elected Alcibiades general, and were so heartened by his words that they wanted to sail on the Piraeus, but Alcibiades opposed this, saying he must first consult with Tissaphernes; he thus, Thucydides says in his own name, made the Athenians fear (*phobein*) Tissaphernes, and Tissaphernes fear the Athenians, which, of course, raised his standing with both (8.82). After dealing with Peloponnesian affairs (8.83–85.3), Alcibiades returned from Tissaphernes to Samos (85.4). The envoys of the Four Hundred had also arrived at Samos and attempt to speak; after some commotion in the navy, they were permitted to do so (86.1–2). They said the Five Thousand would all share in the government, that Chaireas had lied to them, that their relatives were safe, and made a number of proposals: the one that gained the most favor with the navy was to sail on the Piraeus, and Alcibiades was the only man alive, according to Thucydides, who could have stopped them, and he did (86.3–4).

Here we get a remarkable statement from our author:

> Alcibiades seems then to a degree of the first order, and more than anyone else, to have benefitted the city (*kai dokei Alkibiadēs prōtos tote kai oudenos elasson tēn polin ōphelēsai*); for when the Athenians at Samos were bent on sailing against their own people [i.e., full-blown *stasis*], which if they had, the enemy would immediately have been masters of Ionia and the Hellespont; and at that time no other man than he would have been able to restrain the mob, but he stopped them from sailing, and reproaching those who were privately angry at the envoys, he caused them to desist (86.4).

Alcibiades alone saved Athens, and now, with this preeminent service to the city, Athens began to rebound in the war. He then sent word to Athens that he favored the installment of the Five Thousand and economic retrenchment; generally, that if the Athenians showed boldness to the enemy, and the *stasis* parties remained reconciled, they would prevail; otherwise, both parties would be destroyed (86.6–7). Meanwhile, envoys arrived from Argos offering assistance to the Athenian *dēmos* (86.8). Chapter 87 deals with some intrigues of Tissaphernes; Thucydides is uncertain of all the details (87.2), but speculates on his motives (87.4–5). After learning what Tissaphernes has done, Alcibiades sails to him, making great promises, but Thucydides says that he mostly wanted to compromise him with the Peloponnesians (88).

At about the same time, the envoys of the Four Hundred who were sent to Samos return to Athens with Alcibiades' encouraging message, which prompts most of the oligarchs to strengthen their resolve (89.1). A few spoke out, including Theramenes, although the most prominent were too afraid, so they now began to insist on the real establishment of the Five Thousand to place the government on a fairer basis (89.2). Thucydides, however, tells us that this was just playing politics; what each really wanted was to rule over all the others (89.3); most of all they were now jockeying for leadership of the democracy (89.4)! Those most opposed to democracy—Phrynichus (who had quarreled with Alcibiades), Aristarchus, Pisander, and Antiphon are named—sent envoys (including Antiphon) to Lacedaemon to seek peace; they also assiduously built up their fort at Eitonia (90.1–2). Theramenes immediately spoke out against them, and with good reasons: these extremists were willing to go so far as to let the Peloponnesians into the city, if necessary (90.3–4).

When the envoys returned from the Spartans without a peace agreement, Theramenes openly charged his fellow oligarchs with intending to invite the enemy into the city (91.1–2.), which Thucydides says was true (91.3). Now Phrynicus is murdered and the matter is permitted to drop, which emboldens Theramenes and others of the Four Hundred (92.2). Theramenes made charges against other enemies of the Four Hundred (92.3), and they set to work even more earnestly (92.4). After more machinations on both sides, all was in confusion and panic: those in the city expected an imminent attack from the Piraeus; those in the Piraeus expected the same from their enemies in the city (92.5–7). The older men exhorted everyone to calm down: the foreign enemy was nearby, and if they attacked while the Athenians were at one anothers' throats, Athens as a whole could be permanently ruined (92.8); but the hoplites remained furious (92.9), and they and the many (*hoi polloi*) in the Piraeus began to tear down the oligarchs' wall (92.10), wanting a return to full democracy. Their cry was for the Five Thousand to rule, because nobody was certain who the Five Thousand were, or even if they really existed, but in case they did, they refrained from calling for democracy outright; this uncertainty had been fomented by the Four Hundred, since it exploited the mystery about the Five Thousand to their own advantage (92.11).

The next day, the Four Hundred decided to march into the city, but some of the more reasonable men (*epieikeis*, 8.93.2) persuaded them to remain at rest, and the agitated hoplites also eventually agreed to hold an assembly of reconciliation (8.93). But at this point, forty-two Peloponnesian ships arrive nearby, and everything is thrown into confusion again, after which the Athenians *en masse*, seeing the enemy as a worse threat than fighting amongst themselves, hastened to the Piraeus and its walls, and prepared for battle (8.94).

Various battles ensue, some won by the Athenians, some by the Peloponnesians, but the Athenians lose the first one, and at this critical moment, the whole of Euboea revolts (8.95). This sends the Athenians into the greatest panic ever in the war; even more, Thucydides tells us, than after the disaster in Sicily (8.96.1): the fleet at Samos was in revolt, and they might come to battle among themselves (*stasiazontōn*) at any moment, and Euboea was of even greater importance to them than Attica (96.2); the enemy might sail into the Piraeus, which they could no longer defend, with disastrous consequences (96.3–4); but the Spartans, as on so many other occasions, proved the most accommodating of enemies, on account on their habitual slowness and lack of daring (*tolmoi*) (96.5). This permitted the Athenians to recoup: they held an assembly in which they officially deposed the Four Hundred and really established the rule of the Five Thousand; all who could furnish armor for themselves were to be members (97.1). In a remarkable statement, Thucydides judges that, in the first period of this new regime, Athens had the best government they ever had (i.e., better than Pericles' virtual kingship), for it was a measured (*metria*) blending of the oligarchs and the many, and it enabled the city to raise its head up and pursue the war intelligently (97.2). And they recalled Alcibiades and the other exiles (97.3). The *stasis* at Athens is essentially over. Their subsequent victory at the battle of Cynossema gave them renewed confidence that, after the recent series of disasters and their own *stasis*, they could prevail in the war if they pursued it with enthusiasm (*prothumōs*, 106.5).

Full *stasis* never came to Athens, because at critical moments there were "neutral-minded men," or "older men," and especially Alcibiades, whose words carried sufficient weight to forestall it. I take continual presence of such men to be a great Thucydidean compliment to Athens.

The Teaching on *Stasis*

If we allow Thucydides' ideas to unfold as he himself presents them, then there will be no doubt that *stasis* is intimately connected with war. *Stasis* and war alike are intimately related to "motion" (*kinēsis*); political health and prosperity to "rest" or "peace" (*hēsuchia*). When cities are in *stasis*, each faction has a strong incentive to call upon other cities for their aid, which usually brings about war; when cities are at war, they have a strong incentive to foment *stasis* in the enemies' cities. But there is no Hobbesian "individualism" in Thucydides' view of *stasis*, no "war of every man against every man": a group of individuals is always arrayed against another group of individuals. Regime change does not necessarily involve *stasis*. *Stasis* is the complete breakdown of a civilized society: friends conspire against and murder their friends; fathers conspire against and kill their sons; the rule of law disappears, most importantly, divine law. Men lose all hope of salvation in *stasis*, except for resort to evil deeds; words change their meaning, especially those sacred words—oaths—that normally make civilized society stable. What lies behind salutary oaths is trust (*pistis*); in *stasis*, all trust dissipates to nothing. Human beings sink to their lowest possible condition in full-blown *stasis*. In *stasis*, the virtue of "moderation" disappears; "moderation" may be the highest political virtue. For Thucydides, just as there is no "cure" for preventing war, *stasis* is coeval with political life.

Thucydides is interested above all in the relationship between motion (*kinēsis*) and rest (*hēsuchia*), neither of which is primary. Nothing, it seems, is ultimately permanent for Thucydides except this relationship, which is a cosmic one of which the political one is one manifestation. I say "cosmic" because the Greek mind at this time understood the "cosmos" to be the universe as it was visible to man: even Mount Olympus was a place on this earth. Why, then, is Thucydides interested in political philosophy, if we can call his thinking political philosophy, rather than natural philosophy? I suggest it is because Thucydides thinks that man as man can fully understand the human things, but never fully understand the superhuman or "divine" things. Nevertheless, *belief* in the "divine" things is essential to civilized human life. The teaching on the extreme evil of *stasis* is Thucydides' teaching on the extreme importance of piety. Piety—indeed, nothing—will stand in the way of full-blown *stasis* in the worst cases, but piety remains the strongest barrier to that happening. I think this teaching goes a long way toward explaining why Strauss's last writing submitted for publication was "Preliminary Observations on the Gods in Thucydides' Work" (1974), which begins, "These observations 'repeat,' i.e., modify, some observations which I have made in the Thucydides-chapter of *The City and Man*." These observations, then, are not "preliminary" in any normal sense. Rather, they expatiate on the sentences with which Strauss concluded his chapter in *The City and Man* (1964, 240–41):

> It suffices to remember what Thucydides tells us about oracles, earthquakes, and eclipses ... —in brief, all these things for which the modern scientific historian has no use or which annoy him, and to which classical political philosophy barely alludes because for it the concern with the divine has become identical with philosophy ....[W]hat is "first for us" is not the philosophic understanding of the city but that understanding which is inherent in the city as such, in the pre-philosophic city, according to which the city sees itself as subject and subservient to the divine in the ordinary understanding of the divine or looks up to it. Only by beginning at this point will we be open to the full impact of the all-important question which is coeval with philosophy although the philosophers do not frequently pronounce it—*quid sit deus*.

References

Connor, W. R. 1984. *Thucydides*. Princeton: Princeton University Press.
Edmunds, L. 1975. *Chance and Intelligence in Thucydides*. Cambridge: Harvard University Press.
Hornblower, S. 1996. *A Commentary on Thucydides*, 2 vols. Vol. II, Books IV–V.24. Oxford: Clarendon.

Orwin, Clifford. 1994. *The Humanity of Thucydides*. Princeton: Princeton University Press.
Palmer, Michael. 1982a. "Alcibiades and the Question of Tyranny in Thucydides." *Canadian Journal of Political Science* 15: 103–24.
Palmer, Michael. 1982b. "Love of Glory and the Common Good." *American Political Science Review* 76: 825–36.
Palmer, Michael. 1989. "Machiavellian *Virtù* and Thucydidean *Aretē*." *Review of Politics* 51: 365–85.
Palmer, Michael. 1992. *Love of Glory and the Common Good*. Lanham: Rowman and Littlefield.
Palmer, Michael. 2015. "The Spartan Alcibiades: Brasidas and the Prospect of Regime Change in Sparta in Thucydides' War." In *In Search of Humanity: Essays in Honor of Clifford Orwin*, edited by Andrea Radasanu, 65–85. Lanham: Lexington.
Price, Jonathan. 2001. *Thucydides and Internal War*. Cambridge: Harvard University Press.
Strauss, Leo. 1964. *The City and Man*. Chicago: Rand McNally.
Strauss, Leo. 1974. "Preliminary Observations on the Gods in Thucydides' Work." *Interpretation: A Journal of Political Philosophy* 4: 1–16.
Strauss, Leo, 1991. *On Tyranny*, edited by V. Gourevitch and M. Roth. New York: Free Press.
Thucydides. 1976. *Thucydidis Historiae*. Oxford Classical Texts Edition. Oxford: Oxford University Press.
Westlake, H.D. 1968. *Individuals in Thucydides*. Cambridge: Cambridge University Press.

CHAPTER 25

RELIGION, POLITICS, AND PIETY

PAUL A. RAHE

No one who reads Homer's *Iliad* and *Odyssey* and goes on to peruse Herodotus' *Histories* and work through Thucydides' *History* can fail to notice the degree to which the last-mentioned author is out of step with his two predecessors in his assessment of the role played by divine intervention in human affairs. The discrepancy was due in part to Thucydides' purpose. He was not a poet intent on justifying the ways of the gods to man. Nor was he a memorialist, writing to prevent "events" from becoming "evanescent" and "the great and wondrous deeds" of the Hellenes and the barbarians from being "deprived of fame" (Hdt., Pref.). Thucydides was an educator (Rahe 2006).[1]

The book that Thucydides composed as "a possession for all times rather than a contest piece to be heard straightaway" had as its focus statesmanship—chiefly, with regard to foreign affairs. Its author hoped that his *magnum opus* would be "judged useful by those who want to observe clearly the events which happened in the past and which ... will again," he believed, "come to pass hereafter in quite similar ways." To this end, he eschewed "the mythic" or "fabulous (*to muthōdes*)" in a fashion that, he knew, would render his narrative "less delightful (*aterpesteron*)" to some than those on offer from Homer and Herodotus (1.22.4). Oracles and other reports concerning the supernatural he treated with a skepticism foreign to his two great predecessors (2.17.1–2, 21.3, 5.26.3–4, 7.50.3–4, 8.1.1), and he attempted to understand politics and war solely within the horizon of "the human (*to anthrōpinon*)" with an eye to what he called "human nature (*anthrōpeía phusis*)" (1.22.4, 2.50.1, 3.82.2).

The fact that Thucydides thought this secular humanist perspective sufficient is telling. In antiquity, it persuaded Antyllus to call him "a bit godless (*atheos ērema*)" (Marcellinus *Vit. Thuc.* 22). Later, it led Thomas Hobbes, the first to translate Thucydides' *History* from Greek directly into English, to include its author among those in Hellas who "thought not" as his contemporaries "did of their ridiculous religion" but "by the

---

[1] All translations are my own.

light of natural reason" saw "enough in the religion of these heathen to make him think it vain and superstitious; which was enough to make him an atheist in the opinion of the people" (Hobbes 1628, 570–71). In highlighting Thucydides' skepticism, Antyllus and Hobbes are by no means peculiar. The Athenian's silence regarding the divine has caused many a scholar in more recent times to wonder whether he believed in the gods in which his city believed (Marinatos 1981).

It would nonetheless be an error to accuse Thucydides of harboring a "contempt for established religion," and it would be an even greater blunder to suppose that "his prejudice blinded him to [the] historical importance" of religious belief (Badian 1993, 112–13). Of course, where Herodotus is lavish—in discussing religious institutions, practices, and initiatives—the Athenian historian is parsimonious; and this sobriety has annoyed those who think every species of religious propaganda and every consultation of an oracle vitally important for understanding political developments (e.g., Hornblower [1992]; Flower [2009]). But the fact that Thucydides did not believe a full understanding of each and every religious gesture prerequisite for a comprehension of the war as such does not mean that he was insensitive to the role that piety played within the ancient city in shaping human conduct and promoting civic solidarity. As scholars have documented in detail, he touches on religious matters with great frequency (Jordan 1986; Price 2001, 217–36; Furley 2006).

Thucydides' treatment of Sparta is a case in point. In one passage, Herodotus tells us that the Spartans "made the things of the god take precedence over those of men" (5.63.2). In another, he claims that "attending to the affairs of the god was something that the Spartans took with the greatest seriousness" (9.7). Thucydides is more reticent. He makes no such general claim. He simply shows his readers without fanfare, in passage after passage, that the Lacedaemonians were punctilious in everything pertinent to the divine (1.103, 112, 118, 126–34, 2.74, 3.14–15, 92, 4.5, 118, 5.16–18, 23, 30, 49–50, 54, 75–76, 82, 116, 6.95, 7.18, 8.6). He also draws attention to a fact of no mean importance for political developments: that, when they did not fare well in the Archidamian War, the Spartans fell prey to a gnawing suspicion that their travails were due to a grave religious infraction on their part. In refusing Pericles' offer of arbitration on the eve of that war, they had broken the oaths to the gods they had taken in 446 when they agreed to the Thirty Years' Peace (cf. 7.18.2 with 1.78.4, 85.2, 140.2, 141.1, 144.2, 145). Of this violation they were painfully aware. Had they not at the time been promised victory by the oracle of Apollo at Delphi (1.118.3, 123.1, 2.54.4), one must suspect that the Lacedaemonians would have felt compelled to accept Pericles' offer.

Thucydides has considerably less to say about the religious scruples of the Athenians. But, in their regard, he is also alert. The Spartans who appear in his narrative—Pausanias the Regent, Sthenelaïdas, Archidamus, and Brasidas—invoke the gods and sacrifice to them (1.86.5, 2.71.2, 74.2, 4.87.3, 116.2, 5.10.2). Their Athenian counterparts—Pericles, Phormio, Paches, Demosthenes, Lamachus, Hippocrates, Eurymedon, Cleon, Diodotus, and Alcibiades—do nothing of the sort. Among the latter, however, there is one notable exception to the general rule.

Nicias is the only Athenian commander in the entire book alluded to as having conducted a sacrifice before battle (6.69.2). He is the only one of Thucydides' Athenians who advertises his devotion to the gods, who invokes their aid and support, and who contemplates the possibility that a series of setbacks that his compatriots have suffered might be due to a religious offense (7.69.2, 72.2–3, 77.2–3). As it turns out, Thucydides thought this same Nicias "somewhat overly inclined to divination and the like"—for, as a consequence of the interpretation given a lunar eclipse by the seers attendant on Athens' armada, he foolishly and fatally refuses to countenance a timely Athenian withdrawal from Sicily despite his better judgment as a general and that of his colleague Demosthenes (7.50.3–4). At least in this one instance, religion played as important a role in shaping Athenian calculations as it did more generally in shaping those of the Lacedaemonians.

The skepticism that Thucydides evinced did not engender scorn on his part. When he describes the evacuation of the Attic countryside that took place on the eve of the first Peloponnesian invasion, he adopts a tone of melancholy and pauses to relate the legendary history of the unification of Attica, to describe in some detail the city's religious topography, and to lay emphasis on the deep attachment felt by the great majority of Athenians for the country districts they were leaving to the invader, for their homes, their local communities, and their ancestral cult sites. This withdrawal was, he intimates, closely akin to exile. It meant an abandonment of that which was most near and dear. It required that the country folk change their way of life, and it left the Athenians sorely distressed and, we are led to believe, deracinated (2.14–17). This last point needs emphasis. For, as we shall see, Thucydides is deeply sensitive to the manner in which *familiarity* in the most expansive sense of that protean word—which is to say, the amalgam of tradition, sentiment, respect for elders, the love of one's own, and ancestral religion—quiets anxiety, contributes to domestic harmony and civic solidarity, and restrains and channels ambition; and he is alert to the profound political dangers attendant upon uprooting a population.

Athens' Unexpected Defeat

Thucydides' subject was power politics. His vision of that subject was neither narrow nor technical. He admired Pericles. He agreed with his net assessment of the relative strengths and weaknesses of Athens and Sparta as great powers (2.65.5, 13). That the Athenians had the upper hand at the beginning of the war, as Pericles repeatedly asserted (1.141.2–44.1, 2.62, 65.13), Thucydides did not doubt. When he recorded the death of the Athenian statesman, he attributed to him "foresight (*pronoia*) with regard to the war" (2.65.6).

But Thucydides was also aware that Athens eventually lost the war, and he intimates that there was a great deal that the Athenian statesman did not foresee. The latter told his compatriots "that they would prevail if they remained at rest (*hēsuchazontas*) and looked after the fleet and if, during the war, they made no attempt to extend their dominion and refrained from placing the city at risk." While he was alive, they did as instructed. But, when this sexagenarian disappeared from the scene—as, he surely knew, he soon would—"what they did was the contrary in all regards, for they governed themselves and their allies, even in matters seemingly extraneous to the war, with an eye to private ambitions and private profit in a manner quite harmful, pursuing policies whose success would be to the honor and advantage of private individuals, and whose failure brought harm to the city in the war" (2.65.7).

In part because of the respect he commanded, Pericles was able to guide his compatriots. He could rein them in when they became overconfident and buck them up when they were beset with doubt. "Those who came later," Thucydides laments,

> were more on an equal plane with one another, and each desiring to be first, they sought to please the people and to them handed over public affairs. In consequence, as tends to happen in a great city also possessed of an empire, they blundered in many regards, especially with respect to the expedition against Sicily—which failed not so much as a consequence of a mistake in judgment with regard to those against whom it was dispatched, as through the senders' not coming to a proper decision with regard to what suited the needs of those who had gone out, for they chose instead to occupy themselves in private quarrels regarding the leadership of the people, by which they blunted the efforts of those in the camp and became embroiled with one another in matters pertaining to the city. (2.65.8–11)

Even "after losing the better part of their fleet along with their other forces in Sicily," Thucydides tells us, the Athenians nonetheless managed to hold out "despite the fact that they were also caught up in sedition (*stasis*) within the city—until they tripped themselves up" once again "by means of their private differences" (2.65.12).

The implication of Thucydides' brief remarks in this poignant passage is that Athens lost the Peloponnesian War because she defeated herself and that Sparta won the war because she did nothing of the sort. This interpretation leaves open a question that Thucydides did not directly address. What difference accounts for the fact that Athens succumbed to civil strife while Sparta did not? Thucydides' *History* is an extended rumination on this very subject. It explores the manner in which the Athenians squandered the advantages they possessed at the beginning of the war; and, in an oblique manner, it indicates why they did so. There is more to Thucydides' analysis than a lament concerning the damage that political competition can inflict on a democracy. His book is a study of the failure of Pericles' foresight with regard to the political community that, in the preceding decades, he had done so much to shape. As such, it is a stern reminder that statesmen operating in the international arena must always be attentive to domestic affairs and to the tendencies inherent in particular political regimes.

Athens versus Sparta

On the eve of the war, the Corinthians are said to have given a speech at Lacedaemon in which they urged their Spartan allies to reflect on the vast gulf that separated them as a people from their rivals. "The Athenians," they observed,

> are innovators, keen in forming plans, and quick to accomplish in deed what they have contrived in thought. You Spartans are intent on saving what you now possess; you are always indecisive, and you leave even what is needed undone. They are daring (*tolmētai*) beyond their strength, they are risk-takers against all judgment, and in the midst of terrors they remain of good hope (*euelpides*)—while you accomplish less than is in your power, mistrust your judgment in matters most firm, and think not how to release yourselves from the terrors you face. In addition, they are unhesitant where you are inclined to delay, and they are always out and about in the larger world while you stay at home. For they think to acquire something by being away while you think that by proceeding abroad you will harm what lies ready to hand. In victory over the enemy, they sally farthest forth; in defeat, they give the least ground. For their city's sake, they use their bodies as if they were not their own; their intelligence they dedicate to political action on her behalf. And if they fail to accomplish what they have resolved to do, they suppose themselves deprived of that which is their own—while what they have accomplished and have now acquired they judge to be little in comparison with what they will do in the time to come. If they trip up in an endeavor, they are soon full of hope (*antelpisantes*) with regard to yet another goal. For they alone possess something at the moment at which they come to hope (*elpizousin*) for it: so swiftly do they contrive to attempt what has been resolved. And on all these things they exert themselves in toil and danger through all the days of their lives, enjoying least of all what they already possess because they are ever intent on further acquisition. They look on a holiday as nothing but an opportunity to do what needs doing, and they regard peace and quiet free from political business (*hēsuchian apragmona*) as a greater misfortune than a laborious want of leisure. So that, if someone were to sum them up by saying that they are by nature capable neither of being at rest (*echein hēsuchian*) nor of allowing other human beings to be so, he would speak the truth. (1.70)

Thucydides (1.118.2, 4.55.2–4, 8.96) endorses these claims, and subsequent events in the tale he tells confirm their accuracy with regard to both political communities. Moreover, this assessment—though intended by the Corinthians as a criticism of Lacedaemon—bears directly on the reasons for Sparta's success and Athens' ultimate failure in the war. For, as Thucydides' narrative reveals, a people constitutionally "incapable of being at rest (*echein hēsuchian*)" cannot for long be persuaded to do as Pericles advised and "remain at rest (*hēsuchazontas*)"; and the restlessness that characterizes such a people is conducive to "motion (*kinēsis*)," which eventuates in risky martial ventures abroad and in civil unrest and strife at home (1.1.2, 3.82.1).

The reply made by Archidamus the Spartan king to the charges lodged against his fellow Lacedaemonians by the Corinthians deserves attention as well—for, in defending his city and its way of life, he makes two crucial claims. He attributes to his compatriots a "sensible moderation (*sōphrosunē emphrōn*)" and suggests that, because of their sense of shame and moderation, they alone "refrain from giving way to arrogance (*ouk exubrizomen*)" when events turn out well; and after emphasizing that they are both brave in battle and prudent in council, he traces this prudence to the fact that they are not educated to think themselves wiser than their laws and that they are trained to avoid being excessively knowledgeable and intelligent (*xunetoi*) in matters that are of no use (1.84.2–3).

That both claims are true is evident. Neither Thucydides nor Pericles ever attributes *sōphrosunē* to the Athenians. In fact, at Camarina, the Athenian spokesman Euphemus rebuffs those who would presume to teach that virtue to his countrymen and embraces meddlesomeness (*polupragmosunē*) in its stead (Thuc. 6.87.2–4). In contrast, the Spartans are said to have been almost unique in managing to remain moderate (*esōphronēsan*) while enjoying prosperity and flourishing (8.24.4). Underpinning this *sōphrosunē* was an ethos of intense *familiarity* and exaggerated civic piety (Rahe 2016), which Sparta's leaders did nothing to subvert. It is this that explains why the Athenians could truthfully say that in their dealings with foreigners the Lacedaemonians are "conspicuous for thinking the pleasant noble (*kala*) and the advantageous just (*dikaia*)" and why they could then add, without missing a beat, that "in their dealings with one another and in holding to the established laws and customs of the land (*ta epichōria nomima*)" these same Lacedaemonians "display virtue (*aretē*) in the extreme" (5.105.4). The ethos of *familiarity* dictated both that one adopt a posture of loyalty and generosity with regard to those near and dear (*philoi*)—one's family, first of all; then, one's friends and fellow citizens—and that one regard outsiders with suspicion, if not outright hostility, and deal with them strictly as the interests of one's own community dictated.

The Twilight of the Gods

The Athenian response to the Corinthian indictment also deserves attention—for it was a calculated offense, aimed at "providing an indication of the power of their city—at reminding those older of what they knew, and at informing those younger with regard to matters of which they had no experience" (1.72.1). In making their response, the Athenian delegates sought to deter the Spartans from war and to encourage them to remain at rest (*to hēsuchazein*) by demonstrating that they themselves really were, as charged, "daring (*tolmētai*) beyond their strength" (cf. 1.70.3 with 1.72.1). They reminded the Lacedaemonians of the risks that their compatriots had taken when they fought alone against the Mede at Marathon and of the fact that, at the time of Salamis, they had contributed the most ships to the common cause and had provided in Themistocles the most intelligent (*xunetōtatos*) commander. "We displayed a zeal (*prothumia*) most daring by much (*polu tolmērotatē*)," they observe in reference to their remarkable decision to evacuate Attica and to take to the sea. "Had we not been daring (*mē etolmēsamen*)" in this extreme manner, they contend, the battle of Salamis would never have taken place, and events would have progressed in a restful manner (*kath' hēsuchían*)—as the Persians wished (1.73–74).

After reminding the Spartans of the daring that the Athenians had displayed at the time of the Persian Wars, the delegates demonstrate, in their defense of Athens' subsequent acquisition of a maritime empire, a species of intellectual *tolma* suggesting that, when Themistocles had anticipated Pericles in persuading their ancestors to uproot their families from the land and take to the sea, they had become deracinated in more ways than one and that, in the process, they had opened themselves up to radically new ways of thinking about the relationship between justice and necessity. At the outset, the delegates note that their allies had voluntarily sought Athenian hegemony and that the Athenians had been compelled to increase their power above all by fear, then by a love of honor, and later by a legitimate concern for their own interests (1.75). The Spartans, they observe, have certainly paid attention to their own interests in their disposition of affairs within the Peloponnesus (1.76.1). "We have done nothing wondrous," the Athenians insist, "nothing contrary to human ways, in accepting an empire given to us and in not yielding it up, having been conquered by the three greatest things—honor, fear, and self-interest. Nor were we the first such, for it has always been the case that the weaker are subject to those more powerful" (1.76.2).

This was not the last time that Athenian spokesmen would display this particular species of intellectual *tolma*. The species of *Realpolitik* they articulated on this occasion was, in fact, their stock in trade (Romilly 1963). Nowhere, however, in Thucydides' text is the argument advanced in as bald and shocking a fashion as it is in the Melian Dialogue (5.84–113), which took place at the halfway point in Thucydides' war and may have been intended to serve as the centerpiece in his narrative of the whole. For there the Athenians take advantage of a conversation held in private to ostentatiously eschew the attempt to justify their empire and their decision to expand it, dismissing as irrelevant the role they played in defeating the Mede and any wrong the Melians may have done them, and asserting that they and their interlocutors are both aware that "in human disputation assessments of justice pertain only where necessity is equal," while, in all other cases, "the strong do what they can and the weak acquiesce" (5.89). They go on to warn against relying on "hope (*elpis*)," which they deem "by nature costly"; and they urge the Melians not to fall prey to folly like "the many" who, "when they find themselves bereft of visible grounds for hope, turn to the invisible—to prophecy and oracles and the other things of this sort—which, when joined with hope, inflict injury" (5.103). Then, when the Melians piously voice their trust in divine justice (5.104), the Athenians respond,

> Nothing that we assert as just (*dikaioumen*) or do lies outside of what human beings think with regard to the divine and purpose with regard to themselves. Of the gods we believe and regarding humankind we know with clarity that by a necessity of nature, they rule wherever they have the power. And we did not set down this law (*nomos*) ourselves nor were we the first to take advantage of it once it was laid down.

> But having found it in existence and expecting to leave it forever in that condition, we make use of it—knowing that, if you and others possessed the power that we now possess, you would do the same. (5.105)

As this passage suggests, those who serve as spokesmen for the Athenians in Thucydides' narrative are students of the sophists. They draw a sharp distinction between *phusis* and *nomos* that is not to be found in the discourse of Thucydides' Spartans, and there is no discernible difference between the doctrine they advance and that espoused by Callicles in Plato's *Gorgias* (482c–484c) and parodied by Aristophanes in his *Clouds* (889–1104 with Rahe 2010).

If civil strife eventually engulfed Athens, it was in part because those in the political class at Athens recognized that every argument used to justify Athenian imperialism abroad could be applied with equal force to the justification of tyranny at home (Rahe 1995). No one who peruses the Melian Dialogue with Athens' subsequent trajectory in mind can read with equanimity the remark that Euphemus, the Athenian spokesman at Camarina, is said later to have made to the citizens of that Sicilian town: "For a man who is a tyrant or for a city possessing an empire (*archē*), nothing is contrary to the dictates of reason (*alogon*) that is of advantage and no one counts as one's kin except the one who can be trusted" (6.85.1).

What Thucydides writes concerning the revolution that took place at Corcyra early in the war was, as he makes clear (3.82.1), just as applicable to Athens in 411 and 404:

> The cause of all these things was rule pursued out of greed and the love of renown. From these prevailing passions arose as well a keen desire for victory. The leading figures in the cities claimed to be serving the common good—with each of the two sides adopting an attractive slogan, the patrons of the multitude expressing a preference for political equality and their opponents expressing one for a moderate aristocracy—but they were in fact seeking prizes for themselves. In their desire to prevail, they dared to conduct their struggle with one another with no holds barred and proceeded against one another in a terrible fashion and took a revenge greater still, not setting forth as a limit the dictates of justice and the city's advantage but limiting themselves always, on both sides, with an eye to their own pleasure. And they were ready to overpower their opponents either by condemning them on an unjust vote or by seizing them with their own hands and so sought to satisfy immediately their love of victory. And so neither side thought in terms of piety, and they listened more readily to decency of speech on the part of those who found in it the opportunity to do something odious. Those of the citizens in the middle were destroyed by both either because they had not joined in the struggle or by jealousy at their survival. (3.82.8)

The war itself had much to do with this development. "In peace and when matters go well," Thucydides explains, "cities and individuals are better-minded because they have not fallen into the necessity of doing what they do not wish. But war is a violent teacher (*biaios didaskalos*). In depriving them of the means for easily satisfying their daily wants, it assimilates the thinking of the many to their present circumstances" (3.82.1–3).

In the case of Athens, however, something more was at work—for, thanks to the sophistic doctrine embraced by the city's leaders, there had been a relaxation in the traditional ties uniting those of the Athenians in the political class, and they were at the outset already partway down the road where war and hardship would take the Corcyraeans:

> Ties of kinship were less close than those based on one's membership of a political club since those in the latter were readier, without hesitation, to engage in daring action. Such associations were of use not within the context of the established laws (*nomoi*) but for aggrandizement contrary to them. And their members confirmed their trust in one another not by an appeal to the divine law (*theios nomos*) but by a common project of breaking the law. Things nobly said by opponents were greeted, if one had a start on them, not with the generosity of the well-born but by guarding against the deeds that might follow. To take revenge on someone was preferable to avoiding suffering in his stead. And if there were oaths of reconciliation, they were exchanged with regard to an immediate difficulty and remained in force as long as the parties lacked support from elsewhere. And when the opportunity arose, the one anticipating became bold if he caught the other off guard, and he took greater pleasure in exacting vengeance because of the prior establishment of trust than if the deed had been openly done—and he calculated that it was safe because he had gained victory by deceit and in addition had won a contest for intelligence. (3.82.6–7)

If the Spartans won the war, Athens' abandonment of the ethos of *familiarity* was surely one of the reasons.

Periclean Athens

In their speech at Lacedaemon, the Corinthians assert that the Athenians are daring and restless "by nature." Thucydides does not endorse their claim. Instead, he intimates that Pericles bore considerable responsibility for the restless ambition and the spirit of political and intellectual daring that consumed his compatriots, and he allows us to infer that irreligion and a contempt for tradition had something to do with their formation.

The Funeral Oration that Pericles is said to have delivered at the end of the first year of the war is a remarkable document. It eschews what I have called *familiarity*, and it offers little in the way of consolation. It begins with a critique of tradition and an attack on the law specifying that such an oration be delivered (2.35). It gives the accomplishments of the Athenians' ancestors short shrift (2.36). It is entirely silent concerning the gods and heroes of the land; and, despite the annual celebration in Attica of the Eleusinian Mysteries, Pericles never once mentions the afterlife. When he does touch on the athletic contests that took place at Athenian festivals and the sacrifices that were conducted by the city at frequent intervals, he abstracts entirely from their religious significance and treats them solely as forms of recreation and release from toil (2.38.1).

The speech as a whole is focused on the Athenian regime, on the character of the Athenians, and their way of life (2.36.7–46.1); and it praises its audience, as orators are apt to do, for displaying the qualities that the eulogist wants to instill: qualities in this case that really would make of the citizens of Athens "the education of Hellas" (2.41.1). Among these qualities is one that deserves especially close attention here. "*Philosophoumen*," says Pericles regarding his compatriots, "*aneu malakías*" (2.40.1).

The proper rendering of the Greek in this brief passage is controversial, and, until quite recently, translators tended to be incredulous and to dance around the fact that Pericles seems both to be attributing to his compatriots a dedication to philosophy and a love of wisdom and to be offering them as living proof that one can engage in philosophy without incurring cowardice. This is, however, the meaning of his insistence a few lines thereafter that the Athenians "do not regard the making of arguments (*logoi*) as something harmful to the doing of deeds (*erga*) but consider it harmful, instead, to fail to secure instruction in advance through rational speech (*logos*) with regard to that which must be done." This is, moreover, what he has in mind when he insists that his compatriots comport themselves "in a distinctive fashion" by combining in themselves at the same time "daring (*tolman*) of an extreme sort with deliberation (*eklogizesthai*) on a high plane concerning everything that they attempt—while in others ignorance (*amathia*) inspires boldness and calculation (*logismos*), a shrinking from action." It would be "just," Pericles insists, "to regard as strongest in soul those who have a clear knowledge of what is terrible and of what is pleasant and do not because of this turn away from dangers" (2.40.2–4). Pericles' apparent aim is to dispel illusion, promote strength of soul, and teach resoluteness; and it is this that explains this philosophical statesman's ostentatious silence with regard to the gods and heroes and to life after death.

Erōs and *Logos*

Thucydides' Pericles did not, however, think reason's sway sufficient as a replacement for the ethos of *familiarity*. In place of the gods as an object of devotion and a source of civic solidarity, he exalts the city itself, and it he treats as a means for overcoming death. He delivered the Funeral Oration in the Ceramicus, in all likelihood with the Acropolis as a backdrop. In this speech, he sought to induce those in his audience to move beyond traditional patriotism, which was rooted not only in a sober calculation of self-interest but also in sentiment, a sense of belonging, a love for one's own, filial piety, and a profound dedication to, respect for, and awe in the face of the gods and heroes of the land. To this end, knowing that his auditors could not help looking past him to the Parthenon and the other temples on the Acropolis, he encouraged them to continue doing what they were already doing. "Feast your eyes," he said, "every day upon the actual power of the city" (2.43.1). Then he resorted to a surprising sexual metaphor, suggesting that they "become *erastai* of"—which is to say, lovers fixated on—"the city" or "its power" (the Greek is ambiguous). Through Athens and the greatness of its imperial achievement, as he has already suggested, they will secure in fame and glory a species of eternal life: "We inspire wonder now, and we shall in the future. We have need neither for the panegyrics of a Homer nor for the praises of anyone to whose conjecture of events the truth will do harm. For we have forced every sea and every land to give access to our daring (*tolma*); and we have in all places established everlasting memorials of evils [inflicted on enemies] and of good [done to friends]" (2.41.4).

In his final oration (2.60–64), at a time when his compatriots were beleaguered and needed encouragement, Pericles returned to this theme with even greater vigor, magnifying the greatness of Athens, boasting that Athens' empire extends beyond her region of actual control to the maritime world as a whole. Of the sea, he says, "you are in control—not only of the area at present in your power, but elsewhere too, if you want to go further. With your navy as it is today there is no power on earth—not the King of Persia nor any people under the sun—which can stop you from sailing where you wish" (2.62.2). He acknowledges that Athens' empire resembles a tyranny; notes that it may seem to have been unjust to take it up; adds that it is, in any case, now unsafe to let it go (2.63.2); and then returns to his principal theme:

> Remember that this city has the greatest name among all mankind because she has never yielded to adversity, but has spent more lives in war and has endured severer hardships than any other city. She has held the greatest power known to men up to our time, and the memory of her power will be laid up forever for those who come after. Even if we now have to yield (since all things that grow also decay), the memory shall remain that, of all the Greeks, we held sway over the greatest number of Hellenes; that we stood against our foes, both when they were united and when each was alone, in the greatest wars; and that we inhabited a city wealthier and greater than all.

He concedes that Athens is envied and loathed, but argues that such hatred is short lived—since "the splendor (*lamprotēs*) of the present is the glory of the future laid up as a memory for all time" (2.64). It is by encouraging in the citizens a love of the beautiful, focused on Athens and the greatness of its empire, that Pericles attempts to reconcile the citizen's natural interest in his own private welfare with a devotion to the common good.

Pericles' deployment of erotic imagery in this speech is arresting, and it has particular purchase in Thucydides, where *erōs* and its cognates are used sparingly—always to powerful effect. In the Mytilenean Debate, for example, Diodotus (3.45) intimates that, in the funeral oration, Pericles contradicted himself and he asserts that, when inserted in the political realm, *erōs* subverts the human capacity for assessing deeds by way of rational speech. All human beings, he suggests, really are "by nature" inclined to do wrong; law (*nomos*) and the threat of punishment are incapable of imposing restraint since "hope (*elpis*) and the lust for all (*erōs epi panti*)" are more powerful than the fear of death, especially in the case of "cities" concerned "with the greatest of things, freedom and rule over others," in which "each citizen, acting in concert with all," is inclined to overestimate his capacities "in a manner devoid of calculation and impervious to speech (*alogistōs*)."

When he made his first attempt to dissuade his compatriots from launching the Sicilian expedition, Nicias is said also to have resorted to erotic imagery, urging on them a salutary sobriety and warning them against becoming "lustful in a perverse manner (*duserōtas*) for that which is far afield" (6.13.1). In response, Alcibiades, who had been Pericles' ward, reportedly argued that the Athenians had to be forever expanding their dominion if they were to retain what they held and that rest (*hēsuchía*) would be fatal to their city (6.18.2–3, 6). In one of the most telling passages in the entire book, Thucydides then observes that, when Nicias intervened in vain a second time to the same purpose—this time, emphasizing the daunting scale of the endeavor and suggesting that, if the enterprise was to be undertaken, a much larger armada would be required than had hitherto been contemplated (6.19.2–23.3)—his attempt to induce his compatriots to pull back from the brink backfired and "an *erōs* for the expedition fell upon everyone alike."

> To the older men it seemed that they would either subdue the places against which they were sailing or, with so great a force, trip up not at all. Those in their prime felt a yearning for sights and spectacles (*pothos opseōs kai theōrias*) far afield and were of good hope (*euelpides*) that they would be safe. The great mass of people and the soldiers presumed that they would secure silver in the short run and add to their possessions a power whence they would draw wages forever. Because of the excessive desire of the majority, if there was anyone not pleased at the prospect, he feared lest in voting against it he might seem hostile to the city and so he remained at rest (*hēsuchian ēgen*).

In the grips of blind passion, the Athenians then greatly expanded the armada and compounded the danger that they incurred (6.24–26). There can be little doubt that the restlessness and daring inherent in the abandonment of Athens' ancestral religion and the ethos of *familiarity* and in the substitution of an erotic quest for immortal glory and grandeur, which Pericles preached to his compatriots, contributed mightily to their success as imperialists. But, if Thucydides is to be trusted, it also contributed mightily to their demise.

STRESSES AND STRAINS

Passion was not, however, the sole contributor. Early in the war, Athens fell prey to a plague, and Thucydides made much of its impact. He began by describing "the nature" of the disease, using terminology found in the Hippocratic medical texts to describe with great precision its symptoms and trace its trajectory with an eye to enabling men in the future to recognize the malady should it reappear (2.47–50). His chief purpose, however, was to examine the impact of the disease on "human nature" (2.50.1). To this end he explored the manner in which the plague (2.51.4) instilled in human beings a "spiritlessness" that subverted the influence of honor and eliminated the capacity of convention (*nomos*)—whether sanctioned solely by custom or by force of law—to restrain human conduct. As Thucydides put it,

> Overpowered by the violence (*huperbiazomenou*) done by the evil and not knowing what would become of them, human beings became neglectful of things alike sacred and profane. All the *nomoi* that they had formerly observed with regard to burials were confounded and each conducted the rites as best he could. And many, lacking what was required because of the number of those who had died before, resorted to the most shameless methods in disposing of the deceased. To funeral pyres piled up by others, some would add the corpses of their own relatives and, getting in ahead, they would set them afire; others would hurl the bodies they were carrying on top of other corpses already burning and then go away.
>
> In this regard and in others, the plague first gave rise to a marked increase in *anomia*. Seeing the abrupt changes—the unforeseen demise of those who were flourishing and the manner in which the propertyless suddenly came to possess the substance of those who had died—the individual more readily dared to do what he had previously kept hidden and had done in a manner contrary to the dictates of pleasure. And so they thought it worthwhile to reap the fruits quickly with an eye to their own gratification since they regarded their bodies and their money alike as ephemera. And no one was enthusiastic about persisting in what was deemed beautiful and noble since they thought it unclear whether they would die or not before achieving it. So whatever gave immediate pleasure or seemed conducive to it in any way was regarded as both noble and useful. No fear of the gods and no human *nomos* held them back. With regard to the former they judged that it was the same whether they were reverent or not—seeing that all were equally likely to die; with regard to the latter no one expected lives to last long enough for anyone to come to trial and pay the penalty for his offenses since a much greater penalty had been passed on him and was impending—so that it was only fair and reasonable that he enjoy life a bit before that penalty befell him. (2.52–53)

The collapse of morals and manners described in this remarkable passage, the emancipation of individual daring, and the attendant disappearance of all respect for *nomos* (whether human in origin or putatively divine) deserve careful attention.

This plague struck Athens at the very beginning of the war, and Thucydides intimates that it exacted a terrible toll—killing perhaps a quarter or even a third of the population (cf. 3.87.3 with 2.13.6–8), and permanently injuring many of those who survived (2.49.7–8). Although its short-term effect was to undermine morale and loosen all restraints—including those associated with the traditional religion—its long-term impact on the majority of those who survived was to transform religious anxiety into something akin to terror. It was natural and perhaps even inevitable, as the structure of Thucydides' narrative is meant to suggest (Kallet 2013), that many of those who had the time to reflect on what they had been through should suppose that it had been the work of Apollo, whose oracle had promised the Lacedaemonians his support (Thuc. 1.118.3, 123.1, 2.54.4) and was thought to have issued the Athenians warnings long before (2.17.2, 54.2–5). Even Pericles—who was alert to the manner in which "that which is sudden and unexpected and comes to pass largely in defiance of reason" is apt to "enslave the mind and spirit"— catalogues the malady in his last oration among "the things demonic—sent by the gods" (2.61.3, 64.2). If the Athenians later repeatedly succumbed to religious hysteria, their suffering early in the war may well have been a cause (Rubel 2014).

Religious Panic

The deracination described above no doubt compounded the anxiety of the Athenians. The irreligion embraced by Athens' leaders also gave rise in some quarters to flagrant misconduct that was widely regarded as a moral and religious offense. Alcibiades—who, after studying with Socrates and the sophists, emerged as a political force at the end of the Archidamian War—was a case in point. The extravagance and licentiousness that he displayed in his private life inspired in his compatriots a suspicion that he was intent on establishing a tyranny (6.15.2–4).

The explosion took place in 415. One night, shortly before the Sicilian Expedition's departure, a team of vandals defaced the images—scattered throughout the city—of Hermes, the god of travelers. Soon thereafter, it was discovered that others had burlesqued the Eleusinian mysteries in private homes. Fearing that, if the perpetrators were not caught and executed, the city and those about to be dispatched abroad would incur divine wrath, the Athenians demanded an investigation. Those within the political class who were in the grips of an erotic ambition for political power then moved to take advantage of the opportunity that this religious panic afforded them, and suspicion fell on Alcibiades and on other wealthy young aristocrats in his generation known for insolence in their private lives. Alcibiades was recalled from Sicily and escaped execution only by fleeing into exile. At Athens, a bloodbath took place; and the expedition in Sicily was left in the care of a general lacking the audacity requisite for success (6.27–29, 53–61).

Religious hysteria played a role in Sicily not long thereafter at the time of the lunar eclipse mentioned above—where a majority of the Athenians in the expeditionary force reportedly joined Nicias in embracing the advice of the seers accompanying the expedition (7.50.3–4). And an even graver disturbance took place a few years later in the aftermath of the battle of Arginusae—when, at a time when Athens was in desperate straits, unscrupulous, jealous politicians battling for supremacy again took advantage of the fact that their compatriots were caught up in a wave of religious hysteria and this time succeeded in getting them to turn on the city's victorious generals, try them for the religious offense of having failed to recover the bodies of those who had died at sea in the battle, and execute those foolish enough to have returned home.

Thucydides did not live to write about the latter event. But had he lived, he would certainly have discussed it at length—for the elimination of Athens' most experienced generals paved the way for the annihilation of her fleet at Aegospotami two years thereafter and her loss of the war (Kagan 1987, 325–412). If Thucydides' judgment and narrative merit trust, the attempt to turn away from the ethos of *familiarity* and to marginalize Athens' ancestral religion—which Pericles championed—backfired in ways ruinous for Athens.

References

Badian, Ernst. 1993. "Plataea between Athens and Sparta." In *From Plataea to Potidaea: Studies in the History and Historiography of the Pentacontaetia*, 109–23. Baltimore: Johns Hopkins University Press.

Flower, Michael A. 2009. "Athenian Religion and the Peloponnesian War." In *Art in Athens during the Peloponnesian War*, edited by Olga Palagia, 1–23. Cambridge: Cambridge University Press.

Furley, William D. 2006. "Thucydides and Religion." In *Brill's Companion to Thucydides*, edited by Antonio Rengakos and Antonis Tsakmakis, 415–38. Leiden: Brill

Hobbes, Thomas. (1628) 1989. "On the Life and History of Thucydides." Reprinted in Thucydides, *The Peloponnesian War: The Complete Hobbes Translation*, 569–86. Ed. David Grene. Chicago: University of Chicago Press.

Hornblower, Simon. 1992. "The Religious Dimension to the Peloponnesian War, or, What Thucydides Does Not Tell Us." *Harvard Studies in Classical Philology* 94: 169–97.

Jordan, Borimir. 1986. "Religion in Thucydides." *Transactions of the American Philological Association* 116. 119–47.

Kagan, Donald. 1987. *The Fall of the Athenian Empire*. Ithaca: Cornell University Press.

Kallet, Lisa. 2013. "Thucydides, Apollo, the Plague, and the War." *American Journal of Philology* 134, no. 3 (Fall): 355–82.

Marinatos, Nanno. 1981. *Thucydides and Religion*. Königstein: A. Hain.

Price, Jonathan. 2001. *Thucydides and Internal War*. Cambridge: Cambridge University Press.

Rahe, Paul A. 1995. "Thucydides' Critique of *Realpolitik*." *Security Studies* 5, no. 2 (Winter): 105–41.

Rahe, Paul A. 2006. "Thucydides as Educator." In *The Past as Prologue: The Importance of History to the Military Profession*, edited by Williamson Murray and Richard Hart Sinnreich, 95–110. Cambridge: Cambridge University Press.

Rahe, Paul A. 2010. "The Aristophanic Question." In *Recovering Reason: Essays in Honor of Thomas L. Pangle*, edited by Timothy Burns, 67–82. Lanham: Lexington.

Rahe, Paul A. 2016. *The Spartan Regime: Its Origins, Character, and Grand Strategy*. New Haven: Yale University Press.

Romilly, Jacqueline de. 1963. *Thucydides and Athenian Imperialism*. Translated by Philip Thody. Oxford: Blackwell.

Rubel, Alexander. 2014. *Fear and Loathing in Ancient Athens: Religion and Politics during the Peloponnesian War*. Translated by Michael Vickers and Alina Piftor. London: Routledge.

CHAPTER 26

THUCYDIDES ON THE POLITICAL PASSIONS

VICTORIA WOHL

ONE doesn't think of Thucydides as a particularly emotional author. His emphasis on clear-sighted analysis of political realities, his reliance on manifest evidence, and his repudiation of the "mythical" (1.1, 1.21–22) would seem to leave little space for something as apparently subjective and irrational as passion. But this seeming apathy is purely superficial. In fact, the passions—*ta pathē*—are central to Thucydides' analysis of the war and its politics. They are part of the makeup of Athenian democracy and of Thucydides' theorization of it. They are also seminal to his understanding of *to anthrōpinon*, human nature, and therefore to his very conception and practice of history.

THE "TRUEST CAUSE": THE AFFECTIVE HISTORY OF THE PELOPONNESIAN WAR

The importance of emotion for Thucydides' history is indicated early on. At 1.23.6 Thucydides sets out to explain the immediate causes of the Peloponnesian War, but he states that "the truest cause, although least manifest in discourse (*tēn men gar alēthestatēn prophasin, aphanestatēn de logōi*) was that the growth of Athens and the fear (*phobon*) it created in Sparta made the war inevitable (*anankasai*)" (1.23.6; see Robinson, chapter 6 in this volume).[1] This key introductory sentence proposes an underlying emotional causality to the war. Fear is posited both as a historical cause—even a compulsion (*anankasai*)—and a historical effect. This most obscure (*aphanestatēn*) affective substructure will become manifest both in the *logos* (speech, discourse) of Thucydides' historical agents—*pathos* being an inextricable element of political rhetoric—and in his

---

[1] All translations are my own.

own *logos*: the passions pervade both Thucydides' depiction of Greek politics and his historical analysis of them.

This "truest" element of the *History* is "most obscure" for our modern interpretive *logos*, as well. The passions are a difficult object of historical analysis. For one thing, emotions are culturally specific, and the Greeks' *pathē* may not correspond exactly to our own, as David Konstan notes. He compares them to colors: just as we are not sure that the Greeks perceived blue in the same way we do, we can't be certain that the Spartans' *phobos* meant the same thing for them as "fear" means for us (2006, 3–40; see further Shweder 2003). Greek affective vocabulary is not immediately transparent, then. Nor does it necessarily exhaust the text's affect: in addition to the various words we translate as "fear" (from *phobos* and *deos* to the more intense *ekplēxis* and *kataplēxis*), fear can inhere in words like *asphaleia* (security), *hēsuchia* (peace, quiet, quietism), or *tarachē* (disturbance): these words denote objective conditions but also bear an implicit affective charge. The precise nature of that charge is not fixed, however. *Hēsuchia*, for instance, can evoke the confident tranquility of peace or the anxious inactivity of a population during civil war. So affect really is obscure (*aphanes*). It requires and is subject to interpretation, and this not only by modern readers but also by ancient actors, for, as we shall see, the tendentious interpretation and attribution of affect will be a central strategy in the Athenian politics Thucydides describes, as well as in his own textual politics.

The mobility and malleability of emotion are stressed by affect theorist Sara Ahmed. In *The Cultural Politics of Emotion* (Ahmed 2004a; cf. Ahmed 2004b), Ahmed argues that emotion is not a thing that originates or inheres within a subject, although we often speak of it that way. Nor does it inhere within an object, waiting to be released upon contact. Instead, Ahmed understands emotion as a set of relations between subject and object that defines both. Inherently fluid and shaped by power, emotions are not psychological states for her but instead social practices. Thus, she proposes, the question we should ask is not what affect is but what it *does*: how does it circulate within a society and define that society through its circulation? What sort of relations shape it or are shaped by it?

With these questions in mind we might return to the "truest cause" of the war and consider how fear circulates between the Athenians and Spartans, defining each and the relation between them (a process tracked in the Pentacontaetia and throughout Book I of the *History*). In fact, we could say that *phobos* names that relation, on which Thucydides imposes one political interpretation when he identifies Athens as its source and Sparta as its site of manifestation. To say this is to propose, again following Ahmed, that the passions are inherently political, the product of politics as well as their engine. How are various emotions defined? Are they imagined as rational or irrational, active or passive, empowering or disempowering? To whom are they attributed and is that attribution figured as a matter of inherent nature or historical contingency? These questions are arenas of political contest; their answers, its stakes.

Central to this politics of emotion—both for Thucydides and for political theory more broadly—is the question of emotion's relation to reason. At first sight the passions in Thucydides would seem to be antithetical to rational deliberation, and hence to the well-governed polis. So says Diodotus in a famous passage of the Mytilenean Debate in Book 3: "there are two things most inimical to good counsel (*eubouliāi*), haste and anger (*orgēn*): the former is generally accompanied by folly (*anoias*) and the latter by ignorance and lack of intelligence (*gnōmēs*)" (3.42.1). Wise policy for Diodotus is governed by rational calculation and reasoned debate of the polis' self-interest, both of which are clouded by passion (3.42.1–5, 3.48.1). The emotions, in his view, are irrational and lawless: "incurable and overpowering, they lead men into danger" (3.45.4). Intrinsic to human nature (*anthrōpeias phuseōs*, 3.45.7), they drive men to act with no thought of the laws or their own advantage (3.45.3). Above all, he remarks, "hope (*elpis*) and desire (*erōs*) do the most damage, desire leading and hope following; desire devising schemes and hope providing the resources of chance; these invisible forces (*aphanē*) are mightier than visible dangers" (3.45.5), as they lead men and cities alike to self-destruction.

The antithesis Diodotus draws between passion and (political) reason has been pervasive in Western political thought; it is also pervasive, as we shall see, in Thucydides' own political thought. But it was not the only or even the most prevalent way of thinking about the *pathē* in ancient Greece. For Aristotle, as David Konstan (Konstan 2006) and Martha Nussbaum (Nussbaum 2001) have stressed, the passions have a strong cognitive component. Aristotle defines fear, for example, as an evaluation of the likelihood of harm, based on assessment of the power, character, and relative status of the one threatening and the possible checks (practical, moral, or institutional) on his ability to inflict damage (Arist. *Rhet.* 1382a20–83b10; Konstan 2006, 129–55). Fear for Aristotle is "not an instinctive aversion but a socially conditioned response in which relations of power and judgments concerning the status and attitudes of others play a crucial role" (Konstan 2006, 133). Fear "makes people deliberative" (*bouleutikous*, *Rhet.* 1383a7). Likewise, pity is not an automatic reaction to the sight of human misery for Aristotle, but a discerning response to unmerited suffering; it demands appraisal of desert based on social norms and a notion of justice (*Rhet.* 1385b11–86b7; Nussbaum 1996; Konstan 2001; Konstan 2006, 201–18; cf. Lateiner 2005). Aristotle's *pathē* are not the irrational forces imagined by Diodotus. Far from preventing rational judgment, they are in fact inextricable from and indispensable to it.

We see this cognitive understanding of the emotions in Cleon's counter-speech to Diodotus in the Mytilenean Debate. Whereas Diodotus argues against pitying the Mytileneans on the basis of rational self-interest (3.48), Cleon claims that the Mytileneans do not merit the Athenians' pity, because they have brought their suffering on themselves. Emphasizing the *hubris* of the Mytilenean revolt and the contempt it displayed for Athens' superior power (3.39.4–5), he proposes that the Mytileneans deserve not pity but in fact anger (*orgē*). Cleon predicates his argument on assessments of desert and the rhetoric of justice (*dikē*). Accordingly, his appeal to the emotions does not oppose them to reason, as Diodotus does, but instead makes them the basis for reasoned calculation of Athens' interests and its relations—present and future—with its allies (3.40.2–3).

And yet, even as Cleon proposes that the passions are cognitively informed and appropriate to democratic debate, Diodotus accuses his opponent's inflammatory rhetoric of arousing passions that override sound political judgment (3.43), a charge Thucydides seems to second when he introduces Cleon as "most violent and most persuasive to the people" (3.36.6). But Diodotus' position is equally contradictory. His exhortation to dispassionate deliberation would make the Athenian ecclesia a conspicuous exception to his universal law of human nature, that passion drives all men always to act against their own self-interest. It is also complicated by his claim that in Athens the demos' resentment and suspicion force orators to deceive in order to persuade them (3.43.2–3). Perhaps this skillful speech—which advocates a merciful policy by rejecting considerations of mercy—is an example of such deception and the call for dispassion is itself a hidden appeal to the audience's emotions (MacLeod 1978, 73–78; Connor 1984, 85). If so, is it really possible to eliminate the passions from political debate, as Diodotus advocates?

This debate suggests the ambivalence of emotion's connection to political reason (see further Visvardi 2012). It also suggests that this connection is itself political, for whether we deem emotion reason's enemy or ally depends on our response to the prior question of what political reason is and who can most persuasively claim it. Philosophers and cognitive scientists can debate the rationality of the emotions in the abstract; but within Thucydides' *History*, as the Mytilenean Debate suggests, the question is itself fully political. Defining the emotions as rational (or irrational) is not a preliminary to admitting them into (or barring them from) politics, but instead a tactic and outcome of political struggle. The nature of the political passions is thus always already a political issue, a question posed—and tendentiously answered—from within the political sphere.

My paper explores this contention in Athenian domestic and imperial politics. The central section examines how Thucydides uses the antithesis between reason and passion to understand Periclean democracy. Observing how Thucydides uses the demos' passion to construct a specific vision of political rationality, we shall see that articulating emotion's relation to politics is itself a primary political gesture. The final section will examine the irrational passions that propel Athens' empire. The disastrous Sicilian Expedition supports Diodotus' theory that *elpis* and *erōs* drive men to act against their own interests, but whether these destructive passions are intrinsic to democracy, Athens, or human nature in general, remains an open question, and one with significant consequences for Thucydides' politics and historiography.

Affective Leadership: Pericles and the Demos

In his summation of the career of Pericles, Thucydides explains the leader's extraordinary authority:

> The reason for it was that due to his standing, his intelligence (*gnōmēi*) and his manifest immunity to bribery he was able to restrain the majority liberally, and he was not

led by it but rather himself led, and because he did not acquire power through unfitting means, by speaking for pleasure, but, holding power on account of his prestige, he even contradicted [the majority] so as to provoke their anger (*pros orgēn*). When he saw them arrogantly confident beyond due measure (*para kairon hubrei tharsountas*) his speech knocked them down to fear, and again when they were irrationally anxious (*dediotas ... alogōs*), he restored them to confidence once more. It was a democracy in name, but in fact, the rule of the first man. (2.65.8–9)

In this famous passage, Thucydides attributes Pericles' success (at least in part) to his ability to regulate the irrational and excessive moods of the demos. Effective leadership is affective leadership. The passage rests upon the same antithesis Diodotus draws between *orgē* and *gnōmē*. *Orgē* means anger or vehement emotion more generally (Allen 2007). *Gnōmē* denotes rational intelligence, reason, or purposeful resolve (Huart 1973, especially 68–89). It can also bear the more concrete meaning of a political policy. In inscriptions, *gnōmē* is used for motions or decisions in the ecclesia; as such it embodies the judgment of the Athenian demos, and in translating that judgment directly into policy, enshrines the principle of *dēmokratia*, the *kratos* (power) of the demos.

This passage places that affective antithesis at the heart of the relation between Pericles and the demos. *Gnōmē* is "a leitmotif of Pericles in the *History*" (Edmunds 1975, 8; see further Edmunds 1975, 7–88; Farrar 1988, 156–77). This *gnōmē* is represented as virtually passionless: it is immune to the greed and personal ambition that will make later politicians seek office by "unfitting means," including "speaking for pleasure" (*pros hēdonēn*). Pericles' dispassionate intelligence even allows him to contradict the people "so as to provoke their anger" (*pros orgēn*), an anger that defines the demos just as *gnōmē* does the statesman. Against Pericles' steady and steadfast resolve, the demos swing between inappropriate (*para kairon*) and irrational (*alogōs*) emotional extremes. Through his *gnōmē*, Pericles holds the demos' excessive *orgai* in a precarious affective equilibrium that Thucydides sees as definitive of both his leadership and Athens' greatness under it. Just as Sparta's fear is the "truest" cause of the war, so the demos' *orgē* reveals the true nature of Athenian democracy: a democracy in name but in fact the rule of the first man.

The ideas in this passage are so familiar that it is easy to take them for granted: that Pericles is characterized by his rational intelligence; that the people are inherently emotional; that reason naturally does, or normatively should, govern emotion within politics. But these propositions are not inevitable or somehow "natural." Instead, the people's passion emerges out of its relation with its leaders, as an effect of political contest. That contest centers on Pericles' controversial decision (*gnōmē*) to remove the Athenians from their land at the start of the war and gather the whole population within the walls of the city. The Athenians' emotions first become politically salient when they move from the country to the city: in fact, the word *orgē* is used of the Athenians in the first two books of the *History* only in their relation to the land (1.143.5, 2.11.7; cf. 1.74.3).

At 2.14, in a lengthy digression, Thucydides explains their mood. From the time of Cecrops the Athenians had lived in local communities with their own local governments. Theseus united these communities politically, but even after the synoecism the Athenians still mostly lived in autonomous settlements in the countryside. So, he concludes, "They complained and took the evacuation hard (*ebarunonto de kai chalepōs epheron*), leaving their homes and the ancestral temples that had always been theirs from the time of their original communities and facing the prospect of changing their way of life. And each one of them was doing nothing less than abandoning his own city" (2.16.2). The passage offers a genealogy of the demos' collective mood out of the personal experience of each individual Athenian. It describes a sentimental synoecism that completes Theseus' political synoecism (cf. Hornblower 1991, 259) and places the demos' affective unity at the heart of its political identity: "abandoning his own city" each individual will join a collective bound by common feeling. The digression shows that the demos' emotionality has a history and a specifically political history, shaped by the policies (*gnōmai*) of its leaders, first Theseus and now Pericles.

The demos' discontent congeals into an identifiable emotion when it finds Pericles as its object. When the Athenians saw their land being ravaged, they could no longer bear it and wanted to go out to meet the enemy. "The whole city was in a state of excitement and angry at Pericles" (*en orgēi*, 2.21.3). The target of the demos' anger, Pericles is also the first to name it: "Pericles saw that they were upset and were not making the best decisions and trusted that his own decision (*gignōskein*) not to engage was correct. So he did not call an ecclesia or assembly of the people, and by preventing them from committing an error by assembling in anger (*orgēi*) rather than rational judgment (*gnōmēi*), he protected the city and kept peace as much as possible" (2.22.1). The demos' feelings become political when Pericles sets them in contrast to *gnōmē*, both theirs—the familiar antithesis between deliberation in *orgē* and in *gnōmē*—and his own, his correct policy of evacuation.

The demos' emotionality is doubly constructed, then: discursively by Thucydides through his digression, and politically by Pericles, around whom the Athenians' individual discontent sharpens into collective *orgē*. This is a good example of Ahmed's point that emotions are not inherent qualities of subjects or objects, but instead the effect of the relations between them. The political consequences are already clear: defined in opposition to *gnōmē*, the demos' *orgē* not only supports Pericles' policy (*gnōmē*) and his association with political reason (*gnōmē*); it also alienates them from their own decision-making power. Pericles refuses to call an ecclesia, denying the demos a venue in which to express their authoritative *gnōmē*. Neither natural nor inevitable, the antithesis between the demos' *orgē* and Pericles' *gnōmē* is instead thoroughly political, both product and productive of political relations.

The evacuation generates the demos' passion and also defines it. In contemporary comedy, the Athenians' relation to their land is described in the vocabulary of love and longing (*pothos, philia, erōs*; e.g., Aristophanes *Acharnians* 32–33, *Peace* 571–600). In Thucydides, by contrast, the demos' primary feeling about their land is resentment at its loss (*barunesthai, chalepōs pherein*) and anger (*orgē*) at Pericles for that loss. And whereas in Aristophanes the demos' positive passion underwrites its political agency, as the Athenian citizens—individually (in *Acharnians*) or collectively (in *Peace*)—take action to end the war, in Thucydides, the demos' ugly feelings are interpreted as politically disabling (cf. Ngai 2004). In his final speech, Pericles attempts to "release the Athenians from anger (*orgēs*) toward him and lead their minds (*gnōmēn*) away from their terrible circumstances" (2.65.1). He does this not only by arguing that their anger is misplaced and unreasonable (2.60.1, 4–7), but also by detailing its debilitating effect on their political agency. The unexpected "enslaves their minds" (*douloi phronēma*), he tells them, because their anger has rendered their *gnōmē* weak (*asthenei*, 2.61.2) and their judgment debased (*tapeinē*, 2.61.2). It has left them too soft (*malakiāi*) to live up to their glorious reputation and too consumed by private grief to consider the common good (2.61.4; cf. 2.60.2). Interpreting *orgē* as a form of *akrasia* within an ethics of *sōphrosunē* and an ideal of masculine self-mastery, Pericles presents the demos' passion as a sign of weakness, effeminacy, even slavishness.

Pericles' interpretation of *orgē* as emasculating and politically disempowering is not unparalleled, but it was also not the only way to imagine it. Aristotle defines *orgē* as the response to a perceived slight (*oligōria*) and a desire to avenge it: it is an evaluation of relative status and an energetic effort to protect one's position in a highly competitive social world (*Rhet.* 1378a30–80a5; Konstan 2006, 41–76; 2007). From this perspective, it is not getting angry that shows weakness but *not* getting angry: as Aristotle notes, it is considered servile to allow oneself to be insulted (*NE* 1126a7–8). Aristotle limits *orgē* to a response to personal slights, but the Greeks also associated anger with the perception of injustice and righteous indignation in response to it. Not inimical to rational deliberation and prudent policy (as Diodotus would have it), anger is the legitimate impetus toward just decisions (Allen 1999; 2000, 50–72). Thus *orgē* could be conceived as beneficial to democratic politics—indeed, as their very foundation, as Danielle Allen shows in her reading of Aristophanes' *Wasps* (Allen 2000, 128–33; 2007). There *orgē* is valorized as essential to the democratic city, as the Athenian jurors, their stingers raised in righteous anger, buzz in defense of their power to deliver authoritative judgments.

Thucydides hints in places at this more active understanding of *orgē* and the possibility that the demos' anger might be the source of political strength, not weakness. We have already seen how in the Mytilenean Debate, Cleon proposes *orgē* as the alternative to a weak and passive pity and urges the Athenians to abide by their initial angry (*hupo orgēs*, 3.36.2) decision to punish the Mytileneans. For him, *orgē* is an appropriate response to the injustice (3.38.1, 3.39.6) of the Mytileneans' hubristic affront to Athens' rule (3.39.3–4). Associated with manliness and strength, it protects both the city's imperial power and the people's power as judges of imperial policy. "Don't betray yourselves," he concludes, "but return in your mind (*gnōmēi*) as close as possible to your suffering . . . and pay the Mytileneans back without weakening" (3.40.7).

That Thucydides puts this muscular conception of *orgē* in the mouth of the hated Cleon is hardly accidental. He recognizes the cultural association of *orgē* with the demos' political agency but pointedly discredits that agency by continually redefining the demos' passion over their land as sputtering and aporetic. After the second

Peloponnesian invasion, the Athenians, oppressed by plague and war and the destruction of their farms, send ambassadors to Sparta to try to make peace (2.59.1–2). This is an extraordinary moment. As A. W. Gomme says in his commentary on the passage, "Perhaps nothing makes more clear the reality of democracy in Athens, of the control of policy by the ekklesia, than this incident: the ekklesia rejects the advice of its most powerful statesman and most persuasive orator, but the latter remains in office, subordinate to the people's will, till the people choose to get rid of him" (Gomme 1956, 166). But Thucydides interprets this angry agency as a sign not of political strength but of weakness. He depicts the demos here as vacillating in their resolution (*ēlloiōnto tas gnōmas*), ineffectual in their actions (*apraktoi*), and aporetic in their will (*tēi gnōmēi aporoi*, 2.59.1–2). This passage introduces Pericles' final speech, in which, as we saw, he condemns the demos' anger as enfeebling and enslaving. On this, if not universally (see Foster 2010, Chapters 5–6), the statesman and the historian speak in unison, representing the demos' *orgē* as the debilitation of rational judgment (*gnōmē*) and the disqualification from authoritative political judgment (*gnōmē*).

In his summation at 2.65.8–9 Thucydides presents the demos as congenitally passionate and that passion as inherently extreme: without Pericles' wise guidance it veers naturally between hubristic overconfidence and irrational despair. Likewise, Thucydides credits his leadership to Pericles' innate character: his native intelligence and the a-pathy that made him immune to greed or ambition allowed him to lead the demos rather than being led by it. In this way, Thucydides naturalizes the antithesis between demotic *orgē* and Periclean *gnōmē* as a matter of inborn character (*ēthos*). But we have seen that anger is not innate to the demos, but instead is generated by the politician's *gnōmē*, his policy of evacuation. And if Pericles' *gnōmē* produces the demos' *orgē*, the reverse is also true, for it is by adhering steadfastly to his policy in the face of their anger that he proves his superior intelligence: I am always the same man, he says; I always hold the same *gnōmē* (1.140.1, 2.61.2; cf. 2.13.2, 2.22.1, 2.55.2)—a claim tested and proven by the people's vacillating *orgē*. The demos' passion and Pericles' reason are not the source of their political relation, then, but its effect; not the cause, but the affective by-product of the "rule of the first man."

Perhaps it is not surprising then, that Pericles governs not by repressing the people's passions but by arousing and transforming them. Thucydides introduces Pericles' final speech as an attempt "to bolster [the Athenians'] confidence and, drawing off the anger from their minds (*apagagōn to orgizomenon tēs gnōmēs*) to make them more gentle and less fearful" (2.59.3). But the speech that follows does not in fact "draw off" the demos' *orgē*. Instead it disarms it by converting it into a different and complementary affect: contempt (*kataphronēsis*). In Aristotle's discussion of the emotions, contempt (*oligōria, kataphronēsis*) is the typical cause of anger, and anger the appropriate response to contempt (*Rhet.* 1378a30–79a9; Konstan 2006, 45). Pericles urges the Athenians to feel contempt for the enemy, applying *kataphronēsis* as an antidote to their soft and wavering *orgē* (2.62.1). But it is not just the Spartans he wants them to look down upon but their own land. Remember your imperial power, he tells them. That power cannot be measured against the homes and land you have lost. "Nor is it reasonable to take their loss hard, but rather to consider them a mere garden and ornament of wealth in comparison to that power and to feel contempt for them (*oligōrēsai*).... So go against the enemy not only with spirit but with contempt" (*mē phronēmati monon, alla kai kataphronēmati*, 2.62.3).

This last conceit, dismissed by the commentators as empty sophistry (Gomme 1956, 171–72; Rusten 1989, 202–03), gives new meanings to both words. *Phronēma*—a form of cognition often closely associated with *gnōmē*—is dismissed as the ignorant boasting of the lucky. Meanwhile, *kataphronēsis*, which is usually deprecated in Thucydides (e.g., 1.122.4, 2.11.4, 3.83.4, 6.11.5), is here redefined as "relying on one's *gnōmē* to prevail over one's opponents" (2.62.4). It is further glossed as "knowledge born of superiority" (*xunesis ek tou huperphronos*) and "resolution based on existing resources" (*gnōmēi de apo tōn aparchontōn*); contrasted to luck, hope, and *aporia*, it makes foresight more steadfast (*bebaiotera hē pronoia*) and daring more secure (2.62.5).

With this shift from *orgē* to *kataphronēsis*, Pericles brings the demos' emotion into alignment with *gnōmē*, both theirs and his, for *xunesis, pronoia*, and *gnōmē* are all words primarily associated in the *History* with Pericles. Transformed from anger into contempt, their emotion will no longer oppose his policy but will come to approximate his reason. Moreover, contempt itself is a particularly Periclean affect. In Plutarch's biography, *phronēma* and *periphronēsis* (contempt) are the statesman's most conspicuous qualities (e.g., *Per.* 4.6, 5.1, 5.3). Plutarch debates whether this disposition indicated haughtiness or nobility (*Per.* 5.3–4): for him, Pericles' contempt is part of the aristocratic bearing that is his gloss on Thucydides' "rule of the first man" (*Per.* 9.1).

If *kataphronēma* is an affect characteristic of the elite, then Pericles offers the demos a specific way to resemble their social superiors, that is, by giving up their land for the good of the city. When he asks the Athenians to look down on their farms as little pleasure gardens and ornaments of wealth, he invites them to follow his own aristocratic model. Thucydides tells us that before the first Spartan invasion, Pericles, worried that his ancestral guest-friend Archidamus would spare his estates in Attica, promised to make the land public (2.13.1). Thucydides recounts this episode right before the evacuation, as if Pericles' theoretical donation of his vast properties were the equivalent to and model for the demos' deserting the farms that were their sole source of livelihood. Acceding to his policy, the displaced farmers will join Pericles as affective—if not actual—aristocrats. In this way, the demos' passion is brought into alignment with Pericles' *gnōmē*. The *orgē* that might (following Aristotle and Aristophanes) have defended their democratic authority is abandoned along with their farms, for when Pericles incites the demos' contempt toward the land he also demands contempt for their indignation at its loss.

In place of anger for their lost farms, Pericles offers the demos a new passion for a new object: love for the beautiful polis. That affective substitution is effected principally in Pericles' Funeral Oration, which is a "hymn" to that powerful city (2.42.2). Pericles enjoins the Athenians to gaze upon the power of Athens and become her lovers (*erastas*, 2.43.1: see Monoson 2000, 64–87; Ludwig 2002, 121–69, 319–80; Wohl 2002, 30–72; Scholtz 2007, 21–42). This eros marks the endpoint of a sentimental journey that began when the resentful Athenians left their land as if "each of them were doing nothing less than abandoning his own polis" (2.16.2). That individual grief for a lost private polis was, I suggested, the wellspring of the demos' political passion. Here that passion finds its final outlet in shared love for the abstract, idealized city. This transcendent city is completely unified: Pericles' speech eliminates social and economic differences, representing the entire demos as equal in the nobility of their self-sacrifice (Loraux 1986a, 180–92, 279–82; Wohl 2002, 41–55). Political unity is cemented at the affective level by the elimination of all private negative affect. Banning from his imagined polis any suspicion, anger, or offense (*hupopsian, orgēs, lupēras . . . achthēdonas*, 2.37.2–3) among fellow citizens, Pericles produces a public sphere purified of every emotion but a salutary fear (*deos*) of the law and shame (*aischunēn*) at the thought of breaking it (2.37.3). Parents' private grief is replaced by shared glory (2.44) and "the love of honor that alone is unaging" (2.44.4, cf. 2.61.4). Likewise, the individual feelings of the Athenian solider—his desire for profit, his hopes for the future, his fear for his body—are all subsumed at the moment of death: vengeance against the enemy becomes his strongest desire (*potheinoteran*) and victory his greatest hope (*elpidi*), as he leaves his life "at the peak not of fear but of glory" (2.42.4).

This conversion of private affect into patriotic passion is catalyzed by Pericles' redirection of the citizens' eros—arguably the most individual of emotions—toward the city. This eros will bind the Athenians to one another and to the ideal vision of themselves Pericles presents in the speech. It will also bind them to Pericles himself, for he is the living embodiment of the ideal he presents (Wohl 2002, 62–72). In his final speech, Pericles chastises the demos: "you are angry (*orgizesthe*) with a man who is second to none in knowing what is necessary (*gnōnai te ta deonta*) and communicating it, a lover of the city (*philopolis*) and superior to wealth (*chrēmatōn kreissōn*)" (2.60.5). Pericles' *philia* for the city mirrors the patriotic eros he inspires in the demos. In his indifference to wealth he is like the soldiers who sacrificed their hopes of private gain for the city's common good (2.42.4), and his *gnōmē* provides the model for the valiant Athenians who made Athens great by "knowing what was necessary" (*gignōskontes ta deonta*, 2.43.1): to resist the Spartans and die for the polis. Giving up their *orgē* toward Pericles and joining with him in selfless love for an idealized Athens, the Athenians will come to be characterized, as he is, by *gnōmē*, a knowledge of necessities imposed by his policy.

Finally, this *gnōmē* will provide the demos' epitaph as, dying for Pericles' ideal, they enter the utopian geography of eternal glory: "for conspicuous men, the entire world is their tomb, and not inscriptions on *stēlai* in their own land, but in foreign lands the unwritten memory less of their deeds than of their *gnōmē*" (2.43.3). Exchanging their contemptible little farms for the entire world, the demos move from anger to contempt to eros to, finally, a pure, disembodied and deterritorialized *gnōmē* (cf. Bassi 2007). But whose *gnōmē* is this? The *gnōmē* written on their global graves is their own brave resolution but it is also Pericles' policy, the final stage in his evacuation of the land. In the utopia—the perfect nowhere—of glorious death, the Athenians' *gnōmē* and Pericles' become one. But in the process the demos' political authority—that other meaning of *gnōmē*—is left, quite literally, in the Attic dust.

Following this affective trajectory shows how Thucydides uses the demos' *orgē* to construct Pericles' *gnōmē*. The antithesis between reason and emotion defines political rationality and secures the rule of the (first) man who embodies it. Emotion is not an innate quality of the demos, awaiting control by its dispassionate leader. Instead, it is attributed to the demos in the course of and as a means toward establishing that control. This distribution of affect constitutes the politics of Periclean Athens, as Thucydides sees it, but also the politics of his own text, which posits this tendentious "structure of feeling" (Williams 1977, 128–35) as the truth of Athens at its greatest, an affective reality revealed, through the historian's labor and acumen, beneath the surface forms and spurious name of democracy.

Empire of Passion

With Pericles' death the precarious affective equilibrium he achieved is lost. Pericles' dispassion, the immunity to ambition and gain that allowed him to curb the people's excesses, is replaced by the markedly private passions of his successors: "through private ambition and private gain (*kata tas idias philotimias kai idia kerdē*), they pursued policies detrimental themselves and their allies, policies that, if they succeeded, brought benefit and honor to individuals, but if they failed, damaged the city in its war effort" (2.65.7). These private passions run in tandem with and exacerbate the demos' collective desire, driving it toward disastrous ends, both at home and abroad (see Balot 2001, 136–78).

The affective breakdown of post-Periclean Athens will find its fullest illustration in the Sicilian Expedition (as Thucydides hints already at 2.65.11; see Greenwood, chapter 9 in this volume). This fatal mission is framed by precisely the emotional extremes Pericles had held in balance: "When he saw them arrogantly confident beyond due measure (*para kairon hubrei tharsountas*) his speech knocked them down to fear, and again when they were irrationally anxious (*dediotas au alogōs*), he restored them to confidence once more" (2.65.9). The expedition originates in a confidence beyond due measure: Thucydides describes the Athenians seeing off the fleet, their confidence aroused (*anetharsoun*) by the spectacle of the huge force (6.31.1). The mission was conspicuous, he notes, not only for its size and ambition, but also for its disproportionate hope: "it was undertaken in the greatest hope (*elpidi*) for the future in relation to the existing circumstances" (6.31.6). It will end in irrational fear: the total destruction of the Athenian forces (7.87.6) will provoke "fear and extreme terror" back in Athens (*phobos te kai kataplēxis megistē dē*, 8.1.2). This downward spiral from confidence to panic is propelled by a fatal combination of historical action and affective reaction as the despair produced by military failure produces new failures in turn (e.g., 7.47–56, 7.71–75). Emotion plays both an expository role in this narrative, marking its major milestones, and an explanatory role, as affect and event work upon each other to produce history.

From its hopeful beginning to its catastrophic end, the Sicilian Expedition is impelled by passion. The statesman Nicias, in his speech against the excursion, characterizes it as a *duserōs tōn apontōn*, a sick or misguided love of what is absent (6.13.1; see Arrowsmith 1973; Wohl 2002, 171–214). The object of this *duserōs* is obscure. The Athenians were ill informed about Sicily, as Thucydides stresses in his long introductory excursus on the size and population of the island (6.1–6), and the ostensible motive for sailing, to defend the Egestaeans, was merely a pretext for larger desires: the "truest cause" (*alēthestatē prophasis*), says Thucydides in a pointed echo of 1.23.6, was their desire for the conquest of the entire island (6.6.1; cf. 6.8.4) and beyond that, of Carthage (6.15.2). An ever-receding object, Sicily figures Athens' imperial expansion as a dynamic of desire, an insatiable and virtually objectless longing. Supplemented by hope (6.24.3), this imperial passion is resistant to reason. Nicias attempts to impress upon the Athenians the difficulties and dangers of the undertaking. Opposing *pronoia* (foresight) to *epithumia* (desire, 6.13.1), he presents thorough debate and careful examination (6.9.1) as the remedy for a city deliberating its own destruction (6.14.1). And yet his pragmatic arguments against the mission—the cost, the distance, the danger—far from diminishing the Athenians' irrational passion only enflame it the more (6.24). Sicily thus dramatizes Diodotus' theory in the Mytilenean Debate that "hope (*elpis*) and desire (*erōs*) do the most damage," compelling men to act against law, reason, and self-interest. "These invisible forces are mightier than visible dangers," he notes (3.45.5), and the Sicilian narrative bears this out, as the Athenians ignore the manifest risks of dividing their energies and opening a second war-front to pursue the distant object of their imperial longing.

And so, Thucydides writes, "a passion (*erōs*) to sail fell upon them all alike. The older men believed that they would conquer those they were sailing against or at least that such a great force could not fail. The young longed for distant sights and spectacles and were confident that they would be safe" (*euelpides ontes sōthēsesthai*, 6.24.3). This collective passion is the pathological metastasis of Pericles' patriotic eros for the city. Like the latter, it unifies the demos, erasing differences between citizens (here, the division between young and old, which is prominent in the preceding debate, 6.13.1, 6.18.6) and binding them by shared emotion. But whereas for Pericles that emotional unity underpinned the ideal of Athens' democracy (2.37), here it marks its failure: so excessive was the Athenians' desire for the mission that any individual who opposed it was afraid (*dediōs*) to speak out and just kept quiet (*hēsuchian ēgen*, 6.24.4). This anxious *hēsuchia* anticipates the affects that will characterize the Athenian civil war, when pervasive suspicion and fear prevented citizens from speaking out against the oligarchs or taking collaborative action against them (e.g., 8.66; see Zumbrunnen, chapter 28 this volume).

The civil war is also presaged by the individual passion that comes to the fore in Sicily, particularly in the person of Alcibiades. Alcibiades is accused, both by his opponent Nicias and by Thucydides, of promoting the mission out of personal desire for profit and honor (6.12.2, 6.15). A figure closely associated with eros (in Thucydides and beyond: Gribble 1999; Wohl 2002, 124–70), Alcibiades further enflames the demos' desire with his unabashed longing for glory (6.16) and augments their hopes with his predictions of easy victory (6.17). His tyrannical ambition and consumption, his driving passion (*epithumia*) for private (*idia*) gain and glory (6.15) all recall Thucydides' characterization of Pericles' successors as motivated by "private ambition and private gain" (*kata tas idias philotimias kai idia kerdē*, 2.65.7). Alcibiades thus exemplifies Thucydides' insistent distinction between Pericles and later politicians and anticipates the toxic *pleonexia* and *philotimia* that will beset Athens' demagogues during the civil war (8.89.3; Balot 2001, 159–72).

In its deadly combination of the demos' uncontrolled, irrational desire and the demagogues' private ambition and greed, the Sicilian Expedition seems symptomatic of an affective debility endemic to democracy, as Thucydides diagnoses it. This literal "pathology" was suppressed under Pericles, when the democracy wasn't truly a democracy. After his death, democracy and its *duserōs* flourish together, suggesting that the two are inextricably linked. But if *duserōs* is a disease of democracy, it is also, Thucydides suggests, a condition specific to the national *ēthos* of the Athenians, for the passions that drive the Sicilian Expedition—*erōs* and *elpis*, but also *tolmē* (daring), *polypragmosunē* (activity, interventionism), *pleonexia* (greed)—are presented as the defining qualities of the Athenian character throughout the *History* (Arrowsmith 1973; Luginbill 1999, 134–72). Athenians "are daring (*tolmētai*) beyond their capability and run risks beyond reason (*gnōmēn*) and are hopeful (*euelpides*) amidst dangers," say the Corinthians in the debate before the outbreak of war (1.70.3). This confident hope fuels the innate restlessness and acquisitiveness that explain both their astonishing innovation and their aggressive interventionism (1.70.7–9). From this perspective, the Sicilian Expedition's trajectory from confidence to despair appears as a tragic *peripeteia*, the drama of a polis driven to destruction by a fatal overreach, propelled by its own innate passions (Cornford 1965, 79–250).

That the disaster in Sicily is the playing out of the affective pathology of the Athenian character is suggested by Alcibiades when he represents the Sicilian mission as a matter not of desire but of compulsion. It is not in the Athenians' power to limit the extent of their empire, he says, "but it is necessary (*anankē*) in the situation we are in to hold on to the subjects we have and to scheme to add to them, since we risk being ruled by others if we do not rule over others" (6.18.3). A city used to activity (*polin mē apragmona*) will be destroyed by a change to inactivity. Athens' character and customs (*ēthesi kai nomois*, 6.18.7) make it particularly susceptible to the entropy and senescence that Alcibiades sees as the natural result of *hēsuchia* (6.18.6); to curtail its imperial ambition would require changing its entire way of life (6.18.3).

But even as he roots the necessity of Athens' imperial expansion in the city's own passionate character, Alcibiades also offers a different understanding of empire's affective compulsion. The necessity of "rule or be ruled" is repeated numerous times over the course of the *History*. In the Melian Dialogue the Athenians present this principle as an eternal and universal law of human nature (*to anthrōpeion te saphōs dia pantos hupo phuseōs anankaias*, 5.105.2). This universal necessity suggests that the affects driving the Sicilian expedition are endemic not merely to Athens but to human nature in general (see especially Pouncey 1980; Orwin, chapter 21 in this volume). This same universal necessity is stressed by the Athenians in Book I, who justify their imperial growth on the basis of a triple compulsion (*katēnankasthēmen*): "fear first, then honor, then self-interest" (1.75.4). This imperial psychology, as they represent it, is not unique to themselves but instead inheres within both human nature (*anthrōpeiou tropou*) and the very structure of power, inasmuch as rule breeds resentment and hatred, which in turn mean that a polis "is forced (*anankasthentas*) either to rule forcefully over others or to jeopardize itself" (1.76.1–2). This necessity, they say, would bind the Spartans, too, if they were in the same situation.

The argument is obviously self-serving (see Fisher and Hoekstra, chapter 22 in this volume). Nonetheless, it suggests an alternate psychology of empire, in which the tragedy of Sicily is propelled not by the endemic affective imbalance of democracy, or by innate Athenian *erōs* and *elpis*, but by a fear inherent to human nature as a whole. This same imperial fear surfaces again in the Athenian self-justification at Sicily (6.83.3–4) and in the repeated comparison of empire to a tyranny that, as Pericles puts it, may have been unjust to take but is dangerous to give up (2.63.1–2; cf. 3.37.2; Tuplin 1985). Fear—a fear the Athenians insist inheres in relations of power and is intrinsic to mankind as a whole—is both the product of empire and its engine; it is built into its fundamental structure (Romilly 1956, 124–27; Pouncey 1980, 98–104; Desmond 2006, 365–70).

This imperial fear brings us back to Sparta's *phobos* of Athens' imperial growth as the "truest" cause of the war, and the role of affect more generally within Thucydides' historiography. The Athenians' universal pathology of power confirms our intuition at the start of this chapter that this motivating fear lies less in the specific actions of the Athenians or reactions of the Spartans than in the relation of power that binds them. It circulates within that relation in an endless cycle of mutual intensification as fear produces growth produces fear. "Fear" is thus the affect of the Peloponnesian War, the emotion that governs its underlying necessities. It is also the affect of *The Peloponnesian War*. For fear is central not only to the text's historical analysis, but also to its anthropological vision and to its literary tone. Thucydides' vision of human nature is, quite simply, terrifying. In his famous descriptions of the plague in Athens and the civil war in Corcyra, we see *to anthrōpinon* in its naked state (2.50.1, 3.82.2), unprotected by the civilizing veneer of law, religion, or social norms. It is a state of passions unchecked by reason: paralyzing despair and grief (2.51.5); unrestrained greed (3.82.6, 82.8, 84.1) and the desperate gratification of immediate pleasure (2.53.1–3); the suspicion, anger, and resentment that dissolve bonds of trust between fellow citizens (3.82.5–8, 83.1–2, 84.2–3). These lawless passions, which overwhelm more civilizing emotions like shame or religious scruple (2.52.4, 53.4, 3.83.1–2), are both symptom and cause of societal breakdown. "And then, with life thrown into chaos, human nature (*hē anthrōpeia phusis*), always accustomed to commit injustice against the laws (*para tous nomous adikein*), now prevailed over (*kratēsasa*) the laws and happily showed itself unmastered in its passion (*akratēs . . . orgēs*), above justice and inimical to anything superior to itself" (3.84.2).

This horrifying vision of raw human passion evokes fear as the "truest cause" of the war, and that evocation is not just descriptive but performative, not just theoretical but visceral. These dark glimpses of human nature make the reader experience the fear that drives the human agents of the *History* (Desmond 2006, 370–76). This production of affect is more than just a technique of literary *enargeia*: as we saw in "Affective Leadership: Pericles and the Demos," the arousal and attribution of affect is never neutral. Indeed, it is central to Thucydides' historiographical project and his authority as a historian. Thucydides' claim for the prognostic utility of his *History* rests on the constancy of human nature: "if someone wishes to examine clearly (*to saphes skopein*) events that have happened and will happen again in the same or similar ways, human nature (*to anthrōpinon*) being what it is, it will be enough if that person judge my text useful" (1.22.4). The *History*'s status as a "possession for all time" (*ktēma es aiei*) rests upon a particular vision of human nature, and is secured by the feelings that vision arouses in the reader. These same feelings validate Thucydides' authority as "paradigm of the historian" (Loraux 1986b, 141), his self-presentation as the dispassionate investigator of historical truth (1.1, 1.21–22). Finding the "truest causes" (*alēthestatēn prophasin*) through examination of the best evidence, making obscure (*aphanestatēn*) motives clear in speech or lucid through reason (*logōi*), Thucydides presents himself as a figure of pure and passionless *gnōmē*. But this historiographical *gnōmē* is predicated, no less than the political *gnōmē* of Pericles, on a vision of human *orgē*, the horrifying *orgai* that war, that "violent teacher," reduces to the level of men's circumstances (3.82.2). That is to say that historiographical reason, like political, sustains itself by producing emotion as its opposite and enemy, a conflict with enduring consequences for the theory and practice of historiography, and one that reason can never finally win. The truest causes of this conflict are made manifest in the *logos* of Thucydides, whose ostensibly a-pathetic rationalism is secured by the passions it provokes, as well as those it repudiates.

References

Ahmed, S. 2004a. *The Cultural Politics of Emotion*. New York: Routledge.
Ahmed, S. 2004b. "Affective Economies." *Social Text* 79: 117–39.
Allen, D. S. 1999. "Democratic Dis-Ease: Of Anger and the Troubling Nature of Punishment." In *The Passions of Law*, edited by S. A. Bandes, 191–216. New York: New York University Press,
Allen, D. S. 2000. *The World of Prometheus: The Politics of Punishing in Democratic Athens*. Princeton: Princeton University Press.
Allen, D. S. 2007. "Angry Bees, Wasps, and Jurors: The Symbolic Politics of Ὀργή in Athens." In *Ancient Anger: Perspectives from Homer to Galen*, edited by S. M. Braund and G. Most, 76–98. Cambridge: Cambridge University Press.
Arrowsmith, W. 1973. "Aristophanes' *Birds*: The Fantasy Politics of Eros." *Arion* 1: 119–67.
Balot, R. K. 2001. *Greed and Injustice in Classical Athens*. Princeton: Princeton University Press.
Bassi, K. 2007. "Spatial Contingencies in Thucydides' *History*." *Classical Antiquity* 26: 171–218.
Connor, W. R. 1984. *Thucydides*. Princeton: Princeton University Press.
Cornford, F. M. (1907) 1965. *Thucydides Mythistoricus*. London: Routledge and Kegan Paul.
Desmond, W. 2006. "Lessons of Fear: A Reading of Thucydides." *Classical Philology* 101: 359–79.
Edmunds, L. 1975. *Chance and Intelligence in Thucydides*. Cambridge: Harvard University Press.
Farrar, C. 1988. *The Origins of Democratic Thinking: The Invention of Politics in Classical Athens*. Cambridge: Cambridge University Press.

Foster, E. 2010. *Thucydides, Pericles, and Periclean Imperialism*. Cambridge: Cambridge University Press.
Gomme, A. W. 1956. *A Historical Commentary on Thucydides*. Vol. II. Oxford: Clarendon Press.
Gribble, D. 1999. *Alcibiades and Athens: A Study in Literary Presentation*. Oxford: Clarendon Press.
Hornblower, S. 1991. *A Commentary on Thucydides*. Vol. I, *Books I–III*. Oxford: Clarendon Press.
Huart, P. 1973. Γνώμη *chez Thucydide et ses contemporains*. Paris: Éditions Klincksieck.
Konstan, D. 2001. *Pity Transformed*. London: Duckworth.
Konstan, D. 2006. *The Emotions of the Ancient Greeks: Studies in Aristotle and Classical Literature*. Toronto: University of Toronto Press.
Konstan, D. 2007. "Aristotle on Anger and the Emotions: The Strategies of Status." In *Ancient Anger: Perspectives from Homer to Galen*, edited by S. M. Braund and G. Most, 99–120. Cambridge: Cambridge University Press.
Lateiner, D. 2005. "The Pitiers and the Pitied in Herodotus and Thucydides." In *Pity and Power in Ancient Athens*, edited by R. H. Sternberg, 67–97. Cambridge: Cambridge University Press.
Loraux, N. 1986a. *The Invention of Athens: The Funeral Oration in the Classical City*. Translated by A. Sheridan. Cambridge: Harvard University Press.
Loraux, N. 1986b. "Thucydide a écrit la guerre du Péloponnèse." *Mètis* 1: 139–61.
Ludwig, P. W. 2002. *Eros and Polis: Desire and Community in Greek Political Theory*. New York: Cambridge University Press.
Luginbill, R. D. 1999. *Thucydides on War and National Character*. Boulder: Westview.
MacLeod, C. W. 1978. "Reason and Necessity: Thucydides III 9–14, 37–48." *Journal of Hellenic Studies* 98: 64–78.
Monoson, S. S. 2000. *Plato's Democratic Entanglements: Athenian Politics and the Practice of Philosophy*. Princeton: Princeton University Press.
Ngai, S. 2004. *Ugly Feelings*. Cambridge: Harvard University Press.
Nussbaum, M. C. 1996. "Compassion: The Basic Social Emotion." *Social Philosophy and Policy* 13: 27–58.
Nussbaum, M. C. 2001. *Upheavals of Thought: The Intelligence of Emotions*. Cambridge: Cambridge University Press.
Pouncey, P. R. 1980. *The Necessities of War: A Study of Thucydides' Pessimism*. New York: Columbia University Press.
Romilly, J. de. 1956. "La crainte dans l'œuvre de Thucydide." *Classica et Mediaevalia* 17: 119–27.
Rusten, J. S., ed. 1989. *Thucydides: The Peloponnesian War, Book II*. Cambridge: Cambridge University Press.
Scholtz, A. 2007. *Concordia Discors: Eros and Dialogue in Classical Athenian Literature*. Washington, DC: Center for Hellenic Studies.
Shweder, R. A. 2003. "Toward a Deep Cultural Psychology of Shame." *Social Research* 70: 1109–30.
Tuplin, C. 1985. "Imperial Tyranny: Some Reflections on a Classical Greek Political Metaphor." *History of Political Thought* 6: 348–75.
Visvardi, E. 2012. "Collective Emotion in Thucydides." *CHS Research Bulletin* 1 (1). [http://www.chs-fellows.org/2012/11/30/abstract-collective-emotion-in-thucydides/]
Williams, R. 1977. *Marxism and Literature*. Oxford: Oxford University Press.
Wohl, V. 2002. *Love among the Ruins: The Erotics of Democracy in Classical Athens*. Princeton: Princeton University Press.

CHAPTER 27

LEADERS AND LEADERSHIP IN THUCYDIDES' *HISTORY*

MARY P. NICHOLS*

Does history teach lessons that transcend time and place? Thucydides, who was one of our first authors to establish history as a genre, thought so. He wrote his history of the war between the Peloponnesians and the Athenians as "a possession for all time," for in the course of human affairs future events resemble past ones (1.22.4).[1] This essay explores how Thucydides depicts leadership, its opportunities and limits, by looking at the careers of prominent leaders in his *History*. Because leadership is a critical and universal theme of politics, examining particular leaders and the roles they play in Thucydides' *History* allows us to see how Thucydides can find enduring truths in the events of a particular war.

The theme of leadership, moreover, is tied to several other prominent themes in his work: freedom and responsibility, necessity and chance, the different regimes and ways of life, and speech and action. Leaders are constrained by circumstances, including the past, or history itself, by the laws and ways of life of their cities, by the actions of other cities, and even by natural phenomena such as the plague that hit Athens hard early in the war. Thucydides says that the war was made "inevitable" or "necessary" by the growth of Athenian power and Spartan fear (1.23.6). But if human life allowed no scope for human agency, there would, strictly speaking, be no leadership. Those who appear as leaders would be led just as much as their apparent followers, compelled by the various forces that constitute necessity. Leadership demonstrates human freedom, and without freedom, leadership would not be possible. Thucydides

---

* I am grateful to Ryan K. Balot for his editorial suggestions. Portions of this chapter are adapted from *Thucydides and the Pursuit of Freedom*, by Mary P. Nichols. Copyright 2015 by Cornell University (Nichols 2015). Used by permission of the publisher, Cornell University Press.

[1] Translations of Thucydides are my own, based on the Oxford Classical Text of Thucydides (1996–97). I have, however, consulted the translation of Lattimore (1998) and the revised Crawley translation (Strassler 1996).

finds scope for freedom, although its character varies in different regimes and depends on the capacities and virtues of individuals (Ludwig 2002; Johnson, 1991; Rahe 1996; Nichols 2015).

Moreover, Thucydides judges leaders by their success in fostering freedom, for both individuals and peoples. They do so to various degrees through their speeches and their deeds. Although Thucydides indicates that what is said must be tested by what is done (1.21–22), speeches also propose actions and interpret their purposes. Pericles asserts that no one knows better than he does what is necessary and how to convey it (*hermēneuein*) (2.60.5). Pericles also claims that Athenians know that they must be instructed by speech before they act (2.40.2). Thucydides' work is filled with speeches, delivered in direct discourse, especially by leaders, generals, and embassies from cities. The speeches in his work arouse passions, urge or dissuade from action, instruct and mislead. Thucydides' leaders are rhetoricians. The human beings who deliver and hear such speeches weigh alternative courses and choose between what appears better and worse, appreciate the beautiful or noble, and think in terms of justice. In all these ways, Thucydides suggests that freedom is possible for human beings. But he also shows us that freedom must be cultivated, by the speeches and deeds of leaders, as they react to circumstances of time and place, and create them in turn. Leadership is filtered through a city's regime and the way of life it informs, even as regimes and ways of life are modified and sometimes overturned by leaders and those whom they lead, whether toward worthy expressions of their regimes or in flight from them.

I begin my essay with Pericles, the most prominent leader in Athens during the early years of the war, and in some ways the most prominent leader in Thucydides' *History*. Under Pericles, Thucydides tells us, Athens reached its peak of greatness. Thucydides shows that Pericles fosters freedom through his rhetoric, always instructing Athenians about their way of life and what it demands, and implicitly offering himself to them as a model. Pericles serves as Thucydides' model of leadership for free government. Brasidas, the Spartan commander whom I discuss next, also articulates his city's purpose—as the liberator of Hellas from Athenian imperialism—and does more than any other Spartan to achieve that purpose. Brasidas tells the world about Spartan greatness through his words and his deeds, but he does not teach that greatness to the Spartans themselves, or move them toward it. Thucydides' contrast between Pericles and Brasidas shows us that leadership must begin at home, addressing one's community and fostering its virtues. My essay concludes by discussing Alcibiades and Nicias, who share command of Athens' daring expedition to Sicily, and who in different ways contribute to Athens' defeat there. The former asserts his own leadership to the point of betraying his city, while the latter is so dependent on his city that he fails to exercise the leadership that would bring his army safely home. Good leadership must both recognize the particular conditions that make it possible and exercise a capacity for action.

Pericles as the Height of Athens' Greatness

Thucydides claims that Pericles is the most capable Athenian of his time "both in speaking and acting" (1.139.4). Although Thucydides mentions military campaigns that he led (e.g., 1.111.2; 114; 116–17; 2.56.3; and 6.31.2), he portrays Pericles' leadership primarily through the speeches he delivers. Not only in his famous funeral oration, but also in urging policies and defending himself, Pericles asks the Athenian people to understand themselves as free individuals who inhabit a free city, and interprets for them what their freedom means and demands. His success depends on his own character, Thucydides tells us, and his own freedom. He led the people rather than being led by them, for when he saw them overconfident, his speech aroused fear, and when they were unreasonably afraid, he encouraged them. The people had so much respect for his worth and judgment that he could even oppose them when they were angry (2.65.6–11).

We hear Pericles' first speech to the Athenians in Thucydides' work in response to Spartan demands for concessions. Pericles insists that concessions will only be followed by other demands (1.140.4–141.1). War is necessary, he argues, but it is also "necessary that [the Athenians] know" that war is necessary. Their knowledge should influence how they act. Without such knowledge of the war's necessity, the Athenians might vote against war. Yet war is necessary to preserve their freedom. Therefore, the "more willingly" they accept the war, the sooner they will ward off the greatest dangers and achieve the greatest honors (1.144.3). While the Athenian envoys at Sparta earlier explained the growth of the Athenian empire with reference to the "compulsions" of fear, honor, and advantage (1.75.3), Pericles' emphasis is on honor. But to be compelled by honor is not the same as to be compelled by fear. The former might entail risking one's life in order to manifest one's virtue or patriotism. It requires acting in spite of one's fear for one's life, or overcoming pressures to which human beings are vulnerable. Indeed, the necessities of honor lie in living up to ideals that citizens accept and make their own. This "necessary" war, as Pericles presents it, is for the sake of freedom, voluntarily chosen. Only as a result will it bring the greatest honor. However much the actions of human beings respond to circumstances—and Thucydides does not deny that they do—they also come "from within," as Pericles claims of Athenian courage (2.39.1). They are not merely compelled from outside. Freedom is a potential, not a necessity, although it is necessary for full humanity. It must be claimed, taken, and exercised. Freedom requires rule of oneself and therefore of the circumstances with which one is presented, and this will inevitably involve ruling others as well as being ruled by them.

Pericles, moreover, tells the Athenians that if they accept his recommendation for war, they are responsible just as much as he is. Indeed, he "holds it just" for those persuaded now to support their common resolutions later if they meet setbacks, or else not to lay claim to the plan if it meets with success (1.140.1). One cannot claim credit for success, if one does not also accept responsibility for failure. What Pericles tells the Athenians, those who are persuaded, of course applies to himself as well, the one who persuades them. It is a "common" resolution, and the responsibility is shared. Pericles' leadership includes educating the people about what their commitments require of them.

After the Athenian Assembly votes for war, as Pericles urges, and the Peloponnesians invade Attica, the Spartan commander Archidamus sends a herald to Athens for further negotiations. He is turned away in compliance with Pericles' policy that no embassy be admitted from an enemy once he is in the field. When the Peloponnesian forces proceed to ravage the countryside, many in the city want to go out to fight, contrary to Pericles' policy to fight the enemy at sea rather than on land. Pericles refuses to call an assembly lest the Athenians "err by coming together in anger rather than with judgment" (2.21.3–22.1; see also 2.12.1–2). Pericles' "undemocratic" action is necessary to preserve the people's deliberation in the face of passions that arise when war closes in.

Pericles' Funeral Oration occurs toward the end of the first year of the war, in accordance with a law that established the custom. He begins—in a rather daring way—by criticizing the law that requires that a speech be given to honor the fallen, for he himself thinks it sufficient that deeds, the public funeral, honor deeds (see also Strauss 1964, 152; Palmer 1992, 21–22; Orwin 1994, 16). Instead, the law puts "the virtues of many" at risk, dependent on whether "one man speaks well or badly" (2.35.1). In attributing the law to the one who established it, Pericles calls attention to the fact that laws, like speeches, are made by human beings, whether well or badly, and he even refers to "the one" establishing the law, not to the many who are considered legislators in a democracy. At the same time, he speaks in defense of the many, when the law puts their virtue at risk. It is Pericles' speech that fosters Athenian virtue, just as it is he, the man designated to deliver the oration, on whom the virtue of the fallen now depends. Virtue depends on its public interpretation and remembrance, both of which are embodied in the words of a single individual.

In order to understand the achievement of those who gave their lives for Athens, Pericles says, it is necessary to examine the city they served—its regime and way of life—and how it achieved its present greatness. Pericles highlights Athens' democratic principles, which favor the many rather than the few. Athens' "equality" permits merit to rise, according preeminence in the city's affairs to those recognized for virtue, while treating all equally before the law in private matters (2.37.1). Pericles' own preeminence by implication is consistent with Athens' democratic principles—indeed, is due to them, although Perictles does not say so. Once he distinguishes himself from past orators, his emphasis is all on Athens, not on himself.

We Athenians conduct ourselves with freedom, Pericles continues, in both our public and private matters (2.37.2). In the first place, we Athenians share in political affairs, whether propounding or judging them, and consider any who does not do so useless (2.40.2). We also differ from our opponents in the current war by opening our city to all rather than driving out foreigners, preventing no one from seeing or learning about our practices, even though some enemy might benefit from seeing what we do not hide (2.39.1). So too in private life, neighbor does not become angry with neighbor for doing what he pleases (2.37.2). Athens' freedom is thus based on its strength, its self-sufficiency, which carries over into the lives of its citizens (2.36.3 and 41.1). Athenians do not have to hide, and it is the strong who do not have to hide. They are law abiding, to be sure, and heed the rulers and the laws, especially the ones that are for the benefit of those who suffer injustice and the unwritten laws whose violation brings shame (2.37.3). Athenians are moved less by the fear of punishment from violating laws than by their own sense of the shameful—and hence of the noble. Moreover, as Pericles presents them, the Athenians are the protectors of those who suffer injustice; they right wrongs to others.

Consistent with this spirit of largesse, Pericles claims that Athens acquires friends by conferring rather than receiving benefits (2.40.4). He here describes ways of acting that Aristotle was to later attribute to greatness of soul (*Nicomachean Ethics* 1124b10–11). Whereas Aristotle describes an outstanding individual who possesses the peak of virtue (*NE* 1124a1), Pericles is referring to the Athenians in general. It is the Athenians themselves whom Pericles distinguishes "from the many." "We alone are benefactors, not calculating advantage, but confident in our freedom" (2.40.4–5). Pericles' image of Athens is of a city for which an Athenian might understandably give his life, and in doing so justify his life, as he becomes, as Pericles urges, "a lover of his city" (2.43.1). And it is because of this city for which they gave their lives that Pericles praises those fallen in battle. Indeed, he claims that "the whole world" will remember them, as he memorializes his city's achievements before both the citizens and foreigners present in the city (2.43.2; 2.36.4). Pericles closes his speech by asking his hearers to depart, "having finished their lamentations" (2.46.2).

Thucydides' makes clear the demanding, even too demanding, character of Pericles' rhetoric when he turns immediately to the devastating plague that visits Athens. The lamentations that Pericles claimed complete echo during the plague (see 2.51.5). The plague, Thucydides says, was "beyond all accounting" (literally, "stronger than speech"), and its terrors and sufferings were "harsher than human nature could bear" (2.50.1). Scholars have long noted the contrast between Pericles' description of the Athenians and Thucydides' account of the degradations to which they succumb during the plague (Monoson and Loriaux 1998, 289; Palmer 1992, 32; Connor 1984, 63–64). The noble and free Athenians whom Pericles describes become ugly and base, and even slavish (see 2.61.3).

Although Thucydides' juxtaposition of the plague and Funeral Oration suggests the limits of speech, even of Pericles' speech, to overcome suffering, we do hear from Pericles again. When the people, overwhelmed by their sufferings from the war and the plague, blame Pericles for the war, and start negotiating peace with Sparta, Pericles comes forward to answer them. He does not deny that he is to blame for the war, but insists that the people too are responsible because they also supported it (2.64.1). Emphasizing the reasons Athens should remain at war, he takes credit, and shares that credit (cf. Zumbrunnen 2008, 100 and 102). By manifesting his own confidence, he tries to restore the people's confidence and thereby soothe their anger (2.59.1–3). Just as Pericles presents Athens as a model for others to imitate (2.37.1), so he now presents himself as a model for the Athenians. While because of their sufferings, the Athenians have changed and regretted their decision to go to war, Pericles remains "the same" and has not changed (2.61.2). While the Athenians are confounded by domestic afflictions and neglect the common safety, Pericles loves his city (2.60.5). He also shows by his example that the flexibility and willingness to revise that are characteristic of democracy need occasionally to be overridden by the prudent judgment that "staying the course" is best in certain circumstances.

Only if they use Pericles as a model can the distraught Athenians show themselves worthy of the rule they have achieved, and maintain both their rule and their freedom. Although other sources tell us that Pericles lost his son and other relatives to the plague, Pericles does not mention any personal losses in his defense, nor does he recount anything about his family's experience of the plague. He does not, metaphorically speaking, bring his family into court, to appeal to his audience's pity (cf. Plato, *Apology* 34b–d). He stands before the assembly, as self-sufficient as the city he describes in the Funeral Oration (2.36.3; see also 2.41.1).

Pericles in part persuades the Athenians, Thucydides reports, for they decide to persevere in the war, but they remain pained by their suffering, and they eventually fine Pericles out of frustration. Once their anger has ceased, however, they choose Pericles as general again and turn "all their affairs" over to him (2.65.2–4). Whereas Pericles asks them to turn themselves over to the city by becoming its lovers, the people are willing to turn themselves over to Pericles. Pericles mediates their love or devotion to the city. The ways of the city that Pericles recognizes as worthy of love become manifest in the ways of Pericles. He has indeed "sacrificed" himself for his city, for which he receives the city's gratitude. His city's ways are his ways, as he represents Athens to the Athenians through speech that both embodies fundamental Athenian ideals and elaborates those ideals in ways that are appropriate to the circumstances. Whatever reservations Thucydides has about Pericles (see Saxonhouse 1996, 59–71; Mara 2009, 96–97, 105–7, 112, 115–16), no other leader in his work, Athenian or otherwise, comes close to this achievement.

Brasidas's Alienation from His City

At the outset of the war, Thucydides tells us, Sparta proclaimed its goal as liberating the Hellenic world from Athenian domination, and gained the goodwill of many subject to Athens and of others fearing that they would become so (2.8.4–5). Thucydides does not tell us what form that proclamation took, or exactly who made it on behalf of Sparta. Although many of Sparta's allies refer to that city's noble purpose (e.g., 1.69.1; 3.13.7; 3.59.4), Brasidas is the first Spartan to do so. He serves that purpose on his Thracian campaign, as he succeeds in persuading cities in Thrace to break their ties with Athens. Brasidas is "not incompetent at speaking, for a Spartan" (4.84.2). He is also a "force for action" (*drastērion*) (4.81.1). When cities in the Hellenic world see or hear about Brasidas, they are impressed by his virtue, and become more favorable to the Spartan side in the belief that other Spartans will be like him (4.81.2). But no one else like Brasidas comes forth from Sparta in Thucydides' *History* (see Burns 2011, 508–23). The cities that trust Sparta because of Brasidas pay for their mistake (e.g., 5.32.1). Brasidas misrepresents his city to the world. Thucydides accuses him of lying (4.108.5).

When the Chalcideans in Thrace revolt from Athens' rule, they ask Sparta for help, and even request Brasidas, who "wishes" to go. When he and his army arrive in Thrace, Brasidas explains to the cities there that events of the war prevented Sparta from coming previously to liberate them, but now Sparta has sent him to prove true to its purpose (4.85.1). Moreover, Brasidas says, Sparta promises their "autonomy" and will not impose any particular form of government on them. Indeed, Brasidas would not truly offer them freedom if Sparta were to enslave the greater part of their city to the few, or a smaller part to everyone. Such would be harsher than foreign rule, he observes, and the Spartans would be to blame for the very thing for which they blame Athens. Acanthus is the first city to yield to Brasidas, persuaded by his words and fearing his army. Several other cities then come over to Brasidas's side (4.88, 106, 120, 123).

Thucydides gives us reason to doubt much of Brasidas's representation of his city. To Brasidas's claim that Sparta offers the liberated cities autonomy, Thucydides has just provided a counterexample of oligarchic oppression in Megara after the city fell to Spartan forces (4.74.3). Moreover, whereas Brasidas claims that Sparta has sent him to prove true its noble purpose of liberation, Thucydides tells us that the Spartans want to divert the Athenians from operations in the Peloponnesus by threatening them elsewhere. And once Brasidas has succeeded in liberating cities in Thrace, the Spartans are able to exchange the "liberated" cities in their peace negotiations with Athens. Finally, the expedition gives Sparta an excuse to send away some of its subject population, the helots, as hoplites in the army, lest with the war going badly at home the helots start an insurrection. And the Macedonian king Perdiccas offers to pay some of Brasidas's troops, which might serve purposes of his own in Thrace. From Thucydides' account, 700 helots, mercenaries, and one Spartan, Brasidas, go to Thrace as the liberators of Hellas (4.79.2–81.2).

Moreover, although Brasidas promises freedom, he lacks the resources to make good his promises. Sparta refuses to send him reinforcements (4.108.6–7), for example, and after his death his city returns the "liberated" cities to Athens (e.g., 4.81.2 and 5.18). Brasidas cannot succeed without the support of his city, and its actions make a mockery of the words he speaks on its behalf (e.g., 4.123.4–124.1). He acts independently of his city, eventually refusing to follow its orders to suspend his efforts in Thrace (4.122.2–3 and 123.1). Brasidas could hardly go home, although it is not clear that he ever intended to do so. Forcing his way through Thessaly, he in effect cut off his return route to Sparta, at least by land (cf. 4.11.4–12.1). At Amphipolis, the city whose liberation caused the greatest consternation at Athens (4.108.1), Brasidas fights his last battle against Athenian forces, running out in the forefront of his men against the enemy. His side wins the battle, but he dies fighting. He is given a public burial and worshipped as a hero in Amphipolis (5.11). He finds a home elsewhere, but only after his death.

That Brasidas acts without the authority of his city may suggest his freedom, but Thucydides shows us that Brasidas's freedom from his city undermines his ability to accomplish anything lasting. If Athenians are as the Corinthians described them, never at peace, or allowing others to be so, and Spartans are slow to act (1.70.4–9), Brasidas seems to be more like an Athenian than a Spartan. Indeed, he has been called an Athenian among Spartans (Strauss 1964, 213 and 222). But Brasidas is not an Athenian, and Thucydides does not present him for the most part as "among Spartans." The army he leads in Thrace, for example, is composed primarily of helots and mercenaries. Brasidas may be a force for action, but much of what he does becomes undone. His daring thrust against the Athenians at Pylos is repulsed (4.11.4–12.1), for example, and Sparta returns the cities he "liberates" to Athens. Although admiring Brasidas's virtues, Thucydides questions his leadership, for his own city does not follow his lead. His virtues are good, but without support from his political community, they are not entirely good. If what he does becomes undone, he is not a doer at all.

ALCIBIADES' *ERŌS* FOR SAILING AWAY—TO SICILY AND POINTS BEYOND

After Brasidas's death at Amphipolis, the Spartans and Athenians are able to negotiate peace, albeit one so tendentious that Thucydides insists that it did not end the war (5.26.1–3). Shortly after the treaty is in place, Alcibiades, a young man of a distinguished Athenian family, wishes Athens to dissolve its treaty with Sparta in favor of one with Argos, Sparta's long-time enemy. His politics ignores received agreements or laws when better ones become possible (see 1.71.3). But if past agreements do not bind, neither will new ones if better ones become available. A city would be naive to bind itself by an agreement with a city that does not consider its agreements binding. In a world of such flux, can Athens rely on its new allies, or its new allies on it? When Alcibiades binds his city to an alliance with Argos for a hundred years, it might just as well be two hundred, or a thousand. There need be no limit to promises that can be revoked.

Just before the debate over the Sicilian expedition, in which Alcibiades delivers his first public speech in Thucydides' work, Thucydides describes Athens' subjugation of the hitherto neutral island of Melos. Although Alcibiades is not present, his spirit hovers over the Athenians' speech to the Melians. They dismiss considerations of justice and appeal to "a necessity of nature"—by which the strong subdue the weak, and the weak acquiesce. This is a "law" that they did not make, they say, nor were they the first to use it, and they will leave it behind "forever," knowing that Melos and others would follow it as well if they had the opportunity (5.105.1–2). Indeed, this is nothing more than the gods do among themselves, they say, echoing the Unjust Speech in Aristophanes' *Clouds*, which appeals to the ways of the gods to justify human wrongdoing (*Clouds* 1075; 1080–82). That law has little in common with the law that Pericles thinks the Athenians heed out of a sense of shame except that it is unwritten (2.37.3). The Athenians at Melos attempt to imitate the gods, imposing their power on others without limitation, while hiding their hubris behind their appeal to a necessity that applies to god and human alike. They are like the corrupt young man in Aristophanes' play, who also appeals to the necessities of nature to justify his hubristic act of father-beating (*Clouds* 1427–28) (cf. Orwin 1994, 106). In the Athenians' denial of any limits to their actions, they manifest Alcibiades' politics.

Alcibiades speaks in favor of the expedition to Sicily, in response to the cautious advice of the elder statesman Nicias, who had urged the Athenians to stay at home to protect its fragile peace with Sparta rather than to incur the dangers of an enterprise so far away (6.10). The "far away" does not deter Alcibiades. Nor is he deterred from talking about himself to the Athenian people. In fact, he has more to say about himself than he does about the expedition to Sicily, the object of his speech. He even calls attention to his speaking about himself and justifies it: By attacking him, Alcibiades says, Nicias "has compelled" him "to begin" by claiming he deserves to rule (6.16.1). Although others may complain about him, Alcibiades acknowledges, he in fact brings repute to his ancestors and benefits his fatherland (6.16.1). He thus goes a step further than Pericles: whereas Pericles praises the deeds of his contemporaries as greater than those of their ancestors (2.36.2), Alcibiades claims in effect that he shines glory on his ancestors. The effect gives luster to its cause. He does not deny the past; he recreates it. If his reference to Athens as his "fatherland" suggests filial piety, he is a young man who does more for his father than his father does for him (Forde 1989, 79–80; Orwin 1994, 123). Whereas Pericles describes Athens as "brilliant" (2.64.5), Alcibiades refers to his own brilliance (6.16.3).

Alcibiades also takes credit for negotiating Athens' alliance with Argos and other cities of the Peloponnesus. Given Sparta's defeat of this alliance at Mantinea, however, one might suppose that the less he says about it the better. But Alcibiades seems able to convert even defeat into victory: "I brought together the strongest powers on the Peloponnesus without great danger or cost to you and made the Spartans contest everything in a single day at Mantinea." And "even though [the Spartans] prevailed in the battle, their confidence is still not restored to this very day" (6.16.6). Thucydides gave a different account: "by this single deed" the Spartans redeemed the reputation for weakness they incurred previously, and showed themselves to be Spartans still (5.75.3).

When he finally comes to the expedition to Sicily, Alcibiades admits that what he knows about Sicily, he "knows from hearsay" (6.17.6). He is one of the Athenians "without experience" of Sicily whom Thucydides mentions just before his archeology of the island (6.1.1). The cities there are heavily populated with rabble, Alcibiades claims, lack the benefit of established customs, are given to faction, and have no sense of a fatherland (6.17.2–5). From his account, the Sicilian cities seem to have no forms of government or ways of life that give them an identity. Sicily is mere opportunity, a space for Alcibiades' activity. He nevertheless must work to bring the cities there into alliance with the Athenians (6.17.6 and 48). He will use the talents that brought the Peloponnesian cities to ally with Athens against Sparta, the most powerful force on the Peloponnesus, to unite cities on the island of Sicily against Syracuse, the most powerful city there. The world has yielded to his rhetoric and persuasion before, and he supposes it will do so again. He will conquer not by the sword, but by the force of his words, and by the force of the passion underlying them (6.17.1). If the world is essentially unformed, alliances made and easily broken, for example, Alcibiades does not need experience of Sicily.

Echoing the Athenians at Melos, Alcibiades claims that Athens must undertake the expedition to Sicily because unless it rules others it is in danger of being ruled by them. There are only those who rule and those who are ruled, just as the Athenians at Melos deny that there can be neutrals (5.96–98). Alcibiades observes that there is "no reckoning for how far we wish to rule" (6.18.3). The Athenians at Melos imply as much, but they were speaking to the Melians. They were trying to arouse fear. Alcibiades now presents an image of endless or infinite increase to Athens itself. He is like the Athenians at Melos when they warn the Melians that the Spartans could not come to help them, for the Athenians are "commanders of the sea" (*naukratores*). The sea is no wider than their reach. They too verge on asserting command of the unlimited or infinite (5.109–110; and 5.97 and 99; 2.62.1–2). And Nicias, who understands the city as bound by the sea, is incorrect (6.13.1). There are no boundaries.

A "desire for sailing away," Thucydides reports, fell on all alike (6.24.3). Nicias had earlier called Athens' desire for the expedition a "diseased *erōs* [*duserōs*] for the faraway [*aponta*]" (6.13.1). Thucydides confirms that at least the young among the Athenians "long for faraway sights and spectacles" (6.24.3). The "faraway" is, literally, "the absent." Liberated from the restraint of particular purposes and objects that it seeks or loves, without destination or goal, *erōs*, or desire, becomes infinite. Thucydides'—and Nicias's—use of *aponta* echoes the Corinthians' earlier description of the Athenians as "always being away from home" (*apodēmein*) and as believing that "by being away" (*apousia*) they would increase their possessions (1.70.4). Their exaggerated view of the Athenians (see e.g., 2.38) becomes realized in Alcibiades and the Athenians he leads away.

Thus Alcibiades argues that "the quickest way to ruin for an active city is a change to inactivity" (6.18.7). He characterizes Athens and its way of life as motion for its own sake, just as Corinthians claimed that Athenians are bent on "always acquiring" rather than "enjoying" what they acquire (1.70.8). Of course, the Athenians are sailing to Sicily, but the conquest of Sicily opens the imagination to one conquest after another. When Alcibiades reports to the Spartans the purpose of the expedition, he says that after subduing Sicily, the Athenians plan to move against Italy, then Carthage and its empire, and with resources from its conquests subdue Peloponnesus and rule all Hellas (6.90.2–3). But Athens never reaches these points beyond Sicily. The expedition meets ruin in Sicily, and few even return home (7.87.6). It is Alcibiades who reaches points beyond Sicily. When the Athenians send a ship to bring him home to face charges, he escapes by sea. Whereas the Athenians boasted to the Melians that they should not expect aid to arrive because no one could elude the Athenians at sea, Alcibiades escapes them. It is he who masters the sea. Pericles defends himself before the people when they accuse him of causing the war, implicitly acknowledging that they can hold him to account. When Alcibiades is summoned to Athens to answer charges, he does not come. He is the one who arrives in Sparta, in order to escape the Athenians. And when he has a falling out with the Spartans as well, he goes to advise the Persian satrap Tissaphernes on how to play Athens and Sparta against each other. It is Alcibiades who reaches no stopping point in Thucydides' work, for when the *History* breaks off in 411 BCE, before the end of the war, Alcibiades is still alive, negotiating with Tissaphernes, and moving from one place to another. He has still not returned to Athens.

It is when Alcibiades is "away" (*apōn*)—on the expedition to Sicily—that his enemies at home can move against him (6.29.3). He fails to lead, because he has freed himself from his city, which exists in a particular time and place, and thereby serves as a restraint on freedom. We see that this is true not only of Sparta, a city that prides itself on its strict customs and training (1.84.4), but even of Athens, a city that looks up to freedom. When Alcibiades later plots to return to Athens, which he thinks requires a more oligarchic regime that would be more sympathetic to him than a democracy, one of his opponents claims that Alcibiades is indifferent to regimes, and cares only for the one most likely to lend him support. Thucydides claims that this opponent speaks the truth (8.48.2–5; see also 6.89.6). But Alcibiades is not simply indifferent to regimes. He is hostile to all regimes. Regimes establish institutions and determine who is to rule, and those rulers do not merely rule; they are also ruled by their regimes. Regimes stand between the individual and his city, structuring their relationship and interaction. Even when he wants to be recalled from exile and to return home, he is willing to overthrow the regime in order to do so. Unlike Pericles, he has no recognition of the importance of a regime in fostering and protecting freedom.

Nicias's Failure to Lead and the Disaster in Sicily

In spite of offering to resign his command of the expedition to Sicily (6.23.3), Nicias is sent along with Alcibiades and a third general, Lamachus, as commanders. He cannot stop the motion that Alcibiades encourages, but is dragged along. When the Athenians arrive in Sicily, Nicias proposes that they settle the matter with their allies there, display their might, and sail back as soon as possible (6.47–50), but he yields to Alcibiades' more ambitious plan to win over other cities in Sicily to their side against Syracuse (6.47–50). Once again he is dragged along. After Alcibiades is summoned back for trial in Athens and escapes to Sparta, and Lamachus is killed in battle, Nicias becomes sole commander of the Athenian forces.

The tide turns against Athens when Peloponnesian reinforcements arrive (6.88.5; 6.93.4–103; 7.2.1; and 7.6–8). By the following winter, the Athenians are in desperate straits, and Nicias sees no prospect of survival unless they quickly return home or substantial help comes from Athens (7.8.1). Although the commanders were given full authority on the expedition (*autokratores*) (6.26.1), Nicias sends a letter to the Athenians to ask them what he should do (7.8.2–3). Swift action in Sicily is imperative, and of course Athens is some distance away, but Nicias cannot bring himself to act without the backing of the city. Whereas Brasidas does not follow orders that are sent, Nicias asks for orders when he should act on his own. He worries about the reaction of "the crowd," Thucydides says, using the very word for the Athenian people that Alcibiades had used to describe the "rabble" in Sicily (6.17.2). Whereas the "rabble" in Sicily is comforting to Alcibiades—they will be too unorganized to resist the Athenians—the "rabble" in Athens is frightening to Nicias. This is not the first time that we are told that Nicias "fears returning" to Athens with his mission unaccomplished (5.46.4–5). He does not even think about trying to persuade the Athenians, as Pericles did, that the ones who approved the enterprise are as responsible as its leaders for the hardships that result.

When Nicias describes the growing number of enemy troops arriving, the cities of Sicily joining Syracuse, and the deteriorating Athenian navy (7.11.1–14.1), he comes close to telling the Athenians that their cause is lost and that they have no choice but to summon the expedition home. He nevertheless flatters them into supposing that they are free to deliberate and therefore to choose (7.11.1 and 14.4). They must either recall the expedition, he concludes, or send out another just as large, as well as a large sum of money (7.15.2). He had tried a similar tactic before, when he attempted unsuccessfully to dissuade the Athenians from the expedition by telling them the size and expense required (6.19.2). He now implies that it is still possible to conquer Sicily, with requisite force, and that passage home will be possible later as it is now. Thucydides earlier praises Pericles for instilling fear when the people are overconfident and fostering confidence when they are despondent (2.65.9). Nicias, in contrast, tries to do the former and accomplishes the latter, because he himself is moved more by fear of his addressees than by confidence in himself.

The Athenians repeat their earlier decision to go against Sicily, and send another expedition in support of the first one. It is almost as if Alcibiades were still in Athens, influencing its decisions, and Nicias were the one in exile. When Demosthenes arrives with reinforcements and they make a quick assault that fails, he is ready to depart. Nicias refuses on the ground that it would be unacceptable to the Athenians if they did not vote on the matter themselves. If the expedition returns to Athens without being recalled, they will be judged by men who will not be able to see their situation in Sicily as clearly as they themselves can, he says, and who will listen to the criticisms of others (7.7.43–44; 47.3; 48.2–3). However, if the Athenians cannot see clearly enough to judge correctly their generals' decision to withdraw, how can they see clearly enough to make the decision in their place? Those who see their situation as clearly as the generals there do, Nicias inadvertently indicates, would make the more informed decision. Demosthenes has made his call, and Nicias must make his. Refusing to decide will be as consequential as deciding. Nicias must act independently of his city in order to serve it. Nicias is too dependent on his city to go home.

When matters get so bad that the Athenians seem compelled to depart, there is an eclipse of the moon, which the seers interpret to mean they should delay sailing home. The majority of the soldiers want to obey the seers, as does Nicias, who Thucydides says is "overly attached to divination and such things" (7.50.4). Their delay allows their foes to attack once again, and the Athenians' ships are either destroyed or driven to shore. There is no sailing home for them, and they retreat by land, hoping to find refuge somewhere. Nicias's supposedly comforting words to his troops that they will be able to constitute a city wherever they establish themselves (7.77.4) indicate that he does not expect them to return home (see also 6.22–23.2). The speech he delivers to his men as they begin their retreat has the flavor of a funeral oration: they have suffered so greatly that the gods must now feel more pity for them than envy, he tells them. They can therefore hope that the gods will be "kinder" to them now (7.77.4). Nicias has been wrong before, but he is never more wrong than he is now. As they try to cross a river to safety, they trample one another, find the enemy on the opposite bank as well as behind them, and are slaughtered as they seek to quench their thirst in the river. Very soon they are drinking water filled with their own blood (7.84.3).

At last making a decision without considering what Athens might expect of him, Nicias surrenders, telling his foes to do whatever they like with him if only they stop slaughtering his soldiers (7.85.1). The "kindness" he expects the gods to show his long-suffering army (7.77.4) he must render himself. But it is too late to bring his army home. This independent act lies only in yielding to the enemy's superior force. After that he no longer has a say in what happens to him or his men. He is executed, and his soldiers, no fewer than 7,000, are imprisoned in quarries where miserable conditions, including the lack of life's necessities, result in a great number of deaths. The corpses that now pile up unattended in the quarries remind us of Athens during the plague (7.87.1–4).

Thucydides kindly pronounces that of all the Hellenes of his time Nicias was least worthy of the misfortune to which he came, inasmuch as the law-bred practices of his life were directed to every virtue (7.86.5). The virtue that Athens represents for Pericles, in contrast, is not simply law bred, for it comes "from within" (2.39.1). Law-bred virtue asks too much of human beings, when it leaves no room for choice, and too little, when it does not require choice. If Nicias's decision to surrender manifests that he has learned this lesson, it takes him a long time to learn what Pericles knows.

Thucydides' View of Leaders and Leadership

In his *History*, Thucydides illustrates both the opportunities and dilemmas of leadership. Leaders cannot be understood in abstraction from those whom they lead, and in particular from the regimes that inform their actions and that they influence in turn. Pericles holds up to his audience a model of a virtuous and free Athenian, both in the citizen he describes and in his own self-presentation before his city. He is able to interpret Athens to itself as well as to the world. However much his city's deeds fall short of his noble words, he presents Athenians with a view of themselves that they can imagine might be true. Like Pericles, Brasidas depicts a noble view of his city to the world—a liberator of Hellas—but this is only what Sparta claims to be. He interprets Sparta to the world, but not to itself. He delivers no speeches to the Spartan people. When Sparta denies Brasidas's request for reinforcements, Thucydides reports, the denial is due in part to the envy of Sparta's leading men (literally, its "first men") (4.108.7; cf. 1.139.4 and 2.65.9). Sparta has several such men, and Brasidas is not among them. He is in no position to speak for Sparta. We cannot explain his virtue as Thucydides does Nicias's—as law bred. Brasidas is a man without a city. As such he cannot be a leader.

Alcibiades, in contrast to Nicias, seems to represent Athenian freedom. He proclaims the active character of the city and manifests that character in his own life. But if the virtue of Athenians comes from within themselves, those who most exercise that freedom are those who owe least to the regime and most to their own efforts. Just as Alcibiades believes that he can bestow glory on his ancestors, he claims from exile that he wants to "repossess" his city (6.92.4). Repossessing one's city—and thereby making it one's own—is the ultimate demonstration of one's freedom. If Alcibiades could succeed in coming home, he would be an Athenian by virtue of his own act. His homecoming would mean not that he belonged to Athens, but that Athens belonged to him. If Athens could become the home of a man who acts as freely as Alcibiades—and who therefore must repossess his city himself—it would no longer be a free city. The people are correct in suspecting him of plotting tyranny (6.60.1). In Alcibiades, we see the dilemma of being a leader in a free regime. Alcibiades is so free that he cannot lead. In Nicias, we see the other side of that dilemma, for he cannot free himself in order to lead.

Whereas Alcibiades is lawless (6.15.4), Nicias follows orders. He obeys the Athenian Assembly when it appoints him to command in Sicily, even though he opposes the expedition. He asks it for direction when he is in Sicily. Whereas Alcibiades does not understand what his freedom owes to the Athenian regime, Nicias does not exercise the freedom that is its characteristic excellence. He is too dependent on his city to lead the army home when there is still time to withdraw. It is Thucydides' Pericles who held together respect for Athens' regime, laws, and way of life with the freedom for human action that the regime made possible and that made it worthy of respect. Pericles praises the choice of the noble over the pleasant, the just over the advantageous, and the public good over private interest. Indeed, the choice of the former in each case constitutes noble deeds, and manifests freedom. Such choices may serve the pursuit of power, but they also moderate it because they give it a purpose. Purpose both restrains freedom and calls for its exercise. Or so Pericles, and Thucydides, instruct their addressees. Neither Alcibiades nor Nicias was able to find in Athens the home that Pericles did. Alcibiades speaks of his city as unlimited motion (6.18.2–3 and 6–7), whereas Nicias tries to maintain Athens at rest, or at least to do what is necessary to maintain the peace he negotiated and that is still not secure (6.10). And yet they both belong in Athens more than Brasidas does in Sparta. Just as Thucydides prefers Pericles' leadership to that of the other Athenians he describes, he prefers Athens to Sparta. The superior city is the one that not only allows but also demands freedom, and in which leaders can therefore follow its lead.

References

Burns, Timothy. 2011. "The Virtue of Thucydides' Brasidas." *Journal of Politics* 73: 508–23.
Connor, W. Robert. 1984. *Thucydides*. Princeton: Princeton University Press.
Forde, Steven. 1989. *Ambition to Rule: Alcibiades and the Politics of Athenian Imperialism in Thucydides*. Ithaca: Cornell University Press.
Johnson, Laurie M. 1991. *Thucydides, Hobbes, and the Interpretation of Realism*. DeKalb: Northern Illinois University Press.
Lattimore, Steven. 1998. Trans. *The Peloponnesian War, with an introduction, notes, and glossary*. Indianapolis: Hackett.
Ludwig, Paul. 2002. *Eros and Polis*. Cambridge: Cambridge University Press.
Mara, Gerald M. 2009. "Thucydides and Political Thought." In *The Cambridge Companion to Ancient Greek Thought*, edited by Stephen Salkever, 96–125. Cambridge and New York: Cambridge University Press.
Monoson, S. Sara, and Michael Loriaux. 1998. "The Illusion of Power and the Disruption of Moral Norms: Thucydides' Critique of Periclean Policy." *American Political Science Review* 92: 285–97.
Nichols, Mary P. 2015. *Thucydides and the Pursuit of Freedom*. Ithaca: Cornell University Press.
Orwin, Clifford. 1994. *The Humanity of Thucydides*. Princeton: University of Princeton Press.
Palmer, Michael. 1992. *Love of Glory*. Lanham, Maryland: Rowman and Littlefield.
Rahe, Paul A. 1996. "Thucydides' Critique of *Realpolitik*." In *Roots of Realism: Philosophical and Historical Dimensions*, edited by Benjamin Frankel, 105–41. London: Frank Cass.
Saxonhouse, Arlene W. 1996. *Athenian Democracy: Modern Mythmakers and Ancient Theorists*. Notre Dame: Notre Dame University Press.
Strassler, Robert B., ed. 1996. *The Landmark Thucydides. A Newly Revised Edition of the Crawley Translation with Maps, Annotations, Appendices, and Encylopedic Index*. New York: Simon & Schuster.
Strauss, Leo. 1964. *The City and Man*. Chicago: Rand McNally.
Thucydides. *Historiae*. 1996–97 (H.S. Jones, Ed., J.E. Powell Rev.) Oxford: Clarendon.
Zumbrunnen, John G. 2008. *Silence and Democracy: Athenian Politics in Thucydides' History*. University Park: Pennsylvania State University Press.

CHAPTER 28

THUCYDIDES AND CROWDS

JOHN ZUMBRUNNEN

Introduction

In Book 3 of his *Politics*, Aristotle famously suggests that at times the many may in fact be wiser than the one:

> For the many, of whom each individual is not a good man, when they meet together may be better than the few good, if regarded not individually but collectively, just as a feast to which many contribute is better than a dinner provided out of a single purse. For each individual among the many has a share of excellence and practical wisdom...." (Everson 1996, 3.1.1281b)

The increasing significance of "epistemic" arguments in contemporary democratic theory has brought renewed attention to the idea expressed in this passage (Estlund 2008). Broadly speaking, epistemic arguments hinge on the claim that democracy is more likely to produce right decisions, or at least better outcomes, than alternative forms of government.

This claim most often includes an emphasis on the need for a particular set of institutions that embody democratic principles and practices if democracy's epistemic promise is to be fulfilled. In Helene Landemore's version of the epistemic claim,

> democratic institutions such as inclusive deliberation and majority rule with universal suffrage combine their epistemic properties to turn the lead of individual citizens' input into the gold of "democratic reason" and give democracy an epistemic edge over any variant of the rule of the few. (Landemore 2012b, 1; cf. Landemore 2012a)

Josiah Ober has advanced a broadly similar epistemic claim for ancient Athenian democracy. In *Democracy and Knowledge*, Ober surveys Athenian economic and military "performance" and finds it superior to that of other Greek poleis. He explains this superior performance as a consequence of the organization of Athenian social and political life, which produced "innovation" and "learning" that "overbalanced" the admitted "costs of participatory political practices" (2008, 37).

In the popular press, broadly related epistemic arguments draw on the rhetoric of the crowd: witness "the wisdom of the crowd" (Surowiecki 2005) and "crowdsourcing" (Howe 2009; Grier 2013). This rhetoric is of course deliberately provocative. We are to be suitably surprised—perhaps even shocked—that the crowd can have wisdom or that it can be a valuable source of support for innovation, or even of innovation itself. Evocations of the "crowd," that is, serve to highlight the challenge of claims regarding epistemic democracy. In the more familiar rendering, the crowd becomes—in Aristotle's words—"one man" not when it exercises collective intelligence, but when it is seized by collective impulse and its collective passions overwhelm reason and knowledge. Instead, we are told by Aristotle and contemporary epistemic theorists, the crowd can, through the proper institutions and procedures, have its diverse experiences, emotions, and judgments turned into a kind of unified democratic reasoning superior to what the knowledgeable few can muster.

In this essay, I take up the question of the crowd, asking whether Thucydides finds anything like wisdom in it, and so whether he has anything to contribute to discussions of epistemic democracy. As we will see, Thucydides at times echoes traditional claims about the crowd or the "mob" as emotional, unruly, and dangerous. What is more, he shows relatively little interest in the kind of institutional and procedural matters central to the arguments of Ober, Landemore, and others. He instead focuses our attention, first, on questions of leadership—a concept that sits uneasily with the idea of epistemic democracy. I will argue, though, that Thucydides' apparent embrace of leadership by a few is not his final word on the potential wisdom of crowds.

Thucydides and the "Mob"

In his account in Book 6 of the fateful debate among the Athenians about whether or not to sail for Sicily, Thucydides has Alcibiades reassure the Athenians that

> "it is not likely that a mob [*homilon*] like [the people of Sicily] will either listen to proposals with a single purpose or go into action in a common cause." (Lattimore 1998: 6.17.4)[1]

Alcibiades describes the Sicilian "mob" or "crowd" as marked by diversity as well as by corruption. Sicily's "cities," he says "swarm with people of every sort and readily take in and exchange citizens" (6.17.2). In the midst of this civic chaos, every inhabitant stands ever ready to "settle in another land" should "things go wrong" and, in the meantime, to

---

[1] All translations of the *History* are from Steven Lattimore in Thucydides (1998).

take what he can "out of public goods." Perhaps not surprisingly, given what he describes as the diversity of Sicilians, the corrupt seizure of public goods may be a consequence of "faction," but Alcibiades also says that the individual Sicilian may take what he wants "by persuasive speaking." Either self-interest or oratory will on his account lead the ordinary citizen of Sicily not simply to reject any call for unified action, but even to refuse to hear that call at all. In short, the Sicilians are a diverse and ever-shifting mob that makes a great deal of noise. This mob is unable to listen, when listening alone can yield the necessary collective action. From all these weaknesses, Alcibiades promises, the Athenians stand to benefit when they invade the island.

Alcibiades' analysis of the Sicilians is just one of many uses of the language of the crowd or mob—using forms of *ochlos* and *homilos*—throughout the *History*. Many instances of such usage refer to military matters. In 1.49.3, we read of the "crowding [*ochlou*]" of ships together, which makes purposeful movement difficult. In 6.20.4, Nicias, responding to the optimistic estimates that Alcibiades has provided of Sicilian strengths, warns that the cities of Sicily possess many triremes and the "crowds" [*ochlos*] "to man them." At times, Thucydides uses the language of the crowd or mob to refer to an entire military force, but more often that language designates a particular part of a force, usually light-armed troops, as opposed to cavalry, as at 4.65.3, or the "crowd" that follows the army, as at 6.64.1 and 7.78.2. Thucydides relatively rarely refers to crowds or mobs in a political context. He does occasionally (1.80, 6.31, 6.57) use this language to refer to all the Athenians or to an undifferentiated group of Athenians in a public place. Elsewhere, he uses it to mark off a particular segment of the city's population, with the kind of pejorative meaning Alcibiades uses in describing the Sicilians. At 4.28, he reports on the Athenian reaction to Cleon as the demagogue tries to retract his claims about what he would accomplish at Pylos if only he were allowed to command. The gathered Athenians, "as a crowd [*ochlos*] is apt to do," grew ever more excited and "shouted at Cleon to sail."

In general, when Thucydides uses the language of the crowd evaluatively, he does so in ways that fit with what we find often enough in Greek thinkers. Aristotle's insistence on the potential wisdom of the masses contrasts with the more common argument that the many are an unruly mob and the corresponding conclusion that democracy is dangerous. The concerns that Alcibiades expresses about the Sicilians and Thucydides' comment on the behavior of the Athenian crowd that confronted Cleon both resonate, for example, with Plato's portrait of democracy in Book VIII of the *Republic*. There we find Socrates describing democracy's lack of small-mindedness, the toleration that allows for any sort of soul and that makes democracy a "supermarket of constitutions." This diversity is bound up with democracy's lawlessness, which borders on anarchy. In the democratic city, Socrates says, no one is required to rule or to be ruled. (Grube 1992). Though this critique of democracy flows from Socrates' description of kallipolis and its decline, it shares a basic concern about the crowd or mob with Thucydides' Alcibiades. Amid the swarming freedom of the demos—which is, at least in the hands of democracy's elitist critics—another name for the mob or crowd—no one is likely to "listen to proposals," and so it proves impossible even to begin a proper discussion, let alone to establish a proper relationship between rulers and ruled or leaders and led. From this point of view (and, again, various passages in Thucydides suggest something similar), the tendencies of crowds of people render democracy suspect. Democracy as mass collective action can be salvaged only by getting the crowd to listen and perhaps thereby converting the *ochlos* into a proper demos.

After her own comprehensive review of Thucydides' use of the language of the crowd, Virginia Hunter concluded that he focuses our attention squarely on the psychology of the crowd, and ends up at an "entirely" negative judgment about it (Hunter 1988, 26). An unthinking mass, the crowd elides individual distinctions, is moved by collective emotions, ignores reason, and can be manipulated; all the while, it rejects any responsibility for the consequences of its behavior. Hunter cites Thucydides' eulogy of Pericles at 2.65 as providing a "paradigm" for his analysis of crowd psychology. Individual citizens having merged into a crowd in the wake of the plague, the Athenians as a blind, unreasoning mass turn on Pericles. In this context, Thucydides offers what Hunter sees as his basic response to the inevitable tendencies of crowd behavior: social control exercised by a responsible leader:

> Pericles manipulated the masses to his will. In other words, in Thucydides social control is the countervailing force of a single individual who understands crowd psychology and who has the rhetorical skill to make practical use of that understanding. (Hunter 1988: 25)

More recently, Eirene Visvardi has worked with similar evidence but draws a somewhat different conclusion about Thucydides' analysis. Pointing as well to 2.65, she concludes that "Thucydides expresses distrust in the ability of the crowd to self-regulate" (2012, 5). Where Hunter finds Thucydides seeking "social control," Visvardi finds him looking for "competent leaders with a clear and reliable vision of the congruity between individual and collective interest who can create a political culture of trust" (2012, 38).

No doubt we can find connections between the idea of leaders who can exercise "social control" and the idea of leaders who can "create a political culture of trust." Trust can surely be nurtured and manipulated in ways that enable or enhance control. I want here, though, to emphasize the differences between these ways of reading Thucydides' response to the phenomenon of crowds. Hunter's "social control" fits well with the common and longstanding emphasis in the literature on the towering figure of Pericles and, more generally, on the skill or lack of skill exercised by particular individual leaders or would-be leaders (Cornford 1907, 49–50; Cochrane 1929, 32; Jones 1957, 62; Finley 1967, 156–7; Woodhead 1970, 49–51; Orwin 1994, 28). The true leader is a "force" who can reckon with the crowd. Visvardi's "political culture of trust," on the other hand, points less to control by leaders and more toward a reciprocal relationship between leaders and the people. Put differently, understanding Thucydides as admiring a certain sort of political culture and hoping for its preservation in Athens grants more agency to the crowd or mob than does the idea of leaders exercising or failing to exercise control.

The tension between social control and political trust as a response to the dilemmas and challenges posed by the tendency of collectivities to act as crowds runs through the *History*, and it works on multiple levels. The tension appears, at one level, as a question of Thucydides' own stance regarding crowds and crowd control. On another level, it appears as a political question in the Athens Thucydides presents to us. We can accordingly see the tension between social control and political trust in the speeches Thucydides records, which often dwell on the relationship between leaders and people. Even—or perhaps particularly—in the midst of war, Thucydides' Athenians seem preoccupied with questions about the place of prominent individuals in relation to the mass of ordinary citizens. In thinking about social control and political trust as alternative Thucydidean remedies for the problems posed by the crowd, we can usefully begin precisely with Pericles and his place in Athens as both Thucydides and he himself describe it.

Pericles and Social Control

Hunter's claim that Pericles exercised "social control" over the Athenian crowd depends to a considerable extent on the eulogy of the great leader offered by Thucydides in 2.65 (as do many accounts of the centrality of the exceptional Pericles to Thucydides' understanding of Athenian political life). There is, of course, much in the eulogy that points toward Pericles' extraordinary influence. Thucydides goes so far as to describe the time of Pericles' dominance in Athens as an era of "rule by the first man," which rendered the city a democracy in name only. In the central passage upon which Hunter draws, Thucydides does indeed suggest that Pericles could sway the collective emotions of the many. According to Thucydides, Pericles

> exercised free control over the people and was not led by them instead of leading them, because he did not speak to please in order to acquire power by improper means but, since he had this through his prestige, even contradicted them in their anger. Certainly, whenever he perceived that they were arrogantly confident in any way beyond what the situation justified, he shocked them into a state of fear by speaking, and again, when they were unreasonably afraid, he restored them to confidence. (2.65)

Here is the image of a leader with, in Hunter's words, an understanding both of "crowd psychology" and of the rhetoric that can, in the context of that psychology, be used to move the crowd in the right direction.

Other parts of the eulogy, though, point toward the greater complexity suggested by a "political culture of trust." Immediately preceding the lines just quoted, Thucydides describes Pericles as "influential through both reputation and judgment and notable for being most resistant to bribery." Pericles' personal qualities, this suggests, translated into "control" only by means of the relationship he established with the people—a relationship shaped by reputation, undergirded by his being known in a particular way, issuing in influence. What is more, the control his influence enabled was manifestly imperfect; the speech that precedes the eulogy is made necessary by the anger felt by the Athenians toward Pericles in the wake of the plague. Put differently, the speech is necessary only because that anger threatens to get out of control. Moreover, the speech itself does not succeed in reimposing perfect control. Still angry, the Athenians go on to fine Pericles, though soon enough, "as a multitude [*homilos*] is apt to behave, they elected him general and entrusted all their affairs to him."

We might, then, complicate Hunter's story of "social control" by saying that 2.65 describes a highly influential leader who built and sustained a sometimes fragile relationship with the Athenians and that this allowed him to guide them at key moments. This, in fact, fits with how Pericles describes his relationship to the Athenians in his final speech in the *History*. Faced with the anger of the Athenian multitude, Pericles asserts the qualities that mark him as a leader:

> And yet I, the object of your anger, consider myself a man inferior to no one in judgment of what is necessary and explaining it, furthermore, a lover of my country and above money. For one who has ideas and does not instruct clearly is on the same level as if he had not thought of them; the man able to do both but ill-disposed toward his city cannot make any declaration with the comparable loyalty; and if he has that as well but he is conquered by money, for this alone he can be bought in entirety. (2.60)

As Mary Nichols argues (Nichols, chapter 27 in this volume), this passage may well point to a normative model of Thucydidean democratic leadership (see also Pouncey 1980, 78; Finley 1967, 151; Kagan 1974, 358). In the context of the speech in which we find it, though, the passage works as an attempt to re-establish a certain relationship with the Athenians. Pericles offers his "extraordinary self-praise" (Connor 1984, 65) as a reminder to the Athenians of why they have followed him in the past. It follows that they should look elsewhere in placing blame for the course of the war: "if in thinking that I rather than others was endowed with these qualities, however modestly, you were persuaded to go to war, I could not reasonably be charged now with misconduct" (2.60). Again here, to the extent that he exercises control, Pericles does so because the Athenians trust that he has certain qualities suitable for a democratic leader.

Pericles, then, presents himself as possessing certain qualities that form the basis of his relationship with the Athenians; but he is only one party to that relationship. We have seen that Thucydides in 2.65 refers to the Athenians, at least when they are moved by anger against Pericles, as a multitude or crowd. Not surprisingly, Pericles does not use this language to describe his fellow citizens; he does not call them a mob moved by collective emotions. Perhaps his most famous description of the Athenians comes in the Funeral Oration:

> In summary I claim that our city as a whole is an education for Hellas, and that it is among us as individuals, in my opinion, that a single man would represent an individual self-sufficient for the most varied forms of conduct, and with the most attractive qualities. (2.41)

Pericles does not, here, point to the "wisdom of the crowd." He does not, that is, celebrate the potential benefits that might follow from pooling the varied and diverse talents of the many. Instead, he praises the Athenians as individuals. We might indeed read him as suggesting that individual Athenians are interchangeable with one another. Any "single man," possessed of "the most attractive qualities" will serve as well for "varied forms of conduct" as any other man in Athens. There is, then, no need to rely upon the aggregative wisdom of the crowd.

Of course, if every individual Athenian is "self-sufficient for the most varied forms of conduct," then it is unclear why the city should follow the lead of any particular individual like Pericles. Elsewhere in the Funeral Oration, though, Pericles suggests that whatever their self-sufficiency for action of various kinds, there is something of a division of labor in Athenian political life:

> And it is within the capacity of some of us to manage private right along with public business and of the rest, while concentrating on their own occupations, to have no inferior understanding of public affairs. (2.40)

In the context of Pericles' claim about himself in his post-plague speech, we might conclude that those able to manage public affairs are those who, like him, have the sort of knowledge, oratorical skill and honest patriotism necessary to lead. Presumably those other Athenians who have "no inferior understanding" are able—as Pericles says in the next line of the Funeral Oration—to "ratify" even if they cannot "propound proposals."

Pericles points to a similar division of political labor in his first speech in the *History*, at the end of Book 1. Reasserting his defensive strategy for the war, he says that

> and I see now that once more the same identical advice is required of me, and I charge those who stand persuaded that you support our common resolutions, even if there are setbacks, or else not claim their intelligence as a contribution to our successes. (1.140).

Pericles lays preliminary groundwork here for his later insistence on shared responsibility. As we have seen, in his final speech he insists that there are good reasons for the Athenians to have followed him; they should all, therefore, share in the blame rather than direct their frustration and anger at him alone. These claims of collective responsibility rest on the idea that leaders like Pericles make proposals about which the mass of Athenians can, and do, make meaningful judgments. We might think of Pericles as making a weak version of a "wisdom of the crowd" argument. He does not claim that the mass of Athenians can themselves arrive at proper proposals; nor does he suggest that their style of decision-making is superior to alternative processes. He does, though, consistently argue (and seems always to assume) that they can judge wisely about proposals.

Alcibiades says in the Sicily debate that the mob at Sicily is unlikely to listen to proposals. By contrast, in his speeches, Pericles proceeds as if the Athenians did listen and then made decisions based upon what they had heard. His description of Athenian decision-making processes directly claims that they do so. At another level, his rhetorical strategy depends upon the Athenians listening to his often complex arguments, including precisely those claims about collective decision-making in Athens. From a narrow reading of parts of 2.65, we might take all of this as just so much analysis of the rhetorical tools Pericles uses to control the Athenian mob. He may, that is, possess an unusual ability to get his audience to stop and listen to his proposals. I want, though, to complicate matters—first, by suggesting that the Athenians continue to listen even after Pericles departs the scene.

After Pericles

In Pericles' speeches and the Athenians' reactions to them, we find evidence for the existence of a "political culture of trust" that shapes the relationship between the great leader and the people. Thucydides' own summary authorial comments do at times suggest that Pericles "controlled" this relationship, but, again, whatever control he exercised seems dependent upon the prior existence of the rudiments of that relationship. At the very least, Pericles had first to establish himself as someone to whom the people would listen; the people had to be willing in fact to listen. In 2.65, Thucydides makes it plain that a significant change occurred after Pericles' death:

> Those who came later, in contrast, since they were more on an equal level with one another and each striving to become first, even resorted to handing over affairs to the people's pleasure. As a result, many mistakes were made.... (2.65)

We find here a deceptively simple analysis familiar from Thucydides' description of Pericles' dominance. At first glance, Thucydides directs our attention to the failure of the would-be leaders who aimed to succeed Pericles. Unable to match his ability to control the demos, they succumbed to the "people's pleasure."

On another level, though, even this brief excerpt suggests a more complex reality, resting not just upon the skill of leaders in managing or manipulating a potentially unruly mob, but—as with Pericles—on the dynamics of the relationship between leaders and people. The fact that affairs were handed over to the people's pleasure results from the relative equality of the leaders and the resulting competition between them. Put in the terms Thucydides uses to describe the basis of Periclean "control," none of these leaders had the kind of "reputation" or "notability" or "influence" that Pericles enjoyed. Put in the terms I have been using here, no subsequent leader enjoyed the robust—if always tenuous—relationship with the Athenians that Pericles did. Indeed, if we turn to the moments in which Thucydides shows us later Athenian leaders in the Assembly, we find them attempting to negotiate what appears to be a fraying political culture of trust. We can read their attempts in the context of Pericles' description of the qualities that lead the demos to trust him: his knowledge of what should be done; his ability to explain it; his honest commitment to the best interests of the city.

In the midst of their attempts to persuade the demos to their preferred courses of action, subsequent Athenian speakers at times lay claim to these qualities. More strikingly, though, they at times engage in sharp arguments about the relative importance of these qualities. Take first the debate over the fate of the captured inhabitants of the fallen city of Mytilene. Diodotus favors reconsidering the harsh sentence of death passed upon them, while Cleon argues for adhering to that initial sentence. They clash over the relative importance of considerations of justice and expediency in such matters. They also, though, make arguments about leadership that gain significance from Pericles' description of himself, though they never mention him by name.

Speaking first, Cleon takes aim at speech itself. He claims that if anyone rises to call for a reopening of the case of Mytilene,

> it is clear that either he will be striving, out of confidence in his speaking, to demonstrate that what was absolutely decided was not resolved after all, or else he is motivated by profit when he fashions his attractive speech and attempts to mislead." (3.38)

As he thus criticizes the Athenian "habit of approaching words as a spectacle," Cleon apparently rejects one of the three components of Pericles' self-described relationship with the Athenians. The ability to speak persuasively, Pericles had claimed, is necessary to "explain" or "instruct" (2.60). Without it, no relationship with the people is possible.

In his response, Diodotus only briefly mentions Cleon's rejection of speech. He follows Pericles in insisting upon the indispensability of speech, saying that there is no "other way the future and its uncertainty can be considered" (3.42). Diodotus devotes more time to responding to Cleon's suggestion that anyone who opposes him might be "motivated by profit." Cleon's rhetorical tactic here, we should note, fits with Pericles' warning against advisers who are "conquered by money" and so cannot be trusted to offer their best advice to the city. Diodotus, by contrast, rejects this focus on honesty:

> when dishonesty is brought in, he is made suspect if he succeeds and dishonest on top of his incompetence if he fails. The city does not benefit at all in such situations; because of fear, it is deprived of its advisers. (3.42)

Whereas Pericles (and Cleon) had argued that the relationship between leaders and demos was based partly upon considerations of the motives of the former, Diodotus warns that directing scrutiny toward those motives will drive the most valuable advisers from the public arena.

If we move forward to the fateful debate in Book 6 over the Athenian expedition to Sicily, we find Nicias and Alcibiades similarly engaged in an argument over the relevance of the motives of would-be advisers. This argument is, of course, only a small part of their broader clash, in which Nicias warns of the difficulty of conquering Sicily and counsels tending to the existing Athenian empire, while Alcibiades insists that the

Sicilians pose no significant challenge and that, in any event, the Athenian empire must continually expand or it will collapse. Turning to the question of motives, Nicias rather oddly both tries to enhance his position by claiming that he would in fact gain from the expedition he rises to oppose and suggests that it nonetheless does not matter if an adviser stands to gain from the course he recommends:

> And yet I derive honor from such actions and am less fearful than most about my own person, although I think that he who takes his own person and property into account is just as good a citizen; it is exactly that man who would wish for his own sake that the affairs of his city prosper as well. (6.9)

Not the most skillful of democratic leaders—elsewhere in this volume, Mary Nichols charges him with a "failure to lead"—Nicias thus ends up with a confused statement on honesty. Alcibiades, on the other hand, makes things quite clear. As Nichols writes, he "has more to say about himself than he does about the expedition to Sicily" (Nichols, chapter 27 in this volume). To those who would suggest (as Nicias at one point does) that he aims at personal benefit, he responds that "the outcry against me involves things that bring glory to my ancestors and myself but also benefit the country" (2.16). His pursuit of gain and glory redounds to the benefit of the city; it is, in any event, his due as one who produces victory. "Let all submit," he says, "to the arrogance of the successful" (2.16)

Just as Cleon moves decisively away from Pericles in rejecting the importance of speech, so Alcibiades (and before him, Diodotus) overturns Pericles' insistence on the importance of leaders demonstrating themselves to be above self-interest in advising the city. We might well want to think more thoroughly and carefully about these claims regarding the qualities of democratic leaders. The point here, though, is to recognize how both Pericles and those who strive for influence in Athens after his death use speech to try to negotiate the terms of their relationship with the Athenians. This recognition adds weight to the idea that Thucydides is concerned not simply with elite "social control" of the Athenian mob but also with the establishment and maintenance of a political culture of trust in Athens that permits some to exercise influence by offering advice while other citizens remain silent and, in the words of Alcibiades, "listen to proposals." As it appears in the words of Athenian speakers, that culture of trust or shared understanding of the relationship of advisers and people seems to fray over the course of the war; nonetheless, it appears to provide the Athenian alternative to the dangers of the crowd or mob.

At this point, two additional aspects of Thucydides' account of the tenuous relationship between leaders and led in Athens are worth noting. The first concerns a basic implication of the silence of the Athenian people. Thucydides tells us very little about what the Athenian people think of the claims made by their advisers. He of course tells us whose advice they follow. We know that the Athenians end up choosing to follow the path of leniency counseled by Diodotus; and we know that they end up choosing to follow Alcibiades to Sicily. Thucydides does not, though, tell us the particular details of their response to the rhetoric offered in the relevant debates.

Do the Athenians (a few, some, all?) accept Diodotus' embrace of rhetoric? His rejection of the question of motives? Do they agree with Alcibiades that an adviser can pursue his personal glory without compromising the guidance he offers the city? The silence of the mass of Athenians renders the answers to these questions unknowable from the pages of the *History* (see Zumbrunnen 2008). We hear various speakers making claims about the relationship between advisers and people, and we might hope to draw inferences from those claims about the health of Athenian political culture at a particular moment, but Thucydides does not—save in rare direct authorial comments like 2.65—offer his own conclusions.

Perhaps more to the point for thinking about Thucydides and crowds, the silence of the Athenian people abides throughout what appears to us to be the fraying of the culture of trust that Pericles labored mightily to build, maintain, and, when necessary, reconstruct. In all those moments when advisers make claims about the relationship between leaders and led, the Athenians silently listen to proposals. They do not, that is, act like a crowd or mob that will not listen (as Alcibiades says of the Sicilians). It might well surprise us that the Athenians remain silent and listen during the Sicily debate, when Athenian political culture seems so strained. The implications of their silent listening when Pericles speaks are, though, perhaps even more striking. We might take silent listening as a necessary background condition for any claims about the relationship between leaders and led, including those claims Pericles makes about himself and his standing in Athens. Pericles may well have established a relationship with the Athenians that gave him something that looked like "control," but because he could do so only through speech, the Athenians will first have had to listen to him make proposals. More generally, any political culture of trust in Athens emerges in and is negotiated during moments in which the Athenians are already listening to proposals. Before they can participate in such a culture, that is, the Athenians must be something other than an unruly crowd; they must already have grown silent and willing to listen to those who would lead. How might such a thing happen?

SILENCE, *STASIS*, AND THE CROWD

The moments of Athenian politics in the *History* that have drawn the most interest from theorists of democracy—when named speakers rise in the Athenian assembly—occur in the context of the basic silence of the Athenian people. As studies of the *thorubos*—the tendency of Athenian audiences to shout or heckle during speeches—indicate, we should be wary of concluding that the Athenians made no noise whatsoever when Pericles or Cleon or Alcibiades spoke (Balot 2004; Wallace 2004). Nonetheless, Thucydides' account consistently suggests that a certain sort of quiet or silence on the part of the crowd precedes and makes possible the negotiation of a culture of trust between advisers and people. Thucydides traces the stress and strain that culture undergoes, and he seems deeply concerned with its fraying during the course of the war. In the ideal to which Pericles points in his speeches and that works as the backdrop to the claims of later speakers, the silence of the people allows for a kind of interaction through rhetoric that taps into both the special knowledge of particular elites and the ability of the demos to listen to and make sound judgments about rival proposals. When the Athenian crowd grows silent, it turns into a demos that can judge.

If "normal" politics in the *History* is thus marked by a significant silence, we find—at least at first glance—a sharp contrast in times of civil strife or *stasis*. The most noted instance of *stasis* in the *History* is of course the revolution at Corcyra, reported by Thucydides in Book 3. There, famously, *stasis* is attended by a confused and confusing cacophony. Thucydides suggests an atmosphere of constant and reckless claim and counterclaim, accusation and counter-accusation, that no doubt destroyed the possibility of listening and judging:

> ... in self-justification men inverted the usual verbal evaluations of actions. Irrational recklessness was now considered courageous commitment, hesitation while looking to the future was high-styled cowardice, moderation was a cover for lack of manhood, and circumspection meant inaction, while senseless anger now helped to define a true man, and deliberation for security was a specious excuse for deliberation. The man of violent temper was always credible, anyone opposing him was suspect. (3.82)

This account of Corcyra fits broadly with a juxtaposition between healthy politics as involving a certain calm silence and *stasis* as involving noisy tumult. This, in turn, fits with the thematic juxtaposition in the *History* between war and civil war as disruptive movement or *kinēsis* and peace and normalcy as quiet or *hēsuchia*. Thucydides, for example, begins the *History* by describing the war as "the greatest disturbance [*kinēsis*] to affect the Hellenes" (1.1); by contrast, he says that during the Peace of Nicias, "on account of the armistice, matters were quiet [*hēsuchazē*]" (see Carter 1986 and Price 2001).

In broad terms, the disruption of democratic politics in Athens follows those thematic juxtapositions. In Book 8, Thucydides describes the beginnings of Athenian *stasis* as a "movement [*ekinēthē*]" against democracy. Intriguingly, though, silence or quiet or *hēsuchia* continues to play a role throughout the revolutionary moment in Athenian politics. At the outset, for example, Thucydides depicts the silence of the mass of Athenians—whether the ordinary sailors on Samos or in Athens itself—as abetting the anti-democratic movement. When the conspirators on Samos first revealed their plans to appeal to the Persians, Thucydides tells us, "the mob [*ochlos*]" of sailors "kept quiet [*hēchusazēn*]" (8.48). Later at Athens, when the Four Hundred first meets publicly, "the citizens offered no challenge but remained quiet [*hēsuchazon*]" (8.70).

If silence or quiet initially allows the movement of *stasis* to unfold without opposition, it later creates the context in which *stasis* comes to an end with the emergence of the Government of the Five Thousand. In a series of crucial moments, Thucydides tells us that violence is averted and *stasis*-ending arrangements made possible by the advent of quiet among the masses. For example, though the sailors at Samos are inclined to kill envoys from the 400 and sail for Athens to restore democracy, Thucydides tells us that "they managed to quiet down [*hēsuchasantes*]" (8.86). Together with timely and soothing words from Alcibiades (of all people!), Thucydides credits this quieting down with saving Athens from the prospect of its navy leaving the eastern Aegean undefended. Soon thereafter, the Four Hundred move to finish a fort that will dominate the Piraeus and so provide security for the Spartan forces they plan to invite into the city. Athenian hoplites put to work on the fort at this point turn on the Four Hundred and the city stands on the brink of widespread violence. But, Thucydides tells us, certain "older men" intervened and the Athenian people "managed to quiet down [*hesuchasan*] (8.92). The fort is soon torn down, and the hoplites begin to move against the oligarchic conspirators. The city once more on the brink of violence, the Four Hundred send representatives with promises that the Five Thousand will soon be seated, and so succeed in getting the hoplites "to keep quiet" [*hēsuchazein*] (8.92).

I do not pretend here to offer an exhaustive account of the place of quiet or silence during moments of *stasis*, much less in the *History* as a whole. Even this brief review, though, suggests that quiet or silence plays a complex and dynamic role in Thucydides' understanding of revolutionary politics and in the relationship of civil strife to relatively normal political life. It is clear, first, that Thucydides does not point to a simple or uniform assessment of the silence of the masses. On the one hand, the silence of the mob or crowd allows *stasis* to begin; the conspirators can proceed only insofar as the crowd quietly allows them to do so. On the other hand, it is precisely the willingness of the crowd to keep quiet that allows *stasis* to end with what Thucydides describes as the "best government" the Athenians enjoyed "at least in my lifetime" (8.97). Though that government is a "moderate blending of the few and the many" and not a democracy, we might note a certain familiar theme from Thucydides' depiction of democratic politics: the silence of the crowd makes relatively normal political life possible.

That basic conclusion might seem to put Thucydides in league with the Plato of Book VIII of the *Republic* and with many, many others who have bemoaned the mob-like behavior of the crowd and hoped for its silencing in favor of a proper politics. Here, though, it is important to emphasize the complexity of Thucydides' account of how the crowd grows silent. On the one hand, Thucydides at points tells a familiar story of a skillful elite managing to temper the worst inclinations of the mob: hence Alcibiades' intervention at an especially dangerous moment on Samos. At other points, though, he seems to suggest an ability on the part of the crowd to find its own way to quiet or to respond to the urgings of its own members (thus the role of the "older men" in Athens) or even to the appeals of its antagonists (as with the appeal from the envoys of the Four Hundred). The silence of the crowd, which can play a constructive and even pivotal role in concluding stasis, may at times come from somewhere within the crowd itself.

Conclusion

The intriguing place of silence over the course of Athenian *stasis* further complicates any attempt to situate Thucydides in the context of arguments about the "wisdom of the crowd." If we instead focus simply on his account of the revolution at Corcyra, we might well read him as giving voice to fairly straightforward and rather conventional concerns about crowd behavior. Loosed from the constraints of normal social and political life, the ordinary citizens of Corcyra become a mob. In the first of many such instances around Greece, the crowd gave in to a human nature that was "powerless over passion but stronger than justice" (3.84). To be sure, Thucydides places much blame on the Corcyraean oligarchs, who treated the people "abusively" and so primed them to seek revenge. Indeed, the oligarchs themselves were, it would seem, seized by the same mob mentality as the democrats. The broader point, though, is that in his analysis of Corcyra, Thucydides gives full voice to a fearful analysis of crowd psychology.

It is tempting, from this point of view, to return to the centrality of leadership in the *History*, to read Thucydides as consistently telling us that only firm and fair leadership can prevent the horrors of *stasis*. I have aimed here to present a more complex analysis. Thucydides has too many doubts about the behavior of ordinary citizens—and perhaps about human nature in general—to be cast as a full-throated advocate of the wisdom of crowds or its more sophisticated cousin, epistemic democracy. There are, though, aspects of his portrayal of Athenian politics that suggest that its functioning rests not just upon the presence of leaders who can manage the masses but also upon harnessing the potential of the mass of ordinary citizens. On my reading, Thucydides sees Athenian democracy as involving the constant negotiation of the tenuous relationship between a few vocal advisers and the mass of Athenians who remain silent, listen, and at crucial moments, judge between rival courses of action. Leadership is crucial, but so too is the collective ability of ordinary Athenians to judge the claims that would-be leaders make.

In the end, the most striking characteristic of the Athenian "crowd" is its silence. Through most of the *History*, including at particularly dire moments, the Athenians do what Alcibiades says the Sicilians will not: they listen to proposals with an eye toward acting together. Their silence at once makes the practice of persuasive oratory possible and renders the effect of any particular oration, and so the power of any particular speaker, uncertain and so unstable. Silence is hardly a democratic panacea. As the movement of the Four Hundred gets underway, the silence of the Athenian crowd is its undoing, allowing *stasis* to proceed. As we have seen, though, it is the silence of the people that allows for the end of *stasis* and the gradual restoration of moderate government in Athens. From this point of view, as well as from the point of view of their willingness to silently listen to and judge proposals, we might see Thucydides as locating a (perhaps limited) kind of wisdom in the crowd. We might also see him as pointing to complications in our understanding of the place of silence in democracy.

References

Balot, Ryan K. 2004. "Free Speech, Courage, and Democratic Deliberation." In *Free Speech in Classical Antiquity*, edited by Ineke Sluiter and Ralph M. Rosen, 233–60. Leiden and Boston: Brill.

Carter, I. G. 1986. *The Quiet Athenian*. New York: Oxford University Press.

Cochrane, Charles Norris. 1929. *Thucydides and the Science of History*. London: Oxford University Press.
Connor, W. Robert. 1984. *Thucydides*. Princeton: Princeton University Press.
Cornford, Francis M. 1907. *Thucydides Mythistoricus*. London: Edward Arnold.
Estlund, David. 2008. "Introduction: Epistemic Approaches to Democracy." *Episteme: A Journal of Social Epistemology* 5 (1): 1–4.
Everson, S., ed. 1996. *The Politics and the Constitution of Athens*. By Aristotle. Cambridge: Cambridge University Press.
Finley, J. H. 1967. *Three Essays on Thucydides*. Cambridge: Harvard University Press.
Grier, David Alan. 2013. *Crowdsourcing for Dummies*. New York: For Dummies.
Grube, G. M. A., trans. 1992. *Republic*, by Plato. Revised by C. D. C. Reeve. Indianapolis: Hackett.
Howe, David. 2009. *Crowdsourcing: Why the Power of the Crowd Is Driving the Future of Business*. New York: Crown Business.
Hunter, Virginia. 1988. "Thucydides and the Sociology of the Crowd." *Classical Journal* 84 (1): 17–30.
Jones, A. H. M. 1957. *Athenian Democracy*. Oxford: Basil Blackwell and Mott.
Kagan, Donald. 1974. *The Archidamian War*. Ithaca: Cornell University Press.
Landemore, Helene. 2012a. *Democratic Reason: Politics, Collective Intelligence, and the Rule of the Many*. Princeton: Princeton University Press.
Landemore, Helene. 2012b. "Why the Many Are Smarter Than the Few and Why It Matters." *Journal of Public Deliberation* 8 (1): 1–12.
Lattimore, Steven, trans. 1998. *The Peloponnesian War*, by Thucydides. Indianapolis: Hackett.
Ober, Josiah. 2008. *Democracy and Knowledge: Innovation and Learning in Classical Athens*. Princeton: Princeton University Press.
Orwin, Clifford. 1994. *The Humanity of Thucydides*. Princeton: Princeton University Press.
Pouncey, Peter R. 1980. *The Necessities of War: A Study of Thucydides' Pessimism*. New York: Columbia University Press.
Price, Jonathan. 2001. *Thucydides and Internal War*. Cambridge: Cambridge University Press.
Surowiecki, James. 2005. *The Wisdom of Crowds*. New York: Anchor.
Visvardi Eirene. 2012. "Collective Emotion in Thucydides." *CHS Research Bulletin* 1 (1):. http://www.chs-fellows.org/2012/11/30/abstract-collective-emotion-in-thucydides//
Wallace, Robert W. 2004. "The Power to Speak—and Not to Listen—in Ancient Athens." In *Free Speech in Classical Antiquity*, edited by Ineke Sluiter and Ralph M. Rosen, 221–32. Leiden and Boston: Brill.
Woodhead, A. Geoffrey. 1970. *Thucydides on the Nature of Power*. Cambridge: Harvard University Press.
Zumbrunnen, John. 2008. *Silence and Democracy: Athenian Politics in Thucydides' History*. University Park: Penn State University Press.

CHAPTER 29

THUCYDIDES, INTERNATIONAL LAW, AND INTERNATIONAL ANARCHY

ARTHUR M. ECKSTEIN

THE argument of this essay is that ancient Greek city-states existed in a world that was essentially bereft of international law. This lack of international law had profound effects on international relations. The anarchic environment encouraged the development of heavily militarized and diplomatically aggressive societies. The prevalence of such societies, combined with the absence of any overarching authority over them, made wars among polities common. Faced with a conflict of interest, every government independently decided what constituted justice for itself, and—in the absence of international law—all governments had to be ready to use violence or the threat of violence to enforce that view of justice. Hellenic intellectuals—most famously Thucydides, but including thinkers as different as Aristotle and Demosthenes—reacted to the anarchy by hypothesizing that interstate relations were determined above all by relations of power. Thucydides expressed this view of power politics in international life most clearly in what is called the Melian Dialogue (Thuc. 5.84–116). In this essay, however, I will emphasize especially Thucydides' analysis of the outbreak of the Peloponnesian War (1.23), and underline the nature of what he considered "the truest cause" (1.23.6) of that devastating conflict.

ANARCHY

The international environment in the great age of the independent Greek city-state (750–330 BCE) was an "anarchy" under formal definition. That is, the 200 states of the Aegean world recognized no overarching common government or authority, nor any larger interstate organization, that could exercise control over their independent actions. At the same time, there were no formal international laws that were agreed among them that might constrain behavior. Informal customs were few, and there were no enforcement-mechanisms to support the informal customs (see Wight 1977, 50). That the Greeks sometimes thought of themselves as one people with similar customs (for example, the Athenian statement in Herodotus 8.144), made little difference to the overall environment.[1]

The governments of Greek city-states were certainly reluctant to characterize their own behavior as lawless, or even to characterize it overtly as aggressive—though they often made such accusations against others (see Bederman 2001, 276–77). Thucydides does say that the Spartans c. 415 BCE considered their defeats in the first part of the Peloponnesian War the result of their having been the first to break the treaty of peace existing between themselves and Athens: that is, they had broken their oath to the gods to abide by the treaty (Thuc. 7.18.2). But the Spartan case is unusual, and the fact was that the Spartans had consulted Delphi in 432 before going to war and Apollo had given them the go-ahead (see Thuc 1.118.3 with Sommerstein and Bayless 2013, 254–55). Harsh actions could and did result in negative public opinion among the Greeks, and such public opinion was a factor tending toward restraint, as Peter Hunt (2010, 229–30) has noted. But in a world of complexity, and of aggressiveness in interstate interactions, with no recourse to international law available, justifications for one's own decisions were easy to find.

The governments of the Greek *poleis* did accept that, by custom, protection should be afforded to official envoys; that states that were neutral between two warring parties should not be attacked; that minimal protection should be afforded the civilian population of the enemy under certain specific circumstances; and that treaties sworn to the gods should not be violated. The existence of these informal norms, along with the general reluctance to appear simply lawless and aggressive, went some way to ameliorate the widespread conditions of interstate violence (Bederman 2001, 7 and 36; Kokaz 2001, 91–99). But in themselves these minor customary restraints did not constitute major limitations on state conduct (see Nörr 1991 28–41). Moreover, even these customs could not be counted on to be fulfilled. The governments of city-states violated them with impunity—the first in the above list occasionally, the other three often.

For instance, we know of more than 250 written treaties, formally sworn to the gods, between Greek polities in the period we are covering: treaties of peace; of mutual commercial guarantees; of alliance (Bengtson 1975). These treaties clearly represent a considerable effort to regulate interstate relations by means of diplomacy, and the ancients well understood the fact. Thus wrote the orator Isocrates, in 380 BCE:

> Those who created our great festivals are praised, and justly so, for handing down to us a custom that leads us to make treaties with one another, to reconcile the hostilities

---

[1] In what follows, much is based Eckstein 2006, Chapter 3, though it benefits from later thinking and reformulation, and work that has appeared since first publication.

that exist among us.... We are reminded of the original bond of kinship between us, and are more gently disposed toward one another for the future.[2]

Yet even with regard to treaties sanctified by oaths sworn to the gods in solemn public ceremonies and then inscribed on stone to indicate the permanent validity of such agreements, acts and accusations of bad faith among the city-states were common. A recent study of Demosthenes' views of interstate action emphasizes that in the 340s he could state in speeches at Athens, without fear of contradiction, that Greek polities were habitually warlike and faithless with one another (3 *Phil.* 21) and—further—that, "the international rights of Greek states were defined by the strong for the weak" (*On the Crown*, 15.28–29, with Hunt 2010, 159–61). The latter statement is very close to Thucydides' own remarks about international life in the Melian Dialogue (5.89): "In fact the strong exact as much as they can and the weak accept what they have to accept."[3] Similarly, the Corcyraeans in Thucydides could indicate at Athens that treaties among Greek states retained validity only as long as they were congruent with the actual facts of power (1.36.1–2). As both P. J. Rhodes (2008) and Peter Hunt (2010, 227) have emphasized, Greek treaties were complex interstate instruments, containing numerous clauses—some of which could be used to escape the obvious meaning of what one had engaged to do. So it was natural that there was a prevalent atmosphere of distrust (Leppin 1999; Bederman 2001, 179; Adcock and Mosley 1975, 222). As for neutrality, it was often honored in the breach: Robert Bauslaugh's study (1991, 253) concludes that Classical Greek states "all too often seized the first opportunity to assail non-belligerents."

The existence of a limited sense of obligation to refrain from certain types of interstate behavior did help somewhat to alleviate the harsh character of interactions among Greek polities. But this is not the same situation as the rule of international law (see Waltz 1979, 102–14). The latter requires both formally acknowledged rules of interstate conduct and—as Ernst Badian, one of the great modern students of antiquity, has emphasized (1983, 401–5)—guaranteed mechanisms of enforcement. Without a concrete penalty for violating them, international laws cannot be said to exist. Such was the situation in Classical Greece. No outside authority existed that could impose even these limited norms of behavior on the *poleis*. The religious (and sometimes political) pronouncements of the great oracular shrine of Apollo at Delphi had, to be sure, wide influence; but not even Delphi—which one would have thought sacrosanct—was immune from violence by Greek states (see Diod. 16.23–33, 355 BCE).

When informal norms of conduct—or even written agreements sworn to the gods (i.e., treaties)—were violated in the Greek world, it was therefore primarily up to the victimized state itself to punish the perpetrator or gain redress, when and if it could. Self-help was thus a defining feature of ancient interstate culture. Yet often redress was simply impossible. As Thucydides shows, strategic or geopolitical necessity might limit

---

[2] *Panegyricus* 43 (my translation)
[3] Translation of Thuc. 5.89, Chambers (2014, 37). The parallel in thought between Demosthenes and the Melian Dialogue here: Hunt (2010, 160n25).

the response of even a powerful state such as Athens merely to inscribing the fact of violation as an appendix to the publicly displayed text of a treaty (see Thuc. 5.56.3). This was why vengeance played such an important role in Greek interstate relations; it may seem primitive as a motive to us, but the threat of vengeance, or its actual accomplishment, was one way to regulate state behavior. For instance, during the Peloponnesian War, the Eleans, in charge of the great temple of Zeus at Olympia and of the Olympic Games, prevented Spartans from worshipping at the temple or participating in the Games. This was a violation of the rules of neutrality surrounding the Games. The Eleans got away with it—for a while; the Spartans had to wait twenty years before they were able to take revenge. But after they had defeated Athens, the Spartans trumped up an excuse in 399 BCE and invaded Elis, seizing a swath of Elean territory (Xenophon, *Hellenica* 3.21–23 with Lendon 2000, 1–2).

There were, of course, pragmatic benefits to appearing to be a government that took account of justice, one that was a reliable partner in interactions, and this consideration might lead governments to stick to their word.[4] But other than vengeance taken by a victim, the punishment for violations of norms of behavior or even violation of sworn treaties had to be left up to the gods. Again, it is clear that fear of the gods was sometimes a factor in restraining state behavior (Holladay and Goodman 1986; Bederman 2001, 49–73; Rhodes 2008, 11–12; Hunt 2010, 230–31.). But the problem here was that the gods and their actions were to a great extent inscrutable to humans—as Thucydides in a famous passage in the Melian Dialogue (5.104–5) makes clear. Meanwhile, the real-world situations faced by governments were often complex, and "the customs of the Hellenes" were subject to sharply differing interpretations by the Greeks themselves. The latter point is brought out strongly by Thucydides in his detailed depiction of the contradictory appeals to "the customs of the Hellenes" made by the Plataeans and the Thebans after the Thebans captured Plataea early in the Peloponnesian War and wanted to deal harshly with the survivors (3.56.1–3 vs. 3.67.6). Further, it was often possible to find ambiguities (or alleged ambiguities) in the text of an agreement that allowed one an exit if one wished. The same was true with war: justifications could always be found (see Wheeler 1984 on the sophistry sometimes involved). Conversely, even obvious violations of peace treaties might not lead to war if it was not in pragmatic interest of the victim to take vengeance for those violations; thus a treaty would remain in place (Rhodes 2008, 9–11). Even written and sworn treaties on formal public display we might want to think of merely as gestures in a certain direction—even if well-intentioned, subject to change if the circumstances were pressing enough.

The main point is that all such decisions were made by independent governments. As Thucydides has the statesman Hermocrates of Syracuse say to the assembled *poleis* of Sicily, the essence of freedom (*eleutheria*) is the ability of every polity to be the sole arbiter of its own destiny (*autokratōr*: 4.63.2). Pericles at Athens enunciates a similar principle, emphasizing the importance of freedom of action as essential for any *polis*—not to yield to another (2.61.1). And since freedom of decision and action was the essence of

---

[4] See Thuc. 3.54.3; 3.57.1–2; 8.48.1; 8.70.2; cf. 1.42 passim.

freedom, and the maintenance of this freedom was a central value of city-state culture, it is not surprising to find that no powerful ancient state, from the time we have information on them right down to the eventual hegemony of Rome in the second century BCE, ever felt constrained to act in the international arena except exactly as it saw fit (see the comments of Badian 1983, 401–5).

The prevailing anarchic situation meant that frictions and tensions among states were constant and quarrels over clashes of interest accumulated; they could build up into serious political conflicts; and those conflicts tended strongly (though of course there were exceptions) to be resolved through force—outright war. There was no international institutional mechanism to prevent it.

Mediation and/or arbitration of disputes via a neutral third party, chosen by agreement of the interlocutors, did occur on an ad hoc basis. Some sixty cases are known from the period 750–337 BCE. Mediation involved a spectrum of activity from merely providing a venue for talks all the way to suggesting explicit compromises to resolve issues in dispute. Arbitration meant turning the actual decision on an issue over to the representatives of a third party, usually a mutually friendly city-state; but in several cases the interlocutors chose the temple of Apollo at Delphi as arbitrator.[5] This certainly represents a significant Greek effort at the peaceful resolution of conflicts—and such behavior did help to alleviate the prevailing violence of interstate competition (Piccirilli 1973). Yet entry into arbitration or mediation was always voluntary, and the decision to do so arose from pragmatic considerations, not from submission to any general regime of international law or norms of behavior. The prevailing disorder and the total independence of states meant that it was not unusual even for arbitrations of disputes mandated by sworn peace treaties to fail because of the interlocutors' inability even to find a mutually acceptable arbitrator (Hornblower 1996). And sometimes a proposal from one side to engage in arbitration, far from being an attempt at a pacific solution to a conflict, constituted instead merely a propaganda challenge (see Adcock and Mosley 1975, 138). Thucydides offers a good example of the phenomenon in the Athenian refusal in winter 432–431 BCE to rescind the economic boycott of Megara at Spartan demand; the Athenians instead asserted publicly that the terms of the Thirty Years' Peace mandated arbitration of any quarrel, not unilateral concessions by one side (Thuc. 1.145). They were asserting their rights—and refusing to yield (cf. Pericles' maxim at Thuc. 2.61.1).

As for Greek "diplomacy" in general, outbreaks of war between the *poleis* were actually facilitated by its primitive character. At one level, the problem was that no Greek state ever sent a permanent ambassador to any other polity. In the modern world, such permanent ambassadors function as important channels of communication between governments, and thus have an ameliorating impact on international frictions: informing the home government of the concerns of the foreign state, or informing the foreign government of potential problems with the home government before decisions are

---

[5] In a famous case, the Delphic priests in turn suggested that the people of Cyrene choose a citizen of Mantinea to resolve their problems with the Libyans, and their internal disputes as well (Herodotus 4.161).

conclusively made that might exacerbate tensions. But in Classical Greece all diplomatic interactions were ad hoc, with envoys sent out only when there were specific issues. Thus not only were there no international institutions in existence to facilitate negotiation between aggrieved states, but Greek polities in addition had no permanent institutionalized relations with one another (on the negative impact, see Grant 1965, 262). Modern political scientists, when confronted with this fact of interstate life in ancient Greece, have expressed shock at the situation.[6] Given the sporadic nature of diplomatic interactions, it is also not surprising that the *poleis* failed to develop either a specialized corps of experienced diplomats, or (equally important) a specialized diplomatic language employed to soften realities. Instead, Greek diplomatic interactions tended to parallel in tone the blunt tones of bitter private altercations (Grant 1965, 262–263). In sum, the Greek polities existed in an interstate condition one might almost call "prediplomatic" (Aron 1973, 15).

The dangerous impact of the lack of permanent diplomatic missions in Classical Greece was already underlined in the mid-twentieth century (Grant 1965, 50). The low level of Greek diplomatic interaction affected the choices perceived by governments in order to achieve their interests, and even the definition of what those interests were.[7] The prevailing lack of solid information about the capabilities and intentions of other states also tended to work negatively toward increasing the anxiety of governments: this is what modern Realist international-relations theorists call "the uncertainty principle" (on which, see especially Jervis 1976). Indeed, the tendency toward myopia toward the outside world was an aspect of the Greek ideal of autarchy (total independence), including in the economic and military realms.[8]

One important consequence of the primitive level of Greek diplomacy was that when situations developed that did require the dispatch of envoys to another state, they came at a point where friction had already mounted to a dangerous level. Yet when relations with another *polis* were strained over clashes of interest, stern considerations of interstate status and prestige made compromises difficult (Lebow 1991, 144; Kauppi 1991, 119). The fact is that no Classical Greek government ever seriously considered sacrificing important interests merely to preserve the general peace. A state might, of course, sacrifice important interests when confronted by greatly superior power—but the issue then was self-preservation. And on the side of the powerful, diplomacy was not so much a peaceable alternative to war via compromise as an alternative means of pursuing one's agenda: that is, imposing one's will. Indeed, Greek crisis diplomacy very often took the form of what modern political scientists call "compellence diplomacy"—the making of demands. Aquiescence in such demands would avoid war; but the demands, once they

---

[6] See, Lebow (1991, 144–45); Kauppi (1991, 119). The same situation existed in fifth-century BCE China of the Warring States: see Zhang (2001, 48).

[7] On differing regimes of diplomatic process and their impact on the perceived choices available to the governments of states, see Keohane and Nye (1987, especially 745–59).

[8] "Myopia" and its destructive effect on interstate relations: Glaser (1992). The Greek ideal of autarchy: Purnell (1978).

were made, had to be met.⁹ Thus in Thucydides the Spartans in winter 432–431 BCE were willing to avoid war with Athens if the Athenians voted to revoke the economic sanctions the Athenians had imposed on the Spartans' ally Megara; but the Athenians had to make this unilateral concession. The Athenians refused (Thuc. 1.139–145).

Compellence diplomacy like this was customary. And such diplomacy is rarely, nor can it afford to be, a bluff—that is, not backed by a willingness to use force if demands are refused (Ferrar 1981; Stevenson 1997a). The Spartans were not bluffing in winter 432–431 BCE: after the Athenians refused to revoke the Megara decree, war began as soon as the weather permitted it. Greek states making demands on other states were usually ready to fight. Hence crisis diplomacy in Classical Greece was often merely another facet of an interstate system based on power and the prevalence of almost unrestrained competition (see Strauss 1991, 203).

Further, Greek crisis diplomacy was not only coercive, but publicly so (Grant 1965, 262; Lebow 1991, 144–45). When envoys were finally sent out to deal with a crisis that was now so enflamed that envoys were actually dispatched, they usually made their demands for redress of alleged grievances in public, in front of the other side's guiding council or even its people's assembly. Once such demands were so forcefully and publicly made, they were not easily moderated. Indeed, it was rare for envoys in a crisis to have power to modify state demands (Missiou-Ladi 1987). Yet such demands also could not be easily acceded to by the other side, for precisely the reason that, being both coercive and made in public, those demands initiated what modern political scientists term a "contest of resolve" between polities—a contest of resolve, again, played out in public.¹⁰ Thucydidean examples of diplomatic initiatives toward "peace" that soon degenerated into such contests of resolve include the Corcyrean demands at Epidamnus (Thuc. 1.26.3); the Corinthian demands at Athens regarding Corcyra (1.40.3); the Spartan general Brasidas' demands made on the city-state of Acanthus (4.87); and of course the diplomacy between Sparta and Athens in winter 432–431 BCE.

Modern political scientists hypothesize that such threats and/or displays of power, even if momentarily successful in winning concessions, are themselves destabilizing to peace—because they tend to create enduring resentments (Jervis et al. 1985). This was true in the Greek environment, because of the intense competition not only for power but for status. Commitment to independence, to autarchic freedom, to the public assertion of one's rights and hence one's high status, were all central values of *polis*-culture. Demands backed by threats might be seen by one side as an assertion of its right to public respect (in Greek, *timē*), but the other Greek side might easily see those demands—or *any* demands—as damaging to its own honor, worth, and right to respect. Governments might well prefer to risk war rather than risk losing status by giving in. Political compromise for the Greeks was in any case culturally difficult because in a slave-owning

---

⁹ On this type of diplomacy and its detrimental impact in a modern context, see Farrar (1981, especially 194–200).

¹⁰ International crises as "contests of resolve" even in the modern world: Quester (1988, 704–6); Mercer (1993, especially 166–67).

society, concessions to others might well be seen as indicating a "slavelike" mentality—as Pericles in Thucydides (1.141.1) explicitly warns the Athenians (see Rahe 1984; Strauss 1986). The particular cultural characteristics of the *polis* world—a world where Greek elites in public discourse traditionally ranked their cities against one another in *timē*, as if they were Homeric heroes—thus intensified the already powerful pressures deriving (modern political scientists as well as Thucydides would say) from the anarchical environment (see Crane 1998, 66; Lendon 2000, especially 21–22). It is this cultural atmosphere that leads Pericles in Thucydides to praise those men who "would rather perish in resistance than find life through submission" (2.42.2).

In such an atmosphere, making haughty public demands against the other side was likely to lead to rejection—and because no one was bluffing, rejection would mean war. The classic Thucydidean example is the lengthy peace negotiations between Sparta and Athens in winter 432–431 BCE. These diplomatic interactions were unusual in Greek practice, in that several embassies were sent successively by the Spartans to try to resolve the crisis, rather than only one. But every varying Spartan public demand for an Athenian concession brought forth an Athenian public counter-demand along the same lines as the Spartans had brought up: for instance, the Spartan demand that those allegedly under a curse (i.e., Pericles) be exiled because an ancestor had violated the sanctity of a temple (i.e., Megacles, the ancestor of Pericles) received a response pointing to the Spartan violation of a temple in the case of the execution of their general Pausanias. The response did not simply reject the Spartan demand but humiliated the Spartans in public by pointing out their own alleged bad behavior (Thuc. 1.125–135). This diplomatic back and forth went several rounds (see especially Wick 1977, 76–89); there was no one to bring it to resolution. As Pericles said, yielding would in itself be a repugnant act; the Spartans must learn to treat the Athenians as equals. Thus the "negotiations" of winter 432–431—a classic Greek contest of resolve conducted in public between two great states—failed. War began in spring 431.

THUCYDIDES' WORLD OF WAR

Greek writers were usually veterans of inter-*polis* war, and they wrote for an audience of veterans (Hanson 1989, especially 21, 45–46). These writers noted that war among the *poleis* was a prevalent condition, and peace a quite unusual condition; and it is from them that we know that the diplomatic discourse employed by *poleis* focused upon threats. Herodotus shows that not even Persian hegemony in Ionia could prevent the Greek cities there from raiding one another, until the King of Kings in exasperation established by force the arbitration of disputes (6.42). Thucydides of course is famous for the depiction of interstate chaos and violence (see below); Xenophon concludes his continuation of Thucydides in despair at the continual disorder of Greek interstate life (*Hell*. 7.5.27). Demosthenes agrees in underlining how much the Greek states were prone to mutual strife (3 *Phil*. 21). Such conditions explain the statement of the Theban general Epaminondas (Plut. *Mor.* 193E): his city could not hope to maintain its power if its citizens did not maintain their hold on their handgrips (i.e., the grips of their shields). Hence, too, the Spartan maxim that the borders of a polity were "as far as a spear can reach" (Plut. *Mor.* 210 C.).

Thus Jacqueline de Romilly (1968, 27) concludes that in the Greece of the city-states, "war is not only a normal function but a normal condition." Moses Finley's conclusion (1991, 67) is similar: for the Classical Greeks "war was a normal part of life."[11] Thucydides himself perceived that Greece had been riven by warfare from the earliest times up to his own present.[12]

The preeminent Realist theorist Kenneth Waltz would not have been surprised; his most famous dictum is that within an anarchic state system "the state among states conducts its affairs in the brooding shadow of violence.... Among states, the state of nature is a state of war"; within such a system, "war is normal."[13] Waltz's dictum has been confirmed by statistical studies of frequency of warfare in anarchic state systems done in the 1990s at the University of Wisconsin (Geller and Singer 1998).

Such an environment made it natural that *poleis* would develop highly militarized traditions; the anarchic nature of the environment in which they existed forced them in that direction. This was as true of Thucydides' Athens as it was of Sparta. Spartan society famously focused on the production of good soldiers and success in war, but Pericles' Funeral Oration in Thucydides 2.35–46 partakes of the same agonistic spirit; Athenians fought in the battle line in their fifties and sixties, and not only in emergencies (see Ridley 1979; Loraux 1986, 202–20). In almost every campaign Athenian hoplites conscripted "from the hoplite list" (*katalogos*) were joined by substantial numbers of volunteers—perhaps of somewhat lesser social status.[14] Although Greek history writers concentrated on hoplites, evidence suggests that military service during wartime went far down the social scale (van Wees 2001). In many states, laws made the possession of military equipment by citizens compulsory.[15] Cities contained shops for the rich where one could buy the best weapons and armor.[16] At Athens, male citizen orphans when they reached adulthood received, in public ceremony, the state gift of war equipment; it was the essence of citizenship (Raaflaub 2001, 307). Even Aristotle's ideal republic was constructed in part to deal with the threats and perils of war, including extensive military training (*Politics* 1329a, with Purnell 1978, 27).

Peter Krentz's study of known casualty statistics on hoplite battle shows that the victor suffered an average of 5 percent losses in the army in any one engagement,

---

[11] So, too, Grant (1965, 262); Woodhead (1970, 129); JACT (1984, 244); Hanson (1989, 219).

[12] Thuc. 1.2.2–3 and 6; 1.5.1 and 3; 1.7; 1.18. The Greeks, of course, were not alone among ancient states in waging constant war (see Hdt. 7.8); it was the nature of the anarchy.

[13] Waltz (1979, 102; 1988, 620–21 [the quotations]; 2000, 8).

[14] Volunteers: Thuc. 8.24.2; Ar. *Knights*, 1369ff; Lysias 9.4 and 15, and 14.6; Diod. 11.84.4, with Gabrielson (2002, 92 and 22n).

[15] Aen. Tact. 10.7; Hecataeus, FGrHist 264 F 25, with van Wees (2002).

[16] Ar. *Peace*, 1209–64; Xen. *Hell.* 3.4.17 (Ephesus); Lys. 12.19; Dem. 27.9 (Athens). The arms dealer Pasion at one point donated a thousand shields from his workshops to the Athenian State: Dem. 45.85.

and the average was 14 percent losses for the defeated. This reveals how heavily the burden of war lay upon Greek cities (1985). But losses even heavier do not appear to have deterred city-states from war. Thucydides records that in 424 BCE the entire field army of the small city of Thespiae in Boeotia was wiped out in battle —a devastating event (4.133.1); but it broke neither Thespian military spirit nor their long-term ability to wage war, for Xenophon records that thirty years later the Thespians played a valiant role at the battle of the Nemea (*Hell.* 4.2.20). Corinth suffered severe losses against Athens near Megara in 457 (Thuc. 1.106.2); yet the aggressive spirit of the Corinthians was not broken (as Thucydides records in discussing events ten years later: 1.114.1). Again, between 435 and 421 BCE the Corinthians fought annually on land and sea (first against Corcyra, then in the Peloponnesian War); yet despite substantial citizen losses even when victorious in battle, in 421 the Corinthians wanted to continue the fighting, and objected to the Spartans concluding the Peace of Nicias.[17] The Athenians fought on against the Peloponnesians for fully ten years after the horrendous losses they suffered in the Sicilian Expedition (413–403 BCE), and even after the Peloponnesians came to be aided by the Persian Empire; their steadfastness is a theme both in Thucydides and his continuator Xenophon. Indeed, scholars calculate that from 497 BCE down to 338 BCE—that is, during a century and a half—the Athenians went to war in at least two out of every three years, and possibly in three years out of every four (JACT 1984, 246).

The prevalence of war made the state system of the Greeks a world of great danger. Greek city-states (even Athens, the largest) were smaller and more fragile than modern states, and it is simply wrong to assert, as some scholars do (e.g., Adcock and Mosley 1975, 196), that the destruction of states was not usual in the wars of the *poleis*. In fact, we know from a wide range of sources that in the Classical period more than forty cities were destroyed.[18] The primitiveness of ancient technology made total destruction difficult, so it is not clear how complete was the "destruction" referred to so frequently in our sources. Certainly populations were made refugees, and large parts of cities were looted and burned by the victors. As Thucydides' Athenians say to the Melians in 416 B.C., interstate politics was primarily a matter of physical survival (5.101). In the Melian case, of course, the Athenians captured the city, executed all the adult males, and sold all survivors into slavery (Thuc. 5.116); the Athenians had done the same to the people of

---

[17] See Thuc. 5.17.2, 25.1 and 27.2, with Salmon (1984, 324–41).

[18] Examples from Herodotus: the destruction of Priene (1.161), Phocaea (1.163–65), Teos (1.168), Abdera (1.168.), Miletus (6.18–20), many Ionian cities as well as Chios, Lesbos, Tenedos, Chalcedon, and Byzantium (6.31–33); Eretria (6.100–2). From Thucydides: Eion (1.98.1), Scyros (1.98.2), Chaeronea (1.113.1), Hestiaea (1.114.3), Aegina (2.27), Sollium (2.30.1), Amphilochian Argos (2.68.7), Colophon (3.34.1–2), Mytilene (3.50), Plataea (3.68), Potidaea (3.70), Anactorium (4.49), Thyrea (4.57.3), Torone (5.3.4), Leontini (5.4.2)), Megara Hyblaea in Sicily (6.4.2), Zancle, first settlement (6.4.5), Zancle, second settlement (6.4.5), Camarina, first settlement (6.5.3), Camerina, second settlement (6.5.3), Orneae (6.7.2), Hyccara (6.62.3), Mycalessus (7.29–30) From Diodoros: Iasus (13,104.9), Orchomenus (15.79.5–6), Potidaea again (16.8.3–5). From Xenephon: Cedreiae (*Hell.* 2.15); Lampsacus (*Hell.* 2.18). From Pausanias: Plataea again (9.1.8). See Eckstein (2006, 53 and 72n).

Scione, five years previously (Thuc. 5.32). That was destruction indeed—and Thucydides was well aware of it.[19]

The consequences of defeat were not always so fatal. Classical Greek *poleis* rarely seized large areas of territory from defeated enemies; the point of victory was to establish general political domination. But the Athenians sometimes gave confiscated foreign land to their own citizens as private property; these were the Athenian cleruchies that came to exist within the territories of various dependent states (on their impact, see Cawkwell 1997, 102–3), and of course the Spartans had famously seized all of Messenia and its population for their own economic use. The destruction of one's city fortifications was more common for the defeated—and the lack of city walls entailed a sharp restraint on one's independence of decision and action.[20]

Thus for Greek governments in this period, external threats of the gravest sort were real, and occurred often. This is why Thucydides characterized interstate politics as a schooling in danger (1.18.3). Indeed, the term "danger" (Greek: *kindunos*) occurs more than 200 times in Thucydides' work, and appears dozens of times as the deepest concern of state decision-making (Grissom 2012).

Under the conditions imposed by a highly militarized international anarchy—in a world of *kindunos*—it was natural, too, that in Thucydides fear provided a powerful element in the decision-making of most states. There were, of course, other motives, as Thucydides himself has the Athenians say at Sparta in 432 BCE: self-interest (profit, power), the desire for international status (1.76.2). Pride in Athens is a very prominent part of the Funeral Oration Thucydides has Pericles give in honor of the dead of the first year of the war with the Spartans (2.35–46). But Thucydides also emphasizes that the phenomenon of fear existed from earliest times (1.2.2; 1.9.2; 1.9.3). Nothing had changed in his own time. Thus Thucydides attributed the Corcyrean appeal for an alliance with Athens in 433, a crucial step in the quarrels that escalated into the Peloponnesian War, to the Corcyreans' fear of being attacked by Sparta's ally Corinth with no one to help them (1.31.2). Indeed, Thucydides knows that the appeal of fearful polities to the protection of the strong had existed from time immemorial in Greek interstate history, and was a fundamental fact of politics (1.3.2, 1.9.2). But sometimes even the strong were worried. Thus the Mantineans, though allies of Sparta, became allies with Argos in 421 because they feared Sparta would not permit Mantinea to maintain the new power it had established for itself by successful war in Arcadia in the 420s (5.29.1). And Thucydides says that the main reason the Athenians agreed to the alliance with Corcyra was out of fear, too—fear that the naval resources of Corcyra would otherwise fall into the hands of the Peloponnesians (1.44.2). Conversely, many Greek city-states sided with Sparta at the beginning of the war out of fear of Athens (1.77.6: *deos*; cf. *phoboumenoi* at 2.8.5).

---

[19] The Athenians famously considered inflicting the same fate on Mytilene in 427 B.C., as Thucydides discusses in an equally famous and detailed discussion of the debate in the assembly: 3.36–50.

[20] Destruction of city walls: Potidaea (Thuc. 1.56.2); Thasos (Thuc. 1.101.3); Samos (Thuc. 1.117.3); Athens (Xen. *Hell*. 2.2.20 and 23); Elis (*Hell*. 3.2.30–31); Mantinea (*Hell*. 5.1.1–7); Chios and many Ionian cities, evidently by order of Athens: evidence in Meiggs (1972, 149–50). On the importance of city walls as the basis of city-state independence and power, see Ober (2001, 276–79).

Even when Thucydides' Athenians at Sparta acknowledge the motives of self-interest and increased status, they claimed that the primary reason that they had increased their power was out of fear (*deos*: 76.2). This is strongly reiterated in the speech Thucydides has the Athenian Euphemus give later to the Sicilians (6.82–87).

The brutality of that world as Thucydides saw it was of course underlined in his account of the debate between the Athenian generals and the city council of Melos in 416 BCE, when the Athenians attempt to get the Melians to surrender to the superior power of Athens. The Athenians' statements to the Melians on the nature of interstate politics in the late fifth century have become duly famous: questions of justice might occur in discussion between those governments that possess equal power, but otherwise, "the strong exact what they can, and the weak acquiesce in what they must" (5.89). The Athenians were merely following a general law of nature in expanding their power at the Melians' expense (5.105), and indeed the Melians would be doing the same to the Athenians if the Melians had the power of Athens and Athens was as weak as Melos (5.105).

For a certain kind of modern political scientist, such desires for expansion as the Athenians describe appear to be a natural response and indeed even a positive adaptation to a world of anarchy, where the relations between states were regulated merely by power and balances of power, and where the only security comes from strength (see the classic statement of Waltz 1979). Even in the case of Melos, Thucydides has the Athenians say that what motivates them in part is fear of appearing weak before the subject allies they already control were they to let the Melians stay free (5.95–97). There is no need to conclude that this is simply their propaganda. Thucydides in his own voice in fact posits as a general rule that under anarchic conditions every *polis*, fearing the consequences of the highly unstable situation, acts defensively to protect its interests (3.82.2–3)—yet such defensive actions can take the form of aggressive attempts to increase one's power and control over others (3.83.3–4).[21] Numerous other Thucydidean examples of the power of fear could be cited—and have been cited, both by political scientists who study the Thucydidean text, and by traditional Classical historians.[22] And it is instructive that the fears besetting governments are not merely a recurring theme in Thucydides' work, but are actually a more frequent theme as a motivation for state action than is the greedy desire for imperialist expansion (Kauppi 1991, 104).

In sum, as Michael Rostovtzeff concluded long ago, in regard to the most important interstate issues, "in the ancient world, the sole deciding force was might" (Rostovtzeff 1922). It was the basic fact of international life.[23] Some modern scholars argue that the very nature of the discourse that ancient intellectuals developed to describe interstate relations—and which modern Realists employ—contributed to, and even "constructed,"

---

[21] The passage is from Thucydides' famous discussion of internal *stasis* (civil war) on Corcyra, but Connor (1991, 60–65) points out that Thucydides evidently thought of war among the Greek states as a kind of *stasis*.

[22] See Romilly (1956); Kauppi (1991, 104–5); Boucher (1998, 72–74); Crane (1998, 99).

[23] Cf. also Larsen (1962, 233–34); Jehne (1994, 271).

the grim nature of those relations. This is a highly controversial idea (see Eckstein 2006, 29–33). But our topic is Thucydides, and Thucydides certainly saw things in that grim way.

THUCYDIDES 1.23.5–6: THE CAUSES OF THE PELOPONNESIAN WAR

In the absence of international law—either voluntarily accepted or imposed by some overarching power—and given the fragility of informal customs of behavior, interstate relations in fifth century BCE Greece fundamentally depended on balances of power between states. This is true in the modern world as well, and consequently much work has been done on this phenomenon.[24] In Thucydides we frequently find a state fearing that a shift in the balance of power will be to the immediate or eventual detriment of its security, and so it takes action (Kauppi 1991, 104 and n9). The most famous example of this is Thucydides' summary exposition of the decision of the Spartans in the coming of the Peloponnesian War (1.23.5–6). Yet to understand Thuc. 1.23.5–6 requires careful background examination, and careful translation, before its implications are completely clear.

In general, Thucydides often depicts Greek governments as worried that if their polity becomes militarily weak, or even appears to be weak, or becoming weak, this will invite aggression from others. It is an aspect of the heavily militarized anarchy in which all of them existed. Pericles fears this in his speech to the Athenians just before the Peloponnesian War (Thuc. 1.140.5; 1.143.5); the Athenians as a group fear this at 3.16.1; Spartan and Argive statesmen, at war with one another, both fear this at 5.41.2; Nicias fears this in his speech to the Athenians before the Sicilian Expedition (6.10.2, 10.4, 11.4); the Syracusans fear this when they appear to be losing to Athens (6.75.3); the Athenians fear this after the Sicilian defeat, when they appear to be losing to Sparta (8.1.2). And the fear is justified: the Spartans, Thucydides says, became despised by many of their allies for showing weakness in making the compromise Peace of Nicias in 421, and their allies began to desert them (5.28.2). After the Sicilian defeat had weakened Athens, states that had been neutral now prepared to attack (8.2.1; cf. 4.1.3 and 4.25.10).

Sometimes within such an anarchic and therefore war-prone system, however, there occurs a special moment: a truly major shift in the distribution of capabilities among states. This shift can take the form of a dramatic increase in the power of one of the major states—either in absolute or relative terms—or a dramatic decrease in the power of another (again, either in absolute or relative terms), or both developments simultaneously. Political scientists call this phenomenon a "power transition crisis." Moreover, when such a major shift in power occurs, the result is often (though not always) a

---

[24] See, e.g., Sheehan (1996); Vasquez and Elman (2003); Paul et al. (2004).

system-wide war that in turn creates a new configuration of status, privilege, influence, and territory in the system that is more congruent with the new configuration of power. Political scientists call the violence that establishes the new configuration a "hegemonic war." The decline of both Austria-Hungary and Turkey and the rise in power of Czarist Russia leading to World War I is a good example (Stevenson 1997b). Thucydides seems clear that it was a power transition crisis that was the fundamental cause of the outbreak of the Peloponnesian War, a conflict that in turn was a hegemonic war—a "world war" among the *poleis* to determine anew the distribution of influence, status, and privilege within the Greek state-system.

The conundrum for scholars in 1.23.5–6 has been, however, that Thucydides appears to be offering two contrasting or even contradictory reconstructions of the causes of the war simultaneously. In 1.23.5, he states that he is going to present the complaints and disputes (Greek: *tas aitias . . . kai tas diaphoras*), so that no one will ever have to ask why peace was broken among the Greeks and whence arose such a great war. This looks rather like a traditional Greek explanation of conflict as arising from a chain of complaint and counter-complaint, a view of causation one can see as early as Homer's *Iliad* (1.1–430), or the list of complaints and counter-complaints one finds in the first chapters of Book 1 of Herodotus as he explains the origins of the conflict between the Persian Empire and the Greeks (see Sealey 1975). Yet in the very next sentence Thucydides gives his opinion as to the "the truest cause" of the war (Greek: *hē alēthestatē prophasis*)—though, he says, it was not much talked about—and it seems to be not about the quarrels and complaints at all. Rather, he states that the Athenians, by growing great in power (*megalous gignomenous*), caused fear (*phobos*) in the Spartans and forced them toward war. That is, the Peloponnesian war was caused, fundamentally, by a large shift toward Athens in the interstate system of power (a fact about the text emphasized by Lebow 1991).

Major modern historians of antiquity as well as important political scientists have accused Thucydides of fomenting here a profound contradiction in explanation. They also assert that the long narrative of escalation into war that follows 1.23.5–6, that is, the rest of Book 1 of Thucydides' work (especially 1.26–67 and 1.118–146) seems much more to follow the thesis of 1.23.5 (emphasis on specific quarrels and complaints) than it does the "truest cause" thesis of 1.23.6 (emphasis on a structural shift in the balance of power). This view began in the nineteenth century (Meyer 1899, 314–15), and has been asserted continually for more than a century.[25]

The alleged contradictions of concept in Thuc 1.23.5–6 have appeared especially acute to modern political scientists, who naturally are interested in Thucydides in general and in this passage in particular as a precursor to their own theories of interstate action. But since most of them do not read Greek, they must depend on translations. The translations most widely used by political scientists are those of Rex Warner, and Richard Crawley (revised by T. E. Wick). But Warner has Thucydides saying first that the

---

[25] Cf., e.g., Andrewes (1959); Kagan (1969, 357–74); Fornara and Samons (1991, 141). From the perspective of a political scientist, Lebow (1991, 129–30).

quarrels and complaints clearly explain why the war came about, and then saying that these quarrels and complaints *disguise the real reason* for the war, which is the structural change in the balance of power and the fear it caused in Sparta; this structural change in turn made war *inevitable*. In Crawley-Wick, Thucydides appears to depict the quarrels and complaints merely as the *immediate cause of the war*, as opposed to the structural change that caused fear in Sparta, which *is the real cause* of the war, and that—again—made the war *inevitable*.[26]

No wonder that prominent political scientists, depending on these translations, have seen a blatant contradiction between 1.23.5 and 1.23.6.[27] The problem, however, is that none of the phraseology or concepts that I have italicized in the previous paragraph actually exist in Thucydides' Greek.[28] Thucydides does not call the complaints and quarrels wrongly understood causes, nor does he call them merely immediate causes. Thucydides describes the complains and quarrels as events the study of which will explain the war. But then he adds his opinion that the *truest cause* of the war (*hē alēthestatē prophasis*)—that is, not *the true cause* as opposed to false causes, but rather the truest cause among other true causes—was the Spartans' fear, arising from the Athenians' growth in power. This is difficult in English, but one can say it in Greek.[29] Thucydides adds that the Spartan fear consequent on the Athenians' growth in power forced the Spartans toward going to war (Greek: *anankasai eis to polemein*), but the concept of inevitability is not present. Thucydides is not quite as deterministic as that.[30]

Even Classicists, however, have employed the alleged fundamental contradiction between 1.23.5 and 1.23.6: for instance, as an important basis for the argument that Thucydides' work was constructed only in layers, over a long period of time, with Thucydides gradually changing his view on causation. Scholars usually posit Thucydides 1.23.5 as the earlier stratum here, employing a Homeric and Herodotean causal chain of complaint and counter-complaint to explain the origin of the war; Thucydides 1.23.6, which allegedly contradicts it, is the fruit of later (and, it is usually posited, deeper and more sophisticated) thought.[31] Other scholars have turned this hypothesis on its head, arguing that Thucydides later replaced 1.23.6, with its theory of state behavior based solely on changes in the balance of power, by 1.23.5, which (it is said) presents a

---

[26] Translations: Warner (1972, 49); Crawley and Wick (1982, 14); very similar (including *inevitable*): Lattimore (1998, 14–15 and n.)

[27] The Warner translation is used, e.g., by Lebow (1981, 1–3); Doyle (1991, 17); Van Evera (1999, 76 and 102); Copeland (2000, 210–11). The Crawley or Crawley-Wick translation is used by, e.g., Waltz (1979, 127 and 187); Gilpin (1981 1988, especially 596); Wayman (1996 with the Crawley-Wick translation of Thuc. 1.23.6. providing the epigraph for the article).

[28] On what follows, see Eckstein (2003). Because of publication in a journal outside of antiquity and more on the political-science side, this article has often been missed by Classical and Thucydides specialists. This says something about the disciplinary divides.

[29] See Gomme (1945, 154); Heubeck (1980); Heath (1986, 104–5). Missed, however, by Hornblower (1997, 64).

[30] On this, see rightly Gruen (1971). By contrast the political scientist F. W. Wayman (1996, 161) reproves Thucydides, on the basis of the Crawley-Wick translation, for being too deterministic.

[31] Such analysis began with Schwartz (1919); followed by (e.g.) Andrewes (1959); Sealey (1975).

more complex and human-oriented theory of causation (Ober 2001). In the first view, Thucydides progressed from an original and traditional view of causation focused on quarrels and disputes toward a focus instead on structural shifts akin to the Realist or Neorealist tradition in modern political science. But in the second view, Thucydides progressed from a theorist with an elegant but simplistic cause of the war into a true historian who accepted the human complexities involved in any interaction between governments.

The problem, however, is that the alleged contradictions between 1.23.5 and 1.23.6 have been greatly exaggerated all along. That is because every single one of the "complaints and quarrels" between the Athenians and the Spartan side that are referred to in 1.23.5 and discussed in detail in the rest of Thucydides Book 1 are in fact the direct consequences of the growth of Athenian power underlined in 1.23.6.

There were certainly frictions and disputes between Athens and Sparta in the middle and late 430s. But what is essential to note is that in Thucydides the growing pressure of Athenian power emphasized in 1.23.6 is pressure upon the various allies of Sparta, and these incidents with Sparta's allies constitute, precisely, the "complaints and quarrels" of 1.23.5. The complaints and quarrels are (a) the Athenian pressure on Sparta's most important ally Corinth over Corcyra, where the Athenians prevented the Corinthians from winning a war against their Corcyrean enemies, and instead took the island-state into a defensive alliance; (b) the Athenian pressure on Corinth over the Potidaeans, a loyal colony of Corinth but part of the Delian League of Athens, which (in view of the Corcyra conflict) the Athenians ordered to break close relations with Corinth and tear down their fortifications, leaving them vulnerable to Athenian attack; and (c) the Athenian pressure on Sparta's ally Megara, in the form of economic sanctions arising from a boundary dispute.[32] But as Thucydides perceived it, these Athenian pressures on Sparta's allies were, in turn, the consequence of a larger development—namely, the general shift in geopolitical power in the Greek world toward Athens. It was all one complex phenomenon.

It seems to me that Thucydides is clear about this. Two passages are crucial here for helping us to understand Thucydides' meaning at 1.23.5–6: these are his two further general comments, first in 1.88 and then in 1.118.2.

At 1.88 Thucydides again explains the causes of the war. The setting is the complaints at Sparta in summer 432 from Sparta's allies, especially Corinth, concerning Athenian aggression against them, and the resultant debate among the Spartans as to what response to make (1.67–87). At 1.88 Thucydides then sums up why the Spartans decided to declare the Thirty Years' Peace broken: they were persuaded not so much by the complaints of the allies (*ou tosouton* . . .) as by (*hoson*) fear that the power of the Athenians would grow greater. In 1.88, then, the primary cause of the Spartans' decision is their perception of a power-transition threat. But while the complaints of the allies are treated as less significant than the power-transition, these complaints are nevertheless given

---

[32] A clear and careful reconstruction of these escalating quarrels can be found in Kagan (1969, Chapters 13–16).

some weight: *ou tosouton . . . hoson* is a *comparative* evaluation (Westlake 1958, 102–5; Heath 1986, 104). And in any case, in the debate at Sparta the way Athenian power will grow greater is by depriving Sparta of her allies. This is explicit in the speech given the Corinthians: if the Spartans do not provide them aid and instead leave them unsupported (1.68.3; 1.69.1), Corinth will leave the Spartan alliance and find another alliance instead (1.71.4–7). Similarly, the ephor Sthenlaïdas, in successfully urging an immediate declaration of war, dovetails the two concerns found in Thuc. 1.23.5–6: the Athenian threat to Sparta's allies appears in every section of Sthenelaïdas' speech (1.86.1–5), which ends in a warning not to allow the Athenians to become too great in power (1.86.5).[33]

The comments in 1.88 are followed by a long digression (1.89–117) discussing geopolitical developments in Greece in the fifty years after the Persian invasion. Returning finally to his narrative of the events leading immediately to the war, Thucydides then states (1.118.2) that the Spartans, always slow to go to war unless forced into it, had long ignored the growth of Athenian power. But now things changed:

> But at last the power of the Athenians was clearly attaining a
> height, and the Athenians began to lay hands upon Sparta's
> alliance. Then the Spartans could bear it no longer, but
> felt it necessary to attack Athenian power and destroy it
> if they could.

Here we see what "the complaints and quarrels" specifically are, and their relationship to the changing balance of power: the Athenians' growing power was laying hands upon Sparta's alliance.[34] Indeed, all of Thuc. 1.24–67, on the "complaints and quarrels," is a discussion of Athenian pressure on Sparta's allies, especially Corinth—but including Megara and others.[35] Similarly, the description of the last months before the outbreak of the war is focused on Athenian pressure on Sparta's ally Megara (1.118–146), ending with the comment that "these were the complaints and quarrels" that led to the war (1.146.1: an echo of 1.23.5). But Thucydides consistently depicts the Athenians' pressure on Sparta's allies as the specific expression of the general growth of Athenian power; *both* motifs (the "complaints and quarrels," and the growth of Athenian power) are *intermixed* throughout Book 1.

Thucydides's analysis is therefore as follows. Both in 1.88, and then explicitly in 1.118.2, he indicates that the growth of Athenian power—the shift in the balance of power—is the destabilizing element in the interstate system; but this general trend also eventually takes a *specific* form—Athenian actions against Sparta's allies. These are the "complaints

---

[33] In the debate, the Spartans are at first suspicious that their allies' complaints might be motivated by self-interest detrimental to Sparta, and are a way to involve Sparta in an unnecessary war (1.68.2, explicit; cf. 1.88); but discussion of Athenian actions convince them that their allies are right (cf. 1.88); Eckstein (2003, 762 and 770n1).

[34] *hē dunamis Athēnaiōn saphōs ēreto kai tēs xummachias autōn hēptonto*. The translation above of 1.118.2 is mine.

[35] On the latter point see Thuc. 1.67.3–4 and 1.68.2.

and disputes." They led the Spartans, previously passive in the face of growing Athenian power (1.118.2), to feel compelled to risk war.

And this, of course, is also Thucydides' analysis in 1.23.5–6: Athenian pressure on Sparta's allies was a *specific* manifestation of the general growth of Athenian power. After explaining that he is going to lay out in detail "the complaints and disputes," so that everyone will understand "from whence the war arose" (1.23.5), Thucydides then gives his opinion as to "the truest cause" of the war (1.23.6). And this sentence on "the truest cause" begins with the Greek particle *gar* (*tēn men gar alēthestatēn prophasin* . . .) Now, the particle *gar* is not oppositve in meaning ("But . . ."). Rather, *gar* is *explanatory*: "For, indeed . . ." So for Thucydides the "truest cause" *explains* his previous comment about the "disputes and quarrels." And 1.118.2 shows us how: the Athenian actions against Sparta's allies were a manifestation of the shift in the balance of power in the Greek state system in favor of Athens. To Thucydides the quarrels and complaints and the power transition crisis do not appear to be alternatives; he combines them.[36]

One must finally note, however, that for Thucydides the outbreak of the war was *also*, and simultaneously, the result of contingent (if all too natural) decisions made by both the Athenians and the Spartans: there is no "inevitability" in the Greek of 1.23.5–6, because everything comes down to human decision-making. The Athenian assembly could have decided in spring 433 not to aid Corcyra against Corinth (in fact, it was a near-run thing); the Athenians could have decided not to put pressure on Potidaea after the conflict with Corinth over Corcyra, and the Potideaeans and the Corinthians could have decided not to respond by asking Sparta for help (winter 433–432); the complaints of the allies could have met with delay at Sparta, as the Spartan King Archidamus in fact advised (summer 432); the Athenians could have yielded to the Spartans and revoked the economic sanctions on Megara (winter 432–431). Decisive interventions in favor of war were made by individuals: Sthenelaïdas (Thuc. 1.86); Pericles (Thuc. 1.140–44). In that sense, Thucydides' analysis of the causes of the Peloponnesian War is truly complex and multilayered, and includes structural changes in the balance of power, specific complaints and quarrels among polities, and the intervention of important politicians. But complex and multilayered does not mean self-contradictory.

Conclusion

The statesmen who made the decisions—tragic decisions—that led to the outbreak of war between Athens and Sparta in the crisis of 432–431 BCE made those decisions under the pressure of a militarized and lawless international environment. Their decisions were contingent events, and any one of them could have gone the other way; but given the pressures of the anarchy, it was all too understandable that they went the way they did. The Greek culture of honor, and the Greek penchant for the primitiveness of

---

[36] Cf. Cawkwell (1997), *Thucydides and the Peloponnesian War*, pp. 21–23.

compellence diplomacy, aided the spiral of escalation. But one can see why, with all his emphasis on complexity, Thucydides remains the founder of international-systems theory. He invents the concept of the power-transition crisis. And in an environment without law, he points to balances of power as the only regulator of international affairs; hence he privileges the change in the balance of power that he sees with the growth of the power of Athens as a crucial causative variable. That power manifested itself in the mid-430s in consistent pressure on the allies of Sparta (Thucydides' "complaints and quarrels"), and rather than lose major elements in their alliance, the Spartans—in fear—chose to go to war.

Thucydides thus points above all to the lack of international law, the ferocious autarchy of the *poleis*, and the fragility of even basic customs of interstate behavior as the creators of an environment in which serious clashes of interest often led to wars. Statesmen made choices, and convinced their populations, but it would have taken an extraordinary individual to resist the pressures toward war created by the anarchic environment. Thucydides is clear as to how destructive the environment was, and how destructive those wars were. The striking thing is that he offers no solution, no way out of the militarized and anarchic interstate environment he describes. If anything, he predicts the situation will be with us always (*es aiei*: 5.105.2, from the Melian Dialogue). And this is precisely why he declares at 1.22.4 that his historical work will be "a possession for all time" (*ktēma es aiei*).

REFERENCES

Adcock, F. E., and D. J. Mosley. 1975. *Diplomacy in Ancient Greece*. New York: St. Martin's.

Andrewes, A. 1959 "Thucydides on the Causes of the War." *Classical Quarterly* n.s. 9: 223–39.

Aron, R. 1973. *Peace and War: A Theory of International Relations*. New York: Praeger.

Badian, E. 1983. "Hegemony and Independence: Prolegomena to a Study of the Relations of Rome and the Hellenistic States in the Second Century B.C." *Actes du VIIe Congrès de la F.E.I.C.*, 397–414. Budapest.

Bauslaugh, R. A. 1991. *The Concept of Neutrality in Ancient Greece*. Berkeley and Los Angeles: University of California Press.

Bederman, David J. 2001. *International Law in Antiquity*. Cambridge: Cambridge University Press.

Bengtson, H. 1975. *Die Staatsverträge des Altertums I: Die Verträge der griechisch-römischen Welt von 700 bis 338 v. Chr.* 2nd ed. Munich: C. H. Beck Verlag.

Boucher, D. 1998. *Political Theories of International Relations*. Oxford: Oxford University Press.

Cawkwell, G. L. 1997. *Thucydides and the Peloponnesian War*. London: Routledge.

Chambers, M. H. 2014. "The Melian Dialogue and Lorenzo Valla." In *Athenaion Episkopos: Studies in Honor of Harold B. Mattingly*, edited by A. P. Matthaiou and R. K. Pitt, 32–42. Athens: Greek Epigraphic Society.

Chaniotis, A., and P. Ducrey, eds. 2002. *Army and Power in the Ancient World*. Stuttgart: Franz Steiner Verlag.

Connor, W. R. 1991. "Polarity in Thucydides." In *Hegemonic Rivalry: From Thucydides to the Nuclear Age*, edited by R. N. Lebow and B. Strauss, 53–69. Boulder: Westview.

Copeland, D. 2000. *The Origins of Major War*. Ithaca: Cornell University Press.
Crane, G. 1998, *Thucydides and the Ancient Simplicity*. Berkeley and Los Angeles: University of California Press.
Crawley, R., trans., and Wick, T. E. 1982. *History of the Peloponnesian War*, by Thucydides. Rev. and with an introduction by T. E. Wick. New York: Modern Library.
Doyle, M. 1991. "Thucydides: A Realist?" In *Hegemonic Rivalry: From Thucydides to the Nuclear Age*, edited by R. N. Lebow and B. Strauss, 169–88. Boulder: Westview.
Eckstein, A. M. 2003. "Thucydides, the Outbreak of the Peloponnesian War, and the Foundation of International Systems Theory." *International History Review* 25: 757–74.
Eckstein, A. M. 2006. *Mediterranean Anarchy, Interstate War, and the Rise of Rome*. Berkeley and Los Angeles: University of California Press.
Farrar, L. L. 1981. *Arrogance and Anxiety: The Ambivalence of German Power, 1848–1914*. Iowa City: University of Iowa Press.
Finley, M. I. 1991. *Politics in the Ancient World*. Cambridge: Cambridge University Press.
Fornara, C. W., and L. J. SamonsII, eds. 1991. *Athens from Cleisthenes to Pericles* Berkeley and Los Angeles: University of California Press.
Gabrielsen, V. 2002. "The Impact of Armed Forces on Government and Politics in Archaic and Classical Greek *Poleis*." In *Army and Power in the Ancient World*, edited by A. Chaniotis and P. Ducrey, 83–98. Stuttgart: Franz Steiner Verlag.
Geller, D. S., and J. D. Singer. 1998. *Nations at War: A Scientific Study of International Conflict*. Cambridge: Cambridge University Press.
Gilpin, R. 1981. *War and Change in World Politics*. Cambridge: Cambridge University Press.
Gilpin, R. 1988. "The Theory of Hegemonic War." *Journ. of Interdisc. History* 18: 591–613.
Glaser, Charles L. 1992. "Political Consequences of Military Strategy: Expanding and Refining the Spiral and Deterrence Models. *World Politics* 44: 497–538.
Gomme, A. W. 1945. *A Historical Commentary on Thucydides, Vol. I*. Oxford: Oxford University Press.
Grant, J. R. 1965. "A Note on the Tone of Greek Diplomacy." *Classical Quarterly* n.s. 15: 261–66.
Grissom, Daryl Edward. 2012. *Thucydides' Dangerous World: Dual Forms of Danger in Classical Greek Interstate Relations*. Ph.D. diss., University of Maryland.
Gruen, E. 1971. "Thucydides, His Critics and Interpreters." *Journ. of Interdisc. History* 1: 327–37.
Hanson, V. D. 1989. *The Western Way of War: Infantry Battle in Classical Greece*. New York: Knopf.
Heath, M. 1986. "Thuc. 1.23.5–6." *Liverpool Classical Monthly* 11: 104–5.
Heubeck, A. 1980. "*Prophasis* und keine Ende: Zu Thuk. 1.23." *Glotta* 58: 222–36.
Holladay, A. J., and M. D. Goodman. 1986. "Religious Scruples in Ancient Warfare." *Classical Quarterly* 36: 151–71.
Hornblower, S. 1996. "Arbitration (Greek)." In *The Oxford Classical Dictionary*. 3rd ed. Oxford: Oxford University Press.
Hornblower, S. 1997. *A Commentary on Thucydides*. Vol. 1, *Books I–III*. Oxford: Clarendon.
Hunt, Peter. 2010. *War, Peace and Alliance in Demosthenes' Athens*. Cambridge: Cambridge University Press.
JACT (Joint Association of Classical Teachers). 1984. *The World of Athens*. Cambridge: Cambridge University Press.
Jehne, M. 1994. *Koine Eirene: Untersuchungen zu den Befreidungs-und Stabilisierungsbemühungen in der griechischen Poliswelt des 4. Jahrhunderts*. Stuttgart: Franz Steiner Verlag.

Jervis, R. 1976. *Perception and Misperception in International Politics.* Princeton: Princeton University Press.
Jervis, R., J. Stein, and R. N. Lebow. 1985. *Psychology and Deterrence.* Baltimore: Johns Hopkins University Press.
Kagan, D. 1969. *The Outbreak of the Peloponnesian War.* Ithaca: Cornell University Press.
Kauppi, M. V. 1991. "Contemporary International Systems Theory and the Peloponnesian War." In *Hegemonic Rivalry: From Thucydides to the Nuclear Age,* edited by R. N. Lebow and B. Strauss, 101–24. Boulder: Westview.
Keohane, R. O., and Joseph S. Nye, Jr. 1987. "Power and Interdependence Revisited." *International Organization* 41: 723–53.
Kokaz, N. 2001. "Between Anarchy and Tyranny: Excellence and the Pursuit of Power and Peace in Ancient Greece." *Rev. International Studies* 27: 91–118.
Krentz, P. 1985. "Casualties in Hoplite Battle." *Greek, Roman, and Byzantine Studies* 26: 13–20.
Larsen, J. A. O. 1962. "Freedom and Its Obstacles in Ancient Greece." *Classical Philology* 57 (4): 23034.
Lattimore, S., trans. 1998. *Thucydides: The Peloponnesian War.* Indianapolis: Hackett.
Lebow, R. N. 1981. *Between Peace and War: The Nature of International Crisis.* Baltimore: Johns Hopkins University Press.
Lebow, R. N. 1991. "Thucydides, Power Transition Theory, and the Causes of War." In *Hegemonic Rivalry: From Thucydides to the Nuclear Age,* edited by R. N. Lebow and Strauss, 125–65. Boulder: Westview.
Lebow, R. N., and B. Strauss. 1991. *Hegemonic Rivalry: From Thucydides to the Nuclear Age.* Boulder: Westview.
Lendon, J. E. 2000. "Homeric Vengeance and the Outbreak of Greek Wars." In *War and Violence in Ancient Greece,* edited by H. van Wees, 1–30. London: Duckworth.
Leppin, H. 1999. *Thukydides und die Verfassung der Polis.* Berlin: Akademie Verlag.
Loraux, N. 1986. *The Invention of Athens: The Funeral Oration in the Classical City.* Cambridge: Harvard University Press.
McCann, D. R., and B. S. Strauss. 2001. *War and Democracy: A Comparative Study of the Korean War and the Peloponnesian War.* London: Sharpe.
Meiggs, R. 1972. *The Athenian Empire.* Oxford: Oxford University Press.
Mercer, J. 1993. "Independence or Interdependence: Testing Resolve Reputation." In *Coping with Complexity in the International System,* edited by J. Snyder and R. Jervis, 55–71. Boulder: Westview.
Meyer, E. (1899) 2010. *Forschungen zur alten Geschichte II: Zur Geschichte des fünften Jahrhunderts.* Cambridge: Cambridge University Press.
Missiou-Ladi, A. 1987. "Coercive Diplomacy in Greek Interstate Relations." *Classical Quarterly* n.s. 37 (2): 336–45.
Mosley, D. J. 1973. *Envoys and Diplomacy in Ancient Greece.* Wiesbaden: Franz Steiner.
Nörr, D. 1991. *Die Fides im römischen Völkerrecht.* Heidelberg: C. F. Müller Verlag.
Ober, J. 2001. "Thucydides Theoretikos/Thucydides Historikos: Realist Theory and the Challenge of History." In *War and Democracy: A Comparative Study of the Korean War and the Peloponnesian War,* edited by D. R. McCann and B. S. Strauss, 273–306. London: Sharpe.
Paul, T. V., J. J. Wirtz, and M. Fortmann, eds. 2004. *Balance of Power: Theory and Practice in the 21st Century.* Stanford: Stanford University Press.
Piccirilli, L. 1973. *Gli arbitrati interstatali greci. Vol I: Dalle origini al 3338 a.C.* Pisa: Edizioni Marlin.

Purnell, R. 1978. "Theoretical Approaches to International Relations: The Contribution of the Greco-Roman World." In *Approaches and Theory in International Politics*, edited by T. Taylor, 19–31. London: Longman.

Quester, G. 1988. "Crisis and the Unexpected." *Journ. Interdisc. Hist.* 18: 701–19.

Raaflaub, K. 2001. "Father of All, Destroyer of All: War in Late Fifth Century Athenian Discourse and Ideology." In *War and Democracy: A Comparative Study of the Korean War and the Peloponnesian War*, edited by D. R. McCann and B. S. Strauss, 307–56. London: Sharpe.

Rahe, P. 1984. "The Primacy of Politics in Classical Greece." *AHR* 89: 265–93.

Rhodes, P. J. 2008. "Making and Breaking Treaties in the Greek World." In *War and Peace in Ancient and Medieval History*, edited by P. de Souza and J. France, 6–27. Cambridge: Cambridge University Press.

Ridley, R. T. 1979. "The Hoplite as Citizen: Athenian Military Institutions in Their Social Context." *Ant. Class.* 48: 508–48.

Romilly, J. de 1956. "La crainte dans l'oeuvre de Thucydide." *Classica et Medievalia* 17: 119–27.

Romilly, J. de. 1968. "Guerre et paix entre cites." In *Problèmes de la guerre en Grèce ancienne*, edited by J.-P. Vernant, 207–20. Paris: Mouton.

Rostovtzeff, M. (1922) 2009. "International Relations in the Ancient World." In *The History and Nature of International Relations*, edited by E. Walsh. London: BiblioBazaar.

Salmon, J. B. 1984. *Wealthy Corinth: A History of the City to 338 b.c.* Oxford: Oxford University Press.

Schwartz, E. 1919. *Das Geschichtswerk des Thukydides*. Bonn: F. Cohen.

Sealey, R. 1975. "The Causes of the Peloponnesian War." *Classical Philology* 70: 89–109.

Sheehan, Michael. 1996. *The Balance of Power: History and Theory*. New York: Taylor and Francis.

Sommerstein, A. H., and A. Bayless. 2013. *Oath and State in Ancient Greece*. Berlin: De Gruyter.

Stevenson, D. 1997a. "Militarization and Diplomacy in Europe before 1914." *International Security* 22: 125–61.

Stevenson, D. 1997b. *Outbreak of the First World War: 1914 in Perspective*. London: Palgrave-MacMillan.

Strauss, Barry S. 1986. *Athens after the Peloponnesian War: Class, Faction and Policy, 403–396 B.C.* Ithaca: Cornell University Press.

Strauss, Barry S. 1991. "Of Bandwagons and Ancient Greeks." In *Hegemonic Rivalry: From Thucydides to the Nuclear Age*, edited by R. N. Lebow and B. Strauss, 189–210. Boulder: Westview.

Van Evera, S. 1999. *Causes of War: Power and the Roots of Conflict*. Ithaca: Cornell University Press.

van Wees, H. 2001. "The Myth of the Middle Class Army." In *War as a Cultural and Social Force*, edited by T. Bekker-Nielsen and L. Hannestad, 45–71. Copenhagen: Det Kongelige Danske Videnskabernes Selskab.

van Wees, H. 2002. "Tyrants, Oligarchs, and Citizen Militias" In *Army and Power in the Ancient World*, edited by A. Chaniotis and P. Ducrey, 61–82. Stuttgart: Franz Steiner Verlag.

Vasquez, J. A., and Elman, C., eds. 2003. *Realism and the Balancing of Power: The New Debate*. Upper Saddle River: Prentice-Hall.

Waltz, K. 1979. *Theory of Internattonal Politics*. New York: McGraw-Hill.

Waltz, K. 1988. "The Origins of War in Neo-Realist Theory." *Journ. Interdisc. History* 18: 615–28.

Waltz, K. 2000. "Structural Realism after the Cold War." *International Security* 25: 5–41.

Warner, R., trans. 1972. *History of the Peloponnesian War*, by Thucydides. Rev. trans. London: Penguin.
Wayman, F. W. 1996. "Power Shifts and the Onset of War." In *Parity and War*, edited by J. Kugler and D. Lemke, 145–62. Ann Arbor: University of Michigan Press.
Westlake, H. D. 1958. "Thucydides 2.65.11." *Classical Quarterly* n.s. 8: 102–110.
Wheeler, E. L. 1984. "Sophistic Interpretations and Greek Treaties." *Greek, Roman, and Byzantine Studies* 25: 253–74.
Wick, T. E. 1977. "Thucydides and the Megara Decree." *Ant. Class.* 46: 74–99.
Wight, M. 1977. *Systems of States*. Leicester, UK: Leicester University Press.
Woodhead, A. G. 1970. *Thucydides on the Nature of Power*. Cambridge, MA: Harvard University Press.
Zhang, Y. 2001. "System, Empire and State in Chinese International Relations." *Rev. International Studies* 27: 43–63.

CHAPTER 30

XENOPHON AS A SOCRATIC READER OF THUCYDIDES*

PAUL LUDWIG

REALISM is not simply Thucydides' own position; it is a problem he investigates by depicting the successes and failures of realist theories in the speeches and deeds of his protagonists. Realism, his experiments show, occasionally hinders or even destroys itself: for example in the failure of the Athenian envoys to enlighten their counterparts in the Melian dialogue and in Alcibiades' failure to retain popular support from Athenians who find his unconcealed pursuit of self interest threatening. Realist doctrines, such as that the strong do what they can while the weak yield, are not always effective. Despite its name, realism apparently is not fully realistic; it misses something about political reality. This is not to say that traditional morality and piety do not also lead to manifest blunders: the Melians are shown to be utterly deceived in their belief that the gods will come to the aid of righteous men; Nicias' pious interpretation of the eclipse causes the fatal delay that leads to the loss of the Sicilian expedition. Is there a way to have the useful insights of realism while avoiding its blindnesses?

When we turn to Xenophon's *Hellenica*, the picture seems entirely changed. Piety and morality inform the interpretation of events: the gods punish Sparta for the unrighteous act of occupying the Theban acropolis in peacetime (5.4.1). If we sometimes find Xenophon naive (because "politics is not about morality"), that may reflect deeply conditioned tastes on our part rather than an account we have thought through. According to various forms of realism, justice does not exist in international relations where there is no central authority to enforce it, but only domestically where governments punish infractions. Such accounts neglect how radical and deep a problem Thucydides had uncovered. Justice as a whole was called into question: the theoretical critique of justice, which modern realists confine to international politics, in Thucydides contaminates citizen morality and interpersonal ethics (for example, in the speeches and deeds of

---

* I would like to thank Gerald Mara for comments on a draft.

Alcibiades). We lack consistency if we banish morality from international politics while continuing to expect individual citizens to behave altruistically toward one another and self-sacrificially toward their cities. Furthermore, an overemphasis on punishment and external authority seems to slight the contribution of moral character and the internal constraints that individuals place on themselves. Realist arguments accordingly discount the kind of solution Xenophon offers to the problem of justice. In the end, we are brought back to the insight of the *Republic* Book 1 that even a gang of thieves cannot work together without observing some justice toward one another. The roving band of 10,000 mercenaries, or city-on-the-move, in Xenophon's *Anabasis* illustrates in many respects this problem of justice among thieves. Equally clearly, however, a justice motivated by narrow self-interest loses the nobility that contributes to its attractiveness. The *Hellenica* can be seen to respond to the realism depicted in Thucydides by continuing Thucydidean-style investigations into morality and piety, though now in ways less destructive of them. The traditional morality and piety in part associated, in the popular imagination, with Sparta represented an option that was still viable despite its hypocrisy. Such concern for morality can explain some of Xenophon's characteristic evasions and silences that we deprecate today.

As a Socratic, Xenophon may have had further reasons to wish to reset the relation between theory and practice. For example, the incomplete or abortive realism of the Athenian envoys to Melos was not merely a practical failure; their philosophical view of the world must be incomplete if it failed to account for the way the theories would play out in practice. Such Athenians' theories liberated them from traditional constraints but nevertheless did not make their practices fully rational; in addition, the practical outcomes gave a bad name to the theories and to theorizing. In very preliminary ways, the following examines several Socratic themes in the *Hellenica* and, to a lesser extent, in the *Anabasis*: the turn to the human things, *eirōneia* and the defense of Socrates' way, rational piety, and moral agency in the face of natural necessity. In each case Xenophon's differing approaches shed light on Thucydides.

Xenophon's "Continuation" of Thucydides and the Socratic Turn

"After that," begins the *Hellenica*, in the approximate place where Thucydides' narrative breaks off, but with major players in slightly different places from where Thucydides left them, as though there had been a gap. The inexactness could be aristocratic disdain for precision (like the "gentleman's third"). Or the obvious way in which Xenophon made the beginning both a continuation and inexact could be a signal that this continuation will differ from its predecessor. In particular, the opening actions are vague and disordered. We should perhaps compare the closing lines of the *Hellenica*, in which nothing has been settled: "there was even more confusion and disturbance after the battle [of

Mantinea] than before it in Greece." Mere chronology—"after that"—would be appropriate if Xenophon believes history contains no ordering principles of its own.[1] "After that" is neutral about causation, thus differing from "consequently." Political history is one damned thing after another—a stance that may fit the unphilosophic *persona* of the Spartan sympathizer but may also befit a Socratic philosopher. The pre-Socratic principles of motion, rest, and necessity gave order to Thucydides' history. Nature supported certain overarching human tendencies such as the aggregation of power and wealth, which led to greater and greater motions—in fact, to the greatest motion (Thucydides 1.8.3–4, 1.1.2, 3.82.1; cf. 1.69.4, 70.8–9). By contrast, Socrates turned away from natural philosophy to the human things, inquiring after virtue on its own. Brute nature does not teach us sufficiently about ourselves. If, as a pupil of Socrates, Xenophon believed that the human things constitute a realm apart, and that their ordering cannot be deduced by starting from elemental principles, then his narrative might lack this ordering device of nature—as well as the drama attendant on it. On such a view, no single war, however great, could provide us with universal truths, as Thucydides had implied (Dobski 2009, 319). Furthermore, if Xenophon agreed with Socrates that the life of contemplative leisure was more satisfying than the life of political and military activity, the disorder and uncertainty at the beginning and end of the *Hellenica*—and many places in the middle— might provide grounds for that decision. Precisely because political activity is formless and void, participation in it is not the highest aim of man.

History is disordered until strong minds and personalities like Alcibiades, who is imprisoned and escapes, bring some light and order to the chaos.[2] In short order, the map of the Hellespont changes color from Spartan red states to Athenian blue, as the energy and strategy of Alcibiades create success after success. In these early pages, Xenophon keeps up the Thucydidean practice of marking the end of each year, though without any claim of authorship such as "so ended the *n*th year of the war which Thucydides composed." Rather than a whole with a beginning, middle, and end, as Thucydides' (5.26.1) narrative seemed to be, at least in conception, if not in execution, Xenophon's narrative is a succession. Mere succession without order would be in keeping with the very last line, the closest Xenophon comes to Thucydides' repeated claim of authorship: "Up to this point, let it be written by me. Perhaps another will be concerned with what happened *after that*"—echoing the opening words.[3] Tuplin (1993) and others have shown how a morality of anti-imperialism provides an order to the events;[4] but certainly many events recorded escape that order or otherwise evince a messiness in political affairs.

---

[1] Compare Marincola (1999, 311), criticized by Rood (2004, 349–50). Thucydides' own ordering, by summers and winters, also looks initially like mere chronology.

[2] 1.1.6–7, 9–10; Strauss (1968, 664). Rood (2004, 366) points out the historic present tense upon Alcibiades' arrival at 1.1.5.

[3] 7.5.27, emphasis added. All translations from Greek are mine; I have benefited especially from the translation of Ambler (2008), also Brownson (2001), Brownson (2004), Marincola in Strassler (2009), Crawley in Strassler (1996), Smith (1992).

[4] Gray (1989, e.g., 6–7) draws out Xenophon's moralizing and didacticism without distinguishing sharply between Socratic philosophy and conventional morality.

To what degree is Xenophon in control of his subject matter, and do purposes other than morality emerge when a Socratic considers political events?

Understatement and Evasion in Xenophon

Most readers admit that the *Hellenica* must be read between the lines. The question is to what extent we may read in meanings that go beyond the literal (contrast Gray 2011 with Johnson 2012). An example is Xenophon's eulogy of the Athenian cavalry in the early action at Mantinea (7.5.15–17). Among the slain, we know from other sources, was Xenophon's own son Gryllus, who received significant posthumous honors from the Athenians, including being depicted in a public mural (e.g., Dillery 1995, 253–54). Not a word about Xenophon's own pride and loss intrudes upon the narrative. He simply says, "Among them, brave men died." About Gryllus, readers are just supposed to know—and thereby to appreciate Xenophon's tact and reticence. A candidate for further subtlety and, indeed, dramatic flourish, occurs one sentence earlier, in one of the motives attributed to the Athenian cavalry; Xenophon explains why they risked opposing the famous horsemen of the Thessalians and the Thebans in order to save the property and families of the Mantineans left outside the walls. "As soon as they saw the enemy, they charged them, because they felt eros to rescue their ancestral reputation" (*patrōian doxan*). This last phrase could be more literally translated "their paternal reputation" or even "their father's reputation." That is, the phrase could more literally—and poignantly—describe the motivations of Xenophon's two sons, who fought in the battle on Athens' side than it does the Athenian cavalry's as a whole.[5] Xenophon the mercenary had fought for the younger Cyrus, who opposed Athens and sided with Sparta. Xenophon had moreover accompanied his patron Agesilaus to the battle of Coronea, in which Athens was on the opposing side, and he lived for many years under Spartan patronage at Scillus. He was at best a very ambiguous Athenian (e.g., *Anabasis* 3.1.4). But his sons rescued their father's reputation. Perhaps we illicitly infer a paternal artistic touch here, basing it on weak evidence of the etymological association of *patrōia*. But can we put this literary touch past an artist who reveled in his own reticence about Gryllus?

David Thomas reconstructs the flavor of the delight readers who were in the know, insiders, must have felt at reading certain other of his silences and evasions: " 'With what ingenuity ... does old Xenophon avoid specifying Epaminondas' appalling actions in Messenia, and how fitting that the unspeakable should remain unspoken!' "[6]

---

[5] I am indebted to Eric Buzzetti for this point.

[6] Thomas (2009, lxv). Compare Cartledge's (2009, 407) short biography of Lysander: *ex silentio*, Xenophon's failure to mention that Lysander accepted divine honors in his own lifetime "should be taken to signal severe disapproval." A related disapproval of Agesilaus' sacrifice at Aulis, as though he were a new Agamemnon, may have resulted in Xenophon's leaving out that episode (reported in all its abortive

The "old" conjures up an old boys' network: such readers see in Xenophon a great deal of wiliness, slipperiness, and "spin"—prejudice, in sum—a prejudice we now believe we can see through. There is a tendency to think he is only outsmarting himself. Leo Strauss's chosen interlocutor, W. P. Henry, remarks that "the naiveté is contrived." Xenophon wrote the parts of the *Hellenica* about Agesilaus "for those young boys he seems always to have been carrying about with him in his head."[7] We can certainly agree that the *Anabasis*, at least, is initially pitched to the highmindedness of youth. If boy scouts seem also to be the audience of the *Hellenica*, that may say something about us as an audience. It is axiomatic for modern realists, who often trace their lineage to Thucydides, that virtue is not rewarded and vice is not punished (contrast, again, *Hellenica* 5.4.1). For example, the bad end to which the traitor Meno comes in the *Anabasis* is today usually suspected of being a moralism added or created by Xenophon (2.6.21–29). It is simply too coincidental that Meno got what he deserved; the only question is whether Xenophon really believed it himself or was only preaching to his boys. But one can imagine a contemporary audience of adults in whose opinion people do, for the most part, get what they deserve. Xenophon does not assume everyone in his readership is cynical, to put it in a modern way. He may be further concerned not to render them so—certainly not if undercutting their morality would also remove an avenue to the characteristically humanizing realizations of Socratic philosophy (which starts its ascent from the moral opinions commonly held). One thinks of Nicias in the pages of Thucydides: Nicias is a responsible politician and general, "a bit too prone to divination and such" in Thucydides' humorous assessment, who gives various evidences of believing that virtue and law-abiding behavior have cosmic support (e.g., 7.50.4, 77.2–3, 86.5). If the *Hellenica*'s chosen audience were Niciases, well meaning toward Athens as well as toward Sparta but also, like all human beings, self-interested,[8] it would explain why its messages sometimes go astray with modern audiences, for whom a certain realism has become second nature. The question modern audiences rarely ask is whether we continue to harbor Nician assumptions and prejudices, merely on a deeper level or in a way that we disguise from ourselves. As subsequent sections will argue, the persistence of piety or at least moralism among Thucydides' more sophisticated Athenian speakers suggests that "realist" enlightenment is difficult to achieve. At the same time, the *Hellenica* gives many glimpses beneath a certain veneer, though a hidebound or oligarchic, prejudiced and pro-Spartan Xenophon is unlikely to have been what he hid inside. Why a veneer at all?

---

disappointment and anger at *Hellenica* 3.4.4) from his encomium, the *Agesilaus*. See the argument of Proietti (1987, 96–101). Had eulogy exhausted Xenophon's purposes, he might have left the episode out of both works.

[7] Henry (1967, 156–8), quoted in Strauss (1968, 660); cf. Henry (1967, 191). Tuplin (1993, 132) sees "pleasantly understated irony" where readers not "sympathetic to the author" "see only the signs of weakminded *naiveté*." The irony is "almost painfully explicit" for Gray (2011, 335); cf. Johnson (2012, 123).

[8] On 7.48.3–4, see especially Palmer (1982, 120n6): because of his fear for his reputation, Nicias puts Athens at risk. He would rather die in Sicily (that is to say, taking the army down with him) than return home to face charges.

Xenophon may have wished to meet his readers where they were.[9] As a Socratic, Xenophon was familiar with Socratic irony. Disclaiming or minimizing qualities held in high repute is *eirōneia* or irony in a nearly contemporary definition (*Nicomachean Ethics* 4.7, 1127a22–24, b23–26). The *Education of Cyrus* (3.1.14, 38–40) implies that the Athenian fathers put Socrates to death because they envied his influence over their sons (cf. *Memorabilia* 1.2.49). Such envy alone would give Socrates a motive to talk all the time about packasses and leathercutters, as Alcibiades says in Plato's *Symposium* (221d–222a), whereas one must flay the satyr or get inside the speeches to see the images of virtue within. In the *Memorabilia* and other Socratic writings, only Socrates' (failed) student Alcibiades is shown elenchizing someone important, Pericles, in the overt and therefore exciting way that the real Socrates must have been capable of (1.2.39–47). Xenophon's Socrates himself is careful to maintain a surface conventionality or even humdrum character to his speeches, punctuated occasionally by such shocking daring that we tend to think he cannot have meant that (Ludwig 2010, 91–94). In reading any Socratic dialogue, we are sometimes aware that Socrates' interlocutors see through his dissembling. We as readers see through it often or nearly continuously, but his interlocutors see through it intermittently. What if, in reading the *Hellenica*, we are in the position of those Socratic interlocutors whose sophistication enables them to see through the irony only intermittently? A distorted view of what is going on could easily emerge. Xenophon, like Plato, indicates shortcomings of direct-vote democracy and gives serious consideration to regimes with limited franchise.[10] But willingness to think outside the democratic box reinforces the fact that Xenophon is a Socratic, not a Spartan sympathizer in a merely political sense. Sparta remains in one sense a starting point for political philosophy because citizen education was taken so seriously there. But an improved or adequate "Sparta" would somehow have to concentrate on other virtues in addition to what Aristotle called "warlike virtue."[11] When Xenophon the character bows to Spartan pressure at the end of the *Anabasis* he makes at least one of his reasons clear to his fellow mercenaries: it is impractical to oppose the rulers of land and sea (6.6.9, 13–14; 7.1.30).

Some of the evasions of which Xenophon stands accused, such as his minimizing of the achievements of Lysander, can be seen as instances of pointed understatement. A very detailed case has been made that Xenophon viewed Lysander as a Spartan counterpart to the Athenian problem of Alcibiades in Thucydides (Proietti 1987). Briefly,

---

[9] Aristophanes' *Birds* 1277–85 suggests a popular identification of Laconizers with Socratics; perhaps similarities even made the identification inevitable. Cf. Demosthenes 54.34.

[10] For arguments that Xenophon regarded democracy as the least bad of extant regimes, see Gish (2012) and Gish (2009). Thucydides preferred a moderate oligarchy to democracy (8.97.2), but he somehow incurs less blame for being on the wrong side of history in this regard; on the regime of the Five Thousand, see especially Orwin (1994, 189–92), also Dobski (2009, 326–27). Any adequate thinking about Thucydides in the present chapter stems directly or indirectly from Clifford Orwin's teaching and example; the mistakes are mine.

[11] *Politics* 2, 1271a41–b7 on *Laws*, e.g., 625c–38b; see the *Education of Cyrus* 1.2.6–7 for a reimagined Sparta that focuses her education on justice (cf. 1.6.27–34). Compare *Republic* 547d–548c with *Constitution of the Lacedaemonians* 14—such "disappointments" come near the end of many of Xenophon's works; on their pedagogical effect, see Buzzetti (2014, 294).

the burdens of imperialism necessitated regime change for both Athens and Sparta if they wished to expand their empire, in Athens' case, or to assume the helm of a maritime empire, in Sparta's. The private interests, detached from public interests, which Thucydides says contributed to Athens' ruin in the post-Periclean period (2.65.7, 11; 6.15.2–3) could have been brought back into harmony with the public interest by allowing Alcibiades, the most competent general (6.15.4), to rule autocratically. But neither democrats nor oligarchs at Athens could brook such a tyrannical prospect, or not for long (cf. 8.68.4). Thucydides, too, makes the reader work to reconstruct (from a narrative that often seems mere chronology) those patterns to which his selections direct attention; nothing but the reader's own curiosity necessitates that he connect the dots between, for example, Alcibiades' admission to the Athenians of his overweening ambitions and his astounding claim at Sparta that a true patriot must sometimes attack his city (6.16–18, 6.92.4). The *Hellenica* makes the reader work even harder to connect the dots, directing attention to a different but analogous case about the jealousies surrounding Lysander, founder of Sparta's short-lived empire. If Sparta was to flourish in an imperial role, her ancient constitution of dual kingship, limited by heredity rather than open to merit, was an ineffectual instrument. The extraordinary command given to Lysander at 2.1.6–7, shows that Sparta had a dim presentiment of this. But only Lysander fully understands the need, and his imperial policies betray a Spartan version of the primacy of personal self-interest that hurt Athens.[12] Hence neither Alcibiades nor Lysander provided a viable role model, so to speak. These characters represented theoretical problems rather than practical alternatives. On this reading, the "higher criticism" of accounting for Xenophon's biases, such as his dislike of Lysander and his lionizing of Agesilaus, blinds us to more interesting things going on in his text.

THE PERSISTENCE OF PIETY

Despite our modern distaste for it ("religion should be a matter of private conscience"), the importance of piety can hardly be overstated in a war in which one side crippled itself by undertaking a new war of choice—the conquest of a new empire in Sicily—and by getting cold feet at the last minute, accusing and later recalling the instigator of the expedition, Alcibiades, for *asebeia* (Thucydides 6.53). Analogously, Sparta had

---

[12] Proietti (1987, 42) on 2.3.8–9; cf. *Constitution of the Lacedaemonians* 7, 14.2–3 with Plutarch, *Lysander* 17. For ways in which Agesilaus' personal rivalry with Lysander undermined Agesilaus' own prospects and Sparta's, compare *Hellenica* 3.4.9–10 with 3.4.27, 29; one outcome is given at 4.3.10–12, where Agesilaus' nepotistic appointee, his brother-in-law, becomes a new Callicratidas, unable to turn away from a disadvantageous fight (1.6.32). Compare also 4.1.26–28 with 4.2.8; Proietti (1987, 103–5). Cf. Millender (2012, 417–22), Tuplin (1993, 164–5). Thucydides comments late in his last book (8.86.4–5) that only then did Alcibiades first benefit Athens; both realists and moralists must ask why or with what end in view do individuals benefit their polities. For Alcibiades' introduction of realism into domestic politics, see Orwin (1994, 123–26, 194–95) on 6.16–18, especially 6.16.4.

always considered herself in the wrong during the earlier part of the war (7.18.2). She worried that she had broken the treaties. Once she came to consider Athens the guilty party, the treaty breaker, Sparta was able to fight with a better conscience (7.18.3). Quite apart from the accuracy or inaccuracy of Spartan reflections, the morale that undergirds any nation's war effort depends crucially on whether individual citizens believe that, collectively, they are in the right. One thinks of the Churchill posters of World War II: "Deserve Victory!" (cf. *Constitution of the Lacedaemonians* 14.5). If realism is correct that neglecting interest would be superhuman, neglecting justice lays the project open to later doubts and amounts to starting with weak foundations. Thucydides wishes to teach his readers that neither nature nor the divine reward good behavior. However, the majority of Spartans and Athenians of whom he writes believed the contrary.

The more sophisticated among the Athenians may seem to have advanced decisively beyond this traditional notion, for example, when the Athenians at the Peloponnesian conference state that Athens' legality and fairness, far from leading to reward, causes her lots of troubles (1.77). Their point is that Athenian behavior evinces more justice than their power requires and that they hold empire not "unreasonably" (*apeikotōs*, 1.76.3-4, 73.1; cf. 76.2 "worthy"). Though not pious in any traditional sense, these Athenians still believe themselves deserving or worthy of empire. Such a belief bears a resemblance to the traditional notion that merit deserves reward. If this belief constitutes a lapse in their realism, a related lapse can be seen in the would-be enlighteners at Melos (cf. Orwin 1994, 104-5, 114-17). The envoys to Melos advance the claim that the strong are compelled by nature (*hupo phuseōs anankaias*) to rule wherever they can, and they initially set aside questions of justice (5.105.2, 5.89). Such compulsion would appear to rule out the possibility of praise or blame, virtue or vice. However, in implicitly contrasting themselves with Sparta, they, too, seem to accept a (revised) version of the traditional thinking that uncompelled virtues are possible. Spartans merely give their pleasure and self-interest "the names of nobility and justice"; Athenians risk more for their hegemony than the Spartans do for theirs (5.107, 105.4, 91.2; cf. 111.1, where Athens is above fear). The envoys recast traditional views of merit in order to privilege courage or daring. But it is hard to say how natural necessity could permit Athens freely to dare (or deserve) anything. If Athens' daring or justice (at the Peloponnesian conference) amounts to bowing to the constraint of her nature, what merit is there in that? Pragmatically, too, their reasoning constitutes a lapse: by implying that the Athenians themselves can do more or better than natural necessity dictates, the envoys may inadvertently encourage the Melians to attempt to do more, too. The Melians wish to be in the right, to be good men (5.100, 104; cf. 2.63.2). The more the envoys drive home the point that the weak must yield to the strong, the more the Melians perceive that there is nothing righteous or noble about yielding. The Athenian envoys, by recognizing in their own souls the vestiges of this wish to be noble,—that is, to be or do more than necessity dictates—might have been more alive to the desire in their opponents, and constructed a rhetoric that appealed to it. "Realism" would have to take such desires into consideration in order to get its way. This failure of Athenian realism, though not a sufficient condition for the massacre that follows, is certainly a necessary one.

This persistence of the sense of worthiness or desert, even among its most assiduous opponents (e.g., 5.89), raises the possibility that the whole active life, conceived as the statesman's or citizen's participation in the polis and her struggles, requires a belief that good efforts merit reward, perhaps even deserve to succeed—beliefs related to justice and, traditionally, concomitants of piety. To consider why some such belief or hope might be needed, we might examine the thumoeidetic psychology, often assumed to be Platonic because it is found in the *Republic* and other dialogues but which Plato attributes to, or at least puts in the mouth of, Socrates. In Plato at least, the *thumos* or thumoeidetic faculty of soul is especially concerned with deserving (*Republic* 4, 440c–d). It is difficult to imagine anyone competing successfully in life-and-death struggles who believes that his competitors have as good a right to success as he has (or that no one has a right to succeed, strictly speaking). The emotional impetus of righteous indignation, so necessary for physical combat, may be required for mental combat and strategy, for leadership, as well. For example, a leader needs to exact vengeance—paying back injury for injury—if followers are to view him as an adequate safeguard of their interests, a just man who "helps friends and harms enemies" (cf. *Anabasis* 7.7.37–38, 1.9.11–12; also 5.5.21). As we shall subsequently argue, the *Hellenica* takes a particular interest in the morale or confidence of armies and peoples, as a result of which *thumos*-cognates occur frequently. If political activity requires passion, and the passion in question is always potentially indignant about just deserts, then the only way of purifying oneself of this mental vice—the only hope of a realist "enlightenment"—would be to refrain from political activity altogether. Thucydides' (5.26.5) enforced retirement from political activity, and Socrates' refusal to engage in political activity (e.g., *Memorabilia* 1.6.15; cf. *Hellenica* 1.7.15) may now appear necessary to their ability to theorize about events clearly—not merely because of the time afforded by leisure but by its emotional calm or quiet.

All the more remarkable, then, when we see Xenophon the protagonist of the *Anabasis* managing to live the active life, leading the Ten Thousand, while avoiding the characteristic traps of both piety and realism. On the one hand, Xenophon emerges from these pages as the quintessentially pious man. As leader, he spends considerable time sacrificing. On the other hand, Xenophon's rational piety avoids fearful conservatism and can be seen to modify significantly that hopefulness in the face of dire necessities which characterized Nicias as well as the Melians—hope that virtue will be rewarded. Two occurrences in the *Anabasis* suggest rational design in this piety.

The first is Xenophon's initial dream of the burning house, a dream that starts him on his career of leadership (*Anabasis* 3.1.11ff.). The Ten Thousand are at wit's end after their leadership has literally been decapitated. In the middle of hostile territory, leagues upon leagues from the sea, they have no one to lead them. Able to sleep a little, Xenophon sees a dream in which a thunderbolt falls on his father's house (*patrōian oikian*), setting it entirely alight. Xenophon is frightened and immediately wakes up. He recounts his highly peculiar interpretation of the dream:

> He judged the dream good in one way: the fact that, though in toils and perils, he seemed to see a great light from Zeus. But in another way he also feared (since the dream seemed to be from Zeus the King and the fire seemed to shine in a circle) lest he be unable to leave the country of the King and be shut in on all sides by impasses.

Xenophon sees Zeus burning his father's house with a lightning bolt and decides this might be a good thing. The optimism of his interpretation is remarkable. A more likely interpretation would be that his time has come—his own death in the middle of barbarian territory presages the ruin of his whole house.[13] It is time to despair and die. Instead, Xenophon accentuates the positive: fire might be bad, but light is good—and light from the king of the gods cannot be all bad. He deemphasizes the negative: by giving Zeus his epithet of King and noting the circular or surrounding character of the fire, Xenophon perceives that he may get trapped in some other king's (the Persian King's) country. This is a very abstract reading, extracting the notion of king and applying it to something else. The abstraction ensures that the dream contains no negative or demoralizing information except precisely the situation on the ground as Xenophon already knew it (information that must be accommodated in any case). The dream illustrates how Xenophon permits divine phenomena to add nothing to the problems he faces but only, at most, "light," that is, hope for a solution. We recall how many other dreams and omens halt political actors from Nicias to Agesilaus, causing caution and inaction (e.g., *Hellenica* 3.2.24, 3.4.14; contrast 4.7.4 with 4.7.7); instead, Xenophon is galvanized into action.

The random sneeze that occurs during his speech to the multitude helps us get deeper into Xenophon's peculiarly rational piety (3.2.7–10). Xenophon has only just begun the most important speech of his career, likely to determine his own salvation. For the Ten Thousand can save themselves only if they stick together and fight their way out. Xenophon has even dressed for the part. He has begun to point out how punishing Persian treachery can be their salvation, when someone in the audience sneezes. The soldiers are so anxious, and their superstitions accordingly are on such high alert, that as one body they prostrate themselves to the god. Xenophon immediately and extemporaneously interprets the omen as a good omen. It is far from clear that a traditionally pious man could have known for certain, at first glance, that the omen was positive, or that the worried soldiery would have seen it that way without his help.[14] Nor was there time for careful theoretical discussion if Xenophon, like everyone else, had wondered whether it was a good omen or not, and taken the time to consider arguments pro and con. The opportunity would have been lost. Xenophon does not miss a beat: " 'I'm resolved, men,

---

[13] On the improbability of the interpretation, compare Flower (2012, 126–7). For a significantly different symbolism, see Buzzetti (2014, 119–22), who points out ancient sources skeptical about Xenophon's dream: Cicero, *On Divination* 1.25; Lucian, *The Dream* 17.

[14] Penelope shows similar presence of mind at *Odyssey* 17.541–47.

since an omen of Zeus the savior appeared when we were speaking about salvation, to vow to sacrifice thank-offerings for salvation to this god wherever we first arrive in a friendly land. . . .'" (3.2.9). He immediately follows up by gambling the support he has won so far on a single throw: "'And whoever is resolved on these things, let him hold up his hand.'" He runs the risk of men disagreeing with his interpretation of the omen, after which everything would be likely to unravel. None of this could possibly have been part of his planned speech, because the sneeze was a chance event. But he knows his men: the same doubts and fears that might easily have led many to question the goodness of the omen can be turned to incentive to cling to that positive interpretation, especially when they see their fellows raising their hands and do not want to be left out. "And all held up their hands."

Manipulating popular belief in omens may seem to go hand in hand with a total rejection of belief in omens. As a Socratic, Xenophon is unlikely to have accepted the gods as the tradition handed them down. Whatever his religious skepticism may have been like, it was clearly very different from a dogmatic atheism, according to which the question is settled and we should move past religion to more pressing questions, a reflex evident in our own impatience with many passages in Xenophon. His Socratic piety also differs from the "piety" of the envoys to Melos, who do as the gods do, not as they say (Thucydides 5.105.2). Neither the modern nor the ancient stance would be likely to be as sensitive to popular piety as Xenophon evidently was.[15] While Thucydides was experimental as well as didactic about the efficacy of the gods and the effects of piety (sufficiently to puzzle Gomme about his "curious interest"; Strauss 1964, 208, 180), still he left little doubt, in the end, about where he came down (one notes, e.g., the force of "for once" at 5.26.3). In Xenophon, by contrast, experimentation about the gods is carried on beneath a traditionalist exterior. The realism of the envoys is friendly neither to morality nor to philosophy. By contrast, Socratic morality enters the lists with traditional morality in order to contest which is more moral. To explore further the serious basis for Xenophon's Socratic stance, we conclude by more closely examining moral agency.

Moral Agency in the Face of Natural Necessity

The post-"continuation" *Hellenica* (2.3.11–7.5.27), from the end of the Peloponnesian war to the battle of Mantinea, explicitly assumes that occurrences can come from outside nature, from supernatural causes. If they can, and the gods punish actions on the assumption that humans are free to act justly, then divine punishment in one sense valorizes moral agency by dignifying it. Natural necessity, by contrast, removes the dignity

---

[15] For Bowden (2004), in the "scientific study of religion," Xenophon is not a scientist. Dillery (1995) assembles many relevant passages.

of any moral act by removing our responsibility for it. Philosophy insofar as it inquires into natural necessity runs the risk of being literally demoralizing. A real difficulty in Thucydides (7.57, especially 57.3, 7, 9) is to determine in any given case what sort of necessity is present and whether it is truly compulsory. Moreover, discerning what is necessary to do in any given case may still leave the agent morally unfit for or incapable of doing it (e.g., Thucydides 5.111.3).

Several details undercut Xenophon's (5.4.1) assertion that Sparta was punished for occupying the Theban acropolis in peacetime, first and foremost in the events surrounding their defeat at Leuctra itself. It is true that a "divinity was leading on" the Spartan assembly that decided not to disband their army after making a treaty (6.4.3). On the Theban side, however, Xenophon reports that the oracles and portents indicating an impending Spartan defeat may have been manipulated by the Theban leaders for the consumption of the masses (6.4.7). And in the preparations for the battle, he emphasizes a natural cause of defeat: the Spartan cavalry were at their worst, "weakest in body and loving honor least of all" (6.4.10–13). Again, the exactness of the Spartans' comeuppance shows the hand of the gods: "they were punished only by the wronged parties themselves" (5.4.1). Xenophon associates this exactness with the economizing spirit in which the pro-Spartan party at Thebes is also punished: "only seven exiles sufficed to destroy their rule" (also 5.4.1; cf. 5.4.2–9). But if the gods were responsible for any of this, their exactness and economy must have gone astray in other regards. For they also permitted some Spartans to be killed who were no more guilty than those who went free, and they permitted as well the killing of their innocent children (5.4.12; cf. Thucydides 7.29). Similarly with Sparta's later salvation: Epaminondas' descent upon the town itself of Sparta gets sandwiched between two divine explanations of her salvation (7.5.10, 13). But at a crucial turning point of this campaign, Xenophon offers an alternative: "As for what happened next, it is possible to blame the divinity, but it is possible to say that no one can stop desperate men" (7.5.12). The latter possibility picks up Jason of Pherae's earlier advice (6.4.23). Nothing prevents such passages from being studies in the curious way the gods work through secondary causes. But Xenophon was certainly familiar with naturalistic explanations that emphasized the dichotomy; perhaps his alternative—either the gods or desperation—means what it says.[16] The dimmest intelligence at Sparta can discern necessity when backs are literally against the wall. But the same Spartan must still find the inner resources with which to fight rather than crumble.

Whether right has might, supported by the divine, is harder to observe than the fact that rightness and righteous indignation make a soul mighty (see "The Persistence of Piety"). Such a spirited soul naturally thinks it and its friends have divine support. As Thrasybulus stresses, the Athenian oligarchs have put themselves in the wrong; that

---

[16] His downplaying, by modern standards, of another natural cause of Leuctra's outcome—the Thebans' deeper phalanx—highlights divine causality, and this may be the motive for Xenophon's allegedly minimizing the achievement of Epaminondas and the Thebans' innovations with deeper phalanxes (Tuplin 1993, 136–38). Xenophon leaves the reader to apply that information—about the deeper phalanx—which he does in fact supply (4.2.18, 6.4.12, 7.5.22–25).

means the gods are on the democrats' side (2.4.14). Agesilaus rejoices and thanks the Persian satrap for breaking his oaths, since he thereby transferred the gods' allegiance to the Greeks (3.4.11). Similarly with cases of dire necessity: in Xenophon's own pitch to assume the leadership, he stresses how Persian unrighteousness has in a real sense delivered them into the hands of the Ten Thousand (*Anabasis* 3.2.10). Before the truce was broken, doing what many mercenaries desire—looting and plundering—was illegal for the Greeks. Now that the truce has been violated, they can—indeed, should—seize whatever they want without paying money for it: "now these good things lie as prizes in the middle for whichever of us are better men" (3.1.19–22). Such amenities clearly belong to those with stout hearts and sharp swords:

> The gods are the contest's judges, who will be with us, as is likely. For [the Persians] have sworn falsely by them, but we, though seeing many good things, stubbornly abstained from them on account of oaths of the gods. As a result, I think it possible to enter the contest with much higher spirits than they have (*polu sun phronēmati meizoni*, 3.1.21–22; cf. *Hellenica* 5.1.14, 17).

Morale, keeping spirits high, emerges as the crucial factor in practical success (*Education of Cyrus* 1.6.13, *Anabasis* 3.1.36). To maintain morale, money matters a lot (e.g., *Hellenica* 1.1.24, 1.5.7–8, *athumein, prothumoteron, athumōs*), but it is far from the sole factor. Being in the right and getting right with the gods are very important.[17] For the generals and captains (whose spiritedness or dispiritedness the rank and file will imitate, *Anabasis* 3.2.36, 41), Xenophon stresses the opportunity for a beautiful or noble death. Precisely, competitors bent on dying nobly "somehow arrive at old age more" (3.1.43–44)—a curious argument, in that striving for a noble death is made instrumental to longer life. These leaders of the Greeks can fulfill one of two very different desires by one means: showing virtue (cf. 3.2.2–3). In the ensuing pages of the *Anabasis*, Xenophon will counsel the Greeks to get right with god and man and not to commit any act that puts them in the wrong (e.g., 5.7.26–35, 7.1.18–31). As a kind of realist, he knows that if they do wrong and are successful at it, they will ignore or forget about its unrighteousness. But if they are unsuccessful or later fall into misfortunes, the memory of that iniquity will come back to harm them in the form of fear of divine retribution. Thus bad behavior will ultimately undermine morale, which in turn is the absolute prerequisite of their ever escaping their predicament (cf. Thucydides 6.70.1, 7.79.3, *ēthumoun*). Until the Ten Thousand are safe out of harm's way, all enterprises of a purely mercenary, unscrupulous nature are playing with fire (at least until Xenophon is about to leave: 7.8.8–11, 20–24). Good policy is very close to honesty. In other words, on occasions when surrender is not an option, or when necessity makes itself manifest in some other way, a kind of Melianness may be called for (*Anabasis* 3.1.18; 6.3.12–13, 17; 6.5.12–18, 24). Precisely in nobility and morality lies part of the appeal that can render the Ten Thousand effectual,

---

[17] Compare Aristotle, *Rhetoric* 2.5.20–21; Thucydides 7.66.1, 7.68.1, 7.77; *Hellenica* 4.3.10–14 with 1.6.36–37, also 3.1.16–18.

advantageous to themselves. This focus on morality's contribution to morale uncovers another stratum of realist speculation, somewhat in tension with the anti-imperial ethic of the *Hellenica*.

In the "continuation" *Hellenica*, one major occurrence may be said to reinforce a (modified) Athenian realism over Melian piety. The Melians had admonished the Athenian envoys not to destroy the common good in case Athens ever fell from the heights of power, since she would incur the greatest vengeance. The Athenian envoys responded with the forecast that a peer hegemon like Sparta would take no terrible revenge—vengeance would come, instead, from subject peoples' gaining the upper hand (Thucydides 5.90–91). Xenophon relates the outcome of their prediction. The night the news came of the loss of the fleet at Aegospotami, none slept, "thinking they would suffer the sort of things they had done to the Melians, colonists of the Lacedaemonians, whom they had defeated by siege." The Melians merely head a list of guilty actions that undermine Athenian confidence at this low moment, including several other full-blown massacres (*Hellenica* 2.2.3). Lysander had openly identified himself with the vengeful cause of the same newly liberated peoples whom the envoys to Melos especially feared, allies whom he had to court if he was to maintain and increase his unconstitutional sway (2.1.31–32, 2.2.9; Proietti 1987, 30–42). It is possible that a kind of realism about Lysander's personal motive (in siding with the vengeful) eventually informs the fears even of ordinary Athenians. Once they are besieged by land and sea, their fearful thoughts are also clearly moral: "they saw no salvation from suffering the things they themselves had done, not by way of retaliating but rather out of hubris: they had been unjust to people of small cities for no cause other than that they were allied with [the Spartans]" (2.2.10). The Athenians' immediate act to "restore civic rights to those whom they had disfranchised" may increase manpower but also perhaps begins to put Athens in the right, improving her justice, in the belief that right has might (2.2.11; cf. Thucydides 5.32.1). Eventually, their loss of morale (*athumia*, 2.2.14–18) prevents them from negotiating for an advantageous peace, and Theramenes must trick them to get the best deal available. Others of the Greeks, led by the Corinthians and Thebans, initiate the practical step of counseling Sparta to destroy Athens (2.2.19), a destruction the Athenians themselves on some level appear to agree they deserve. Instead, Sparta saves them, very much as the envoys at Melos had predicted (2.2.20). The public language of Spartan magnanimity, recognizing Athenian service during the Persian wars, should not obscure what a weapon Athens could be if, deprived of the long walls that make her proof against any land-based interference in her affairs, she will "follow the Lacedaemonians both on land and on sea wherever they lead" (2.2.20; cf. 2.3.41, Thucydides 5.109). It is hard to see what comparable advantage the Melians could have offered the Athenians. In a final twist, the morality of service in the Persian wars, which the Athenian envoys had dismissed as "fine names" (Thucydides 5.89), actually does turn out to contribute to their salvation, in the sense of providing the moral camouflage behind which Sparta can do what interest dictates rather than give her allies the justice they desire (Rood 2004, 355–56).

The new, improved kind of realism on offer in the *Hellenica* and the *Anabasis* takes better account of the passions that animate all or most human hearts, whether sophisticated or not, than the Athenian envoys to Melos had done. Such a modified "moral realism" is aware of the way morality remains inextricably bound up with political and military actions even, or especially, when they most seem to lack morality. It raises the further question whether natural necessity might be behind the ironical point at the end of the "continuation": contrary to Greek hopes, Sparta no better than Athens could resist the siren call of empire (*Hellenica* 2.2.23; cf. Thucydides 1.77.6). Such moral realism seems certain to be closer to Thucydides' own view (perhaps, e.g., 3.42–48) than is that of his Athenian envoys. Thucydides was a realist especially sensitive to morality, and Xenophon's dialogue with him is made possible by the latter's being a moralist of an especially realistic type. The perspective on Thucydides that emerges from this very preliminary comparison makes us wonder what further riches their dialogue may help to unlock.

References

Ambler, Wayne, trans. 2008. *The Anabasis of Cyrus*, by Xenophon. Ithaca: Cornell University Press.

Bowden, Hugh. 2004. "Xenophon and the Scientific Study of Religion." In *Xenophon and His World: Papers from a Conference Held in Liverpool in July 1999. Historia: Journal of Ancient History*, edited by C. Tuplin, 172. Stuttgart: Franz Steiner Verlag.

Brownson, Carleton, trans. 2001. *Anabasis*, by Xenophon. Edited by J. Dillery. Cambridge: Harvard University Press.

Brownson, Carleton, trans. 2004. *Hellenica*, by Xenophon. 2 vols. Cambridge: Harvard University Press.

Buzzetti, Eric. 2014. *Xenophon the Socratic Prince*. New York: Palgrave MacMillan.

Cartledge, Paul. 2009. "Lysander." In *The Landmark Xenophon's Hellenika*, edited by R. B. Strassler, 407. New York: Anchor.

Dillery, John. 1995. *Xenophon and the History of His Times*. London: Routledge.

Dobski, Bernard J. 2009. "Athenian Democracy Re-Founded: Xenophon's Political History in the *Hellenika*." *Polis* 26 (2): 316–38.

Flower, Michael A. 2012. *Xenophon's Anabasis, or, the Expedition of Cyrus*. New York: Oxford University Press.

Gish, Dustin. 2009. "Spartan Justice: The Conspiracy of Kinadon in Xenophon's *Hellenika*." *Polis* 26: 339–69.

Gish, Dustin. 2012. "Defending *Dēmokratia*: Athenian Justice and the Trial of the Arginusae Generals in Xenophon's *Hellenika*." In *Xenophon: Ethical Principles and Historical Enquiry*, edited by F. Hobden and C. Tuplin, 161–212. Leiden: Brill.

Gray, Vivienne. 1989. *The Character of Xenophon's Hellenica*. Baltimore: Johns Hopkins University Press.

Gray, Vivienne. 2011. *Xenophon's Mirror of Princes*. New York: Oxford University Press.

Henry, William Patrick. 1967. *Greek Historical Writing: A Historiographical Essay Based on Xenophon's Hellenica*. Chicago: Argonaut.

Johnson, David M. 2012. "Strauss on Xenophon." In *Xenophon: Ethical Principles and Historical Enquiry*, edited by F. Hobden and C. Tuplin, 123–59. Leiden: Brill.

Ludwig, Paul. 2010. "Educating the Perfect Wife: Piety and Rational Control in Xenophon's *Oeconomicus*." In *The Pious Sex*, edited by A. Radasanu, 77–100. Lanham: Lexington.

Marincola, John. 1999. "Genre, Convention and Innovation in Greco-Roman Historiography." In *The Limits of Historiography: Genre and Narrative in Ancient Historical Texts*, edited by C. S. Kraus, 281–323. Leiden: Brill.

Millender, Ellen. 2012. "Spartan 'Friendship' and Xenophon's Crafting of the *Anabasis*." In *Xenophon: Ethical Principles and Historical Enquiry*, edited by F. Hobden and C. Tuplin, 377–425. Leiden: Brill.

Orwin, Clifford. 1994. *The Humanity of Thucydides*. Princeton: Princeton University Press.

Palmer, Michael. 1982. "Alcibiades and the Question of Tyranny in Thucydides." *Canadian Journal of Political Science* 15 (1):103–24.

Proietti, Gerald. 1987. *Xenophon's Sparta: An Introduction*. Supplements to Mnemosyne 98. Leiden: Brill.

Rood, Tim. 2004. "Xenophon and Diodorus: Continuing Thucydides." In *Xenophon and His World: Papers from a Conference Held in Liverpool in July 1999. Historia Einzelschriften*, edited by C. Tuplin, 172. Stuttgart: Franz Steiner Verlag.

Smith, C. F., trans. 1992. *History of the Peloponnesian War*, by Thucydides. 4 vols. Cambridge: Harvard University Press.

Strassler, Robert B., ed. 1996. *The Landmark Thucydides*. New York: Touchstone.

Strassler, Robert B., ed. 2009. *The Landmark Xenophon's Hellenika*. New York: Anchor.

Strauss, Leo. 1964. *The City and Man*. Chicago: University of Chicago Press.

Strauss, Leo. 1968. "Greek Historians." *Review of Metaphysics* 21: 656–66.

Thomas, David. 2009. "Introduction." In *The Landmark Xenophon's Hellenika*, edited by R. B. Strassler, ix–lxvi. New York: Anchor.

Tuplin, Christopher. 1993. *The Failings of Empire*. Stuttgart: Franz Steiner Verlag.

CHAPTER 31

POLITICAL PHILOSOPHY IN AN UNSTABLE WORLD

Comparing Thucydides and Plato on the Possibilities of Politics

GERALD MARA[*]

DIFFERENT TEXTS, DIFFERENT WORLDS?

For many readers, the perspectives of Plato and Thucydides are fundamentally incompatible. Plato's authentic philosophers allegedly occupy an unchanging world of intellectual forms or ideas existing, in the language of the *Republic*'s cave story, above and in the light, far removed from darker politics "down here" (*Republic* 521a). In contrast, Thucydides' world is passionate and disrupted, diagnosed with frightening intensity by the character Diodotus in Book 3's debate on Mytilene. "Hope and *erōs* [which] are everywhere ... extend human nature relentlessly toward [some] action (*tēs anthrōpeias phuseōs hormōmenēs prothumōs ti praxai*)"[1] (3.45). Nietzsche (1954) acknowledges these diverging worlds in *Twilight of the Idols*, "What I Owe to the Ancients." "It is courage before reality that at last distinguishes natures like Thucydides and Plato. Plato is a coward before reality, consequently, he flees into the ideal; Thucydides has himself in control, consequently he also keeps control of things." Though offered for its own complex purposes, Nietzsche's judgment is seconded by many of our contemporaries. Among classical scholars, Jacqueline de Romilly (1963, 362 and 365) and Gregory Crane (1989, 324–25) contrast abstract Platonic idealism with gritty Thucydidean realism. Philosophically, Raymond Geuss asks, "[w]ho is a better guide to human life, Plato or

---

[*] With thanks to Ryan K. Balot, Jill Frank, Melissa Lane, Paul Ludwig, and Rachel Templer.
[1] Translations of passages from Thucydides rely on those of Lattimore (1998) and Smith (1962–1988) though I have made some changes. Translated passages from the *Republic* are Bloom's (1968) with small changes.

Thucydides?" and answers the latter, precisely because of his engagement with the real world (2005, 219–233).

If we agree with these assessments, we find two authors speaking such different languages that prospects for dialogue between them seem impossible. In spite of the discursive approaches of both writers, many readers find these texts eventually dominated by rigid theorizing. Though the Platonic corpus represents the human world through a series of dialogues, many commentators interpret the conversations as venues for a Platonic theory that demonstrates moral imperatives philosophically (Reeve 1988, 234). While Thucydides narrates speeches and practices of political agents, these are often read as confirming lawlike statements on the causes of political disorder (Romilly 1963, 322–39). Thus, the "Melian Dialogue" in Book 5 becomes a parody of dialogue, limited by compulsions of power (Athenian military superiority—5.86) and distorted by attachments to political imaginaries (Melian visions of an ordered world ruled by the divine—5.104—and Athenian acceptance of the imperatives of empire—5.95, 97, 105). Even the parody unravels as the substitutes for dialogue, Melian appeal to kinship and just gods and Athenian recognition of a natural law subordinating the weaker to the stronger (5.105), collapse in the narrative that follows.

According to such readings, neither Plato nor Thucydides offers a resource for any conversational political theory. Plato's transparently monologic dialogues at best approximate the decisive clarity of a philosophy absorbed in the ideas. Thucydides' dialogic possibilities are overcome by compulsions that he can diagnose but not remedy. Thus read, each author rejects conversation in the name of a conclusive frame of reference that dismisses alternative views of the world and discourages attempts at practical change. Guided by a seriously "Platonic" philosophical project, we are directed to an enduring but distant space where ordinary politics are invisible or irrelevant. Instructed by Thucydides, our frame of reference becomes an unending turbulence whose dynamics may be explained by science but not placed under the scrutiny of thoughtfulness and care of agency. If we reconsider Geuss's earlier question—which thinker is a better guide to human life?—the right answer might be "neither."

I want to challenge that conclusion by suggesting that we can read Thucydides and Plato more dialogically. Beyond expanding our understanding of these authors, such mutual readings help us to appreciate their contributions to conversational political theory. I try to show how each author opens possibilities for dialogic engagement with his own text and then I indicate areas of plausible exchange between them. This interactive reading avoids the binary frames of reference of abstract and illusory peace or ongoing and inescapable war, drawing attention to experiences in need of continued intellectual negotiation and opening spaces for practical improvement.

Texts and Contexts

This reading begins by appreciating how both authors complicate relations of texts to their contexts. Plato's philosophical dialogues are not simply responses to the political events of Athens' fifth-century history; they inscribe those events, particularly those surrounding the Peloponnesian War, within their dramatic structures. While Thucydides' narratives are not explicitly philosophical, they gesture toward philosophical concerns and invite philosophical reflection.

Socrates' practices within the dialogues largely parallel the war. He makes his first public impression in the *Protagoras*, historically set (in 432) just before the war's outbreak. Seth Benardete (1991, 7) notes that textual references in the *Gorgias* extend virtually through the war's entire course. In the *Meno* (set circa 401), the angry encounter with Anytus, Socrates' principal accuser in his capital trial, reflects Athens' internal political disturbance after its defeat by Sparta (404), when the oligarchy of the thirty tyrants (404–403) was overthrown by a returning democracy involving Anytus. Even dialogues more overtly philosophical are politically situated. The sweeping cosmology offered by the Locrian Timaeus is the first of a series of responses to Socrates' request to see a regime resembling the *Republic*'s city in speech at war. The program is organized by Critias, the eventual leader of the Thirty, and is designed to precede Critias' revelation that such a city existed historically as ancient Athens (*Timaeus* 26 c–d).

In the *Republic*, we find reminders and images of the war that implicitly engage portions of Thucydides' narrative (Bloom 1968; Nails 2002). The dialogue's interlocutors, some of whom will become the Thirty's victims, anticipate the tyranny. The conversation's physical location connects by contrast to the democratic restoration that will be decided in a battle fought near the temple of Bendis (Frank 2007), the Thracian goddess whose festival prompts Socrates' and his companion Glaucon's visit, "down to the Piraeus" (327 a). Socrates' eventual representation of a philosophy "making no use of anything sensed in any way, but [only] forms themselves, through forms to forms, . . . ending in forms" (511 b–c) reveals "a life better than ruling" (520 e–521 a) to Glaucon, who is addressed, in the language of oligarchic political clubs, as a *hetairos* and thus as someone potentially attracted to the Thirty. Just as his uncle Critias proclaims the historical existence of a Socratic city in speech, Glaucon demands to be shown how the *Republic*'s city can be realized (471 d–e). Identifying a life better than ruling is a speech act within a conversation in which a different kind of ruling and being ruled connects the partners (427 c–e).

Reversing direction, Thucydides moves from the anxieties and agendas of particular individuals and regimes to broader ways of understanding and engaging the world. Here, we should revisit Donald Kagan's judgments about the place of the characters' speeches in the narrative. For Kagan (2009, 17), Thucydides either reports the speeches as accurately as possible or violates objective history. In his own methodological sketch (1.22), Thucydides notes that he aims to be as accurate as possible about the war's deeds (*erga*) and, as to the speeches (*logoi*), because "recalling precisely what was said was difficult" he offers what "seemed . . . each would have said [as] especially required (*ta deonta malist' eipein*) on the occasion, [while] maintaining as much closeness as possible to the general sense (*gnōmēs*) of what was truly said." This might indeed mean reporting the *logoi* as factually as possible. Yet another possibility is that the book's speeches represent the most appropriate speeches to be given on *these* occasions, by *these* speakers, before *these* audiences. This does not mean that Thucydides fabricates speeches (Nichols 2015, 16) but it does recognize his authorial discretion in crafting *logoi* that most clearly reveal the priorities or identities of the speaker or regime in question. Differing from straightforwardly factual reports, such representations invite a critical scrutiny that Thucydides applies through a range of narrative strategies. Thus, the speeches are also speech acts with their own pragmatic intentions (achieved or not) and consequences (foreseen or not). Each *logos* is an *ergon* connected to other narrated *erga*. Pericles' Funeral Oration strikes a different tone after the plague narrative. His last speech proclaiming (2.64) that the daring exhibited by Athens' multiple wars will forge a name persisting in eternal memory (*aieimnēstos*) must be critically reassessed in light of the severe Athenian distress caused by its fighting two wars at once (7.28).

Though politically situated, Thucydides' speeches show the limits of those situations by gesturing beyond them, as in the Athenian statements on Melos about the significance of nature and the gods as contexts for their political aggressiveness (5.105). In pointing beyond immediate political horizons such appeals acknowledge that cultural meanings are insufficient justifications for practice. Yet the pragmatic character of these appeals implies that visions of nature, the gods, and the human things (*ta anthrōpeia*) generally, emerge within pragmatic contexts. When Athenian (1.76; 5.105) and Syracusan (4.61) speakers say that nature mandates the domination of the weak by the strong, they speak within powerful regimes that construe imperatives of nature as validations.

Interpreting the speeches as more than factual reports means reading them as representations of political, ethical, and epistemic alternatives that are scrutinized within a broader narrative. Critically examining *logoi* of all sorts may be Thucydides' core intellectual project. The war's deeds are accessed through investigations of others' accounts (Ober 1998; Saxonhouse 2006) and the speeches offer distinctive and controversial possibilities for politics. In this light, the book is multivocal and Thucydides' own *logos* takes other *logoi* seriously, while nonetheless subjecting them to a critical examination that is more provocative than decisive. This ongoing multivocality allows dialogic intersections with the *Republic* that are both illuminating and critical.

In what follows, I test this intuition by considering two questions. The first is epistemically foundational, asking whether extremity clarifies or distorts our understanding of *ta anthrōpeia*. The second is politically controversial, examining allegations of the necessity of war. In both cases, Thucydides' frame of reference seems to exclude serious engagement with Platonic political philosophy. I will try to smooth some of these edges by uncovering Thucydidean/Platonic interactions that are more mutual, creating possibilities for a more conversational form of political theory.

Politics and Extremes

Speaking in what may be his darkest voice, Thucydides implies that *ta anthrōpeia* are clearest during times of what Jeremy Mynott (2013, 3) calls upheaval. Concerning the *stasis* in Corcyra, Thucydides writes, "And so many hardships fell upon the cities on account of *stasis*, things that happen and will always happen as long as human beings have the same nature (*hē autē phusis anthrōpōn*) . . . In peace and good circumstances (*agathois pragmasin*), cities and individuals hold better thoughts (*ameinous tas gnōmas*) because they do not have to confront involuntary necessities, but war (*polemos*), generally depriving [human beings] of daily resources is a violent teacher (*biaios didaskalos*), making the dispositions of both [cities and individuals] like that [harsh] condition" (3.82).

We might clarify this position by comparing it with those of Carl Schmitt and Thomas Hobbes. In emphasizing the explanatory power of the extreme, Thucydides may anticipate Schmitt's understanding of politics as "the most intense and extreme antagonism, and every concrete antagonism becomes that much more political the closer it approaches the most extreme point, that of the friend enemy grouping" (2007, 27). Yet differences between Thucydides and Schmitt eventually overwhelm similarities. While Schmitt's extreme telescopes politics, Thucydides' destroys it. Under the escalating violence of Corcyra's factions, politics itself disintegrates. In Corcyra, the party allegiances of the Athenian-leaning democrats and the Spartan-inclined oligarchs overcome kinship relations, sacred reverence, and civic membership. Brother citizens kill one another in the name of a party loyalty (*philetairos*) that has become all consuming (3.82). This is only the beginning. While the terms of these contentions initially center around democratic/oligarchic competitions, the progression of factional conflict may disrupt even these. As the Corcyrean narrative unfolds, Thucydides moves from hostility among parties (still presupposing political organization) to deadly clashes wherein participants are described in increasingly individualistic terms, strength and weakness, categories whose own meanings become increasingly unpredictable (3.83). Hyperpoliticization spawns radical depoliticization (Orwin, 1994, 178–80). If this extreme reflects nature, then the establishment and exercise of political power are not, as some of Thucydides' characters allege, natural but counter-natural.

Seeing politics as resisting natural chaos seems more Hobbesian. Yet this parallel, too, is limited. The inhabitants of Hobbes's "natural condition" do not, as in Diodotus' diagnosis, extend themselves relentlessly toward action; they are paralyzed by anxiety blocking any effective action (1994, *Leviathan* 13.9). While Hobbes presents *Leviathan*'s institutional designs as remediation (29.1), Thucydides makes no such claim. Instead, attempts at political stabilization are often self-undermining. The same drives for gain and honor that converged to create stability prior to the Trojan war (1.8) are the roots of political disintegration (3.83). Though the hegemonies established by Athens and Sparta after the Persian wars ordered Hellenic political life (1. 8–19), their competition now threatens to destroy it. The civic disruption in Corcyra previews a condition that progressively threatens all of the Greek cities (Price 2001).

Such a political narrative could not be further from a *Republic* structured by idealist metaphysics. Yet this judgment ignores the ways that historically recognizable political extremes frame discourses within the dialogue. This influence is observable not only in the regime-driven narratives of Books 8 and 9 (which draw so heavily on the disruptions of 404/403 BCE) but also in portions of the work that seem more philosophically analytic. Take one example: in his characterization of the appetitive part of the soul in Book 4, Socrates insists that the desires (*epithumiai*) aim only at their appropriate satisfactions, disregarding concerns for quality. "Let no one make an uproar if [we are] inattentive ... that no one desires drink but good drink (*chrēstou potou*), not food but good food (*chrēstou sitou*), for all, of course, desire good things (*tōn agathōn*) ... [A] particular kind of thirst is for a particular kind of drink, but thirst itself is neither for much nor little, good or bad, nor, in a word, for any particular kind, but thirst by itself is naturally only for drink" (438 a; 439 a).

Some commentators read this as a logical analysis of the character of desire as such (Reeve 1988, 138). Yet even this "analytic" section is part of a dramatic trajectory, as Socrates attempts to identify psychic justice by constructing images of civic justice and injustice (368 d–369a). If desire is blind to satisfaction's quality, calculative rationality (439 c–d) is needed for the just governance of the soul (Weiss 2006, 175). This psychic order parallels the just city's stratified political structure, reinforcing the claim that cities should be ruled (or dominated—*kratoumenas*) by the *epieikesteroi*, translated in Bloom (1968) as "the more intelligent" (431 c–d). Yet though it is presented as analogic, the civic/psychic comparison has deep fault lines. This representation of a stratified psychic structure disconnects desire *qua* desire from any concern for the good, splitting emotional and rational psyches. However, this severity is challenged by Socrates' own choices of words. In its yearning (*orexis*) and urge (*hormē*) for satisfying drink, the thirsting soul also takes counsel (*bouletai*) (439 a–b), implying deliberation. The *epieikesteroi* are identified by both their desires (*epithumiōn*) and their prudence (*phronēseōs*). Eventually, the framing analogy of soul/city itself becomes provisional and controversial (434c–435 a), introducing questions, not demonstrating solutions. In the revised account of Book 9 each of the soul's parts is distinctively appetitive, characterized by its particular desire, now intensified into love (580 d ff).

Since Book 4's analytic of desire is misleading, are there alternative readings? Taking the dialogue's underlying polemical drama seriously, may we interpret desire's separation from quality as a representation of desires experienced under extreme circumstances, during which concerns for survival render judgment about quality otiose? Survival becomes an imperative for those afflicted by war and *stasis*. Looking to Thucydides helps us to grasp this point. Focusing on pure thirst, both the plague narrative of Book 2 and the account of the slaughter of Nicias' army in Book 7 offer images of intense thirst absent any concern for quality. As the horrific retreat from Syracuse ends, "the Athenians pushed on to the Assinarus river ... partly because of their weariness and desire to drink (*piein epithumia*).... The Syracusans hurled missiles down upon the Athenians most of whom were drinking greedily.... The Peloponnesians went down to the water's edge and butchered them, most of all those in the river. The water at once became foul but was drunk all the same, though muddy and full of blood, it was fought over by many" (7.84). We can extend this parallel to extreme hunger. During the siege of Potidaea, the inhabitants had "sometimes eaten one another" (2.70). In anticipating the Thirty, the *Republic* presumes the decisive siege of Athens. When Xenophon extends Thucydides' time horizon through the city's eventual defeat in *Hellenica* 2.2, he underscores starvation and famine. Read in these contexts, the divide between desire and rationality is far from abstract, and the psychic scenario wherein calculation masters desire becomes a disturbing commentary on political extremes. Rationality is most needed when its effectiveness is least likely. Subsequently, Socrates imagines warring (*polemein*) and faction (*stasiazontoin*) between calculation and appetite (that by which the soul loves—*era*, the *hetairos* of satisfactions and pleasures) in his story of Leontius (439 e–440 b). Calculation loses, leaving anger (*orgē*) in its wake.

According to this reading, Socrates' representation of desire in Book 4r implies that politics influences even the most basic psychological functions. The significance of warlike politics is anticipated earlier in Socrates' account of how the city constructed thus far will fight (422 a). Pressed by Adeimantus, he proposes that it exploit the cleavage within its competitors, each of which sounds like a potential Corcyra, "two [cities] warring with each other, one of the poor, the other of the rich." Making *stasis* go viral is the key to victory (422 e–423 b). For someone obsessed with defending the imperative of justice (354 b–c), Socrates is remarkably clinical about the consequences of this strategy for Greek political life. Yet the destructive influence of cultural forces, one exploiting, the other vulnerable to *stasis*, highlights the politically created character of extremity and the possibility, though hardly the guarantee, that things could be otherwise.

Socrates gradually softens extreme polemicism in a second war narrative, offered in Book 5 (Kochin 1999; Frank 2005). This section is a seeming digression within his attempt to show Glaucon how their city in speech could be realized (471e). While the eventual outcome may confirm that this achievement is impossible (Roochnik 2009), a more pragmatic implication is that the violent wars waged both among Greeks and with barbarians can be moderated. Socrates distinguishes wars (*polemoi*) with barbarians from internal conflicts (*staseis*) among Greek cities. Unlike Pericles, he does not see Greek wars as theaters of renown. Abandoning Book 4's cynicism, he envisages ways in which wars among Greeks would be less devastating. Both linking and revising Thucydides' plague and Corcyrean narratives, *stasis* is curable disease, not inevitable collapse (470 c–d). Socrates next imagines that Greeks might fight barbarians the way that they now fight one another (471 b), opening the possibility of moderating wars with barbarians as well.

Such moderation presumes a distinctively non-Periclean regime. In honoring "those who have been judged exceptionally good in life when dying of old age or in some other way" in the same fashion as it memorializes those dying on campaign (469b), this regime does not base its reputation on the scope of its wars; its funeral orations would revise conceptions of conspicuous men (2.43–6). Eventually, the principal condition of this city's emergence is the coincidence (473c) of philosophy and political power, an association that is, while neither natural nor necessary, not impossible (497 a). If nature does not simply order things for the best—one implication of Timaeus' ambitious cosmology—neither is it the nightmarish chaos of Corcyra. Human nature might instead be understood as indeterminate, offering possibilities as well as hazards. In recognizing extremes without surrendering to them, the *Republic* encourages deeper inquiry.

Can this reading of the *Republic* reflexively enrich readings of Thucydides? Speculatively, a byplay between the distortion and insight offered by extreme statements may help to identify the controversial place of Chapter 84 in Book 3. There, *stasis* is said to reveal "human nature (*hē anthrōpeia phusis*) dominating (*kratēsasa*) the laws and inclined even against the laws to do injustice, well pleased to show its passion (*orgēs*) as uncontrollable, stronger than justice, enemy to distinction." Because "the language has a more rhetorical character [and] the criticism of human nature ... [is] less nuanced than in 3.82" (Lattimore 1998, 171), commentators have sometimes read the chapter as spurious. Alternatively, while it may be Thucydidean in authorship, it is part of an earlier draft (Connor 1984, 102; Mynott 2013, 219). However, since the chapter itself seems extreme, it could be read as a textual acknowledgment of both the distorting consequences and stark clarity of seeing "human things" extremely. Perhaps Thucydides' treatment of nature shares some of Plato's ambiguities. Three of the very few Thucydidean references to women may illustrate the point. Within the Funeral Oration, Pericles advises the women hearing his encomium to conspicuous males (2.43) to respect nature's standard (*huparchousēs phuseōs*) by avoiding manly *kleos* (2.45). Yet by speaking in nature's (authoritative) name within the context of a controversial view of the human good, Pericles' rhetoric acknowledges that there may be counter-possibilities framed by alternative views of nature. Concerning Corcyra, Thucydides comments (3.74) that *stasis* drove the city's women to a boldness and endurance (the political behaviors of Athens and Sparta) counter to nature (*para phusin*). Nature may include a gentleness violated by political extremities that may nonetheless be moderated. Is it accidental that a sequel narrates the peaceful festivals of the old Ionians, with a focus on the women's chorus (3.104)? Those told to avoid *kleos* by a statesman dismissing Homer (2.41) receive Homeric praise.

In backing away from his revised Corcyrean narrative with a revised Periclean narrative, Socrates' voice in *Republic*, Book 5, encourages reconsideration of Thucydides' authorial narrative. In saying why the war is most worthy of being spoken about (*axiologōtaton*) in 1.1, Thucydides points to the scope and intensity of its motion, drawing on criteria valorized in Pericles' praise of daring and energy. "For this was the greatest motion (*kinēsis ... megistē*) that had come to be among Greeks and even [among] portions of the barbarians, indeed one may speak of [the involvement of] most of humanity" (*pleiston anthrōpōn*) (1.1.2). Yet in 1.23 the war's greatness (*megiston*) shows another side, "such sufferings as came to afflict Hellas unlike those [experienced] in any [length of] time. For never had there been so many cities seized and abandoned, some by barbarians and others by the Hellenes warring against each other (and some even changed population after they were overpowered), nor were there so many human beings dislocated or slaughtered, both on account of the war itself and because of factional fighting (*stasiazein*)." Both explanations of the war's significance offer visions of extremes (*erga megista*) that challenge better thoughts in peace and good circumstances. The appropriate response may not be retreat to those better thoughts, but critical judgment applied to extreme prospects, including the extremes of idealism and realism. By following *kinēsis* with *stasiazein* across his explanations of the war's importance, Thucydides implies that the extremism of the Corcyrean narrative should become part of a critical examination of Pericles' Athenian narrative. We can begin that critique by considering the origin of war.

The Necessity of War and the Possibility of Logos

The proposal to moderate wars in *Republic* Book 5 presumes regime functions beyond the resistance to disorder. In addition to exercising power, political cultures influence choices of justice or injustice and the discursive practices that can inform critical judgment. Judgment and *logos* are linked by Socrates in Book 9 when he asks "[b]y what must things that are going to be finely judged (*kalōs krithēsesthai*) be judged? Isn't it by experience, prudence, and *logos*?" (582 a.) The *Republic* as a whole interrogates *logoi* about justice and injustice. What *logos* means is not obvious of course, yet on first view prospects for its exerting the influence envisaged by Socrates seem discounted by Thucydides. The actions and deeds represented in his book appear, at least, to illustrate the subordination of *logos* to passion (*orgē*) or power (*dunamis*). When rationality does appear, it is only as Thucydides' rigorous, though disheartening, analysis. Yet I believe that this impression misleads. The importance and fragility of *logos* within political judgment emerges thematically within Thucydides' complex treatment of the necessity of the war.

In his last speech, Pericles considers whether this war was chosen or necessary, answering the latter. "For those in good fortune and [able to make] a choice, waging war is altogether thoughtless, but when from necessity they must [either] submit by giving way to their neighbors or prevail by running risks, those who flee from dangers are more blameworthy than those who stand up to them" (2.61). Thucydides seems to agree when he comments, twice (1.23; 5.25), that the Athenians and Spartans were compelled (*anankasai*) to war. However, both Pericles and Thucydides provoke questions. For Pericles, war is necessary when cities confront the alternatives of subjection or prevailing; running risks is necessitated by the starkness of the alternative. Yet in his first speech, running risks is valorized as the source of "the greatest honors (*megistai timai*) for both cities and individuals" (1.144). Submitting to Lacedaemonian demands is dishonorable slavery for a regime of Athens' stature (1. 141). Consequently, the meaning of compulsion (*anankē*) becomes a question within Thucydides' narrative and his own judgment about the war's necessity is not settled.

The Athenians' speech at Sparta in Book 1 (1.73–78) traces the creation of their empire to necessity, the three compelling (*katēnankasthēmen*) or conquering (*nikēthentes*) forces of fear, honor, and interest. Thucydides' representation of this claim, both within the speech and across the narratives that follow, raises questions about its validity. The speech is intended (1.72) to show Athens' power (*dunamis*), deterring hasty Spartan reactions to warnings about a growing Athenian threat. Yet the Athenians' confidence in their power's ability to restrain may ignore its propensity to distress, making war more, not less, likely. In the broader context of the narrative, Athenian greatness and Spartan fear are identified (1.23) as the truest *prophaseis* of the war, where *prophasis* means neither scientific cause nor cosmetic pretext, but perhaps Hobbes's "true quarrel." By explicitly referencing regime characteristics, Thucydides suggests that *ananke* can be interpreted not as a sequence dictated by inexorable laws but as a controversial thesis (Orwin 1994, 64) made within and across regimes. The allegedly conquering forces are variably ordered (1.75–6); a second statement gives primacy not to fear but to honor, implying different perceptions of necessity and shifting priorities for practice. If fear dominates, then reputation is valued principally as deterrence. If honor prevails, then the greatest fear may be loss of reputation.

Yet the Athenians also say that they deserve their empire because of their decisive role against the Persians (1.75). The city is especially worthy of praise (*epaineisthai te axioi*) because it treats its subject cities more equally and more justly (*dikaioteroi*) than its superior military power requires (1.76–7). This justice is not Thrasymachus' advantage of the stronger (*Republic* 337 c), but works to the advantage of the weaker. Complications nonetheless persist. Claims to distinctive merit fit uneasily with exonerations conferred by necessity. By representing their regard for equality as discretionary, the speakers give the generosity of the powerful literal pride of place. Yet the speech also implies a countervailing dynamic between power and justice. While Athens' justice is enabled by its power, this same justice can criticize power in the name of an equality beyond balances of power. The outcomes of such criticism cannot be presumed, of course; influences of fear, honor, and interest persist. Yet the possibility of judgment attentive to a justice not dictated by power acknowledges the potential integrity of *logos*. For such a *logos*, "realism," including the later (5.89) Athenian claim that justice holds only when material powers are balanced, is a discourse to be interrogated.

Logos is thematized politically in Book 3 by Diodotus, as he argues for the prudently humane treatment of Mytilene, whose defeated rebellion has prompted Athenian outrage (3. 35). He defends speech (*logos*) and deliberation (*bouleusis*) against the accusations of Cleon, the architect of a previous decision to execute the Mytilenean men and enslave the women and children (3.37–8). *Logos* is presented as the resource of the good citizen (*agathos polites*) who encourages wise decisions, not "by intimidating one's opponents but by a speaking (*legonta*) on equal terms (*apo tou isou*) that makes the better [course] apparent" (3.42). Yes, Diodotus indicts practices of the Assembly that block good citizenship. To be successful in the current climate, any proposal, whatever its character, must "lie to gain trust (*pseusamenon piston genesthai*)" (3.43). One consequence of this admission is that we should not take Diodotus' claim that moderation toward Mytilene is only a matter of expedience as his last word (Orwin 1994, 151–53; Saxonhouse 2006, 160–3; Mara 2008, 58–59). The crucial point, though, is that Diodotus identifies the persuasive work of the good citizen as the standard by which Athenian political practices should be judged.

The importance of *logos* allows political comparisons. While the debate over Mytilene (3. 36–50) is highly flawed, its *logoi* matter. This Athenian debate contrasts sharply with the longer antilogy before the Spartan judges deciding the fate of defeated Plataea, an episode that follows closely in Book 3 (3. 52–68). Though the desperate Plataeans and accusing Thebans speak at great length, Thucydides' final comment is that the outcome, fatal to Plataea, was settled in advance. "[I]t was almost entirely because of Thebans that the Lacedaemonians came to turn against the Plataeans, thinking that the Thebans were useful to them in the war that was now beginning" (3.68; Mara 2009, 121; Nichols 2015, 73–74). To the extent that Athens supports a serious, though always fragile, attention to *logos*, it is closer than Sparta to a community that Diodotus—and Socrates—might identify as political.

The place of *logos* plays a critical role within Thucydides' comments on Pericles' leadership (2.65). "[W]henever he perceived that [the Athenians] were arrogantly confident in any way . . . he shocked them into a state of fear by his speaking, and again, when they were unreasonably afraid, he restored them to confidence." Pericles' Funeral Oration prizes Athenian *logos*, as instructing, not impeding, action (2.40). This implicitly distinguishes Athens from Archidamus' (1.80–85) Sparta, where shame (*aischunē*) and deference (*aidōs*) fostered by harsh education ensure subordination to the laws (1.84; Balot 2014, 207–9). Eventually, however, Pericles' rhetoric also subordinates *logos*, not to deferential *aidōs*, but to energetic *ergon*. Athens needs no Homer because the city's actions, leaving remembrances of harm and good everywhere (2.41), speak for themselves. Athens' standing as an "education to Greece" (*paideusin tēs Hellados*) is "not boastful speaking (*logon*) for the occasion but the factual truth (*ergōn alētheia*) [as] shown by the power (*dunamis*) of the city." However, this appeal to factual dynamism needs its own rhetoric to succeed. Pericles may imply that Athens has replaced Homer as Greece's educator, but its memory may persist through the enduring *logos* of Thucydides.

Within the Thucydidean *logos*, Pericles' political speaking and leadership depart from the discursive practices of the good citizen as presented by Diodotus. In all of his direct speeches, Pericles attempts to silence views of the human good different from his own. Those offering alternatives are dismissed as do-nothings (2.64) who, when thought of at all, are considered useless (2.40). While explicitly complimenting Athens' *logos*, Pericles' speaking is performatively non-discursive; Thucydides does not pair his speeches with any others. Under Pericles' influence, what was in name a democracy was "in fact the rule by the first man (*archē tou prōtou andros*)" (2.65). His success in taming and encouraging the city as first man is troublingly followed by a political failure caused by the machinations of would-be successors, who "strove each to become first (*oregomenoi tou prōtos hekastos gignesthai*) [and] resorted to handing over the city's affairs to the pleasure of the *dēmos*." Though this behavior is generally consistent with Athens' competitive political culture, the status of Pericles and the destructive ambition of those following are expressly connected by the adjacent references to first positioning, contrasting dramatically with the civic practice endorsed by Diodotus.

Even at its best, however, *logos* is vulnerable. In 4.108 Thucydides comments on how rationality can be obscured by passion or ambition when he traces how the revolt against Athens, inspired by the Spartan Brasidas' successes in Chalkidice, spread across the peninsular cities. "[They] secretly sent proposals to [Brasidas] . . . . each wanting to start the first revolt. It seemed to them they could do so with impunity, a mistake about Athenian power as great as the obviousness of that power later on, but their judgments were based on vague wishes not on clear foresight, according to the human habit of giving desire over to thoughtless hope, while using sovereign reason (*logismōi autokratori*) to dismiss anything unattractive" (4.108). Here, the sovereignty of *logos* can only be ironic, for it is not a resource for critical judgment, but a ruling power sweeping judgment aside.

Finally, even the most well-intentioned political *logos* may eventually do harm. Commentators (Johnson 1993, 107–110; White 1984, 75) note that Diodotus' advising Athens to consider only its advantage in deciding about Mytilene returns within the harsh ultimatum delivered to Melos. Absent a Thucydidean narrative of the Assembly's debate, we cannot connect its brutal disposition of Melos directly to the words of the envoys (Zumbrunnen 2008, 104–5). Still, this disquieting linkage points to the unpredictability of politics. What rescues in one context executes in another. Once embedded in politics, *logos* can neither escape its hazards nor control its uncertainties. In spite of its limitations, however, *logos* as interpreted by Diodotus remains the best resource for the citizen confronting political contingencies (Mara 2015). The pragmatic character of Thucydides' book may lie in its aspiration to instruct under conditions of uncertainty.

Building on this reading of Thucydides, we can revisit Socrates' narrative of war's origin (*genesis*) in *Republic* 2. His first city in speech (*logō*) is of "the most extreme necessity" (*anankaiotatē*—369 d) meeting only basic needs. At Glaucon's insistence, Socrates adds adornments making the city luxurious (*truphōsan*). Conflicts begin. Because its territory is no longer adequate, "we must [now] cut off a piece of our neighbor's land, if we are going to have enough for grazing and growing, and they in turn from ours, if they give in to the acquisition of money, overstepping the boundary of the necessary" (373 d). While different motivations allegedly drive the needy city and its avaricious neighbor, the comparison itself emerges within a regime already grown luxurious. Calling its competitor's motivations aggressive and its own necessary may describe the same phenomenon from two different perspectives. Notably, this account of the genesis of war does not include a Periclean promise of renown. In contrastive parallel to Pericles' first speech (1.144), Socrates comments, "Let's not yet say whether war works evil or good . . . but only this much, that we have in turn found the origin of war—in those things whose presence in cities most of all produces evils both private and public (*idea kai dēmousia kaka gignetai*)" (373 e). In the categories of Thucydides' Athenians, Socrates traces war to interest and fear but is silent about honor.

The story of war's origin is followed by the introduction of a philosophy that is philosophically unrecognizable. If wars must be fought, then the regime requires a class of specialized warriors qualified by both strength and spiritedness (*thumos*). By recognizing *thumos*, Socrates introduces the psychic home for a love of honor (581 a) that can be both useful and destructive. "[W]ith such natures how will [the warriors] not be savage to one another and the other citizens?" (375 b.) In order to target their hostility only on outsiders, Socrates proposes that the warriors be made philosophical, led to "define one's own and the other by intelligence (*sunesei*) and ignorance (*agnoia*)" (376 b). Constructed by familiarity, this philosophy cannot turn a critical eye within; its presumptive justice is the discredited "helping friends and harming enemies" (334c–335 a). Yet by calling this orientation *philosophia*, the love of wisdom, not the love of the city, Socrates points to other possibilities. Intelligence may be enlisted for the advancement and justification of one's own but it also may be self-critical and open to the other.

This second possibility arises with the recast philosophy of Book 5 whose philosophers love learning of all sorts. "[O]ne who is willing to taste every sort of learning ... and is insatiable we shall justly (*en dikē*) say is a philosopher" (475 c). By noting that this philosophy is present by coincidence, Socrates acknowledges contingency, so while this regime might fight moderately, wars will not vanish. In response, this philosophical city employs resources that its premise mistrusts, reintroducing a drive toward honor tied to *erōs*. Erotic rewards are promised to "the man who has been best and earned good repute" so that he will "be more eager (*prothumoteros*) to win the rewards of valor" (468 b–c). Here, the love of honor is motivational tool, not consummate goal. Yet as the narrative progresses, the erotic love of honor does not remain auxiliary. Socrates' tragic point of reference is Ajax (468 d), the hero driven insane by a destructive need for recognition. This regime's philosophy carries no assurances against abuse or pathology as long as wars are engaged, however just or necessary they might be. As Jill Frank notes (2005, 454; though see Pritchard 2010, 20), Socrates' attempts to soften the waging of wars in Book 5 recall traditional restraints that were, at the time of the dialogue's performance, already being shattered by the Peloponnesian War. The inability of philosophy to control *erōs* is eventually confirmed by the emergence of a faction that disintegrates the apparently perfect polis (546 a ff)

One reason for this failure is that the philosophy introduced in Book 5 is deeply flawed. As others have noted, its pretenses to closure are exposed as hopeless and dangerous, especially when compared with the aporetic philosophy of Socrates (Frank 2007; Roochnik 2009; Mara 1997; Nichols 1987; Weiss 2012; Zuckert 2009). The flaws intensify as the training of philosophers becomes the overarching purpose of this city. Yet the drama of the *Republic* suggests that no coincidence of political power with philosophy, however corrected, can eliminate the persistence of war and its threatening implications. Philosophy's vulnerability to violence is reinforced by reminders of Athens' turbulent politics in Books 8 and 9, returning to Thucydidean themes, if not immediately to the Thucydidean narrative. The futures of the interlocutors signal the Thirty's harsh control of the city following the defeat. Though Thucydides' book ends prior to these events, there is some justification for seeing, as Simon Hornblower (2008, 850) does, the "seed" of a judgment on the Thirty sown in Thucydides' account of the violence of the Four Hundred (in 411) and his comments on oligarchy generally (8.66, 68, 89). Plato may go further historically and anticipate the democratic removal of the Thirty, perhaps represented in Book 8's account of democracy's victory over oligarchy (556 d–557 a). Within the continuing narrative, however, victory is unstable. The disorder of the democratic man parallels the deterioration of a city under conditions of *stasis* where *logos* or language is perverted by uncontrolled ambition. Tyranny reemerges from democracy's "extreme freedom" (*akrotatēs eleutherias*—564 a). The hypothetical tyrant's political success story parallels some events in the early career of the historical tyrant Pisistratus (*Republic* 566 a–b; Aristotle, *Athēnaiōn Politeia*, 14). In hinting at these connections, Socrates not only challenges democratic triumphalism but also rejects the prospect of any end of history. Political time horizons now seem fluid and contestable, paralleling Thucydides' complex narrative arcs (Mara 2009). By acknowledging a lingering Pisistratid or tyrannical narrative in Athens, Socrates might be read as critically engaging the democratic fear sketched in Thucydides' Book 6. Instead, however, he advises Glaucon to construct a regime within himself (592 b), refocusing on soul, not city.

However, any sense that self-construction can avoid politics is challenged in a concluding myth that represents what Socrates calls "the whole risk for a human being (*ho pas kindunos anthrōpō*)" (618 b), the ongoing need for pragmatic choice amidst a welter of contingencies. Risk is not an opportunity to achieve a name that will persist eternally but an anxiety surrounding the ongoing need to examine one's life, not escaping time, but always recurring in times, not decisive, once and for all, but uncertain, again and again. The indeterminacy of such choices is reinforced in Socrates' final, ironic exhortation to his conversation partners. "[I]f we are persuaded by me . . . we shall practice justice with prudence. . . . And here and in the thousand year journey that we have described we shall do well (*eu prattōmen*)" (621 c–d). The immediate interlocutors and witnesses will not unambiguously "do well." That the *Republic* occurs in the midst of a war destined to be lost, followed by a tyranny with murders close to home is a dramatic reminder of dark risk, continuing across times and spaces. The ending of the dialogue may be as inconclusive—or as textually arbitrary—as that of Thucydides' book, prompting us to consider whether the Thucydidean ending is circumstantially accidental or authorially chosen.

Different Texts in a Shared World

Beyond existing in common historical space (Ober 1998), Thucydides' and Plato's texts share an intellectual space where they might interrogate and instruct both one another and their readers. Guided by Hunter Rawlings and Jeffrey Rusten (Romilly 2012, ix), we can interpret Thucydides' "possession forever," *ktēma te es aiei*, not as a conclusive last word, but as a resource to be listened to repeatedly. Listening to this book means speaking about it within attempts to uncover what things are *axiologōtaton* and why, implying readjusted interpretations and indefinite receptions. In offering his *logos* of a war thus worthy, Thucydides presents its *logoi* and *erga* so that they may be listened to and spoken about reflectively, pointing to the educational condition of a certain kind of peace.

By recalling and reconstructing Thucydidean themes, the *Republic* dramatizes a kind of conversation able to take Thucydides' book seriously. Socrates' revisions of the Corcyrean and Periclean narratives are themselves provisional and incomplete, not least because they invite Thucydides' involvement as interlocutor. The broader historical and cultural inscriptions of the dialogue remind us that no such conversations can avoid dangers and abuses, occurring, as they do and will, amidst the interested agendas and passionate attachments of individuals and regimes. Consequently, both texts presume that their readers occupy a space of anxious leisure. Without anxiety there would be no good reason to turn our attention, one way of describing *theōria*, toward the deeply disturbing images of Corcyra, Melos, Sicily, and Mycalessus. Absent a leisure capable of resisting both charming distractions (the *Republic*'s promised torch race on horseback, eventually forgotten, 328 a) and paralyzing terrors (devastating war and violent tyranny, eventually inescapable), we are driven to dismiss attempts at *theōria* as luxuries or denials.

These pragmatic features of the texts have epistemic consequences for political theory. By representing ways in which politically situated human beings attempt to make sense of and to respond to their circumstances within dialogic spaces located between peace and war, Thucydides and Plato validate a conversation that should not be limited by either abstract (and pretended) serenity or immediate (and overwhelming) disruption. We can therefore deepen and correct Nietzsche's judgments about both authors. In exhorting his listeners to "practice justice with prudence in every way" Socrates does not preach the lessons of what Geuss (2005, 230) calls a hypermoralized philosophy but pragmatically responds to "the whole risk for a human being." And in attempting to provide a work to be heard and spoken about again and again, Thucydides does not face harshness resolutely without offering a potential resource for gentling it. Notably, Diodotus' image of the seemingly inevitable destructiveness of *prothumia* is articulated as a part of his offering *euboulia*, political good counsel. As different as they surely are, both authors validate the Socratic insight offered at the end of the *Protagoras* (361 c–d) and thus at the very brink of a devastating war. Courage within turbulence is another description of philosophy.

References

Balot, Ryan. 2014. *Courage in the Democratic Polis*. Oxford: Oxford University Press.
Benardete, Seth. 1991. *The Rhetoric of Morality and Philosophy*. Chicago: University of Chicago Press.
Bloom, Allan, trans. 1968. *The Republic of Plato*. New York: Basic Books.
Brownson, C. L., trans. 1918. *Hellenica*, by Xenophon. Cambridge: Harvard University Press.
Connor, W. Robert. 1984. *Thucydides*. Princeton: Princeton University Press.
Crane, Gregory. 1998. *The Ancient Simplicity*. Berkeley: University of California Press.
Frank, Jill. 2005. *A Democracy of Distinction: Aristotle and the Work of Politics*. Chicago: University of Chicago Press.
Frank, Jill. 2007. "Wages of War: Judgment in Plato's Republic." *Political Theory* 35: 443–67.
Geuss, Raymond. 2005. *Outside Ethics*. Princeton: Princeton University Press.
Gomme, A. W., A. Andrewes, and K. J. Dover. 1945-1981. *A Historical Commentary on Thucydides*. Vols. I-V. Oxford: Clarendon Press.
Hobbes, Thomas. 1994. *Leviathan*, edited with an introduction by E. M. Curley. Indianapolis: Hackett.
Hornblower, Simon. 2008. *A Commentary on Thucydides*. Vol. III, *Books 5.25–8.109*. Oxford: Clarendon.

Johnson, Laurie. 1993. *Thucydides, Hobbes and the Interpretation of Realism*. DeKalb: Northern Illinois University Press.

Kagan, Donald. 2009. *Thucydides: The Reinvention of History*. New York: Penguin.

Kochin, Michael. 1999. "War, Class and Justice in Plato's *Republic*." *Review of Metaphysics* 53: 403–23.

Lattimore, Steven, trans. 1998. *Thucydides: The Peloponnesian War*. Indianapolis: Hackett.

Mara, Gerald. 1997. *Socrates' Discursive Democracy*. Albany: State University of New York Press.

Mara, Gerald. 2008. *The Civic Conversations of Thucydides and Plato*. Albany: State University of New York Press.

Mara, Gerald. 2009. "Thucydides and Political Thought." In *The Cambridge Companion to Ancient Greek Political Thought*, edited by Stephen Salkever, 96–125. Cambridge and New York: Cambridge University Press.

Mara, Gerald. 2015. "Thucydides and the Problem of Citizenship." In *A Handbook to the Reception of Thucydides*, edited by Christine Ming-Whey Lee and Neville Morley, 313–31. Malden: Wiley-Blackwell.

Mynott, Jeremy, trans. 2013. *The War of the Peloponnesians and the Athenians*. Cambridge and New York: Cambridge University Press.

Nails, Debra. 2002. *The People of Plato*. Indianapolis: Hackett.

Nichols, Mary. 1987. *Socrates and the Political Community*. Albany: State University of New York Press.

Nichols, Mary. 2015. *Thucydides and the Pursuit of Freedom*. Ithaca: Cornell University Press.

Nietzsche, Friedrich. 1954. "What I Owe to the Ancients," *Twilight of the Idols*. In *The Portable Nietzsche*, translated by Walter Kaufmann, 556–63. New York: Viking.

Ober, Josiah. 1998. *Political Dissent in Democratic Athens*. Princeton: Princeton University Press.

Orwin, Clifford. 1994. *The Humanity of Thucydides*. Princeton: Princeton University Press.

Price, Jonathan. 2001. *Thucydides and Internal War*. Cambridge: Cambridge University Press.

Pritchard, David. 2010. "The Symbiosis between Democracy and War." In *War, Democracy and Culture in Classical Athens*, edited by David Pritchard, 1–62. Cambridge and New York. Cambridge University Press.

Reeve, C. D. C. 1988. *Philosopher Kings*. Princeton: Princeton University Press.

Romilly, Jacqueline de. 1963. *Thucydides and Athenian Imperialism*. Translated by Philip Thody. Oxford: Blackwell.

Romilly, Jacqueline de. 2012. *The Mind of Thucydides*. Translated by Elizabeth Trapnell Rawlings; edited with an Introduction by Hunter R. Rawlings III and Jeffrey S. Rusten. Ithaca: Cornell University Press.

Roochnik, David. 2009. "The Political Drama of Plato's *Republic*." In *The Cambridge Companion to Ancient Greek Political Thought*, edited by Stephen Salkever, 156–77. Cambridge and New York: Cambridge University Press.

Saxonhouse, Arlene. 2006. *Free Speech and Democracy in Ancient Athens*. Cambridge and New York: Cambridge University Press.

Schlatter, Richard, ed. 1975. *Hobbes's Thucydides*. New Brunswick: Rutgers University Press.

Schmitt, Carl. 2007. *The Concept of the Political*. Translated by George Schwab with a Foreword by Tracy B. Strong. Chicago: University of Chicago Press.

Smith, Charles Forster, trans. 1962–1988. *Thucydides*. 4 vols. Cambridge: Harvard University Press.

Weiss, Roslyn. 2006. *The Socratic Paradox and Its Enemies*. Chicago: University of Chicago Press.
Weiss, Roslyn. 2012. *Philosophers in Plato's Republic*. Ithaca: Cornell University Press.
White, James Boyd. 1984. *When Words Lose Their Meaning*. Chicago: University of Chicago Press.
Zuckert, Catherine. 2009. *Plato's Philosophers*. Chicago: University of Chicago Press.
Zumbrunnen, John. 2008. *The Silence of Democracy: Athenian Politics in Thucydides' History*. University Park: Pennsylvania State University Press.

SECTION IV

CONTEXTS AND ANCIENT RECEPTION OF THUCYDIDEAN HISTORIOGRAPHY

CHAPTER 32

THUCYDIDES' PREDECESSORS AND CONTEMPORARIES IN HISTORICAL POETRY AND PROSE

LEONE PORCIANI

IN the days of Herodotus and Thucydides, the Greeks were well aware that the past could be nothing more than a world of words. In a digression in the fifth book of his *Histories* Herodotus recounts certain events that took place in Magna Graecia at the end of the sixth century BCE: excluded from the dynastic succession, Dorieus, one of the sons of Anaxandridas, king of Sparta, leaves his homeland and embarks on a series of peregrinations that take him from Africa to Sicily, where the oracle of Delphi had authorized him to found a colony. He thus sets out "toward Italy" (Hdt. 5.43), an obvious direction for someone traveling to Sicily from the Peloponnesus. And here the historian's tale takes two separate paths, following the versions of the inhabitants of both Sybaris and Croton. According to the former, Dorieus and his Spartan companions collaborated with Croton in the expedition against Sybaris; the latter, however, maintain that no foreigner, except the Elean soothsayer Callias, helped them (5.44). What follows is an exposition of the supporting evidence of the two differing versions (*marturia ... apodeiknuousi tade*): the Sybarites cite an extra-urban sanctuary near the Crathis River, dedicated to Athena, which they claim was founded by Dorieus himself, and as ultimate proof (*marturion megiston*) they adduce the unfortunate end that he later met in Sicily: apparently he paid rather dearly for the lack of observance of the Delphic Oracle that he demonstrated by not going immediately to his destination, but instead allowing himself a "distraction" on the Ionian coast (5.45.1). The Crotoniates, on the other hand, point out (*apodeiknusi*) that many valuable lands were given to Callias of Elis—the soothsayer's descendants were still in possession of them during Herodotus' time—while nothing of the sort can be attributed to Dorieus or his family: Dorieus, therefore, did not help Croton. "Each side advances these attestations (*marturia apophainontai*); and it is possible to subscribe to the version one would like to believe," concludes Herodotus in his sovereign wisdom (5.45.2).

These chapters of the fifth book of the *Histories* are an exceptional testimony to the workings of social memory in fifth-century BCE Greece. Through Herodotus' exposition we witness the unfolding of a veritable dialectic *agon* around a historical problem, the participation of a Spartan in the war between two Achaean cities in 511/0 BCE. The communities defend differing points of view: the Crotoniates respond de facto to the Sybarites, whose accusation is dismantled with proofs of an almost cadastral nature. Something escapes us, and we cannot fully understand why it is so important for Croton to eliminate suspicion of collaboration with Dorieus and his men (this was perhaps part of an attempt to "obliterate" Dorieus, who may have been expelled by the Crotoniates and prevented from founding his colony on the site of Sybaris: Pugliese Carratelli 1976, 374); but we can clearly see the evolution of the discussion and the argumentative techniques that are employed. The concept of *marturion*, "proof," is pervasive, as is the act of "showing" and "demonstrating" (*apodeiknumi*), which indicates passion for a documented argument, founded on the concreteness of things that are still visible decades later, such as a sanctuary and land lots belonging to a family. We also get a glimpse of the vehicles of local tradition and the environments in which they thrived for so long: a sanctuary, that of Athena Crathia, and a family of *manteis*. As is often the case in Ancient Greece, administration of the sacred and familiarity with the past appear to go hand in hand.

In this chapter we shall try to observe the classical landscape of historical memory through the very eyes of Thucydides. In the complex topography that comes into sight, different forms of oral memory alternate, as we shall see, with early attempts to apply writing to the description of the past. Every element of the fifth-century memory landscape (Herodotus, oral history, local historians, poetry, *epitaphios logos*) played a precise role in forging Thucydides' view and practice of history, and forced him to find his place, take a stand against other genres, and discover new ways of composing a work of prose about human events.

The Perspective on Herodotus and Oral Traditions

The historian Thucydides wrote during the last thirty years of the fifth century BCE, starting not much later than Herodotus, and was immersed in the same world of tales and events. He undoubtedly preferred the events, the facts of his own time, but on occasion he was called on to confront the traditions of a distant past. After having laid out a framework for archaic history—the *archaiologia*—which demanded a great reconstructive effort on his part, Thucydides observes that "people indiscriminately hand down the oral traditions on past events, even when they are those of their own region" (1.20.1).

And he uses a trenchant example, due to the relevance of the city in question: in Athens most people (*to plēthos*) believe that Hipparchus, one of the sons of Pisistratus, was in power as a tyrant himself when killed by Harmodius and Aristogiton. But the tyrant was not Hipparchus, but rather his elder brother, Hippias (1.20.2). In this way, an essential part of the historical conscience of the Athenians is called into question: so strong was their reverence for this supposed act of tyrannicide that they commissioned a commemorative statue group from Antenor and erected it in the *agora*. And when the first sculptures were carried away by the Persians, a new set by the hands of Critius and Nesiotes took their place.

For Thucydides, the verbal realm of politically oriented and local knowledge is a place of confusion and error, just as the oral testimonies of the contemporary war (*ho polemos houtos*, object of his historiographical reflection from 1.21.2 forward) are undermined by contradictions (1.22.3). According to the historian, not only the Athenians, but also "the other Greeks" (1.20.3) are susceptible to false beliefs. To support this judgment, he relates two details: the first regards the presumed right of the kings of Sparta to two votes (in the *gerousia*), the other the existence of a "company of Pitane," one of the districts that constituted the community of Sparta (*ōbai*). These examples of "errors" evoke a Peloponnesian context: traditions, therefore, belonging to "other Greeks" in regard to those of Athens. But local traditions are only one of Thucydides' targets. It is often noted that the same two historical details are found in Herodotus' text (cf. e.g. Hornblower, *Comm. on Thuc.*, i. 57–58; Corcella [2006, 49]; a cautious Asheri in Asheri, Corcella, and Vannicelli [2006, 246]): indeed, in Hdt. 6.57.4 we read that when the kings do not participate in the meetings of the elders (*gerontes*), their closest relatives enjoy their prerogatives, or *gerea*, as kings and are allowed two votes (apiece: most likely each of the two kings' next of kin, cf. Stein [1893–1908, iii. 163]; in the text, the equivalence "*gerea* = two votes apiece" is clear); in 9.53 we find the story of Amompharetus, commander of the company of Pitane, in tactical disagreement with the Spartan commander Pausanias. Herodotus, whom Thucydides never mentions by name, seems to be the focus of his attention: he speaks of errors in the oral tradition, but he is also implicitly referring to the historical text that contains those falsehoods. The striking conciseness of his reference to the kings' votes, which makes more sense if the allusion is to a written text, is one indication of this. But above all, the entire context is Herodotean (Herodotus, too, speaks of Hipparchus, "brother of the tyrant Hippias" and of the tyrannicide incident in 5.55 and in 6.123, this time without "error"), and Thucydides' famous comment on "the investigation of truth" (*zētēsis tēs alētheias*) that is "taken lightly" (*atalaipōros*) and on the many who accept "that which is readily available" (*ta hetoima*, 1.20.3) can not but have specifically historiographical resonance and allude to a predecessor; a predecessor whose name is as avoided by Thucydides as it is obsessively present in his considerations on history (on other features in which a response to Herodotus is apparent, see Stadter [2012]; on occasion, the relationship between the two may perhaps be reversed: Hornblower [2011, 277–85]).

Thus, the oral traditions on the one hand, and Herodotus on the other, are almost placed on the same level, and they stand out as fundamental presences on Thucydides' horizon. They are the first predecessors and contemporaries of Thucydides whom we meet: anonymous depositories of news and stories (the level of passive oral history, which in its simplest form is the widely diffused knowledge of events of varying degrees of importance that regard a community's past, as the local memories of resistance to Nazi fascism can be in Europe today), or active processors of traditions (forged or distorted with the aim of political bias, for example). And then a specific name, the Greek from Asia who shortly before Thucydides began to put into writing his ethnographic *logoi* and the history of the Persian wars. Ancient biographical tradition has created a brilliant snapshot of the relationship between Herodotus and Thucydides: while attending a performance by the elder historian, Thucydides was purportedly moved to tears by his stories, and upon seeing those tears, Herodotus remarked on the young man's thirst for knowledge (Marcellin., *vit. Thuc.*, 54). The story is of course apocryphal, but the link between the two historians and their respective views was very close. Herodotus is ever-present in the chapters on methodological reflection in Thucydides' Book 1: he is certainly behind Chapter 23, on the battles and horrors of war, in which the constant comparison is between Thucydides' subject—the Peloponnesian war—and the Persian wars; he is also, naturally (for all cf. Hornblower, *Comm. on Thuc.*, i. 61), the main target of 1.22.4, where the "contest essay intended for an ephemeral listening," in contrast to the "everlasting possession," is usually and rightfully considered a polemic reference to the Herodotean *Histories*. Finally, he is very present, as a foil, in the structure of Thucydides' first book: the *archaiologia* is a general outline of the most ancient Greek history up until the Persian wars, or better, a study of the levels of military and economic power achieved in the past (1.1.3–18.2). This introduction is innovative, moreover, with respect to Herodotus, due to its focus on "that which today is called Greece" (1.2.1; in Herodotus, on the other hand, archaism endures on a largely Mediterranean scale, or in relation to profiles of large, individual *poleis*). The *etē pentēkonta malista* or, less appropriately, *pentēkontaetia* (Thuc. 1.89–118.2: a development of 1.18.2–19) examine the phases of the Athenian empire and the tensions between Athens and Sparta in the roughly fifty years between Xerxes' withdrawal and the outbreak of the Peloponnesian war, and are clearly the narrative link between the end of Herodotus' *Histories* and the beginning of Thucydides: that is, they represent a *supplementum Herodoti*. Thucydides' operation therefore consists in building the structure of Greek history—the same one, *mutatis mutandis*, that we still conceive as such—upon the cornerstone of what for us are Books 5–9 of Herodotus (Ionian revolt and Persian wars: chronologically, the first twenty years of the fifth century). From this foundation of Greek history, Thucydides casts his gaze backward (*archaiologia*) and forward (*etē pentēkonta malista* and Peloponnesian war), and from this approach derive, among other things, the metaphors "to look" (*skopein*) and the consequent "to find" (*heuriskein*), characteristic of Thucydides' lexicon from the very first lines of the *Histories* (1.1.3; see De Vido and Mondin [2015] and Gengler [2015], with an excellent discussion of other views on *heuriskein* in Thucydides).

Inside and Outside the Genre: Hellanicus, Antiochus

From "The Perspective on Herodotus and Oral Traditions" above we draw a significant conclusion: with Thucydides following in Herodotus' footsteps, we see the formation of a true historical genre that focuses on Panhellenic history, recent or contemporary (the one preferred by the "good" historians: Momigliano [1978, 5]; cf. Momigliano [1977]), and is characterized by consecutive narrative blocks, to which successors would add their contributions. This can be called the main line of ancient historiography. Drawing on all of the implications of Herodotus' innovation with regard to genealogies, Thucydides establishes a canon of rules. The borders of the new historiographical genre are now defined, and it is also clear who is left out: they are the regional and local historians, such as Hellanicus, inasmuch as he was the author of the *Atthis*, the first local history of *Attica*, which was finished after 407/6 (events of this year were treated in detail, judging by two fragments: *FGrH* 323a FF 25–26; perhaps the work ended with the epoch-marking year 404/3). Unlike Herodotus, Hellanicus has the privilege of being specifically mentioned by Thucydides, who in 1.97.2 states that he is devoting a digression to the period between the end of the Persian wars and the beginning of the war because it is a "field" or "territory abandoned" by all of his predecessors (*tois pro emou hapasin eklipes . . . chōrion*), who wrote about "either Greek history prior to the Persian wars or the Persian wars themselves." Here the predecessors in question are Herodotus and probably authors such as Hecataeus, who in his *Genealogies* (around 490 BCE), a prose elaboration of the epic's subject matter, dealt with a long-distant past, but still a form of "Greek history" (perhaps Charon of Lampsacus as well, if we allow an early chronology for this author: see Porciani [2001, 33 and n. 67, 61–63]; for the *Persica*, in addition to Herodotus, we can cite Dionysius of Miletus and Hellanicus; for later writings about Persia, see Stevenson [1997]). And he immediately adds: "and the one who even touched upon these events, Hellanicus in his work on Attica, mentioned them briefly and with little regard to chronological precision." This seems to be an addition that makes up for the shot taken in the preceding sentence, where it is asserted that no one prior to Thucydides had treated the fifty-year ascent of the Athenian empire; it is possible that he made this addition during the late stages of composition, while "bibliographically" updating, as it were, a passage that had in fact been written earlier, perhaps even much earlier (Ziegler [1929, 66n2]; Jacoby, *FGrH*, IIIb Suppl., i. 5–6; Dover, *HCT*, v. 410). But upon close examination, the text presents no real contradiction and lends itself easily to a different interpretation: Thucydides' predecessors are Herodotus and probably the genealogists, authors of *Hellenica*, or "Greek histories," with a different chronological focus; Hellanicus as author of the *Atthis*, on the other hand, is not a true predecessor, because he writes about *local*, not general, history. His "brevity" may also have been due to an insufficient framing of Athenian events in the overall context of inter-*poleis* relations, which itself could have been a consequence of the limited scope of the work. In brief, Thucydides *continues* Herodotus because he operates on the grand scale of historiography, while he *supersedes* a "local" Hellanicus (this very fitting formulation comes from Jacoby [1909, 100n2]; the historiographical genres of the Greeks "were constantly dependent upon change and innovation," as Marincola [1999, 320] has stated, but this must not be pressed in the sense that genres and subgenres did not exist at all, or did not significantly affect the historians' choices).

Hellanicus was a slightly older contemporary of Thucydides': an expert such as Apollodorus of Athens, in the Hellenistic age, estimated him to be sixty-five at the outbreak of the Peleponnesian war (*FGrH* 244 F 7b) and therefore put his birth at 496/5; but ostensibly this date should be lowered to c. 480—an ideal context for the attribution of a name deriving from *Hellanonikos* and evoking the "Greek victory"—unless one chooses to believe that Hellanicus was still busy writing *Atthis* at ninety years of age (on the problems with Apollodorus' chronology, cf. Porciani [2001, 135–38]). He was a prolific author, and the whole of his output can not be labeled "local history," a category that is nevertheless well-represented among his works (*Aiolica, Argolica, Peri Arkadias, Boiōtica, Lesbiaca,* and *Thettalica,* in addition to *Atthis*). Genealogical monographs (*Phōronis* and *Trōica,* among others) or ethnographies (on Persia, as already mentioned, as well as on Egypt and Scythia; his *Origins of Peoples and Cities* and *Barbarian Customs* must have shared an ethnographic nature) are also attributed to Hellanicus, but his most significant contribution to the historical culture of his time was the *Priestesses of Hera at Argos*. This latter work was an extensive chronicle covering at least three books that avails itself of the solid documentary anchoring provided by a list of the ancient temple priestesses, complete with the years during which each one held the position (*FGrH* 4 FF 74–84). For example, according to Hellanicus, the arrival of Sicelus and his Ausones in Sicily occurred "in the third generation before the Trojan war, during the 26th year of Alcyone, priestess at Argos" (*FGrH* 4 F 79b): the historian dated non-local events based on the chronological backbone provided by the succession of the Argive priestesses, in a Greece that, because it lacked political unity, also lacked any homogeneity in the calculation of time. Further, Hellanicus compiled a list of victors at the Carnea, an important Dorian festival (*Karneonikai*). The great openness of Hellanicus' horizon and especially the exceptional Panhellenic significance of the *Priestesses* explain why Thucydides, launching into the actual narration of his war in 2.2.1, gives the date of the Theban attack at Plataea as the year in which "Chrysis had been priestess at Argos for 48 years, Ainesias was ephor in Sparta and in Athens there were two [or four] months remaining in the arconship of Pythodorus." The dates with the eponymous magistrates of the large *poleis* involved in the conflict are preceded by an indication that is by all appearances purely ornamental, and would not merit a prominent position had Hellanicus—with his chronicle published after 421—not endowed the Argive priestesses with a fundamental chronological function (on the reference to Hellanicus see also Hornblower [2011, 144]). Thucydides therefore continues Herodotus, supersedes Hellanicus, inasmuch as author of the *Atthis*, but pays homage to the very same Hellanicus as the builder of a Panhellenic chronological structure. Historiographical genres count more than the personalities of the authors.

Some scholars maintain that Hellanicus appears elsewhere in the Thucydidean text as well. If we consider his numerous works on the Peloponnesus (*Karneonikai*, for instance, or of the genealogical works *Phorōnis*, which traced the great Peloponnesian lineages back to the Argolic hero Phorōneus, and, in part, *Trōica*) and the fragment on Pelops and the murder of his son Chrysippos (*FGrH* 4 F 157, cf. 155), it is easy to see why he is assumed to be the one to whom Thucydides particularly refers in 1.9.2, where he addresses the issue of the origin of Agamemnon's military power as leader of the Trojan campaign ("Hellanicus and other writers": Gomme, *HCT*, i. 109; Hornblower, *Comm. on Thuc.*, i. 32). Pelops, says Thucydides, was the first to acquire political strength because of the wealth he had brought with him from Asia: "those who through oral transmission have had the most trustworthy Peloponnesian traditions handed down to them by their predecessors." Thus the text is normally interpreted (*hoi ... mnēmēi para tōn proteron dedegmenoi*), where the word that should designate "oral transmission" is *mnēmē*. As early as 1452, Lorenzo Valla translated *qui exploratissime Peloponnensium gesta a maioribus natu sibi per manus tradita cognoverunt* (see Chambers [2008, 6]), from which no one has veered since. But in Greek the specific term for this concept is *akoē*. The word *mnēmē*, on the other hand, means "memory," as in an individual engaged in the act of remembering. And thus it is intended in this passage, which simply means "those who through memory have inherited the most trustworthy Peloponnesian traditions from their predecessors," or, more plainly, "have learned by heart from their predecessors" (full illustration in Porciani [2001, 117–24]). These are truly masters of local knowledge (*logioi andres*: Jacoby [1949, 50–51, 215–219, 389n.5, 391n10]; Evans [1991, 94–98], Porciani [2001, 117–24]), whose capacity for memory is socially recognisable because it is built on a chain of transmission ("from their predecessors": this is the most convincing definition of *hoi proteron*, meaning not "ancestors," "forefathers," or "ancients," but rather "those who came before them" in developing a discourse on the past or performing the same "formal" task). It is possible that Thucydides did not consult these *mnēmēi dedegmenoi* directly, but that he instead took the reference from Hellanicus or another author who had already cited them; in any case, the passage is extremely significant for its illustration of the key role that oral sources play in the workshop of the fifth-century BCE Greek historian. Indeed, they appear in the foreground even where the relationship with orality has presumably been mediated by a *logographos* (or "author of narrative/historical prose," a term used by Thucydides at 1.21.1; cf. *logopoios* in Hdt. 2.134.3, 2.143.1, 5.36.2, 5.125; *logos* has the meaning of "narrative" several times and, most memorably, in Herodotus' introduction: 1.5.3; the Thucydidean *logographoi* are not "orators," as Grethlein [2013, 127–28, with earlier bibliography], has proposed: the idea that, in the fifth century BCE, a word whose basic rhetorical sense is "speech-*writer*" could have designated the public speakers, beginning with those who pronounced the *epitaphioi logoi* at Athens, is not convincing).

If we examine the relationship with another contemporary of Thucydides', the historian Antiochus of Syracuse, we see a similar picture emerge. Thucydides does not name him, of course (the "privilege" of being cited is reserved for Hellanicus), but since Niebuhr (1847–1851, i. 309, from his Bonn courses 1826–1830) modern scholars have been convinced that the beginning of Thucydides' Book 6, the so-called Sicilian *archaiologia*, derives from Antiochus. Antiochus was the author of the nine-volume *Sicelica* (from the time of the Sicanian king Cocalus to the peace of Gela in 424: there is one remaining fragment, cited by Paus. 10.11.3: *FGrH* 555 F 1, on the colonization of Lipara) and of a *Peri Italiēs*—if they were indeed, as is commonly thought, two distinct works. The Sicilian *archaiologia* appears as a significant historical digression (Thuc. 6.2–5) that introduces one of the most important episodes of the Peloponnesian war: the great Sicilian Expedition undertaken by the Athenians during the years 415–413, which would prove to be a catastrophic defeat for Athens. The majority of Athenians, observes the historian, "had no concept of the size of the island, nor the number of its inhabitants, Greek and barbarian" (6.1.1); Sicily is separated from the continent by straits roughly the size of twenty stadia (6.1.2). The historical digression opens with a description of the earliest population of the island by barbarians (6.2) and Greeks (6.3–4). The latter is well known for providing the basis of our entire ancient Greek chronology (e.g., Murray 1993, 113) and begins with the news of the founding of Naxos (734 BCE) by settlers from Chalcis in Euboea, led by Thucles: they are the "first among the Greeks" to settle on the island, and even dedicate an altar to Apollo Archēgetēs (meaning "leader" and "founder" together), on which all *theōroi* departing from Sicily lay sacrifices (6.3.1; on the altar, see Malkin [2011, 101–7]). The following year Archias of Corinth founds Syracuse (6.3.2), after which the Chalcidians, once again, give birth to Leontinoi and Catane. The Megarians, for their part, face a complex sequence of events that leads them to found Megara Hyblaea on the coast between Catane and Syracuse (6.3.3–4), and so on.

This passage is unusual for Thucydides, not only because it deals with archaic history, but also because it does so by displaying a chronological precision that suggests the possibility of a written source. Antiochus is the most plausible name, though Hellanicus—preferred by Jacoby (1949, 352–53n2), still thought-provoking—cannot be excluded (and, as an alternative, may deserve further reflection). It is entirely possible that Thucydides decided to rely on a contemporary/predecessor when writing the history of a region and a chronological period that fell outside of his usual domain. Sicily was a region of complex status, being at once barbarian and Hellenized, and writing about its history in the fifth century BCE meant doing something halfway between ethnography and local history of Greek *poleis* and regions. Thucydides did not consider it a "field abandoned" as he did the *etē pentēkonta malista*; on the contrary, it had been well ploughed by Antiochus. But he decides to draw on his contemporary's work, very likely adding observations such as the ones on the poetic tradition found in 6.2.1; and in fact he supersedes Antiochus too, merging material from his investigation into a digression from the principal subject matter, which focuses on contemporary political facts: what in Antiochus was a specific object of inquiry, in Thucydides becomes accessory material. He reclassifies Antiochus' topic, placing it in a different framework. Thucydides would have most likely disagreed with Jacoby's assertion that Antiochus was a western Herodotus (e.g., 1949, 118: "he intended from the first to supplement Herodotos' work of universal history in regard to the West"). He viewed Antiochus, rather, as a regional historian and a useful source of eccentric knowledge.

The question of how this "local" writer worked is a matter that we cannot address here, but one that does merit attention because it ties into the chronological precision that characterizes the first pages of Book 6. If Thucydides did in fact use a *logographos* such as Antiochus, the meticulous calculation of the years between one founding and the other would certainly have been one of the things that struck him the most. How had Antiochus obtained these dates? By listening to the learned locals (*logioi tōn ekei katoichountōn*), like the Greeks or the Hellenized indigenous people who, according to a probable excerpt from Antiochus' *Peri Italiēs* (Jacoby, FGrH IIIb Komm., i. 611, 36–7; ii. 355n30), told tales of Italus and the origins of the toponym *Italia* (*phasi gar hoi logioi . . .*, FGrH 577 F 13; cf. the famous proem, 555 F 2, mentioning *archaioi logoi* whose nature, oral or written, is debated: Marincola [1997, 100n181])? Or perhaps we should take into account the possibility that Antiochus modified more fluid traditions: for example, by converting into years the generations typical of oral memory (Murray [2014, 454–57] refutes this hypothesis, but we cannot exclude it for the 245 years of Megara Hyblaea until the taking of the city by Gelon in 484/3—Thuc. 6.4.2—that were the equivalent of seven generations of thirty-five years each: a seemingly very similar case to the seven kings of Rome). The impression that the sanctuary of Apollo Archēgetēs, the divine *oikistēs* of Sicily, might have been the source for these colonial data is strong (Murray 1993, 113; 2014). However, the Thucydidean page on the Greeks who reach Sicily still bears traces of a sort of competition between local memories: the distance of barely a year between Naxos and Syracuse (6.3.2), or the clarification by the inhabitants of Catane on the name of the *oikistēs* (not Thucles as in Naxos and Leontinoi, but Euarchos, a speaking name that honors a "good beginning": 6.3.3), makes it evident that the text is an intersection of divergent versions, which must have been rooted in each city, in a framework of competition—at least among the most influential ones. Competitive recollection, a form of oral memory, can almost be seen backlit behind the written page.

Poetry, History, and the *Epitaphios Logos*

The theme of rivalry between local traditions, with which we began, reappears here, re-evoking the duel between Crotoniates and Sybarites over Dorieus. *Logographoi* and *poiētai*, the two categories that are critically addressed in 1.21.1, are only the tip of the iceberg of Greek memory. The orality that stirs under the surface, however, has undeniable connections, especially with poetry, or better yet, with the poetic genres, which in archaic times and well into the fifth century have a very strong oral dimension (not only regarding the diffusion, but also to a certain extent the composition of the text, given the connection with social institutions such as the symposium). In the fifth century CE, the rhetor Marcellinus explained that Thucydides had imitated Homer in the organization of his subject matter and Pindar in his high, obscure style (*vit. Thuc.*, 35). However, if we consider the way in which Thucydides himself—as was inevitable for any Greek author—regards Homer, it appears clear that the great epic poems do not constitute a model for him. The poet par excellence is not a true predecessor for Thucydides. He treats Homer as an oral witness of the most ancient times of Greece: some famous passages from the *archaiologia* in which he evokes Homer—the one on the inexistence of a unifying ethnic name for all Greeks (1.3.3–4) or the one in which the historian ruminates about the "greatness" of the Trojan war (1.10)—demonstrate this. Homer can offer clues (*tekmērioi*, 1.3.3), but he is under special observation precisely because he is a poet and therefore he tends to exaggerate, particularly with regard to the number of military forces on the field (1.10.3–5). An illustrious tradition of studies dealt with the relationship between epic and historiography (Jacoby [1913, 502–4]; Huber [1965]; Strasburger [1982]; Rutherford [2012]): it is in the epic, for example, that the narrative object is expressed through discourse and facts (*logoi, erga*); the *Odyssey* and the *Iliad* identify the main themes (the journey, war) that orient the great historiography (Herodotus 1–5 on the one hand, Herodotus 5–9 and Thucydides on the other); and these are the poems that inaugurate the Panhellenic perspective "consciously followed" by historians (Jacoby 1949, 199). What is most interesting, however, is that the conscience of a historian like Thucydides highlights the differences rather than the similarities, and in so doing delimitates the historiographical field, an act that cannot be ignored if one wishes to understand ancient historiography *iuxta propria principia*. Homer is fundamental for Thucydides, but he is a source of information, exactly as he is for historians today who study ancient trade and scrutinize epic poems in search of useful *tekmēria*.

His true predecessors, Hecataeus and Herodotus, are not named by Thucydides; this "honor" lies with those who represent genres and subgenres different from his own, namely, Homer and Hellanicus of the *Atthis* (they themselves being different from each other, but that is another matter). To name is to delimit. Thucydides lays the foundations of great historiography on the contemporary—Jacoby's *Zeitgeschichte*—digging a furrow that excludes both the narrative expertise of the epic singers and different approaches to writing history. The prose writers that we have had occasion to mention (Hecataeus, Herodotus, Hellanicus, Antiochus) are likely the only ones that Thucydides could have known, or nearly. We could add to the list a handful of others: two "old" genealogists (Acusilaus and Pherecydes); Dionysius of Miletus, author of *Persica*; perhaps Xanthus with his *Lydiaca*; and finally a very few writers of local history in a broad sense or in particular of *horoi*, "chronicles" (cf. Corcella [2006, 38–39]; on Ion's *Foundation of Chios*, datable to around the mid-fifth century BCE; see especially Porciani [2001, 32n63]). But that is the extent of Thucydides' historiographical horizon. Dionysius of Halicarnassus has left us a double list of Herodotus and Thucydides' predecessors in the treatise *De Thucydide*, 5, the result of erudite hypotheses that has been the subject of numerous recent analyses (for terms of the discussion, Porciani [2001, 13–63], and Fowler, *EGM* ii. 673–74). Whether Charon of Lampsacus, whom we have already encountered, had already published the *Prytaneis of the Lacedaemonians* when Thucydides wrote the text of 2.2.1, where he cites the ephor Ainesias, is very uncertain, all the more so because of the possibility that the work was, in fact, not about Sparta at all, but about Lampsacus (Fowler, *EGM* ii. 642).

The poets are a more complex matter, because of course there was not only Homer for Thucydides. According to Marcellinus' biography there was also Pindar, and today some learned and detailed studies interpret entire narrative sequences in Thucydides through the lens of the Pindaric epinikion: one example of this is Thucydides' recounting of the Great Sicilian Expedition of 415, found in Books 6 and 7, which according to Hornblower (2004, 327–53) corresponds to the Argonautic section in Pindar's *Pythic* 4. The "desire" for foreign lands that takes the young Athenians to Sicily (*pothos*, 6.24.3, a Thucydidean *hapax*) is parallel to the "desire" for the ship *Argō* that Hera instils in the heroes, in order to incite them to adventure (Pi. *Pyth.* 4.184–5); the agonistic lexicon (*agōn*, *agōnisma*), borrowed from epinician poetry, appears frequently in the second part of Thucydides' Book 7 (49–87), and the list goes on; Sicily appears to be the Athenians' golden fleece (Hornblower [2004, 331]). Parallels have also been drawn between historiographical narrative structures and epic, especially regarding situation reversals: a famous example of this, explicitly noted by Thucydides, is the destruction of the Athenian fleet in Syracuse, which "reverses" the episode of Pylos and Sphacteria in 425, where the Athenians were the ones who destroyed the enemy ships and spread panic, even among those who were on land (7.71.7; cf. 4.14.2); and the epic models of situation reversal are now examined by Richard Rutherford (2012). Understanding what is to be deduced from these analogies is essential: has Thucydides constructed his episodes in a certain way because he has read Pindar and Homer and is competing with them at the literary level, or is he simply more susceptible to certain lexical choices or narrative structures because athletics and the epic are part of the culture of his time and inevitably shape the way he interprets the world? Are we certain that a Thucydidean poetic workshop actually exists?

What surely does exist is poetry's contribution to historical thought. This applies to Herodotus even more than to Thucydides, however, and we can touch on it only briefly: from the seventh/sixth century to the end of the fifth century BCE, many are the poets who treated recent and contemporary history, in elegiac couplets or in hexameter: Mimnermus of Colophon in the *Smyrneis*, on the conflict between the Lydian king Gyges and the Greek cities of Asia Minor in the seventh century BCE; Xenophanes in the *Migration to Elea*; Simonides in his elegies, such as the one for the battle of Plataea (frags. 10–18 West, 2nd ed. [West²]; see Boedeker and Sider 2001; Vannicelli 2007); and Choerilus of Samos in his poem *Persica* (*Suppl. Hell.* 314–23; alternative titles: *Barbarica*, *Mēdica*), to name but a few. Moreover, it is well known that even the tragic poets occasionally turned to the themes of their day, abandoning myth, from Phrynicus (*Sack of Miletus*, *Phoenician Women*) to Aeschylus (*Persians*); Anaxion of Mytilene with his *Persai Satyroi*, *TrGF* 202, is of uncertain chronology; but neither should we forget comic poets such as Epicharmus (frags. 110–11), Chionides (test. 1) or Pherecrates (or Pseudo-Pherecrates: frags. 132–41 KA). It is easy to understand how Mimnermus or the "new" Simonides differ from Herodotus and Thucydides: heroization of the endeavor (e.g., Mimnermus' exalting the courage of him who was seen routing the Lydian cavalry: frag. 14, 1–4 West^2) or superposition between the legendary past and the present (e.g., Simonides' evoking the great epic hero Achilles at the beginning of the elegy for the Battle of Plataea, frags. 10–11 West^2) are among the typically poetic characteristics that historiography tends to avoid, control, or repress (on the representation of the Battles of Salamis and Plataea in poetry, cf. LeVen 2014, 194–202). But as Santo Mazzarino illustrated many years ago, Mimnermus also wondered *why* the Greeks and the Eastern kings were in conflict, which is undoubtedly an expression of historical thought (Mazzarino 1965–1966, i. 40).

Rather than asserting that Thucydides' text has poetic characteristics, we would prefer to bring the relationship between poetry and history back down to earth by pointing out that the poets, even prior to Thucydides, sometimes think like historians (or have been influenced by them, as Pindar who in *Pyth.* 4 exhibits a thorough knowledge of the genealogy of the Battiadai: Corcella [2006, 37]; even as early as 476 BCE, a passage like *Ol.* 1.28–29 on the *dedaidalmenoi . . . muthoi*, "the stories embellished with embroidered lies, speech of mortals going beyond the true account, are deceptive," shows the effects of the myth revision conducted by Hecataeus in particular). This is not surprising, and it does not mean that historians like Thucydides do not possess genre-based specificities that identify them as such. Historians were not the first to think in historical terms; politicians, merchants, or common people wondered about the world around them and about the temporal and causal connections between events. But the responsible account, or the analysis of facts selected for their pertinence to a certain area and chronological period, are characteristics that are found neither prior to, nor outside of historiography, and nowhere are they more highly defined than in Thucydides' work. Between oral history, practiced at the most diverse of levels and on the most diverse of occasions, and a highly formalised *xungraphē*, such as Thucydides', there is at once continuity and a methodological leap. This leap—a true epistemological fracture—consists in: focusing on the present (which becomes the favoured object of research, mostly because it is considered to be more important than the *palaia*, or more ancient events), and on war and painful current events in particular; the resulting temporal articulation that separates the past from the present, in which history culminates; the conception of a responsible subjectivity in the recounting of events; and finally the ambition to transform the historical account into an exhaustive rendering of contemporary reality, in such a way that the account itself becomes the equivalent or *Ersatz* of historical reality, and as such demands to be continued, but not replaced, by a successor. All of these elements are very much present in Thucydides' work and, as has been illustrated (Porciani [2001, 65–117]), are intrinsic to an exceptional form of the oral memory of Athens, namely, the *epitaphios logos*, or the eulogy to fallen citizens, which the city entrusts each time to a man of recognized intellect and prestige (Thuc. 2.34.6). It is very likely that this *logos*, as part of a wider and highly ritualized funeral ceremony (the *patrios nomos*), was regularly held in Athens starting around the seventies of the fifth century BCE (Diod. *Sic.* 11.33.3; Thomas [1989, 207–8]): the *polis* that is constantly at war evolves, as a social system, a specific way of exalting the present through a historical perspective. It was a new way of viewing historical events, and one by which the Athenian Thucydides was inevitably influenced.

We owe to Cicero the memory of the ancient connection between historiography and *mortui laus*: the rule of the latter is "tell the whole truth and nothing but the truth," as we gather from *De leg.* 2.63 Büchner (*quom siquid veri erat praedicatum—nam mentiri nefas habebatur—iusta confecta erant*, regarding private ceremonies that later develop into eulogies *in publicis sepulturis*, 2.65). According to the famous wording of one of Cicero's other works, they are the same rules that apply to history (*ne quid falsi dicere audeat . . . ne quid veri non audeat, De orat.* 2.62). Based on this, the points of intersection that we have listed prove to be relevant, starting with the highlighting of contemporary history that is found both in Pericles' discourse for fallen soldiers in 431 (Thuc. 2.36.3 and 2.41.2–5, on the power of Athens) and in the parts in which Thucydides expresses his personal judgment as historian on the present as a culminating phase—in terms not of moral values but of factual magnitude (1.1, 1.21.2, 1.23.1–3; full illustration in Porciani [2001, 65–85]; similar echoes are differently assessed by Grethlein [2013 and elsewhere], according to whom Pericles' oration serves as a foil for the historian's own approach to history, but the interpretation rests upon a questionable translation of *logographoi* in Thuc. 1.21.1 as "orators": see above, 557).

For us, it is not a matter of Thucydides lending Pericles his own ideas. That Thucydides is our sole source of fifth-century epitaphs is not cause to doubt that Pericles' oration, like the other discourses in Thucydides, retraces the *gnōmē*, that is, the logical sequence of the speech that was actually given (Porciani [2007]; on the historical context of the funeral oration, Bosworth [2000]); and the centrality of the contemporary in the *epitaphios logos* is part of the epitaphic tradition, as evidenced by fourth-century epitaphs, and especially by Hyperides' (cf. *Epit.* 10 ff. on the glorious events of the first year of the Lamiac War). Pericles' account of history from the days of the *progonoi*, or "ancestors," who defend Attica's freedom with valor (2.36.1), and the *pateres*, or "fathers," who conquer the *archē*, or "empire" (2.36.2), is the exact parallel of the chronological division employed by Thucydides, in whose writing the *palaia* or *archaiologia* (which also include the Persian wars: 1.1.3–18.2) are followed by the *etē pentēkonta malista*, which open with Xerxes' retreat after Salamis (480: 1.118.2). The theme of *logos isorropos* or *isos* and *metriōs eipein*, or the commitment to make discourse conform to reality, both by avoiding reductiveness and by refraining from disproportionate praise (Thuc. 2.35.2; 2.42.2; [Dem.] 60.1; [Lys.] 2.1; Hyp. *Epit.* 2), becomes in Thucydides the requirement of a style that does not embellish or exaggerate events and that distances itself from the *muthōdes* (1.21.1; 1.22.4), and whose purpose is to achieve the solidity that is typical of historical reality (*ktēma te es aiei*, 1.22.4; *mnēmeia kakōn te kagathōn aidia*, 2.41.4).

Oral sources usually offered historians like Thucydides, or even Herodotus or Antiochus, a significant amount of the raw material with which they worked, but their contribution in terms of "form of content" was negligible. But the contrary could be said of the *epitaphios logos*: this verbal tradition was lacking in content (dates, information, news), but represented a leap in quality as far as the categories that permitted the re-evaluation of historical processes and events were concerned. The *epitaphios logos* incubated these categories (i.e., focus on the present, temporal articulation, responsible subjectivity, historical account as an equivalent of reality) and transmitted them to historiography: in other words, it offered the categorizing mediation that was necessary in order for history to become what it did in the second half of the fifth century BCE. It was Athenian society and its political leaders who placed contemporary war at the center of their own political and oratory *logos*. The Athenian perspective, because of the importance of the *polis*, was bound to develop by spreading to the entire Greek world. Indeed, from Thucydides onward, the great Greek historians followed no other path, creating a discourse free of local and municipal limitations. The "man chosen by the city" to deliver the *epitaphios logos* (Thuc. 2.34.6) passed the torch to a man to whom "it befell a twenty-year exile from his homeland" (5.26.5).

References

Asheri, David, Aldo Corcella, and Pietro Vannicelli, eds. 2006. *Erodoto, Le Storie. Libro IX: La battaglia di Platea*. Milan: Fondazione Valla.

Boedeker, Deborah, and David Sider, eds. 2001. *The New Simonides: Contexts of Praise and Desire*. Oxford: Oxford University Press.

Bosworth, Albert Brian. 2000. "The Historical Context of Thucydides' Funeral Oration." *JHS* 120:1–16.

Chambers, Mortimer. 2008. *Valla's Translation of Thucydides in Vat. Lat. 1801, with the Reproduction of the Codex*. Vatican City: Biblioteca Apostolica Vaticana.

Corcella, Aldo. 2006. "The New Genre and Its Boundaries: Poets and Logographers." In *Brill's Companion to Thucydides*, edited by A. Rengakos and A. Tsakmakis, 33–56. Leiden and Boston: Brill.

De Vido, Stefania, and Luca Mondin. 2015. "zeteō." In *Lexicon historiographicum Graecum et Latinum*, diretto da C. Ampolo, U. Fantasia, L. Porciani, iii. 235–43. Pisa: Edizioni della Normale.

Evans, James Allan Stewart. 1991. *Herodotus, Explorer of the Past: Three Essays*. Princeton: Princeton University Press.

Gengler, Olivier. 2015. "heuriskō." In *Lexicon historiographicum Graecum et Latinum*, diretto da C. Ampolo, U. Fantasia, L. Porciani, iii. 224–27. Pisa: Edizioni della Normale.

Grethlein, Jonas. 2013. "Democracy, Oratory, and the Rise of Historiography in Fifth-century Greece." In *The Greek Polis and the Invention of Democracy: A Politico-cultural Transformation and Its Interpretations*, edited by J. P. Arnason, K. A. Raaflaub, and P. Wagner, 126–43. Chichester: Wiley-Blackwell.

Hornblower, Simon. 2004. *Thucydides and Pindar: Historical Narrative and the World of Epinikian Poetry*. Oxford: Oxford University Press.

Hornblower, Simon. 2011. *Thucydidean Themes*. Oxford: Oxford University Press.

Huber, Ludwig. 1965. "Herodots Homerverständnis." In *Synusia: Festgabe für Wolfgang Schadewaldt zum 15 März 1965*, edited by H. Flashar and K. Gaiser, 29–52. Pfullingen: Neske.

Jacoby, Felix. 1909. "Ueber die Entwicklung der griechischen Historiographie und den Plan einer neuen Sammlung der griechischen Historikerfragmente." *Klio* 9: 80–123.

Jacoby, Felix. 1913. "Herodotos." 7. In *RE*, Suppl. ii: 205–520.

Jacoby, Felix. 1949. *Atthis: The Local Chronicles of Ancient Athens*. Oxford: Clarendon.

LeVen, Pauline A. 2014. *The Many-Headed Muse: Tradition and Innovation in Late Classical Greek Lyric Poetry*. Cambridge: Cambridge University Press.

Lloyd-Jones, Hugh, and Peter J. Parsons (edd.). 1983. *Supplementum Hellenisticum*. Berlin.

Malkin, Irad. 2011. *A Small Greek World: Networks in the Ancient Mediterranean*. Oxford: Oxford University Press.

Marincola, John. 1997. *Authority and Tradition in Ancient Historiography*. Cambridge: Cambridge University Press.

Marincola, John. 1999. "Genre, Convention and Innovation in Greco-Roman Historiography." In *The Limits of Historiography: Genre and Narrative in Ancient Historical Texts*, edited by C. S. Kraus, 281–324. Leiden: Brill.

Mazzarino, Santo. 1965–1966. *Il pensiero storico classico*, i–ii.1–2. Rome and Bari: Laterza.

Momigliano, Arnaldo. 1977. "Tradition and the Classical Historian." In *Essays in Ancient and Modern Historiography*, 161–77. Oxford: Blackwell [*Quinto contributo alla storia degli studi classici e del mondo antico*, Rome: Edizioni di storia e letteratura, 1975, i. 13–31].

Momigliano, Arnaldo. (1978) 1980. "Greek Historiography." *H&T* 17:1–28 [*Sesto contributo alla storia degli studi classici e del mondo antico*, Rome: Edizioni di storia e letteratura, 1980, i. 33–67].

Murray, Oswyn. 1993. *Early Greece*. 2nd ed. Cambridge: Harvard University Press.

Murray, Oswyn. 2014. "Thucydides and the Altar of Apollo Archēgetēs." *ASNP* s. 5, 6:447–473.

Niebuhr, Barthold Georg. 1847–1851. *Vorträge über alte Gechichte, an der Universität zu Bonn gehalten*, edited by M. Niebuhr, i–iii. Berlin: G. Reimer.

Porciani, Leone. 2001. *Prime forme della storiografia greca. Prospettiva locale e generale nella narrazione storica*. Stuttgart: Steiner.

Porciani, Leone. 2007. "The Enigma of Discourse: A View of Thucydides." In *A Companion to Greek and Roman Historiography*, edited by J. Marincola, ii. 328–35. Malden, Oxford, and Carlton: Blackwell.

Pugliese Carratelli, Giovanni. 1976. *Scritti sul mondo antico: Europa e Asia—Espansione coloniale—Ideologie e istituzioni politiche e religiose*. Naples: Macchiaroli.

Rutherford, Richard B. 2012. "Structure and Meaning in Epic and Historiography." In *Thucydides and Herodotus*, edited by E. Foster and D. Lateiner, 13–38. Oxford: Oxford University Press.

Stadter, Philip A. 2012. "Thucydides as 'Reader' of Herodotus." In *Thucydides and Herodotus*, edited by E. Foster and D. Lateiner, 39–66. Oxford: Oxford University Press.

Stein, Heinrich, ed. 1893–1908. *Herodotos*, i–v. 4th–6th ed. Berlin: Weidmann.

Stevenson, Rosemary B. 1997. *Persica: Greek Writing about Persia in the Fourth Century BC*. Edinburgh: Scottish Academic Press.

Strasburger, Hermann. 1982. *Homer und die Geschichtsschreibung*. In *Studien zur alten Geschichte*, edited by W. Schmitthenner and R. Zoepffel, ii. 1057–97. Hildesheim and New York: Olms.

Thomas, Rosalind. 1989. *Oral Tradition and Written Record in Classical Athens*. Cambridge: Cambridge University Press.

Vannicelli, Pietro. 2007. "To Each His Own: Simonides and Herodotus on Thermopylae." In *A Companion to Greek and Roman Historiography*, edited by J. Marincola, ii. 315–21. Malden, Oxford, and Carlton: Blackwell.

Ziegler, Konrat. 1929. "Der Ursprung der Exkurse im Thukydides." *RhM* n.F. 78: 58–67.

CHAPTER 33

THUCYDIDES AND HIS INTELLECTUAL MILIEU

ROSALIND THOMAS[*]

Introduction

How can we approach such an original writer as Thucydides and delineate his intellectual milieu when the writers and thinkers of the period notoriously defy attempts to pigeonhole them? One of the most striking phenomena in this period is the interaction and interflowing of ideas, methods, and theories amongst a group of thinkers and writers who cannot be neatly divided up into philosophers, orators, historians, tragedians, and doctors. The individuals conventionally characterized as "sophists" differed widely from one another (it was Plato who attempted to unify the sophists as teachers of the art of rhetoric, and we have been left with Plato's legacy). Thrasymachus, for example, was known mainly for his systematization of rhetoric, but was also notoriously connected with a theory of justice as self-interest (*Republic* I), and his tombstone was said to have claimed that his profession (*technē*) was wisdom (DK 85, A8). Several sophists had interests in aspects of natural philosophy (Prodicus, Gorgias); Antiphon tried to square the circle, and Gorgias, though known above all for rhetoric, also engaged in philosophical speculation. Hence it is perhaps best to talk of intellectual affinities, of intellectual experiments, and of the "sophistic generation" in general. Techniques of argument and rhetoric swept the board, and can be found in Euripides' tragedies, parodied in Aristophanes, experimented with in live speeches, reproduced in Thucydides, and used to a greater or lesser extent by the medical essays. Doctors needed and used the arts of persuasion. Techniques of argument were examined as valid or invalid among the more philosophical; used by medical writers to buttress their theories or to make up for the painful lack of hard understanding of the nature of the human constitution; and used and misused by speakers who simply wished to persuade, regardless of any inherent truth or validity

[*] My warmest thanks to Tim Rood, Michael Drolet, and the editor for their perceptive comments.

in what they said. Plato's *Symposium* threw together a group of writers and intellectuals, including a poet and a doctor, and, while fictional, this captures the fluidity of interaction. Thucydides' masterly analysis of the early development of Greek society (1.2ff.) used theory, assumptions, and general ideas about how human society would progress, and is in many ways comparable to Protagoras' theory of the development of political society in the *Protagoras*, or to *Ancient Medicine*: part theory, part observation of the world, filtered through ideas of early human development.[1] The Melian Dialogue used arguments that reappear in somewhat different form in Plato's *Republic* and that have roots in Gorgias' *Helen*.

The love of argument and counterargument was a particular hallmark of this period, which saw the refinement of argument and modes of refutation: modes of argument were developed so that authors did not simply offer an opposing picture, but openly refuted the views of their opponents. Hippocrates' *Nature of Man*, for instance, objected to sweeping theories about the "nature of man"—such as that man is air, or fire, or water or earth—adding that they did not produce convincing evidence or proofs, and convincing arguments that could win in debate (chap. 1). Similarly, Thucydides criticized Athenian ignorance, and set out in detail exactly what the real truth about the tyranny was (1.20; 6.53.3–59). The difference is that he was trying to give a convincing account of past history. Thucydides and Herodotus both resort to this mode occasionally, Herodotus more strikingly throughout the *Histories*.[2] This explicit method of refuting could stoke the development of careful science and philosophy and also that of rhetoric and political persuasion; it could turn into the chop-logic of the ambitious youth parodied in the *Clouds* (of 423 BCE). It is therefore often unclear if a certain mode of argument may be assigned to forensic rhetoric, philosophy or early science, since such methods crossed over the genres;[3] perhaps, rather, we should think of common, shared features that could have differing uses and functions in various authors.

Given these features, it is therefore potentially misleading and difficult to talk of Thucydides' intellectual milieu, unless we agree that he is in, but not of, any one milieu. We should also note Hornblower's valuable warning against seeking to isolate a Thucydidean debt to another writer—or the other way round—rather than admitting a wider circulation of shared ideas and theories from which both drew.[4] Despite these fluid boundaries, it is nevertheless useful for the sake of clarity to consider Thucydides in relation to the medical writers and rhetoricians and/or sophists in turn. In each area, we shall see that Thucydides was not merely reflecting but also participating actively and critically in the current debates on a wide range of topics. These include methods

---

[1] See Romilly (1966b), especially 147 ff. On individual sophists, Guthrie (1971); Kerferd (1981), Wallace (1998); Solmsen (1975); Nestle (1948; orig 1914) with wide-ranging examples and comparison; for Antiphon, Gagarin (2002) and Pendrick's new edition (2002).

[2] Herodotus should strictly enter a discussion of intellectual milieu; cf. Thomas (2000).

[3] Thus Plant's focus on forensic rhetoric is too narrow (1999): this style of argument had a far wider popularity and force. See above all Lloyd (1979, 1987) for proof and argument in Greek science.

[4] Hornblower (1987, 111); cf. also Winton's salutary remarks (2000).

of inquiry, causation, the nature of law, and the claims of justice versus self-interest in human and state relations.

Often when we are in a position to understand the context, Thucydides seems to appropriate, assimilate, and move on. It is hard to think of Thucydides merely "borrowing" or imitating, and indeed this makes it essential to think in terms of intellectual milieu in the most general terms. This is particularly evident when we consider his relation to the ideas and methods of the medical writers. They are especially significant in this context because we have several complete essays, whole arguments, and a variety of authors collected under the name of Hippocrates, while we lack complete texts for the famous sophists except for Gorgias and a couple of anonymous writers (*Anon.Iamblichi, Dissoi Logoi*), and must see them through the filter of later, hostile, thinkers (but note the papyri and probably the speeches of Antiphon if the sophist and orator are identical). The medical writers were themselves a variegated group, though their various essays were ultimately collected under the name of a single great representative, Hippocrates. The early works dating to the late-fifth-century range from the very rhetorical, to the minutely exact delineation of daily symptoms in the *Epidemics I and III*; from the grand theory of the humors in *Ancient Medicine*, to the highly sophistic argument of *On the Art*. The philosophical arguments and underpinnings in some are so prominent that some highly theoretical essays seem more akin to "philosophy" than what we think of as medical research; whilst others tend to exact "proto-scientific" observation (Jouanna 1992).

We turn first to medical writers and medical theory; then to rhetoric and theories of justice and self-interest as seen through certain sophists and Thucydides' speeches.

Medicine and *Akribeia*

Thucydides showed that he was well aware of one of the major theories of the early Hippocratics, as he patiently explained that the "change" of temperature in the Syracusan quarries made many Athenians prisoners ill (7.87.1). Shocking as this piece of medical diagnosis is in the midst of this tragic narrative, it is a pure piece of Hippocratic theory: change in temperature is a classic cause of illness according to their theories.[5] In the Plague narrative, Thucydides goes out of his way to explain that the plague also struck animals and birds as well as humans (2.50.1–2): here we have the opposite phenomenon, when Thucydides knows and contradicts a common medical theory. For as Demont points out, the general educated view must have been that disease attacked only one species: this can be deduced from an imagined counterargument provided by the Hippocratic *Breaths* to elucidate the author's theory (chap. 6), the imagined objection being that such diseases affect only one species.[6] When Thucydides points out that birds

---

[5] Cf. *Alcib.* at 6.18.7, on change from *polupragmosunē*, with Jouanna (1980), perhaps part of the same complex of ideas.

[6] See Demont (1983) for detailed discussion.

and animals were also affected, he is implicitly, then, countering a medically favored view, and he is doing so with the authority of his own lived experience. He implies that the plague did not conform to the commonly held categories and expectations.

But that is only one aspect among several in which Thucydides' account of the plague serves to undermine and improve upon the theories of the medical writers. As the most sustained piece of medical description in Thucydides' *History*, the plague has been closely scrutinized and it provides the best evidence that Thucydides was very well versed in current medical terminology and theory. Page's work is fundamental in its meticulous examination of the medical terms used by Thucydides (Page 1953). It is true that many of these medical terms were also the standard Greek terms in use for such symptoms as sneezing, and Parry emphasizes the other aspects of the plague description, which indicated that it was not meant simply as pure science (Parry 1969). The tragic elements here are clear, as the plague struck at the moment of Athens' greatest power and confidence, but this does not negate the "medical flavor" of the Plague description. The two go hand in hand, and the unremitting accuracy of the description is itself "tragic akribeia."[7] Moreover, it can be somewhat misleading to talk of technical terms in medicine at this early stage, since by and large the medical works were using the vocabulary of ordinary Greek, and had not developed much of a specialized technical vocabulary (Eijk 1997). The more significant point is that Thucydides thought to give a blow-by-blow account of symptoms at all, in a form and detail that was similar to those visible in *Hippocratic Epidemics*. The very inclusion of this prolonged description implied a degree of specialized knowledge of the fledging *technē* of medicine, and Thucydides shows that he was familiar with this. As for the vocabulary, the 1986 concordance of the Hippocratic Corpus by J.-H. Kühn and U. Fleischer makes comparison of vocabulary far more secure and Page's analysis stands up extremely well: the various types of burning sensations, for instance, occur in the plague description and in the medical works—cf. *thermai ischurai* (in the plural), in Thuc. 2.49.2 as in the medical works.[8]

Yet when we examine exactly how Thucydides treats *diaita*, or "regimen," the word and concept dear to the early Hippocratic writers, or bile (*cholē*), the essential humor of several colors in the Hippocratic scheme of humors, we can suspect that Thucydides is doing something somewhat different. He mentions "all kinds of purging of bile named by the doctors" (2.49.3: ἀποκαθάρσεις χολῆς πᾶσαι ὅσαι ὑπὸ ἰατρῶν ὠνομασμέναι), and somewhat later, he mentions "those tended by every type of regimen" (2.51.3: τὰ πάσῃ διαίτῃ θεραπευόμενα) as equally prone to die at the hands of the plague. There is, then, a sly dig at medical expertise here: yes, the doctors can distinguish and name all sorts of different purges of bile, and they tried to cure with different types of diet/regimen, but none worked. What was the point of minute descriptions of different processes, when virtually all died?

---

[7] To use Hornblower's phrase (1987, 35), denoting the use of simple factual description for tragic effect.
[8] See Thomas (2006, 95 ff,) for further details, with Page (1953) and Parry (1969).

This phraseology may partly be explained as a deliberate avoidance of excessive technicality, as Parry argued, though we should prefer to speak of incipient technicality as doctors sought to argue that they were in fact an art/*technē*. More interesting, however, is the implication that Thucydides both knew much of the medical parlance and despised its lack of efficacy and unrealistic technicality. He could describe the disease exactly to help later generations recognize the plague if it should strike again (2.48.3), but the doctors were of little or no help. Indeed he stated this emphatically toward the start: the doctors were unable to find cures and died themselves (2.47.2), "nor was any other human art (*technē*)" able to alleviate the disease. Here Thucydides used the language of the *technē* much beloved by the doctors—the early Hippocratic essays were much concerned to prove that medicine was an art, a *technē*. But here the *technē* could not be much avail. He reiterated at the end the inability of anyone to find a cure: "people died, both those who were neglected and those who received a lot of care. No single remedy, as it were, established itself; for what was beneficial for one harmed another" (2.51.2).

Here we can discern several implications: for one, he states that doctors and care had no effect, or at least no predictable effect, for one treatment harmed one and helped another. Thus, it is implied, the plague was terrifying because it did not appear to follow a predictable process (having a standard set of symptoms, but with variants). It is also a critique of the doctors and their elaborate theories or special names and terms, all of which were powerless. Above all, this serves to put the plague itself in center stage as a phenomenon really beyond human understanding, and particularly beyond the understanding of the medical *technē*. Let us elaborate:

It is also not susceptible to any *explanation* or cause, as Thucydides explains. To be precise, he states that he will leave to others any theories about its nature and cause: "Let others, doctors or laymen, speculate where it originated and the causes which each thinks might be sufficient to cause so great a disturbance (*metabolē*). But for myself I will set down its nature, and the symptoms by which anyone who knows them beforehand should recognize it if it should ever strike again. These I shall demonstrate (δηλώσω) having myself suffered the disease and having watched other people suffering it" (2.48.3). We can read this as a way of saying that others may wish to discuss causes but it is impossible to know where it came from and what caused it. Later he endorses this by adding that there was no cause or explanation (49.2: ἀπ' οὐδεμιᾶς προφάσεως). This is markedly different from the Hippocratic discussions of what caused disease— and indeed from Thucydides' confidence in diagnosing the causes of the war: different authors argued for different causes of illness, it is true, but they were certain that there *were* causes and they claimed with all the confidence of an early science to know what they were—imbalance of the four humors in *On Ancient Medicine*; excessive heat and damp, linked to "airs, waters and places" in *Airs, Waters, Places*; air in *Breaths*.[9] For instance, *Nature of Man*, chap. 15 opens with "most fevers come from bile (*cholē*)," and

---

[9] Cf. *Breaths* Chapter 6, init.: "There are two kinds of fevers; one is epidemic, called plague. Both of these fevers, however, are caused by air."

there are four types of them; or chap. 9, on diseases attacking many at once, where regimen/*diaitē* or *diaitēmata* is therefore not the cause, but unhealthy air. This cheerful certainty must have seemed vain to those living through the plague.

Thucydides also came up with the theory of acquired immunity, noting that if someone managed to survive the disease, as he himself had, he did not fall ill again, or if he did, it was not fatal (2.51.5). This observation has no counterpart in the Hippocratic Corpus—and perhaps could not have one, since they believed disease was primarily caused by humoral imbalance and regimen, unless from miasmata in air (*Breaths*). We thus see Thucydides presenting a theory from observation and his own personal experience, which serves again to improve upon the doctors. This too offers a fundamental difference from the medical writers: he has autopsy, and still better, he lived through it, like the war.[10] This is an altogether different level of knowledge—not from books, not from the *technē*, but from experience. It is reminiscent of what Thucydides later said about the Corcyrean stasis and the effect of the war: the war itself was a "harsh teacher," a βίαιος διδάσκαλος (3.82.2). No need for Hippocrates if you experienced and learned from that experience. It seems an entirely understandable reaction to undergoing and surviving such an ordeal, but Thucydides also had the intellectual and medical tools with which to analyze and describe it and to make original observations. For instance we note his confidence in describing the main features of the disease, "setting aside many other peculiarities in particular cases" (2.51.1).

The Plague section is so famous that we need to remind ourselves how remarkable it is that Thucydides felt it desirable to offer a sustained description of the disease at all. Two questions then arise: 1.) Does the medical description suggest a wholly human history with human and scientific explanations? 2.) Does his emphasis on social effects situate his work in any particular intellectual milieu?

First, the very presence of this detailed medical description instantly implied that old-fashioned and religiously based views of disease or plague as divine visitations were out of place. By giving a detailed analysis of its course, even if no cure existed, Thucydides indicated that it was susceptible to human description and therefore (one might guess tentatively) perhaps one day (if not now), to human understanding: this was history based on human experience, not divine will or divine intervention. Experience was important: even if most died, the fact that survivors went on to resist the disease might also be seen as a blow to any view that the plague was caused by Apollo. This signals a radical break from poetic traditions and from Herodotus, whose complex views of causation did also allow for the divine affecting the human world. So even though Thucydides left explanations to others, the sheer fact of the description aligned his work with the more secular human-based view of history.

A recent interesting argument has been put forward that the structure of the narrative surrounding the plague might allow the possibility that Thucydides did, after all, think it *possible* that Apollo sent the Plague (Kallet 2013). Among other elements, Kallet notes the

---

[10] The medical writers used autopsy, of course; but this stresses experience of the actual illness as well as observation of others.

close juxtaposition of the Spartan invasion and the Plague's arrival (2.47), the Plague's unprecedented immensity (2.47.2), the impossibility of suggesting a cause, the catastrophes that were also unprecedented during the war (1.23.1–3; 3.87), the recent oracle to Sparta mentioned alongside the plague at Athens (2.54.4–5).[11] All this might just leave open the possibility. It is certainly true that the narrative is hung about with almost paradoxical remarks such as "the year was otherwise unusually free from disease" (2.49.1). At 2.50.1, it is κρεῖσσον λόγου, literally "stronger than *logos*" (reason, rational understanding),[12] and quite different from other diseases. He justifies this statement carefully (τά γάρ . . . τεκμήριον δέ . . .) with the exact argument that birds and beasts also caught it or abstained from the corpses; the proof of this was the absence of the birds you would expect. It is the plague that effects social breakdown at this point, not the war, just as the stasis in Corcyra effected it there. But perhaps the Plague as a medical and secular phenomenon takes the place of the divinely wrought disasters of Greek epic and tragedy? The Hippocratic essay *On the Sacred Disease* argued repeatedly that epilepsy "was no more sacred than any other disease": that is, the author did not deny the gods, but strove to point out non-divine causes behind epilepsy. We might be tempted to say that Thucydides was doing the same with the Plague, providing a resolutely human and physical analysis for something that many (most?) Greeks would say was brought by Apollo. The problem with this idea is that he effectively dismissed the possibility of identifying a cause, and that could be dismissing divine as much as other more scientific causes. Besides, he stressed that religious rituals were no help against the plague; he left out the purification of Athens that later sources mentioned (see Hornblower 1992). A more plausible possibility was argued by Demont (2013) in a complex nest of arguments, stressing among other things the combination of *limos* and *loimos* (famine and plague): thus Thucydides' narrative was constructed in part to deny what many Athenians would have believed, which is that Pericles was responsible for bringing the Plague upon Athens. This seems more compelling.

It might be best, then, to suggest that he left the cause or possible cause horrifyingly ambiguous, dangling in the air, possibilities hinted at but a kind of aporia left at the end in the face of its terrible devastation. He was not a Herodotus, willing to assert that yes, indeed the gods do occasionally intervene—as for the rumor of victory at Plataea (9.100), and for the Bacis oracle (8.77), though we should note that Herodotus implied here that the question was debatable. In any case, humanly caused devastation is equally visible in Thucydides' parallel treatment of the devastating social effects of the stasis at Corcyra, and—he adds—these were replicated all over Greece and brought about by the dynamics of the war itself (8. 82–3). In this sense, Thucydides was every bit a historian of the sophistic revolution, with the sophistic emphasis on the human world.[13] We recall that Thucydides' remark about the usefulness of his *History* for the future as well as

---

[11] Kallet stresses Thucydides' didactic intention. It seems to me that 2.54.4–5, and so on are compatible with (merely) other people connecting the Plague with Apollo's help to Sparta: see Demont (2013).

[12] Cf. Lattimore's translation, "an occurrence beyond all accounting"; Mynott, "defied all reason."

[13] Cf. Solmsen (1975, Chapter 5) for discussion of human psychology. Note the emphasis on demoralization in the Plague, the psychology affecting people's resistance (2.51).

understanding the past depended on the sentiment that affairs were likely to be more or less similar, κατὰ τὸ ἀνθρώπινον—"according to human nature," as this is widely understood (1.22.4).

One final comparison with the Hippocratics connects with this. Unlike the medical writers, Thucydides was interested in the wider social and political effects of the plague and gave more description to the breakdown of social and religious norms than to the course of the disease itself. Here it is analysis of social change, change in fundamental beliefs and forms of ritualized behavior, as well as fundamental attitudes to life, that seems to interest Thucydides more. Compare the following, for instance:

> The sacred places also in which they had quartered themselves were full of corpses of persons that had died there, just as they were; for as the disaster passed all bounds, men, not knowing what was to become of them, became utterly careless (ἐς ὀλιγωρίαν ἐτράποντο) of everything, whether sacred or profane. All the burial rites before in use were entirely upset, and they buried the bodies as best they could. (2.52.3: translated by Crawley)

Similarly in the Corcyrean stasis, he analyzed change or contortions in basic Greek values and priorities, as well as in the values expressed though language (3.82.4):

> The sufferings which revolution entailed upon the cities were many and terrible, such as have occurred and always will occur, as long as the nature of mankind (ἡ αὐτὴ φύσις ἀνθρώπων) remains the same; though in a severer or milder form (*eidesi*), with every new combination of circumstances. (3.82.2: N.B. αἱ μεταβολαὶ τῶν ξυντυχιῶν)[14]

Hippocratic texts certainly can show awareness of wider psychological effects and (in *Airs*) of individuals' health as a function of the larger environment, but their focus was of course on health and illness, and not the large-scale impact on human society. And yet the idea of a larger overarching phenomenon (disease, stasis) with differing effects according to local circumstances, is reminiscent of doctors' struggles with varying human constitutions: we note the way Thucydides expresses the constants of human nature above (3.82.2) that create sufferings, while the appearances or forms (*eidesi*) will be greater or lesser according to particular cases or circumstances. The analysis is entirely original to Thucydides, but he seems to have been helped by the way Hippocratic doctors tried to express how an illness could have different manifestations in different people, and the use of *eidos*, and *metabolai* indicate this: thus *Epidemics* I 23 or *Breaths* chap. 6.[15]

---

[14] Hornblower (1991, 481) has an important note on Thucydides' originality here. Note that medical writers also share this conception of variation (and see below).

[15] See Weidauer (1954, 21ff) for *eidos*. *Eidos* is a favorite Hippocratic word and idea: eg., *Sacr. Dis.* I 10 J, "for each form of the disease"; *Anc.Med.* 7.3, 12.2, 15.1 etc.; very common in *Airs*, and cf. the idea of "local" diseases (*epichōria*)—"endemic," prevalent in particular regions and environments, e.g., 3.3.

We may, however, be seeing ideas and methods shared between a larger group of intellectuals—to which doctors, so-called sophists, and the practitioners of the new *technē* of history belonged. Let us turn to the concept of "*akribeia*," literally, accuracy or precision. Thucydides is famous for his devotion to *akribeia*, and we do not need to discuss here his attempt at accuracy of dating, or facts. We note only that alongside his criticism of others for accepting traditions and accounts uncritically (1.20), he half-apologized for his treatment of speeches thus (very literally): "it was difficult for me to recall the exact form (*akribeia*) of what was said, both of those speeches I heard myself, and for those reported to me" (1.22.1). A little later, he expressed his intention not to recount events (*erga*) merely from one account or from his own experience, but to test each report as far as it was possible with *akribeia* (22.2, ἀκριβείᾳ περὶ ἑκάστου ἐπεξελθών).

Akribeia thus lies at the heart of his methodological statements, and denotes here "in accordance with reality," as Hornblower notes.[16] This is in the context of a historical work: the basic meaning must be to convey accuracy and precision more generally. It is interesting that *akribeia* is a term relatively commonly used in the early Hippocratic texts in relation to strictures on method. It does not occur at all in Herodotus when he is underlining his method or criticizing others.[17] Herodotus and Thucydides shared other conceptions of method: for instance, the stress on careful argument, proof, and deduction at the start of Thucydides' *History* can be paralleled in Herodotus (n. 17), but *akribeia* stands out. In his emphasis on *akribeia* Thucydides was either sharing or signaling an adherence to precision which was also followed by the less rhetorical of the early Hippocratics when they discussed method. I suspect this indicates that Thucydides and the more exact edges of medical research shared a similar outlook and vocabulary for method.

In *Epidemics III*, the author declares that you need to scrutinize (*skopein*) the written accounts, know the conditions of the seasons precisely (ἀκριβῶς), as well as the disease, and then produce a prognosis and treat the patient (chap. 16). *Sacred Disease* 16.4J uses "*akribēs*" of air, within his theory about the brain, to denote the quality of being "precise" or "distinct" (Jouanna 2003). Most reminiscent of Thucydides is *Ancient Medicine*, chap. 12, where the idea of *akribeia* appears three times in connection with advances in method. Arguing generally against those who make a single substance the cause of illness, the author says this: "It is difficult, even with such a pitch of exactness (*akribeia*) in the art [of medicine] to reach always the truest precision (τοῦ ἀτρεκαστάτου). Many forms of medicine have reached this pitch of exactness (*akribeia*), about which I will speak later. I say that we should not reject the ancient art [of medicine] as non-existent ... just because it has not attained accuracy (*akribeia*) in everything." There is an

---

[16] 1991, 60; 1987, 37.
[17] See Thomas (2000, ch. 6). *Akribōs* occurs only at Hdt. VII 32, but excised in the Oxford Classical Text. Gagarin (2002, 27f) sees *akribeia* as generally sophistic, citing Antiphon and Gorgias DK 82, B6. Alcidamas, however, associated *akribeia* with written speeches (*On Those Who Write Written Speeches*), a stylistic quality. Antiphon, *Second Tetral.* 2.1, uses it of the past.

interplay here between *akribeia* and "truth" (τοῦ ἀτρεκαστάτου appears twice), where the expression "the most true" seems to denote a very high degree of precision in the sense of "being true," as well.[18] A similar conjunction occurs in a passage criticizing bad doctors: because of the complexity of nourishment, good and bad food, and the dangers of not eating, the doctor needs a lot of *akribeia* in his treatment, and "it is laborious to acquire knowledge so exact (οὕτω καταμαθεῖν ἀκριβῶς) that only small mistakes are made here and there" (9.3J).[19] *Akribeia* does not occur in the more rhetorical essays, *Breaths* and *On the Art*, or in *Airs*. *Akribeia* is, then, a mark of the superior and more effective doctor, as they claimed. The claim to respect from patients, and to truth as part of the *technē*, depends in part on the striving for *akribeia*.[20]

It is likely, then, that Thucydides' stress on *akribeia* not only signalled his most careful research and skepticism on his own account, but also tapped into a vocabulary and a discourse that was probably familiar to those medical enquirers who prided themselves on doing proper research, avoiding baseless hypotheses, and examining case studies: case studies such as those listed in *Epidemics*. Precision/*akribeia* was an important aspiration and distinguished one kind of doctor from those who "simply" engaged in clever rhetoric or abstract philosophical speculation. It was perhaps a catchword (like "*orthos*"), specifically espoused by those opposed to flashy rhetoric.

Performance, Speeches, and the Rhetoric of Justice

One of the primary features of the sophistic generation of the late fifth century was the vogue for rhetorical displays and performances that in Plato are associated with the main sophists. All the major sophists—Protagoras, Prodicus, Hippias—are portrayed by Plato with more or less criticism, as giving performances of lectures about their theories. Hippias, the least sophisticated, gave lectures to the Spartans about "archaiologia," a reminder that certain "sophists" also treated the past: he is mocked for preferring set performances that gave no allowance for questions (or change of mind) (see Thomas 2003). Others, like Prodicus or Protagoras, gave display lectures (the *epideixis*), and the language of epideictic display is very common indeed in Plato's portrayal of them—usually critical. There were also question-and-answer sessions, the so-called *brachylogia* (e.g., *Protagoras* 334e–335a); there were dialogues and contests with opposed speakers pitted against each other. Thucydides' relation to this mode of intellectual activity

---

[18] Jouanna's text with note (1990, 180) and Jones's text (1923) rejects Littré's acceptance of μὴ after χαλεπὸν: the point is that there is already a degree of "accuracy" but there is still a way to go.

[19] Note also 20.2J, in connection with precise knowledge, research, and enquiry about the nature of man.

[20] The *Nature of Man* castigates the lack of correct understanding: the phrase is *orthos ginōskein* (chap. 1), but one sees a similar exasperation with unfounded theories, lack of accuracy.

was notoriously distant. He managed to write his entire *History* without mentioning a single sophist, with the striking exception for Antiphon in Book 8, mentioned as a hidden architect and strategist of the oligarchic coup of 411 (8.68.1–2: this Antiphon of Rhamnous may not be identical to Antiphon the sophist, though Gagarin 2002 argues cautiously for identity). He composed speeches but was well aware of their specious effects at persuasion. Famously, he declared that his work was a possession for all time rather than an *agōnisma* for the immediate gratification of the listeners (1.22.4). Often taken mainly as a rejection of the Herodotean mode (flowing style, lively anecdotes, entertaining information), it is more likely to be criticizing more widely the agonistic fashion of display pieces, competitors in rhetorical displays, orators, and specious purveyors of entertaining listening. The poets and *logographoi* are criticized, too, separately (1.21)—logographers pay excessive attention to pleasing the audience and give stories about the past that tend to "the mythical"[21]—but we need not equate the targets of his superior claim to produce a "possession for ever" to be Herodotus alone, or only those writing about the past. Herodotus also shared the epideictic mode.[22]

The "*epideixeis* of the sophists" are mentioned once by Thucydides in the speech of Cleon (3.38.7): supporting the death penalty already voted for the Mytileneans, the demagogue turns on his audience and accuses them of listening to political speeches on policy as if they were hearing the sophists' *epideixeis*, "carried away by the pleasure of listening (*akoēs hēdonē*), like spectators of the sophists," rather than citizens deliberating about the polis. This significant antithesis is no less powerful for being in a speech that is also just such a display. It is ironic that Cleon is made to criticize the citizens for behaving like these other audiences awaiting rhetorical entertainment while at the same time he was arguing that the Athenians should not reconsider their decision, but just (blindly) continue their course without further thought. There is much anti-intellectualism in this speech.

As is well recognized, Thucydides was familiar with all the tricks of contemporary rhetoric, the ways to persuade;[23] he could write a brilliant *antilogia* between an unconvincing speech trying to convey valid points by Nicias, and a slick and superficially plausible one by Alcibiades (Nicias versus Alcibiades in 6.9–18); or equally he could put into Alcibiades' mouth a smooth set of sophisms and reinterpretations of the past (6.89 ff.). The Melian dialogue may be his version of the "question and answer" session in the sophistic mode, but set in the darker circumstances of real time (Macleod called it a "travesty" of dialectic[24]). There is abundant evidence both within the speeches and in the way speeches interact with narrative that he was acutely aware of the duplicitous character (or potential) of rhetoric. Thucydides never mentioned Gorgias, but Gorgias' idea that words are like medicines, both evil or good, is often present[25]. For example,

---

[21] *Logographoi* I take to be prose writers who treated the past, including various *muthoi* and geography.
[22] See Thomas (2000).
[23] Dion. Hal. *Thuc.* 24, 46 for Gorgianic influence; Finley (1942, 1967); for *ta deonta* of 1.22.1 as Gorgianic, see Macleod (1983, 68).
[24] Macleod (1983, 52–67, with 109n12); "travesty," p. 109. Cf. Nestle (1948, 352) on dialogue form.
[25] *Helen* 14 (and cf. 12–13): the power of speech on the soul is like that of medicines on the body.

there is the specious Athenian claim to the Camarineans during the Sicilian expedition that they will not use fine words, οὐ καλλιεπούμεθα . . . (6.83.2–3); Hermocrates of Syracuse warned the Sicilians against believing the present *sophismata* (sophisms) of the Athenians, that is, the claim to be helping Leontinoi and Egesta (677.1).[26] Thrasymachus was introduced as a prominent teacher of rhetoric in the highly critical discussion of rhetoric in Plato's *Phaedrus*: "Is not rhetoric, taken generally, a universal art of enchanting the mind by arguments," asked Socrates (261a), and continued, having mentioned Thrasymachus by name, "And a practitioner of the art [of persuasion] will make the same thing appear to the same persons to be at one time just, at another time, if he is so inclined, unjust?" (261c-d). Similar skills are attributed to Tisias and Gorgias (267 a–b); and to Protagoras. No wonder Thucydides might wish to distance himself from the *agōnisma* and the art of rhetoric. Yet he himself composed some of the most rhetorically sophisticated speeches in Greek literature.

There are elements in the speeches within the *History* that seem to comment implicitly on the baleful or dangerous effects of rhetoric (as well as much else) and the concepts such rhetoric employs, and I wish to explore whether we can probe these for further use of, or comment on, current debate and central Greek values. They display many arguments about the key concepts and theoretical preoccupations of the period—*nomos*: law/custom, justice, human nature, the relation between *nomos* and *phusis*. It is thus through the speeches and their relation to the surrounding narrative that we can perhaps get nearer to understanding Thucydides' relation to certain sophistic ideas: can we read the speeches while bearing in mind the doctrines of Antiphon, who emphasized the bonds of the laws and customs of society, as well as the importance of τὸ συμφέρον, self-interest or advantage (frag. 44)? Or the more extreme views of Thrasymachus, portrayed in Plato's *Republic* I as arguing that men are governed by self-interest and that justice is merely the interests of the stronger? Even if we doubt that Plato's Thasymachus replicated his exact views, others voiced similar views with variations (e.g., Antiphon, Callicles), and tragedy experimented with such ideas (cf. the Nurse's arguments, *Hippolytus* 433ff.). In any case such theories are found in Thucydides' speeches, showing at least a familiarity with certain extreme ideas of the time, the "immoralists." The speeches do not necessarily echo Thucydides' views, of course,[27] yet we are made to watch through the surrounding narrative whether such arguments have any purchase on the course of decision-making and events. We can surely discern some comment on the sophistic preoccupations with the relation of laws, individual and the state.

A particularly rich case study is the debate between Plataeans and Thebans that took place before the Spartans (3.53–68).[28] A debate about a relatively small town,

---

[26] Cf. Flory (1990), especially p. 198 for the pleasure of speeches: Flory's overall argument on *to muthōdes* is unconvincing. Note Romilly (1966b).

[27] Cf. Nestle's suggestion that the greater profundity of Thucydides' thought explained why the *nomos/phusis* antithesis was less marked in Thucydides than the sophists (1948, 347–49).

[28] Much discussed: see particularly Macleod (1983, chap.11); Hornblower (1991), Comm. ad loc.; Debnar (1996); Price (2001, 103 ff.); Grethlein (2012), seeing a programmatic contrast with Thucydides' method.

it is resonant with sophistically flavored concepts and reasons for action, high ideals, and a tragic end. We concentrate here on the claims to justice, law, convention, and "Greek laws."

The background is important: the Thebans attacked Plataea in peacetime, just before the outbreak of hostilities, in order to capture their inveterate enemy and ally of Athens (2.2 ff.); there followed a messy narrative of betrayal and parley, and then in the midst of negotiations with Thebans, the Plataeans turned and killed many Thebans. As another Theban party approached, more negotiations ensued, with contradictory accounts from each side, and the remaining Theban prisoners were killed (2. 5). This attack was the first overt rupture of the treaty in the preparations for war (2.7). The small town of Plataea had a special relationship with Athens but was situated within Boeotian territory. The Spartans marched against Plataea and began the siege shortly after the plague hit Athens (2.71ff.). The Plataeans appealed to the Spartans to desist on the grounds that after the Persian Wars, Pausanias the Spartan had declared Plataea independent and inviolate in recognition of the Plataeans' recent courage. They appealed to history, to the "gods to whom the oaths were made," to the gods of the Spartan ancestors, and to those of Plataea. The Spartans accused them of not remaining neutral (2.72) and being on the Athenian side. The Plataeans felt squeezed between Thebes and Athens; the Spartans suggested that they should hand over their city for the duration of the war, an impossible option, and the massive siege began. Archidamus appealed to the gods and declared that the Spartans were not the aggressors, because the Plataeans had already broken the oaths (2.74). After some months some Plataeans made a dramatic escape (3.21–24). The next year the desperate Plataeans still within the walls accepted voluntary surrender to the Spartans, and the Spartans promised them a trial before judges, the punishment of the guilty but "no one contrary to justice" (3.52.2: τούς τε ἀδίκους κολάζειν, παρὰ δίκην δὲ οὐδένα). At this point the Plataean debate starts, ten full pages in the OCT (3.53–67). It is rich in arguments based on law and "the laws," justice, and the presumed importance of the past.

The Plataean defense can be shown, point by point, both to use conventional techniques of trials and in circumstances that offer only a travesty of a trial, as Macleod (1983) showed brilliantly. He also thought it illustrated the shifting senses and distortions of *nomos* characteristic of wartime; more recently; Price saw it as illustrating the distortion of values and of meaning resulting from stasis (2001). But equally it shows the distortions of rhetoric itself and stages the ineffectiveness of justice and law against self-interest.

Arguments invoking justice and injustice recall the conventional techniques of rhetoric.[29] The Plataeans claimed that when the Thebans invaded and took Plataea in time of peace, the Plataeans merely followed "the universal law" of resisting the invader (3.56.2).

---

[29] See above all, Macleod (1983, chap. 11). *Pace* Price (2001), I find it hard to distinguish clearly the specious arguments of rhetoric from the (possible) distortions of meaning borne of war (while not denying the latter). The point is that the war and desperate situations make the attempts at persuasion all the more strained.

Spartans should consult justice, not only their own immediate interests/advantage (56.3: "If you let your idea of justice be fixed by your own immediate advantage and the Theban hostility"[30]). The slaughter of prisoners of war who had surrendered voluntarily is forbidden by Greek law, so they should be spared (3.58.3) (but this is exactly what Plataeans had done to the Thebans in Book 2). They make much of the common Greek resistance against the Persians, the Plataean help in this, the tombs of the ancestors of so many Greeks near Plataea, and the freedom which is embodied there, evoking a shared heritage and shared values, the "common customs of the Hellenes" (τὰ κοινὰ ... νόμιμα). They called on the "gods of the Hellenes" and the great claim of Sparta that they were now the liberators of Greece, just as Spartans, Plataeans, and Athenians were liberators in the Persian Wars. Though disordered by emotion, the speech is almost a paian to the common resistance of the Greeks to the Persian invaders—the Thebans being the notorious exception; and to common Greek gods, and universal Greek law.[31] This uplifting claim is reminiscent of the resonant appeal to the common gods and customs of the Greeks, a common Hellenism, uttered by the Athenians in Herodotus' narrative (8.144), and the echo is surely deliberate. It is a sentiment and rhetorical ploy many Greeks could give in their defence; the appeal to common Hellenic laws and the heroic resistance to Persia puts the Plataeans on the moral high ground.

The Thebans' counter-speech to the Spartans accused Plataea of making much of irrelevances (3.61.1), only to stress with equal obstinacy their past dealings with the Plataeans, the origin of the quarrel, and the tricky problem of Theban medizing (3.62). The speech may possibly be read as illustrative of Theban incompetence in speaking.[32] They justify their medizing on the extraordinary grounds that they were not running themselves at the time but were in the hands of a "*dunasteia* of the few" (62) (exactly the kind of constitution they still had!).[33] They then contradict Plataean claims that Plataea had supported the general Greek cause, insisting that they did this only because they were Athenian allies. A set of grievances include Plataea's "willful atticizing," which linguistically serves to put Plataean freedom fighting in a slot parallel to "medizing";[34] and the Thebans claim that they attacked Plataea recently not on their own account but because invited in by certain Plataeans who wished to restore Plataea to its proper Boeotian place (65). The Plataeans lawlessly (παρανόμως) butchered those captured Thebans whose lives were spared (66.2); there were three injustices (*adikias*), broken promises; the Plataeans think they should escape justice. "You [the Plataeans] say *we* are the ones who acted against custom (παρανομῆσαι) and should pay the penalty" (66.3). "Vindicate the Hellenic law which they have broken" (67.6)—and they finally appeal to

---

[30] Hornblower's translation (1991).

[31] The speech is exceptional in Thucydides for its stress on the past: (Hornblower 1991, 445).

[32] Debnar (1996); more sympathetically, Macleod (1983, 113 ff.), seeing it as a function of the "parody of legality which this whole 'trial' is" (118).

[33] Perhaps cf. Epicharmus' αὐξανόμενος λόγος, frag. 136 (= Plut. *De Sera numinis vindicta* 559 a–b, the fallacy that change renders one not responsible for past deeds: with thanks to Prof. A. C. Cassio for this suggestion.

[34] Macleod (1983, 116).

the Spartans not to listen to speeches at all, not to be deceived by the Plataeans' fine words, but to put one short question (67.6–7). "Where wrong is done, speeches adorned with words are needed to veil it" (67.6: ἁμαρτανομένων δὲ λόγοι ἔπεσι κοσμηθέντες προκαλύμματα γίγνονται).

What happened after all this speech-making? The Spartans simply asked each Plataean if he had helped the Spartans in the (current) war. They then killed them all and completely destroyed Plataea, reusing the materials to honour Hera. They behaved like this, according to Thucydides, simply to please the Thebans for the immediate war (3.69).

Why, then, is the debate staged at all? It seems to dramatize precisely the grand words and sentiments, the claims and counterclaims to justice, to law, "laws of the Greeks," admirable achievements in the past, past contributions to Greek liberty, and the conflict between justice and self-interest. But it also illustrates devious and unscrupulous arguments, and the fact that all these are useless in the face of expediency. The Plataeans invoke one universal law (3.56.2) and in the same breath almost accuse the Spartans of conflating justice and self-interest (like the Thrasymachean theory). However, it is not absolutely clear that their two senses of *nomos* in 56.2 and 58.3 are contradictory, as Macleod argued.[35] Rather, they are two different and separate "laws," both equally powerful and compelling, the first very general (general human response to invasion). We see not so much distortion of meaning as the clever selection of whatever "laws" could justify their behavior, and disagreement about key facts. It is striking that even the Plataeans do not quite tell the truth, for in the main narrative the Theban intruders were just beginning to negotiate when the Plataeans decided to massacre them (2.3), and later there were serious disagreements on each side about why the second group of Thebans were killed (2.5).[36] The speech seems to enhance Plataean claims to sympathy, their pitiful and dangerous situation between Thebes and Athens, their contribution to the Persian Wars, but in the end this counts for nothing at all. The Spartans decided the single question was fair, since their offer of neutrality had been refused. In other words, the claims to justice, common Greek laws, and the common Greek past, are irrelevant against the single question of immediate expediency. The Spartans had said initially that they would not act *para dikēn*, but when it came to it, they acted (in Thucydides' view) simply out of immediate self-interest. *Dikē* did not come into it; or perhaps this *was* Spartan *dikē*? Perhaps, we begin to think, Spartan self-interest is completely conflated with what they think is *dikē*—the Spartans at this point precisely illustrative of the Thrasymachus doctrine[37]. At least in the Mytilenean debate,[38] the Athenians debated whether to reopen the question of Mytilene, and what to do (though we note both speakers focus on interest rather than justice, separating the two), whereas the Spartans

---

[35] Macleod (1983, 108): partly because war justified reciprocal violence, and therefore made the second "law" weak; followed by Price (2001, 113). Note ὅσιον, however, in 3.56.2, which hints at a different level (with thanks to Tim Rood).
[36] The Thebans claimed the Plataeans promised to give up the prisoners if the Thebans retired.
[37] Indeed, the Athenians say this is the Spartan idea of justice in the Melian Dialogue, 5.105.
[38] See e.g., Macleod (1983, chap.11); Hornblower (1991 ad loc., 462f).

were totally uninterested in any discussion. We note also how irrelevant history is as well as rhetoric.

It is hard not to envisage that Thucydides intended a deliberate contrast with Herodotus' main Persian theme, and Herodotean trails of causation involving revenge or reciprocal help in return for some past action (e.g., Hdt. III 47, on why Sparta helped the Samians); or where claims to status and consideration are so often presented in terms of the past. Of course Herodotus was aware of false claims, but Thucydides seems to offer here a carefully constructed set of scenes that reveal that the Persian Wars, along with various categories of good, are now no longer relevant at all for current action.[39] It is shortly after this that the yet grimmer narrative of the Corcyrean revolution unfolds in which values, social norms, and words were all subverted in stasis and war. Again, we might contrast this moral upheaval with the rational and positive affirmation in Herodotus that "*nomos* is king" to emphasize Herodotus' belief in the priority and significance of a society's own laws and customs (3.38).

If speeches, fine sentiments, and concepts are paraded and then emphatically shown to be dismissed, we seem to see a Thrasymachean vision working out in practice, in real time. Thrasymachus in the *Republic* stated that he thought human behavior was dominated by self-interest; right or justice was simply the interest of the stronger, or of the stronger party (*Rep.* 338 c–e); Antiphon, at least, entertained a similar if more nuanced view (frag. 44). But rather than see a linear link or relationship between Thrasymachus or Antiphon and Thucydides, we may be seeing a sentiment that was debated and experimented with by several thinkers, of which Thucydides was one, Thrasymachus another.[40] Thucydides claimed that war was a violent teacher (3.82.2), that is, it taught new methods by itself, which might imply that the conditions for perversions of justice were not permanent. One perhaps did not need sophistic theories to see this development, but they could have helped to crystallize ideas and formulate the building blocks of analysis. Moreover, he hints that rhetoric did not always hold the seductive charm that Gorgias promised; it could be powerless—its grand ideals as well as more self-serving constructions—against the elements of expediency.

Can we go further on the valuation of *nomos* and *nomoi* here? The use of various appeals to *nomos* here of course implies that *nomos* (however defined, perhaps left undefined) is a good, a common ideal that will have force in a rhetorical argument. This is not necessarily the Thucydidean view, but in any case the realism of the narrative then shows that neither justice nor *nomoi* have a hold on the Spartans. The speeches imply a normative position on *nomos*—that it should be upheld; the narrative implies that it is upheld only when convenient (and different interpretations of the same events and promises also come into the mix). All this seems to have an oblique or distant relationship to the numerous discussions about law, justice, and nature and the relations among

---

[39] Rood connects this lesson, interestingly, with the more general absence in Thucydides of the past being used in political decisions (2006, 246).

[40] Guthrie (1971, 85) is rather bland: Thucydides' speeches "supply the necessary background to an outburst like that of Thrasymachus."

them that were prominent in various sophistic debates and that have such importance in Antiphon, Anonymus Iamblichi, and Plato's dialogues. Antiphon discussed this and argued that it was advantageous and necessary to keep to the law when in public view, but that it might be advantageous to disobey the laws in secret if you could evade detection (frag. 44 A col. 1):

> Justice, then, is not to transgress the *nomima* of whatever city one lives in. Now a man would make use of justice in a way most advantageous (ξυμφ[ε]ρόντως) to himself, if he were to regard the laws as great in the presence of witnesses, but nature as great when deprived of witnesses. For the laws are imposed (ἐπίθ]ετα), whereas nature is necessary.

Nevertheless, he does not seem to have equated this disobeying of law with "justice," in contrast to the Thrasymachean line as portrayed in the *Republic*.[41] The author of the Anonymus Iamblichi was more cautious and conventional. Yet the Plataeans and Thebans conform to popular morality and approval of the laws. The implication in Thucydides is that if laws go, what is left is human nature.

It seems implausible to think of direct influence from one writer to another, but rather a sharing of interests, terms of argument, and debate. Thucydides' formulation so sharply in terms of law, laws and their dismissal in counter-arguments, can belong only in a period when much theoretical interest was evinced in law and its value, but he goes his own way. It was symptomatic of an intellectual climate in which enormous energy was apparently given to theoretical debate about the relations between law, nature, and justice. These could enter rhetorical argument, speeches in trials, and *epideixeis*, as well as more theoretical discussion. Antiphon and Thrasymachus produced a normative theory—should *nomoi* be obeyed, what is justice? Thucydides observed the reality, or perhaps better, described and analyzed what he saw as the reality with the help of these sharpened concepts. Then he showed the destructive effects of such behavior. The descriptions of the collapse of values and social norms as a result of plague and stasis suggest he appreciated with Protagoras the cohesive strength of social nomoi, and was certainly not a moral relativist.[42] His condemnation of *pleonexia* (greed) in the stasis analysis contrasts with Callicles and Thrasymachus.[43] In the Melian Dialogue, the Athenians declare that "the strong do what they can and the weak suffer what they must" (5.89). Yet they prohibit justice from the debate, saying that the two sides must only debate about what is advantageous, *sumpheron*. This confirms that Thucydides thought the two were not identical (5.89: justice is relevant only between equals in power—and cf. 5.90); yet it was possible to speculate about when and where justice could have a tangible role.

---

[41] See edition by Pendrick (2002), with Introduction, especially 53 ff.
[42] For Protagoras: Plato, *Protag.*, Kerferd (1981, chap. 12), Guthrie (1971, chap. 5); cf. Bett (1989, 2002). Gomme et al. (1945–1981), comm. on 3.82f, 386 notes Thucydides' disapproval of moral relativism here. Thomas (2011) on *anomia* in Thucydides and sophistic ideas of progress.
[43] 3.82.8; cf. *Gorgias* 483 c–d; *Rep.* I, 343d–344a.

Much more could be discussed. We have seen enough to show that Thucydides must have had a profound and constantly developing and critical relationship to the other writers and thinkers of his age. This was an intellectual and political world in which *dikē*/justice was being dissected from many angles—its relation to nomos, convention, in legal frameworks, in rhetorical arguments in trials. Rather than offering a "background" to the sophists (*pace* Guthrie), Thucydides offered a profound contribution to the debates and theoretical concerns of his age—though he did this apparently through a narrative of realism. The fascinating possibility is that his ideas influenced the next generations in abstract as well as historical thought.

References

Allison, J. W. 1983. "Pericles' Policy and the Plague." *Historia* 32: 14–23.
Bett, R. 1989. "The Sophists and Relativism." *Phronesis* 34: 139–69.
Bett, R. 2002. "Is There a Sophistic Ethics?" *Ancient Philosophy* 22: 235–62.
Brock, R. 2000. "Sickness in the Body Politic: Medical Language and the Greek Polis." In *Death and Disease in the Ancient City*, edited by V. M. Hope and E. Marshall, 24–34. London and New York. Routledge.
Crawley, R., trans. and Thucydides 1910. History of the Peloponnesian War. London.
Cochrane, C. 1929. *Thucydides and the Science of History*. Oxford: Oxford University Press.
Debnar, P. 1996. "The Unpersuasive Thebans (Thucydides 3.61–67)." *Phoenix* 50: 95–110.
Demont, Paul. 1983. "Notes sur le récit de la pestilence athénienne chez Thucydide at sur ses rapports avec la médicine grecque de l'époque classique." In *Formes de pensée dans la Collection hippocratique, Actes IVe colloq. Internat. Hippocratique 1981 (Lausanne)*, edited by F. Lasserre and P. Mudry, 341–53. Geneva.
Demont, Paul. 2013. "The Causes of the Athenian Plague and Thucydides." In *Thucydides between Literature and History*, edited by A. Tsakmakis and M. Tamiolaki, 73–87. Berlin and Boston, De Gruyter.
Diller, H. 1955. "Review of Weidauer (1954)." *Gnomon* 27: 9–14.
Eijk, Ph. J. van der. 1997. "Towards a Rhetoric of Ancient Scientific Discourse: Some Formal Characteristics of Greek Medical and Philosophical Texts (Hippocratic Corpus, Aristotle)." In *Grammar as Interpretation: Greek Literature in Its Linguistic Contexts*, edited by E. J. Bakker, 77–129. Leiden: Mnemosyne Supplement.
Finley, John. 1942. *Thucydides*. Cambridge, MA: Harvard University Press.
Finley, John. 1967. *Three Essays on Thucydides*. Cambridge: Harvard University Press.
Flory, S. 1990. "The Meaning of τὸ μὴ μυθῶδες (I 22.4) and the Usefulness of Thucydides' History." *CJ* 85: 193–208.
Gagarin, M. 2002. *Antiphon the Athenian*. Austin: University of Texas Press.
Gomme, A. W., A. Andrewes, and K. Dover. 1945-1981. *An Historical Commentary on Thucydides*. 5 vols. Oxford: Clarendon.
Grethlein, J. 2012. "The Use and Abuse of History in the Plataean Debate (Thuc. 3.52–68)." In *Time and Narrative in Ancient Historiography: The "Plupast" from Herodotus to Appian*, edited by J. Grethlein and C. Krebs, 57–75. Cambridge: Cambridge University Press.
Guthrie, W. K. C. 1971. *The Sophists*. Cambridge: Cambridge University Press.

Hawthorn, G. 2014. *Thucydides on Politics. Back to the Present*. Cambridge: Cambridge University Press.
Heinimann, F. 1945. *Nomos und Physis: Herkunft und Bedeutung einer Antithese im griechischen Denken des 5. Jahrhunderts*. Basel: Reinhardt.
Holladay, A. J. 1987. "Thucydides and the Recognition of Contagion: A Reply." *Maia* 39: 95–96.
Holladay, A. J., and J. C. F. Poole. 1979. "Thucydides and the Plague of Athens." *CQ* 29: 282–300.
Hornblower, S. 1987. *Thucydides*. London: Duckworth.
Hornblower, S. 1991. *A Commentary on Thucydides*. Vol. I, *Books I–III*. Oxford: Clarendon.
Hornblower, S. 1992. "The Religious Dimension to the Peloponnesian War, or, What Thucydides Does Not Tell Us." *HSCP* 94: 169–97.
Hornblower, S. 2004. *Thucydides and Pindar*. Oxford: Oxford University Press.
Hornblower, S. 2008. *A Commentary on Thucydides*. Vol. III, *Books 5.25–8.10*. Oxford: Clarendon.
Jones, W. H. S., trans. 1944. *Hippocrates*. Vol. 1. Cambridge MA: Harvard University Press.
Jouanna, J. 1980. "Politique et médecine: La problématique du changement dans le *Régime des maladies aiguës*, et chez Thucydide (Livre VI)." In *Hippocratica. Actes du colloque hippocratique de Paris, 1978*, edited by M. D. Grmek, 299–318. Paris.
Jouanna, J. 1984. "Rhétorique et médecine dans la Collection Hippocratique." *REG* 97: 26–44.
Jouanna, J. 1990. *Hippocrate. L'Ancienne Médecine*. Paris: Belles Lettres.
Jouanna, J. 1992. *Hippocrate*. Paris: Fayard.
Jouanna, J. 2003. *Hippocrate. La Maladie Sacrée*. Paris: Belles Lettres.
Jouanna, J. 2005. "Cause and Crisis in Historians and Medical Writers of the Classical Period." In *Hippocrates in Context: Papers Read at the XIth. Intern. Hippocratic Colloquium: Univ. of Newcastle, 27–32 Aug, 2002*, edited by P. van der Eijk, 3–27. Leiden.
Kallet, L. 2013. "Thucydides, Apollo, the Plague and the War." *AJP* 134: 355–82.
Kerferd, G. B. 1981. *The Sophistic Movement*. Cambridge: Cambridge University Press.
Kühn, J.-H., and U. Fleischer. 1986. *Index Hippocraticus*. Göttingen: Vanderhoeck & Ruprecht.
Lattimore, S., trans. 1998. *The Peloponnesian War*, by Thucydides. Indianapolis and Cambridge.
Lloyd, G. E. R. 1979. *Magic, Reason and Experience: Studies in the Origins and Development of Greek Science*. Cambridge: Cambridge University Press.
Lloyd, G. E. R. 1987. *Revolutions of Wisdom. Studies in the Claims and Practice of Ancient Greek Science*. California: University of California Press.
Longrigg, J. 1992. "Epidemics, Ideas and Classical Athenian Society." In *Epidemics and Ideas: Essays on the Historical Perception of Pestilence*, edited by T. O. Ranger and P. Slack, 21–44. Cambridge: Cambridge University Press.
Longrigg, J. 1993. *Greek Rational Medicine: Philosophy and Medicine from Alcmeon to the Alexandrians*. London: Routledge.
Macleod, C. 1983. *Collected Essays*. Oxford: Oxford University Press.
Mansfeld, J. 1980. "Theoretical and Empirical Attitudes in Early Greek Scientific Medicine." In *Hippocratica: Actes du colloque hippocratique de Paris, 1978*, edited by M. D. Grmek, 371–90. Paris.
Mynott, J., trans. and ed. 2013. *Thucydides. The War of the Peloponnesians and the Athenians*. Cambridge: Cambridge University Press.
Nestle, W. (1914) 1948. "Thukydides und die Sophistik." *Neue Jahrbücher f.d. Klass. Altertum* 17, 649–81; repr. in his *Griechische Studien* (Stuttgart, 1948), 321–73.
Nicolai, R. 2014. "At the Boundary of Historiography: Xenophon and His Corpus." In *Between Thucydides and Polybius: The Golden Age of Greek Historiography*, edited by G. Parmeggiani, 63–87. Washington, D.C.: Center for Hellenic Studies.

Page, D. L. 1953. "Thucydides' Description of the Great Plague at Athens." *CQ* 47: 97–119.
Parry, Adam. 1969. "The Language of Thucydides' Description of the Plague." *BICS* 16 (106–18.
Pendrick, G. J. 2002. *Antiphon the Sophist: The Fragments*. Cambridge: Cambridge University Press.
Plant, I. M. 1999. "The Influence of Forensic Oratory on Thucydides' Principles of Method." *CQ* 49: 62–73.
Price, Jonathan. 2001. *Thucydides and Internal War*. Cambridge: Cambridge University Press.
Rengakos, A., and A. Tsakmakis, eds. 2006. *Brill's Companion to Thucydides*. Leiden: Brill
Romilly, J. de. 1966a. "La condemnation du plaisir dans l'oeuvre de Thucydide." *W.Stud.* 79, 142–48.
Romilly, J. de. 1966b. "Thucydide et l'idée de progress." *Annali della Scuola normale superiore di Pisa. Lettre, storia, e filosofia* 35: 143–91.
Rood, T. 1998. *Thucydides: Narrative and Explanation*. Oxford: Oxford University Press.
Rood, T. 2006. "Objectivity and Authority: Thucydides' Historical Method." In *Brill's Companion to Thucydides*, edited by A. Rengakos and A. Tsakmakis, 225–49. Leiden: Brill.
Solmsen, F. 1975. *Intellectual Experiments of the Greek Enlightenment*. Princeton: Princeton University Press.
Swain, S. 1994. "Man and Medicine in Thucydides." *Arethusa* 27: 303–27.
Thomas, R. 2000. *Herodotus in Context: Ethnography, Science and the Art of Persuasion* Cambridge: Cambridge University Press.
Thomas, R. 2003. "Prose Performance Texts: *Epideixeis* and Written Publication in the Late Fifth and Early Fourth Centuries." In *Written Texts and the Rise of Literate Culture in Ancient Greece*, edited by H. Yunis, 162–88. Cambridge: Cambridge University Press.
Thomas, R. 2006. "Thucydides' Intellectual Milieu and the Plague." In *Brill's Companion to Thucydides*, edited by A. Rengakos and A. Tsakmakis, 87–108. Leiden: Brill.
Thomas, R. 2011. "Thucydides and Social Change: Between *Akribeia* and Universality." In *Unfounding Time in and through Ancient Historical Thought*, edited by A. Lianeri, 229–46. Cambridge: Cambridge University Press.
Tsakmakis, A. and M. Tamiolaki, eds. 2013. *Thucydides between History and Literature*. Berlin and Boston: De Gruyter.
Wallace, R. 1998. "The Sophists in Athens." In *Democracy, Empire and the Arts in Fifth-Century Athens*, edited by D. Boedeker and K. Raaflaub, 203–22. Cambridge: Harvard University Press.
Weidauer, K. 1954. *Thukydides und die hippokratischen Schriften*. Heidelberg: Winter.
Winton, R. 2000. "Herodotus, Thucydides and the Sophists." In *The Cambridge History of Greek and Roman Political Thought*, edited by C. Rowe and M. Schofield, 89–121. Cambridge: Cambridge University Press.

CHAPTER 34

THUCYDIDES, EPIC, AND TRAGEDY

TOBIAS JOHO[*]

COMPETITION and rivalry tend to go hand in hand with emulation and admiration in Greek literature, and criticism can coexist with profound indebtedness. Thucydides' stance vis-à-vis Homeric epic and Attic tragedy belongs to this tradition of tangled relationships. Thucydides criticized Homer and the "ancient poets" in the *Archaeology*, citing their dubious relationship with the truth as a major shortcoming (1.5.2, 9.4, 10.1, 10.3, 21.1). This standoff notwithstanding, Thucydides shared with Homer and the tragedians the serious subject matter and the profound awareness, pointed out by Colin Macleod (1983, 157–58), of suffering as the central benchmark in human experience. This agreement led him to base important aspects of his own work on models that were derived from Homer and the tragedians.

Most readily conspicuous is the indispensability of speeches in direct discourse, which due to Homer's authority were considered the medium of choice for higher-order reflections of general application.[1] Homer's example was also partly responsible for both Herodotus and Thucydides choosing war as their chief subject. For Homer, war, the fountainhead of κλέος, was the topic most worthy of a grand heroic narrative. The Trojan War, comprising the anger of Achilles and its ensuing consequences, provided the paradigmatic example. Strasburger observed that Thucydides implemented this *Iliadic* model with much greater rigor than Herodotus (Strasburger 1966, 61–63): whereas Herodotus was more open to the comparatively domestic aspects of the *Odyssey*, Thucydides, in an act of grandiose one-sidedness, adopted the *Iliad* as his primary point of reference and focused his work very sharply on the exceptional state of crisis or, in Thucydides' words, "the greatest convulsion" that ever happened (κίνησις μεγίστη; Thuc. 1.1.1).

---

[*] I am happy to thank Edith Foster and Christopher Pelling for reading drafts of this paper, which benefited greatly from their advice and insight.
[1] On Speeches in Thucydides, see Tsakmakis, chapter 16 in this volume.

Beyond these large-order influences, Homer and the tragedians left a deep imprint on several specific features of Thucydides' text. Thucydides followed epic and tragic models in three areas: he adopted aspects of their narrative technique, he modeled his ethos and narrative voice on Homer and the tragedians, and he used allusions to bring out parallels between his account and specific epic or tragic episodes.

Narrative Technique

The Interlace Method

In choosing the Peloponnesian War as his topic, Thucydides set himself to describe events that were taking place simultaneously in different arenas throughout the eastern Mediterranean, so that he had to find a way to deal with the problem of synchronicity, that is, the representation of simultaneous events in narrative form. Homer provided Thucydides with a model for the solution of this problem.

Homer's way of representing simultaneous events has been labeled the "interlace technique" or "desultory method" (Rengakos 2006a, 289; de Jong 2001, XIV, 589–90). If Homer sets out to narrate two separate yet contemporaneous chains of events, he usually proceeds in the following way: he tells the first narrative strand until the initial events cohere and he can break off, and then begins again, building the second narrative strand up to a similar point; then he switches back to the first strand, picking it up where he left off, and so forth. The alternation between the account of the battle before the Greek ships and the scenes in which Patroclus obtains permission from Achilles to lead the Myrmidons to the rescue provides a characteristic Homeric example (*Il.* 15.592–746, 16.1–101, 16.102–123, 16.124–256).

In Thucydides, an especially elaborate instance of this method is provided by the narrative concatenation of the unsuccessful secession of Mytilene and the downfall of Plataea in Book 3.[2] One can detect four narrative strands. First, the Mytilenaean sequence, which in turn contains two separate strands: (1a) relates the secession of Mytilene, the Athenian counter measures, the city's eventual surrender, and the Athenians' decision concerning the fate of Mytilene (2–6, 16–19, 27–28, 35–50); (1b) relates the Spartans' half-hearted attempts to send relief to Mytilene (8–15, 25–26, 29–34). Strand two tells the story of the siege of Plataea, which culminates in the city's surrender, the Spartan mock trial, and the execution of the defenders of Plataea (20–24, 52–68); Strands three and four offer two separate brief reports of Athenian diversionary attacks (7 and 51).

---

[2] For other examples, see Gomme (1954, 134–37) on the alternating narrations of the Athenian campaign to Boeotia and of Brasidas' advance in northern Greece, and Romilly (2012, 30–31 = 1956, 56–58) on Gylippus' journey to Sicily.

The interlacing of the separate strands allows Thucydides to infuse his account with subtle shades of meaning. For instance, the arrangement enables the reader vividly to experience Sparta's ineffectiveness. Thucydides tends to juxtapose lengthy reports of Spartan attempts to support Mytilene (8–15 and 29–34) with much shorter segments containing efficient Athenian countermeasures (16–19 and 27–28). By spending much less narrative time on the Athenian exploits than on the simultaneous Spartan actions, Thucydides enables the reader to grasp how much less real time the Athenians take to accomplish their aims. This experience is made possible through the sudden shifts between narrative strands and the attribution of segments of disproportionate length to each side.[3]

One particular use of illustratively disproportionate narrative segments warrants further attention. In light of the increasing pressure on Plataea, of which the reader is reminded through an extended episode at 3.20–24, the two smaller Athenian incursions provide important information. The first (3.7) appears immediately after the segment that reports the beginning of the Mytilenaean secession (3.2–6), thus indicating that the Athenians enjoy, despite the sudden trouble at Mytilene, enough scope of action to send out a fleet of thirty ships to harass the Peloponnesians. Thucydides places the second episode, his report of the trivial Athenian excursion to Minoa (3.51), immediately before the monumental account of Plataea's downfall (52–68). The proportion brings out the absurd inverse relationship: from the Athenian point of view, the expedition to Minoa is paramount, but measured by the yardstick of impartial Thucydidean historiography the sad fate of Plataea merits much greater interest.

Schadewaldt pointed out (1966, 77) that Homer derives three major benefits from the interlace method: (1) it helps to avoid pauses, (2) it enables the reader to be aware of simultaneous events, and (3) it uncovers the causal chains that connect one sequence of events with another. As our analysis of the arrangement of the earlier half of Book 3 shows, Thucydides likewise achieves these three effects. Moreover, he intensifies certain aspects of Homer's use of the interlace method. The extremely short accounts of the two diversionary attacks go beyond what one usually finds in Homer. The effect of these segments resides in their extreme abbreviation and the contrast with the ample scope of the narratives concerning Mytilene and Plataea. Such opposition between an episode reduced to mere outlines and an adjacent one of monumental dimensions would be atypical for Homer's more evenly distributed arrangement, which springs from Homer's habit of lingering over individual episodes so as to give each detail its due. Thucydides, on the other hand, mines the effects produced by abrupt contrasts of scale.

Suspense: Step-by-Step Clarification and Retardation

For the purpose of heightening suspense, Thucydides adopts a number of strategies that can again be traced back to Homer. Both epic and historiography had to reckon with an audience that was already familiar with many of the reported events. Therefore,

---

[3] On narrative scale in Thucydides, see Connor, chapter 12 in this volume.

suspense was usually not based on the audience's uncertainty about the outcome of an event; instead it tended to revolve around the question of how a certain outcome was to be realized.

Rengakos uses the term "step-by-step clarification" to describe one way of achieving suspense during the narration of a known course of events (2006a, 295). Schadewaldt stressed the central importance of this device for the *Iliad* (1966, 112–13): as a given narrative strand unfolds, the poet tends to give the reader clues as to what will happen in the future; yet, instead of revealing all the details at once, he provides just enough information to prepare the reader for what is coming, thus inducing suspense about how exactly the expected course of action will come to pass. The progressively more detailed disclosures of the plan of Zeus in the *Iliad* provide a suitable example (cf. Schadewaldt 1966, 113; Rengakos 1999, 321–22).

Connor found the same principle applied in Thucydides' report of the initial phase of the Pylos episode (4.2–15, cf. Connor 1984, 110–12), and Rengakos (2006, 295) draws attention to a movement from vague references to full-fledged disclosure in the account of Brasidas' advance in Thrace (4.70.1, 71.2, 78, 79, 81). To these examples, one could add Thucydides' gradual revelation in the early phase of the Sicilian narrative that the money promised to Athens by the city of Egesta did not exist. The incessant nagging and grandiloquent promises of the Egestaeans (twice at 6.6.2 and twice at 6.6.3), who had come to Athens to plead for Athenian support for their wars in Sicily, make the reader, and indeed the Athenians themselves (6.6.3), immediately suspicious about the substance of the Egestaean pronouncements. The Athenians send a fact-finding mission, and when the Athenian envoys return, they and the Egestaean envoys tell the Athenians, according to Thucydides, "things that were enticing and eminently untrue" (τά τε ἄλλα ἐπαγωγὰ καὶ οὐκ ἀληθῆ; 6.8.2). This explicit acknowledgement of the falsehood of the information provokes the reader to wonder how the statements of the Athenian envoys could possibly be false, given that they went to Egesta and therefore must surely have seen the large quantities of money with their own eyes. After this, Nicias casts further doubt on the reliability of the Sicilians in general (6.12.2) and the Egestaeans in particular (6.22) in the course of his speeches in the Sicilian Debate. Thucydides has therefore laid recurring hints. However, the actual Egestaean trick is revealed only after the Athenian fleet has already arrived at Rhegium. Until this moment, Thucydides keeps the reader in suspense about the full scope of the Egestaean deceit, but now he offers a vivid story, a flashback that shows how the Athenian envoys were fooled (6.46.1–4). Although many readers will have known the outcome of the story, Thucydides' parsimonious management of the crucial information creates suspense about how, exactly, this end was accomplished.

Still more widespread is Thucydides' use of another Homeric method to enhance suspense: retardation, that is, slowing down the narrative in order to put off reaching the end. Reichel distinguishes three types of narrative retardation, all of which can be found in Homer (1990, 131): interruption, the temporary inversion of the direction of the action, and deceleration.

An example of the first variety is Homer's postponement of the report of Briscis' removal from Achilles' tent in the first book of the *Iliad*: instead of reporting this event immediately after the assembly of the Greek leaders has been broken up, Homer inserts the description of the preparations for Odysseus' trip to the island Chryse (*Il.* 1.308–317). The second type of retardation, temporary inversion of the narrative, can be illustrated with the celebrated example of Agamemnon's failed trial of the Greek army (cf. Reichel 1990, 131–32). Zeus' promise to Thetis (*Il.* 1.524–27) that the Greeks would endure a period of devastating defeat has induced the reader to expect an imminent battle. Nevertheless, in the wake of Agamemnon's failed attempt to test the fighting spirit of the Greeks, the Greek army sets out to leave Troy and the narrative direction is temporarily inverted (*Il.* 2.109–210). Finally, deceleration of the narrative is typically achieved through increased specification of detail. Rengakos has analyzed this procedure in Homer's account of Odysseus' delayed encounter with the Cyclops in the *Odyssey* (1999, 313–15). Through the enumeration of a variety of predominantly visual details, the narrator causes the relation to linger for about sixty lines (*Od.* 9.196–251) and thus postpones the encounter between Odysseus and the Cyclops.

In both Homer and Thucydides, interruption of the narrative, the first variety of retardation, often occurs in connection with the interlace method. The aforementioned alternation between the equally dramatic Mytilenaean and Plataean narratives in Book 3 is a case in point: while the reader learns about the course of events in one arena, he is kept in suspenseful anticipation about the simultaneous events of the other narrative strand.

Thucydides' account of the Athenians' delay after their defeat in the Great Harbor of Syracuse provides a good example of temporary inversion of the narrative. Before the beginning of the battle, the Athenians had already decided that they would retreat by land if the battle went poorly (7.60.3). Once the battle has been lost, the reader expects an immediate retreat. Indeed, just after the defeat, the Athenians are collectively resolved to retreat instantaneously (7.72.5). Yet they easily let themselves be tricked by the mendacious claim of Hermocrates' messengers that the Syracusans have blocked the roads (7.73.1–4). As a result, the first night after the defeat is left unexploited. Moreover, after this the Athenians waste yet another day, which they spend packing up their belongings (7.74.1), so that they do not depart until the third day after the battle (7.75.1).

Extreme narrative deceleration is a distinctive quality of Thucydides' subsequent report of the Athenians' ill-fated retreat on Sicily. His account covers eight days, each explicitly referenced. Through this framework, Thucydides applies an especially tight grid to this portion of the narrative and obliges himself to spell out the events of every single day separately. As long as the Athenians make relatively good progress during the first two days (7.78.2–4), Thucydides' narrative advances rapidly. The narrative of the third (7.78.5–7), fourth (7.79.1–5), and fifth day (7.79.5–6) becomes more detailed and is slowed down considerably: on each day, the Athenians encounter heavy opposition and make merely insignificant advances. At this point, Thucydides momentarily passes over from a day-by-day scheme to an even tighter grid of day and night: faced with a lack of basic necessities and the sorry plight of their army, Nicias and Demosthenes decide to change their route and to resume the retreat during the night between the fifth and sixth day in order to evade the Syracusan watches (7.80.2–7). At sunrise of the sixth day, the

Syracusans realize that the Athenians have escaped and set out in pursuit at breakneck speed (7.81.1). Soon the Syracusans encircle Demosthenes' army within a walled olive grove (7.81.2–5) and eventually force it to surrender (7.82.1–3). On the next, seventh, day, Nicias is already encircled. At this point, the story is practically over. But the day-by day-pattern enables Thucydides to draw out this final stretch of the report; for, despite the desperate situation, Nicias will surrender only on the eighth day. Through reporting a range of drastic details, Thucydides manages to achieve a final climax of deceleration in the narrative of these last two days (seventh day: 7.83.1–5; eighth day: 7.84.1–85.4). Because Thucydides takes progressively longer to narrate the events of a given day, the reader has the impression that time passes ever more slowly.

Retardation was also a favorite device of Herodotus. For instance, Rengakos points out (2006b, 192–94) that all three varieties of retardation occur in the narrative of the Persian advance against Greece in Herodotus' Book 7. Retardation is but one example of a series of epic narrative devices that came to Thucydides through the Herodotean filter.[4] Against the background of this tradition, distinctive Thucydidean characteristics become manifest: the tight day by day grid and the carefully calibrated retarding pace in the account of the Athenian retreat attest to Thucydides' dramatic intensification of strategies that he found in the works of Homer and Herodotus.

Narrative Patterning: Juxtaposition

Both Homer and the tragedians link separate parts of their narrative through verbal or thematic parallels. This device is called narrative patterning. Juxtaposition is a particular variety of patterning by which entire episodes, mostly directly adjacent ones, are made to respond to each other.

Juxtaposition already appears in Homer: for example, in the contrast, pointed out by Schadewaldt (1966, 146–48), between the quarrel on earth and the quarrel on Olympus in Book 1 of the *Iliad*. The effects achieved by such linked scenes were considerably heightened by the Attic tragedians. Two inherent character traits of the tragic genre made this intensification possible: first, the alternation of stage action and choral odes made it easier to highlight parallel situations by placing them at corresponding junctures within the unified whole; second, staging opened up the possibility of underscoring parallels by visual means.

Perhaps the most celebrated example of such a mirror scene is the parallelism between the culminating moments of the *Agamemnon* and the *Libation Bearers*. The climax of each play is identical: the murder of a member of the house of Atreus (Agamemnon and Clytemnestra) at the hands of a close relative (Clytemnestra and Orestes). As Taplin has pointed out, the staging of each incident powerfully underscores the parallelism between the two scenes (1978, 125–26): on both occasions, the central door of the *skēnē*

---

[4] The intermediary role of Herodotus is stressed by Macleod (1983, 157), Hornblower (1987, 28, 113), and Rengakos (2006a, 303).

is thrown open, the *ekkyklēma* with the blood-spattered corpse is rolled out, and the murderer stands towering over the victim. Taplin (1978, 126) also points out the contrasts. While Clytemnestra, sword in hand, stands over the dead body of Agamemnon in exuberant, ecstatic triumph, Orestes, who likewise carries a sword in his hand, but also holds a suppliant's branch and wreath, is painfully aware of his guilt: as the suppliant branch makes visible, he is asking for the protection of Apollo, who commanded him to carry out the killing (*Cho.* 1034–36).

Thucydides contrasts scenes in ways that recall such techniques. His most characteristic procedure, aptly described by Gomme, is the direct juxtaposition of large-scale episodes that illuminate each other (1954, 142–44). For instance, he juxtaposes the Funeral Oration and the excursus on the plague, the Mytilenaean Debate, and the Plataean Debate, and the Melian Dialogue and the Sicilian Debate at Athens. Let us look at the second pair in some detail.

As pointed out in the section entitled "Narrative Technique: The Interlace Method," above, Thucydides separates the monumental accounts of the downfalls of Mytilene and Plataea by one brief chapter, in which he recounts an unremarkable Athenian diversionary expedition (3.51). The interposition of this chapter creates a gap, similar to the interruption between separate plays of a tragic trilogy. The two accounts are thus juxtaposed, and the reader is called upon to reflect on the similarities and differences between them. On each occasion, one of the two Greek superpowers has undertaken a protracted siege of a smaller city, the small city has been forced to surrender, and the superpower has come to sit in judgment over the conquered. Thus, both stories culminate in extended debates in which the fate of the smaller city is sealed. Each time, an initial procedure is revised: after their severe initial sentence on Mytilene, the Athenians experience pangs of conscience and decide to discuss the case of Mytilene anew (3.36.2–5); similarly, the Spartans revise their initial procedure, which consisted simply in asking each Plataean individually whether he had rendered any services to Sparta during the ongoing war (3.52.4–5), and allow the Plataeans to give a speech in their defense. Within the parallel arrangement, not only similarities, but also salient differences are brought to light. At Athens, the second meeting of the assembly involves a genuine second debate and miraculously results in a mitigation of the sentence over Mytilene (3.49.1). No such miracles happen where the Spartans are in charge: they listen patiently to the conflicting speeches of the Plataeans and the Thebans, only to reiterate their original question (3.68.1–2). Since the Plataeans cannot possibly answer it in the affirmative, they are killed man by man (3.68.2).

Although the scope of Thucydides' work recalls the vast dimensions of the *Iliad* much more than those of a Greek tragedy, Thucydidean mirror episodes are nonetheless closer to the juxtapositions of Greek tragedy than to Homer. Compared with Homer, Thucydides tends to make a greater effort to anchor the relevant episodes in relationships of structural correspondence, thus creating the kind of symmetrical parallelism that the tragedians like to set up. He also, again like the tragedians, makes a greater effort to carve out a series of precise parallels.

Ethos and Tone

Some of the methods that Thucydides adopted from Homer and the tragedians are geared toward evoking a specific tone. The following aspects of Thucydides' ethos are paramount examples: the disquieting awareness of uncanny ironies, a vivid awareness of the thin dividing line between a fortunate outcome and utter catastrophe, and an objective pathos achieved through the dispassionate acknowledgment of suffering.

The Irony of Hidden Implications: Anticipation, Tragic Irony, and Reversal

The notion of irony, as it is usually applied to Homer, the tragedians, and Thucydides, is premised on a hidden connection between two or more events. It revolves around the discrepant awareness that distinguishes the limited perspective of the characters from the higher level of comprehension enjoyed by the narrator and usually by the audience.[5] From this definition, it follows that irony is based on narrative patterning: through specific verbal or thematic cross-references, a parallel between two events is established, which however is usually not made explicit, but left to the reader or spectator to discover. In most cases, the later event does not simply recall the earlier, but is connected with it through a developmental logic: it represents an enhancement of the earlier event or a radicalization or its underside, which is initially invisible, yet nonetheless momentous.

Anticipatory irony, for instance, is created when there is some disparity between a character's forecast, whether correct or false, of future events and the audience's antecedent knowledge of the actual outcome. A Homeric example of ironic anticipation is to be found in the contrary predictions of Polydamas and Hector: the former correctly anticipates the outcome of the Trojan advance against the Greek ships (*Il.* 12.211–28) whereas Hector's confident forecast turns out to be false (*Il.* 12.231–50). Such ironic anticipations represent another clear instance of Herodotus' mediation between a Homeric principle and its adoption in Thucydides. As Rengakos has pointed out (2006b, 202–7), Herodotus makes ample use of this procedure when reporting in Book 7 the predictions of various characters, such as Artabanus, Mardonius, and Demaratus, about the chances of Xerxes' campaign against Greece. Thucydides follows Homer and Herodotus in setting up a clear-cut and direct opposition between speakers who anticipate, usually in great detail, the actual course of events, and those who predict its direct opposite with similar precision. Examples cluster with particular frequency during the run-up to the onset of the Peloponnesian War and on the eve of the Sicilian Expedition: Pericles

---

[5] This disparity is the broadest definition of the term dramatic or tragic irony. As will become clear below, we will use the term tragic irony in a more restricted sense for which Sophoclean tragedy is the prime example. On the various senses of the term tragic irony, see Rutherford (2012, 323–24).

and Nicias offer correct predictions (Pericles: 1.143.5, 144.1; Nicias: 6.20.4, 21.1, 21.2, 22), the Corinthians and Alcibiades provide a number of forecasts that will prove to be false (Corinthians: 1.120.3; Alcibiades: 6.17.2, 17.3, 18.5). The effect achieved by these instances of exact anticipation is double edged. Pericles and Nicias come to occupy, at least momentarily, an Olympian perspective, comparable to that of the narrator or of Zeus in Homeric epic. Yet the speakers' general inability, with the partial exception of Pericles, to derive lasting practical benefits from their accurate forecasts leaves the impression of human limitation and of events following an irrevocable necessity.

Thucydides also draws on the type of irony for which Sophocles' *Oedipus Tyrannus* provides the *locus classicus*, and which is premised on the following principle: an utterance that a character overtly and consciously makes about situation X turns out to have a more vital application to situation Y, of which the speaker, unlike the audience, is completely unaware. The following words of Oedipus offer a characteristic example (Soph. *OT* 137–141):

> Not on behalf of distant friends, but for my very own sake will I drive away this pollution. For whoever the killer was may well wish to inflict the same kind of violence on me, too: thus, in defending that man [that is, the dead king Laius] I am helping myself.

Almost every assertion in this passage has an ironic flipside: the murdered Laius is indeed Oedipus' φίλος, but far from being a "distant friend," he is Oedipus' own father; Oedipus will in fact drive away the pollution "for his very own sake"—yet not as he means it here, but because he himself is that pollution; "the killer," who of course is Oedipus himself, will in truth inflict violence on Oedipus, but this will happen in a way unimaginable to Oedipus at this point, namely, through an act of self-mutilation; and in finding Laius' murderer, Oedipus will "help himself" in a chillingly ironic way, namely by turning himself into a polluted outcast.

From the standpoint of verisimilitude, it is incredible that Oedipus makes these obliquely self-referential statements by pure chance. Yet if one allows for the daemonic atmosphere of the *Oedipus Tyrannus* and for the possibility that the god himself, unbeknownst to the characters on stage, comes to speak through human beings, Sophocles' device ceases to seem forced. However, it is truly surprising that Thucydides is drawn to this type of uncanny irony, which seems to presuppose the hidden presence of divine forces. The Melian Dialogue offers the most striking example. Several observations made by the Athenians about the Melians' alleged folly apply with equal if not greater justification to subsequent behavior of the Athenians themselves:[6] on both occasions hope (ἐλπίς) confounds people's perceptions of the present situation and intoxicates them with the charm of uncertain possibilities (twice at 5.103, 111.2, 113 ~ 6.15.2, 24.3,

---

[6] Two of the following instances of irony, namely, the prominence given in both episodes to ἐλπίς and the Athenians' dependence on the justice of the victors at the end of the Peloponnesian War, were pointed out by Liebeschuetz (1968, 75–76).

30.2, 31.6), and each time this infatuation amounts to a fascination with the "invisible" (5.103, 113 ~ 6.9.3). The Melians, too, touch on issues that will be painfully relevant to Athens as the war goes on: their emphasis on maintaining the principle of justice (5.90) looks forward to the Athenians' dependence on the justice of the victors at the end of the war in 404; their warning about inducing hostility in neutrals (5.98) is relevant to the Athenian failure to gain support from neutrals in Sicily; their anticipation of a Spartan attempt upon the territory of the Athenian allies (5.110.2) will become true in the wake of the defeat at Sicily; and, finally, the Melians' self-designation as "a country that never belonged to you" (5.110.2) refers with equal justification, as Emily Greenwood pointed out (2006, 86), to Sicily.

With unnerving exactness, each of these statements fits into an entirely different frame of reference, of which the speakers, unlike the author and the reader, cannot possibly be aware. One could demonstrate the workings of the same type of irony, again anticipating the Athenian obsession with Sicily, in some of Cleon's and Diodotus' statements in the Mytilenaean Debate (3.38.4–7; 3.45.5–6). Thucydides' account of the Sicilian Expedition turns out to be framed by a type of irony whose tragic counterpart implies the involvement of sinister divine agents. The exactness of the anticipation, combined with the speakers' total ignorance, suggests that the course of events is shot through with an eerie inevitability.

Reversal, the third type of ironic device, represents another hallmark of the Sicilian narrative. A reversal consists in the symmetrical inversion of an earlier situation that had the appearance of being stable and secure. Aristotle called this structure περιπέτεια and considered it to be one of the basic components of a complex tragic plot (Arist. Poet. 1452a22–24). It often manifests itself in a steep and sudden downfall from a moment of exceptional flourishing. The ironic component has to do with the retrospective realization that the earlier boon was the inverse anticipation of the eventual calamity. The *Oedipus Tyrannus* also offers the paradigm case for a consummate tragic reversal. Jean-Pierre Vernant has pointed out the relentlessly exact symmetry through which Sophocles impresses the vehemence of Oedipus' reversal on the audience (1990, 123-24): the man who was considered "equal to the gods" (Soph. *OT* 31) at the outset is now "equal to nothingness" (Soph. *OT* 1187–88), and he who clairvoyantly solved the riddle of the Sphinx and saved the city has become a blind man and a bane for the city.

Thucydides exploits the structure of tragic reversal to the full at the conclusion of the Sicilian narrative. Not only did the Athenians suffer a downfall from the height of their previous success, but also the Syracusans come to acquire exactly the characteristics that had distinguished the Athenian ἀκμή on the eve of the expedition (7.12.3, 14.1). At the outset, the Athenians were buoyed by confident hope (6.15.2, 24.3, 30.2, 31.6), whereas the Peloponnesians were, according to Alcibiades, in a state of utter hopelessness (6.17.8). However, as things go ever more poorly at Sicily, the Athenians come to experience, as Avery has shown (1973, 2–6), states of increasing hopelessness (7.4.4, 47.2, 71.7, 75.2, 8.1.1), in correspondence with which their opponents experience a steep upswing of hope (7.7.4, 25.1, 25.9, 46, 66.3, 67.1; 8.2.4). The same lesson can be drawn from the reversal of Athenian splendor. Both Alcibiades and the Athenians in his wake emanate dazzling splendor during the run-up to the expedition (6.12.2, 16.3, 16.5, 31.6); yet in the course of the campaign this splendor, as Jordan observed (2000, 78), changes sides and comes to attach itself to the Syracusans (7.55.1, 71.5, 75.6, 87.5). A further instance of this type of reversal has to do with the deceptive tricks of the Egestaeans: whereas Alcibiades prides himself on his grand display at Olympia, by which he induced an exaggerated conception of Athenian strength in the other Greeks (6.16.3: φαίνεται), the Egestaeans trick the Athenians about their strength through an even more shameless act of display (6.46.3: φαινομένων). Just as hope and splendor shift from the Athenians to the Syracusans, so the power of deception bids farewell to the Athenians and comes to ally itself with the Egestaeans. Instead of being passive attributes, hope, splendor, and make-believe play the role of independent agents. Such a conception of passions, character traits, and situations as objectified, independent entities is typical of tragedy and exemplified by the *Oedipus Tyrannus*.

Rutherford (2012b, 30) has pointed out that Thucydides' report of the decisive Athenian defeat in the battle in the Great Harbor at Syracuse reverses, as Thucydides himself remarks (7.71.7), an earlier stunning Athenian success, namely, their triumph over the Spartans at Pylos. A close verbal echo highlights the resemblance between the situations: on each occasion, the Athenians find themselves in the paradoxical situation of "fighting a land-battle from ships" (4.14.3: ἀπὸ νεῶν ἐπεζομάχουν; 7.62.4: πεζομαχεῖν ἀπὸ τῶν νεῶν). The phrases that immediately surround this echo reveal a fundamental reversal: at Pylos, the Athenians engaged in this peculiar type of warfare of their own free will (βουλόμενοι 4.14.3) whereas at Sicily they "have been compelled" to do so (ἠναγκάσμεθα; 7.62.4). Moreover, further parallels emphasize that the Athenians have come to play the sorry role that the Spartans had at Pylos: both at Sicily and at Pylos, the original besiegers end up being besieged (4.14.5; 7.75.5), and each time one of the two Greek superpowers is defeated in its distinctive sphere of excellence, Sparta on land and Athens at sea (4.12.3; 7.55.2, 66.2–3). The reversal of the Athenian victory at Pylos is not coincidental. The earlier humiliation of the Spartans had tempted the Athenians to contemn their opponents, and this disdain paved the way for the high-risk adventure at Sicily (6.17.8). Far from belonging to fundamentally different spheres, the poles of success and disaster are mysteriously connected, an insight that attests, as Colin Macleod observed (1983, 143), to the strong affinity between Thucydides' outlook and the ethos of Greek tragedy.

Thucydidean irony tends to revolve around precise verbal echoes and exact symmetrical correspondences; his obsessive systematization stands out, whereby his relentless focus on salient details bears considerable resemblance to the ironic style of Sophoclean tragedy. This affinity, together with the objectified representation of passions and ways of behavior, creates a daemonic atmosphere, which could be taken to hint at the involvement of mysterious superhuman forces. Yet Thucydides carefully refrains from making such a possibility explicit. In light of this failure to consider the possibility of divine intervention, the daemonic resonance in Thucydides may be taken to suggest that in his *History*, human nature fulfills part of the role that the divine fulfils in epic and tragedy: it is a mysterious force that is not fully understood by human beings, escapes the control of individual agents, and is likely to plunge them into misguided, self-destructive adventures.

Almost Episodes: What Nearly Happened

Homer sometimes pauses for a moment at a specific juncture to acknowledge that events might have taken a different course if there had been a slight change in the constellation of relevant factors. These episodes have become known as Homeric "Almosts" or "If-Nots" (cf. Nesselrath 1992, 1–4). Some of these episodes are more playful and others more tragic. Karl Reinhardt calls the former category ironic, and the latter, which usually occurs in situations of combat, heroic (1961, 110). Agamemnon's ridiculously unsuccessful trial of the Greek army in the second book of the *Iliad* is an example of the ironic Almost: the war would have been over if Hera had not sent Athena to incite Odysseus' resolute intervention (*Il.* 2.155–56). The heroic Almost, by contrast, is exemplified by the high point of Patroclus' *aristeia*: Patroclus would have led the Achaeans to the capture of Troy if Apollo had not repulsed him from the city wall three times and upon his fourth onslaught commanded him to pull back (*Il.* 16.698–709).

Thucydidean Almost episodes invariably occur in connection with military events and are thus modeled on the heroic type. Twice such episodes deal with the possibility of capturing the Piraeus. The Peloponnesian fleet under the leadership of Cnemus and Brasidas would have captured Salamis and entered the Piraeus if they had been capable of a somewhat more unflinching determination (2.94.1). Years later, the revolt of Euboea becomes the occasion for the same Almost: if they had just been a bit bolder, the Peloponnesians could easily have caused severe trouble for the Athenians by attacking the undefended Piraeus (8.96.4). Another Almost that relates to the near capture of a city appears in the account of the siege of Plataea: the Spartans kindle a fire that threatens to destroy the Plataeans, but the sudden outbreak of a thunderstorm quenches it in the nick of time (2.77.5–6). True to its role as the great analogue to the Plataean account, the narrative of the downfall of Mytilene also contains an Almost, which is the most dramatic one in Thucydides' entire work. Paches, the Athenian commander at Mytilene, has received orders to execute *en masse* the male population of the city. He is about to put these instructions into action when at the very last moment a second ship puts in and informs him about the reversal of the Athenian decision. Thucydides closes the narrative strand with the remark "to such an extreme of danger had Mytilene come" (3.49.4). The same remark returns at the turning point of the Sicilian narrative, which becomes the occasion for a double "Almost": Gylippus arrives at the very moment when the Syracusans are on the cusp of giving up their war effort (7.2.2) and just before the Athenians finish building their encircling wall (7.2.4). Thucydides concludes with the remark familiar from the story of Mytilene: "to such an extreme of danger had the Syracusans come" (7.2.5). The recurring phrases in these Almost episodes ("to such an extreme of danger": 3.49.4, 7.2.5; "greater fear than ever": 2.94.1, 8.96.1) create links between the passages and reinforce the impression that a methodical ambition motivates their inclusion: while ignoring the more playful ironic Almost, Thucydides is drawn to the tragic variety, which allows him to articulate the recurring experience of escape by the skin of one's teeth.

An awareness of the fragility of human affairs invariably crystallizes around Thucydides' relation of this type of episode: a mere modicum of greater boldness, speed, or delay would have caused the downfall of Athens, Syracuse, Plataea, and Mytilene. These episodes also enable Thucydides to make a systematic point about the Spartan and the Athenian character. The course of events at Mytilene shows how Athenian impetuousness brings the Mytilenaeans to the brink of the abyss. In Almost episodes involving Sparta, the opposite character trait, namely, overcautious hesitancy, tends to stand out. Athens and Sparta represent opposite modes of being in paradigmatic perfection. Yet, this deep-seated antithesis notwithstanding, the Athenians and the Spartans are similarly subject to the same basic experience: events elude their efforts to exercise reliable stewardship over them. It is no coincidence that Thucydides seeks out the potential of the "Almost" in connection with the superlatively consequential situation of the sack of a city: he forces his reader to confront the awe-inspiring inverse proportion between sheer accident and the most far-reaching consequences. While the reader holds his breath, Thucydides retains his usual calm composure. Much of this effect is achieved through an invocation of the Homeric tone, marked as it is by sobriety and simple grandeur: through the mere assertion of the "almost," the reader is made to grasp how fragile the ground is on which human endeavors hope to stand.

Pathos through Objective Precision

One of the hallmarks of the Homeric poems is the evocation of a distinctive kind of pathos. Instead of being based on the expression of heightened emotional states, Homeric pathos is evoked through the sober acknowledgement of an objective fact: for instance, a numerical detail. The relation of this fact reveals the weight of a specific situation in a restrained yet powerful manner. Instead of excluding an emotional response, Homer's factual, objective simplicity lets the event speak for itself, thus enabling it to appear in its true, awe-inspiring dimensions.[7] Thucydides follows this Homeric method, thus infusing his account with a tone of "tragic akribeia" (Hornblower 1987, 35).

A frequently employed instance of this procedure is the habit of naming exact numbers of casualties. For example, Homer enumerates how many of Odysseus' companions are killed by the Cyclops (*Od.* 9.289–90, 310–11, 343–44) and by Scylla and Charybdis (*Od.* 12.245–46), and how many maidservants out of the total number of fifty were unfaithful and consequently suffered capital punishment (*Od.* 22.421–25). In like manner, Thucydides provides the exact number of the Theban prisoners killed at Plataea (2.5.7), the Mytilenaeans executed at Athens (3.50.1), the Plataeans executed by the

---

[7] On the pathos typical of Homer's representation of sad events, Jasper Griffin remarks: "Simplicity and brevity in such expressions heighten their effect, conveying a sort of understatement, a noble restraint which allows the event to speak for itself" (1980, 121).

Spartans (3.58.3), and the Athenian losses during Demosthenes' hapless campaign in Aetolia (3.98.4). The sober indication of numerical facts contrasts sharply with the light that they cast on human affairs: the quantitative specifications suggest a solid grasp on reality, but the results thus recorded highlight dire mortality. Again the comparison with Herodotus is instructive. At the conclusion of the narrative of the Battle of Marathon, Herodotus mentions that, while 6,400 Persians fell, only 192 Athenians died (6.117.1). This specification of numerical details does owe something to Homer's tragic precision. But its sadness notwithstanding, the death of the 192 men at Marathon acquires an uplifting heroic luster, both through the Athenian victory and through the direct juxtaposition of the Athenian casualties with the much higher Persian losses. While Herodotus does not shrink from placing sorrow and buoyancy side by side, Thucydides typically avoids mitigating the tragic facticity of numerical precision through the admixture of brighter colors.

The same ethos of tragic precision manifests itself in Thucydides' habit, pointed out by Grant (1974, 82), of referencing the superlative character of specific events, either the unparalleled scope of a military campaign or a climactic military catastrophe. In highlighting the immensity of suffering, the superlatives contribute to Thucydides' tragic tone: for instance, Thucydides writes that "among the events that happened in this war" the Ambraciot losses in Acarnania were "the greatest affliction that befell a single Greek city in an equal number of days" (3.113.6); the slaughter of the population of Mycalessus was "an affliction that was, considering the size of the city, less deplorable than none of the things that happened in the course of the war" (7.30.3); the Athenian defeat in Sicily, the most comprehensive Thucydidean superlative of all, was "the greatest event of all that occurred in the course of this war, and, as it seems to me, of all Greek events of which we know through report: for the victors most splendid, for those destroyed most disastrous" (7.87.5). Striving for precision manifests itself in Thucydides' pausing to spell out that a specific event marks a distinct peak of suffering. Moreover, it finds expression in Thucydides' repeated effort, attested by all three passages, to spell out the exact terms within which the superlative is valid. Homer again provides the ultimate model for Thucydides' employment of superlatives to emphasize an apogee of misfortune. When describing how Scylla devoured six of his comrades, Odysseus calls this event "most pitiful" (οἴκτιστον δή; *Od.* 12.258) of all the things that he beheld on his travels. The lost comrades were "best in strength and in might" (χερσίν τε βίηφί τε φέρτατοι; *Od.* 12.246). The sad pathos evoked by this superlative has an especially close Thucydidean parallel: combining numerical detail and attention to the specific culminating moment of disaster, Thucydides calls the approximately 120 Athenian hoplites killed in Aetolia "truly the best men" (βέλτιστοι δὴ ἄνδρες; 3.98.4) that Athens lost in the Peloponnesian War. While the tone of the Thucydidean superlatives evidently goes back to Homer, Thucydides leaves his characteristic imprint on the Homeric material: Thucydides' frequent specification of the exact parameters under which the superlative holds true signals his conscientious effort to justify his ascertainment of a climactic moment. This procedure is meant to differentiate him from the ungrounded hyperboles that he considers a typical shortcoming of the poets.

Allusions to Homer and Tragedy

Thucydides' account of the Sicilian Expedition stands out for its unmatched frequency of allusions to specific passages in Homer and Greek tragedy. The abundance of references suggests that Thucydides found the Sicilian Expedition particularly congenial to the perspective of his epic and tragic models.

One organizing principle underlying these allusions is the Odyssean theme. By way of an obvious reference to Books 9 and 10 of the *Odyssey*, Thucydides mentions the Cyclopes and the Laestrygonians as the earliest inhabitants of Sicily (6.2.1). As Mackie has shown, the Sicilian Expedition represents a replay of the *Odyssey* in reverse order, starting out from home and ending in the jaws of Sicilian menaces (1996, 110–12). In addition, the Athenians' excitement about the sight of faraway lands (6.9.3, 13.1, 24.3), a major motivation for the expedition, recalls, as Frangoulidis observes (1993, 97–98), a central Odyssean theme, namely, Odysseus' curiosity about the inhabitants of distant lands, which prompts him to visit the Cyclops and the Laestrygonians (*Od.* 9.172–74, 10.100–101). Moreover, Mackie has observed several parallels between the character of Alcibiades and that of Odysseus (Mackie 1996, 112): among other things, both men possess a versatile intelligence, and each of them has the astonishing capacity to adapt to alien environments and thereby survives dangers against all odds.

There is also another mythological lens through which Thucydides looks at the Sicilian Expedition: the erotic desire of Paris and his role in unleashing the Trojan War. Alcibiades, like Paris, implicates his city in a large-scale and disastrous war for the sake of satisfying his personal desire: just as the Trojan War is caused by Paris' abduction of Helen, for whom he has conceived an overwhelming passion (*Il.* 3.441–46), so Thucydides emphasizes that personal desires motivated Alcibiades in his agitation for the expedition (6.15.2, 15.3, 15.4). Several other characteristic Alcibiadean attitudes bear comparison to Homer's Paris. Alcibiades' disarming charm bears a resemblance to Paris' indestructible good-naturedness: just as Paris manages to dull the edge of Hector's reprimand in Book 6 by announcing his eagerness to return to battle together with Hector (*Il.* 6.340–41), so Alcibiades counters Nicias' personal attack by urging the Athenians to appoint them both as generals and thus to capitalize on each man's distinctive qualities (Thuc. 6.17.1). Both Paris and Alcibiades take a naive delight in splendor and personal display: while the war is raging outside, Paris sits in his chamber and delights in his beautiful weapons (*Il.* 6.321–22), and not much later he returns to battle "gleaming in his armor like the shining sun" (*Il.* 6.513); throughout all of this, Paris is concerned with his personal splendor (*Il.* 3.392: κάλλεΐ τε στίλβων καὶ εἵμασιν, 6.513: τεύχεσι παμφαίνων ὥς τ' ἠλέκτωρ). Alcibiades is likewise infatuated with putting on a dazzling display, and Thucydides repeatedly describes his appearance in terms that suggest shiny splendor (Thuc. 6.12.2: ἐλλαμπρύνεσθαι; 6.16.2: τῷ ἐμῷ διαπρεπεῖ; 6.16.5: λαμπρότητι). Another common feature is their enmeshment in ambiguity: while their excellence in military matters is beyond question, they are nonetheless unreliable and give reason for offense

(*Il.* 6.521–23; Thuc. 6.15.4); moreover, despite their evident charm, their relationship with the population of their home city tends to be tense (*Il.* 3.451–55; Thuc. 6.15.4, 16.5). Alcibiades' conspicuous obsession with expensive racehorses (Thuc. 6.12.2, 15.3, 16.2) makes one think of a buoyant simile by which Homer likens Paris, as he returns to battle, to a frisky horse in high spirits (*Il.* 6.506–11). Finally, Paris has the good fortune simply to disappear from the battlefield when he is on the verge of being killed by Menelaus, since Aphrodite clouds him in a mist and carries him back to Troy (*Il.* 6.379–382). After his recall to Athens, Alcibiades disappears with similar mysteriousness at Thurii in southern Italy and makes his way across the sea to Cyllene in the Peloponnesus, whence he soon goes to Sparta (Thuc. 6.61.6, 88.9). The effortless speed with which Alcibiades leaps across considerable distances is reminiscent of Paris' swift transplantation from the battlefield into his own chamber; and just as Alcibiades disappears and leaves Menelaus in a frantic search (*Il.* 3.449–50), so Alcibiades magically ceases to be "visible" (Thuc. 6.61.6, 61.7) and his appointed guards look for him in vain.

Alcibiades' desire for conquest of Sicily is mirrored by a collective ἔρως that has seized the Athenian population at large. It is probably no coincidence that the two most pointed expressions of this collective Athenian infatuation bear close resemblance to passages in Greek tragedy. Thucydides' phrase "Upon all alike there fell a desire to sail" (ἔρως ἐνέπεσε τοῖς πᾶσιν ὁμοίως ἐκπλεῦσαι; 6.24.3) recalls, as Connor pointed out (1984, 167–68), the same combination of ἔρως and ἐμπίπτω in Aeschylus' *Agamemnon*, where it suggests the Greek desire, sure to incur divine retribution, to ravage the sacred shrines of Troy (Aesch. *Ag.* 341–342). Nicias also uses a word with tragic resonance when he urges the Athenians "not to be madly in love with absent things." (μηδ'... δυσέρωτας εἶναι τῶν ἀπόντων; 6.13.1). The rare word δυσέρως, combined with the striving for what is out of reach, recalls the occurrence of the same terms in a famous passage from Euripides' *Hippolytus*, where it is used in connection with Phaedra's illicit desire for her stepson (Eur. *Hipp.* 183–85 and 191–94). Thucydides' allusions to tragic ἔρως on the eve of the Sicilian Expedition make one think of a daemonic power that drives people into ruin.

The resemblances between Alcibiades and Paris and the emphasis on tragic ἔρως as the principal motivation behind the Sicilian Expedition look ahead to Thucydides' somber concluding statement that the Athenians suffered "total destruction" (πανωλεθρίᾳ; 7.87.6), a word that alludes, as Marinatos and Rawlings (1978) have shown (331–34), to Herodotus' use of the same word for the destruction of Troy (2.120.5). Yet the Homeric echoes link the Athenians not only with the Trojans but also with the Greeks. In the same concluding passage, Thucydides remarks that "few out of many returned home" (ὀλίγοι ἀπὸ πολλῶν ἐπ' οἴκου ἀπενόστησαν; 7.87.6). Scholars have observed that the verb ἀπονοστέω represents an allusion to the *Odyssey*, whose central theme is νόστος, "home-coming" (Hornblower 1987, 116; Allison 1997, 512–15). The sequence, from tragic ἔρως to the "total destruction" of Troy and the "home-coming," full of suffering, of few survivors, lends considerable support to Cornford's interpretation of the Sicilian narrative. According to Cornford, Thucydides saw the expedition progressing through a tragic sequence from ἄτη and ἀπάτη, consequent ὕβρις, and eventual νέμεσις (1907,

234–36, 242). Cornford based his view on a wide range of (primarily) tragic parallels in both thought and language, of which the passages from the *Agamemnon* and *Hippolytus* quoted above are eminent examples. On this view, at Athens just as much as at Troy, the eternal tragedy of human folly and self-undoing runs its course. Even if Thucydides does not commit himself to the outlook of traditional mythology and religion, he does seem to regard ἔρως as a pervasive cosmic power that easily brings entire states, notwithstanding their immense power, to ruin.

The abundance of Homeric and tragic echoes in the Sicilian narrative, in combination with the frequent employment of epic and tragic narrative devices, may seem hard to reconcile with Thucydides' self-proclaimed aversion to the adornments with which the poets magnify their accounts (1.21.1). To some extent, therefore, we may conclude that Thucydides has sacrificed consistency of principle to literary artistry and depth of interpretation. Yet the tragic and epic material also enables him to make a point about the character of the Sicilian Expedition: in resolving to follow Alcibiades and to attack Sicily, the Athenians have chosen to erase a fundamental distinction by merging the sphere of politics and the realm of myth. Beguiled by Alcibiades' intriguing splendor, which in turn evokes exciting mythological models, the Athenians try to act out their fantasies and to become just as excitingly grand as the mythical seducers, city-sackers, and seafarers. If we judge from the outcome of the expedition, this mentality is an unsuitable guide in political decision-making. If Homer and the tragedians are to be their guiding lights, the Athenians must act out the tragic and epic script until the very end and experience what is the hallmark of these genres: suffering and reversal on a grand scale.

References

Allison, J. W. 1997. "Homeric Allusions at the Close of Thucydides' Sicilian Narrative." *AJP* 118: 499–516.
Avery, H. C. 1973. "Themes in Thucydides' Account of the Sicilian Expedition." *Hermes* 101: 1–13.
Connor, W. R. 1984. *Thucydides*. Princeton: Princeton University Press.
Cornford, F. M. 1907. *Thucydides Mythistoricus*. London: E. Arnold.
Frangoulidis, S. A. 1993. "A Pattern from Homer's 'Odyssey' in the Sicilian Narrative of Thucydides." *Quaderni Urbinati* n.s. 44: 95–102.
Gomme, A. W. 1954. *The Greek Attitude to Poetry and History*. Berkeley: University of California Press.
Grant, J. R. 1974. "Toward Knowing Thucydides." *Phoenix* 28: 81–94.
Greenwood, E. 2006. *Thucydides and the Shaping of History*. London: Duckworth.
Griffin, J. 1980. *Homer on Life and Death*. Oxford: Oxford University Press.
Hornblower, S. 1987. *Thucydides*. London: Duckworth.
Jong, I. J. F. de. 2001. *A Narratological Commentary on the Odyssey*. Cambridge: Cambridge University Press.
Jordan, B. 2000. "The Sicilian Expedition Was a Potemkin Fleet." *CQ* 50: 63–79.
Liebeschuetz, W. 1968. "The Structure and Function of the Melian Dialogue." *JHS* 88: 73–77.
Mackie, C. J. 1996. "Homer and Thucydides: Corcyra and Sicily." *CQ* 46: 103–13.

Macleod, C. 1983. "Thucydides and Tragedy." In *Collected Essays*, by C. Macleod, 140–58. Oxford: Oxford University Press.

Marinatos, N., and H. R. Rawlings III. 1978. "Panolethria and Divine Punishment. Thuc. 7.87.6 and Hdt. 2.120.5." *Parola del Passato* 33: 331–37.

Nesselrath, H.-G. 1992. *Ungeschehenes Geschehen: 'Beinahe-Episoden' im griechischen und römischen Epos von Homer bis zur Spätantike*. Stuttgart: Teubner.

Reichel, M. 1990. "Retardationstechniken in der Ilias." In *Der Übergang von der Mündlichkeit zur Literatur bei den Griechen*, edited by W. Kullmann and M. Reichel, 125–51. Tübingen: Narr.

Reinhardt, K. 1961. *Die Ilias und ihr Dichter*. Göttingen: Vandenhoeck and Ruprecht.

Rengakos, A. 1999. "Spannungsstrategien in den homerischen Epen." In *Euphrosyne. Studies in Ancient Epic and Its Legacy in Honor of D. N. Maronitis*, edited by J. N. Kazazis and A. Rengakos, 308–38. Stuttgart: Steiner.

Rengakos, A. 2006a. "Thucydides' Narrative: the Epic and Herodotean Heritage." In *Brill's Companion to Thucydides*, edited by A. Tsakmakis and A. Rengakos, 279–300. Leiden: Brill.

Rengakos, A. 2006b. "Homer and the Historians: The Influence of Epic Narrative Technique on Herodotus and Thucydides." In *La poésie épique grecque: métamorphoses d'un genre littéraire. Entretiens sur l'antiquité classique* 52, edited by F. Montanari and A. Rengakos, 183–214. Vandoeuvres –Geneva: Fondation Hardt.

Romilly, J. de. 2012. *The Mind of Thucydides*. Ithaca: Cornell University Press. (= 1956. *Histoire et raison chez Thucydide*. Paris: Les Belles letters)

Rutherford, R. B. 2012a. *Greek Tragic Style: Form, Language and Interpretation*. Cambridge: Cambridge University Press.

Rutherford, R. B. 2012b. "Structure and Meaning in Epic and Historiography." In *Thucydides and Herodotus*, edited by E. Foster and D. Lateiner, 13–38. Oxford: Oxford University Press.

Schadewaldt, W. 1959. *Von Homers Welt und Werk*. Stuttgart: Koehler.

Schadewaldt, W. 1966. *Iliasstudien*. Berlin: Akademie-Verlag.

Strasburger, H. 1966. *Die Wesensbestimmung der Geschichte durch die antike Geschichtsschreibung. Sitzungsberichte der Wissenschaftlichen Gesellschaft an der Goethe-Universität Frankfurt* Bd. 5, Nr. 3. Wiesbaden: Steiner.

Taplin, O. 1978. *Greek Tragedy in Action*. Berkeley: University of California Press.

Vernant, J.-P. 1990. "Ambiguity and Reversal: On the Enigmatic Structure of *Oedipus Rex*." In *Myth and Tragedy in Ancient Greece*, by J.-P. Vernant and P. Vidal-Naquet, 113–40. New York: Zone Books. (= 1972. "Ambiguité et renversement. Sur la structure énigmatique d'Oedipe-Roi." *Mythe et Tragédie en Grèce ancienne* vol. I, 99–132. Paris: Maspero).

CHAPTER 35

THUCYDIDES AND ATTIC COMEDY

JEFFREY HENDERSON

As students of fifth-century Athens, Thucydides and the Old Comic poets are separated by differences as broad as their subject. The famously abstract and sober-sided Thucydides, in pursuit of what for him qualified as facts, clarity, and truth, abjures the kinds of gratification (*terpsis*) afforded by traditional storytelling (*to muthōdes*, 1.22.4), commemorative poetry (2.41.4), crowd-pleasing oratory (3.40.3), or festivals and the arts, which his Pericles deemed holidays from the pain and struggle of the real world (2.38); is more interested in large historical patterns and forces than individuals, least of all their character per se or their private lives; mostly ignores the internal political, judicial, and intellectual life of Athens; regards intelligence and chance, not the gods, as the limiting factors in human endeavor; and considers popular knowledge and belief to be generally ill founded, untrustworthy, and thus rarely worth crediting.

Those who have trusted Thucydides as the objective historian of *wie es eigentlich war* accept these emphases and exclusions and do not worry that they also differentiate him from (therefore less trustworthy) historiographic contemporaries like Herodotus, the "Old Oligarch," Stesimbrotus of Thasos, and Ion of Chios (Porciani, chapter 32 in this volume); from the historians, memoirists, and apologists of the following generations, for example, Ephorus, Duris of Samos, Theopompus, Plato, Xenophon, Aristotle, and the Peripatetics, who looked to comedies as important complementary sources, not only reflections of Athenian life and opinion but also vehicles for the poets' own views (Gray, chapter 36 in this volume); and from historians (Polybius, Plutarch) and scholars from Hellenistic times onward. Historical utility, not least for the era treated by Thucydides, was indeed a major factor in the circulation, preservation, and canonical selection of Old Comic plays. But in recent decades faith in historiographic objectivity has been effectively challenged, so that Thucydides' *History* may once again be read and interrogated as but one narrative, however impressive, among others. And as alternative, especially comic, narratives come into better focus we can see that Thucydides himself was not above taking them into account when formulating his own narrative.

Although Old Comic poets show no awareness of historiography (Aristophanes' *Acharnians* 523–29 is not a parody of Herodotus, cf. Henderson 2012), and Thucydides, generally reticent about identifying sources, only seldom indicates that he is countering an opposing view and never cites comedy, he does seem to respond to the sort of material that was picked up, cooked up, argued, and popularized by comic poets: for example, in his construction of Pericles as the ideal democratic leader, which like the ideal Socrates of Plato and Xenophon includes a rebuttal of comic portrayals that exemplified and channeled contrary popular views; or when he claims that as a leader Pericles differed fundamentally from his successors (especially 2.65), that the war with the Peloponnesians was one war, exceptionally great, inevitable, and necessary, and that Pericles' war strategy was honest and (had it been followed after his death) sound.

There are also areas of agreement, not merely incidental or documentary but also interpretive. At the broadest level Thucydides and the comic poets share an essentially coherent narrative of Athenian acme and decline that proved immediately convincing and has generally remained so: how exceptional achievement, general prosperity, unity of purpose, and infinite promise in laws and institutions, government, warfare, international power, culture, and the arts were squandered after the death of Pericles, when the sovereign demos began to choose leaders who no longer brought out its best qualities but played to its worst, thus imperiling the viability of the democracy itself.

COMIC WITNESS AND ENGAGEMENT

Recent scholarship has significantly enhanced our understanding of drama as an institution of and witness to Athenian society and thus as a source for historians. Fresh approaches to lost dramas are revealing a rich and varied terrain beyond our familiar extant examples, most significantly for comedy, long an Aristophanocentric field, in the wake of the Kassel and Austin edition of the fragments (1983–), the appearance of new translations (Henderson 2008, Storey 2011, Rusten 2011), the first systematic commentaries (Olson 2007, Zimmermann 2013–), general studies (Harvey and Wilkins 2000), and book-length treatments of the major poets Eupolis (Storey 2003) and Cratinus (Bakola 2010). Our understanding of comic witness and engagement (or not) with society and politics has been correspondingly refined (Olson 2010, Henderson 2013b), as has our sense of comic typology and chronology (Rusten 2006: 557–58) from the beginning of our attestation c. 440, when comedy was introduced into the newly established Lenaea festival—more parochial than the Dionysia and thus better suited to political comedy (*Ach.* 502–8)—to the momentous generational change coinciding with the death of Pericles in 429, and through the eventful three decades to follow.

When Thucydides has Pericles situate festivals and the arts among life's refreshing diversions (2.38), he both associates the cultural acme of Athens with the "Age of Pericles" and justifies largely ignoring a significant crucible of public opinion that bedeviled the real-life Pericles: the theater and its poets, especially though not exclusively the comic poets. Like other protégés of the Muses, still the principal custodians of communal memory and normative verities, the dramatic poets framed individual and society, including Athens' relatively novel democratic society, largely in terms of myth, tradition, and timeless polis values. But it is now clear that the dramatic festivals were not wholly a time-out from reality: they had at once a religious/festive and a civic character and served uniquely large, unrestricted, and self-selecting audiences. Nor were the plays, though entertaining and in the case of comedy also humorous, exempt from the legal standards governing public speech generally (Henderson 1998a, Sommerstein 2004a) or incapable of impact on the real world, tragedy by moral and historical example and comedy by topical criticism and honest advice, as Aristophanes regularly asserts.

It has often been assumed that comic poets engaged with society and politics through free-form mockery, which only notices and does not constitute a coherent narrative or explanation, that is, a view. It is true that explicit mockery (ὀνομαστὶ κωμῳδεῖν) was a hallmark of fifth-century comedy (ancient scholars noted as exceptional its avoidance by certain poets and its absence in particular plays) and that it was for the most part incidental, not systematic, a stylistic ingredient suitable for any type of play. Incidental mockery ranged across the broadest spectrum of celebrity, from mere foibles, physical abnormalities, or character flaws—centered mainly on money, eating, drinking, and sex—to activity with political or social impact, but it took the form mostly of drive-by jokes trafficking in the news of the day: asides, references, or brief songs, unconnected with the main plot or themes of the play, and thus easily inserted or detached. Most of the targets (*komoidoumenoi*) were men associated with politics and the courts, their friends and favorite courtesans, the rest mainly associated with the arts (especially theater), and the trades or professions (Sommerstein 1996).

But beyond mockery there was a politically engaged type of comedy: these were not simply plays that contained a lot of mockery or certain kinds of mockery—*Lysistrata*, for example, is fully engaged politically but contains only one fleeting reference to an identifiable politician (490)—but rather plays that focused on current public issues, took a recognizable and more or less coherent political stance, and expected to have a real-life impact, as their *parabasis*-speeches on behalf of the poet regularly assert. Such plays engaged with individuals and/or civic/political issues in a sustained thematic way; criticized or admonished the spectators; and could involve the poet himself as a partisan, at least in the case of Aristophanes in his series of plays frontally attacking Cleon, from *Babylonians* in 426 to *Wasps* in 422. The engaged type of comedy may contain free-form mockery and its humor and satire may aim in all directions, including at the poet himself, but this does not confuse, as it would in an academic or political tract: the main thrust of the argument is always clear and the poet's appeal to his audience, almost always in accord with real-life partisans, is earnest. By contrast with incidental mockery, this engaged or forensic thrust was not generically characteristic of comedy (Edwards 1993 speaks of hijacking) but rather was produced relatively infrequently by a small subset of poets in specific political environments: when populist politicians were ascendant (Pericles followed by "demagogues") and/or Athens was at war with Sparta, particularly when the fighting came to Attica, that is, c. 440–c. 417 (ostracism of Hyperbolus),

412–411, 405–404. The anti-populist trigger seems also to account for the appearance of politically engaged comedies in the fourth century (Henderson 2014: 184–90).

The terms of engagement are clearest in the extant Aristophanes, but in essentials they seem to be shared (or adopted) by his rivals. In personal *parabases* and through sympathetic characters or choruses, Aristophanes espouses the social, moral, and political sentiments of contemporary upper-class conservatives, showing consistent bias in his choice of political figures to criticize and not to criticize: all of his political targets were on the left, whereas traditionalists like Nicias, Laches, Alcibiades, those implicated in the scandals of 415, and the oligarchs disenfranchised after the oligarchic *coup d'état* of 411 are entirely spared, and occasionally even defended (e.g., *Lysistrata* 581, *Frogs* 686–705). The wealthy as a class are never criticized, whereas the poor often are (though this attitude is mitigated in the postwar plays). Wealthy individuals were satirized in a subtype of comedy that Eupolis may have invented (*Spongers* [*Kolakes*] of 421, *Autolycus* of 420), but its focus was on family and friends, not politics or civic life. There is attention to the culture wars and generational conflict: disapproval of the popular intellectual movements associated with the sophists (including Socrates) and of such vulgar novelties in poetry and music as those of Euripides and the new dithyrambic poets. There is hostility to such populist institutions as the subsidy enabling the poor to serve on juries (but not to the equipment subsidy for the wealthy knights). There is criticism of the manipulation by demagogues and "sycophants" of the Council, the Assembly, and the courts against the wealthy in Athens and the empire. And there is disagreement with the rationale behind, and the leadership of the wars of 431–421 and 413–404 (not one war, e.g., *Lysistrata* 513–14), which had ended the Cimonian dream of joint Athenian-Spartan hegemony, thrown the Greek world into turmoil, encouraged barbarian aggression, and rewarded the selfish ambitions of demagogues, as earlier the ego of a tyrannical Pericles; but when Sparta was not involved the plays either say nothing about the war or positively support it (e.g., *Birds* on the campaign in Sicily: 186, 640, 813–816, 1360–1369). In general there is a belief that the daring and progressivism for which Pericles congratulated the Athenians in his Funeral Oration dangerously disrupted wholesome traditional norms (cf. the Old Oligarch and the Corinthians at Thuc. 1.68–71).

Like Thucydides and other contemporary writers, Aristophanes frequently criticizes the demos; *Knights*, *Wasps*, and *Lysistrata* run the gamut of complaints. He also criticizes the operation (but not the rightness) of its institutions, especially the jury system (as manipulated by demagogues to harass the wealthy and enrich themselves), and he occasionally even champions views held by oligarchs, though never oligarchy itself, unlike Thucydides (8.97.2 on the Five Thousand). But like orators and litigants he was addressing his criticism and advice to the demos (as theater audience), so that he hewed to democratic parameters: the stated intent was not to undermine the democracy but to help the demos achieve or restore a better version of itself (Sommerstein 2009a). His expression of conservative, elitist, or oligarchic views no doubt reflects their current strength among the public (cf. Olson 2012 on *Lysistrata*) or tests it, as in the appeals in *Frogs* to reinfranchise the culprits of 411 and to turn on Cleophon (Sommerstein 2009c). Aristophanes is careful never to portray the demos as intrinsically unfit for sovereignty but puts all the blame on its demagogic, that is, deceptive leaders: all would be well (again) if the demos turned once more to "the best" as its advisors, as in the good old days (often represented by elderly characters or choruses) of Aristides and Miltiades (*Knights* 1326), before Pericles eclipsed Cimon and then Thucydides son of Milesias, when a united demos had been able to repel the Persian invaders, win a great empire, and lift Athens to unprecedented heights of prosperity.

Aristophanes and Thucydides portray a sovereign and volatile demos—unlike the docile followers of Plato's philosopher-king, Xenophon's Cyrus, or Isocrates' Evagoras, who abide in ideal(ized) states of *homonoia*—a demos that, if it is to make good decisions, must get good advice. But from whom? In comedy, from no particular living candidate (as distinct from "the best" as a notional category) but most often a fantastic hero(ine), typically a fictional every(wo)man with a brilliant plan, respect for tradition, and community spirit, whose good sense, practical skill, strength of purpose, and persuasive power magically create or restore an ideal way of (Athenian) life. Sometimes the candidate is a dead poet or statesman whom the hero might resurrect: *Frogs* (405) offers a choice of Euripides or Aeschylus, Eupolis' *Demes* (probably 417) Solon, Miltiades, Aristides, or Pericles (how this turned out is unclear). Thucydides does something similar, casting Pericles as a selfless and enlightened leader in order to contrast "the Periclean Athens which might have been with the non-Periclean Athens which came into being" (Rhodes 2006: 541). But in light of the comic Pericles, Thucydides had to furnish his hero with some fantastic features of his own.

THE AGE OF PERICLES

While Thucydides portrays Pericles only as a public figure in connection with the Peloponnesian War, comic poets seem to have assailed his character, politics, and private life from the time of the Samian War (440–439), Cratinus leading the way (Bakola 2010: 181–208) for Hermippus (also an iambic poet) and Telecleides; the evidence, much of it from Plutarch's *Life*, is collected in Schwarze 1971. The poets apparently worked by re-purposing or allegorizing myth-comedy, a prominent type of comedy at the time, that is, by using a mythological plot and characters to represent contemporary politics, especially Trojan War mythology involving Helen: for example, Cratinus' *Dionysalexander*, where Dionysus impersonated Paris in the Judgment and Pericles was somehow "comedized very convincingly by implication (*emphasis*: the technical term) for bringing the war on the Athenians" (T 1: 44–48), and *Nemesis*, where Zeus (suggesting Pericles: F 118) seduces Nemesis in Attica and the Helen-egg is hatched by Leda in Sparta (Henderson 2012). This technique was perhaps inspired by Euripides' sensational *Telephus* of 438, which apparently assimilated the Trojan War to the Samian War and which Aristophanes later re-purposed in *Acharnians* to fit the Peloponnesian War (Wright 2007); the technique may (also) have been a way to finesse the Decree of Morychides (in force 440/9 to 438/7: scholia on *Ach.* 67), which somehow limited comic freedom of expression; or these first political comedies may simply have treaded cautiously: some degree of *emphasis* or allegory characterizes political comedy until Cleon's death in 422, when poets begin to attack a politician undisguisedly (Plato's *Peisander* in 421).

The comic portrayal of Pericles reflects the attitudes of the traditional elite: he was an Olympian strongman whose power to sway the demos, ascendancy over fellow aristocrats, dissolute personal life, and coercive tactics amounted to tyranny, for example, Cratinus' *Cheirons* of c. 436–432, "Stasis and ancient-born Time (*codd.*: Cronus *anon.*) came together and begat the greatest tyrant, whom the gods indeed call Head-Gatherer (κεφαληγερέταν)" (F 258); "Depravity (Καταπυγοσύνη) bore him a Hera, a bitch-faced concubine" (F 259), referring to Aspasia (who was also assimilated to Helen, Omphale, and Deianeira), actually a free-born Milesian who could possibly have been Pericles' wife. He was a "new Peisistratus" (Teleclides F 45, Plu. *Per.* 16, cf. Hdt. 1.59) who had achieved his power by trickery (Cratinus F 240), forceful oratory (Cratinus F 327, Plu. *Per.* 8.4, cf. *Acharnians* 530–31), even spells (Eup. 102, cf. X. *Mem.* 2.16.3), though action did not invariably follow (Cratinus F 326 from late 440s, on completing the South Long Wall). He had questionable and possibly manipulative associates like Anaxagoras, Pheidias (cf. *Peace* 605), Damon, and Aspasia (cf. Pl. *Menexenus*); in Cratinus' *Wealths* unjustly enriched associates (among them Hagnon) will be punished "now that the rule of tyranny is undone and the people have the power" (F 171.22–23), likely cheering Pericles' deposition in 430. He controlled institutions through friends like Metiochus (*comica adespota* F 741, cf. Plu. *Mor.* 811F). He lacked sexual restraint, scandalously consorting not only with Aspasia but also with a Corinthian, Chrysilla (Teleclides F 18), with free-born women in liaisons arranged by Aspasia (Plu. *Per.* 32.1: that Hermippus prosecuted her for this [T 2] may be an inference from comedy), and even with his own daughter-in-law (Stesimbrotus *FGrH* 107 F 10b). In Cratinus' *Thracian Women* he sponsored and introduced new gods (F 118), and when he came onstage while he was wearing the Odeum as a crown (F 73), the point was that his building program was for the greater glory of Pericles, not the people. Aristophanes would recall such criticisms even after Pericles' death (*Ach.* 530–34, *Pax* 604–14) and expressed sympathy with Thucydides son of Milesias, who had led the opposition to him (*Ach.* 703–12).

Thucydides characterizes the Periclean era as "in theory a democracy but in fact the rule (*archē*) of its first man" (2.65.9). He rejects the tyrant label, stressing that it was the people who held the power and indeed were collectively a tyrant (2.63.2, cf. *Knghts* 1111–14); after all, the demos could and did punish even Pericles. He led not by deceptive or meretricious oratory but in good democratic fashion (unlike the aristocratic and allegedly tyrannical Alcibiades) by offering good advice; like a comic hero (or an Antiphon: 8.68.1) he was not afraid to upbraid the demos, whose interests he served, not his own: he was entirely devoted to the common good, and urged the Athenians too to be "lovers (*erastai*) of the polis" (2.43.1, a notion boisterously ridiculed by Aristophanes as demagogic flattery in *Knights* 732 ff.); throughout the *History* care for the common good is a touchstone of any good government. Thus Thucydides may ignore the friends, relatives, concubines, courtesans, lovers, and private interests so prominent in comedy, even if a politician's means, background, personality, and conduct were in reality always important factors in leadership and in stasis along with civil or class conflict. Thucydides plays down political division by picturing an almost monolithic unity of the demos under Pericles: even when the demos is "changeable" (2.59.1, cf. 65.4) it is vis-à-vis Pericles, nothing to do with enemies or competitors like Thucydides son of Milesias, who succeeded Miltiades' son Cimon, and Cleon (Plu. *Per.* 33.8), who would succeed Pericles as "first man": these are ignored along with the democratic principle of *isēgoria* itself, so important in Herodotus but insignificant when only one man's views counted. Political competition was rather for the lesser men who succeeded Pericles (2.65).

Historians tended to take the comic rather than the Thucydidean line on Periclean leadership—Plutarch characterizes his polity as "aristocratic and monarchic" (*Per.* 15.2)—until the eighteenth century, when the idea of an "Age of Pericles" resurfaces, followed by the great-man portrayal by Grote (1861), who also tried to redeem Cleon.

THE GREATEST WAR

Thucydides claims that he expected from the start that "the war between the Peloponnesians and the Athenians would be great and more notable than any preceding it" (1.1) and that it was precipitated not by issues that might have been resolved by diplomacy (in particular the Megarian Decree) but by large and inevitable historical forces, its "truest cause" being Spartan fear of the growth of Athenian power (1.23.6), which Pericles understood and convinced the Athenians to accept: the decision was between war or a surrender of power too dangerous for a tyrant polis to consider (2.63), though the winning strategy must include exposing the Attic countryside to enemy devastation and relocating its inhabitants to the city; it was a good plan that ultimately failed because Pericles' successors lacked his discipline, resolve, and unifying leadership (2.65).

Comic poets did not recognize a single long war against the Peloponnesians and opposed the fighting only when it involved the Spartans over arguably negotiable differences and/or afflicted the Attic countryside and thus the property of landowners (cf. Thuc. 2.65.2), that is from 431–21 and 413–11. In *Birds* of 414, for example, the Sicilian expedition is not associated with a wider struggle and reflects the broad popular enthusiasm that Thucydides characterized as lustful (6.24.3), while in 411, Lysistrata, who dates the current fighting to the Athenians' "stupid" repudiation of the terms of the Peace of Nicias in 418 (513–14) and traces the Sicilian expedition to a chaotic and ill-omened meeting of the Assembly (387–98), reminds the Athenians and Spartans that there are plenty of barbarians available if they want a war (1133–34, echoing Athena in Aeschylus' *Eumenides* 864). Aristophanes supplied detailed and plausible arguments in support of his appeals to renormalize relations with Sparta (e.g., *Acharnians* 513–56, *Lysistrata* 1125–56), though he is careful to qualify them (*Acharnians* 510–12) or soften them with condescending humor (*Lysistrata*), and he makes light of the fashion for things Spartan among some oligarchic Athenian youths (e.g., *Wasps* 475–77, *Birds* 1281 ff., cf. Pl. *Protagoras* 342b–c, *Gorgias* 515e).

Nor in the comic view were the wars with Sparta inevitable or necessary: they were rather a senseless disruption of the long and prosperous era following the Persian wars, foisted upon the Athenians by Pericles for trivial and personal reasons—border violations with Megara leading to the mutual abduction of whores, two of whom were Aspasia's, by drunken wastrels (*Acharnians* 515–38), much as a decade earlier the Samian War was allegedly instigated by Aspasia—and then prolonged by demagogues despite repeated Spartan offers to negotiate, in both cases distracting attention from malfeasance: Pericles from the scandal involving Pheidias (*Peace* 605–27), Cleon from extortion of the allies and general criminality (*Knights* 801–4). The Spartan offer of peace in return for repeal of the Megarian Decree must have raised the issue of its triviality, which Thucydides moots by having Pericles argue that accepting the offer would only invite more serious demands (1.140.4–5). In Thucydides, Pericles convinces the whole city—contrast his report of dissension in the Assembly after Pericles' death, for example, about Mitylene, Sphacteria, and the Sicilian Expedition, and his disapproval of its rejection of Sparta's peace overtures after Sphacteria, with which Aristophanes concurs: Thuc. 4.15–22, cf. 41.3–4, *Knights* 794–6, *Peace* 667—whereas in *Acharnians* Dicaeopolis/Telephus/Aristophanes reminds the Acharnians, united at this time by desire for vengeance on the Spartans, of the war's trivial origins and continued exploitation by self-serving leaders. It is noteworthy that Thucydides reports Archidamus as factoring into his prewar calculations the possibility that the Acharnians might change their bellicose stance (2.20.4).

Thucydides ennobles the war's first casualties by having Pericles place their sacrifice beyond words and for a cause greater than the present action (2.35–36), but there must have been mixed feelings: Cratinus in *Dionysalexander* and Hermippus in *Fates* portray Pericles and his defensive strategy as cowardly (in tune with significant public opinion: Thuc. 2.21.3), and military leadership (though not the valor and skill of the rank and file, cf. *Acharnians* 595–619) continued as an issue that comic poets might enlist in criticizing the war. In *Peace* Aristophanes holds Pericles, and then Cleon and Brasidas (the "mortar and pestle" of the war, 269–74), responsible for continuing the war to the detriment of good people on every side (compare Thucydides 5.16.1, though he favorably contrasts Brasidas with Cleon as a general: 4.81.2); in *Acharnians* the general Lamachus is caricatured as self-important and pampered, brave and dutiful in an unworthy cause; the taxiarch described in *Peace* 1172–84 fears battle; Cleon in *Knights* is a coward who stole the victory at Pylos from others; in *Lysistrata* the old men (chorus, proboulos) are given no arguments for continuing the war, only stubborn bluster; according to Aeschylus in *Frogs*, inspiration to bravery is absent, discipline and good order have broken down; and Eupolis in *Taxiarchs* and *Draft-Dodgers* (dates uncertain) will have made similar criticisms.

Politics After Pericles

The death of Pericles in 429 was a turning point both in Athenian politics and on the comic stage. "New politicians," the first from commercial rather than landed and military backgrounds and thus lacking established family or political alliances, competed with one another for ascendancy on the strength of their individual prowess in assembly and court, taking a novel populist line that included attacks on the now sidelined traditional elite; even if there was more continuity in policy and procedure than Thucydides allows (2.65), the ensemble of changes in family background, civic values, rhetorical style, and class affiliation was real enough, and is reflected even in contemporary tragedy: for example, Euripides' *Supplient Women* 399–456. At the very same time a new generation of comic poets made their debuts, including Eupolis (429), Aristophanes (427), and Plato (mid-420s), and took the subgenre of politically engaged comedy in fresh directions by portraying the new politicians as "demagogues": the Olympian-tyrant persona attached to Pericles did not suit these "men of the marketplace," for "leadership of the people (δημαγωγία) is no longer a job for a man of education and good character, but for the ignorant and disgusting" (*Knights* 191–93, cf. 128–37, 213–22), though these demagogues could trick and wheedle the demos into ceding them its proper tyrannical powers (Henderson 2003).

Aristophanes led the way with four plays—*Babylonians* (Dionysia 426, focusing on imperial policy), *Acharnians* (Lenaea 425, the war), *Knights* (Lenaea 424, demagoguery), and *Wasps* (Lenaea 422, corruption of the courts and class conflict)—connected by a sustained attack on the popular leader Cleon. These plays transformed the vehicle for political comedy from myth-allegory and *emphasis* to straightforwardly topical satire and criticism, though myth is still an ingredient in *Babylonians* and *Acharnians* and *emphasis* in *Knights* (Cleon appears as a Paphlagonian slave) and *Wasps* (as an extortionate dog): not until after Cleon's death in 422 were demagogues portrayed *in propria persona*, first in Plato's *Peisander* in 421 (Lenaea), though at the same festival Eupolis followed Aristophanic precedent in *Marikas* (a Persian slave representing Hyperbolus). Subsequent demagogue comedies were Hermippus' *Breadwomen* (420?) and Plato's *Hyperbolus* (419?) against Hyperbolus; after Hyperbolus' ostracism c. 417 (degraded by its very use against such a man: Plato F 203), no demagogue comedy was produced until the Lenaea of 405, when Plato's *Cleophon* competed with Aristophanes' *Frogs*, which all but calls for Cleophon's death (678–85, 1532–33), soon to become a reality with his judicial murder in 404 by anti-democratic conspirators (Lysias 13.7–12, 30.10–14), as also Androcles and many lesser "miscreants" (*ponēroi*, a standard comic and elite slur used also by Thucydides of Hyperbolus, 8.73.3).

Aristophanes prided himself on the originality of these plays and on his courage in attacking Cleon and not a lesser figure like Hyperbolus (*Clouds* 545–62, *Wasps* 1029–37, *Peace* 748–61). His artistic ambition was rewarded by three consecutive first prizes—*Babylonians* was the first Dionysian victory by a new poet in ten years—and one second prize (*Wasps*), and his claim to civic impact was affirmed by Cleon himself, whose legal actions against the poet after *Babylonians* and again after *Knights* made the conflict not only political but personal, if it had not been personally motivated all along: the poet and the politician were fellow demesmen. Aristophanes would later express gratitude to "certain gentlemen" for their early sponsorship (*Clouds* 528–33) and solidarity with the elite corps of knights, also targets of Cleon (*Acharnians* 299–302, *Knights* 507–11); Callistratus produced both *Babylonians* and *Acharnians*, suggesting at least sympathy for the young poet's stance; and Philonides, another fellow demesman and father of the comic poet Nicochares, produced *Wasps*. The artistic success of these plays together with Cleon's rising to the bait fulfilled Aristophanes' hope that they would live on for future ages to enjoy (*Clouds* 561–62).

The plays also immortalized Cleon as the exemplary demagogue, as he was for Thucydides, too, though there were other candidates (cf. Rhodes 1981: 344–61 on [Arist.] *Ath.* 28 and the various traditions). Thucydides describes Pericles' successors as "more on an equal footing one to the other" (ἴσοι μᾶλλον αὐτοὶ πρὸς ἀλλήλους, 2.65.10), and the motive oracle in *Knights* 127–43 specifies a dynastic succession of demagogues each worse (and thus better) than the last, with an oakum seller and a sheep seller preceding the tanner (Cleon) who is overthrown in the play by a sausage seller. At the same time, both Aristophanes and Thucydides consider other demagogues hardly worth noticing (*Clouds* 551–59 and Thuc. 8.73.3 on Hyperbolus). Ancient scholars identified the oakum seller and the sheep seller from other allusions in comedy as Eucrates and Callias or Lysicles, and from this paucity of evidence Dover concluded that "presumably Aristophanes has exaggerated, for the sake of the oracular climax, whatever part they played in politics" (1972, 93), but it is equally likely that he exaggerated Cleon, too. Personal enmity, an avowed motive for Aristophanes, is likely also for Thucydides, who treats Cleon with special animus: both Cleon and Thucydides were first elected *stratēgos* for 424/3 (Nicias and Lamachus were among their colleagues), and Cleon (harrier of generals: *Knights* 166, 288, *Wasps* 240–44, 836–1008) may well have played a role in Thucydides' exile, as Marcellinus' *Life* states (46.3–4). Nor were the comic poet and the historian the only Athenians who felt aggrieved or threatened, if there is truth in Aristophanes' insistence that no decent citizen, wealthy or poor, was safe from the violence and rapacity of Cleon (*Knights* 225–29) and politicians like him (*Wasps* 655–712).

The model of post-Periclean degeneracy also answered thematic purposes. Aristophanes elides Pericles in order to emphasize the novelty of the new politicians, although they were not really parvenus (e.g., Cleon's father, Cleaenetus, was a liturgist and Cleon himself had been noteworthy among Pericles' opponents: Hermippus F 47) and they hardly introduced class antagonism to Athens, even if their self-identification with the demos was novel. Thucydides portrays Pericles as the ideal military/political leader from which the new politicians represented a decline, although there was considerable continuity in policies, especially those involving internal administration, that Thucydides plays down or ignores (e.g., jury pay; ideological, political, and financial feuds in the courts; the basic strategy of the war, followed until the unexpected breakthrough at Sphacteria; the distribution of public funds; imperial administration; and fiscal operations generally), and few radical changes.

As regards the empire, Thucydides and the comic poets show similar complementarity. Both Aristophanes and Thucydides' Pericles embrace the notion of Athens as a "tyrant city." For Aristophanes, the Athenians benefit handsomely and rightly by exploiting their subjects (e.g., *Wasps* 707–11) while the subjects are ever ready to betray their masters (e.g., *Peace* 619–22). Apparently Eupolis expressed the same high-handed attitude: *Cities* (probably Dionysia 422) had a chorus representing the allies as women subject to various forms of mishandling by Athenians. Even in 411, when allied defection was a serious problem, the need to consult them on the issue of peace (and it was an issue with some allies both in 421 and 404: Thuc. 5.17.2, Xenophon *Hellenica* 2.2.19–20) is laughed off (*Lysistrata* 1176–81). Thucydides has Pericles express pride in the empire (2.36, giving the impression that its acquisition had been a solidary Athenian project all along) and warn of the danger in letting it go "even if it was wrong to acquire it" (2.63), and he illustrates the (mainly political) complexities of disciplining it in the debates about Mytilene (showcasing Cleon's hard line: the poet's appeal in the *parabasis* of *Acharnians* 630–32 to the Athenians as both "quick to decide" and "quick to change their minds" must recall this debate) and about Melos (ominous in Thucydides, good for a laugh at *Birds* 186). He is less interested in the legal and administrative dimensions that show up in comedy ("how the people in the allied cities are democratically governed": *Acharnians* 642, recalling the poet's exposé in *Babylonians*), notably the trying of serious cases in Athenian courts, the (fawning and deceptive) lobbying of the demos by allied envoys (cf. *Acharnians* 630–46), and the exaction of tribute.

When Aristophanes does speak of the allies sympathetically (as in *Babylonians*, where they are portrayed as enslaved barbarians) it is only as an argument against demagogues like Cleon, who allegedly exploited them for his own enrichment at the expense of the Athenians generally: for example, *Eq.* 313 (tribute), 326–7 (milking rich foreigners), 801–2, 1196–7 (bribes), 1030–4 (profiteering). By contrast, Thucydides does not note the role of Athenian leaders in the domination of the allies, already an issue in the 430s: for example, Teleclides F 45 = Plutarch's *Life* 16.2 (the Athenians have ceded to Pericles) "the tribute from the cities and the cities themselves, some to bind and some to raze, to erect stone walls and pull them down again, treaties, power, might, peace, wealth, and prosperity," perhaps because it would align Pericles with Cleon. Nor does he mention the upward reassessment of tribute in 430, 428 (probably), and 425 (*IG* i^3 79 = ML 69), perhaps because the rapid exhaustion of Athenian reserves by 428 (*IG* i^3 369) would have belied Pericles' assurances that the Athenians had enough financial reserves to outlast the Peloponnesians.

SICILY AND REVOLUTION

After the Peace of Nicias, celebrated at the Dionysia of 421 in *Peace* along with the deaths of Cleon and Brasidas, Aristophanes turned from politically engaged comedy to other subjects, as did his fellow political poets after Hyperbolus' ostracism c. 417, when elite

(Alcibiades, Critias) or traditional (Nicias) politicians, with little to fear from the comic stage, returned to ascendancy. The major events for Thucydides, the Sicilian expedition (Greenwood, chapter 9 in this volume) and the oligarchic revolution (Wolpert, chapter 10 in this volume), register in comedy only indirectly or incidentally, and then not in essentially negative fashion. The resurgence of populist politics could still trigger the usual comic responses—in 411 *Lysistrata* presses for a negotiated end of the war, still blamed on "thieving" politicians like Peisander (490), and in 405 *Frogs* champions a return to traditional (martial) values and leadership by re-enfranchising men who had "made a mistake" by joining the oligarchy and repented (686–737) and perhaps even by recalling Alcibiades (1422–32)—but after 413 the tone is more sombre: the question is no longer how best to manage Athenian power and prosperity, as in the days of Pericles and Cleon, but how to recover them.

For Thucydides the Sicilian Expedition illustrates the *pleonexia* that Pericles had warned against and is presented as a climactic event that follows a virtually tragic arc and leaves shock and recrimination in its wake (Thuc. 8.1–2). The comic poets avoid mentioning the outcome (pointedly at *Lysistrata* 590–91), and the one specific comic reminiscence—*Lysistrata* 387–98 recalling the deliberations to authorize the expedition—emphasizes the ill-omened forebodings of war-weary Athenian women and the improvidence of the men, exemplified by a hot-headed speaker (Demostratus, unnamed in Thucydides' account), and rather more lightheartedly than would be expected in a traumatized atmosphere. *Sicily*, a comedy by Demetrius produced after the war and possibly reflecting knowledge of Thucydides, seems to include Athenians travelling to Sicily and reminiscing about the invasion, thus reflecting less painful memories than Thucydides leads us to expect (Storey 2012: 317–19). Indeed, Aristophanes' *Birds* (Dionysia 414) may well allegorize the expedition as a success under Alcibiades, as if he had not been removed from its command *in absentia* by enemies playing on popular fears of elite tyranny (e.g., Thuc. 6.15.4, 53.3, 61.1–2) and stoking a religious scandal that awakened old paranoia (Henderson 1998a).

In *Birds* the hero, Peisetaerus, who has left Athens in search of a place free of ceaseless lawsuits and botheration, takes to the sky, where he has the brilliant idea of unifying the scattered and apathetic but once-great birds into a united and powerful demos, displacing the usurping Olympians and reclaiming a mighty empire, himself replacing Zeus as *tyrannos* of all creation. For Thucydides the Sicilian expedition was hubristic, ill advised, and then bungled, and if that was also Aristophanes' opinion, then Peisetaerus' success must be ironic, a kind of warning to the audience about hubris such as Thucydides wrote up for Pericles. But Aristophanes offers no such encouragement: on any straightforward reading *Birds* not only reflects the self-confidence and high expectations of the great majority of Athenians in the expedition, as in Thucydides' account, but also impatiently awaits its success (e.g., 186, 640, 813–816, 1360–1369). After all, Aristophanes never expresses qualms about Athenian imperialism or about warfare that did not involve Sparta and/or aggrandize demagogues. And Peisetaerus seems a new kind of hero befitting a time of elite re-emergence: earlier heroes (like Thucydides' Pericles or Aristophanes' Dicaeopolis) could steer the demos in the right direction by sheer honesty, intelligence, and eloquence; now Peisetaerus operates as a benign *tyrannos* outside conventional politics and structures, as does Lysistrata a few years later. The earlier model is about wise leadership of a powerful but disorganized demos, the latter is about rescuing a floundering demos from its own disorganization. Comic heroes, unlike comic villains, are always fictitious and never portraits, but they may channel actual individuals, and if Peisetaerus recalled any leader in particular it was (the popular fantasy of) Alcibiades.

Libanius' statement that Alcibiades was ubiquitously featured in comedy (frag. 50 β 2) is not supported by the surviving evidence: except for Eupolis' *Baptai*, in which Alcibiades may have been ridiculed on private but not political grounds, the notices are few and the political ones positive, much as for Thucydides it was as much the demos' suspicions as Alcibiades' behavior that caused the trouble and left the expedition's command weaker for his absence (6.15.3–4). For years Aristophanes had been debunking the threat of elite tyranny as merely a demagogic smear, though it is clear from references in *Knights* and *Lysistrata* that (*pace* Thucydides) the spectators were aware that Hippias, not Hipparchus, had been tyrant (6.54.2) but not that it was the Spartans, rather than the Athenians and Harmodius, who had played a decisive role in expelling him (cf. Rhodes 2006: 527–29, Henderson 2012: 159).

The Eleusinian scandal that provided the grounds for recalling Alcibiades—an event whose importance obliged the historian to register it—is not noticed by comedy, though anti-Eleusinian sentiment combined with suspicion of tyrannical ambition had been ridiculed as a demagogic slur already in *Wasps* (377–78), nor are the c. 65 people implicated, three of whom indeed seem to have been the comic poets Archippus, Aristomenes, and Cephisodorus. It is not impossible that this silence was involuntary, related to a decree attributed to the politician Syracosius (*PAA* 853435) and protested by the comic poet Phrynichus in *Monotropos*, produced in 414 (F 27), as limiting comic freedom of abuse. But more likely it is another example of the overall rarity of comic references to figures on the right. Figures on the left continue to be ridiculed in this period: for example, Syracosius himself, a career politician who fits the profile of the demagogues who succeeded Pericles: first mentioned in 429 in Eupolis' *Prospaltians* (F 259.72), who when on the podium, according to Eupolis in *Cities* (probably 422), ran about yapping like a little dog (F 220; cf. *Birds* 1297, where he is compared to a jay).

Thucydides chronicles the oligarchic coup of 411 and evaluates it in generally positive terms, speaking well of the participants both collectively and individually (Antiphon, Phrynichus, Theramenes: 8.27.5, 68), portraying the democrats as unable to muster effective opposition, and deeming the initial stages of the moderate or mixed democracy of the Five Thousand "one of the periods when the affairs of Athens were conducted best" (8.97). By contrast, the comic poets, as public and sometimes partisan voices, were more reticent or cautious: as they freely ridiculed populist fears of elite aspiration to tyranny, they avoided explicit acknowledgement of oligarchy, the real and perennial threat. They mention *hetaireiai* only rarely and without identifying political stripe (*Lysistrata* 577–78, Eupolis *Demes* F 99.28), and even as the campaign of terror preceding the coup took hold, Aristophanes' allusion to the threat, though clear enough, is inexplicit

(*Thesmophoriazusae* 1136–47). The *Frogs* parabasis sympathizes with those who had participated in the conspiracy but not *qua* oligarchs: they are simply good men "tripped up" by the demagogue-turned-conspirator Phrynichus (Thuc. 8.68.3, 90.1, Lysias 25.9; his assassins received civic honors after the war, *IG* i^3 102) and should not live in fear of reprisals (686–705), which by the Decree of Demophantus in 410 could be deadly for anyone deemed an aspiring tyrant (Andocides 1.96–8; for the decree's authenticity see Sommerstein 2014, Teegarden 2014); the chorus immediately turns to ridicule of Cleigenes, one of the sponsors of the decree (cf. Storey 2012: 312–13).

Aristophanes may nevertheless have anticipated in an indirect way, à la *Birds*, an oligarchic change of constitution in *Lysistrata*, where the heroine and her helpers are characterized as upper-class Athenian matrons, loyal patriots, and closely aligned with Athena Polias, while their opponents, the old men of the chorus, are parasitic democrats who squander what their great Athenian forebears bequeathed the city while making no contributions of their own (638–57) and who persist in a senseless war out of irrational hatred of Spartans, misguided patriotism, and sheer stubbornness. The women intend to force the men, for their own good, to negotiate a peace whether they like it or not (498–501) in "a fantasy of active subversion of the allegedly failed democratic state for what is presented as the true popular good" (Olson 2012: 77). It is true that Lysistrata's conspiracy involves the women of all the warring states and is only temporary, but as in Thucydides its focus is on breaking through the democratic gridlock in Athens from outside the normal process.

Official Athens is represented in *Lysistrata* by an unnamed Proboulos (cf. Thuc. 8.1.3), one of a board that in usurping functions previously held by the Council could be thought oligarchic rather than democratic (cf. Aristotle, *Politics* 1298b, 99b, 1329a) and indeed may have later helped implement the oligarchy ([Arist.] *Ath.* 29.2), though neither Thucydides (8.67.1) nor the comic poets mention this. But the harsh portrayal of the Proboulos is not inconsistent with rightist modeling in *Lysistrata*: in the dangerous political climate of early 411, darkly described by Thucydides, the play's arguments were best advanced by characters outside the political establishment: citizen women (apparently represented for the first time in comedy) versus an elderly, unnamed member of an extraordinary board, who after all was carrying out, and thus prolonging the viability, of the allegedly failed democratic policy.

After the war politically engaged comedy was largely abandoned, quite possibly because of its "perceived contribution ... to the overthrow of democracy" (Sommerstein 2000: 444–45) but surely also because of the return to leadership by the familiar elite and the diminished popular appeal of demagogic politics, as during the subgenre's earlier eclipse after Hyperbolus' ostracism. Thus it was resurrected in the fourth century in periods of democratic restoration by Timocles, Archedicus, and Philippides; and even Menander revisits the trial scene in *Orestes* in *Sicyonian(s)*, thus probably dating that play after 307 (Henderson 2014). But as *Ecclesiazusae* illustrates, comic exploration of democratic and other constitutions in the abstract was alive and well in the fourth century in ways that would have interested Thucydides.

References

Bakola, Emmanuela. 2010. *Cratinus and the Art of Comedy*. Oxford: Oxford University Press.
Boedeker, Deborah, and Kurt Raaflaub, eds. 1998. *Democracy, Empire and the Arts in Fifth-Century Athens*. Cambridge: Harvard University Press.
Cairns, Douglas L., and Ronald A. Knox. 2004. *Law, Rhetoric and Comedy in Classical Athens*. London: Duckworth; Swansea: Classical Press of Wales.
Dobrov, Gregory W. 1998. *The City as Comedy: Society and Representation in Athenian Drama*. Chapel Hill: University of North Carolina Press.
Dover, Kenneth J. 1972. *Aristophanic Comedy*. Berkeley and Los Angeles: University of California Press.
Edwards, Antony T. 1993. "Historicizing the Popular Grotesque: Bakhtin's *Rabelais* and Attic Old Comedy." In *Theater and Society in the Classical World*, edited by R. Scodel, 89–117. Ann Arbor: University of Michigan Press.
Fontaine, Michael, and Adele Scafuro. 2014. *The Oxford Handbook of Greek and Roman Comedy*. Oxford: Oxford University Press.
Grote, George. 1861. *History of Greece*. Vol. VI. New York: Harper and Brothers.
Harvey, David and John Wilkins, eds. 2000. *The Rivals of Aristophanes: Studies in Athenian Old Comedy*. London: Duckworth; Swansea: Classical Press of Wales.
Henderson, J. 1998a. "Mass versus Elite and the Comic Heroism of Peisetairos." In Dobrov 1998, 135–48. Chapel Hill: University of North Carolina Press.
Henderson, J. 1998b. "Attic Old Comedy, Frank Speech, and Democracy." In *Democracy, Empire and the Arts in Fifth-Century Athens*, edited by D. Boedeker and K. Raaflaub, 255–73. Cambridge. Harvard University Press.
Henderson, J. 2003. "Demos, Demagogue, Tyrant in Attic Old Comedy." In *Popular Tyranny*, edited by K. A. Morgan, 155–79. Austin: University of Texas Press.
Henderson, J. 2008. *Aristophanes V: Fragments*. Loeb Classical Library. Cambridge: Harvard University Press.
Henderson, J. 2012. "Old Comedy and Popular History." In *Greek Notions of the Past in the Archaic and Classical Eras: History without Historians*, edited by J. Marincola et al., 144–59. Leventis Studies 6. Edinburgh: Edinburgh University Press.
Henderson, J. 2013a. "The Comic Chorus and the Demagogue." In *Choral Mediations in Greek Tragedy*, edited by Renaud Gagné and Marianne Hopmann, 278–96. Cambridge: Cambridge University Press.
Henderson, J. 2013b. "A Brief History of Athenian Political Comedy (c. 440–c.300)." *Transactions of the American Philological Association* 143: 249–62.
Henderson, J. 2014. "Comedy in the Fourth Century II: Politics and Domesticity." In *The Oxford Handbook of Greek and Roman Comedy*, edited by M. Fontaine and A. Scafuro, 181–98. Oxford: Oxford University Press.
Kassel, Rudolf, and Colin Austin, eds. 1983–. *Poetae Comici Graeci (PCG)*. 12 vols. Berlin and New York: De Gruyter.
Marincola, J., L. Llewellyn-Jones, and C. Maciver. eds. 2012. *Greek Notions of the Past in the Archaic and Classical Eras: History without Historians*. Leventis Studies 6. Edinburgh: Edinburgh University Press.
Markantonatos, Andreas, and Bernhard Zimmermann, eds. 2012. *Crisis on Stage: Tragedy and Comedy in Late Fifth-Century Athens*. Berlin and Boston: De Gruyter.

Marshall, C. W., and George Kovacs, eds. 2012. *No Laughing Matter: Studies in Athenian Comedy*. London: Bristol Classical Press.

Olson, S. Douglas. 2010. "Comedy, Politics, and Society." In Dobrov, 35–69.

Olson, S. Douglas. 2012. "Lysistrata's Conspiracy and the Politics of 412 BC." In *No Laughing Matter: Studies in Athenian Comedy*, edited by C. W. Marshall and G. Kovacs, 69–81. London: Bristol Classical Press.

Olson, S. Douglas, ed. 2007. *Broken Laughter: Select Fragments of Greek Comedy*. Oxford: Oxford University Press.

Rengakos, A., and A. Tsakmakis, eds. 2006. *Brill's Companion to Thucydides*. Leiden and Boston: Brill.

Rhodes, Peter J. 1981. *A Commentary on the Aristotelian* Athenaion Politeia. Oxford: Oxford University Press.

Rhodes, Peter J. 2006. "Thucydides and Athenian History." In *Brill's Companion to Thucydides*, edited by A. Rengakos and A. Tsakmakis, 523–46. Leiden and Boston: Brill.

Rusten, Jeffrey. 2006. "Thucydides and Comedy." In *Brill's Companion to Thucydides*, edited by A. Rengakos and A. Tsakmakis, 547–58. Leiden and Boston: Brill.

Rusten, Jeffrey, et al., eds. 2011. *The Birth of Comedy: Texts, Documents, and Art from Athenian Comic Competitions, 486–280*. Baltimore: Johns Hopkins University Press.

Schwarze, Joachim. 1971. *Die Beurteilung des Perikles durch die attische Komödie und ihre historische und historiographische Bedeutung*. Munich: C. H. Beck.

Scodel, Ruth, ed. 1993. *Theater and Society in the Classical World*. Ann Arbor: University of Michigan Press.

Sluiter, Ineke, and Ralph M. Rosen, eds. 2004. *Free Speech in Classical Athens*. Leiden: Brill.

Sommerstein, Alan H. 1996. "How to Avoid Being a Komodoumenos." *Classical Quarterly* 46: 327–56.

Sommerstein, Alan H. 2000. "Platon, Eupolis, and the Demagogue-Comedy." In Harvey and Wilkins, 437–51.

Sommerstein, Alan H. 2004a. "Comedy and the Unspeakable." In *Law, Rhetoric and Comedy in Classical Athens*, edited by D. L. Cairns and R. A. Knox, 205–22. London: Duckworth; Swansea: Classical Press of Wales.

Sommerstein, Alan H. 2009a. "An Alternative Democracy and an Alternative to Democracy in Aristophanic Comedy." In Sommerstein 2009b, 204–22.

Sommerstein, Alan H., ed. 2009b. *Talking about Laughter and Other Studies in Greek Comedy*. Oxford: Oxford University Press.

Sommerstein 2009c. "Kleophon and the Restaging of *Frogs*." In Sommerstein 2009b, 254–71.

Sommerstein, Alan H. 2014. "The Authenticity of the Demophantus Decree." *Classical Quarterly* 64: 49–57.

Storey, Ian. 2003. *Eupolis: Poet of Old Comedy*. Oxford: Oxford University Press.

Storey, Ian. 2011. *Fragments of Old Comedy*. 3 vols. Loeb Classical Library. Cambridge: Harvard University Press.

Storey, Ian. 2012. "Comedy and the Crises." In *Crisis on Stage: Tragedy and Comedy in Late Fifth-Century Athens*, edited by A. Markantonatos and B. Zimmermann, 303–19. Berlin and Boston: De Gruyter.

Teegarden, David. 2014. *Death to Tyrants! Ancient Greek Democracy and the Struggle against Tyranny*. Princeton: Princeton University Press.

Wright, Matthew. 2007. "Comedy and the Trojan War." *Classical Quarterly* 57: 412–31.

Zimmermann, Bernhard, ed. 2013–. *Fragmenta Comica*. Berlin: Antike Verlag.

CHAPTER 36

THUCYDIDES AND HIS CONTINUATORS

VIVIENNE J. GRAY

Introduction

THE last sentence of Thucydides' history of the Peloponnesian War leaves the story incomplete. It tells us that Tissaphernes arrived *first of all* at Ephesus on his way to the Hellespont in 411 BCE, but not where he went next.[1] Several historians did describe what happened next, in "completions" of Thucydides' history down to his envisaged endpoint in the defeat of Athens (Thuc. 5.26.1), and they attached to these their "continuations" of what happened even after that. Ancient testimony mentions Cratippus of Athens, Xenophon of Athens, and Theopompus of Chios,[2] and modern discoveries add the author of the *Hellenica Oxyrhynchia* ("P"). The dates of their completions are discussed below, but they are all from the fourth century BCE.

This chapter will discuss each of the continuators in turn, establishing as much as the evidence allows of the main features of their completions, as well as the detail, in order to illuminate their reception of Thucydides.[3] Xenophon is fully extant, but the others are in fragments, and the amount of text we have to work on determines the order and extent of the discussion. The continuation of a predecessor has precedent in the epic cycle, and

---

[1] Modern editors bracket the final reference in manuscripts to the end of the winter of the twentieth year of the war: (Canfora 1970, 75–76). Thucydides survived the end of the war, perhaps until 397 BCE: see Hornblower (2008) on 5.26.

[2] Xenophon and Theopompus are named in Marcellinus 45 (trans. Burns 2010) and D.S. 13.43. Cratippus is named in D.H., *Thucydides* 16. Cf. Canfora (1970, 62–73) who interprets the evidence to prove that Xenophon alone started from 411 BCE.

[3] Among those who have written other chapters on the continuators, Nicolai (2006) focuses on the program of Xenophon's *Hellenica* (on which also see Gray [2003, 2011]), Hose (2006) reviews sources for the whole war, and Nicolai (2009) takes Thucydides' comment on speeches and the work as a possession for all time as a test of reception.

Xenophon invites another writer to continue his own *Hellenica* at the end of his account (7.5.27),[4] but the continuators of Thucydides completed an unfinished history and that raises special questions beyond their general reception of his authority, such as how they connected their work to his and whether they imitated his style or followed his conception of the war. The problem is that they are mostly fragmentary and rarely make explicit reference to Thucydides, so that most of the time we have to infer their reception from indirect evidence that is also incomplete: Xenophon's is the only text we have showing the connection to Thucydides, for instance. The two explicit references they make to Thucydides' work indicate that their reactions varied: Cratippus criticized Thucydides' balance of speech and action, while the *HO* made a back reference to him that points to acceptance of his authority. But one strong general impression is that though the continuators took their starting point from Thucydides, they went their own way. There are exceptions, but they did not systematically adopt the narrative features that we most immediately associate with Thucydides or his outlook on the war. There are some signs that this constituted rejection of Thucydides, but it could also just reflect temperaments and ambitions that were different from his.

Cratippus

We have nothing but secondhand reports about the work of Cratippus. Dionysius of Halicarnassus, *On Thucydides* (16) says that he "was [Thucydides'] contemporary and wrote up the events he left unwritten (*ta paraleiphthenta*, the regular phrase for the completions)".[5] His status as a contemporary gives him a claim to be the first of the continuators of Thucydides, rivaling Xenophon for that position (see below). Some rule this out, on the grounds that Marcellinus 33 has Cratippus consult a Zopyrus whom they identify as Zopyrus of Magnesia, c. 300 BCE (Plutarch, *Moralia* 314e–f); but an earlier Zopyrus could be involved (one is recorded by Plutarch as the tutor of Alcibiades): Hornblower 2008, 52–53, Chambers 1993, XXIII. Cratippus also seems to have continued Thucydides as well as completing him, according to the summary of the contents of his history in

---

[4] Canfora (1970, 196–97) cites the epic cycle, on which now see West (2013), and then how Demophilus continues Ephorus (*FGH* 70 T 9a); Diillus continues Ephorus (70 and 73), Psaon continues Diillus (*FGH* 78), Athanas continues Philistus (*FGH* 556 F 562). Tuplin (2007) discusses the wider phenomenon of continuous history outside the continuators.

[5] Jacoby *FGH* 64 assembles the meager evidence about Cratippus. For the translation of *ta paraleiphthenta*, cf. Usher (1974) ("editor of the history as he left it"); Pritchett (1975) ("the matters passed over by him"). This may sound as if he filled in gaps in Thucydides' text, but *LSJ* allows the translation of matters "left remaining" and "left to others," which would capture how Thucydides "left to others to write" events he failed to complete (Jacoby 115 Fr. 5). Some manuscripts of Xenophon even entitle his completion "the *paraleipomena* of Thucydides" (the present tense participle of *paraleiphthenta*): Breitenbach (1967, 1674); Canfora (1970, 57), confirming that it means a sequel. Plutarch *Moralia* 345 c–e describes his contents only as events after Thucydides' endpoint (notwithstanding any "editing" he may have also done to Thucydides' text).

Plutarch, *Moralia* 345 c–e, which indicates that he covered the period 411–394 BCE. The ending of the history in 394 BCE would also accord with an early date for Cratippus—if he wrote about his own times.

The most noteworthy feature of Cratippus is that, according to Dionysius in that same passage (16), Cratippus considered Thucydides' speeches to be distractions from the action and annoyances to the reader. He thought Thucydides did not complete his work, because he was attending to weaknesses in the existing speeches, and he praised their absence from the eighth book. This chimes with our view that Thucydides is not out to entertain his audiences, but not with the admiration we feel for the high level of intellectual analysis in his speeches. Cratippus apparently went on to compare the first and eighth books, the first abounding in speeches but not action, the latter abounding in action without speeches. If Dionysius gives an accurate report (and he does imply that everything previous did come from Cratippus when he goes on to give his own opinion about the speeches, section 17), Cratippus must have written a sustained critique of Thucydides, which makes him unique among the other continuators, whose remains mention Thucydides only in one other place, but we do not know where it figured in his work, perhaps in a preface, perhaps a digression.

Cratippus did not just complete Thucydides, but went beyond his envisaged endpoint, as did all the other continuators. This might mean that he was critical of the endpoint; perhaps it was too pessimistic. Thucydides 5.26.1 envisaged the end as the destruction of the Athenian empire and the capture of the Long Walls and Piraeus, whereas Cratippus' continuation is said to have gone down to the Athenian recovery of her walls and her sea power c. 394 BCE. This was an uplifting endpoint of the kind that was approved by Dionysius of Halicarnassus. In fact, Dionysius criticized Thucydides in his *Letter to Pompey* (3.2) for not taking his story down to the return of the exiles from Phyle and the recovery of freedom for Athens after their Civil War, and he praised Xenophon in section 4 for continuing his work through to that recovery and the rebuilding of their walls. (Xenophon in fact goes further but Dionysius cuts him short because he is arguing the case for positivity.) They do not make it explicit then, but the continuators may have anticipated Dionysius' criticism. Cratippus seems also to have glorified Athens, an act that might have countered Thucydides' harsher picture of their moral decline in the Peloponnesian War. This glorification is implied by Plutarch, *Moralia* 345 c–e, who describes the topics Cratippus covered in a work that is specifically about the glory writers achieve by writing about glorious subjects: "[You will have no Cratippus if you] take away the dashing deeds of Alcibiades around the Hellespont and of Thrasyllus against Lesbos and Theramenes' overthrow of the oligarchy and Thrasybulus and Archinus and those from Phyle rising up against the hegemony of Sparta and Conon taking Athens again to the sea." His glorification of events may be the reason that Plutarch chose Cratippus as the historian who covered these events, even though Xenophon also wrote about them in his *Hellenica* 1–2, 4.8. The fact that Cratippus continued the War beyond the defeat of Athens might also mean he rejected Thucydides' monographic concept of a single war as the focus of a history: Rood 2007; his later experience might have made the War seem just a stage in an ongoing story: Tuplin 2007, 165. We could say on this fragmentary basis that Cratippus' reception of Thucydides was generally antipathetic.

Theopompus

Theopompus wrote many works, including a *Hellenica*, which is thought to have completed and continued Thucydides' history,[6] but he makes no reference to Thucydides and there is nothing to suggest that he was indebted to him for his historiography. Certainly his focus on a single individual (Philip of Macedon) in his major work, the *Philippica*, is un-Thucydidean and so is his love of blame, which Dionysius of Halicarnassus identified in his *Letter to Pompey* 5 as his major and unique feature. Thucydides does not figure as an influence either in the fragments we have of his *Hellenica* in twelve books, published before 343/2 BCE and covering 411 to 394 BCE (D.S. 13.42.5, 14.84.7, cf. Shrimpton 1991, 27–28, 39–41). We could in fact find signs of rejection if we press the matter of his endpoint. The reports we have that his *Hellenica* went down to the battle of Cnidus, where the Spartans lost control of the sea, while the Athenians recovered their naval power and liberated Asiatic Greece in alliance with the Persians, might indicate that he, like Cratippus, was also dissatisfied with Thucydides' ending for Athens, but equally he might just have wanted to complete the story of Spartan naval hegemony, especially if that was the central theme of his *Hellenica*: Tuplin (2007, 167), Schepens (2007, 69–71).

In one of the few citations we have from his completion, Theopompus praises Lysander, a key player in ending the war after the events described by Thucydides:

"He loved toil and was able to court private men and kings, being modest and superior to all pleasures. Proof is that when he became ruler of almost all of Greece, he will appear in none of the cities to have had an impulse toward sexual pleasures or an indulgence in untimely drinking and eating sessions (*FGH* 115 F. 20)."

In considering the tradition behind such characterization in historical writing, Thucydides could come to mind (he characterizes Pausanias and Themistocles, Pericles, Cleon, Hermocrates and Nicias, Hyperbolus), but Thucydides' motive is mostly to assist political understanding, whereas Lysander's characterization reflects more purely moral interests: Flower (1994, 150–53). We might rather look for influence from characterization such as we find in Xenophon's encomium *Agesilaus* (e.g., 5 on that king's love of toil and mastery of pleasures): Porphyrius (frag. 21) indicates that Xenophon was a considerable influence on Theopompus when he says that Theopompus in "many places" reworked passages from Xenophon: for instance, the meeting between Agesilaus and Pharnabazus (*Hell.* 4.1.29ff.), in which Theopompus destroyed Xenophon's liveliness by overelaborating the conversation. This meeting is from Xenophon's continuation rather than his completion, but the self-promotion Theopompus displays in the preface to his *Philippica* (frag. 25) makes competition with Xenophon's completion likely enough as

---

[6] See Shrimpton (1991) and Flower (1994) for his life and works; the fragments are in Jacoby, *FGH* 115.

well (see below). Theopompus is said to have adapted other authors too (frag. 70, 102), but they do not include Thucydides.

In another fragment from Theopompus' completion, about the helots (frag. 13), he makes a unique contribution in naming some of them "Heleatics" from Helos in Laconia and credits them with a savagery that reflects Xenophon (*Hell.* 3.2.6) as much as Thucydides. There is also the un-Thucydidean conversational anecdote that illustrates the disdain of the Spartan King Agesilaus for the fancy food offered him by the Thasians (frag. 22): he tells them to take it to his helots, indicating that it is fit only for slavish appetites, a thought that we find in Xenophon's philosophical works and in his description of Agesilaus' mastery of his appetite and his waiving of his share of food to others (*Ages.* 5.1). Xenophon also liked conversational anecdotes.

Lack of evidence, as in the case of Cratippus, prevents our saying whether Theopompus' completion had features we consider unique to Thucydides, such as his interest in mass psychology, his antithetical debates, or the generalizations that constitute his lessons for all time. He does not imitate Thucydidean language any more than the other continuators. His linguistic style in the characterization of Lysander, if the citation is exact, is rather plain, but his laboring of Xenophon's conversation suggests a more ponderous and artificial style. We have two grandly phrased extracts from his speeches in his *Philippica* (frag. 164, 166) but not enough to judge the presence of Thucydidean qualities and none from the completion. Hornblower (1995, 56–57) notes an echo of Thucydides' funeral speech in Theopompus' continuation (2.45.1, frag. 395), but this is a commonplace thought, as its source Theon, *Progymnasmata*, shows when he puts Theopompus and Thucydides alongside other authors who expressed the same sentiment. Echoes need to be more individual to sustain engagement. Theopompus (frag. 96) is certainly not acknowledging Thucydides when he describes Hyperbolus' fate in such a different way (cf. 8.73.3).

The Hellenica Oxyrhynchia

The author of the *HO* wrote before 346 BCE and has been identified as Cratippus and Theopompus, but his identity does not affect our assessment of his reception of Thucydides.[7] There are substantial fragments from his completion in the surviving papyri. We do not have his beginning, but his earliest event is from late 411 BCE: Timolaus' sea battle against the Athenians near Amphipolis, which he says he "has mentioned before" (*HO* 10.4). The fragments from his completion include a version of the campaigns of Thrasyllus in Asia, on the same scale as Xenophon's (*HO* 1–3, *Hell.*1.2), the battle of the Horns (Ta Kerata) (*HO* 4; cf. D.S. 13.65—which Xenophon does not record), and the battle of Notion (*HO* 8, *Hell.* 1.5.11–14). The back-reference to Thucydides for Pedaritus (*HO* 5.39–40: "concerning which Thucydides has said": 8.55.3)

---

[7] Text and commentary in Bruce (1967) and Chambers (1993).

indicates that he has read Thucydides closely and did not re-describe the events he had already covered. In his continuation the last events he mentions are from 395 BCE, but we cannot identify his end point, unless he was a source for Ephorus/D.S. down to 387/6 BCE (Accame 1938; see also 1950, 1978). He seems to admire Conon, the early architect of the recovery of Athenian power even if he was working with the Persians (*HO* 9–12, 18, 22–23 esp. lines 641–644).

The language of the *HO* is not generally Thucydidean, and is often called dull, but one striking passage recalls Thucydides in a context that reflects also his characteristic attitude to the Athenian demos. This is the description of the unstable psychology of the Athenians, who are "mad with joy" (περιχαρεῖς) over their victory at the Horns, but blame the generals for their '"rashly" (προπετῶς) taking a risk and "gambling" (κυβεῦσαι) on the polis. "Mad with joy" is found in Herodotus, but Thucydides 2.51.6 and 7.73.2 uses it in contexts of mass hysteria. On the other hand, the *HO* avoids the startlingly abstract phrasing so characteristic of Thucydides: "the immediate overjoyedness" in their freedom from plague or in victory, and his "rashly" and "gambling" are not found in Thucydides, though they and their cognates do figure in Xenophon (*Cyrop.* 1.3.8, *Hell.* 6.3.16). The battle of the Horns also has the colourful προτροπάδην for headlong retreat (never in Thucydides, once in Xenophon *Mem.* 1.3.13). The *HO* does use litotes, alliteration, and word play (Chambers, XIX), but these need no Thucydides to authorize them.

The author does seem to have used Thucydides' chronology of seasons and years of war in his continuation. This was an appropriate structure for a monographic focus. Dionysius of Halicarnassus, *On Thucydides* 9, says it was unique to Thucydides, but *HO* 12.1 refers to the "most important events of the year," to "summer" (see also 11.34, 20.8, 21.35 for seasons) and how the "eighth year had begun": Bruce (1967, 9). The reference to the eighth year indicates that the *HO* covered a period of time with a monographic focus in his continuation, as Thucydides did, and this has been defined as the period of Athenian recovery or of Spartan hegemony: Chambers (1993, XV–XVI). Yet in these same chronological references the *HO* uses language that is not Thucydidean, such as the unusual *hadrotata* for "the most important," and *eneistekei* for the "beginning" of a new year, which weakens the impression of a debt, and makes one wonder whether such dating was not in fact more regular than we suppose.[8] His conception of "the Decelean War" (10.3, 22.2) may originate in Thucydides (7.27.2: "the war from Decelea"), but if he made it last twelve years down to the end of the Civil War, he would differ from Thucydides: Schepens 2007, 74–7.

The fragments preserve only one speech (18.2), which consists of a one-liner, and that is more typical of Xenophon in his battle narrative (*Hell.* 4.2.22, *An.* 1.8.26 and further examples below) than of Thucydides. If the Michigan Papyrus is from the *HO*, we also have a speech from Theramenes on the subject of the peace that ended the War (Chambers 1993, XVII) that may be compared with Xenophon *Hell.* 2.2.16, but there

---

[8] Canfora (1970, 209) argues that the restoration might include archon or ephor dating, which is not Thucydidean.

are no obvious Thucydidean features there either. Digressions giving explanatory background, such as the one on the Boeotian constitution (*HO* 19: Bruce 1967, 11–15), are found in Thucydides and may indicate his influence, but they are also found in Herodotus, which suggests a wider debt. In the digression on the Boeotian constitution (19.4–5) the description of how the Boeotians profited from their occupation of Decelea by taking the wood and clay fixtures from the fine country houses in Attica could be a pastiche of Thucydides (2.65.2 for the richness of the houses, 2.14 for the Athenians taking their own woodwork as they evacuate Attica), but the *HO* could have his own sources of information.

Xenophon

Xenophon's *Hellenica* has the merit of surviving whole.[9] He has a claim to be the first of the continuators according to Canfora (1970, 2006), who supposed that Xenophon first published and edited Thucydides' manuscript and wrote his completion from Thucydides' notes. Canfora's case rests on Diogenes Laertius 2.57, who says that Thucydides' books "had escaped attention," and that Xenophon published them to make Thucydides famous, though Xenophon could have taken them for his own. Yet connections between writers can be forced, such as the tradition that Xenophon wrote Thucydides' Book 8 (other candidates are an ailing Thucydides, his daughter, or Theopompus). Marcellinus 43–44 commented on this: "that [Book 8] is not by Xenophon, the style itself almost shouts aloud." That makes us think harder before accepting Diogenes' testimony on Xenophon's role. We know little about publication in Thucydides' times, but the model of prepublication circulation through friends or pupils that we find in Isocrates, *Panathenaicus* 200–272, who suggests the possibility (Hornblower 2008, 31) that parts of his work were known prior to Thucydides' death, even from his residence in Thrace. But if Xenophon was the first to bring his work to public attention, it is likely that he was also the first to complete Thucydides, in spite of the competing claims of Cratippus (above).

The abrupt beginning of his *Hellenica* ("*after these events* not many days later") suggests that he is completing Thucydides in a way meant to be seamless, and that might mean endorsement or even reflect the generosity to his predecessor that Diogenes Laertius points to when he says that Xenophon's publication of Thucydides (2.57) was designed to promote the glory of Thucydides; it has a certain charm as a positive form of reception. But once again he goes beyond Thucydides' envisaged endpoint by attaching a continuation to his completion, and then cuts himself completely loose of Thucydidean practices: for instance, by demonstrating a notion of "greatness" in history that is not the magnitude of Thucydides' War, but an ethical greatness that reflects the philosophy he learned as a pupil of Socrates. He shows this in authorial statements in the work,

---

[9] Krentz (1989) is the main modern commentary. The text is Marchant's *OCT*.

starting with the comment on the courage of Theramenes at 2.3.56: Gray (2003). In the completion (*Hellenica* 1.1.1–2.3.9) his concepts are not so obvious, because there are no such comments, but its beginning already anticipates the commitment to the notion of continuous history that is confirmed in the ending of his history as a whole ("Let this be the limit of my account; as to what happened *after these events*, this will be the concern of another": 7.5.27—henceforth unmarked references are to the *Hellenica*). It is not clear whether this means he rejected the monographic focus of Thucydides, or whether he was just dealing with events for which it was inappropriate.

His completion appears to soften the defeat that Thucydides proposed as his ending. It does describe the occupation of Piraeus, the return of the exiles, and the demolition of the walls that he forecast (2.2.23), and it emphasizes Athenian fears of enslavement (2.2.3, 10, 14, 16), but it does this in order to highlight how the Spartans release them from such fears in refusing to enslave them or occupy their land (2.2.19–20—see below). That lightens the darkness in a way that the ancient critics found characteristic of Xenophon: Demetrius, *On Style* 134–5, an assessment that we see also in reaction scenes that mingle joy with tears: 7.1.32, 7.2.9. The light continues when the demos resolves to elect thirty men to write a new constitution, Agis evacuates Decelea and disbands the Peloponnesian army, Samos is returned to its original inhabitants, and Lysander evacuates Piraeus and returns to Sparta with his spoils (2.3.1–9). Xenophon then tells the story of the imposition of tyranny on Athens and their liberation (2.3–4) and the rebuilding of their walls and their sea power (4.8), a narration that ancient critics found so uplifting a counterpoint to Thucydides (above), and he points positively to their moral regeneration (6.3.10–17) and their impulse to help others (3.5.16, 6.5.45–9). The main focus of his continuation, however, is the rise and fall of Sparta, and his ultimate endpoint is the anarchy that followed the failure of all the major powers (Athens, Sparta, Thebes, Thessaly, and Arcadia) to maintain hegemony down to the battle of Plataea (362 BCE). Xenophon's allusion there to "even more confusion" after the battle than before is a new pessimism, but it may also soften the Athenian failure in the completion by making it only the first in a series of hegemonies falling throughout the *Hellenica*, and the only one that had learned through defeat not to oppress others.

There is a possibility that Xenophon originally published his completion as a stand-alone work. He published his continuation after 357 BCE (6.4.37), but stylistic and other differences have been argued for that leave open the possibility of an earlier date and separate publication for the completion: MacLaren (1934); cf. Dover (1981).[10] This would mean that Xenophon did originally complete Thucydides' War as a monograph. But Xenophon's reference to the reasons for the election of the Thirty in the completion (2.3.1–2) seems to me to anticipate their failure to carry out the terms of their election at the beginning of the continuation (2.3.11) and this works against the idea of separation. It may also be significant that the manuscript tradition regularly includes the completion alongside the

---

[10] How early is debated and depends on whether he was born around 430–425 BCE or 440 BCE, as Canfora (1970, 63) suggests. Neither is unlikely.

continuation.[11] The matter must remain open, but the differences between his completion and continuation might yet be explained in ways that do not involve separate publication: (Dover 1981; Gray 1991).

There are few Thucydidean features in Xenophon's completion: (Dover 1981). Any reader can see that Xenophon's language is not Thucydidean, and ancient critics were right to differentiate their styles (including Marcellinus on Xenophon's authorship of Thucydides Book 8 above). Thucydides wrote in a grand and difficult style: D.H., *On Thucydides* 24, but Xenophon is more varied, simple, and charming, as well as grand, as seen in the analyses in Pontier (2014). For instance, Euryptolemus' speech has grand thought and phrasing (1.7.16–33), but the letter announcing the defeat at Cyzicus has laconic dialect and brevity (1.1.23), and this style, along with the Athenian reaction to disaster at 2.2.3, can be contrasted with the much grander reactions to disaster in Thucydides: (Gray 2014). Xenophon's completion is also on a much smaller scale than Thucydides, more comparable to the *HO*: for instance, on the battle of Notion (*HO* 8). The speeches in the completion include reported speech (1.3.19; 1.4.13–17), shorter single speeches (1.6.5, 8), the laconic letter (1.1.23), the appeal of Euryptolemus above, and tart one-liners (1.1.14, 28; 1.5.6; 1.6.2, 15, 32; 2.1.26), but the completion has no big debates such as we find in Thucydides (at least in Books 1–7). In the continuation we find the paired speeches of Critias and Theramenes debating the definitions of friend and traitor (2.3.24–56), but even these show an ethical rather than political interest, which reflects Xenophon's Socratic training. His completion has none of the other features we associate most with Thucydides, like the predictive speech that analyzes the subsequent action, and the short story of the mutiny at Chios, with the punchline "he was carrying a cane" (2.1.1–4), recalls Herodotus more than Thucydides.

Xenophon's chronological markers look Thucydidean because they mark the passing of seasons and years and synchronize events outside the main theatre of war, but they are inconsistent, sometimes wrong, and they use un-Thucydidean language: the verb for when the year "ended," for instance, is different (*elēgen*). They also go beyond Thucydidean practice in using Olympiad and archon and ephor dating, and in summarizing events in Sicily and Persia that had nothing to do with the war. For reasons like these many think that they are interpolated,[12] but some go back to the early papyri,[13] and editors are selective in what they print. For instance Marchant prints the year ending and events in Sicily (1.1.37), but brackets the Olympiad, archon, and ephor dating at 1.2.1; he prints the year ending and events in Persia (1.2.19), as well as the change of season and the archon and ephor dating and the number of years of war at 1.1.3.1, and the year ending and events in Sicily (1.5.21), but he brackets the archons and ephors and numbers of the years of war at 1.6.1. On another point, Schepens (2007, 68–9) defends

---

[11] Pellé (2010, 39–42), with Thucydides' text in L (Parisinius Coislisianus 317) and T (Matritensis 4561), and Neopolitanus XXII 1.
[12] Mazzini (1971) confirms two interpolators, one the summarian and the other the synchronist, put in after the publication of *Cyropedia* 8.8 in 361/0 bce.
[13] Pellé (2010) 50 prints a papyrus from the third century CE, containing 1.2.19 with all interpolations intact: Col XV.

the authenticity of the reference to twenty-eight and a half years as the duration of the war (2.3.9). And so forth. The fact that this is in a completion of Thucydides makes us look for his influence, as we do with the *HO*, but if we had other histories from this era, we might see that such dating was more common than we suppose. Dionysius, *On Thucydides* 9, says no one imitated Thucydides' system, but he says that dismissively in order to support his own argument that it was confusing.

History is not, of course, just a series of annals. There is also thematic focus. If Xenophon's completion has a unifying theme, it is the exploits of Alcibiades in the first half and those of Lysander in the second. Alcibiades gives the Athenians hopes of survival from his first appearance (1.1.5), even increasing them after his return from exile (1.4.8–23) but he then disappoints their hopes and disappears from view (1.5.17). Even so, his relative Euryptolemus (1.4.19) delivers the longest speech in the completion, and his final appearance at Aegospotami (2.1.25) reminds us of what the Athenians lost in putting him aside. From 1.5.1, Alcibiades is eclipsed by Lysander and his Persian ally Cyrus. Lysander's competition with Callicratidas keeps him in view even where he is not in command (1.6.2), and he returns to win the battle of Aegospotami (2.1.7) and carry the spoils back to Sparta (2.3.9). These focuses may be reflected in the ancient book divisions, where Book 1 ended with the eclipse of Alcibiades at 1.5.8 and Book 2 with Lysander's victorious return to Sparta at 2.3.9: Pellé (2010, 55). Alcibiades was a major focus of Thucydides, too: Rood (2004, 365–69), but before we see Xenophon's interest as a reflection of his predecessor, we recall that Cratippus also made a feature of Alcibiades and might then conclude that no historian of the period could fail to make him a focus.

The connections back to Thucydides' text from Xenophon's are sometimes exact, sometimes inexact, so that sometimes he seems to have read Thucydides closely, but sometimes not at all. This is one reason that has led to the idea that we have lost the original opening of his completion (Defosse 1968); the other is that we might ordinarily expect a prefatory comment of the kind that we find in the nearest model we have of one historian taking up from another, which is Thucydides' continuation of Herodotus (1.89.1). The lost opening is believed to have been an account of the catastrophe around Euboea that we find in D.S. 13.41. MacLaren (1979) argues against this that Xenophon is just showing his usual carelessness with continuity, which can be even within his completion. For instance, Xenophon does not explain how the Athenians got to occupy Calchedon (1.3.2–11, 2.2.1). A lacuna might also spoil the impression of continuity that we find in the ending.

His treatment of the movements of Tissaphernes is a case of good connection: Thucydides left Tissaphernes on his way to the Hellespont to stop the rumors Alcibiades was spreading about his preference for Alcibiades and the Athenians. Xenophon opens his completion with the report that Thymochares (last seen at Thuc. 8.95.2) came to the Hellespont "after this not many days later," that the Spartans met and defeated him, that Dorieus (last seen at Thuc. 8.84.2) came from Rhodes and the Athenians fought him, that Mindarus (Thuc. 8.104.3) intervened but Alcibiades (last seen at Thuc. 8.108.1–2) came to the rescue, that the Spartans fled to Abydos and the protection of Pharnabazus, and that the Athenians then retired and left the Hellespont to collect money, while Thrasyllos (last seen at Thuc. 8.105) went to Athens for troops and ships. The report of these events gives Tissaphernes time to arrive and, as anticipated in Thucydides, stop Alcibiades' rumours about his close relations with Tissaphernes (1.1.9): "After these events Tissaphernes came to the Hellespont, and when Alcibiades came to him in a single trireme with friendly overtures and gifts, he arrested him and shut him up in Sardis, repeatedly asserting that the king ordered him to war against Athenians." Xenophon does not say explicitly "angered that Alcibiades was saying these things..." but takes this for granted.

Elsewhere it seems that Xenophon is working from memory rather than close reading. Thucydides indicates at 8.107 that the Athenians recovered Cyzicus and collected money from them while the Peloponnesians sent Hippocrates and Epicles to bring back ships from Euboea. In Xenophon, we hear that Alcibiades again captures Cyzicus and again takes money from them (1.1.19–20) but nothing about its previous capture in Thucydides, and then Hippocrates reappears (1.1.23) without notice of his return from Euboea. Xenophon has also apparently not remembered that Thucydides 8.85 had already dealt with the exiling of Hermocrates because he gives another version of it (1.1.27–31). This highlights Hermocrates' good relations with his followers, while Thucydides underlines Hermocrates' dislike of Tissaphernes' double-dealing and his preference for Pharnabazus, which Xenophon confirms only at the end of his account, and when he then sends Hermocrates on a mission to Pharnabazus (1.3.13). The repetition might be explained as no repetition at all if Thucydides' reference to the exile was proleptic, but Hornblower (2008) on 8.85.3 rules that out. In another case, Xenophon's treatment of Thasos (1.1.32) reveals a discontinuity with Thucydides' focus of interest as well as his information. Thucydides 8.63 presented Thasos as a classic case of how Athenian-backed oligarchic rule pleased the allies no more than Athenian-backed democratic rule. This is typical of his interest in mass faction politics and his generalizing from the one case. In Xenophon Thasos is no test case, and Eteonicus and the laconizing party lose control of the city without a description of how they won it (this is not in Thucydides), or of how Eteonicus got there from his last location in Thucydides 8.23.4.

In considering the unevenness of this continuity we should not overlook the physical circumstances of reading in antiquity, which made close reading of texts difficult. Our assumption that ancient authors had the text in front of them at every turn is probably false: Small (1997), Dorandi (2000, 2007). Their rolls of papyrus lacked book and paragraph numbers, making "information retrieval" difficult (Hornblower 1995, 49) and exact citation a rarity. We could fall back on the idea that Xenophon did not complete his completion, but only a very odd kind of incompletion would explain his repeat of the exile of Hermocrates. We should not rule out the possibility either, remote as it may seem, that the text Xenophon was not the one we now use, but that is too problematic to contemplate.

The inconsistencies described above may make it seem unlikely that Xenophon would enrich his completion by inviting his readers to recall details in Thucydides, but he might well engage with his larger ideas. This is reception in its most interesting form, involving not just imitation or rejection of the predecessor, but dialogue. The case for such engagement has been made by Rood (2004). Rood's analysis deserves more attention than can be given here, but, in what follows, my approach will be to read such passages from the completion on their own terms first, and then consider how allusion to Thucydides might enrich them, since allusion must always be predicated on existing meaning. There are implications for audience knowledge of Thucydides' text in crediting Xenophon with allusion of this kind: the audience would need to know Thucydides' text quite well to appreciate it.

One passage of interest is what happened to Athens at the end of the war. Here, Xenophon says that, under siege from the Peloponnesians after defeat at Aegospotami, the Athenians expected to suffer the same treatment as they had previously inflicted on places they took by siege: "the Melians, colonists of Sparta, the Histiaeans and Scioneans and Toroneans and Aeginetans and many other Greeks" (2.2.3). This meant expectation of execution, enslavement, or occupation (Thuc. 1.114, 2.27, 5.4.1, 5.116.4). He repeats their expectation at 2.2.10 (also 14 and 16), making them recognize their hubris in treating small cities so viciously just for being on the Spartan side. The specific mention of Melos in particular is said to recall Thucydides' Melian Dialogue, especially because of the Athenians' brief mention of Melos as a Spartan colony, a factor that is emphasized in the Dialogue (Thuc. 5.84–113): (Rood (2004), 351–58).

Read on its own terms without allusion to Thucydides, the passage anticipates the generosity of the eventual outcome, in which the Spartans do not inflict the expected punishment (2.2.20), but refuse to enslave the Athenians (*andrapodiein*)—even though many other Greeks expressed a strong desire to destroy them utterly—on the grounds that Athens did great good for Greece "in the greatest perils for Greece." It seems Xenophon has deliberately raised Athenian fears in order to emphasize this generosity through contrast. Some would find the real reason for their withholding of punishment in their fear that with Athens gone there would be no buffer against Thebes, but whatever their motive, they do release the Athenians from their greatest fears. Subsequently, Lysander sailed into Piraeus, the exiles returned, and they pulled down the walls, "thinking that day was the beginning of freedom for Greece (2.2.23).

This raising of expectation of punishment and generous resolution is very Xenophontic. It fits into of a series of patterned stories in Xenophon's narrative where the dominant party shows mercy even where the punishment is deserved and even when others urge him to inflict it: (Gray 2011, 212–32). It also fits into the theory of self-knowledge we find in Xenophon's other works, where ignorance leads to overestimation of your capacities and defeat, and where defeat leads to recognition of your lesser capacities, which is self-knowledge (*Mem.* 4.2.25–9, *Cyrop.* 7.2.23–4). In this theory the victors can withhold punishment because fear of punishment is sufficient punishment in itself to make the defeated party more moderate than before and a valuable ally thereafter (*Cyrop.* 3.1.15–25, where the doctrine is associated with Socrates in eastern disguise: 3.1.14, 38–40). Xenophon is applying this thought to the Athenians after their defeat at Aegospotami, when their fear of punishment is very great. Their acquisition of the moderation that comes from self-knowledge is confirmed by Callistratus in the continuation when he tells the Spartans that the Athenians have learned that "grasping for more" (beyond their capacities) produced defeat and he hopes that the Spartans have learned from their failures, too, as the Athenians have, to be more moderate in their relations with others (6.3.10–11). We find another victorious party remembering the good and sparing opponents at the end of the Civil War at Athens (2.4.40–43), mirroring in domestic politics what happened at the international level. Here the victorious democratic leader Thrasybulus explicitly tells the defeated oligarchs to "know themselves" as men who tried to rule the demos, but overestimated their capacities and found themselves defeated, deserted, and handed over to the demos they had wronged, which had shown superior capacities in their struggle. His comment that the Spartans have handed them over to the demos they have wronged "like muzzled dogs" foreshadows punishment, but he withholds it and reconciles the two parties to live in peace, swearing "not to remember wrongs" in the future (2.4.43).

Xenophon's message is then coherent in its own terms, but allusion to Thucydides could enrich it through contrast. For instance, the cynical view of the Athenians in the Melian Dialogue that the Spartans would not rescue their colony might contrast with their new and morally better expectation that they would now punish the Athenians for treating it so badly (5.106–110). But Xenophon's brief mention of Melos need not imply engagement: (Hornblower 1995, 50). Xenophon has his own reasons to mention the status of Melos as a colony (to make the Spartans' generosity more remarkable). Moreover Isocrates shows that knowledge of these atrocities no longer drew directly on Thucydides but was widespread when Xenophon was writing (*Pan.* 100, 110, and later *Panath.* 63, 89, referring to "accusers" in his own times who go on about the suffering of Melos, Scione, Torone, and other little cities). It might be added that Xenophon's list as a whole does not map well onto Thucydides, because he says so little about Aegina (2.27) or Histiaea/Hestiaia (1.114). So, the "clash of temporal perspectives" (Rood 2004, 354), where Xenophon credits the Athenians with more moral attitudes than Thucydides, may not be a deliberate echo, but simply reflect Xenophon's general tendency to accentuate the positive in human nature, as he shows in his leadership theory in *Hellenica* and other works: (Gray 2011).

Still, we might say of his own presentation of these events that Xenophon is softening Thucydides' forecast ending, which was nothing but defeat, by stressing their release from their greatest fears. The recall of Thucydides' account of their reaction to Syracuse (Thuc. 8.1) would also bring attention to the difference in Xenophon's account, which is their recognition of the wrong they did other cities, a narration that would again enhance Xenophon's more positive outlook (cf. Rood 2004, 352). Readers too who thought that the "many other Greeks" who wanted to annihilate Athens included their subjects (2.2.19), might recall the Athenians' prediction in the Dialogue that they had more to fear from their subjects than the Spartans (Thuc. 5.91); and they would then be even more impressed by the unexpected way in which the Spartans do prove to be the lesser threat—by refusing to allow Corinth and Thebes and those erstwhile subjects to destroy Athens as they desired.

Moving on to the end of the siege, Xenophon, it has been said, recalls Thucydides' references to Sparta's crusade for freedom (e.g., 2.8.4 5.26) and his "beginning of misfortunes for Greece" (2.12.3: Rood 2004, 348–51), when he comments that those who pull down the walls of Athens expect "that day was the beginning of freedom for Greece" (2.2.23). It seems to me more likely that Xenophon is reflecting the Homeric formula "day of freedom" (*Iliad* 6.455, 16.831, 20.193) or Herodotus' reference to "the day of freedom for Greece" in the famous oracle that predicts liberation from the Persians (8.77). Thucydides also echoes Herodotus' "beginning of ills for Greece" (5.97). If there is an echo of Thucydides in Xenophon, then by contrast it again enhances Xenophon's different outlook. Thucydides' Athenians predicted that the Spartans, quite contrary to their claims of liberation, would be as oppressive as the Athenians (1.77.6), but here Xenophon's Spartans confirm their commitment to freedom by refusing to enslave the Athenians. Freedom can mean many things. Spartan liberation gone sour was a theme for later ages (Hornblower 1995, 66–68), and they do deny political autonomy to Greeks in the later *Hellenica*, but the juxtaposition of the "day of freedom" with enslavement in this passage (2.2.20, 23) makes it mean freedom from the enslavement the Athenians inflicted on Melos and the others. Xenophon's subsequent narrative does not dent their commitment to freedom in this sense. Lysander puts a garrison into Samos but does not occupy the land (2.2.6–7), he wishes to destroy Athens when called into in the Civil War (2.4.28–30), but King Pausanias engineers a peace that preserves Athenian freedom to such an extent that the democratic leader Thrasybulus can say that the Spartans have deserted the oligarchs (2.4.40–42). The Spartans are next seen answering the appeal from the Greeks in Asia to preserve their freedom and their land against the Persians (3.1.3ff.). We can question their motives but not their liberating effects.

Xenophon has been thought to echo Thucydides' phrasing elsewhere, too, but these instances are also problematic. The comment of Xenophon's generals when they reject Alcibiades' good advice at Aegospotami that "they were now the generals, not he" (2.1.25–26) is less likely to recall Cleon's comment in Thucydides 4.28.2: "he was not general but Nicias" when it is recognized as a trope of strained relations between generals that Xenophon credits also to Lysander: "he will not meddle where another is in charge" (1.6.3). Likewise, the "mourning" of Hermocrates for his exile could echo Alcibiades' slightly different word of "mourning" for his (1.1.27, *apolofuronto*, Thuc. 8.81.2–3, *anolofuronto*), but similar words are not always echoes: Thucydides 2.46 uses the *apo*-compound of lament for the dead in his funeral speech, where it cannot recall Hermocrates. Perhaps too, if Xenophon describes Hermocrates' exile as if he had not read Thucydides' account, it is unlikely to echo Thucydides.

One of the longer passages thought to recall Thucydides is Xenophon's account of the trial of the generals of Arginusae. Here, Theramenes' deception of the demos, their rage against due process of law, their unlawful execution of their generals, and their regret for their unlawful decision (1.7) is said to match Thucydides' idea that self-interested leaders caused the fall of Athens (2.65), and that the demos was emotional and gullible and inconstant: Rood (2004, 374–80). (The *HO* reflects this same inconstancy when it describes the demos as overjoyed after the victory of the Horns but still blaming the generals.) Xenophon does reflect these notions, but he sends his own message about them. The speech of Euryptolemus, which is the longest episode in the trial, makes obedience to the laws its central theme in insisting that the generals should be tried according to the laws. This reflects Xenophon's Socratic views about the benefits of obeying the laws, as expressed at *Memorabilia* 4.4.15–17, which starts by praising Socrates' resistance to lawlessness at this very trial (*Mem.* 4.4.2; also 1.1.18). He gives Socrates' resistance at this trial (*Hell.* 1.7.15) further significance by crediting him with one of those trenchant one-liner speeches for which he was famous (above, and see Demetrius, *On Style*, 6, 137). (Xenophon shows the same interest in obedience to the laws in the first episode of his continuation (2.3.10–56), which describes the lawless rule of the Thirty Tyrants.) Euryptolemus mentions one episode that Thucydides had previously mentioned, which is the treachery of Aristarchus, but Xenophon again serves his own theme by focusing on the point not found in Thucydides, which is that the demos gave Aristarchus a trial according to the laws even though he was a traitor (1.7.28; cf. Thucydides 8.98). In the description of the regret that the demos subsequently felt for their unjust execution of the generals (1.7.35), we might expect an allusion to how the demos regretted their death sentence on the Mytileneans in Thucydides (3.36–50), but there is none. The execution of the unnamed "blameless" individual, which Euryptolemus seems to say the demos regretted (1.7.27: the text is faulty), cannot mean the Mytileneans, because that sentence involved more than one individual and was in any case revoked. Overall, readers familiar with Thucydides would find Xenophon's ideas to be very different from those of his predecessor in episodes such as those discussed above.

Diodorus Siculus

Diodorus may provide more evidence about the continuators in his account of events after Thucydides. Rood (2004, 380-90) discusses his echoes of Thucydides, while Schepens (2007) shows how his source Ephorus used the continuators, especially the *HO*, in his response to Thucydides. If we could isolate the changes made by Diodorus and Ephorus to the *HO*, we might discover more about the *HO*'s use of Thucydides. That is a large "if" however, since though Diodorus uses the *HO* for the battle of the Horns, he omits the only Thucydidean element: the Athenian reaction to the victory (above). Our findings would be restricted to the *HO* alone if Accame (1938) is correct and Diodorus uses Ephorus throughout his completion of Thucydides' War, but he may have used other continuators as well—such as Theopompus. Diodorus 14.11 shows that Ephorus is not his main source for the death of Alcibiades, and that opens up the possibility that he does not monopolize Diodorus' completion of Thucydides. Xenophon may not be a direct source,[14] but Diodorus names Theopompus as a continuator alongside

---

[14] D.S. does preserve Xenophon's basic order of events: 13.45–47.2 the battle involving Dorieus and Mindarus (*Hell.* 1.1.1–10), 13.49–51 the battle of Cyzicus (1.1.11–26), 13.63.1–2 the exile of Hermocrates (1.1.27–31), 13.64.1 the campaigns of Thrasyllus (called Thrasybulus) (1.2.1–17), and Xenophon's tax on the Hellespont, which Xenophon places in the aftermath of Cyzicus (1.1.22, 13.64.2–4), 13.66–7 Calchedon and Byzantium (1.3.2–21), 13.68–69 the homecoming of Alcibiades (1.4.8–23), 13.70–71 Lysander and

Xenophon, and some of his episodes rework Xenophon, as Theopompus was known to do (above). These episodes were not treated by Thucydides, but if Theopompus is their source, they give an insight into his working methods that may illuminate the nature of his relations with Thucydides as well.

For instance in the battle of Arginusae, Diodorus replaces the helmsman's warning about the superior numbers of ships that we find in Xenophon (1.6.32) with a seer's omens predicting Callicratidas' death (D.S.13.97.4–98.1). This retains the saying of Callicratidas in Xenophon: "Sparta will be no worse off if he dies," but not his point that flight in the face of greater numbers is dishonorable, because it has omitted the point about inferior numbers. Diodorus 13.98.1 then goes beyond Xenophon in referring to a full speech, citing the ending only, where Callicratidas encouraged others to die, too, by announcing his self-sacrifice, and appointed his successor. In another unhappy adaptation, when Alcibiades comes to Aegospotami, rather than pointing out the tactical difficulties as he does in Xenophon (2.1.25–6), he offers a Thracian alliance in exchange for command (D.S.13.105). As with Callicratidas, this characterizes Alcibiades' morality but omits his tactical advice. Accame (1938, 394–95) sees Ephorus behind this, but it reflects Theopompus' priorities too, and in both incidents the source has replaced Xenophon's effective brevity with something longer-winded, in the manner of Theopompus' adaptation of the meeting of Agesilaus and Pharnabazus (above).

Some of the elaborations concern Socrates. Diomedon, on the way to unjust execution in the trial of the generals, plays out the role of Socrates in remembering his vow (of a cock to Aesclepius) in Plato, *Phaedo*: he asks the Athenians to see to the victory vows of the generals of Arginusae (D.S. 13.102.2–3). Accame (1938, 406) sees the source again as Ephorus, but in the later account of Theramenes' death, in which Xenophon may himself recall Socrates and the hemlock (2.3.56), Diodorus elaborates Xenophon's account of Theramenes' leap to the altar and his speech about Critias' impiety (D.S. 14.4.6–7, cf. 2.3.52–3: editing out his lawlessness), by adding that his fortitude came from his Socratic training and that Socrates and two attendants tried save him (D.S. 14.5.1–4). He also reproduces the thought Xenophon attributes to Theramenes, that the Thirty can violate others as they violated him (2.3.53), but he attributes it to the people in order to underline Theramenes' virtue (D.S. 14.5.4). Diodorus shows no interest in Socrates elsewhere, but Theopompus admired Antisthenes (D.L. 6.14) and challenged Plato (frag. 275, 259), which suggests he had an interest in Socrates, too.

In another elaboration, when Callixeinus escapes to Decelea, as he does in Xenophon (1.7.35), he becomes a negative moral example thereafter for the part he played in the execution of the generals of Arginusae (D.S. 13.103), and the demos exemplifies another negative moral when it is punished for its part in the trial by being made subject to the rule of the Thirty. Accame (1938, 405) says "Ephorus" again, but when Lysander sends

---

Notion (1.5), 13.72–73 capture of Thasos and Agis' attack on Athens (not in Xenophon's order, cf. 1.1.33–36, 1.4.9), 13. 73.3–74 the exile of Alcibiades, 13.76–79, 97–100 the battle of Arginusae (1.6), 13.100–103 the trial of the generals (1. 7), 13.104–6 Aegospotami (2.1.15–32), 13.107 the siege and surrender of Athens (2.2).

the booty of Athens back to Sparta (2.3.7–9, D.S. 13.106.8–10), and Gylippus steals the money and is judged as the man who spoiled his excellent record with one unjust act, like his father, Clearchus, who took a bribe in the Archidamian War, we might say "Theopompus," who also highlighted the corrupting effect on Spartan virtue of the wealth Lysander sent back to Sparta (frag. 332–33) and may have told this tale as an elaboration on Xenophon's plainer account (2.3.8–9). Diodorus also uses a word especially associated with Theopompus (*antipoliteuesthai*) in the exile of Hermocrates (D.S. 13.63.1, 65.4)—though Chambers (1993, XXI–XXII) is unimpressed.

There is one episode in which Diodorus' source seems to use Thucydides alongside Xenophon. This is the Spartan peace appeal after Cyzicus, where the response to the appeal (D.S.13.53) has been read as a pastiche of Thucydidean thoughts (Rood 2004, 386–89), but part of the appeal itself (D.S.13.54.6) rehashes Xenophon (7.1.2–11). Accame (1938, 362) says "Ephorus," but we might see in Diodorus' advertisement of the laconic nature of the appeal (D.S. 13.52.2) Theopompus' rivalrous response to Xenophon's laconic letter (1.1.23), which the appeal seems to replace. This would again have Theopompus destroy Xenophon's effective brevity and cannibalize Thucydides, perhaps in the same kind of way.

Conclusion

It is not easy to reach general conclusions about the continuators' reception of Thucydides. Their number, for instance, might suggest that Thucydides was much read in the fourth century but Hornblower (1995) shows that he is not so much known in other authors of that time. The continuators make little explicit reference to Thucydides, so we largely rely on inferences about matters of interest to ourselves, such as their reactions to his monographic focus and his endpoint, their use of features we associate especially with Thucydides, and their engagement with his ideas. The fact that they did not rewrite Thucydides may suggest that they largely accepted his authority for the events he had described, but it is possible that this acceptance was of a passive kind. They felt the need to complete his account because the events were so significant, but none of them copies what we consider Thucydides' unique features, such as his language, his antithetical debates or his generalizations about human nature and power, and they often adopt new narrative forms such as conversational anecdotes and moralizing characterizations. These departures could constitute rejection of Thucydides, but perhaps the continuators went their own way without such deliberation. A quite sustained engagement with Thucydides' ideas has been found in Xenophon, whether he intended it or not, and the main effect there is to show how different his ideas were. And we might yet enlarge our knowledge of how the continuators did or did not grapple with Thucydides through further analysis of Diodorus Siculus, who used them as sources.

References

Accame, Silvio. 1938. "Le fonti di Diodoro per la guerra deceleica." *Rendiconti Accademia Nazionale dei Lincei*, s. vi, 14: 347–453.

Accame, Silvio. 1950. "Trasibulo e i nuovi frammenti delle Elleniche di Ossirinco." *Riv. di Filol.* 28: 30–49.

Accame, Silvio. 1978. "Ricerche sulle Elleniche di Ossirinco e Cratippo." *Misc. gr. e rom.* 6: 125–83.

Breitenbach, H. R 1967. "Xenophon von Athen," *RE IX A* 2 1569–2052.

Bruce, I.A.F. 1967. *An Historical Commentary on the Hellenica Oxyrhynchia.* Cambridge: Cambridge University Press.

Burns, Timothy. 2010. "Marcellinus' Life of Thucydides." *Interpretation* 38 (1): 3–26.

Canfora, L. 1970. *Tucidide Continuato.* Padova: Antenore.

Canfora L. 2006. "Biographical Obscurities and Problems of Composition." In *Brill's Companion to Thucydides*, edited by A. Rengakos and A. Tsamakis, 3–31. Leiden and Boston: Brill.

Chambers, Mortimer. 1993. *The Hellenica Oxyrhynchia.* Stuttgart and Leipzig: Teubner.

Defosse, P. 1968. "A propos du début insolite des Helléniques." *Revue belge de Philologie* 46: 5–24.

Dorandi, T. 2000. *Le stylet et la tablette: Dans le secret des auteurs antiques.* Paris: Belles Lettres.

Dorandi, T. 2007. *Nell' Officina dei classici: Come lavoravano gli autori antichi.* Rome: Carocci.

Dover, K. J. 1981. Appendix 2. In *A Historical Commentary on Thucydides, Vol. 5*, edited by A. W. Gomme et al., 431–44. Oxford: Clarendon.

Flower, Michael. 1994. *Theopompus of Chios: History and Rhetoric in the Fourth Century B.C.* Oxford: Oxford University Press.

Gomme, A.W., A. Andrewes, and K. J. Dover. 1981. *A Historical Commentary on Thucydides, Vol. 5.* Oxford: Clarondon.

Gray, V. J 1991. "Continuous history and Xenophon *Hellenica* 1–2.3.10." *AJPh.* 112: 201–28.

Gray V. J. 2003. "Interventions and Citations in Xenophon, Hellenica and Anabasis." *CQ* 53: 111–23.

Gray, V. J. 2011. *Xenophon's Mirror of Princes.* Oxford: Oxford University Press.

Gray, V. J. 2014. "Le style simple de Xénophon: Du rabaissement de la grandeur." In *Xénophon et la Rhétorique*, edited by P. Pontier, 319–37. Paris: Presses de l'Université Paris-Sorbonne.

Hornblower, S. 1995. "The Fourth Century and Hellenistic Reception of Thucydides." *JHS* 115: 47–68.

Hornblower S. 2008. *A Commentary on Thucydides.* Vol. III, Books 5.25–8.109. Oxford: Clarendon.

Hose, Martin. 2006. "The Peloponnesian War: Sources Other than Thucydides." In *Brill's Companion to Thucydides*, edited by A. Rengakos and A. Tsakmakis, 669–90. Leiden and Boston: Brill.

Jacoby, F. 1923. *Die Fragmente der griechischen Historiker.* Leiden: Brill.

Kendrick Pritchett, W., trans. 1975. *On Thucydides*, by Dionysius of Halicarnassus. Oakland, CA: University of California Press.

Krentz, P. 1989. *Xenophon, Hellenica I–II.3.10.* Warminster: Aris and Phillips.

MacLaren, Malcolm. 1934. "On the Composition of Xenophon's *Hellenica*." *American Journal of Philology* 55: 121–39, 249–62.

MacLaren, M. 1979. "A Supposed Lacuna at the Beginning of Xenophon's Hellenica." *AJPh* 100: 228–38.
Marincola J., ed. 2007. *A Companion to Greek and Roman Historiography*, Vol. 1. Oxford: Oxford University Press.
Mazzini, Innocenzo. 1971. 'Struttura e stile delle interpolazioni al primo e secondo libro delle Elleniche di Senofonte." *Quaderni Urbinati di Cultura Classica* 11: 77–95.
Nicolai, Roberto. 2006. "Thucydides Continued." In *Brill's Companion to Thucydides*, edited by A. Rengakos and A. Tsakmakis, 693–719. Leiden and Boston: Brill.
Nicolai, Roberto. 2009. "Ktêma es aei: Aspects of the Reception of Thucydides in the Ancient World." In *Oxford Readings in Classical Studies: Thucydides*, edited by J. Rusten, 381–404. Oxford: Oxford University Press.
Pellé, Natascia. 2010. *I frammenti delle opere di Senofonte*, Vol. 8 of *Corpus dei papiri storici greci e latini*. Pisa and Rome: Fabrizio Serre Editore.
Pontier, Pierre, ed. 2014. *Xénophon et la Rhétorique*. Paris: Presses de l'Université Paris-Sorbonne.
Rengakos, Antonios, and Antonis Tsakmakis, eds. 2006. *Brill's Companion to Thucydides*. Leiden and Boston: Brill.
Rood, Tim, 2004. "Xenophon and Diodorus: Continuing Thucydides." In Tuplin 2004, 341–95.
Rood, Tim. 2007. "The Development of the War Monograph." In *A Companion to Greek and Roman Historiography*, Vol.1, edited by J. Marincola, 147–58. Oxford: Oxford University Press.
Rusten, Jeffrey S., ed. 2009. *Oxford Readings in Classical Studies: Thucydides*. Oxford: Oxford University Press.
Santi Amantini, Luigi, ed. 2007. *Il Dopoguerra nel mondo Greco: Politica, propaganda, storiografia*. Rome: L'Erma di Bretschneider.
Schepens, Guido. 2007. "Tucidide 'in controluce': La Guerra del Peloponneso nella storiografia greca del quarto secolo a. C. In *Il Dopoguerra nel mondo Greco: Politica, propaganda, storiografia*, edited by L. Santi Amantini, 57–99. Rome: L'Erma di Bretschneider.
Shrimpton, G.S. 1991. *Theopompus the Historian*. Montreal: McGill-Queen's University Press.
Small, J. P. 1997. *Wax Tablets of the Mind: Cognitive Studies of Memory and Literacy in Classical Antiquity*. New York: Routledge.
Tuplin C., ed. 2004. *Xenophon and His World*. Stuttgart: Franz Steiner.
Tuplin, C. 2007. "Continuous Histories." In *A Companion to Greek and Roman Historiography*, Vol.1, edited by J. Marincola, 159–70. Oxford: Oxford University Press.
Usher, S., trans. 1974. *Critical Essays*. 2 vols., by Dionysius of Halicarnassus. Cambridge, MA: Harvard University Press.
West, M. L. 2013. *The Epic Cycle: A Commentary on the Lost Troy Epics*. Oxford: Oxford University Press.
Worthington, I., ed. *Brill's Jacoby* (online edition). Leiden: Brill.

CHAPTER 37

DIONYSIUS OF HALICARNASSUS ON THUCYDIDES

CASPER C. DE JONGE

Introduction

> Philosophers and rhetoricians, if not all of them, yet most of them, bear witness to Thucydides that he showed the greatest concern for the truth, the high-priestess of which we desire history to be.
>
> Dionysius of Halicarnassus, *On Thucydides* 8.1[1]

THE ancient reception of Thucydides was rich, diverse and wide ranging. Historians continued his work, imitated his style, or followed his idea of historiography; scholars wrote learned commentaries that explained his difficult vocabulary and syntax; and rhetoricians found inspiration in the speeches, which they analyzed as models of stylistic writing.[2] While readers of different periods and disciplines had their own interests and approaches, they generally shared their admiration for one aspect of the work: Thucydides was regarded as a champion of the truth. The point of departure of such portrayals was the historian's criticism of colleagues who did not care about "the search after the truth" (ἡ ζήτησις τῆς ἀληθείας, Thuc. 1.20.3). Thucydides' methodological statements on his careful investigation of the events of the war, the absence of the fabulous

---

[1] References to the rhetorical works of Dionysius of Halicarnassus in this chapter follow the edition of Aujac (1991 and 1992). Translations of Dionysius' *On Thucydides* are adapted from Usher (1974) and Pritchett (1975). Translations of Dionysius' other rhetorical treatises are adapted from Usher (1974 and 1985). Citations and translations of the *Roman Antiquities* follow Cary (1937).

[2] On the reception of Thucydides in Roman and late antiquity, see Canfora (2006).

from his narrative, and the usefulness of his work as "a possession for all time" (κτῆμα ἐς αἰεί, Thuc. 1.22.4) deeply shaped and guided the ancient reception of Thucydides. In his essay *On How to Write History*, Lucian (2nd century CE) presents Thucydides as the sort of man the historian should be: fearless, incorruptible, free, and "a friend of freedom of speech and truth" (παρρησίας καὶ ἀληθείας φίλος, 41–42). Following the admonition of their great predecessor, later historians again and again emphasize the truthfulness of their own narratives. "Truth," however, could mean different things. It could be impartiality, as in Lucian, or it could refer to the close correspondence between historical facts and narrative; and truth could also mean the rejection of myth and unverifiable stories.

For modern readers, it can be difficult to understand how this emphasis on truthfulness relates to the rhetorical character of ancient historical writing.[3] Ancient historians constantly emphasize that truth is their primary aim, their best friend, or their "goddess" (see Avenarius 1956, 40–46). At the same time, however, their histories adopt all sorts of rhetorical forms, such as the artistic arrangement of narrative, polished speeches, and vivid accounts of reported events (ἐνάργεια), which might seem to detract from their historical accuracy in the eyes of a modern audience. One ancient author who perfectly embodies this complex relationship between historiography and rhetoric is Dionysius of Halicarnassus (first century BCE), who was a historian, a rhetorician, and also a critic of Thucydides. Dionysius' readings of his predecessor constitute a fascinating chapter in the reception of Thucydides, in which the notion of "truth" plays an important role.

In his *Letter to Pompeius Geminus* (3.15) Dionysius points out that "the attitude (διάθεσις) of Thucydides is outspoken and bitter, revealing the resentment that he felt against his native city for his exile." How does this judgment relate to the idea, expressed in the same author's *On Thucydides* (8.1) that Thucydides was "most careful of the truth, the high-priestess of which we desire history to be"? Starting from a general discussion of Dionysius' reception of Thucydides, which will be explained within the context of rhetorical culture at Rome, this chapter will examine the two passages in context. It will be argued that Dionysius' ideas on Thucydides' anti-Athenian attitude on the one hand and truthfulness on the other can be reconciled, if we take into account the critic's concept of "truth," the intended audience of his writings, and his rhetorical, pragmatic view on the writing of history. A close analysis of the statement on Thucydides' honouring of the truth (*Thuc.* 8.1, cited above) will reveal that Dionysius' praise of his predecessor is more ambiguous than a first reading might suggest. The final part of this chapter will concentrate on Dionysius' self-fashioning in his treatise *On Thucydides*: Dionysius presents himself as a critical historian of Thucydidean historiography, who claims to be writing nothing but the truth—that is, the truth *about Thucydides*.[4]

---

[3] Woodman (1988) and Fox and Livingstone (2010) examine the connections between Greek rhetoric and historiography.

[4] This part of my argument builds on the astute observations in Weaire (2005, 255–56).

Dionysius on Thucydides

Dionysius of Halicarnassus came to Rome in 30 BCE, where he worked at least until 8 BCE. His extant works demonstrate in various ways that he, like most of his contemporaries, regarded rhetoric and historiography as a harmonious and productive couple (Fox 1993; Fox and Livingstone 2010). While writing his history of early Rome in twenty books, of which the first ten and part of the eleventh are preserved, he was also active as a rhetorician. In that capacity he constantly urged his students and colleagues to read, to study, and to imitate the orators, poets, and historians of classical Greece. Deeply engaged as he was in the Greek literature of the classical past, Dionysius was well connected with the intellectual elite of the Roman world in which he lived. His extensive treatise *On Thucydides* is addressed to the Roman lawyer and historian Quintus Aelius Tubero, the father of two consuls, who seems to have had a particular interest in the subject (see below). More generally, Dionysius composed this work "for the special benefit of those who would wish to imitate Thucydides" (*Thuc.* 25.2). In adopting this practical perspective, *On Thucydides* follows the framework of Dionysius' treatises *On Imitation* and *On the Ancient Orators*, which includes separate essays on Lysias, Isocrates, Isaeus, and Demosthenes. All those works aim to guide students of rhetoric and writers of prose to the creative imitation and emulation of the best elements of classical Greek literature.

Apart from *On Thucydides*, Dionysius wrote several critical works that contain observations on Thucydides.[5] The *Letter to Pompeius* presents an extensive comparison between Herodotus and Thucydides in terms of subject matter and style, which results in a clear victory for the historian of Halicarnassus (*Pomp.* 3: see below, "Thucydides' anti-Athenian Attitude: the *Letter to Pompeius*"). The criticism of Thucydides in the *Letter to Pompeius* is repeated and somewhat mitigated in *On Thucydides*, which takes a slightly more balanced view of Thucydides' subject matter. In the technical treatise *On Composition* Dionysius analyses some passages of Thucydides as examples of the so-called austere type of word arrangement (σύνθεσις αὐστηρά). The *Second Letter to Ammaeus*, finally, is an appendix to *On Thucydides*, which examines and illustrates the grammatical peculiarities of Thucydides' style, which are rejected as unnatural and close to solecism (see De Jonge 2011).

Dionysius cites a total of sixty-nine passages from Thucydides in his treatise *On Thucydides*; in his other works, he quotes another seventy-five passages. Not surprisingly, the rhetorician has a particular interest in the speeches, but he also offers detailed analyses of a number of narrative passages. While Dionysius deeply admires his fellow townsman Herodotus, he has some serious reservations about Thucydides. His objections against Thucydides concern both the contents of the narrative (discussed in *Thuc.* 9–20) and his obscure style (*Thuc.* 21–49), which he finds unfit for creative imitation

---

[5] For Dionysius' theory of historiography, see Halbfas (1910) and Sacks (1983). For discussions of Dionysius' criticism of Thucydides, see Pavano (1936); Grube (1950); Pavano (1958); Wiater (2011, 130–65) and Hunter, in preparation. For general discussions of Dionysius, see De Jonge (2008) and Wiater (2011).

(μίμησις). He criticizes Thucydides' narrative for a variety of reasons that have raised the eyebrows of modern scholars. According to Dionysius, his predecessor has chosen an unworthy topic for his history, he has selected the wrong beginning and end for his narrative, he has devoted too much space to unimportant events while passing over more important ones, and he has assigned some of the speeches to the wrong moments in his narrative. Pericles' monumental funeral speech (Thuc. 2.35–46), to mention one example, comes after the first invasions of the Peloponnesians, which were relatively insignificant; the speech would have been much more appropriately placed after an important battle with many victims: "any book that one might choose would be a more suitable place for the funeral oration than the second book" (*Thuc.* 18.1). Notorious is Dionysius' criticism of the arrangement of the first book of the *Histories*. He claims that the work would have been much improved if Chapters 2–20 had been left out, and he actually rewrites the passage by first citing Chapter 1.1 and then immediately moving on to Chapters 1.21–23 (*Thuc.* 20).

In his discussion of Thucydides' style, Dionysius praises the description of the battle of Syracuse (Thuc. 7.69–72 in Dion. Hal. *Thuc.* 26–27) as "worthy of emulation and imitation" (ἄξια ζήλου τε καὶ μιμήσεως), demonstrating such qualities as elevation (μεγαληγορία), elegance (καλλιλογία), and forcefulness (δεινότης). The narrative of the revolution at Corcyra (Thuc. 3.81–83 in Dion. Hal. *Thuc.* 28–31) on the other hand is characterized by "the obscure and involved style, in which the charm is far exceeded by the confusion that obscures the sense" (*Thuc.* 33.1).

Dionysius' Criticism in Context: Historiography and Rhetoric in Rome

Some of Dionysius' objections to both the contents and the style of Thucydides sound bizarre, if not ridiculous in the ears of a modern audience, and they have indeed provoked the scorn of many readers. When Dionysius prefers Herodotus' choice of subject matter to that of Thucydides on the ground that the former historian deals with the glorious deeds of the past whereas the latter describes a war "that had best never happened at all, or should have been consigned to silence and oblivion" (*Pomp.* 3.3–4), Thomas Hobbes reacts by stating that "there was never written so much absurdity in so few lines."[6] It is not difficult to criticize Dionysius from a modern perspective on what historiography should be. But Dionysius' reception of Thucydides must be understood in its historical context, more particularly the context of historiography and rhetorical teaching in Rome.

In the course of the first century BCE Thucydides had become quite popular in Rome, especially after 83 BCE when Sulla brought the library of Apellicon of Teos, including copies

---

[6] Burns (2014) discusses the dispute between Hobbes and Dionysius on Thucydides.

of Thucydides, from Athens to Rome. In different ways Thucydides' writing inspired such Roman writers as Lucretius, Nepos, and especially Sallust, the Roman Thucydides (cf. Quint. 10.1.101; on Thucydides in Rome, see Leeman [1955]; Canfora [2006]; Weaire [2005, 256–57]; Wiater, chapter 38 in this volume). There were also Roman orators who took Thucydides as their stylistic model in composing speeches. Cicero took exception to these "Thucydideans," because he considered their artificial style incomprehensible and hence self-defeating in forensic or deliberative oratory: "Thucydides gives us history, wars and battles—fine and dignified, I grant, but nothing in him can be applied to the court or to public life. Those famous speeches contain so many dark and obscure sentences (*obscuras abditasque sententias*) as to be scarcely intelligible, which is a prime fault in a public oration" (*Orator* 30, trans. Hubbell). Cicero's evaluation of Thucydides is echoed in Dionysius' observations on the historian's obscure style and "unnatural" syntax in *On Thucydides* and the *Second Letter to Ammaeus*. It is clear that the criticism of Thucydides in both Cicero and Dionysius formed a reaction to the popularity of the Greek historian among Roman rhetoricians and historians.

One of the fervent supporters of Thucydides in Rome seems to have been the prominent historian Quintus Aelius Tubero, the addressee of Dionysius' treatise *On Thucydides*. As he was not satisfied with Dionysius' treatment of Thucydides in *On Imitation* (which is preserved in the *Letter to Pompeius*), Tubero asked Dionysius for a separate essay on the Greek historian (*Thuc.* 1.4) whose archaic style appears to have inspired Tubero's own history of Rome in Latin.[7] Dionysius accepted the invitation, but we may wonder whether his friend, possibly his patron, was entirely happy with the result. At first reading, the work commissioned by Tubero appears to adopt a slightly more positive view of Thucydides than the *Letter to Pompeius*, since it praises certain aspects of the narrative and tones down some of the negative comments presented in the earlier work (see Weaire 2005); but its general message nevertheless comes down to a severe warning *against* the imitation of Thucydides.

If we wish to understand Dionysius' criticism of Thucydides' subject matter and style, we must take into account his own concept of historiography, which is closely related to his rhetorical program of classicism. Dionysius' works are invariably based on the crucial concept of μίμησις, the eclectic and creative imitation of admirable examples from the past (Delcourt 2005, 43–47). In his rhetorical works he asks his students to adopt the best elements of classical writing; in his *Roman Antiquities* he holds up the earliest inhabitants of Rome, who were in fact Greek (1.5.1), as excellent models of a noble lifestyle, to be imitated by the readers of the *Roman Antiquities* (1.6.4).[8] This approach to historiography implies that the historian presents, or rather shapes and constructs, the past as a useful framework that inspires a good life in the present (Fox 1993; Wiater 2011,

---

[7] On Tubero, see Bowersock (1965, 132). Tubero wrote a history of Rome in archaizing, Thucydidean style: see Fromentin (1998, xv) and the references in Weaire (2005, 255 n. 27), whose reading of *On Thucydides* rightly draws attention to the role of Tubero and the sensitivities of Dionysius' Roman audience.

[8] On the intended audience of Dionysius' *Roman Antiquities* (Greek, Roman, or both), see Luraghi (2003). Weaire (2005, 246) persuasively argues that Dionysius' works were written for "a Greek-literate readership, both Greek and Roman, with particular strategies adopted at different points in the work to appeal to particular segments within that readership."

165–223). It also means that for Dionysius a historiographical work should be organized in such a way that it facilitates the process of imitation, which has direct consequences for the choice of topic, the portrayal of characters, and the arrangement of the narrative. Dionysius' objections to Thucydides' treatment of subject matter should be understood from this rhetorical perspective on historiography.

Dionysius' stylistic criticism of Thucydides is likewise grounded in his program of classicizing rhetoric. Faithful as he is to the principles of Atticism, Dionysius constantly draws attention to the importance of stylistic clarity (σαφήνεια). For students and orators who aim at a clear and lucid style, the work of Thucydides is a dangerous model: Dionysius points to his exotic vocabulary, his unnatural syntax (which borders on solecism), and his obscure composition and figures of speech. These criticisms are repeated and illustrated with numerous examples in the *Second Letter to Ammaeus*, for which Dionysius made use of a philological commentary on Thucydides, an indispensable tool, as the Greek critic claims: "Very few people can understand the whole of Thucydides and even they do not understand him without a linguistic commentary" (*Thuc.* 51.1: see De Jonge 2011). It might surprise us that Thucydides, being an Attic writer, receives such negative feedback from an Atticist critic. In Dionysius' perception, however, Thucydides seems to have turned from an Athenian citizen into an anti-Athenian outsider, an isolated figure, who lost the connection with his Attic roots when he was banished from Athens (cf. Wiater 2011, 142–144).

In the treatise *On Thucydides* (50.2-3), Dionysius concludes that Thucydides' style is not only inappropriate for political debate, but also for historical works, despite the claims made by "some professors of repute" (τινες οὐκ ἄδοξοι σοφισταί), who think that Thucydides' grandeur, solemnity, and impressiveness are at home in the writing of history. While some scholars have suggested that Dionysius here refers to the views of his contemporary colleague Caecilius of Caleacte (Leeman 1955, 198; Aujac 1991, 161), he may as well be alluding to the reception of Thucydides by Roman admirers (Weaire 2005, 261–62). The view that Thucydides is suitable as a model for historiography but not oratory is reminiscent of Cicero's statement that "everyone praises Thucydides, but as an intelligent, serious and dignified commentator on events, one to describe wars in history, not to handle cases in law-courts" (*Orator* 31, trans. Hubbell; see De Jonge 2008, 214–15).

Dionysius' objections to Thucydides' style and narrative thus reflect his program of rhetorical education as well as his rhetorical perspective on historiography. This background will help us to understand Dionysius' views on Thucydides' biased attitude in the *Letter to Pompeius* and his statements on the historian's commitment to the truth in *On Thucydides*.

Thucydides' anti-Athenian Attitude: The *Letter to Pompeius*

In the third chapter of the *Letter to Pompeius* Dionysius presents a systematic comparison between Herodotus and Thucydides, which he reproduces from his earlier work *On*

Imitation.[9] In the discussion of style (*Pomp.* 3.16–21), Thucydides is said to be superior in conciseness, the representation of emotions, and in force and intensity; Herodotus wins points for the portrayal of character, persuasion and delight, and appropriateness; the two historians divide the points for purity of language (Ionic versus Attic dialect), vividness, and grandeur and impressiveness. "The beauty of Herodotus is gay, while that of Thucydides is awe-inspiring," Dionysius concludes (*Pomp.* 3.21: τὸ μὲν Ἡροδότου κάλλος ἱλαρόν ἐστι, φοβερὸν δὲ τὸ Θουκυδίδου). We will here concentrate on his discussion of subject matter (*Pomp.* 3.2–15), where Herodotus defeats Thucydides on all accounts.

The first task for a historian is to select a subject that is fine and pleasant (καλὴ καὶ κεχαρισμένη, *Pomp.* 3.2). Herodotus, who records "wonderful deeds" (θαυμαστὰ ἔργα) of Greeks and barbarians, has succeeded, whereas Thucydides has failed, for the Peloponnesian war was "neither glorious nor fortunate" and hence should have been forgotten altogether (*Pomp.* 3.4). The second task for a historian is to decide where to begin and where to end. Again Herodotus wins: his narrative starts with the earliest origins of the conflict between Greeks and barbarians and ends with the Persian defeat. The starting point of Thucydides' *History*, however, is "the moment when Greek affairs started to decline." Dionysius argues that "Thucydides, being a Greek and an Athenian" (*Pomp.* 3.9), should not have shown his native city in such bad light. He ought to have started his narrative directly after the Persian wars, when Athens was flourishing, and instead of ending his story abruptly with the sea-battle at Cynossema in the twenty-second year of the war, Thucydides should have carried his narrative down to the end of the war and the liberation of Athens. Herodotus also beats Thucydides in the selection of events, which is the third task of the historian: Dionysius tells us that Herodotus' account has a pleasant variety, whereas the narrative of Thucydides is uniform, so that the audience's mind is quickly exhausted. The fourth duty concerns the distribution and arrangement of the material. Thucydides adopts a purely chronological structure, which makes his narrative obscure. Herodotus follows the divisions that the events themselves suggested to him and thereby manages to bring many subjects together into one harmonious body (σύμφωνον ἓν σῶμα, *Pomp.* 3.14). The final category of subject matter concerns the historian's "attitude" (διάθεσις) toward the events that he describes (*Pomp.* 3.15):

> ἡ μὲν Ἡροδότου διάθεσις ἐν ἅπασιν ἐπιεικὴς καὶ τοῖς μὲν ἀγαθοῖς συνηδομένη, τοῖς δὲ κακοῖς συναλγοῦσα· ἡ δὲ Θουκυδίδου διάθεσις αὐθέκαστός τις καὶ πικρὰ καὶ τῇ πατρίδι τῆς φυγῆς μνησικακοῦσα. τὰ μὲν γὰρ ἁμαρτήματα ἐπεξέρχεται καὶ μάλα ἀκριβῶς, τῶν δὲ κατὰ νοῦν κεχωρηκότων ἢ καθάπαξ οὐ μέμνηται, ἢ ὥσπερ ἠναγκασμένος.

> The attitude of Herodotus is fair throughout, showing pleasure in the good and distress at the bad. That of Thucydides on the other hand is outspoken and harsh, revealing the grudge that he felt against his native city for his exile. He recites a catalogue of its mistakes, going into them in minute detail; but when things go according to plan he either does not mention them at all, or only like a man under constraint.

---

[9] See *Pomp.* 3.1 with Fornaro (1997, 163–65); Heath (1989, 71–89); and Wiater (2011, 132–54) offer useful discussions of Dionysius' comparison of Herodotus and Thucydides.

A century later, Plutarch reverses this judgment when he accuses Herodotus of malice (κακοήθεια), which consists among other things in reporting something discreditable that is irrelevant to the narrative and in "the omission of good things" that deserve a place in the narrative (*On the Malice of Herodotus* 855c–d). In Dionysius' view, however, it is Thucydides who is guilty of such faults, including μνησικακία ("the remembrance of wrongs"). His negative attitude toward Athens comes to light in the decisions that he has made in choosing his subject, in determining the beginning and end of his narrative, and in the selection of events: all these aspects of his work present the Greek world, and Athens in particular, in a bad light. The past that Thucydides presents to his readers is unworthy to be remembered, let alone to be studied or imitated by later generations.

Herodotus' work, on the other hand, is both useful and entertaining. It is useful because it offers admirable exempla of human behaviour; and it is entertaining because the reader will enjoy a varied, unbroken narrative about his brave compatriots with a happy ending, namely, the Greek defeat of the Persians. Dionysius' praise of Herodotus and criticism of Thucydides is echoed in the introduction of the *Roman Antiquities* (1.1.2–3), which emphasizes that history should deal with admirable subjects that will be morally useful for the reader:

> For I am convinced that all who propose to leave such monuments of their minds to posterity as time shall not involve in one common ruin with their bodies, and particularly those who write histories, in which we have the right to assume that truth, the source of both prudence and wisdom, is enshrined (ἐν αἷς καθιδρῦσθαι τὴν ἀλήθειαν ὑπολαμβάνομεν ἀρχὴν φρονήσεώς τε καὶ σοφίας οὖσαν), ought, first of all, to make choice of noble and lofty subjects (ὑποθέσεις ... καλὰς καὶ μεγαλοπρεπεῖς) and such as will be of great utility (ὠφέλειαν) to their readers, and then with great care and pains, to provide themselves with the proper equipment for the treatment of their subject. For those who base historical works upon deeds inglorious or evil or unworthy of serious study (...) are neither admired by posterity for their fame nor praised for their eloquence; rather, they leave this opinion in the minds of all who take up their histories, that they themselves admired lives which were of a piece with the writings they published, since it is a just and a general opinion that a man's words are the images of his mind (εἰκόνας εἶναι τῆς ἑκάστου ψυχῆς τοὺς λόγους).

The contrast between Thucydides and Dionysius is enormous. Thucydides famously states that, while the absence of storytelling might render his work "less pleasing" (ἀτερπέστερον) to the ear, he wishes his history to be intellectually "useful" to his readers for the understanding of the events that happened in the past as well as similar events that will happen in the future (Thuc. 1.22.4). Dionysius by contrast is not so much interested in intellectual as in moral usefulness: his history will make his readers better citizens. Hence, for Dionysius usefulness and entertainment go hand in hand, as Wiater (2011, 135) has pointed out, because history can only be practically useful if the reader is able to identify with the protagonists. Dionysius believes that history must be truthful—truth being the "origin of both prudence and wisdom" (ἀρχὴν φρονήσεώς τε καὶ σοφίας)—but not every truth is appropriate to being treated in historiography (cf. Goudriaan 1989, 279). Here we arrive at the central problem that Thucydides poses to Dionysius. Within the discourse of Dionysius' classicism, Athens represents the glorious model of all political oratory, art, and literature (Delcourt 2005, 157–173). A narrative that brings out Athenian failures, like Thucydides' account of the Peloponnesian War, cannot be reconciled with that idealized image (Wiater 2011, 147–149).

The High Priestess of Truth: *On Thucydides*

Let us now turn to *On Thucydides*. In the light of the objections that Dionysius raised against Thucydides in his *Letter to Pompeius*, his praise of the historian's devotion to the truth in the treatise might come as a surprise to his readers (*Thuc.* 8.1–2):

> Μαρτυρεῖται δὲ τῷ ἀνδρὶ τάχα μὲν ὑπὸ πάντων φιλοσόφων τε καὶ ῥητόρων, εἰ δὲ μή, τῶν γε πλείστων, ὅτι καὶ τῆς ἀληθείας, ἧς ἱέρειαν εἶναι τὴν ἱστορίαν βουλόμεθα, πλείστην ἐποιήσατο πρόνοιαν, οὔτε προστιθεὶς τοῖς πράγμασιν οὐδὲν ὃ μὴ δίκαιον οὔτε ἀφαιρῶν, οὐδὲ ἐνεξουσιάζων τῇ γραφῇ, ἀνέγκλητον δὲ καὶ καθαρὰν τὴν προαίρεσιν ἀπὸ παντὸς φθόνου καὶ πάσης κολακείας φυλάττων, μάλιστα δ' ἐν ταῖς περὶ τῶν ἀγαθῶν ἀνδρῶν γνώμαις. καὶ γὰρ Θεμιστοκλέους ἐν τῇ πρώτῃ βύβλῳ μνησθεὶς τὰς ὑπαρχούσας αὐτῷ ἀρετὰς ἀφθόνως ἐπελήλυθε, καὶ τῶν Περικλέους πολιτευμάτων ἁψάμενος ἐν τῇ δευτέρᾳ βύβλῳ τῆς διαβεβοημένης περὶ αὐτοῦ δόξης ἄξιον εἴρηκεν ἐγκώμιον· περί τε Δημοσθένους τοῦ στρατηγοῦ καὶ Νικίου τοῦ Νικηράτου καὶ Ἀλκιβιάδου τοῦ Κλεινίου καὶ ἄλλων στρατηγῶν τε καὶ ῥητόρων ἀναγκασθεὶς λέγειν, ὅσα προσήκοντα ἦν ἑκάστῳ, δεδήλωκε.

> It is confirmed by all philosophers and rhetoricians, or at least by most of them, that Thucydides showed the greatest concern for the truth, the high priestess of which we desire history to be. He adds nothing to the facts that should not be added, and takes nothing therefrom, nor does he take advantage of his position as a writer, but he adheres to his purpose without wavering, leaving no room for criticism, and abstaining from envy and flattery of every kind, particularly in his appreciation of men of merit. For in the first book, when he makes mention of Themistocles, he unstintingly mentions all of his good qualities, and in the second book in the discussion of the statesmanship of Pericles, he pronounces a eulogy such as is worthy of a man whose reputation has penetrated everywhere. Likewise, when he was compelled to speak about Demosthenes the general, Nicias the son of Niceratus, Alcibiades the son of Clinias, and other generals and speakers, he has spoken so as to give each man his due.

Various scholars have pointed out that there is a tension, if not a contradiction, between this praise of Thucydides as the guardian of truth and the passage in the *Letter to Pompeius* on his anti-Athenian attitude (Pritchett 1975, 58; Goudriaan 1989, 289–290; Weaire 2005, 253–255). How should we explain this tension? Two approaches to this problem have been suggested: one is based on the relative chronology, the other on the different audiences of the two works.

Some scholars have explained the differences between the *Letter to Pompeius* and *On Thucydides* as resulting from a development in Dionysius' critical thinking. The comparison between Herodotus and Thucydides was originally presented in *On Imitation*, one of Dionysius' earlier works. The *Letter to Pompeius* (which reproduces the passage from *On Imitation*) has been assigned to the essays of the "middle period," whereas *On Thucydides* belongs to the later works (Bonner 1939). So, did Dionysius change his mind about Thucydides? That is what Pritchett (1975, 58) suggests when he qualifies the *Letter to Pompeius* as the "earlier and less mature" work. This solution however is not satisfactory, for many of Dionysius' points of criticism in the *Letter to Pompeius* are actually repeated in *On Thucydides*, including comments on the chronological method, the treatment of the beginning and the end of the work, and the distribution of speeches. More importantly, if we read carefully, we will see that Dionysius complains about Thucydides' negative portrayal of the Athenians in *On Thucydides* just as much as in the *Letter to Pompeius* (Goudriaan 1989, 289–90; Weaire 2005, 254). He points out that the words of the Athenians in the Melian Dialogue are those of barbarian kings rather than Greeks (*Thuc.* 39.1). And he objects to the superficial treatment of the Athenian embassy to Sparta in 430 BCE, which Thucydides (2.59) presents as a minor event, omitting the speeches as well as the names of the ambassadors. When the Spartans send an embassy to Athens in 425 BCE, however, Thucydides devotes much attention to the event, by citing the Spartan speeches at length (4.15–22). Dionysius is displeased (*Thuc.* 15.2):

> (… I cannot imagine why he attached more importance to the Spartan than to the Athenian embassy (πρεσβείαν), more to the later embassy than to the earlier, to the embassy of strangers (τὴν ἀλλοτρίαν) rather than that of his own city (τῆς ἰδίας), to the one sent because of lesser sufferings rather than the one sent because of greater sufferings.

This passage, which criticizes Thucydides for a lack of chauvinism, shows the continuity in thought between the *Letter to Pompeius* and *On Thucydides*. The language used in the two relevant passages reveals that same continuity. In the *Letter to Pompeius*, Dionysius complains that Thucydides focuses on the failures of the Athenians, while ignoring their successes, mentioning them only reluctantly—as if he is "forced" to do so (ἠναγκασμένος, *Pomp.* 3.15). In the treatise, he praises Thucydides' fair portrayals of noble men. But Dionysius then proves his point by offering a list of Athenian generals who are presented favourably by Thucydides: Themistocles, Pericles, Demosthenes, Nicias, and Alcibiades all received the treatments that they deserved (προσήκοντα)—and also other generals about whom he was "forced to speak" (ἀναγκασθεὶς λέγειν,

Thuc. 8.2). The language of "being forced" (ἀναγκάζεσθαι) connects this passage with the one from the *Letter*. This echo suggests that Dionysius has not at all changed his mind about Thucydides—the truthfulness of the historian is here "proven" by the fact that "when forced" to speak about the most important Athenian leaders he did not yield to his anti-Athenian bias. According to this interpretation, then, the tone of the two passages is different, but the underlying view of Thucydides as an anti-Athenian writer is present in both, although more implicitly in the later passage.

Weaire (2005) has suggested a more fruitful approach to this difference in tone, which focuses on Dionysius' professional situation and intended audience. We know nothing about Demetrius, the addressee of *On Imitation*, or about Pompeius Geminus, the addressee of the *Letter to Pompeius*, but they seem to have been Greek intellectuals who worked in similar conditions as Dionysius himself.[10] In writing his treatise *On Thucydides*, however, Dionysius had to take into account the important position of his Roman addressee Quintus Aelius Tubero, who was obviously impressed by Thucydides and dissatisfied with Dionysius' earlier comments in *On Imitation*. In addressing his influential Roman friend, Dionysius had to acknowledge that Thucydides was highly admired at Rome. In "an unusually lengthy and defensive *captatio benevolentiae*" (Weaire 2005, 252) he defends himself against readers who will censure him for stating that "the greatest of historians (τὸν ἁπάντων κράτιστον τῶν ἱστοριογράφων) was occasionally at fault in his choice of subject matter and weak in his powers of expression" (*Thuc.* 2.2). It is plausible that the positive remarks about Thucydides' ἀλήθεια (*Thuc.* 8) are part of the same strategy to win the favour of Tubero and other die-hard fans: before raising his objections against the historian's use of subject matter and style, he first had to acknowledge the generally accepted opinion that Thucydides was a respectable historian, who surpassed his predecessors.

DIONYSIUS ON THE HISTORY OF HISTORIOGRAPHY: FROM MYTH TO TRUTH

So, what does "concern for the truth" mean for Dionysius, if it is not an impartial attitude? In order to understand his praise of Thucydides' ἀλήθεια, we must consider the structure of *On Thucydides* (cf. Grube 1950, 95–100; Pritchett 1975, xxxv):

Chapters 1–4 Dionysius' right to criticize Thucydides
5   The predecessors of Thucydides: early historians and Herodotus
6–7   Thucydides' originality: his focus on one war and his rejection of myth

---

[10] No evidence proves or disproves conjectures that Pompeius Geminus was a freedman of Pompeius the Great (Rhys Roberts 1901, 38) or that he was the author of the treatise *On the Sublime* (Richards 1938), although some of his views are indeed close to those of "Longinus" (De Jonge 2012, 292–95).

8	Thucydides' devotion to the truth
9–20	Subject matter
	(9 chronological arrangement; 10–12 beginning and end; 13–20 elaboration)
21–49	Style
	(22–24 general; 25–33 detailed criticism of passages; 34–48 speeches; 49 conclusion)
50–51	Arguments in favor of Thucydides and their refutation
52–55	Demosthenes' imitation of Thucydides

Chapter 8 forms the end of the introductory part of the treatise, which establishes Thucydides' place in the history of historiography (see Toye 1995). Dionysius first lists the early historians, including Hecataeus, Charon, Xanthus, and Hellanicus (*Thuc.* 5.3):

> (…) they all had the same aim: to make generally known the traditions of the past as they found them preserved in local monuments and religious or secular records, in the various tribal and urban centres, without adding to or subtracting from them. (…) These accounts contained some stories (μῦθοι) that had been believed from remote antiquity, and many dramatic tales of changing fortunes which men of today would think quite silly.

Next came Herodotus, who "enlarged the scope" of historiography: he did not record the history of one city or nation, but numerous events in Europe and Asia, which he brought together in a single narrative (*Thuc.* 5.5). Dionysius then introduces Thucydides, who is said to differ from his predecessors in two respects (*Thuc.* 6.4–5):

> Thus Thucydides differed from the earlier historians firstly in the choice of his subject, which was neither completely monothematic nor divided up into a number of disconnected topics, and secondly by his exclusion of all legendary material (τὸ μηδὲν … μυθῶδες) and his refusal to make his history an instrument for deceiving and captivating the common people, as all his predecessors had done when they wrote stories like those of female monsters at Lamia rising up out of the earth in the woods and glades (…); and other stories which seem incredible (ἀπίστους) and largely ridiculous to us in these days.

This characterization of Thucydides' work and its rejection of myth clearly echoes the historian's own *Methodenkapitel* (τὸ μὴ μυθῶδες, 1.22.4). Dionysius in fact cites that famous passage (*Thuc.* 7.3), immediately before recording the general admiration for Thucydides' devotion to the truth (*Thuc.* 8.1, quoted at the head of this chapter): (almost) all rhetoricians and philosophers testify for the historian that he has been most careful of the truth. In Chapter 9 Dionysius then opens his attack, criticizing the chronological arrangement of the *Histories*, its starting point, and the distribution of the speeches. The context of Dionysius' "praise" of Thucydides (*Thuc.* 8.1–2) tells us that the primary meaning of "truth" in this context is not "impartiality" or "being unbiased," but the rejection of legendary tales: Thucydides' history of the Peloponnesian War honors truth because it omits the incredible stories that his predecessors had included in their histories.

Dionysius' Ambiguous Praise of Thucydides

We have seen that there is no substantial development between the *Letter to Pompeius* and *On Thucydides*: Dionysius has not actually changed his mind about Thucydides' anti-Athenian attitude, even if he presents his case more cautiously in the treatise. On closer inspection, his praise of Thucydides' truthful historiography appears to be subject to various qualifications: the compliment to Thucydides, which concerns the rejection of myth rather than impartiality, forms part of Dionysius' rhetorical strategy to please Tubero and the Thucydideans. A close reading of the opening statement of Chapter 8 will in fact demonstrate its ambiguity (*Thuc.* 8.1):

> Μαρτυρεῖται δὲ τῷ ἀνδρὶ τάχα μὲν ὑπὸ πάντων φιλοσόφων τε καὶ ῥητόρων, εἰ δὲ μή, τῶν γε πλείστων, ὅτι καὶ τῆς ἀληθείας, ἧς ἱέρειαν εἶναι τὴν ἱστορίαν βουλόμεθα, πλείστην ἐποιήσατο πρόνοιαν, . . .
>
> It is confirmed by all philosophers and rhetoricians, or if not, at least by most of them, that Thucydides showed the greatest concern for the truth, the high priestess of which we desire history to be (. . .).

The remarkable formulation of this sentence raises three questions. Firstly, who are these philosophers and rhetoricians who agree on Thucydides' truthfulness?[11] Secondly, why does Dionysius appear to correct himself by claiming that perhaps not "all" agree, but "at least most of them"? And finally, who are "we" who desire history to be "the priestess of truth"?

As to the identity of 'the philosophers and rhetoricians', scholars have offered different opinions. Aujac (1991, 148) believes that Dionysius must be thinking of Demosthenes, whom he presents at the end of his treatise as an early imitator of Thucydides. Canfora (2006b, 746–47) points to the Peripatetic school of Aristotle and Theophrastus. But given the fact that Thucydides was quite popular in Rome, we should not exclude the possibility that he is in fact thinking of Roman rather than Greek writers. In this context, we should recall Cicero's statement (*Orator* 31, cited above) that "Thucydides is praised by everyone" (*laudatus est ab omnibus*). It is possible that Dionysius is likewise alluding to the Roman imitators of Thucydides, including his addressee Aelius Tubero.

---

[11] Diodorus Siculus 1.37.4 observes that Xenophon and Thucydides are "praised for the accuracy of their histories" (ἐπαινούμενοι κατὰ τὴν ἀλήθειαν τῶν ἱστοριῶν).

Let us now look at our second question, concerning Dionysius' self-correction. He states that Thucydides' care for the truth is confirmed "by all philosophers and rhetoricians, or if not, at least by most of them" (ὑπὸ πάντων . . . , εἰ δὲ μή, τῶν γε πλείστων). By correcting his use of the word "all" (πάντων) Dionysius might be seen to undermine his praise of Thucydides, for his correction raises the question as to who would be the few rhetoricians and philosophers who do *not* agree. It is attractive to suppose that Dionysius is here making an exception for himself: by using the passive voice (μαρτυρεῖται, "it is confirmed," "it is testified") in the first part of the sentence and then correcting "all" into "most" men, Dionysius leaves open the possibility that he himself is not one of the rhetoricians who praises Thucydides' truthfulness.

In the second part of the sentence, however, Dionysius switches to the first person plural: "we desire" (βουλόμεθα) that history should be the high priestess of truth. This brings us to the third question, concerning the identity of the "we" who hold this belief. Whereas Dionysius does not commit himself to the first claim about Thucydides, he does include himself in the group of people who believe that history should honor the truth. We have indeed seen that this position agrees with Dionysius' statements at the beginning of his *Roman Antiquities* (1.1.2) about histories, "in which we assume that truth, being the source of prudence and wisdom, should be enshrined" (ἐν αἷς καθιδρῦσθαι τὴν ἀλήθειαν ὑπολαμβάνομεν ἀρχὴν φρονήσεώς τε καὶ σοφίας οὖσαν).

Who else belongs to "we"? The religious discourse that portrays truth as a goddess and history as her priestess resonates with the language of several voices in the ancient theory of historiography (Avenarius 1956, 40–46). Cicero (*De oratore* 2.36) refers to history as *lux veritatis*, "the illuminator of reality," but Dionysius' words correspond more closely to Diodorus Siculus' characterization of history as the "prophetess of truth" (προφῆτις τῆς ἀληθείας): it is noteworthy that Diodorus (1.2.2) introduces this analogy in a passage that aims to bring out the differences between myth and history—both the formulation and its context are thus very similar to the statement in Dionysius' *On Thucydides*. The theme of truth as the goddess of history culminates in Lucian's essay *How to Write History*. Lucian's goddess of history is still called Truth (ἀλήθεια), but her role seems to have shifted. Unlike Dionysius, Lucian does not understand truth merely as the rejection of myth and folk tales. For him truth seems to be precisely that impartial and unbiased attitude of the historian that Dionysius did not discover in Thucydides: "Even if the historian personally hates certain people he will think the public interest far more binding, and regard the truth as worth more than enmity, and if he has a friend he will nevertheless not spare him if he errs. This (. . .) is the one thing peculiar to history, and only to Truth must sacrifice be made (μόνῃ θυτέον τῇ ἀληθείᾳ)" (*Hist. Conscr.* 39–40, trans. Kilburn).

Dionysius and the Truth about Thucydides

On Thucydides can be read as an evaluation report, which mixes positive and negative criticism. Dionysius emphatically presents himself as a fair critic, who suggests that his balanced judgment pays respect to both strengths and weaknesses in his predecessor's history. This is where we encounter another dimension of "truth" in Dionysius' treatise: by presenting himself as a critic who is, unlike his colleagues, devoted to the truth—the truth about Thucydides—Dionysius adopts the role of the unbiased historian, thereby suggesting that he can defeat Thucydides as a priest in the religious cult of Alētheia (cf. Weaire 2005, 255–56).

At the beginning of his treatise, Dionysius defends himself against potential protests of readers who admire Thucydides. He assures his addressee (*Thuc.* 2.1) that "I do this not with you in mind and those like you, who are completely honest in your judgments and value nothing more highly than the truth (ἀλήθεια), but on account of all those others who take great delight in finding fault (...)." Dionysius then claims that he has the right to criticize Thucydides: some readers will censure him for daring to find fault with "the greatest of historians." But Dionysius emphasizes that his criticism should not be misunderstood as "malice" (κακοήθεια), and he tells his addressee (*Thuc.* 2.4) that "you and other scholars must each judge for himself whether my arguments are true and fair" (ἀληθεῖς καὶ προσήκοντας). Dionysius plays the role of a sincere critic who is devoted to the truth about Thucydides: he will praise the good and disapprove of the bad aspects of the ancient historian's work. In this respect he is different, he claims, from the contemporary imitators of Thucydides: those who admire the historian immoderately are enchanted by their blind admiration. They are no longer able to see the shortcomings of his narrative, as if they have fallen in love with a pretty face (*Thuc.* 34.4–7):

> They are suffering from the same sort of infatuation as a man overcome with an almost frantic love of some face or other. He thinks that the face that has captivated him possesses all the charms that go with a comely form; and those who attempt to criticize any blemishes that it has he accuses of slander and backbiting. In the same way Thucydides' admirers, hypnotized by this single virtue [sc., the invention of arguments and ideas] also claim for him all the qualities that he does not possess: each man thinks what he wants to think about the object of his love and admiration. But those who keep an impartial mind (ἀδέκαστον τὴν διάνοιαν) and examine literature in accordance with correct standards, (...) do not praise everything alike or find fault with everything, but give due recognition to correct usage and withhold praise from any part that is seriously at fault.

Whereas Dionysius criticizes Thucydides for his bitter attitude, which would reveal his resentment against Athens, he claims for himself an impartial mind: as a historian of historiography, Dionysius presents himself as unbiased and fair. His self-fashioning might surprise some of his modern readers—for it would not be difficult to argue that Dionysius is in fact not always fair towards Thucydides, for instance, when he criticizes the abrupt ending of the *Histories*. But the more important point here is that in writing about Thucydides Dionysius himself adopts the Thucydidean language and discourse of ἀλήθεια, thereby suggesting that he is more impartial and more devoted to truth than the classical historian—Dionysius becomes in other words "the better Thucydides" (Weaire 2005, 255). This strategy wonderfully culminates in the final words of the treatise, where Dionysius once more alludes to Thucydides' famous *Methodenkapitel*, referring to the familiar contrast between entertainment and truth (*Thuc.* 55.5: see also Weaire 2005, 255–256 and Hunter, in preparation, who notes that Dionysius' formulation also echoes Nicias' words in Thuc. 7.14.4):

> I might have written you more pleasant things (ἡδίω) about Thucydides, my dearest Quintus Aelius Tubero, but nothing that would be more true (ἀληθέστερα).

The concluding word of Dionysius' *On Thucydides* is "more true" (ἀληθέστερα). It is not only the fitting climax to a theme that has been prominent throughout the treatise, but it also concludes the competition that Dionysius has entered with Thucydides from the first pages of his work. The final sentence of the treatise concludes a complex game of intertextuality. Alluding to Thucydides' well-known characterisation of his history as "less pleasing" but "useful" for future generations (Thuc. 1.22.4), Dionysius claims that his own work is likewise useful rather than pleasant for his Roman addressee. The readers who have studied his treatise carefully, however, will understand that the climactic comparative ἀληθέστερα may carry a second, more suggestive meaning: in comparison with Thucydides' history, Dionysius' own history of historiography turns out to be "more true."[12]

References

Aujac, G., ed. 1991. *Denys d'Halicarnasse: Opuscules Rhétoriques*. Vol. 4. Paris: Les belles lettres.
Aujac, G., ed. 1992. *Denys d'Halicarnasse: Opuscules Rhétoriques*. Vol. 5. Paris: Les belles lettres.
Avenarius, G. 1956. *Lukians Schrift zur Geschichtsschreibung*. Meisenheim: Hain.
Bonner, S. F. 1939. *The Literary Treatises of Dionysius of Halicarnassus: A Study in the Development of Critical Method*. Cambridge: Cambridge University Press.
Bowersock, G. W. 1965. *Augustus and the Greek World*. Oxford: Clarendon/Oxford University Press.
Burns, T. W. 2014. "Hobbes and Dionysius of Halicarnassus on Thucydides, Rhetoric and Political Life." *Polis. The Journal for Ancient Greek Political Thought* 31: 387–424.
Canfora, L. 2006. 'Thucydides in Rome and Late Antiquity." In *Brill's Companion to Thucydides*, edited by A. Rengakos and A. Tsakmakis, 721–53. Leiden and Boston: Brill.
Cary, E., trans. 1937–1950. *The Roman Antiquities of Dionysius of Halicarnassus*. London and Cambridge: Harvard University Press.
Delcourt, A. 2005. *Lecture des Antiquités romaines de Denys d'Halicarnasse, Un historien entre deux mondes*. Brussels: Classe des Lettres, Académie Royale de Belgique.
Fornaro, S. 1997. *Dionisio di Alicarnasso, Epistola a Pompeo Gemino: Introduzione e commento*. Stuttgart and Leipzig: Teubner.
Fox, M. A. 1993. "History and Rhetoric in Dionysius of Halicarnassus." *JRS* 83: 31–47.

---

[12] This chapter was written during a research stay at the Hardt Foundation at Vandoeuvres. I am very grateful to Daniël den Hengst for his helpful comments.

Fox, M. A. 2001. "Dionysius, Lucian, and the Prejudice against Rhetoric in History." *JRS* 91: 76–93.
Fox, M. A., and N. Livingstone. 2010. "Rhetoric and Historiography." In *A Companion to Greek Rhetoric*, edited by I. Worthington, 542–61. Malden and Oxford: Blackwell.
Fromentin, V., trans. 1998. *Denys d'Halicarnasse. Antiquités Romaines*. Tome 1: *Introduction générale et livre 1*. Paris: Les belles lettres.
Goudriaan, K. 1989. *Over classicisme: Dionysius van Halicarnassus en zijn program van welsprekendheid, cultuur en politiek*. PhD Diss., Amsterdam.
Grube, G. M. A. 1950. 'Dionysius of Halicarnassus on Thucydides." *Phoenix* 4: 95–110.
Halbfas, F. 1910. *Theorie und Praxis in der Geschichtsschreibung bei Dionys von Halikarnass*. PhD Diss., Münster.
Heath, M. 1989. *Unity in Greek Poetics*. Oxford: Clarendon / Oxford University Press.
Hendrickson, G. L., and H. M. Hubbell., trans. 1952. *Cicero, Brutus; Orator*. London and Cambridge: Harvard University Press.
Hunter, R., in prepraration. "Dionysius of Halicarnassus and the Idea of the Critic." In *Dionysius of Halicarnassus: History and Criticism in Augustan Rome*, edited by C. C. de Jonge and R. Hunter.
de Jonge, C. C. 2008. *Between Grammar and Rhetoric: Dionysius of Halicarnassus on Language, Linguistics and Literature*. Leiden and Boston: Brill.
de Jonge, C. C. 2011. "Dionysius of Halicarnassus and the Scholia on Thucydides' Syntax." In *Ancient Scholarship and Gramma: Archetypes, Concepts and Contexts*, edited by S. Matthaios, F. Montanari, and A. Rengakos, 451–78. Berlin and New York: De Gruyter.
de Jonge, C. C. 2012. "Dionysius and Longinus on the Sublime: Rhetoric and Religious Language." *AJP* 133: 271–300.
Kilburn, K., trans. 1959. *Lucian*. Vol. 6. London and Cambridge: Harvard University Press.
Leeman, A. D. 1955. "Le genre et le style historique à Rome: Théorie et pratique." *REL* 33: 183–206.
Luraghi, N. 2003. "Dionysios von Halikarnassos zwischen Griechen und Römern." In *Formen römischer Geschichtsschreibung von den Anfängen bis Livius: Gattungen—Autoren—Kontexte*, edited by U. Eigler, U. Gotter, N. Luraghi, and U. Walter, 268–86. Darmstadt: Wissenschaftliche Buchgesellschaft.
Pavano, G. 1936. "Dionisio d'Alicarnasso critico di Tucidide." *Memorie della Reale Accademia delle Scienze di Torino* (Parte seconda, Classe di Scienze di morali, storiche e filologiche) 68: 1–43 [251–93].
Pavano, G. 1958. *Saggio su Tucidide*. Palermo: Priulia.
Pritchett, W. K., trans. 1975. *Dionysius of Halicarnassus: On Thucydides*. Berkeley, Los Angeles and London: University of California Press.
Rhys Roberts, W., trans. 1901. *Dionysius of Halicarnassus: The Three Literary Letters*. Cambridge: Cambridge University Press.
Richards, G. C. 1938. "The Authorship of the Περὶ ὕψους." *CQ* 32: 133–34.
Sacks, K. S. 1983. "Historiography in the Rhetorical Works of Dionysius of Halicarnassus." *Athenaeum* 61: 65–87.
Toye, D. L. 1995. "Dionysius of Halicarnassus on the First Greek Historians." *AJP* 116: 279–302.
Usher, S., trans. 1974. *Dionysius of Halicarnassus: The Critical Essays*. Vol. 1. London and Cambridge: Harvard University Press.
Usher, S., trans. 1985. *Dionysius of Halicarnassus: The Critical Essays*. Vol. 2. London and Cambridge.

Weaire, G. 2005. "Dionysius of Halicarnassus' Professional Situation and the *De Thucydide*." *Phoenix* 59: 246–66.

Wiater, N. 2011. *The Ideology of Classicism: Language, History, and Identity in Dionysius of Halicarnassus*. Berlin and New York: De Gruyter.

Woodman, A. J. 1988. *Rhetoric in Classical Historiography: Four Studies*. London and Sydney: Croom Helm.

CHAPTER 38

POLYBIUS AND SALLUST

NICOLAS WIATER

Polybius

Polybius' debt to Thucydides is not immediately obvious. His style, which is characterized by long, usually well-balanced periods and a predilection for periphrasis, as well as a certain verbal abundance that sometimes borders on pleonasm (Ziegler 1952, 1569–72; de Foucault 1972, especially 107–9, 166, 209–11; Wiater 2014, 129–30), is a far cry from the brevity and provocatively dense expression for which Thucydides was famous already in antiquity (Quint. *Inst.* 10.1.73, 16, below). And Polybius' strong authorial presence stands in sharp contrast to the artfully designed "disappearance" behind the events that is so typical of Thucydides' narrative (Loraux 1986).

An analysis of individual passages, however, reveals that Thucydides did, in fact, have a formative influence on Polybius: Polybius developed fundamental elements of his own approach to the past, in particular his conceptual vocabulary and principles of historical interpretation, by way of a close engagement with the concepts and methods of his Athenian predecessor. Thucydides' influence on Polybius' historical method has long been recognized by scholars (e.g., Walbank 1972, 40; cf. Ziegler 1952, 1522–24), even though the extent to which Polybius critically engages with and rethinks Thucydides' ideas, concepts, and methods has not always been adequately appreciated: as the first part of this section will show, Polybius stands for far more than simply "a return to the aims and methods of Thucydides" (Walbank 1972, 40).

While Thucydides' influence on Polybius' historical method has been fairly well understood, scholars have only recently begun to examine Polybius' engagement with Thucydides also in the narrative structures of his work. Even though these inquiries are, as yet, based on a relatively limited amount of material, they have revealed the various ways in which the themes, design, and structure of larger passages and episodes of Polybius' *Histories* evoke and adapt the work of his predecessor. Their results will be the focus of the second part of this section.

Thucydides' Influence on Polybius' Historiographical Method

Even though Polybius explicitly mentions Thucydides' name only once, at 8.11.3, where he characterizes Theopompus as Thucydides' (not very successful) continuator, Polybius' frequent statements detailing his approach to history writing often hark back to his Athenian predecessor, both in terms of the ideas, concepts, and principles Polybius espouses, and also (albeit less frequently) through verbal echoes.

The most significant of these passages is 3.6.7, where Polybius develops his own concept of historical causation by way of a profound rethinking and rewriting of Thucydides' famous analysis of the causes of the war between Athens and Sparta (cf. Pédech 1964, 88; Walbank 1957, 305–06; most recently, Longley 2012, 72–73, with further literature). The passage is central to our understanding of Polybius' conceptual vocabulary of historical interpretation as well as of his engagement with Thucydides, and deserves to be quoted in full. Criticizing his historical predecessors, Polybius introduces a strict distinction between beginnings, causes, and justifications. Historians who dealt with the causes of the Hannibalic War before him, Polybius states, were

> [ἀλλ' ἔστιν ἀνθρώπων τὰ τοιαῦτα] μὴ διειληφότων ἀρχὴ τί διαφέρει καὶ πόσον διέστηκεν αἰτίας καὶ προφάσεως, καὶ διότι τὰ μέν ἐστι πρῶτα τῶν ἁπάντων, ἡ δ' ἀρχὴ τελευταῖον τῶν εἰρημένων. ἐγὼ δὲ παντὸς ἀρχὰς μὲν εἶναί φημι τὰς πρώτας ἐπιβολὰς καὶ πράξεις τῶν ἤδη κεκριμένων, αἰτίας δὲ τὰς προκαθηγουμένας τῶν κρίσεων καὶ διαλήψεων· λέγω δ' ἐπινοίας καὶ διαθέσεις καὶ τοὺς περὶ ταῦτα συλλογισμοὺς καὶ δι' ὧν ἐπὶ τὸ κρῖναί τι καὶ προθέσθαι παραγινόμεθα.

> ... unable to see in what way and to what extent a beginning differs from a cause and a justification (προφάσεως), and that the cause (αἰτία) is the very first, but the beginning (ἀρχή) is last of all the factors mentioned here. By the beginning of anything I mean the first attempt to execute and put in action plans on which we have decided, by its causes [I mean] what is leading up to decisions and judgments, that is, our notions of things, our state of mind, our reasoning about these, and everything through which we reach decisions and embark on projects" (translation Paton-Walbank-Habicht, adapted).

In many ways, this passage recalls Thucydides 1.23.4–6:

> The Athenians and the Spartans began (ἤρξαντο) the war when they broke the Thirty Year Truce which they had made after the capture of Euboea. The reasons (τὰς αἰτίας) why they broke the truce I have set out first along with the specific disputes between them: this is in order that no one will ever have to enquire again about what led to this great war falling upon the Hellenes. I consider its truest cause (ἀληθεστάτην πρόφασιν), though least openly stated, to be the growth of Athenian power and the fear (φόβον) which this caused in Sparta. As for the reasons (αἰτίαι) for breaking the truce and declaring war which were openly expressed (ἐς τὸ φανερὸν λεγόμεναι) by each side, they were as follows" (translation Warner, adapted)

In this famous passage, Thucydides distinguishes the beginning of the Peloponnesian War (ἤρξαντο, 23.4), namely the political and diplomatic crisis over Epidamnus and Corcyra, which in turn *caused* the breach of the Thirty Years' Peace and, thus, the outbreak of the Peloponnesian War (τὰς αἰτίας, 23.5), from the psychological cause, the ἀληθεστάτη πρόφασις (23.6) that lay behind these political events, namely the Spartans' fear (φόβον) of the Athenians' growing power (cf. further below).

The terms used by Polybius (ἀρχή, αἰτία and πρόφασις) clearly evoke these crucial elements of Thucydides' explanation of the causes of the Peloponnesian War, but Polybius invests his predecessor's concepts with significantly different meanings. To begin with, he narrows down the coexistence of psychological (Thucydides' ἀληθεστάτη πρόφασις) and political causes (Thucydides' αἰτίαι) to psychological factors only. While Thucydides had ascribed "genuine explanatory force" (Heath 1986; cf. Hornblower 1991, 65) to the political and legal conflicts that caused the breach of the Thirty Years' Peace and, thus, the beginning of the war, Polybius accepts only psychological factors as "causes" and marks his departure from his predecessor by adopting Thucydides' term for political and legal conflicts, αἰτίαι, exclusively for the psychological factors. At the same time, he redefines Thucydides' αἰτίαι as mere "beginnings" (ἀρχαί) and denies that they have any explanatory force.

Finally, Polybius rejects Thucydides' use of πρόφασις for the psychological motivations of historical actors and appropriates it for a separate explanatory category, namely the "alleged reason" or "justification" overtly and "officially" pronounced by historical actors (cf. Pédech 1964, 88–91; Baronowski 2011, 75, 77). In so doing, Polybius is both elaborating on and criticizing the Thucydidean concepts and terminology. He is elaborating on Thucydides inasmuch as Thucydides mentions only that historical actors spoke about their disputes and quarrels, that is, the political causes (αἰτίαι), which, Thucydides says, were "openly expressed" (ἐς τὸ φανερὸν λεγόμεναι), while the deeper causes of the war, the "truest cause" (ἀληθεστάτην πρόφασιν) was "least openly stated" (ἀφανεστάτην δὲ λόγῳ, Thuc. 1.23.6, cited above). Polybius, by contrast, establishes the historical actors' "justifications" (πρόφασις) as a category of historical analysis in its own right alongside "beginnings" and "causes": Polybius is not only interested in the psychological motivation lying behind the historical figures' actions; he also wants to understand how individuals managed to convince others to adopt their personal "notions of things, state of mind and reasoning about these" (3.6.7, cited above) and thus gain support for their own plans and projects. This is the decisive step through which individual designs and desires gain traction, as it were, and become forces that shape the course of history (see, e.g., 3.7.2–3; 15.8–13). By defining the "justification" (πρόφασις) as a separate category on a par with the cause (αἰτία) and the beginning (ἀρχή), Polybius draws the reader's attention to the importance of this process. It is tempting to see Polybius' rethinking of the Thucydidean concepts as a reaction to the political and religious importance that the Romans attributed to proper (and properly communicated) justifications, especially for their military campaigns (cf. Pol. frag. 99 with Derow 1979, especially 13–5).

At the same time, Polybius' clear tri-partite division seems to imply criticism of Thucydides' confusing use of πρόφασις: (probably) derived from πρό-φημι (Hornblower 1991, 25), the term originally means something like "announcement," or "declaration." Thucydides, however, used the term for the *hidden*, underlying cause that was *least* talked about (ἀφανεστάτην [...] λόγῳ, above). It is almost as if Polybius was deliberately correcting the divide between etymology and meaning introduced by Thucydides' use of the term by redefining it in such a way as to realign the meaning ("officially declared cause") and the etymology.

But Polybius' rewriting of Thucydides goes even further and extends well beyond the redefinition of terms and concepts: Polybius also engages with the way in which Thucydides had implemented his causal analysis of the Peloponnesian War into his narrative: Thucydides announces at 1.23.4 that the breach of the Thirty Years' Peace of 446 constituted the "beginning" of the Peloponnesian War (ἤρξαντο δὲ αὐτοῦ Ἀθηναῖοι καὶ Πελοποννήσιοι λύσαντες τὰς τριακοντούτεις σπονδάς) and that his own narrative will begin precisely with an account of the political "quarrels" that were the "causes" of this breach (1.23.5). His subsequent narrative, beginning with the famous phrase Ἐπίδαμνός ἐστι πόλις [...], implements this program, detailing the events lying behind the breach of the peace (the αἰτίαι in Thucydides' definition) and, hence, the outbreak of the Peloponnesian War. Polybius, too, "begins" (3.5.9) his narrative with an exploration of the "causes" of the Hannibalic War. But unlike Thucydides, he does not do so by way of the narrative of the events, but turns what had been merely a few theoretical statements in Thucydides (1.23.5–6) into a substantial analysis and reinvestigation of the existing theories about the causes of the war (3.6–12). The actual narrative of the events (the part corresponding to Thucydides' Ἐπίδαμνός ἐστι πόλις), by contrast, does not begin until 3.13, with Polybius' account of Hannibal's conquests in Spain. The structure of the first part of Polybius' narrative is rewriting the structure of the first part of Thucydides' narrative, just as Polybius' definition of historical causes rewrites that of his Athenian predecessor.

Part of this extensive process of rewriting Thucydides' narrative and theory of causation is certainly Polybius' desire to prove himself a worthy successor of Thucydides. This desire to be associated with his great predecessor also lies behind other crucial elements of Polybius' approach to historical writing, namely his programmatic disapproval for history written merely for the sake of pleasure and his emphasis on the usefulness of historical accounts. Polybius' statement at 3.31.12 is particularly significant in that respect. Here he links the usefulness of history with the thorough investigation of the causes, circumstances, and consequences of actions and events—qualities that he regards as the essence of any proper work of history and that, moreover, recall Thucydidean principles (cf. Samotta 2012, 363)—while evoking Thucydides' contrast between the use of his work for future generations and its lack of short-term gratification at 1.22.4 (cf. Longley 2012, 70): "For if we remove from history the discussion of why, how, and to what purpose each thing was done, and whether the result was what should have been reasonably expected, what is left is a clever show-piece (ἀγώνισμα), but not a lesson (μάθημα), and while pleasing for the moment (τέρπει) of no possible benefit (οὐδὲν ὠφελεῖ) for the future" (Pol. 3.31.12; translation Paton-Walbank-Habicht, adapted).

Compare Thucydides 1.22.4: "Perhaps the absence of the element of the fable in my work may make it seem less easy on the ear (ἀτερπέστερον); but it will have served its purpose well enough if it is judged useful (ὠφέλιμα) by those who want to have a clear view (τὸ σαφὲς σκοπεῖν) of what happened in the past and what—the human condition being what it is—can be expected to happen again some time in the future in similar or much the same ways. It is composed to be a possession for all time and not just a performance piece (ἀγώνισμα) for the moment" (translation Mynott).

The strong verbal echoes (ἀγώνισμα, μάθημα, τέρπει and ὠφελεῖ evoke ἀτερπέστερον, τὸ σαφὲς σκοπεῖν, ὠφέλιμα, and, particularly, ἀγώνισμα in the Thucydides passage) make the reference to Thucydides virtually certain. As with his own concept of historical causation, however, Polybius seeks to develop an approach to pleasure, historical explanation, and truth that goes beyond his predecessor. While pleasure and truth/usefulness are opposites in Thucydides, Polybius goes one step further: not only does he, too, condemn historical writing that sacrifices historical accuracy to mere entertainment (see Polybius' severe criticism of the "tragic historiography" of Phylarchus, 2.56.7–16); he also redefines an accurate, truthful historical account itself as pleasurable (Wiater 2016). Truth, usefulness, and pleasure thus form a new, complex unity.

This tendency to elaborate on, and, indeed, correct, Thucydides is characteristic of Polybius' engagement with his predecessor in general. Thus Polybius' criticism of Timaeus' use of invented speeches and his demand that historians ensure the historical accuracy of the speeches inserted into their works at 12.25a–b has been convincingly argued to have been directed not only at Timaeus, his primary target, but also at Thucydides' famous and much debated statement at 1.22.4 (above; cf. Rood 2012, 53 n14; Wiater 2014, both with further literature; Pédech 1964, 257). This tendency is also visible in Polybius' rationale for writing the first two books (the so-called προκατασκευή) as he explains it at 1.3.9. His emphasis on "motives, powers, resources" as the "tools of success," in particular, echoes "Thucydides' explanatory schemes," especially Thuc. 1.23.5, and "answers to a Thucydidean preoccupation," but varies the words and terms of his predecessor so as to make them suitable for Polybius' "different shape of story" (Pelling 2007, 246). And Polybius' emphasis on historiography as providing concrete, practical lessons that will have an essential and immediate impact on his readers' success in their own political and military endeavors (especially 12.25b.2–3; but see Maier [2012a, 2012b] on the importance of contingency and unpredictability in Polybian thought) may well be seen as a response to Thucydides' notoriously vague remarks about the practical usefulness of his work (1.22.4, 2.48.3; cf. Rood 2012, 63–64).

The passages discussed above demonstrate that Polybius developed essential aspects of his thinking about history in close, and often critical, engagement with Thucydides. Polybius conceived of himself as a successor of the famous Athenian in the sense of being a historical writer who continued the self-reflexive, analytical kind of historical writing established by Thucydides. But the discussion has also demonstrated, I hope, the inadequacy of the view that Polybius simply "returned" to the "aims and methods of Thucydides" (Walbank 1972, 40, cited above). This falls short of appreciating the complexities and subtleties of Polybius' relationship with Thucydides: Polybius was

Thucydides' successor also in the sense that he continuously attempted to develop further the latter's concepts, methods, and principles in order to identify and correct his weaknesses and create the novel kind of historiography that alone would be capable of dealing with the challenges presented by the unprecedented rise of Roman power that distinguished Polybius' own time (1.1.5–6; Wiater 2016).

Thucydides' Influence on the Themes, Structure, and Design of Polybius' Narrative

Thucydides' influence on Polybius' historical narrative is still largely uncharted territory. It was only recently, in an important paper by Tim Rood (2012), that a first, systematic attempt has been made to explore this aspect of Polybius' engagement with Thucydides. As will become apparent, Polybius employed here the same method of selective and critical adaptation of central aspects of Thucydides' narrative as in the development of his own historical method.

As Rood demonstrated conclusively, Thucydides' analysis of the causes of the Peloponnesian War and his account of the Athenian invasion of Sicily influenced Polybius' narrative of the First Punic War and his famous analysis of the Roman constitution (2012, 51). At the most general level, Polybius evokes Thucydides' account of the Sicilian Expedition through "the structuring opposition of land-and sea-fighting," his frequent gesturing "towards Thucydides' account of naval tactics" (58), his emphasis on the "shifting fortunes experienced by both sides" during the first war and the "vocabulary of shock and awe" designed to illustrate the emotional impact of the events: Rood (59) notes the unusual clustering of the passive of ἐπιρρώννυμι, "recover strength, pluck up courage" (LSJ s.v.), that is distinctive of both Thucydides' and Polybius' accounts.

But Thucydides also seems to loom large behind concrete episodes. Rood (2012, 54–55) argues convincingly, for example, that Polybius' account of the escalation of events that resulted in the First Punic War—the Mamertines' takeover of Messene and their appeal to the Romans for military support, their subsequent additional appeal to Carthage, and the Romans' concerns about growing Carthaginian power prompted by that appeal, which led to their decision to support the Mamertines (1.10.2–11.1)—follows, in a compressed manner, the three stages of the escalation that led to the war between Athens and Sparta: the civil dispute in Epidamnus, Epidamnus' appeals to both Corcyra and Corinth, the conflict between Corinth and Corcyra that resulted from these appeals, and the Peloponnesian War which, in turn, resulted from this conflict when the Athenians decided to support Corcyra against the Spartan ally, Corinth. Further examples of "Thucydidean overtones" in Polybius' narrative are his description of the first sea battle of the First Punic War (Pol. 1.27–29) as well as the striking similarity between the role played by the Spartan Xanthippus in the war against Carthage (Pol. 1.32–35) and that of the Spartan Gylippus whose intervention alleviated the dire situation of Syracuse in Thucydides 7.2 (Rood 2012, 60).

Even more significant than these structural parallels are important thematic similarities: at several points of Polybius' narrative, intertextual references evoke Thucydides' characterization of the Athenians as an important point of comparison to Polybius' characterization of the Romans. The same comparison had been employed already by the very first Roman historiographer, Quintus Fabius Pictor (Samotta 2012, 352), and a century after Polybius, Sallust would find it a tool of historical interpretation congenial to the aims and purposes of his works (see below). The most striking similarity between Polybius' and Thucydides' analyses is perhaps the motive of one superpower's fear of the other, which is central to the narratives of both (cf. Pol. 1.10.6 and Thuc. 1.23.6): the Romans' fear of Carthaginian expansion evokes Thucydides' "truest cause" (ἀληθεστάτην πρόφασιν, 1.23.6) of the Peloponnesian War, namely Spartan fear of Athens' growing power. This parallel is reinforced by an allusion (including verbal echoes) to a concrete passage: Polybius' description of the Romans' fear of the Carthaginians (1.10.5) seems to evoke Alcibiades' description of the Athenian imperial ambitions at Thuc. 6.90.2: "By analogy with Thucydides' Athenians, Polybius' Carthaginians (at least as the Romans perceive them) are also cast as greedy and doomed to defeat" (Rood 2012, 56).

Another important theme that informs Thucydides' characterization of the Athenians, especially in the speech of the Corinthians in Book 1 (1.68–71), is the role of determination, bravery, and the ability to adapt quickly to new situations as the foundations of their power and success. In the same way, Polybius' Romans adapt quickly to the challenge of having to fight the Carthaginians at sea, and Polybius emphasizes the εὐψυχία that allowed the Romans to prevail in that endeavor despite the Carthaginians' superior skill and experience in naval warfare (ἐμπειρία, 6.52.1, 8–9) in a way that recalls Hermocrates' encouragement to his Syracusan countrymen to pursue the war at sea despite the ἐμπειρία of the Athenians (Thuc. 7.21.3; Rood 2012, 64).

Intertextual references to Thucydides are an important element of Polybius' characterization of the Romans also elsewhere in his account. Polybius' sketch of the Carthaginians' desperate fight for their existence against the rebelling mercenaries (1.71.5–6), for example, evokes Thucydides' description of the Athenians' dismal state after their defeat in Sicily (8.1.2), and Polybius' character sketch of the Romans at 1.37.7 alludes to the Corinthians' characterization of the Athenians at Thuc. 1.70.7. The full significance of Polybius' comparison of the Romans with Thucydides' Athenians becomes apparent in the third book of his *Histories*: at 3.75.8, in a "thoughtful continuation of [the] pattern [...] already found in the account of the First Punic War" (Rood 2012, 60–63, the quote at 62), Polybius describes how the Romans overcame their shock at the horrible defeat at Cannae in 216 BCE and managed to turn their fear into a source of strength and the basis of their future success (cf. Thuc. 8.1.4).

Ultimately, as Rood (2012, 53) rightly notes, it must remain uncertain "how much Polybius had read Thucydides." We must also remain conscious of the influence of Hellenistic historiography and philosophy on Polybius, which, in many cases, might have been an important intermediary stage between Polybius and Thucydides (cf. Gelzer [1955] 1964, 160; *pace* Samotta 2012, 363; the most extensive discussion of Polybius' place in Hellenistic writing and thought is Pédech 1964; concise overview in

Samotta 2012, 348–50). Theopompus in particular, whose interest in the psychology and motives of historical actors was famous already in antiquity (Dion. Hal. *Pomp.* 6.7–8), might have been an important influence on Polybius (Polybius' criticism at 8.11.3 notwithstanding); and Polybius himself refers to the historian Ephorus as the only writer who successfully wrote "universal history" before him (5.33.1–2; cf. Miltsios 2013, 10–11 with n13). However, the lacunose state of Theopompus' and Ephorus' works makes certainty impossible. Nevertheless, taken together, these passages do constitute compelling evidence that the design and some key themes of Polybius' narrative and characterization of the Romans were influenced by Thucydides.

As pointed out in this section, Polybius' engagement with Thucydides in the design and structure of his narrative, his characterization of historical actors, and the various techniques through which he seeks to represent the events of the past are much less well understood than Thucydides' influence on Polybius' historical method. Only a future systematic, large-scale analysis of the narrative parts of the *Histories* will enable us fully to appreciate the intricacies, subtleties, and different layers of Polybius' relationship with his Athenian predecessor.

Sallust

Even though Sallust never refers to Thucydides by name, the connection between the two historians was firmly established as early as the first century BCE. The Roman historian Velleius Paterculus called Sallust a "rival of Thucydides" (*aemulum Thucydidis*, 2.36.2) and the famous rhetorician and literary critic Quintilian stated categorically that "our history writing [. . .] need not yield the prize to the Greeks. I should have no hesitation in matching Sallust with Thucydides" (*Inst.* 10.1.101; translation Russell, adapted). The influence of these ancient judgments on modern scholarship can hardly be overestimated: the view that Sallust drew heavily on Thucydides in a variety of ways is now commonplace, and generations of scholars have collected and compared passages to bear out and refine the somewhat general remarks of Quintilian and Velleius (e.g., Dolega 1871; Robolski 1881; Perrochat 1949; Syme 1964, 54, 245–48; Scanlon 1980; Nicols 1999; Grethlein 2006).

Precisely because Thucydides' influence on Sallust has received so much attention in ancient and modern scholarship, however, the argument offered here needs to start with a cautionary note: the sheer quantity of studies on that subject must not give rise to the erroneous assumption that Sallust was simply some sort of "imitator" of Thucydides, or that the design, style, scope, and purpose of his work can be understood simply by analyzing his relationship with Thucydides. To begin with, for all the similarities, there are also significant differences (Grethlein 2006). Moreover, other influences were equally formative, most notably the Roman historiographical tradition, especially the works of Cato the Elder (Syme 1964, 267–69; Levene 2000). Sallust also drew on the rich historiographical practice and popular philosophical thought that had developed in Hellenistic times (Perrochat 1949, 40–45; Avenarius 1957; overview and further literature in Koestermann 1971, 23–26; Paul 1984, 10–11). To complicate things even further, Hellenistic as well as Roman historiography were themselves deeply shaped by Thucydides (Samotta 2012, on Roman republican historiography). This makes it sometimes difficult to determine whether certain features of Sallust's texts hark back to Thucydides specifically or simply result from the more general tradition of historical writing that had developed after, albeit in close engagement with, Thucydides (cf. the previous section on Polybius). We might also be dealing with "two-tier references," "double allusions" referring back to Thucydides *via* the work of an author who was influenced by him, "carrying with it some of the connotations of both" (Levene 2000, 183, on Sallust referring to the Greek orator Lycurgus via Cato). Finally, we must not forget that Sallust was a brilliant and innovative author in his own right who drew selectively on these various strands of historical and philosophical traditions, adapted them to his own purposes and integrated them into works that were profoundly original in design, thought, and style. While exploring the way in which Thucydides influenced Sallust's thinking and writing, we therefore need to keep in mind that his relationship with Thucydides is only one aspect of what defines Sallust as a complex historical and literary figure.

"Sallust," as Ronald Syme (1964, 56) put it, "exploits Thucydides in two ways. First, translation or adaptation of phrases. Second, and much more important, to produce an equivalence of manner and atmosphere." Even though Syme's distinction falls short of appreciating the full depth of Thucydides' influence on Sallust's historical thinking and interpretation of history and does not do justice to the importance of Thucydides to Sallust's authorial "self-fashioning" (Greenblatt 1980, 2; see below), style, manner, and atmosphere are indeed important aspects of Sallust's engagement with Thucydides and were identified as such already by Sallust's ancient readers. Given that they also constitute the most basic level of this engagement, we shall begin with them before proceeding to more complex phenomena.

Features of Sallust's Style and Narrative Technique Evoking Thucydides

Following Syme's distinction, we can identify general features of Sallust's style and narrative technique that are typical of, and therefore evoke, Thucydides' work (Syme's "manner and atmosphere"), as well as phrases, expressions, and whole passages that obviously adapt specific passages of the *Histories* (Syme's first category). We shall consider the general features first, followed by a discussion of concrete passages that hark back to the *Histories*. This will lead us to the bigger question of Sallust's interest in specific themes and also to the specific outlook on and interpretation of the past that he shared with Thucydides.

The one feature that has been identified since antiquity as the most distinctive of Sallust's style is his "brevity," a highly concentrated mode of expression that pares sentences down to the absolute minimum, often deliberately defying immediate intelligibility (Perrochat 1949, 34–38; Kroll 1927, 283–284; Syme 1964, 265; Scanlon 1980, 65–66, 70–73, 186–188). Seneca the Younger describes Sallust's phrases as "lopped off": "words came to a close unexpectedly, and obscure conciseness was equivalent to elegance" (*amputatae sententiae et verba ante exspectatum cadentia et obscura brevitas fuere pro cultu*, *Ep*.114.17, translation Gummere). Likewise, Quintilian warns the budding orator of "the famous 'Sallustian brevity'" (*illa Sallustiana* [...] *brevitas*) and "the abrupt sort of language" (*abruptum sermonis genus*), which can be detrimental in a trial even though "in Sallust himself" they "coun[t] as a virtue" (*virtutis optinet locum*; *Inst*. 4.2.45, translation Russell); in another passage Quintilian praises the "immortal rapidity" of his expression (*inmortalem Sallusti velocitatem*, *Inst*. 10.1.102, translation Russell). The same "concentrated expression" and "speed" were also recognized as being among the most characteristic features of the style of Thucydides: Quintilian characterizes it as "close-textured, concise, always pressing himself hard" (*densus et brevis et semper instans sibi Thucydides*, *Inst*. 10.1.73, translation Russell), and the Greek literary critic and historiographer Dionysius of Halicarnassus, who was active in Rome in the first century BCE (see de Jonge, chapter 37 in this volume), emphasizes Thucydides' "effort to express as much as possible in the fewest possible words, and to combine many ideas into one, and to leave the listener still expecting to hear something more"; "these," he adds, "help to make his brevity obscure" (*Thuc*. 24.10, edited by Aujac; translation Usher). He then goes on to characterize Thucydides' style as "compact and solid" (τὸ στριφνὸν καὶ πυκνόν) and emphasizes the "rapidity" of his expression (τὸ τάχος τῆς σημασίας). Seneca the Elder even pronounced Sallust superior (*vicit*) to Thucydides "in that very brevity that is so peculiar (*praecipua*) to him [that is, Thucydides]" (*Controv*. 9.1.13).

Examples of Sallust's "brevity" include Sallust's use of *in* with the comparative of a neuter adjective (cf. *Iug*. 73.5: *in maius celebrare*, with Thuc. 1.21.1: ἐπὶ τὸ μεῖζον κοσμοῦντες; Perrochat 1949, 34–35); *ad sensum* constructions (that is, constructions determined by the sense of a word, rather than its grammatical form, for example, in English, "the team *were* beaten" instead of "the members of the team"), which are frequent in both authors (examples in Perrochat 1949, 28–29; Kroll 1927, 288–289); the "pregnant sense in adverbs or in neuter abstract nouns" (cf. *Cat*. 41.1: *in incerto habuere* with Thuc. 1.25.1: ἐν ἀπόρῳ εἴχοντο; *Cat*. 52.12: *in obscuro*; Thuc. 1.42.2: ἐν ἀφανεῖ; Scanlon 1980, 71–72, the quotation at 71); and the frequent omission of words, which requires readers to extrapolate appropriate terms from the context (brachylogy; examples in Perrochat 1949, 36–37). A particularly interesting case of Sallust's brevity is his account of the battle of Zama (*Iug*. 60.4). Sallust here clearly evokes the last naval battle between Syracusans and Athenians in *Histories* 7.70–1 (cf. esp. *Iug*. 60.4 with Thuc. 7.71.3; Perrochat 1949, 18–19) but manages to produce an even more condensed and concise account than that of Thucydides (Scanlon 1980, 151). Given that this passage of Thucydides was famous already in antiquity (Dion. Hal., *Thuc*. 27.1), Sallust's passage is clearly meant to be a demonstration that he, as an *aemulus Thucydidis* (above), was not only on a par with, but, as Seneca the Elder had so aptly observed (above), even surpassed his predecessor.

Another generally Thucydidean feature of Sallust's style and narrative technique is his predilection for *variatio* or *inconcinnitas*, that is, "the lack of congruity or harmony in grammatical structures and a tendency to the unusual, unexpected, and asymmetrical,"[1] which is often produced by *ad sensum* constructions and chiasmus (Perrochat 1949, 30–34; Scanlon 1980, 189–190; Kroll 1927, 285–288, 300). Sallust also frequently employs certain figures of style, especially sharp antitheses and parallelism, paronomasies ("word play": e.g., *Iug.* 63.3: *stipendiis faciundis, non Graeca facundia*) and homoeoteleuta (the combination of different words with the same ending), which Dionysius of Halicarnassus identifies as typical of Thucydides' style as well (*Thuc.* 24.2–9, especially 9; Perrochat 1949, 29–30).

In addition to these stylistic features, some important structural elements of Sallust's work establish strong ties between his and Thucydides' works:

(1) Like Thucydides, Sallust employs speeches "as a means of extended political analysis" (Kraus and Woodman 1997, 36; Scanlon 1980, 89–92). The speeches of Adherbal, Memmius, and Marius in the *Bellum Iugurthinum* (chaps. 14, 31, 85, respectively) belong to this category (cf. Kraus and Woodman 1997, 24–25). The most famous examples, however, are the speeches of Cato and Caesar at *Cat.* 51-2 (Perrochat 1949, 9–10), which recall the debate between Cleon and Diodotus about the fate of the Mytileneans in Thuc. 3.37–48 (Scanlon 1980, 89) and where Sallust adopts Thucydides' habit of pairing speeches that discuss a question from contrasting angles (*antilogiai*).

(2) The description of the morals of the early Romans (*Cat.* 6–13) recalls Thucydides' "archaeology" of Athenian naval power (1.2–19) and contains a direct comparison with the Athenians (8.2–3) which Scanlon (1980, 11) regards as a reference to Thucydides' work. At the same time, however, Sallust's "archaeology" is a "two-tier reference" in that it also recalls Cato's *Origines* (Levene 2000, 174–180).

(3) Seneca the Elder credits Sallust with the introduction of "death notices," designed to give a concise account of an important individual's life and achievement after his or her death, and specifically links this practice with Thucydides (*Suas.* 6.21) (Perrochat 1949, 2); at the same time, this (just like Sallust's interest in the psychology of historical figures, Perrochat 1949, 5) places Sallust firmly in the tradition of Hellenistic historical writing (e.g., Polybius: see Pomeroy 1986; Pédech 1964).

(4) Finally, Thucydides and Sallust are distinguished by the conscious effort to create a vocabulary and diction that was profoundly original and markedly and provocatively different from anything their contemporaries (and future generations, see Dion. Hal. *Thuc.* 24.1; *Amm. II* 3.2) were familiar with (Perrochat 1949, 27–38; Syme 1964, 260 and 266–267; but note Kraus and Woodman 1997, 11, and Syme 1964, 264 on Sisenna and Cato as important precedents). They both deliberately

---

[1] http://www.thelatinlibrary.com/sallust/style.html (accessed 12 June 2015).

"de-familiarize" (cf. Shklovsky [1917] 1998) not only the established historical but also, and especially, the dominant oratorical and political discourse (Kraus and Woodman 1997, 12–13). I will argue below that this was one of the reasons why Sallust found Thucydides' work so congenial to his own historical projects.

Passages Adapted from Thucydides

Some typical expressions and numerous more complex passages clearly evoke specific passages of Thucydides' *Histories*, thus inviting the reader to gain a deeper understanding of the events which Sallust describes by bringing his text into dialogue with Thucydides. These passages have been repeatedly compiled and discussed by scholars. Perrochat (1949, 13–22; helpful list on 22) is the best place to start because he prints the Latin and Greek passages side by side and thus enables direct comparison. Scanlon's (1980, helpful index on 257–260) discussion, on the other hand, explores the larger themes that inform Sallust's engagement with Thucydides. While Sallust engages with Thucydides in all three of his works, the number of such adapted passages decreases noticeably from the *Bellum Catilinae* to the *Bellum Iugurthinum* (Perrochat 1949, 22).

Sallust's adaptations from Thucydides range from simple phrases, especially *fieri amat* (cf., e.g., *Iug.* 34.1, with Thuc. 3.81.5: οἷον φιλεῖ ἐν τοιούτῳ γίγνεσθαι), to longer, complex passages. It is the latter that illustrate best how Sallust engaged with and adopted key ideas and themes of Thucydides' *Histories*. Thanks to Perrochat's and Scanlon's detailed discussions, we can limit ourselves here to some of the most significant examples. Sallust's account of the battle of Zama (*Iug.* 60.4) and the debate between Cato and Caesar (*Cat.* 51–2), for which Sallust drew on Thuc. 7.71.3 and 3.37–48, respectively, have already been mentioned. Two other Thucydidean episodes are evoked most often in Sallust's texts: the famous Funeral Oration of Pericles in 2.35–46.1, and Thucydides' striking "pathology" of civil strife at Corcyra in 3.81–84.

Sallust evokes the Funeral Oration at the very beginning of the *Bellum Catilinae*. When describing how difficult it is for the historian to create an adequate account of men's deeds (*Cat.* 1.5), he draws on the opening statement of Pericles' Funeral Oration, which makes a similar point (Thuc. 2.35.2). Other passages also draw inspiration from the Funeral Oration: Sallust's explanation of the foundations of Roman power and influence in early Roman history at *Cat.* 6.5 (*magisque dandis quam accipiundis beneficiis amicitias parabant*) evokes Pericles' explanation of fifth-century Athenian power (Thuc. 2.40.4), and Pericles' statement of the Athenians' obligation to honor and preserve their political and moral-ideological heritage (Thuc. 2.62.3) looms large behind Memmius' characterization of the Romans' obligation to preserve the *libertas* which their ancestors (*maiores*) fought so hard to establish (*Iug.* 31.17).

On the other hand, Thucydides' description of the reason (αἴτιον) for the civil unrest that befell Greece in 427 (Thuc. 3.82.8) informs Sallust's analysis of the course of moral degeneration that followed the initial period of Roman political and moral superiority (*Cat.* 10.3). The same context is evoked later in the work, in Cato's analysis of the complete breakdown of the traditional meaning of words that characterizes contemporary Roman political culture, including the famous statement that "we have long since lost the true names for things" (*vera vocabula rerum amisimus*, *Cat.* 52.11, translation Rolfe and Ramsey. Cf. Thuc. 3.82.4: τὴν εἰωθυῖαν ἀξίωσιν τῶν ὀνομάτων ἐς τὰ ἔργα ἀντήλλαξαν τῇ δικαιώσει), and again in Sallust's description of how the crisis brought upon the Roman state by the conflict with Jugurtha "tore apart" the Roman citizenry at *Iug.* 41.5 (cf. Thuc. 3.82.8).

The Meaning of Style: Language, History and Politics

As Scanlon (1980) has well demonstrated, Sallust's frequent recourse to Thucydides is an expression of a shared concern for the same topics and questions. Sallust looked to Thucydides because he recognized in the development of Roman politics and power since the fall of Carthage (*Cat.* 10.1) the symptoms and causes of change and decline described by Thucydides. Sallust's view of the past was deeply informed by Thucydidean ideas and categories, and Thucydides provided him with a model of diction along with the conceptual vocabulary that he needed in order to express this view in his own writings.

At the heart of both authors' interpretation of the past lies the complex interrelationship of politics, language, and morals: Pericles' Funeral Oration is a large-scale attempt to define the essence of Athenian identity at the beginning of a war that would bring almost all the fundamental elements of this self-definition into question, and both the debate about the fate of the Mytileneans at 3.37–48 (above) and the speech of the Corinthians at 1.68–71, which Sallust evokes repeatedly in the speech of Lepidus (*Hist.* 1.55; Maurenbrecher; Perrochat 1949, 16–17), debate crucial questions regarding the nature of Athenian power, its foundations, and the obligations and responsibilities that come with it. Thucydides' description of civil strife in the third book, on the other hand, is centered precisely on the way in which social upheaval goes hand in hand with an upheaval of the usual moral and political concepts and their expression in language (esp. Thuc. 3.82.4, cited above): Thucydides enabled Sallust to diagnose and describe that "slipperiness of words [that] at once reflects and creates a moral and political chaos that is ultimately as labile and invasive as any disease" (Kraus and Woodman 1997, 24). In a way, then, Sallust actualizes Thucydides' hope that his work would enable future generations to "understand clearly the events which happened in the past and which (human nature being what it is) will, at some time or other and in much the same ways, be repeated in the future" (Thuc. 1.22.4; translation Warner).

The most concise expression of Sallust's view of the political situation is Cato's statement that *vera vocabula rerum amisimus* (*Cat.* 52.11, above), which establishes a direct link between language (semantics), morals, and politics (Batstone 1990, 125). Cato's words echo Sallust's own description of the political climate of his time, especially the greed and ambition that ultimately corrupted him and to which he attributed the failure of his career in active politics (*Cat.* 3.3–4). Consequently, Sallust's style has been seen as an attempt to create "a linguistic atmosphere imitating the contradictions and hypocrisies in the 'real world'" and to reflect the "lack of coherence between words and reality by writing in a way that similarly deceives expectations" (Kraus and Woodman 1997, 12).

Kraus and Woodman have made an important contribution to our understanding of the significance of Sallust's style. One wonders, however, whether Sallust's diction is really meant to *represent* the chaotic realities of contemporary Roman politics—it might present the reader with numerous challenges, but is not itself "chaotic" or contradictory. Quite to the contrary, Sallust's style is a carefully designed linguistic work of art of which Sallust is in complete control: every challenge to the reader is deliberate. As Syme (1964, 260) put it, Sallust's diction might be "peculiar," but it is "in no way enigmatic. What he was trying to do is clear enough."

I would therefore suggest that we should conceive of Sallust's style as a statement, rather than the reflection of an ideology (Kraus and Woodman 1997, 12), let alone of the chaotic disorder of Roman politics and society. Sallust's style sends a message: the traditional political-cum-moral discourse of his time, which is based on such concepts as *mos maiorum* and *virtus*, no longer provides either reliable guidance for an unambiguous assessment of the situation or a secure basis for conceiving an appropriate response to it. This "diagnosis" is exemplified by the debate between Caesar and Cato (above), which "reveals [...] a fragmentation of varying dimensions which is the result of virtues themselves in conflict with each other and an underlying conceptual failure which produces an opposition between the traditional Roman virtues of action and the traditional intellectual categories by which those virtues are known, named and understood" (Batstone 1988, 2; cf. Sklenár 1998, 217–218; Batstone 2010). Caesar and Cato both fail to offer a viable and convincing solution to the problem (the punishment of Catiline and the other conspirators), because they are both operating from within a language and concomitant set of concepts that have lost their original significance. Any attempt to restabilize the meaning of these terms and to re-endow them with their original significance is futile and will only aggravate the discrepancy between language and meaning (cf. Batstone 1990, 120; 125).

Sallust's effort to draw on a Greek author to create a new, startling, and "defamiliarizing" style, can thus be seen as an attempt to step outside the hopelessly entangled contemporary discourse and enable readers to take an "outside" perspective on their own language and the moral and political values that are bound up with it. Rather than reflecting it, Sallust's style creates critical distance to contemporary political reality, prompting readers to recognize and examine the misguided concepts and values (*malae artes*, *Cat.* 3.4) to which they have fallen prey just as Sallust had in his youth, and, thus, to free themselves from these errors, just as Sallust did. It is the mind (*ingenium*, *Cat.* 1.3; 2.1–2; *Iug.* 4.1; *animus*, *Cat.* 1.2, 5; *Iug.* 1.3; 2.3), Sallust says, that controls the body and enables people to do great deeds (*ingeni egregia facinora*, *Iug.* 2.2; cf. Sklenár 1998, 209–211). He believed that one's "condition" (*fortuna*) changes with one's "character" (*mores*; *Cat.* 2.5; but see Batstone 1990, 125, for a more pessimistic reading). The peculiar and startling style of Sallust's work is designed to facilitate precisely such a change of character: it enables readers to see what kind of values have been defining their lives and actions and, thus, to make a conscious effort to return to the *bonae artes* (*Cat.* 2.9; *Iug.* 1.5; cf. *Iug.* 4.5–6; Kraus and Woodman 1997, 10–11).

At the same time, Sallust's diction contributes to defining and representing his own role in the contemporary system, his "self-fashioning." In the preface to the *Bellum Catilinae* (esp. 3.3–4.2) he programmatically defines himself as an "outsider within," somebody with firsthand experience of the political culture who has realized its dangers and shortcomings and has therefore decided to withdraw from politics (*a re publica procul*, 4.1). This "self-styled 'decision' to leave public life" (Kraus and Woodman 1997, 13) finds its expression in Sallust's deliberately "noncontemporary" style (Syme 1964, 260; 271), which defines his privileged position as a "reformed" man with well-founded insight into the system who is therefore uniquely qualified to criticize it and who alone might be able to change it (cf. Syme 1964, 272).

Sallust's style thus simultaneously creates and expresses a stance toward contemporary public life that corresponds to the real-life position of an outside critic with privileged knowledge and unique insight that distinguished Thucydides in his actual exile (Thucydides' critical stance towards his fellow Athenians and the "alienating" (ἠλλοτριῶσθαι, *Pomp.* 3.5) effect of his work is connected explicitly with his exile by Dionysius of Halicarnassus, *Pomp.* 3.15; Wiater 2011, 137–147). Sallust, to be sure, remained in Rome and remained part of Roman society. But his works allowed him (and his readers) to be "exile[s] in [their] own environment" (Syme 1964, 272). Rather than representing a transition "from politics to history" (Syme 1964, chap. 5), then, Sallust's works re-define "politics": they seek to establish historical writing as an alternative kind of political discourse "away from" (*procul*) and against the corrupted discourse of politics and state language. Mastering Thucydides' diction and thought and creating an equivalent in Latin plays a crucial part in this process: this is the great achievement of Sallust's own *ingenium* that, he believed, might just save the *res publica*.

References

Avenarius, W. 1957. "Die griechischen Vorbilder des Sallust." *SO* 33: 48–86.
Baronowski, D. W. 2011. *Polybius and Roman Imperialism*. Bristol: Bristol Classical Press.
Batstone, W. W. 1988. "The Antithesis of Virtue: Sallust's 'Synkrisis' and the Crisis of the Late Republic." *CA* 7: 1–29.
Batstone, W. W. 1990. "Intellectual Conflict and Mimesis in Sallust's *Bellum Catilinae*." In *Conflict, Antithesis, and the Ancient Historian*, edited by J. W. Allison, 112–32. Columbus: Ohio State University Press.
Batstone, W. W. 2010. "Catiline's Speeches in Sallust's *Bellum Catilinae*." In *Form and Function in Roman Oratory*, edited by D. H. Berry and A. Erskine, 227–46. Cambridge: Cambridge University Press.
Derow, P. 1979. "Polybius, Rome, and the East." *JRS* 69: 1–15.
Dolega, S. 1871. *De Sallustio imitatore Thucydidis*. Vratislaviae (https://archive.org/stream/desallustioimitaoodole#page/n3/mode/2up)
Foucault, J.-A. de. 1972. *Recherches sur la langue et le style de Polybe*. Paris: Les Belles Lettres.

Gelzer, M. (1955) 1964. "Die pragmatische Geschichtsschreibung des Polybios." In *Kleine Schriften*, ed. by H. Strasburger and C. Meier, 3.155–56. Wiesbaden: Steiner.
Greenblatt, S. 1980. *Renaissance Self-Fashioning: From More to Shakespeare*. Chicago: University of Chicago Press.
Grethlein, J. 2006. "The Unthucydidean Voice of Sallust." *TAPA* 136: 299–327.
Gummere, R. M., trans. 1925. Seneca: *Epistles 93–124*. Cambridge and London: Harvard University Press.
Heath, M. 1986. "Thucydides 1.23.5–6." *LCM* 11: 104–105.
Hornblower, S. 1991. *A Commentary on Thucydides*. Vol. I, *Books I–III*. Oxford: Clarendon.
Koestermann, E. 1971. *C. Sallustius Crispus, Bellum Iugurthinum: Erläutert und mit einer Einleitung versehen*. Heidelberg: Winter.
Kraus, C. S., and A. J. Woodman. 1997. *Latin Historians*. Greece and Rome: New Surveys in the Classics 27. Oxford: Oxford University Press.
Kroll, W. 1927. "Die Sprache des Sallust." *Glotta* 15: 280–305.
Levene, D. 2000. "Sallust's *Catiline* and Cato the Censor." *CQ* 50: 170–91.
Longley, G. 2012. "Thucydides, Polybius, and Human Nature." In *Imperialism, Cultural Politics, and Polybius*, edited by C. Smith and L. M. Yarrow, 68–84. Oxford: Oxford University Press.
Loraux, N. 1986. "Thucydide a écrit La Guerre du Péloponnèse." *Mètis* 1: 139–61.
Maier, F. K. 2012a. "Learning from History παρὰ δόξαν: A New Approach to Polybius' Manifold View of the Past." *Histos* 6: 144–68.
Maier, F. K. 2012b. *"Überall mit dem Unerwarteten rechnen": Die Kontingenz historischer Prozesse bei Polybios*. Vestigia 65. Munich: Beck.
Miltsios, N. 2013. *The Shaping of Narrative in Polybius*. Trends in Classics Suppl. 23. Berlin: de Gruyter.
Mynott, J., trans. and ed. 2013. *The War of the Peloponnesians and the Athenians*. Cambridge: Cambridge University Press.
Nicols, J. 1999. "Sallust and the Greek Historical Tradition." In *Text and Tradition: Studies in Greek History and Historiography in Honour of Mortimer Chambers*, edited by R. Mellor and L. Tritle, 329–44. Claremont: Regina.
Paton, W. R., trans. 2010. Polybius: *The Histories*. Rev. ed. by F.W. Walbank and C. Habicht. Cambridge and London: Harvard University Press.
Paul, G. M. 1984. *A Historical Commentary on Sallust's* Bellum Jugurthinum. Liverpool: Cairns.
Pédech, P. 1964. *La methode historique de Polybe*. Paris: Les Belles Lettres.
Pelling, C. 2007. "The Greek Historians of Rome." In *A Companion to Greek and Roman Historiography*, edited by J. Marincola, 1.244–58. Malden: Blackwell.
Perrochat, P. 1949. *Les modèles grecs de Salluste*. Paris: Les Belles Lettres.
Pomeroy, A. J. 1986. "Polybius' Death Notices." *Phoenix* 40: 407–23.
Robolski, J. 1881. *Sallustius in conformanda oratione quo iure Thucydides exemplum secutus esse existimetur*. Halis Saxonum (https://archive.org/stream/sallustiusinconfoorobo#page/n5/mode/2up).
Rolfe, J. C., trans. 2013. Sallust: *The War with Catiline; The War with Jugurtha*. Revised by J.T. Ramsey. Cambridge and London: Harvard University Press.
Rood, T. 2012. "Polybius, Thucydides, and the First Punic War." In *Imperialism, Cultural Politics, and Polybius*, edited by C. Smith and L. M. Yarrow, 50–67. Oxford: Oxford University Press.
Russell, D. A., trans and ed. 2001. Quintillian: *The Orator's Education*. Cambridge and London: Harvard University Press.

Samotta, I. 2012. "Herodotus and Thucydides in Roman Republican Historiography." In *Herodotus and Thucydides*, edited by E. Foster and D. Lateiner, 345–78. Oxford: Oxford University Press.

Scanlon, T. F. 1980. *The Influence of Thucydides on Sallust*. Heidelberg: Winter.

Shklovsky, V. (1917) 1998. "Art as Technique." In *Literary Theory: An Anthology*, edited by J. Rivkin and M. Ryan, 17–23. Malden: Blackwell.

Sklenár, R. 1998. "Le République des Signes: Caesar, Cato, and the Language of Sallustian Morality." *TAPA* 128: 205–20.

Smith, C., and L. M. Yarrow, eds. 2012. *Imperialism, Cultural Politics, and Polybius*. Oxford: Oxford University Press.

Syme, R. 1964. *Sallust*. Berkeley: University of California Press.

Walbank, F. W. 1957. *A Historical Commentary on Polybius* 1. Oxford: Clarendon.

Walbank, F. W. 1972. *Polybius*. Berkeley: University of California Press.

Warner, Rex, trans. 1972. *History of the Peloponnesian War*. With an introduction and notes by M. I. Finley. Revised, with a new introduction and appendices. Harmondsworth: Penguin.

Wiater, N. 2011. *The Ideology of Classicism. Language, History, and Identity in Dionysius of Halicarnassus*. Berlin: de Gruyter.

Wiater, N. 2014. "Polybius on Speeches in Timaeus: Syntax and Structure in *Histories* 12.25a." *CQ* 64: 121–35.

Wiater, N. 2016. "The Aesthetics of Truth: Narrative and Historical Understanding in Polybius' *Histories*." In *Truth and History in the Ancient World: Pluralising the Past*, edited by L. Hau and I. Ruffell. London: Routledge.

Ziegler, K. 1952. "Polybios (1)." *RE* 21.2: 1440–578.

CHAPTER 39

WRITING WITH POSTERITY IN MIND

Thucydides and Tacitus on Secession

CYNTHIA DAMON

INTRODUCTION: A PROPOSITION AND A PROBLEM

I begin with a proposition and a problem. Here's the proposition. Seen from a distance Thucydides and Tacitus have much in common: they are both uncomfortable authors whose unsparing commitment to revealing the truth results in grim depictions of the amoral deployment of political power—power for the sake of power—in idiosyncratic and difficult idioms.[1] Kurt Raaflaub juxtaposes the two as prime examples of historians with a "desire to unmask ideology," while Ronald Martin's alignment highlights the pair's intellectual and stylistic mastery, giving Thucydides a small edge in the former category and Tacitus a clear victory in the latter: Martin speaks of Tacitus' exercise of "a penetration that rivals Thucydides' . . . and a pungency unequalled by any writer, Greek or Roman."[2] One can even draw content-based parallels between Thucydides' *History* and Tacitus' surviving historical works: the former treats the self-inflicted defeat of Athens and, more generally, the derogation of the Greek world from its Persian War past, the latter treats the self-inflicted collapse of the Julio-Claudian dynasty and, more generally, the derogation of Rome from its Republican past. The two historians also share a wide-ranging interest in the nature of empire and a pronounced humorlessness, except in "jokes" of the darkest variety. Furthermore, in recent years Thucydides has come to

---

[1] This paper benefited materially from comments by members of the audience on the occasions of its presentation at Columbia, Georgetown, Indiana, Toronto, and UVA.
[2] Raaflaub (2010, 194); Martin (1981, 213).

seem more and more like Tacitus: intense, rhetorically manipulative, adept in the use of tragic structures, emotionally powerful, even "postmodern."[3]

But here's the problem. Tacitus never announces a program of Thucydides-imitation, whether pertaining to methodology, like Josephus, or theme, like Sallust.[4] Nor do ancient commentators point to any resemblance between Tacitus and his Greek predecessor, as they do for Sallust and even Cato.[5] A further obstacle to assessing Tacitus' debt to Thucydides is the uncertainty about the extent to which Sallust is an intermediary, an uncertainty that the loss of (most of) Sallust's *Histories* makes particularly intractable.[6] There are of course motifs or moments in Tacitus' works for which a Thucydidean original has been suggested, but most of these are better understood as historiographical topoi and type-scenes.[7] However, the broad similarities outlined above involve important aspects of the historiographical achievement of both authors, so it is worth trying to understand their relationship.

Thucydides of course invites the future to align its experiences with those he describes, both by predicting the recurrence of historical processes (1.22.4, 3.82.2) and by suppressing or neutralizing "variables" when depicting those processes; his bedrock is *to anthrōpinon*, human nature. Apropos of the suffering caused by stasis in Corcyra, for example, he says that "it happened then and will for ever continue to happen, as long as human nature remains the same, with more or less severity and taking different forms as dictated by each new permutation of circumstances" (3.82.2). Tacitus, too, writes with the expectation that his readers will find elements of his narrative of the past in their present. Justus Lipsius was one reader who did precisely that, particularly in Tacitus' treatment of autocratic power and resistance thereto.

> He presents kings and monarchs to you, in a word, the theater of our life today. I see in one place a ruler attacking the laws and constitution, and in another subjects rebelling against the ruler. I find the ways and means of destroying liberty; I find ill-fated efforts to recover lost liberty . . . Tacitus, good God! is a great and useful writer.[8]

---

[3] See, e.g., in addition to the relevant chapters in the present volume, Connor (1977) for an overview and Walker (1993) for some specifics.

[4] Jos. *BJ* 1.1 ≈ Thuc. 1.1.1; *BJ* 1.2, 7–8, 30 ≈ Thuc. 1.22.2–4, on which see recently Price (2010). Sall. *Cat.* 52.11 ≈ Thuc. 3.82.4, *Cat.* 38.3 ≈ Thuc. 3.82.8 (on which see Wiater, chapter 38 in this volume). Early discussions of the topic, those of Kornemann (1904) and Strebel (1935, 33), allow Thucydides only an indirect influence on Tacitus. Nicolai (1995, 12) presumably includes Tacitus when he dismisses all ancient emulation of Thucydides (but see also the more cautious assessment in Gowing 2009, 17). Tacitus is not mentioned in recent surveys of the Roman reception of Thucydides (Canfora, 2006; Dziuba 2008). There is a brief discussion of the relationship in O'Gorman (2000, 14–22).

[5] E.g., for Sallust, Vell. 2.36.2, Sen. *Contr.* 9.1.13–14; for Cato, Plu. *Cat.mai.* 2.4. For a recent study of traces of Thucydidean influence in early Roman historiography, see Samotta (2012).

[6] For a possible Sallustian intermediary between the secession episodes considered in the present paper see note 39 below.

[7] E.g., Tac. *H.* 5.23.3 ≈ Thuc. 2.13.1 ≈ Liv. 2.39.5, 22.23.4. Strebel 1935, 33 n. 124 gives further examples. For Roman awareness of Thucydides as the originator of prominent features of contemporary historiography, see, for example, Sen. *Suas.* 6.21.

[8] Justus Lipsius, from the preface to his 1581 commentary on the *Annals*. Quoted and translated in Morford (1993, 138).

However, any alignment between the universalizing Thucydides and the oh-so-Roman Tacitus is not going to be perfect.[9] A pair of episodes in which the two historians treat one of history's "repeating events"—secession from an imperial power—offers a promising terrain in which to explore Tacitus' debt to Thucydides. Due attention will be given to "each new permutation of circumstances," the important proviso that Thucydides attaches to his prediction about recurrence (3.82.2).

On Secession: The Mytilenean and Batavian Revolts

It is precisely in connection with secession that Thucydides and Tacitus are paired by two giants of the American Revolution in an exchange of letters from 1812, when Thomas Jefferson and John Adams were looking back with some satisfaction on the colonies' secession from Britain and looking forward with some trepidation for the security of the new nation. Jefferson expresses his detachment from current affairs by saying that he has given up reading newspapers and turned instead to "Thucydides & Tacitus ... Newton & Euclid." Adams' reply suggests that reading the first two, at least, doesn't get one very far from the fray:

> I have read Thucidides and Tacitus, So often and at Such distant Periods of my life, that elegant, profound and enchanting as is their style, I am weary of them. When I read them I Seem to be only reading the History of my own Times and my own Life.[10]

The colonial secession in which Jefferson and Adams played such leading roles turned out very differently from the Mytilenean revolt against the Athenian empire in 428–27 BCE, or the Batavian revolt from the Roman empire in 69–70 CE, but the ancient secessions as described by Thucydides and Tacitus have many similarities of form and content.

In each author the defection of a privileged and island-dwelling ally at a moment of uncharacteristic weakness on the part of the imperial power is the subject of a substantial narrative that contributes to a general analysis of how empires work.[11] Each author

---

[9] See, for example, O'Gorman (2000, 19). For formal differences see Levene (2009a, 213; 2009b, 227).

[10] Jefferson's letter is dated 12 January 1812, Adams' reply 3 February 1812. Quoted from the texts published at http://founders.archives.gov (accessed 5 August 2014). I am grateful to Tim Joseph for the reference.

[11] Privileged status for Mytilene: Thuc. 3.10.5, 3.36.2, 3.39.2, 5; for the Batavi: Tac. H. 4.12.3, 4.17.2, 5.25.2. Tacitus comments on the rarity of this kind of privileged alliance with a stronger power (H. 4.12.3 *rarum in societate validiorum*). Mytilene as an island: Thuc. 3.13.5, 3.39.2; the Batavians' island homeland: Tac. H. 4.12.3, 4.15.1, 5.19.1. Weakness of Athens: Thuc. 3.9.3, 3.13.3, 3.39.2; weakness and division of Rome: Tac. H. 4.13.1, 4.14.4, 4.15.3, 4.17.5, 4.55.4. On the diagnostic value of the Batavian revolt, Timpe (2005, 175–87, especially 178). For an analysis that integrates the (speeches of) the Batavian revolt into the *Histories*' political themes, see Keitel (1993).

emphasizes the scope and complexity of the defection he describes by devoting to it a series of episodes, four in the case of Mytilene, at least four for the Batavian revolt, and numerous substantial speeches, as follows. In Thucydides' first panel, Mytilene revolts and Athens declares war on her ally after the failure of a preemptive strike and negotiations (3.2–6). In the second, the Peloponnesian League is persuaded to support Mytilene (3.8–18; this panel includes a speech by the Mytileneans). In the third, Mytilene capitulates after Peloponnesian assistance proves dilatory and the demos refuses to fight for the city (3.25–33, including an ineffective speech to the Peloponnesian commander by "a man from Elis," Teutiaplus). In the fourth panel, the punishment of Mytilene is debated in the Athenian Assembly and carried out with moderation (3.35–50, with speeches by Cleon and Diodotus).

In the first panel of Tacitus' narrative, the Batavian cohort commander Civilis initiates a revolt by tribes subject to Rome. They are encouraged by a Roman faction and tribes from free Germany. Civilis then lays siege to a Roman fortress after the Roman response proves dilatory and divided (4.12–37, with two speeches by Civilis). In the second panel, the widening rebellion spawns a Gallic empire, Roman generals are murdered, and Roman legions and cities defect to the rebels (4.54–67, with an ineffective speech by a Roman commander and a debate over the fate of Cologne). In the third panel, Rome's response begins in earnest (4.68.5–4.79, including two speeches by the new Roman commander, Cerealis). In the fourth, after inconclusive fighting, the inducements offered by Cerealis tempt Civilis' backers to abandon the revolt (5.14–26, with a fragment of a speech by Civilis). And at this point the narrative of the Batavian revolt breaks off, not quite complete.

Tacitus' decision to use a discontinuous format is particularly striking, since this feature of Thucydides' work was singled out for criticism by the Augustan-era literary critic Dionysius of Halicarnassus (*Thuc.* 9):

> In the third book (for I shall limit myself to this, needing no other) the author starts to write about the Mytilenaeans, but before completing the narrative passes on to Lacedaemonian affairs. Yet, without bringing these to a head, he mentions the siege of Plataea. Leaving this also unfinished, he speaks of the Mytilenaean war.... The whole book has been chopped up into small bits and has lost the continuity of the narrative.... It is plain, then, that the Thucydidean canon is not suited to history. (Pritchett 1975 translation)

Thus Dionysius. But Tacitus begs to differ, if one is to judge by the chopped-up structure of his own secession narrative, where the panels on the Batavian revolt are interleaved among narratives of events at Rome and elsewhere in the empire within the framework of the years 69–70 CE.[12]

---

[12] Likewise Rood (1998, 111–21). For discussion of the episodic format of Tacitus' narrative of the Batavian revolt, but without reference to Thucydides (or Dionysius), see Timpe (2005, especially 156–64), and, apropos of the speeches, Keitel (1993).

Besides structure, the two episodes we are considering also share an interest in the abuse of power by the dominant party in an alliance, and they pay concomitant attention to the issue of equality among allies, which the Mytileneans idealistically posit as a defining feature of successful alliances and the Roman general Cerealis claims—not altogether persuasively, but with surprising insistence—as a feature of Rome's alliances.[13] Furthermore, the status divide between the pro-Athenian (or pro-capitulation) populace at Mytilene and the pro-resistance elite is reflected in that between the pro-Vitellius (or pro-capitulation) legionaries and pro-resistance (or at least pro-Vespasian) commanders, although in Tacitus' narrative the situation is complicated by the fact that there are two empires, the Roman and the Gallic, competing for the loyalties of Roman allies and soldiers.[14] There are also similarities in more circumstantial details, such as the fact that the beginnings of each secession were aided by willful neglect or indifference on the part of the imperial power,[15] or the show of self-reliance by those imperial powers when threatened: Athenians crew their own triremes (Thuc. 3.16.1) and Roman legions fight their own battles after dismissing Gallic auxiliaries (Tac. *H*. 4.71.2).[16]

If we look beyond these broad and significant similarities of form and content to some particularly close alignments of language and incident, the differences between the two narratives come into clearer focus, which suggests that Tacitus wanted his reader to see "new permutations of circumstances" as well as the patterns identified by Thucydides.

Closest of all, perhaps, is the expression *duplex . . . seditio* at *Histories* 4.35.4, which seems to recall the Mytilenean "double secession" (Thuc. 3.13.1 διπλῆν ἀπόστασιν). Both expressions are so unusual that their authors gloss them. For the Mytileneans, the doubleness is a consequence of what the Athenian empire has become since the Persian War, namely, an oppressor of other Greek states. They consider that their secession will be a secession "from the Greek alliance, to join in their liberation rather than the Athenians' oppression of them, and [a secession] from the Athenians, to forestall their future attempts to destroy us."[17] As the gloss and the context make clear, to secede from one alliance is to join another, in this case the coalition of Athens' enemies, the Peloponnesian League. The Tacitean expression seems simpler, at first glance anyway. His "twofold sedition" arises in an embattled legionary camp in Germany when disaffected troops resist a general's handling of their difficult predicament in two different ways: some tell the general not to leave to get reinforcements, others refuse to stay (4.35.4). One might even dismiss this as phrase making for the sake of a closural antithesis, since the next sentence

---

[13] Abuses of power by Athens: Thuc. 3.10.4, 3.37.2, 3.39.2, 3.40.4, 3.46.5; by Rome: Tac. *H*. 4.14.1–2, 4.32.2. Equality among allies: Thuc. 3.9.2, 3.10.4–5, 3.11.1, 3.12.3, 3.45.6; Tac. *H*. 4.74.1.

[14] Faction along status lines: Thuc. 3.27.3, 3.39.6, 3.47.2–4; Tac. *H*. 4.22.2, 4.24.3, 4.31.2, 4.37.2, especially 4.27.3 *haud dubie gregarius miles Vitellio fidus*, and 4.13.3, 4.19. 3, 4.36.2, 4.37.2, 4.56.1, especially 4.27.3 *splendidissimus quisque in Vespasianum proni*.

[15] Neglect and indifference: Thuc. 3.3.1; Tac. *H*. 4.18.1, 4.22.1.

[16] Neither Athens nor Rome actually forgoes the support of its allies: Thuc. 3.5.1, 3.6.1, 3.19.1; Tac. *H*. 4.79.4 (see also note 20 below).

[17] Here and elsewhere I quote Hammond's translation (2009) of Thucydides, unless otherwise indicated.

begins with "meanwhile," signaling a change of venue (4.36.1 *Interim*).[18] Furthermore, if we are meant to align these two defections, it is the Batavians, not the disaffected Roman legions, that are the obvious counterpart to Thucydides' Mytileneans. But this is where the possibility of a "new permutation" becomes relevant: these soldiers will themselves defect from Rome within a few weeks; indeed, they will declare loyalty to the Gallic empire (4.59.2–3; 4.60.2; 4.70.3). Why? Precisely because of how Rome has changed since the civil war began. These troops had put Vitellius on the throne, and they now, post-Vitellius, prefer a foreign ruler to the current incumbent in Rome, Vespasian (*H.* 4.54.1). So their sedition *is* twofold in the Thucydidean sense, at least in prospect: their insubordination toward a single Roman general will become a defection from Rome herself and involve participation in an alliance of Rome's former subjects that aims "to join in their liberation rather than [Rome's] oppression of them."[19]

This adaptation of Thucydidean language to characterize the Batavian-inspired revolt seems justified by the fact that the prehistory, too, of the revolt aligns neatly with that of Mytilene. Just as the Mytileneans cooperated with Athens in the suppression of the revolt at Samos in 440 BCE (Thuc. 1.116.2, 1.117.2), so Rome deployed Gallic tribes to suppress a revolt in Gaul in 68, a revolt that indirectly precipitated Nero's fall that same year. As the Batavian commander Civilis boasted in one of his exhortations, Rome was dependent on provincial manpower, including Batavian manpower: "to those who consider the matter in a true light," he says, "Gaul succumbed to her own strength."[20] In fact the Batavian revolt goes further toward realizing the aims expressed by the Mytileneans than the Mytileneans did, since the latter were defeated by Athens almost immediately.

Another element present in both narratives is the idea of avenging defection by wholesale destruction. In Thucydides the target is of course Mytilene, whose destruction is the subject of an extended debate in the Athenian Assembly (3.35–50). The arguments both for and against speak to the need to maintain the empire. Severity, it is argued on the one side, will be a deterrent to future defections. Moderate punishment, says the other, will be an investment in their expedient resolution. The vote(s) are close, but moderation wins and Mytilene is punished selectively, not wholesale (Thuc. 3.46.4 μετρίως κολάζοντες): the ringleaders are executed, the city walls are demolished, and the city's ships are confiscated (3.50).

In the narrative of the Batavian revolt we have several "new permutations" relevant to this exemplary Thucydidean incident. First, it is the nascent Gallic empire, not Rome,

---

[18] Thucydides' phrase, too, is part of what has been called a "somewhat forced antithesis" (Hornblower 1996 ad loc.), but also "significantly complex" (Macleod 1978, 66–67).

[19] The doubleness itself doubled and given a negative spin by the general in question, Dillius Vocula (4.58.5 *transfugae e transfugis et proditoribus e proditoribus*). On *libertas* as the aim of the Batavian revolt see, for example, Tac. *H.* 4.17.1, 5, 4.25.3, 4.32.3, 4.54.3, 4.55.4, 4.65.1, 4.67.2, 4.78.1, 5.25.2.

[20] Tac. *H.* 4.17.3 *provinciarum sanguine provincias vinci. . . . Batavo equite protritos Aeduos Arvernosque . . . vereque reputantibus Galliam suismet viribus concidisse*. Cf. Civilis' argument that the Belgae provide Rome's *robor* (*H.* 4.76.1), and the long list of passages where Rome deploys or recruits provincial troops during this rebellion: 4.18.1 (Ubii, Treveri, Batavi), 4.20.2 (Belgae), 4.24.1 (*per Gallias*), 4.25.2 (*per Gallias, Britanniamque et Hispanias*), 4.33.2–2 (Nervii, Vascones), etc.

that debates avenging defection. The leaders of the revolt discuss eliminating the seditious legions completely, but settle on a policy of executing the officers (*H.* 4.56.1; cf. 4.59.1–3, 4.61.2, 4.70.5). Here again the argument for moderation wins on grounds of expediency, "lest by removing hope of a pardon they arouse obstinacy" (*H.* 4.56.1 *vicit ratio parcendi, ne sublata spe veniae pertinaciam accenderent*). The reference to *pertinacia* in particular evokes Diodotus' argument that defectors "will hold out to the very last," if they know that there is no hope for clemency (3.46.2 παρατενεῖσθαι ἐς τοὐσχατον). As was the case with the double sedition, however, the alignment is imperfect, since the legions defected from Rome, not from the Gallic empire. But the language may cause us to see the new empire against a Thucydidean backdrop.[21]

There is a comparable cue a little later in the passage, when representatives of a Gallic tribe begin a speech about their defection from Rome with an echo of the Mytilenean representatives at Olympia. The Mytileneans open with "our secession ... has proceeded faster than we would wish, and left us unprepared" (Thuc. 3.13.2; cf. 3.2.1). The Gallic representatives begin, "We have seized our first opportunity of freedom with more haste than prudence" (*H.* 4.65.1 *quae prima libertatis facultas data est avidius quam cautius sumpsimus*). The defection of this tribe is in fact quite unlike that of the Mytileneans, in that it is coerced and insincere; they are biding their time rather than pressing for a preemptive strike like the Mytileneans.[22] And yet Tacitus has already hinted that this tribe *has* made a preemptive strike in a different and more significant sort of defection.

The tribe in question is the Ubii, a Romanized German tribe that had moved to the "Roman" side of the Rhine a hundred years earlier. This defection too needed avenging, since the Gallic empire, like the (early stages of the) Athenian empire, boasted a unifying ethnic ideology (*H.* 4.64), something that the Roman empire conspicuously lacked.[23] The Ubii lived in a city with walls and Roman priesthoods and merchants and taxes and fleets, a city, moreover, that was the birthplace and namesake of a Roman emperor's mother. The Ubii/Agrippinenses were an irritating anomaly, "in that a people of Germanic origin was called 'the citizen body of Agrippa's town' after disowning their fatherland for a name belonging to the Romans" (*H.* 4.28.1 *quod gens Germanicae originis eiurata patria Romanorum <in> nomen Agrippinenses vocarentur*). In the very brief "Ubian debate" at 4.63 the leaders of the nascent Gallic empire consider eradicating this symbol of Roman imperialism. Once again the prudential argument wins: "a reputation for clemency," it is argued, "[is] useful for those initiating a new empire" (*H.* 4.63.1 *novum imperium inchoantibus utilis clementiae fama*). They decide instead to invite the Ubii to join the alliance of Rome's opponents and to prove their loyalty to that alliance by themselves destroying the Roman features of their city: walls, Roman inhabitants,

---

[21] Also, later in the episode, to assess the old (Roman) empire, whose representatives are avid for the destruction of Trier, the capital of the defecting Treveri; the moderate alternative wins again (Tac. *H.* 4.72.1–2).

[22] For the pro-Roman position of the Ubii see, for example, Tac. *H.* 4.18.1, 4.28.2, 4.55.3.

[23] For another Gallic echo of the early days of the Athenian empire, see Tac. *H.* 4.66.2, where the Batavian leader Civilis denies having imperialistic ambitions. Tacitus, of course, believed otherwise (4.17.6).

private property, luxurious habits (4.64.2–3).[24] The "new permutation of circumstances" plays out differently when the Ubii temporize successfully (4.65) until an opportunity arises to declare their loyalty to Rome by murdering their German garrison individually and in gruesome fashion *en masse* (4.79.1–2). Speaking broadly one might say that this episode of the revolt combines the issue and arguments of the Mytilenean debate, the loyalty test at Plataea, and the atrocities of Corcyrean stasis.

Summing up so far, one can say that Thucydides established analytical categories and benchmarks that constitute a useful shorthand for Tacitus' narrative and that can be combined with suggestive results. In a narrative that evokes Thucydides' exemplary treatment of the defection of one element of Athens' empire, Tacitus gives us three defections from two imperial systems. Furthermore, the rise and fall of the Gallic empire replays over the course of a few months the transformation of an idealistic alliance into a profitable conglomerate that took fifty years in the Greek world.[25] At fast-forward speed the process looks almost farcical, of course, and there are no compensatory cultural achievements. However, despite its chaotic nature, the Batavian revolt was more efficacious than that of Mytilene: the Batavians recruited to their cause not only foreign allies from free Germany but also a number of tribes from within Rome's empire and, as was already mentioned, Rome's own disaffected legions. The help that Mytilene received from the Peloponnesian League, by contrast, was modest at best (the dispatch of a military expert, Salaethus, 3.25.1) and a travesty at worst (an invasion that stopped at the Isthmus, 3.15–16, and the chaotic mission of Alcidas, 3.29–33), and the revolt itself caused no immediate cracks in the Athenian empire.

Furthermore, the backdrop of the Mytilenean revolt allows Tacitus to explore systemic as well as outcome differences between imperial Rome and Athens. The comparison between the external power to which the Mytileneans appealed, the Peloponnesian League, and the tribes of free Germany, for example, is instructive.

In Book 3 of the *Histories*, before the secession narrative proper begins, Tacitus had previewed the danger that turbulence in Germany represented for Rome: "Germany was disturbed," he reported, "and ... the Roman state nearly shattered" (*H.* 3.46.1 *turbata ... Germania, et ... prope adflicta Romana res*). But despite this attention-getting preview, and despite the startling betrayal of Rome by her own legionaries, as the story plays out it becomes clear that the free Germans, a loose coalition of tribes with a reclusive female priestess at their head, are not an adequate makeweight for Rome.[26] First, their motives for

---

[24] The threat of provincial reprisals against Romans and Romanness naturally evokes the attack ordered by Mithridates in the province of Asia in 88 BCE (see, e.g., Appian, *Mith.* 3.22). But an allusion to the Republican-era contest between Rome and a foreign king does not preclude an allusion to Thucydidean scenarios, which have different points of contact with the Tacitean narrative.

[25] Civilis' disaffection goes back at least to his arrest in 68 CE, but the Gallic defection does not get under way until after Vitellius' death in December 69. It is all but over by the fall of 70. For the chronology and the distribution of events in *H.* 4–5 see Timpe (2005, 166–72).

[26] The revolt involves more than a dozen German tribes. For Veleda see Tac. *H.* 4.61.2, 4.65.3–4, 5.24.1, 5.25.2, and more generally *Germ.* 45.6 on female rulers. For a historical perspective on these factors see Brunt 1960, 504 with n. 1. And for Tacitus' attribution of "Germanness" to tribes resident in the Gallic provinces see Timpe (2005, 177).

supporting Civilis are short sighted: in essence, booty or bribes. Second, they don't have any tenacity in the face of setbacks or any organization adequate to a sustained campaign. And finally, they are uncontrollable: the Germans, a Gallic leader complains, "do not submit to orders or governance but conduct affairs as they please" (4.76.2 *Germanos . . . non iuberi non regi sed cuncta ex libidine agere*).[27] In the case of the Mytilenean revolt one feels that, even before the hard-fought debate on the fate of the defeated, the situation was nicely balanced. If Sparta's allies had joined them at the Isthmus so that the invasion could proceed (3.15–16), or if the Athenians had been less convincing in their show of strength (3.16), or if an unnamed individual had not succeeded in giving the Mytileneans timely warning of the arrival of the Athenian fleet (3.3.5), things might have turned out differently. In the Roman context, however, as Tacitus' Batavians put it, "one people cannot ward off a servitude that encompasses the whole world" (5.25.1 *nec posse ab una natione totius orbis servitium depelli*).[28]

The real causes of Civilis' success were Roman factionalism and the tribes of Roman Gaul.[29] His movement was initially supported by the Flavians in order to undermine the Vitellians, and for a long time he proclaimed himself a supporter of the Flavian cause.[30] The extent of these civil war divisions can be gauged from the attitude of the legions of Germany, former Vitellians, which preferred a foreign master to a Flavian one (4.54.1) and murdered a legionary legate who tried to keep them loyal to Vespasian's Rome (4.58, 4.59.1). And news of the most dramatic result of Rome's internecine conflict, the burning of the Capitoline temple, sets a fire, so to speak, under her Gallic subjects, who come to believe that the empire's end is at hand, a notion embroidered by Druids who foretell that the demolition left undone by their ancestors in the fourth century BCE will soon be complete, and that mastery over human affairs will move to their side of the Alps (4.54, especially *ut finem imperio adesse crederent*).

The defection of these Gallic tribes dominates the second panel of Tacitus' narrative, in which the "contagion" that Thucydides' Cleon had warned about shows its power when the Gallic leaders join their forces to those of Civilis and his German allies (4.57.1 *cum ducibus Germanorum pacta firmavere* [sc. *Tutor et Classicus*]).[31] In the first panel the defections had been piecemeal, with individual army units deserting or failing their

---

[27] Motives: Tac. *H*. 4.21.2, 4.23.3, 4.37.3; 4.76.2, 4.78.1. Lack of tenacity: 4.37.3, 5.24–25; lack of organization: 4.37.3, 4.76.1. Uncontrollable: 4.60.2–3, 4.63.2–63, esp. 4.76.2 *Germanos . . . non iuberi non regi sed cuncta ex libidine agere*.

[28] Further comments on the magnitude of Rome by comparison with the scale of the defection can be found at Tac. *H*. 4.21.1–2 and 4.25.1.

[29] At *H*. 3.46.1 Tacitus lists four factors as responsible for Rome's danger in this episode: *turbata per eosdem dies Germania, et socordia ducum, seditione legionum, externa vi, perfidia sociali prope adflicta Romana res*. I do not discuss here the first, the slackness of her generals, which is everywhere on display in this episode (see, e.g., 4.20.1–2, 4.25.2, 4.35.3–4, 4.36.2).

[30] Civilis and the Flavian cause: Tac. *H*. 4.13.2–3. 4.14.4, 4.17.4, 4.21.1, 4.32.1, especially 5.26.3.

[31] For Cleon's prognostications see Thuc. 3.37.2 "your empire is a tyranny, exercised over unwilling subjects who will conspire against you," 3.39.7 "Consider now the effect on our other allies. . . . do you not think that all will revolt on the slightest pretext?", 3.40.7 "set a clear example to the rest of the allies that the penalty for revolt will be death. When that is understood, you will be less distracted . . . by the need to fight your own allies." An echo of Cleon's argument appears at Tac. *H*. 4.57.2, where a Roman commander

Roman commanders, but in this panel whole tribes defect.[32] The Treveri and Lingones, who had been part of the Roman empire since the time of Julius Caesar, led the conspiracy. Their plan was to block the Alpine passes and set up a Gallic empire independent of Rome (4.55.4). The combined forces of Batavians, Germans, and Gauls achieve the capitulation of one of the seats of Roman administration in Gaul, Cologne, and of virtually the entire Roman garrison.[33] At the high water of success one of the Gallic leaders, a Lingonian named Julius Sabinus, "toppled all of the monuments of the alliance with Rome and—Tacitus enjoys this irony—ordered men to address him as Caesar" (4.67.1 *Julius Sabinus proiectis foederis Romani monumentis Caesarem se salutari iubet*).[34] However, the tide begins to turn against the defectors when the Sequani, a tribe whose involvement with Rome figures prominently in the first book of Caesar's *Gallic War*, remain loyal to Rome (4.67.2; cf. 4.73.2). Another tribe with a long pro-Roman track record, the Remi, then takes the lead in a debate by an assembly of representatives of Gaul on the question of whether they want freedom or peace (4.67.2).[35] And then, after a quick narrative jaunt to Rome (4.68.1–4), it's back to business as usual for the Roman empire in the episode's third and fourth panels (see, e.g., 4.68.5, 4.69.1). As I mentioned earlier, the Batavian revolt is not quite over when the *Histories* fall silent, owing to the loss of everything after 5.26.3, but the end appears to be in sight thanks to the restoration of unity under the Flavians, an event that allows them to mobilize Rome's military might more effectively and to encourage the Gauls' aforementioned desire for peace.[36]

The Flavian loyalist Josephus presents the conflict between Rome and Civilis as a foreign war (*BJ* 7.75–88), but Tacitus is more interested in the war's mixed quality: it is both foreign and civil (*H.* 4.12.1, 4.16.2, 4.22.2; cf. 2.69.1, 3.46.2).[37] Even more fundamental to his analysis is its capacity to serve as a diagnostic tool for the health of the Roman empire. Despite the fact that alternatives to Rome are insignificant, that there is no Sparta for Civilis, defection is possible when Rome herself is split.[38] If the Batavian revolt was more successful than that of Mytilene, one must conclude that the civil wars consequent on

---

maintains that the desertion of the Treveri and Lingones resulted from the preferential treatment they had received from the Romans (cf. Cleon at Thuc. 3.39.5 "From the first we should never have treated the Mytileneans with greater regard than the others, and then we would not have seen this degree of presumption.")

[32] Individual unit defections: Tac. *H.* 4.16.2–3, 4.18.3, 4.19.1, 4.20.2–3, 4.25.3, 4.33.2.; defecting tribes: 4.55, 4.66.1, 4.66.2–3.

[33] Admittedly, a severely depleted garrison (Tac. *H.* 1.61.2, 4.15.3; cf. 4.14.4, 4.20.2, 4.22.3).

[34] Sabinus was given to boasting that Julius Caesar had an affair with his great-grandmother (Tac. *H.* 4.55.2). At 4.59.2 another Gallic leader, Julius Classicus, adopts other Roman insignia of power.

[35] "Their friendship with Rome was notorious and of long standing. It is surprising that they have not hitherto been mentioned" (Chilver and Townend, 1985, *ad* 4.67.2).

[36] Restoration of unity at Rome: Tac. *H.* 4.44.1, 4.45.1, 4.46.3, 4.53 (cf. also 4.72.2 *posito civium bello ad externa modestiores*); military resources: 4.68.4–5; Gauls' desire for peace: 4.69.1.

[37] On Josephus' approach see Brunt 1960, 504. The question of how the war was framed by Pliny the Elder, whose *Bella Germaniae* is the source presumed to underlie Tacitus' account, is much debated. For an overview see Hose (1998).

[38] Factions: Tac. *H.* 4.17.5, 4.54.3.

the collapse of the Julio-Claudian dynasty did more damage to the Roman empire than invasion and plague and military expenditure did to the Athenian.

In his narrative of the Batavian revolt Tacitus is not emulating Thucydides, exactly, but rather using his predecessor's account and analysis as a source of informative and sometimes ironic parallels. As the alignments prompted by the various verbal and situational cues show, Tacitus enriches the historical record on questions of self-determination and empire by setting the "new permutations of circumstances" in 69–70 CE against the backdrop of the Greek past.[39] And the resulting confection, as Lipsius urges, can itself be used as a backdrop in "the theater of our life today." For, as John Adams wearily reflects, "When I read [Thucydides and Tacitus] I Seem to be only reading the History of my own Times and my own Life."

κτῆμα ... ἐς αἰεί VERSUS *CURA POSTERITATIS*

Both Thucydides and Tacitus adopt the policy that would later be formulated by Lucian as the key to successful historiography, namely, writing with posterity in mind (Luc. *Hist.Conscr.* 41).[40] But their interpretations of what it means to write "with posterity in mind" are quite different. More precisely, they envisage "posterity" differently.

Thucydides' "possession for all time" is offered to "all those who will want to see a clear picture of what happened" (1.22.4 ὅσοι δὲ βουλήσονται τῶν τε γενομένων τὸ σαφὲς σκοπεῖν). That is, he writes for a self-selecting intellectual posterity; ὅσοι and σκοπεῖν are both important.[41] As is the fact that he defers to their judgment: if they judge his work useful, that is enough for him (1.22.4).

When Tacitus speaks of posterity, however, as he often does, he uses a term with a much higher affective content, *posteri*, "those who come after."[42] After what? "After us." Thus at one of the few spots where the historian speaks positively about his contemporaries, he says "Our age too has produced much merit, many attainments worthy of imitation by posterity (*posteris*). Long may this honorable competition with our ancestors (*maiores*) persist!" (*Ann.* 3.55.5). The link from ancestors to posterity

---

[39] An earlier "new permutation" may have appeared in Sallust's apparently substantial narrative, in the scantily preserved *Histories*, of the secession of Sertorius and the Spanish provinces in 78–72 BCE; Sertorius is mentioned at *H.* 4.13.2. The topic deserves further study, but for the moment I see no reason to assume that the Sallustian account would have occluded that of Thucydides.

[40] On Thucydides in particular see Greenwood (2006, chap. 6).

[41] As Hornblower (1991 notes ad loc.), "Thucydides' aim is purely intellectual." For an exploration of how Thucydides' program might pertain to future historians see Kallet (2006). Rood (2006, 239) stresses the self-selecting readership. Raaflaub sees the identification of recurrent patterns as a key component of the historian's legacy, and names Tacitus as "Thucydides' closest successor" in this endeavor (2013, especially 21n65).

[42] See, for example, Tac. *Ag.* 1.1 *clarorum virorum facta moresque posteris tradere*; *H.* 2.50.5 *fama apud posteros*, 4.17.1 *in posterum usui*; *Ann.* 1.32.2 *memoria apud posteros*, 3.55.5 *imitanda posteris*.

passes through the present, and both historical actors and historians bear it in mind when making choices, or at least they should do.[43] For example, historians who write biased narratives are faulted by Tacitus for their lack of *cura posteritatis*: "Truth," he says in his assessment of post-Actium historiography, "was crippled in many ways, first by ignorance of public affairs (now in somebody else's control), eventually by the passion for flattery or on the other hand by hatred of the rulers; and among hostile or subservient authors no one had any concern for posterity" (*H.* 1.1.1). The *posteri* in Tacitus' works are expected to pass judgment on the past itself, as well as on historians. Tacitus' Otho, for example, chooses suicide over prolonging a civil war, saying "Let this be the basis of posterity's judgment of Otho" (*H.* 2.47.2 *hinc Othonem posteritas aestimet*). And such judgments even become the stuff of history: Tacitus' own last word on Otho is that "the reputation he earned with posterity (*apud posteros*) contained as much good as bad" (*H.* 2.50.1).[44] What's more, posterity's judgment, as Tacitus frames it, pays a debt imposed by the past: "everyone receives due honor from posterity" (*Ann.* 4.35.3 *suum cuique decus posteritas rependit*). The self-selecting readers into whose hands Tacitus' historical works come, works that he calls his *cura* (*Ann.* 4.11.3) will, he expects, share his definition of terms such as "good," "bad," and "honor." It is hard to see any such common moral ground in Thucydides, at least in anything more specific than the "human decency" (τὸ εὔηθες, 3.83.1; cf. ὠμόν τὸ βούλευμα, 3.36.4) that he uses as a standard against which to measure the inhuman brutality contemplated against the Mytileneans and exercised against fellow citizens in Corcyra.

However, historical circumstances may have exaggerated the differences due to authorial disposition and historiographical program. When Thucydides was writing with posterity in mind, at least in the final stages of his work, the Athenian empire had collapsed. Another empire, no doubt, would arise in the course of human events, but perhaps not very soon given the fundamental differences between Athenian power and that of the city that defeated her.[45] When Tacitus was writing, however, some four decades after the Batavian revolt, the Roman empire was more stable than ever and indeed expanding aggressively under Trajan. Gaul "wobbled" in 69–70 CE, as Tacitus says in the *Histories*' "table of contents" (*H.* 1.2.1 *Galliae nutantes*), but the *Schreckenszenario* of internal dissent and external disaffection did not in fact dissolve "the fabric of the empire" in the chaos that followed Nero's suicide, as it threatened to do.[46] So the posterity for whom he narrated the Batavian revolt included his contemporaries, who still had an empire to manage. Thucydidean detachment was not an option.

How, then, is one to describe the relationship between Tacitus' historical works and Thucydides' *History*? The best answer I can give is borrowed from Seneca, from his

---

[43] Choosing with posterity in mind: Tac. *Ag.* 32.5, *Dial.* 23.6, *H.* 1.21.2, 1.84.4, 2.47.2, *Ann.* 15.59.3, 16.25.2.

[44] Verdicts: Tac. *H.* 5.17.2, *Ann.* 3.65.1, 4.38.2, 6.32.4.

[45] On the other hand, if Raaflaub (2013, 9–12) is right about Thucydides' anachronistic critique of Sparta's "imperial impulses," perhaps the historian expected a recurrence sooner rather than later.

[46] Timpe (2005, 170) and Syme (1958, 1.172).

84th *Letter*, to be precise. In that essay on the relationship between reading and writing Seneca offers an analogy from the natural world: just as bees convert the nectar they collect from flowers into an entirely different substance, honey, by a kind of fermentation process, so should the writer do with the fruits of his reading. Literary raw material may be perceptible in the new work, just as the sweetness of nectar is perceptible in honey, but the work itself should be something different. "The intellect," Seneca says, "should conceal the things by which it has been helped, and display only this, the product" (*quod effecit, Ep.* 84.7). In Tacitus' account of the Batavian revolt you have a product. I have argued that one can taste Thucydides' Mytilenean revolt in it, but I don't insist: *de gustibus non est disputandum*.

References

Brunt, P. A. 1960. "Tacitus on the Batavian Revolt." *Latomus* 19: 494–517.
Canfora, L. 2006. "Thucydides in Rome and Late Antiquity." In *Brill's Companion to Thucydides*, edited by A. Rengakos and A. Tsakmakis, 721–53. Leiden: Brill.
Chilver, G. E. F., and G. B. Townend. 1985. *A Historical Commentary on Tacitus' Histories IV and V*. Oxford: Oxford University Press.
Connor, W. R. 1977. "A Post-modernist Thucydides?" *Classical Journal* 72: 289–98.
Gowing, A. 2009. "From the Annalists to the *Annales*: Latin Historiography before Tacitus." In *The Cambridge Companion to Tacitus*, edited by A. J. Woodman, 17–30. Cambridge: Cambridge University Press.
Greenwood, E. 2006. *Thucydides and the Shaping of History*. London: Duckworth.
Hammond, M., trans. 2009. *Thucydides: The Peloponnesian War*. Oxford: Oxford University Press.
Hornblower, S. 1987. *Thucydides*. Baltimore: Johns Hopkins University Press.
Hornblower, S. 1991–2008. *A Commentary on Thucydides*. 3 vols. Oxford: Clarendon Press.
Hornblower, S. 1996. *A Commentary on Thucydides*. Vol II, *Books IV–V.24*. Oxford: Clarendon.
Hose, M. 1998. "'*Libertas an pax*': Eine Beobachtung zu Tacitus' Darstellung des Bataveraufstandes." *Hermes* 126: 297–309.
Kallet, L. 2006. "Thucydides' Workshop of History and Utility outside the Text." In *Brill's Companion to Thucydides*, edited by A. Rengakos and A. Tsakmakis, 335–68. Leiden: Brill.
Keitel, E. 1993. "Speech and Narrative in *Histories* 4." In *Tacitus and the Tacitean Tradition*, edited by T. J. Luce and A. J. Woodman, 39–58. Princeton: Princeton University Press.
Kornemann, E. 1904. "Thukydides und die römische Historiographie." *Philologus* 63: 148–53.
Levene, D. S. 2009a. "Speeches in the *Histories*." In *The Cambridge Companion to Tacitus*, edited by A. J. Woodman, 212–24. Cambridge: Cambridge University Press.
Levene, D. S. 2009b. "Warfare in the *Annals*." In *The Cambridge Companion to Tacitus*. edited by A. J. Woodman, 225–38. Cambridge: Cambridge University Press.
MacLeod, C. 1978. "Reason and Necessity: Thucydides III.9–14, 37–48." *Journal of Hellenic Studies* 98: 64–78.
Martin, R. 1981. *Tacitus*. Berkeley: University of California Press.
Morford, M. 1993. "Tacitean *prudentia* and the Doctrines of Justus Lipsius." In *Tacitus and the Tacitean Tradition*, edited by T. J. Luce and A. J. Woodman, 129–51. Princeton: Princeton University Press.

Nicolai, R. 1995. "ΚΤΗΜΑ ΕΣ ΑΙΕΙ: Aspetti della fortuna di Tucidide nel mondo antico." *Rivista di filologia e di istruzione classica* 123: 5–26.

O'Gorman, E. 2000. *Irony and Misreading in the Annals of Tacitus*. Cambridge: Cambridge University Press.

Price, J. 2010. "Josephus' Reading of Thucydides: A Test Case in the *Bellum Judaicum*." In *Thucydides: A Violent Teacher?* edited by G. Rechenauer and V. Pothou, 79–98. Göttingen: V&Runipress.

Pritchett, W. K. 1975. *Dionysius of Halicarnassus: On Thucydides*. Berkeley: University of California Press.

Raaflaub, K. A. 2010. "Ulterior Motives in Ancient Historiography: What Exactly, and Why?" In *Intentional History: Spinning Time in Ancient Greece*, edited by L. Foxhall, H.-J. Gehrke, and N. Luraghi, 189–210. Stuttgart: Steiner.

Raaflaub, K. A. 2013. "*Ktêma es aiei*: Thucydides' Concept of 'Learning through History.'" In *Thucydides between History and Literature,* edited by A. Tsakmakis and M. Tamiolaki, 3–21. Berlin and Boston: De Gruyter.

Rood. T. 1998. *Thucydides: Narrative and Explanation*. Oxford: Oxford University Press.

Rood, T. 2006. "Objectivity and Authority: Thucydides' Historical Method." In *Brill's Companion to Thucydides,* edited by A. Rengakos and A. Tsakmakis, 225–49. Leiden: Brill.

Samotta, I. 2012. "Herodotus and Thucydides in Roman Republican Historiography." In *Thucydides and Herodotus*, edited by E. Foster and D. Lateiner, 345–78. Oxford: Oxford University Press.

Strebel, H. G. 1935. *Wertung und Wirkung des thukydideischen Geschichtswerks in der griechisch-römischen Literatur*. Speyer: Pilger Druckerei.

Syme, R. 1958. *Tacitus*. 2 vols. Oxford: Oxford University Press.

Timpe, D. 2005. "Tacitus und der Bataveraufstand." In *Gegenwärtige Antike—antike Gegenwarten,* edited by T. Schmitt, W. Schmitz, A. Winterling, 151–87. Munich: R. Oldenbourg Verlag.

Walker, A. 1993. "*Enargeia* and the Spectator in Greek Historiography," *Transactions of the American Philological Association* 123: 353–77.

CHAPTER 40

THUCYDIDES, PROCOPIUS, AND THE HISTORIANS OF THE LATER ROMAN EMPIRE

CONOR WHATELY

When the newly promoted—to *magister militum per Orientem*—Roman general Belisarius set off against Persia in 527 CE, he took along with him a lawyer from Caesarea named Procopius as his assessor, that is, his secretary. That lawyer would stay with Belisarius for the better part of twenty years, and besides carrying out whatever legal duties his job entailed, he seems to have been involved in activities like the collection of intelligence in Sicily and the procuring of supplies in central Italy. Procopius' experiences undoubtedly made a profound impression on his mind, for he turned his hand to writing, and composed a history of the wars of the reigning emperor Justinian. We call Procopius' work, which survives to this day, the *History of the Wars of Justinian*, or simply the *Wars*.

Although Procopius had plentiful historiographical examples at his disposal, he decided to write in the manner of Thucydides, in terms of both the content and the form of his work. In this chapter we therefore take a look at Thucydides' influence on Procopius, and more generally on the writing of history in late antiquity. We shall focus primarily on Procopius, since he is not only one of the best preserved classicizing historians, but also the most successful of Thucydides' late antique imitators, and arguably the most interesting, though we shall frequently reference the works of Dexippus, Priscus, Agathias, and other historians. By the end of the chapter we will have discussed some important examples of their engagement with Thucydides, and the implications of this engagement for the tradition of historiography in late antiquity.

Since these historians are less familiar to most readers of Thucydides, this overview will begin with a brief look at the writing of history in late antiquity, together with an initial overview of the traces of Thucydides' influence on classicizing historians of this era. It will continue with a discussion of the role that education in the rhetorical arts played in extending Thucydides' influence into late antiquity, and an examination of the place of Thucydides' account of the siege of Plataea for our understanding of Thucydides' influence in this period. Why Plataea? A closer look at this particular siege narrative and its afterlife in the late antique historians will allow us to delve into a number of pertinent issues, from its pride of place in the *progymnasmata*[1] and use as a model by historians like Dexippus, Priscus, and Procopius, to the manner in which these historians attached themselves to specific Thucydidean phrases. In the last section of this chapter, we focus almost exclusively on Procopius, examining additional evidence for Thucydides' influence on late antiquity's most successful classicizing historian.

Writing History in Late Antiquity

Historiography in the classical style, often billed as classicizing historiography, continued to attract an audience well into the end of antiquity, though writers were increasingly drawn to other sub-genres. Eusebius, for example, writing in the first half of the fourth century, wrote two works that had a marked impact on later writers, his *Chronicle* and his *History of the Church*. Many later writers, like Jerome (b. c. 350 CE) and Jordanes (sixth century CE), wrote chronicles of their own. These works often provided little more than lists of persons (say consuls or bishops) and events arranged chronologically, and they were invariably Christian in outlook. Related works called chronographs, such as that of Malalas, written in the sixth century, included not only the same sorts of lists of persons and events found in the chronicles, but also some extended narrative passages drawn from known literary sources (see Jeffreys 2003). The church histories written by later writers such as Theodoret (b. c. 393 CE), Socrates (b. c. 380 CE), Sozomen (b. c. 400 CE), and Evagrius (b. c. 536 CE), were in turn inspired by Eusebius' ecclesiastical history (cf. Leppin 2003 and Whitby 2003). In addition there were a host of short histories in Latin, such as those of Aurelius Victor (b. c. 320 CE) and Eutropius (second half of the fourth century CE).

Although much of this history writing—the chronicles, chronographs, and ecclesiastical histories—was primarily concerned with matters that had some bearing on the church, it did, over time, increasingly tend to turn to secular material, and though this secular material never supplanted the Christian material, it certainly complemented it, with this process becoming particularly noticeable from the fifth century onward (Blockley 1981, 86–94). Evagrius, who wrote near the end of the sixth and beginning of the seventh century, for instance, provided a detailed account of the Battle of Melitene in 576 CE (Evag. 5.14; cf. Theophylact Simocatta at 3.12.12–14.11 and John of Ephesus at

---

[1] The *progymnasmata* were rhetorical handbooks, and were a fundamental component of the ancient Roman educational system. They contained student exercises on upwards of fifteen different models ranging from fable to narrative and comparison, invective, and description. Note the texts collected, translated, and discussed in Kennedy (2003).

6.8–9). In general, however, the language and subject matters of these works were a far cry from that of earlier classical and even contemporary classicizing histories.

Despite the abundance and apparent popularity of such works, secular, classical, or classicizing history (scholars have used all three terms) in the manner of Thucydides remained popular. However, classicizing historians of this period faced two problems that divided them from their ancient Greek and Roman predecessors, namely, the advent of Christianity and the continuing evolution of the Greek language. For those who chose to write classicizing history in Greek, the Greek that was to be adopted was the Attic Greek of Thucydides. This meant coming to grips with terms and ideas that did not exist in Thucydides' day, especially religious ones—and this is where the two problems, Christianity and language, come together. To counter them, classicizing historians often employed circumlocutions, describing Christian matters in Thucydidean language, and often in the way that Herodotus might use in order to comment on a people's unusual customs (Cameron and Cameron 1964). Because of their employment of Atticizing language, their regular use of circumlocutions, and their general avoidance of church matters, scholars have questioned the religious leanings of these historians (as in the long-running debate about Procopius' religious preferences; cf. Whitby 2007), and expressed doubt about their abilities as historians. What is more, scholars have argued that late antique classicizing historians had only a superficial familiarity with Thucydides, and that whatever familiarity they did possess arose as a result of reading late antique compendia, such as that of Hesychius, or lexica, such as that of John Stobaeus. Overall, their predilection for imitation and apparent lack of originality has meant that these historians are often belittled (Marrou 1956, 201; Jenkins 1963; Mango 1975; 1980, 243; and Wilson 1983, 5). Others have questioned the degree to which classicizing historians reflected their age, effectively arguing that they were outliers, in stark contrast to authors like Malalas (Scott 2013). We are led to the view that in late antiquity Thucydides' influence was best seen in the works of lesser historians, who were inferior in terms of the content of their works and those works' importance for our understanding of late antiquity, and who were unable to think for themselves and therefore slavishly imitated Thucydides. Is this a fair assessment?

Thucydidean Borrowings

It is not difficult to spot signs of Thucydides' influence on classicizing late antique histories. The very subject matter of classicizing works points towards a Thucydidean influence. Eunapius, Olympiodorus, Priscus, Malchus, Procopius, Agathias, Menander Protector, and Theophylact Simocatta all make war a part of their works, though the vagaries of their texts' survival means that the proportion of their writing devoted to war narrative is not always known. The emphasis on war is much clearer in Procopius' *Wars*, Agathias' *Histories*, and Theophylact's *Histories*, all of which survive in their entirety. For instance, Thucydides famously opened his *Histories* with, "Thucydides of Athens wrote about the war between the Peloponnesians and Athenians" (Thuc. 1.1.1). Procopius echoed those statements and their main theme (Procop. *Wars* 1.1.1): "Procopius of Caesarea wrote about the wars which Justinian, the emperor of the Romans, began against the barbarians of the east and the west." Agathias, on the other hand, does not get to his subject matter until well into his preface (pr. 20). His preface thus has a different shape from Procopius', and is much less Thucydidean in that regard. However, Agathias expressly states that he is picking up where Procopius left off (pr. 22), which meant a focus on war and politics. The works of Eunapius, Olympiodorus, Priscus, and Malchus are lost; for all we know their prefaces might have been along the same lines as Procopius'. Priscus, for instance, did write about matters related to war and politics, which we know because much of what survives of Priscus' work relates the story of an embassy to Attila, in which Priscus himself participated (the passage is preserved in Constantine Porphyrogenitus' *Excerpts on Roman Embassies to Foreigners*). What is more, from the *Suda* (Pi, 2301) we learn that Priscus "wrote a Byzantine history, and about the affairs concerning Attila." Although we lack that sort of information in the *Suda* about Eunapius, Olympiodorus, and Malchus, there seems no reason to doubt, at least on the basis of the surviving fragments, that they wrote about political and military affairs (Blockley 1981); the same holds true for Menander Protector (Blockley 1985).

For imitation of other large order elements of Thucydidean narrative, we can again find evidence in the more complete histories of Agathias and Procopius. Procopius, for instance, begins to adopt Thucydides' dating formula in the *Gothic Wars* (books 5 to 7 of the *Wars*, which is divided into eight books) and book eight. For example, at 2.103 in the *Histories* we read, "so ended this winter and so ended the third year of this war recorded by Thucydides," and at 5.7.37 of the *Wars* we read, "the winter drew to a close, and thus ended the first year of this war, the history of which Procopius has written." Agathias, once again, did not adopt this practice. One other particularly marked feature of Thucydides' *History* is the abundance of speeches. Here, Thucydides' influence on both Agathias and Procopius appears to be quite strong. For instance, Agathias imitates parts of Thucydides' account of Pericles' funeral oration (Thuc. 2.36—Agathias 3.9.19), the Mytilenean debate (Thuc. 3.39.5—Agathias 3.9.3), and the speech of the Corcyraeans (Thuc. 1.34.3—Agathias 4.8.21) (Cameron 1964, 49). Procopius also imitates Thucydides' speeches, as we shall discuss.

Evidence of this kind reveals Thucydides' influence on the larger narrative structures in the works of late antique classicizing historians. But what happens if we delve into details? How did Thucydides influence the historians' use of language? Before we look at some examples of Thucydides' literary influence, some discussion of the impact of a rhetorical education is warranted because of the role it played in fostering an appreciation of Thucydides' writing among classicizing historians.

Rhetoric and Education

If we want to know why Thucydides influenced late antique historiography, perhaps we need not look any further than the character of late antique higher education, especially with respect to the teaching of rhetoric, for the two authors cited most often in the *progymnasmata* were Homer and Thucydides (Webb 2009, 19). The education of writers like Priscus and Procopius would have been eerily familiar to earlier writers like Lucian and Strabo. By late antiquity, its features had long been established. As is well known, in its later stages students would very likely study some sort of rhetorical handbook, such as any one of the four treatises of Hermogenes of Tarsus (the *peri staseon*, the *peri ideon*, the *peri heureseos*, and the *peri methodon deinotetos*). In the course of his or her training, the student would be required to compose and deliver his or her own speeches based on general moral or political topics.[2] This level was the most demanding of the whole training, with those students who completed their rhetorical education taking anywhere from six to ten years to do so (Cribiore 2001, 56).

One of the fundamental features of this training was the dominance of Attic Greek. This was not the Greek spoken on the streets of Constantinople in late antiquity; the Greek of that time and place was perhaps more akin to the Greek found in Malalas' *Chronograph*, but rather the Greek perhaps spoken, and certainly written, during the classical period of ancient Athens in the fifth century BCE. The continued dominance of the literary form of the language was largely due to the reactionary writers of the second Sophistic. In the words of Swain, "Atticizing Greek was about the repristination of linguistic features, phonological, morphological, or syntactical, that were becoming or had become obsolete" (1996, 34–35; Cf. Marrou 1956, 201).

Writing Attic Greek was surely not easy, and by late antiquity a large number of lexicographical guides were available to the aspiring writer (Wilson 1983, 5). One example was the anthology of John Stobaeus, who was probably writing in the fifth century. The anthology included excerpts from various poets and prose writers from Homer to Themistius listed under a variety of different headings. The existence of such anthologies has brought into question the degree to which late antique writers—historians amongst them—were actually familiar with their ancient predecessors, whom they often quote. As already noted, some scholars have even gone so far as to suggest that in many instances the obvious mimesis was superficial (Mango 1975, for instance; cf. Cresci 1986). A closer look at some examples will help determine whether those carrying out the imitations seemed to know what they were doing. We will focus on ekphrastic descriptions of military action.

Ekphrasis is a Greek (Latin *ecphrasis*) term denoting an exercise in description that involves the speaker and/or writer in bringing (by means of description) something before the eyes of the listener or reader. Subjects might include anything from persons and places to events and objects. The authors of the various *progymnasmata*, such as Pseudo-Hermogenes, Aelius Theon, Aphthonius, and Libanius, tend to consider war, combat, and the construction of siege engines, ships, and weapons of war as suitable subject matter for *ekphrasis* (Aelius Theon, Spengel p. 118; Pseudo-Hermogenes 10.2; Aphthonius 12.1). The example provided by Aphthonius is Thucydides' account of the night battle at Syracuse (Aphthonius 12.2; Thuc. 7.43–44; cf. Pseudo-Hermogenes 10.3).

---

[2] See the insightful discussion of Gibson (2004).

Aphthonius calls this a case of "mixed" *ekphrasis*, where "mixed" refers to the inclusion of both an event, in this case Thucydides' description of the battle itself, and the occasion, here Thucydides' description of the night-time setting in which the battle took place. Unfortunately, apart from broad recommendations of good examples to imitate, the rhetoricians do not specify what particular elements or themes an orator or historian should include in a description of a war or battle. While discussing the education of the young, Aelius Theon simply refers to Thucydides' descriptions of the siege of Plataea, and then to assorted cavalry actions and naval battles without identifying them (Aelius Theon, Spengel 1854, 118). When he turns to the subject of *ekphrasis* he again singles out the siege at Plataea, and Thucydides' description of the preparation of a siege engine, as well as the making of Achilles' arms from Homer (Aelius Theon, Spengel 1854, 118. Cf. Hom. *Il*. 18.478–614; Thuc. 3.21, 4.100). When it comes to the description of combat as an *ekphrasis*, if there is one thing that the *progymnasmata* have in common in this regard, it is that Thucydides serves as an exemplary model; moreover, it is Thucydides' siege narratives that stand out to these rhetoricians. What these discussions do not, unfortunately, say much about is how, exactly, Thucydides' *ekphrases* are so exemplary; the *progymnasmata* often give quite precise references without providing explication, the implication being that the student would be familiar enough with the passage in question not to need explanations (Cribiore 2001, 225; Pernot 2005, 150).

Thucydides Narrative of the Siege of Plataea and Its Afterlife

Thucydides' account of the siege of Plataea seems to have had a greater demonstrable impact on the descriptions of sieges in late antique classicizing histories than any other siege narrative in his *History*. Scholars have long commented on the parallels between Thucydides' Plataea story and Dexippus' description of the siege of Philippopolis, Priscus' of the siege of Naissus, Procopius' of the siege of Naples (among others—the siege stories of Amida, Edessa, and Antioch all include imitation, in part, of Procopius' Neapolitan account), and Agathias' of the siege of Onoguris. It is worth noting, however, that the Plataea story had been famous in the Roman imperial period as well, with Josephus (*Ant*. 4.55), Arrian (*Anab*. 2.18, 21, 23, 27), and Cassius Dio (Cass. Dio 66.4.2) drawing parallels to the Plataea story in siege accounts of their own and so possibly providing some of the impetus for these late antique imitations (Cameron 1964, 50). Thus, Thucydidean influence may have been direct, transmitted through intervening historians, or both.

As Hornblower (1991) noted (357), Thucydides devoted incredibly detailed chapters of descriptions to the Plataea story (Thuc. 2.71–78, especially 75–78), a fact that goes some way toward explaining Dexippus' and Priscus' tendency to imitate those parts of

Thucydides' account.[3] We cannot conclude any more than this about the accounts of Dexippus and Priscus, for whom but one fragment each survives.[4]

We can know more about the better-preserved historians. For instance, Thucydides' account opens with negotiations. Although Agathias does represent some deliberation between key parties in the buildup to the siege of Onoguris, there is nothing like the discussion between the Spartans and Plataeans that we find in Thucydides (2.71–74). Indeed, in Agathias' case the discussion, presented between Gubazes of the allied Lazi and a host of Roman generals, involves not the attackers and the besieged, but the leading figures among the attackers alone, and it concerns how to attack the Persians at Onoguris (3.4.1–4). Agathias, then, did not choose to imitate Thucydides' negotiation scene. In contrast, Procopius does include a negotiation between the Roman general Belisarius and the Neapolitan Stephanus (5.8.7–18) in his account of the siege of Naples, a parallel to Thucydides that has attracted some attention (Bornmann 1974, 147–150; Pazdernik 2000, 173). Procopius' dialogue echoes Thucydides' account of the negotiation between Archidamus and the Plataeans, though there are also hints of Brasidas' speeches in Thrace (Thuc. 4.87–88; see Pazdernik 2000, 176).

Thucydides' Plataeans and Procopius' Neapolitans both stress the injustice of the attacks and the nature of their relationship with the larger powers. Both sets of speakers make a series of ultimately unsuccessful pleas. Yet it is also clear that Procopius does not bend his story to fit the Thucydidean model, for in Thucydides the exchange at Plataea takes place over a few days (the Plataeans send envoys to Athens to discuss matters), while in Procopius the exchange at Naples is a much briefer affair and lacks the concomitant armistice. In addition, while Thucydides' Plataeans request an armistice to discuss the conditions so that they might deliberate with Athens, in Procopius the Neapolitans sneakily dispatch envoys to Theodohad in Rome to ask for help. The emerging pattern then, in Procopius at least, is that while the parallels with Thucydides are evident, these do not seem to come at the expense of the individuality of Procopius' account.[5] Procopius is not a slavish imitator, but an interpreter of Thucydides who stands in a long tradition (see, for instance, Ludwig, chapter 30, Wiater, chapter 38, and Damon, chapter 39, in this volume).

The core parallels, however, involve the siege itself. As Blockley (1972, 21) notes, Dexippus makes a number of verbal allusions to Thucydides. He quotes the manner in which Thucydides described the construction of the siege mound (Dexippus frag. 27.7, 27.8, 27.11; Thuc. 2.75.1, 75.4, 75.6) and the deployment of various beams, though in Dexippus the beams themselves are used differently than in Thucydides (Dexippus frag.

---

[3] Blockley (1972, 18) singles out Thucydides 2.75–78; Braun (1885, 47) also highlights 2.75–78, with 3.20–24 and 52 as the most imitated parts of Thucydides' description of Plataea.
[4] For Dexippus, frag. 20 deals the siege of Philippopolis, and Priscus's frag. 1b deals with the siege of Naissus.
[5] Cf. Matthews (1989, 298) on the individuality of Ammianus' descriptions of combat.

27.6; Thuc. 2.76.4). Priscus and Naissus reference not only Thucydides (Priscus frag. 1b; Thuc. 2.75.5), but also Dexippus (frag. 27.6).[6]

Some Thucydidean phrases became common parlance among these historians. When describing the wooden wall that the Plataeans constructed to counter the Peloponnesian mound, Thucydides notes that the building had a defensive covering of skins and hides (δέρσεις καὶ διφθέρας) that served to protect the wooden structure from fire and keep the men safe (2.75.5). Priscus notes that when the Huns attacked Naissus, they brought wheeled machines and rams to bear on the city, the former covered with skins and hides (δέρρεις καὶ διφθέρας) to protect the items from fire and to keep the men safe (1b.3). Agathias, in his account of Onoguris, notes the use of so-called wicker roofs, which have layers of skins and hides (δέρρεις δὲ ὕπερθεν καὶ διφθέρας) placed overtop to protect the men and the machine from missile fire (3.5.10). Procopius uses the same terms for skins and hides, "δέρρεις τε καὶ διφθέρας" (6.20.14), though not in his account of the siege of Naples. What is more, although he uses the terms in the context of a siege (the siege of Orvieto), they do not offer protection, but serve as a source of sustenance when the inhabitants of the city find themselves starving and besieged by the general Belisarius. In all these instances, then, Thucydides would seem to have been the inspiration for the use of these terms for skins and hides.[7] Arrian's description of the siege of Tyre (Arr. *Anab.* 2.18.6) is the only other case besides those already mentioned, and Arrian, who might himself be considered a classicizing historian, significantly uses the phrase, like Thucydides, Priscus, and Agathias, to refer to a form of protection from flaming missiles for siege machine and attacker alike. All three classicizing historians then—four if we include Arrian—have used this phrase (δέρρεις . . . διφθέρας), first found in Thucydides in his account of the siege of Plataea and its attendant defensive mechanisms, as part of their own siege descriptions. It should come as no surprise that each writer used the phrase in a different way.

Procopius' use of phrases from Thucydides' Plataea narrative is both more subtle and more frequent than the uses we can perceive in the other classicizing historians. Pazdernik (2000, 164n36) notes that Procopius' use of συνελευθεροῦτε at 3.16.14 (Justinian to the Vandals) parallels the form used (ξυνελευθεροῦτε) by Thucydides' Archidamus at Plataea at 2.72.1 (the only use of this verb in the imperative in Thucydides). Two books later, Procopius' account of the calculations for the height of the wooden towers during the opening stages of the first siege of Rome alludes to Thucydides' account of the Plataeans' repeated counting of the courses of brick forming

---

[6] His reference to the dropping of heavy stones imitates both (Priscus frag. 1b.6). As Blockley (1972, 24) notes, however, while there certainly is some parallelism, the practice (dropping stones) and term used (ἀμαξιαῖος) is common enough (Xen. *Hell.* 2.4.27; Dion. Hal. *Ant. Rom.* 3.67.4; Diod. Sic. 17.68.2). In general, Priscus tends to transplant Thucydides' words or phrases into his own scenarios (Blockley 1972, 24).

[7] The word δέρσεις ("skins") appears only once in the *Thesaurus Linguae Graecae* with the sigma, and that is in Thucydides' account of Plataea. The form δέρρεις is not terribly common; it very rarely appears with διφθέρας ("hides") in the works of the classical and late antique periods, and then invariably in the context of a siege.

the Spartan siege wall (Proc. 5.21.3; Thuc. 3.20). One last example: while besieged at Osimo, Procopius' Goths decide to send word to Wittigis, a Gothic king: "They first put in readiness the men whom they intended to send to Wittigis and then waited for a moonless night" (6.24.3). Similarly, Thucydides had written of his besieged Plataeans that "when everything was ready, they waited for a stormy night with wind and rain and no moon, and then they slipped out of the city, led by the men who had been the originators of the plan" (3.22.1). Overall, Procopius' use of Thucydides and Plataea is of a much larger order than that exhibited by the other classicizing late antique historians we have looked at. On the basis of the surviving evidence, where historians like Dexippus and Priscus tend to limit their use of Thucydides' account of Plataea to select phrases, Procopius goes further, incorporating not only Thucydidean words and phrases, but also entire scenes, like the negotiation scene from the beginning of his account of the siege of Plataea.

Why the interest in sieges? In Procopius' case, sieges make up a good chunk of the subject matter of the *Wars*; moreover, in his *Buildings* Procopius also devoted a great deal of attention to the sites of sieges, namely, the empire's varied fortifications, and to their construction.[8] This emphasis is a product of his experiences. Sieges were part and parcel of warfare in the east in late antiquity, and Procopius was intimately acquainted with the realities of siege warfare (Petersen 2013; Whitby 2013). His service on Belisarius' staff exposed him to a number of protracted sieges, particularly those in Italy. It is easy to imagine that he was called upon to participate in the defense of those cities. Indeed, he was sent to procure supplies when Belisarius and the Romans were besieged in Rome (Procop. *Wars* 6.4.1ff.). Thus, we need look no further than Procopius' life experiences to find an explanation for his interest in Thucydides' siege narratives.[9]

It is also worth remembering the influence of the educational practices we have discussed. As we have seen, Thucydides was one of the two most cited authors in the *progymnasmata*, the other being Homer, and it is no coincidence that the two authors spend a considerable amount of time on war. What is more, when it came to *ekphrasis*, of the four subject categories the rhetoricians mention (persons, places, times, events—see Webb 2009, 62–67), actions or events, such as battles and sieges, were central (Webb 2009, 67).

Thus, by taking a closer look at the siege of Plataea and its afterlife, not only are we able to understand something of the reasoning behind the interest in war and politics

---

[8] In this context it is worth noting that building and construction narratives in the *Wars* can be modeled on Thucydides: Procopius seems to have molded his description of the construction of the Appian Way at 5.14.9 on Thucydides' account of the construction of the walls of Piraeus at 1.93.5: the stones for the Appian Way were, in Procopius' eyes, fastened together without adding concrete or anything else, just as Thucydides notes that the space between the outer surfaces of the Piraeus was not filled in with rubble or clay.

[9] As little as we know about Procopius, we know even less about Dexippus and Priscus, for obvious reasons—though we do know something about Agathias. Thus while we cannot say whether any experience on the part of Dexippus or Priscus—though Priscus did travel into the heart of Attila's kingdom—might have impelled them to devote attention to sieges; Agathias, so far as we know, had none.

among late antique historians, but we can also appreciate more fully the impact of a rhetorical education on their writing, while getting a sense for some of the varied ways (the shared phraseology, for instance) in which these late antique historians have engaged with Thucydides. Wherever we have evidence of this engagement they are doing more than slavishly cutting and pasting Thucydidean phrases. On the other hand, Procopius seems to be the most independent minded of them all, at least on the basis of the surviving evidence, an issue that merits further consideration. In the next section we look for additional evidence of deeper engagement with Thucydides, with a particular emphasis on Procopius.

Thucydides and Procopius

To this point we have looked at Thucydides' influence on a handful of late antique historians. In this section, in which we delve more deeply into the sticky world of intertextuality, we shall concentrate on Procopius, who has attracted far more attention than his successor Agathias. Before we jump in wholeheartedly and explore the depths of Procopius' intertextual relationship with Thucydides, some caution is in order, given the subject's complexity, a point well made for earlier Greek historiography in Hornblower (1995b, 54–69). Many scholars, though acknowledging the arguments put forward by Pazdernik, who has explored Procopius' intertextual relationship with Thucydides in some detail (1997; 2000; 2015), tend to dismiss the possibility of an intertextual relationship between Procopius' text and that of another author such as Thucydides. It is true that the gaps in the literary record make determining an unambiguous intertextual relationship between an author like Procopius and his predecessors a difficult task, a point often made by Kelly (2008) in his study of Ammianus. Not all texts from antiquity survive, nor are those that do necessarily complete, with the result that lines of influence can be difficult to discern. Cassius Dio is particularly troublesome in this regard (see Potter 1999, 70–78). Indeed, it can be difficult to determine where we should perceive a direct relationship, such as the relationship between Procopius and Thucydides discovered by Adshead (1990) in Procopius' narrative of the siege of Rome, and where we should see a common intellectual debt that was the product of the long-standing and shared Hellenistic educational system, combined with the staying power of the genre of classical and classicizing historiography.

It seems clear that Procopius engaged with historians other than Thucydides, since a variety of historiographical influences coexist in his work. For instance, when Procopius expounds Belisarius' virtues after his departure at *Wars* 7.1.8, his discussion of the rewards implemented to bolster troop loyalty is faintly reminiscent of Polybius' discussion of the Roman practices of punishment and reward described at length in book six of his *Histories* (6.19.1–42.6). Polybius' emphasis on *tychē* also springs to mind (see Evans 1972, 119, 133; Walbank 1972, 58–65; Kaldellis 2004, 19–21, 174, 218). Procopius' diction, as was already suggested, sometimes also seems to betray Herodotean influence. We find, for example, a handful of references to "warlike men," or to "the most warlike men," μαχιμώτατοι (Proc. *Wars* 1.15.2, 7.5.1, 7.15.2, 7.19.6), as opposed to soldiers, in Procopius' *Wars*. Perhaps here we ought to be reminded of Herodotus, though Herodotus prefers "warlike" to "most warlike" (Hdt. 3.102.5 for "most warlike"; Hdt. 2.164.2, 7.185.14, and 9.32.8, for example, for "warlike"). Thucydides, however, also makes ready use of "the most warlike men": where there is one reference in Thucydides to "warlike men" (Thuc. 1.10.4), there are five references to "most warlike men" (Thuc. 1.110.2, 2.81.4, 2.98.4, 3.108.2, 6.90.3).

Thus, not only Thucydidean influences are visible in Procopius. However, such intertextual relationships are difficult to interpret. As we have seen, some scholars have seen strong Thucydidean echoes in the *Gothic Wars* (Adshead 1990; Pazdernik 1997; 2000), but others have discounted any such suggestions, and instead argue that any similarities are little more than superficial (Kouroumali 2005). As noted, caution is indeed warranted: not all are convinced by supposed examples of Thucydidean, Herodotean, or Polybian intertexts.

In my view, Thucydidean influence on Procopius' writing is evident. Our focus shall be on the *Wars*, although it is worth pointing out that Procopius' *Secret History* also alludes to Thucydides (note, for example, Procop. *SH* 13.12 and Thuc. 2.89). Procopius never names Thucydides, but some scholars have recognized the Thucydidean character of Procopius' *Wars* (e.g., Cameron 1985, 3; Brodka 2004, 15–16; and Treadgold 2007, 177), and we have already seen many examples of Procopius' large order, thematic, and linguistic borrowings from Thucydides. One particular Thucydidean episode has attracted a great deal of attention: Procopius' account of the plague in 542 CE (Cameron 1985, 40; Meier 1999, 2004; cf. Little 2007). In his imitation of the plague, Procopius was not alone, for there are similarities between Thucydides' account and that of the fourteenth century Byzantine historian John Kantakouzenos, though Kantakouzenos may be alluding both to Thucydides and to Procopius, who served as one of John Kinnamos' models (Brand 1976, 7; Scott 1981, 66; cf. Hunger 1976; 1978, 45; Miller 1976; Scott 1981, 72). On the other hand, though Agathias describes an instance of plague at Leutharis (2.3.69–70), the description is not particularly Thucydidean (Cameron 1964, 50). In addition to the plague narrative, Adshead has argued that Procopius' siege accounts are greatly indebted to those found in Thucydides (Adshead 1990, 93–104). Indeed, as we saw, Procopius' description of the siege of Naples and Thucydides' of the siege of Plataea exhibit a number of parallels; however, they are, in Adshead's words, only "the curtain raisers for the *pièces de résistance*," namely, Procopius' stories of the siege of Rome and the siege of Syracuse. Procopius also engaged with Thucydides' powers of characterization. Pazdernik has laid out a detailed set of correspondences between Thucydides and Procopius in regard to Procopius' casting of Belisarius in the mold of Thucydides' Brasidas (Pazdernik 2000, 149–187), and the partial fashioning of Totila as a latter-day Pericles, if an unsuccessful one (Pazdernik 2015). Also worth noting are the parallels Kaldellis (2004, 198) draws between Belisarius at the start of the *Wars* book seven and the obituary of Pericles.

Other responses to Thucydides' characters are not difficult to find.[10] For instance, Procopius' comments on John the Cappadocian at 1.24.12 echo those of Thucydides on Themistocles at 1.138.3: both John and Themistocles are highlighted for their natural intelligence, an intelligence not fostered by careful study. At the dawn of the *Vandal War* (books three and four of the *Wars*), Belisarius is characterized as quick at forming a plan and tireless in his execution at 3.9.25, an allusion to the Corinthians' characterization of the Athenians at 1.70.2, where they too are considered quick at forming plans and inexhaustible at carrying them out. When he turns to Theoderic early in his *Gothic War*, Procopius, our narrator, models his eulogy of the Gothic general at 5.1.25–31 on Thucydides' eulogy of Pericles at 2.65.1–13. Especially noteworthy is Procopius' comment that Theoderic was in name a usurper, while in reality an emperor (5.1.29), and Thucydides' comment that what was in name a democracy (Athens) was in fact under the power of the first citizen (Pericles—2.65.9). Procopius also responds to Thucydidean themes like freedom, slavery, and treason. Pazdernik (1997), for instance, has argued for the interplay between freedom and slavery in domestic and international political contexts in the works of both historians. In addition, a Thucydidean cast on treason and treachery colors Procopius' account of a plot against Justinian. From 7.32.7 on, Procopius describes Artabanes' conspiracy against Justinian and his subsequent fall, an episode that borrows language from Thucydides' account of the fall of the Spartan king Pausanias at 1.131–133.

As already noted, Procopius also imitated the content and form of Thucydidean speeches. The dialogue between Belisarius and the Goths at 6.6.3ff. in the *Wars* is modeled on the Melian Dialogue at 5.84–111 in the *Histories*. Aspects of Totila's speech to the Goths at 7.25.4–5 allude to parts of Pericles' speech to the Athenians at 2.59.3 and 2.64.3. For a final, closely related example, Belisarius' letter to Justinian in the early stages of the *Gothic War* at 5.24.1 is modeled on Nicias' letter to Athens during the siege of Syracuse (Thuc. 7.10–15), although Procopius' letter reverses Thucydides' (Kaldellis 2014, 305n549). Where Belisarius' letter opens with some words on the early success of the Roman invasion of Italy (5.24.1–2) and with the Romans on the offensive, Nicias' letter opens with the Athenians finding themselves the besieged rather than the besiegers (7.11.2–3). However, in both letters the writer/sender of the letter (Belisarius and Nicias) is desperate for supplies from home. The content of a number of Procopius' speeches and speech-like episodes, then, bears witness to Procopius' debt to Thucydides.

It could also be argued that classicizing historians like Procopius modeled not only particular speeches on the words and themes of Thucydides' speeches, but also their very approach to constructing speeches, with the pre-battle speeches (also called military exhortations or *paraineseis*) being perhaps the most notable example. While Agathias devoted a limited amount of space to pre-battle speeches, Procopius devoted a great

---

[10] Many of these parallels come from the notes in Kaldellis's revised translation of the *Wars*, and a number of others can be found scattered throughout the book (Kaldellis 2014).

deal. The existence of military exhortations in both Thucydides and Procopius is not sufficient evidence to posit Thucydides' influence on the latter. However, it is certainly suggestive that Procopius' pre-battle speeches often follow the same historiographic logic as Thucydides'. Romilly (Romilly 1956, 144–150) closely analyzed Thucydides' speech and battle episodes and demonstrated that the generals giving the speeches laid out what they thought would be the integral elements of the battle to follow. Inevitably, one general would demonstrate a better grasp of the military reality than the other, and his speech would effectively predict the outcome of the battle, as happens with the naval battle at Naupactus (Thuc. 2.86–90). Kaldellis (2004, 29-31) applied de Romilly's model to the Battle of Mammes in the *Vandal War* and found that Procopius imitated this literary strategy. It happens that Procopius also wrote up other battles, such as the Battle of Dara, in this way (Whately 2016, 80–84).

As this section draws to a close it is worth returning to the discussion at the start of this chapter, and in particular to the concerns of some scholars about the level of Thucydides' effect in late antiquity. In my view, there is considerable evidence for Thucydides' influence on select classicizing historians, and on Procopius in particular. Thucydides' influence on characterization, on the opening and ordering of classicizing histories, on their speeches, subject matter, and themes is far from superficial (cf. Moore 2014, 54–80). However, what is most striking about Procopius' intertextual relationship to Thucydides is his ability to make the evidence work for his own aims.

The Age of Historiographical Dinosaurs

As this chapter draws to a close, it remains to discuss the reasons for this influence and its wider implications. As we saw, there is little doubt that authors like Priscus, Procopius, and Agathias were well read. It seems unlikely that those historians and others like them sat with lexica while composing their works, and picked episodes and phrases from Thucydides at random with little regard for the context of those phrases in their own work or in the work of Thucydides. The passages to which they refer seem too well chosen for this to be the case, with Procopius forming a particularly noteworthy example in this regard. Their penchant for alluding to Thucydides is unsurprising, given his prominence in Greek education; moreover, he was long held up as the benchmark for ancient historiography.

When it comes to the fragmentary historians like Dexippus, Priscus, and Menander, it is difficult, if not impossible, to come to a conclusion about what level of success they achieved in their engagement with Thucydides, let alone any other classical author. Our assessments of Agathias' (Cameron 1970; Cameron and Cameron 1964) and Theophylact's (Whitby 1988) engagements with the classics, Thucydides included, have revealed that those historians left something to be desired,[11] even if Kaldellis (Kaldellis 1997; 1999) has made a strong case that Agathias deserves more credit as an historian than he is usually afforded. That leaves Procopius, and though we have barely scratched the surface in this chapter, there seems little doubt that he was the most successful of those late antique historians who engaged with Thucydides. In fact, it would not be unreasonable to argue that Procopius was one of the most successful of any of Thucydides' ancient, late antique, or medieval readers.

With that in mind, was Thucydides a reasonable model historian for the late antique world? In other words, should we see the classicizing historians as historiographical dinosaurs, stuck in the past and stubbornly unwilling to engage more fully with newer and more vibrant sub-genres of historiography and ways of seeing the world? The simple answer is no. Following Turquois (2013, 16), it is perhaps better to think of these late antique historians not as antiquarians stuck in the past, but rather as participants in a rich, vibrant, and continuous tradition of classicizing prose narrative. War and politics remained integral and pervasive aspects of late antique life, and Thucydides provided a ready model for those interested in these important topics. Other modes of history writing, such as chronicles, lacked the means adequately to describe and explain war and politics (Whately 2016, 219-235), and although Thucydides had his detractors, like Dionysius of Halicarnassus and John Tzetzes, among ancient and medieval readers, there seems to have been universal agreement that Thucydides was capable of writing a vivid tale of political and military events. Indeed, perhaps a better indication of Thucydides' usefulness is the fact that Thucydides' impact on classicizing historiography extended well into the Byzantine era. Although the Arab invasions of the seventh and eighth centuries brought an end to writing history in the manner of historians like Procopius, Agathias, and Theophylact Simocatta, classicism re-emerged a century or two later, and the same Thucydidean influence prevalent in works like the *Wars* manifests itself in works like Anna Komnene's *Alexiad*. What is more, for some of those later writers, like Leo the Deacon, it is often the works of historians like Procopius and Agathias that had an impact—we have, then, evidence for both a direct influence (Anna read Thucydides), and an indirect Thucydidean one (Leo might not have).

Furthermore, in time the most Thucydidean of late antique historians seem to have supplanted, at least to some degree, Thucydides himself: for all that Thucydides had an effect beyond the late antique period, it happens that some of his late antique imitators took on his role in the medieval Byzantine period. Besides becoming a model for rhetoric, Procopius, and to a lesser degree Agathias, had become models for describing battle, at least for the historians Leo the Deacon and John Kinnamos (Brand 1976, 7; Russell 1998, 40; Kelso 2003; Kalli 2004, 161–62; Talbot and Sullivan 2005, 23). In the end, it is

---

[11] One author whom we have not discussed, but who very likely shared the education and outlook of historians like Procopius and Agathias, and who also hailed from the sixth century, was John the Lydian. Though his history (assuming he completed it) does not survive, a number of his other works do, works that are full of learned allusions to classical texts and culture (Maas 1992, 6).

perhaps a mark of Thucydides' success and lasting influence that his most esteemed late antique successors managed to fill his role among later Byzantine historians.

References

Adshead, K. 1990. "Procopius' Poliorcetica: Continuities and Discontinuities." In *Reading the Past in Late Antiquity*, edited by G. Clarke, 93–119. Canberra: Australian National University Press.
Blockley, R. C. 1972. "Dexippus and Priscus and the Thucydidean Account of the Siege of Plataea." *Phoenix* 26: 18–27.
Blockley, R. C. 1981. *The Fragmentary Classicising Historians of the Later Roman Empire: Eunapius, Olympiodorus, Priscus and Malchus.* Vol. I. Liverpool: Francis Cairns.
Blockley, R. C. (ed. and trans.) 1985. *The History of Menander the Guardsman.* Liverpool: Francis Cairns.
Bornmann, F. 1974. "Motivi tucididei in Procopio." *A & R* n.s. 19: 138–50.
Brand, C. M., trans. 1976. *Deeds of John and Manuel Comnenus.* New York: Columbia University Press.
Braun, H. 1885. *Procopius Caesariensis quatenus imitatus sit Thucydidem.* Erlangen: Typis Jungii et filii.
Brodka, D. 2004. *Die Geschichtsphilosophie in der spätantiken Historiographie.* Frankfurt am Main: Peter Lang.
Cameron, A. 1964. "Herodotus and Thucydides in Agathias." *BZ* 57: 33–52.
Cameron, A. 1970. *Agathias.* Oxford: Oxford University Press.
Cameron, A. 1985. *Procopius and the Sixth Century.* London: Duckworth.
Cameron, A., and A. Cameron. 1964. "Christianity and Tradition in the Historiography of the Later Roman Empire." *CQ* 14: 316–28.
Cresci, L. R. 1986. "Ancora sulla ΜΙΜΗΣΙΣ in Procopio." *RFIC* 114: 449–57.
Cribiore, R. 2001. *Gymnastics of the Mind: Greek Education in Hellenistic and Roman Egypt.* Princeton: Princeton University Press.
Evans, J. A. S. 1972. *Procopius.* New York: Twayne.
Gibson, C. A. 2004. "Learning Greek History in the Ancient Classroom: The Evidence of the Treatises on Progymnasmata," *CP* 99: 103–29.
Hornblower, S. 1991. *A Commentary on Thucydides.* Vol. 1, *Books I–III.* Oxford: Clarendon.
Hornblower, S. 1995. "Introduction." In *Greek Historiography*, edited by S. Hornblower, 1–72. Oxford: Oxford University Press.
Hunger, H. 1976. "Thukydides bei Johannes Kantakuzenos: Beobeachtungen zur Mimesis." *JÖB* 25: 181–93.
Hunger, H. 1978. *Die hochsprachliche profane Literatur der Byzantiner.* Munich: Beck.
Jeffreys, E. 2003. "The Beginnings of Byzantine Chronography: John Malalas." In *Greek and Roman Historiography in Late Antiquity*, edited by G. Marasco, 497–527. Leiden: Brill.
Jenkins, R. 1963. "The Hellenistic Origins of Byzantine Literature." *DOP* 17: 37–52.
Kaldellis, A. 1997. "Agathias on History and Poetry." *GRBS* 38: 295–305.
Kaldellis, A. 1999. "The Historical and Religious Views of Agathias: A Reinterpretation." *Byzantion* 69: 206–52.
Kaldellis, A. 2004. *Procopius of Caesarea: Tyranny, History, and Philosophy at the End of Antiquity.* Philadelphia: University of Pennsylvania Press.

Kaldellis, A., trans. 2014. *The Wars of Justinian*. Indianapolis: Hackett.
Kalli, M. 2004. *The Manuscript Tradition of Procopius' Gothic Wars*. Munich: De Gruyter.
Kelly, G. 2008. *Ammianus Marcellinus: The Allusive Historian*. Cambridge: Cambridge University Press.
Kelso, I. 2003. "Artillery as a Classicizing Digression." *Historia* 52: 122–25.
Kennedy, G. A., trans. 2003. *Progymnasmata: Greek Textbooks of Prose Composition and Rhetoric*. Leiden: Brill.
Kouroumali, M. 2005. *Procopius and the Gothic War*. DPhil diss., University of Oxford.
Leppin, H. 2003. "The Church Historians (I): Socrates, Sozomenus, Theodoretus." In *Greek and Roman Historiography in Late Antiquity*, edited by G. Marasco, 219–54. Leiden: Brill.
Little, L. K. 2007. *Plague and the End of Antiquity: The Pandemic of 541–750*. Cambridge: Cambridge University Press.
Maas, M. 1992. *John Lydus and the Roman Past: Antiquarianism and Politics in the Age of Justinian*. London: Routledge.
Mango, C. 1975. *Byzantine Literature as a Distorting Mirror*. Oxford: Clarendon.
Mango, C. 1980. *Byzantium: The Empire of New Rome*. London: Weidenfeld and Nicolson.
Marrou, H. G. 1956. *A History of Education in Antiquity*. Translated by G. Lamb. New York: Sheed and Ward.
Matthews, J. F. 1989. *The Roman Empire of Ammianus*. London: Duckworth.
Meier, M. 1999. "Beobachtungen zu den sogenannten Pestschilderungen bei Thukydides II 47–54 und bei Prokop, *Bell. Pers.* II 22–23." *Tyche* 14: 177–210.
Meier, M. 2004. "Prokop, Agathias, die Pest und das 'Ende' der antiken Historiographie." *HZ* 278: 281–310.
Miller, T. S. 1976. "The Plague in John VI Cantacuzenus and Thucydides." *GRBS* 17: 385–95.
Moore, J. 2014. *Procopius of Caesarea and Historical Memory in the Sixth Century*. Unpublished PhD diss. University of Wisconsin-Madison.
Pazdernik, C. F. 1997. *A Dangerous Liberty and a Servitude Free from Care: Political Eleutheria and Douleia in Procopius of Caesarea*. Unpublished Phd diss. Princeton University.
Pazdernik, C. 2000. "Procopius and Thucydides on the Labors of War: Belisarius and Brasidas in the Field." *TAPha* 130: 149–87.
Pazdernik, C. 2015. "Belisarius' Second Occupation of Rome and Pericles' Last Speech," In *Shifting Genres in Late Antiquity*, edited by G. Greatrex and H. Elton, 207–18. Farnham: Ashgate.
Pernot, L. 2005. *Rhetoric in Antiquity*. Translated by W. E. Higgins. Washington, DC: The Catholic University of America Press.
Petersen, L. I. R. 2013. *Siege Warfare and Military Organization in the Successor States (400–800 AD): Byzantium, the West and Islam*. Leiden: Brill.
Potter, D. S. 1999. *Literary Texts and the Roman Historian*. London: Routledge.
Romilly, J. de. 1956. *Histoire et Raison chez Thucydide*. Paris: Les Belles Lettres.
Russell, D. 1998. "The Panegyrists and Their Teachers." In *The Power of Propaganda. The Role of Panegyric in Late Antiquity*, edited by M. Whitby, 17–50. Leiden: Brill.
Scott, R. 1981. "The Classical Tradition in Byzantine Historiography." In *Byzantium and the Classical Tradition*, edited by M. Mullett and R. Scott, 61–74. Birmingham: Centre for Byzantine Studies, University of Birmingham.
Scott, R. 2013. *Byzantine Chronicles and the Sixth Century*. Farnham: Ashgate.
Spengel, L. ed. 1854. *Rhetores Graeci*. Vol. 2. Leipzig: Teubner.

Swain, S. 1996. *Hellenism and Empire: Language, Classicism, and Power in the Greek World, AD 50–250*. Oxford: Oxford University Press.
Talbot, A. M., and D. F. Sullivan, trans 2005. *The History of Leo the Deacon: Byzantine Military Expansion in the Tenth Century*. Cambridge: Harvard University Press.
Treadgold, W. 2007. *The Early Byzantine Historians*. Basingstoke: Palgrave MacMillan.
Turquois, E. 2013. "Envisioning Byzantium: Materiality and Visuality in Procopius of Caesarea." Unpublished DPhil diss. University of Oxford.
Walbank, F. W. 1972. *Polybius*. Berkeley: University of California Press.
Webb, R. 2009. *Ekphrasis, Imagination and Persuasion in Ancient Rhetorical Theory and Practice*. Farnham: Ashgate.
Whately, C. 2016. *Battles and Generals: Combat, Culture, and Didacticism in Procopius'* Wars. Leiden: Brill.
Whitby, M. 1988. *The Emperor Maurice and His Historian: Theophylact Simocatta on Persian and Balkan Warfare*. Oxford: Oxford University Press.
Whitby, M. 2003. "The Church Historians and Chalcedon." In *Greek and Roman Historiography in Late Antiquity*, edited by G. Marasco, 449–95. Leiden: Brill.
Whitby, M. 2007. "Religious Views of Procopius and Agathias," *Electrum* 13: 73–93.
Whitby, M. 2013. "Siege Warfare and Counter-Siege Tactics in Late Antiquity," In *War and Warfare in Late Antiquity: Current Perspectives*, edited by A. Sarantis and N. Christie, 433–59. Leiden: Brill.
Wilson, N. G. 1983. *Scholars of Byzantium*. London: Duckworth.

Index Locorum

Abydenos, *FGrH* 685 F 5, 54n9
Aelian, *Various Histories*, 4.22, 42n2
Aelius Theon, Spengel 118, 695–96
Aeneas Tacticus
   10.7, 499n15
   17.2–4, 154
Aeschines, 2.175, 136, 140
Aeschylus
   3.183–85, 69
   Agamemnon, 592, 603
      341–42, 602
   Choephoroe (Libation Bearers), 592
      1034–36, 593
   Eumenides, 864, 611
   Persae, 293, 376
   Persians, 561
   Suppliants, 60–68, 260n6
Agathias, *Histories*, 693
   2.3.69–70, 701
   2.103, 694
   3.5.10, 698
   3.9.3, 694
   3.9.19, 694
   4.8.21, 694
   preface 20, 694
   preface 22, 694
Alcidamas, *On Those Who Write Written Speeches*, 575n17
Anaxion of Mytilene, *Persai Satyroi*, *TrGF* 202, 561
Andocides
   1.96–98, 618
   2.11, 112
   3.8, 137
   3.8–9, 140
   3.9, 136
   Against Alcibiades
      4, 155
      4.22, 155
Antiochus, *Peri Italiēs*
   FGrH 555 F 2, 559
   FGrH 577 F 13, 559
   FGrH IIIb *Komm.*, i. 611, 36–37, ii., 559
Antiphon
   8.68.1, 610
   frag. 44, 578, 582
   frag. 44a, 583
   Second Tetral., 2.1, 575n17
Aphthonius
   12.1, 695
   12.2, 695
Apollodorus of Athens, *FGrH* 244 F 7b, 556
Appian, *Mithridates*, 3.22, 684n24
Archilochus,
   frag. 3 West, 59
Aristophanes
   Acharnians, 119, 609, 612–14
      32–33, 448
      67, 609
      197, 126
      299–302, 614
      425, 126
      502–508, 606
      504, 103
      510–12, 611
      513–56, 611
      515–38, 612
      515–39, 119
      523–29, 606
      530–31, 610
      530–34, 610
      595–619, 612
      630–32, 615
      630–46, 615
      642, 615
      703–12, 610

Aristophanes (*cont.*)
　Babylonians, 607, 613–15
　Birds, 103, 175, 611, 616, 618
　　186, 608, 615–16
　　640, 608, 616
　　813–16, 608, 616
　　1021–57, 101
　　1054, 102
　　1277–85, 520n9
　　1281 ff., 612
　　1297, 617
　　1360–69, 608, 616
　Clouds, 466, 568
　　528–33, 614
　　545–62, 613
　　551–59, 614
　　561–62, 614
　　889–1104, 434
　　984–85, 42n2
　　1075, 466
　　1075–82, 378
　　1080–82, 466
　　1427–28, 467
　Ecclesiazusae, 618
　Equites
　　313, 615
　　326–27, 615
　　465–67, 152
　　801–802, 615
　　1030–34, 615
　　1196–97, 615
　Frogs, 608, 612, 618
　　363, 106
　　405, 609
　　678–85, 613
　　686–705, 608, 618
　　686–737, 616
　　1422–32, 616
　　1532–33, 613
　Knights, 608, 612–14, 617
　　30–35, 368
　　54–57, 126
　　127–43, 614
　　128–37, 613
　　166, 614
　　191–93, 613
　　213–22, 613
　　225–29, 614
　　288, 614
　　424, 126
　　507–11, 614
　　595–610, 126
　　732 ff., 610
　　794–96, 612
　　801–804, 612
　　1052–53, 126
　　1058–59, 126
　　1111–14, 610
　　1166–67, 126
　　1201, 126
　　1303–304, 49n4
　　1324–34, 42n2
　　1326, 609
　　1369 ff., 499n14
　Lysistrata, 608, 612, 617
　　387–98, 611, 616
　　390–92, 175
　　490, 607, 616
　　498–501, 618
　　513–14, 608, 611
　　577–78, 617
　　581, 608
　　590–91, 616
　　638–57, 618
　　1125–56, 611
　　1133–34, 611
　　1176–81, 615
　Peace, 615
　　242–43, 126
　　269–74, 612
　　312, 126
　　421, 126
　　571–600, 448
　　601–27, 119
　　604–14, 610
　　605, 610
　　605–27, 612
　　619–22, 615
　　664–67, 126
　　667, 612
　　748–61, 613
　　1172–84, 612
　　1209–64, 499n16
　Thesmophoriazusae, 1136–47, 618

Wasps, 449, 607–8, 613–14
  210, 126
  240–44, 614
  377–78, 617
  422, 126
  475–77, 612
  655–712, 614
  656–60, 136
  707–11, 615
  836–1008, 614
  1029–37, 613
Aristotle
  Athēnaiōn Politeia, 184
    14, 544
    22.7, 60
    24.2, 73
    24.3, 101
    28, 614
    28.5, 187
    29.2, 181, 184, 188, 618
    29.3, 188
    30–31, 184
    30.1, 184
    32.1, 184
  frag. 98 Rose, 59
  frag. 611.20 Rose, 54
  Nicomachean Ethics
    4.7
    1127a22–24, 520
    1127b23–26, 520
    1124a1, 463
    1124b10–11, 463
    1126a7–8, 449
  Poetics
    9.1451b11, 271
    1452a22–24, 596
  Politics, 320
    2.3 1265b35–40, 397
    2.9.1271b1–11, 333
    2.1271a41–b7, 520n11
    3, 475
    3.1.1281b, 475
    3.4.1279a26–1279b10, 400
    5.1.1302a7–10, 399n19
    5.2.1302a24–31, 335
    5.1304a, 154
    7.14 1333a3, 405

    7.14.1333b5–40, 333
    1254b–1255a, 356
    1255b, 356
    1289b38–39, 59
    1298b, 618
    1299b, 618
    1305a7–15, 58
    1329a, 499, 618
  Problēmata, 7.886b 33 ff., 218
  Rhetoric
    2.5.20–21, 527n17
    2.18.4, 215
    1378a30–79a9, 450
    1378a30–80a5, 449
    1382a20–83b10, 445
    1383a7, 445
    1385b11–86b7, 445
  Rhetoric for Alexander, 1425b 37, 215
Arrian, *Anabasis*
  2.18, 696
  2.18.6, 698
  2.21, 696
  2.23, 696
  2.27, 696
Asios frag. 13 West, 42n2
Athenaeus, 512bc, 42n2
Athēnaiōn Politeia. see Aristotle, *Athēnaiōn Politeia*; Xenophon, *Athênaiôn Politeia*
The Athenian Tribute Lists (ATL)
  3, 74
  3.334, 136
  iii.69–70, 136
  iii.352, 136

Berossos, *FGrH* 680 F 7c, 54n9

Caesar, *Gallic War*, 1, 686
Cassius Dio, 66.4.2, 696
Cato, *Origines*, 669
Charon of Lampsacus, *Prytaneis of the Lacedaemonians*, 560
Chionides, test. 1, 561
Choerilus of Samos
  Barbarica, 561
  Medica, 561
  Persica Suppl. Hell. 314–324, 561

Cicero
  De divinatione, 1.25, 524n13
  De legibus
    2.63, 563
    2.65, 563
  De oratore
    2.36, 654
    2.62, 563
  De oratore (Hubbell)
    30, 645
    31, 646, 653
Constantine Porphyrogenitus, *Excerpts on Roman Embassies to Foreigners*, 694
Constitution of the Athenians. see Aristotle, *Athēnaiōn Politeia*; Xenophon, *Athēnaiōn Politeia*
Cratinus
  Cheirons, 610
    F 240, 610
    F 258, 610
    F 259, 610
    F 327, 610
  Dionysalexandros, 612
    T 1:44–48, 609
  Nemesis, F 118, 609
  Thracian Women
    F 73, 610
    F 118, 610
  Wealths, 610
    F 171.22–23, 610
    F 741, 610

Demetrius
  Sicily, 616
  On Style
    6, 635
    19, 227
    54, 216
    63, 216
    134–35, 628
    137, 635
    208, 219
Demosthenes
  1.27, 137
  20.106, 332
  27.9, 499n16
  45.85, 499n16
  60.1, 563
  On the Crown, 15.28–29, 493
  Third Philippic, 21, 493, 498
Dexippus
  frag. 20, 697n4
  frag. 27.6, 697–98
  frag. 27.7, 697
  frag. 27.8, 697
  frag. 27.11, 697
Diodorus Siculus
  1.2.2, 654
  1.37.4, 653n11
  11.33.3, 562
  11.84.4, 499n14
  12.38–39, 119
  12.58.6, 139
  12.74–76, 145
  12.75.1, 146
  12.75.2, 148
  12.75.4, 148
  12.75.5, 148
  12.75.6–7, 148
  12.75.7, 153–54
  12.77.4, 146
  12.78–79, 145
  12.78.4–6, 153
  12.79.1, 153
  12.80.2, 153
  12.80.2–3, 154
  13.5.1, 150
  13.8, 145
  13.9.1, 158
  13.14.4–16.7, 164
  13.41, 630
  13.42.5, 624
  13.43, 621n2
  13.45–47.2, 635n14
  13.49–51, 635n14
  13.52.2, 636
  13.53, 636
  13.54.6, 636
  13.63.1, 636
  13.63.1–2, 635n14
  13.64.1, 635n14
  13.64.2–4, 635n14
  13.65, 625
  13.65.4, 636

13.66–67, 635n14
13.68–69, 635n14
13.70–71, 635n14
13.72–73, 635n14
13.73.3–74, 635n14
13.76–79, 635n14
13.97–100, 635n14
13.97.4–98.1, 636
13.98.1, 636
13.100–103, 635n14
13.102.2–3, 636
13.103, 636
13.104–106, 635n14
13.104.9, 500n18
13.105, 636
13.106.8–10, 636
13.107, 635n14
14.5.1–4, 636
14.5.4, 636
14.11, 635
14.84.7, 624
15.79.5–6, 500n18
16.8.3–5, 500n18
16.23–33, 493
17.68.2, 698n6
Diogenes Laertius
  2.57, 627
  3.37, 227
  6.14, 636
Dionysius of Halicarnassus
  On the Ancient Orators, 643
  On Composition, 643
    25, 227
  On Imitation, 643, 645–47, 650–51
  Letter to Ammaeus, 16, 225
  Letter to Ammaeus II, 643, 645–46
    3.2, 669
  Letter to Pompeius
    Geminus, 645–51, 653
    3, 643
    3.1, 647n9
    3.2, 623, 647
    3.2–15, 647
    3.3–4, 644
    3.4, 647
    3.5, 673
    3.9, 647

    3.14, 647
    3.15, 642, 647, 650, 673
    3.16–21, 647
    3.21, 647
    4, 623
    5, 624
    6.7–8, 666
  Roman Antiquities, 645
    1.1.2, 654
    1.1.2–3, 648
    1.5.1, 645
    1.6.4, 645
    3.67.4, 698n6
  On Thucydides, 641–56
    1–4, 651
    1.4, 645
    2.1, 655
    2.2, 651
    2.4, 655
    5, 560, 651
    5.3, 652
    5.5, 652
    6–7, 651
    6.4–5, 652
    7.3, 652
    7.72.2–4, 52
    8, 20n1, 651–53
    8.1, 641–42, 652–53
    8.1–2, 649, 652
    8.2, 651
    8.24, 31
    9, 22, 626, 630, 652, 680
    9–20, 643, 652
    10, 118
    10–12, 652
    11, 64
    13, 211
    13–20, 652
    15, 217
    15–16, 276
    15.2, 650
    16, 621n2, 622–23
    17, 623
    18.1, 644
    19–20, 39
    20, 644
    21–49, 643, 652

Dionysius of Halicarnassus (cont.)
    22–24, 652
    24, 577n23, 629
    24.1, 669
    24.2–9, 669
    24.10, 668
    25–33, 652
    25.2, 643
    26–27, 644
    27.1, 668
    28–31, 644
    33.1, 644
    34–48, 652
    34.4–7, 655
    39.1, 650
    46, 577n23
    49, 652
    50–51, 652
    50.2–3, 646
    51.1, 646
    52, 225
    52–55, 652
    55, 225
    55.5, 656
    249, 669
Dionysius of Miletus, *Persica*, 555, 560

Ephorus, *FGrH* 70 F 179, 54
Epicharmus
    frag. 136, 580n33
    frags. 110–111, 561
Eupolis
    102, 610
    Autolycus, 608
    Baptai, 617
    Cities, 615
        F 220, 617
    Demes, 609
        F 99.28, 617
    Draft-Dodgers, 612
    Prospaltians, F 259.72, 617
    Spongers, 608
    Taxiarchs, 612
Euripides
    Hippolytus, 602–3
        183–85, 602
        191–94, 602
        319, 377

    Phoenissae
        382, 376
        1763, 376
    Suppliant Women, 399–456, 613
    Telephus, 438, 609
    Trojan Women
        886, 377
        906–1032, 377
        946–50, 377
Eusebius
    Chronicle, 692
    History of the Church, 692
Evagrius, 5.14, 692
Die Fragmente der griechischen Historiker,
    i–iii (*FGrH*)
    4 F 79b, 556
    4 F 155, 557
    4 F 157, 557
    4 FF 74–84, 556
    70 F 179, 54
    90 F 58.3, 54
    105 F 1, 58
    107 F 10b, 610
    244 F 7b, 556
    323a FF 25–26, 555
    555 F 1, 558
    555 F 2, 559
    566 F 71, 56
    577 F 13, 559
    680 F 7c, 54n9
    685 F 5, 54n9
    IIIb *Komm.*, i. 611, 36–37, 559
    IIIb *Komm.*, ii., 355n30, 559
    IIIb *Suppl.*, i. 5–6, 555
Die Fragmente der Vorsokratiker, 6th edition (*DK*)
    22 B 53, 322
    80 B 6a, 279
    82 B 6, 575n17
    82 B 11.13, 279
    85 A8, 567

Gorgias
    82 B 11.13 DK, 279
    DK 82, B6, 575n17
    Helen, 568
        2, 386
        12–13, 577n25
        14, 577n25

*Greek Epic Fragments from the Seventh
    to the Fifth Century*
    (West)
  frag. 3, 59
  frag. 13, 42n2
*Greek Epic Fragments from the Seventh to the
    Fifth Century* (West), 2nd edition
  frags. 10–18, 561
Greek Historical Inscriptions (RO) 22, 109
  line 24, 104

Hecataeus
  FGrHist, 264 F 25, 499n15
  Genealogies, 555
Hellanicus
  Aiolica, 556
  Argolica, 556
  Atthis, 556
    FGrH 323a FF 25–26, 555
  Barbarian Customs, 556
  Boiotica, 556
  FGrH 4 F 155, 557
  FGrH 4 F 157, 557
  frag. 164 Fowler, 44
  Karneonikai, 557
  Lesbiaca, 556
  Origins of Peoples and Cities, 556
  Peri Arkadias, 556
  Persica, 555
  Phoronis, 556–57
  Priestesses of Hera at Argos
    FGrH 4 F 79b, 556
    FGrH 4 FF 74–84, 556
  Thettalica, 556
  Troica, 556–57
Hellenica Oxyrhynchia, 14, 621, 625–27,
    629–30, 634–35
  1–3, 625
  4, 625
  5.39–40, 625
  8, 625, 629
  9–12, 626
  10.3, 626
  10.4, 625
  11.34, 626
  12.1, 626
  18, 626

18.2, 626
19, 627
19.4–5, 627
20.8, 626
21.35, 626
22–23, 626
22.2, 626
Heracleides of Pontus, Athenaeus 512bc;
    Aelian *Various Histories* 4.22, 42n2
Heraclitus, DK 22 B 53, 322
Hermippus
  Breadwomen, 613
  F 47, 614
  Fates, 612
Herodotus
  Histories, 21, 427, 551, 554, 568
    1, 504
    1–5, 560
    1.1, 148
    1.1–5, 259
    1.5–6, 41
    1.5.3, 557
    1.15.3, 59
    1.22.4, 56
    1.27.5, 56
    1.59, 610
    1.64, 58
    1.64–67, 55
    1.64.2, 55
    1.67, 48
    1.68.6, 57
    1.82, 148
    1.141, 58
    1.141.4, 56
    1.143–47, 55
    1.143.1, 55
    1.151, 55
    1.152, 58
    1.153.3, 55
    1.161, 500n18
    1.161–62, 55
    1.163–64, 57
    1.163–65, 500n18
    1.163.2, 55
    1.165.1, 56
    1.166–67, 55
    1.166.1, 55–56

Herodotus (cont.)
- 1.168, 500n18
- 1.169.2, 56
- 1.171.2–5, 44
- 2.1, 56
- 2.116, 261n7
- 2.118.1, 41
- 2.120.5, 602
- 2.123.1, 195
- 2.134.3, 557
- 2.143.1, 557
- 2.156.2, 239
- 2.159, 54
- 2.164.2, 701
- 3.1, 56
- 3.13.1, 57
- 3.14.4–5, 57
- 3.34.4, 57
- 3.38, 582
- 3.39, 55, 57
- 3.39.2, 56
- 3.40–43, 56
- 3.41, 57
- 3.44, 56–57
- 3.45–46, 58
- 3.47, 582
- 3.48–53, 54
- 3.49, 54
- 3.54–56, 58
- 3.102.5, 701
- 3.115.1–2, 239
- 3.122.2, 41, 55
- 3.124, 57
- 3.125.2, 55, 59
- 3.148, 58
- 4.97, 57
- 4.137, 57
- 4.161, 495n5
- 5, 552
- 5–9, 554, 560
- 5.2, 56n10
- 5.10, 56n10
- 5.11, 56n10, 57
- 5.14–16, 56n10
- 5.26, 57
- 5.28, 56
- 5.30–34, 56n10
- 5.30.1, 267n3
- 5.32–3, 57
- 5.36.2, 557
- 5.37, 57
- 5.38, 57
- 5.43, 551
- 5.44, 551
- 5.45.1, 551
- 5.45.2, 552
- 5.49–51, 58
- 5.55, 553
- 5.63, 58
- 5.63.2, 428
- 5.77, 59
- 5.78, 58
- 5.90–103, 58
- 5.91, 58
- 5.92α1–2, 57
- 5.92η5, 57
- 5.94, 58, 259
- 5.97.3, 267n3
- 5.99, 59
- 5.124–26, 56n10
- 5.125, 557
- 6.8, 57
- 6.15.1, 46
- 6.18–20, 500n18
- 6.31–33, 500n18
- 6.34–39, 45
- 6.37, 57
- 6.41, 57
- 6.42, 56, 498
- 6.57.4, 553
- 6.76, 58
- 6.89, 53
- 6.100–102, 500n18
- 6.108, 58
- 6.123, 553
- 7, 206, 592, 594
- 7–9, 166
- 7.5–25, 268
- 7.8, 499n12
- 7.32, 575n17
- 7.102–104, 94
- 7.134, 48
- 7.144.2, 59
- 7.150, 259

7.159, 48, 259
7.161.3, 259
7.185.14, 701
8, 206
8.1, 59
8.3.2, 66
8.43, 59
8.43–48, 59, 164
8.66, 69
8.77, 573, 634
8.82, 59
8.94, 53
8.112, 69
8.121, 69
8.137.1, 248
8.144, 492
9.7, 428
9.25, 259
9.25–26, 259
9.26, 260
9.32.8, 701
9.53, 553
9.100, 573
9.106, 67
9.116, 259
9.121, 68
Persica, 555
Hesiod
  frag. 23(a)
    17, 50
    165.14, 50
    198.16, 50
    204.47, 50
  frag. 130 M.-W., 50
  Works and Days
    22, 43n3
    527–28, 50
    650–60, 59
    651–53, 50
    780–81, 43n3
Hippocrates
  Airs, 571, 574, 576
    3.3, 574n15
  On Ancient Medicine,
    568–69, 571
    7.3, 574n15
    9.3, 576

12, 575
    12.2, 574n15
    15.1, 574n15
    20.2, 576n19
  On the Art, 569, 576
  Breaths, 569, 571–72, 576
    6, 571n9, 574
  Epidemics, 570, 576
    I, 569
    I 23, 574
    III, 569, 575
    III 16, 575
  Nature of Man
    1, 568, 576n20
    9, 572
    15, 571
  Places, 571
  On the Sacred Disease, 573
    1.10 J, 574n15
    16.4 J, 575
  Waters, 571
Hobbes, Thomas
  Leviathan
    1.8, 535
    1.8–19, 535
    3.83, 535
    10.58, 339
    13.9, 535
    29.1, 535
    120, 396
    lvi, 401
  The Peloponnesian War. Thucydides: The Complete Hobbes Translation (1628/1989), 8, 197–98, 208
    570–71, 428
  The Peloponnesian War. Thucydides: The Complete Hobbes Translation (1975)
    15, 321, 321n2
Homer
  Iliad, 4, 45, 163, 267, 379, 427, 560, 587, 590, 593
    1, 592
    1.1–430, 504
    1.2, 50
    1.8, 28, 30
    1.30, 50
    1.308–17, 591

Homer (*cont.*)
    1.524–27, 591
    2.42–47, 51
    2.109–210, 591
    2.115, 50
    2.155–56, 598
    2.404, 50
    2.510, 45
    2.720–21, 45
    3.392, 601
    3.441–46, 601
    3.449–50, 602
    3.451–55, 602
    6.321–22, 601
    6.340–41, 601
    6.379–82, 602
    6.455, 634
    6.506–11, 602
    6.513, 601
    6.521–23, 602
    7.73, 50
    8.56, 375
    8.57, 375
    9.301, 50
    9.328–29, 45
    9.410–16, 379
    12.211–28, 594
    12.231–50, 594
    15.592–746, 588
    16.1–101, 588
    16.102–23, 588
    16.124–256, 588
    16.698–709, 598
    16.831, 634
    18.478–614, 696
    18.597–98, 51
    20.193, 634
    23.685, 52
    23.710, 52
    Odyssey, 4, 163, 427, 560, 587, 591, 602
        1.90, 50
        1.239, 50
        2.2–14, 51
        3.71–74, 51n5
        3.105–106, 45
        3.263, 50
        4.99, 50
        4.307–11, 51
        7.211–12, 379
        8.403–406, 51
        9, 601
        9.172–74, 601
        9.196–251, 591
        9.252–55, 51n5
        9.289–90, 599
        9.310–11, 599
        9.343–44, 599
        10, 601
        10.100–101, 601
        12.245–46, 599
        12.246, 600
        12.258, 600
        14.369, 50
        17.541–47, 524n14
        18.67, 52
        18.76, 52
        20.124–57, 51
        21.119, 51
        22.74, 51
        22.421–25, 599
        24.32, 50
    Homeric Hymn to Apollo, 452–55, 51n5
    Homeric Hymn to Demeter, 147, 376
Hyperides, *Epitaphs*
    2, 563
    10 ff., 563

Ion of Chios, *Foundation of Chios*, 560
Inscriptiones Graecae (*IG*)
    VII.52.5–6, 52n6
    Volume I, 3d edition
        15, line 38, 101
        21, 108
        21, lines 5–6, 102
        41, 103
        62, lines 5–6, 101
        71, 135
        79, 615
        83, 111, 150
        86, 154
        102, 618
        282, B.I., lines 11–12, 101
        285, fr. 1, 74
        364, lines 19–21, 128

369, 135, 615
1454, 110
Volume II, 2d edition
   174, 112
   5224, 112
Isocrates
   Archidamus
      6.84, 56
   Panathenaicus
      63, 633
      89, 633
      200–72, 627
   Panegyricus
      43, 493n2
      100, 633
      110, 633
   On the Peace, 166
      2.84–85, 167

John of Ephesus, 6.8–9, 693
Josephus
   Antiquitates Judaicae, 4.55, 696
   Bellum Judaicum
      1.1, 678n4
      1.2, 78, 30, 678n4
      7.75–88, 686

Libanius, frag. 50 β 2, 617
Livius Andronicus, *Odyssia*
   2.39.5, 678n7
   22.23.4, 678n7
Logistai Inscription (*IG* I^3 369 = ML #72), 135
   ML #72, 217, 136
Longinus, *On the Sublime*, 651n10
   15.2, 218
   22.4, 223
Lucian
   The Dream, 17, 524n13
   On How to Write History, 20n1, 642, 654
      41–42, 642
   Quomodo historia conscribenda sit
      39–40, 654
      41, 687
Lycurgus, *Against Leocrates*, 1.112, 185
Lysias
   2.1, 563
   9.4, 499n14

9.15, 499n14
12.19, 499n16
12.65, 181
13.7–12, 613
13.70–72, 185
14.6, 499n14
22.14, 131
25.9, 618
30.10–14, 613

Machiavelli, *The Prince*, Chapter 25, 371
Marcellinus, *Life of Thucydides*
   22, 427
   33, 622
   35, 560
   43–44, 627
   45, 621n2
   46.3–4, 614
   54, 554
Menander, *Sicyonians*, 618
Mimnermus of Colophon
   frag. 14, 1–4 West^2, 562
   Smyrneis, 561

Nepos, *Themistocles*, 2.2, 60
Nicolaus of Damascus, *FGrH* 90 F 58.3, 54
Nietzsche, Friedrich, *Twilight of the Idols*,
   "What I Owe to the Ancients", 531

Old Oligarch. *see* Xenophon, *Athēnaiōn Politeia*
Ovid, *Metamorphoses*, 6.424–84, 260n6

Pausanias
   1.44.1, 52n6
   2.20.2, 154
   4.26.2, 134
   5.23.4, 148
   9.1.8, 500n18
   10.8.6, 56
   10.11.3, 558
   10.18.7, 55
Pherecrates, frags. 132–41 KA, 561
Philistus, *Sikelika*, 175
Phrynichus
   Monotropos, F 27, 617
   Phoenician Women, 561
   Sack of Miletus, 561

Pindar
   Olympian, 1.28–29, 562
   Pythian
      4, 561–62
      4.14.2, 561
      4.184–85, 561
Plato
   Apologia, 34b–d, 464
   Crito, 272n11
   Gorgias, 533
      482c–484c, 434
      483c–d, 583n43
      515e, 612
   Laws
      625c–638b, 333, 520n11
      625d–e, 321
      IV 722a f., 222
   Menexenus, 260, 610
      242 c–e, 140
   Meno, 533
   Parmenides, 127b–d, 199
   Phaedo, 636
      97bc–98b, 199
   Phaedrus, 578
      228a–b, 199
      234e6, 386
      261a, 578
      261c–d, 578
      267a–b, 578
      267 b, 211
   Politicus, 277c, 218
   Protagoras, 533, 568
      3.82f, 386, 583n42
      334e–335a, 576
      342b–c, 612
      361c–d, 545

   Republic, 227, 361, 523, 531, 533–34, 536–38, 544, 568, 583
      1, 516, 567
      1.327a, 227, 533
      1.338c–e, 582
      1.343d–344a, 583n43
      2, 542
      2.334c–335a, 543
      2.369d, 542
      2.373d, 542
      2.373e, 542
      2.375b, 542
      2.376b, 542
      2.382c–d, 416
      2.581a, 542
      4, 536
      4.354b–c, 537
      4.368d–369a, 536
      4.422a, 537
      4.422e–423b, 537
      4.427c–e, 533
      4.431c–d, 536
      4.433 ff., 578
      4.434c–435a, 536
      4.438a, 536
      4.439a, 536
      4.439a–b, 536
      4.439c–d, 536
      4.439e–440b, 537
      4.440c–d, 523
      4.469b, 537
      4.470c–d, 537
      4.471b, 537
      4.473c, 537
      4.497a, 537
      5, 538–39
      5.337c, 540
      5.452cd, 52n6
      5.468b–c, 543
      5.468d, 543
      5.471d–e, 533
      5.471e, 537
      5.475c, 543
      5.546a ff., 543
      5.582a, 539
      6.511b–c, 533
      7.520e–521a, 533
      7.521a, 531
      8, 477, 487, 535, 543
      8.328a, 545
      8.547d–548c, 520n11
      8.556d–557a, 543
      8.564a, 543
      8.566a–b, 544
      8.592b, 544
      8.618b, 544
      8.621c–d, 544

9, 535, 543
9.580d ff., 536
10.17b–e, 376
Symposium, 568
  221d–222a, 520
Theaetetus, 199
Timaeus, 26 c–d, 533
Plato Comicus
  Cleophon, 613
  Hyperbolus, 613
    F 203, 613
  Peisander, 610
Pliny the Elder, *Bella Germaniae*, 686n37
Plutarch
  Alcibiades, 145
    14.2, 150
    15.1, 154
    15.2, 154
    15.4–5, 154
    16.6, 155
  Aristides
    23, 67
    24.3–5, 136
    25.3, 74
  Cato Maior, 2.4, 678n5
  Cimon
    6, 67
    7.4–6, 69
    8.3–6, 44
    9, 68
  De Sera Numinis Vindicta, 599a–b, 580n33
  On the Glory of the Athenians
    3, 218
    347a, 20n1
  Lysander, 17, 521n12
  On the Malice of Herodotus
    21, 58
    855c–d, 648
  Moralia
    760e–761a, 59
    153f, 59
    193E, 499
    210C, 499
    314e–f, 622
    345c–e, 622n5, 623
    347a, 218

    811F, 610
    859a, 58
  Nicias
    1, 176
    4.1–2, 290
    9.6–97, 140
    23.1–24.1, 290
    28.4, 176
    29, 176
    30, 176
  Pelopidas, 23.4, 94
  Pericles, 609
    4.6, 451
    5.1, 451
    5.3, 451
    5.3–4, 451
    8.4, 610
    9.1, 451
    12, 78
    12.1, 74
    15.2, 611
    16, 610
    16.2, 615
    17.1, 44
    20.3, 49n4
    25.8, 107
    31–32, 119
    32.1, 610
    33.8, 611
  Themistocles, 4.2, 60
Polybius, *Histories*, 15, 659
  1.1.5–6, 664
  1.3.9, 663
  1.10.2–11.1, 664
  1.10.5, 665
  1.10.6, 665
  1.27–29, 664
  1.32–35, 664
  1.37.7, 665
  1.71.5–6, 665
  2.56.7–16, 663
  3, 665
  3.5.9, 662
  3.6–12, 662
  3.6.7, 660–61
  3.7.2–3, 661
  3.13, 662

Polybius, Histories (*cont.*)
   3.31.12, 662
   3.75.8, 665
   5.33.1–2, 666
   6, 700
   6.19.1–42.6, 700
   6.52.1, 665
   6.52.8–9, 665
   8.1.4, 665
   8.11.3, 660
   12.25a–b, 663
   12.25b.2–3, 663
   15.8–13, 661
   frag. 99, 661
Porphyry, frag. 21, 624
Priscus
   frag. 1b, 697n4, 698
   frag. 1b.3, 698
   frag. 1b.6, 698n6
Procopius
  Buildings, 699
  Gothic War, 701
   5–7, 694
   5.1.25–31, 702
   5.1.29, 702
   5.24.1, 702
   5.24.1–2, 702
   8, 694
  History of the Wars of Justinian, 15, 691, 693, 704
   1.1.1, 694
   1.15.2, 701
   1.24.12, 702
   1.70.2, 702
   1.93.5, 699n8
   3–4, 702–3
   3.9.25, 702
   3.16.14, 698
   5.7.37, 694
   5.8.7–18, 697
   5.14.9, 699n8
   5.21.3, 699
   6.4.1 ff., 699
   6.6.3 ff., 702
   6.20.14, 698
   6.24.3, 699
   7, 701
   7.5.1, 701
   7.15.2, 701
   7.19.6, 701
   7.25.4–5, 702
   7.32.7, 702
  Secret History, 701
   13.12, 701
Protagoras, DL 9.51 = 80 B 6a DK, 279
Pseudo-Hermogenes
   10.2, 695
   10.3, 695

Quintilian, *Institutio oratoria*
   4.2.45, 668
   6.2.30 ff., 218
   8.3.48, 215
   8.6.64, 227
   9.2.41, 217
   10.1.73, 659, 668
   10.1.101, 645, 666
   10.1.102, 668

Sallust
  Bellum Catilinae, 670
   1.2.5, 672
   1.3, 672
   1.5, 670
   2.1–2, 672
   2.5, 672
   2.9, 673
   3.3–4, 671
   3.3–4.2, 673
   3.4, 672
   4.1, 673
   6–13, 669
   6.5, 670
   10.1, 671
   10.3, 670
   38.3, 678n4
   41.1, 668
   51–52, 669–70
   52.11, 671, 678n4
   52.12, 668
  Bellum Iugurthinum, 670
   1.3, 672
   1.5, 673
   2.2, 672

2.3, 672
4.1, 672
4.5–6, 673
14, 669
31, 669
31.17, 670
34.1, 670
41.5, 671
60.4, 668, 670
63.3, 669
73.5, 668
85, 669
Histories, 678, 687n39
7.70–71, 668
A Selection of Greek Historical Inscriptions: to the End of the Fifth Century B.C., 2nd edition (ML)
17, 111
31, 76, 110
37, 75
40, 74, 75, 103, 109
40, lines 13–14, 101
45, 103, 108
45, §1, 101
45, §3, 101
45, §4, 102
45, §9, 101
46, 76, 108
46, lines 41–43, 103
52, 74, 103, 109
55, 73
65, 110
68, 105
69, 105, 107, 108, 135, 615
69, lines 4–6, 101
69, p. 193, 136
72, 135
72, p. 217, 136
73, 108
73, line 14, 103
87–88, 104
p. 120, 108
Seneca the Elder
Controversiae
9.1.13, 668
9.1.13–14, 678n5
Suasoriae, 6.21, 669, 678n7

Seneca the Younger, *Epistulae*
84, 689
84.7, 689
114.17, 668
Simonides
frag. 10–11 West^2, 562
frag. 10–18 West^2, 561
frag. 549 Page, 48
Sophocles
Antigone, 33
Oedipus Tyrannus, 595–97
31, 596
137–41, 595
1187–88, 596
Philoctetes, 1316–17, 376
Standards Decree
(ML) 45, 103, 108
§1, 101
§3, 101
§4, 102
§9, 101
State Archives of Assyria, 19 025, 54n9
Stesichorus frag. 216, 48
Stesimbrotus of
Thasos, *FGrH* 107 F 10b, 610
Strabo, 10.1.12, 59
Suda (Pi, 2301), 694

Tacitus
Agricola
1.1, 687n42
32.5, 688n43
Annals, 678n8
1.32.2, 687n42
3.55.5, 687, 687n42
3.65.1, 688n44
4.11.3, 688
4.35.3, 688
4.38.2, 688n44
6.32.4, 688n44
15.59.3, 688n43
16.25.2, 688n43
Dialogus de oratoribus, 23.6, 688n43
Germania, 45.6, 684n26
Histories
1.1.1, 688
1.2.1, 688

Tacitus (*cont.*)
    1.21.2, 688n43
    1.61.2, 686n33
    1.84.4, 688n43
    2.47.2, 688, 688n43
    2.50.1, 688
    2.50.5, 687n42
    2.69.1, 686
    3, 684
    3.3.5, 685
    3.13.1, 681
    3.15–16, 684–85
    3.16, 685
    3.16.1, 681
    3.25.1, 684
    3.29–33, 684
    3.46.1, 684, 685n29
    3.46.2, 683, 686
    4–5, 684n25
    4.12–37, 680
    4.12.1, 681n15, 686
    4.12.3, 679n11
    4.13.1, 679n11
    4.13.2–3, 685n30
    4.13.3, 681n14
    4.14.1–2, 681n13
    4.14.4, 679n11, 685n30, 686n33
    4.15.1, 679n11
    4.15.3, 679n11, 686n33
    4.16.2, 686
    4.16.2–3, 686n32
    4.17.1, 682n19, 687n42
    4.17.2, 679n11
    4.17.3, 682n20
    4.17.4, 685n30
    4.17.5, 679n11, 682n19, 686n38
    4.17.6, 683n23
    4.18.1, 681n15, 682n20, 683n22
    4.18.3, 686n32
    4.19.1, 686n32
    4.19.3, 681n14
    4.20.1–2, 685n29
    4.20.2, 682n20, 686n33
    4.20.2–3, 686n32
    4.21.1, 685n30
    4.21.1–2, 685n28
    4.21.2, 685n27

4.22.2, 681n14, 686
4.22.3, 686n33
4.23.3, 685n27
4.24.1, 682n20
4.24.3, 681n14
4.25.1, 685n28
4.25.2, 685n29
4.25.3, 682n19, 686n32
4.27.3, 681n14
4.28.1, 683
4.28.2, 683n22
4.31.2, 681n14
4.32.1, 685n30
4.32.2, 681n13
4.32.3, 682n19
4.33.2, 686n32
4.33.2–2, 682n20
4.35.3–4, 685n29
4.35.4, 681
4.36.1, 682
4.36.2, 681n14, 685n29
4.37.2, 681n14
4.37.3, 685n27
4.44.1, 686n36
4.45.1, 686n36
4.46.3, 686n36
4.53, 686n36
4.54–67, 680
4.54.1, 682, 685
4.54.3, 682n19, 686n38
4.55, 686n32
4.55.2, 686n34
4.55.3, 683n22
4.55.4, 679n11, 682n19, 686
4.56.1, 681n14, 683
4.57.1, 685
4.57.2, 685n30
4.58, 685
4.58.5, 682n19
4.59.1, 685
4.59.1–3, 683
4.59.2, 686n34
4.59.2–3, 682
4.60.2, 682
4.60.2–3, 685n27
4.61.2, 683, 684n26
4.63, 683

4.63.1, 683
4.63.2–63, 685n27
4.64, 683
4.64.2–3, 684
4.65, 684
4.65.1, 682n19, 683
4.65.3–4, 684n26
4.66.1, 686n32
4.66.2, 683n23
4.66.2–3, 686n32
4.67.1, 686
4.67.2, 682n19, 686
4.68.1–4, 686
4.68.4–5, 686n36
4.68.5, 686
4.68.5–4.79, 680
4.69.1, 686, 686n36
4.70.3, 682
4.70.5, 683
4.71.2, 681
4.72.1–2, 683n21
4.72.2, 686n36
4.73.2, 686
4.74.1, 681n13
4.76.1, 682n20, 685n27
4.76.2, 685, 685n27
4.78.1, 682n19, 685n27
4.79.1–2, 684
4.79.4, 681n16
5.14–26, 680
5.17.2, 688n44
5.19.1, 679n11
5.23.3, 678n7
5.24–25, 685n27
5.24.1, 684n26
5.25.1, 685
5.25.2, 679n11, 682n19, 684n26
5.26.3, 685n30, 686

Telecleides
  F 18, 610
  F 45, 610, 615

Theon, *Progymnasmata*, 625

Theophylact Simocatta, *Histories*, 693
  3.12.12–14.11, 692

Theopompus
  frag. 259, 636
  frag. 275, 636

frag. 332–33, 636
Hellenica, 14, 624
  FGH 115 F 20, 624
Philippica, 624
  frag. 22, 625
  frag. 25, 624
  frag. 70, 625
  frag. 96, 625
  frag. 102, 625
  frag. 164, 625
  frag. 166, 625
  frag. 395, 625

Thucydides, *History of the Peloponnesian War*
  1, 29, 156, 171, 200–202, 344, 393, 403, 444, 455, 481, 504, 507, 539, 554, 644, 665
  1–7, 629
  1.1, 20–22, 169–70, 195, 228, 257, 296, 314, 443, 457, 486, 538, 563, 611, 644
  1.1–19, 200, 208
  1.1–21, 2
  1.1–23, 6, 40n1, 49–60, 264, 296, 339, 343n3, 344–45, 347, 350, 395, 397, 409–10, 587
  1.1.1, 22, 32, 39–40, 99, 320, 380, 587, 678n4, 693
  1.1.1–2, 39, 223
  1.1.2, 40, 146, 247, 320, 367, 380, 391, 431, 517, 538
  1.1.3, 22, 39, 264, 554
  1.1.3–18.2, 554, 563
  1.1.5, 517n2
  1.1.6–7, 517n2
  1.2, 23, 323
  1.2–11, 260
  1.2–12, 323
  1.2–19, 64, 241, 669
  1.2–20, 228, 321, 644
  1.2.1, 43, 53n7, 248, 258, 554
  1.2.2, 43, 340, 501
  1.2.2–3, 499n12
  1.2.3–6, 48
  1.2.4, 43, 260n5, 395, 409
  1.2.5, 44
  1.2.6, 43–44, 48, 499n12
  1.2 ff., 568
  1.3, 23
  1.3.1, 53n7, 258–59
  1.3.1–2, 340

Thucydides, *History of the Peloponnesian War (cont.)*
  1.3.2, 47, 501
  1.3.2–3, 47
  1.3.3, 47, 248, 261, 400, 560
  1.3.3–4, 560
  1.3.4, 43, 259, 341
  1.4, 43, 47, 248
  1.4.1, 258
  1.4.5, 341
  1.5–6, 23
  1.5.1, 43, 499n12
  1.5.1–2, 43
  1.5.1–6.2, 43
  1.5.2, 51n5, 261, 587
  1.5.3, 28, 400, 499n12
  1.6, 397, 400
  1.6.1, 43, 341
  1.6.3, 44, 247, 261n8, 341
  1.6.4, 42, 341, 395, 399–400
  1.6.5, 42, 51
  1.6.6, 42, 400
  1.7, 43–44, 342, 499n12
  1.7.1, 43
  1.8, 261
  1.8.1, 51n5, 264n14
  1.8.2, 43, 47, 341
  1.8.2–4, 259
  1.8.3, 29, 44, 47, 341
  1.8.3–4, 517
  1.9–11, 328
  1.9.1, 47, 261
  1.9.1–4, 248, 259
  1.9.2, 230, 261, 501, 557
  1.9.2–3, 47
  1.9.3, 29, 47, 248, 261, 501
  1.9.4, 47, 53n7, 342, 587
  1.10, 78, 321, 560
  1.10.1, 22, 319, 587
  1.10.1–2, 24
  1.10.2, 48, 260, 336, 343
  1.10.3, 24, 261, 341, 587
  1.10.3–5, 560
  1.10.4, 45, 701
  1.10.5, 22, 44, 53n7, 196
  1.11, 53n7
  1.11–12.1, 259

  1.11.1, 44–45
  1.11.2, 45, 260
  1.12–14, 322
  1.12.1, 45
  1.12.1–3, 48
  1.12.2, 45
  1.12.4, 45, 48
  1.13, 257
  1.13–15, 83
  1.13.1, 43, 45–46, 342, 400
  1.13.1–2, 46
  1.13.2, 52
  1.13.2–4, 53
  1.13.3, 52, 53n7, 342
  1.13.4, 52
  1.13.5, 43, 45, 53, 342
  1.13.6, 48, 55
  1.14.1, 45, 53, 53n7, 55
  1.14.2, 46, 58, 400
  1.14.3, 45–46
  1.14.6, 342
  1.15, 57
  1.15.1, 48, 342
  1.15.2, 48, 342
  1.16, 56
  1.16.3, 342
  1.17, 48, 57–58, 400
  1.18, 499n12
  1.18.1, 49, 51, 58, 332, 335–36, 343, 397, 399–401, 403, 414
  1.18.2, 46, 48–49, 83
  1.18.2–19, 554
  1.18.3, 47, 321, 501
  1.19, 47, 49, 68, 104, 397, 398n13
  1.20, 24, 248, 273, 328, 568, 575
  1.20–22, 125, 241
  1.20–23, 195, 200
  1.20.1, 22–23, 257, 262, 552
  1.20.2, 230, 262, 553
  1.20.3, 22–23, 195, 410, 553, 641
  1.21, 40n1, 577
  1.21–22, 21, 39, 147, 380, 443, 457, 460
  1.21–23, 644
  1.21.1, 22–23, 32, 196, 257, 260, 261n7, 268n4, 273, 380, 557, 559, 563, 587, 603, 668
  1.21.2, 39–40, 169, 196, 257, 273, 553, 563
  1.22, 7, 272, 533

1.22.1, 22, 25–27, 273, 386, 575, 577n23
1.22.1–2, 257
1.22.2, 23, 174, 195, 244, 575
1.22.2–3, 129
1.22.2–4, 257, 678n4
1.22.3, 22, 25, 553
1.22.4, 7, 22, 29, 31, 174, 196, 249, 258, 261,
    284, 297, 314, 320, 322, 340, 352, 378,
    380, 386, 388, 392, 410, 427, 457, 459,
    509, 554, 563, 577, 605, 648, 652, 656,
    662–63, 671, 678, 687
1.22.5, 574
1.23, 28, 223, 241, 251, 254, 322, 491,
    538–40, 554
1.23.1, 214, 239
1.23.1–2, 380
1.23.1–3, 39, 169, 223, 263, 563, 573
1.23.1–4, 164
1.23.2, 40n1
1.23.2–3, 30, 32, 34
1.23.3, 40n1, 240, 368
1.23.4, 661–62
1.23.4–6, 660
1.23.5, 28, 196, 504–8, 661–63
1.23.5–6, 64, 68, 115, 125, 503–8, 662
1.23.6, 28, 63–65, 68, 117, 173, 215, 243, 248,
    258, 332–33, 374, 388, 443, 454, 459, 491,
    504–6, 508, 611, 661, 665
1.24–28, 302
1.24–55, 28, 200
1.24–67, 507
1.24.2, 54
1.25, 54
1.25.1, 668
1.25.4, 259
1.26–67, 504
1.26.3, 497
1.29–30, 302
1.31, 302
1.31–55, 53
1.31.2, 501
1.32–36, 201
1.32–43, 269
1.34.3, 694
1.36.1–2, 493
1.37–43, 201
1.37.1, 386

1.40.3, 497
1.40.5, 54
1.41.2, 53–54
1.42, 494n4
1.42.2, 215, 668
1.44.2, 501
1.46–55, 302
1.49.3, 477
1.50.1, 307n2
1.51.2, 128
1.55, 671
1.56–61, 303
1.56–65, 28
1.56–66, 200
1.56.2, 501n20
1.57.2, 400
1.57.2–5, 304
1.62.3–4, 303
1.66–88, 81
1.67–87, 506
1.67–88, 200
1.67.3–4, 507n35
1.68–69, 140
1.68–70, 332
1.68–71, 76, 82, 148, 201, 293, 378, 608,
    665, 671
1.68–78, 270
1.68–87, 270
1.68.1, 403
1.68.2, 507n33, 507n35
1.68.3, 507
1.69, 82
1.69.1, 345–46, 464, 507
1.69.4, 345, 517
1.69.5, 42, 82
1.70, 78, 330, 393, 397, 431
1.70.1–4, 404
1.70.1–9, 397
1.70.2, 345, 379
1.70.2–4, 83
1.70.3, 432, 455
1.70.4, 345–46, 468
1.70.4–9, 466
1.70.5–6, 181
1.70.7, 346, 350, 665
1.70.7–9, 455
1.70.8, 345–46, 379, 468

Thucydides, *History of the*
　　Peloponnesian War (cont.)
　1.70.8–9, 517
　1.70.9, 367
　1.71, 82, 367
　1.71.1, 345
　1.71.2, 345
　1.71.2–3, 82, 90
　1.71.3, 83, 403, 466
　1.71.4, 140
　1.71.4–5, 82
　1.71.4–7, 92, 507
　1.71.5, 82
　1.72, 539
　1.72–86, 120
　1.72.1, 432
　1.73–74, 334, 433
　1.73–75, 42
　1.73–78, 109, 111, 201, 539
　1.73–86, 123
　1.73.1, 260, 522
　1.73.2–75.2, 47
　1.74, 333, 348
　1.74.1, 46
　1.74.2, 83
　1.74.3, 447
　1.75, 433, 540
　1.75–76, 325, 540
　1.75.1–3, 382
　1.75.2, 47, 65, 382
　1.75.3, 356–57, 382, 461
　1.75.4, 382, 456
　1.75.5, 381
　1.76, 336, 534
　1.76–77, 540
　1.76.1, 433
　1.76.1–2, 456
　1.76.2, 110, 258, 325, 340, 356–57, 382, 433,
　　　501–2, 522
　1.76.2–4, 325
　1.76.3–4, 356, 383, 522
　1.77, 76, 103, 522
　1.77.1, 103
　1.77.1–5, 356
　1.77.6, 501, 529, 634
　1.78, 332
　1.78.1–2, 171

　1.78.4, 428
　1.79, 140
　1.79.1, 270
　1.79.2, 40, 284, 398
　1.80, 216, 477
　1.80–81, 84
　1.80–85, 76, 201, 284, 284n2,
　　　331, 541
　1.80–85.2, 83, 286
　1.80–86, 270
　1.80.1, 86
　1.80.3, 40–41
　1.80.3–4, 84, 345n4
　1.80.4, 41
　1.81.1, 41
　1.81.2, 304
　1.81.2–6, 84, 86
　1.81.3, 304
　1.81.3–4, 84
　1.81.4, 41
　1.81.6, 140
　1.82.1, 41, 84
　1.82.2, 41
　1.82.2–4, 84, 86
　1.82.5, 41
　1.82.5–6, 41
　1.83.2, 41, 84
　1.83.2–3, 84
　1.84, 398, 403, 541
　1.84–85.1, 84–85
　1.84.1–2, 85, 331
　1.84.2–3, 432
　1.84.3, 84, 331
　1.84.3–4, 332
　1.84.4, 84, 403, 469
　1.85, 332
　1.85.1, 85–86
　1.85.2, 428
　1.86, 77, 85, 140, 201, 284, 508
　1.86–87, 332
　1.86–88, 332, 335
　1.86.1–5, 507
　1.86.2, 398
　1.86.3, 41
　1.86.5, 428, 507
　1.87, 270
　1.87–88, 85, 334

1.88, 29, 64, 116, 243, 270, 332–33, 350, 506–7, 507n33
1.88.1, 374
1.89, 343
1.89–117, 21, 507
1.89–118, 200, 270
1.89.1, 243, 630
1.90–92, 120, 343
1.93.3, 402
1.93.3–4, 46
1.93.3–8, 324
1.94, 65
1.94–95, 415
1.94–97.1, 49
1.95, 66
1.95.1, 66, 197
1.95.4, 67
1.95.5, 67
1.95.7, 400
1.96, 100
1.96.1, 67
1.96.1–2, 68, 104
1.96.2, 104
1.97, 22, 64
1.97.1, 68, 100–101
1.97.2, 22, 243, 555
1.98.1, 500n18
1.98.2, 44, 500n18
1.98.4, 70, 110
1.99, 68, 70, 75
1.99.1, 387
1.100, 69–70
1.100.1, 214
1.100.2–101.2, 214
1.100.3, 69
1.101, 335
1.101–102, 335
1.101–103, 345n4
1.101.3, 69, 501n20
1.103, 428
1.103.3, 133
1.103.4, 53, 77, 121, 133
1.104, 71
1.105.3–4, 307n2
1.106.2, 500
1.106.3, 231
1.107–108, 77, 313

1.107.4, 326
1.108.3, 133
1.109.1, 35
1.110, 71
1.110.2, 701
1.111.2, 285n3, 461
1.112, 72, 428
1.113, 325
1.113–14, 133
1.113.1, 500n18
1.113.4, 34
1.114, 72n2, 313, 461, 632
1.114.1, 285n3, 500
1.114.2, 130
1.114.3, 103, 107, 285n3, 500n18
1.115–17, 107
1.115.1, 148
1.115.2–117, 72
1.115.3, 103
1.115.5, 102
1.116–17, 461
1.116.1, 285n3
1.116.2, 131, 682
1.116.3, 285n3
1.117.2, 285n3, 682
1.117.3, 501n20
1.118, 71, 428
1.118–46, 504, 507
1.118.1, 72
1.118.2, 64, 116, 243, 431, 506–7, 507n34, 508, 563
1.118.3, 245, 332, 368, 428, 439, 492
1.119–25, 200
1.120–24, 85, 201
1.120.1, 41
1.120.2, 41
1.120.3, 595
1.121, 330, 332
1.121–23, 130
1.121.2, 41, 86
1.121.3, 41, 85
1.121.4, 41, 88
1.121.5, 41, 85
1.122, 333
1.122–24, 332
1.122.1, 85
1.122.2, 41

Thucydides, *History of the Peloponnesian War (cont.)*
- 1.122.3, 400n21
- 1.122.4, 140, 451
- 1.123, 332
- 1.123.1, 428, 439
- 1.124.1, 41
- 1.124.3, 400n21
- 1.125, 86
- 1.125–35, 498
- 1.125.2, 41
- 1.126–34, 428
- 1.126–39, 200
- 1.126.6, 401
- 1.127, 324
- 1.127.1, 401n23
- 1.127.2–3, 285
- 1.128–30, 67
- 1.128.1, 335
- 1.128.2–35.1, 415
- 1.130, 334
- 1.130.1–2, 400
- 1.130.2, 67
- 1.131, 335
- 1.131–33, 334, 702
- 1.132, 334
- 1.132.2, 400
- 1.132.4, 335
- 1.133, 236
- 1.134, 334
- 1.135.2–38, 250
- 1.138, 402
- 1.138.2, 294n10
- 1.138.3, 249, 264n16, 274, 702
- 1.138.4, 297n14, 402
- 1.138.6, 335
- 1.139, 119, 121
- 1.139–45, 119, 497
- 1.139.3, 140
- 1.139.4, 244, 250, 264n16, 285, 374, 461, 472
- 1.140, 64, 123, 481
- 1.140–41, 324–25
- 1.140–44, 200–201, 275, 284n2, 508
- 1.140.1, 262n11, 264n16, 278, 285, 383, 399, 450, 461
- 1.140.2, 383, 428
- 1.140.2–41.1, 140
- 1.140.4–5, 612
- 1.140.4–41.1, 461
- 1.140.5, 123, 503
- 1.141, 539
- 1.141.1, 383, 428, 498
- 1.141.2–44, 83
- 1.141.2–44.1, 130, 429
- 1.141.3, 41, 86, 344
- 1.141.4–7, 345
- 1.141.5, 41
- 1.141.6, 41
- 1.141.7, 41
- 1.142.1, 41
- 1.142.5–9, 41
- 1.142.6–9, 86, 88
- 1.142.7, 41, 345
- 1.143.1, 345
- 1.143.2, 41
- 1.143.4, 84, 130–31
- 1.143.5, 41, 447, 503, 595
- 1.144, 539, 542
- 1.144.1, 106, 132–33, 595
- 1.144.2, 49, 140, 428
- 1.144.3, 373, 461
- 1.144.3–4, 324
- 1.145, 428, 495
- 1.145–2.1, 200
- 1.145.1, 285
- 1.146.1, 507
- 1.171, 259n3
- 2, 189, 202, 302, 392, 393n5, 536, 580
- 2–5.24, 206
- 2.1, 22, 179, 201, 321
- 2.1–5.24, 130
- 2.2–3, 326
- 2.2–7, 309
- 2.2.1, 556, 561
- 2.2 ff., 579
- 2.3, 581
- 2.5, 573n13, 579, 581
- 2.5.7, 599
- 2.6, 336
- 2.7, 579
- 2.7.2, 41, 131
- 2.8, 314
- 2.8.1, 322
- 2.8.4, 140, 332

INDEX LOCORUM   731

2.8.4–5, 322, 325, 336, 464
2.8.5, 501
2.9–94, 333
2.10, 86
2.10–23, 86
2.11, 86, 284, 284n2, 332
2.11.1, 86
2.11.2, 86
2.11.4, 262n11, 451
2.11.6–8, 86, 130
2.11.7, 447
2.11.9, 41, 86
2.12–13, 275
2.12.1–2, 462
2.12.1–4, 86
2.12.3, 267n3
2.13, 201, 284n2
2.13.1, 86, 286, 326, 401, 451, 678n7
2.13.2, 132, 450
2.13.2–5, 41
2.13.2–8, 286
2.13.3, 75, 104, 135–36
2.13.6–8, 41, 439
2.14, 86, 448, 627
2.14–16, 322
2.14–17, 286, 429
2.14.2, 263
2.14.2–15, 263–64
2.15, 21
2.15.1, 263
2.15.1–2, 44
2.15.2, 41, 249, 264, 324, 387, 401–2
2.15.3–5, 263
2.15.3–6, 323
2.16, 484
2.16.1, 264
2.16.1–2, 264
2.16.2, 86, 448, 452
2.17.1–2, 427
2.17.2, 246, 440
2.18, 333–34
2.18–20, 284
2.18.2–5, 86, 92
2.18.3, 86
2.18.3–4, 86
2.19.1, 35
2.20, 87

2.20.1–22.1, 41
2.20.4, 612
2.21, 328
2.21.1, 333–34
2.21.1–22.1, 130
2.21.2–22.1, 86–87
2.21.2–22.2, 130
2.21.3, 427, 448, 612
2.21.3–22.1, 462
2.22, 327
2.22.1, 448, 450
2.23, 87, 284
2.24.1, 135
2.25, 295, 334
2.25.2, 415
2.26.2, 133
2.27, 106–7, 213, 500n18, 632
2.28, 369
2.29.3, 247, 249n14, 260n6
2.29.3–4, 400
2.30.1, 400, 500n18
2.31.2, 216
2.31.3, 132
2.32, 44
2.33.1, 132, 400
2.34.4, 250
2.34.6, 264n16, 562, 564
2.35, 435
2.35–36, 612
2.35–36.2, 260
2.35–46, 201, 268, 284n2, 286, 323, 499, 501, 644
2.35–46.1, 670
2.35–65, 5
2.35.1, 197, 324, 462
2.35.2, 212, 563, 670
2.36, 324, 435, 615, 694
2.36.1, 260n5, 278n21, 563
2.36.2, 467, 563
2.36.3, 351, 463–64, 563
2.36.4, 393, 463
2.36.7–46.1, 436
2.37, 323, 328, 454
2.37–40, 323
2.37–41, 204
2.37.1, 278n21, 324, 398, 462–63
2.37.2, 400, 462–63

Thucydides, *History of the*
    Peloponnesian War (cont.)
  2.37.2–3, 452
  2.37.3, 452, 463, 466
  2.37.4, 225
  2.38, 468, 605–6
  2.38–40, 324
  2.38.1, 436
  2.38.2, 369
  2.39, 332
  2.39.1, 400, 403, 461–62, 471
  2.40, 333, 481, 541
  2.40.1, 398, 436
  2.40.2, 347, 404, 460, 462
  2.40.2–3, 330
  2.40.2–4, 436
  2.40.4, 463, 670
  2.40.4–5, 463
  2.41, 324, 480, 538, 541
  2.41.1, 85, 204, 311, 436, 463–64
  2.41.2–5, 563
  2.41.4, 260–61, 437, 563, 605
  2.42.2, 451, 498, 563
  2.42.4, 230, 452
  2.43, 357, 538
  2.43–6, 537
  2.43.1, 361, 436, 451–52, 463, 610
  2.43.1–2, 228–29
  2.43.2, 352, 463
  2.43.3, 452
  2.44, 452
  2.44.1, 250
  2.44.4, 452
  2.45, 538
  2.45.1, 625
  2.46, 634
  2.46.2, 463
  2.47, 573
  2.47–50, 438
  2.47–54, 138, 325, 330, 368
  2.47–59, 392
  2.47.2, 87, 571, 573
  2.47.2–54, 286
  2.47.3, 368
  2.48, 195, 368
  2.48.2, 368
  2.48.3, 196, 296, 571, 663
  2.49, 138, 330
  2.49.1, 573
  2.49.2, 570–71
  2.49.3, 138, 570
  2.49.7–8, 439
  2.50, 368
  2.50.1, 378, 427, 438, 456, 463, 573
  2.50.1–2, 569
  2.51.1, 572
  2.51.2, 571
  2.51.3, 204, 570
  2.51.4, 439
  2.51.5, 139, 456, 463, 572
  2.51.6, 139, 626
  2.52, 574
  2.52–53, 327, 439
  2.52.2, 217–18, 221
  2.52.3–4, 33
  2.52.4, 138, 331, 456
  2.53, 138, 331
  2.53.1–3, 456
  2.53.4, 456
  2.54.2, 245
  2.54.2–5, 440
  2.54.3, 245
  2.54.4, 245, 368, 428, 439
  2.54.4–5, 573, 573n11
  2.55–56.1, 87
  2.55.2, 450
  2.56, 137
  2.56–57, 330
  2.56.1–2, 131
  2.56.3, 461
  2.56.5, 126, 131
  2.57, 87, 137
  2.58.3, 138
  2.59, 328, 650
  2.59–65.3, 86
  2.59.1, 611
  2.59.1–2, 450
  2.59.1–3, 399, 463
  2.59.2, 119, 286
  2.59.3, 450, 702
  2.60, 480, 483
  2.60–64, 201, 275, 284n2, 286, 437
  2.60.1, 262n11, 383, 449
  2.60.2, 449

2.60.2–4, 396
2.60.4–7, 449
2.60.5, 272, 274, 452, 460, 464
2.60.5–6, 286, 289
2.61, 322, 539
2.61.1, 383–84, 494–95
2.61.2, 449–50, 464
2.61.3, 440, 463
2.61.4, 324, 449, 452
2.61.5–7, 401
2.62, 429
2.62.1, 450
2.62.1–2, 468
2.62.2, 346, 437
2.62.2–3, 83–84
2.62.3, 451, 670
2.62.4, 451
2.62.5, 451
2.63, 108, 611, 615
2.63–64, 324
2.63.1, 346, 383–84
2.63.1–2, 456
2.63.1–3, 382
2.63.2, 112, 248, 347, 383, 400n21, 420, 437, 522, 610
2.63.3, 347
2.64, 330, 437, 534, 541
2.64.1, 463
2.64.2, 287, 376, 440
2.64.3, 287, 351, 381, 383, 702
2.64.3–5, 384
2.64.4–5, 384
2.64.5, 467
2.64.6–5, 352
2.65, 22, 107, 117, 179, 201, 250, 253–54, 262, 286–87, 293, 324, 399, 478–80, 482, 485, 541, 611, 613
2.65.1, 449
2.65.1–4, 399
2.65.1–13, 702
2.65.2, 611, 627
2.65.2–4, 464
2.65.3, 297, 328
2.65.4, 399, 611
2.65.5, 264n16, 321, 388, 429
2.65.5–13, 381
2.65.6, 402, 429

2.65.6–11, 461
2.65.7, 106, 130, 132, 253, 350, 430, 453, 455, 521
2.65.7–10, 132
2.65.7–11, 393n5
2.65.7–13, 396
2.65.8, 286, 374, 388, 399
2.65.8–9, 324, 447, 450
2.65.8–10, 140
2.65.8–11, 430
2.65.9, 401, 418, 453, 470, 472, 610, 702
2.65.10, 614
2.65.10–11, 326, 402
2.65.10–12, 230, 295
2.65.11, 133, 162, 167, 253, 351, 453, 521
2.65.11–12, 171
2.65.11–13, 72, 286
2.65.12, 230, 252–53, 298, 330, 381, 430
2.65.12–13, 179
2.65.13, 429
2.66, 87, 132
2.67, 111, 324
2.67.4, 324, 336
2.68, 21
2.68.3–5, 248
2.68.7, 500n18
2.69, 106, 330
2.69.1, 44
2.70, 329, 536
2.70.1, 218, 387
2.71–74, 267n3, 697
2.71–78, 696
2.71.2, 428
2.71 ff., 579
2.72, 579
2.72.1, 284n2, 698
2.72.3, 284n2
2.74, 336, 428, 579
2.74.2, 284n2, 428
2.75–77, 309
2.75–78, 336, 696, 697n3
2.75.1, 697
2.75.4, 697
2.75.5, 698
2.75.6, 697
2.76.4, 698
2.77.5, 314

Thucydides, *History of the Peloponnesian War (cont.)*
- 2.77.5–6, 598
- 2.78, 336
- 2.79, 308n5
- 2.79–94, 330
- 2.80, 303
- 2.80–81, 42
- 2.80–82, 91
- 2.80–92, 87–88, 302
- 2.81.4, 701
- 2.83–92, 132, 308n5
- 2.84.2, 88, 303
- 2.84.2–4, 88
- 2.85–93, 295
- 2.85.1, 88–89
- 2.85.2, 88, 334
- 2.86–90, 703
- 2.86.6, 334
- 2.87, 274n16
- 2.87.2, 88
- 2.87.3, 88
- 2.87.3–9, 88–89
- 2.87.4–5, 333
- 2.87.4–59, 332
- 2.87.9, 88
- 2.89, 312, 701
- 2.89.2, 88, 333
- 2.89.8, 89
- 2.90, 89
- 2.90.1, 89
- 2.91, 89, 333
- 2.91.4, 89
- 2.91.4–92.1, 308n4
- 2.92.1, 89
- 2.92.1–2, 89
- 2.92.3, 89
- 2.93–94, 89, 331
- 2.93.1, 89
- 2.93.3, 89
- 2.93.4–94.3, 90
- 2.94.1, 90, 598
- 2.95–101, 42
- 2.95–102, 246
- 2.95.2, 247
- 2.96.1, 246–47
- 2.96.2, 246
- 2.96.3, 247
- 2.97.1, 246
- 2.97.2, 189, 189n7
- 2.97.4, 246
- 2.97.4–5, 246
- 2.97.5, 42
- 2.97.6, 42
- 2.98.3, 246
- 2.98.4, 246, 701
- 2.99.3–6, 248
- 2.101.5–6, 247
- 2.102, 21, 369
- 2.102.5–6, 248
- 3, 202, 204, 208, 212, 216, 224, 302, 393, 445, 486, 531, 540, 588–89, 591
- 3.1, 87, 217
- 3.1–3, 87
- 3.2–6, 588–89, 680
- 3.2.1, 322, 683
- 3.2.1–4.2, 375
- 3.2.3, 48
- 3.3.1, 681n15
- 3.4.1–4, 697
- 3.5.1, 681n16
- 3.6.1, 681n16
- 3.7, 588–89
- 3.8–15, 588–89
- 3.8–18, 680
- 3.9–14, 109, 325
- 3.9.2, 681n13
- 3.9.3, 679n11
- 3.10.3, 65
- 3.10.4, 681n13
- 3.10.4–5, 681n13
- 3.10.5, 679n11
- 3.11.1, 681n13
- 3.12.3, 681n13
- 3.13.2, 683
- 3.13.3, 330, 679n11
- 3.13.5, 679n11
- 3.13.7, 464
- 3.14–15, 428
- 3.15–16, 87, 90
- 3.16, 137
- 3.16–17, 330
- 3.16–19, 588–89
- 3.16.1, 503

3.16.3, 90
3.17, 46, 135, 137
3.18.5, 131
3.19, 137
3.19–24, 336
3.19.1, 137, 681n16
3.20, 699
3.20–22, 309
3.20–24, 334, 588–89, 697n3
3.21, 696
3.21–24, 579
3.22.1, 699
3.24–33, 680
3.25–26, 87, 588
3.25–33.1, 87, 90
3.26, 87
3.26.1, 90
3.27, 333–34
3.27–28, 588–89
3.27–33, 336
3.27.1, 90
3.27.3, 109, 681n14
3.28, 207
3.29, 90, 333
3.29–33, 131
3.29–34, 588–89
3.29.1, 90
3.30, 90
3.31, 90, 333
3.31.1–2, 90
3.31.2–33.1, 90
3.32, 336
3.33, 333
3.33–36, 333
3.34.1–2, 500n18
3.35, 207, 540
3.35–50, 588, 680, 682
3.36, 207, 275
3.36–50, 501n19, 540, 635
3.36.2, 449, 679n11
3.36.2–5, 593
3.36.4, 688
3.36.5, 446
3.36.6, 26–27, 275, 278, 287, 325
3.37, 108, 347
3.37–38, 540
3.37–40, 198, 287

3.37–48, 669–71
3.37.2, 248, 382, 400n21, 456, 681n13, 685n31
3.37.3, 403
3.38, 483
3.38.1, 449
3.38.4–7, 596
3.38.7, 275, 577
3.39, 104
3.39.2, 679n11, 681n13
3.39.2–6, 385
3.39.3–4, 449
3.39.4–5, 445
3.39.5, 679n11, 694
3.39.6, 449, 681n14
3.39.7, 685n31
3.40, 325
3.40.1, 385
3.40.2–3, 445
3.40.3, 605
3.40.4, 681n13
3.40.7, 449, 685n31
3.42, 483, 540
3.42–48, 287
3.42.1, 445
3.42.1–5, 445
3.43, 446, 540
3.43.2, 386
3.43.2–3, 446
3.43.3, 399
3.45, 337, 437, 531
3.45.3, 360, 445
3.45.4, 445
3.45.5, 445, 454
3.45.5–6, 596
3.45.6, 681n13
3.45.6–7, 360
3.45.7, 445
3.46.4, 682
3.46.5, 681n13
3.46.5–6, 325
3.47.2–3, 395n9
3.47.2–4, 681n14
3.48, 445
3.48.1, 445
3.49, 112
3.49–50, 325
3.49.1, 593

Thucydides, *History of the*
    Peloponnesian War (cont.)
    3.49.4, 107, 598
    3.50, 103, 207, 500n18, 682
    3.50.1, 213, 599
    3.51, 106, 133, 588–89, 593
    3.51.2, 131
    3.52, 335, 697n3
    3.52–68, 541, 588–89
    3.52.2, 579
    3.52.4, 336
    3.52.4–5, 593
    3.53–67, 579
    3.53–68, 578
    3.54.3, 494n4
    3.54.5, 335
    3.55, 58, 336
    3.56, 336
    3.56.1–3, 494
    3.56.2, 579, 581, 581n35
    3.56.3, 580
    3.57, 336
    3.57.1–2, 494n4
    3.58.2, 277
    3.58.3, 580–81, 600
    3.59.1, 277
    3.59.4, 464
    3.60–67, 366
    3.60.1, 197
    3.61, 58
    3.61–67, 268
    3.61.1, 580
    3.62, 335, 580
    3.65, 580
    3.66.2, 580
    3.66.3, 580
    3.67.6, 494, 580–81
    3.67.6–7, 581
    3.68, 333, 335, 500n18, 541
    3.68.1, 230, 336
    3.68.1–2, 593
    3.68.2, 593
    3.68.3, 336
    3.68.4, 336
    3.68.5, 58, 216
    3.69, 87, 90, 295, 581
    3.70, 500n18
    3.70–80, 295
    3.70–84, 393
    3.70.1, 410
    3.70.3, 410
    3.70.4–5, 410
    3.70.6, 102, 410
    3.70 ff., 217
    3.71–72.3, 410
    3.72.2, 420
    3.72.3, 217
    3.73, 398n14, 410
    3.73.1, 217
    3.74, 410, 538
    3.74.1, 217
    3.74.1–2, 217
    3.75–81, 240
    3.75.1, 217, 410
    3.75.3, 411
    3.75.4, 411
    3.75.5, 411
    3.76, 411
    3.76–80, 132
    3.76–81.1, 88, 90
    3.77.1, 411
    3.77.2, 411
    3.77.3, 411
    3.78.1, 411
    3.78.2, 411
    3.78.3–4, 411
    3.80.2, 411
    3.80.2–81.1, 132
    3.81–83, 644
    3.81–84, 670
    3.81.1, 90, 411
    3.81.2, 411
    3.81.2–5, 399
    3.81.3, 411
    3.81.4, 411
    3.81.4–3.82, 327
    3.81.5, 35, 216, 411, 670
    3.82, 198, 321, 413, 486, 535, 538
    3.82–83, 331, 337, 367
    3.82–84, 117, 198
    3.82.1, 109, 240, 322, 356, 362, 367,
        395, 395n9, 397, 411, 431,
        434, 517
    3.82.1–3, 435

3.82.2, 107, 321, 378, 387, 399, 412, 427, 456–57, 572, 574, 582, 678–79
3.82.2–3, 502
3.82.3, 412
3.82.4, 198, 412, 574, 671, 678n4
3.82.5, 412
3.82.5–8, 456
3.82.6, 395, 403, 412, 456
3.82.6–7, 435
3.82.8, 362, 393, 398n13, 412, 434, 456, 583n43, 670–71, 678n4
3.83, 535
3.83.1, 35, 403, 410n2, 412, 688
3.83.1–2, 456
3.83.2, 149, 412
3.83.3, 412
3.83.3–4, 502
3.83.4, 413, 451
3.84, 413, 488, 538
3.84.1, 413, 456
3.84.2, 378, 413, 456
3.84.2–3, 456
3.84.3, 413
3.85, 413
3.85.1, 413
3.85.2, 413
3.85.3, 413
3.85.4, 413
3.86, 303
3.86.4, 30, 131, 240, 242
3.87, 573
3.87–88, 330
3.87.1–3, 138, 240
3.87.2, 125
3.87.3, 138
3.87.4, 30, 239–40
3.88.1, 240
3.88.3, 240
3.88.4, 240
3.89, 333
3.89.1, 87, 239–40
3.89.1–5, 370
3.89.3, 239
3.89.4, 239
3.89.5, 239, 376
3.90.1, 22, 30, 213, 242
3.91.1–3, 106, 133

3.91.2, 155
3.92, 88, 428
3.94–98, 51
3.94.2–5, 303
3.94.3–98, 133
3.94.4, 51
3.96.1, 21
3.96.5, 393
3.97.1, 51
3.98, 219, 329
3.98.1, 219
3.98.3, 35, 219
3.98.3–4, 307n2
3.98.4, 219, 600
3.98.5, 219
3.99, 106
3.100, 93
3.102, 133
3.102.1, 212
3.102.5–7, 91–92
3.103, 106
3.104, 30, 51n5, 139, 538
3.104.2, 55
3.104.3–6, 321
3.105–13, 91–92
3.105–14, 302
3.107.1–114.2, 133
3.107.3, 303
3.108, 92
3.108.2, 701
3.108.3, 93, 307n2
3.109, 333
3.109–11, 92
3.109.1, 93
3.109.1–2, 92
3.110–12, 92
3.112–13, 325
3.112.7, 307n2
3.113, 32, 267n3
3.113.4, 33
3.113.6, 33, 92, 249, 328, 600
3.115, 242
3.116.1–2, 240
3.116.3, 240
3.122, 259n3
4, 150, 208, 541
4.1.3, 503

Thucydides, *History of the*
    Peloponnesian War (cont.)
  4.2–6, 303
  4.2–15, 590
  4.2–41, 302
  4.2.1, 87
  4.2.2–4.41, 303
  4.2.3, 87–88, 132
  4.3–15, 91
  4.3.1, 88
  4.3.3, 335
  4.5, 428
  4.8.2, 132
  4.8.7, 129
  4.10, 312
  4.11.4–12.1, 465–66
  4.12, 333
  4.12.1, 306n1
  4.12.2–3, 91
  4.12.3, 91, 131, 597
  4.13, 333
  4.13.4, 129
  4.14.3, 597
  4.14.5, 597
  4.15, 93
  4.15–22, 612, 650
  4.16, 155
  4.16–23.1, 93
  4.16.1, 132
  4.17–20, 111
  4.17.2, 331
  4.18, 334
  4.20.1, 156
  4.21–23, 325
  4.21.3, 278, 287
  4.22, 275
  4.22.3, 93
  4.23.1, 132
  4.24.5, 21
  4.25.10, 503
  4.25.12, 242
  4.27–28, 275
  4.27–29, 325
  4.27.3–4, 288
  4.27.3–5, 287
  4.27.3–28, 326
  4.27.5, 325
  4.28, 477
  4.28–40, 91
  4.28.2, 634
  4.28.3, 289
  4.28.5, 325
  4.29–31, 303
  4.30.1, 197
  4.32.3–4, 323
  4.34.1, 308n4, 332
  4.34.2, 218
  4.34.2–3, 306n1
  4.35.1, 308n4
  4.36, 323, 335
  4.36.1, 134
  4.39.3, 325
  4.40, 93, 331–33
  4.41, 335–36
  4.41.1, 137, 313
  4.41.3, 93, 134
  4.41.3–4, 612
  4.41.4, 303
  4.42–44, 126
  4.45.2, 133
  4.46–48, 399
  4.49, 500n18
  4.50, 127
  4.52.1, 30, 369
  4.53–54, 131, 133, 308n5
  4.55, 305, 335
  4.55–57, 334
  4.55.1, 134
  4.55.2, 91
  4.55.2–4, 431
  4.56–57, 213
  4.57, 141
  4.57.3, 500n18
  4.57.4, 213
  4.58–65, 244
  4.59–64, 284n2
  4.59.2, 322
  4.61, 534
  4.61.3–6, 325
  4.61.5, 376
  4.62, 322, 360
  4.63.2, 494
  4.64.4–5, 396
  4.65, 329

4.65.3, 297, 477
4.65.3–4, 303
4.65.4, 49, 242, 314
4.66, 303
4.66–74, 133
4.66.1, 132
4.67.1, 313
4.67.3, 131
4.68.5, 313
4.69.1, 233
4.70–74.1, 295
4.70.1, 414, 590
4.71.1, 236
4.71.2, 233, 590
4.72.2, 313
4.73, 233–35
4.74, 335
4.74.3, 465
4.75.2, 371
4.76, 303, 326
4.76–5.10, 301–14
4.76–81, 302–3
4.76–116, 302
4.76.1, 303
4.76.4, 303
4.76.5, 303
4.77.1, 303
4.77.2, 303
4.78, 590
4.78.1, 304
4.78.3, 304
4.78.4, 304
4.78.5, 295, 304
4.79, 590
4.79–80, 414
4.79.1, 295, 304
4.79.2–81.2, 465
4.80, 134, 335
4.80.1, 304
4.80.2, 134
4.80.3, 304, 398–99, 403
4.80.4, 335
4.80.5, 134
4.81, 91, 295, 334–35, 416, 590
4.81.1, 464
4.81.2, 334, 402, 465, 612
4.81.2–3, 296, 415

4.81.3, 334
4.84, 312, 331
4.84.2, 91, 274, 296n12, 415, 464
4.85, 312
4.85–87, 109, 284n2, 296, 312, 332
4.85.1, 465
4.85.2, 120, 140
4.85.7, 236, 313
4.86, 335
4.86.1–5, 312
4.86.2, 416
4.87, 335, 497
4.87–88, 697
4.87.2–3, 312
4.87.3, 428
4.87.4, 415
4.88, 312, 465
4.88.1, 274, 296n12
4.89, 305
4.89–92, 278
4.89–101.2, 133
4.89.1, 307n2
4.90.1–3, 305
4.90.2–3, 314
4.90.4, 130, 305
4.91, 276
4.92, 283, 306
4.92.6, 313
4.93.1, 306
4.93.2, 306
4.93.3, 306
4.93.4, 306
4.94.1, 306
4.94.2, 276
4.95.2, 313
4.95.3, 313
4.96.1, 306
4.96.2, 307
4.96.3, 307n2
4.96.3–4, 307
4.96.4, 307
4.96.5, 307, 307n2
4.96.6–9, 307
4.96.8, 307
4.97.1, 307
4.98.6, 385
4.100, 696

Thucydides, *History of the Peloponnesian War* (cont.)
- 4.100.2–4, 314
- 4.101.1, 307
- 4.101.2, 283
- 4.101.2–103.3, 134
- 4.102, 314
- 4.102–108, 329
- 4.102.3, 259
- 4.103–106, 296
- 4.103.5, 314
- 4.104.4–107.1, 296
- 4.105.1, 297
- 4.106, 69, 283, 415, 465
- 4.108, 330, 335, 541–42
- 4.108.1, 134, 465
- 4.108.2, 361
- 4.108.2–3, 416
- 4.108.3, 322, 325, 415
- 4.108.4, 296n12, 314, 337
- 4.108.4–7, 325
- 4.108.5, 236, 313, 416, 465
- 4.108.6, 91
- 4.108.6–7, 417, 465
- 4.108.7, 93, 335, 472
- 4.109, 314
- 4.110–12, 308
- 4.110.1, 314, 326
- 4.110.2, 309
- 4.111.2, 309
- 4.112.2, 309
- 4.113.1, 308
- 4.113.2, 314
- 4.114, 309
- 4.114.3, 312–13
- 4.114.3–5, 296n12
- 4.114.4, 336
- 4.115.3, 218
- 4.116.2, 309, 314, 428
- 4.117, 93, 137, 139, 156, 302
- 4.117–5.11, 302
- 4.117–5.83, 156
- 4.117.2, 139
- 4.118, 428
- 4.120, 314, 465
- 4.120.1, 259
- 4.120.3, 214, 296n12, 312–13
- 4.121, 325, 335
- 4.121.1, 296n13
- 4.122.2–3, 465
- 4.123, 325, 465
- 4.123.1, 465
- 4.123.4–124.1, 465
- 4.124–28, 308
- 4.126, 214, 284n2, 312
- 4.126.1–2, 312
- 4.126.2, 333
- 4.126.5, 313
- 4.129–33, 126
- 4.130.6–7, 324
- 4.132.3, 313, 335
- 4.133.1, 500
- 4.133.2, 148
- 4.134, 93
- 4.135.1, 309
- 5, 29, 120, 149, 154–56, 165, 208, 213, 268n4, 302, 532
- 5.1–10, 325n4
- 5.3.4, 314, 500n18
- 5.4.1, 632
- 5.4.2, 500n18
- 5.6–8, 310
- 5.7, 325n4
- 5.7–10, 139
- 5.7.2, 335
- 5.7.3–4, 310, 323
- 5.8.2, 311
- 5.9, 284n2, 310, 312
- 5.9.9, 332–33
- 5.10.2, 428
- 5.10.3, 310
- 5.10.4, 310
- 5.10.5, 310
- 5.10.8, 311
- 5.10.11, 310, 402
- 5.10.12, 310
- 5.11, 296, 335, 465
- 5.11.1, 259, 311
- 5.11.2, 311
- 5.11.3, 311
- 5.13–15, 334
- 5.14, 139
- 5.14–15, 139
- 5.14–17, 310

5.14.1, 283
5.14.1–2, 137
5.14.3, 120, 134, 140, 172, 335
5.14.4, 93, 148–49
5.14 ff., 302
5.15, 93
5.15–17, 335
5.16, 140
5.16–17, 139, 333–34
5.16–18, 428
5.16.1, 288, 310, 326, 367, 612
5.17.2, 93, 231–32, 500n17, 615
5.18, 465
5.18.11, 148
5.20, 195
5.20.1–2, 22
5.20.2, 196
5.22.1, 93
5.22.2, 93, 149
5.23, 428
5.23–24, 146
5.23.3, 335
5.24.2, 146
5.24.2–26.4, 50
5.25, 146, 539
5.25–26, 141, 145
5.25–116, 206
5.25.1, 93, 146, 500n17
5.25.1–3, 146
5.25.2, 146
5.25.3, 146, 157
5.26, 22, 146–47, 159, 195–96, 199, 296, 321, 367
5.26.1, 147, 517, 621, 623
5.26.1–3, 466
5.26.1–4, 168
5.26.2, 147, 152, 196
5.26.2–3, 140
5.26.3, 147, 196, 369, 525
5.26.3–4, 30, 427
5.26.4–5, 21
5.26.5, 25, 27, 149, 154, 174, 296, 321, 523, 564
5.26.5–6, 174, 329
5.26.6, 146–47
5.27, 148, 155
5.27–30, 93
5.27–38, 121
5.27–43, 147
5.27.2, 93, 151, 500n17
5.27.6, 151
5.28, 148
5.28.2, 91, 93, 95, 503
5.29, 148
5.29–31, 93, 148
5.29.1, 93, 501
5.29.2, 150
5.29.2–3, 93
5.29.3, 148
5.30, 93, 428
5.30.2, 132n2
5.31, 151
5.31.1–5, 148
5.31.6, 148, 151
5.32, 501
5.32.1, 296n12, 314, 324, 465, 528
5.32.5–7, 93
5.33, 93
5.33.1, 148
5.34.1, 151
5.34.2, 336
5.35, 148
5.35.2, 146, 148
5.35.2–4, 148
5.35.3, 93
5.35.8, 148
5.36, 149
5.36–38, 93
5.37–38, 149
5.39, 335
5.40, 149
5.40.1, 149
5.40.3, 149
5.41, 149
5.41.2, 503
5.41.3, 149
5.42–43, 327
5.43, 150, 158, 291–92, 326–27
5.43.1, 149
5.43.2, 285
5.43.2–3, 150
5.43.3, 291
5.43.3–48.1, 93
5.44, 150
5.44–46, 327

Thucydides, *History of the*
    Peloponnesian War (cont.)
  5.45, 150
  5.46, 150, 326
  5.46.1, 326
  5.46.4, 327
  5.46.4–5, 470
  5.46.5–47, 327
  5.47, 111, 150
  5.48, 151
  5.49–50, 327, 428
  5.50, 332
  5.50.5, 152
  5.51.1–52.2, 151
  5.52–53, 327
  5.52–56, 152
  5.52.1, 22
  5.52.2, 151–52
  5.53, 152
  5.54, 428
  5.54–55, 332, 334
  5.55.1, 152
  5.56.3, 111, 152, 494
  5.57, 303
  5.57–60, 153
  5.57–75, 305
  5.57–83, 153
  5.57.1, 22, 94
  5.57.2, 94
  5.58–60, 302
  5.59.5, 112, 153
  5.60, 333–34
  5.60.1, 94, 153
  5.60.5–6, 153
  5.61.1–2, 153
  5.61.2, 154
  5.62, 153
  5.63, 58, 153, 333–34
  5.64, 58, 153, 302
  5.64–74, 333
  5.64.1, 94
  5.64.2, 94
  5.65, 333–34
  5.65–73, 302
  5.65.4, 303
  5.66, 153
  5.66–74, 94
  5.66.3–4, 27
  5.67, 153
  5.67.2, 94
  5.68, 154
  5.68.1–2, 196
  5.68.2, 27, 328, 378
  5.68.2–3, 27
  5.69.1, 94
  5.69.2, 332
  5.70–74, 154, 291
  5.71, 306n1
  5.71–73, 94
  5.72, 58
  5.72.2, 332–33
  5.73, 335
  5.73.3, 94–95
  5.74–76, 58
  5.74.1, 27, 153
  5.74.3, 27, 154
  5.75, 327
  5.75–76, 428
  5.75.3, 91, 95, 140, 154, 334, 467
  5.75.6, 153
  5.76, 154
  5.76–80, 95
  5.76.2, 153
  5.76.3, 112
  5.77, 154
  5.78, 95, 268
  5.79, 111, 154
  5.80, 154
  5.81, 95
  5.81.2, 153–54
  5.81.6, 364
  5.82, 325, 334, 428
  5.82.2–6, 154
  5.82.3, 333
  5.83, 333
  5.84–111, 702
  5.84–113, 433, 632
  5.84–116, 491
  5.84.1, 154–55
  5.84.2, 155
  5.85–111, 267n3
  5.85–113, 155
  5.85–116, 112
  5.86, 532

5.89, 29, 260, 433, 493, 493n3, 502, 522–23, 528, 540, 583
5.89.1, 384
5.90, 165, 583, 596
5.90–91, 528
5.90.1, 386
5.91, 202, 336, 633
5.91.1, 384
5.91.2, 522
5.95, 532
5.95–97, 502
5.95.1, 384
5.96–98, 468
5.97, 468, 532, 634
5.97.1, 384
5.98, 596
5.99, 468
5.100, 522
5.101, 500
5.103, 433, 595–96
5.104, 155, 165, 433, 522, 532
5.104–105, 494
5.105, 259n4, 434, 502, 532, 534, 581n37
5.105.1 2, 466
5.105.2, 325, 340, 356, 376–77, 455, 509, 522, 525
5.105.3–4, 336
5.105.4, 432, 522
5.107, 522
5.109, 528
5.109–110, 468
5.110.2, 596
5.111.1, 522
5.111.2, 595
5.111.3, 526
5.111.3–4, 358
5.111.4, 356–57
5.112–13, 336
5.112.2, 165
5.113, 165, 595–96
5.116, 333, 336, 428, 500
5.116.2–4, 155, 324
5.116.3, 326
5.116.4, 107, 632
6, 156–57, 161–63, 161n1, 165–74, 176, 200–202, 206, 208, 262, 284, 302, 311, 347, 393, 401, 476, 544, 558–59, 561

6–7, 242
6.1, 157
6.1–5, 21, 52, 200, 322
6.1–6, 328, 454
6.1.1, 158, 169, 263, 314, 467, 558
6.1.2, 24, 558
6.2, 558
6.2–5, 162, 558
6.2.1, 21, 163, 263, 558, 601
6.2.3, 48, 263
6.2.5, 48
6.3–4, 558
6.3.1, 558
6.3.2, 54, 558–59
6.3.3, 559
6.3.3–4, 558
6.4.2, 500n18, 559
6.4.5, 500n18
6.5.3, 500n18
6.6, 71
6.6–7, 200
6.6.1, 68, 71, 166, 173, 314, 454
6.6.2, 590
6.6.3, 590
6.7.2, 500n18
6.8, 111
6.8–26, 162, 200
6.8.2, 288, 590
6.8.4, 26, 454
6.9, 484
6.9–14, 157, 201, 284n2, 289
6.9–18, 367, 577
6.9–23, 216, 289
6.9.1, 350, 454
6.9.2, 289
6.9.3, 174, 289, 350, 596, 601
6.10, 230, 467, 472
6.10.1, 157
6.10.2, 503
6.10.2–3, 157
6.10.4, 503
6.11.4, 168, 503
6.11.5, 451
6.12.2, 157, 292, 327, 454, 590, 597, 601–2
6.13.1, 168, 438, 454, 468, 601–2
6.14, 277
6.14.1, 454

Thucydides, *History of the Peloponnesian War* (cont.)
    6.15, 49n4, 292–93, 327, 454–55
    6.15–16, 150, 327
    6.15.2, 157, 166, 292, 326, 454, 595–96, 601
    6.15.2–3, 521
    6.15.2–4, 393, 440
    6.15.3, 601–2
    6.15.3–4, 157, 292, 400, 617
    6.15.4, 22, 291, 294–95, 298, 326, 472, 521, 601–2, 616
    6.15.5, 602
    6.16, 454
    6.16–18, 157, 284n2, 292–93, 521, 521n12
    6.16–28, 201
    6.16.1, 293, 467
    6.16.2, 601–2
    6.16.3, 467, 597
    6.16.4, 521n12
    6.16.5, 597, 601
    6.16.6, 95, 154, 157, 467
    6.17, 454
    6.17.1, 468, 601
    6.17.2, 470, 476, 595
    6.17.2–5, 467
    6.17.3, 595
    6.17.4, 476
    6.17.6, 467
    6.17.8, 157, 596–97
    6.18.2–3, 384, 438, 472
    6.18.3, 347, 384, 455, 468
    6.18.4, 162, 351
    6.18.5, 595
    6.18.6, 351, 438, 454–55
    6.18.6–7, 472
    6.18.7, 351, 455, 468, 569n5
    6.19, 71, 111
    6.19–25, 326
    6.19.2, 470
    6.19.2–23.3, 438
    6.20–23, 157, 201, 284n2, 289
    6.20.4, 477, 595
    6.21.2, 595
    6.21.2–22, 45
    6.22, 590, 595
    6.22–23.2, 471
    6.23.3, 289, 469
    6.24, 274, 322, 365, 454
    6.24–26, 438
    6.24.3, 293, 361, 454, 468, 561, 595–96, 601–2, 611
    6.24.4, 325, 454
    6.26.1, 469
    6.26.2, 137
    6.27–28, 327
    6.27–29, 162, 293n9, 326, 440
    6.27–32, 200
    6.27.3, 157
    6.28.2, 157, 292n8, 393
    6.29, 327
    6.29.3, 152, 158, 469
    6.30.2, 596
    6.30.2–31.1, 162
    6.31, 477
    6.31.1, 314, 453
    6.31.2, 461
    6.31.6, 453, 596–97
    6.32.3, 27
    6.32.3–41.4, 163
    6.33–34, 201, 284n2
    6.33–41, 200
    6.33.1, 173
    6.33.2, 166
    6.33.5–6, 42
    6.34.3, 157
    6.35.2, 278
    6.36–40, 201, 393
    6.36.1–2, 398
    6.38.2–5, 398
    6.39, 328, 398n13
    6.39.1–2, 398
    6.40.1–2, 398
    6.41, 201, 276
    6.42–52, 200
    6.43.1, 230
    6.46, 328
    6.46.1–4, 590
    6.46.3, 597
    6.47–50, 469
    6.48, 467
    6.53, 326, 328, 521
    6.53–61, 200, 203, 328, 440
    6.53–61.4, 293n9
    6.53.1–3, 393

6.53.2, 327
6.53.3, 24, 58, 262, 616
6.53.3–59, 568
6.54, 325n3
6.54–55, 125
6.54–59, 21, 24, 175, 195, 248, 361
6.54–60, 195
6.54.1, 174, 262, 319
6.54.2, 617
6.54.5, 58, 401
6.55.1, 24, 174, 196
6.55.1–2, 24
6.57, 477
6.59.4, 58
6.60, 326
6.60.1, 24, 157, 262, 472
6.60.1–2, 393
6.60.2, 262, 327
6.60.5, 328
6.61, 155
6.61.1, 393
6.61.1–2, 616
6.61.3, 150, 152
6.61.5, 158
6.61.6, 602
6.61.7, 602
6.62–75, 200
6.62.3, 500n18
6.64.1, 477
6.68, 284n2
6.68.1, 275
6.69–71, 244
6.69.1, 244
6.69.2, 429
6.69.3, 164
6.70.1, 527
6.72.2, 244, 402
6.72.3–4, 244
6.72.4–5, 244
6.73.1, 244
6.73.1–2, 157
6.74.1, 293
6.75.3, 503
6.75.4, 244
6.76–80, 201, 284n2
6.76–88, 200
6.76.1–80.5, 163

6.76.2, 166
6.77.1, 578
6.80.1, 157
6.81.87, 358
6.82–87, 107, 201, 270, 502
6.82.3, 348
6.82.4, 348
6.83, 325
6.83.1, 348
6.83.2, 260
6.83.2–3, 578
6.83.3–4, 456
6.83.4, 349
6.84.1, 157
6.85.1, 400n21, 434
6.87.1, 157
6.87.2–4, 432
6.87.3, 325
6.88, 365
6.88.5, 469
6.88.7–8, 157
6.88.9, 158, 602
6.88.10, 157
6.89, 150, 326–27
6.89–92, 158, 200–201, 272, 284n2, 293, 326, 335n6
6.89.1, 386
6.89.3–6, 366
6.89.6, 469
6.89 ff., 577
6.90, 49n4
6.90.2, 166
6.90.2–3, 468
6.90.3, 701
6.91.1, 173–74
6.91.6, 158
6.92.2–4, 272
6.92.4, 472, 521
6.93, 200, 335n6
6.93.1–2, 174
6.93.2, 158
6.93.4–103, 469
6.94, 201
6.95, 333, 428
6.98, 302
6.100, 302
6.101–103, 302

Thucydides, *History of the Peloponnesian War (cont.)*
  6.117.1, 600
  7, 34, 156–57, 161–62, 161n1, 165, 167–73, 176, 179, 181, 202, 206, 224, 284, 302, 311, 349, 403n28, 536, 561
  7.2, 664
  7.2.1, 167, 469
  7.2.2, 598
  7.2.4, 167, 598
  7.2.5, 598
  7.3–4, 302
  7.3.4, 269
  7.4.4, 596
  7.5.27, 517n3
  7.6–8, 469
  7.7.4, 596
  7.7.43–44, 470
  7.8, 278n21
  7.8–10, 195
  7.8.1, 469
  7.8.2, 26, 174
  7.8.2–3, 469
  7.10–15, 702
  7.11–14, 174
  7.11–15, 201, 284n2
  7.11.1, 470
  7.11.1–14.1, 470
  7.11.2, 174
  7.11.2–3, 702
  7.12.3, 596
  7.14.1, 596
  7.14.4, 174, 290, 470, 656
  7.15.1, 174, 289–90
  7.15.2, 470
  7.18, 332, 428
  7.18.2, 64, 120, 140, 169, 321, 403n28, 428, 492, 522
  7.18.3, 111, 522
  7.19.1, 158
  7.21.3, 665
  7.25.1, 596
  7.25.9, 596
  7.26–31, 203
  7.26.2, 203
  7.27–28, 164, 330
  7.27.2, 626
  7.27.3–5, 158
  7.27.3–28.4, 203
  7.28, 105, 158, 534
  7.28.3, 120, 140, 158, 169–70, 172
  7.28.3–4, 169
  7.28.4, 349
  7.29, 164, 526
  7.29–30, 34–35, 203, 249–50, 325, 500n18
  7.29.3, 219, 349
  7.29.3–5, 349
  7.29.4, 220, 250
  7.29.5, 164, 220, 249n14
  7.29f, 219
  7.30, 325
  7.30.1, 220
  7.30.3, 164, 220, 250, 600
  7.31.1, 203
  7.42, 303
  7.43–44, 695
  7.43.7, 308
  7.44, 321
  7.44.1, 175
  7.44.3–8, 306n1
  7.44.7, 307n2
  7.46, 308n4, 596
  7.47–56, 453
  7.47.2, 596
  7.47.3, 470
  7.48, 329
  7.48–49, 326
  7.48.2–3, 470
  7.48.3–4, 519n8
  7.49–87, 561
  7.50, 368
  7.50.3–4, 427, 429, 440
  7.50.4, 290, 369, 470, 519
  7.55.1, 597
  7.55.2, 109, 163, 597
  7.56.4, 164, 170
  7.57, 104, 334, 364–66, 526
  7.57–58, 366
  7.57–59.1, 164
  7.57.1, 364
  7.57.2, 365
  7.57.3, 526
  7.57.5, 48, 364
  7.57.7, 364, 526

7.57.9, 526
7.57.11, 364
7.58.3, 364
7.58.4, 365
7.59, 175
7.59.3, 129
7.60.3, 591
7.61–64, 201, 284n2
7.61.3, 165
7.62.4, 597
7.66, 312
7.66–68, 274n16
7.66.1, 527n17
7.66.2, 166
7.66.2–3, 597
7.66.3, 596
7.67.1, 596
7.67.4, 165, 174
7.69–72, 644
7.69.2, 201, 400, 429
7.69.3–7.72, 311
7.70, 218
7.70–71, 163, 171–72, 302
7.71–75, 453
7.71.3, 668, 670
7.71.3–7, 311
7.71.5, 597
7.71.7, 561, 596–97
7.72.2–3, 429
7.72.3–4, 308n4
7.72.5, 591
7.73–87, 220–22
7.73.1–4, 591
7.73.2, 626
7.74.1, 220, 591
7.75, 171
7.75.1, 220, 591
7.75.2, 596
7.75.2–3, 172
7.75.4, 221
7.75.5, 163, 221, 597
7.75.6, 597
7.75.7, 173
7.76, 276
7.76.1, 221
7.77, 201, 221, 278, 284n2, 527n17
7.77.2, 290–91, 363

7.77.2–3, 429, 519
7.77.3–4, 363
7.77.4, 471
7.77.7, 171, 290
7.78–87, 307n2
7.78.2, 477
7.78.2–4, 591
7.78.5–7, 591
7.79.1–5, 591
7.79.3, 527
7.79.5–6, 591
7.80.2–7, 591
7.81.1, 592
7.81.2–5, 592
7.82.1–3, 592
7.83.1–5, 592
7.84, 536
7.84–85.1, 171
7.84.1–85.4, 592
7.84.2, 222
7.84.3, 471
7.84.3–5, 221
7.85.1, 221, 471
7.85.4, 32, 221
7.86, 201
7.86–87, 325
7.86.2, 222
7.86.4, 232
7.86.5, 250, 290, 471, 519
7.87, 171, 325–26
7.87.1, 569
7.87.1–2, 222
7.87.1–4, 471
7.87.2, 218, 222
7.87.5, 32, 170, 222, 322, 597, 600
7.87.5–6, 251, 369
7.87.6, 162, 170, 206, 291, 453, 468, 602
8, 4, 6, 156, 172, 179–81, 189–90, 202, 206, 213, 251–54, 268n4, 275–76, 319, 393, 398, 418–19, 486, 577, 627, 629
8.1, 158, 330, 418, 633
8.1–2, 616
8.1–3, 72
8.1–4, 303
8.1.1, 427, 596
8.1.1–3, 181
8.1.2, 328, 453, 503, 665

Thucydides, *History of the Peloponnesian War* (cont.)
- 8.1.3, 184, 618
- 8.1.4, 330
- 8.2, 87
- 8.2–3, 669
- 8.2.1, 172, 503
- 8.2.1–2, 180
- 8.2.4, 596
- 8.3.1, 67
- 8.4, 330
- 8.5–28, 106
- 8.5.1, 172
- 8.5.6, 182
- 8.6, 428
- 8.6.3, 152, 326
- 8.6.5, 333
- 8.8–11, 182
- 8.11.3, 147, 334
- 8.12–22, 182
- 8.14, 337
- 8.14.1–2, 326
- 8.15, 330
- 8.21, 420
- 8.23–25, 182
- 8.23.4, 631
- 8.24, 251, 337
- 8.24.2, 499n14
- 8.24.4, 334, 398, 403, 432
- 8.24.4–5, 337
- 8.24.5, 337
- 8.26–27, 182
- 8.27, 327, 358
- 8.27.5, 182, 189, 617
- 8.32, 183
- 8.38.3–4, 183
- 8.39.2, 183
- 8.40, 183, 337
- 8.40.2, 398, 403
- 8.43.3–4, 183
- 8.45–46, 183, 294
- 8.45–98, 326
- 8.46, 418
- 8.46.1, 253
- 8.47, 185, 327, 418
- 8.47–48, 326
- 8.47.1, 150, 294
- 8.47.1–2, 418
- 8.48, 486
- 8.48.1, 185, 494n4
- 8.48.2–5, 469
- 8.48.3, 185
- 8.48.4, 294, 399n16, 418
- 8.48.4–6, 185
- 8.48.4–7, 325
- 8.48.6, 398n13, 399
- 8.48.6–8, 393
- 8.49, 418
- 8.50–51, 186n5, 326–27
- 8.50.1, 418
- 8.50.2–4, 418
- 8.50.5, 419
- 8.51, 419
- 8.52, 419
- 8.53–54, 186
- 8.53.1, 419
- 8.53.2, 419
- 8.53.3, 419
- 8.54.1, 419
- 8.54.2, 419
- 8.54.3, 419
- 8.54.4, 419
- 8.55.3, 625
- 8.56, 419
- 8.56.2, 253
- 8.57.1, 183
- 8.58, 183
- 8.63, 150, 631
- 8.64, 251
- 8.65, 186
- 8.65.2, 419
- 8.65.3, 419
- 8.66, 419, 454, 543
- 8.67, 186
- 8.67–68.1, 419
- 8.67.1, 184, 618
- 8.68, 251, 327, 405, 543, 617
- 8.68.1, 420
- 8.68.1–2, 189, 274, 577
- 8.68.2, 320, 420
- 8.68.3, 186, 393, 420, 618
- 8.68.4, 420, 521
- 8.69, 420, 543
- 8.69.1, 186

8.69.3–4, 186
8.70, 486
8.70.1, 420
8.70.2, 420, 494n4
8.71, 420
8.72, 420
8.73, 420
8.73.3, 127, 613–14, 625
8.74, 421
8.74.1, 421
8.75.1, 421
8.75.1–2, 187
8.75.2–3, 421
8.76, 421
8.76.2–3, 187
8.77, 421
8.81.1, 421
8.81.2–3, 294, 421, 634
8.82, 104, 421
8.82–83, 573
8.83–85.3, 421
8.84.2, 630
8.85, 631
8.85.3, 631
8.85.4, 421
8.86, 251, 327, 487
8.86.1–2, 421
8.86.3–4, 421
8.86.4, 187, 189, 327, 421
8.86.4–5, 294, 521n12
8.86.6–7, 422
8.86.8, 422
8.87, 422
8.87.2, 252, 422
8.87.4, 253
8.87.4–5, 422
8.88, 422
8.89, 187
8.89.1, 422
8.89.2, 184, 422
8.89.3, 187, 399, 422, 455
8.89.4, 422
8.90.1, 236, 618
8.90.1–2, 422
8.90.1–3, 187
8.90.3–4, 422
8.91.1–2, 422

8.91.3, 422
8.92, 188, 487
8.92.2, 185, 422
8.92.3, 422
8.92.4, 422
8.92.5–7, 422
8.92.8, 422
8.92.9, 422
8.92.10, 422
8.92.11, 184, 189, 422
8.93, 422
8.93.2, 184, 422
8.94, 330, 423
8.95, 423
8.95.2, 630
8.96, 112, 188, 333–34, 431
8.96–97, 330
8.96.1, 251, 423, 598
8.96.1–2, 172
8.96.2, 251, 423
8.96.3–4, 423
8.96.4, 252, 598
8.96.5, 163, 334, 378–79, 397, 404, 423
8.97, 8, 487, 617
8.97–98, 188
8.97.1, 423
8.97.2, 251, 320, 393, 404, 423, 520n10, 608
8.97.3, 423
8.98, 635
8.98.1–3, 252
8.98.4, 252
8.99, 236
8.99.1, 375
8.100.3, 48
8.103, 112
8.104.3, 630
8.105, 631
8.106, 330
8.106.5, 423
8.107, 631
8.108.1–2, 630
8.109, 268
8.144, 580
Timaeus, *FGrH* 566 F 71, 56
Tragicorum Graecorum fragmenta, i–ii², iii–v (*TrGF*) 202, 561

Tribute Reassessment Decree of 425
  ML 69, 105, 107–8, 135, 615
    lines 4–6, 101
    p. 193, 136

Velleius Paterculus, 2.36.2, 666, 678n5

Xanthus, *Lydiaca*, 560
Xenophanes, *Migration to Elea*, 561
Xenophon
  Agesilaus, 519n6
    5, 624
    5.1, 625
  Anabasis, 516, 523, 528
    1.8.26, 626
    1.9.11–12, 523
    2.6.21–29, 519
    3.1.4, 518
    3.1.11 ff., 523
    3.1.18, 527
    3.1.19–22, 527
    3.1.21–22, 527
    3.1.36, 527
    3.1.43–44, 527
    3.2.2–3, 527
    3.2.10, 527
    3.2.36, 527
    5.5.21, 523
    5.7.26–35, 527
    6.3.12–13, 527
    6.3.17, 527
    6.5.12–18, 527
    6.5.24, 527
    6.6.9, 520
    6.6.13–14, 520
    7.1.18–31, 527
    7.1.30, 520
    7.7.37–38, 523
    7.8.8–11, 527
    7.8.20–24, 527
  Athēnaiōn Politeia, 99
    1.16, 103
  Cyropaedia
    1.2.6–7, 520n11
    1.3.8, 626
    1.5.10, 43n3

    1.6.13, 527
    1.6.27–34, 520n11
    3.1.14, 520, 632
    3.1.15–25, 632
    3.1.38–40, 520, 632
    6.3.10–11, 633
    7.2.23–24, 632
    8.8, 629n12
  Hellenica, 14, 515–20, 523, 528, 621n3, 622, 627
    1, 630
    1–2, 623
    1.1.1–2.3.9, 628
    1.1.1–10, 635n14
    1.1.3.1, 629
    1.1.5, 630
    1.1.9, 631
    1.1.11–26, 635n14
    1.1.14, 629
    1.1.19–20, 631
    1.1.22, 635n14
    1.1.23, 629, 631, 637
    1.1.24, 527
    1.1.27, 634
    1.1.27–31, 631, 635n14
    1.1.28, 629
    1.1.32, 631
    1.1.33–36, 636n14
    1.1.37, 629
    1.2, 625
    1.2.1, 629
    1.2.1–17, 635n14
    1.2.19, 629, 629n13
    1.3.2–11, 630
    1.3.2–21, 635n14
    1.3.13, 631
    1.3.19, 629
    1.4.8–23, 630, 635n14
    1.4.9, 636n14
    1.4.13–17, 629
    1.4.19, 630
    1.5, 636n14
    1.5.1, 630
    1.5.6, 629
    1.5.7–8, 527
    1.5.8, 630
    1.5.11–14, 625

INDEX LOCORUM 751

1.5.17, 630
1.5.21, 629
1.6, 636n14
1.6.1, 629
1.6.2, 629–30
1.6.3, 634
1.6.5, 629
1.6.8, 629
1.6.15, 629
1.6.32, 521n12, 629, 636
1.6.36–37, 527n17
1.7, 634, 636n14
1.7.15, 523, 635
1.7.16–33, 629
1.7.27, 635
1.7.28, 635
1.7.35, 635–36
1.17, 76
1.114, 633
2, 630
2.1.1–4, 629
2.1.6–7, 521
2.1.7, 630
2.1.15–32, 636n14
2.1.25, 630
2.1.25–26, 634, 636
2.1.26, 629
2.1.31–32, 528
2.2, 536, 636n14
2.2.1, 630
2.2.3, 109, 165, 314, 528, 628–29, 632
2.2.6–7, 634
2.2.9, 528
2.2.10, 528, 628, 632
2.2.11, 528
2.2.14, 628, 632
2.2.14–18, 528
2.2.16, 626, 628, 632
2.2.19, 528, 633
2.2.19–20, 615, 628
2.2.20, 501n20, 528, 632, 634
2.2.23, 501n20, 529, 628, 632, 634
2.3–4, 628
2.3.1–2, 628
2.3.1–9, 628
2.3.7–9, 637
2.3.8–9, 637

2.3.9, 630
2.3.10–56, 635
2.3.11, 628
2.3.11–7.5.27, 525
2.3.24–56, 629
2.3.41, 528
2.3.53, 636
2.3.56, 628, 636
2.4.14, 527
2.4.27, 698n6
2.4.28–30, 634
2.4.40–42, 634
2.4.40–43, 633
2.4.43, 633
2.8.4, 633
2.12.3, 634
2.15, 500n18
2.18, 500n18
2.27, 633
2.65, 634
3.1.3 ff., 634
3.1.16–18, 527n17
3.2.6, 625
3.2.7–10, 524
3.2.9, 525
3.2.10, 43n3
3.2.24, 524
3.2.30–31, 501n20
3.4.4, 519n6
3.4.9–10, 521n12
3.4.11, 527
3.4.14, 524
3.4.17, 499n16
3.4.27, 521n12
3.4.29, 521n12
3.5.16, 628
3.15–21, 95
3.21–23, 494
3.42–48, 529
4.1.26–28, 521n12
4.1.29 ff., 624
4.2.8, 521n12
4.2.9–23, 95
4.2.18, 526n16
4.2.20, 500
4.2.22, 626
4.3.10–12, 521n12

Xenophon (*cont.*)
    4.3.10–14, 527n17
    4.7.4, 524
    4.7.7, 524
    4.8, 623, 628
    5.1.1–7, 501n20
    5.1.14, 527
    5.1.17, 527
    5.4.1, 111, 515, 526
    5.4.2–9, 526
    5.4.12, 526
    5.26, 633
    5.106–110, 633
    6.1.4–16, 270n7
    6.3.10–11, 633
    6.3.10–17, 628
    6.3.16, 626
    6.4.3, 526
    6.4.7, 526
    6.4.10–13, 526
    6.4.12, 526n16
    6.4.23, 526
    6.4.37, 628
    6.5.45–49, 628
    7.1.2–11, 637
    7.1.32, 628
    7.2.9, 628
    7.5.10, 526
    7.5.12, 526
    7.5.13, 526
    7.5.15–17, 518
    7.5.22–25, 526n16
    7.5.27, 498, 622, 628
  Lakedaimoniōn Politeia
    7.14.2–3, 521n12
    13.5, 94
    14, 520n11
    14.5, 522
  Memorabilia
    1.1.18, 635
    1.2.39–47, 520
    1.2.49, 520
    1.3.13, 626
    1.6.14, 199
    1.6.15, 523
    2.16.3, 610
    4.2.25–29, 632
    4.4.2, 635
    4.4.15–17, 635

Subject Index

abstraction, 205, 274, 524
Acamas, 45
Acanthus, 214, 302, 308–309, 312–313, 416, 465, 497
Acanthus of Sparta, 52
Acarnania, 32–33, 51, 91–92, 132, 248, 302, 365–366, 369, 600
Accame, S., 635
accuracy. *See* historical accuracy
Achaea, 4, 50, 77, 163, 259, 375, 552, 598
Acharnae, 87
Achilles, 28, 30, 376, 379–380, 415, 562, 587–588, 590, 696
Adams, John, 198, 679
Adshead, K., 701
advisors (*probouloi*), 181–182, 184
the Aegean, xvii (*map*)
Aegina, 60, 71, 77, 107, 152, 155, 344, 410, 632–633
　annexation of, 106
　fortifications of, 71
　scale of coverage of, 212–213
Aegospotami, 165, 182, 190, 441, 528, 630, 632, 634, 636
Aeolians, 56, 90
Aeschines of Sicyon, 58
Aeson, 149
Aetolians, 51
afterthoughts, 249–251
Agamemnon, 28–30, 44–45, 47–48, 52, 261, 341–342, 344
Agathias, 691, 693–694, 696–704
Agis II (Spartan king), 94, 153, 158, 182–183, 240, 298, 334, 420, 628
agriculture, 43–45, 87, 118
Ahmed, S., 444
akoe (hearsay) as evidence, 23–25
akribeia (precision), 575–576

Alcaeus, 146
Alcibiades, 95
　Agis II and, 182–183
　architectural parallelism and, 199–202
　characterization of, 291–295, 293n9
　critique of imperialism by, 166
　on crowds, 476–477, 483–484
　Eleusinian Mysteries, 157
　Endius and, 150
　Epidaurus and, 152
　leadership of, 181, 466–469, 472
　mutilation of the herms and, 157–158, 162
　narrative art and, 150–159
　on necessity of empire, 384–385
　Nicias and, 162
　occupation of Decelea and, 157–159
　the Peloponnesus and, 152–154, 157
　Phrynichus and, 185–186, 186n5
　Plutarch on, 145
　political theory and, 326–327
　removal of the Four Hundred and, 187
　revolt of Chios and, 181, 336–337
　Sicilian expedition and, 203, 350–351
　Sparta and, 158
　speeches of, 173–174, 272, 275, 278
　stasis and, 418–423
　Tissaphernes and, 185–186
Alcidas, 90, 411
Alciphron, 153
Alcmaeon, 369–370
Alexiad (of Anna Komnene), 704
alibi, nature as, 355–357
alliances. *See* international relations; Quadruple Alliance
allusions, 601–603
almost episodes, 598–599
ambassadors. *See* international relations
Ambracia, 32–33, 58, 93

Ameinocles, 53–54, 342
Amorges, 182
Amphilochia, battle in, 32–35, 91–92
Amphipolis. *See* Ennea Hodoi (Amphipolis)
anankē, 374–375
anarchy, 491–498
Anaxandridas (king of Sparta), 58
Androcles, 186, 419, 613
Andros, 69
anticipation (*prolepsis, anticipatio*), 242, 594–595
Antimachus, 45
Antiochus, 24, 557–559
Antiphon, 187, 189, 418–420, 422, 577
Antyllus, 427
aparchai, 74–75
Arcadia, 93
the "Archaeology," 64, 200–201
   characterization of Athenians in, 83
   compression and, 214
   Dionysius of Halicarnassus on, 39
   myth and, 257–264
   power and, 39–60, 39n1, 339–352
   purpose of, 39–40, 39–40n1
   ring composition and, 40n1, 202–203
Archidamian War, 81, 82–83, 86, 91, 95, 111, 125–141
   Athenian leadership and, 132–133
   campaigns in Sicily and, 127
   expansion of Athenian Empire during, 106
   financial resources and, 134–137
   helots and, 133–134
   historical accuracy and, 125–129
   infantry and, 130–132
   inscriptions re, 128
   literary evidence re, 126–127
   narrative art and, 129–141
   naval power and, 130–132
   Peace of Nicias and, 139–141, 146
   Persian ambassador and, 127
   plague narratives in, 138–139
   topography and, 126, 128–129
   units of action and, 206
Archidamus II of Sparta, 40, 76, 92, 146, 331–336
   speech of, 83–87, 123, 270, 278

Archippus, 617
architectural parallelism, 199–202
archon/archontes, 101–102
Argos, 50, 77, 82, 91, 92, 94–95
   Alcibiades and, 150–151
   Corinth and, 149
   infantry and, 58
   internal troubles of, 153–154
   narrative art and, 153–154
   Olympic crisis of 420 and, 151
   Peace of Nicias and, 148
   Quadruple Alliance and, 93, 95, 111, 148, 150–151, 154, 158
   Sparta and, 149, 153–154
Aristarchus, 187
Aristides, 67
Aristogiton, 24, 262
Aristomenes, 617
Aristophanes, 607–617
   on Athenian officialdom, 101–103
   on causation, 119
   on the demos, 449
   as evidence, 118, 123, 126–127
   on the necessities of nature, 377–378
   on Sicilian expedition, 175
   on taxation, 106
Aristotle
   compression and, 215
   on crowds, 475–477
   on historiography, 271
   irony and, 596
   on Lelantine War, 59
   on nature, 355–356, 358
   on vividness, 218
armament, 40–42
   bearing arms in daily life and, 51–52
   consequences of, 39–40n1
   financial resources and, 44–45
   long-range missiles and, 59
   Spartan technology and, 83–87
   stagnation of Sparta and, 81–82
   warfare as normal part of life and, 498–503
army. *See* infantry
Artabanus, 269
Artaphernes, 127
Artaxerxes, 77, 127
Artemisium, 69

Artobazanes, 269
asides, 244–249
assembly debates, 26–27
Assyrian expansion, 54
Astyochus, 182, 186n5, 418
asymmetry, 669
Athenagoras, 276
Athēnaiōn Politeia, 184–185, 187–188
Athenian development. *See also* Athens/Athenian Empire
  criteria of, 40–42
  expansion and, 70–72
  imperial, 99–113
  process of, 43–50
  revolts and, 72–74
  Sparta as facilitator of, 49
Athenian Empire (Meiggs), 74
Athens/Athenian Empire, 32–33. *See also* Athenian development; Delian League; Greece
  alliances of (*see* international relations)
  assembly debates at, 26–27, 162, 269
  attitudes toward, 108–110
  causes of war and (*see* causation)
  changing nature of, 106–108
  characterization of, 8, 83, 105, 323–331
  critique of imperialism of, 165–168
  discord within, 179–180, 183–187
  expansion of, 106–108, 118
  fall of, 179–190, 251–253, 427–441
  finance and (*see* financial resources)
  the Five Thousand and, 184, 187–190
  fortification of (*see* fortification)
  the Four Hundred (*see* the Four Hundred)
  Greek interstate relations and, 110–112
  inaccuracy in histories from, 24
  judicial regulations of, 103–104
  leadership and, 132–133
  management of, 100–104
  naval power of (*see* naval power)
  necessity and, 381–385
  officials of, 100–104
  oligarchy and (*see* the Four Hundred; oligarchy)
  origins of war and (*see* causation)
  political theory and, 323–331
  Quadruple Alliance and, 93, 95, 111, 148, 150–151, 154, 158
  refusal to fight by, 130–131
  religion and (*see* religion/divine intervention)
  Sicily and (*see* Sicily/Sicilian expedition)
  stability of, 44, 106–109, 341
  stasis and, 418–423
  the Thirty and, 187–188
  trade and (*see* trade)
  tribute and (*see* tribute)
athletic nudity, 51–52
Atossa, 269
Attica, 69, 86, 87, 91, 92, 120
  agriculture and, 87
  occupation of Decelea in, 34
  Theseus' unification of, 44
Attic comedy. *See* comedy
Attic tragedy. *See* tragedy
audience, 14, 196
  Dionysius and, 14–15
  drama and, 33
  influencing, 173
  interpretation and, 173
  response of, 207–209
Aujac, G., 653
authorial comments, 6, 239–254
  as afterthoughts, 249–251
  as asides, 244–249
  on fall of Athens, 251–253
  on instability, 248–249
  programmatic, 242–244
authorial control, 6–7
authorial vision, 206–207

Bacchiads, oligarchy of the, 54
Badian, E., 119–120, 493
Bakker, E., 169, 171
balance. *See* objectivity/impartiality
Balot, R., 8
Barker, E., 174–175
Batavian revolt, 679–680, 682–689
battle narratives. *See* campaign/battle narratives; *specific battles*
Bauslaugh, A., 493
Bay of Navarino, 128–129
Bearzot, C., 4

Belisarius, 691, 697–702
Benardete, S., 533
blockade of trade, 131
Boeotia, 71, 93, 94
   campaigns in, 301–314
   migration and, 48
   Peace of Nicias and, 148
Bolmarcich, S., 95
Brasidas, 89, 91, 151
   characterization of, 207, 295–296
   leadership of, 464–466, 471–472
   narrative art and, 134, 140
   political theory and, 334–337
   speeches of, 134, 274, 278, 414–417
   stasis and, 411, 414–417
   Thracian campaign and, 302–314
brevity. *See* compression of episodes
brutality of war, 33, 502
burial rites. *See* funeral customs
Byzantium, 65, 110

Caecilius of Caleacte, 646
Cambyses, 55–57
campaign/battle narratives, 7, 301–314. *See also specific battles*
   introductions to, 302–305
   speeches in, 311–313
   topography and, 126, 128–129
Canfora, L., 147, 627, 653
Capreedy, J., 93
Caria, 106
Carians, 47, 51n5
Carthage, 49, 55–56
Cassius Dio, 700
catalogues, 164, 364–366
Cato the Elder, 666
causation, 27–30, 115–124
   Athens and, 118–120, 122–123
   Corinth and, 120–121
   expansion and, 118
   Herodotus and, 28
   international relations and, 503–508
   Megarian Decree and, 119–123
   nature and, 355–372
   the Pentecontaetia on, 68
   political passions and, 440–446
   rank as, 122–123

   Sicilian expedition and, 173–175
   Sparta and, 120–123
   superficial *vs.* true, 28–30
Cephisodorus, 617
Chaireas, 421
Chalcis, 59, 66n1, 77
Chalcis decree, 74
character. *See* characterization; human nature
characterization, 7, 279, 283–298. *See also specific individuals*
   of Athens, 8, 83, 105, 323–331
   gossip and, 284
   interpretation and, 275
   lack of, 283–284
   of Sparta, 8, 76–77, 84
   through speeches, 284
the Chersonese, 45, 57
Chilon, 58
Chios, 57, 73, 76
   revolt of, 181–182, 337–338
   Sparta and, 181–182
chronology. *See* dating systems
Churchill, Winston, 35
Cicero, 563, 645–646, 653
Cilicia, 72
Cimon, 67, 72, 74
citizenry. *See* crowds
civil war. *See stasis*
Clazomenae, 182
Cleobulos, 149
Cleon, 91, 107, 120
   Aristophanes on, 126, 129
   characterization of, 278, 287–288
   on crowds, 483–484
   Mytilene revolt and, 104, 207–208
   narrative art and, 139–140
   speeches of, 198, 275, 278, 445–446
Cnemus, 88, 89
coinage, 103
Collingwood, R. G., 225
colonization, 65
comedy, 14, 99, 126, 448, 605–618
   comic witness and, 606–609
   engagement and, 606–609
   mockery and, 607
   Pericles as subject of, 609–611
   politics as subject for, 613–615

revolt as subject of, 611–618
  Sicily as subject of, 611–618
  war as subject for, 611–618
compression of episodes, 211, 213–215, 225, 668
conciseness, 212
Connor, W. R., 5, 13, 164, 167, 189, 202–203, 207, 590
contemporary history, 20–22
context, 532–534, 644–646
contingents, catalogue of, 364–366
continuation of Thucydides, 621–637
  by Cratippus, 622–624
  by Diodorus Siculus, 635–637
  in *Hellenica Oxyrhynchia*, 625–627
  by Theopompus, 624–625
  by Xenophon, 516–518, 621–622, 627–635
Corcyra, 72, 87–88, 90, 107, 116
  Athenian alliance with, 53–54, 119–120
  murder of Peithias by, 102
  stasis and, 35, 409–414
Corinth, 53–54, 58, 87, 89, 94, 96, 151
  Argos and, 93, 149
  Aristophanes on, 126
  Athenian power and, 77
  Athenian response to, 432–435
  causation and, 120–121
  dating of naval history of, 52–54, 54n8
  history of, 52–54
  Megara and, 71
  narrative art and, 132, 132n2
  naval power of, 45–46, 48, 52–55, 59, 342
  Peace of Nicias and, 148
  Sicily and, 167–168
  Sparta and, 76, 82–86, 90, 92, 151
  speeches of, 345–346, 431–432
  trade and, 52, 118
  war against the tyrants and, 58
Cornford, F. M., 181, 602–603
Coronea, 95
Crane, G., 531
Cratinus, 606, 611
Cratippus, 14, 622–624
Crawley, R., 504–505
critical reasoning. *See* judgment
crowds, 10–11

instability of, 262
Pericles' leadership and, 479–485
political theory and, 475–488
Sicilian expedition and, 476–477
stasis and, 485–487
wisdom of, 475–477, 481, 487–488
The Cultural Politics of Emotion (Ahmed), 444
culture/custom, 42, 50–52, 110. *See also* funeral customs

Damon, C., 15
Danaos, 50
Darius, 57, 269
dasmos. *See* tribute
dating systems, 21–22
  of cultural history, 50–52
  of Diodorus, 65
  of Hellanicus, 64
  inscriptions and, 74–76
  Lelantine War and, 59–60
  narrative art and, 146
  naval history of Corinth and, 52–54, 54n8
  in the Pentecontaetia, 65
  seasonal, 22, 196–197
day-by-day narrative, 217, 220–222
de Bakker, M., 6
Decelea, 34, 157–159, 203
de Jonge, C., 14–15
Delian League, 49. *See also* Athens/Athenian Empire
  campaigns of, 69–70
  decision-making in, 100
  dues of (*see* tribute)
  leadership of, 66
  Persian Empire and, 70
  rank in, 122–123
  treasury of, 2, 68, 74, 78, 104
deliberative speeches, 268
Delium, battle at, 305–308
Delos, 68, 74, 78, 90, 104
  purification of, 30, 51n5, 55, 139
Demetrius, 219, 616
democracy, 109–110, 122
  advisors and, 181–182
  crowds and, 475–488
  distrust and, 148

democracy (*cont.*)
    the Four Hundred and, 183–188
    mutilation of the Herms and, 157–158
    Pericles' leadership and, 446–453
    regime and, 188, 394–399
    stability of, 394–399
Democracy and Knowledge (Ober), 475
Demosthenes, 91–92, 133–134
de Ste.-Croix, G. E. M., 120–121
Deucalion, 47
development. *See* Athenian development
Dewald, C., 206, 213
Dexippus, 691–692, 696–699, 703
dialogues, 33, 155, 204, 216, 267, 267–268n3.
    See also speeches
    Melian (*see* Melian Dialogue)
    Platonic, 272n11, 523, 532
    Socratic, 520, 523
Dickens, Charles, 19
Diïtrephes, 34, 164
Diodorus Siculus, 14, 139
    continuation of Thucydides by, 635–637
    dating systems of, 65
    as evidence, 118, 123
    on the interwar years, 145
    on Sicily, 163–164
Diodotus, 326, 337
    on crowds, 483–485
    on nature, 359–362
    speeches of, 445–446
Dionysius of Halicarnassus, 14–15, 641–656, 680, 704
    on anti-Athenianism, 646–649
    on the "Archaeology," 39
    audience and, 14–15
    on causation, 118
    context of, 644–646
    on Cratippus, 622
    on expansion of episodes, 216–217
    on Herodotus, 643–644, 646–648, 650–652
    on the Pentecontaetia, 64
    on Sallust, 668
    on scale, 211
    on style, 31
    truth and, 651–653
diplomacy. *See* international relations
diptych structures, 233–236

direct discourse. *See* speeches
divine intervention. *See* religion/divine intervention
Dolopians, 44
domestic politics, 392–394
Dorians, 48, 52
double war motif, 162, 168–172
dress, 51–52

earthquakes, 32, 65, 239–240, 376
Eckstein, A. M., 11
eclipses, 32
Edmunds, L., 394, 396
Egesta, 71, 75
Egypt, 54, 56, 65, 70–72, 74
Eion, 69
eklogeis, 105
the Eleusinian Mysteries, 157
Elis
    Lepreum and, 153
    Olympic crisis of 420 and, 151
    Peace of Nicias and, 148
    Quadruple Alliance and, 93, 95, 111, 148, 150–151, 154, 158
Embatum, 90
embellishment, 22, 32
emotion, 10, 19, 31–35. *See also* suffering
    anger (*orgē*) and, 449–450, 452
    erōs and, 436–438
    mimesis and, 222–224
    political passion and, 443–457
Endius, 150
engagement, 606–609
Ennea Hodoi (Amphipolis), 65, 69, 126, 139–140, 296–297, 308–314
Ephorus, 14, 65, 635–637, 666
Epidamnus, 28, 116
Epidaurus, 152–154
epideictic genre of speeches, 268
epigraphy. *See* inscriptions
episkopoi, 101
Erechtheis, 72
Eretrians, 59
erōs. *See* emotion
Erythrae, 90, 101, 109, 182
Erythrae decree, 74, 75–76
ethnography, 246–247, 263–264

Euben, P., 9
Euboea, 59, 69, 75, 88, 172, 188
Eunapius, 693–694
Euphemus, 107, 157, 347–349
Eupolis, 126, 606, 617
Euripides, 377–378, 613
Eurylochus, 92
Eurymedon, battle of, 65, 70, 72
Eusebius, 692
Eustrophos, 149
Evagrius, 692
evasion, 518–521
evidence, 22–24
   dearth of facts and, 23, 173–175
   differing versions of events and, 551–552
   hearsay as, 23–25
   Homeric poetry as, 23–24, 560–562
   inscriptions as, 24, 74–76, 99–100, 128, 135
   literary, 23–24, 99–100, 118, 123, 126–127
   oral tradition as, 23–24, 552–554, 562–564
   physical, 24
   truth and, 22–25, 651–653
exaggeration. *See* embellishment; hyperbole
exile
   appeals to Athens from, 71
   of Thucydides, 25, 49, 147, 149, 174, 185, 296–297
expansion of Athenian Empire, 70–72, 106–108, 118
expansion of episodes, 211, 215–217, 220–222
expeditions, 65
eyewitness accounts, 22, 25

famines, 32
fiction. *See* narrative art
figures of speech, 216
financial resources. *See also* taxation; tribute
   after Sicilian expedition, 181
   armament and, 44–45
   loans and, 135–137
   monetary policy and, 103
   narrative art and, 134–137
   public, 43–47, 49, 57
   Trojan War and, 44–45
First Sacred War, 59
Fisher, M., 9
the Five Thousand, 184, 187–190, 319–320

   regime and, 404–405
   stasis and, 419, 421–423
Fleischer, U., 570
Flory, S., 89
focalization, 163–164, 207–209
forensic oratory, 268
formal speeches. *See* speeches
Forsdyke, S., 1–2
fortifications, 342–343
   Aeginetan, 71
   the Long Walls as, 21, 41, 66n1, 71, 77, 126, 130–131
   Thasian, 69
Foster, E., 7
the Four Hundred, 179–190, 420–423. *See also* oligarchy
Frangoulidis, S., 163, 601
freedom of speech, 277
funding. *See* financial resources
funeral customs, 33–34, 138–139
   juxtaposition of, 203–204
   Pericles' funeral oration and (*see* Pericles)
Furley, W., 139

Gelon, 58
genealogy, 553, 555
Genette, G., 208
Geuss, R., 531, 545
global political theory. *See* international relations
gnōmē. *See* judgment
gods. *See* religion/divine intervention
Gomme, A. W., 72, 100, 450, 593
Gongylus, 167–168
gossip, 284
Gray, V., 14
Greece, 200–201, xvii (*map*).
   See also Athens/Athenian Empire
   absence of word "Hellenes" in Homer and, 23
   agriculture and, 43–45
   anarchy under, 491–498
   Barbarians and, 28
   civil war and, 43, 45
   diplomacy and, 492, 495–497
   early art and, 51
   early history of, 39–60

Greece (*cont.*)
  identity of (*see* Hellenic identity)
  interstate relations in, 110–112
  Italy and, 52
  migration and, 43, 45, 48
  naval power of, 43–47
  Olympic crisis of 420 and, 151
  Pausanias and, 66
  power of, 39–60
  Sicily and, 52
  on Sparta, 93
  stagnation of, 57–60
  trade and, 43–45
  warfare as normal part of life in, 498–503
Greek tragedy, 33
Greenwood, E., 4
Grethlein, J., 171, 241
Griffin, J., 599n7
Gryllus, 518
Gylippus, 167–168, 171
  critique of imperialism by, 166
  speeches of, 165, 174

Hagnon, 181
Hanson, V. D., 122
harbors, 69
Hard Times (Dickens), 19
Harmodius, 24, 262
Harris, E. M., 185
Hawthorn, G., 166
hearsay (*akoe*) as evidence, 23–25
Hecataeus, 25, 25n3
Hellanicus, 22, 64, 65, 555–557, 560
Hellen (Hellenos), 47
Hellenica Oxyrhynchia, 625–627
Hellenic identity, 23, 47, 50–51
Hellenic League. *See* Delian League
Hellenotamiai, 68, 74, 78, 100.
  See also tribute
helots, 65, 94, 120–121, 133–134
Henderson, J., 13–14
Henry, W. P., 519
Heraclea Trachinea, 88
heralds (*kerukes*), 33–34, 101
Hermippus, 611, 613, 614
Hermocrates, 157, 163
  critique of imperialism by, 166
  on nature, 359–362
  speeches of, 173–174, 244, 276
Hermogenes of Tarsus, 695
the herms, mutilation of, 157–158, 162
Herodotus
  authorial comment by, 240
  on Cambyses, 56–57
  catalogues of, 164
  causation and, 28
  on differing versions of events, 551–552
  Dionysius of Halicarnassus on, 643–644, 646–648, 650–652
  on divine intervention, 30, 427–428
  eyewitness accounts and, 25
  on freedom of speech, 277
  hearsay and, 25
  on Homer, 261n7
  Homer and, 587
  on Ionians, 55
  irony and, 594
  judgment of, 25
  on Karystos, 69
  legend and, 245
  on Lelantine War, 59
  methods of, 195
  myth and, 6, 258–260
  on naval power, 56
  oral tradition and, 25, 552–554
  parallels with, 206
  on Pausanias, 66
  on Persian Empire, 71, 166
  Persian War and, 21
  Plutarch on, 648
  poetry and, 561
  on Polycrates, 55
  proclamation of identity by, 21
  on Sparta, 57–58
  speeches in, 267, 268–269, 577, 582
  structure of, 196–197
  suspense and, 592
  treatment of legend by, 41
  use of fiction by, 35
  on war against the tyrants, 58
Hesiod, 50, 59
Hestiaeans, 107
Hesychius, 693
Hiero, 58
Hipparchus, 24, 175, 553
Hippias, 24, 57–58, 175, 553

Hippocrates, 568–575
 death of, 283
 speech of, 276
Histiaeus of Miletus, 56n10
Histoire et raison chez Thucydide (Romilly), 205
historical accuracy, 2–4, 22–25
 myth and, 257
 of speeches, 272–273
historical method, 1–2, 19–36, 195–196
 narrative art as part of, 31, 35–36
historiography, 4–7, 559–564. *See also* narrative art
 Aristotle on, 271
 authorial comments and (*see* authorial comments)
 campaign/battle narratives and (*see* campaign/battle narratives)
 characterization and (*see* characterization)
 compression of episodes and, 211, 213–215, 225
 conciseness and, 212
 contemporary history and, 20–22
 day-by-day narration and, 217, 220–222
 expansion of episodes and, 211, 215–217, 220–222
 focalization and, 207–209
 irony and, 203–204
 juxtaposition and, 203–204
 late antique, 15, 692–693
 late nineteenth century reception of, 19
 method of Polybius and, 660–664
 mimesis and, 222–224
 myth and, 257–264
 reception of, 12–16, 19–20
 refined structuring and, 195–209
 reprise and, 219–220
 ring composition and, 40n1, 202–203
 Roman republican, 15
 scale and, 211–224
 sentence length and, 225–236
 speeches and (*see* speeches)
 twentieth century reception of, 20
 units of action and, 206–207
 verbal linkages and, 205
 vividness and, 217–222
Hobbes, Thomas, 8, 197–198, 208, 339–341, 396, 413, 427–428, 535, 644

Hoekstra, K., 9
Homer, 587, 695
 allusions to, 601–603
 almost episodes and, 598–599
 bearing arms in daily life and, 51
 catalogues of, 164
 dress in, 52
 evidence of, 23–24, 560–562
 Hellenic identity and, 23, 50–51
 Herodotus and, 587
 interlace technique and, 588–589
 irony and, 594
 juxtaposition and, 592–593
 myth and, 258, 260–261, 261n7
 narrative style of, 587–603
 objective pathos and, 599–600
 on rank, 122
 as rival, 27
 on Sicily, 162–163
 speeches in, 267, 268
 suspense and, 589–592
 Trojan War and, 21
hoplites, 84, 87–90, 138
Hornblower, S., 100, 117, 128, 168, 181, 568, 637, 696, 700
hortatory speeches, 268
hubris. *See* piety/hubris
human nature, 29–30
 judgment and, 30
 necessity and, 378–381
 nonhuman nature and, 371–372
 political theory and, 322, 355–372
 power and, 339–341
Hunt, P., 3–4, 493
Hunter, V., 478–480
hyperbaton, 216, 225–226
hyperbole, 32, 34–35, 216
Hyperbolus, 126–127
ideal state, 319–321
Imbros, 57
impartiality. *See* objectivity/impartiality
imperialism.
 See Athens/Athenian Empire; Persian Empire
implicit meaning, 197–202
Inaros, 71
individuals. *See* characterization; narrative art; *specific individuals*

infantry, 48–49, 56n10, 58, 91–93
   Archidamian War and, 130–132
   attacks by, 66n1
   hoplites and, 84
   narrative art and, 130–132
   unification and, 48–49
inscriptions as evidence, 24, 74–76, 99–100, 128, 135
instability. *See* stability/instability
interlace technique, 588–589
international relations, 11, 53–54, 111–112, 119–120, 149, 150, 180–183
   anarchy and, 491–498
   capture of Persia and, 127
   causation and, 503–508
   Greek, 492, 495–497
   interwar years and, 147–149
   mediation and, 495
   political theory and, 491–509
   power and, 506–508
   Quadruple Alliance, 93, 95, 111, 148, 150–151, 154, 158
   realism and, 496–506
   stability and, 320, 322, 335
   transcription of documents and, 155–156
   war and, 498–503
interpretation, 275. *See* judgment
interwar years, 145–159
   Alcibiades and, 150–152
   Argos' internal troubles during, 153–154
   diplomacy and, 147–149
   instability during, 146–148, 156
   instability of truce and, 146–147, 168–170
   Olympic crisis of 420 and, 151
   the Peloponnesus and, 152–154
   Sicilian expedition and, 157
Ionia, 90
   growth of, 55–57
   migration and, 48, 52
   naval power of, 55–57, 58
   Pausanias and, 66
   revolt of, 57
irony, 203–204, 594–598
Isocrates
   critique of imperialism by, 166–167
   literary evidence of, 99
   on tribute, 104

Jacoby, F., 560
Jaffe, S., 9
Jefferson, Thomas, 679
Jerome, 692
John Kinnamos, 704
John Stobaeus, 693, 695
John Tzetze, 704
Joho, T., 13–14
Jordanes, 692
judgment (*gnōmē*), 19, 20, 23–24, 449–453
   of character, 243–244, 249–251
   of Herodotus, 25
   human nature and, 30
   of imperialism, 165–168
   of leadership, 460
   Plato on, 539–544
   Sicilian expedition and, 173–175
   speeches and, 27
judicial regulations of Athens, 103–104
justice, 381–385, 576–584
Justus Lipsius, 678
juxtaposition, 203–204, 592–593

Kagan, D., 119, 134, 533
Kaldellis, A., 703–704
Kallet, L., 2, 105, 136, 164
Kantakouzenos, J., 701
Karystos, 69, 70
Kelly, G., 700
Kelly, T., 87, 88
Kerameikos, 138
kerukes. *See* heralds
kinēsis, 8, 11, 40, 223, 367, 380, 431, 486, 538
   interwar years and, 146–147
   political theory and, 339–340, 344–346
   stasis and, 410, 423–424
King's Peace, 96
Kleinias, 76
Komnene, A., 704
Komon, 134
Konstan, D., 444
Kraus, C. S., 672
Krentz, P., 499
Kühn, J.-H., 570

Lacedaemonians, 82, 84, 88, 90, 94–95
Laches, 126, 150

Lamachus, 126
land army. *See* infantry
Landemore, H., 475
Lapis Primus, 74
late antique historiography, 15
law, 491–509
    anarchy and, 491–498
    causation and, 503–508
    rule of, 403–404
    stability and, 403–406
leadership, 132–133
    of Alcibiades, 181, 466–469, 472
    of Brasidas, 464–466, 471–472
    of Delian League, 66
    judgment of, 460
    of Nicias, 469–472
    of Pericles, 189, 429–430, 435–436, 446–453, 460–464, 471–472, 479–482
    political theory and, 459–472
legend, 21, 41–42, 245, 247–249
Lelantine War, 57, 59–60
Lemnos, 57, 73
Lendon, J. E., 122–124
Leon, 150
Leontini, 71
Leo the Deacon, 704
Lepreon/Lepreum, 148, 151, 153
Lesbos, 57, 73, 87, 182–183
Leuctra, battle of, 96
Libya, 71
Lichas, 182
linkages, verbal, 205
literary evidence, 23–24, 99–100, 118, 123, 126–127
litotes, 216
loans, 135–137
Logistai inscription, 135
logos. *See* judgment
Longinus, 218, 223
long-range missiles, 59
long ships, 45
Loraux, N., 169
Low, P., 3
lowering style, 215
loyalty oaths, 101
Lucian, 687, 695
Ludwig, P., 11

Macedonia, 107, 110
Machiavelli, 319, 322
Mackie, C. J., 601
Macleod, C., 386, 581, 581n35, 587
Malalas, 693
Malchus, 693–694
Mantinea, 83, 92–93, 95
    battle of, 27, 94–96, 153–154, 333–334
    Peace of Nicias and, 148
    Quadruple Alliance and, 93, 95, 111, 148, 150–151, 154, 158
    Tegea and, 153
Mara, G., 11–12
Marinatos, N., 602
Martin, R., 677
Massalia, 55–56
Mattingly, H., 75
Mazzarino, S., 562
meaning, 197–202, 205
mediation, 495
medical writings, 29, 138, 567, 569–576
the Mediterranean, xxiii (*map*)
Megabazus, 56n10
Megara, 72, 72n2, 77, 89–90, 93
    Corinth and, 71
    Peace of Nicias and, 148
    revolt of, 75
Megarian Decree, 64, 119–123
Meiggs, R., 74, 136
Melian Dialogue, 165, 202, 433–434
    juxtaposition of, 204
    parody and, 531
Melos, 29, 106, 107
    capture of, 154–155
    narrative art and, 154–155
    scale of coverage of, 213
memory, 22, 350–352
    deficits in, 25–27
Menander, 618
Menander Protector, 693–694, 703
Menedaïus, 92
mercenaries
    Persian Empire and, 73
    Thracian, 34–35, 164–165, 203
merchant shipping.
    See naval power; trade
Messenians, 71, 77

764   SUBJECT INDEX

method. *See* historical method
Methone, 75, 110
Methymna, 182
migration, 43, 45, 48, 52, 55–56
Miletus, 56–57, 58, 72
   archon of, 102
   blockade of, 182–183
   restrictions on, 108
military resources. *See* armament; technology
military skill. *See* armament
Millender, E., 2–3
mimesis, 222–224
Mimnermus, 561–562
Minoa, 106
Minos of Crete, 51
   evidence and, 52
   naval power of, 29, 43–44, 46, 341
   as peacemaker, 44
   unification of Greece and, 47
Minotaur, 44
Mitchell, L., 393n4
mobs. *See* crowds
mockery, 607
modernity, 41–42
monetary policy, 103
morality, 515–516, 525–529. *See also* piety/hubris; religion/divine intervention
movement. *See kinēsis*
Müller, D., 128
Munson, R., 6
Mycalessus, 34–35, 164–165, 203, 349–350. *See also* Boeotia
Mycenae, 24
Mynott, J., 534
Myrcinus, 56n10
myth, 6, 257–264. *See also* religion/divine intervention
Mytilene, 57
   Cleon and, 207–208
   juxtaposition of, 204
   revolt of, 31, 90, 103, 104, 106–107, 109, 182, 207–208, 679–686, 688–689
   scale of coverage of, 212–213
   Sparta and, 66

narrative art, 19–20, 30–35, 73, 117–123. *See also* historiography
   Alcibiades and, 150–159
   allusions and, 601–603
   almost episodes and, 598–599
   the "Archaeology" and, 39
   Archidamian War and, 129–141
   architectural parallelism and, 199–202
   asymmetry and, 669
   authorial comment and (*see* authorial comments)
   causation and, 115–124
   characterization and (*see* characterization)
   comic witness and, 606–609
   conveying historical insight through, 35–36
   day-by-day, 217, 220–222
   disaster and, 173–175
   early Greek history and, 39–60
   engagement and, 606–609
   focalization and, 163–164, 207–209
   the Four Hundred and, 179–190
   historical method and, 1–2, 19–36
   imperial development and, 99–113
   incompleteness and, 4, 146–147, 149, 156, 171, 179–181, 190
   influences on, 664–671
   interlace technique and, 588–589
   interpretive problems and, 161–163
   interwar years and, 145–159
   irony and, 203–204, 594–598
   juxtaposition and, 203–204, 592–593
   location of the Pentecontaetia and, 64
   objective pathos and, 599–600
   as part of historical method, 31, 35–36
   patterning and, 594–598
   Peloponnesian League and, 81–96
   the Pentecontaetia and, 63–79
   raising abstract questions through speeches and, 271–272
   retardation and, 590–592
   rhetorical necessity and, 385–387
   ring composition and, 40n1, 202–203
   Sicilian expedition and, 161–176
   Sparta and, 81–96
   speeches and (*see* speeches)
   stasis in, 409–424
   step-by-step clarification and, 590
   style and, 659–673
   suspense and, 170–172, 589–592

of tragedy, 172–173
  tragedy and, 587–603
  transcription of documents and, 155–156
narratives. *See* campaign/battle narratives; plague narratives
nature
  as alibi, 355–357
  defectiveness of, 358–359
  divine law and, 370–371
  necessity of, 375–378, 525–529
  as obstacle, 355–357
  political theory and, 355–372
  worthiness of Athens and, 357–358
Naupactas, 71, 77
naval power, 41–60, 56n10, 78. *See also* trade
  Archidamian War and, 130–132
  of Athens, 66n1, 70, 78, 86, 131–132
  Delian League and, 69–70
  hoplites and, 87–90
  narrative art and, 130–132
  of the Peloponnese, 131–132
  of Phoenicia, 73
  political theory and, 340–352
  removal of the Four Hundred and, 187–188
  of Sparta, 87–90
Naxos, 58, 66n1
  enslavement of, 110
  revolt of, 65, 70, 72, 78
necessity
  choice and, 374–375
  human nature and, 378–381
  imperialism and, 381–385
  injustice and, 381–385
  natural, Xenophon on, 525–529
  of nature, 375–378, 525–529
  responsibility and, 378–381
  rhetorical, 385–387
  of war, 373–389, 539–544
Necho, 54
Nemea, 95
Nichols, M., 10, 480, 484
Nicias, 25–26
  Alcibiades and, 150, 162
  architectural parallelism and, 199–202
  characterization of, 202, 288–291
  critique of imperialism by, 168
  on crowds, 483–484
  leadership of, 469–472
  letter from, 25–26, 174, 278n21
  narrative art and, 140
  the Peloponnesus and, 157
  on piety, 363–364
  religion and, 429
  speeches of, 165, 171–172, 174, 201, 274–275, 278
Nicostratus, 410–411
Nietzsche, Friedrich, 531, 545
Nisaea, 90
non-human nature, 371–372
nudity, 51–52

oaths, 29, 92, 187, 336–337, 341, 527
  international relations and, 492–493
  interstate relations and, 101, 111
  interwar years and, 150, 152
  myth and, 261
  religion and, 428
  stasis and, 412, 414, 416, 421, 424
  tragedy and, 579
Ober, J., 475–476
objectivity/impartiality, 25, 117, 120, 599–600
observation. *See* eyewitness accounts
obstacle, nature as, 355–357
Oenoe, 86
Oenophyta, battle of, 71
"Old Oligarch", 99
oligarchy. *See also* the Four Hundred
  Athēnaiōn Politeia on, 184–185
  portrayal of, 183–184
  stability of, 394–399
  tyranny and, 58
oligarchy of the Bacchiads, 54
Olympic crisis of 420, 151
Olympiodorus, 693–694
omens, 368–369
oracles, 245–246
oral tradition
  as evidence, 23–24, 552–554, 562–564
  Hecataeus and, 25
  Herodotus and, 25, 552–554
oratory. *See* funeral customs; speeches
orgē. *See* emotion
The Origins of the Peloponnesian War (de Ste.-Croix), 120

Orwin, C., 8–9, 379, 394
Ostwald, M., 117, 375
Ozolian Locrians, 51

Paches, 207–208
Page, D. L., 570
Pagondas, 283
Palmer, M., 9
Pamphylia, 70
Pan-Achaeans, 50
Panhellenes, 50
Paralos (ship), 411
parody, 157, 531
Paros, 69
Parry, A., 198, 570–571
passions. *See* emotion; suffering
pathos, 224, 599–600
patterning, 594–598
Pausanias, 66–67
Pazdernik, C., 700, 702
Peace of Callias, 78
Peace of Nicias, 49, 51, 53, 82, 111, 145–159
    Archidamian War and, 146
    instability of, 146–147, 168–170
    narrative art and, 139–141
    ratification of, 148
    transcription of documents and, 155–156
Peiraeus, 89–90
Peisistratus, 55, 58
Peithias, murder of, 102
Peloponnesian League, 2–3, 71, 93
    Congress of, 270
    rank in, 122–123
    secessions from, 121
    Sparta and, 81–96
    speeches held before, 81–82
Peloponnesus, 70, 90, xix (*map*).
    See also Sparta
    agriculture and, 118
    Alcibiades and, 152–154, 157
    diplomacy in, 147–149
    earthquake in, 65
    instability in, 94–95
    migration and, 48
    narrative art and, 147–149, 157
    naval power of, 41, 131–132, 182–183
    self-interest and, 48
    Sicilian expedition and, 157
    subjection of, 71, 148
Pentecontaetia, 21, 63–79
    Athenian power and, 116
    Athens' imperial power and, 106
    campaign narrative in, 69–70
    on causation, 68
    on Corinth, 77
    dating systems in, 65
    evidence and, 74–76
    on expansion, 70–72
    narrative location of, 64
    on origins of empire, 65–66
    on Pausanias, 66–67
    on power of Athens, 70–77
    power of Athens and, 66n1
    purpose of, 63–65
    on revolt, 72–74
    on Sparta, 76–77
    on tribute, 67–68
pentekontors, 45–46, 57, 59–60
Perdiccas (Macedonian king), 107
performance of speeches, 576–584
Periander (tyrant of Corinth), 54, 58, 59
Pericles
    Aristophanes on, 126
    on armament, 41
    on Athens, 86
    causation and, 118–119
    characterization of, 285–287
    death of, 107
    first speech to the Athenians of, 88
    funeral oration and, 139, 201, 203–204, 260, 268, 323–331, 347, 351–352, 435–436
    leadership of, 189, 429–430, 435–436, 446–453, 460–464, 471–472, 479–485
    Megarian Decree and, 64
    on military tactics, 83–84
    narrative art and, 130–133, 135, 139–140
    on necessity of empire, 383–384
    on necessity of war, 373–374, 387–389
    parallelism and, 199–202
    restraint of, 107
    Samos revolt and, 73
    on scale, 212
    speeches of, 88, 119, 122–123, 274–275, 344–347, 436–438

strategy of, 182
as subject of comedy, 609–611
on tribute, 75
perioikic revolt, 65
Perrochat, P., 670
Persian Empire
    Athens and, 49
    collaboration with, 57
    dasmos and, 68
    Delian League and, 70
    diplomatic relations with, 111–112, 127
    expansion of, 56
    funding of navies by, 49
    invasions of, 166
    Lacedaemonians and, 82
    naval power and, 42, 55–57, 56n10
    Samian revolt and, 73
    Sparta and, 181–183
    tribute and, 104
Persian War, 21, 55
personal observation. *See* eyewitness accounts
Pharnabazus, 182
Phaselis, 76
Pheidon of Argos, 58, 59
Philistus, 175–176
Philocharidas, 150
Phliasians, 94
Phocaea, 55–57, 77
Phocis, 58
Phoenicia, 70, 72–73
Phormio, 88, 132
phoros. *See* tribute
phrourarchos, 101
Phrynichus, 182, 185–187, 186n5, 189, 418–419
phusis, 355–356, 358
physical evidence, 24
piety/hubris, 8, 11. *See also* religion/divine intervention
    nature and, 356, 363–364, 369
    Plato on, 523
    political philosophy and, 332–333, 335–336
    political theory and, 427–441
    Xenophon on, 515–516, 521–525
Pindar, 561
piracy, 23, 43–46, 51, 51n5, 55–56
Piraeus, 69, 118, 188
Pisander, 186–188, 418–420, 422

plague narratives, 31–33, 138–139, 204, 438–440, 569–574
Plataea, 31, 696–700
    defense speech, 277–278
    justice and, 578–581
    juxtaposition of, 204
    Theban attack on, 64
Plato, 11–12
    comedy in, 609, 613
    context and, 532–534
    dialogues and, 272n11, 523, 532
    on judgment, 539–544
    on nature, 355, 358, 361
    on necessity for war, 539–544
    on piety, 523
    political theory and, 531–545
    realism and, 538, 540
    on scale, 211
    on upheaval, 534–539
Pleistoanax, 77, 130, 140
Pleistolas, 146
pleonasm, 216
Plutarch
    on Alcibiades, 145
    on Aristides, 67
    characterization and, 284
    on Delos, 74
    as evidence, 118
    on Herodotus, 648
    Hobbes on, 198, 208
    on the interwar years, 145
    on Sicilian expedition, 176
    on Skyros, 69
    on war against the tyrants, 58
poetry, 559–562. *See also* specific poet
polemics, 242–243
politeia. *See Athēnaiōn Politeia*; regime (*politeia*)
political theory, 7–12, 319–337
    Athens and, 323–331
    comedy and, 613–615
    crowds and, 475–488
    global (*see* international relations)
    human nature and, 322, 355–372
    ideal state and, 319–321
    instability and, 531–545
    international relations and, 491–509

political theory (*cont.*)
   leadership and, 459–472
   nature and, 355–372
   naval power and, 340–352
   necessity and (*see* necessity)
   passion and, 443–457
   Pericles' funeral oration and, 323–331
   power and, 339–352
   principles of political rule and, 401–405
   realist (*see* realism)
   regime and, 391–406
   religion and, 427–441
   Sparta and, 331–336
   stasis and, 409–424
   utopianism and, 319–321
   war and, 321–322
   Xenophon and, 515–529
Polybius, 15, 659–666
Polycrates, 48, 55–58
polysyndeton, 222
Pontier, P., 629
Pope, M., 395
Porciani, L., 12–13
portents, 368–369
Potidaea, 28, 72, 116, 119, 120
power
   analysis of, 39–40
   the "Archaeology" and, 39–60, 39n1, 339–352
   of Athens, 24, 28–29, 64, 66n1, 70–77, 339–352
   as cause of war, 115–124
   of Greece, 39–60
   human nature and, 339–341
   international relations and, 506–508
   memory and, 350–352
   naval (*see* naval power)
   political theory and, 339–352
   realism and, 336–337
   of Sparta, 343–346
   suffering and, 39n1
praeteritio, 260
Prasia, 126
precision (*akribeia*), 575–576
Price, J., 410n2, 411n3
Priene, 72
Priscus, 691–699, 703
Pritchett, W. K., 128, 650

probouloi (advisors), 181–182, 184
Procopius, 15, 691–705
Prodicus, 212
"Prospectus" of multilateral alliance, 109
proxenos, 102, 110, 112
public finance, 43–47, 49, 57. *See also* tribute
purification, 30, 51n5, 55, 139
Pylos, 93
   Aristophanes on, 126, 129
   battle of Mantinea and, 154
   geography of, 128–129
   occupation of by Athenian Demosthenes, 91

Quadruple Alliance, 93, 95, 111, 148, 150–151, 154, 158
Quintilian, 215, 218, 666, 668
Quintus Aelius Tubero, 645, 651, 653
Quintus Fabius Pictor, 665

Raaflaub, K., 35, 166, 394, 396, 677
Rahe, P., 9–10
raids, 34–35
rank, Spartan–Athenian relations and, 122–123
rationalism, 25n3
rationality, 10
Rawlings, H. R., III, 5, 13, 544, 602
realism, 11, 366, 409, 531
   international relations and, 496–506
   Plato and, 538, 540
   power and, 336–337
   speeches and, 278
   tragedy and, 582–584
   Xenophon and, 515–529
reasoning. *See* judgment
reception of historiography, 12–16, 19–20
refined structuring, 195–209
regime (politeia)
   democratic, 188, 394–399
   domestic politics and, 392–394
   the Five Thousand (*see* the Five Thousand)
   importance of, 391–392
   kingship and, 400–401
   oligarchy and, 394–399
   political theory and, 9, 391–406
   principles of political rule and, 401–405
   rule of law and, 403–404

Spartan, 85, 396–398
tyranny and, 395, 400–401
wisdom and, 402–403
Reichel, M., 590
Reinhardt, K., 598
religion/divine intervention, 9–10, 28, 30, 32.
    See also myth
  divine law and, 370–371
  First Sacred War and, 59
  funeral customs and (*see* funeral customs)
  late antique historiography and, 692–693
  loans from sacred treasuries and, 135–137
  Olympic crisis of 420 and, 151
  omens and, 368–369
  panic over, 440–441
  participation in, 110
  piety and (*see* piety/hubris)
  plague narratives and, 572–573
  political theory and, 427–441
  Second Sacred War and, 77
  Third Sacred War and, 151
  Xenophon on, 521–525
Rengakos, A., 590–592
reprise, 219–220
responsibility, 378–381
retardation of narrative, 590–592
reversal, 596–598
revolt
  Athenian development and, 72–74
  of Batavia, 679–680, 682–689
  of Chios, 181–182, 337–338
  of Clazomenae, 182
  of Egypt, 71
  of Erythrae, 182
  of Euboea, 75, 188
  helot, 65, 120–121
  Ionian, 57
  of Megara, 75
  of Messenians, 71
  of Methymna, 182
  of Mytilene, 31, 90, 103, 104, 106–107, 109,
    182, 207–208, 679–686, 688–689
  of Naxos, 65, 70, 72, 78
  perioikic, 65
  of Rhodes, 182
  of Samos, 72–73, 77, 107
  Sparta's encouragement of, 181–182

  as subject of comedy, 611–618
  Tacitus on, 679–687
  of Thasos, 65, 69, 78
  tribute and, 75
rhetoric, 273–275, 694–696. *See also* speeches
  of justice, 576–584
  necessities of, 385–387
  performance of speeches and, 576–584
Rhodes, 182
Rhodes, P. J., 493
ring composition, 40n1, 202–203
risk-taking, 223
rivals of Thucydides, 20–21, 27, 31, 666
Robinson, E., 3
Roisman, J., 90
Roman republican historiography, 15
Romilly, J. de, 5, 205, 340, 499, 531, 703
Rood, T., 207–208, 241, 250, 632, 635, 664, 665
Roscher, W., 19
Rostovtzeff, M., 502
Rubel, A., 139
Rusten, J., 5–6, 208, 544

Sacred War. *See also* religion/divine
    intervention
  First, 59
  Second, 77
Saïd, S., 393n4, 394
Salaminia (ship), 158, 411
Salamis, 67, 69, 89
Sallust, 15, 665–673, 677
Samons, L., 129
Samos, 53–54, 59, 66n1, 76
  alliance with Athens and, 182
  naval power of, 48, 57
  removal of the Four Hundred and, 187
  revolt of, 72–73, 77, 107
  stasis in, 73, 76
  war against the tyrants and, 58–59
Saxonhouse, A., 8
scale, 211–224
Scanlon, T. F., 670
Schadewaldt, W., 589
Schepens, G., 629
Schiller, Friedrich, 267
Schmitt, C., 535
Scione, 126

Scyros, 44
seasonal dating systems, 22, 196–197
secession. *See* revolt
Second Preface, 147
Second Sacred War, 77
self-interest, 48
sentence length, 225–236
Sestos, 68
Shear, J. L., 185
shipping. *See* naval power; trade
ships/shipping. *See* naval power
Sicily/Sicilian expedition, 30, 31, 34, 49, 71, 107, 161–176, 200–201, xxi (*map*)
   accuracy re, 127
   Alcibiades and, 203
   Aristophanes on, 175
   authorial vision and, 206–207
   catalogue of the contingents and, 364–366
   colonization of, 54
   critique of imperialism and, 165–168
   crowds and, 476–477
   Diodorus Siculus on, 163–164
   diplomatic relations with, 111–112
   as disaster, 173–175
   double war motif and, 162, 168–172
   early history of, 21
   Euboea and, 172
   Greek expansion and, 52
   Homer on, 162–163
   juxtaposition of, 204
   narrative art and, 157
   naval power of, 48
   the Peloponnesus and, 157
   Philistus on, 175–176
   Plutarch on, 176
   political passion and, 453–457
   the Sikanoi and, 24
   as subject of comedy, 611–618
   as tragedy, 172–173
   tribute and, 104
   tyrants of, 48, 57–59
   unpredictability of war and, 170–172
Sicyon, 58, 77
Sigeion, 58
signs, 368–369
the Sikanoi, 24
Skyros, 69
slavery, 134
   capture of Melos and, 155
   Naxos and, 110
   in the Pentecontaetia, 47, 49, 69, 70, 78
social control. *See* crowds
social status, 109, 138
Socrates/Socratics, 520, 523
   on nature, 355–372
   Xenophon and, 515–529
Song of Wrath (Lendon), 122
the Sophists, 212, 576–577
Sophocles
   as advisor, 181
   irony and, 595–597
   tragedies of, 33
Sparta. *See also* the Peloponnesus
   Agamemnon and, 47–48
   Alcibiades and, 150, 158
   Ambraciots and, 32
   Argos and, 149, 153–154
   Aristophanes on, 126
   Assembly speeches of, 81–82
   Athenian power and, 65, 70–72, 76–77, 115–124
   attitudes toward Athens and, 109
   capture of Melos and, 154–155
   causation and, 120–121, 122–123
   characterization of, 8, 76–77, 84
   Chios and, 181–182
   collapse of, 111
   Corinth and, 76, 82–86, 90, 92, 151
   Delian League and, 66
   diplomacy and, 147–149
   discord within, 182
   Euboea and, 88
   as facilitator of Athenian development, 49
   geographical errors re, 128–129
   Greece on, 93
   Herodotus on, 57–58
   infantry of (*see* infantry)
   Mytilene and, 66
   narrative art and, 147–149
   naval power of, 87–90, 181–182
   occupation of Decelea by, 34
   Olympic crisis of 420 and, 151
   Pausanias and, 67
   Peloponnesian League and, 81–96
   Persian Empire and, 181–183
   political theory and, 331–336

power of, 343–346
power of Athens and, 24, 28–29, 66n1
refusal of arbitration by, 64
regime and, 85, 396–398
religion and (*see* religion/divine
  intervention)
revolts against, 65
secrecy of, 27
size of army of, 27
stagnation of, 81–82
stasis at, 414–417
strategy of, 181–182
technology and, 83–87
truce with Athens and, 93
war against the tyrants and, 57–59
speeches, 7, 25–27, 33, 267–279, 270n7, 271n9.
  See also specific speakers
  attitudes toward Athens in, 109
  in campaign/battle narratives, 311–313
  characterization through, 284
  composition of, 26
  deliberative, 268
  diversity of, 276
  epideictic genre of, 268
  exhortative, 268
  forensic oratory and, 268
  in Herodotus, 577, 582
  historical accuracy of, 272–273
  judgment and, 27
  Peloponnesian League and, 81–82
  performance of, 576–584
  raising abstract questions through, 271–272
  realism and, 278
  rhetoric and, 273–275
  Sicilian expedition and, 157
  silence during, 485–487
  sound effects in, 278n21
  at Spartan Assembly, 81–82
  stasis and, 414–417
  topics of, 276–277
Sphacteria, 91, 93
Spiraeum, battle of, 182
stability/instability, 367, 370
  of Athens, 44, 106–109, 341
  authorial comments on, 248–249
  of crowds of, 262
  of democracy, 394–399
  international relations and, 320, 322, 335

during interwar years, 146–148, 156
of language, 393n4
law and, 403–406
migration and, 48
of oligarchy, 394–399
in the Peloponnesus, 94–95
political theory and, 531–545
stasis and, 417
unification and, 49
Stadter, P., 7
Stahl, H.-P., 5, 167
Standards Decree, 102–103, 108
stasis, 9–10, 13, 362
  Athens and, 418–423
  Corcyra and, 409–414
  crowds and, 485–487
  political theory and, 409–424
  rule of law and, 403–404
  in Samos, 73, 76
  Sparta and, 414–417
  stability and, 417
  teaching on, 423–424
step-by-step clarification, 590
Sthenelaïdas, 77, 85, 123
  speech of, 270, 278
Strabo, 59, 695
Strasburger, H., 5, 587
Strauss, L., 357, 370–371, 394, 409, 424
structure, 5–6, 196–197
  diptych, 233–236
  refined, 195–209
  syntactical, 197–199
Strymon River, 56, 56n10, 65, 69, 70
Studies in Ancient Greek Topography
  (Pritchett), 128
subjection
  Aeginetans and, 71
  of the Peloponnesus, 71, 148
  tribute and, 68, 75–76, 104
subjugation. *See* subjection
subordination, 226
suffering, 32–35. *See also* emotion
  the "Archaeology" and, 39
  mimesis and, 222–224
  power and, 39n1
sungrapheis, 181, 184, 186
supernatural. *See* myth; religion/divine
  intervention

superstition. *See* myth; religion/divine intervention
surplus, 43–47
suspense, 170–172, 589–592
Swain, S., 695
Sybaris, 59
Syme, R., 667, 672
syntactical structure, 197–199
Syracuse, 58, 59
   focalization on, 163–164
   withdrawal from, 220–222

Tacitus, 15, 677–689
Tanagra, 71, 77
Taplin, O., 592
taxation. *See also* tribute
   narrative art and, 137
   Periander (tyrant of Corinth) and, 54
   replacement of tribute with, 105–106
   tyrants and, 58
technology, 83–87
Tegea, 94, 153
Telecleides, 611, 615
teleology, 171, 355–356, 359, 361
Ten-years war. *See* Archidamian War
Teutiaplus, 90
Thasos, 58, 66n1, 77
   fortifications of, 69
   revolt of, 65, 69, 78
Thebes, 64, 578–581
Themistocles, 59, 66n1, 67, 69, 130, 152, 342
Theophylact Simocatta, 693, 703–704
Theopompus, 14, 624–625
Theramenes, 181, 187–188
Theseus, 44–45
Thessalians, 48, 151
Third Sacred War, 151
the Thirty, 187–188
Thirty Years' Peace, 119–120
Thomas, R., 13
Thrace, 70–71, 91, 106–107
   campaigns in, 301–314
   mercenaries from, 34–35, 164–165, 203
   naval power and, 42
   Peace of Nicias and, 148
Thrasybulus, 187, 420–421
Thrasyllus (Thrasylos), 153, 187, 420–421

Thucydides
   controversies re, 117–123
   exile of, 25, 49, 147, 149, 174, 185, 296–297
   proclamation of identity by, 21
   rivals of, 20–21, 27, 31, 666
   unitarian *vs.* separatist views of, 117–118, 146–147, 156
Tissaphernes, 182–183, 185–186, 418–419, 421–422
Topographisch-geographisches Bildlexikon zum Geschichtswerk des Thukydides (Müller), 128
topography, 126, 128–129
Torone, 155, 214, 302, 305, 308–309, 312–314, 632–633
trade, 76. *See also* naval power
   blockade of, 131
   competition for, 118
   Corinth and, 52, 54
   early Greeks and, 43–45
   merchants in Piraeus and, 118
   the Strymon River and, 69
tragedy
   allusions to, 601–603
   Greek, 33
   irony and, 594–598
   juxtaposition in, 592–593
   narrative style of, 587–603
   necessity and, 378–381
   objective pathos and, 599–600
   realism and, 582–584
   Sicilian expedition as, 172–173
   Sophoclean, 33
transcription of documents, 155–156
transparency, 26–27
treasury, 2, 68, 74, 78, 104
tribute (*phoros*), 68, 74–75. *See also* taxation
   Athens and, 71, 73, 78, 100–101, 104–106
   Delian League and, 67–68
   Hellenotamiai and, 68, 74, 78, 100
   narrative art and, 136–137
   Persian Empire and, 104
   revolt and, 75
   subjection and, 68, 75–76, 104
Tribute Quota Lists, 100, 104–106, 109
triremes, 46, 53–55, 57–60, 131
Trojan War, 21, 44–45, 261, 341–342

Tsakmakis, A., 7
tsunami, 239–240
Turquois, E., 704
tyranny, 262. *See also specific individual*
    Athenians on, 24
    naval power and, 46
    oligarchy and, 58
    regime and, 395, 400–401
    rise of, 54
    taxation and, 58
    wars against, 57–59

understatement, 518–521
unification, 44, 47–50
unitarian *vs.* separatist views, 117–118, 146–147, 156
uniting of wars, 146–147, 168–170
universality, 7–8
unpredictability of war, 170–172
upheaval, 534–539
utopianism, 319–321

van Wees, H., 2
Velleius Paterculus, 666
verbal linkages, 205
verbs, 227–232
Visvardi, E., 478
vividness, 31–35, 217–222. *See also* emotion
Voltaire, 267
von Ranke, L., 19

walls. *See* fortifications
Waltz, K., 499
war
    brutality of, 33, 502
    causes of (*see* causation)
    international relations and, 498–503
    necessity of, 373–389, 539–544
    political theory and, 321–322, 373–389
    as subject for comedy, 611–618
Warner, R., 504–505
weights and measures, 103
Westlake, H. D., 184–185
Whately, C., 15
Wiater, N., 15, 648
Wick, T. E., 504–505
wisdom, 402–403
    of crowds, 475–477, 481, 487–488
Wohl, V., 10
Wolpert, A., 4
Woodman, A. J., 212, 218, 672

Xenares, 149
Xenophon, 11, 14, 129
    on attitudes toward Athens, 109
    authorship of Second Preface and, 147
    continuation of Thucydides by, 516–518, 621–622, 627–635
    evasion in, 518–521
    on morality, 515–516, 525–529
    on necessity, 525–529
    on piety, 515–516, 521–525
    political theory and, 515–529
    realism and, 515–529
    on retribution, 165
    on Sparta, 94, 111
    speeches in, 267
    understatement in, 518–521
Xerxes, 166, 197, 206, 268–269

Zacynthus, 87
Zanker, G., 218
Zumbrunnen, J., 10–11

Lightning Source UK Ltd.
Milton Keynes UK
UKHW031827080821
388496UK00004B/42